Skype for Business

UNLEASHED

800 East 96th Street, Indianapolis, Indiana 46240 USA

Skype for Business Unleashed

ISBN-13: 978-0-672-33849-6
ISBN-10: 0-672-33849-1

Library of Congress Control Number: 2016943460

1 16

Trademarks

All terms mentioned in this book that are known to be trademarks or service marks have been appropriately capitalized. Que Publishing cannot attest to the accuracy of this information. Use of a term in this book should not be regarded as affecting the validity of any trademark or service mark.

Warning and Disclaimer

Every effort has been made to make this book as complete and as accurate as possible, but no warranty or fitness is implied. The information provided is on an "as is" basis. The authors and the publisher shall have neither liability nor responsibility to any person or entity with respect to any loss or damages arising from the information contained in this book.

Special Sales

For information about buying this title in bulk quantities, or for special sales opportunities (which may include electronic versions; custom cover designs; and content particular to your business, training goals, marketing focus, or branding interests), please contact our corporate sales department at corpsales@pearsoned.com or (800) 382-3419.

For government sales inquiries, please contact governmentsales@pearsoned.com.

For questions about sales outside the U.S., please contact intlcs@pearson.com.

Editor-in-Chief
Greg Wiegand

Acquisitions Editor
Trina MacDonald

Development Editor
Mark Renfrow

Managing Editor
Sandra Schroeder

Senior Project Editor
Tonya Simpson

Copy Editor
Bart Reed

Indexer
Cheryl Lenser

Proofreader
H. S. Rupa

Technical Editor
Tim Harrington

Contributing Writers
Adam Berns
Adam Jacobs
Iain Smith
Ken Lasko
John Cook
Stale Hansen
Tom Arbuthnot
Fabian Kunz
Shawn Harry
Tom Morgan

Editorial Assistant
Cindy Teeters

Cover Designer
Chuti Prasertsith

Compositor
codeMantra

Contents at a Glance

Table of Contents

Part VII Integration with Other Applications

Part X Planning for Deployment

Foreword

When I work with customers, I find it's sometimes useful to put the current set of technology into a bit of a historical context—essentially how the solutions they are evaluating fit into a long-term timeline. There are a bunch of ways to look at the evolution of the business communications industry, and this model I've just found to be moderately helpful.

One can think of the first generation of business communications to be all about the on-premises circuit-switched PBX. This really started with the advent of deregulation, where it was now permitted to attach third-party equipment to the public network, and companies wanted a piece of that in their own environment. This was a big step—the birth of the heterogeneous network—and in many ways foretold a sliver of the power we would see in later years with the Internet.

The Internet also gave us the technical foundations for the next generation—the digital PBX. Now where we once had two wires coming into the office—one for data and one for voice—we could have a single wire with both. Yay progress! Of course as this generation of technology advances, we get some more benefits. Off-the-shelf hardware brings some cost and operational efficiencies. SIP brings some level of interoperability, although not nearly as much as HTTP, its signaling protocol inspiration.

What SIP does provide, though, is a way to think about sessions generically, leading to the third generation of business communication—that of on-premises unified communications. Now instead of consolidating wires, we're consolidating experiences—bringing media and applications together across different form factors and providing end users with communications capability in everything they do. Gurdeep Singh Pall, the long-time leader of Microsoft's UC engineering, compared this to salt in a cooking recipe—integrated, expected, and missed when it's not there.

I've been fortunate to help customers understand the technology options from Microsoft, which have matured in complexity and adoption over the last few years. This has been quite a set of products—from Communicator to Lync to Skype for Business. This set of clients spans nearly eight meaty server releases, each with new scenarios, additional capabilities, and lots to know about planning, deployment, and operations. We've dedicated entire conferences to the study of how the ever-increasing set of clients operates with the ever-increasing set of diverse server deployment options.

Now we're getting into the next generation—that of cloud-based UC. In one way this is a big simplification, to have the on-premises complexity of operating spindles, cycles, and bits, and the software requiring those resources all provided as a subscription service. This also opens up the opportunity for customers to make strategic decisions about how to operate UC workloads—whether it makes more business sense to have the global multitenant cloud do the work or to have those functions operate on on-premises servers. With every generation, more and more scenarios, clients, and features are available to customers. Now we're adding the hybrid concept on top of this as well, with servers operating in concert with the cloud.

Each generation builds on the last, so in this volume you'll see everything from circuits to SIP interop to multimedia meetings. The task of cataloging all the technology and packaging it into a set of words and diagrams folks can make sense of is really, really big. The authors have combined some 50-plus years of experience, and it shows. So whether you're just getting started in your UC journey or are a seasoned veteran ready to make the transition to the next generation, you'll find tons of great insights here to light the way.

Thanks for being here and participating in the next huge change in business communications.

Jamie Stark
Senior Product Manager, Microsoft

About the Authors

Alex Lewis, MCITP, CISSP, has a mixed background in technology and business spanning 20 years. He has worked with a wide range of environments, from small organizations to large enterprises requiring complex or custom communications solutions, and is responsible for architecting and implementing some of the largest Lync and Skype for Business deployments in the world. Alex is a strong believer in aligning technology to business goals to create a competitive business advantage. Including titles on Active Directory and Exchange, and three on Lync, Alex has participated in writing nine books from 2004 to present. He is currently Vice President at Event Zero, the global leader in real-time analytics for Skype for Business. In his spare time Alex enjoys scuba diving and beach volleyball.

Pat Richard is a Unified Communications consultant and PowerShell Developer who began working with Microsoft Exchange and evolved into working with the full Microsoft Unified Communications stack. He has been involved in some of the best-known deployments and migrations in the world, including those in the defense, finance, government, real estate, manufacturing, and services fields. Pat maintains the renowned ehloworld.com blog, which focuses on solutions, ideas, scripts, and information centered on PowerShell and Unified Communications. His PowerShell scripts, Excel design calculators, and other tools have been used by many of the major consulting firms, large enterprises, small- and medium-sized shops, and even Microsoft Consulting Services to deploy and manage millions of seats on Exchange Server, Lync Server, and Skype for Business Server. Pat is the host of the popular Exchange/Lync/Skype for Business/Office 365 focused podcast "The UC Architects" and has been recognized by Microsoft and awarded the Microsoft MVP award more than 10 times across three products. He has contributed to several books, spoken at international conferences, and has been spotlighted by some Microsoft marketing campaigns.

Phil Sharp is a Unified Communications consultant with over 10 years of experience working with Microsoft Unified Communications solutions. His career in Microsoft UC began with one of the first Office Communications Server 2007 voice deployments in the U.S. He has extensive experience architecting, implementing, and supporting Microsoft Active Directory, Office Communications Server 2007/R2, Lync Server 2010/2013, Skype for Business, and Exchange for organizations of all sizes and verticals. In Phil's current role at Modality Systems, he leads a world-class team of Microsoft UC consultants who specialize in telephony integration of Lync and Skype for Business.

Rui Maximo started in the Microsoft Skype for Business product team at Microsoft since the early days of RTC in 2003. As a lead program manager, he managed multiple areas of responsibility on the server side, including AD schema, topologies, management, setup, Enterprise Voice, and CWA. Rui has authored over 40 technical articles, training videos, whitepapers, and multiple books.

In addition to writing technical books, Rui is the principal software architect of the Security Filters (www.lync-solutions.com), a suite of seven security products that protect Skype for Business Server against denial-of-service (DoS) and over 20 different types of attacks, provide granular control of federation traffic, and restrict access to only authorized mobile devices. He consults and does contract work for clients looking to integrate their products with Skype for Business Server 2015.

Dedications

Kate Hudson, I dedicate this to you for all your love and support over the years and for the years to come. You are and always will be my rock.

—Alex Lewis

Every adult has that one person who is a sounding board about life, who mentors and answers without judging. For me, that person is Joe Ferrera. Life wouldn't be the same without you, buddy.

—Pat Richard

This book is dedicated to my wife, Michelle, who inspires me beyond words.

—Phil Sharp

To my wife, Anne, who has patiently stood by me: Your strength in battling cancer the past 15 years is nothing short of inspiring. To my kids, Marie, Mathew, and Chloe: You never cease to amaze me how brilliant you are.

—Rui Maximo

Acknowledgments

Alex Lewis

First of all, thank you to the Sams team for all your patience and hard work to make this book a success. It wasn't always smooth, but I'm very proud of the end product we've all produced. Thank you to Dave Tucker for building a world-class company in Event Zero and letting me be a small part of it! And, thank you to Rand Morimoto of CCO for your ongoing mentorship and always being available for a chat.

To all my friends, thank you for your endless understanding of all the nights I couldn't go out, all the trips I couldn't join you for, and all the fun I missed. Although you sufficiently rubbed it in, I love you all and I couldn't ask for better friends. Finally, thank you to Pugsley and Freya, my pups that provided endless companionship, love, and entertainment throughout the process!

Pat Richard

Thanks to the Pearson team and Alex Lewis for bringing us together and pushing us to get this book written. It took quite a bit of effort to write about a constantly evolving product. Thanks to the team at Microsoft, especially Jamie Stark and Derek Whittle, who work tirelessly on getting us information about the product. And thanks to the MVP community for being a great resource and sounding board for ideas, issues, and suggestions. I'm honored to be a part of that group. Thanks to my colleagues, past and present, who continue to challenge me to excel, and who keep me laughing while doing it. And thanks to Rui Maximo and Phil Sharp for working on this project with me. And lastly, thanks to John Cook and Ståle Hansen for chipping in on some of the content.

To my close friends and immediate family, thanks for understanding the long hours required to bring this project together. There were many times when I wished I could have just hung out with you, but I had to stay engaged in writing. There are also some people who either test my sanity or help me maintain it (or both). That includes, among others, Karen Lopez, Beth Rubus, Julie Rosen, and Mike Floerkey (our plucky comic relief). I offer sincere appreciation to all of them. And to my grandson Nathan, who always reminds me it's important to have fun and be a kid once in a while.

To the social media followers, thanks for understanding that I set aside working on scripts, podcasts, and blog posts while I worked on this. Life should get back to normal now.

Phil Sharp

To my wife Michelle, and daughters, Ava and Alexandra: Thank you for your patience and encouragement throughout this journey. Your love and support mean more to me than I could ever express.

Thank you to the entire team who brought this all together and got it across the finish line. I know there were a lot of long nights to get us here. And a special thanks to Alex Lewis for providing the opportunity to work on this amazing project.

Rui Maximo

Thank you to Sams for publishing this book. Many hours from the team were put into this work. Thank you to my co-authors, and to Alex Lewis for inviting me to work on this book. Hard to believe this is my sixth one. I also want to recognize my contributing writer, Tom, and technical reviewers, Fabian and Shawn. You've been great technical resources and friends to me. Thank you!

To my colleagues and the professionals in the ever-growing Skype for Business community, I've made wonderful friends the past 13 years, and continue to meet fantastic individuals from all over the world. I'm grateful for your kindness and help. Do not hesitate to reach out to me. I'm always looking to make new friends.

We Want to Hear from You!

As the reader of this book, *you* are our most important critic and commentator. We value your opinion and want to know what we're doing right, what we could do better, what areas you'd like to see us publish in, and any other words of wisdom you're willing to pass our way.

We welcome your comments. You can email or write to let us know what you did or didn't like about this book—as well as what we can do to make our books better.

Please note that we cannot help you with technical problems related to the topic of this book.

When you write, please be sure to include this book's title and author as well as your name and email address. We will carefully review your comments and share them with the author and editors who worked on the book.

Email: feedback@samspublishing.com

Mail: Sams Publishing
ATTN: Reader Feedback
800 East 96th Street
Indianapolis, IN 46240 USA

Reader Services

Register your copy of *Skype for Business Unleashed* at quepublishing.com for convenient access to downloads, updates, and corrections as they become available. To start the registration process, go to quepublishing.com/register and log in or create an account*. Enter the product ISBN, 9780672338496, and click Submit. Once the process is complete, you will find any available bonus content under Registered Products.

*Be sure to check the box that you would like to hear from us to receive exclusive discounts on future editions of this product.

CHAPTER 1

What Is Skype for Business?

IN THIS CHAPTER

- ▶ Skype for Business Server Overview
- ▶ Skype for Business Server Terms and Acronyms
- ▶ Versions and Licensing
- ▶ Integration with Other Microsoft Applications

For more than 10 years, Microsoft has been focused on a vision of providing an integrated software suite that allows users to communicate and collaborate in new and innovative ways. Skype for Business Server 2015 represents the latest iteration in the product line that has been designed to fulfill that vision. Previously called Lync Server, the name was changed to Skype for Business Server as Microsoft brings the enterprise unified communications platform and the existing consumer Skype product into the same family.

As an alternative to traditional voice-only systems such as private branch exchanges (PBXs), Skype for Business Server instead offers a software-based infrastructure that combines voice, video, instant messaging, conferencing, and collaboration managed from a single interface. The end result is a unified communications system that can easily adapt to the changing needs of an organization and can be extended to provide new functionality as it becomes available.

In this new world of unified communications, users are no longer tied to a single device as a communication endpoint. They can choose to use a traditional-style desk phone, a headset attached to a laptop, a desktop, a tablet, or a mobile device to place and receive calls. In addition, plenty of flexibility exists in how these devices are provisioned to users. For example, instead of being assigned a phone that is tied to a specific phone number, a user can simply log in to any supported phone with appropriate credentials and make use of that device for communications. Incoming calls are then routed to this device and can also be routed to any other device that the user is logged into, simultaneously. Optional forwarding settings also allow timers to forward to voicemail or other configured numbers, such as a mobile device. At the same time, Presence information is published to allow a user to determine whether another user is available even before the caller picks up the phone to call the other user.

Skype for Business Server allows users to choose and change their forms of communication seamlessly as the situation demands, using a single interface. For example, Julie and Don are collaborating on a project, and Julie has a question for Don. Julie looks at her Skype for Business client and sees that Don is listed as available. Julie sends Don an instant message asking whether he has a moment to answer a question. Don replies, "Sure." After a few messages, Don determines that the subject is a bit too complicated to be explained via IM, and suggests that they have a voice conversation. Julie then escalates the session to a voice call with a single click, and Julie and Don are able to speak directly. After a few minutes, Julie determines that she would like to see a document that Don has referred to, and asks whether Don could show her the document. At this point, Julie adds video to the call, and Don uses application sharing to display the document as he continues talking.

The communication session just described could just as easily take place with the two individuals being at coffee shops or at the beach using Internet-connected laptops, as opposed to a traditional corporate setting. Skype for Business Server doesn't require participants to reserve or schedule video conferencing resources ahead of time, nor does it require users to be in a specific location, or even to use specific hardware. Skype for Business Server allows users to dynamically control their own communications and to be available almost anywhere they can get an Internet connection, at almost any time.

Skype for Business Server Overview

Skype for Business Server is an integrated suite of communication tools that enable point-to-point or point-to-multipoint communications across various mediums. Even the most basic Skype for Business Server implementations include several core features that are useful for almost any organization. For example, all Skype for Business Server deployments enable instant messaging between two or more users for simple text-based communications, as well as point-to-point voice and video chat between clients. Also included in this core set of features is full-featured web conferencing, combining audio, video, application and desktop sharing, remote control, file transfer, and more.

An additional core functionality that exists with all Skype for Business implementations is the concept of Presence, in which one can view the status of other users in real time. Although Presence is a feature that has been widely adopted for use with the majority of communications software on the market, Skype for Business Server presents an advantage in that the Presence information published by Skype for Business is extended into other popular Microsoft applications, such as Microsoft Office, Exchange, and SharePoint. As an example, it is possible to view a document created by a coworker that is stored in SharePoint, quickly determine the status of the document owner, and then contact that document owner with a single click, leading to an IM conversation or a voice call.

Moving beyond the basic features of Skype for Business Server, this functionality can be extended in various ways depending on the needs of an organization. For example, through the use of media gateways or a qualified PBX, Skype for Business users can participate in voice conversations with users of other voice systems, including the Public Switched Telephone Network (PSTN). Skype for Business Server also enables extended methods of conferencing, such as calling in to a conference from a PBX or the PSTN (dial-in conferencing) and integration with dedicated video conferencing systems. For larger conferences, Skype for Business Server has the ability to provide most if not all of an enterprise's conferencing needs.

Instant Messaging and Presence

Although instant messaging (IM) and Presence are two different functions, together they form the most basic functionality available in Skype for Business. In fact, it is not possible to deploy one without the other. IM describes the now-ubiquitous function of engaging in a conversation with another user using simple text-based messaging. The previous version, Lync Server 2013, provided access to public IM connectivity (PIC) with several more popular IM providers such as AOL and Yahoo! In Skype for Business Server 2015, that feature has been removed and can now be provided by third-party Unified Communications Exchange providers. These providers can also connect Skype for Business Server 2015 with disparate systems such as IBM Sametime, Cisco, Unify, and others. Skype for Business Server 2015 also provides for connecting to the consumer Skype service for peer-to-peer (P2P) audio and video conversations. This is monumental as more than 560 million people have used Skype, all of whom can use a plethora of clients, including PC, tablets, smartphones, as well as the more than 50 million Skype-enabled televisions. In addition, Skype for Business Server allows organizations to federate with other organizations that are also using Skype for Business, extending the IM capabilities beyond corporate borders.

Federation effectively sets up a connection between multiple implementations of Skype for Business, Lync, or Office Communications Server, allowing both sides to selectively share Presence information with one another and use the core features of Skype for Business for communication. This is an especially useful feature for business partners who are required to frequently and quickly contact one another. Rather than the inherent delays involved in sending single sentences or short emails to one another, federated partners can simply exchange instant messages in real time.

NOTE

Although this might seem like a small distinction in methods of communications, administrators who manage email systems are quite satisfied to offload communications to alternate methods such as IM. This is largely due to the realization that a large percentage of the data stored in mail systems consists of nonessential conversations along the lines of "Where do you want to meet for lunch?"

Although on the surface it might seem minor, being informed as to a user's availability and willingness to communicate can be useful for both parties. For example, often a user won't bother to call another individual if it is evident that the other person is not likely to answer the call. At other times, a user might choose to intentionally call someone who is listed as not available so that the user can simply leave a quick message and avoid a lengthy conversation. These examples are common uses of Presence and illustrate the usefulness of this feature.

These are some of the more commonly used Presence states within Skype for Business:

- Available
- Offline
- Away
- Busy
- Do Not Disturb

Skype for Business can update a user's Presence status based on information available in other applications. One of the most useful examples of this is the client-side integration between Skype for Business and Microsoft Outlook. If Microsoft Outlook is installed on the same client workstation as the Skype for Business client, Skype for Business will automatically update the user's Presence status based on information in the user's Outlook calendar.

Peer-to-Peer Audio

Peer-to-peer (P2P) audio is a core feature of all Skype for Business Server deployments, and is very simple to configure and support because it doesn't involve integration with any other systems. Much like IM, P2P audio involves a point-to-point conversation between Skype for Business endpoints; however, in this case the network communications include audio codecs rather than simple text. This audio communication requires more bandwidth than IM and is also much more sensitive to network latency. However, P2P audio still generally requires relatively little in the way of system resources. Because P2P audio communications traverse the data network only, generally good quality can be expected even across a wide area network (WAN) or the Internet.

Web, Audio, and Video Conferencing

Skype for Business Server 2015 includes a comprehensive set of conferencing capabilities as an important core feature of the product. Web conferencing provides users with document collaboration and application sharing, along with whiteboard, remote control, session recording, and other useful collaboration tools. This is a key adoption feature because it allows users who are not provisioned in Skype for Business Server 2015, including those in other organizations, to participate in Skype for Business Server 2015 conferences. These features, combined with audio and video conferencing, provide a powerful set of features, all of which are made available via the Skype for Business client software. Meetings can be either scheduled or ad-hoc, and through automatic integration with Microsoft Outlook they can be scheduled using a single click. All the Skype for Business conferencing capabilities can be leveraged seamlessly in an on-demand fashion without interrupting a meeting and without requiring separate software, resulting in a conferencing experience that is extremely user friendly.

In the last few years, Microsoft has introduced purpose-built hardware solutions for conferencing, including the Lync Room System and the Surface Hub. Both extend Skype for Business functionality into conference room hardware that improves the meeting experience.

While some organizations may already have investments in video conferencing technology from other providers such as Cisco/Tandberg solutions, Skype for Business Server 2015 can leverage those solutions in Skype for Business conferencing via a new feature called Video Interop Server.

NOTE

Web, audio, and video conferencing features are available with all Skype for Business Server 2015 deployments and do not require additional components beyond the Skype for Business Front End Server. However, PSTN connectivity, as well as dial-in conferencing, which allows users to join a conference using a PSTN phone, requires a PSTN gateway along with the Skype for Business Mediation Server role before it can be used.

Enterprise Voice

Enterprise Voice describes the set of features that allow Skype for Business Server to be leveraged as a complete telephony solution for an organization. This includes connectivity to the PSTN, as well as PBX and IP-PBX systems using media gateways and Session Initiation Protocol (SIP) trunks. It also includes voice features that are common to many voice platforms, such as call forwarding, hold, transfer, call parking, enhanced 9-1-1, call admission control, branch office survivability, distinctive ringing, and many more. Traditional voice management functions are also included, such as dial plans, call authorization, and call detail records.

The Enterprise Voice features included with Skype for Business Server are on par with and in many cases exceed the functionality provided by a traditional PBX system. For this very reason, Skype for Business Server can be considered a viable replacement for PBX systems, which can be accomplished either through attrition or via a greenfield replacement.

NOTE

Remote Call Control (RCC) allows integration between Skype for Business Server 2015 and a PBX, such that RCC-enabled users can use the Skype for Business interface to control calls on their PBX phone. This can be an option for organizations that want to evaluate Skype for Business Server while maintaining their existing telephony investment, or as an effective method of gradually introducing Skype for Business into the environment while retiring an older voice platform.

In Skype for Business Server 2015, RCC is deprecated, but will continue to be supported as a coexistence option. However, the feature is completely removed in the Skype for Business 2016 client, and is inaccessible from the Lync 2013 client when using the Skype for Business skin.

For many organizations, an important benefit of using a VoIP system such as Skype for Business Server is the ability to bypass long-distance toll charges through the use of call routing, which is also referred to as toll bypass. For example, if a company has offices in San Francisco and New York, and these two locations are connected via a WAN link, calls between the sites can be routed internally via Skype for Business Server, which makes the call effectively free since the data network is being utilized.

If, on the other hand, a user in San Francisco needs to call an external user in New Jersey, there are two ways this call can be routed. Either the VoIP call from San Francisco can directly exit the local PSTN gateway to the long-distance provider, or the call can first traverse the WAN to the New York office and then exit the PSTN gateway at that location. This would likely result in a cost savings because the toll charges for a call to New Jersey are likely lower from New York than from San Francisco. Through the use of effective dial plans and call routing, a Skype for Business Server administrator can leverage toll bypass to ensure that the least expensive call path is used for a given scenario. These rules are typically configured based on area codes so that the number of required rules remains manageable.

Persistent Chat

Persistent Chat is a Skype for Business Server 2015 feature that allows users to create chat rooms that contain persistent conversations based on specific topics and categories. In contrast, a Skype for Business IM conversation between three or more users is considered an IM conference; however, when all parties leave the conversation, the content of that conversation cannot be retrieved or reviewed. With Persistent Chat, conversations remain even after all users involved in a conversation leave the chat room. The persistent nature of the messages allows Skype for Business users to view ongoing conversations at their leisure, and also search for information within the chat rooms. Additionally, keyword alerting can draw attention to conversations about a given subject. Many organizations find that ongoing persistent conversations provide a valuable and effective tool for collaboration that can be leveraged by teams of users.

Remote Access

Offices are shrinking as the corporate workforce is becoming increasingly mobile. Once outside the confines of the corporate network, users often must rely on solutions such as virtual private networks (VPNs) to connect to company resources. With Skype for Business Server 2015, this is not the case. A Skype for Business Server 2015 deployment can include an Edge Server or Edge Server pool to provide secure access to remote users. Users are free to utilize the same features and functionality as when they are within the company network.

Connecting with coworkers and partners is unchanged as remote users appear just as internal users. A user who wishes to communicate with another user does not need to know if that user is internal or external, or what type of device they are using. This feature is also beneficial because it enables a seamless work-from-home capability. Whether users work from home daily, or just on a sick day or weather-related day, they maintain functionality to communicate with coworkers.

NOTE

When using a VPN for Skype for Business traffic, it is highly recommended that a split tunnel be configured, with Skype for Business traffic *not* traversing a VPN connection. This is to ensure optimal quality.

Skype for Business Server Terms and Acronyms

In the world of unified communications, many terms and acronyms are routinely used that might be unfamiliar to those new to the Skype for Business product line. This book contains many references to these terms and acronyms; therefore, becoming familiar with the most common ones allows you to more quickly absorb the information in the remaining chapters. Following are some of the common terms and acronyms that will be used throughout this publication:

- **Call Admission Control (CAC)**—A method of preventing oversubscription of VoIP networks. Unlike QoS tools, CAC is "call aware" and acts as a preventive congestion control by attempting to route calls across other media before making a determination to block a call. Ultimately, the result of a properly implemented CAC configuration is that the quality of existing calls is preserved, even when bandwidth is scarce.

- **Call detail record (CDR)**—A record produced by a phone system containing details of calls that have passed through it. Each record includes information such as the number of the calling party, the number of the called party, the time of call initiation, the duration of the call, the route by which the call was routed, and any fault condition encountered. These records might be used for billing, for tracking of an employee's usage of the system, or for monitoring system uptime and issues.

- **Client Access License (CAL)**—A software license that entitles a user to access specific systems or specific features in a system. A CAL is typically offered in several flavors: Standard, Enterprise, and Plus.

- **Direct Inward Dialing (DID)**—Also know in Europe as Direct Dialing Inward (DDI). A service offered by phone carriers wherein a block of telephone numbers is provided to a customer for connection to the customer's internal phone system (including Skype for Business Server or a traditional PBX). Incoming calls to the DID block are routed to internal destination numbers, which allows an organization to have significantly more internal lines than external lines.

- **Dual-Tone Multi-Frequency (DTMF)**—A method for providing telecommunication signaling over analog telephones lines in the voice frequency band. DTMF is also referred to as *touch tone*. This technology enables users to initiate events in the phone system by simply pressing a button on a keypad.

- **Extensible Markup Language (XML)**—A set of rules for encoding documents in a machine-readable format. The goal of XML is to be a simple and open standard for representing arbitrary data structures, and it is most often used in web services.

- **Extensible Messaging and Presence Protocol (XMPP)**—An open, XML-based protocol designed to provide near-real-time extensible IM and Presence information. XMPP has more recently expanded into VoIP and file transfer signaling.
- **Hardware load balancing (HLB)**—A method of distributing a workload across multiple computers to optimize resource utilization, increase throughput, and provide a level of redundancy through the use of an external hardware device.
- **Instant messaging (IM)**—A form of real-time, direct, text-based communication between multiple parties. IM is sometimes referred to as *online chat.*
- **Interactive Voice Response (IVR)**—A technology that enables a system to detect voice and dual-tone multifrequency inputs. IVR is often used in telecommunications as an input for automated decision trees. For example, IVR technology is used behind the scenes with voice menu prompts that are frequently heard, such as "press 1 for English."
- **Mean opinion score (MOS)**—In multimedia, MOS provides a numerical indication of the perceived quality of a call after compression and/or transmissions. MOS is expressed as a single number ranging from 1 to 5, with 1 being the lowest perceived audio quality and 5 being the highest perceived audio quality.
- **Network Address Translation (NAT)**—A method of modifying network address information when packets pass through a traffic routing device. NAT effectively remaps a packet from one IP space to another, and is common in home usage when there are multiple computers with a private IP addressing site behind a router or firewall that holds a publicly routable address. NAT maps a port back to the initiating internal host and reroutes responses back to the originating host.
- **Network load balancing (NLB)**—A method of distributing a workload across multiple computers to optimize resource utilization, increase throughput, and provide a level of redundancy through the use of software running in the Windows operating system.
- **Plain Old Telephone Service (POTS)**—Another term for PSTN.
- **Public Switched Telephone Network (PSTN)**—The global network consisting of the world's public circuit-switched telephone systems. The first company to provide PSTN services was Bell Telephone.
- **Private branch exchange (PBX)**—A telephone system that serves a particular business or office as opposed to a common carrier or a system for the general public. A PBX is what traditionally provides voice services to companies that are connected to a local exchange, and provides external connectivity to the PSTN for users in that organization.
- **Quality of experience (QoE)**—A subjective measure of a customer's experiences with a vendor or service.
- **Quality of service (QoS)**—A mechanism to control resource reservation in a system; typically, it is a method to prioritize various traffic types to ensure a minimum level of performance for a particular type of traffic.

- **Realtime Transport Protocol (RTP)**—A standardized format for delivering audio and video over the Internet. A noted advantage of RTP is its ability to handle large amounts of packet loss before the impact on the call becomes noticeable.
- **Remote Call Control (RCC)**—A method of utilizing a phone resource on one system with a resource on another. Typically, in the context of Skype for Business Server, this is the capability to use a Skype for Business client to place a call through a desk phone that is controlled by a PBX rather than by Skype for Business Server.
- **Role-based access control (RBAC)**—An approach to restricting system access to authorized users by granting the rights based on the role served by the user. This normally results in granular permissions with the goal of granting the minimum level of rights needed to perform a task.
- **Session border controller (SBC)**—Often a physical appliance but also seen in virtual form, this product resides in the signaling and/or media path between a Voice over IP (VoIP) infrastructure such as Skype for Business Server 2015 and a SIP trunk from either a trunk provider or a trunk connected to another PBX system. It provides many features, including security, SIP normalization, advanced SIP message, and header manipulation.
- **Session Initiation Protocol (SIP)**—An Internet Engineering Task Force (IETF) defined protocol used for controlling multimedia communications sessions. The goal of SIP is to provide a common signaling and call setup protocol for IP-based communications.
- **SIP for Instant Messaging and Presence Leveraging Extensions (SIMPLE)**—An open standard protocol suite that provides for the registration of Presence information and the receipt of Presence status notifications.
- **Survivable Branch Appliance (SBA)**—A physical appliance that combines the Skype for Business Registrar, Mediation Server, and PSTN gateway services in one compact unit; it is designed to maintain most voice services for a branch site that has lost connectivity to the main Skype for Business Server site.
- **Transmission Control Protocol (TCP)**—One of the core protocols of the Internet, TCP is a protocol that provides reliable ordered delivery of a stream of packets from one device to another. TCP has the advantage of sending an acknowledgment of receipt of a packet back to the sender, resulting in increased reliability. This acknowledgment, however, comes at a performance price and can therefore serve to limit the scalability of TCP.
- **Uniform Resource Identifier (URI)**—A string of characters used to identify a name or a resource on the Internet. This allows interaction with representations of the resource over a network, often the Internet, using various protocols.
- **User Datagram Protocol (UDP)**—Another one of the core protocols of the Internet, UDP delivers a stream of packets from one device to another, but does not attempt to order or verify delivery of packets. UDP also does not need to first initiate a

conversation with a destination host via a handshake. This behavior makes it faster and more scalable than TCP, but ultimately it is less reliable.

- **Virtual private network (VPN)**—A method of passing packets across a public network in a secured and authenticated manner. VPNs enable users to access their private corporate networks through connections to the public Internet.
- **Voice over IP (VoIP)**—A generic term for transmission technologies that deliver voice communications over IP-based networks. VoIP is also referred to as *IP Telephony* or *Internet Telephony*.

Versions and Licensing

Like previous versions, Skype for Business Server 2015 comes in two flavors: Standard Edition and Enterprise Edition. The two versions present a variety of deployment options for organizations of all sizes. A Skype for Business Server topology can be relatively simple or as complex as needed to meet the requirements and budget of even the largest organizations. Features between the two editions are very similar, with Enterprise providing more scalability, along with high availability and disaster recovery options that aren't available in the Standard Edition. However, to leverage these additional options, Enterprise Edition represents a more significant investment and requires higher-end components than Standard Edition. For example, a dedicated backend SQL server is required for Enterprise Edition rather than a local installation of SQL Express, which is automatically used and required with Standard Edition. Hardware load balancers (HLBs) are also required, as DNS load balancing cannot be used for HTTP traffic.

Skype for Business Server Standard Edition

The Standard Edition of Skype for Business Server provides a relatively simple way for small-to-medium-sized organizations to introduce unified communications into a network. It offers a relatively low cost of entry based on the fact that all internal components are hosted on a single server, with the option of adding an Edge Server to support external connectivity.

Standard Edition utilizes a local SQL Server Express Edition database to store Skype for Business Server 2015 information, and the database is installed automatically by the deployment wizard. Although Standard Edition does not provide all the high-availability options available with the Enterprise Edition, Skype for Business Server 2015 can leverage functionality that was added in Lync Server 2013 in the form of Front End Pool Pairing. This feature allows Standard Edition pools to be designed for a level of resiliency, even across multiple sites. For this reason, many organizations will find that installing multiple Standard Edition servers across several sites will result in an ideal combination of low cost, site resiliency, and a solid set of features. The primary disadvantage to Standard Edition is that it is designed to handle relatively low user loads, because the all-in-one nature of the system limits scalability in terms of performance. At the same time, the consolidated design of a Standard Edition server makes it simpler to deploy and maintain than an Enterprise Edition topology, and the performance characteristics will be more than adequate for many small-to-medium-sized organizations.

A typical Standard Edition deployment would involve a single system acting as a Front End Server, which might include additional collocated roles depending on the requirements, such as Mediation Server, Archiving Server, Monitoring Server, and Persistent Chat Server. To round out the deployment, a PSTN gateway can be used to enable Enterprise Voice, and an Edge Server can be installed to provide external connectivity. An additional system hosting the Director role can optionally be used to redirect incoming user requests to the Front End Server. This configuration is sufficient to provide IM, voice, and video services for a small-to-medium-sized organization, as well as external connectivity for remote users, A/V conferencing, federation with other organizations, and more.

NOTE

Although Skype for Business Server Standard Edition is typically used in small-to-medium-sized deployments, it is also quite common for both editions to be used within the same architecture. For example, some larger organizations deploy Enterprise Edition Skype for Business Server 2015 pools in primary data centers, and use Standard Edition pools to service smaller, regional offices. The Enterprise and Standard editions of Skype for Business Server can easily be mixed and matched as needed within a network to accommodate different levels of service and budget for different locations.

Skype for Business Server Enterprise Edition

The Enterprise Edition of Skype for Business Server provides a scalability jump compared to Standard Edition, and provides additional high-availability options. The increase in scalability results from the separating of roles onto separate systems for better performance, and also the use of more robust components in certain areas. For example, whereas Standard Edition can use only a local SQL Express database, Enterprise Edition requires the use of a full SQL instance installed on a dedicated system. In this one area alone, scalability is improved not only by using a more robust database, but also by isolating the database load from other systems.

In terms of high availability, Enterprise Edition provides several advantages compared to Standard Edition. Although the Front End Pool Pairing feature is available with either edition, only Enterprise Edition allows for the failure of a Front End Server with no resulting loss of functionality for the pool users. This is possible because Enterprise Edition allows the installation of separate Front End Servers for the same pool within a particular site. An additional resiliency advantage is that Enterprise Edition requires a separate database for backend data storage, which presents the opportunity to leverage native SQL high availability for the Skype for Business Server 2015 data. Skype for Business Server 2015 supports SQL Always On, which requires two backend SQL servers and uses data synchronization between the two systems. Both SQL mirroring and clustering are still fully supported. Unlike SQL clustering, neither Always On nor mirroring require shared storage.

Of course, the additional scalability and high availability provided by Enterprise Edition come at a higher cost, in terms of both additional systems and licensing. A typical Enterprise Edition deployment at a given site consists of at least two Front End Servers (up to a maximum of 12 per pool), with hardware load balancers (or a combination of hardware load balancers and DNS load balancing) used to distribute the load between the systems. At least one SQL server system would be used to store the backend data, although two such systems with SQL Always On or mirroring would be recommended for redundancy. On the Front End Server systems, several other Skype for Business Server roles can be collocated, including Mediation Server, Monitoring Server, and Archiving Server. The Mediation Server role can also be installed separately from the Front End Server to increase performance. Other systems that can be added to provide increased functionality with an Enterprise Edition deployment include one or more PSTN gateways to enable Enterprise Voice features, Persistent Chat Server, and an Edge Server or Edge Server pool to support external connectivity.

NOTE

With Lync Server 2010, the Monitoring Server and Archiving Server roles were always installed separately from the Front End Server, and the A/V Conferencing Server role could be installed separately if desired. This behavior changed in Lync Server 2013, and continues in Skype for Business Server 2015. Each of these roles is collocated with the Front End Server with all deployments. The Persistent Chat Server can also be collocated with the Front End Server in a Standard Edition deployment, but must be installed separately from the Front End Server with an Enterprise Edition deployment. The Mediation Server role can either be collocated with the Front End Server or installed separately, depending on the specific Enterprise Voice requirements of the deployment.

Client and Server Licensing

Microsoft licensing for Skype for Business includes both client and server licensing. Whereas the server licensing is straightforward, the client licensing can be challenging to absorb. With regard to servers, all Front End Servers installed in a Skype for Business deployment must be licensed. Other roles, such as Edge Server, Persistent Chat Server, and Mediation Server, do not require server licensing for Skype for Business Server 2015.

As for client licensing, one Client Access License (CAL) is required for each user to access the services of a Skype for Business server. However, there are three types of CALs available for Skype for Business Server 2015:

- Skype for Business Server 2015 Standard CAL
- Skype for Business Server 2015 Enterprise CAL
- Skype for Business Server 2015 Plus CAL

The Standard CAL is the base CAL, which is required for all users and grants access to a standard set of Skype for Business Server 2015 features, including IM and Presence and peer-to-peer audio and video communications. The Enterprise and Plus CALs are additive CALs that grant access to additional Skype for Business Server 2015 features. Whereas the Enterprise CAL grants access to audio, video, and web conferencing features, the Plus CAL includes Enterprise Voice features. To enable access to the entire feature set provided with

Skype for Business Server 2015, a user must be licensed with all three CALs. Note that this is the case regardless of the server edition installed on the Skype for Business servers that the user connects to.

The CAL types mentioned can all be purchased individually as part of a standalone Skype for Business deployment, and the Skype for Business Standard and Enterprise CALs in particular can also be purchased as part of a volume licensing arrangement. For example, the Skype for Business Standard CAL can be purchased as part of the Microsoft Core CAL Suite (CCAL), and the Skype for Business Standard or Enterprise CAL can be purchased as part of the Microsoft Enterprise CAL Suite (ECAL). Many organizations purchase Skype for Business licensing as part of a larger volume licensing agreement in order to save on overall licensing costs. Note that the Plus CAL must be purchased as standalone license, because it is not included in either the CCAL or the ECAL volume license offerings. There is also a licensing requirement for the Skype for Business client software. The client software can be purchased as a standalone application, or it is included as part of the Office Professional Plus 2013 suite. Microsoft continuously updates the licensing features and costs. Licensing can be complex, and it is recommended that you check with Microsoft to determine the proper licensing strategy for the deployment scenario.

Integration with Other Microsoft Applications

One of the primary advantages of Microsoft Skype for Business Server 2015 over competing products in the unified communications arena is integration with other Microsoft applications. Not only do other Microsoft applications provide functionality within Skype for Business, but Skype for Business was also designed to create hooks into other popular Microsoft software. The end result is that information stored in other applications such as Exchange Server and SharePoint Server can be accessed within Skype for Business Server 2015, and on the other end, rich Presence information stored within Skype for Business Server 2015 can be shared with other applications. With Skype for Business Server 2015, Microsoft is continuing to leverage integration points within its portfolio to provide additional value across the software stack.

Integration with Exchange Server

Skype for Business Server 2015 will continue to provide the integrations with Exchange Server that existed in previous versions, and will introduce several additional integrations as well.

NOTE

All of the Exchange Server integration features offered with Skype for Business Server 2015 also require Exchange Server 2013 or later. Therefore, an organization must upgrade both products in order to use all the Exchange Server integration features.

Continuing in Skype for Business Server 2015 is integration with Exchange Outlook Web App (OWA). Skype for Business Server 2015 and OWA integration allows Presence and IM capabilities within an OWA session, and includes the following useful features:

- Presence for internal and federated Skype for Business Server contacts
- The capability to start and maintain chat sessions directly from OWA
- Skype for Business Server contact list integration, including adding and removing contacts and groups
- The capability to control Skype for Business Presence states from OWA

As in previous versions, Skype for Business Server integrates with the Unified Messaging role in Exchange, which allows Skype for Business Server to use Exchange as a replacement for traditional voicemail systems. Voice messages stored in Exchange can then be retrieved from the Skype for Business client as well as from the user's Exchange mailbox.

Skype for Business Server 2015 Archiving integration is a feature that integrates the Skype for Business Server 2015 Archiving role with the Exchange In-Place Hold feature, resulting in a common repository of archival data that simplifies compliance and eDiscovery tasks across the two communications platforms.

An additional integration feature between Skype for Business Server 2015 and Exchange Server 2013 is the Unified Contact Store, which presents a common repository for user contacts that is shared between the Skype for Business Server 2015 and Outlook clients. When enabled, the Skype for Business client connects to Exchange Web Services (EWS) to read and maintain contacts instead of using SIP to connect to the Skype for Business Front End Server for contacts, as in previous versions.

NOTE

Unified Contact Store requires both Skype for Business Server 2015 and Exchange Server 2013 or later; however, it is an optional feature that can be enabled or disabled, even after required versions of both products are deployed.

Rounding out the integration features between Skype for Business and Exchange is the storage and retrieval of high-resolution photos that are shared between the two platforms. Both Skype for Business Server 2015 and Exchange Server 2013 support photos of up to 648 × 648 pixels, which are stored in Exchange Server 2013 and are added to contacts within the Skype for Business and Outlook clients. The photos are stored as a hidden item in the root of a user's Exchange mailbox. Having the option to store these photos in Exchange is an improvement from previous Lync Server versions, since the photos were typically stored in Active Directory, which presented some limitations due to potential problems with replication.

Integration with SharePoint

Similar to Exchange, Skype for Business Server 2015 continues to offer integrations with SharePoint that were available with previous versions of the two products, and provides some additional functionality that is available with SharePoint 2013 and later. Whenever a contact is shown in a SharePoint page, Skype for Business presents Presence information along with the associated contact card for the user, and Skype for Business functions can be initiated via a simple click on the Presence icon.

An interesting SharePoint integration feature that was introduced with Lync Server 2010 and will continue to be supported in the on-premises version of Skype for Business Server 2015 is Skill Search. With Skill Search, the Skype for Business client can be used to search SharePoint My Site pages to find individuals with a specific skill set. With SharePoint integration, users are also able to access their SharePoint My Site profile page from the Options dialog box within the Skype for Business client.

A feature introduced in Lync Server 2013 and SharePoint 2013 and continuing in Skype for Business Server 2015 is the ability to use SharePoint to search Skype for Business Server 2015 archives using an eDiscovery site collection. The Skype for Business Server 2015 archive data must first be integrated with Exchange Server 2013 or later to form a common repository for archive data to allow this search functionality within SharePoint.

This type of bidirectional integration presents many options for organizations to allow productive and efficient communication for the user base. For example, it can be challenging for new employees in a large organization to find the right resource to handle a particular question. With Skype for Business and SharePoint integration, that employee can use Skill Search to display a list of employees who have a particular expertise, quickly determine whether they are available to communicate, and then initiate the communication using various methods. All of this can be accomplished using a single interface, compared to searching a company intranet, looking for the appropriate department, digging up contact information for individuals with the right skill set, and then manually contacting each one until someone is available.

Integration with Microsoft Office

On the client side, integration between Skype for Business and Microsoft Office has provided valuable features with previous versions of Lync, and that will continue to be the case with Skype for Business Server 2015. Here are some of the more compelling features provided through the integration of Skype for Business and Microsoft Office:

- Skype for Business automatically updates the user's Presence status based on information in the user's Outlook calendar.
- The Online Meeting Add-in for Skype for Business allows users to create a Skype for Business conference from the Outlook client and automatically schedule the meeting in the user's calendar, providing a single interface to service all meeting requirements.
- Presence information is automatically displayed wherever mail recipients are shown in Outlook.
- Skype for Business IM conversations are recorded in the Conversation History folder in Outlook, and can be viewed and searched along with other Outlook data.

- The Skype for Business client can be used to record personal notes regarding a meeting that are stored in a OneNote 2013 or later notebook.
- The Skype for Business client can be used to open a shared OneNote 2013 notebook and distribute a link to connect to the shared notebook for all meeting participants.

Integration with Third-Party Applications

Microsoft has not forgotten about line of business applications that don't carry the Microsoft moniker. By supplying comprehensive software development kits, organizations can extend their applications with Skype for Business features and connectivity. The most common adaptation is the inclusion of IM and Presence into applications.

Organizations can also build complete clients and solutions around Skype for Business, adding features and functionality not already available in the Skype for Business server and client applications. These include Attendant Consoles, web-based applets, information dashboards, help desk tools, and more.

Summary

Microsoft Skype for Business Server 2015 is the latest chapter in Microsoft's unified communications story, offering a powerful suite of communication and collaboration tools that can be leveraged using a single interface. The core features of IM, Presence, conferencing, and peer-to-peer audio and video are included in all deployments, and additional features such as Enterprise Voice, archiving, monitoring, external access, and federation can be added as necessary. Several editions and a number of topology options are available to scale a Skype for Business Server deployment to meet the needs of even the largest organizations. Skype for Business Server 2015 can be used for anything from a simple IM platform to a full PBX replacement, to a distributed VoIP implementation. Microsoft continues to enable integrations between Skype for Business and other popular Microsoft products such as Exchange, SharePoint, and Office, which presents new ways for users to communicate and provides additional value for the investment. Microsoft Skype for Business Server 2015 enables users to simplify communications and expand the ways in which they can collaborate.

CHAPTER 2

What's New in Skype for Business?

IN THIS CHAPTER

- Animated Emoticons ... and Consumer Integration
- New Topologies and Supported Architectures
- Hybrid and Online Features
- Enhanced Mobile Experience
- In-place Upgrades

Microsoft offered a mixed message with the launch of Skype for Business Server 2015. The story of "in-place upgrades" and "it's nothing more than a service pack" starkly contrasted with messages of "revolutionary cloud-first approach" and "significant changes to transform the way people work." It can't be both, can it? After all, Microsoft did bring animated emoticons to the product, including the ever-popular "mooning guy" in the beta versions of the product.

First, let's address the concept that not a whole lot has changed. For the first time ever, administrators can perform an in-place upgrade of their Lync Server 2013 servers to Skype for Business Server 2015. There are a number of caveats, covered in Chapter 15, "Migrating from Lync Server 2010/2013," but it's certainly possible for many organizations. Under the covers, many of the components are the same; even almost all of the services have the same name.

Despite the "nothing's changed" message, Microsoft Skype for Business Server 2015 has also introduced a number of significant improvements from its predecessor, Lync Server 2013, and made yet another compelling case for organizations to consider upgrading. The largest change is the shift to a cloud-first focus for Microsoft. This means all deployments will need to have some level of Office 365 cloud integration to take advantage of the new and upcoming features. Microsoft promises a regular cadence of updates and features through its cloud-first strategy.

Server-side conversation history, for example, makes it easy to take your conversations on the go, seamlessly transitioning from PC to smartphone without missing a beat. Speaking of mobile devices, there are a number of enhancements for the mobile experience as well.

This chapter covers the major changes and improvements most organizations try to leverage in their business case for upgrading servers.

Animated Emoticons ... and Consumer Integration

While platforms like Yahoo IM were among the first to have emoticons, Skype (consumer) took them to a new level with a wide range of choices and entertaining animations. Skype for Business added a number of new emoticons, blending popular consumer animated icons with more traditional business ones as well.

The Consumerization of Lync

Previous versions of Lync have been laser-focused on providing a professional, enterprise experience for business users. With Skype for Business, the lines have been notably blurred between the business and consumer versions of Skype. For traditional businesses, including the dozens I've spoken with, the reaction is overwhelmingly negative; however, for newer, millennial-based companies the reaction has been very positive. It wouldn't be a surprise to see a converged client between Skype Consumer and Skype for Business in the near future.

In talking of emoticons, Skype for Business has a number of animated non-business emoticons (see Figure 2.1 for an example). This can blur the line between business communication and casual conversation. In regulated environments, this may become a significant barrier to adoption.

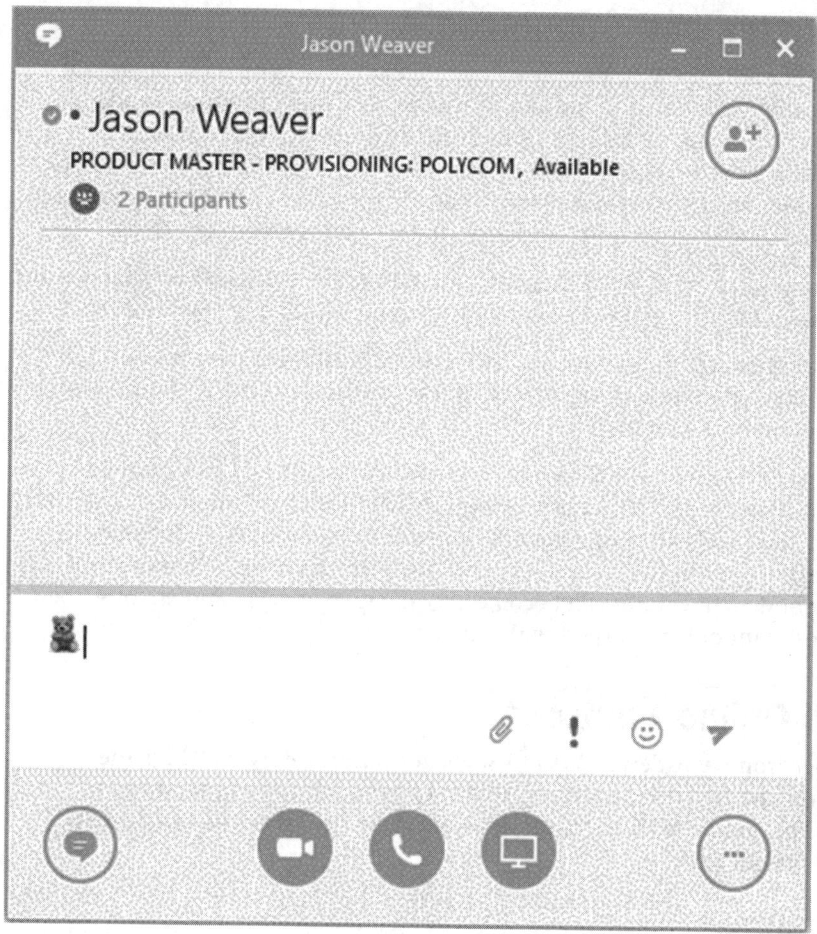

FIGURE 2.1 New emoticons in Skype for Business.

A significant enhancement to Skype for Business is the ability to search the Skype directory for contacts. This truly allows universal communications between business users and casual Skype consumer users. A Skype for Business user can search for a Skype user either by Microsoft ID or by Skype ID, a late-added enhancement.

Skype carries more Voice over IP traffic than all other services in the world combined. Bringing that together with Skype for Business creates a powerful universal communications tool for businesses of all sizes.

New Topologies and Supported Architectures

The key focus of Microsoft's new strategy is strongly "cloud first." The most important nuance for most current customers is the idea that they need to be in hybrid mode to take advantage of most, or all, of the new features of the product. This is in stark contrast to the message of the last 10+ years of "deploy Microsoft UC on premises." This may be barrier to adoption for less agile organizations in the Microsoft ecosystem. They may feel left out as new features are "cloud only" and drive them to competitive solutions.

However, for customers where "cloud" integration in an option, Microsoft offers a number of options. Not much has changed with on-premises options from Lync Server 2013.

With the release of Microsoft Cloud PBX and PSTN access, customers can choose a fully cloud solution for their communications needs, at least in the U.S. (Other countries are promised this solution in the future.)

More interesting is the host of hybrid options available to customers. Users hosted in Office 365 can use on-premises PSTN egress using a "Cloud Connect" appliance available from a number of approved partners, including Sonus and AudioCodes. A deployment might also have some users in the cloud and others on-premises using different PSTN egress options. Hybrid architectures can become very complex quickly and are often best designed by a consultant or other expert with extensive experience.

Hybrid and Online Features

The biggest change from Lync Server 2013 to Skype for Business Server 2015 is the addition of features and functions only available to cloud or cloud-hybrid customers. These features are *not* available to customers who decide to deploy Skype for Business Server 2015 on-premises only.

Broadcast Meetings

Prior to Skype for Business Server 2015, large meeting support was little more than the ability to check a box on an RFP for Microsoft. It required dedicated A/V server pools, dedicated accounts, and offered a clunky user experience. Even then, it had some significant limitations and was rarely adopted in the industry. The answer, according to Microsoft, is broadcast meetings in Office 365.

Skype Meeting Broadcasts are made up of four roles, offering different levels of participation in the meeting:

- **Organizer**—Creates the meeting invite and sends it to other presenters and attendees. Can also review post-meeting reports and metrics.
- **Producer**—Controls the meeting, including content, audio, video, and presentations. Also has recording capabilities.
- **Event Team**—The main presenter role for the broadcast. Can present all types of content and answer questions.
- **Attendee**—Watches the event, usually through an approved web browser.

Skype for Business Online Broadcast Meetings can be as large as 10,000 attendees, with even larger capacity planned for the future!

Cloud PBX

Cloud PBX is exactly what it sounds like—PBX features hosted in Microsoft's Office 365 cloud. Note that Cloud PBX is distinctly different from PSTN access. PSTN access is an add-on license whereas Cloud PBX is available with the Microsoft "E5" license. Although it doesn't currently have feature parity with an on-premises Skype for Business Server 2015 deployment, it does have an impressive feature list for a first-release platform. Here is the full list of functions available at launch:

Feature	Cloud PBX
Phones	Yes
Mobile	Yes
PSTN calling and on-premises PSTN connectivity	Yes
Call hold/retrieve	Yes
Call transfer	Yes
Call forwarding	Yes
Camp On	Yes
Distinctive ringing	Yes
Simultaneous ringing	Yes
Voicemail	Yes
USB peripherals	Yes
Delegation (boss/admin)	Yes
Team call	Yes
Basic Call Policy support	Yes

PSTN Calling

PSTN calling is another new function of Skype for Business in Microsoft's Office 365 cloud. It provides users hosted in Office 365 with the ability to make and receive PSTN phone calls.

NOTE

On-premises users cannot leverage Office 365 PSTN calling for PSTN access.

Currently PSTN calling is only available in the U.S.; however, it is planned for many more countries around the world in coming years. There is a lot of confusion around the licensing for PSTN calling. It can be assigned to any Standalone 2 or Enterprise 1, 3, or 5 plan, but is not included in any of them by default. It's an add-on license and needs to be assigned to users through the Office 365 Administration console or remote PowerShell.

What if you already have dozens, hundreds, or even thousands of DIDs? You can port them to Office 365 as part of the migration process. Office 365's process for this is simpler and more transparent than a standard port between tradition telecom carriers.

Enhanced Mobile Experience

Skype for Business Mobile is an iterative update to the mobile clients on Windows Phone, iPhone, iPad, and Android. It's not revolutionary but rather a solid evolutionary update to bring the mobile experience closer to the desktop experience. However, Microsoft's mobile client still lags significantly behind others in the market and has a lot of work to do to catch up to market demands.

The biggest addition is the ability to view and participate in content sharing. Previously, mobile users have been relegated to audio and video only, with nearly all participants using only the audio modality. This change finally makes Skype for Business mobile a legitimate client for collaboration.

Another change that has filtered down to the Lync 2013 mobile client is anonymous join. Now, even those without a Skype for Business account can download the mobile client and have a rich meeting experience.

In-place Upgrades

For the first time in the lifetime of Microsoft's real-time communications platform, in-place upgrades are a possibility. There are a number of caveats, covered later in this book, but in-place upgrades are possible for many deployments, especially those with paired enterprise pools.

Summary

Skype for Business provides iterative improvements on Lync Server 2013. Far and away, the biggest changes come in the online and hybrid functions. For existing on-premises users, the upgrade is similar to a service pack or "R2" release. This release will force enterprises to consider a cloud strategy for communication and collaboration as many new functions will only be available in Microsoft's cloud.

CHAPTER 3

Business Case for Skype for Business?

IN THIS CHAPTER

- Why Unified Communications
- Return on Investment (ROI)
- Why Skype for Business Server 2015 for Unified Communications

In this chapter we will explore common business cases for Skype for Business Server 2015. Before we cover the business cases for Skype for Business Server 2015, it is important to understand some fundamentals about *unified communications*, which has become a standard term in the Voice over IP (VoIP) industry. Unified communications (UC) is defined as the integration of real-time communication services such as instant messaging, Presence, telephony, video conferencing, data sharing, call control, and unified messaging (integrated voicemail, email, and fax). The term is pretty self-explanatory, as it aims to unify your existing communication tools over the IP network. A common approach to UC is to consolidate all communication tools into a single-vendor solution. This chapter outlines why many people believe that Microsoft Skype for Business Server 2015 is the go-to product for unified communications, and it covers the following topics:

Why Unified Communications—Gives an overview of why UC is beneficial to all types of organizations.

Return on Investment—Describes how you define ROI and how UC provides ROI.

Why Skype for Business Server 2015 for Unified Communications—Explains why, based on what we know about UC, Skype for Business Server 2015 is the ideal solution for UC.

Why Unified Communications

Communication that occurs in silos poorly replicates the richness of an in-person meeting. Individuals share ideas orally, visually, and in writing. The digital analogs are audio, video, application sharing, white boarding, IM collaborating on documents, and more. Communication that can seamless integrate all of these modalities comes closer to replicating that in-person interaction that sparks the best ideas and enables frictionless team collaboration. Skype for Business Server 2015 integrates these modalities to provide that level of remote collaboration.

There are four key components to UC:

- Instant messaging and Presence
- Web, audio, and video conferencing
- Enterprise telephony (traditional PBX functionality)
- Unified messaging

This section gives a brief description of each of the key UC components and explains why moving to a UC solution can be beneficial for organizations.

Instant Messaging and Presence

Instant messaging (IM) is the capability to communicate instantaneously between two or more people with text-based messages. Presence conveys the ability and willingness of a user to communicate. These two capabilities combine to be the most commonly used UC components in nearly every organization. Understanding how Enterprise IM and Presence evolved will help you understand why it is the core of any UC solution.

IM and presence has been around since the 1990s. You might remember ICQ and AOL Instant Messenger (AIM). A lot of companies followed suit, and soon there was an explosion of consumer IM providers, all with different protocols and clients. Consumers started to use these consumer IM services for business communications, which was very risky for organizations. Business users were using third-party tools that often were not secured in any form. Usage could not be tracked or controlled, and these tools were being used for day-to-day business on company PCs. When users were communicating through public networks, the exposure to malware increased, as well as the possibility of valuable company information leaving company PCs or being intercepted going over unencrypted traffic to public networks on the Internet. Because of those risks, there was a need to develop an enterprise-grade solution that would allow business users to securely communicate the way they were used to communicating outside of work.

In 1998, IBM launched Lotus Sametime, the first enterprise instant messaging product. Shortly after that, Microsoft released Exchange Instant Messaging, which would later evolve into Live Communications Server, then Office Communications Server, then Lync Server, before finally becoming what is Skype for Business to reflect the evolving integration of Lync Server with the Microsoft acquisition of Skype. IM has evolved into an integral business-critical communications tool for most organizations. In fact, many organizations consider IM more critical than email, and some consider it even more critical than dial tone.

Benefits of Instant Messaging and Presence

IM and Presence are the core of all UC solutions. These two features are often packaged together, and sometimes are simply referenced as only "instant messaging." IM is a feature most organizations will implement on day one of a UC deployment. Presence is one of the major drivers for UC, because it is at the core of providing an increase in productivity to end users. Presence introduces the real-time availability of users, which allows organizations to benefit from increased productivity through more efficient communications, particularly when face-to-face meetings are not possible or are inconvenient, as in the case of remote work scenarios. This benefit is best described in the scenario that follows.

Assume that Randy and Alex both work for CompanyABC. The company does not have a UC solution deployed today. Randy works in the Manhattan office and Alex works in the San Francisco office. If Randy wants to get in touch with Alex, he has two options: He can either send Alex an email or call him on the telephone. The problem starts here: Randy does not know when Alex will respond to that email or whether Alex will be around to answer the phone when he calls. Most likely, time will be wasted with missed calls and emails while Randy is attempting to reach Alex. This type of inefficient communication impacts their overall business productivity.

Now, introduce a UC solution that leverages IM and Presence. When Randy wants to communicate with Alex, he simply needs to look at his Presence indicator. If Alex shows as available, Randy can send an IM to Alex and ask whether he is available to talk. In some cases, an IM might be all that is needed to cover what Randy originally needed to talk to Alex about. If they need to communicate through voice, this is often a quick escalation in the same Skype for Business client. If Alex is showing as not available, Randy will know what the most efficient way to communicate with him is. Randy could tag Alex's contact for status alerts, which would alert Randy when Alex becomes available. Randy could also communicate either through an email or a phone call to voicemail, or Randy could simply wait until Alex is available to start an IM conversation.

The scenario just described clearly outlines why IM and Presence are critical components for UC and are major drivers for organizations to introduce a UC solution to their environment.

Web, Audio, and Video Conferencing

Conferencing is not new to most organizations; however, a unified conferencing experience remains relatively new despite growing adoption. Many organizations have web, audio, and video conferencing through separate third-party providers. For web and audio conferencing, organizations are typically charged a monthly fee per user in addition to a per-minute fee for using these services. For video conferencing, some organizations have large deployments of video conferencing equipment on their network, whereas others might be using a third-party hosted solution.

The services available in each of these areas can vary greatly. Some audio conferencing solutions are simply PSTN dial-in bridges, in which all users in a conference will dial a

PSTN phone number and be placed into a conference hosted by the provider. Some web conferencing solutions provide a web browser application for conferencing functionality, whereas others require a desktop application to be installed. Which service options are available to organizations is not entirely important for this section; however, it is important that these services are usually not interoperable with each other. This leads to a disjoined conferencing experience, and organizations are not able to realize the true benefits of conferencing.

Benefits of Web, Audio, and Video Conferencing

When an organization deploys a unified communications solution that supplies all conferencing workloads as part of the solution, the most recognized benefit is leveraging a single vendor for its conferencing solutions. This often leads to a consistent user experience as well as reduced costs to deploy and operate such a solution.

Providing users with a unified conferencing solution that is easy to use and that provides benefits to their productivity means that they are more likely to use it. Because end users are actually using this solution more often, the ROI is realized faster, and the organization benefits from increased productivity. In the "Unified Communications Return on Investment (ROI)" section, we explore these benefits in greater detail.

Enterprise Telephony

Enterprise telephony has evolved greatly over time. Most commonly this functionality is referenced using the term *private branch exchange* (PBX), which was first used when switchboard operators were manually operating company switchboards. It now is used to describe complex telephony switching systems of all types.

Enterprise telephony refers to the capability of making and receiving voice calls between users across the Public Switched Telephone Network (PSTN) and all the complex features that many organizations demand of a PBX system. These features can include the following:

- Auto attendants
- Automatic call distribution (ACD)
- Call accounting
- Call forwarding
- Call park
- Call pickup
- Call transfer
- Call waiting
- Music on hold
- Voicemail
- Emergency call handling (911 and E911)

The features listed are commonly used to determine whether a modern telephony system is capable of performing PBX features. Many new systems are not marketed as PBXs. They are called PBX replacements with UC functionality instead. Microsoft's Skype for Business Server PBX replacement is called Enterprise Voice.

Understanding the Benefits of Enterprise Telephony as Part of a UC Solution

Many UC solutions are designed to replace PBXs. Because of this, the benefits of introducing enterprise telephony as part of a UC solution is just that—to remove your PBXs. Many organizations have a PBX deployment with the following characteristics:

- There are many vendors across many locations.
- If the same vendor is used, there are many software versions.
- Each system has a separate maintenance contract.
- Each system has a local PSTN ingress/egress.
- Systems typically require specialized engineers to perform basic tasks.

When you introduce a UC solution like Microsoft Skype for Business Server, you integrate voice communication as another modality into the same client used for IM, application and desktop sharing, file transfer, and web meetings. The user experience is integrated, making it more efficient for users to collaborate seamlessly. This convenience enabled by Skype for Business Server spans the Microsoft Office suite and can be easily integrated into customer line of business applications.

Skype for Business Server eliminates the need to configure internal dial plans. By routing based on the SIP URI, all internal calls initiated by dialing the user's phone number are translated into the callee's SIP URI and routed that way. Administrators, for the most part, only need to concern themselves with configuring dial plans and routing to the PSTN via a gateway. This significantly simplifies the configuration of Enterprise Voice in Skype for Business Server 2015 compared to a traditional PBX environment.

Unified Messaging

The term *unified messaging* (UM) is used to describe the integration of different messaging systems. This can include email, fax, and voicemail. This integration typically means that you can access all of these messages from the same interface and on different devices. The most common use of unified messaging is to combine voicemail and fax into an organization's email system.

Microsoft Exchange Server UM is the voicemail solution for Skype for Business Server 2015. UM functionality was introduced in Exchange 2007. Exchange UM provides voicemail, Outlook voice access, and inbound fax functionality. Many other solutions typically deliver voicemail and fax messages to a user's Exchange email inbox as an email attachment, or through the use of an add-in. Modern UM systems offer functionality such as the following:

- **Interactive Voice Response (IVR)**—The capability for the caller to interact with the UM system through voice commands.
- **Find me, follow me**—The capability to ring other telephone numbers before leaving a voicemail.
- **Voicemail transcription**—The capability for the UM system to transcribe voice messages and provide voicemail preview as a text transcription in an email to the end user.
- **Secure voice messaging**—The ability for the UM system to encrypt voice messages and restrict the users who are able to listen to them.
- **Auto attendants**—Often leveraging IVR, UM systems are able to act as a receptionist, receiving calls coming into the organization and directing callers to end users.

Understanding the Benefits of Unified Messaging as Part of a UC Solution

Deploying unified messaging as part of a UC solution has similar benefits to deploying enterprise telephony. Many organizations today have a separate voicemail system deployed with each PBX. Introducing a single UM solution using Exchange UM can reduce costs as well as increase user productivity by providing enhanced features in a single interface.

Unified messaging is a key part of deploying UC in any organization. For many organizations, UM is considered "low-hanging fruit." Exchange UM can often be deployed rather quickly, replacing legacy voicemail systems, and integrate with Skype for Business Server 2015, resulting in a quicker ROI. Exchange UM provides additional benefits such as call logs, server-side conversation history, visual voicemail, calendar integration, and unified contact cards.

Unified Communications Return on Investment (ROI)

When organizations choose to deploy a new technology, there is always an investment that must be made. This investment is commonly referred to as a *capital investment* or *capital expenditure* (capex, for short).

Return on investment is the performance measurement of how an organization will see a benefit on the investment made. When a UC solution is deployed, there are various types of cost savings, and these savings make up the ROI. This next section outlines what investments an organization must make when deploying a full UC solution as well as the factors for realizing ROI.

Unified Communications Investments

Some organizations will have invested in UC prior to making the decision to move to a UC solution; however, it is still important to understand what these investments are and ultimately how they can be paid for (ROI).

Consider the Capital Investments

The term *capital investment* in terms of UC is described as the cost to deploy the solution. When UC is deployed, many components can contribute to a capital investment. Some organizations will categorize certain purchases. For example, some organizations will spread purchases out over five or more years, resulting in a distributed capital investment, or amortization. Regardless of how an organization chooses to categorize its purchases, the following expenses are most commonly referred to as "capital expense" (or capex):

- Licensing
- Data center hardware (servers, storage, and so on)
- Media gateways (PSTN gateways, Session Border Controller [SBC], and so on)
- End-user hardware (headsets, IP phones, cameras)
- Implementation costs (staff and professional consulting services)
- Network upgrade investments (hardware and other "setup" fees for network upgrades)

The capital investments will vary depending on the organization. Regardless of the size of the company, these investments will be significant.

Consider the Operating Expenses

In addition to capital expenses, organizations also have to consider an increase in certain operating expenses (or opex, for short). Although UC solutions reduce operating expenses overall, it is common for organizations deploying UC to increase IT operating expenses.

When organizations consider capital and operating expenses for UC, there will be a common theme: an increase in network costs. Network investments tend to make up the most significant capital and operating investment for organizations deploying UC. In a worst-case scenario, existing enterprise telephony is not IP based, and because of this, organizations are not equipped to run real-time voice over their IP networks. This results in a major investment in network expansion.

In an optimal scenario, the organization is already using an IP-based telephony system, and the new network investment must now account for increased usage such as conferencing and video.

The first scenario often requires a complete network overhaul. Multiprotocol Label Switching (MPLS) circuits and Internet connections must be increased, and that often comes with upgraded hardware. The second scenario involves network optimization. This is a combination of increasing bandwidth and optimizing connections to provide priority to UC traffic (quality of service).

Monitoring for quality of experience (QoE) and quality of service (QoS) should be a mandatory step in managing a successful rollout of Skype for Business Enterprise Voice.

Consider the Committed or "Dual-Run" Costs

One factor in calculating ROI that is often overlooked is committed costs. These costs can also be referred to as dual-running costs. In most scenarios, an organization cannot simply turn off a legacy system and immediately stop paying for it. Not only is there a transition period between systems, but there are often committed costs associated with a contract or lease. These committed costs can be attributed to hardware leases as well as support and service contracts. Many organizations will also choose to amortize capital investments over any number of years. Hardware investments must be depreciated before they can leave the books. Organizations typically have the following committed costs when deploying a new UC solution:

- **Investment depreciation**—Many organizations depreciate hardware over five years in order to spread out that capital investment.
- **Hardware lease costs**—Some organizations lease PBX hardware and PBX endpoints instead of purchasing them. These can have committed lease periods.
- **Dual-running solutions**—Costs to run legacy equipment and the new UC solution while migrating off the legacy solution to the new UC solution.
- **Support contracts**—Support contracts typically include a multiyear agreement between the organization and the vendor.

Before return on investment can be realized, these costs must be accounted for.

In summary, a UC solution is not purely cost savings. There will always be a significant investment to successfully deploy UC. However, the benefits of a true UC solution can lead to a rapid ROI, which ultimately makes UC worth the investment.

Audio Conferencing Return on Investment

It is common for many large organizations to spend millions of dollars a year on audio conferencing from a third-party provider. When deploying a UC solution that includes audio conferencing functionality, organizations tend to see a significant cost savings. This cost savings is typically the largest UC ROI factor for businesses.

When deploying a UC solution like Skype for Business Server 2015, organizations can bring all of their audio conferencing internally instead of using a third-party audio conferencing provider. Previously, organizations would pay per-minute audio conferencing charges for services that provided a dial-in conferencing bridge and audio conferencing. When this is brought in-house, those costs are reduced. The costs for audio conferencing are replaced by the costs to maintain the UC system and the inbound PSTN trunks for dial-in conferencing users. Many organizations are leveraging SIP trunks for this functionality to further reduce costs. On average, organizations will reduce their dial-in conferencing usage by 85%. That 85% reduction accounts for users who are now leveraging a UC client to join a conference using IP audio. The remaining 15% accounts for users who are still dialing in to the audio conference through the PSTN.

When the ROI of a UC solution is evaluated, it is important to not completely remove audio conferencing costs from the total cost of ownership (TCO). A small portion of the costs that are removed are replaced by new costs. This can include PSTN trunks, PSTN gateways, bandwidth, and additional server hardware if needed. Additionally, many organizations require the use of a third-party audio bridge for advanced conferencing scenarios. This functionality is often referred to as *managed conferencing*. These scenarios include operator-assisted meetings, or very large audio conferences with more than 1000 participants.

Realizing ROI with Centralized Telephony

As mentioned in earlier sections, most organizations have a distributed PBX system. When an organization is considering UC, one option is to replace the distributed PBX systems with a centralized UC telephony platform. The centralization of the telephony platform can have many benefits.

Reduced Hardware Footprint

When an organization chooses to centralize its telephony platform, the hardware footprint is greatly reduced. This can provide ROI by reducing hardware purchase costs, hardware maintenance costs, and facility run costs.

Reduced Support Costs

Often when organizations move to a centralized telephony environment, the costs to support the environment are much smaller than the costs of a distributed system. If support of the legacy telephony solution was outsourced before, the outsourcing contract might be reduced. If this was completely supported by internal staff, staffing can often be reduced or allocated to other tasks.

SIP Trunk Opportunity

Using SIP trunks is a relatively new trend in telephony. They provide the capability to purchase PSTN services and have them delivered over IP connections rather than traditional T1/E1 PRI connections. Although SIP trunks do not require a centralized deployment model, a centralized telephony deployment does introduce the opportunity to deploy SIP trunks more easily. The combination of centralized telephony and SIP trunks is ideal for realizing cost savings.

Many organizations have a vast number of PRI connections delivering PSTN services. The problem with PRIs is that they come in only one size (23 voice channels per trunk in the U.S.). SIP trunks allow organizations to have more control over how many channels are purchased. In simple terms, if you were a mid-size organization that needed 40 voice channels to support your call load, this would result in two PRIs. Those two PRIs would require two T1 connections. The end result is double the cost for a very small capacity increase.

These are the three ways in which SIP trunks allow you to reduce your PSTN costs:

- **Reduction in the number of voice channels**—Organizations that deploy SIP trunks typically see a 40% reduction in the number of actual voice channels, because the capacity is much easier to predict and control. This reduction in voice channels also comes with a cheaper, more flexible delivery method: IP. Many times this is delivered through an MPLS connection from the provider directly to the organization's data center, but there are services that target small- and mid-market customers that also deliver these services over the Internet.
- **Shared usage**—Organizations can reduce their voice channels even more in a centralized telephony model. When the PSTN trunks are centralized, they can be shared across all of your sites. This works very well in organizations spread across multiple time zones. In fact, SIP trunks can be optimized based on time zones to provide capacity where it is needed, resulting in a large amount of cost savings.
- **Flexibility**—SIP trunks introduce the ability to increase or decrease capacity as needs change. Time-division multiplexing (TDM) connections often require additional physical line configurations to accommodate capacity changes. With SIP trunks, this simply becomes a matter of provisioning by the provider in many cases. SIP trunk providers are also able to offer advanced functionality, including failover routing as well as multiple area codes and international numbers on the same connection, something that TDM trunks are simply not able to do.

The areas previously described are the most common areas in which organizations can realize cost savings and ROI from deploying a UC telephony solution. The level at which ROI is realized will depend on how willing the organization is to adopt the centralized and shared model for the telephony infrastructure.

Productivity Improvements

When any UC solution is being introduced, an increase in productivity is one major selling point. How this increase in productivity influences ROI can be more difficult to calculate. Productivity increases are often referred to as soft *costs*, meaning that you cannot put a definitive dollar amount next to them. However, it is practical to make educated estimates based off of common scenarios that result in productivity increases. After the solution is deployed and used, it is possible to monitor usage and identify productivity cost savings.

A key scenario in which productivity increases can translate directly to dollar amounts is the task of checking voicemail. When you consider the process for listening to voicemail on a legacy voicemail system, it becomes clear how tedious this process is. Assume that you have a billable resource. This resource makes the company money at $300 per hour. If it takes that person three minutes per day to listen to his voicemail, it seems to be a small cost (under $2 per day). However, you must now multiply that number by all resources in your organization, say 10,000 users. That quickly turns into $20,000 dollars per day, or $100,000 per week.

When evaluating UC ROI, organizations should also consider time that is wasted for travel. Many organizations have resources that must travel to and from the office, as well as to and from clients. If you were to use similar logic as that used previously with a resource that can make the company $300 per hour, removing that travel time and replacing it with billable work will save the company money. Many organizations will charge customers travel time for such resources; however, if a business no longer has to charge for travel because moneymaking resources can work remotely with UC, that organization is now more attractive to do business with.

UC presence makes it possible for users to spend less time on common tasks and allows users to increase productivity in many other areas. When users have the real-time availability of their peers, their communications are more efficient, less time is lost, and similar logic to that used previously can be applied to calculate soft cost savings.

Reduced Travel Costs

The preceding section mentions cost savings due to travel reduction. That section outlines the increased productivity and potential "billability" of users based on less travel. This next section explains how organizations can reduce their overall travel costs.

Many organizations with a global footprint spend millions of dollars per year on travel between their sites. Today, even completely U.S.-based organizations require their employees to travel between sites. In recent years, Telepresence video was introduced as a way to reduce those travel costs. However, the complexity and cost of Telepresence systems has resulted in many organizations not realizing travel cost savings. A new and more reliable trend for travel cost reduction is to deploy a common UC solution across the organization that targets each and every end user.

Not all in-person meetings can be replaced with a conference, even if HD video is involved, but the industry is realizing that the majority of these trips can be replaced with a highly intuitive collaboration experience. When an organization empowers its end users with a tool that allows them to seamlessly collaborate with peers across the world, money is saved.

The process to calculate this savings varies across the different types of organizations. This is another cost that is hard to place a solid number on before the product is deployed and used for some time. However, as with the productivity increase, you can take estimates for common situations. Consider the travel expenses and the lost time associated with traveling for meetings and then estimate the savings when these meetings are moved to a UC conference.

There are also many tools in the industry that allow organizations to monitor the usage of their UC systems and then use that data to calculate estimated cost savings. Look for these tools to help you back up your original cost-saving estimates and show true contribution to the UC ROI.

Office Space Reduction

Another interesting trend in the industry is a cost reduction related to real estate. Many organizations are exploring the idea of a "modern work space." These modern work spaces typically are less formal and provide more of a shared environment. The idea is that fewer users will actually be in the office, and therefore you can reduce the size of your offices, or remove some offices altogether. It is absolutely critical to have a true UC solution deployed to allow for this workspace transformation. Many organizations can save millions by moving to modern work spaces and remote work from home, thus reducing their real estate footprint.

This approach is not typically started with UC, but is driven by UC. In my experience, organizations that are exploring the benefits of this solution have already been working on this for quite some time. The amount of money that can be saved varies greatly across regions and business verticals.

Why Skype for Business Server 2015 for Unified Communications

Now that you know what makes up a UC solution and how UC can drive cost savings in an organization, let's talk about why you should choose Skype for Business Server 2015 as a UC solution.

With Skype for Business Server 2015, organizations are given more deployment options, greater resiliency, and enhanced voice, video, and web conferencing features. Skype for Business Server 2015 introduces advanced UC features into a single platform, with a single client software. This section outlines why Skype for Business Server 2015 is the superior UC solution in the market.

Software-Based Unified Communications

The key to a true UC solution is software. Without intuitive, user-friendly software, a UC solution cannot be successfully deployed. When compared on paper, the UC solutions from companies such as Microsoft, Cisco, Avaya, and ShorTel have nearly the same features. These solutions can perform the functionality that any organization needs for UC. The key difference between Microsoft and the competition is the software. If you look at the list of companies, which one is a software company and not a hardware company? Microsoft.

Hardware vendors are getting better at creating software, either through acquisition or through experience with development. However, these companies are playing catch-up with Microsoft. Since Microsoft Lync Server 2010, all UC functionality has been available in a single client UI. Even in the latest versions of Cisco's UC suite, functionality is spread across multiple applications. The complexity that this introduces to end users is a major deterrent to the successful deployment of UC.

For organizations to realize the full benefits of UC, there must be a high rate of adoption. Users are less likely to take advantage of a UC solution that is not user friendly. Microsoft is the only company that can provide a truly unified communications experience and allow organizations to reach their full potential with UC. Cisco is typically the biggest competitor of Microsoft Skype for Business Server 2015. The basic scenario that follows outlines the differences between Microsoft and other vendors' UC solutions, including Cisco. These differences can have a major impact on user productivity and overall user satisfaction. User satisfaction is critical to the success of UC deployments.

When you are using Microsoft Skype for Business Server 2015, not only are all modalities (IM, audio, video, and sharing) provided in a single application, but the conferencing experience for these modalities is in the same application. When you want to hold a conference, that conference is held in Skype for Business Server 2015. If you are in a peer-to-peer session and want to escalate to a conference, you can simply turn that call into a conference in Skype for Business Server 2015. Cisco, on the other hand, leverages two applications: Jabber for peer-to-peer functionality and WebEx for conferencing. This leads to two separate applications for end users to learn, resulting in a disjointed experience when escalating between peer-to-peer and conference. When you want to turn a peer-to-peer session into a conference, a web page to the WebEx site must be opened. This is where the problem starts for end-user productivity.

In addition to the more intuitive user experience provided in Skype for Business, the integration with Microsoft Office applications cannot be overlooked. Microsoft Office is the primary business application for many end users across the world. Having communication capabilities integrated into your business applications is a major factor for driving usage and enhancing productivity. Microsoft Skype for Business integrates UC capabilities into Office applications, reducing the amount of effort required for end users to collaborate with their peers. Although other vendors can leverage APIs to show presence and allow click-to-call capabilities from Microsoft Outlook, they cannot integrate at a deeper level. Examples of this include the following:

- **SharePoint skill search**—The capability to search SharePoint and view results based on skills and other user information, without leaving the Skype for Business client.
- **Exchange distribution list expansion**—The capability to add Exchange Server distribution lists directly to the Skype for Business client contact list as contact groups. These lists will query information directly from Exchange Server, so users do not have to worry about adding new contacts manually.
- **Exchange integration**—The Skype for Business client has the capability to display out-of-office messages that are configured by the user in the Outlook client and stored in Exchange Server.
- **Conversation history search in Outlook**—The Skype for Business client has the capability to store conversation history in the user's Exchange mailbox. Users can also search this conversation history in the Skype for Business client as well as in Outlook or the Outlook Web App with their mail.

The preceding examples show certain areas that competitors simply do not provide integration for. Office, SharePoint, and Exchange are deployed in nearly every organization, and that is why these features are important.

In addition to integrating with other Microsoft applications, Skype for Business Server 2015 also allows for easy integration with other line-of-business applications. One major benefit to Skype for Business Server 2015 is the development platform it is built on. The software APIs for the client and server are available to developers and are currently heavily utilized for many custom solutions. The simplest form of this development is integrating functionality, such as Presence and click to call, into line-of-business applications. Many organizations have also taken advantage of the Skype for Business Server APIs to build custom solutions that enhance business processes. This concept is known as *communications-enabled business processes* (CEBPs) and is a major differentiator in the market. This ecosystem, which is open and "partner driven," has led many organizations to be more successful with UC than they ever could have imagined.

In summary, a UC deployment relies heavily on the software experience that is provided to users. Although UC includes telephony, and IP phones are important to telephony, the true value of UC is seen through the software application providing anywhere access and collaboration. Microsoft Skype for Business Server 2015 is a superior choice for UC because it is a software-based UC platform.

Lower Total Cost of Ownership

Lower Total Cost of Ownership (TCO) refers to the cost of purchasing, licensing, deploying, and maintaining an equipment (in our case, the equipment is a telephony solution) over the lifetime of the solution's use. Various solutions have components that are cheaper than others, but what is really important is TCO. Just because one software license is cheaper doesn't mean that the overall cost to purchase and run a solution is cheaper. Microsoft claims a lower TCO than the competition.

Microsoft offers key advantages that contribute to a lower TCO:

- **Hardware flexibility**—Skype for Business Server 2015 allows organizations to choose the server platform as well as the endpoints to be used. This allows organizations to deploy whatever server hardware is right for them, at the right price. This includes the capability to virtualize across the different platforms available to organizations. Other UC systems will leverage IP phones as the primary endpoint. Not only does Microsoft offer an IP phone solution through certified partners (Polycom, AudioCodes, and others) that is cheaper than the competition, but has high-quality headsets available at low prices. Many Skype for Business–optimized wired headsets are under $50, and that does not include bulk purchase discount.
- **Leveraging Microsoft investments**—Skype for Business Server 2015 leverages Exchange for Unified Messaging and Active Directory for identity management, domain name service (DNS), and public key infrastructure (PKI). Leveraging the customer's existing infrastructure helps drive a lower cost of investment and management because user identity is not dispersed across multiple independent identity systems.
- **Conferencing cost savings**—Skype for Business Server 2015 offers a great level of cost savings on audio conferencing. When directly compared, the architecture and, sometimes, the additional licensing required will make Microsoft up to 50% less expensive than the competition in this area.
- **Rapid ROI**—The fact that Skype for Business Server 2015 is an integrated solution, as opposed to other vendors' solutions, allows organizations to realize ROI much faster than when deploying a competing UC solution.

The factors just described contribute to Skype for Business Server 2015 having a lower TCO when compared to the competition.

Deployment Flexibility

The statement "Give us speed where we need it" highlights a common theme among many organizations evaluating Skype for Business Server 2015 and other UC solutions. Deployment flexibility is a key area in which Microsoft provides greater value than the competition through Skype for Business Server 2015. The following points highlight some of the aspects where Skype for Business Server 2015 provides greater value as a solution in a Microsoft-centric infrastructure:

- **Integration with existing systems**—Microsoft believes in integrating with existing systems and augmenting functionality through deep integration, not ripping and replacing. This allows organizations to utilize their existing investments to their full potential, and then replace when necessary.
- **Hybrid solutions**—Microsoft allows organizations to leverage cloud solutions from Office 365 to integrate with their on-premises Skype for Business Server 2015 infrastructure, creating hybrid deployments. Hybrid deployments integrate the Skype for Business experience whether users are homed on-premises or on Office 365. In the same timeframe of the Skype for Business Server 2015 release, Office 365 offers the following advantages:
  - **Skype Meeting Broadcast**—This allows organizations to host very large meetings in the cloud for up to 10,000 participants. Skype for Business Server 2015 and Lync Server 2013 support meetings with up to 1,000 participants with a dedicated Front End pool configuration.
    - **Cloud PBX with PSTN calling**—Office 365 users can make and receive calls from the PSTN without using an on-premises PSTN gateway.
    - **PSTN conferencing**—Participants can join a Skype meeting hosted on Office 365 from the PSTN.
- **"Speed where you need it"**—Microsoft allows organizations to choose at which speed they deploy their solution. If an organization has a desire to rapidly deploy the solution, it can easily be done. However, Microsoft does not force organizations to rip and replace or into upgrade scenarios. Many organizations will treat the core capabilities of UC as a more immediate need (IM, peer-to-peer A/V, conferencing) and then choose to opportunistically deploy enterprise telephony. With the features and flexibility of the on-premises and Microsoft cloud solutions, organizations can truly move at whatever speed they need to, and can be successful with their UC deployment.

Remote Access and Federation

To provide the best ROI, organizations must be able to offer UC solutions to end users anywhere, on any connection, at any time. More and more organizations are adopting the "living on the net" motto, meaning that their users must be able to do their job seamlessly from any Internet connection. Microsoft Skype for Business Server 2015 is without a doubt the superior solution for remote access in the UC industry. Microsoft Skype for Business Server 2015 was built with the Internet in mind. Not only does it provide users with all functionality over the Internet, securely, without a VPN, but with the acquisition of Skype, the SILK media codec, which provides a superior audio quality used by millions across the Internet, has been integrated into Skype for Business Server 2015.

Many organizations can mistakenly discount the importance of choosing a UC solution that was developed for the Internet. Traditional IP telephony relied only on the LAN/WAN networks that were controlled by the organization. However, UC cannot be restricted to the same network conditions as traditional IP telephony. For UC to be successful in an organization, it must provide access to all functionality, from any connection, on any device. This is how organizations will see increased usage of the solution and, ultimately, rapid ROI.

Following on the remote access story, federation with other organizations is a trend in UC technology. Microsoft Skype for Business Server 2015 offers organizations the capability to communicate seamlessly with other organizations that are running Lync Server or Skype for Business Server 2015, as well as communicate with consumers on the public networks (Skype). Although competitors can provide IM and Presence federation to other organizations, no other solution provides Presence, IM, audio, video, and conferencing federation natively like Microsoft Skype for Business Server 2015 does. The capability to seamlessly collaborate with business partners and customers (Skype) makes many organizations treat federation as a critical requirement.

CAUTION

When deciding between UC products, organizations should dig deeper than the "check box" for functionality. Federation is a good example: Cisco allows XMPP federation to other XMPP systems for just IM and Presence functionality. An XMPP gateway is required on both ends to provide this federation. In Skype for Business Server 2015, XMPP and SIP federation are native to the Edge Server.

Skype federation was introduced in Lync Server 2013, and Skype for Business Server 2015 expands this integration to include directory search and video to the millions of current Skype users around the world. This includes both businesses and consumers, which means a user can search the Skype network for another user from within their Skype for Business client and establish a video session with them. The flexibility this provides organizations for establishing communications with partners and customers is a feature that many users cannot live without. Some critics will discount the importance of UC federation over Internet connections. We are definitely not at the point where federation is going to replace the PSTN; however, many people do believe that this is the path the industry is going down.

Summary

IM and Presence provide organizations with increased user productivity, and they are the key to providing more efficient communications across organizations.

Web, audio, and video conferencing allow organizations to increase productivity, reduce costs, and provide users with a more immersive collaboration experience, no matter where they are in the world.

Enterprise telephony allows organizations to the break the mold of traditional, distributed telephony systems. Organizations can realize major cost savings by centralizing enterprise telephony.

Unified messaging allows organizations to enhance the traditional messaging capabilities that users are stuck with. By introducing UM, organizations can reduce costs and increase user productivity.

Organizations that choose to invest in unified communications are able to achieve return on investment in five key areas:

Audio conferencing—Many organizations are paying millions in audio conferencing fees per year. UC allows organizations to change their audio conferencing model and see significant cost savings.

Centralized telephony—Organizations are able to reduce their telephony hardware footprint, reduce their support costs, and introduce the opportunity to deploy centralized SIP trunking.

Productivity—UC introduces productivity increases that can be translated into real dollar amounts.

Travel costs—UC functionality and UC conferencing allow organizations to reduce travel costs and become more attractive business partners.

Real estate—UC allows organizations to explore reducing real estate footprint through the use of modern workspaces.

Finally, Microsoft Skype for Business Server 2015 is considered by many to be the preferred UC solution for organizations large and small for the following reasons:

Software-based UC—Microsoft is a software company that develops software targeted at the end-user experience. The end-user experience is absolutely critical for UC and requires a truly software-based UC approach, which Microsoft Skype for Business Server 2015 follows.

Lower TCO—Microsoft has proven to have a lower total cost of ownership than the major competitors in the industry.

Deployment flexibility—Not only does Microsoft Skype for Business Server 2015 integrate with an existing solution by adding value instead of replacing the system, but the combination of cloud and on-premises services allows organizations to choose at which pace they want to deploy UC.

Remote access and federation—The capability to communicate from anywhere, on any device, to nearly anyone in the world is thought by many to be one of the most important features of UC. Microsoft is the leading UC provider when it comes to remote access and federation.

CHAPTER 4

Skype for Business Server 2015 Front End Server

IN THIS CHAPTER

- ▶ Front End Server Overview
- ▶ Active Directory Preparation
- ▶ Front End Server Installation
- ▶ Front End Server Configuration
- ▶ Front End Server Administration
- ▶ Front End Server Troubleshooting
- ▶ Front End Server Best Practices

Skype for Business Server 2015 has various server roles. These can be combined in a number of ways to produce a myriad of architecture options. Even the collocation of services for a given role can be split out for added flexibility.

The Front End role in Skype for Business Server 2015 is similar in architecture to a Lync Server 2013 Front End. If you are upgrading from Lync Server 2010, there are three significant architecture changes related to the Front End Server role that should be understood. First of all, the AV Conferencing role can no longer be split out as a separate role. It *always* exists on the Front End Server. Next, on a Standard Edition Server, the Persistent Chat role can be collocated with the Front End Server. Finally, the Monitoring and Archiving roles, if deployed, are also now always collocated on the Front End Servers. This is true for Standard Edition servers and Enterprise Edition pools.

As in previous versions, a single Front End Server and multiple Front End Servers are organized into logical pools. A Standard Edition Server exists as the only server in a pool, whereas multiple Enterprise Edition Servers can exist in a pool to provide redundancy and scalability. In an Enterprise Edition pool, HTTP traffic should still be load-balanced by a dedicated load balancing solution; however, other Skype for Business services are often load-balanced via DNS. This architecture moves complex traffic (SIP and media) off of load balancers traditionally designed solely for HTTP traffic and simplifies the overall design.

NOTE

Assuming that all clients are Lync 2010 or higher, DNS load balancing is the preferred method, leaving only HTTP services to a hardware load balancer.

This chapter highlights the full life cycle of the Front End Server role. Because the Front End Server is deployed first, this chapter also reviews the steps necessary to prepare Active Directory. Then it moves on to the installation of the Standard and Enterprise Editions of the Front End Server role, followed by configuration and administration. Finally, the chapter concludes with troubleshooting and best practices.

Front End Server Installation

Microsoft Skype for Business Server 2015 heavily leverages Active Directory. This results in tight integration across the Microsoft stack, including Microsoft Exchange Server and Microsoft SharePoint Server. However, first Active Directory must be prepared before installation can begin. All the Active Directory preparation steps can be performed in either the Deployment Wizard GUI or the Skype for Business Server Management Shell, a customized version of PowerShell. This chapter reviews both methods.

The first step is to ensure that your Active Directory environment meets the minimum requirements for Skype for Business Server 2015. The requirements are outlined here:

- All domain controllers in the forest where Skype for Business Server 2015 will be deployed must be Windows Server 2003 SP2 or higher.
- All domains where you deploy Skype for Business Server 2015 must have a functional level of Windows 2003 native or higher.
- The functional level for the forest must be Windows 2003 native or higher.

After the Active Directory prerequisites have been met, the next step is to extend the Active Directory schema to support Skype for Business Server 2015. The schema-preparation process adds new classes and attributes to Active Directory that are required for Skype for Business Server 2015. This process must be run as a user that is a member of the Schema Admins group and is a local administrator on the server that holds the Schema Master FSMO role.

NOTE

To run the preparation steps from another domain member server other than the Schema Master, ensure that the remote registry service is running and the appropriate registry key is set on the Schema Master. In addition, the Active Directory Remote Server Administration Tools (AD DS) feature must be installed on the server where the preparation steps will run.

Active Directory Schema Extension in Skype for Business Server 2015

To extend the Active Directory schema using the Skype for Business Server Deployment Wizard, as shown in Figure 4.1, follow these steps:

1. From the Skype for Business Server 2015 installation media, run `Setup.exe`.

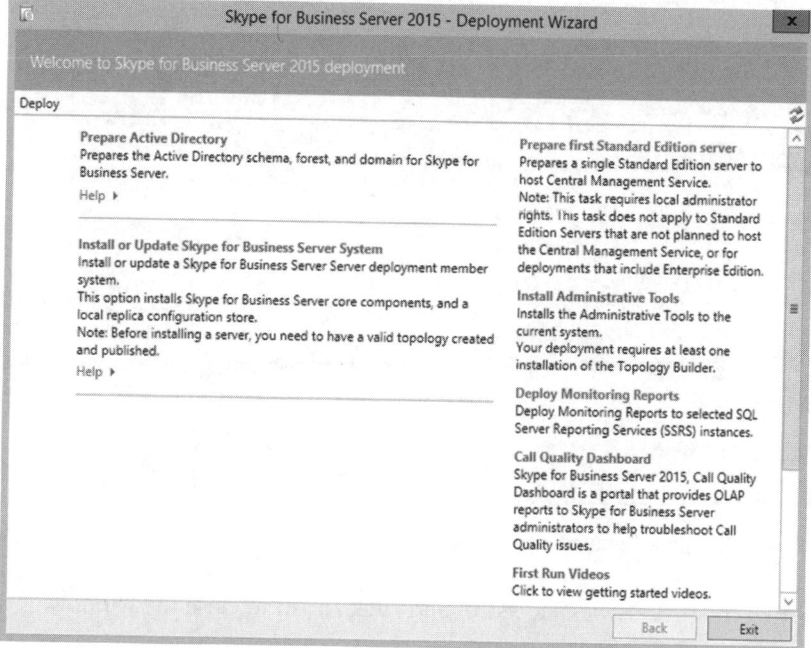

FIGURE 4.1 Skype for Business Server 2015 Deployment Wizard.

2. Click Prepare Active Directory.
3. For Step 1: Prep Schema, click Run.

4. At the Prepare Schema screen, click Next. You'll see the Management Shell command that is being executed, as shown in Figure 4.2.

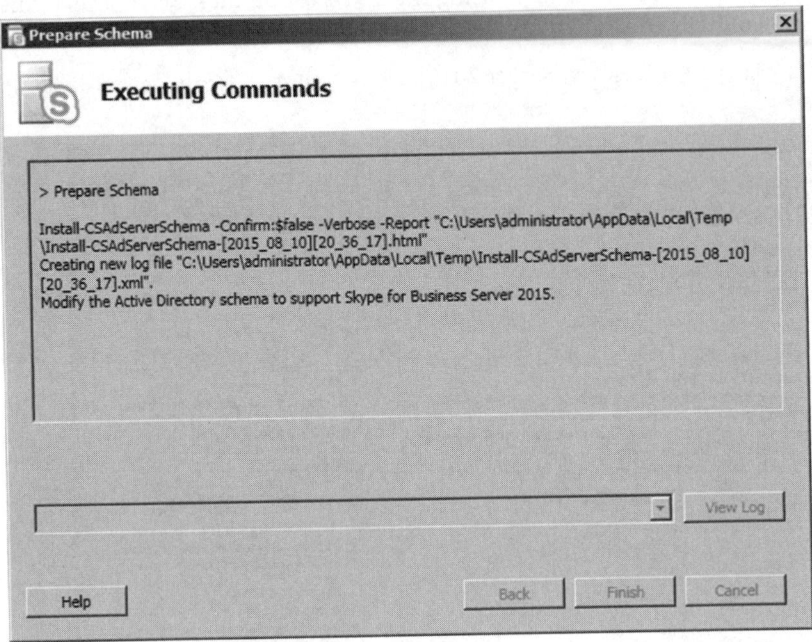

FIGURE 4.2 Prepare Schema command.

5. Ensure that the process was successful and click Finish to close the window.
6. Ensure that the information has replicated to all domain controllers before continuing to the next step.

NOTE

If upgrading from Lync Server 2013, you may notice that the Prepare Active Directory task already has a green check mark. This is because there are no additional Active Directory changes or objects created for Skype for Business Server 2015. This is expected, and you can move on to the "Installation" section of this chapter.

To prepare the Active Directory schema using the Skype for Business Server Management Shell, open the shell and run the `Install-CsAdServerSchema` cmdlet. The proper syntax for the command is `Install-CsAdServerSchema -LDF <full directory path where the ldf files are located>`. Here's an example:

```
Install-CsAdServerSchema -LDF "C:\Program Files\Skype for Business Server
➥2015\Deployment\Setup"
```

The Skype for Business Server schema-extension process adds the following attributes to Active Directory:

- **msExchUserHoldPolicies**—Shared with Exchange 2013 and will already be in place if the schema has already been extended for Exchange 2013. It is a multivalue attribute that holds identifiers for user hold policies applied to a given user.
- **msRTCSIP-UserRoutingGroupId**—Defines the SIP routing group ID. The SIP routing group ID defines which Front End Server a user will register to.
- **msRTCSIP-MirrorBackEndServer**—Used to store the information for the mirrored SQL Server backend used by the Front End pool.

Additionally, Active Directory Classes are updated as shown in Table 4.1.

TABLE 4.1 Active Directory Classes Modified by Skype for Business Server 2015

Class	Change	Class or Attribute
User	Add: mayContain	ProxyAddresses
	Add: mayContain	msRTCSIP-UserRoutingGroupId
Contact	Add: mayContain	ProxyAddresses
	Add: mayContain	msRTCSIP-UserRoutingGroupId
Mail-Recipient	Add: mayContain	msExchUserHoldPolicies
msRTCSIP-GlobalTopologySetting	Add: mayContain	msRTCSIP-MirrorBackEndServer

Active Directory Forest Preparation in Skype for Business Server 2015

The next step is to prepare the Active Directory forest. This process must be run by a user of the enterprise admins group or domain admins for the root domain. Forest preparation creates global objects and sets the appropriate permissions and groups to complete the installation process. Note that in a new deployment, the global settings are automatically stored in the Configuration partition. If you are upgrading from an older version of Lync Server, you can still store the settings in the System container, as was standard during previous versions' installation.

The Deployment Wizard should still be up from the preceding set of steps. If not, run the Skype for Business Server Deployment Wizard and it will pick up where you left off. Follow these steps to prepare the forest:

1. For Step 3: Prepare Current Forest, click Run.
2. At the Prepare Forest screen, click Next. You'll see the Management Shell command that is being executed, as shown in Figure 4.3.

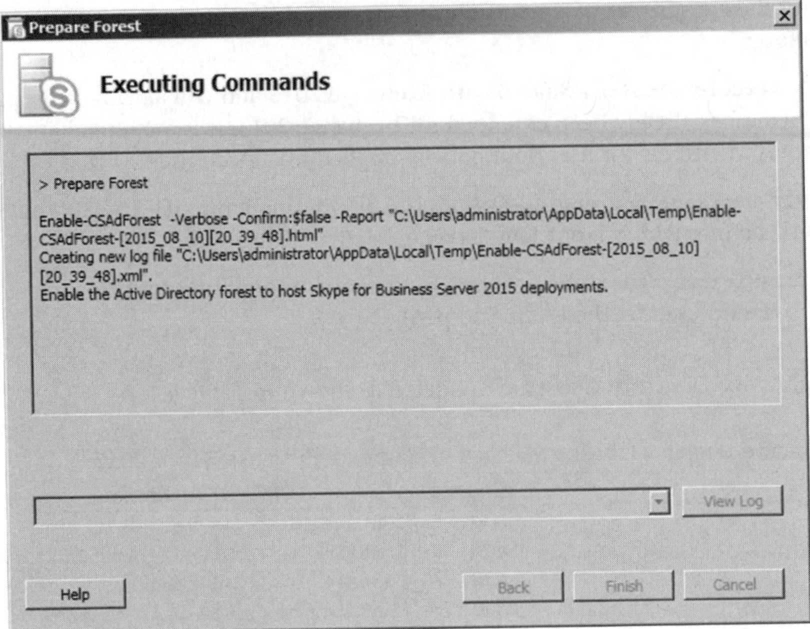

FIGURE 4.3 Prepare Forest command.

3. Ensure that the process was successful and click Finish to close the window.
4. Ensure that the information has replicated to all domain controllers before continuing to the next step.

To prepare the Active Directory forest using the Lync Server Management Shell, open the shell and run the `Enable-CsAdForest` cmdlet. The proper syntax for the command is `Enable-CsAdForest -GroupDomain <FQDN of the domain to create the universal groups>`. Here's an example:

```
Enable-CsAdForest -GroupDomain skypeunleashed.com
```

Following is a list of Active Directory Administration groups created by the preparation processes. They are referenced throughout the book and are good to be familiar with.

Service groups:

- **`RTCHSUniversalServices`**—Includes service accounts used to run Front End Server and allows servers read/write access to Lync and Skype for Business Server global settings and Active Directory user objects.
- **`RTCComponentUniversalServices`**—Includes service accounts used to run conferencing servers, web services, Mediation Server, Archiving Server, and Monitoring Server.

- **`RTCProxyUniversalServices`**—Includes service accounts used to run Lync and Skype for Business Server Edge Servers.
- **`RTCUniversalConfigReplicator`**—Includes Lync and Skype for Business servers that participate in Central Management Store (CMS) replication.
- **`RTCSBAUniversalServices`**—Grants read-only permission to Lync and Skype for Business Server settings and allows for the configuration of survivable branch appliances (SBAs) and servers (SBSs).

Administration groups:

- **`RTCUniversalServerAdmins`**—Allows members to manage server and pool settings.
- **`RTCUniversalUserAdmins`**—Allows members to manage user settings and move users from one server or pool to another.
- **`RTCUniversalReadOnlyAdmins`**—Allows members to read server, pool, and user settings.

Infrastructure groups:

- **`RTCUniversalGlobalWriteGroup`**—Grants write access to global setting objects for Lync and Skype for Business Server.
- **`RTCUniversalGlobalReadOnlyGroup`**—Grants read-only access to global setting objects for Lync and Skype for Business Server.
- **`RTCUniversalUserReadOnlyGroup`**—Grants read-only access to Lync and Skype for Business Server user settings.
- **`RTCUniversalServerReadOnlyGroup`**—Grants read-only access to Lync and Skype for Business Server settings. This group does not have access to pool-level settings, only to settings specific to an individual server.
- **`RTCUniversalSBATechnicians`**—Grants read-only permission to the Lync and Skype for Business Server configuration, and members of this group are placed in the local administrator group of the survivable branch appliance during installation.

Forest preparation then adds service and administration groups to the appropriate infrastructure groups, as described here:

- `RTCUniversalServerAdmins` is added to `RTCUniversalGlobalReadOnlyGroup`, `RTCUniversalGlobalWriteGroup`, `RTCUniversalServerReadOnlyGroup`, and `RTCUniversalUserReadOnlyGroup`.

4

- RTCUniversalUserAdmins, RTCSBAUniversalServices, and RTCUniversalSBATechnicians are added as members of RTCUniversalReadOnlyAdmins.
- RTCHSUniversalServices, RTCComponentUniversalServices, and RTCUniversalReadOnlyAdmins are added as members of RTCUniversalGlobalReadOnlyGroup, RTCUniversalServerReadOnlyGroup, and RTCUniversalUserReadOnlyGroup.

Forest preparation creates the following role-based access control (RBAC) groups:

- CSAdministrator
- CSArchivingAdministrator
- CSHelpDesk
- CSLocationAdministrator
- CSPersistentChatAdministrator
- CSResponseGroupAdministrator
- CSResponseGroupManager
- CSServerAdministrator
- CSUserAdministrator
- CSViewOnlyAdministrator
- CSVoiceAdministrator

Forest preparation grants the RTCUniveralGlobalReadOnlyGroup the following public access control entries (ACEs):

- Read root domain System Container (not inherited)
- Read configuration's DisplaySpecifiers container (not inherited)

Additionally, forest preparation performs the following tasks on the Configuration container, under the Configuration naming context:

- Adds the entry {AB255F23-2DBD-4bb6-891D-38754AC280EF} for the RTC property page under the adminContextMenu and adminPropertyPages attributes of the language display specifier for users, contacts, and InetOrgPersons (for example, CN=user-Display,CN=409,CN=DisplaySpecifiers).

- Adds an `RTCPropertySet` object of type `controlAccessRight` under `Extended-Rights` that applies to the User and Contact classes.
- Adds an `RTCUserSearchPropertySet` object of type `controlAccessRight` under `Extended-Rights` that applies to the User, Contact, OU, and DomainDNS classes.
- Adds `msRTCSIP-PrimaryUserAddress` under the `extraColumns` attribute of each language organizational unit (OU) display specifier (for example, `CN=organizationalUnit-Display,CN=409,CN=DisplaySpecifiers`) and copies the values of the `extraColumns` attribute of the default display (for example, `CN=default-Display, CN=409,CN=DisplaySpecifiers`).
- Adds `msRTCSIP-PrimaryUserAddress`, `msRTCSIP-PrimaryHomeServer`, and `msRTCSIP-UserEnabled` filtering attributes under the `attributeDisplayNames` attribute of each language display specifier for Users, Contacts, and InetOrgPerson objects (for example, in English: `CN=user-Display,CN=409,CN=DisplaySpecifiers`).

Active Directory Domain Preparation in Skype for Business Server 2015

The final step is to prepare the Active Directory domain or domains. You'll need to run this in every domain where you plan to deploy Skype for Business 2015 servers or host user accounts that will be enabled for Skype for Business. This step adds to universal groups the necessary ACEs (access control entries). As in the two previous steps, this can be done through the Skype for Business Server Deployment Wizard or the Skype for Business Server Management Shell.

Using the Deployment Wizard, perform the following steps. Note that if you closed the Deployment Wizard, you'll need to run it again.

1. For Step 5: Prepare Current Domain, click Run.
2. At the Prepare Domain screen, click Next. You'll see the Management Shell command that is being executed, as shown in Figure 4.4.

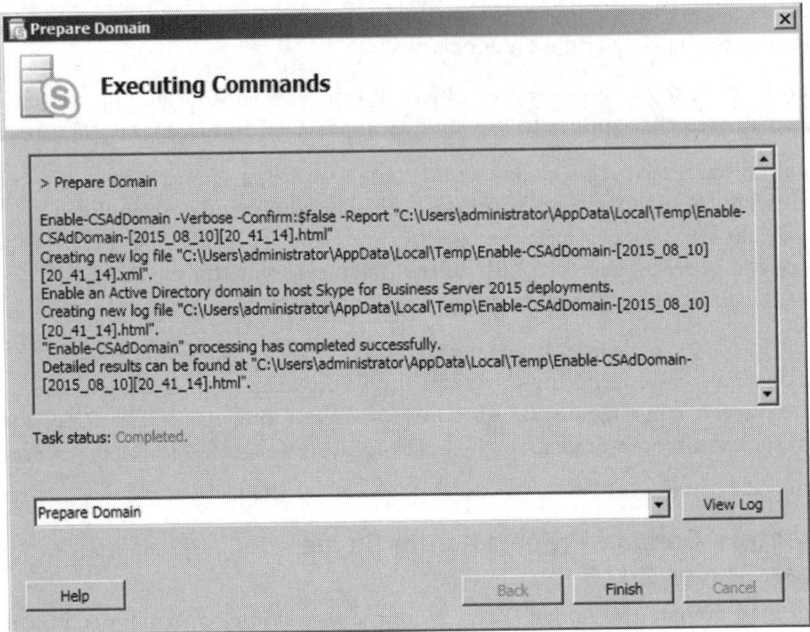

FIGURE 4.4 Prepare Domain command.

3. Ensure that the process was successful and click Finish to close the window.
4. Ensure that the information has replicated to all domain controllers before continuing to the next step.

To prepare an Active Directory domain using the Lync Server Management Shell, open the shell and run the `Enable-CsAdDomain` cmdlet. The proper syntax for the command is `Enable-CsAdDomain -Domain <current domain FQDN> -GroupDomain <FQDN of the domain where the Universal groups were created>`. Here's an example:

```
Enable-CsAdDomain -Domain companyabc.com -GroupDomain skypeunleashed.com
```

During Domain preparation, several access control entries (ACEs) are applied to grant privileges to several of the Administration groups created during the forest preparation process. All ACEs are applied on the domain root and inherited unless otherwise indicated in Table 4.2.

TABLE 4.2 Active Directory ACEs Applied to the Domain Root by Skype for Business Server 2015

ACE	RTCUniveralUser Read-OnlyGroup	RTCUniversalServer Read-OnlyGroup	RTCUniversal UserAdmins	RTCUniversal Services	Authenticated Users
Read Container (not inherited)	**Yes**	**Yes**	No	No	No
Read User PropertySet User-Account-Restrictions	**Yes**	No	No	No	No
Read User PropertySet Personal-Information	**Yes**	No	No	No	No
Read User PropertySet General-Information	**Yes**	No	No	No	No
Read User PropertySet Public-Information	**Yes**	No	No	No	No
Read User PropertySet RTCUserSearchProperty-Set	**Yes**	No	No	No	**Yes**
Read User PropertySet RTCPropertySet	**Yes**	No	No	No	No
Write User Property Proxy-Addresses	No	No	**Yes**	No	No
Write User PropertySet RTCUserSearchProperty-Set	No	No	**Yes**	No	No
Write User PropertySet RTCPropertySet	No	No	**Yes**	No	No
Read PropertySet DS-Replication-Get-Changes of all Active Directory objects	No	No	No	**Yes**	No

In addition to the ACEs applied to the Domain Root, the "Read Container" (not inherited) ACE for `RTCUniveralUserReadOnlyGroup` and `RTCUniversalServerReadOnlyGroup` are applied to the three built-in containers: Users, Computers, and Domain Controllers.

NOTE

Note that the PowerShell method is the only way to perform the domain, forest, and schema preparation steps when only 32-bit domain controllers are available.

Installation

This section outlines the steps for installing both the Standard and the Enterprise Edition of Skype for Business Server 2015. Standard Edition is generally used for small deployments, whereas Enterprise Edition offers significant benefits for redundancy and scalability. The largest difference between the Standard Edition and the Enterprise Edition of Skype for Business Server 2015 is that the Standard Edition uses SQL Server Express, previously known as MSDE, whereas Enterprise Edition uses a full version of SQL 2008 R2, 2012, or 2014. In addition, a Standard Edition Server can also host the Persistent Chat service, whereas an Enterprise Edition Front End pool requires Persistent Chat to be hosted on a dedicated server.

Skype for Business Server 2015 Topology Builder

After you have prepared Active Directory, the next step is install the Skype for Business Server 2015 Topology Builder. As in previous versions of Lync, this tool is front and center for all new Skype for Business infrastructure additions. With a single tool, an administrator can design and validate a Skype for Business Server 2015 topology and then publish it to CMS. This process is very similar to Lync Server 2010 and 2013, but offers a bit more flexibility inline with the improved feature set and additional server roles in Skype for Business Server 2015.

Installation of the Topology Builder does come with some prerequisites and requirements. First, the administrator must be a member of the Domain Admins account in Active Directory. The right to install the Topology can be delegated, but only by a user that is a member of both the Domain Admins and `RTCUniversalServerAdmin` groups. The other requirements and prerequisites are outlined here:

- 64-bit edition of one of the following:
    - Windows Server 2008 R2
    - Windows Server 2012
    - Windows Server 2012 R2

  - Windows 7
  - Windows 8/8.1
  - Window 10
- .NET Framework 4.5
- Microsoft Visual C++ 2013 Redistributable x64 12.0.21005. The Deployment Wizard will automatically install this package if it is not already installed.

After the prerequisites are installed, the actual installation of the Topology Builder tool can begin.

1. Run `setup.exe` from the installation media. It is located at `\setup\amd64\setup.exe`.
2. When prompted to check for updates, select Connect to the Internet to Check for Updates, as shown in Figure 4.5. This will tell the installer to download the latest Skype for Business Server 2015 application updates and apply them as part of the installation process. If the server doesn't have Internet access, select Don't Check for Updates Right Now. Click Next.

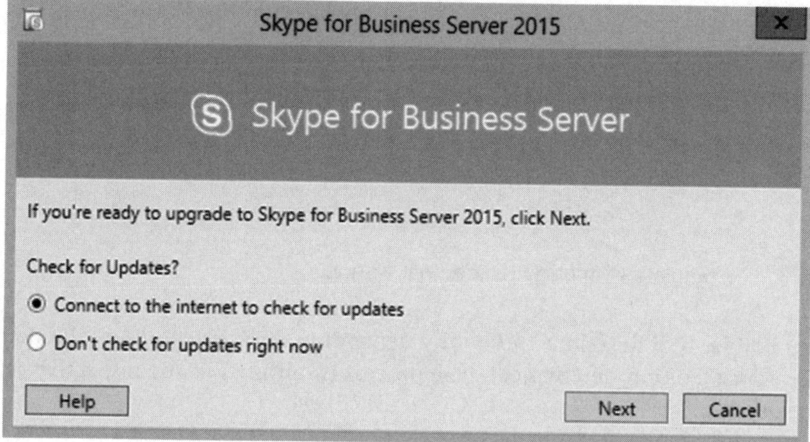

FIGURE 4.5 Skype for Business Server 2015 installer prompt to check for updates.

3. If prompted for the license agreement, click I Accept Terms in the license agreement, and then click OK.
4. After the installer checks for updates, click Next.
5. The installer will install the Microsoft Visual C++ 2013 Redistributable automatically.

6. Click Install Administrative Tools from the right-column menu of the Deployment Wizard. This installs all the tools, including Topology Builder.
7. After installation is complete, there should be a green check mark next to the Install Administrative Tools link, grayed out, as shown in Figure 4.6.

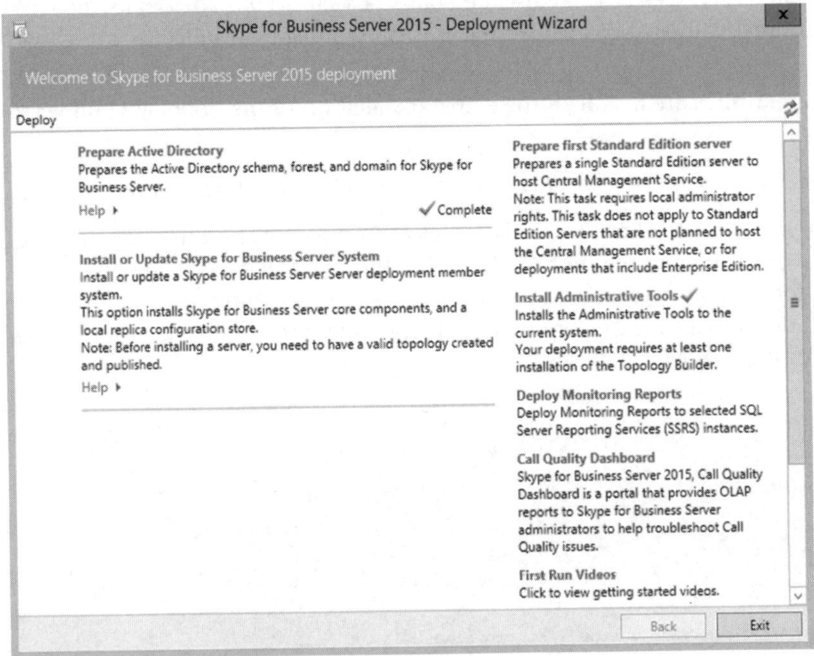

FIGURE 4.6 Completed Topology Builder installation.

The Topology Builder tool functions differently depending on your choice of Standard Edition or Enterprise Edition deployment. The process is outlined in the respective sections that follow.

Standard Edition Installation

As noted previously, Skype for Business Server 2015 Standard Edition is designed for smaller deployments. Standard Edition deployments can have only one server per pool and use SQL Server Express on the same server as the Front End. This results in limited scalability and limited high-availability options. For this reason, Standard Edition is recommended only for small deployments. If this will be the first Skype for Business Server 2015 Front End pool deployed, the first step is to prepare the server as a Central Management Store and prepare the database:

1. From the main Deployment Wizard screen, click Prepare the First Standard Edition Server in the right pane.
2. Click Next at the first screen.

3. The window displays the actions being performed to prepare the server as the first Standard Edition Server, including setting up the Central Management Store. Wait as this process takes a few minutes to complete.

4. When the process is done, ensure that it completed successfully and then click Finish.

The next step is to define the topology with Topology Builder.

Topology Builder for Standard Edition Deployments

Skype for Business Server 2015 uses the published topology to process traffic and maintain overall topology information. To ensure that the topology is valid, it is required to run the Topology Builder before your initial deployment and publish an updated topology after each topological change. This example shows a Standard Edition topology. Remember, if you change the topology later, it must be republished to ensure consistency.

When you first launch Skype for Business Topology Builder, you'll be presented with three options, as shown in Figure 4.7.

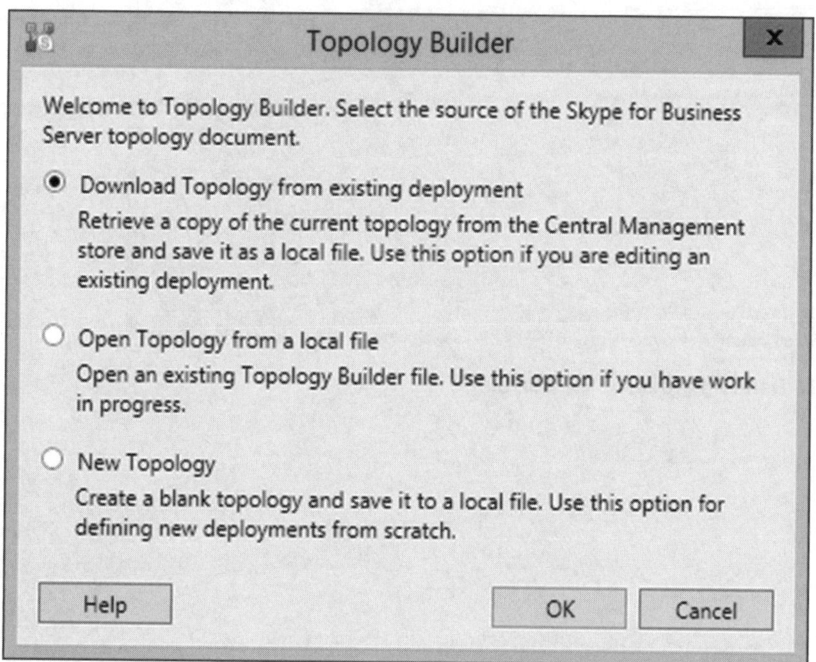

FIGURE 4.7 Initial prompt when opening Topology Builder.

Because we will be deploying the first Front End pool in the environment, select New Topology and click OK.

To begin using Topology Builder, perform the following steps:

1. Enter a filename for the local Topology file, and then click Save.
2. Define the default SIP domain. In many deployments this is simply your domain name, as shown in Figure 4.8. In more complex deployments you can add SIP domains by clicking the Add button. When you are done defining SIP domains, click OK.

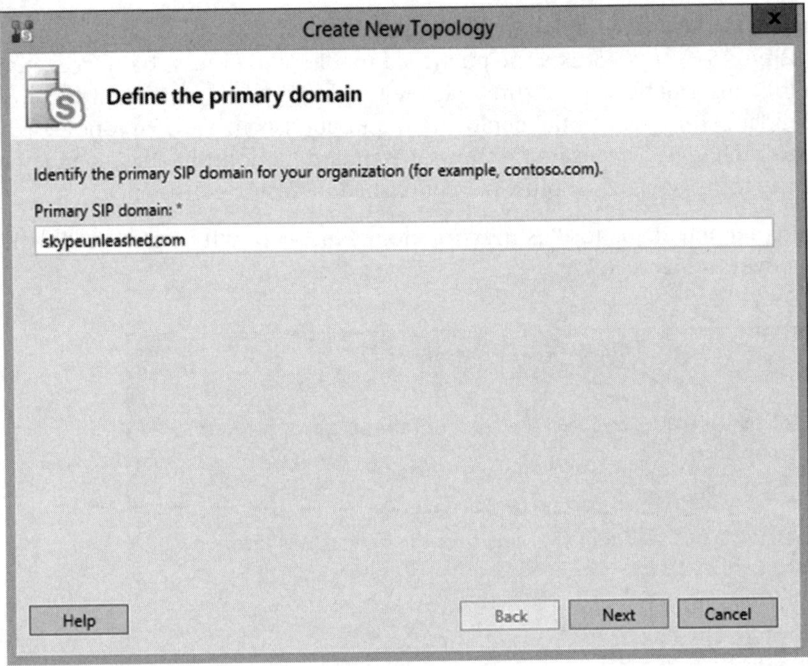

FIGURE 4.8 Define the default SIP domain.

3. Enter a name for the first Central Site in your deployment. This can be virtually anything, but once entered it cannot be changed without significant effort, so choose wisely. Most commonly, Central Sites are named on a location basis (HQ, SEA, Redmond, and so on). Enter the appropriate information, as shown in Figure 4.9, and click Next.

NOTE

Note that Skype for Business Server sites have no relation to Active Directory sites. They are completely separate and unique to Skype for Business Server.

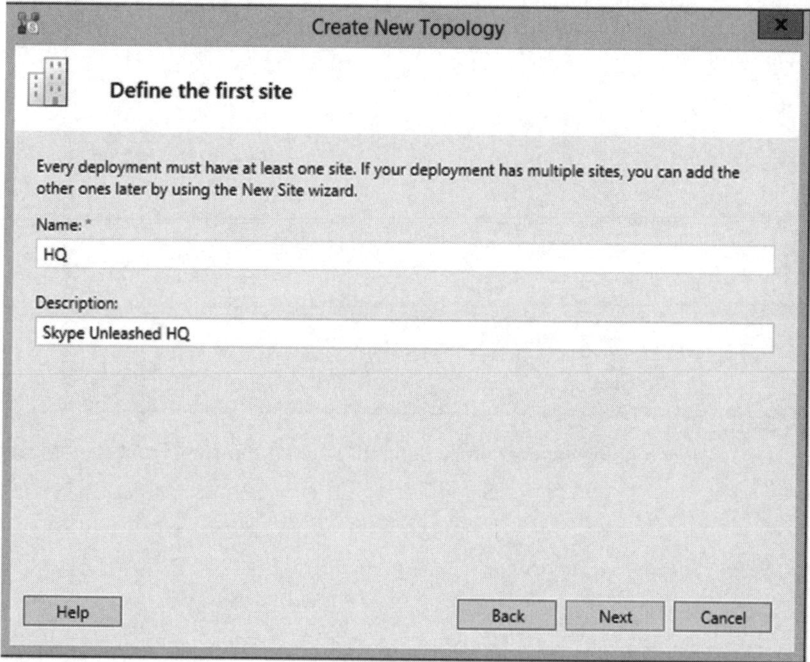

FIGURE 4.9 Define the site.

4. Once the site information has been entered, you will be given the option to open the New Front End Wizard when this wizard closes. Leave this box checked and then click Finish, as shown in Figure 4.10.

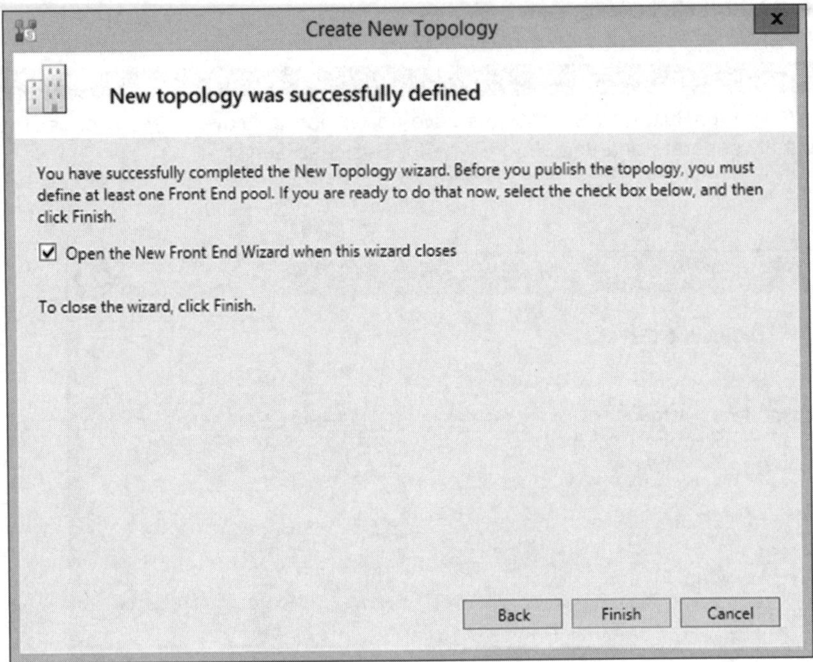

FIGURE 4.10 New topology successfully defined. Launch the New Front End Wizard.

5. Click Next on the initial screen. Select the radio button for Standard Edition Server. Define the System FQDN, as shown in Figure 4.11. For a Standard Edition deployment, the server name will also be the FQDN. When you are done, click Next.

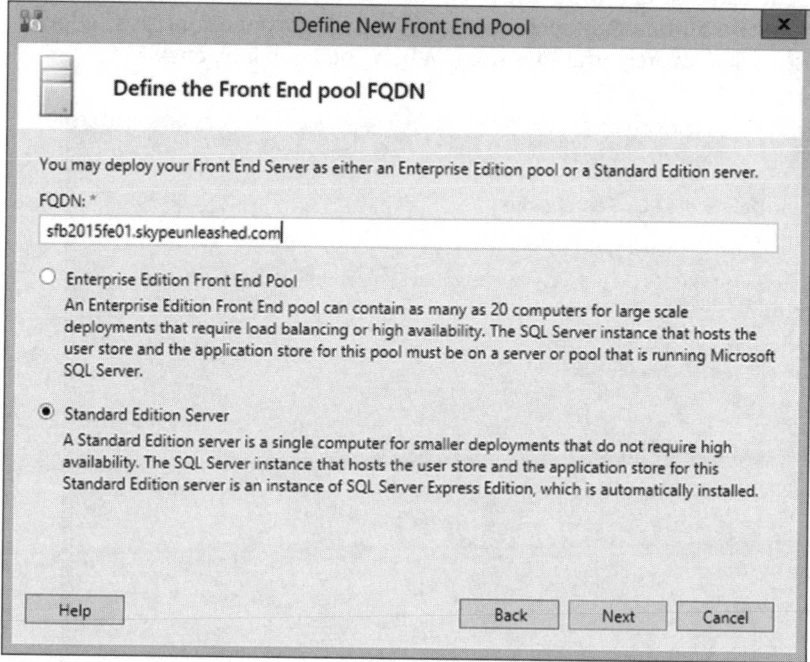

FIGURE 4.11 Define the Front End server.

6. Choose the appropriate workloads for your deployment.

7. If you choose to enable archiving and/or monitoring, select the appropriate check box here as well. When complete, click Next.

8. If you are deploying Enterprise Voice, click the check box to enable the Mediation Server role collocated with the Front End Server. Click Next.

9. You will be prompted to associate the Front End pool with an Edge pool. Leave this box unchecked for now. We will cover the deployment of the Edge Server role in Chapter 5, "Skype for Business Server 2015, Edge Server."

10. Define the database and file share to be used by the pool, as shown in Figure 4.12. For a Standard Edition deployment, the SQL box is grayed out because a local instance of SQL Express is always used. When you are ready, click Next.

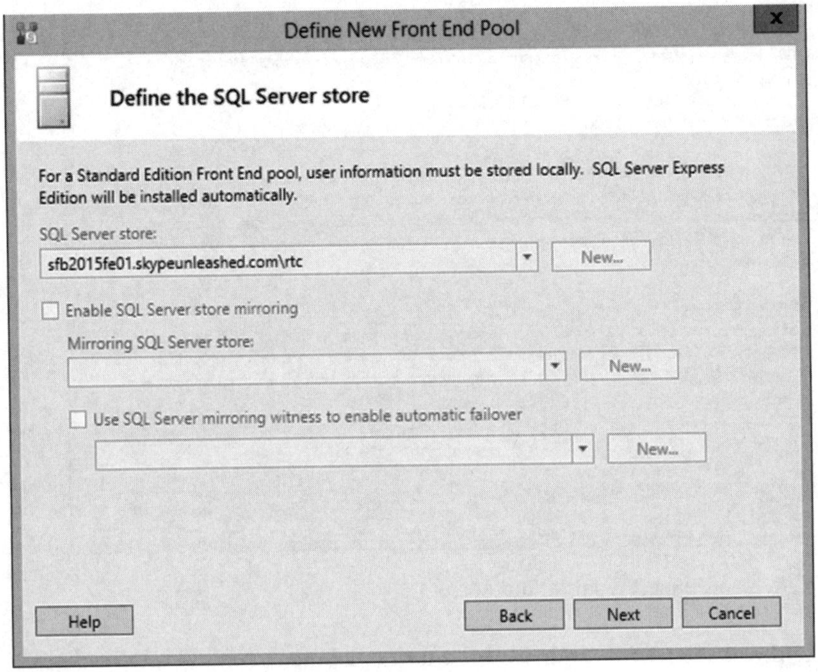

FIGURE 4.12 Define the SQL instance.

11. Note that you'll need to manually create the share on the Front End before progressing past this step. After the share is created, Skype for Business Server assigns the appropriate permissions when you publish the topology.

Define the file store, as shown in Figure 4.13. In general, this is created on the Front End Server in a Standard Edition deployment.

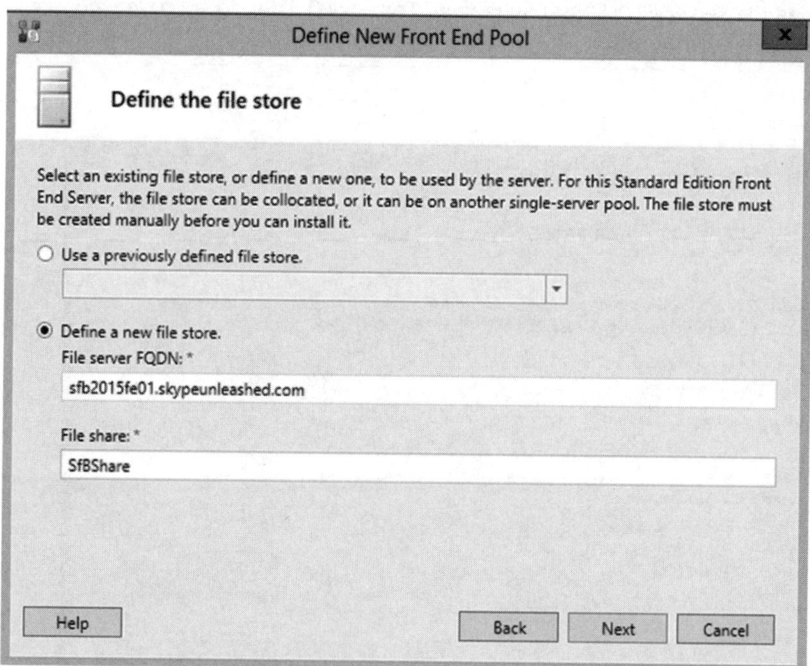

FIGURE 4.13 Define the file store.

12. Define the web services URLs for the pool. The internal and external URLs should be different, as shown in Figure 4.14. They can be defined here. When complete, click Next.

NOTE

When deploying a Standard Edition Front End pool, the internal web services URL must be the same as the server FQDN. For this reason, Topology Builder does not let you modify the internal web services URL.

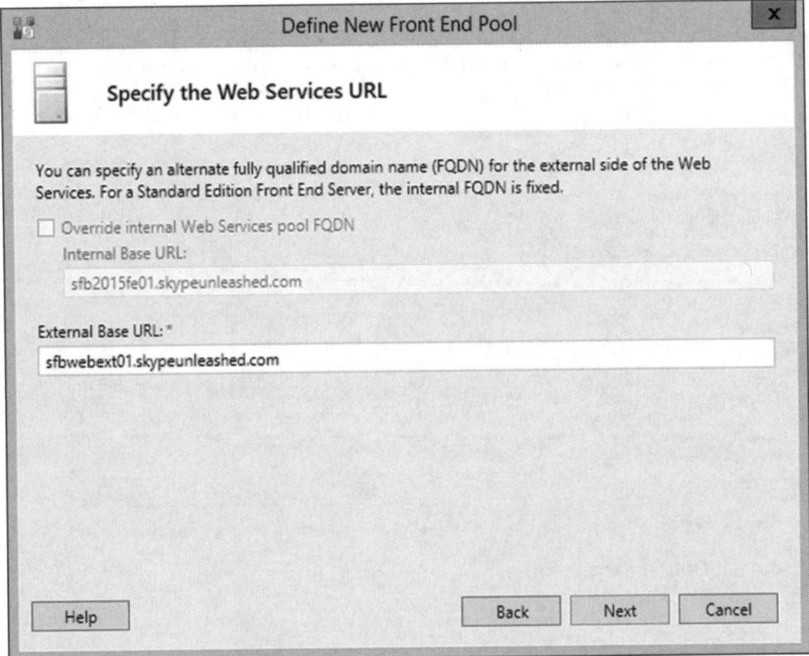

FIGURE 4.14 Web services URLs.

13. Define an Office Web Apps Server. Note that this server must be deployed in advance and pre-existing to define it here.

This completes the initial topology definition. However, there are additional steps to complete a fully functional topology. The next step is to define easy-to-remember URLs for common Skype for Business Server 2015 functions:

1. From the main Topology Builder page, right-click the top-level Skype for Business Server node and choose Edit Properties. Select Simple URLs in the left pane, as shown in Figure 4.15, and enter your preferred simple URLs.

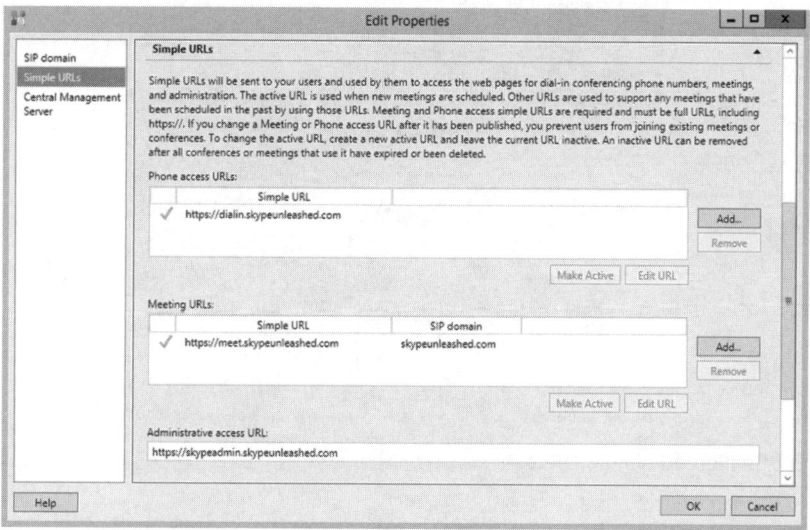

FIGURE 4.15 Expand the Simple URLs item.

TIP

It is recommended to leave the Phone Access and Meeting URLs at their default values. For the Administrative Access URL, define an easy-to-remember FQDN that is not already in use. Be sure to create this record in DNS pointing to the same IP address as the web services internal FQDN.

2. Enter easy-to-remember URLs for Phone Access, Administrative Access, and Meeting services, as shown in Figure 4.16. Note that the following three examples are all valid for Skype for Business Server simple URLs:

   - **https://<function>.<domain _fqdn>** (for example, https://meet.skypeunleashed.com)
   - **https://<prefix>.<sip_domain>/<function>** (for example, https://skype.skypeunleashed.com/meet)
   - **https://<prefix>.<publicdomain>/<sip_domain>/<function>** (for example, https://skype.skypeunleashed.com/skypeunleashed.com/meet)

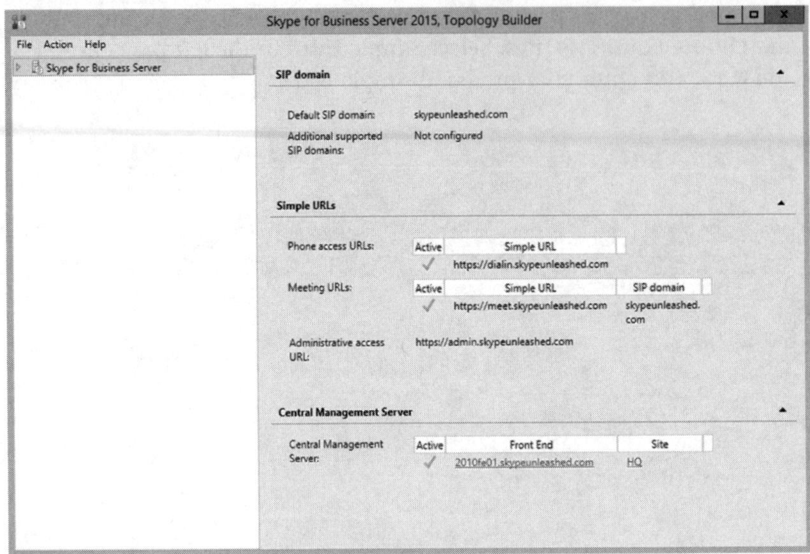

FIGURE 4.16 Configured simple URLs.

Note that these are the only allowed syntaxes. Port information, such as https://dialin.skypeunleashed.com:443, is invalid. If you choose the first or second option, FQDNs for each SIP domain will need to be included as SANs on your certificates. If you choose the third option, note that the following virtual directory names are reserved and cannot be used as part of a simple URL:

- `ABS`
- `Conf`
- `LocationInformation`
- `RequestHandler`
- `AutoUpdate`
- `cscp`
- `OCSPowerShell`
- `RGSClients`
- `CertProv`
- `GetHealth`
- `ReachWeb`
- `RGSConfig`

- `CollabContent`
- `GroupExpansion`
- `RequestHandlerExt`
- `WebTicket`

The final step is to publish the topology to the Central Management Store. In a Standard Edition deployment, this is the first Front End you define. Perform the following steps to publish your topology:

1. From the Topology Builder Tool, right-click the top-level menu item in the left pane, Skype for Business Server, as shown in Figure 4.17.

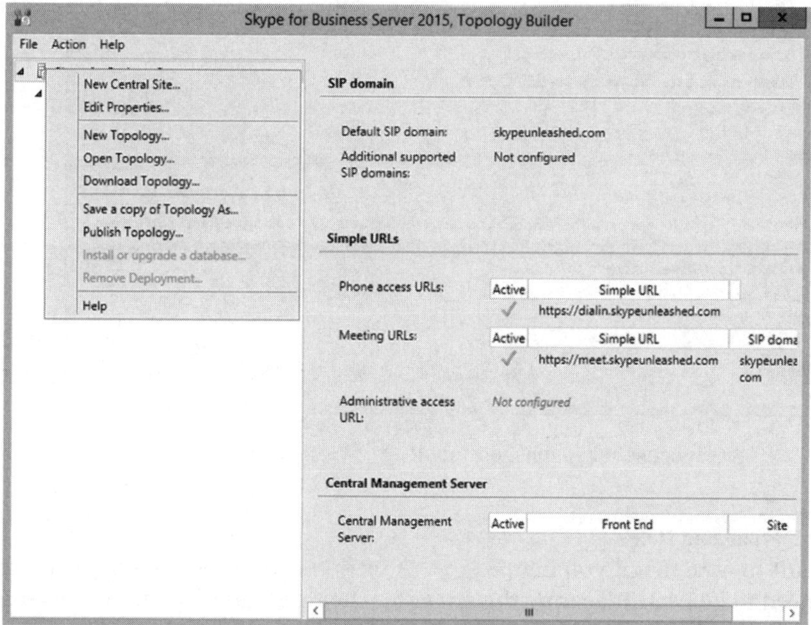

FIGURE 4.17 Publishing the Skype for Business Topology.

2. Select Publish Topology, as shown in Figure 4.17.
3. At the opening screen, click Next.

4. This starts the publishing process and overwrites any existing topologies.
5. The Publish Topology window displays the actions being performed. Ensure that all steps say "Success" when it is finished, as shown in Figure 4.18, and then click Finish.

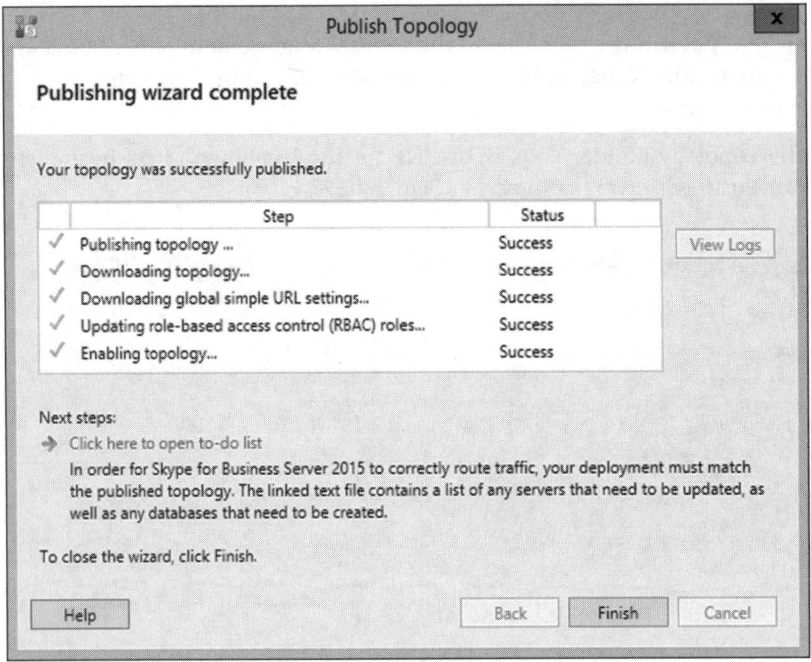

FIGURE 4.18 Successfully published topology.

Installing the Front End Role

It is important to note that if you jumped to this section before completing the preceding steps, you need to go back. Preparing the server for the first Standard Edition Server and building a valid topology in the Topology Builder tool are both prerequisites to installing the Front End role. It should be familiar if you've already installed Lync Server 2010 or 2013. Administrators new to Skype for Business Server 2015 are advised to review the new features, requirements, and prerequisites before beginning the installation process. The following prerequisites are required to install the Standard Edition Front End role:

The following items (some items were installed prior to Administrative Tools installation):

- Windows PowerShell 3.0
- Microsoft .NET Framework 3.5

- Microsoft .NET Framework 4.5
    - WCF Services
    - HTTP Activation
  - Windows Identity Foundation 3.5
  - Remote Server Administration Tools
    - Role Administration Tools
      - AD DS and AD LDS Tools
  - Silverlight
- IIS with the following options:
  - Common HTTP Features
    - Default Document
    - HTTP Errors
    - Static Content
  - Health and Diagnostics
    - HTTP Logging
    - Logging Tools
    - Tracing
  - Performance
    - Static Content Compression
    - Dynamic Content Compression
  - Security
    - Request Filtering
    - Client Certificate Mapping Authentication
    - Windows Authentication
  - Application Development
    - .NET Extensibility 3.5
    - .NET Extensibility 4.5
    - ASP .NET 3.5
    - ASP .NET 4.5
    - ISAPI Extensions
    - ISAPI Filters

- Management Tools
  - IIS Management Console
  - IIS Management Scripts and Tools

Note that this can also be done in PowerShell using the following command:

```
Add-WindowsFeature NET-Framework-Core, RSAT-ADDS, Windows-Identity-Foundation,
Web-Server, Web-Static-Content, Web-Default-Doc, Web-Http-Errors, Web-Dir-Browsing,
Web-Asp-Net, Web-Net-Ext, Web-ISAPI-Ext, Web-ISAPI-Filter, Web-Http-Logging,
Web-Log-Libraries, Web-Request-Monitor, Web-Http-Tracing, Web-Basic-Auth,
Web-Windows-Auth, Web-Client-Auth, Web-Filtering, Web-Stat-Compression,
Web-Dyn-Compression, NET-WCF-HTTP-Activation45, Web-Asp-Net45, Web-Mgmt-Tools,
Web-Scripting-Tools, Web-Mgmt-Compat, Server-Media-Foundation, BITS
```

TIP

If your Front End server is not connected to the Internet, make sure you have the Windows Server 2012 or 2012 R2 mounted on the server in order to install .NET Framework 3.5. You will also need to provide additional syntax for the source media in the preceding command. Simply add `-source D:\sources\sxs` to the end of the command, where "D:" is the drive letter for the source media.

Once the Role and Feature prerequisites are installed, run Windows Update to ensure that updates are applied to the newly enabled features. If required, apply the following updates specific to the operating system indicated:

- **Windows 2012**—Microsoft KB2858668, "PLA data collector sets stop after 72 hours on a Windows Server 2012-based computer."
- **Windows 2012 R2**—Microsoft KB2982006, "IIS crashes occasionally when a request is sent to a default document in Windows 8.1 or Windows Server 2012 R2." (KB2919355 and KB2969339 must be installed prior to installing KB2982006.)

After you've completed the steps previously outlined, the server is ready to install the Front End role. From the main Skype for Business Deployment Wizard screen, click Install or Update Skype for Business Server System from the main pane.

Follow these steps to complete the installation process:

1. For Step 1: Install Local Configuration Store, click Run.
2. On the next screen, select Retrieve Directly from the Central Management Store, as shown in Figure 4.19. Then click Next.

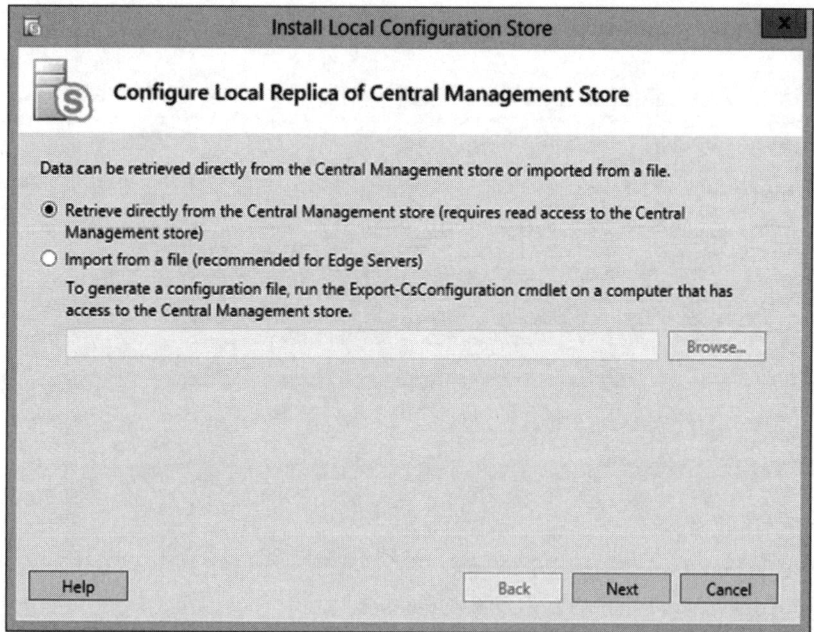

FIGURE 4.19 Retrieve the topology directly from the Central Management Store.

3. You will see the installation of the RTCLocal databases, and an initial copy of the topology will be replicated to the Front End server, as shown in Figure 4.20. Click Finish.

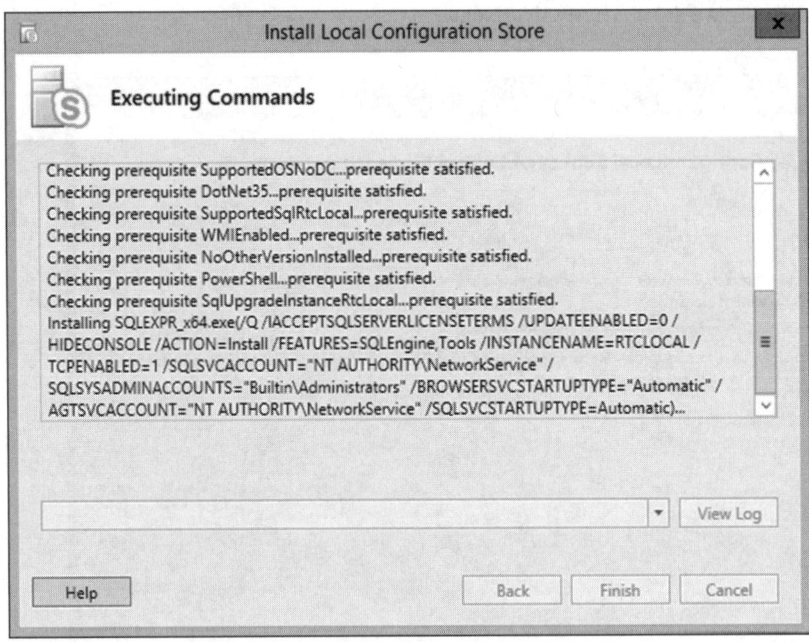

FIGURE 4.20 Installation of RTCLocal databases.

4. For Step 2: Set Up or Remove Lync Server Components, click Run.

5. At the screen that pops up, click Next.

6. The next screen shows the actions being performed, as shown in Figure 4.21. This process takes several minutes to complete.

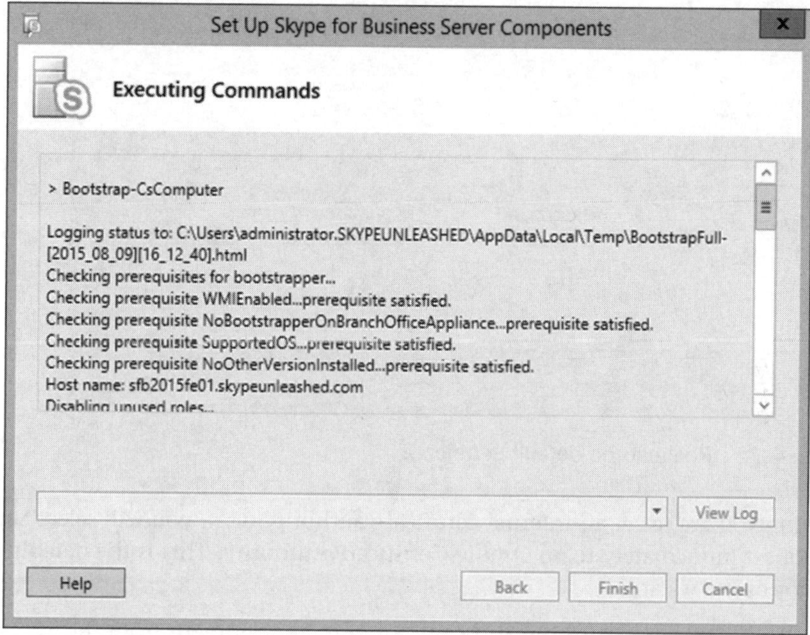

FIGURE 4.21 Installing the Front End role.

7. After the task completes, click Finish and you are brought back to the Install or Update Member System screen of the Deployment Wizard.
8. Review Step 3: Request, Install or Assign Certificates, and then click Run.
9. At the next screen, highlight Default Certificate.

10. Click Request, as shown in Figure 4.22.

FIGURE 4.22 Request the default certificate.

11. Assuming you are using an internal certificate authority (CA), you will select Send the Request Immediately to an Online Certificate Authority. This is the default behavior of the wizard.

12. Select the appropriate certificate authority for your environment from the drop-down list. By default, for a Front End certificate, a friendly name will be automatically entered, the key length set to 2048, and the certificate's private key will not be exportable.

13. Enter your Organization Name and Organizational Unit, select your country from the drop-down menu and then enter your state/province and city/locality. Remember that full names must be entered; abbreviations are not considered valid for certificate requests.

14. Be sure to select each SIP domain that the certificate should contain a "sip.doman.com" SAN for. The Deployment Wizard also automatically adds the SANs required based on the published topology. Unless you have special requirements, bypass the Advanced Wizard.

15. Once the Certificate Request Wizard is completed, as shown in Figure 4.23, click Next.

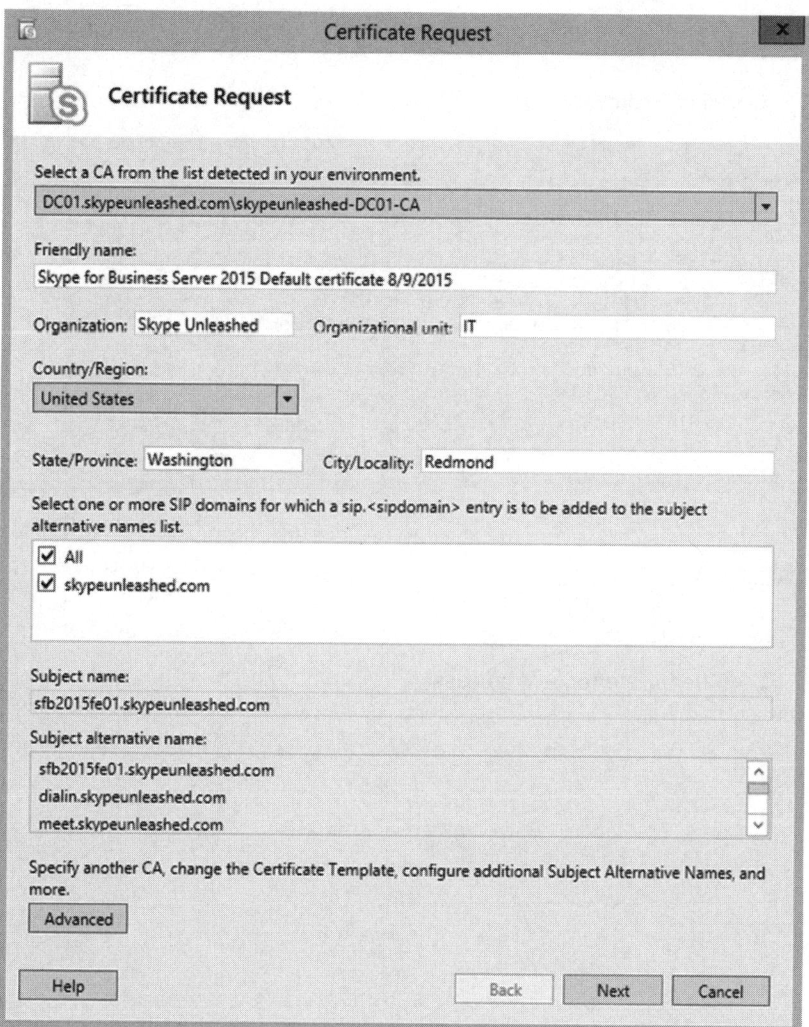

FIGURE 4.23 Certificate request settings.

16. Review the information to ensure that it is correct and click Next. The following screen shows the commands to be executed, as shown in Figure 4.24.

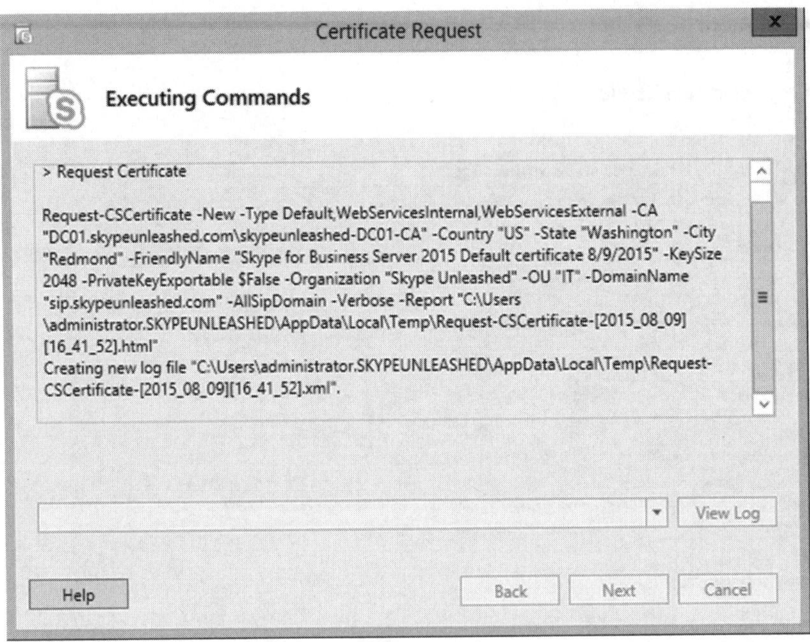

FIGURE 4.24 Certificate request process.

17. Upon completion of the request, click Next. You will be presented with a screen and given the option to assign this certificate to Skype for Business Server certificate usages. This option is checked by default, as shown in Figure 4.25.

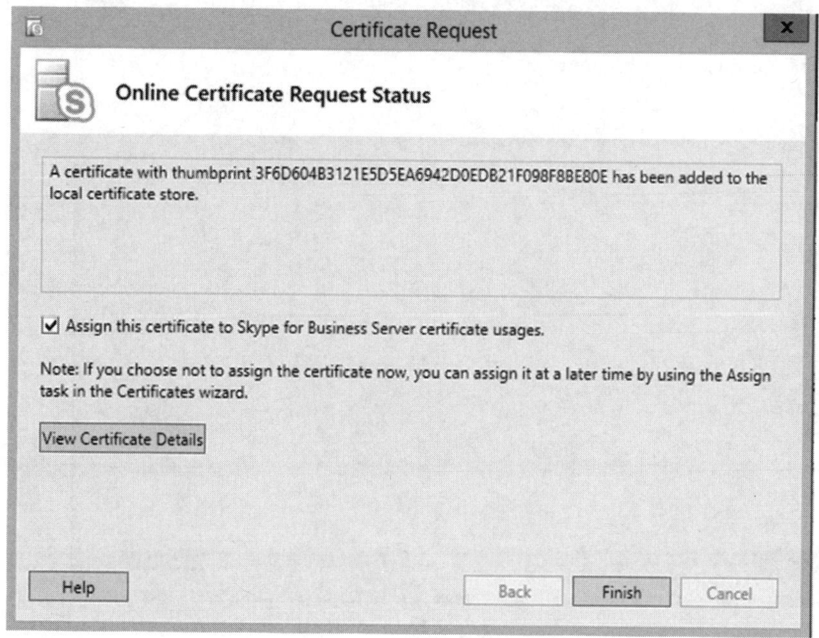

FIGURE 4.25 Certificate request process (continued).

18. Click Finish, and the Certificate Assignment Wizard will be launched, as shown in Figure 4.26.

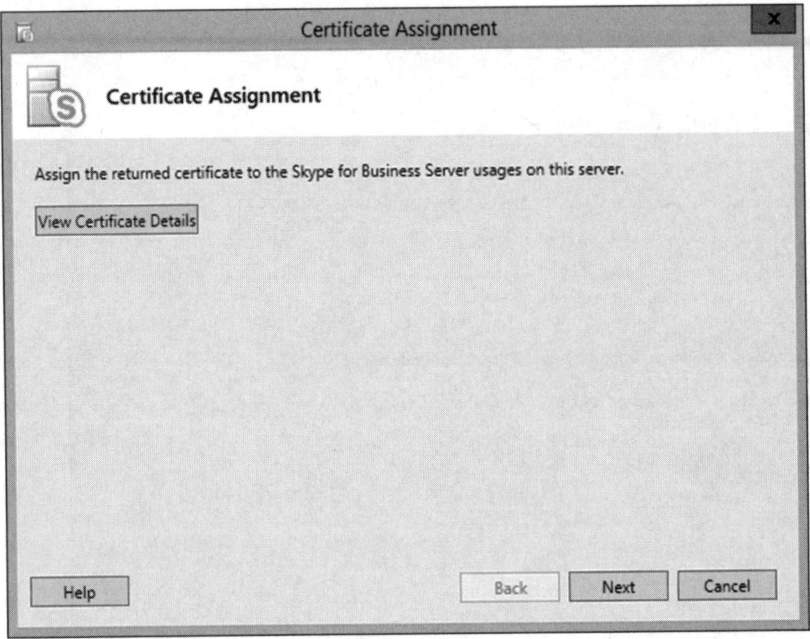

FIGURE 4.26 Certificate Assignment Wizard.

19. Click Next.

20. Verify the details of the certificate to be assigned and then click Next. The commands will be executed to assign the certificate, as shown in Figure 4.27.

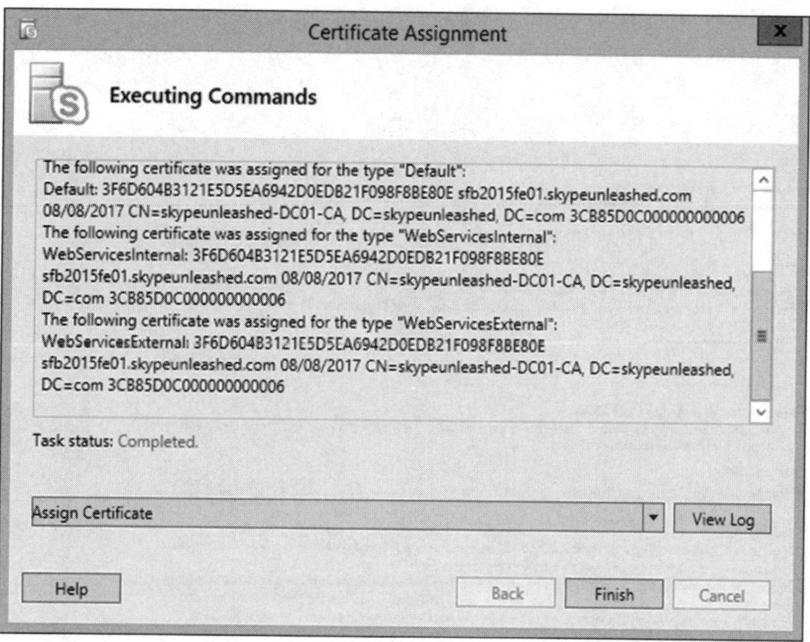
Certificate Assignment
Executing Commands
The following certificate was assigned for the type "Default":
Default: 3F6D604B3121E5D5EA6942D0EDB21F098F8BE80E sfb2015fe01.skypeunleashed.com
08/08/2017 CN=skypeunleashed-DC01-CA, DC=skypeunleashed, DC=com 3CB85D0C000000000006
The following certificate was assigned for the type "WebServicesInternal":
WebServicesInternal: 3F6D604B3121E5D5EA6942D0EDB21F098F8BE80E
sfb2015fe01.skypeunleashed.com 08/08/2017 CN=skypeunleashed-DC01-CA, DC=skypeunleashed,
DC=com 3CB85D0C000000000006
The following certificate was assigned for the type "WebServicesExternal":
WebServicesExternal: 3F6D604B3121E5D5EA6942D0EDB21F098F8BE80E
sfb2015fe01.skypeunleashed.com 08/08/2017 CN=skypeunleashed-DC01-CA, DC=skypeunleashed,
DC=com 3CB85D0C000000000006
Task status: Completed.
Assign Certificate
View Log
Help
Back
Finish
Cancel

FIGURE 4.27 Certificate assignment process.

21. Click Finish, and you will be returned to the main Certificate Wizard.

22. Perform the same steps to request the `OAuthTokenIssuer` certificate.

NOTE

There is a single `OAuthTokenIssuer` certificate in each environment. This certificate only needs to be requested or renewed from a single server. The `OAuthTokenIssuer` certificate will be published to the CMS and replicated to all other Skype for Business servers through the CMS replication process.

23. Click Close on the main Certificate Wizard screen after completing and assigning all certificates.

24. After all the certificates have been assigned, there will be a green check mark by Step 3, as shown in Figure 4.28. If there is not a check mark, recheck your process because it's likely you skipped a step.

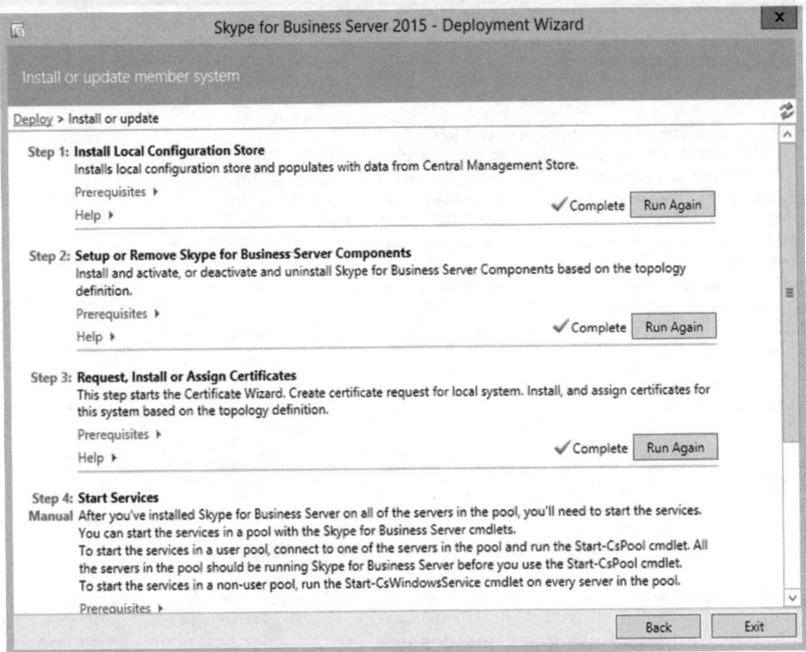

FIGURE 4.28 Certificate process completed.

25. Start the Skype for Business services by launching the Skype for Business Server Management Shell with administrative privileges. Issue the `Start-CsPool` command, as shown in Figure 4.29.

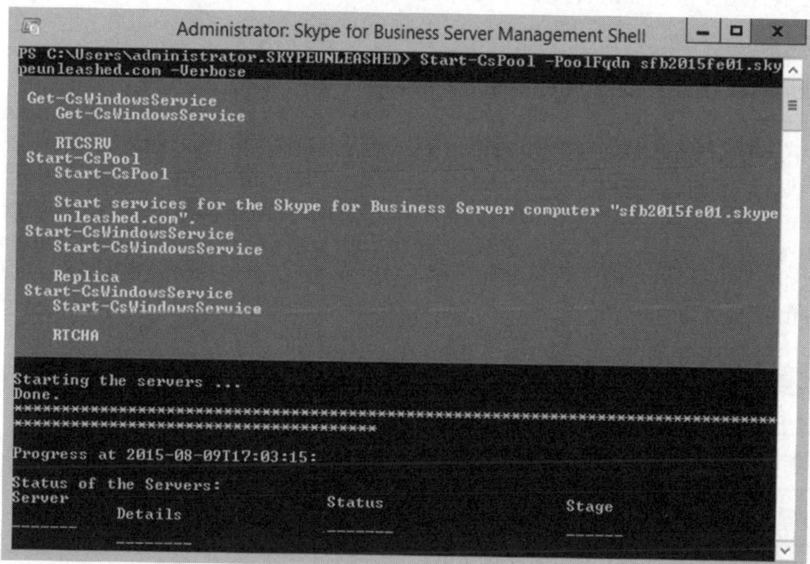

FIGURE 4.29 Starting the Front End pool after installation.

26. Ensure the command finished successfully. You can also check the status of services in the Services MMC console found in the server administrative tools.

27. Click Exit to leave the Deployment Wizard.

The Standard Edition Front End is now installed and ready for further configuration using the Skype for Business Server Control Panel.

Note that the client autoconfiguration requirements are still the same as previous versions of Lync Server. The following DNS records are required for client autoconfiguration:

- `lyncdiscoverinternal.<sip_Domain>` pointing to the IP address assigned to your Front End pool or Director internal web services.
- SRV record of `sipinternaltls._tcp.<sip_Domain>` for port 5061 pointing to the FQDN of your Front End pool or Director.
- `sip.<sip_Domain>` pointing to the IP address assigned to your Front End pool or Director.

Enterprise Edition Installation

Skype for Business Server 2015 Enterprise Edition is designed for larger deployments or those that require high availability or redundancy. Enterprise Edition allows for multiple Front End servers in a pool and scales to support larger user counts with an outboard SQL database.

Topology Builder for Enterprise Edition Deployments

Skype for Business Server 2015 uses the published topology to process traffic and maintain overall topology information. It is especially important to ensure that all information included in the Topology Builder is correct because it sets all the initial configuration information for the deployed server roles. To ensure that the topology is valid, it is required that you run the Topology Builder before your initial deployment and publish an updated topology after each topological change. This example shows an Enterprise Edition topology. Remember, if you change the topology later, it must be republished to ensure consistency.

When you first launch Skype for Business Server 2015 Topology Builder, you'll be presented with three options, as shown in Figure 4.30.

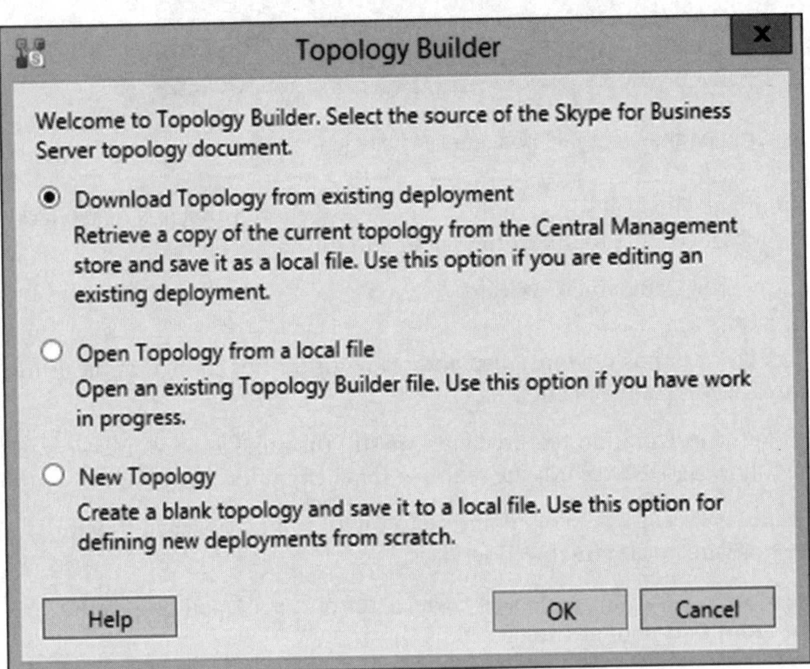

FIGURE 4.30 Initial prompt when opening Topology Builder.

Because we will be deploying the first Front End pool in the environment, select New Topology and click OK.

To begin using Topology Builder, perform the following steps:

1. Enter a filename for the local Topology file and then click Save.
2. Define the default SIP domain and then click Next. In many deployments this is simply your domain name, as shown in Figure 4.31. In more complex deployments, you can add SIP domains on the following screen by clicking the Add button. When you are done defining SIP domains, click Next.

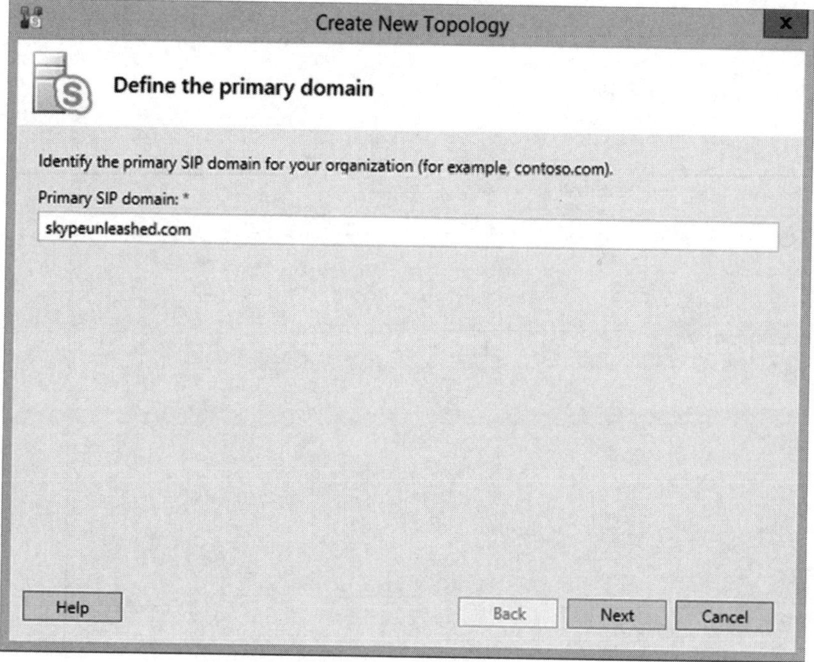

FIGURE 4.31 Define the default SIP domain.

3. Enter a name for the first Central Site in your deployment. This can be virtually anything, but once entered it cannot be changed without significant effort, so choose wisely. Most commonly Central Sites are named on a location basis (HQ, SEA, Redmond, and so on). Enter the appropriate information, as shown in Figure 4.32, and click Next. Note that Skype for Business Server sites have no relation to Active Directory sites. They are completely separate and unique to Skype for Business Server.

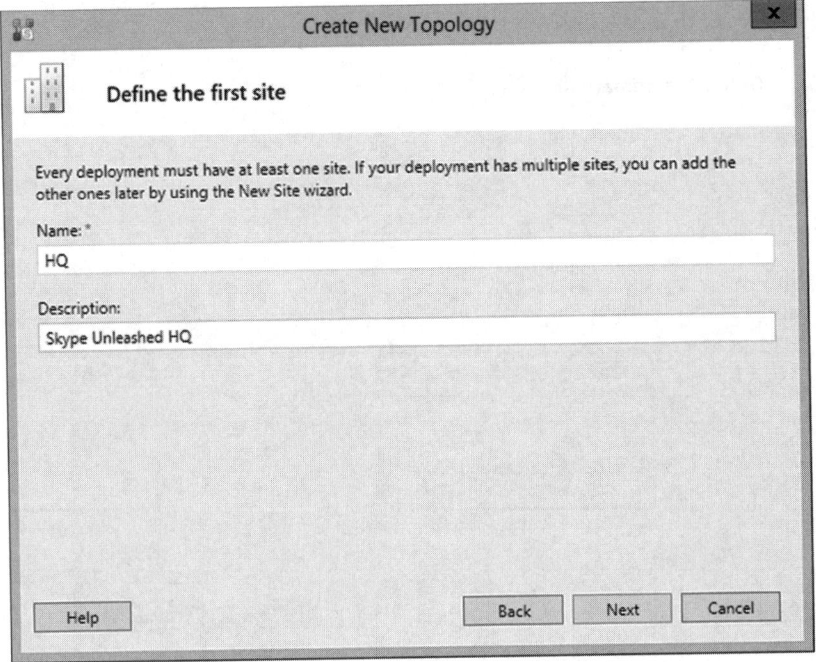

FIGURE 4.32 Define the site.

4. Once the site information has been entered, you will be given the option to open the New Front End Wizard when this wizard closes. Leave this box checked and then click Finish, as shown in Figure 4.33.

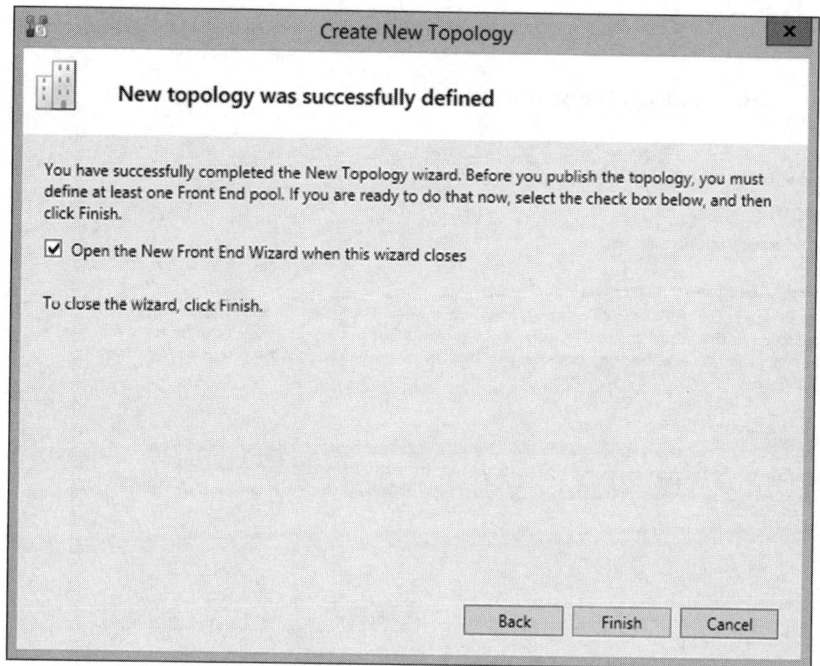

FIGURE 4.33 New topology successfully defined. Launch the New Front End Wizard.

5. Click Next on the initial screen. Select the radio button for Enterprise Edition Front End Pool. Define the Pool FQDN, as shown in Figure 4.34. When you are done, click Next.

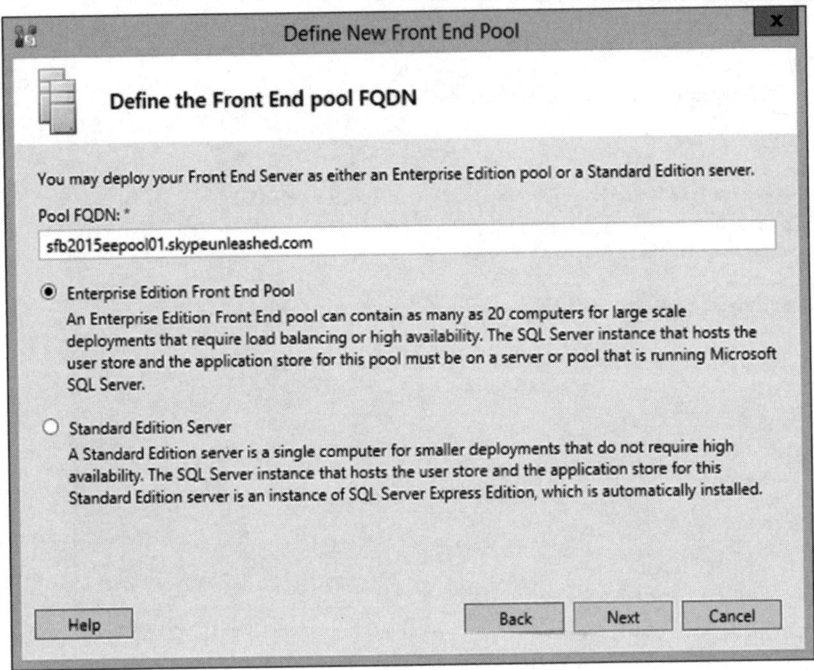

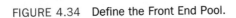

FIGURE 4.34 Define the Front End Pool.

6. Define the servers that will make up the Front End pool by adding their FQDNs and clicking Add, as shown in Figure 4.35. When you are done, click Next.

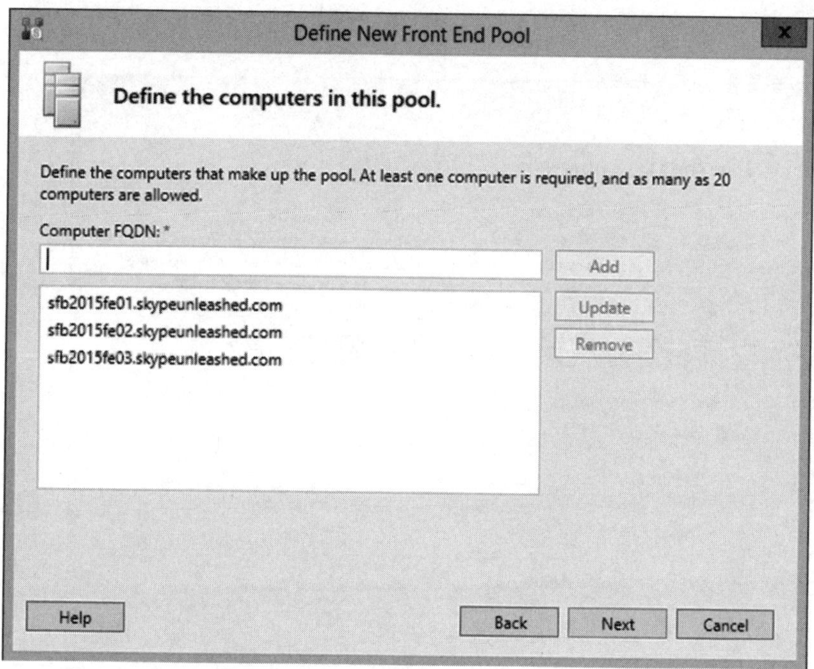

FIGURE 4.35 Add servers to the Front End Pool.

7. Choose the appropriate workloads for your deployment and click Next. Then choose whether you'd like to collocate the Mediation Server role on your Front End Servers and click Next.

8. You will be prompted to associate the Front End pool with an Edge pool. Leave this box unchecked for now. We will cover the deployment of the Edge Server role in Chapter 5.

9. Define the database and file share to be used by the pool, as shown in Figure 4.36. For an Enterprise Edition pool, SQL cannot be collocated on one of the Front End Servers. If you know how SQL will be configured for high availability, you can configure those settings as well. When you are ready, click Next.

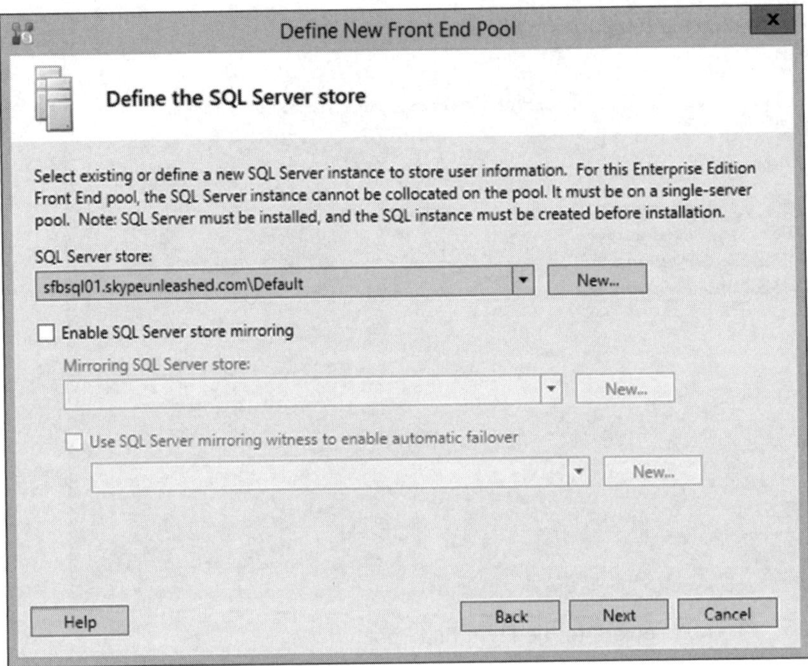

FIGURE 4.36 Define the SQL instance for the Front End Pool.

10. Define the file share to be used by the pool, as shown in Figure 4.37. You'll need to manually create the share on a server other than the Front End Servers before progressing past this step. After the share is created, Skype for Business Server assigns the appropriate permissions when the topology is published. When you are ready, click Next.

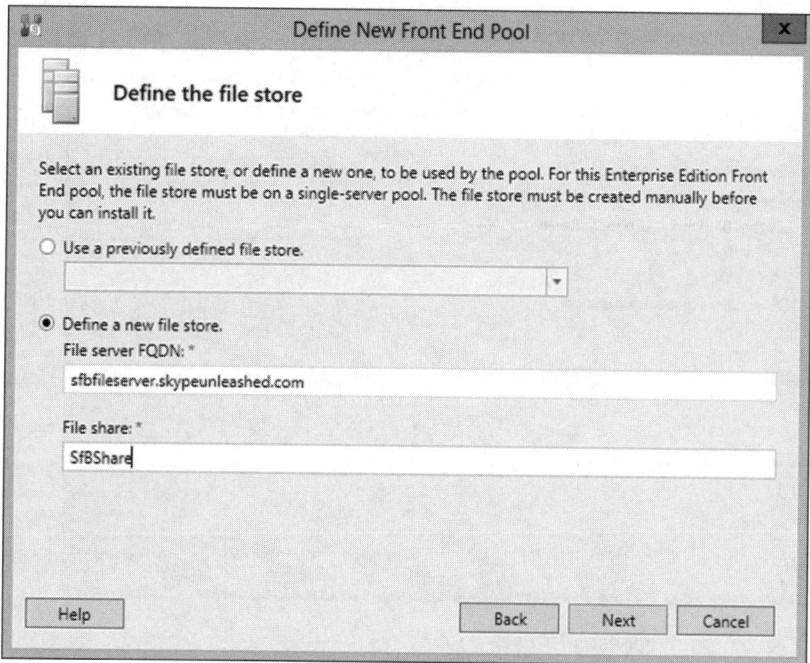

FIGURE 4.37 Define the file share for the Front End Pool.

11. Specify the web services URLs. It is highly recommended that you override the default settings for the internal URL, as shown in Figure 4.38. This should be an FQDN that resolves to a VIP on an HTTP load balancer. Click Next.

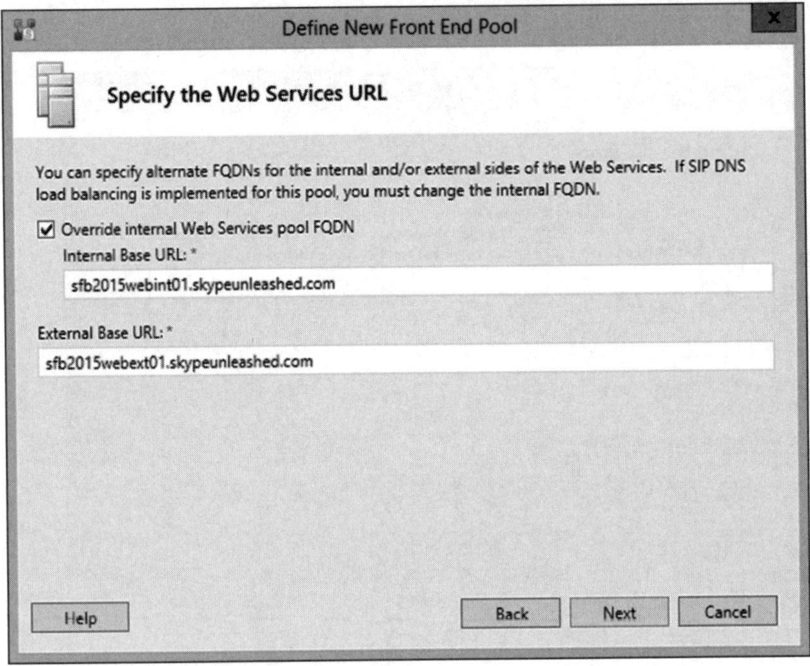

FIGURE 4.38 Web services URLs.

12. Decide whether this Front End pool will be associated with an Office Web Apps server/pool. You can choose an existing server or define a new one. When complete, click Finish.

This completes the initial topology definition. However, there are additional steps to complete a fully functional topology. The next step is to define easy-to-remember URLs for common Skype for Business Server 2015 functions:

1. From the main Topology Builder page, right-click the top-level Skype for Business Server node and choose Edit Properties. Select Simple URLs in the left pane, as shown in Figure 4.39, and enter your preferred simple URLs.

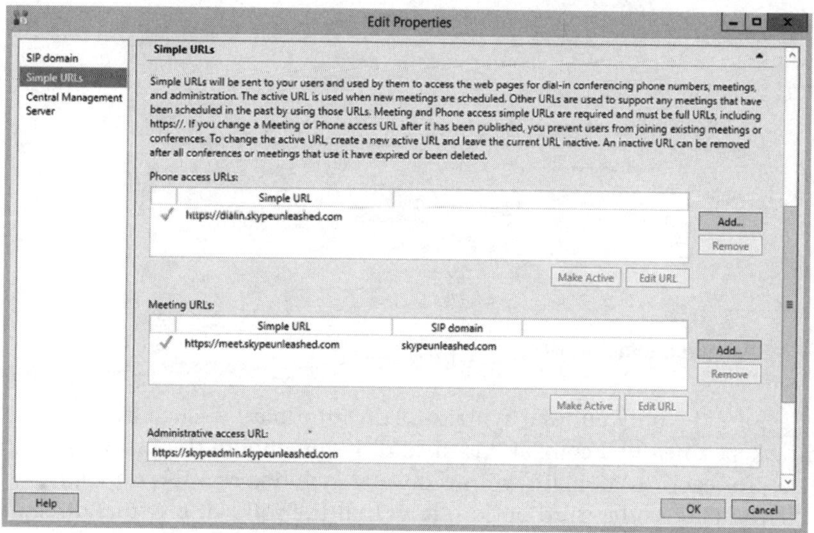

FIGURE 4.39 Expand the Simple URLs item.

2. Enter easy-to-remember URLs for Phone Access, Administrative Access, and Meeting services, as shown in Figure 4.40. Note that the following three examples are all valid for Skype for Business Server simple URLs:

   - **https://<function>.<domain _fqdn>** (for example, https://meet.skypeunleashed.com)
   - **https://<prefix>.<sip_domain>/<function>** (for example, https://skype.skypeunleashed.com/meet)
   - **https://<prefix>.<publicdomain>/<sip_domain>/<function>** (for example, https://skype.skypeunleashed.com/skypeunleashed.com/meet)

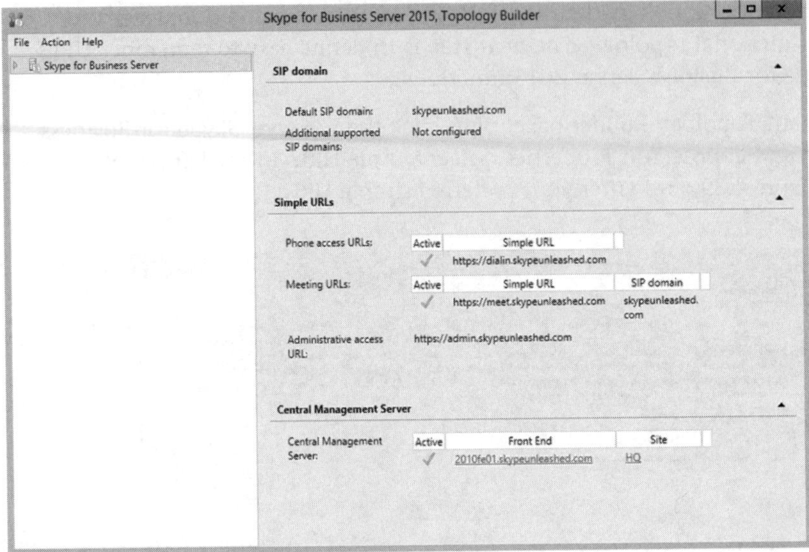

FIGURE 4.40 Configured simple URLs.

Note that these are the only allowed syntaxes. Port information, such as https://dialin.skypeunleashed.com:443, is invalid. If you choose the first or second option, FQDNs for each SIP domain will need to be included as SANs on your certificates. If you choose the third option, note that the following virtual directory names are reserved and cannot be used as part of a simple URL:

- `ABS`
- `Conf`
- `LocationInformation`
- `RequestHandler`
- `AutoUpdate`
- `cscp`
- `OCSPowerShell`
- `RGSClients`
- `CertProv`
- `GetHealth`
- `ReachWeb`
- `RGSConfig`

- `CollabContent`
- `GroupExpansion`
- `RequestHandlerExt`
- `WebTicket`

The final step is to publish the topology to the Central Management Store. In an Enterprise Edition deployment, this is the first SQL Server store you define. Perform the following steps to publish your topology:

1. From the Topology Builder Tool, right-click the top-level menu item in the left pane, Skype for Business Server, as shown in Figure 4.41.

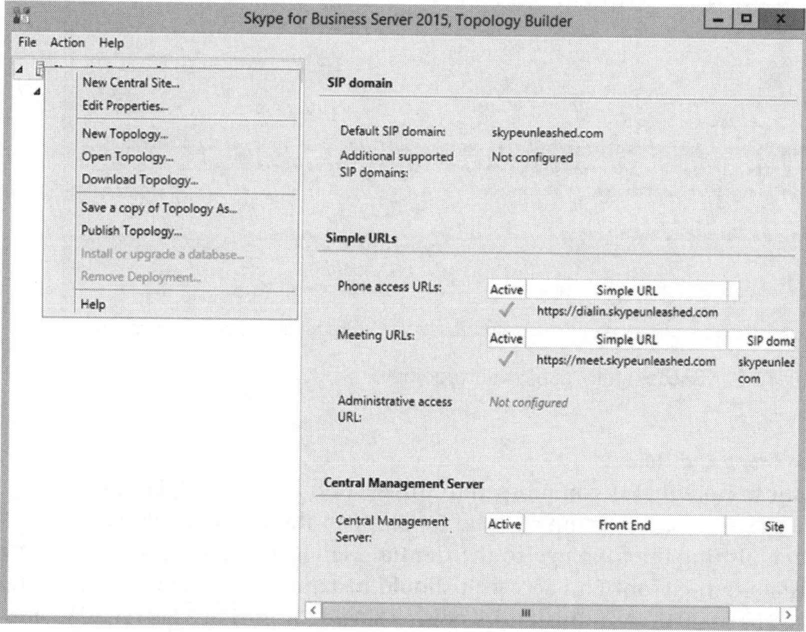

FIGURE 4.41 Publishing the Skype for Business Topology.

2. Select Publish Topology, as shown in Figure 4.41.
3. At the opening screen, click Next.
4. Select the Front End pool that will host the Central Management Store and click Next.
5. Ensure that the database selections are correct and then click Next. This begins the topology publishing process.

6. The Publish Topology window displays the actions being performed. Ensure that it completes successfully, as shown in Figure 4.42, and then click Finish.

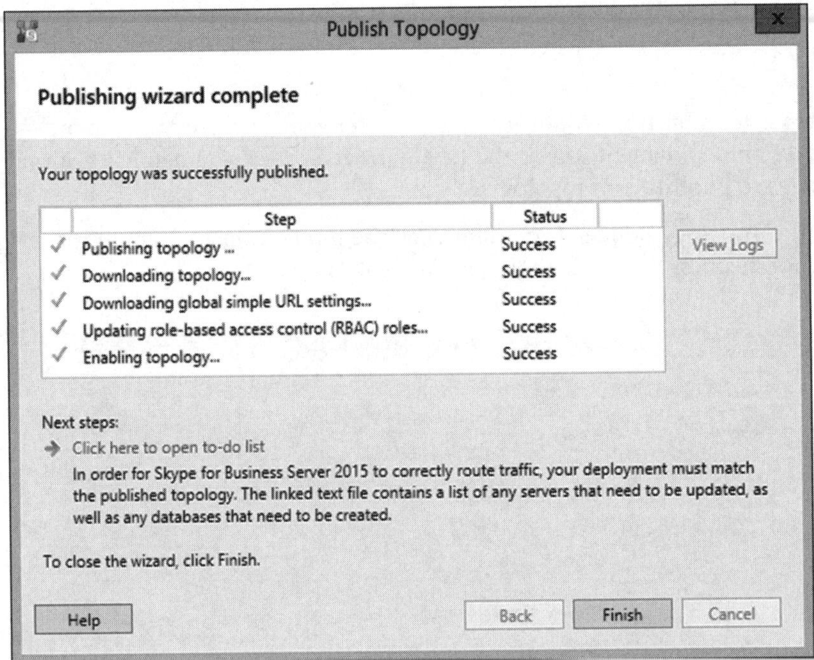

FIGURE 4.42 Successfully published topology.

Installing the Front End Role

It is important to note that if you jumped to this section before completing the preceding steps, you need to go back. Building a valid topology in the Topology Builder tool and successfully publishing the topology to the Central Management Store are both prerequisites to installing the Front End Server. It should be familiar if you've already installed Lync Server 2010 or 2013. Administrators new to Skype for Business Server 2015 are advised to review the new features, requirements, and prerequisites before beginning the installation process. The following prerequisites are required to install the Enterprise Edition Front End role:

- The following items (some items were installed prior to Administrative Tools installation):
    - Windows PowerShell 3.0
    - Microsoft .NET Framework 3.5

    - Microsoft .NET Framework 4.5
        - WCF Services
            - HTTP Activation
    - Windows Identity Foundation 3.5
    - Remote Server Administration Tools
        - Role Administration Tools
            - AD DS and AD LDS Tools
    - Silverlight
- IIS with the following options:
    - Common HTTP Features
        - Default Document
        - HTTP Errors
        - Static Content
    - Health and Diagnostics
        - HTTP Logging
        - Logging Tools
        - Tracing
    - Performance
        - Static Content Compression
        - Dynamic Content Compression
    - Security
        - Request Filtering
        - Client Certificate Mapping Authentication
        - Windows Authentication
    - Application Development
        - .NET Extensibility 3.5
        - .NET Extensibility 4.5
        - ASP .NET 3.5
        - ASP .NET 4.5
        - ISAPI Extensions
        - ISAPI Filters

- Management Tools
    - IIS Management Console
    - IIS Management Scripts and Tools

Note that this can also be done in PowerShell using the following command:

```
Add-WindowsFeature NET-Framework-Core, RSAT-ADDS, Windows-Identity-Foundation,
Web-Server, Web-Static-Content, Web-Default-Doc, Web-Http-Errors, Web-Dir-Browsing,
Web-Asp-Net, Web-Net-Ext, Web-ISAPI-Ext, Web-ISAPI-Filter, Web-Http-Logging,
Web-Log-Libraries, Web-Request-Monitor, Web-Http-Tracing, Web-Basic-Auth,
Web-Windows-Auth, Web-Client-Auth, Web-Filtering, Web-Stat-Compression,
Web-Dyn-Compression, NET-WCF-HTTP-Activation45, Web-Asp-Net45, Web-Mgmt-Tools,
Web-Scripting-Tools, Web-Mgmt-Compat, Server-Media-Foundation, BITS
```

TIP

If your Front End Server is not connected to the Internet, make sure you have the Windows Server 2012 or 2012 R2 mounted on the server in order to install .NET Framework 3.5. You will also need to provide additional syntax for the source media in the preceding command. Simply add `-source D:\sources\sxs` to the end of the command, where "D:" is the drive letter for the source media.

Once the Role and Feature prerequisites are installed, run Windows Update to ensure that updates are applied to the newly enabled features. If required, apply the following updates specific to the operating system indicated:

- **Windows 2012**—Microsoft KB2858668.
- **Windows 2012 R2**—Microsoft KB2982006. (KB2919355 and KB2969339 must be installed prior to installing KB2982006.)

After you've completed the steps previously outlined, the server is ready to install the Front End role. From the main Skype for Business Server Deployment Wizard screen, click Install or Update Skype for Business Server System in the main pane.

Follow these steps to complete the installation process:

1. For Step 1: Install Local Configuration Store, click Run.
2. On the next screen, select Retrieve Directly from the Central Management Store, as shown in Figure 4.43. Then click Next.

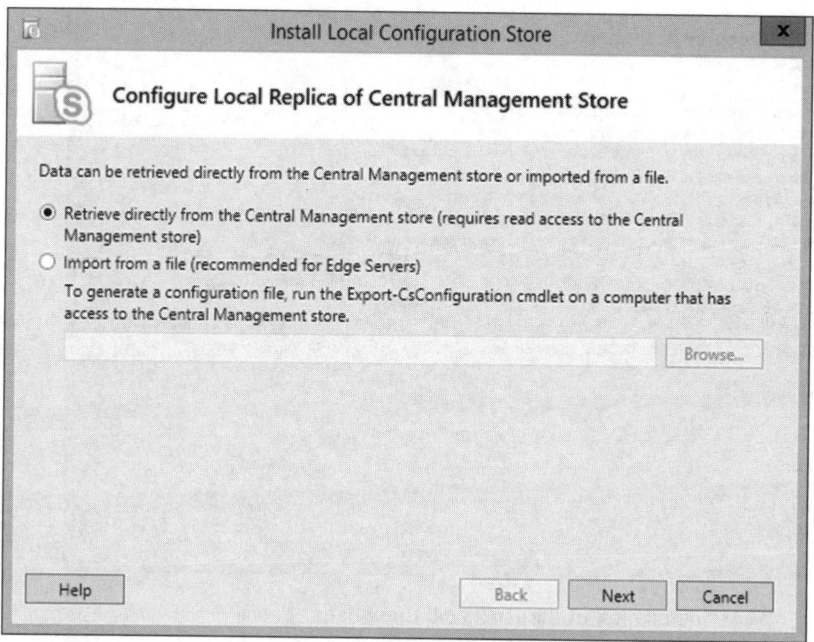

FIGURE 4.43 Retrieve the topology directly from the Central Management Store.

3. You will see the installation of the RTCLocal databases, and an initial copy of the topology will be replicated to the Front End server, as shown in Figure 4.44. Click Finish.

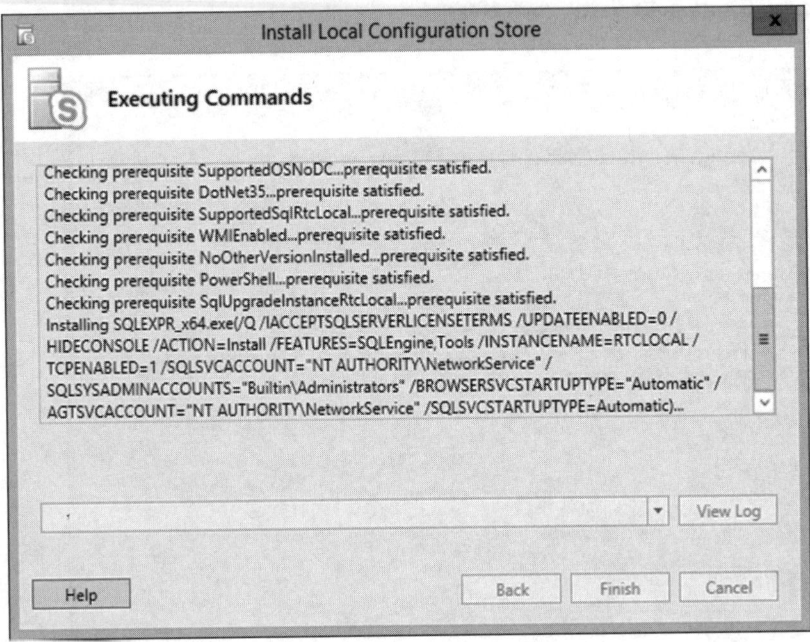

FIGURE 4.44 Installation of the RTCLocal databases.

4. For Step 2: Set Up or Remove Lync Server Components, click Run.

5. At the screen that pops up, click Next.

6. The next screen shows the actions being performed, as shown in Figure 4.45. This process takes several minutes to complete.

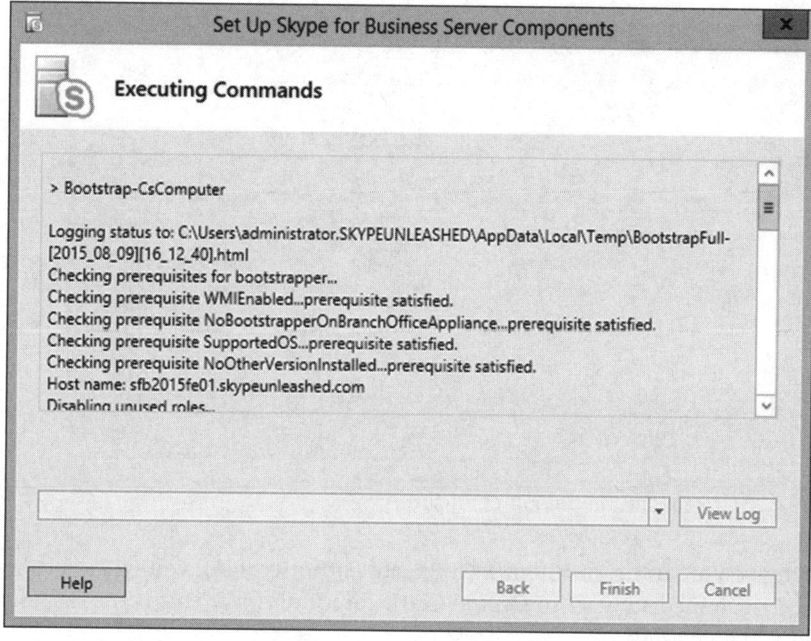

FIGURE 4.45 Installing the Front End role.

7. After the task completes, click Finish. You are brought back to the Install or Update Member System screen of the Deployment Wizard.

8. Review Step 3: Request, Install, or Assign Certificates, and then click Run.

9. At the next screen, highlight Default Certificate.
10. Click Request, as shown in Figure 4.46.

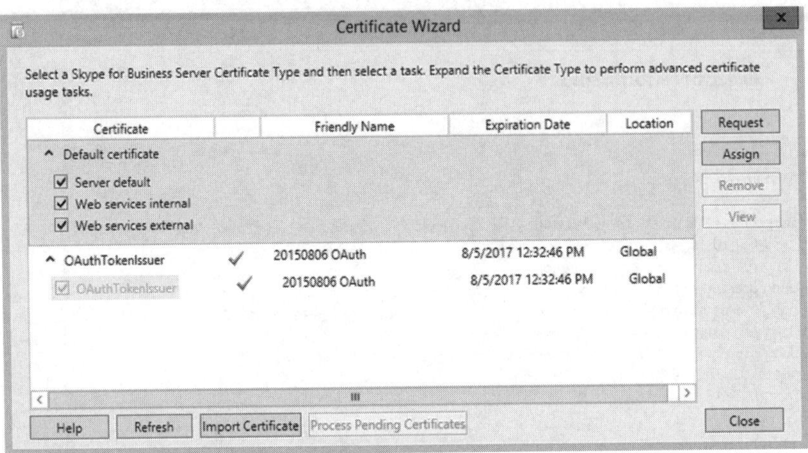

FIGURE 4.46 Request the default certificate.

11. Assuming you are using an internal certificate authority (CA), you will select Send the Request Immediately to an Online Certificate Authority. This is the default behavior of the wizard.
12. Select the appropriate certificate authority for your environment from the drop-down list. By default, for a Front End certificate, a friendly name will be automatically entered, the key length set to 2048, and the certificate's private key will not be exportable.
13. Enter your Organization Name and Organizational Unit, select your country from the drop-down menu, and then enter your state/province and city/locality. Remember that full names must be entered; abbreviations are not considered valid for certificate requests.
14. Be sure to select each SIP domain that the certificate should contain a "sip.doman.com" SAN for. The Deployment Wizard also automatically adds the SANs required based on the published topology. Unless you have special requirements, bypass the Advanced Wizard.

15. Once the Certificate Request Wizard is completed, as shown in Figure 4.47, click Next.

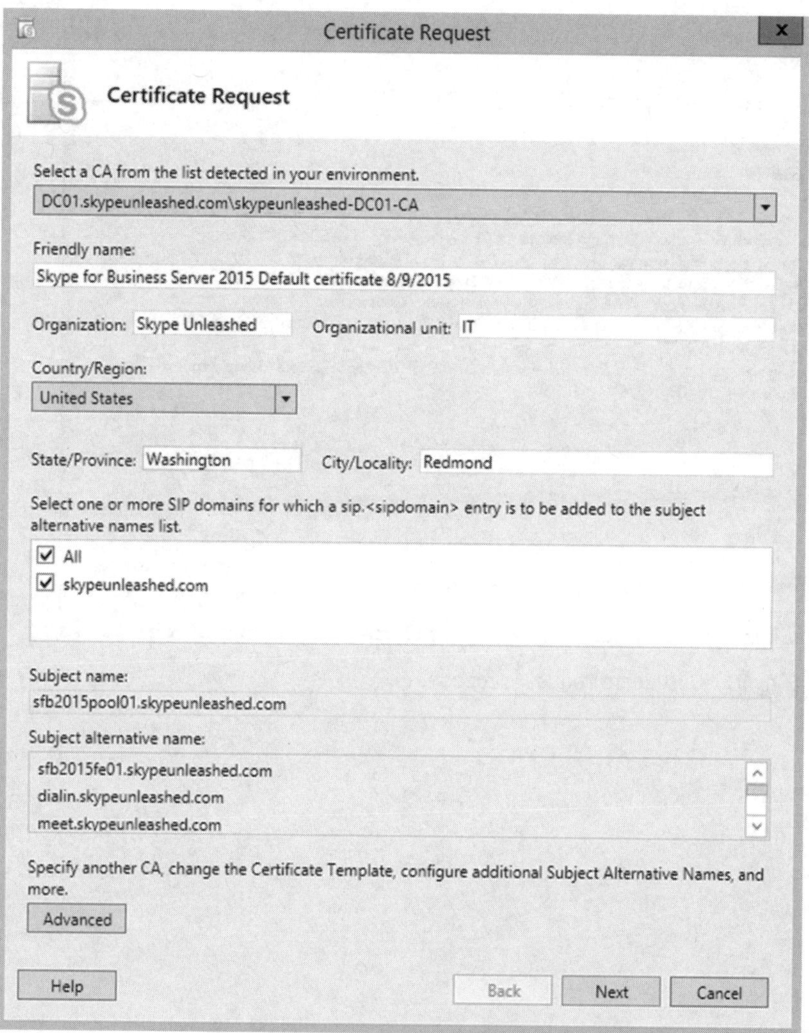

FIGURE 4.47 Certificate request settings for a Standard Edition Front End Pool.

16. Review the information to ensure that it is correct and click Next. The following screen shows the commands to be executed, as shown in Figure 4.48.

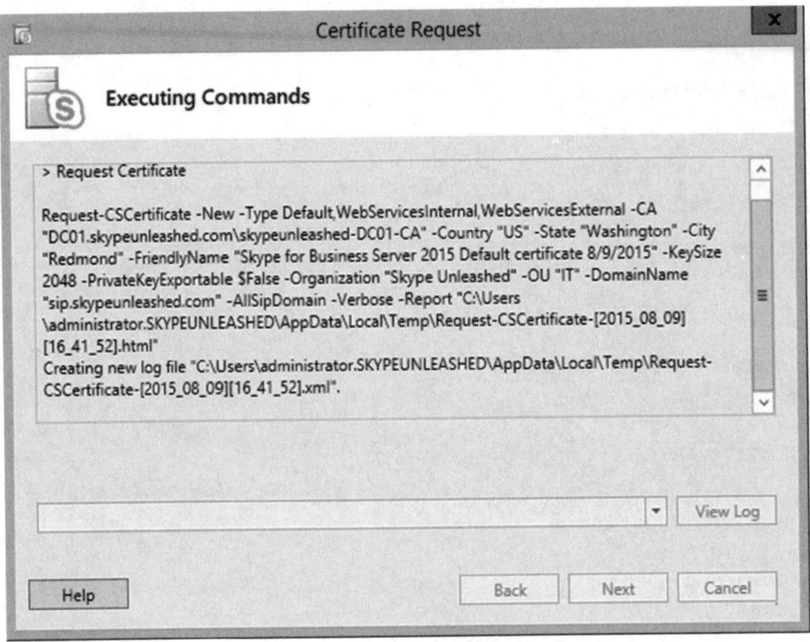

FIGURE 4.48 Certificate request process.

17. Upon completion of the request, click Next. You will be presented with a screen and given the option to assign this certificate to Skype for Business Server certificate usages. This option is checked by default, as shown in Figure 4.49.

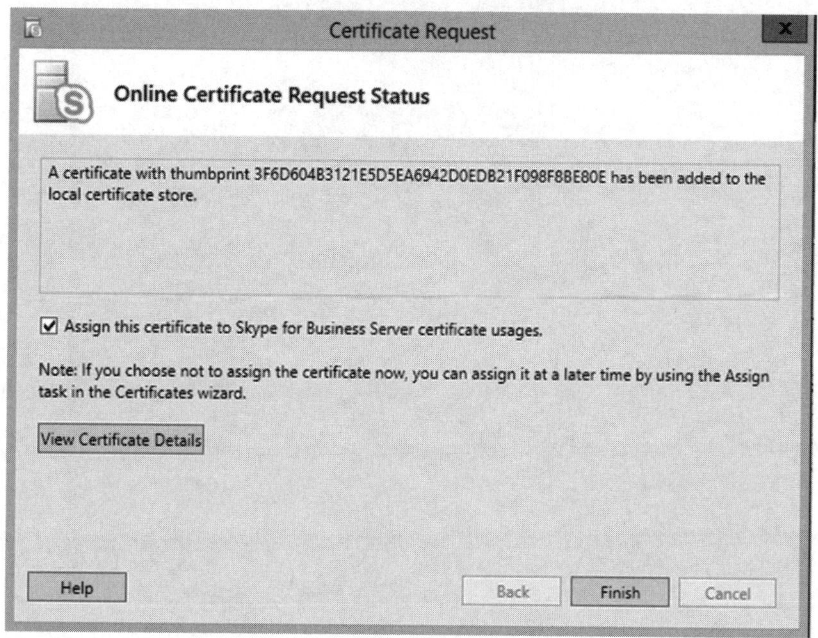

FIGURE 4.49 Certificate request process (continued).

18. Click Finish, and the Certificate Assignment Wizard will be launched, as shown in Figure 4.50.

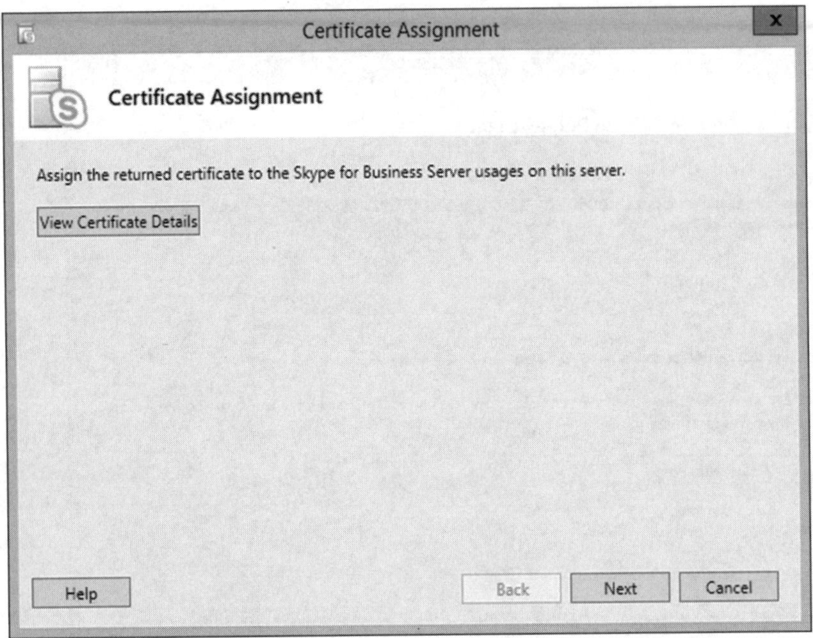

FIGURE 4.50 Certificate Assignment wizard.

19. Click Next.

20. Verify the details of the certificate to be assigned and then click Next. The commands will be executed to assign the certificate, as shown in Figure 4.51.

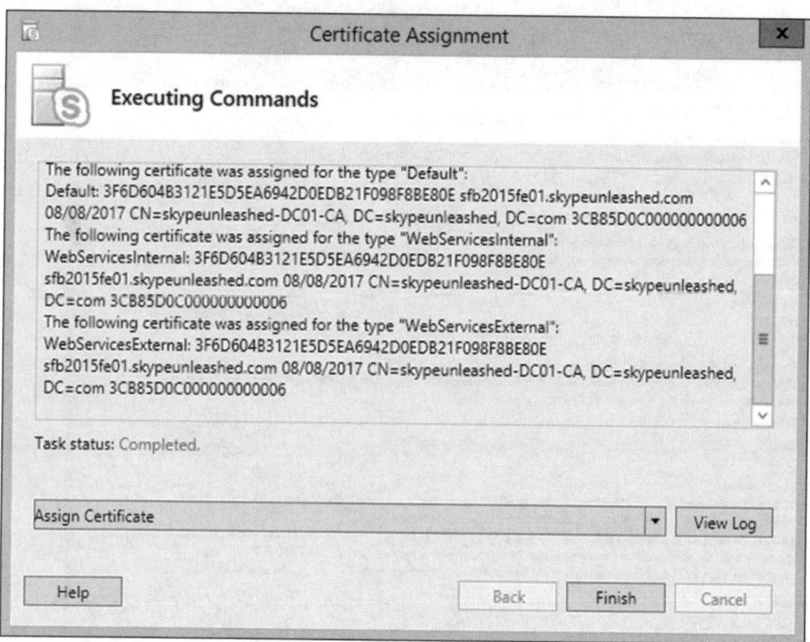
Certificate Assignment
Executing Commands
The following certificate was assigned for the type "Default":
Default: 3F6D604B3121E5D5EA6942D0EDB21F098F8BE80E sfb2015fe01.skypeunleashed.com 08/08/2017 CN=skypeunleashed-DC01-CA, DC=skypeunleashed, DC=com 3CB85D0C000000000006
The following certificate was assigned for the type "WebServicesInternal":
WebServicesInternal: 3F6D604B3121E5D5EA6942D0EDB21F098F8BE80E sfb2015fe01.skypeunleashed.com 08/08/2017 CN=skypeunleashed-DC01-CA, DC=skypeunleashed, DC=com 3CB85D0C000000000006
The following certificate was assigned for the type "WebServicesExternal":
WebServicesExternal: 3F6D604B3121E5D5EA6942D0EDB21F098F8BE80E sfb2015fe01.skypeunleashed.com 08/08/2017 CN=skypeunleashed-DC01-CA, DC=skypeunleashed, DC=com 3CB85D0C000000000006
Task status: Completed.
Assign Certificate
View Log
Help
Back
Finish
Cancel

FIGURE 4.51 Certificate assignment process.

21. Click Finish, and you will be returned to the main Certificate Wizard.

22. Perform the same steps to request the `OAuthTokenIssuer` certificate.

23. Click Close on the main Certificate Wizard screen after completing and assigning all certificates.

24. After all the certificates have been assigned, there will be a green check mark by Step 3, as shown in Figure 4.52. If there is not a check mark, recheck your process because it's likely you skipped a step.

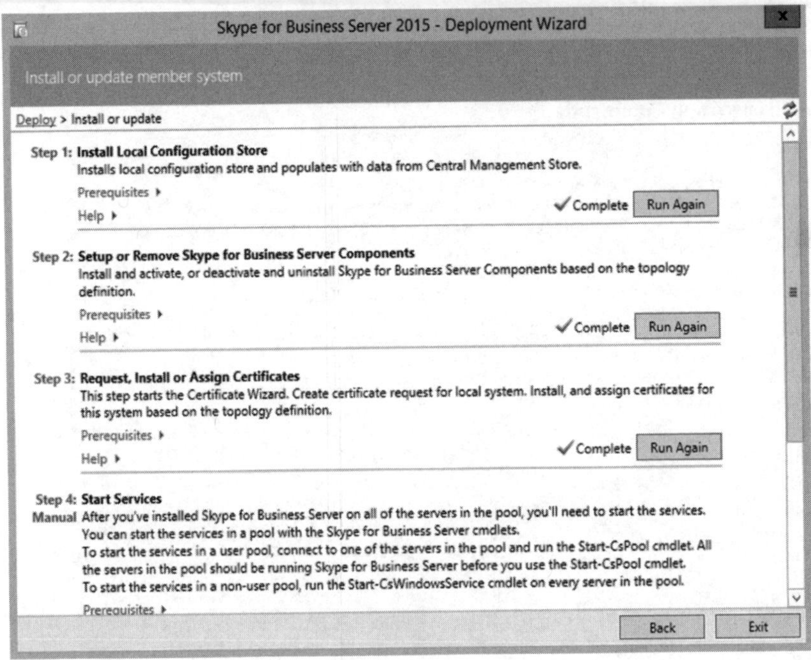

FIGURE 4.52 Certificate process completed.

25. Repeat all of the preceding steps on each server that will be a member of this Front End pool. Note that the `OAuthTokenIssuer` certificate only needs to be requested and assigned on the first Front End server in the topology. The `OAuthTokenIssuer` certificate will be automatically replicated to each additional server in the topology.

26. Once all servers have had the Skype for Business Server application installed, start the Skype for Business services by launching the Skype for Business Server Management Shell with administrative privileges. Issue the Start-CsPool command, as shown in Figure 4.53.

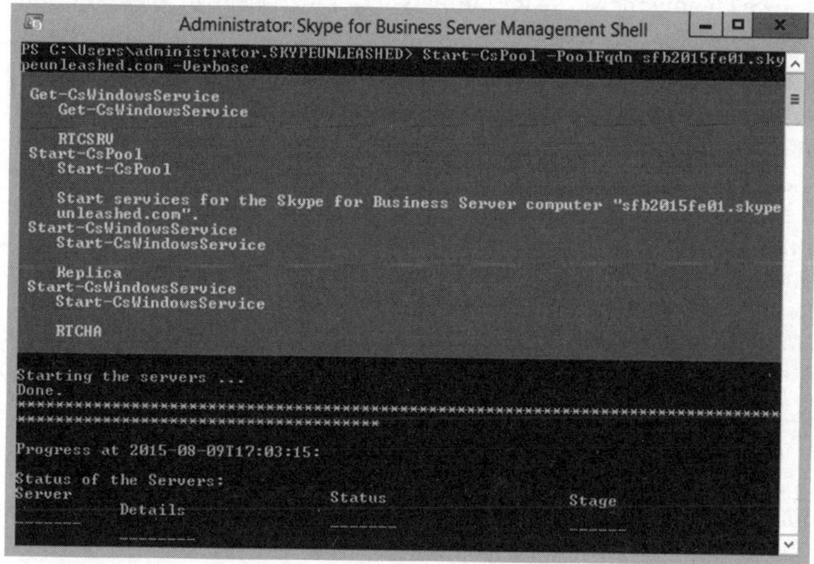

FIGURE 4.53 Starting the Front End pool after installation.

27. Ensure the command finishes successfully. You can also check the status of services in the Services MMC console found in the server administrative tools.

28. Click Exit to leave the Deployment Wizard.

The Enterprise Edition Front End pool is now installed and ready for further configuration using the Skype for Business Server Control Panel.

Note that the client autoconfiguration requirements are still the same. The following DNS records are required for client autoconfiguration:

- lyncdiscoverinternal.<sip_Domain> pointing to the IP address assigned to your Front End pool or Director internal web services.
- SRV record of sipinternaltls._tcp.<sip_Domain> for port 5061 pointing to the FQDN of your Front End pool or Director.
- sip.<sip_Domain> pointing to the IP address assigned to your Front End pool or Director.

Configuration and Administration Overview

The good news about Skype for Business Server 2015 is that with the Topology Builder tool, much of the infrastructure configuration is done automatically. Although both configuration and administration can be done from the Silverlight web GUI, there are many tasks for which only the Skype for Business Server Management Shell will suffice.

First, an introduction to the Skype for Business Server Control Panel: This section briefly covers the tabs and options in the Silverlight Control Panel web application. Before opening the Control Panel for the first time, ensure that the server is included in the list of trusted sites or the local intranet zone on the server or your client. Without this setting, the Control Panel will fail to launch. To launch the Control Panel on a Skype for Business Server 2015, select the Skype for Business Server Control Panel link from the Start menu under the Skype for Business Server 2015 program group. To launch the Control Panel from another system, enter the Admin simple URL you entered during the initial installation or https://<poolFQDN>/cscp. In the example environment this would be either https://skypeadmin.skypeunleashed.com/ or https://sfb2015fe01.skypeunleashed.com/cscp/. Either URL will bring you to the Control Panel.

When you first log in, you're brought to the Control Panel home page. The navigation bar is on the left and includes options for Home, Users, Topology, IM and Presence, Persistent Chat, Voice Routing, Voice Features, Response Groups, Conferencing, Clients, Federation and External Access, Monitoring and Archiving, Security, and finally Network Configuration.

On the Home page you'll see a link to a quick-start guide and other informational links in the center pane as well as shortcuts to common tasks in the main pane. Explanations of these functions and more are covered in detail in Chapter 13, "Administration of Skype for Business Server 2015."

Troubleshooting

As with every version of Skype for Business Server so far, there are two major gremlins with the Front End role installation: certificates and DNS. The Deployment Wizard takes most of the guesswork out of certificate generation by automatically filling the SAN fields with the appropriate FQDNs for a given deployment. However, in more complex environments, manual configuration might be necessary. The added convenience of the Deployment Wizard doesn't lessen the importance of certificates. They are still core to all server and server-client and server-server communications. DNS, on the other hand, is not automated. For each pool created, the administrator will need to create an A record for each pool pointing to the load-balanced VIP for multiple server pools or to the Front End IP address for single-server pools.

The Lync Server event log (yes, it is still referred to as "Lync Server" here!) is also a good place to check for errors. From the Start Menu, select Administrative Tools and then select Event Viewer. Expand the Applications and Services Logs item and select Lync Server. All events related to Skype for Business Server functions reside here. Often the error description is enough to identify the problem and make clear the resolution.

As with Lync Server 2013 before it, Skype for Business Server 2015 offers centralized logging as a feature. The Centralized Logging Service (or CLS for short) can be a tremendous timesaver when tracking down complex issues. For anyone who has had to troubleshoot a large deployment, this is especially true. Not only is logging for all servers centralized, but a base form of logging is always running by default. This means most errors do not need to be manually reproduced; they are likely already captured in the logs. For details on how to use these advanced management and troubleshooting tools, refer to Chapter 13.

Best Practices

The following are the best practices from this chapter:

- Use DNS load balancing for SIP traffic. A hardware load balancer is still required for web services such as the address book service.
- Explore the pool failover functions of Skype for Business Standard Edition before assuming that Skype for Business Enterprise Edition is the right architecture. A full description of both is included in Chapter 14, "High Availability and Disaster Recovery."
- Although the Skype for Business Server Control Panel might seem more familiar at first, there are many functions that can be accomplished only in the Management Shell.
- Always install the SQL backward-compatibility pack to ensure that all cmdlets run correctly.
- Use the RBAC controls to delegate administration rights. Delegate only the minimum rights needed to accomplish the required tasks.
- Always publish an updated topology before making changes or installing a new server role.
- It is recommended that you close Topology Builder when not making changes. This prevents conflicting topology changes, especially in large environments with multiple Skype for Business administrators.
- When deploying an Enterprise Edition Front End pool, deploy a minimum of three member servers. An odd number of servers in the pool is recommended.

Summary

The Skype for Business Server 2015 Front End Server role is the single most important role in the Skype for Business Server infrastructure. All core platform capabilities and features are dependent upon the Front End Server role. Whether installing Skype for Business Server in a "greenfield" deployment or performing an upgrade from a previous version of Lync Server, the Front End role will be the first server deployed in the environment. If you're planning a migration from Lync Server 2010, be sure to note the key architectural changes and supported server collocations in Skype for Business Server 2015. When considering whether to deploy a Standard Edition or Enterprise Edition Front End pool, keep in mind that both types of pools support all the same end-user features and workloads. However, the two most common reasons for choosing an Enterprise Edition pool are increased scalability and redundancy. By following Front End Server best practices and using this chapter as a guide, you will be well on your way to having a new Skype for Business Server 2015 environment up and running in no time!

CHAPTER 5

Skype for Business Server 2015 Edge Server

IN THIS CHAPTER

- Edge Server Overview
- Edge Server Installation
- Edge Server Configuration
- Edge Server Administration
- Edge Server Troubleshooting
- Edge Server Best Practices

The Skype for Business Server 2015 Edge Server enables remote access to the internal Skype for Business Server infrastructure. In addition to providing feature parity for external or remote users, the Edge Server can enhance a deployment by federating with partner organizations or public providers. These federation features help organizations use rich communication methods securely with each other across the Internet.

This chapter focuses on the Edge Server role installation and configuration. It covers how to deploy each of the Edge roles both in a standalone scenario and in a high-availability deployment where multiple Edge Servers are used.

Edge Server Overview

The Skype for Business Server 2015 Edge Server consists of four separate services: Access Edge Server, Web Conferencing Edge Server, A/V Edge Server, and the XMPP Gateway. Each service provides slightly different functionality, and depending on the organization's requirements, it might not be necessary to use all services. In Skype for Business Server 2015, all services are automatically deployed on every Edge Server.

The Edge Server only uses SQL Express to store the Local Configuration Store replica from the Central Management Store. Because the Edge Server is designed to be deployed in a network perimeter or DMZ, it runs a limited set of services to make it as secure as possible. Edge Servers are also typically not joined to the internal Active Directory (AD) Directory Services. The different Edge Server roles provide unique features, as shown in Figure 5.1.

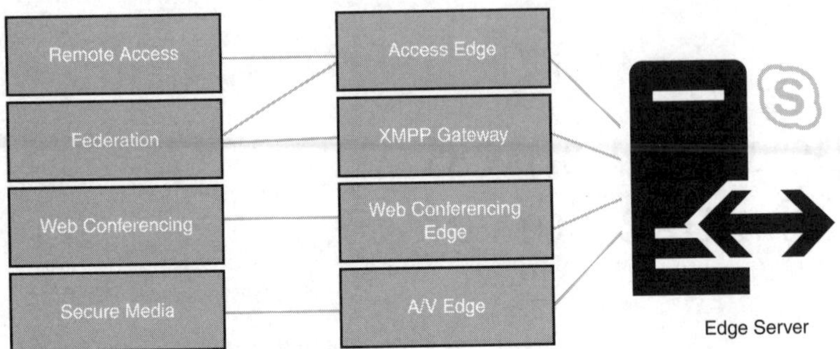

FIGURE 5.1 Edge Server services.

In addition to the Skype for Business Server 2015 Edge Server services, a reverse proxy solution is required to publish web services, including Mobility. For more information on reverse proxy requirements, see Chapter 32, "Firewall and Security Requirements."

Access Edge

The Access Edge service serves as a secure proxy for signaling traffic with external Edge Servers from other organizations as well as external endpoints of remote users. Without the Access Edge service deployed, all other Edge roles would not be able to function. The Access Edge provides remote access, federation, and public provider connectivity in Skype for Business Server 2015.

Remote Access

One function of the Access Edge is to provide remote access capabilities to a Skype for Business Server infrastructure. Once Skype for Business Server is deployed internally, the next step is usually to allow external access to the Skype for Business Server infrastructure so remote users can sign in across the Internet.

As long as the appropriate SRV records are created in the external DNS or the client is manually configured correctly, a user can connect to the Skype for Business Server infrastructure in and out of the office without ever making a change to their endpoint. This enables users to have full access to Skype for Business 2015 regardless of location.

NOTE

Because 443 is a standard, well-known port, it is used for remote access by the Access Edge Service.

The Access Edge use certificates and Mutual TLS (MTLS) to secure the signaling traffic (SIP) between the Edge Server and the internal Skype for Business Server as well as between the Edge Server and the partner Edge Server or remote endpoints. This ensures that instant messaging and Presence traffic is never transmitted in plain text.

SIP Federated Domains

The Access Edge also provides the capability to federate with other organizations that have deployed Lync or Skype for Business Server, meaning users from both organizations can communicate with each other seamlessly.

Unless media ports used for audio, video, and application sharing are blocked by the external firewall of either organization, users will be able to communicate with federated users in the same way they communicate with other internal users, depending on the version of Lync or Skype for Business Server the partner has deployed. The only exception is directory search. Users do not have directory search capabilities of the federated partner's user directory. This means users in companyabc.com cannot search the directory of companyxyz.com by keyword, assuming these two organizations are federated. To find a federated partner, a user needs to know the SIP URI of the federated user in order to search for them.

NOTE

Port 5061 is the standard port used by the Access Edge to communicate with federated partners.

SIP Federated Providers

A special form of federation is the capability to use Skype for Business Server to communicate with contacts on the public IM networks, referred to as SIP federated providers. The only federated provider supported is Skype. AOL and Yahoo! are no longer supported providers. To communicate with users from these public networks, Skype for Business users need to add the SIP address to their contact lists.

Skype for Business Server users can see Presence and exchange instant messages with their Skype contacts when the Skype provider is provisioned. The conversations are limited to person-to-person communication and cannot include three or more participants, unlike conversations within the organization or with federated contacts. Audio support with Skype was added in Lync Server 2013. Video support was added in Skype for Business Server 2015.

Web Conferencing Edge

The Web Conferencing Edge service enables remote users and external participants to participate in web conferences with internal users. The Web Conferencing Edge enables remote users to participate in collaboration sessions that involve application sharing, desktop sharing, whiteboarding, and polling. Before a remote user can join a web conference, the remote user must first authenticate with the Access Edge.

Organizations can also elect to allow anonymous or unauthenticated users to join web conferences. Web conferencing uses Microsoft's Proprietary Shared Object Model (PSOM) protocol over HTTPS port 443. It is secure and resilient to proxy servers. For more information on web conferencing functionality, see Chapter 18, "Skype for Business Native Video and Data Conferencing."

A/V Edge

The A/V Edge service is responsible for securely relaying audio and video media among internal, external, and federated contacts. The A/V Edge uses the Interactive Connectivity Establishment (ICE), Simple Traversal Utilities for NAT (STUN), and Traversal Using Relay NAT (TURN) protocols to enable endpoints to traverse firewalls and communicate from nearly any network with Internet connectivity.

When possible, endpoints attempt to use a peer-to-peer connection for media streams, but when an endpoint is behind a NAT device such as a home router, the A/V Edge can act as a relay point between the endpoints to facilitate communication. The A/V Edge uses a combination of TCP port 443 and UDP port 3478 to negotiate and establish the media stream network path.

To support media traffic between internal and external users, an additional service exists on the Edge Server called the Media Relay Authentication Service (MRAS). This service is responsible for authenticating media requests from internal users to external contacts. When a user wants to initiate an A/V conversation with an external participant, the external user is provided with a temporary media token that the user then uses to authenticate to MRAS before media traffic can flow through the A/V Edge.

XMPP Gateway

The Edge Server integrates the XMPP gateway functionality. The XMPP gateway service translates SIP to XMPP, and vice versa. It is a gateway between the two protocols, which allows Skype for Business to federate with XMPP partners. XMPP federation provides Presence information and instant messaging integration for XMPP networks such as Google's GTalk. The Edge Server listens for XMPP federation traffic on port 5269.

Collocation

All Edge services (Access Edge, A/V Edge, Web Conferencing Edge, and XMPP Gateway) are collocated on the Edge Server and installed together. The Edge Server cannot be collocated with any other Skype for Business Server role. The Edge Server does not require access or being joined to Active Directory because it is deployed in the perimeter network.

Edge Server Installation

The rest of this chapter focuses on the actual installation and configuration of the Edge Server. The next sections discuss the Edge Server hardware, operating system, and software prerequisites.

Hardware Requirements

The Edge Server processor requirements are as follows:

- ▶ 64-bit dual-processor, quad-core, 2.26 GHz or faster

CAUTION

Skype for Business Server is a 64-bit application only and requires a 64-bit-capable processor. This is generally not an issue with modern hardware, but be sure to verify that legacy hardware supports a 64-bit operating system before attempting to use it for an Edge Server.

The Edge Server memory requirement is as follows:

- ▶ 16GB RAM

The Edge Server disk requirements are as follows:

- ▶ Local storage, minimum 10,000 RPM hard disk drives or solid state drives (SSD), with at least 72GB of free space in a 2× RAID 1 configuration

The Edge Server network requirements are as follows:

- ▶ Two network interfaces that are dual-port network adapters, 1Gbps or faster. NIC teaming with a single MAC address and a single IP address per interface is supported.

TIP

When teaming multiple network adapters, use them only for fault tolerance. This means network adapters should be used for failover only and should not be combined for greater throughput.

Operation System Requirements

The Edge Server supports the following operating systems:

- ▶ Windows Server 2012 R2 Standard or Enterprise Edition 64-bit version with all latest updates installed (including KB article 2982006)
- ▶ Windows Server 2012 with KB article 2858668 installed

Software Requirements

The Edge Server requires the following software to be installed prior to installing the Edge Server:

- Microsoft .NET Framework 4.5
- Windows Identity Foundation

The Edge Server installs the following software:

- Microsoft Visual C++ 2013 Redistributable (x64) – 12.0.21005

Configure Networking

After the required components are installed, you must configure the DNS suffix of the Edge Server. To configure the DNS suffix of the Windows Server, perform the following steps:

1. Open the server's System Properties (Control Panel, System and Security, System).
2. Click the Change button.
3. Click the More button.
4. In the Primary DNS Suffix of This Computer field, enter the DNS suffix. The DNS suffix appended to the server name must match the FQDN of the Edge Server in Skype for Business Topology Builder.

It is important to configure the Edge Server networking before installing Skype for Business Server 2015 Edge Server. An Edge Server must have at least two network adapters: one for external traffic and one for communicating with internal servers or clients. Figure 5.2 provides an overview of the Edge Server network adapter configuration.

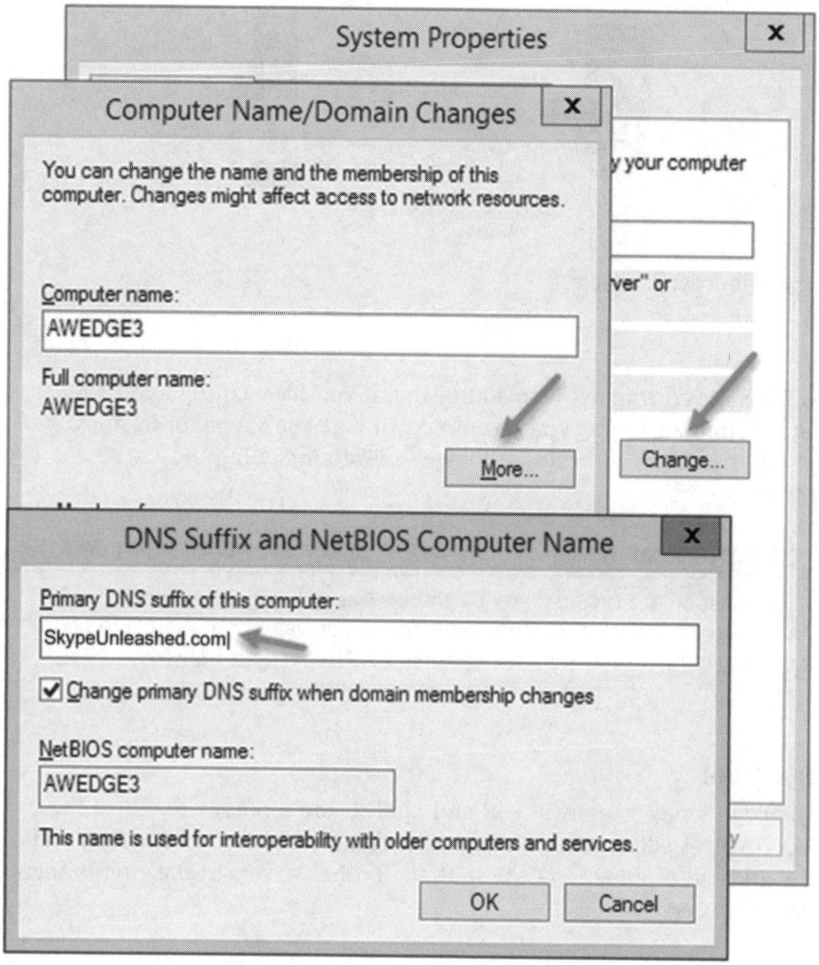

FIGURE 5.2 Edge Server network adapter configuration.

TIP

Make sure the necessary routing statements are entered on each Edge Server so that the traffic for internal clients and servers uses the correct adapter. As shown in Figure 5.3, only the external facing adapter should have a default gateway assigned in the IP network settings to ensure consistent routing behavior. If your clients or internal servers are on a subnet separate from your Edge Server internal network interface, persistent routes must be added in Windows. Use the `netsh interface ipv4 add route` command for this configuration.

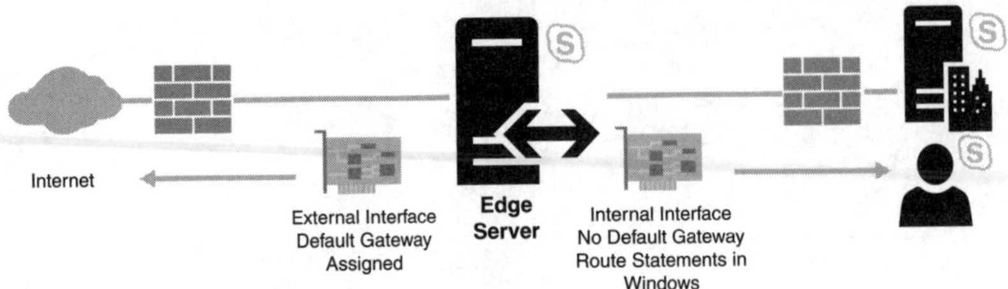

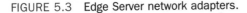

FIGURE 5.3 Edge Server network adapters.

IPv6 Support

Skype for Business Edge Server supports IPv6 addressing. If you have configured IPv6 addresses on the host Windows Server, you can now configure the Skype for Business Server Topology to use these IPv6 addresses. All Edge services, including the XMPP Gateway, support IPv6.

TIP

To support IPv6, you must create DNS records for the IPv6 addresses. These host records are defined as AAAA records. The DNS records required are consistent between IPv4 and IPv6. For details on required DNS records, see Chapter 10, "Dependent Services."

Create the Edge Pool

Before installing the Edge Server, you must edit and publish the topology to reflect the new Edge pool. This involves editing the existing topology, adding a new Edge role, and then publishing the updated topology to CMS so that all other servers in the environment are aware of the new Edge Server.

Editing the Topology

The next step in deploying an Edge Server is to edit the existing Skype for Business Server topology. This task must be performed from a Skype for Business Server on the internal network such as a Front End Server. To edit the topology, perform the following steps:

1. Open the Skype for Business Server Topology Builder.
2. When prompted to download a topology from an existing deployment, click OK.
3. Save your topology file as appropriate.
4. Expand the Site node where the Edge Server will be deployed.
5. Expand the Skype for Business Server 2015 node.
6. Right-click the Edge pools node and then select New Edge Pool.
7. Click Next to begin the wizard.

8. In the Pool FQDN field in the wizard, specify the fully qualified domain name (FQDN) of the internal edge of the Edge pool.

9. Follow the appropriate subsequent sections depending on whether a single Edge Server or a pool of load-balanced Edge Servers will be deployed.

Deploying a Single Edge Server

If you are deploying a single Edge Server, follow these steps:

1. Select the option This Pool Has One Server, and then click Next.

2. If federation will be used, check the Enable Federation box.

3. If XMPP federation will be used, check the Enable XMPP Federation box, and then click Next.

4. If a single public IP address will be used for the Access Edge, Web Conferencing Edge, and A/V Edge services, check the box Use a Single FQDN and IP Address. This requires using ports other than 443 for the Access Edge and Web Conferencing services.

NOTE

It is recommended that you use separate unique IP addresses for each of the services: Access, Web Conferencing, and Audio/Video.

5. Check valid IP options as they relate to your deployment. If your deployment is using IPv6, check the IPv6 boxes for the internal and external interface. If not, ensure that only the IPv4 boxes are checked.

6. If the IP address used for the A/V Edge uses NAT, check the box The External IP Address of This Edge Pool Is Translated by NAT. Click Next when complete.

7. Under the Access Edge Service field, enter the external FQDN and port of the Access Edge. Typically, this is similar to sip.companyabc.com and port 443.

NOTE

If you elected to use a single FQDN and IP address for your public Edge services, you will be permitted to enter only a single FQDN, and the default ports will be set to 5061, 444, and 443.

8. In the Web Conferencing Edge Service field, enter the external FQDN and port of the Web Conferencing Edge. Typically, the name and port are similar to webconf.companyabc.com and port 443.

9. In the A/V Edge Service field, enter the external FQDN and port of the A/V Edge. Typically, the name and port are similar to av.companyabc.com and port 443. Click Next when complete.

NOTE

If you are using IPv6 in your environment and have selected to enable IPv6 on the Edge Server, you will be required to enter the IPv6 and/or IPv4 address for each Edge Server.

10. Enter the internal-facing IP address for the Edge Server and click Next.
11. In the External IP Address field, enter the address of the external Edge. Click Next.
12. Select a next-hop pool to be used by the Edge Server to route network traffic internally to. Click Next. If a director is deployed, you should select the director as the next hop.
13. Associate any Front End pools and Mediation pools that will use this Edge Server for external media traffic. These Front End pools and Mediation pools will route traffic to the Edge Server that is not routable internally. Click Finish to complete the wizard.

Deploying a Load-Balanced Edge Pool

If you are deploying multiple Edge Servers in a pool configuration, referred to as an *Edge pool*, follow these steps:

1. Select the option This Pool Has Multiple Servers, and then click Next.
2. If federation will be used, check the Enable Federation box.
3. If XMPP federation will be used, check the Enable XMPP Federation box, and then click Next.
4. If a single public IP address will be used for the Access Edge, Web Conferencing Edge, and A/V Edge services, check the box Use a Single FQDN and IP Address. This requires using ports other than 443 for the Access Edge and Web Conferencing services.

NOTE

It is recommended that you use separate unique IP addresses for each of the services: Access, Web Conferencing, and Audio/Video.

5. Check valid IP options as they relate to your deployment. If your deployment is using IPv6, check the IPv6 boxes for the internal and external interface. If not, ensure that only the IPv4 boxes are checked.
6. If the IP address used for the A/V Edge uses NAT, check the box The External IP Address of This Edge Pool Is Translated by NAT. Click Next when complete.
7. In the Access Edge service field, enter the external FQDN and port of the Access Edge. Typically, this is similar to sip.companyabc.com and port 443.

8. In the Web Conferencing Edge Service field, enter the external FQDN and port of the Web Conferencing Edge. Typically, the name and port are similar to webconf.companyabc.com and port 443.
9. In the A/V Edge Service field, enter the external FQDN and port of the A/V Edge. Typically, the name and port are similar to av.companyabc.com and port 443. Click Next when complete.
10. Define the information for all Edge Servers that will be part of this Edge pool. Click Add.
11. Enter the internal IP address of the Edge Server and the internal server FQDN. Click Next.

NOTE

Each member of the Edge Server pool must have a unique external IP address for each public service, as well as a unique internal IP address. Your load-balancing method will distribute traffic to each member on the designated IP addresses. In the wizard, make sure you are entering the IP addresses assigned to the pool member, not that of the pool.

12. In the Access Edge Service field, enter the external IP address assigned to the Edge Server.
13. In the Web Conferencing Edge Service field, enter the external IP address assigned to the Edge Server.
14. In the A/V Edge Service field, enter the external IP address assigned to the Edge Server and then click Finish.
15. Repeat the previous steps for each Edge pool member and then click Next.
16. Select a next-hop pool to be used by the Edge pool to route network traffic internally to. Click Next. If a director is deployed, you should select the director as the next hop.
17. Associate any Front End pools and Mediation pools that will use this Edge Server for external media traffic. These Front End pools and Mediation pools will route traffic to the Edge Server that is not routable internally. Click Finish to complete the wizard.

Publishing the Topology

After the topology is modified to include the new Edge pool, the configuration must be published. This step publishes the changes to the Central Management Store. All Skype for Business and Lync Servers in the topology will update their local configuration stores to match to recognize the new Edge pool.

1. From the Skype for Business Server Topology Builder where the new Edge pool was defined, click the top node of the Topology Builder.
2. Click the Action menu and select Publish Topology. Alternatively, you can select Publish Topology from the Actions pane on the right side of the console.
3. Click Next to begin publishing the topology.
4. When the log indicates a successful update, click Finish to complete the wizard.

Install the Edge Server

At this point, the target server is ready to be installed as an Edge Server.

Exporting the Topology

The process for installing a local configuration store on an Edge Server varies depending on whether an Edge Server is part of the Active Directory domain and can access the configuration store directly. Typically, the Edge Server is isolated and requires a few extra manual steps to read the topology. These steps involve exporting the entire topology to a ZIP file and copying it to the Edge Server.

1. On an internal Skype for Business Server, such as a Front End Server, open the Skype for Business Server Management Shell.
2. Run the following command:

   ```
   Export-CSConfiguration -FileName C:\Config.zip
   ```

3. Copy the exported file to the target server that will be the new Edge Server.

Installing a Local Configuration Store

To install any Skype for Business Server role, the target server must first have a local configuration store installed and populated with the topology information.

1. Insert the Skype for Business Server 2015 media on the Edge Server and launch `Setup.exe`, found in the `Setup\amd64` folder.
2. Enter a location for the installation and then click Install.
3. Click Install or Update Skype for Business Server System.
4. Under Step 1: Install Location Configure Store, click Run.
5. Because the Edge Server is part of a workgroup and cannot access the Central Management Store, select Import from a File and then click Browse. If the Edge Server is part of the same domain as your internal Skype for Business Servers, it will be able to read the Central Management Store directly.
6. Select the ZIP file that was exported earlier and then click Next.
7. Click Finish when the topology is imported successfully.

Installing the Skype for Business Server Components

The following steps will read topology information from the local configuration store and then install any prerequisites and Skype for Business Server role identified for this server.

1. Under Step 2: Setup or Remove Skype for Business Server Components, click the Run button.

2. Click Next to begin the Edge Server installation.

3. When prompted to install the Microsoft Network service, click the Install button.

4. Click Finish when the installation completes.

Creating Certificates

Like all other roles in Skype for Business Server, the Edge Server communicates to other servers in the organization using Mutual Transport Layer Security (MTLS). The Edge Server requires two certificates. At a minimum, the Edge Server always requires a certificate with its internal fully qualified domain name (FQDN) for communication to other internal servers, and a certificate for external Edge services. The internal certificate's subject name (SN) must specify the Edge pool's internal FQDN. The external certificate must specify all public FQDNs used by the Edge Server.

The certificate used for the Access Edge should adhere to the following guidelines:

- The subject name should be the published name for the Access Edge.
- All supported SIP domains must be entered as a subject alternative name (SAN) in the format sip.<SIP domain>.

The certificate used for the Web Conferencing Edge should adhere to the following guideline:

- The subject name should be the published name for the Web Conferencing Edge.

The certificate used for the A/V Edge is a self-signed certificate automatically generated by the Edge Server. As the administrator, you won't need to create it. This certificate is used only to generate encryption keys, but the name used by the wizard matches the internal Edge pool FQDN.

See Chapter 10 for a more detailed explanation of certificate requirements.

NOTE

The Certificate Wizard in Skype for Business Server automatically populates the subject name and required subject alternative names based on the published topology. This greatly simplifies certificate confusion created by prior versions. As long as the published topology is accurate, changing the certificate names or adding subject alternative names in the Certificate Wizard is unnecessary.

Use the following steps to request the necessary Edge Server certificates:

1. Under Step 3: Request, Install, or Assign Certificate, click the Run button.
2. Highlight the Edge Internal option and click the Request button.
3. Click Next to begin the wizard.
4. Select either Send the Request Immediately to an Online Certification Authority or Prepare the Request Now, but Send It Later (Offline Certificate Request). Click Next.

TIP

The option to send a certificate request immediately is usually reserved for internal servers. This requires communication between the Edge Server and an internal Certificate Authority (CA). If your server has access, you can choose this option and enter the URL and credentials required. However, for Edge Servers it is more common to generate offline requests for internal certificates because the Edge Server doesn't have network connectivity to the internal CA.

5. Click the Browse button and select a file location for the certificate signing request (CSR) file to be saved. Click Next.
6. To use the standard Web Server template, click Next on the Specify Alternate Certificate Template page.

TIP

Many organizations with managed internal Certificate Authority deployments are not using the built-in Web Server templates. You should check with your CA administrator to verify the certificate temple that should be used for your Edge Server requests.

7. Enter a friendly name for the certificate, such as `Edge Server Internal`. This is only a display name for the certificate.
8. Select a key bit length for your certificate: 2048 or 4096.
9. If the certificate should be exportable, select the Mark Certificate Private Key as Exportable check box and then click Next.

TIP

If this is the first server in an Edge pool, the internal and external certificates must be exportable. All Edge Servers in the Edge pool must share the same internal and external certificates. If this is not the first Edge Server in the pool, you should cancel the wizard and instead import the two certificates from the first Edge Server and then follow the steps to assign certificates.

10. Through the next few steps, enter all organization information that applies to your organization. Click Next to continue.

11. Click Next after reviewing the automatically populated subject and subject alternative names.
12. For the internal certificate, you should not configure additional subject alternative names, because they are not needed. For the external certificate, it is possible to enter additional SAN entries if they are required. Click Next.
13. Click Next to complete the request, and then click Finish to complete the wizard.

After completing the wizard, you must run it one more time to generate a CSR for the External Edge Server certificate. Repeat all the preceding steps, but choose the External Certificate as part of step 1.

Importing Offline Certificate Requests

After you have processed an offline certificate request from the Certificate Authority, a certificate file will be issued. The certificate file must be imported to your Edge Server. The easiest way to import this certificate is through the Skype for Business Server Deployment Wizard.

1. Under Step 3: Request, Install, or Assign Certificate, click the Run button.
2. In the Certificate Wizard window, choose Import Certificate.
3. Choose the certificate file issued by your Certificate Authority and finish the Import Wizard.
4. This certificate should now be available to assign to your Edge Server. See the next section for more information.

Assigning Certificates

After the necessary certificates have been created, they must be assigned to the internal Edge and external Edge of the Edge Server. This process binds each certificate to a specific Edge service. To assign a certificate, perform the following steps:

1. Under Step 3: Request, Install, or Assign Certificate, click the Run button.
2. Highlight Edge Internal and click the Assign button.
3. Click the Next button to begin the wizard.
4. Select Assign an Existing Certificate and then click Next.
5. Select the correct certificate issued by the internal CA for this usage. Certificates will not appear here unless they can be verified to a Trusted Root Certification Authority and have a private key associated. Click Next.
6. Verify that the certificate is selected and then click Next.
7. Click Finish when the process is complete.

Repeat the previous steps to assign the certificate issued by the public CA to the external Edge of the Edge Server.

Starting the Services

After the necessary certificates are requested and assigned, the Edge Server services can be started.

1. Under Step 4: Start Services, click the Run button.
2. Click Next to start the Skype for Business Server services.
3. Click Finish to complete the wizard.

At this point, the Edge Server installation is complete and functional.

Edge Server Configuration

This section outlines common configuration tasks for Edge pools. Major changes to the Edge Server configuration must be carried out using the Skype for Business Server Topology Builder. This includes changing IP addresses, changing DNS names, or changing Front End or Mediation pool associations. Any topology changes will require running the Skype for Business Server Deployment Wizard again to ensure that the changes are reflected on the Edge Server.

Other configuration changes, such as enabling certain features or configuring federation, can be carried out in the Skype for Business Server Control Panel or the Skype for Business Server Management Shell. Common configurations are outlined in this section as well as the section on administration.

Enabling Edge Server Features

To enable Edge Servers to process remote access and federation requests, the Access Edge configuration must be updated to enable these features. Figure 5.4 shows a sample policy configuration. Use the following steps to enable Access Edge features to the Skype for Business Server infrastructure:

1. Open the Skype for Business Server Control Panel.

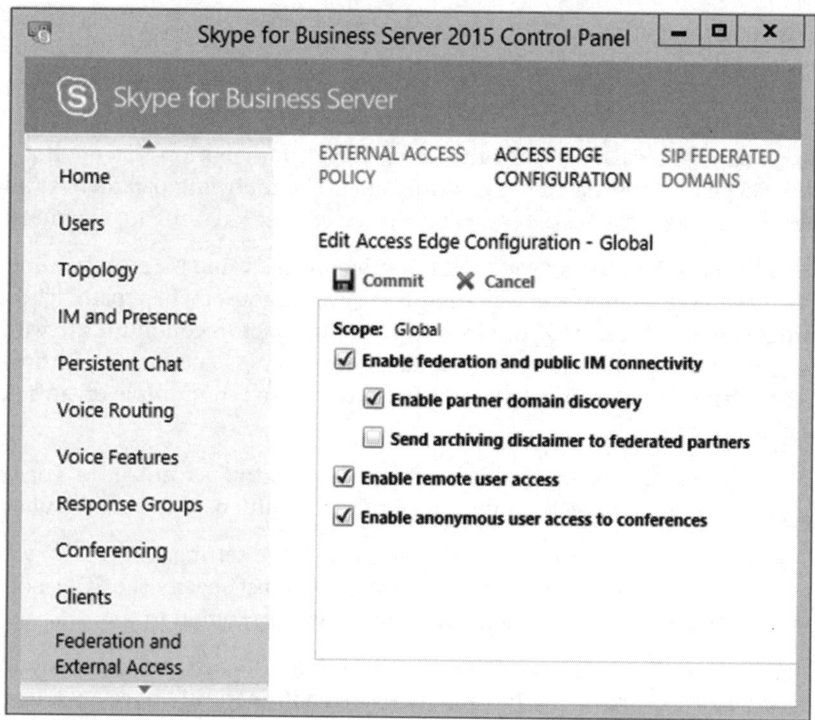

FIGURE 5.4 Access Edge Configuration.

2. Select Federation and External User Access in the navigation pane.
3. Click Access Edge Configuration.
4. Highlight the Global policy; then click Edit and then Modify.
5. Check the Enable Federation and Public IM Connectivity box.
6. If DNS SRV lookups are allowed to discover federated partners, check the Enable Partner Domain Discovery box.
7. If an archiving disclaimer should be sent to federated contacts when initiating an IM conversation, check the Send Archiving Disclaimer to Federated Partners box.
8. Check the Enable Remote User Access box.
9. If the Web Conferencing service should allow anonymous external participants, check the Enable Anonymous User Access to Conferences box.
10. Click Commit to accept the changes.

Alternatively, the Skype for Business Server Management Shell can be used to configure these settings:

```
Set-CSAccessEdgeConfiguration -AllowOutsideusers $true -AllowFederatedUsers $true
➥-EnablePartnerDiscovery $true -EnableArchivingDisclaimer $true
➥AllowAnonymousUsers $true
```

Some additional options are available for the Access Edge configuration that are not exposed in the Skype for Business Server Control Panel. The following parameters can also be used as part of the `Set-CSAccessEdgeConfiguration` cmdlet to configure external access:

- **`BeClearingHouse`**—This has a `true` or `false` value. If this value is `true`, then the Edge Servers serve as a federation gateway (that is, a clearinghouse) where participating companies connect directly to your infrastructure in order to communicate with other organizations participating in your Skype for Business network. A clearinghouse Edge Server can be used to support direct federation between multiple organizations. Typically, this value is `false`.

- **`CertificatesDeletedPercentage`**—This setting controls the percentage of Trusted Certificate entries that are deleted during certificate maintenance. Default value is 20.

- **`DefaultRouteFQDN`**—This setting should only be set if the setting, `UseDefaultRouting`, is set to `true`. When you enable default routing, you must specify the FQDN of the external Edge Server where all federation requests will be routed to.

- **`EnableDiscoveredPartnerContactsLimit`**—This has a `true` or `false` value. By default, any federated partners that are discovered automatically have a contact limit imposed. This setting can be used to disable that contact limit by default.

- **`UseDefaultRouting`**—This has a `true` or `false` value indicating whether the Edge Servers will use a manually entered default route FQDN. This value is `false` by default, which enables Edge Servers to use DNS SRV records to discover where to route federation requests.

- **`KeepCRLsUpToDateForPeers`**—This has a `true` or `false` value indicating whether the Edge Servers will periodically check whether a partner's certificate is still valid based on the CRL. This parameter is `true` by default.

- **`MarkSourceVerifiableOnOutgoingMessages`**—This has a `true` or `false` value indicating whether the Edge Servers mark outgoing messages from a verified source. This enables partners to assign a higher level of trust to messages they receive from an organization marking messages as verifiable. This parameter is `true` by default.

- **`MaxAcceptedCertificatesStored`**—This setting allows administrators to control the maximum number of trusted certificates that are stored on each Edge Server. The default value is `1000`.

- **`MaxContactsPerDiscoveredPartner`**—By default, any federated partners that are discovered automatically have a contact limit of 1000 imposed. This setting can be used to decrease or increase that limit.
- **`OutgoingTLSCountForFederatedPartners`**—This is a numeric value from 1 to 4 indicating the maximum number of connections that can be used for a federated partner. The default value is `4`, but if connections should be more limited, this value can be reduced.
- **`VerificationLevel`**—If you are using default routing (`UseDefaultRouting`), the `VerificationLevel` property is used to monitor and assess the verification level of incoming messages. Here are the valid values:
    - **`AlwaysVerifiable`**—All requests received on the default route are marked as verified. If a verification header is not present, it automatically is added to the message.
    - **`AlwaysUnverifiable`**—Messages are passed only if the addressee (the user the message is intended for) has configured an Allow ACE (access control entry) for the person who sent the message.
    - **`UseSourceVerification`**—Message verification is based on the verification level included with the message. If no verification header is present, the message is marked as unverified.

Introducing High Availability

Redundancy for Edge Servers requires just adding more Edge Servers to an Edge pool. There is no logical limit on the number of Edge Servers that can be part of an Edge pool. Load balancing can be done either with DNS load-balancing requests or by using a hardware load balancer.

DNS load balancing is achieved by entering multiple host records in DNS for the Edge pool FQDN, one entry for each Edge Server in the Edge pool. For example, if an Edge pool with the FQDN access.skypeunleashed.com has three Edge Servers, there would be three host records. Each host record (access.skypeunleashed.com) would point to one of the three Edge Servers' IP addresses. When clients and servers attempt to reach a server that is unavailable, they attempt to use an alternative server.

A hardware load balancer can be used instead of DNS load balancing for Edge pools. Refer to your hardware load balancer vendor's documentation. Confirm that it can load-balance SIP traffic.

TIP

This method is best achieved using a single VIP for the internal-facing services. From an external perspective, all three services should be load balanced, but they should all use a separate VIP.

Adding Edge Servers to a Pool

Adding an Edge Server to an Edge pool requires updating and publishing the topology to reflect the change. Use the following steps to add another Edge pool member:

1. Expand the Edge Servers node.
2. Right-click the Edge pool name and select New Server.
3. Enter the internal IP address and FQDN IP address of the Edge Server's internal interface. Click Next.
4. Enter the external IP addresses for the Edge Server's Access Edge, Web Conferencing Edge, and A/V Edge services. Click OK.
5. Click OK when complete.

Next, publish the topology and proceed with the new Edge Server installation.

To complete installation of the Edge Server, follow the steps defined in the "Install the Edge Server" section earlier in this chapter.

After installing the new Edge Server, if you're using DNS load balancing, be sure to add a host record in DNS for the Edge pool pointing to the IP address of the new Edge Server. If you are using hardware load balancing, add the IP address of the new Edge Server in the hardware load balancer configuration so that traffic can start flowing to the new Edge Server.

Edge Server Administration

Administration of Edge pool features is done through either the Skype for Business Server Control Panel or Skype for Business Server Management Shell. Much of the administration involves configuring various external access and conferencing policies for the users.

Editing the Global External Access Policy

For users to connect to your Skype for Business Server infrastructure remotely (that is, from the Internet), their Active Directory accounts must be enabled for external access. This can be done at a global level so that it applies to all users, or it can be configured on a per-site or per-user basis. The following steps show how to enable external access for all users in the organization.

1. Open the Skype for Business Server Control Panel.
2. Select Federation and External User Access in the navigation pane.
3. Click External Access Policy.
4. Highlight the Global policy, click Edit, and click Modify.

5. Check the Enable Communications with Federated Users box to allow federation with other organizations.
6. Check the Enable Communications with XMPP Federated Users box if you want to federate with external XMPP networks.
7. Check the Enable Communications with Remote Users box to allow users external access.
8. Check the Enable Communications with Public Users box to allow users to communicate with consumers on public networks such as Skype.
9. Click Commit when complete. A sample configuration is shown in Figure 5.5.

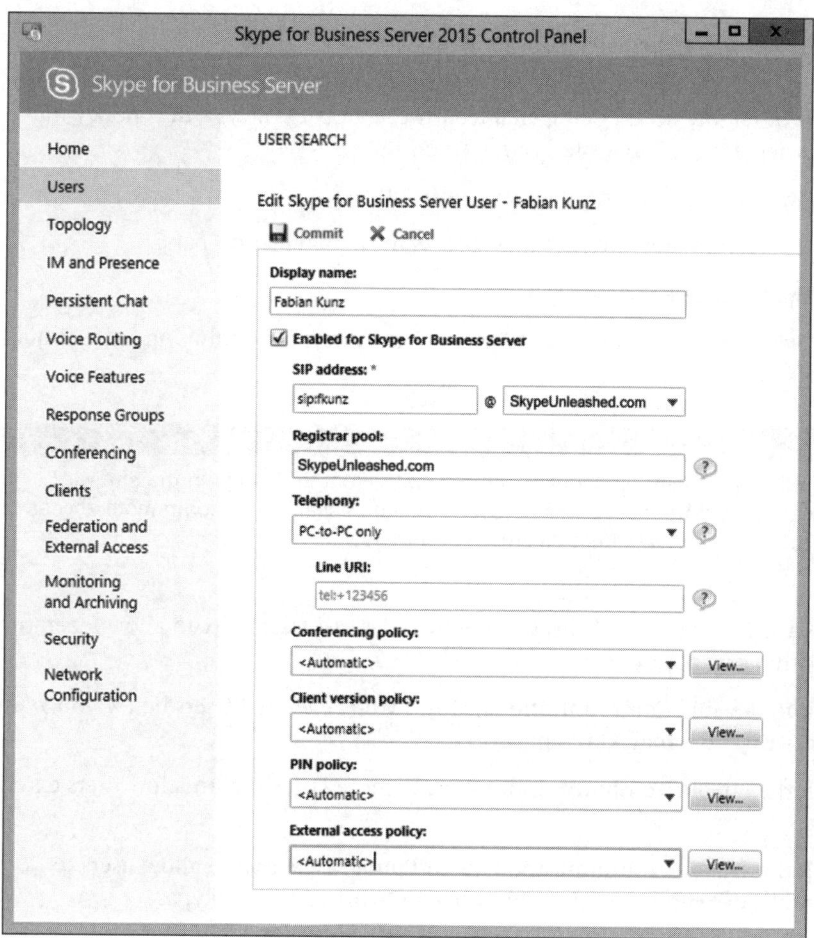

FIGURE 5.5 Edit the global external access policy.

Alternatively, the Skype for Business Server Management Shell can also be used to configure these settings:

```
Set-CSExternalAccessPolicy Global -EnableOutsideAccess $true
➥-EnableFederationAccess $true -EnablePublicCloudAccess $true
➥-EnablePublicCloudAudioVideoAccess $true -EnableXMPPAccess $true
```

TIP

The `EnablePublicCloudAudioVideoAccess` parameter in the preceding example enables audio and video communication to Skype.

Creating a New External Access Policy

In some scenarios, it is best to enable these features only for a select group of users or sites. Instead of remote access being enabled on the global policy, a new policy must be created and then assigned to a site or user accounts.

1. Open the Skype for Business Server Control Panel.
2. Select Federation and External User Access in the navigation pane.
3. Click Access Edge Policy.
4. Click New and then select Site Policy or User Policy, depending on what should be targeted.

NOTE

If a site policy is defined, all users associated with Front End pools in the site will automatically inherit the policy. This is used to automatically provision remote access features to some sites while not allowing it to others.

5. Check the Enable Communications with Federated Users box to allow federation with other organizations.
6. Check the Enable Communications with XMPP Federated Users box if you want to federate with external XMPP networks.
7. Check the Enable Communications with Remote Users box to allow users external access.
8. Check the Enable Communications with Public Users box to allow users to communicate with consumers on public networks such as Skype.
9. Click Commit when complete.

Alternatively, the Skype for Business Server Management Shell can also be used to create the new policy:

```
New-CSExternalAccessPolicy -identity "Allow All Features"
➥-EnableOutsideAccess $true -EnableFederationAccess $true
➥-EnablePublicCloudAccess $true -EnablePublicCloudAudioVideoAccess $true
➥-EnableXMPPAccess $true
```

TIP

To create a policy with site scope using the Skype for Business Server Management Shell, name the policy with a "`Site:`" prefix followed by the site name. For instance, if a site called `SF` existed, the preceding sample policy should be named `Site:SF` to apply only to that site.

Assigning External Access Policies

After the new user policy is created, it must be assigned to a user account. If the external policy is created with a site scope, this step is not required.

1. Open the Skype for Business Server Control Panel.
2. Select Users in the navigation pane.
3. Search for a user, highlight the account, click Modify, and click Assign Polices.
4. In the External Access Policy section, select the new external access policy and click OK. An example of this configuration was shown earlier in Figure 5.5.

The Skype for Business Server Management Shell can also be used to assign a policy to a user:

```
Grant-CSExternalAccessPolicy user@SkypeUnleashed.com -PolicyName "Allow all features"
```

Managing Federation

After enabling user accounts for federation, administrators can manage the organizations with which they want to federate. If federation partner discovery lookups are allowed on the Edge Server configuration, all domains are automatically allowed. Manually adding allowed domains can still be done to grant a higher level of trust to partners, but is not required. If partner discovery is not allowed, administrators must manually add all federated partners to the allow list.

Blocking a federated domain can be used to prevent internal users from communicating with specific partners. This is used in situations where federation should be allowed globally, but blocked to only a few specific SIP domain names.

Skype for Business Server 2015 only allows or blocks federated users at the SIP domain level. This means you cannot allow a subset of your users to communicate with users from a federated partner or allow only a subset of users from a federated partner to communicate with your users. Skype for Business Server 2015 does not provide this level of granular control of federation. You would need to investigate third-party options.

To allow or block a federated domain, use the following steps:

1. Open the Skype for Business Server Control Panel.
2. Select Federation and External User Access in the navigation pane.
3. Click SIP Federated Domains.
4. Click New and then select either Allowed Domain or Blocked Domain.
5. Enter the SIP domain name of the federated domain allowed or blocked, as shown in Figure 5.6, and click OK.

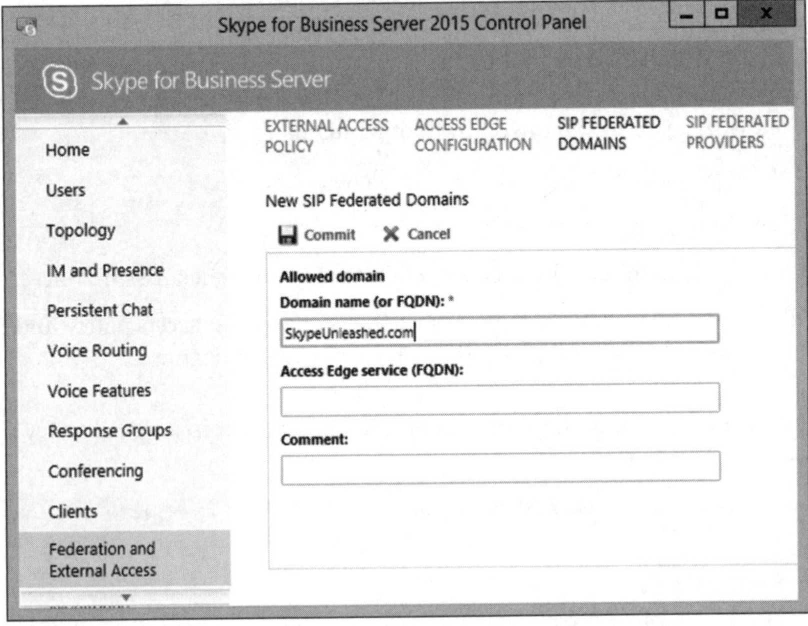

FIGURE 5.6 Adding an allowed SIP domain for federation.

CAUTION

When you are adding an allowed federation SIP domain, the option exists to add the partner's Access Edge FQDN. This field is not required, but when it is used it grants a higher level of trust to the domain by allowing more requests per second from that federated domain. Be careful when using this field because if a partner changes its FQDN later, the configuration for this federated domain will no longer be valid.

The Skype for Business Server Management Shell can also be used to perform these tasks. To allow a new federated domain, use the following command. The only required parameter is the SIP domain name, but a comment and partner's Access Edge FQDN can also be specified. In addition, the `MarkForMonitoring` parameter can be set to enable quality monitoring to this federated domain by a Monitoring Server role.

```
New-CSAllowedDomain -Domain <federated SIP Domain Name> -Comment <Comment string>
➥-ProxyFQDN <Partner Access Edge FQDN> -MarkForMonitoring <True|False>
```

To block a domain from sending or receiving messages, use the following command:

```
New-CSBlockedDomain -Domain <federated SIP Domain Name>
```

Managing XMPP Federation

The XMPP gateway service is available on the Edge Server as well as the Front End Server or Front End pool. To federate with XMPP networks, you must specify an XMPP domain. To add an XMPP domain, perform the following steps:

1. Open the Skype for Business Server Control Panel.
2. Select Federation and External Access in the navigation pane.
3. Select XMPP Federated Partners.
4. To create a new configuration, click New.
5. Define a primary domain; this is the base domain of the XMPP partner.
6. Provide a description.
7. Define additional domains, if necessary. This can include any other domains that are available through this partner. You must do this for all available domains, including subdomains of the primary domain.
8. Select a partner type. You have the option of Federated, Public Verified, or Public Unverified. Many organizations will be using XMPP for public connections. The primary difference is that in a Public Verified configuration, the partner contact is allowed to invite your Skype for Business users to conversations. In a Public Unverified configuration, your Skype for Business users must add the XMPP user to their contact list before any communications can occur.
9. You must identify security methods for connections to this partner. First, choose whether TLS negotiation or SASL negotiation is required.

CAUTION

Each XMPP configuration will have unique requirements for TLS and SASL. It is recommended that you identify these requirements from the partner or public provider before configuring these settings.

10. Identify whether dial-out negotiation is enabled. The dial-out process uses DNS and an authoritative server to verify requests from an XMPP partner. This is another configuration that needs to be identified with the partner or provider before configuration.

11. Click Commit when completed. Figure 5.7 shows a sample configuration.

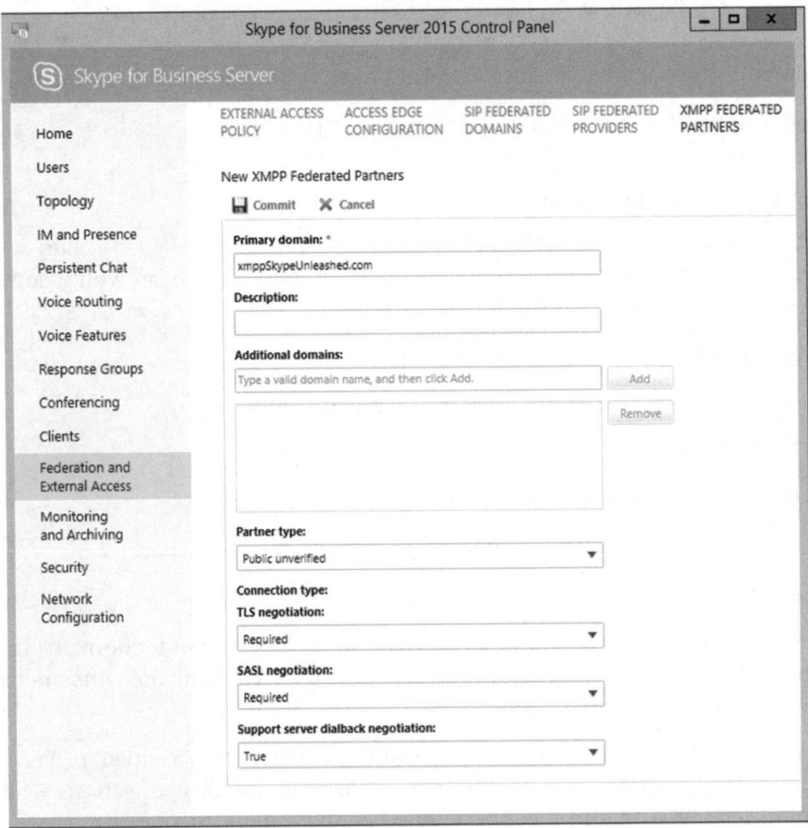

FIGURE 5.7 XMPP Partner configuration.

Alternatively, the Skype for Business Server Management shell can be used to configure XMPP domains. See the following command example:

```
New-CsXmppAllowedPartner xmppSkypeUnleashed.com -TlsNegotiation optional
➥-SaslNegotiation NotSupported -EnableKeepAlive $false
➥-SupportDialbackNegotiation $false
```

Managing Public Providers

Similar to managing federation, the Public IM providers can be allowed or blocked when you're configuring an Edge Server. By default, all the included providers are disabled and must be enabled before users can communicate with contacts in these domains.

Skype for Business Server 2015 does not provide the ability to allow only a specific subset of users from the public provider to communicate with your organization or block specific users from the public provider from communicating with your Skype for Business users while allowing everyone else. This level of granular control is not available. You would need to research third-party solutions.

The following additional options are available when dealing with the public IM providers:

- **Allow Communications Only with Users Verified by This Provider**—This is the default setting and it means the Edge Server trusts the public IM provider's determination of valid or invalid users trying to send messages to your Skype for Business users.
- **Allow Communications Only with Users on Recipients' Contact Lists**—This setting limits communication only to users explicitly added to the contact list of the Skype for Business user. If a contact who was not added to the Skype for Business user's contact list tries to initiate a conversation with the internal user, the message is rejected by the Edge Server.
- **Allow All Communications with This Provider**—This setting enables all incoming communication from the provider regardless of whether the provider indicates that the message should be trusted.

To manage access to the public networks, use the following steps:

1. Open the Skype for Business Server Control Panel.
2. Select Federation and External User Access in the navigation pane.
3. Click SIP Federated Providers.
4. Highlight one of the providers, click Edit, and click Show Details.
5. Check the Enable Communications with This Provider box and then click Commit.
6. Repeat for enabling additional providers.

Figure 5.8 displays the default SIP Federated Provider configuration for a Skype for Business Server 2015 deployment.

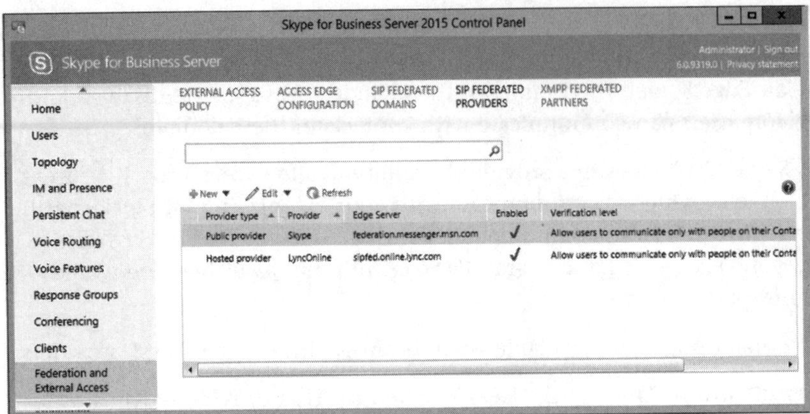

FIGURE 5.8 Configuring SIP federated providers.

To perform these steps in the Skype for Business Server Management Shell, use the following command:

```
Set-CSPublicProvider <Provider Name> -Enabled $true
```

To enable federation with Skype, use the following command:

```
Get-CSPublicProvider | Set-CSPublicProvider -Enabled $true
```

You can view the status of the public IM providers by running the `Get-CSPublicProvider` cmdlet. The following is the output from this command:

Identity:	Skype
Name:	Skype
ProxyFQDN:	sipfed.online.lync.com
VerificationLevel:	UseSourceVerification
Enabled:	True

Managing External Web Conferencing Features

Enabling remote access to the web conferencing features of Skype for Business Server is actually performed with the remote access policies. As long as a user is associated with a policy that enables remote access, the user has web conferencing capabilities through the Edge Server from the global conferencing policy.

After the Edge Servers are deployed, the option to invite anonymous users to join web conferences becomes available. Anonymous users are considered individuals who are not federated partners or internal users connecting from the Internet (that is, remote users). These users cannot authenticate to your Skype for Business Server infrastructure. Therefore, they are considered anonymous users.

To configure the external access rules and anonymous access, the conferencing policy must be edited:

1. Open the Skype for Business Server 2015 Control Panel.
2. Select Conferencing in the navigation pane.
3. Highlight the global policy, click Edit, and click Show Details.
4. Verify that the Allow Participants to Invite Anonymous Users check box is selected (see Figure 5.9).

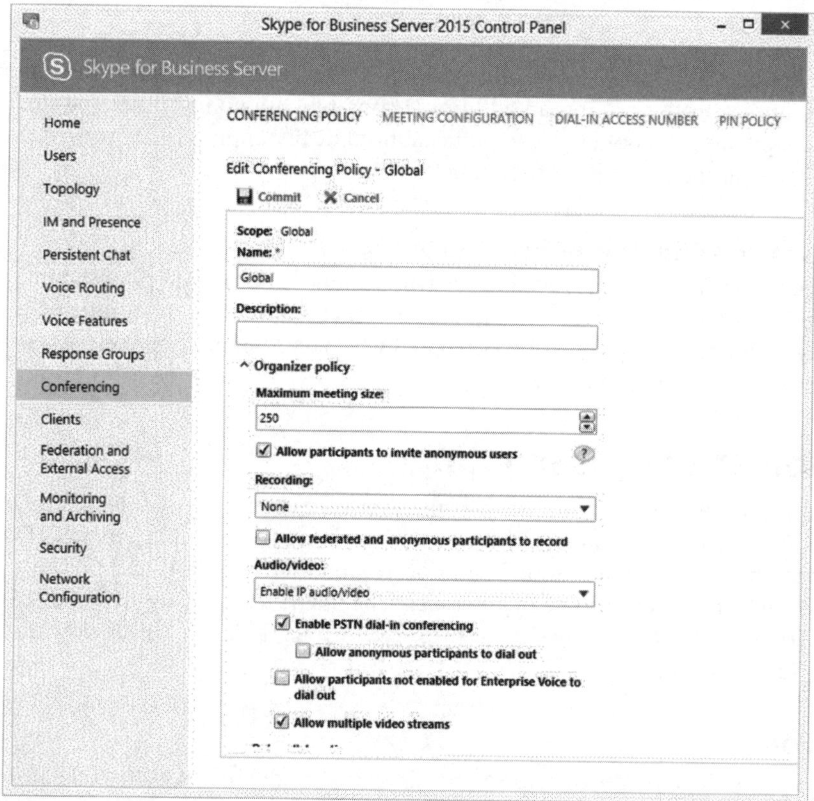

FIGURE 5.9 Editing Web conferencing policies.

5. If external users should be allowed to control shared applications or desktops, ensure that the Allow External Users to Control Shared Applications check box is checked.
6. Click Commit.

To enable anonymous access and external sharing control for the global policy through the Skype for Business Server Management Shell, use the following command:

```
Set-CSConferencingPolicy Global -AllowAnonymousParticipantsInMeetings
➥$true -AllowExternalUserControl $true
```

NOTE

Selecting the Enable Recording option in a meeting policy presents an additional check box, Allow External Users to Record Meeting, which lets an administrator control whether only internal users may record a meeting.

If you are enabling anonymous access and external user control features must be limited to specific locations or user groups, an additional conferencing policy should be created. As with the external access policy, a site policy automatically applies to an entire location, and user policies can be assigned to individual users.

Managing A/V Edge Features

After an Edge Server has been deployed, users will be able to do peer-to-peer audio and video through the Edge Server without additional configuration. To support A/V conferencing features, the user must be associated with a conferencing policy that enables audio, video, and application sharing.

Edge Server Troubleshooting

Troubleshooting Edge Servers is necessary in the event that users are unable to sign in or some features become unavailable. This section discusses the key components of an Edge Server to check when issues arise. Common troubleshooting tools and tips are also provided, which should resolve many issues. The Skype for Business Server 2015 Debugging Tools can be downloaded from http://www.microsoft.com/en-us/download/details.aspx?id=47263.

Firewall Ports

Connectivity to an Edge Server or reverse proxy can be limited by firewalls and can be tricky to troubleshoot because the connections generally cross a few network boundaries. See Chapter 11, "Firewall, Reverse Proxy, and Security Requirements." Check firewalls between remote clients, Edge Servers, and internal Skype for Business Servers. Also, check whether the Windows Firewall is blocking connections.

Routing

Any time a server has multiple network adapters, it can be problematic to make routing work correctly. Ensure that requests destined for the internal network are routed out the correct network adapter by using tools such as packet sniffers and traceroute. Packet capture tools have the capability to monitor a specific adapter, so it should be easy to determine whether traffic is flowing through an adapter. It is important to make sure you have properly configured Windows persistent routes. Use the `ROUTE PRINT` command to verify routes on each of your Edge Servers.

Certificates

Incorrectly issued certificates are a potential issue with Edge Server configuration. It is common for intermediate and root certificates to be missing from Edge Server deployments. This will cause intermittent or even complete failures on most connections to the Edge Server. Confirm that you have all required certificates installed from your public Certificate Authority. DigiCert offers a free certificate-checking utility online that can verify the proper installation of certificates. This tool can be found at http://www.digicert.com/help.

TIP

As a best practice, always use the built-in Certificate Wizards because they automatically generate the correct names for a server role. Only the Access Edge and Web Conferencing Edge certificates need to be issued by a public Certificate Authority. The internal Edge certificate and A/V Authentication certificates are used only by internal clients.

Follow these guidelines to rule out certificate issues:

- **Key bit length**—The certificate bit length must be 2048, or 4096, to be supported by Skype for Business Server.
- **Template**—The template used to issue the certificate should be based on the Web Server template. If the Skype for Business Server Certificate Wizard is used, the correct template is automatically applied.
- **Private key**—The server certificate must have the private key associated to be used by Skype for Business Server. In situations where certificates are exported or copied between servers, export the private key with the certificate.
- **Certificate chain**—The Edge Server must be able to verify each certificate up to a Trusted Root Certification Authority. Additionally, because the server presents the certificate to clients, it must contain each intermediate certificate in the certificate chain.
- **Certificate store**—All certificates used by the Edge Server must be located in the Personal store of the local computer certificate store. A common mistake is to place certificates in the Personal store of the user account certificate store.
- **Certificate trust**—Be sure that the clients and servers communicating with the Edge Server all contain a copy of the top-level Certificate Authority of the chain in their Trusted Root Certification Authority local computer store. When the Certificate Authority is integrated with Active Directory, this generally is not an issue. When using an offline or nonintegrated Certificate Authority, install root certificates on clients and servers.

Additionally, each service has slightly different requirements for the subject and subject alternative names.

Edge Internal Certificate Names

The required name for the Internal Edge certificate is as detailed here:

- **Subject name**—Ensure that the subject name matches the internal Edge pool FQDN entered in the Topology Builder.
- **Shared certificate**—Remember that in a load-balanced Edge pool, all Edge Servers in that Edge pool must share the same internal certificate with the same private key.

Access Edge Certificate Names

The required names for an Access Edge certificate are described here:

- **Subject name**—Ensure that the subject name matches the Access Edge FQDN entered in the Topology Builder.
- **Subject alternative names**—The SAN field must contain all supported SIP domains in the `sip.<SIP Domain>` format.

Web Conferencing Edge Certificate Names

The required name for a Web Conferencing Edge certificate is detailed here:

- **Subject name**—Ensure that the subject name matches the Web Conferencing Edge FQDN entered in the Topology Builder.

TIP

Instead of requesting a separate certificate for the Web Conferencing Edge, you have the option to include the Web Conferencing Edge FQDN as a SAN entry in the certificate for the Access Edge. This would save on the cost of purchasing public certificates.

A/V Authentication Certificate Names

The Media Relay Authentication Service (MRAS) certificate does not have any specific name requirements. It is auto-generated by the Edge Server.

Wildcard Certificates

Some organizations attempt to use wildcard certificates or a single certificate with subject alternative names that attempt to cover all possible names. There are certainly some cases in which this configuration might work, but in the end the simplicity of following the actual name requirements tends to outweigh any small cost savings achieved by using fewer certificates. Wildcard certificates are not supported for Edge Servers. They are only supported for Skype for Business web traffic over the reverse proxy.

DNS Records

Successfully signing in to an Edge Server is heavily dependent on correctly configuring the DNS. The NSLookup tool can be used to verify that the necessary DNS records are in place, as described in Chapter 10.

TIP

When you are troubleshooting any Edge Server issue, it is important to check that all necessary DNS records exist and are resolving to the correct IP addresses.

The following sample NSLookup sequence within a command prompt checks the host record of the pool:

```
nslookup
set type=a
edgepool.SkypeUnleashed.com
```

A successful query returns a name and an IP address. Verify that the IP returned matches the IP addresses assigned to the Edge Servers or hardware load balancer and that no extra (or surprise) IP addresses are returned.

To verify the SRV record required for automatic client sign-in externally, specify the type to be SRV. The following is another sample NSLookup sequence:

```
nslookup
set type=srv
_sip._tls.SkypeUnleashed.com
```

A successful query returns a priority, weight, port, and server hostname. Verify that the server name matches the Access Edge FQDN and that the correct port is returned.

Use the same steps to verify that the following services resolve correctly in public DNS:

- Access Edge FQDN
- Web Conferencing Edge FQDN
- A/V Edge FQDN

For internal DNS, verify that clients can resolve the Internal Edge pool FQDN.

TIP

Ensure that the Edge Server can resolve internal DNS names of all Skype for Business Servers. It must be able to properly resolve these DNS entries to communicate with internal servers and users.

Windows Event Logs

A good source of information when troubleshooting any server issue is the event logs. Skype for Business Server creates a dedicated event log for informational activities, warnings, and errors within the standard Windows Server Event Viewer console. To view this event log, perform the following steps:

1. Open the Event Viewer Microsoft Management Console.
2. Expand the Applications and Services Logs folder.
3. Click the Lync Server log.
4. Examine the log for warning or error events that might provide additional insight into issues.

Skype for Business Centralized Logging Service

Every Skype for Business Server runs the centralized logging service (CLS), which can receive commands from any other Skype for Business Server to enable logging for troubleshooting scenarios. CLS can be managed from PowerShell. Introduced in Skype for Business Server 2015, a graphical interface called CLS Logger is available.

For Edge Servers, you must make sure that TCP ports 50001 to 50003 are open between your Front End Servers and Edge Servers. These ports are used to communicate centralized logging commands. Windows Firewall is modified as part of the installation; however, these ports must be opened on any other firewalls in the environment that may impact this traffic. The following example uses centralized logging to collect data on an Edge pool:

1. Open the Skype for Business Server Management Shell.
2. Type the following command to determine the current CLS configuration. You can add the parameter `-LocalStore` to retrieve the configuration for the local computer.

   ```
   Get-CsClsConfiguration
   ```

3. Type the following command to enable logging for the Instant Messaging and Presence scenario:

   ```
   Start-CsClsLogging -scenario im -pools edgepool.SkypeUnleashed.com
   ```

4. After the logging is enabled, reproduce the issue you are trying to troubleshoot.
5. From the same command prompt, run the following command to stop logging on the Edge pool:

   ```
   Stop-CsClsLogging -stop -scenario -im
   -pools edgepool.SkypeUnleashed.com
   ```

6. Type the following command to search the logs from the Edge pool. If required, you can filter by specific components; however, this example will simply export data for all tracing components.

```
Search-CsClsLogging -outputfilepath c:\EdgeLog.TXT
-pools edgepool.SkypeUnleashed.com
```

7. Use Snooper.exe (available from the Skype for Business Server 2015 Debugging Tools) or Notepad to examine the log file.

Skype for Business Server Management Shell

The Skype for Business Server Management Shell provides several cmdlets that test various functions of a server. A useful cmdlet for verifying the overall health of a server is `Test-CSComputer` server, which verifies that all services are running, that the local computer group membership is correctly populated with the necessary Skype for Business Server Active Directory groups, and that the required Windows Firewall ports are open.

The `Test-CSComputer` cmdlet must be run from the local computer and uses the following syntax:

```
Test-CSComputer -Report "C:\Test-CSComputer Results.xml"
```

After running the cmdlet, open the generated XML file to view a detailed analysis of each check.

Telnet

Telnet is a simple method of checking whether a specific TCP port is available. From a computer that has trouble connecting to an Edge Server, use the following steps to verify connectivity to the Access Edge or Web Conferencing services:

TIP

The Telnet client is not installed by default starting with Windows Vista and Windows Server 2008. On a Windows desktop computer, it must be installed by using the Turn Windows Features On or Off option found in Programs and Features. On a Windows server, it can be installed through the Features section of Server Manager.

1. Open a command prompt.
2. Type the following command:

```
telnet <Access Edge FQDN> <443 or 5061>
```

Here's an example:

```
telnet sip.SkypeUnleashed.com 5061
```

5

If the Telnet window goes blank, leaving a flashing cursor, the connection was successful and the specified port can be contacted without issue. If the connection fails, an error is returned. Check that the services are running on the Edge Server and that no firewalls are blocking the traffic.

Troubleshooting Skype for Business Services

Basic troubleshooting begins with making sure that the Skype for Business Server services are all running. When services are in a stopped state, users will notice many issues such as being unable to sign in or connect to the Edge Server. Verify that the following Windows services are configured to start automatically and are running:

- Skype for Business Server Access Edge
- Skype for Business Server Audio/Video Authentication
- Skype for Business Server Audio/Video Edge
- Skype for Business Server Centralized Logging Service Agent
- Skype for Business Server Replica Replicator Agent
- Skype for Business Server Web Conferencing Edge
- Skype for Business Server XMPP Translating Gateway Proxy (if installed)
- SQL Server (RTCLOCAL)

Best Practices

The following are the best practices from this chapter:

- Use Edge Servers to provide secure remote access for Skype for Business Server.
- Place the Edge Servers in a perimeter or DMZ network.
- Use DNS load balancing or a hardware load balancer to provide high availability for Edge Server pools.
- Create external access policies with site-level scopes to apply automatically to users.
- Plan to use a reverse proxy server to publish external web services.
- Use DNS SRV records for routing federation requests to reduce management overhead with federation.
- Use certificates from a public Certificate Authority for the Access Edge and Web Conferencing Edge roles so that they are trusted automatically by remote clients and federated partners.

Summary

The Edge Server is a big element of why Skype for Business Server is such a compelling product. The fact that users can be inside or outside the office with complete access to the same features drives productivity and collaboration. With the way the Edge services work regardless of location, users have no need to change their workflows, whether they are in the office, at home, or traveling halfway around the world.

On the less glamorous side, the Edge Server is a safe and stable role designed to be a secure gateway to the Skype for Business Server infrastructure. The granular external access and conferencing policies give administrators complete control over what features are deployed and who is allowed to use them.

The federation and public IM features enable an organization to extend the reach of their unified communications platform to partners or customers without additional products. Organizations considering Skype for Business Server should include Edge services within the deployment to take full advantage of the features it offers.

CHAPTER 6

Skype for Business Server 2015 Monitoring and Archiving Best Practices

IN THIS CHAPTER

- Monitoring Components Installation
- Monitoring Configuration
- Monitoring Administration
- Monitoring Troubleshooting
- Call Quality Dashboard Components Installation
- Call Quality Dashboard Configuration
- Call Quality Dashboard Administration
- Call Quality Dashboard Troubleshooting
- Archiving Components Installation
- Archiving Configuration
- Archiving Administration
- Archiving Troubleshooting
- Best Practices

Both the Monitoring role and the Archiving role changed significantly since Lync Server 2010. The biggest change is that neither of them is a dedicated server role any longer. Although they remain logically separate, they are collocated with the Skype for Business Server 2015 Front End role. In fact, they are simply listed as an option in the Front End Wizard in Topology Builder. As such, there won't be traditional "installation steps" in this section as you'll find in the other chapters. Instead, this chapter covers both roles at a high level and discusses how they apply to the Skype for Business 2015 environment as a whole.

The Monitoring role in Skype for Business Server 2015 has evolved from previous versions. For those new to Skype for Business Server 2015, the Monitoring role is actually an agent that lives on each Front End Server in a pool and collects and manages information from the Front End, Mediation, and other server roles and stores it in a database separate from the one used by the Front End. It leverages SQL Server Reporting Services to create reports related to call quality and metrics. These reports are often used for ROI (return on investment) justification. For example, if the legacy conferencing provider charged $0.10 per minute and after conferencing was moved to Skype for Business Server 2015 the current report showed 100,000 minutes of usage, then the company saved $10,000 in conferencing costs for that month. It's often found that most companies can achieve 100% ROI in one to three months after deployment, even in large, highly redundant deployments.

The Call Quality Dashboard, or CQD, is an add-on IIS-based portal that provides for creating and editing reports based on quality of experience (QoE) data. CQD is not meant to be a replacement of the Monitoring Server role, but as an addition to it. Utilizing a SQL Server Analysis Services (SSAS) cube, data from the QoE Metrics database is replicated to an archive database, where the cube performs aggregation to allow for fast access and analysis for display in the portal for further investigation. Reports can be viewed, created, and edited to allow for greater information and analysis—and better yet, more helpful reporting into usage and quality in a Skype for Business Server 2015 environment.

The Archiving role in Skype for Business Server 2015 primarily serves the purposes of legal compliance. That said, other companies might want to have a centrally searchable archive for other purposes because the Archive server role is able to archive communications across both IM and meetings. Similar to the Lync Server 2013 generation of products, Skype for Business archiving data can be stored in a central repository with archived email in an Exchange 2013 environment; however, that is beyond the scope of this chapter. For more information on integrating Skype for Business Server 2015 with Exchange Server, see Chapter 20, "Unified Contact Store, Exchange, and SharePoint Integration." This chapter focuses on the native Skype for Business Server 2015 tools as related to archiving.

The Archiving role scales well with the Front End collocated service capable of handling all the users hosted by the pool.

The Archiving Server role can archive the following content:

- Peer-to-peer instant messages.
- Multiparty instant messages.
- Web conferences, including uploaded content and events (for example, join, leave, upload).
- Metadata (only) for audio/video for peer-to-peer instant messages and web conferences. Media is not included.
- Web conferencing annotations and polls.

Organizations should decide before the implementation of the Archiving role how archiving will be configured. Decisions around site and user-based archiving must be made. It is also critical to determine how archive data will be managed. The archiving database was not meant to be a long-term retention solution, and as such, Skype for Business Server 2015 does not provide an eDiscovery solution for archived data. Various third-party solutions, however, are optimized for eDiscovery within archived Skype for Business data. This data should optimally be moved to other storage or collocated with Exchange 2013.

TIP

When you're deciding how to configure the Archiving Server topology, the obvious question might be, "How much bandwidth does my Archive Server need?" The answer depends on your archiving configuration, policy, and user load. The user load should be monitored during your pilot implementation to get a feel for how much load it will generate.

Installing Monitoring Components

Although this section doesn't cover the simple "check box" to add the monitoring components to the Front End Server, it does cover the other items that are required for a fully functional Skype for Business Server 2015 Monitoring deployment. The Monitoring role allows administrators to collect, trend, and review quantitative data related to audio calls, video calls, and IM messages. The Monitoring Server leverages the Lync Storage Service framework, known as LYSS, to collect information and deposit it in the monitoring database. Then it leverages SQL Server Reporting Services to display various canned and custom reports.

Installing Microsoft SQL Server 2012 Reporting Services

The Skype for Business Server 2015 Monitoring Server leverages Microsoft SQL Server Reporting Services to provide rich reports related to usage and quality of experience data. This section assumes you've already installed SQL and are familiar with the process. Small installations that choose to use the Enterprise edition of Skype for Business Server 2015 can use the same SQL Server as the Front End pool; however, most larger deployments require a separate SQL Server and, in very large installations, a separate SQL Reporting Services server. In the steps that follow, you'll walk through the installation process and post-installation steps for SQL Reporting Services.

In the SQL Server 2012 Installation Wizard, ensure that the Reporting Services box is checked and continue through the wizard. See Figure 6.1 for an example.

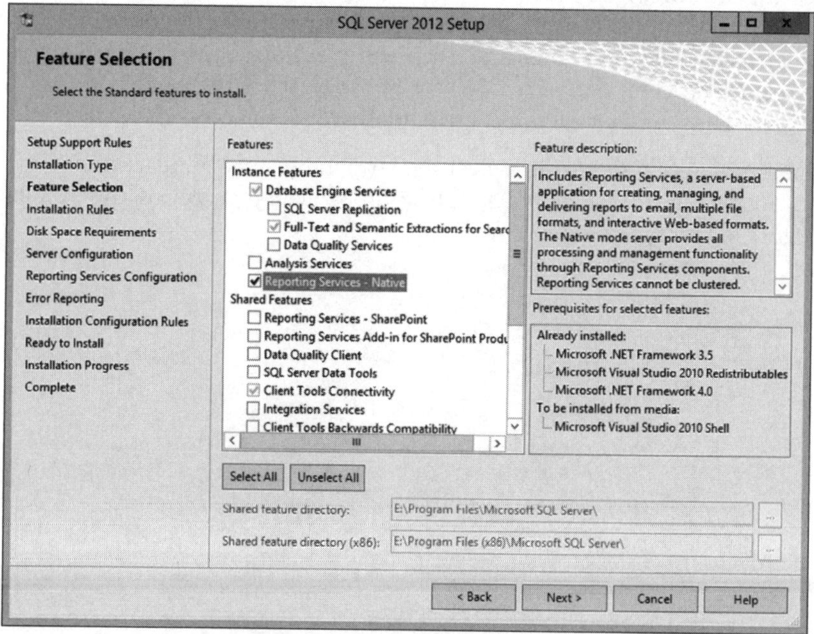

FIGURE 6.1 Selecting Reporting Services—Native.

Be sure to examine the scalability requirements for your environment to determine whether the Reporting Services role should be placed on the SQL database server or on a dedicated server. The administrator must also decide where to install the Reporting Services database, either on an existing SQL server or on the Reporting Services server. In general, it is recommended to collocate the Reporting Services database on the Reporting Services server. After the SQL Reporting Services role is installed, it needs to be configured before the Monitoring Server can use it.

Configuring Microsoft SQL Server 2012 Reporting Services

From the Start Menu, navigate to All Programs, Microsoft SQL Server 2012, Configuration Tools and then select Reporting Services Configuration Manager. Ensure that the appropriate server and instance are selected and click then Connect. To finish installing the Monitoring components, follow these steps:

1. Click the Server Account button in the left column and set the appropriate report server service account.
2. Click the Web Service URL button. Review the settings. Usually the default settings are acceptable. However, if you want to use SSL, you'll need to pick the certificate to be used. A certificate can be requested from the IIS console. Once the desired settings are in place, click Apply.
3. Click the Database button. Ensure that the proper database server is set. If not, or no database is listed, click Change Database. Select the server name and authentication type. Generally, the default values are sufficient. Click Next. Verify the database name, temp database name, and language. Like the server information, the default values are generally sufficient here. Click Next. Choose Next for the database credentials screen. Ensure that the correct credentials are set to access the database.
4. Click the Report Manager URL button. Select the virtual directory to be used to access reports. By default, this is "Reports." Click Apply, even if accepting the default values. See Figure 6.2 for an example.

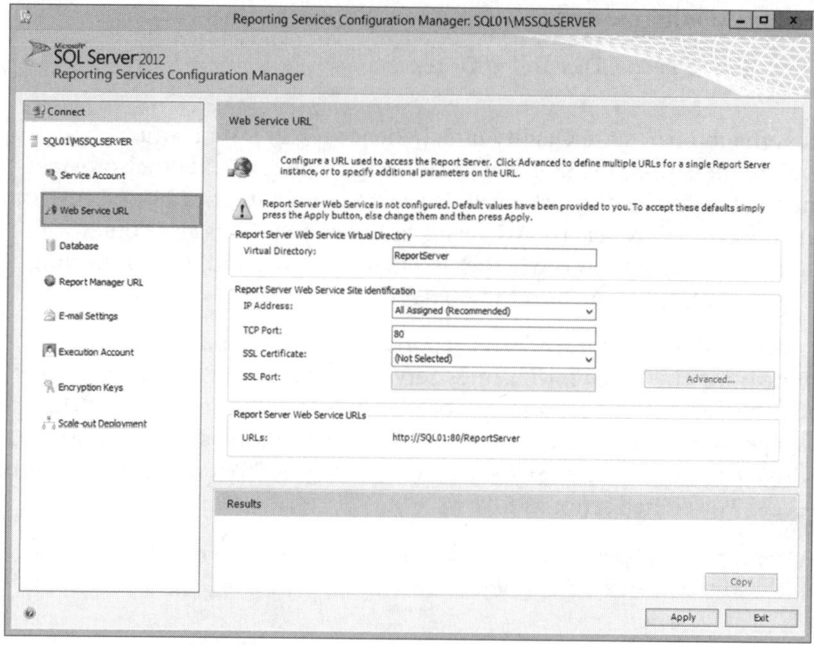

FIGURE 6.2 Report Manager URL virtual directory.

Now the SQL Reporting Services server is almost ready. After the Monitoring Server is installed, you'll need to deploy the Monitoring Server Report Pack to the SQL Reporting Services server, as reviewed in the following text.

Monitoring Configuration

The good news about Skype for Business Server 2015 is that with the Topology Builder tool, much of the configuration is done automatically. Although both configuration and administration can be done from the Silverlight web GUI or the Skype for Business Server Management Shell, the configuration section focuses on the former and the administration section focuses on the latter, to avoid duplication of concepts.

Open the Skype for Business Server 2015 Control Panel. For reference, it can be found at the short URL you defined earlier (https://skypeadmin.skypeunleashed.com/ in the sample environment, or https://<pool_FQDN>/Cscp/).

Scrolling down in the left bar, click the Monitoring and Archiving button. This brings up the settings menus for the Monitoring and Archiving Server roles. By default, there is only one Call Detail Recording policy. Select it and click Edit and then Modify. Here are the available options:

- Name (the name of the policy)
- Enable Monitoring of Call Detail Records (CDRs)

- Enable Purging for Monitoring Servers
- Options for duration to keep CDRs and error reports

The next item across the top bar is the Quality of Experience (QoE) Data menu. Microsoft's approach to measuring the user experience is through QoE data that provides qualitative and quantitative analysis of every call. It provides some metrics around instant messaging and network type (VPN versus LAN versus WAN) as well. This also comes with one policy by default. The only option is whether to enable purging and, if so, how long to keep QoE data. By default, this value is set to 60 days.

The next step is to deploy the Monitoring Server reports to the SQL Reporting Server. This step can be done using the Skype for Business Server Management Shell or from the main screen of the deployment wizard. From any of the Skype for Business Server 2015 servers, open the Skype for Business Server Management Shell and run as administrator. With `C` being the drive letter from where Skype for Business Server 2015 was installed, run the `DeployReports.ps1` PowerShell script as follows:

```
C:\Program Files\Skype for Business Server 2015\Deployment\Setup\DeployReports.ps1
➥-storedUserName <domain\user> -storePassword <password>
```

This is the most minimal version of the command. The full syntax, including optional items, is outlined here:

```
DeployReports.ps1 -storedUserName <domain\user> -storedPassword <password>
➥-readOnlyGroupName <ReportReadOnlyGroupName> -reportServerSQLInstance
➥<ReportServerSQLInstance>
```

Here is an explanation of each option presented:

- **`storedUserName`**—The username used to access the Monitoring Server store.
- **`storedPassword`**—The password for the value of `storedUserName`.
- **`readOnlyGroupName`**—The domain group that will be granted read-only access to the Monitoring Server reports. This group must already exist in Active Directory for the action to complete successfully.
- **`reportServerSQLInstance`**—The SQL instance that is hosting SQL Reporting Services. If this is left blank, the script assumes that it is the same server that holds the Monitoring Server databases.

Run the `Get-CsReportingConfiguration` cmdlet and pay special attention to the `ReportingURL` field. This is the URL where you'll access the Skype for Business Server 2015 reports. For the sample environment, it would be this:

> http://SQL01:80/ReportServer/Pages/ReportViewer.aspx?%2fLyncServerReports%2fReports+Home+Page

The reports themselves are covered in detail in the following section.

Monitoring Administration

This section reviews common administration tasks for the Skype for Business Server 2015 Monitoring role. In general, there isn't much day-to-day administration of the Skype for Business Server 2015 Monitoring components. Instead, this section focuses on the reports generated by the Monitoring Server.

Once the Monitoring reports are deployed, a link is automatically inserted into the Home screen of the Skype for Business Server 2015 Control Panel. Simply expand the View Monitoring Reports link, as seen in Figure 6.3.

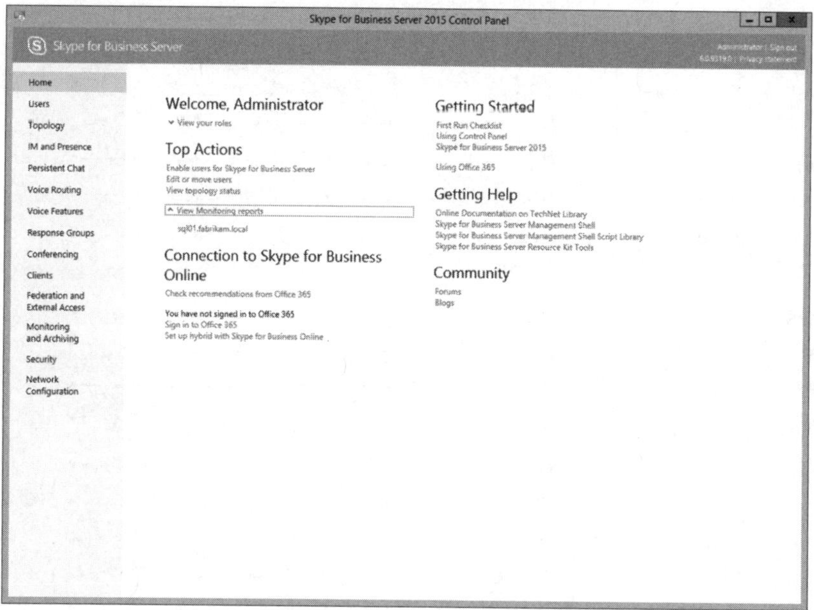

FIGURE 6.3 View Monitoring Reports link in Control Panel.

Clicking the link will open the Monitoring reports in a web browser.

The most important page is the Dashboard. The Dashboard is broken up into four distinct areas or panes: System Usage, Per-User Call Diagnostics, Call Reliability Diagnostics, and Media Quality Diagnostics. By default, the Dashboard shows "this week" and a "6 week" view. However, a monthly view is also available via a link in the upper-right corner of the screen.

System Usage is the first section (see Table 6.1). Many of the fields are self-explanatory, and they are very useful for at-a-glance looks at the environment. For example, the total A/V Conference Minutes item is great for "back of the napkin" ROI on the savings Skype for Business Server 2015 provides over outsourced conferencing services. Possibly even more important, it gives a snapshot of how your users are using Skype for Business Server 2015. Are they using Skype for Business as a softphone? How about for application sharing? Has overall collaboration time increased since Skype for Business Server 2015 was implemented? This report isn't the end-all for these answers, but it does provide an insightful view.

TABLE 6.1 The System Usage Section of the Dashboard

System Usage		
Registration		
Unique user logons	1	
Peer-to-Peer		
Total sessions	186	
IM sessions	0	
Audio sessions	186	
Video sessions	0	
Application sharing	0	
Total audio session minutes	954.37	
Avg. audio session minutes	5.13	
Conference		
Total conferences	21	
IM conferences	9	
A/V conferences	11	
Application sharing conferences	0	
Web conferences	0	
Total organizers	0	
Total A/V conference minutes	216.48	
Avg. A/V conference minutes	19.68	
Total PSTN conferences	0	
Total PSTN participants	0	
Total PSTN participant minutes	0.00	

The next section is Per-User Call Diagnostics (see Table 6.2). This is a great at-a-glance view for overall health of your voice deployment. It also makes for great bragging rights in a well-planned deployment.

TABLE 6.2 Per-User Call Diagnostics Section of the Dashboard

Per-User Call Diagnostics		
Users with Call Failures		
Total users with call failures	0	
Conference leaders with call failures	0	
Users with Poor-Quality Calls		
Total users with poor-quality calls	0	

The Call Reliability Diagnostics section (see Table 6.3) provides a deeper view into the health of your UC deployment and a window into the end-user experience. This is a very valuable resource to administrators of Skype for Business Server 2015.

TABLE 6.3 Call Reliability Diagnostics Section of the Dashboard

Call Reliability Diagnostics		
Peer-to-Peer		
Total failures	0	
Overall failure rate	0.00 %	
IM failure rate	0.00 %	
Audio failure rate	0.00 %	
Application sharing failure rate		
Conference		
Total failures	0	
Overall failure rate		
IM failure rate		
A/V failure rate		
Application sharing failure rate		

The last section is Media Quality Diagnostics (see Table 6.4). This table gives information about quality of calls in terms of total poor-quality calls and percentage of poor-quality calls compared to the total number of calls. It also offers the same metrics for conferences.

TABLE 6.4 Media Quality Diagnostics Section of the Dashboard

Media Quality Diagnostics		
Peer-to-Peer		
Total poor-quality calls	0	
Poor-quality call percentage		
PSTN calls with poor quality	0	
Conference		
Total poor-quality calls	1	
Poor-quality call percentage	1.10 %	
PSTN calls with poor quality	0	
Top Worst Servers by Poor-Quality Call Percentage		
No server has media quality data based on current period.		

From the main Monitoring Server reports page, you can find a plethora of reports to review. The next section summarizes each report in the order in which it is presented on the main page. Also, here is a full list of the available reports. You'll see that they are a deeper dive into the snapshots presented in the Monitoring Server reporting Dashboard.

System Usage Reports

- User Registration Report
- Peer-to-Peer Activity Summary Report
- Conference Summary Report
- PSTN Conference Summary Report
- Response Group Service Usage Report
- IP Phone Inventory Report
- Call Admission Control Report

Per-User Diagnostics Reports

- User Activity Report

Call Reliability Diagnostics Reports

- Call Diagnostic Summary Report
- Peer-to-Peer Activity Diagnostic Report
- Conference Diagnostic Report
- Conference Join Time Report
- Top Failures Report
- Failure Distribution Report

Media Quality Diagnostics Reports

- Media Quality Summary Report
- Media Quality Comparison Report
- Server Performance Report
- Call Leg Media Quality Report
- Location Report
- Device Report

- **User Registration Report**—This report shows user registrations over time. This can be useful to determine peak login times and AD authentication requirements.
- **Peer-to-Peer Activity Summary Report**—This report shows peer-to-peer activity, including IMs, application sharing, and file transfers.
- **Conference Summary Report**—The Conference Summary Report measures conference metrics, including Communicator conferences and PSTN conferences, number of organizers, and total conference minutes.
- **PSTN Conference Summary Report**—This report contains data specific to PSTN Conferences in Skype for Business Server 2015.
- **Response Group Service Usage Report**—Metrics for Response Groups, including agent response and number of calls answered by the response group.
- **IP Phone Inventory Report**—Statistics about the number and type of IP phones in the Skype for Business Server 2015 deployment. Includes all Lync Phone Edition devices.
- **Call Admission Control Report**—Information about peer-to-peer and conferencing sessions that were conducted under restrictions set in place by Call Admission Control.
- **User Activity Report**—This report reviews user-focused call failures for person-to-person calls and conferences. This report is useful for measuring the overall health of your conferencing deployment.
- **Call Diagnostic Summary Report**—This gives a high-level view of failed calls, total call minutes, and other call metrics.
- **Peer-to-Peer Activity Diagnostic Report**—This report contains information about failures in peer-to-peer activity, including IMs and collaboration activity.
- **Conference Diagnostic Report**—This report contains information on failures during IM, peer-to-peer, and PSTN conferences.
- **Conference Join Time Report**—The report shows the average join time (in milliseconds) and also provides a breakdown that lets you know how many users were able to join a conference in 2 seconds or less, how many users required between 2 and 5 seconds to join the conference, and so on.
- **Top Failures Report**—This report gives a snapshot view of the top failures in the organization. It can reveal systemic problems and configuration issues.
- **Failure Distribution Report**—This report provides statistics about the failures related to site or pool. It is a great troubleshooting tool for finding error conditions.
- **Media Quality Summary Report**—This report provides an overall high-level view of media quality across the whole environment. It should be referenced often to review the overall health of your voice deployment.

- **Media Quality Comparison Report**—This report enables you to compare call quality values for different types of audio calls (for example, calls made over a wireless network vs. calls made across a wired connection).
- **Server Performance Report**—This report breaks down media quality metrics by server. This is especially important in deployments that utilize separate mediation servers.
- **Call Leg Media Quality Report**—This report enables administrators to compare call volumes and call quality for audio calls made across the Public Switched Telephone Network (PSTN).
- **Location Report**—The Location Report reviews media quality statistics by location defined in Skype for Business Server 2015 or by individual users.
- **Device Report**—Similar to the Location Report, the Device Report pivots media quality data by type of device used when a failure is experienced.

Although some of the reports might initially seem similar, they all examine the data from a different, unique angle. These reports are critical in proactively monitoring the health of your Skype for Business Server 2015 environment. A wise administrator will leverage these reports along with a monitoring platform like Microsoft System Center Operations Manager. For information on utilizing System Center Operation Manager, see Chapter 12, "Monitoring Skype for Business Server 2015."

Monitoring Troubleshooting

The Monitoring role is fairly straightforward; however, there are a few things that commonly go wrong during deployment. This section covers the common issues and areas to check should you find your Monitoring Server deployment not going smoothly.

Because a lot of server-to-server connections are involved in a Monitoring Server deployment, the most obvious problem area is in ensuring proper permissions. Also, ensure that usernames and passwords are typed correctly. When in doubt, reenter the usernames and passwords used for database access for the Monitoring Server and the Reporting Server. Also, ensure that the accounts aren't subject to password expiration in Active Directory. There's no "D'oh" feeling like having a service account's password expire 30 or 90 days into your deployment.

If you've chosen to use SSL for your Reporting Services URLs, ensure that the subject name (SN) of the certificate matches the site name you've chosen. Note that this might or might not be the same as the FQDN of your server, depending on your reporting server configuration.

The Lync Server event log is also a good place to check for errors. From the Start Menu, select Administrative Tools and then Event Viewer. Expand the Applications and Services Logs item and select Lync Server. All events related to Skype for Business Server 2015 functions reside here. Often the error description is enough to identify the problem and determine the resolution.

Installation of Call Quality Dashboard Components

Before installing CQD, ensure that a Monitoring SQL Server Store has been defined in the topology, and the topology has been published. The Monitoring SQL Server Store is defined at the Front End pool level. See Figure 6.4 for an example of Topology Builder.

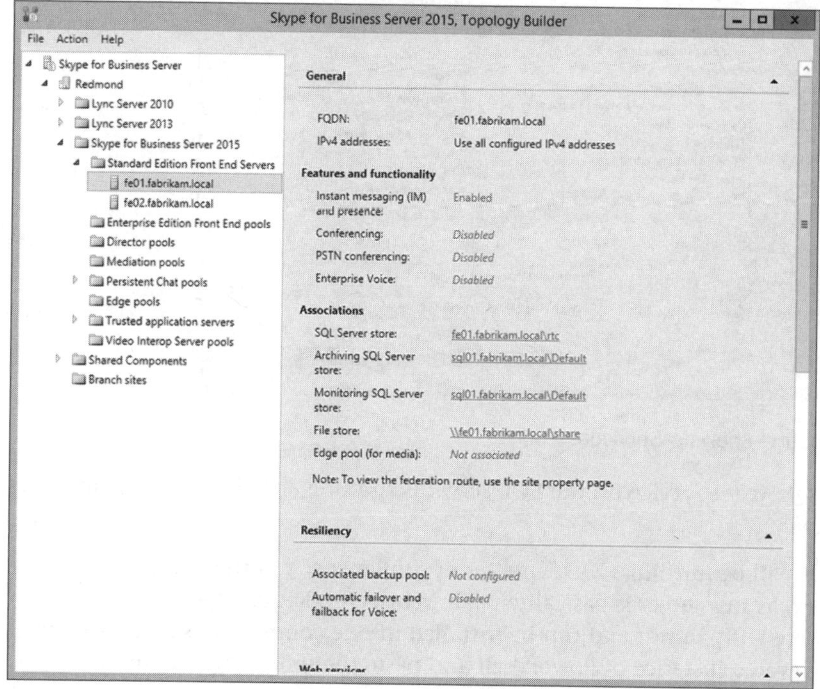

FIGURE 6.4 Monitoring SQL Server store defined in Topology Builder.

CQD can exist on the same server that is running SQL Server Reporting Services (SSRS) and is supported. However, both default to using the Default Web Site. Should you wish to use both on the same server, you'll have to change the Default Web Site binding port in IIS. However, CQD should be installed on a dedicated server to achieve the best performance.

SQL Server versions supported for a SSAS Cube include SQL Server 2008 R2, 2012, and 2014. The Business Intelligence or Enterprise Edition of SQL is recommended for performance reasons, but Standard Edition can also be used.

If using SQL Server 2012, and if the SQL Server 2012 SP1 Feature Pack is not installed, you will get prompted that CQD needs SQL Server Analysis Services (SSAS). SSAS is composed of two components—SQL Server 2012 ADOMD.NET, and SQL Analysis Management Objects—which are available in the SQL Server 2012 SP1 Feature Pack.

During the SQL Server Installation Wizard, ensure that the Analysis Services box is checked and continue through the wizard. An example is shown in Figure 6.5.

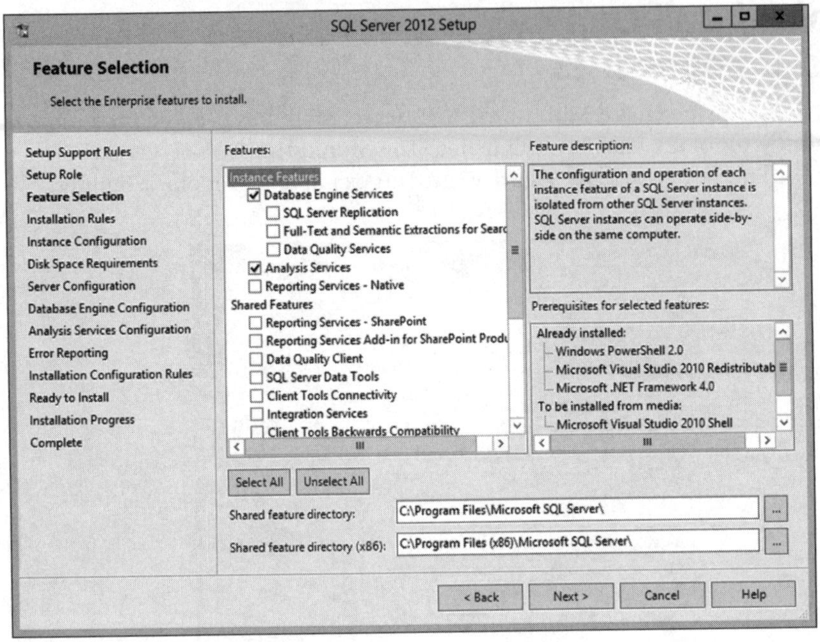

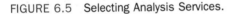

FIGURE 6.5 Selecting Analysis Services.

Ensure that the SQL Agent Service on the SQL server is running and that the Startup Type is set to Automatic.

For the server that will be running CQD, a server of similar spec to other resources is generally sufficient, as this server is basically just a web server. Requirements for the operating system are fairly minor and can be installed in one command using PowerShell. Simply open an elevated instance of PowerShell and paste the following two lines:

```
Import-Module ServerManager
Add-WindowsFeature Web-Server, Web-Static-Content, Web-Default-Doc, Web-Asp-Net,
➥Web-Asp-Net45, Web-Net-Ext, Web-Net-Ext45, Web-ISAPI-Ext, Web-ISAPI-Filter,
➥Web-Http-Logging, Web-Url-Auth, Web-Windows-Auth, Web-Mgmt-Console
```

The installation package for CQD is a separate installer available for download from Microsoft at https://www.microsoft.com/en-us/download/details.aspx?id=46916. Once launched, there are several configuration pages to complete before data processing can proceed. The first is the QoE Archive Configuration. Each of the fields is described next:

- **QoE Metrics SQL Server**—SQL instance (data source) where the QoE Metrics DB is located.
- **QoE Archive SQL Server Name**—This is the Archive DB name and can only be installed on the local machine. This is a read-only field and fixed to the fully qualified domain name of the local machine.
- **QoE Archive SQL Server Instance**—A local SQL Server instance name for where the Archive DB is to be created. For the default SQL Server instance, leave this blank. For a named SQL instance, specify just the instance name.

- **QoE Archive Database**—This option is set to Create New Database by default. Because Archive DB upgrade is not supported, the only circumstance under which the Use Existing Database option can be used is if the existing Archive database has the same schema as the build to be installed.
- **Database File Directory**—Path to where the database files (.mdf and .ldf) for the Archive DB will be placed. This should be on a different drive from the OS. For simplicity sake, use an empty folder.
- **Use Multiple Partitions**—For SQL Server Standard edition, select the Single Partition option. For Business Intelligence edition or Enterprise edition of SQL Server, select the default option Multiple Partition. For best cube processing performance, use Multiple Partition.
- **Partition File Directory**—Path for the partition files for the QoE Archive database. This should be on a drive separate from the OS drive and SQL database log files drive. As with the Database File Directory, it is recommended that an empty folder be specified.
- **SQL Agent Job User–User Name & Password**—Domain service account credentials used to run the "QoE Archive Data" step of the SQL Server Agent job. UPN format for User Name is not supported, so use the DOMAIN\USERNAME format. Because these credentials are used to run stored procedures that retrieve data from the QoE Metrics database and that insert data in the Archive database, ensure that this account has read access to the QoE Metrics DB as well as a login to the QoE Archive SQL instance. See Figure 6.6 for an example of the QoE Archive Configuration screen.

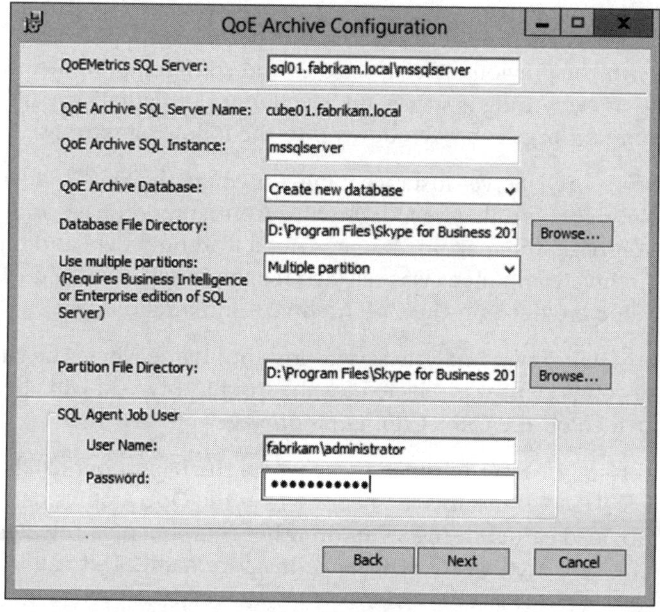

FIGURE 6.6 QoE Archive Configuration.

Once this is completed, click Next, and the installer will complete the required validation checks. Resolve any issues before continuing. Once you're done, the Cube Configuration page appears.

- **QoE Archive SQL Server Name—**This is a read-only field and fixed to the FQDN of the local machine. Cube can be installed only from the machine that contains the QoE Archive database.
- **QoE Archive SQL Server Instance—**Name of the SQL instance where the QoE Archive DB is located. For a default SQL Server instance, leave this blank. To specify a named SQL Server instance, enter the instance name (for example, the name after the "\"). If the QoE Archive component was selected for the install, this field will default to the value provided on the QoE Archive Configuration page.
- **Cube Analysis Server—**SQL Server Analysis Service instance name where the cube will be created. This can be a different machine, but the installing user has to be a member of Server administrators of the target SQL Server Analysis Service instance.
- **Use Multiple Partitions—**The default is set to Multiple Partition, which requires the Business Intelligence edition or Enterprise edition of SQL Server. For Standard edition, select the Single Partition option. Note that cube processing performance may be impacted if Single Partition is used.
- **Cube User–User Name & Password—**Domain service account credentials that will trigger the cube processing. If the QoE Archive component was selected for the install, this field will already contain the values provided on the Archive Configuration page for the SQL Agent Job User. However, it is recommend that a different domain service account be specified so that Setup can grant the least required privilege.

Click Next to proceed. As with the previous screen, settings and configurations are validated before proceeding. If everything is successful, the Portal Configuration page appears. The Portal Configuration page is broken down into the following settings:

- **QoE Archive SQL Server—**SQL Server instance name for where the QoE Archive database is located. Note, that, unlike the QoE Archive Configuration page and the Cube Configuration page, the machine name is not a read-only field and must be provided. If QoE Archive component was selected for the install, this field will already contain the value provided on the QoE Archive Configuration page.
- **Cube Analysis Server—**SQL Server Analysis Service instance name where the cube is located. If the Cube component was selected for the install, this field will already contain the value provided on the Cube Configuration page.
- **Repository SQL Server—**SQL Server instance name where the Repository database will be created. If the SQL Server instance name for where the QoE Archive database is located has been provided earlier in the setup (in other components), this field will already contain the QoE Archive DB SQL Server instance name. This can be any SQL Server instance.

- **Repository Database**—By default, the option is set to Create New Database. Since Repository DB upgrade is not supported, the only circumstance under which the Use Existing Database option can be used is if the existing Repository DB has the same schema as the build to be installed.
- **IIS App Pool User–User Name & Password**—The domain service account that the IIS application pool should execute under. Note that the User Name and Password fields will be grayed out if built-in system accounts are selected.

Clicking Next will perform the final set of validation tests. Once those tests are completed, the installer will begin the actual setup. Once that setup is completed, the initial set of QoE data will be loaded and cube processing will begin. Depending on the amount of data, this can take some time. To verify the status of the data ingestion, browser to http://computername/CQD/#/Health. Once data ingestion is completed, the portal page can be viewed at http://computername/CQD.

Enabling CQD in Skype for Business Online

Setting up CQD in Skype for Business Online is very simple. First, sign in to your Office 365 tenant with administrative credentials and choose the Admin tile.

Under Admin in the left pane, click Skype for Business. Once in the Skype for Business Admin Center, click the Skype for Business Online Call Quality Dashboard link. If asked to log in again, make sure you use the Global Admin account credentials. Once this is completed, the Call Quality Dashboard will begin collecting and processing data; however it may take several hours before any relevant data is available.

Call Quality Dashboard Configuration

By default, all users will have access to the CQD portal because URL Authorization component is inherited by the default URL Authorization, which is Allow All Users. To adjust authorization to the CQD dashboard for users, the URL Authorization component of IIS Manager can be used. Authorization can be restricted by going into URL Authorization for the CQD Home website. Remove the inherited rules and create new rules, adjusting accordingly. This can be individual users and/or roles (groups).

Once the authorization settings are in place, some simple file permissions must be granted for the CQD directory. Traditional methods of using the Security tab of the folder are possible, but the official recommendation is to use the Configuration Editor for the /CQD Home site in IIS Manager. Upon opening the Configuration Editor, use the drop-down option to go to system.webServer/serverRuntime. Change authenticatedUserOverride to UseWorkerProcessUser and then click Apply.

Call Quality Dashboard Administration

By browsing to the portal site at http://computername/CQD, you'll see that the first report is visible.

To see the status of the CQD System Health, click the gear icon in the upper-right corner and then select System Health, as shown in the example in Figure 6.7.

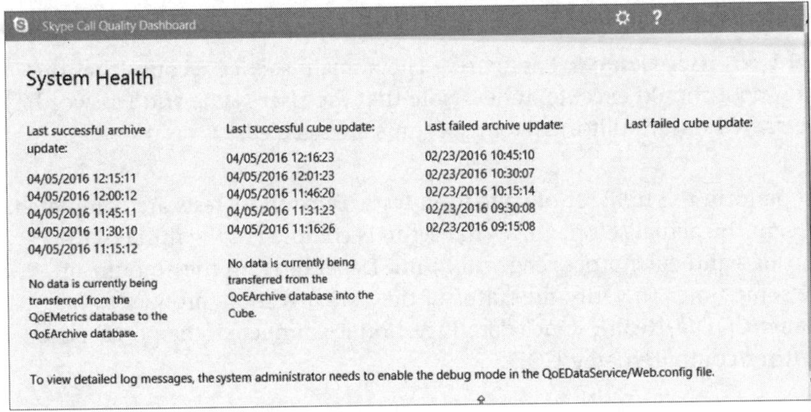

FIGURE 6.7 CQD System Health.

The Call Quality Dashboard contains many reports already available. And clicking the title of the report will drill down to deeper reports. Hovering over any particular area of a report will show a more exact breakdown of the details. See Figure 6.8 for an example.

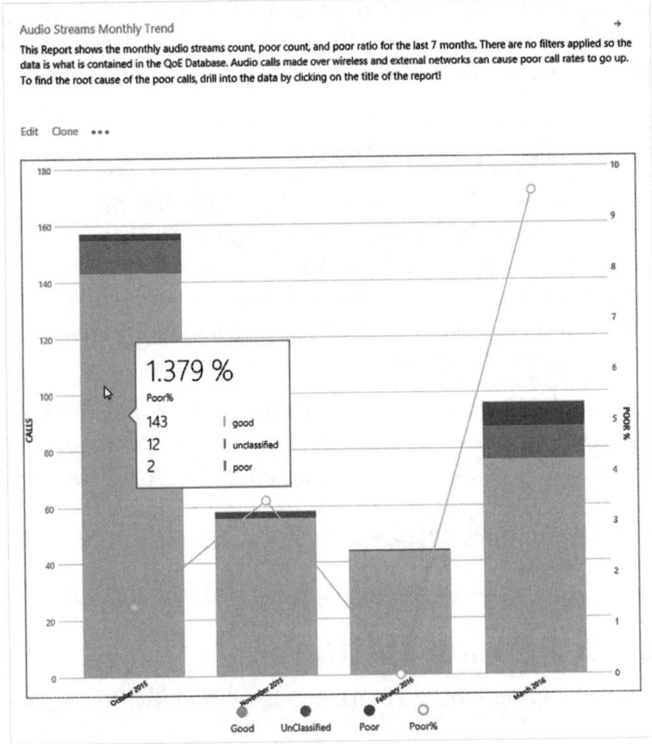

FIGURE 6.8 CQD with greater detail.

Each report can be customized to fit particular requirements. Each report can be edited, or even cloned to create a new report, with the original service as a starting point. Simply click the appropriate link to edit or clone. This brings up the Query Editor. Chart types, trends, time span, description, and so on can all be added/removed/updated. An option to include sparklines in tables cells shows even greater dimension. An example of the Query Editor is shown in Figure 6.9.

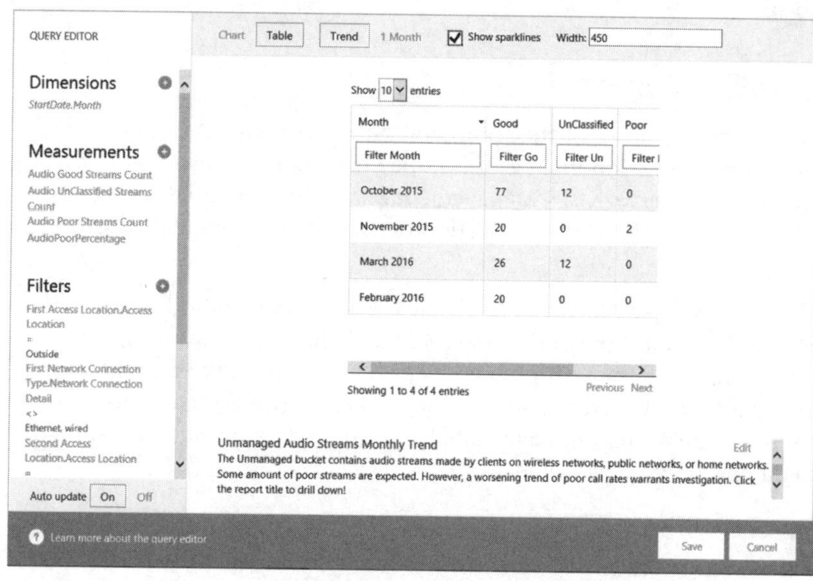

FIGURE 6.9 CQD Query Editor.

Archiving Components Troubleshooting

Once deployed, you may see the following message on the CQD portal:

> "We couldn't perform the query while running it on the Cube. Use the Query Editor to modify the query and fix any issues. Also make sure that the Cube is accessible."

To resolve this, open SQL Management Studio and connect to Analysis Services. Next, expand Databases, expand the QoE Cube, and then under Cubes choose QoE Metric.

Right-click the QoE Metric cube and click Process. Once processing is finished, right-click the QoE Metric cube again and select Browse. This should open a page that allows for browsing. If no errors are displayed, using a web browser to access the CQD portal page should not be successful.

Archiving Components Installation

The only component needed for Skype for Business Server 2015 Archiving, outside of choosing to add it to all the Front End Servers during the topology building process, is the installation of SQL Server. SQL Server 2008 R2, SQL Server 2012, and SQL Server 2015 are supported for Skype for Business Server 2015. Standard and Enterprise editions are required because the Express edition is not supported. The SQL installation process is covered in detail in Chapter 10, "Dependent Services."

Archiving Configuration

With the Topology Builder tool, most of the configuration is done automatically. Although both configuration and administration can be done from the Silverlight web GUI or the Skype for Business Server 2015 Management Shell, the configuration section focuses on the former and the administration section on the latter, to avoid duplication of concepts.

Open the Skype for Business Server 2015 Control Panel, which can be found at https://<pool_FQDN>/Cscp/. Scroll down in the left bar and click the Monitoring and Archiving button. This brings up the settings menus for the Monitoring and Archiving server roles. Because Call Detail Recording and Quality of Experience Data are Monitoring functions, skip directly to the Archiving Policy tab. Here, you see the default global policy. Select it and click Edit and then Show Details.

Here are the available options:

- Name (the name of the policy)
- Description (your own notes to identify the policy)
- Archive Internal Communications check box
- Archive External Communications check box

Now move to the Archiving Configuration tab. Again, you see the default global policy. Select it and click Edit and then Show Details. The available options are listed here:

- Name (the name of the policy)
- Archiving settings, including three options in the drop-down list:
    - Disable Archiving
    - Archive IM Sessions
    - Archive IM and Web Conferencing Sessions
- Block Instant Messaging (IM) or Web Conferencing Sessions If Archiving Fails check box
- Enable Purging of Archiving Data check box

If purging is enabled, there are two radio button options:

- Purge Exported Archiving Data and Stored Archiving Data After Maximum Duration (Days)
- Purge Exported Archiving Data Only

If the "Days" option is selected, the administrator has the option to define how many days the archived data is stored.

Creating Site and User Policies

In addition to modifying the default global policy, administrators can create additional policies. To create a site policy, follow these steps:

1. From the Monitoring and Archiving window, click the Archiving Policy tab and click New.
2. Choose either Site Policy or User Policy.

   A site policy can be associated with specific sites to allow their behaviors to be different from the default global policy. User policies are assigned directly to users and allow them to bypass the default global policy. This is useful when archiving is needed only for select users who are distributed across the environment.
3. For this example, choose a site policy. When prompted to select a site, choose it from the list and click OK.
4. Now, the policy is named after the site—this cannot be modified. Input a description and choose whether internal and external communications will be archived. Click Commit.

Administrators can also create user policies that can be assigned to individual users instead of at a site level. To create a user policy, follow these steps:

1. For a user policy, repeat steps 1 and 2 but choose User Policy.
2. Enter a name for the user policy.
3. Enter a description for the policy.
4. Choose whether internal and external communications will be archived. Click Commit.

This results in the creation of multiple policies that can be used to manage archiving.

To apply a user-based archiving policy to a user, perform the following steps:

1. From the Skype for Business Server 2015 Control Panel, click Users in the left pane.
2. Click Find in the search area to view the list of enabled users.

3. Double-click the user you want to modify.
4. Scroll down to Archiving Policy and choose the policy you want to apply from the drop-down list.

NOTE

It is worth highlighting the Archiving Configuration option Block Instant Messaging (IM) or Web Conferencing Sessions If Archiving Fails. This is what Microsoft refers to as "critical mode." If archiving this content is deemed critical by an environment, usually due to regulatory compliance, this option prevents unarchived IMs or web conferences from occurring.

For administrators who prefer to do all their configuration tasks through PowerShell, Skype for Business Server 2015 supports the capability to read and modify the archive policy and archive configuration through the following cmdlets:

```
Get-CsArchivingConfiguration

Identity                      : Global
EnableArchiving               : ImAndWebConf
EnablePurging                 : True
PurgeExportedArchivesOnly     : False
BlockOnArchiveFailure         : True
KeepArchivingDataForDays      : 120
PurgeHourOfDay                : 2
ArchiveDuplicateMessages      : True
CachePurgingInterval          : 24
EnableExchangeArchiving       : False
```

The `ArchiveDuplicateMessage` value is important in multipool environments because that setting controls whether conversations between users on separate pools are archived on each pool. Setting this to `false` will cause the conversation to only be archived on one pool, making it more time consuming to find and archive desired conversations.

Using Cmdlets for Configuration Tasks

As one might logically expect, the policies and configurations can also be created through cmdlets; here's an example:

```
New-CsArchivingConfiguration -Identity "site:Redmond" -EnableArchiving
➥ImAndWebConf -EnablePurging $True
➥-KeepArchivingDataForDays 120
➥-ArchiveDuplicateMessages $False
```

Notice the last argument set in this command: `ArchiveDuplicateMessages`. This is a good example of where there are options available through the cmdlets that aren't exposed to the GUI tools.

The power of using cmdlets to manage an application, such as Skype for Business Server 2015, becomes readily evident when you are dealing with a large implementation. By scripting the configuration of the entire environment, you are able to eliminate the human error introduced by having a distributed group of people perform repetitive tasks. Similarly, the script written to perform the configuration immediately becomes the documentation of the configuration. If later changes need to occur, you can perform queries to find the objects and modify them at the same time. If you plan to manage the environment in this manner, it becomes helpful to put some thought into a logical naming convention for policies and configurations. This enables you to search on some common value in the policies and configurations to select them for modification.

In a similar manner, PowerShell-based cmdlets make it easy to pull configuration reports from a large implementation. For example, imagine that your company announced a policy that all IMs will be retained for at least 30 days. More than likely, someone will ask you to make sure that all your configurations retain messages for at least 30 days. Rather than scrolling through the GUI to find configurations with values under 30, you could simply run a cmdlet like the following to produce a report of all configurations in which the `CachePurgingInterval` is less than 30 days:

```
Get-CsArchivingConfiguration | Where-Object {$_.CachePurgingInterval
➥-lt 30} | Select-Object Identity
```

However, if you were going to do that, why not fix it all at once?

```
Get-CsArchivingConfiguration | Where-Object {$_.CachePurgingInterval -lt 30} |
Set-CsArchivingConfiguration -CachePurgingInterval 30
```

This report searches all configurations in the topology and sets any that have a `CachePurgingInterval` of less than 30 to 30 without touching any that were already equal to or higher than 30.

Archiving Administration

This section reviews common administration tasks for the Skype for Business Server 2015 Archiving role, including Data Export and Purge Mode.

In general, there isn't much day-to-day administration of the Skype for Business Server 2015 Archiving Server role. Instead, this section focuses on the management of data stored in the Archiving database.

One of the most common tasks an administrator will perform against the Archiving Server is exporting content from the Archive database. This is performed through the Skype for

Business Server 2015 Management Shell using the `Export-CsArchivingData` cmdlet as follows:

```
Export-CsArchivingData -Identity sql01.fabrikam.local -StartDate 12/15/2015
➥-OutputFolder "C:\Archiving" -UserUri MFloerkey@SkypeUnleashed.com
```

This command exports all sessions pertaining to the `UserURI` defined in the cmdlet. Omitting the `UserURI` will export all conversations in the database that began on or after the `StartDate` value. The output is a series of .eml files, one for each conversation, that are created in subfolders in the `OutputFolder` path. The first subfolder is the FQDN of the SQL server, with a subfolder under that in yyyymmdd format. The files contained in that subfolder have names based on the time and date that the conversation took place. Opening one in an application such as Microsoft Outlook will show an HTML-formatted conversation. See Figure 6.10 for an example.

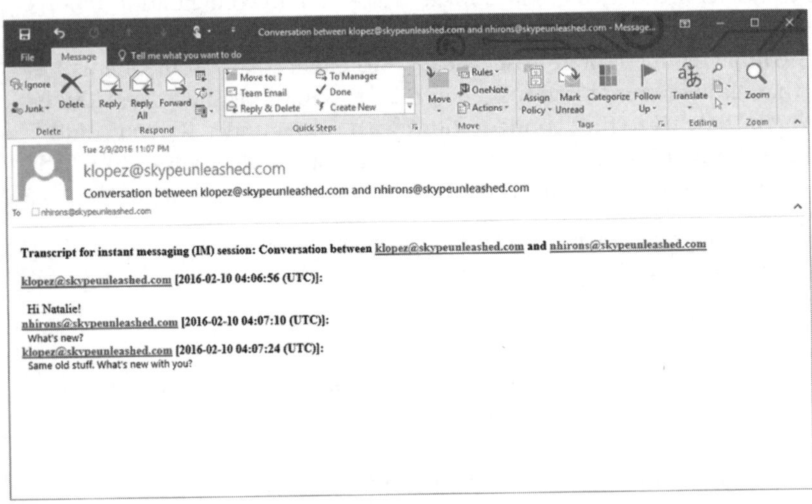

FIGURE 6.10 Archived conversation.

Archiving Disclaimer

If an organization is going to archive communications from Skype for Business Server 2015, it is wise to notify the users of this policy. However, there is also the issue with communicating with external (or federated) contacts and properly notifying those contacts that the conversations are being archived. Fortunately, a solution is built in to the Access Edge configuration of Skype for Business Server 2015. By using the `Set-CsAccessEdgeConfiguration` cmdlet, you can set the parameter `EnableArchivingDisclaimer` to `$True`. By default, it is set to `$False`. Once this is set, federated contacts will see a disclaimer reading, "Warning: Parties in this conversation may be archiving the instant messages." You can see an example in Figure 6.11.

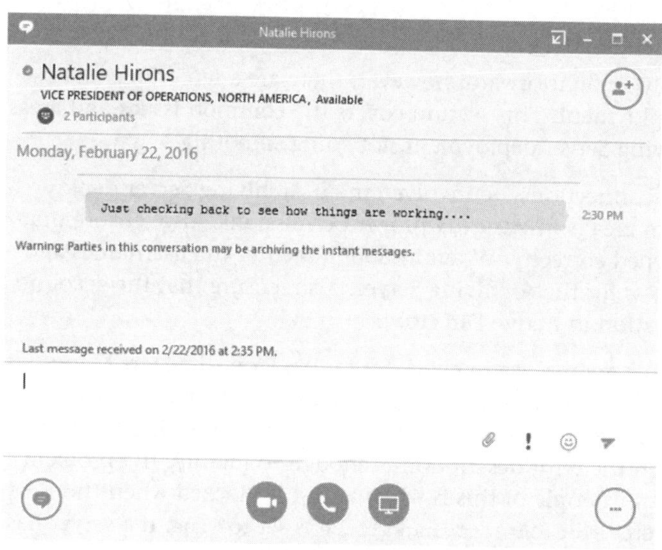

FIGURE 6.11 Archiving disclaimer in an instant message.

Purging Archived Data from the Database

Because all conversations are initially archived, some conversations between users who are not assigned archiving policies will make their way into the archive. If no member of the conversation is assigned an archiving policy, those conversation transcripts are removed automatically. The frequency of that process is due to an Archiving Configuration parameter called `CachePurgingInterval`, which, by default, is every 24 hours.

Data that is intended to be maintained in the database can also be purged. In the Archiving Configuration, a parameter called `EnablePurging` determines if data should be eliminated as part of routine maintenance. Several parameters determine what and when purging takes place. The first is the `PurgeHourOfDay` value, which is based on a 24-hour clock. This is the time of day when data that exceeds the value set by `KeepArchivingDataForDays` is removed from the archive. Additionally, a parameter called `PurgeExportedArchivesOnly` sets whether only data that was exported by the process mentioned earlier in this section is removed. If set to `False`, then all data exceeding the `KeepArchivingDataForDays` threshold is removed.

To manually purge data from the archive database, you can use the `Invoke-CsArchivingDatabasePurge` cmdlet. Here is an example of purging all data that is more than 24 hours old, regardless of whether it has been exported:

```
Invoke-CsArchivingDatabasePurge -Identity
➥"service:ArchivingDatabase: sql01.fabrikam.local"
➥-PurgeArchivingDataOlderThanHours 24 -PurgeExportedArchivesOnly
➥$False
```

6

Archiving Troubleshooting

The Archiving Server role is fairly straightforward; however, there are a few things that commonly go wrong during deployment. This section covers the common issues and areas to check if you find your Archiving Server deployment not going smoothly.

Because a lot of server-to-server connections are involved in an Archiving Server deployment, the most obvious problem area is in ensuring proper permissions. Also, ensure that usernames and passwords are typed correctly. When in doubt, reenter the usernames and passwords used for database access for the Archiving Server. Also, ensure that the accounts aren't subject to password expiration in Active Directory.

The Lync Server event log is also a good place to check for errors. From the Start Menu, select Administrative Tools and then select Event Viewer. Expand the Applications and Services Logs item and select Lync Server. All events related to Skype for Business Server 2015 functions reside here. Often the error description is enough to identify the problem and determine the resolution. An example of this is when an IM is blocked when the Archiving Configuration parameter `BlockOnArchivingFailure` is set to `True`. If a server has been rebooted and the local storage database on the Front End Server isn't yet initialized, users will see their IMs fail, but seconds later, they will succeed. Reviewing the Lync Server event log will show an Event ID 56717, as shown in Figure 6.12.

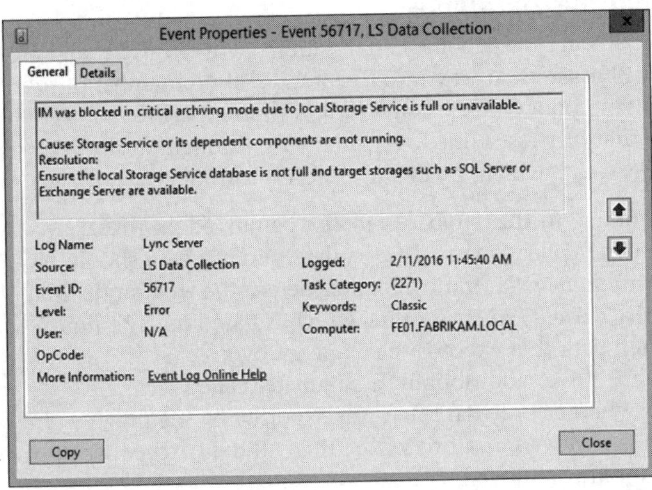

FIGURE 6.12 Event log showing blocked conversation.

Note that Front End Servers use lazy writes to send the archiving data to SQL. Therefore, it can take several minutes before messages arrive in the archive, depending on server activity. The contents of the archive can be viewed in SQL Management Studio. Expand the LcsLog database and expand Tables. Right-click the Message table and choose Select Top 1000 Rows. Rows with the same SessionIdTime are part of the same conversation, and the row with the Body that begins with "<Span" is the first message in the conversation. See the example in Figure 6.13.

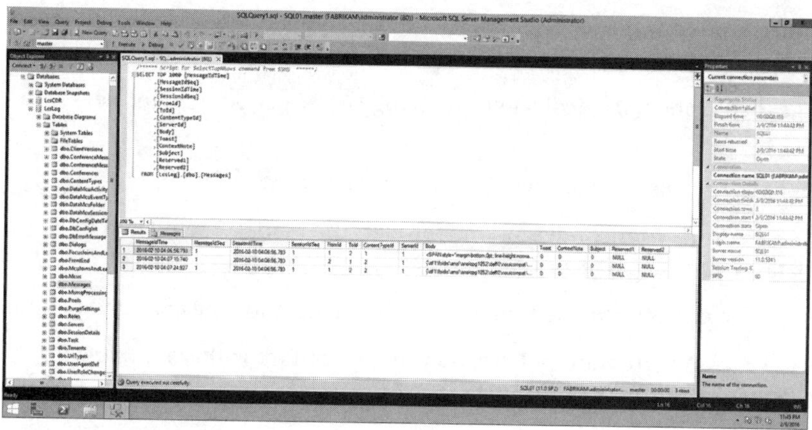

FIGURE 6.13 Archived messages in SQL.

Although it's not terribly easy to read the contents of the conversation by viewing the rows in the database, using SQL Management Studio can be key in determining if/when data is making it into the archive.

Best Practices

The following are the best practices from this chapter:

- Leverage the Monitoring reports to keep a close eye on the overall and ongoing health of your deployment and to troubleshoot user-experience quality issues.
- Although the Skype for Business Server 2015 Control Panel might seem more familiar at first, there are many functions that can be accomplished only in the Management Shell.
- For larger deployments, use a dedicated SQL Reporting Services Server.
- Before running the `DeployReports.ps1` script, ensure that the group you specify for read-only access already exists in Active Directory.
- Always publish a new topology before making changes or installing a new server role.
- Test your SQL Reporting Services deployment before loading the Monitoring Server Report Pack.
- New reports are often included in Skype for Business Server 2015 cumulative updates. Be sure to redeploy the Monitoring reports following the same process as you did initially to add the new or updated reports.
- The Call Quality Dashboard can be used to see trends of usage and quality.
- Leverage the Archiving Server to record messages for key employees.

- Be sure to understand compliance regulations around archiving that you might need to follow in Skype for Business Server 2015.
- For some larger deployments, a dedicated Archiving Server per pool might be required.
- For larger deployments, use a dedicated SQL Archiving Server.
- When possible, perform your configurations through the Management Shell to simplify bulk tasks and keep a record of what changes were made.
- Make sure you have enough storage to maintain the Archive for the expected period.
- Be aware of any existing retention policies that might conflict with your plans for archiving in Skype for Business Server 2015.

Summary

Monitoring a Skype for Business Server 2015 environment is quite important. Microsoft has provided free tools and features to help ensure organizations can see the status of their deployment to address user issues. With the Monitoring role, quality and other data, such as trending, is always close by to review. This can be further augmented by the Call Quality Dashboard.

With the archiving features, there are several options to allow an organization to keep data for regulatory, legal, and/or ethical purposes. Between the built-in database and Exchange archiving, flexibility exists without the need for third-party solutions.

CHAPTER 7

Skype for Business Server 2015 Mediation Server

IN THIS CHAPTER

The Microsoft Skype for Business Server 2015 Mediation Server is a critical component that facilitates Enterprise Voice and Dial-In Conferencing services. The Mediation Server acts as a back-to-back user agent, translating signaling and media between your internal Skype for Business infrastructure and the Public Switched Telephone Network (PSTN).

This chapter focuses on the Mediation Server role and how it interacts with other components of the Skype for Business Server 2015 infrastructure. An overview of how the Mediation Server provides connectivity to the PSTN is provided. Additionally, supported Mediation Server configurations are outlined.

This chapter also discusses the steps required to prepare a server for the Mediation Server role and how to install the Mediation Server role. The components of a Mediation Server role are examined, and guidelines for troubleshooting common issues with a Mediation Server are provided for reference.

Mediation Server Overview

The Mediation Server in Microsoft Skype for Business Server 2015, although referred to as a server, is really a service or component that by default is deployed and collocated with the Front End Server but can also be deployed as a dedicated server. Similar to other Skype for Business components, more than one Mediation Server can be deployed into a pool for additional capacity and resiliency.

Its role is to connect your Skype for Business users and Skype for Business Servers to the Public Switched Telephone

Network (PSTN), the global telephony network, and/or existing internal phone systems, called private branch exchange (PBX) systems. This allows Skype for Business users to make voice calls to PSTN and PBX users using normal telephone numbers (referred to as Enterprise Voice) and to allow PSTN users to dial in to conferences. When this chapter refers to the Mediation Server connecting to the PSTN, it could equally refer to connecting to an existing PBX.

When organizations are planning to deploy Enterprise Voice or Dial-In Conferencing, a Mediation Server must be deployed. There are various ways to connect to the PSTN, including a PSTN gateways or Session Border Controllers (SBCs), via an IP-PBX, or by routing directly to a Carrier SIP trunk. For simplicity in Skype for Business topologies, these are all referred to as "PSTN gateways." In this chapter, we will use the term *gateways* to refer to all these types of devices that the Mediation Server talks to.

Details on planning and designing PSTN connectivity for your infrastructure can be found in Chapter 33, "Planning for Voice Deployment."

Understanding Trunks

A Mediation pool can connect to one or more gateways for multiple routing options and resiliency. Similarly, a gateway can connect to more than one mediation pool. The relationships are distinguished by using different ports for each pairing. A "trunk" is a configuration object that represents an association between a mediation server and specific listening port number and a gateway and listening port number. Trunks are defined in the Skype for Business Server 2015 Topology Builder, as shown in Figure 7.1.

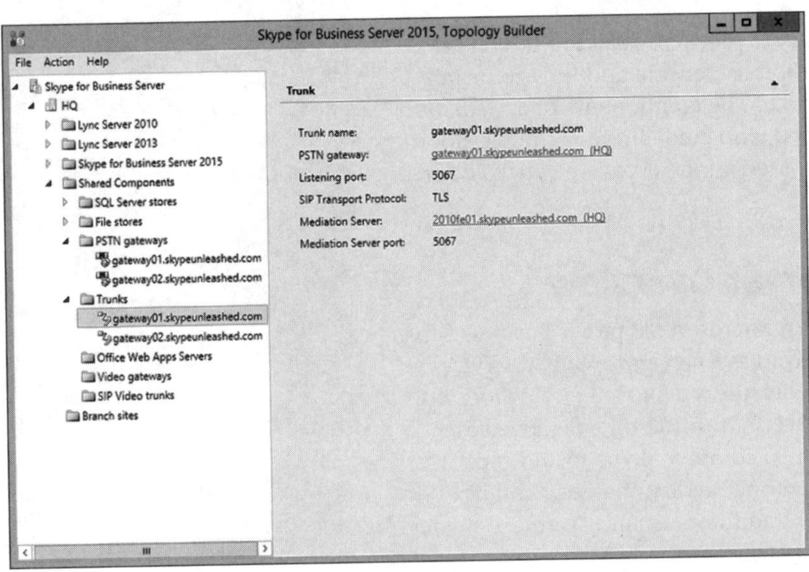

FIGURE 7.1 Topology Builder trunk example.

When defining call routes in Skype for Business, you choose a trunk to route your calls to, which defines the Mediation server and gateway pair the call routes through.

Mediation Server Traffic Flows

The Mediation Server is a back-to-back user agent (B2BUA). A B2BUA operates between both endpoints in a SIP call to facilitate communications—in this case, MTLS to Skype for Business and TLS or TCP to the gateway. All qualified gateways will support TLS. In non-media bypass scenarios, the Mediation Server is responsible for transcoding media from Microsoft Real Time Audio (RTA) to standards-based G.711, a codec that nearly all PSTN/PBX providers support.

SIP signaling will always route via the Mediation Server. Media Bypass, introduced in Lync Server 2010, allows Skype for Business clients to send G.711 media (voice traffic) direct from the client to the gateway. The media "bypasses" the Mediation Server. Previous to this, all media had to route via the Mediation Server. The bypass reduces network hops and latency, reduces Mediation Server CPU usage, and improves scaling. Your gateway must support Media Bypass for this feature to work. Signaling still routes via the Mediation Server.

As an example, the Mediation Server receives a PSTN call request from Skype for Business clients. The communication consists of a signaling and a media session. The Mediation Server then initiates a call through the PSTN gateway based on the trunk definition. During PSTN calls, all SIP signaling routes through the Mediation Server. Media can route through the Mediation Server or route directly from the PSTN gateway to the user if Media Bypass is enabled. Figure 7.2 outlines a sample call flow between a Skype for Business client and the PSTN with and without Media Bypass.

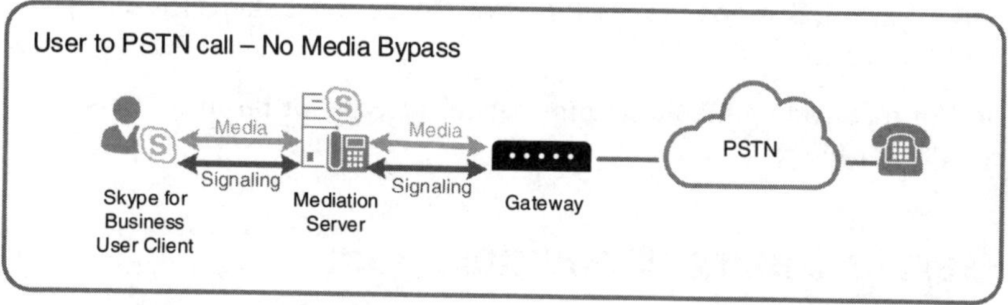

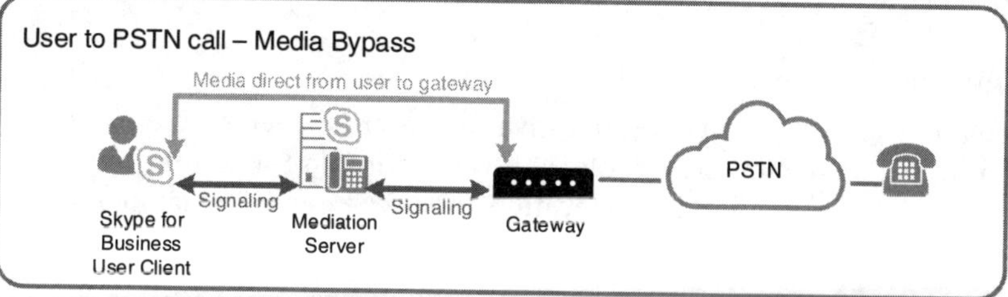

FIGURE 7.2 Mediation Server media flow with and without media bypass.

Media Bypass is a particular benefit in branch site scenarios. When a branch site is connected to a centralized Skype for Business infrastructure and that branch site has its own PSTN gateway connectivity, Media Bypass can allow Skype for Business users in the branch site to send media directly to the local media gateway, greatly reducing bandwidth requirements over the WAN.

The Mediation Server can also provide PSTN connectivity to remote users through the Skype for Business Edge Server, as shown in Figure 7.3. When remote users make PSTN calls, they will be connected to a Mediation Server through the Edge Server. The signaling and media flow will be handled as if the users were on the corporate network, with the exception of Media Bypass, which is not enabled in Edge Server scenarios.

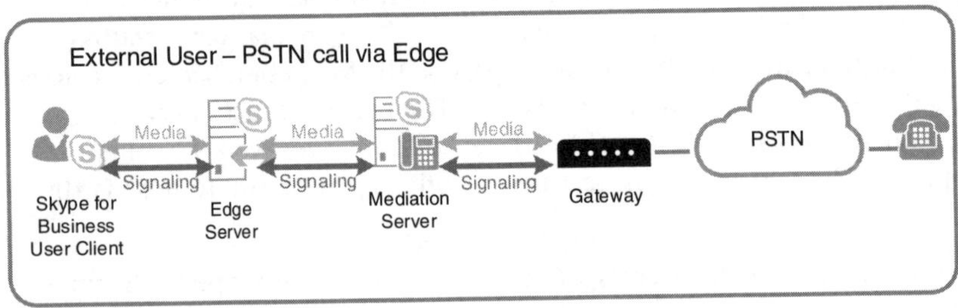

FIGURE 7.3 Mediation Server media flow for an external user making a PSTN call.

As a summary, the Mediation Server is responsible for the following functions in Skype for Business Server 2015:

- Encrypting/decrypting media from Skype for Business users to a legacy PBX or the PSTN
- Maintaining SIP signaling sessions over TCP and/or TLS between Skype for Business users and the PBX or PSTN
- Translating and/or transcoding media streams between Skype for Business users and servers and the PBX or PSTN

Mediation Server Design Considerations

This section covers some key design considerations when deploying Mediation Servers.

Sizing and Topology

By default, the Mediation Server role is collocated with the Front End Server role. Microsoft supports collocation of the Mediation Server role with the Front End Server role, but no other server roles. Although it is supported, collocation should be carefully planned for based on the following:

- The number of gateway peers the Mediation Server will be connected to
- The amount of traffic through those gateways
- The percentage of calls enabled for Media Bypass

Media traversal and transcoding through the Mediation Server can be processor intensive in some scenarios. Often, small organizations can collocate the Mediation Server role; however, many larger organizations will require dedicated Mediation Servers for capacity purposes. Media Bypass also has a major impact on the number of calls a Mediation Server can support. Media transcoding is the most CPU-intensive job the Mediation Server does; if Media Bypass is enabled, the Mediation Server can scale to a higher number of concurrent calls. Details on capacity planning for all roles, including the Mediation Server, can be found in Chapter 31, "Planning for Basic Skype for Business Server 2015 Services." However, keep the capacity numbers included in Table 7.1 in mind when planning for Mediation Server collocation.

TABLE 7.1 Mediation Server Collocated Capacity Numbers

Configuration	Maximum Calls
Collocated Mediation Server with Media Bypass disabled	150
Standalone Mediation Server with Media Bypass disabled	1100

High Availability

Redundancy for the Mediation Server role is provided in a similar fashion as with Front End Servers: multiple Mediation Servers can be added to a pool. Load balancing is achieved via DNS load balancing, where the IP address of each server in the pool resolves to the pool name. If one IP address is unavailable, the endpoint will attempt to connect to another IP address provided for the pool based on the DNS lookup. More than one Mediation pool can be deployed, and users can be aligned to try multiple Mediation server/trunks for resiliency.

Remember that a single gateway can be connected to more than one Mediation pool for additional resiliency.

TIP

Plan for high availability in the environment from the start; even if you are deploying a single Mediation Server initially, you can deploy it as a pool of one. Adding more servers for high availability to the environment later simply becomes a matter of adding the new servers to the topology and creating the DNS records.

Mediation Server Installation and Configuration

Installing the Mediation Server role is similar to deploying any other role in Skype for Business Server 2015. Much of the installation process is actually completing the prerequisite work, and installing the actual server can be done fairly quickly. A Mediation Server can be introduced into the environment at any time and does not necessarily need to be deployed from the start.

If you are deploying the Mediation Server collocated with a Front End Server, it will be automatically deployed as part of the Front End Server deployment. This section details the deployment of a standalone Mediation pool.

Prerequisites

A Mediation Server requires the same basic prerequisite software as all other Skype for Business Server roles. The hardware, operating system, and software prerequisites are discussed in this section.

Hardware Recommendations

This section gives the hardware recommendations for Skype for Business Server 2015 servers.

Here are the Skype for Business Server 2015 Mediation Server processor recommendations:

- 64-bit dual processor, quad-core, 2.26 gigahertz (GHz) or higher.

NOTE

Skype for Business Server 2015 is a 64-bit application only and requires a 64-bit-capable processor. All modern server CPUs will be 64-bit compatible.

Here is the Skype for Business Server 2015 Mediation Server memory recommendation:

- 16GB RAM

These are the Skype for Business Server 2015 Mediation Server disk recommendations:

- Four or more 10K RPM HDD (2×RAID 1 configuration)
- Or solid state drives (SSDs) able to provide the same free space and similar performance to 4×10K RPM HDDs

These are the Skype for Business Server 2015 Mediation Server network recommendations:

- Dual 1Gbps network adapters (teamed with a single MAC and IP address, recommended for resiliency)
- Single 1Gbps network adapter (supported)

NOTE

When you're using multiple network adapters, it is recommended to use them only for fault tolerance. This means network adapters should be used for failover only and should not be combined for greater throughput.

Operating System Requirements

The Skype for Business Server 2015 Mediation Server supports the following operating systems:

- Windows Server 2012 R2 Standard or Data Center
- Windows Server 2012 Standard or Data Center

NOTE

Windows Server 2008 R2 is supported as part of an in-place upgrade, but is not supported for new deployments. With Windows Server 2012/R2, Microsoft removed the Enterprise Edition.

Software Requirements

The Skype for Business Server 2015 Mediation Server requires the following components to be installed:

- Microsoft .NET Framework 4.5
- Windows Management Framework 3.0
- Windows Identity Foundation
- Visual C++ 13 Redistributable

Server Roles and Features

The Mediation Server does not require that any additional Windows Server roles and services be deployed.

Create a Mediation Server Pool

After the server has been fully prepared for installation, the topology must be edited to add the new Mediation Server pool and then it must be published.

Steps to Edit the Existing Topology

The next step in deploying a Mediation Server is to edit the existing Skype for Business Server topology. To edit the topology, follow these steps:

NOTE

If the Topology Builder is not already installed on the local computer or another computer in the environment, it can be installed from the Skype for Business Server 2015 media.

1. Open the Skype for Business Server Topology Builder.
2. When prompted to select the source topology, select Download Topology from Existing Deployment to retrieve the current topology.
3. Enter a location to which to save the temporary topology file.

4. Expand the Site node where the Mediation Server will be deployed.
5. Expand the Skype for Business Server 2015 node.
6. Right-click the Mediation Pools node and select New Mediation Pool.
7. If you're deploying a pool of servers, leave Multiple Computer Pool selected and enter the fully qualified name of the Mediation Server pool in the Pool FQDN field. If you are deploying a single server, select Single Computer Pool and enter the FQDN of the server. Click Next.
8. Enter the fully qualified name of the Mediation Servers in the Computer FQDN field, click the Add button, and then click Next.
9. Select a next-hop server. This Front End pool will be where the Mediation Server will route all inbound calls for lookup. Click Next.
10. Select an Edge Server Pool to be used for Media Relay. Click Finish.

Steps to Publish the Updated Topology

After the topology has been modified to include the Mediation Server pool, the topology can be published. This process publishes the changes to the Central Management Store, and all existing Skype for Business Server 2015 servers will update their local configuration stores to match. Follow these steps to publish the updated topology:

1. Ensure that the Skype for Business Server Topology Builder is still open and contains the Mediation Server pool recently added.
2. Click the Action menu, select Topology, and then select Publish.
3. Click Next to begin publishing the topology.
4. Review the Publishing Wizard log for any errors or warnings and remediate as necessary.
5. When the log indicates a successful update, click Finish to complete the wizard.

Install Skype for Business Mediation Server Components

At this point the target server should be fully prepared and meet all prerequisites. Refer to the "Prerequisites" section earlier in this chapter for a full list of the Mediation Server requirements.

Cache Installation Files

The first step of the Skype for Business installation process will be to cache the setup files locally on the server:

1. Insert the Skype for Business Server 2015 media on the server to be used as a Mediation Server and launch Setup.exe, found in the Setup\amd64 folder.
2. Enter a location for the installation files to be cached and click Install. The default location is C:\Program Files\Skype for Business Server 2015.

3. When prompted to check for updates, select Connect to the Internet to Check for Updates. If the server doesn't have Internet access, select Don't Check for Updates Right Now. Click Next.

4. Select I Accept the Terms in the Licensing Agreement and then click OK.

NOTE

After you've browsed to the setup folder using Windows Explorer, the install window might appear behind the current Explorer window. It can be easy to miss this fact, so check the taskbar for the Skype for Business install icon if some time has passed without any screen activity.

Install Local Configuration Store

To install any server role in Skype for Business Server 2015, the target server must first have a local configuration store installed and populated with the topology information. The Skype for Business Deployment Wizard will automatically open after the installation files have been cached on the system.

1. Click Install or Update Skype for Business Server System.
2. Under Step 1: Install Local Configuration Store, click Run.
3. Select Retrieve Configuration Automatically from the Central Management Store and then click Next.
4. Click Finish after the local store is successfully created.

Install Skype for Business Server Components

The following steps will allow the server to read the topology information from the local configuration store and then install the server roles matching its own FQDN:

1. Under Step 2: Setup or Remove Skype for Business Server Components, click the Run button.
2. Click Next to begin the Mediation Server installation published in the topology.
3. Click Finish when the installation completes.

Create Certificates

Like all other roles in Skype for Business Server 2015, the Mediation Server communicates with other servers using TLS/Mutual Transport Layer Security (MTLS). To leverage MTLS, the Mediation Servers will need a single certificate for each server in the Mediation Server Pool. This certificate is very basic and has the following requirement:

- The subject name should contain the pool's fully qualified domain name (FQDN).
- The server and pool names should be included as a subject alternative name.

NOTE

The Certificate Wizard in Skype for Business Server 2015 will automatically populate the subject name and any required subject alternative names based on the published topology, which greatly simplifies certificate confusion created by prior versions.

Follow these steps to request and assign the necessary certificates:

1. Under Step 3: Request, Install, or Assign Certificate, click the Run button.
2. Highlight the Default certificate and click the Request button to start the Certificate Request Wizard.
3. Click Request to continue.

NOTE

The following steps here assume that an internal Certificate Authority is used to generate the request.

4. Select the appropriate Certificate Authority for your environment from the drop-down list. By default, for a Mediation certificate, a friendly name will be automatically entered, the key length set to 2048, and the certificate's private key will not be exportable.
5. Enter your organization name and organizational unit, select your country from the drop-down menu and then enter your state/province and city/locality. Remember that full names must be entered; abbreviations are not considered valid for certificate requests.
6. The Deployment Wizard will automatically set the subject name as the Mediation pool name. The Deployment Wizard also automatically adds the SANs required based on the published topology. Unless you have special requirements, bypass the Advanced Wizard.
7. Once the Certificate Request Wizard has completed, click Next.
8. Review the Certificate Request Summary screen for accuracy and when satisfied click Next.
9. The Skype for Business Management Shell commands are displayed and the user can optionally review the certificate request log. Unless the request failed, this is not necessary. Click Next.
10. Leave the Assign This Certificate to Skype for Business Server Certificate Usages check box selected to skip straight to the Certificate Assignment Wizard. Click Finish to complete the request process.

NOTE

It might not seem intuitive, but to process a response to an offline certificate request, use the Import Certificate button found at the bottom of the Certificate Wizard. If a request to an online Certificate Authority is in a pending state, the Process Pending Certificates button will be available to complete those requests.

Certificates issued from an online Certificate Authority will be installed automatically. If an offline request was performed, first copy the Certificate Authority response to the server. Then use the Import Certificate button found at the bottom of the wizard to complete the process. Follow these steps to import the completed request:

1. Click Browse and select the Certificate Authority response.
2. Uncheck the Certificate File Contains the Certificate's Private Key check box. Click Next.
3. Review the import certificate summary and click Next.
4. Click Finish to complete the process of associating the private key and Certificate Authority response.

Assign Certificates

After creating the necessary certificates, you must ensure the Mediation Server services have certificates assigned to them. To assign a certificate, follow these steps:

1. Under Step 3: Request, Install, or Assign Certificate, click the Run button.
2. Highlight the Default certificate and click the Assign button to start the Certificate Request Wizard.
3. Click Next to continue.
4. Select the certificate to be assigned and click Next. It's possible to view each certificate in more detail by highlighting it and clicking the View Certificate Details button.

NOTE

If a certificate is not available on this screen, that usually means a private key is not associated with the certificate. Be sure to complete any pending or offline requests before this step.

5. Click Next on the Certificate Assignment Summary screen.
6. The Skype for Business Management Shell commands are displayed and the user can optionally review the certificate request log. Unless the request failed, this is not necessary. Click Next.
7. Click Finish to complete the wizard.

Start Services

After the necessary certificates have been requested and assigned, the Skype for Business Server 2015 Mediation Server services can be started:

1. Step 4 will direct you to run `Start-CSWindowsService`.
2. Alternatively, you can run `services.msc` and start the services manually.
3. Click Exit to complete the wizard.

The wizard does not actually wait for the services to complete startup. Use the Services MMC to view the actual service state.

At this point the Mediation Server installation is complete and it should be functional.

Adding Mediation Servers to an Existing Pool

Adding a Mediation Server to a pool is much like creating the initial pool. The topology must first be updated and published to reflect the change. Follow the steps described previously to import the existing topology in Topology Builder, and then follow these steps to add another pool member:

1. Expand the Mediation Pools node.
2. Right-click the Mediation Pool name and select New Server.
3. Enter the fully qualified domain name of the new Mediation Server.
4. Select either Use All Configured IP Addresses or Limit Service Usage to Selected IP Addresses and enter the IP addresses to be used by the Skype for Business Server 2015 services.
5. Optionally, select the IPv6 check box if IPv6 is in use on the network.
6. Click OK when complete.

Now simply publish the topology again and proceed with the Mediation Server installation using the same steps defined in the "Install Skype for Business Mediation Server Components" section earlier in this chapter. After installation, be sure to add the corresponding Mediation pool DNS record so that clients can locate the new Mediation Server.

Mediation Server Configuration

After a Mediation Server pool has been installed, there generally is not much configuration left to do. You will likely want to deploy one or more gateways and associate them with the mediation server pool by configuring one or more trunks. At the trunk level, you can configure the following:

- Whether the gateway supports TLS encryption or just TCP
- Media Bypass support
- Advanced features such as SIP REFER support and session timers

Mediation Server Administration

Administration of the Mediation Server role in Skype for Business Server 2015 can be performed through a combination of the Skype for Business Server Control Panel and the Skype for Business Server Management Shell. This section discusses management of the Mediation Server services.

Services

Installing a Mediation Server in Skype for Business Server 2015 deploys only a minimal number of Windows services. The following services will be visible within the Services MMC after the Mediation Server installation:

- Skype for Business Server Centralized Logging Service
- Skype for Business Server Mediation Server
- Skype for Business Server Replica Replicator Agent
- SQL Server (RTCLOCAL)
- SQL Server Agent (RTCLOCAL)

NOTE

The SQL Server Agent services are installed but set to disabled.

The Skype for Business Management Shell can also be used to check the current service status. Open the Skype for Business Management Shell and run the following command:

```
Get-CsWindowsService -ExcludeActivityLevel
```

Review the status report:

- `Status    Name`
- `------    ----`
- `Running   REPLICA`
- `Running   RTCCLSAGT`
- `Running   RTCMEDSRV`

The state of a Mediation Server can also be viewed through the Skype for Business Server Control Panel. To check the status of a Mediation Server Pool, perform the following steps:

1. Open the Skype for Business Server Control Panel.
2. Click Topology.
3. Highlight the server in question and click Properties.
4. Make sure that the green play button appears in the Service Status column. A red square indicates that a required service is not running.

7

Services Management

Managing the Skype for Business Server services is fortunately about the extent of administration involved with a Mediation Server after it's installed and configured. However, Enterprise Voice requires a fair bit more administration. The Mediation Server is just a supporting role of Enterprise Voice; for details on how to manage Enterprise Voice features, see Chapter 17, "Advanced Skype for Business Voice Configuration."

Administrators can start, stop, or drain the Mediation Server services either from the Skype for Business Server Control Panel or from the Skype for Business Server Management Shell. Stopping the services ends all user sessions, but draining the services allows existing connections to continue but prevents new connections from being accepted. This enables an administrator to prepare a server for maintenance.

To manage the Skype for Business Server services, perform the following steps:

1. Open the Skype for Business Server Control Panel.
2. Click Topology.
3. Highlight the server to be modified.
4. Click Action and select one of the following: Start All Services, Stop All Services, or Prevent New Connections for All Services.
5. Alternatively, double-click the server to drill down further and manage the individual services.

Topology Replication Status

A relatively easy method of checking the health status of a Mediation Server or pool exists through the Skype for Business Server Control Panel. To check the status of a Mediation Server pool, perform the following steps:

1. Open the Skype for Business Server Control Panel.
2. Click Topology.
3. Highlight the server in question and view the Replication column. A green check mark indicates that the Mediation Server has an up-to-date copy of the topology. A red X indicates that it does not have the most recent topology change.

The Skype for Business Management Shell can also be used to validate the topology status. Open the Skype for Business Management Shell and run the following command:

```
Get-CsManagementStoreReplicationStatus -ReplicaFQDN MEDIATIONSERVER.skypeunleashed.com
```

Check for the `UpToDate` parameter to report `true`:

- `UpToDate : True`
- `ReplicaFQDN : MEDIATIONSERVER.skypeunleashed.com`
- `LastStatusReport : 9/8/2012 3:34:09 PM`
- `LastUpdateCreation : 9/8/2012 3:34:06 PM`

Mediation Server Troubleshooting

Troubleshooting a Mediation Server might become necessary in the event that users are unable to make or receive calls to or from the PSTN. This section discusses the key components of a Mediation Server to check when issues arise. Common troubleshooting tools and tips are also provided that should resolve many issues.

Connectivity to Gateways

Given the Mediation Server's role of providing PSTN connectivity through a gateway, ensuring that connectivity is healthy is important in all troubleshooting scenarios. Skype for Business Server 2015 maintains health monitoring of these connections by default, and it does so in two ways:

- **SIP OPTIONS requests**—The Mediation Server continuously communicates with the gateway(s) through SIP OPTIONS requests. These exchanges are a method of validating a healthy connection between the two services. If these messages fail to be exchanged, Skype for Business Server 2015 will alert administrators through the Lync Server event log. For information on checking this log, see the "Event Logs" section.
- **Routing timeouts**—Skype for Business Server 2015 identifies issues with a Mediation Server and gateway after a number of failed calls. If a Mediation Server is not able to route calls to a gateway, it is marked as down. When this occurs, Skype for Business Server routes calls through alternative routes if available; if not, users receive errors when making outbound calls and event logs are recorded identifying the error.

Whenever troubleshooting PSTN call issues, always ensure that a healthy connection between the Mediation Server and the gateway is active. Look for the errors described previously, and also validate IP routing connectivity between the Mediation Server and the gateway(s) utilizing tools such as Ping and Telnet.

Connectivity to Edge Servers

When Skype for Business Edge Servers are deployed in the environment, the Mediation Server service requires constant communication with the Edge Server. The Mediation Server acts much like a Skype for Business client in regard to Edge Server connectivity. When the Mediation Server is establishing any call, it will request Media Relay ports with the Edge Server to be ready in the event that a remote user might be involved. Even when the call is made from an internal user, this process is still followed. If the Mediation Server cannot contact the Edge Server, the actual call might not fail but a delay in call setup time can occur.

A common issue with call setup delays is connectivity between Mediation Servers and Edge Servers. Ensure that the Mediation Server can communicate with the Edge Server on port 3478 UDP and 443 TCP for port allocation. If that network connection is not available or the Edge Servers are having issues, a delay of several seconds might be incurred at call setup time. Additionally, if remote Skype for Business users are not able to make calls to the PSTN, Edge Server connectivity is a key component to analyze.

DNS Records

Skype for Business Server 2015 Mediation Server DNS requirements are fairly simple. However, because Mediation Server Pools rely on DNS load balancing, it is important to validate the DNS configuration. A Mediation Server Pool requires a DNS entry for each server in that pool. For every Mediation Server in the pool, ensure that there is an A record of the FQDN of the pool pointing to the IP of the server.

Event Logs

A good source of information in troubleshooting any server issue is the Windows event logs. Skype for Business Server 2015 creates a dedicated event log for informational activities, warnings, and errors within the standard Windows Server event log. To view this event log, follow these steps:

1. Click Start.
2. Type **eventvwr.msc** and press Enter to open the Event Viewer Microsoft Management Console.
3. Expand the Applications and Services Logs folder.
4. Click the Lync Server log.
5. Examine the log for any warning or error events that might provide additional insight into any issues.

Skype for Business Server Management Shell

The Skype for Business Server 2015 Management Shell provides several cmdlets that can be used to test various functions of a server. A useful cmdlet for verifying the overall health of a server is `Test-CSComputer`, which verifies that all services are running, that the local computer group membership is correctly populated with the necessary Skype for Business Server Active Mediation Server groups, and that the required Windows Firewall ports have been opened. The `Test-CSComputer` cmdlet must be run from the local computer and it uses the following syntax:

```
Test-CSComputer -Report "C:\Test-CSComputer Results.xml"
```

After running the cmdlet, open the generated XML file to view a detailed analysis of each check.

Synthetic Transactions

A really useful feature first introduced in Lync Server 2010 is synthetic transactions. These are PowerShell cmdlets that can simulate actions taken by servers or users in the environment. These synthetic transactions allow an administrator to conduct tests against a service. In the case of a Mediation Server, the two most useful synthetic transactions are `Test-CSOutboundCall` and `Test-CSPSTNPeertoPeerCall`.

When `Test-CSOutboundCall` is run, a full outbound call is made to a phone number the administrator provides. This transaction tests the policies as well as the signaling and media connectivity to the PSTN. After the signaling path has been established, the transaction sends DTMF tones to validate media connectivity. Running this cmdlet requires a user account to authenticate and register to Skype for Business Server 2015, as well as a valid destination phone number. The user credential parameter's username and password must be collected by an authentication dialog and saved to a variable, as seen in this command:

```
$Credential = Get-Credential "SKYPEUNLEASHED\skypeadmin"
```

After the credentials have been collected, the cmdlet can be run with the user credential variable previously saved:

```
Test-CsPstnOutboundCall -TargetFqdn <Front End Pool FQDN>
➥-TargetPstnPhoneNumber "+15551234567" -UserSipAddress "sip:tom@skypeunleashed.com"
➥-UserCredential $credential
```

Here's a Test-CSPSTNOutboundCall example:

- TargetFQDN : SfBpool1.skypeunleashed.com
- Result : Success
- Latency : 00:00:10.9506726

As seen in the output, the call was successful.

`Test-CSPSTNPeertoPeerCall` is very similar; however, it establishes a call between two Skype for Business users over the PSTN. This transaction authenticates two Skype for Business users and makes a call between them but forces it through the PSTN gateway rather than peer to peer. The call is established, media connectivity is validated, and then the call terminates. To run this cmdlet, you must provide two valid user accounts in Skype for Business Server 2015. An example is provided next.

The user credential parameter's username and password must be collected by an authentication dialog and saved to a variable, as seen in the following command:

```
$Credential1 = Get-Credential "SKYPEUNLEASHED\tom"
$Credential2 = Get-Credential "SKYPEUNLEASHED\anna"

Test-CsPstnPeerToPeerCall -TargetFqdn <FRONT END POOL FQDN>
➥-SenderSipAddress "sip:tom@skypeunleashed.com" -SenderCredential $credential1
➥-ReceiverSipAddress "sip:anna@skypeunleashed.com" -ReceiverCredential $credential2
```

Here's a Test-CSPSTNPSTNPeertoPeerCall example:

- TargetFQDN : SfBpool1.skypeunleashed.com
- Result : Success
- Latency : 00:00:10.9506726

As seen in the output, the call was successful.

Telnet

Telnet is a simple method of checking whether a specific TCP port is available from a client machine. From a machine that is having trouble contacting a Mediation Server, follow these steps to verify connectivity to the Mediation Server service:

> **TIP**
>
> The Telnet client is not installed by default in modern Windows operating systems. On a desktop operating system it must be installed by using the Turn Windows Features On or Off option found in Programs and Features. On a server operating system it can be installed through the Features section of Server Manager.

1. Open a command prompt.
2. Type the following command:

```
telnet <Mediation Server pool FQDN> 5061
```

If the window goes blank and only a flashing cursor is seen, it means the connection was successful and the port can be contacted without issue. If the connection fails, an error is returned. Check that the services are running on the Mediation Server and that no firewalls are blocking the traffic.

System Time

A key component of any service running successfully in Skype for Business Server 2015 is the system time. Be sure to verify that the clocks on any Skype for Business Server 2015 servers are correctly set and have the appropriate time zones configured. If the clocks between a server and a client are off by more than five minutes, Kerberos authentication will begin to fail and TLS negotiations may be impacted.

Best Practices

The following are best practices from this chapter:

- Mediation Servers are required for connectivity to the PSTN and PBXs.
- Deploy Mediation Server pools for redundancy and scalability.
- Carefully consider collocating the Mediation Server with the Front End Server role. Media Bypass will enable higher concurrent call scaling. If Media Bypass is not available, a standalone Mediation pool may be more appropriate.
- When deploying Mediation Server roles, be sure to configure a DNS A record for each server in the pool for the pool FQDN.
- The Mediation Server must be able to connect to the Edge Server pool if deployed for all calls. If the Mediation Server cannot route to the Edge Server, you may see call setup delays.

Summary

The Mediation Server in Skype for Business Server 2015 remains a critical component for providing Enterprise Voice and Dial-In Conferencing to Skype for Business users. Deploying Mediation Server pools that are paired with gateways can provide organizations of any type with redundant and scalable voice connectivity.

The Mediation Server also provides critical functionality required for interoperability with legacy PBXs, and should be deployed by any organization considering Skype for Business Enterprise Voice.

The Mediation Server connects to many other Skype for Business Server components, including the Front End Server, the Edge Server, and Conferencing Servers as well as the PSTN gateway(s). Because of this, troubleshooting Mediation Server issues often results in validating other components.

CHAPTER 8
Persistent Chat

IN THIS CHAPTER

- Persistent Chat Overview
- Persistent Chat Deployment
- Configuring Persistent Chat
- Persistent Chat Administration
- Lync Online and Hybrid Environments
- Persistent Chat Troubleshooting

For many organizations, the primary focus of a new Skype for Business deployment is the adoption of IM and Presence. This is understandable because the brief and simple nature of IM, along with the dynamic nature of Presence information, makes for an efficient and flexible means of communication. However, organizations are also increasingly finding that ongoing, persistent communication provides valuable benefits as well, particularly for teams of users who collaborate on projects and share knowledge on specific topics. Skype for Business Server 2015 provides for this form of communication as well, in the form of the Persistent Chat Server role.

Persistent Chat Overview

Persistent Chat is a Skype for Business Server role that enables administrators and/or users to create chat rooms containing persistent conversations based on specific topics and categories. The persistent nature of the messages enables Skype for Business users to view ongoing conversations at their leisure, and also search for information within the chat rooms. The benefits of Persistent Chat become evident when there is a need to share information with multiple people on a specific topic and that data needs to be available at a later time and be easily searchable. Although this can be accomplished to some degree using other forms of communication, none of these other forms is as effective as Persistent Chat for these specific requirements. Some of the primary uses for Persistent Chat are project communications, group discussions, meetings, and knowledge bases.

NOTE

Persistent Chat was available as a third-party trusted application with Lync Server 2010, and was known as Group Chat. With Lync Server 2013, Persistent Chat was included as part of the Lync topology along with other Lync Server roles for the first time. For this reason, along with other important architectural changes, Persistent Chat will likely find more widespread adoption than ever before with Skype for Business Server 2015.

Like several other Skype for Business Server roles, Persistent Chat consists of a front-end component as well as a back-end SQL database component. As further detailed in later chapters, these components can in some cases be collocated with other Skype for Business Server 2015 Server roles, depending on the Skype for Business topology and the requirements for Persistent Chat.

Persistent Chat Deployment

In Lync Server 2013, Persistent Chat was included as part of the Skype for Business topology; this made the deployment process more streamlined compared to that of previous versions. This section provides the details on installation of the Persistent Chat Server role into an existing Skype for Business Server 2015 environment.

Topology Options and Scaling

Several topology options are available with Persistent Chat, and these are dependent on the overall Skype for Business deployment. Similar to the Skype for Business Front End services, an instance of Persistent Chat is referred to as a pool, even if just a single server is used. As with other Skype for Business Server roles, both front-end and back-end components are included in a Persistent Chat pool. The front-end components include the Persistent Chat service and the Compliance service. Back-end databases for Persistent Chat include the Persistent Chat Store and the Persistent Chat Compliance Store.

With a Standard Edition deployment, the Persistent Chat Server role can be collocated with the Front End Server. The single-server deployment can support up to 20,000 users. However, since all Skype for Business services are hosted using a single system with this topology, Persistent Chat performance will be entirely dependent on the resource usage requirements for all Skype for Business services. With an Enterprise Edition deployment, Persistent Chat cannot be collocated with the Skype for Business Front End services, and therefore dedicated systems are required. However, the Persistent Chat databases can be collocated on the same SQL Server, or even the same SQL instance, as the Skype for Business Back End databases. Hosting the Persistent Chat Stores on a dedicated SQL Server is of course also an option, and is recommended particularly for larger Skype for Business implementations to ensure the best performance.

NOTE

The requirement to install Persistent Chat on dedicated systems with an Enterprise Edition deployment is better understood when considering the differences in how resiliency is handled between a Persistent Chat pool and a Front End pool. When Enterprise Edition

Front End pools are configured for Front End pool pairing, the Skype for Business Server Backup service replicates the databases between the pools for high availability. In contrast, to achieve high availability with Persistent Chat, a single pool is stretched across two locations, and SQL log shipping is used to replicate database information between SQL systems at the two locations.

Persistent Chat also includes support for multiple-server topologies, with several high availability and disaster recovery options. Up to eight Persistent Chat Servers can be installed into a single pool, and these servers can be installed across multiple locations for site resiliency. Up to four Persistent Chat Servers in a pool can be active at any time, and each active server can support up to 20,000 concurrent connected endpoints, for a total of 80,000 users. The load is automatically distributed evenly across the active servers, and in the event of a server failure, users are automatically transferred to a remaining active server. When multiple Persistent Chat Servers are used, the file stores and databases are shared among the servers, and the servers freely communicate with each other as needed to form a cohesive Persistent Chat system. The end result is that all chat history is available to any of the servers in the pool, and users connected to different Persistent Chat Servers can freely chat with each other.

TIP

It is not possible to add additional servers to a Persistent Chat pool if the first Persistent Chat Server is collocated with a Standard Edition Front End Server. If there is any question as to whether multiple servers will eventually be needed for Persistent Chat, it is recommended that you install the first server as a standalone instance to allow the pool to grow accordingly.

Intra-site high availability can be achieved with the installation of multiple SQL servers in a datacenter and using SQL mirroring, clustering, or AlwaysOn to replicate the data between them. For cross-site disaster recovery, at least one set of Persistent Chat Front End Servers and dedicated Back End database servers must be installed at each location. SQL log shipping is then used to replicate Persistent Chat database information between the two locations. For more detailed information regarding high availability and disaster recovery options with Persistent Chat, see Chapter 14, “High Availability and Disaster Recovery.”

Prerequisites

The infrastructure requirements for a Persistent Chat pool are very similar to the requirements for a Front End pool. For example, the Active Directory requirements are identical with one small exception: At least one AD global catalog server must exist in the forest root domain for Persistent Chat to be installed in that forest. Also similar to the Front End pool, a file store must be defined for use with Persistent Chat, which serves as a repository for files that are uploaded using the chat rooms. With a single-server deployment, the file store can be defined as a local file path on the Persistent Chat Server. For multiple-server deployments, a UNC path location must be specified. If desired, the same UNC path location can be used as a file store for both the Front End pool and the Persistent Chat pool.

To facilitate in-place upgrades from Lync Server 2013, the system requirements for a Persistent Chat Server are the same, as summarized here:

- Windows Server 2008 R2 with SP1 is supported, but only recommended in in-place upgrade scenarios. Windows Server 2012 (Standard, Enterprise, or Datacenter Editions) and 2012 R2 (Standard or Enterprise) are supported operating system platforms for new installations.
- For Windows Server 2012 R2, the hotfix from KB 2982006.
- For Windows Server 2012, the hotfix from KB 2858668.
- For Windows Server 2008 R2, the hotfix from KB 2533623.
- .NET Framework 4.5 (included with Windows Server 2012).
- .NET Framework 3.5.
- Windows PowerShell 3.0 (included with Windows Server 2012) or later.
- Windows Identity Foundation (included with Windows Server 2012).
- The Message Queuing feature (including Directory Service Integration) included with Windows Server is required if the Persistent Chat Compliance service is enabled.
- Microsoft Visual C++ 2013 x64 redistributable (automatically installed from the Skype for Business media if not present when starting the Skype for Business installation).
- One standard SSL certificate is required, from either a third party or an internal Certificate Authority (no subject alternative names are required).

Hardware guidelines for a Persistent Chat Server are the same as for other Skype for Business Server roles and are summarized here:

- Hex-core 64-bit dual processor (2.26 GHz or higher).
- 32GB RAM.
- Eight or more 10,000 RPM hard disk drives with at least 72GB of free space, or a RAID 1 or RAID 10 volume on a storage area network. Solid state drives (SSDs) capable of providing the same level of performance are also supported.
- One dual-port network adapter, 1Gbps or higher. (NIC teaming with a single MAC address and single IP address are supported.)

NOTE

Microsoft's listed hardware guidelines are based on a user pool of 80,000 users and can therefore be scaled back appropriately as needed.

For the Persistent Chat database server, SQL Server 2008 R2, SQL Server 2012, and SQL Server 2014 are the only supported database platforms. For two-node clusters or mirroring, the Standard edition of SQL Server is sufficient. For up to 16-node solutions, the Enterprise edition is required. In either case, the latest updates for each should be installed. Skype for Business Server supports SQL Server AlwaysOn in both AlwaysOn Availability Groups and AlwaysOn Failover Cluster instances. These are both features of SQL Server 2014.

The hardware guidelines for a Persistent Chat database server are the same as for other Skype for Business database servers, as summarized here:

- Hex-core 64-bit dual processor (2.26 GHz or higher).
- 32GB RAM.
- Eight or more 10,000 RPM hard disk drives with at least 72GB of free space, or a RAID 1 or RAID 10 storage area network with four dedicated LUNs.
- One network adapter, 1Gbps or higher. (NIC teaming with a single MAC and single IP address is supported.)

Topology Update

As with all Skype for Business Server roles, the Topology Builder must be updated to include Persistent Chat before the server role is installed. Follow these steps to update the Skype for Business topology to include Persistent Chat:

1. Log on to a system where the Skype for Business Server 2015 administrative tools are installed using an account that is a member of the `Domain Admins` and `CsAdministrator` groups, and then open the Skype for Business Server Topology Builder.
2. At the prompt, select Download Topology from Existing Deployment to retrieve the current topology from the Central Management Store.
3. At the Save Topology As prompt, select a name and location for the Topology Builder file and click Save.
4. In the left pane, expand Skype for Business Server, expand the Skype for Business site where Persistent Chat will be installed, expand Skype for Business Server 2015, and then right-click the Persistent Chat pools node and select New Persistent Chat Pool.
5. At the Define the Fully Qualified Domain Name (FQDN) screen, enter the FQDN that will be used for the Persistent Chat pool. If Persistent Chat will be collocated with a Standard Edition Front End, the FQDN entered here must be the FQDN of the Front End Server. If Persistent Chat will be deployed using separate servers, the FQDN entered will be new to the topology. After the FQDN is entered, choose either the Multiple Computer Pool or Single Computer Pool option and then click Next.

TIP

Although a new FQDN is created in the topology for Persistent Chat pools that are deployed on separate hardware, it is not necessary to enter the FQDN of the Persistent Chat pool as an internal DNS record. The Front End Server handles all the routing for Persistent Chat without requiring DNS queries.

6. If the Multiple Computer Pool option was selected on the preceding screen, the Define the Computers in This Pool screen appears. Enter the FQDN of each system that will be added as a Persistent Chat Server and then click Add to add each to the pool. When finished, click Next.

NOTE

If the Single Computer Pool option was selected, the Standard Edition Front End Server is automatically chosen as the Persistent Chat Server because this is the only option.

7. At the Define Properties of the Persistent Chat Pool screen, enter a display name for the pool, and keep the default Persistent Chat port number of 5041. Select from among the listed options to enable compliance or to define this pool as the default for the Skype for Business site. If the Multiple Computer Pool option was selected earlier, the option to enable disaster recovery is also presented. After the desired options are selected, click Next.
8. At the Define the SQL Server Store screen, several SQL options are presented, as shown in Figure 8.1. To use a SQL Server that is not currently part of the topology, click New, enter the FQDN of the new SQL Server, enter the instance name if the default instance is not being used, and select the SQL mirroring option if high availability will be used. To use a SQL Server that is already part of the topology, use the drop-down menu to select the SQL Server that will be used. If SQL mirroring will be used for high availability with this server, select this option and then click New to enter the information for a new SQL store for this purpose, or use the drop-down menu to select one that is already part of the topology. If automatic failover will be used, thus requiring a SQL Server mirroring witness, enable this option as well and then click New to enter the information for a new system to act as a SQL witness, or you can use the drop-down menu to select one that is already part of the topology. After the SQL Server store options have been selected, click Next.

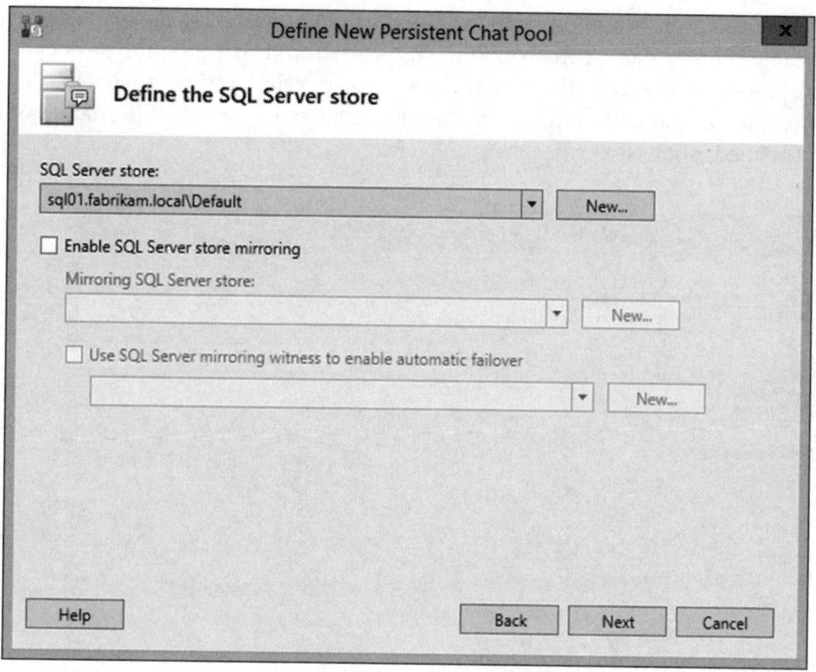

FIGURE 8.1 Persistent Chat SQL Server store options.

9. If the compliance option was enabled on an earlier screen, the Define the Compliance SQL Server Store screen appears, presenting the same SQL options for the compliance store that were presented for the Persistent Chat Store. To use a SQL Server for compliance that is not currently part of the topology, click New, enter the FQDN of the new SQL Server, enter the instance name if the default instance is not being used, and select the SQL mirroring option if high availability will be used. To use a SQL Server for compliance that is already part of the topology, use the drop-down menu to select the SQL Server that will be used. If SQL mirroring will be used for high availability with this server, select this option and click New to enter the information for a new SQL store for this purpose, or you can use the drop-down menu to select one that is already part of the topology. If automatic failover will be used, requiring a SQL Server mirroring witness, enable this option as well. Click New to enter the information for a new system to act as a SQL witness, or use the drop-down menu to select one that is already part of the topology. After the compliance SQL Server store options have been selected, click Next.

10. The Define File Store screen appears, as shown in Figure 8.2. If you are using a file store that is already part of the topology, use the drop-down menu to select the existing file store. If a new file store will be defined, select Define a New File Store and enter the fully qualified name of the file server as well as the file share name. When finished, click Next.

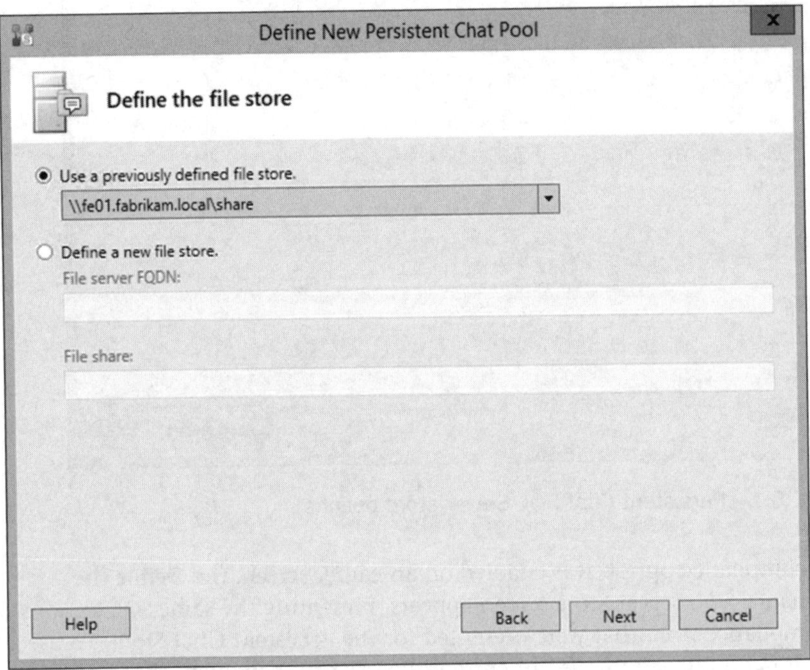

FIGURE 8.2 Persistent Chat file store options.

TIP

When you are using a new file store for Persistent Chat, the file store does not need to be created before it is defined in Topology Builder. However, it must be created before the topology is published.

11. If the option to install the Persistent Chat pool using separate servers was chosen on an earlier screen, the Select the Next Hop Server screen will appear. Use the drop-down menu to select the next-hop pool for traffic sent from this Persistent Chat pool, and then click Finish to complete the wizard and return to the Topology Builder.

12. The Persistent Chat pool details are now displayed in Topology Builder, as shown in Figure 8.3.

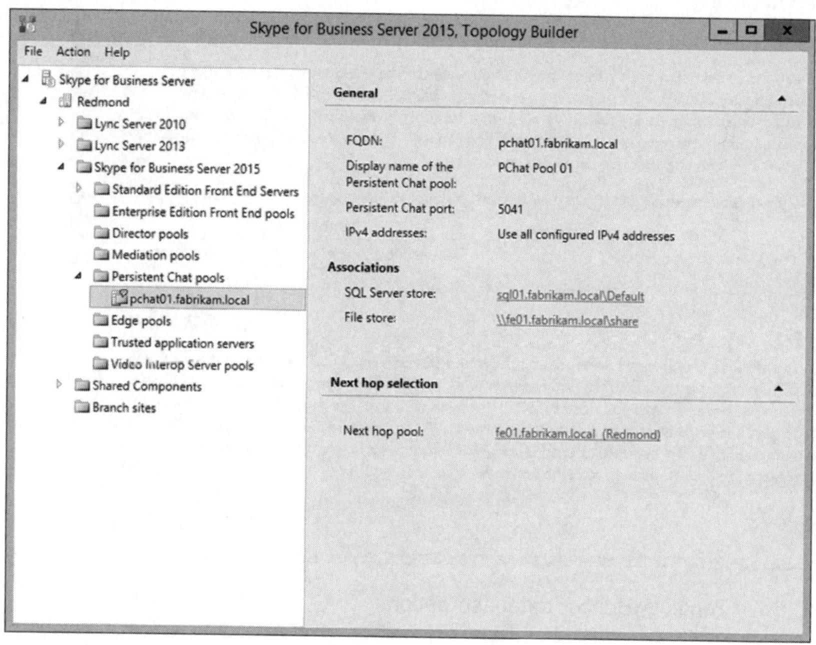

FIGURE 8.3 Persistent Chat pool in the Topology Builder.

13. From the Action drop-down menu, select Topology and then select Publish.

14. At the Publish Topology screen, click Next to continue.

15. If the option to define a new SQL Server store was chosen on an earlier screen, the Select Databases screen now appears, as shown in Figure 8.4. Verify that the correct target database server for the Persistent Chat pool is selected. Note that the wizard defaults to the option of automatically determining the file locations for the Persistent Chat database. If alternative database paths are needed (for example, if dedicated volumes have been created on the target SQL Server for database and log files), then select the target store in the wizard and click the Advanced button. The Select Database File Location dialog box is then presented. To specify alternative paths for the database files, select the option titled Use These Paths on Target SQL Server; then enter the specific paths to the database files and the log files on the target server, and then click OK. Click Next to continue.

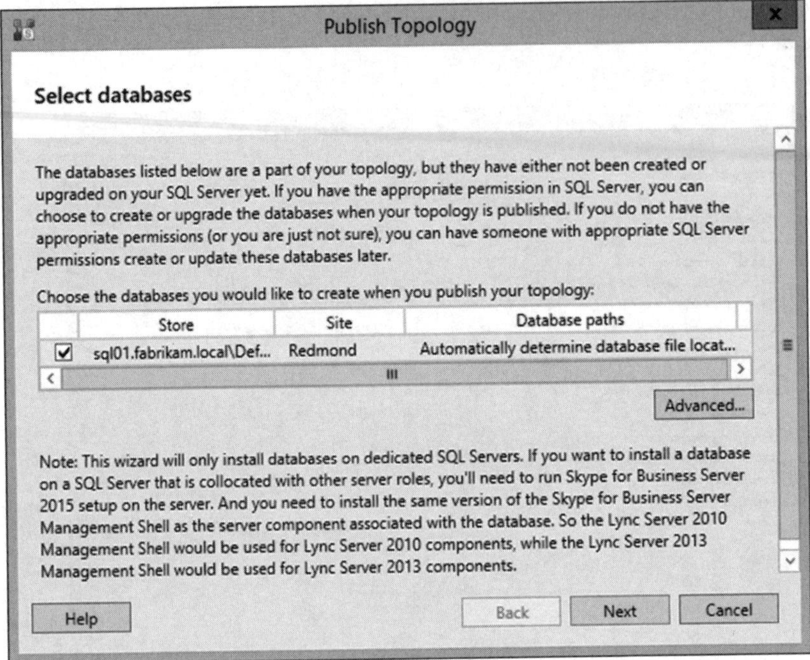

FIGURE 8.4 Topology Builder database options.

16. The topology updates are now published, and the new Persistent Chat databases are created on the target SQL Server. When the topology has been successfully published, click Finish to complete the topology update for Persistent Chat.

Installing the Persistent Chat Server Role

After the Skype for Business topology has been updated to include the Persistent Chat pool, the Skype for Business Server role installation can be run on each Persistent Chat server that has been added to the topology. The following procedure is used to install Persistent Chat on one of the servers that has been defined in the topology:

1. Log on to the server using an account that has local administrative rights on the system, and execute the setup.exe file from the Setup\amd64 folder of Skype for Business media.
2. If it's not already installed, a prompt appears regarding the installation of Microsoft Visual C++ X64 Minimum Runtime as a prerequisite. Click Yes to install the software.
3. When the wizard displays, select the option Connect to the Internet to Check for Updates. Then, either browse to your intended installation location or accept the default location. Click Install.

4. When prompted, read the software license terms, click the I Accept the Terms in the License Agreement option if you agree to the terms, and click OK.
5. If the option to check online for updates was selected in the previous step, the wizard will now check online and download any relevant updates. A results screen will be displayed. Review the results and click Next.
6. The core components of Skype for Business Server 2015 are now installed, which includes the Skype for Business Management Shell and the Skype for Business Deployment Wizard. After the Deployment Wizard launches, click Install or Update Skype for Business Server System.
7. The wizard now determines the current state of the local system and provides links to various installation options as needed. At Step 1: Install Local Configuration Store, click Run.
8. At the Configure Local Replica of Central Management Store screen, keep the default option of Retrieve Directly from the Central Management Store and then click Next.
9. The commands required to install a local configuration store are executed. After the installation is complete, click Finish to return to the Deployment Wizard.
10. At Step 2: Setup or Remove Skype for Business Server Components, click Run.
11. At the Set Up Skype for Business Server Components screen, click Next.
12. The commands required to install the Persistent Chat software are now executed. After the installation is complete, click View Log to determine whether any errors occurred during the software installation process. When finished, click Finish to return to the Deployment Wizard.

After the software is installed, a certificate needs to be installed for the Persistent Chat Server. As with other Skype for Business Server roles, Persistent Chat supports certificates issued by a third party or an internal CA. Continuing with the Deployment Wizard, the following steps are used to request and assign an SSL certificate from an online internal CA:

1. At Step 3: Request, Install or Assign Certificates, click Run to begin the certificate request.
2. When the Certificate Wizard screen appears, a single certificate type is displayed for the Default certificate. Click Request.
3. The Certificate Request Wizard now launches. Click Next.
4. At the Delayed or Immediate Requests screen, online and offline request options are presented. Because this request will be sent to an internal CA, select Send the Request Immediately to an Online Certificate Authority and then click Next.

5. At the Choose a Certification Authority (CA) screen, the online Certificate Authority systems that have been detected by the wizard are listed, as shown in Figure 8.5. Keep the default option of Select a CA from the List Detected in Your Environment. If you would like to change the friendly name, which makes it easier to identify later, enter a friendly name for the certificate. Enter the name of the organization and organizational unit into the corresponding fields. Select the country from the drop-down menu and then enter the information into the State/Province and City/Locality fields. The names that are automatically populated into the certificate by the wizard are now displayed. The opportunity to enter additional subject alternate names (SANs) outside those automatically determined by the wizard is available via the Advanced button. For a Persistent Chat Server, typically no additional names are needed. Also available in the Advanced Wizard is the ability to supply alternative credentials, or use a template other than the default WebServer (SSL) template. If those options are not required, click Next.

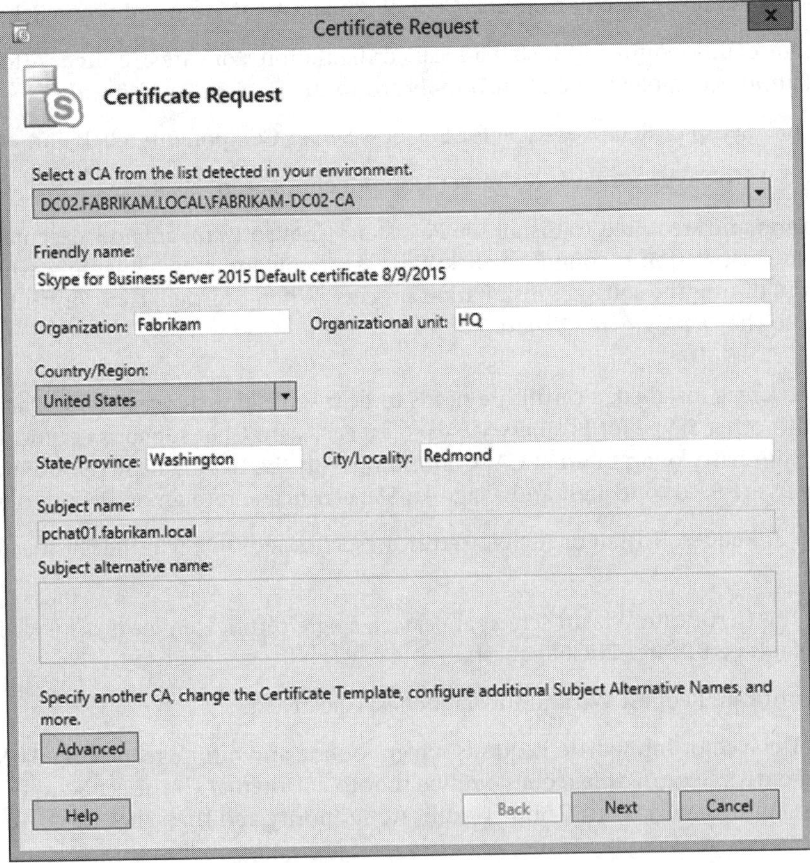

FIGURE 8.5 Internal Certificate Authorities detected.

6. At the Certificate Request Summary screen, review the values for accuracy and then click Next.

7. The commands required to generate the certificate request file are now executed. Click View Log to determine whether any errors occurred during the certificate request process. When finished, click Next.
8. At the Online Certificate Request Status screen, the results of the certificate request are shown. To view the properties of the certificate, click View Certificate Details. At this point, the certificate has been installed to the local certificate store on the system, but it has not been assigned to Skype for Business. To immediately assign the certificate to Skype for Business, keep the default selection of Assign This Certificate to Skype for Business Server Certificate Usages and then click Finish.
9. At the Certificate Assignment screen, click Next.
10. At the Certificate Assignment Summary screen, review the summary information and then click Next.
11. The commands required to assign the certificate are now executed. Click View Log to determine whether any errors occurred during the certificate assignment process. When finished, click Finish to return to the Certificate Wizard.
12. The default certificate is now assigned to the server, as shown in Figure 8.6. Click Close to exit the Certificate Wizard.

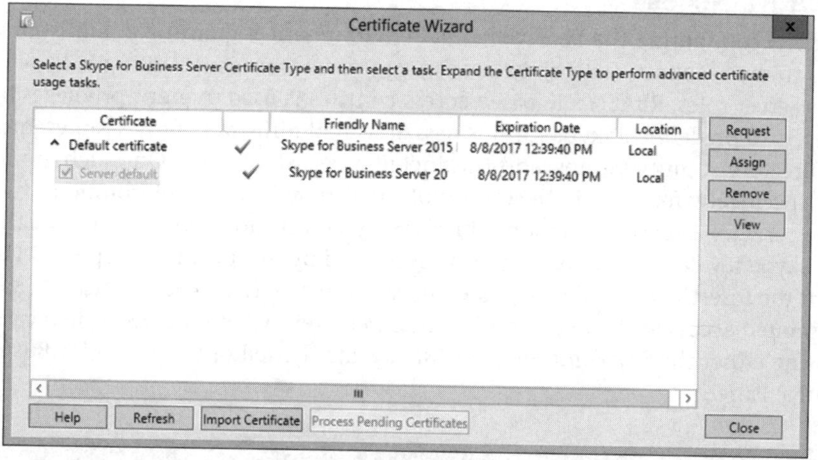

FIGURE 8.6 Viewing the assigned certificate.

Now that the software has been installed and the certificate has been assigned, the final step is to start the Persistent Chat services for the first time. Continuing with the Deployment Wizard, the Persistent Chat services are started as shown here:

1. At Step 4: Start Services, click Run.
2. The Services MMC snap-in will now open. Find the Skype services, right-click each one, and choose Start. Verify each is in a Running state and then close the Services tool.
3. Click Exit to close the Deployment Wizard.

In-place Upgrading the Persistent Chat Server Role

The process for performing an in-place upgrade of an existing Lync Server 2013 Persistent Chat Server is the same as that for a Front End Server role, with one exception. Because users aren't homed on Persistent Chat Servers, there is no need to move them before upgrading. The Persistent Chat service will be offline while the server is upgraded. For more information on performing in-place upgrades see, Chapter 4, "Skype for Business Server 2015 Front End Server."

Group Chat Servers that are part of a Lync Server 2010 topology cannot be upgraded in place.

Configuring Persistent Chat

With Skype for Business Server 2015, Persistent Chat configuration is performed using the standard Skype for Business Server administration tools, greatly simplifying the entire process of configuring and maintaining the Persistent Chat environment. Both the Skype for Business Server Control Panel and the Skype for Business Server Management Shell can be used to perform Persistent Chat configuration tasks. The following sections provide details on the primary tasks that are necessary for a Persistent Chat deployment.

Administrative Access

The first task in configuring the Persistent Chat environment is granting administrative permissions to the accounts that will be managing the environment. With all Skype for Business Server roles, RBAC (role-based access control) is used to grant privileges by assigning users to predefined Skype for Business Server administrative roles represented by Active Directory security groups, and this includes Persistent Chat. One such group is provided specifically for the administration of the Persistent Chat environment, the `CsPersistentChatAdministrator` group. This security group, along with the rest of the predefined Skype for Business security groups, is located by default in the top-level Users container in the forest root AD domain. Members of the `CsPersistentChatAdministrator` group are granted access to the Skype for Business Persistent Chat cmdlets, which can be executed using either the Skype for Business Management Shell or the Skype for Business Server Control Panel.

NOTE

While the `CsPersistentChatAdministrator` group grants specific access to the Persistent Chat portion of the Skype for Business environment, two other groups also have administrative access to much of the Persistent Chat configuration as part of their broader administrative scope: `CsAdministrator` and `CsUserAdministrator`. Therefore, in smaller organizations where one group of administrators manages the entire Skype for Business environment, including Persistent Chat, it might not be necessary to populate the `CsPersistentChatAdministrator` group.

By default, there are no members of the `CsPersistentChatAdministrator` group, and therefore the group must be populated with user accounts to delegate administrative rights to the Persistent Chat configuration.

Persistent Chat Policies

Persistent Chat policies are used to determine which Skype for Business users are enabled for Persistent Chat. Four levels of policies can be used: global, pool, site, and user. There is only one global policy, which is automatically created when Persistent Chat is deployed, and it is simply named Global. This default global policy does not need to be used, but it cannot be deleted.

Only one Persistent Chat pool policy can be created per Skype for Business pool, and it affects all users within that pool. Similarly, one Persistent Chat site policy can be created per Skype for Business site, and it affects all users in that site. On the other hand, multiple Persistent Chat user policies can be created and applied on a user-by-user basis as needed. Pool and site policies override the global policy, and user policies override the pool and site policies.

TIP

Only a single setting exists in a Persistent Chat policy; it simply allows users that are assigned to the policy to be enabled for Persistent Chat. For this reason, at most only a few Persistent Chat polices are typically needed. If it is determined that all users in the environment will be enabled for Persistent Chat, this can be accomplished using just the global policy. If, on the other hand, Persistent Chat will be assigned to specific users, then the pool, site, and user policies will be useful.

The following example shows the steps for creating a user policy and then assigning the policy to a user:

1. Log on to a system where the Skype for Business administrative tools are installed using an account that is a member of the `CsAdministrator` or `CsPersistentChatAdministrator` security group, and then open the Skype for Business Server Control Panel.
2. In the left pane, select Persistent Chat and then click the Persistent Chat Policy tab at the top.
3. From the New drop-down menu, select User Policy.

8

4. At the New Persistent Chat Policy screen, enter a name and description for the policy and then select the Enable Persistent Chat setting, as shown in Figure 8.7.

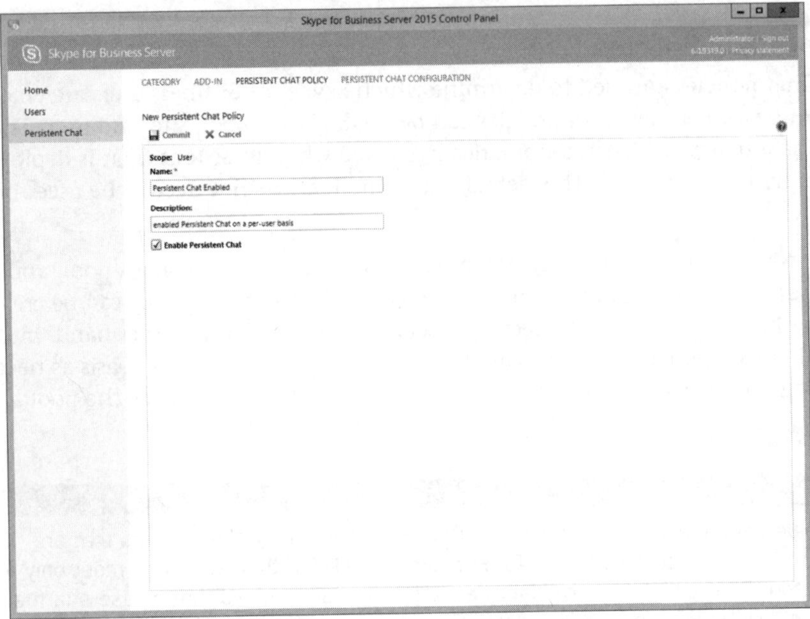

FIGURE 8.7 Creating a Persistent Chat user policy.

5. Click Commit to save the policy.
6. In the left pane, select Users.
7. Type a portion of the target user's name in the search field at the top of the screen, and then click Find to list all users that meet the search criteria.
8. Select the target user account in the bottom pane; then, from the Edit drop-down menu, click Show Details.
9. Scroll down to the bottom of the user properties and then use the Persistent Chat Policy drop-down menu to select the user policy created previously.
10. Click Commit to save the setting.

Persistent Chat Server Options

Skype for Business Server 2015 provides the capability to create a set of server options that can be applied globally to all Persistent Chat pools; alternatively, these same server options can be applied to a specific site or pool. There is only one global configuration, which is automatically created when Persistent Chat is deployed, and it is simply named Global. This default Global configuration contains default settings that can be changed as needed, but the configuration itself cannot be deleted. A configuration that is applied at the pool or site level overrides the same settings that are configured at the global level. Persistent Chat server option settings include the following:

- **Default Chat History**—The number of chat messages that are immediately available for each chat room upon first request (the global default is 30 chat messages).
- **Maximum File Size (KB)**—The maximum size of a file that can be uploaded to or downloaded from a room (the global default is 20MB).
- **Participant Update Limit**—The maximum number of participants in a given room for which Persistent Chat will send roster updates (the global default is 75). Roster updates are used to inform connected clients about who is present in the chat room.
- **Room Management URL**—The URL used for custom chat room management. This is an optional setting that allows the use of a custom room management solution. For example, an organization can develop its own web application used to manage Skype for Business chat rooms. If the URL for the custom web application is specified as the room management URL within the Persistent Chat options, then users will be redirected to the custom room management site when they create or manage a chat room using the Skype for Business client.

Use the following steps for creating and applying server options to a specific Persistent Chat pool:

1. Log on to a system where the Skype for Business administrative tools are installed using an account that is a member of the `CsAdministrator` or `CsPersistentChatAdministrator` security group, and then open the Skype for Business Server Control Panel.
2. In the left pane, select Persistent Chat and then click the Persistent Chat Configuration tab at the top.
3. From the New drop-down menu, select Pool Configuration.
4. In the Select a Service dialog box, select the Persistent Chat service from the list and click OK.

5. The New Persistent Chat Configuration screen now appears. The name for the configuration is automatically chosen based on the name of the Persistent Chat pool, as shown in Figure 8.8.

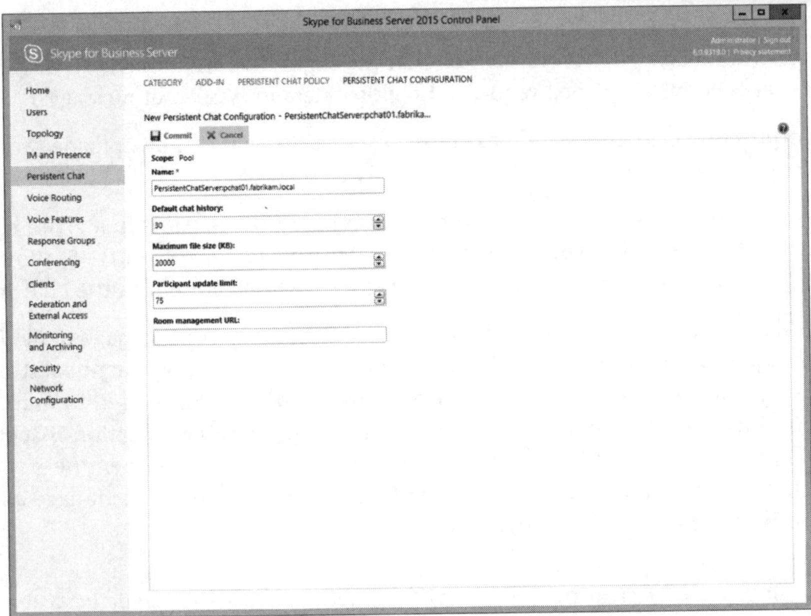

FIGURE 8.8 Creating a new Persistent Chat configuration.

6. The Default Chat History, Maximum File Size, and Participant Update Limit fields are automatically populated with the same default values used in the Global policy. Enter new values for these fields to meet the Persistent Chat requirements of the pool.

7. If a custom room management site will be used, enter the URL for the site in the Room Management URL field.

8. When finished, click Commit to save the configuration.

Chat Room Categories

Chat room categories are used to develop a logical structure for the organization of chat rooms, and they also serve as a mechanism for controlling which users and groups are permitted to create or join the chat rooms within those categories. Each category also contains properties that determine the options available for the chat rooms within that category.

Each chat room has only one parent category. For each category created, Persistent Chat administrators can allow or deny membership to rooms that belong to that category, and they can also assign users to be creators for the category. A user who is assigned as a creator for a category has permissions to create chat rooms, assign members, and assign managers for the chat rooms within that category. Assigning creator rights at the category level is therefore an effective means for Persistent Chat administrators to delegate chat room management to responsible users—typically department heads or power users. Users who have creator rights can then in turn assign other users to be managers of individual chat rooms. Chat room managers can configure many aspects of their assigned chat rooms, including chat room membership.

Categories that are well designed result in an effective chat room structure that meets the needs of the users and at the same time simplifies delegated administration of the Persistent Chat environment. Figure 8.9 shows an example of a category and chat room structure that might be used to model an organization's departmental structure.

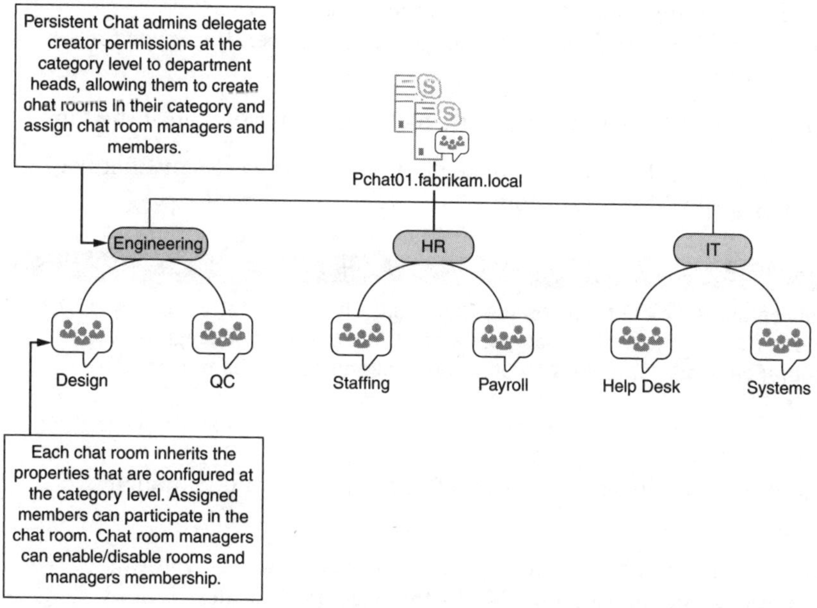

FIGURE 8.9 Example of a Persistent Chat category and chat room structure.

Following are the options available for configuration with each category:

- **Enable Invitations**—Controls whether chat rooms within the category will support invitations, which are used to notify users when they have been added as chat room members.
- **Enable File Upload**—Determines whether file uploads are permitted for chat rooms within the category.
- **Enable Chat History**—Determines whether chat history will be maintained for chat rooms within the category. Disabling chat history at the category level effectively makes chat nonpersistent for all chat rooms in that category.
- **Allowed Membership**—Determines which users are allowed to be members of chat rooms in the category.

TIP

Adding Active Directory objects to the allowed membership at the category level does not automatically cause the affected users to become members of any chat room. It simply allows those users to be added as members to the chat rooms in that category, which is configured at the chat room level. Users who are denied at the category level cannot be members of any chat room in that category.

The following steps would be used to create one of the Persistent Chat categories shown earlier in Figure 8.9:

1. Log on to a system where the Skype for Business administrative tools are installed using an account that is a member of the `CsAdministrator` or `CsPersistentChatAdministrator` security group, and then open the Skype for Business Server Control Panel.
2. In the left pane, select Persistent Chat and then click the Category tab at the top.
3. Click New; then, at the Select a Service dialog box, select the Persistent Chat pool that will be associated with this category. Click OK.

NOTE

The Select a Service dialog box determines the Persistent Chat pool that will be used by Skype for Business clients to identify which pool a particular category belongs to. After it has been created, a category can belong to only one pool and cannot be moved to a different pool.

4. At the New Category screen, enter the name for the category and, optionally, enter a description.
5. Select the chat room options that will be enabled for the chat rooms in this category: invitations, file upload, and chat history (see previous description).
6. In the Allowed Members section, click Add.
7. The Select Allowed Members dialog box now appears, which allows the option to search for four types of Active Directory objects that can be added as allowed members: organizational units, distribution groups, domains, and individual user accounts. Enter the name of an AD object to search and click Find.
8. After the object appears in the list, select the object and click OK.

9. The New Category screen now shows the AD object as an allowed member for the category, as shown in Figure 8.10. Repeat steps 6 through 8 as needed to add additional allowed members.

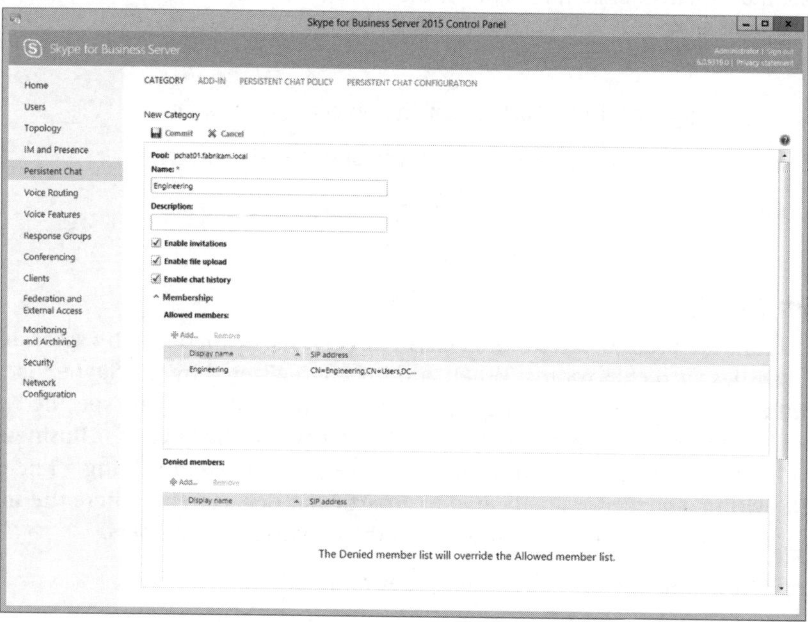

FIGURE 8.10 New Persistent Chat category.

10. Scroll down farther in the New Category screen to bring the Denied Members and Creators sections into view.
11. In the Denied Members section, click Add.
12. The Select Denied Members dialog box now appears, which allows the option to search for Active Directory objects that can be added as denied members. Enter the name of an organizational unit, a distribution group, a domain, or an individual user account and then click Find.
13. After the object appears in the list, select the object and click OK.
14. Repeat steps 11 through 13, as needed, to add additional denied members.
15. In the Creators section, click Add.
16. The Select Creators dialog box now appears, which allows the option to search for Active Directory objects that can be added as creators. Enter the name of an organizational unit, a distribution group, a domain, or individual user account and then click Find.

NOTE

Each user who is added as a creator must first be added to the allowed member list for the category, either explicitly or via membership in an organizational unit or a distribution group. Also, a user must not be a member of the denied member list for the category to be added as a creator.

17. After the object appears in the list, select the object and click OK.
18. Repeat steps 15 through 17, as needed, to add additional creators.
19. When finished, click Commit to save the new category.

Chat Room Add-Ins

Chat room add-ins are used to extend the Persistent Chat user experience by associating customized websites with chat rooms. When add-ins are registered by the Skype for Business administrator and associated with chat rooms, the content of the specified websites is embedded in the conversation extensibility pane of the Skype for Business client. A good example of how an add-in might be used would be embedding a Microsoft OneNote URL within a chat room dedicated to a particular department, where the site provides information that would be of interest to the department members.

The following steps would be used to create a chat room add-in:

1. Log on to a system where the Skype for Business administrative tools are installed using an account that is a member of the `CsAdministrator` or `CsPersistentChatAdministrator` security group, and then open the Skype for Business Server Control Panel.
2. In the left pane, select Persistent Chat and then click the Add-in tab at the top.
3. Click New; then, at the Select a Service dialog box, select the Persistent Chat pool that will be associated with this add-in. Click OK.
4. At the New Add-in screen, enter a name for the add-in, enter the URL that will be associated with the add-in, and then click Commit to save the configuration.

After an add-in has been registered, it is associated with a chat room using the Skype for Business Server Management Shell. The following procedure would be used to associate an add-in named Engineering Design Add-in with the Engineering chat room shown earlier in Figure 8.9:

1. Log on to a system where the Skype for Business administrative tools are installed using an account that is a member of the `CsAdministrator` or `CsPersistentChatAdministrator` group and the `RTC Local Administrators` group on the Persistent Chat Server, and that has administrative rights on the local system.

2. Open the Skype for Business Server Management Shell and execute the following cmdlet:

```
Set-CsPersistentChatRoom -Identity pchat01.fabrikam.local
➥-Add-in Engineering Design Add-in
```

Chat Rooms

After categories have been created, chat rooms can be created within those categories, and they will inherit the options that have been configured at the category level. Chat rooms can be created either by a Persistent Chat administrator or by another user who has been assigned as a creator for one or more categories. Unlike the other Persistent Chat configuration tasks described previously, the creation and configuration of chat rooms is not performed using the Skype for Business Server Control Panel. There are two ways to create a chat room: using the Skype for Business Server Management Shell and using the Skype for Business client. Both methods are described next.

Creating a Chat Room Using the Skype for Business Server Management Shell

The first method that can be used to create a chat room is using the Skype for Business Server Management Shell, which would typically be used by Skype for Business administrators or other IT personnel who have been delegated administrative permissions to the Persistent Chat deployment. To execute Persistent Chat PowerShell cmdlets remotely, a user must be a member of the `RTCUniversalServerAdmins` group, must be explicitly listed as a member of the RTC Local Administrators group on the Persistent Chat Server, and must also have local administrative rights on the system where the Management Shell is used.

Following is the procedure for using the Skype for Business Server Management Shell to create one of the chat rooms shown earlier in Figure 8.9:

1. Log on to a system where the Skype for Business administrative tools are installed using an account that is a member of the `RTCUniversalServerAdmins` group in AD, a member of the RTC Local Administrators group on the Persistent Chat Server, and has administrative rights on the local system.

2. Open the Skype for Business Server Management Shell and execute the following cmdlet to create a chat room named Design within the Engineering category:

```
New-CsPersistentChatRoom -Name Design -PersistentChatPoolFqdn
➥pchat01.fabrikam.local -Category pchat01.fabrikam.local\Engineering.
```

3. If the command is successful, the chat room is created and the properties of the new chat room are displayed, as shown in Figure 8.11.

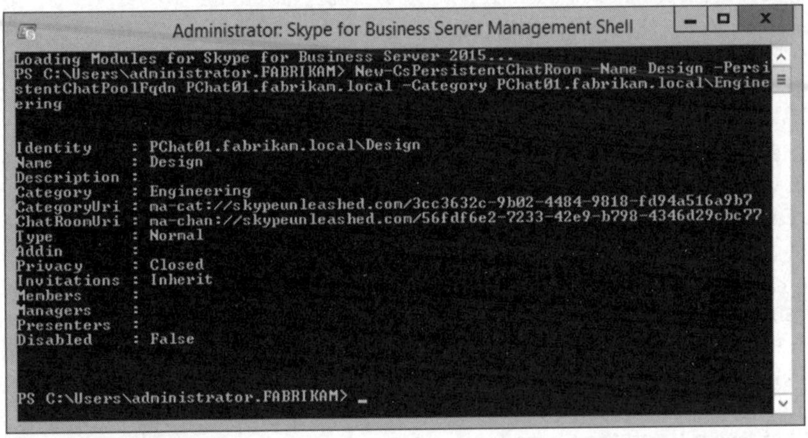

```
Administrator: Skype for Business Server Management Shell
Loading Modules for Skype for Business Server 2015...
PS C:\Users\administrator.FABRIKAM> New-CsPersistentChatRoom -Name Design -Persi
stentChatPoolFqdn PChat01.fabrikam.local -Category PChat01.fabrikam.local\Engine
ering


Identity     : PChat01.fabrikam.local\Design
Name         : Design
Description  :
Category     : Engineering
CategoryUri  : ma-cat://skypeunleashed.com/3cc3632c-9b02-4484-9818-fd94a516a9b7
ChatRoomUri  : ma-chan://skypeunleashed.com/56fdf6e2-7233-42e9-b798-4346d29cbc77
Type         : Normal
Addin        :
Privacy      : Closed
Invitations  : Inherit
Members      :
Managers     :
Presenters   :
Disabled     : False


PS C:\Users\administrator.FABRIKAM> _
```

FIGURE 8.11 Creating a chat room using the Management Shell.

NOTE

Note from Figure 8.11 that when the room is initially created, there is no membership. Additional commands can then be used to configure various properties of the room, including room type, membership, managers, and more. For details on the configuration of chat rooms, see the "Persistent Chat Administration" section, later in this chapter.

Creating a Chat Room Using the Skype for Business Client

The second method that can be used to create a chat room is using the Skype for Business client, which would typically be used by a user who has been assigned creator permissions to one or more categories. To create a chat room using the Skype for Business client, a user must first be enabled for Persistent Chat via a Persistent Chat policy, in addition to being assigned as a creator.

Following is the procedure for using the Skype for Business client to create one of the chat rooms shown earlier in Figure 8.9:

1. Log on to the Skype for Business client using an account that has been enabled for Persistent Chat and has been assigned as a creator in a Persistent Chat category.

2. If the user has been enabled for Persistent Chat, the Chat Rooms icon automatically appears as the second icon from the left, as shown in Figure 8.12. Click the Chat Rooms icon to display the Chat Rooms section of the Skype for Business client.

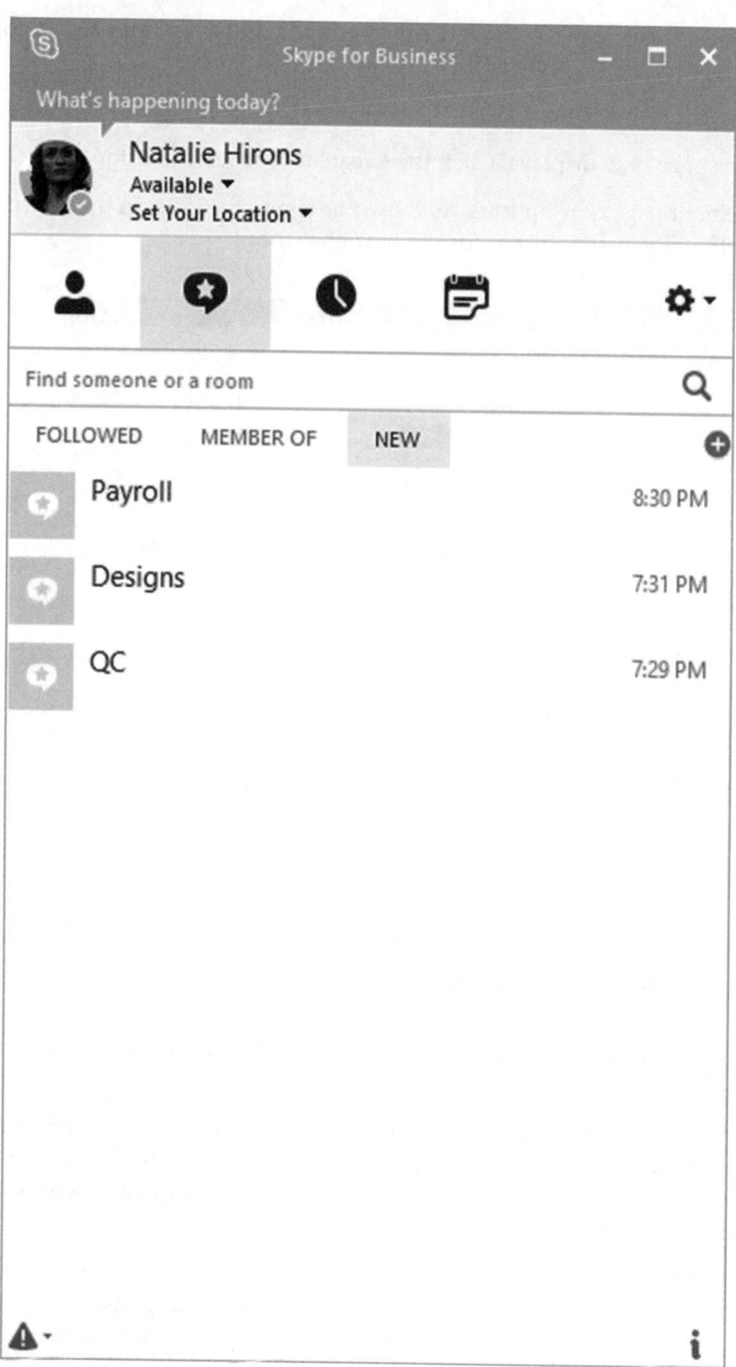

FIGURE 8.12 Chat Rooms section of the Skype for Business client.

3. On the right side of the window, click the plus symbol, and then from the list of options that appears, click Create a Chat Room.
4. At the prompt, enter the credentials of the user with creator rights.
5. The My Rooms page now displays. Click the Create a New Room option.
6. The Create a Room page now appears, as shown in Figure 8.13. Begin by entering a name and, optionally, a description for the new chat room.

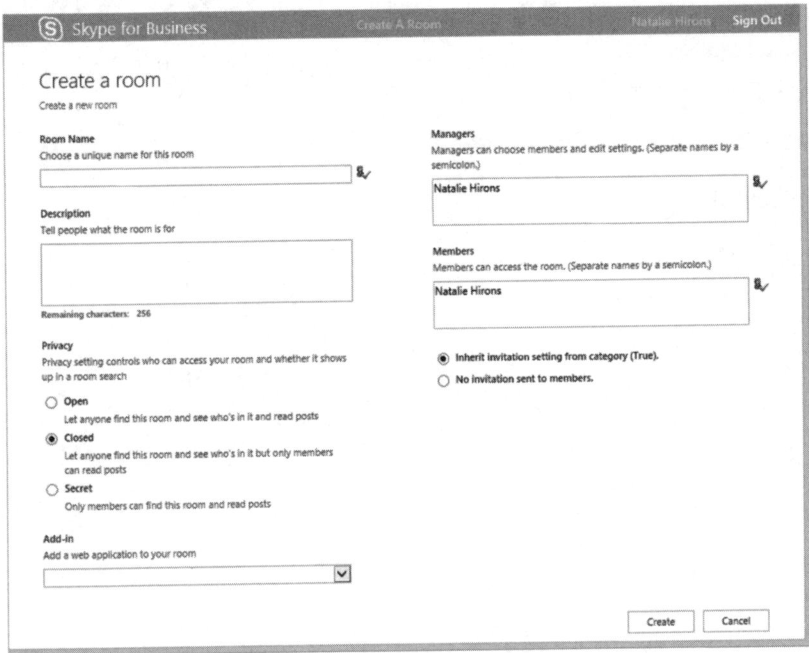

FIGURE 8.13 Creating a chat room using the Skype for Business client.

7. Additional properties that can be configured when the chat room is created include the following:
   - **Privacy**—Select Open, Closed, or Secret. Open rooms can be searched and accessed by anyone. Closed rooms can be searched by anyone, but can be accessed only by members. Secret rooms can be searched and accessed only by members of the room.
   - **Add-in**—Use the drop-down menu to associate an add-in with the chat room, which allows URL content to be viewed by members while participating. Add-ins must be previously approved by a Persistent Chat administrator in order to appear in this list.

- **Managers**—The creator of the chat room is listed by default as the initial chat room manager; however, this can be changed as needed. If a different user will be assigned as the manager, or if additional chat room managers will be assigned, enter one or more names within the Managers box, with multiple names separated by a semicolon. The check mark icon at the right of the Managers box can be used to verify the accuracy of the manager names entered.
- **Members**—If the chat room privacy setting is configured as Closed or Secret, individual names can be entered within the Members box, with multiple names separated by a semicolon. The check mark icon at the right of the Members box can be used to verify the accuracy of the member names entered.
- **Invitations**—If the chat room privacy setting is configured as Closed or Secret, the invitations setting can be configured to either inherit the invitation setting from the parent category or disable invitations for the chat room. Invitations are used to notify users when they have been added as chat room members.

8. When finished, click Create to create the new chat room.

Compliance Configuration

Persistent Chat compliance allows Skype for Business administrators to maintain an archive of Persistent Chat messages as well as activities. For example, the activities that can be recorded and archived through compliance include new messages, new events such as a user entering a chat room, and searches that are performed against chat history. The compliance information can then be retrieved from the Compliance SQL database as needed.

After the Persistent Chat compliance feature has been enabled using the Topology Builder, it can then be configured using the Skype for Business Server Management Shell. The cmdlet used to configure Persistent Chat compliance is `Set-CsPersistentChatCompliance-Configuration`. The parameters that can be set using this command include the following:

- **`AdapterType`**—An adapter is a third-party product that converts the data in the compliance database to a specific format. Adapter types include Akonix, Assentor, Facetime, and XML (the default).
- **`OneChatRoomPerOutputFile`**—This parameter allows separate reports to be created for each chat room.
- **`AddChatRoomDetails`**—When enabled, this records additional details about each chat room in the database. This setting can greatly increase the size of the database, and therefore is disabled by default.
- **`AddUserDetails`**—When enabled, this records additional details about each chat room user in the database. This setting can greatly increase the size of the database, and therefore is disabled by default.

8

- **RunInterval**—This parameter dictates the amount of time before the server outputs the next compliance output file (the default is 15 minutes).
- **Identity**—This setting allows compliance settings to be scoped for a particular collection, including the global, site, and service levels. If no identity is specified, the settings will apply to the global collection.

Additional parameters are also available, and you can view them by executing the following command in the Management Shell:

```
Get-Help Set-CsPersistentChatComplianceConfiguration -Detailed
```

The following example sets the compliance properties for the global collection, specifying that separate reports be created for each chat room, and reducing the run interval to 10 minutes:

```
Set-CsPersistentChatComplianceConfiguration -OneChatRoomPerOutputFile $true
➥-RunInterval 00:10:00
```

Persistent Chat Administration

Administration of the Persistent Chat environment is largely focused on managing the individual chat rooms. From the Skype for Business administrator's perspective, chat room management is performed using the Skype for Business Server Management Shell. However, management of chat rooms can also be delegated to responsible users (for example, department heads or other personnel). Chat room management by end users is typically handled simply by use of the Skype for Business client. This section provides details on some of the more common administrative tasks that are required to maintain the Persistent Chat environment.

Chat Room Management by Administrators

The basic procedure for creating a chat room using the Skype for Business Server Management Shell was covered earlier in the "Configuring Persistent Chat" section. Although it is possible to configure some chat room parameters when the room is created using the `New-CsPersistentChatRoom` cmdlet, these same parameters and more can be configured after the chat room is created using the `Set-CsPersistentChatRoom` cmdlet. Parameters that can be configured using this cmdlet include the following:

- **Disabled**—Allows the status of the chat room to be disabled or enabled using the value `$true` or `$false`.
- **Type**—Allows a chat room to be specified as either a normal chat room, which accepts messages posted by any member, or an auditorium chat room, which allows only the presenter to post messages that other members can only read.

- **Addin**—Associates a previously configured add-in with a chat room, which allows URL content to be viewed by members while participating.
- **Privacy**—Allows a chat room to be configured as Open, Secret, or Closed. Open rooms can be searched and accessed by anyone. Secret rooms can be searched and accessed only by members of the room. Closed rooms can be searched by anyone, but can be accessed only by members. By default, each new room is initially configured as Closed.
- **Invitations**—Allows enabling or disabling of chat room invitations, which are used to notify users when they have been added as chat room members. The default setting for invitations is inherit, which causes the chat room to adopt the invitation setting configured on the category it belongs to. Configuring the invitations setting to `false` at the chat room level allows the category setting to be overridden.
- **Members**—Configures membership for the chat room. You can add or remove either individual or multiple members using a single cmdlet by specifying the SIP address of the users. To allow users to be added in bulk, Active Directory organizational units or distribution groups can also be specified.
- **Managers**—Allows managers to be assigned to the chat room. Managers have the permissions to define membership of a chat room along with other settings.
- **Presenters**—Allows presenters to be assigned to an auditorium chat room.

Using one of the sample chat rooms shown earlier in Figure 8.9, the following command would be used to temporarily disable the chat room:

```
Set-CsPersistentChatRoom -Identity pchat01.fabrikam.local\Staffing
➥-Disabled $true
```

The following command would be used to change the privacy setting to Secret, assign members using a distribution group, and assign an individual as a manager:

```
Set-CsPersistentChatRoom -Identity pchat01.fabrikam.local\Staffing
➥-Privacy secret -members @{Add="CN=HR Staff,OU=Groups,DC=fabrikam,DC=local"}
➥-Managers @{Add="sip:HRlead@skypeunleashed.com"}
```

Note that only members under the scope of the Persistent Chat category allowed members can be specified.

If the command is successful, the updated parameters for the chat room are listed, as shown in Figure 8.14.

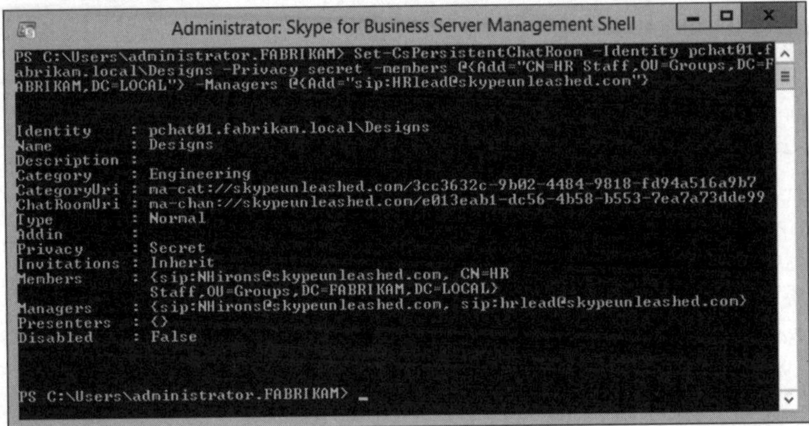

FIGURE 8.14 Adjusting chat room parameters using the command line.

You can view the complete syntax of the `Set-CsPersistentChatRoom` cmdlet along with helpful examples by executing the following command using the Management Shell: `Get-Help Set-CsPersistentChatRoom -Detailed`. It is also simple to view the parameters for an existing chat room by executing the `Get-CsPersistentChatRoom` cmdlet, specifying the identity of the room.

After a user has been assigned as a member of a chat room, the room automatically appears in the Skype for Business client, as shown earlier in Figure 8.12. From here, participation in a room is simply a matter of double-clicking one of the listed rooms to view existing chat messages and adding new messages.

NOTE

The message history initially presented to the user when viewing a chat room is based on the Default Chat History setting configured by the administrator, as described earlier in the "Persistent Chat Server Options" section. However, this does not prevent a user from searching the chat room for additional messages that are maintained within the chat history for the room.

After chat rooms become available within the Skype for Business client, the user can configure topic feeds, notifications, and more. For details on the client-side aspects of Persistent Chat, see Chapter 26, "Windows and Browser Clients."

From time to time, it might be necessary for a Skype for Business administrator to clear messages from a room, which can be accomplished with the `Clear-CsPersistentChatRoom` cmdlet. The clearing of messages from a room always starts with the oldest messages, but it is possible to specify an end date to provide a range of messages to be cleared. For example, the following command would be used to clear all of the messages from a chat room that are older than a specific end date:

```
Clear-CsPersistentChatRoom -Identity pchat01.fabrikam.local\Designs
➥-EndDate "9/28/2015"
```

On occasion it might also be necessary for an administrator to remove individual messages from a chat room, perhaps because they are deemed inappropriate. This can be accomplished via the `Remove-CsPersistentChatMessage` cmdlet. To assist in finding messages to be removed, multiple keywords can be specified in the cmdlet as search criteria. For example, the following command would be used to search the Payroll chat room and remove any messages that contain both of the words "executive" and "salaries":

```
Remove-CsPersistentChatMessage -Identity pchat01.fabrikam.local\Payroll
➥-Filter "executive salaries" -MatchClause And
```

If one or more matches are found, the removed messages are replaced with a notification that the message has been removed by a Persistent Chat administrator, as shown in Figure 8.15.

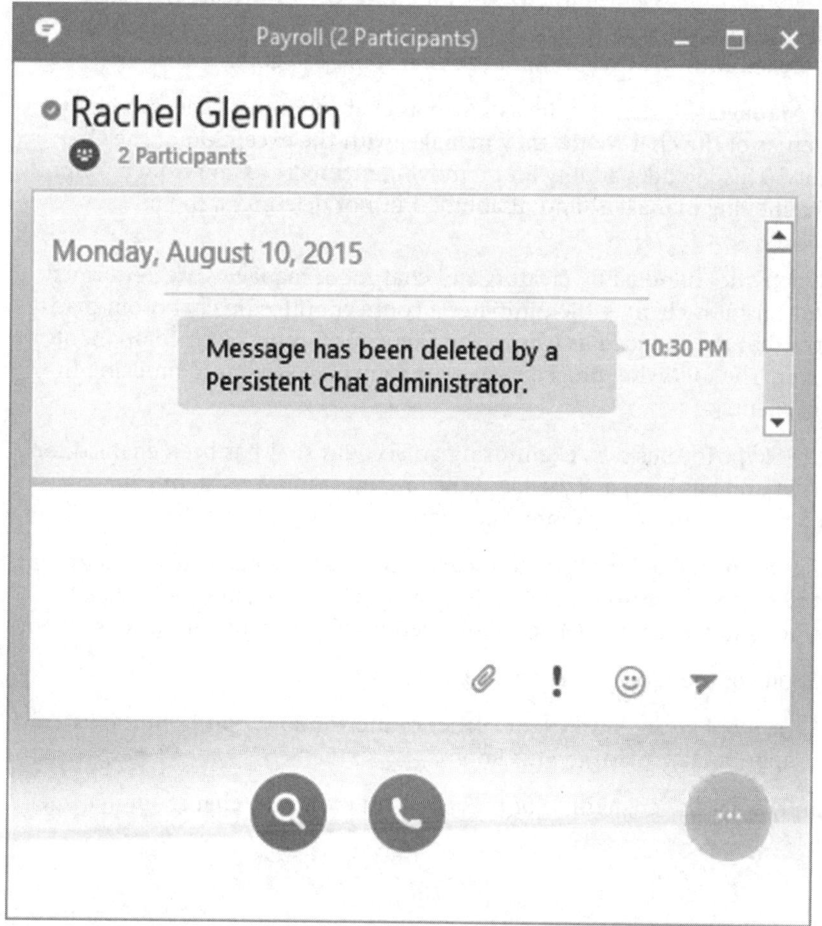

FIGURE 8.15 Chat message removed by an administrator.

TIP

Unless otherwise specified, removed messages are replaced with the default text shown in Figure 8.15. However, it is also possible to specify different replacement text using the `-ReplaceMessage` parameter. Additional parameters are also available, including date ranges for the search. You can find further details by executing the following command in the Management Shell: `Get-Help Remove-CsPersistentChatMessage -Detailed`.

Chat Room Management by End Users

As noted previously, chat room management can be handled not only by Skype for Business administrators, but also by end users who are delegated low-level administrative permissions to the chat room configuration. This level of administration can be performed simply by using the Skype for Business client. End users can be delegated permissions to manage various aspects of the chat room configuration by being assigned the following roles:

- **Creator**—Users who are assigned as creators for a category can create new chat rooms within that category, and they can change all the properties of the chat rooms they create, with the exception of the chat room category.
- **Chat Room Manager**—Users who are assigned as chat room managers can change all the properties of the chat rooms they manage, with the exception of the chat room category. This includes adding and removing members to and from a room, adding and removing managers, and disabling (but not deleting) a room.

The management activities handled by creators and chat room managers are performed using the Skype for Business client, which initiates a connection to the chat room management web pages that are included as part of the Skype for Business web components on the Front End Server. The following procedure is used to manage a chat room using the Skype for Business client:

1. Log on to the Skype for Business client using an account that has been enabled for Persistent Chat and has been assigned as either a creator in a Persistent Chat category or a manager of one or more chat rooms.
2. If the user has been enabled for Persistent Chat, the Chat Rooms icon automatically appears as the second icon from the left, as shown earlier in Figure 8.12. Click the Chat Rooms icon to display the Chat Rooms section of the Skype for Business client.
3. Double-click one of the rooms from the list to open it.
4. Click the (...) symbol at the lower-right corner of the window, and from the list of options that appear, click Manage This Room.
5. At the prompt, enter the credentials of the user with creator or chat room manager rights.

6. The Edit a Room page now appears, as shown in Figure 8.16. Adjust the properties of the room as needed (see a description for each property in the "Creating a Chat Room Using the Skype for Business Client" section, earlier in this chapter).

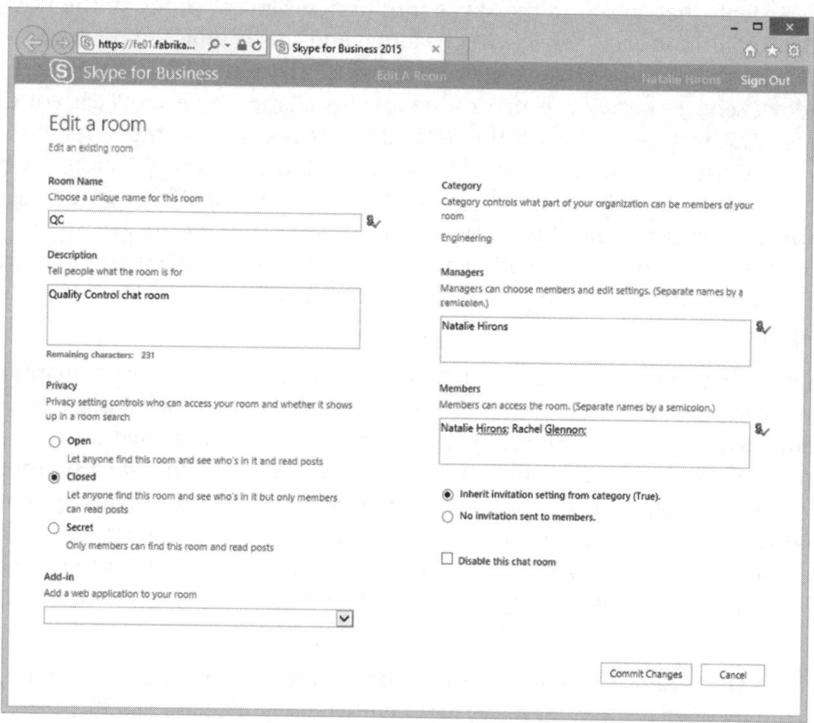

FIGURE 8.16 Editing a chat room using the Skype for Business client.

7. When finished, click Finish to save the changes to the chat room.

Skype Online and Hybrid Environments

Organizations that utilize Lync Online/Office 365 will find that Persistent Chat is not available with any licensing plans, including E1-E5. There has not been any publicized plans for bringing Persistent Chat to the service. The speculation is that, in addition to the infrastructure that would be required to bring Persistent Chat to the service, Microsoft is also leveraging its Yammer web-based collaboration solution to fulfill some of the features. Although feature parity does not exist between Persistent Chat and Yammer, mobile users can use Yammer but not Persistent Chat.

For organizations that are in a hybrid configuration, Persistent Chat servers will need to be on-premises. Users who are on-premises can be enabled for Persistent Chat, but cloud-based users cannot.

Persistent Chat Troubleshooting

Troubleshooting for Persistent Chat starts with the basics, which consist of the Event Viewer and the Services console on the Persistent Chat Server. Error messages that are logged for Persistent Chat appear in the Skype for Business Server portion of the Event Log under the Applications and Services log heading, and this is typically the first place to look when you are experiencing problems with Persistent Chat. There are also several Windows services installed as part of the role installation on each Persistent Chat Server. Two of these services are specifically related to Persistent Chat: the Skype for Business Server Persistent Chat service and the Skype for Business Server Persistent Chat Compliance service. Both of these services are set to start up automatically when the system is turned on, and they need to remain started continually for the Persistent Chat service to function. Additional information about the Persistent Chat environment can also be quickly retrieved by executing the following command using the Skype for Business Server Management Shell: `Get-CsService -PersistentChat`.

If the Persistent Chat services are started and the Event Log does not provide helpful clues as to the cause of an issue, an additional useful tool for troubleshooting a Persistent Chat problem is synthetic transactions. Synthetic transactions can be used to test sending and receiving messages in a chat room between two users. You can initiate a synthetic transaction using the Skype for Business Server Management Shell by executing the `Test-CsPersistentChatMessage` cmdlet. Sender and receiver credentials are supplied as parameters, and you obtain these by first using the `Get-Credential` cmdlet to store the credentials in variables that are referenced within the `Test-CsPersistentChatMessage` cmdlet.

The following example shows the commands used to execute a synthetic transaction, testing the sending of chat room messages between two users who are members of the chat room named Design. The `Test-CsPersistentChatMessage` cmdlet requires the `ChatRoomUri` value for the desired chat room. This can be achieved by using the `Get-CsPersistentChatRoom` cmdlet, like so:

```
Get-CsPersistentChatRoom -Identity "Design"
```

Note the `ChatRoomUri` value (which in this instance is `ma-chan://skypeunleashed.com/56fdf6e2-7233-42e9-b798-4346d29cbc77`):

```
$cred1 = Get-Credential "fabrikam\nhirons"
$cred2 = Get-Credential "fabrikam\rglennon"
Test-CsPersistentChatMessage -TargetFqdn fe01.fabrikam.local
➥-ChatRoomUri "ma-chan://skypeunleashed.com/56fdf6e2-7233-42e9-b798-4346d29cbc77"
➥-SenderSipAddress "sip:nhirons@skypeunleashed.com"
➥-SenderCredential $cred1 -ReceiverSipAddress "sip:rglennon@skypeunleashed.com"
➥-ReceiverCredential $cred2.
```

The first and second commands cause interactive prompts for the password of the sender and receiver users, respectively. After these credentials are entered, they are stored in the variables that are referenced in the third command. The end result is then displayed as either Success or Failure, as shown in Figure 8.17. If the transaction fails, an error message is displayed to assist in further diagnosing the cause of the issue.

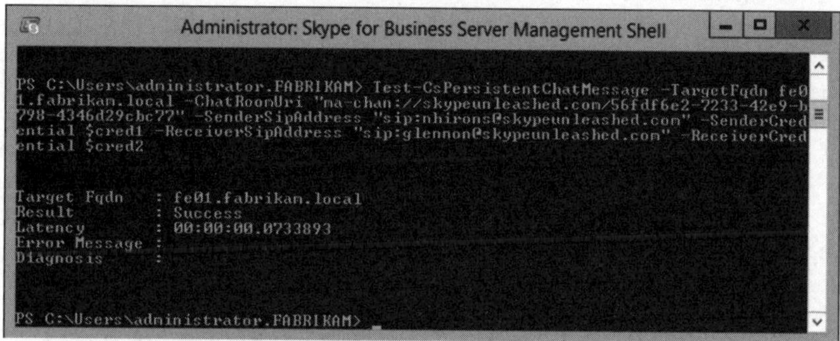

FIGURE 8.17 Persistent Chat synthetic transaction used for troubleshooting.

Best Practices

Following are some best practices from this chapter:

- If there is any question as to whether multiple Persistent Chat servers will be needed, install the first server as a standalone instance. If the first Persistent Chat server is collocated with a Standard Edition Front End, no additional servers can be added to the pool.
- If ethical walls are required to prevent conflict of interest in the organization, configure Persistent Chat categories to meet these requirements, where the allowed members for each category are limited to specific groups of users.
- In smaller businesses or when no ethical walls are required, a single category can be used for all chat rooms. The allowed members of the category would include all users, and then membership lists can be used to grant or restrict access to the chat rooms.
- If a central support team such as the help desk will be used to create new rooms, assign the members of this team as creators on each category using a distribution group or an organizational unit containing all the members. This will make it easy to maintain the appropriate permissions when members of the team change.
- The category names are not visible to the end users; only the chat room names are. With that in mind, choose category names that are meaningful to the administrators, whereas the chat room names need to be meaningful to the users. A description can also be assigned to each chat room for further clarity if needed.

- Assign appropriate add-ins to chat rooms to enhance the overall Persistent Chat experience for end users. If the organization maintains websites that provide useful business data to specific teams, these can be assigned as approved add-ins by the administrator, which will allow chat room creators and managers to associate these with chat rooms under their control.

- If there is a requirement for an "announcement style" chat room that is read-only for the majority of users, create a chat room with auditorium as the type. Assign one or more users as presenters for the room so that these users can post announcements and other information to be read by the members.

Summary

With Persistent Chat being included in the Skype for Business topology, as was Lync Server 2013, this technology will likely get much more exposure with Skype for Business than ever before. No doubt many organizations will find that having the combination of ongoing, persistent communication alongside IM and Presence will provide valuable benefits to the various teams of users that share knowledge on specific topics. With the added architectural changes that Microsoft has introduced with this version, Skype for Business administrators will also find Persistent Chat to be relatively easy to deploy and manage, and Skype for Business users will appreciate the capability to use a single client to access all features of Skype for Business, including Persistent Chat.

CHAPTER 9

Network Requirements and Best Practices

IN THIS CHAPTER

- ▶ Managed and Unmanaged Networks
- ▶ Network Discovery
- ▶ Edge and Interactive Connectivity Establishment
- ▶ Bandwidth Estimation
- ▶ Wireless Considerations
- ▶ Call Admission Control
- ▶ Quality of Service
- ▶ Software Defined Networking

It can take months to deploy a Skype for Business infrastructure. You can have the newest servers, latest OS, most recent patches, and have everybody trained. All that work can be destroyed by one single incident of a poor phone call. All of this because the network cannot handle the additional overhead that is now being placed on it. If you already have some kind of IP-based telephony system, you may have a good idea of what to expect. But can your wide area network or metropolitan area network handle it? Perhaps your wireless network needs to be investigated. Knowing how your network has been performing, what to expect, and how to plan for these changes can make the difference between a successful and an unsuccessful deployment.

Managed and Unmanaged Networks

There are two types of networks in any company: the one you manage and the one you do not. A managed network is anything within your building walls: your wired and wireless networks, their ports, and their cables. Then there is the unmanaged network. This is the home network, or a Wi-Fi hot spot at a coffee shop, and even in some cases your WAN network, especially if you are using a site-to-site VPN over the Internet. For the purposes in this chapter, a managed network will be anything considered owned and supplied within your corporate offices and datacenter, and an unmanaged network is either a home or public hot spot. The difference between these two is critical when troubleshooting poor call quality. If a user is on a call from a public hot spot and then later calls in stating the call quality was poor, you can use the call detail reporting to assess the user's location and determine whether they were calling from an unmanaged network.

Within the managed network there are typically two types of connections: wired and wireless. A wired connection is pretty straightforward. However, a wireless-based connection has additional complexities that need to be taken into account that will be discussed in this chapter.

From an unmanaged network there are three methods of connection: carrier, wireless, wired. How these connect back to your company are also discussed in this chapter. A cellular carrier is a wireless provider for your mobile device, and they could be utilizing Edge, G4, and other protocols to make an IP connection. Wireless and wired networks may seem like the same technology that you would use in your office, but they will use consumer-grade equipment in most cases. Most companies utilize 802.11 AC for wireless, while most homes may still be using 802.11 N. The Internet connection from a home office is also not to the same performance standard as an enterprise will have. In many homes you have multiple devices all sharing the same router, which manages both wired and wireless traffic. It is very easy to consume the entire home network, taking into account streaming movies, online games, a Skype for Business meeting, and other resources.

The bandwidth to any location is either symmetric or asymmetric. A symmetric link is where the inbound and outbound traffic have equal bandwidth; this is typical of an enterprise Internet connection. Most consumer connections are asymmetrical, meaning that the inbound bandwidth is greater than the outbound. This comes into play for home users when the client is determining what codec to use for a conference.

NOTE

When you are making a call from a mobile device with the Skype for Business client, it is important to be in a good location for IP traffic. Just because your cell phone may show a great connection to your provider, this does not mean you will have a good data experience. Along with bandwidth; latency and packet loss can also affect your call quality. Because there is no network quality of service (QoS) over a Skype for Business call, any one of those three metrics can cause a poor call.

IPv6 Support

In Skype for Business Server 2015, both IPv4 and IPv6 are supported. You can also run both, which is known as *dual stack*. If your company is not currently running IPv6 internally, you should disable the IPv6 protocol. There is more to it than just unchecking the box: a registry setting must be made that requires a reboot. To disable IPv6, follow these steps:

1. Within the network connection properties, uncheck the box for Internet Protocol Version 6 (TCP/IPv6).
2. Open Regedit and go to the subkey HKEY_LOCAL_MACHINE\SYSTEM\CurrentControlSet\Services\Tcpip6\Parameters\.

3. Back up that registry subkey.
4. Double-click DisabledComponents.
5. If DisabledComponents does not exist, create a new DWORD (32-bit). It is case sensitive
6. Set the value to 0xff.

To understand more about how IPv6, IPv4, and dual stack work within Skype for Business, read the TechNet article at https://technet.microsoft.com/en-us/library/jj204624.aspx.

Network Discovery

Before starting on any deployment of Skype for Business Server 2015, having a clear understanding of your entire network is critical. Network congestion can cause dropped calls and poor audio in a conference call. It only takes one person with a poor experience to put a black mark on the entire project. This is not just about your wide area or metropolitan area connections, but your local network, too (for example, all of your DHCP ranges and settings, any quality of service already being used, and redundancy).

Historical Data and Metrics

One of the best ways to understand your network is to look over how the network has been performing in the past. Not just from statistics from a network monitoring tool, but also within your ticketing system. When looking through historical data, take into account the following:

- Link speed and type
- Bandwidth monitoring per link
- Number of traffic queues and queue sizes
- Number of users per site
- Internet utilization; spikes and conferencing
- The patch versions of your switches and access points

Those are just the basics of your network. Other services come into play that may not correlate directly to your internal network. Here are some of the aspects that come into play that affect these:

- Number of phone calls between users and between sites.
- Number of conferences and endpoints internally and externally.
- What modalities are used, such as IM, screen sharing (for example, with remote desktop support), and video conferences.
- PSTN calls (if you plan on moving to SIP), if you replace your PBX with Skype for Business Enterprise Voice.

- How backups are done and over which connections.
- Home and remote users. (Do they connect to the office for voice? Do they have a desktop phone?)

In general, three months of statistics can give you a good insight to your network. Three months is used because in that time frame you will usually have at least a quarterly financial close as well as a few large meetings. This will represent not only a good average but also show spikes. If your company has a remote office, but does a great deal of large file transfers once a month, a short amount of statistics will not show that. If at the same time you have executives trying to make an important call while a large file copy is happening, they may experience a poor call.

Topology

Having a clear diagram of your overall topology is vital to the success of the deployment. The plan may call for a Front End Server or SBA in a location; however, that location may not have the network bandwidth, or even the server infrastructure, to support it. This information can give you the vision to what can be deployed with what you have and what may need to be upgraded. You will need to know each region (North America, EMEA, or APAC) and each site in those regions (for example, each office building in San Jose, CA, USA). Even though your initial plans may not include infrastructure at some sites, services such as Call Admission Control will require it. It's not just networking you will want to gather, but also headcount, growth, number and size of meetings, quantity of phone calls, and more. If you have a site with a slow network connection to its central site, and the site makes a lot of phone calls or has several conferences with external customers, you may want to increase the network between the sites or deploy an SBA or Front End Server with Edge services at that site. On the other hand, if they have a lot of internal-only conferences, it may be better to not have services at their location.

WAN Optimizers

WAN optimizers or packet shapers are not supported in Skype for Business. This is because of the real-time communications. All Skype for Business traffic must be configured to avoid any WAN optimizers. If your WAN network does not have the bandwidth to support Skype for Business, you could deploy Call Admission Control (CAC), which is a feature built into Skype for Business. This determines whether to enable audio/video sessions based on available network capacity. CAC is able to reroute call flows by using your PSTN network.

Virtual Private Networks

Most likely you utilize a VPN of some kind. When you're deploying Skype for Business within a VPN, extra steps need to be made on your VPN services during your deployment. Data from a Skype for Business endpoint is already encrypted to the Front End Server. This means that if your VPN does not support split tunneling, the data is being double-encrypted, which can cause poor call quality, latency, jitter, and additional overhead of client and VPN server resources. It is considered a best practice to use split tunneling when using a VPN to prevent all Skype for Business traffic over a VPN, site to site, or at home. When you're using a VPN solution and Skype for Business, a policy should be placed on the VPN client to force all Skype for Business traffic to traverse over the Internet.

NOTE

When a network connection resets or changes, the Skype for Business client will detect this and log off the user and then log back in with the new network information. Many VPN clients make changes to the routing table; this does not force the client to disconnect, even though there is a new path. If this does happen, the user should sign out of the Skype for Business client and log back in.

Firewalls

Skype for Business uses a variety of workloads, from audio and video to Presence and web conferencing. These workloads use a variety of protocols: SIP, SDP, SRTP, SRTPC, Persistent Shared Object Model (PSOM), ICE, and HTTPS. Because of this variety, the firewall needs to be able to handle all of this without any performance impact. The scale of the firewall is based off the utilization of external access.

CAUTION

If you have a web proxy that is between your users' endpoints and the Edge Servers, you will need to create a policy to have all traffic to the internal interface of the Edge Servers bypassed. When a web proxy inspects the packets, in many cases it will either cause a delay for real-time media or edit the packets in a way that the Edge Server cannot use.

Edge: Interactive Connectivity Establishment and External Communications

Interactive Connectivity Establishment (ICE) is what allows for a Skype for Business or Lync client to traverse a firewall. This comes into play for any peer-to-peer communications that are not within your company's network requiring a Network Address Translation (NAT) traversal. ICE consists of two protocols: Session Traversal Utilities for NAT (STUN) and Traversal Using Relays around NAT (TURN). It is the job of the Edge Server to provide the list of candidates to both clients. STUN is used when the media will flow between the two endpoints directly. TURN is used when there is no direct path between the two external endpoints and all media must be relayed through the Edge Server. ICE, STUN, and TURN are industry standards not specific to Skype for Business. This means that there are three possibilities for two clients to communicate. They are in a specific order from highest to lowest preference. A client will always try to connect to another client (or candidate) in this order. Even though the preference is in order, it will try to make a connection to all three and then choose the most efficient route. If none of these methods is available, the connection cannot be completed.

- **Host or local candidate**—The actual IP address that will be used for communications is directly associated to the client (for example, if it is located on the same network internally).
- **Reflexive or STUN candidate**—The public IP address assigned to the client's firewall that performs NAT translation (for example, a home network router).
- **Relay or TURN candidate**—This would be the public IP address of the A/V service on the edge server. This would be when the Edge Server public interface is translated behind a firewall.

Calls Between Internal People

A conversation between two clients internally will be initiated using a direct connection to that endpoint, as illustrated in Figure 9.1.

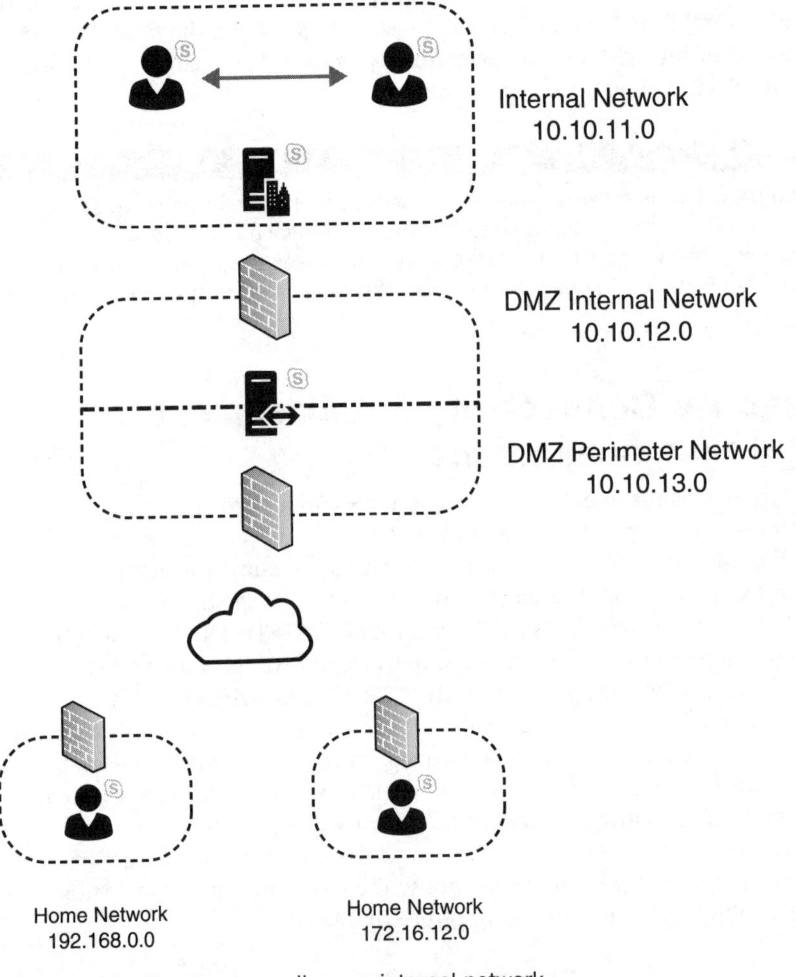

FIGURE 9.1 Peer-to-peer call on an internal network.

Calls Between External People

This scenario involves a peer-to-peer conversation between clients located on separate external networks outside your company. In this case, there is no direct connection between the two clients. The clients would use STUN because it is the most direct connection between them. Figure 9.2 shows an example of how STUN works.

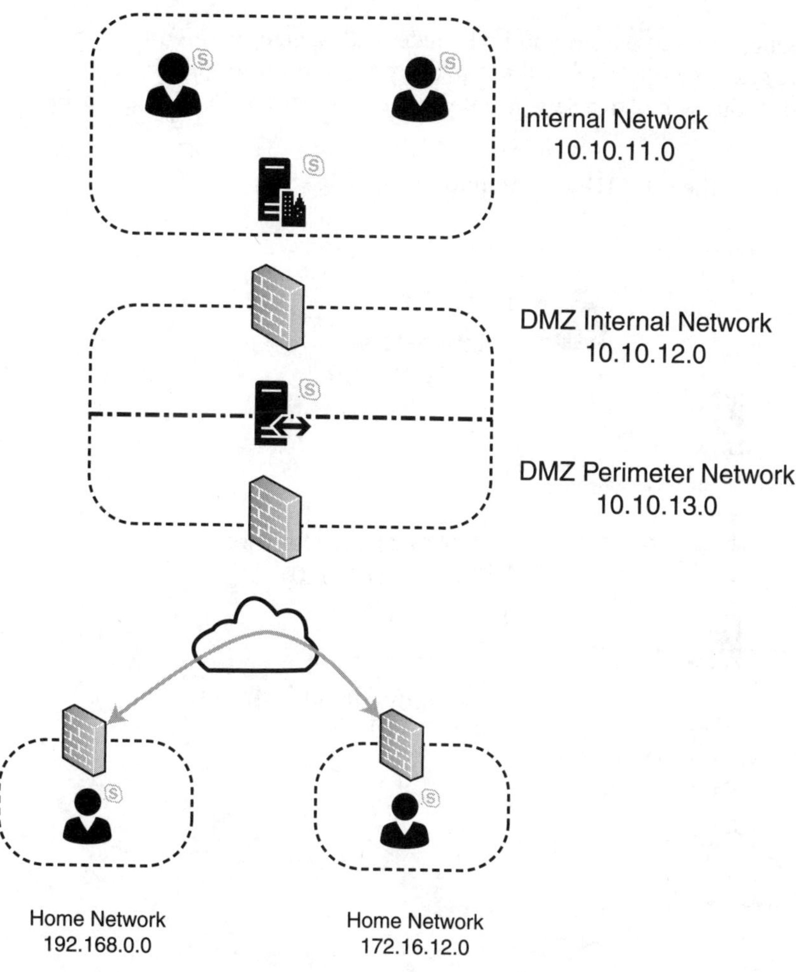

FIGURE 9.2 The use of STUN when the two users are external.

If all your users are located in Office 365, all communication, except for peer-to-peer communication, will travel through the Office 365 Edge services, just like it would on-premises.

Calls Between an External User and Internal User

In many cases a connection is attempted by an internal user from their home office to a client within the corporate network. This would utilize the TURN protocol because the home user client does not have a direct connection to the internal client, and therefore all media must be relayed through the Edge Server, which can access both the internal and external clients.

This would be the same scenario used if you had a federated domain with Office 365, where your users are synced with Azure Active Directory Synchronization. All communications go through the Edge Server, unless you have Express Route or a virtual private network.

In Figure 9.3, notice how the call "TURNS" around on the Edge Server.

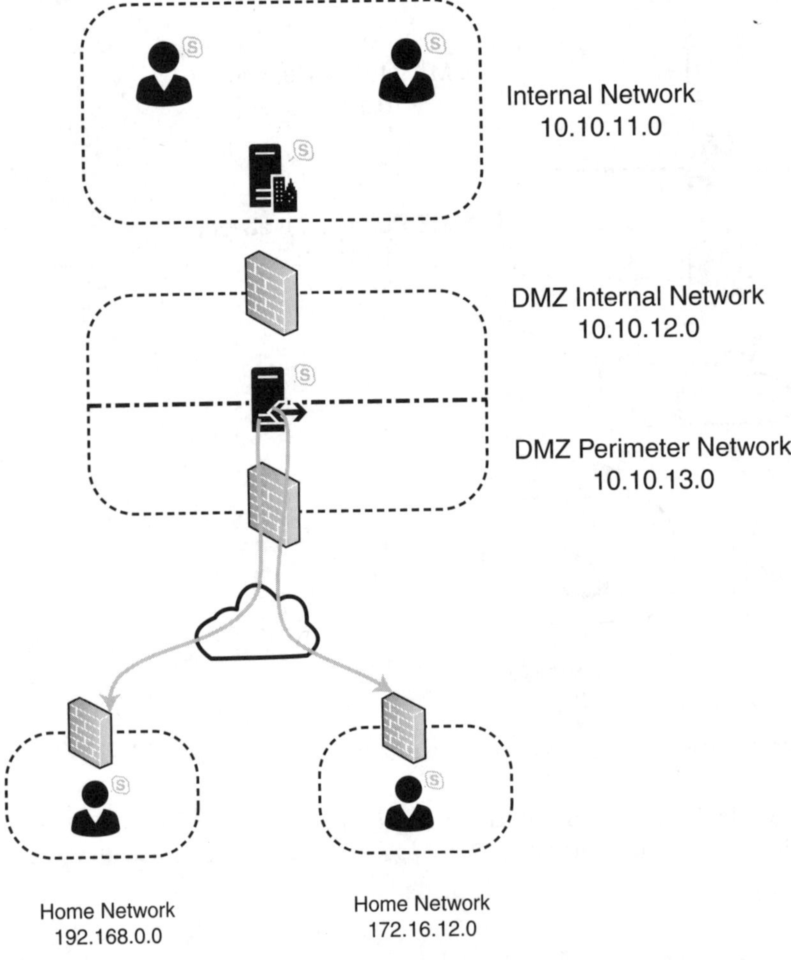

FIGURE 9.3 The use of TURN when there is no direct connection between users.

Conferences

In a conference, the Front End Server hosting the conference becomes the "client," meaning that the external or internal endpoint wants to make a connection to that Front End Server. A conference will utilize the STUN protocol for external users in most cases. An internal user will always connect directly to the Front End Server.

Office 365

Office 365 works no different than on-premises. You will still go through whatever edge the other peer is set for. The catch, however, is if the conference is based out of a user in Office 365, all users attending that meeting will go through the Office 365 edge, which could have a large impact on your Internet connection.

Calculating Bandwidth Requirements

Calculating estimated bandwidth is a tough challenge. There are many factors to consider, including average bandwidth usage, peak bandwidth usage, and various spikes such as "end of month finance review" that might skew estimates. This section reviews the basic requirements; however, ensure you cover the niche cases for your organization.

Call Flows

Skype for Business utilizes a wide range of scenarios, including peer-to-peer calls, conference calls, and PSTN/PBX calls. Each scenario has different media paths and utilize a different load requirement.

A *peer-to-peer session* is any communication between only two endpoints within the corporate network or federation partner. All media is exchanged directly between those two endpoints.

A *conference session* is any call that originates at an endpoint and terminates at the Skype for Business Server pool that hosts the audio/video conferencing service. Multiple sessions will terminate on the A/V service.

A *PSTN session* is any communication that originates at a Skype for Business endpoint and terminates on the Mediation Server for relay to a PSTN gateway, assuming that Media Bypass is not enabled. The physical location between these two systems needs to be understood because the more hops and the longer the distance could affect PSTN call quality.

Bandwidth Utilization

The following tables summarize the general network utilization for different common protocols. This information includes the overhead for IP, UDP, RTP, and SRTP. This may look higher than other vendors because most do not include this additional overhead in their details. The following tables do not include Forward Error Correction (FEC) overhead. FEC is a mitigation technique that is enabled when the network suffers unusually high packet loss, which is not practical for planning purposes. The G722 codec is only used for Lync Room Systems, which utilize a single stereo microphone or a pair of mono microphones.

Content Sharing

Content sharing utilizes a new protocol—Video-based Screen Sharing (VbSS)—to share an application or your desktop. PowerPoint sharing (not through application sharing but through the SharePoint Web Services) does not use this protocol. The following tables give some general guidance for content sharing.

Video Resolution Bandwidth

Table 9.1 shows the video usage of each resolution that can be used by Skype for Business.

TABLE 9.1 Video Usage of Each Resolution Used by Skype for Business

Video Codec	Resolution and Aspect Ratio	Maximum Video Payload Bitrate (Kbps)	Minimum Video Payload Bitrate (Kbps)
H.264	320×180 (16:9)		
212×160 (4:3)	250	15	
H.264/RTVideo	424×240 (16:9)		
320×240 (4:3	350	100	
H.264	480×270 (16:9)		
424×320 (4:3)	450	200	
H.264/RTVideo	640×360 (16:9)		
640×480 (4:3)	800	300	
H.264	848×480 (16:9)	1500	400
H.264	960×540 (16:9)	2000	500
H.264/RTVideo	1280×720 (16:9)	2500	700
H.264	1920×1080 (16:9)	4000	1500
H.264/RTVideo	960×144 (20:3)	500	15
H.264	1280×192 (20:3)	1000	250
H.264	1920×288 (20:3)	2000	500

Audio and Video Codec Bandwidth Peer-to-Peer

Table 9.2 summarizes the audio and video codec usage when making a peer-to-peer call. In Skype for Business Server 2015, a new codec is introduced called SILK. This codec offers improved audio quality but also causes an increase in network utilization.

TABLE 9.2 Audio and Video Codec Usage for Peer-to-Peer Calls

Media	Codec	Typical Stream (Kbps)	Maximum Stream (Kbps)
Audio	RTAudio Wideband	39.8	62
Audio	RTAudio Narrowband	29.3	44.8

Audio	SILK Wideband	44.3	69
Main video when calling Skype for Business Server endpoints	H.264	460	4010 (for maximum resolution of 1920×1080)
Main video when calling Lync 2010 or Office Communicator 2007 R2 endpoints	RTVideo	460	2510 (for maximum resolution of 1280×720)
Panoramic video when calling Skype for Business Server endpoints	H.264	190	2010 (for maximum resolution of 1920×288)
Panoramic video when calling Lync 2010 endpoints	RTVideo	190	510 (for maximum resolution of 960×144)
Audio (PSTN)	G.711	64.8	97
Audio (PSTN)	RTAudio Narrowband	30.9	44.8

Audio and Video Codec Bandwidth Conferences

In a conference call, different combinations of audio and video codecs are used. Table 9.3 lists the codecs used in a conference. Notice that SILK is no longer used, and in Skype for Business Server 2015 each client will request the optimal stream for the network and screen resolution available.

TABLE 9.3 Bandwidth Usage by Codec for Conference Calls

Media	Typical Codec	Typical Stream (Kbps)	Maximum Stream (Kbps)
Audio	G.722	46.1	100.6
Audio	Siren	25.5	52.6
Main video receive	H.264 and RTVideo	260	8015
Main video send	H.264 and RTVideo	270	8015
Panoramic video receive	H.264 and RTVideo	190	2010 (for maximum resolution of 1920×288)
Panoramic video send	H.264 and RTVideo	190	2515

Bandwidth Calculations

The numbers listed in the preceding tables don't really mean much until everything is all put together into a client experience to see what it means to the network. In the next few examples, we investigate different scenarios and the formulas behind them. Even though the November 2015 version of the Bandwidth Calculator has been updated for Skype for Business Server 2015 (https://www.microsoft.com/en-us/download/details.aspx?id=19011), it can be a little daunting to understand. Although it is difficult to always calculate the average bandwidth, planning for the maximum is easier and will provide a better solution.

Audio Peer to Peer

A peer-to-peer call is the simplest case to understand. It uses just a single stream for any modality. We will assume that the call is made internally so neither STUN nor TURN is used and that each client is using the Skype for Business client, and thus the SILK codec. The SILK codec uses 69 Kbps per call. Typically, you might think to double this due to having two clients. However, unless both users are talking at the same time, you only need to calculate for one stream at a time. If they are making a PSTN call, that typically will use G.711, which is 97 Kbps. To start, you would want to get existing information about your current call system in your company—especially calls that would take place over a slow network link.

Audio Conferencing

Calculating conferencing is more complex because all media goes through the front end and then back to the client. By default, conferencing will use G.722 or Siren (G.722 will always be the preferred choice). Before we start the calculations, an understanding of the scenario needs to be determined. To simplify the process, let's say the company Bernsian Devices has a conference with 20 attendants. Adam is hosting the conference on a Front End Server in San Jose. Although there are users in San Francisco, all these users are accessing the conference with voice only. We now know that using SILK would require 10 users × 69 Kbps (Stereo), or a total of 690 Kbps. The following has been established by Microsoft: In an average conference, 80% of the time there is a single speaker, 7% of the time there are two speakers, and 13% of the time there is silence. This, then, becomes the formula:

$$(1 \text{ user} \times 690 \text{ Kbps} \times 80\%) + (2 \text{ users} \times 69 \text{ Kbps} \times 7\%) + (0 \text{ users} \times 69 \times 13\%) = 560$$

This is pretty much near our estimation of 690 Kbps for the SILK codec.

Video Conferencing

Adding video to a conference increases the complexity of the network requirements. Because a peer-to-peer call is an easy calculation, we will focus strictly on what happens in a conference. A single attendant at any one time could be seeing a panoramic video of a conference room, an instance of desktop sharing, five people in the gallery view, plus their own picture as well as static pictures of everybody else. This means five video streams starting off in a small view (for example 212×160), which means each feed will consume 250 Kbps or 1250 Kbps, plus an additional 250 Kbps for the stream, for 1500 Kbps total stream to the client.

Because the pictures of people are pretty small, the users will most likely want to see a larger video. If five people go to a size of 424×320, that would now be 5×450 Kbps = 2250 Kbps. However, they also have to send their stream of the lower quality 250 Kbps + 450 Kbps, so an additional 700×5 users, or 3500 Kbps, will be consumed per client. That is just for video, and media such as a shared desktop experience adds overhead to that. You can see that even with a small conference, a lot of bandwidth can easily be used. In this example, if the people in the remote office in San Francisco were on a 1Mb connection, they would not have a good conference experience.

Wireless Networks

In today's enterprise, Wi-Fi is a necessity. Even if you are not running it in your enterprise, it is being used on the road, in public hot spots, or in the home. Each one of these scenarios comes to a single point: Will the user have a good experience on Skype for Business? You already know that in a public situation there is not much that can be done from an IT standpoint to make the experience better, outside of letting the users know that you have no control over that network and that using it may result in a poor experience. You may have more control over a home user, though. If your company deploys remote access points, you can make sure that you are providing the ones with the latest firmware and the best coverage. You can equally guide the users to a better home router or provide additional ones to make sure there is enough coverage. The enterprise network is where the most time and budget is spent. Therefore, you should make sure that the access points (APs) have a good connection back to the core network, the firmware is updated, and they are all properly placed.

Planning Access Points

In most cases, when access points are deployed, they are spread out to minimize the number of APs and maximize coverage. Although this works fine for Internet and file transfers, it is not optimal for real-time media traffic. Figure 9.4 demonstrates what a typical AP deployment might look like. Figure 9.5 is more aligned for what is needed for real-time media: capacity. This translates to having a better signal strength over fewer APs to provide a better experience with Skype for Business. Here are two points to note:

- If one AP fails, the surrounding ones can now take that traffic without being oversubscribed.
- Although this will decrease the number of devices connected to an AP, it allows for more data to be passed between endpoints and APs.

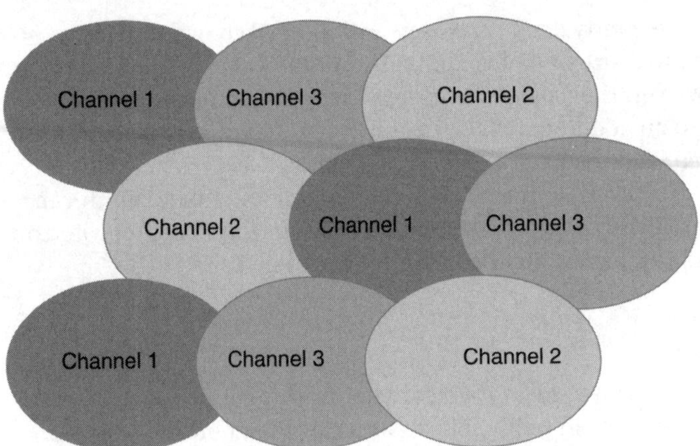

FIGURE 9.4 A typical access point layout designed for coverage.

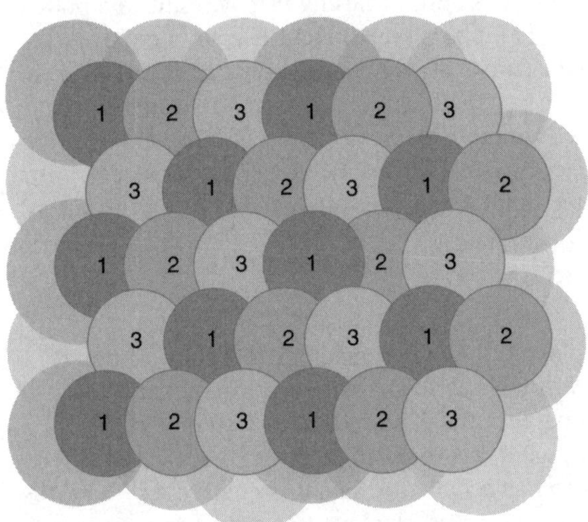

FIGURE 9.5 Wireless coverage for density.

Notice in Figure 9.4 how there are fewer APs, but they cover more area.

Figure 9.5, though exaggerated, shows the same coverage area but more access points. This allows for more bandwidth usage in an environment where Skype for Business is used for making calls over a wireless network.

Endpoints

In many cases, drivers (especially the network ones) have not been updated since a machine was deployed or an image was made. Network drivers are updated more often now that real-time media is becoming a major standard in organizations. Updates may include performance improvements to simple transmission rates while moving between APs.

In many cases, there are issues with inconsistencies in the client choosing which band to use: 2.4 GHz or 5 GHz. It is important to have tested all your wireless network drivers and firmware before rolling out Skype for Business to your clients, and in some cases this may require firmware and driver updating.

Call Admission Control

Call Admission Control (CAC) is a mechanism that determines whether there is sufficient network bandwidth to provide a high-quality experience for calls. CAC is purely configured within the Skype for Business infrastructure and has no information about the underlying network. It relies on the engineer to configure and identify potential network limitations between sites. CAC will provide a better experience to the end user by rejecting or rerouting the call rather than allowing for a poor call experience. CAC does not replace the need for quality of service; instead, it works alongside with it. CAC can be utilized to configure maximum bandwidth for a single call. CAC can only manage Skype for Business audio traffic. It does not apply to traffic going through the Internet with the ICE protocol; it is only used for internal and known networks. It may be better to deploy QoS or increase bandwidth. Having a CAC configuration that is wrong can cause poor call quality.

Configuring CAC is a long process that requires a great deal of network analysis. This process can be reduced by having a defined and completed network topology. The following is an example of the basic steps on how to configure CAC. Full details of the step-by-step instructions can be found at https://technet.microsoft.com/en-us/library/gg398529.aspx.

- Identify all your network regions that have a central site. A region may be identified as North America, APAC, and/or EMEA.
- Identify a central site for each CAC region. For example, the North America region may have a central site in San Jose, California.
- Identify the network sites that are connected to each region. Here, you are identifying sites that have constraints on network bandwidth. For example, a small regional site using an SBA in Santa Cruz, California. There may be another site within that region (for example, Palo Alto, California) that does not have any constraints.
- Describe the bandwidth constraints for each site.
- Associate each subnet to a site. This must be the subnet that is used by DHCP for the client. For example, if you have a region that is 10.1.0.0/16 but have a DHCP range of 10.1.1.0/24, you must use the /24 range for configuring CAC, using the super subnet will not work.
- Define a route between each pair of regions.

As you can see, just making all the requirements for a large network can take a lot of time. Once everything has all been gathered, the topology has been identified, and a plan has been developed, you can start building out the CAC topology.

Quality of Service

Quality of service (QoS) is basically prioritizing certain traffic over a network corridor. For example, take two people making a Skype for Business call between two buildings on two different subnets. Also in that same connection they are sharing streaming video, file share copies, and email data. We know that network availability for voice is key for a good call. Using QoS will prioritize, or give more bandwidth to, that voice call. At the same time, however, it will reduce the available bandwidth for the other services that are not as critical to real-time data transfer.

Quality of service is not built in to Skype for Business by default; however, it supports QoS using Differentiated Services Code Point (DSCP). At the highest level it classifies traffic into priority groups. Each packet is then marked with a group. For example, a packet with a DSCP value of 0 is given best effort, meaning the network switches will do their best to deliver the packet. At the opposite side, if you have a DSCP value of 46, this is considered to be extremely important and must be delivered with priority over everything else. This level of importance is known as Expedited Forwarding (EF). Between these two extremes you also have Assured Forwarding (AF). Assured Forwarding has its own subclassifications as well. There is also Class Selector (CS), which is simply a legacy format used mostly for signaling for the user in Skype for Business. For example, video is more important than a file transfer, both of which are part of the AF classification. So when you think about how important each protocol is, you need to consider the importance of the traffic. Audio is by far the most important, then usually video, and then application sharing. Then there is SIP traffic, which uses TCP, which by nature can handle packet loss. However, too much packet loss can cause delayed call setup or even delays with holding and transfers. For this reason, SIP signaling is usually placed with a higher priority.

CAUTION

Before you go and start deploying QoS on your infrastructure, you need to get the network team involved. It could be that they already have QoS in place and are using DSCP tags that are common to Skype for Business with a different purpose. You also need to make sure QoS is deployed end to end. If any single switch or router between the two points (for example, your laptop and the Front End Server), strips the DSCP tag, the QoS will be dropped and performance may suffer.

Table 9.4 contains the common DSCP settings used in Skype for Business.

TABLE 9.4 Common DSCP Settings Used in Skype for Business

DSCP Value	Meaning	Error Probability	Usage
0	Best effort	High	Standard traffic
14	AF13	High	File transfer
24	CS3	Medium	SIP signaling
26	AF31	Medium	Application sharing
34	AF41	Low	Video
46	EF	None	Audio

CAUTION

Not all endpoints support QoS. Windows OS and some desktop phones are the only platforms that currently support Skype for Business QoS.

Client Ports

By default, the client application uses any ports between 1024 and 65535. Here's how to enable QoS to use range ports:

```
Set-CsConferencingConfiguration -ClientMediaPortRangeEnabled $True
```

The preceding command enables the setting at a global level; if you want to enable it per site, add `-Identity` to the command:

```
Set-CsConferencingConfiguration -ClientMediaPortRangeEnabled $True
➥-Identity "Site:SanJose"
```

In general, 20 ports per modality will suffice. Remember, this is for the client communications to the servers. Table 9.5 reviews the standard port ranges for audio and video.

TABLE 9.5 Standard Port Ranges and DSCP Values for Audio and Video

Modality	Starting Port	Ending Port	Port Count	DSCP Value
Client Audio	40803	40843	40	46 (EF)
Client Video	49152	49192	40	34 (AF41)
Client Application Sharing	57501	57541	40	26 (AF31)
Client File Transfer	20000	2040	40	14 (AF13)
Client SIP	20080	20120	40	24 (CS3)

The following command will apply these ports to the clients:

```
Set-CsConferencingConfiguration -Identity global -ClientAudioPort 40803
➥-ClientAudioPortRange 40 -ClientVideoPort 49152 -ClientVideoPortRange 40
➥-ClientAppSharingPort 57501 -ClientAppSharingPortRange 40
➥-ClientFileTransferPort 20000 -ClientFileTransferPortRange 40
➥-ClientMediaPortRangeEnabled $true -ClientMediaPort 20041
➥-ClientMediaPortRange 40
```

9

Front End Server Ports

The first step is to find the ports already in use by running the following commands:

```
Get-CsService -ConferencingServer | Select-Object Identity, AudioPortStart,
➥AudioPortCount, VideoPortStart, VideoPortCount, AppSharingPortStart,
➥AppSharingPortCount
```

```
Get-CsService -ApplicationServer | Select-Object Identity, AudioPortStart,
➥AudioPortCount,VideoPortStart,VideoPortCount,AppSharingPortStart,
➥AppSharingPortCount

Get-CsService -MediationServer | Select-Object Identity, AudioPortStart,
➥AudioPortCount
```

You will want to modify the port range for the Application Server and the Mediation Server. There should be a minimum of 8349 ports for each audio and video and 8033 ports for application sharing (make sure that there is no overlap). Table 9.6 shows the commonly used set of port ranges.

TABLE 9.6 Common Port Ranges

Modality	Starting Port	Ending Port	Port Count	DSCP Value
Server Audio	40803	49151	8348	46 (EF)
Server Video	49152	57500	8348	34 (AF41)
Server Application Sharing	57501	65533	8033	26 (AF31

NOTE

Remember that the ports used for clients are much smaller in count because this is point to point. The ports used on the server for conferencing are larger because in a conference all media goes through the Front End pool and is not point to point.

To set these ports, run the following commands to set it on all the conferencing servers. Very seldom would you want to make these settings different among all your servers. After setting these values, you will need to restart the services.

```
Get-CsService -ConferencingServer | ForEach-Object {Set-CsConferenceServer
➥-Identity $_.Identity -AppSharingPortStart 57501 -AppSharingPortCount 8033
➥-AudioPortStart 40803 -AudioPortCount 8348 -VideoPortStart 49152
➥-VideoPortCount 8348}

Get-CsService -ApplicationServer| ForEach-Object { Set-CsApplicationServer
➥-Identity $_.Identity -AppSharingPortStart 57501 -AppSharingPortCount 8033
➥-AudioPortStart 40803 -AudioPortCount 8348 -VideoPortStart 49152
➥-VideoPortCount 8348 }

Get-CsService -MediationServer| ForEach-Object { Set-CsMediationServer
➥-Identity $_.Identity -AudioPortStart 40803 -AudioPortCount 8348 }

Set-CsMediaConfiguration -Identity global -EnableQoS $true
```

```
Get-CsService -EdgeServer| ForEach-Object { Set-CsEdgeServer -Identity
➥$_.Identity -MediaCommunicationPortStart 50000
➥-MediaCommunicationPortCount 10000}
```

Using Defined Ports When Using a Site-to-Site VPN

As mentioned previously, having your Skype for Business traffic traverse over a VPN may result in a poor call experience. By having all the ports defined, you can help prevent calls from traversing through VPN by blocking those ports and the internal IP addresses of your servers. In the configuration used by blocking ports 2000–2081 and 40803–65534, you will force clients to use the Internet connection to access all Skype for Business Server 2015 services. In addition to blocking the port ranges, you also need to make sure that the lyncdiscover service has an ANAME record on internal DNS that points to the public IP address and that hair pinning is configured.

Configure DCSP Markings

Now that we have configured Skype for Business to use DCSP tagging, the servers and clients need to be told to use those ports for DSCP tagging. This can all be done through PowerShell. In this example, the Mediation services are collocated on the Front End Pool.

NOTE

When applying these group policies, it is best to create separate OUs for each role, Front End, Edge (if it is domain joined), Mediation (if not collocated), and Back End. Each policy should be applied at the proper OU. This will make sure that you do not have conflicting DCSP by not placing the policy at the top level of the OU. If all of your computers are in the default container, you will need to place the client policies at the root because containers do not support group policies.

Use the following command to import the Active Directory and Group Policy cmdlets:

```
Import-module ActiveDirectory,GroupPolicy
```

Windows Client

A Group Policy object must first be created, and then all settings after that are added to that object:

```
New-GPO -Name "SfB QoS Client" -Comment "DSCP markings for Skype for
➥Business Clients"
```

This first setting, Do Not Use NLA, tells the system to apply DCSP tagging on all network adapters. It is very seldom that you would apply DCSP to one interface and not all of them.

```
Set-GPPrefRegistryValue -Name "SfB QoS Client" -Context Computer
➥-Key "HKLM\SYSTEM\CurrentControlSet\Services\Tcpip\QoS"
➥-ValueName "Do not use NLA" -Value "1" -Type String -Action Update
```

Configure the Audio DCSP:

```
Set-GPRegistryValue -Name "SfB QoS Client"
➥-Key "HKLM\SOFTWARE\Policies\Microsoft\Windows\QoS\SfB Audio QoS"
➥-ValueName "Version", "Application Name", "Protocol", "Local Port",
➥"Local IP", "Local IP Prefix Length", "Remote Port", "Remote IP",
➥"Remote IP Prefix Length", "DSCP Value", "Throttle Rate" -Type String
➥-Value "1.0", "lync.exe", "*", "40803:40842", "*", "*", "*", "*", "*",
➥"46", "-1"
```

Configure the Video DCSP:

```
Set-GPRegistryValue -Name "SfB QoS Client"
➥-Key "HKLM\SOFTWARE\Policies\Microsoft\Windows\QoS\SfB Video QoS"
➥-ValueName "Version", "Application Name", "Protocol", "Local Port",
➥"Local IP", "Local IP Prefix Length", "Remote Port", "Remote IP",
➥"Remote IP Prefix Length", "DSCP Value", "Throttle Rate" -Type String
➥-Value "1.0", "lync.exe", "*", "49152:49191", "*", "*", "*", "*", "*",
➥"34", "-1"
```

Configure Application DCSP:

```
Set-GPRegistryValue -Name "SfB QoS Client"
➥-Key "HKLM\SOFTWARE\Policies\Microsoft\Windows\QoS\SfB Application
➥Sharing QoS" -ValueName "Version", "Application Name", "Protocol",
➥"Local Port", "Local IP", "Local IP Prefix Length", "Remote Port",
➥"Remote IP", "Remote IP Prefix Length", "DSCP Value", "Throttle Rate"
➥-Type String -Value "1.0", "lync.exe", "*", "57501:57540", "*", "*",
➥"*", "*", "*", "26", "-1"
```

Configure File Transfer:

```
Set-GPRegistryValue -Name "SfB QoS Client"
➥-Key "HKLM\SOFTWARE\Policies\Microsoft\Windows\QoS\SfB File Transfer QoS"
➥-ValueName "Version", "Application Name", "Protocol", "Local Port",
➥"Local IP", "Local IP Prefix Length", "Remote Port", "Remote IP",
➥"Remote IP Prefix Length", "DSCP Value", "Throttle Rate" -Type String
➥-Value "1.0", "lync.exe", "*", "20000:20039", "*", "*", "*", "*", "*",
➥"14", "-1"
```

Configure SIP:

```
Set-GPRegistryValue -Name "SfB QoS Client"
➥-Key "HKLM\SOFTWARE\Policies\Microsoft\Windows\QoS\SfB SIP QoS"
➥-ValueName "Version", "Application Name", "Protocol", "Local Port",
➥"Local IP", "Local IP Prefix Length", "Remote Port", "Remote IP",
➥"Remote IP Prefix Length", "DSCP Value", "Throttle Rate" -Type String
➥-Value "1.0", "lync.exe", "*", "20080:20119", "*", "*", "*", "*",
➥"*", "24", "-1"
```

UC Phone Edition

The UC phone edition does not contain all of the other features. You can retrieve the current configuration by running the command

```
Get-CsUCPhoneConfiguration
```

The basic command to set the DCSP for a UC phone is

```
Set-CsUCPhoneConfiguration -VoiceDiffServTag 46
```

You can also set it per site, like so:

```
Set-CsUCPhoneConfiguration -Identity "site:San Jose" -VoiceDiffServTag 46
```

Or you can set it on all configurations:

```
Get-CsUCPhoneConfiguration | Set-CsUCPhoneConfiguration -VoiceDiffServTag 46
```

Windows Store App

The Windows Store App, also known as the Skype for Business Metro App, is similar in many ways to the standard Windows desktop application. The following commands show how to correctly set QoS for the Windows Store App.

Configure Audio:

```
Set-GPRegistryValue -Name "SfB QoS Client"
➥-Key "HKLM\SOFTWARE\Policies\Microsoft\Windows\QoS\SfB Windows Store App
➥Audio QoS" -ValueName "Version", "Application Name", "Protocol", "Local Port",
➥"Local IP", "Local IP Prefix Length", "Remote Port", "Remote IP", "Remote IP Prefix
➥Length", "DSCP Value", "Throttle Rate" -Type String -Value "1.0",
➥"lyncmx.exe", "*", "40803:40842", "*", "*", "*", "*", "*", "46", "-1"
```

Configure Video:

```
Set-GPRegistryValue -Name "SfB QoS Client"
➥-Key "HKLM\SOFTWARE\Policies\Microsoft\Windows\QoS\SfB Windows Store App
➥Video QoS" -ValueName "Version", "Application Name", "Protocol", "Local Port",
➥"Local IP", "Local IP Prefix Length", "Remote Port", "Remote IP", "Remote IP Prefix
➥Length", "DSCP Value", "Throttle Rate" -Type String -Value "1.0", "lyncmx.exe",
➥"*", "49152:49191", "*", "*", "*", "*", "*", "34", "-1"
```

9

Windows Server

All of these commands are exactly the same—the difference being the port numbers and the port count. In these configurations, the services are referenced as conferencing because the modality will only be used in a conference of three or more people. Less than that, and it is peer-to-peer and will just use the client DCSP markings.

The GPO Object:

```
New-GPO -Name "SfB QoS Server" -Comment "DSCP markings for Skype for
➥Business Servers"
```

Configure "Do Not Use NLA":

```
Set-GPPrefRegistryValue -Name "SfB QoS Server" -Context Computer
➥-Key "HKLM\SYSTEM\CurrentControlSet\Services\Tcpip\QoS" -ValueName "Do not
➥use NLA" -Value "1" -Type String -Action Update
```

Configure Audio:

```
Set-GPRegistryValue -Name "SfB QoS Server"
➥-Key "HKLM\SOFTWARE\Policies\Microsoft\Windows\QoS\SfB Conferencing
➥Audio QoS" -ValueName "Version", "Application Name", "Protocol", "Local Port",
➥"Local IP", "Local IP Prefix Length", "Remote Port", "Remote IP", "Remote IP
➥Prefix Length", "DSCP Value", "Throttle Rate" -Type String -Value "1.0",
➥"avmcusvc.exe", "*", "40803:49151", "*", "*", "*", "*", "*", "46", "-1"
```

Configure Video:

```
Set-GPRegistryValue -Name "SfB QoS Server"
➥-Key "HKLM\SOFTWARE\Policies\Microsoft\Windows\QoS\SfB Conferencing Video QoS"
➥-ValueName "Version", "Application Name", "Protocol", "Local Port", "Local IP",
➥"Local IP Prefix Length", "Remote Port", "Remote IP", "Remote IP Prefix Length",
➥"DSCP Value", "Throttle Rate" -Type String -Value "1.0", "avmcusvc.exe", "*",
➥"49152:57500", "*", "*", "*", "*", "*", "34", "-1"
```

Configure Application Sharing:

```
Set-GPRegistryValue -Name "SfB QoS Server"
➥-Key "HKLM\SOFTWARE\Policies\Microsoft\Windows\QoS\SfB Application Sharing
➥QoS" -ValueName "Version", "Application Name", "Protocol", "Local Port",
➥"Local IP", "Local IP Prefix Length", "Remote Port", "Remote IP", "Remote IP
➥Prefix Length", "DSCP Value", "Throttle Rate" -Type String -Value "1.0",
➥"asmcusvc.exe", "*", "57501:65533", "*", "*", "*", "*", "*", "26", "-1"
```

Configure Response Groups:

```
Set-GPRegistryValue -Name "SfB QoS Server"
➥-Key "HKLM\SOFTWARE\Policies\Microsoft\Windows\QoS\SfB Response Group QoS"
➥-ValueName "Version", "Application Name", "Protocol", "Local Port", "Local IP",
➥"Local IP Prefix Length", "Remote Port", "Remote IP", "Remote IP Prefix Length",
➥"DSCP Value", "Throttle Rate" -Type String -Value "1.0", "OcsAppServerHost.exe",
➥"*", "40803:49151", "*", "*", "*", "*", "*", "46", "-1"
```

Configure Conference Announcement:

```
Set-GPRegistryValue -Name "SfB QoS Server"
➥-Key "HKLM\SOFTWARE\Policies\Microsoft\Windows\QoS\SfB Conference
➥Announcement Service QoS" -ValueName "Version", "Application Name", "Protocol",
➥"Local Port", "Local IP", "Local IP Prefix Length", "Remote Port", "Remote IP",
```

```
➥"Remote IP Prefix Length", "DSCP Value", "Throttle Rate" -Type String -Value
➥"1.0", "OcsAppServerHost.exe", "*", "40803:49151", "*", "*", "*", "*", "*",
➥"46", "-1"
```

Configure Call Park:

```
Set-GPRegistryValue -Name "SfB QoS Server"
➥-Key "HKLM\SOFTWARE\Policies\Microsoft\Windows\QoS\SfB Call Park QoS"
➥-ValueName "Version", "Application Name", "Protocol", "Local Port", "Local IP",
➥"Local IP Prefix Length", "Remote Port", "Remote IP", "Remote IP Prefix Length",
➥"DSCP Value", "Throttle Rate" -Type String -Value "1.0", "OcsAppServerHost.exe",
➥"*", "40803:49151", "*", "*", "*", "*", "*", "46", "-1"
```

Configure UCMA Audio:

```
Set-GPRegistryValue -Name "SfB QoS Server"
➥-Key "HKLM\SOFTWARE\Policies\Microsoft\Windows\QoS\SfB UCMA Applications
➥Audio QoS" -ValueName "Version", "Application Name", "Protocol", "Local Port",
➥"Local IP", "Local IP Prefix Length", "Remote Port", "Remote IP", "Remote IP
➥Prefix Length", "DSCP Value", "Throttle Rate" -Type String -Value "1.0",
➥"OcsAppServerHost.exe", "*", "40803:49151", "*", "*", "*", "*", "*", "46", "-1"
```

Configure UCMA Video:

```
Set-GPRegistryValue -Name "SfB QoS Server"
➥-Key "HKLM\SOFTWARE\Policies\Microsoft\Windows\QoS\SfB UCMA Applications
➥Video QoS" -ValueName "Version", "Application Name", "Protocol", "Local Port",
➥"Local IP", "Local IP Prefix Length", "Remote Port", "Remote IP", "Remote IP
➥Prefix Length", "DSCP Value", "Throttle Rate" -Type String -Value "1.0",
➥"OcsAppServerHost.exe", "*", "49152:57500", "*", "*", "*", "*", "*", "34", "-1"
```

Configure Mediation

```
Set-GPRegistryValue -Name "SfB QoS Server"
➥-Key "HKLM\SOFTWARE\Policies\Microsoft\Windows\QoS\SfB Mediation Audio QoS"
➥-ValueName "Version", "Application Name", "Protocol", "Local Port", "Local IP",
➥"Local IP Prefix Length", "Remote Port", "Remote IP", "Remote IP Prefix Length",
➥"DSCP Value", "Throttle Rate" -Type String -Value "1.0", "MediationServerSvc.exe",
➥"*", "40803:49151", "*", "*", "*", "*", "*", "46", "-1"
```


Edge Server

The policy for Edge Servers requires only a destination port range, hence you cannot simply apply the Application Servers QoS policies to your Edge Servers. Instead, you must create new policies and apply those policies to your Edge Servers only. If your Edge Servers are not part of the domain, you can use Local Group Policy instead of Active Directory Group Policy: The only difference is that you must create these local policies using the Local Group Policy Editor, and you must create the same set of policies on each Edge Server individually. Edge servers only use three modalities. The processes are the same, and the ports and DCSP tagging are the same; however, the application is different.

```
New-GPO -Name "SfB QoS Edge Server" -Comment "DSCP markings for Skype for
➥Business Edge Servers"
```

Configure "Do Not Use NLA":

```
Set-GPPrefRegistryValue -Name "SfB QoS Edge Server" -Context Computer
➥-Key "HKLM\SYSTEM\CurrentControlSet\Services\Tcpip\QoS" -ValueName "Do
➥not use NLA" -Value "1" -Type String -Action Update
```

Configure Audio:

```
Set-GPRegistryValue -Name "SfB QoS Edge Server"
➥-Key "HKLM\SOFTWARE\Policies\Microsoft\Windows\QoS\SfB Conferencing Audio
➥QoS" -ValueName "Version", "Application Name", "Protocol", "Local Port",
➥"Local IP", "Local IP Prefix Length", "Remote Port", "Remote IP", "Remote
➥IP Prefix Length", "DSCP Value", "Throttle Rate" -Type String -Value "1.0",
➥"MediaRelaySvc.exe", "*", "40803:49151", "*", "*", "*", "*", "*", "46", "-1"
```

Configure Video:

```
Set-GPRegistryValue -Name "SfB QoS Server"
➥-Key "HKLM\SOFTWARE\Policies\Microsoft\Windows\QoS\SfB Conferencing
➥Video QoS" -ValueName "Version", "Application Name", "Protocol", "Local Port",
➥"Local IP", "Local IP Prefix Length", "Remote Port", "Remote IP", "Remote IP
➥Prefix Length", "DSCP Value", "Throttle Rate" -Type String -Value "1.0",
➥"MediaRelaySvc.exe", "*", "49152:57500", "*", "*", "*", "*", "*", "34", "-1"
```

Configure Application Sharing:

```
Set-GPRegistryValue -Name "SfB QoS Edge Server"
➥-Key "HKLM\SOFTWARE\Policies\Microsoft\Windows\QoS\SfB Application
➥Sharing QoS" -ValueName "Version", "Application Name", "Protocol", "Local
➥Port", "Local IP", "Local IP Prefix Length", "Remote Port", "Remote IP",
➥"Remote IP Prefix Length", "DSCP Value", "Throttle Rate" -Type String
➥-Value "1.0", " "MediaRelaySvc.exe", "*", "57501:65533", "*", "*", "*",
➥"*", "*", "26", "-1"
```

That completes all of the Skype for Business settings and Group Policy objects. Notice how all of the settings used in the application settings match those used in the Group Policy objects. Once all of these settings have been deployed, you either need to reboot each system (client and server) twice or run following command and reboot once:

```
Gpupdate.exe /force
```

NOTE

You can download a spreadsheet that contains all of this information and allows for an easy customization from http://www.ehloworld.com/2821.

Software Defined Networking

With the Skype for Business Software Defined Networking (SDN) API, software can now interact directly with the network infrastructure, so QoS and services can be dynamically adjusted to always deliver the best possible experience. The servers and clients can inform the network about a call, ongoing state changes, latency, jitter, packet loss, and other quality metrics. These metrics also inform the network's diagnostics system about call issues, which can be visualized in real time and archived for reporting purposes.

In a network environment, the API obtains call setup information, endpoints, URIs, ports, media, and the protocols used. This information can help ensure that traffic streams are prioritized correctly (QoS).

The SDN API can also work within monitoring tools to collect data about calls, from end to end (at least within your managed network) in real time to assist in your overall Skype for Business voice quality. This data can be stored for historical reporting or near-real-time incident management.

How SDN Works

There are three components to SDN: listener, manager, and the management system. The listener is the service that is waiting for a Skype for Business call to set up. Once the call has been set up, the listener then sends XML data to the manager about that call. The manager then forwards that data to a management system. Once this process has been completed, QoE data is then sent from the client to the listener, which forwards this all to the final endpoint: the network tools. All of this is done over HTTP or HTTPS traffic.

The listener is always installed on a Front End Server. It does not install on any other servers. The manager can be installed on the Mediation Server or on a separate server.

NOTE

Although it is acceptable to install the manager on the Mediation Server, this is not recommended. Doing so will limit your flexibility and scale, and increase the configuration needed on the manager and the management system. The manager can be installed on a server running other applications. The amount of utilization the manager uses is proportional to the amount of calls made. If you have just a single Standard edition Front End, you may want to install the manager on the Front End as well.

Figure 9.6 demonstrates how each component works. In this example, Stella is calling Gavin, and both users are on the company's internal wireless network. The call starts with the signaling to the Mediation Server. The LDL sends the SDN data to the manager, which sends the data to the network controller, which in turn ensures the call between the two has proper QoS and routing, as well as collects historical data in the network management system.

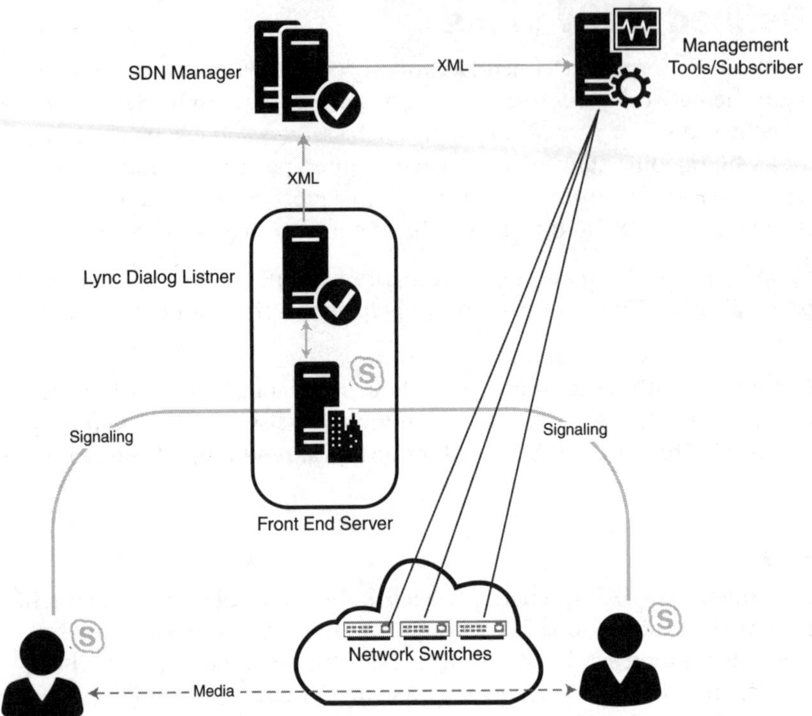

FIGURE 9.6 The SDN API call flow.

NOTE

The data used by SDN is not stored in the QoE database. It is managed by the network hardware and software in its own system. The data can be tied together, but that is dependent on third-party network tools.

What the SDN API Does Now

The SDN API has several features that are available currently. However, the two most distinctive aspects are its increased visibility on Skype for Business traffic and how it can help correlate network data with call information. We know that from the QoE database we can retrieve a great amount of information about a call. It is missing one component, though: the network behind the call. It has no access into the switches and routers that move the data. With the SDN API, you can correlate the full call from end to end inside your company network. Depending on your network management tools, the QoE data is fed directly into the toolset for the complete view. Some toolsets go even further and can retrieve data from the device making the call, such as WMI information.

The SDN API current has three primary use cases:

- **Diagnostics**—By using the data from the API, network monitoring systems can then correlate between media flows in Lync and activities in the network that may have an impact on quality.
- **Automatically provisioning quality of service (QoS)**—When the controller gets information about a media flow starting up, it can instruct the network to assign the appropriate marking to those packets in real time.
- **Orchestration**—This is just what it sounds like. Imagine all the different instruments of the network from Layer 1 to Layer 7 all singing along in harmony.

Installing the SDN API

With the latest version of the SDN API, you have four ways to install the SDN API topology. The choice comes down to the scalability and redundancy required. The following lists the four options, from most desirable to least:

NOTE

The SDN API is not required. Even if you have installed it and the service stops, calls will still continue as normal. Your users will not notice a difference, except for maybe call quality.

- The Lync dialog listeners connect to a pool of DNS load-balanced LSMs. This option does require SQL Express. In a large deployment, you may want to use a pair of SQL Enterprise Servers for maximum availability. This also requires specific DNS SRV records to be created.
- LSM primary/secondary failover (redundant LSM).
- LSM and LDL collocated.
- Single LSM. This is the most basic deployment type. All LDLs send data to a single LSM. There is no fault tolerance, and it designed for smaller deployments.

During the installation process you will be prompted for the location of the SDN logs (by default this is the temp directory of the current user). This can make it difficult for other users to review the logs. It is recommended that you locate the logs in a common location (for example, C:\SDNLogs).

Because the LDL accesses the QoE database, it will need permissions into the database. If your SQL instance that the QoE is running under is the Network Service, when installing the LDL, choose the Network Service Account. If SQL is running under a service account, you will want to choose an account that has access to the QoE database as well as is a member of the CSAdministrator and CSServerAdministrator groups.

After the initial install, logging is turned on for almost all the services. You should decrease the logging level once you have all the services and management interfaces installed.

Summary

The information in this chapter has given you an overview of some of the network requirements to make that first call a success. By knowing the network requirements for the different codecs, you can estimate if your current network will have available bandwidth. By deploying quality of service and wireless access points designed for density, calls will be prioritized correctly and be completed with great video and audio clarity. When you start your Skype for Business deployment, make sure you take into account not just the servers, endpoints, and conference rooms, but your network as well—and analyze what you have and prepare for what you may need.

CHAPTER 10
Dependent Services

IN THIS CHAPTER

- Active Directory Dependencies
- Domain Name Server Dependencies
- Server Certificates Dependencies
- Network Dependencies
- Office Web Apps Server Dependencies
- SQL Server Dependencies

Skype for Business Server 2015, like many other Microsoft applications, depends on a number of infrastructure services to function properly. Skype for Business Server 2015 integrates with Active Directory to store configuration information on user objects. DNS is used for Skype for Business Server 2015 fully qualified domain name (FQDN) resolution (that is, A records) and SRV records. Skype for Business Server 2015 uses certificates to secure network connections between server-to-server and server-to-client communications. Network dependencies also impact both the performance and functionality of Skype for Business Server 2015.

Skype for Business Server 2015 uses SQL Server as a database to store configuration information, deploy the Central Management Store (CMS), and synchronize a copy of user information from Active Directory. Skype for Business Server 2015 also leverages other servers, such as Office Web Apps Server for PowerPoint sharing and Exchange Server for calendar information, contact card information, and unified messaging. Finally, Skype for Business Server 2015 uses third-party reverse proxies to publish Skype for Business Server 2015 web services to the Internet.

This chapter provides details on each of these dependencies and helps Skype for Business Server administrators understand and configure these items to ensure a healthy Skype for Business environment.

Active Directory Dependencies

Like many other Microsoft applications, Skype for Business Server 2015 has a high level of dependency on Active Directory (AD) Directory Services. Skype for Business Server 2015 must be installed in an Active Directory environment, and certain attributes must be available in the AD schema for Skype for Business Server to install. For these reasons, Microsoft includes a set of wizards with the Skype for Business Server 2015 media to assist administrators in preparing Active Directory to support Skype for Business Server 2015. Using these AD preparation wizards in the appropriate order makes this aspect of the Skype for Business Server 2015 installation quite simple. However, because the health of the Skype for Business Server 2015 environment is highly dependent on the health of Active Directory, it makes sense for administrators to perform a basic health check of AD prior to running the Skype for Business Server 2015 AD wizards.

AD requirements for Skype for Business Server 2015 are the same as for Lync Server 2013. In fact, you'll notice that the Skype for Business Server 2015 Deployment Wizard does not require you to run the AD preparation wizards when upgrading from Lync Server 2013.

The AD requirements are as follows:

- All domain controllers in the forest must run Windows Server 2003 or higher.
- The functional level for domains where Skype for Business Server is deployed must be Windows Server 2003 native or higher (not Windows Server 2003 mixed).
- The functional level for the forest must be Windows Server 2003 native or higher (not Windows Server 2003 mixed).

Schema Extensions

Before you can install Skype for Business Server 2015, it is necessary to extend the AD schema. This process is typically easiest to run on a system that will be a Skype for Business Front End Server, and it must be run using an Active Directory domain account that is a member of the Schema Admins group. If an installer user account is temporarily added to the Schema Admins group in preparation for installing Skype for Business Server, it will be necessary to log off of the system and then log back on to reflect the group membership change. Before you can extend the schema, the following components must first be installed on the system:

- Remote Server Administration Tools (AD DS and AD LDS tools only, available as integrated Windows Features)
- Microsoft Visual C++ x64 redistributable (automatically installed from the Skype for Business Server 2015 media if not present when starting the Skype for Business installation)

NOTE

To avoid permissions issues, be sure that the domain controller hosting the Schema Master role is online and that the installer account has Schema Admin credentials before using the Deployment Wizard.

Forest Prep

After the schema has been updated, the Deployment Wizard enables the remaining AD preparation steps. The next step is to prepare the forest for the Skype for Business Server installation, which creates global configuration settings and universal security groups required for the Skype for Business Server deployment. The forest prep step must be performed by a user who is currently a member of the Enterprise Admins group.

TIP

Replication of the forest prep changes can be verified by simply using the Active Directory Users and Computers console to determine whether the Skype for Business security groups have been created. In the Users container at the domain root, 11 new groups named with the "CS" prefix should be present (for example, CSAdministrator).

Domain Prep

After the forest is prepared, the final AD preparation task is to prepare the domain for Skype for Business Server 2015. Unlike the previous two steps, domain prep must be performed on every domain that will host either Skype for Business Servers or users who will be enabled for Skype for Business. The domain prep step configures the permissions required for the universal security groups created in the forest prep step, and it must be performed by a user who is currently a member of the Domain Admins group for the domain that the tool is run against.

TIP

Replication of the domain prep changes can be verified using the Skype for Business Server 2015 Management Shell, using the following command: `Get-CsAdDomain`. If the domain prep changes have replicated successfully, the cmdlet returns a value of `LC_DOMAIN_SETTINGS_STATE_READY`.

Skype for Business Server 2015 Security Groups

After the Active Directory preparation steps previously described have been completed, a number of new AD security groups are introduced. The groups can be divided into four primary categories: service groups, administration groups, infrastructure groups, and role-based access control (RBAC) groups. The purpose of each security group is described next.

Skype for Business Server 2015 service groups include the following:

- **RTCHSUniversalServices**—Includes service accounts that can be used to run the Front End services and grants Skype for Business servers read/write access to Skype for Business Server global settings and Active Directory user objects
- **RTCComponentUniversalServices**—Includes service accounts that can be used to run Skype for Business conferencing and web components services

- **RTCProxyUniversalServices**—Includes service accounts that can be used to run a Skype for Business proxy service
- **RTCSBAUniversalServices**—Grants read access to the Skype for Business deployment for survivable branch appliance installation

Skype for Business Server 2015 administration groups include the following:

- **RTCUniversalServerAdmins**—Allows members to manage server and pool settings
- **RTCUniversalUserAdmins**—Allows members to manage user settings and move users from one server or pool to another
- **RTCUniversalReadOnlyAdmins**—Allows members to read server, pool, and user settings
- **RTCUniversalSBATechnicians**—Grants read access to the Skype for Business 2015 deployment as well as local administrative access to a survivable branch appliance during installation

Skype for Business Server 2015 infrastructure groups include the following:

- **RTCUniversalConfigReplicator**—Allows Skype for Business servers to participate in replication of the Skype for Business configuration
- **RTCUniversalGlobalWriteGroup**—Grants write access to global settings for Skype for Business Server
- **RTCUniversalGlobalReadOnlyGroup**—Grants read-only access to global settings for Skype for Business Server
- **RTCUniversalUserReadOnlyGroup**—Grants read-only access to Skype for Business Server user settings
- **RTCUniversalServerReadOnlyGroup**—Grants read-only access to individual Skype for Business Server settings

Skype for Business Server 2015 RBAC groups include the following:

- **CSAdministrator**—Grants full administrative access to the Skype for Business 2015 environment
- **CSArchivingAdministrator**—Grants access to the archiving-related Skype for Business settings and policies
- **CSHelpDesk**—Grants read-only access to Skype for Business user properties and policies, along with access to specific troubleshooting functions
- **CSLocationAdministrator**—Grants access to the E911 management functions of Skype for Business

- **CSPersistentChatAdministrator**—Grants access to the Skype for Business Persistent Chat admin cmdlets
- **CSResponseGroupAdministrator**—Grants access to configure the Response Group application within Skype for Business
- **CSResponseGroupManager**—Grants access to manage limited configuration of Skype for Business Response Groups that have been assigned
- **CSServerAdministrator**—Grants access to manage, monitor, and troubleshoot Skype for Business servers and services
- **CSUserAdministrator**—Grants access to enable, disable, and move Skype for Business users as well as assign existing policies
- **CSViewOnlyAdministrator**—Grants read-only access to the Skype for Business deployment for monitoring purposes
- **CSVoiceAdministrator**—Grants access to create, configure, and manage voice-related Skype for Business settings and policies

Domain Name System Dependencies

Skype for Business Server 2015 heavily relies on Domain Name System (DNS) for name resolution and service lookups. Because Skype for Business Server 2015 is always installed in an Active Directory environment, which also requires DNS, this service is typically already in production before the installation of Skype for Business Server 2015, and therefore simply needs to be configured to meet Skype for Business requirements.

Skype for Business Server 2015 utilizes DNS for several purposes. First, there is the requirement for hostname-to-IP-address lookups, which is the typical use of DNS. However, Skype for Business Server 2015 also uses specialized DNS records to identify particular services. Skype for Business Server 2015 also leverages DNS round robin to provide load balancing for specific Skype for Business Server 2015 functions. Here are the DNS record types that are primarily used by Skype for Business Server 2015:

- A (host) records
- SRV (service location) records

A very basic Skype for Business Server 2015 deployment involving only the core services requires only a few DNS records. However, as additional Skype for Business Server 2015 features and services are deployed in the environment, quite a few additional DNS records might be required. For this reason, the DNS requirements for each Skype for Business feature will be detailed in the various chapters of this book corresponding to that particular feature. For example, Edge services, the Device Update Web service, and Skype for Business Mobility all have specific DNS requirements. In this section, the DNS records required to allow basic Skype for Business functionality are covered.

Skype for Business Server 2015 requires registration of the hostname for each Skype for Business server as an internal A record. For Standard Edition, a DNS A record that resolves the fully qualified name of the pool to the IP address of the Front End server is also needed. For Enterprise Edition Front End pools involving a hardware load balancer, a DNS A record that resolves the fully qualified name of the pool to the virtual IP address of the load balancer is needed.

DNS Load Balancing

For SIP traffic, Skype for Business Server 2015 provides the option to employ DNS load balancing or hardware load balancing for distributing traffic load across all Front End Servers in an Enterprise pool. For HTTP traffic, Skype for Business Server 2015 requires a hardware load balancer to distribute web traffic across the web services on all Front End Servers in an Enterprise pool.

To configure DNS load balancing for SIP traffic, DNS A records are manually created to resolve the fully qualified name of the pool to the IP address of each of the Front End Servers in the pool.

When configuring hardware load balancing for HTTPS traffic, in addition to configuring the hardware load balancer, you must manually create a DNS A record to resolve the fully qualified name of the pool web components service to the virtual IP (VIP) address of the hardware load balancer.

The following is a sample DNS configuration that leverages both DNS load balancing for SIP traffic and hardware load balancing for HTTPS traffic for an Enterprise pool:

```
EntFE1.skypeunleashed.com     A  10.1.1.2  Standard host record
EntFE2.skypeunleashed.com     A  10.1.1.3  Standard host record
Pool.skypeunleashed.com  A  10.1.1.2  DNS load balancing for SIP and media traffic
Pool.skypeunleashed.com  A  10.1.1.3  DNS load balancing for SIP and media traffic
Web.skypeunleashed.com   A  10.1.1.4  Hardware load balancing for HTTP traffic
```

Automatic Client Sign-In

Most organizations rely on the Lync and Skype for Business client's capability to automatically discover the user's organization Skype for Business infrastructure both inside the corporate network and outside (if deployed). Once the client discovers the user's Skype for Business environment, it signs in the user. To provide this automatic and seamless client sign-in experience, Skype for Business 2015 uses the DNS A record, `lyncdiscover.<SIP domain>`, to discover the Skype for Business Server 2015 environment when connecting from the Internet (externally). If the LyncDiscover DNS record is not resolvable, the Skype for Business 2015 client will attempt to resolve the DNS SRV record, `_sip._tls.<SIP domain>`. If this DNS SRV record is not resolvable, the client will attempt to resolve the A record, `sip.<SIP domain>`.

When the Skype for Business 2015 client signs in internally, it will attempt to resolve the DNS A record, `lyncdiscoverinternal.<SIP domain>`, first. If this DNS query fails, the client will attempt to resolve the DNS SRV record, `_sipinternaltls._tcp.<SIP domain>`.

NOTE

If you are configuring Skype for Business Server 2015 Hybrid, the clients must also be able to resolve the DNS A record, `lyncdiscover.<SIP domain>`, internally as well as externally.

SRV records hold information that is not used with other types of DNS records, such as priority, weight, and port number. In addition to specifying the location of the service, this information provides a means to influence how the incoming traffic load will be shared or directed.

TIP

For Skype for Business deployments that use several SIP domains, one SRV record is required for each SIP domain to support automatic client sign-in.

Simple URLs

An additional Skype for Business Server 2015 feature that affects the DNS configuration is simple URLs. Simple URLs are used to provide access to common Skype for Business web services using names that are intended to be easy to remember by users. Skype for Business Server 2015 provides the capability to configure simple URLs for three services: web conferencing, dial-in conferencing, and administrative access to the Skype for Business Server Control Panel. Several options are available for the configuration of simple URLs, and each requires the configuration of at least one DNS A record for the simple URL to function. For the majority of Skype for Business deployments, the option to use a separate base URL for each simple URL is used, because this configuration results in a naming convention that is typically the easiest for users to remember.

For the internal DNS, each of the simple URLs requires an A record that resolves the URL to either the Front End Server (for Standard Edition) or the virtual IP (VIP) address of the hardware load balancer (for Enterprise Edition). For the external DNS, each of the URLs should resolve to the external reverse proxy.

The following is an example of a DNS configuration that might be used to add simple URLs for the `skypeunleashed.com` Skype for Business deployment in the internal network:

```
meet.skypeunleashed.com       A  10.1.1.4   Simple URL for web conferencing
dialin.skypeunleashed.com     A  10.1.1.4   Simple URL for dial-in access to meetings
admin.skypeunleashed.com  A  10.1.1.4   Simple URL for access to the Skype for
➥Business Server Control Panel
```

10

Server Certificates Dependencies

Microsoft has adopted a "secure out of the box" approach for both operating system and application releases. Skype for Business Server 2015 continues with that same approach, requiring SSL certificates to protect communications between Skype for Business servers, as well as between the client and server. In addition, a second type of certificate was introduced with Lync Server 2013: the Open Authentication (OAuth) certificate. While the SSL certificates will continue to be used to encrypt communications, the OAuth certificates will be used to establish trust across the Office 2013 and above family of server applications. The OAuth certificates allow the exchange of security tokens that grant access to resources for a period of time. Server-to-server authentication and authorization using OAuth is supported between Lync Server 2013 and Skype for Business Server 2015, as well as among Exchange Server 2013, SharePoint Server 2013, and Office 365 for integration scenarios.

The certificates applied to Skype for Business Server systems can be either public certificates issued by a third-party Certificate Authority (CA) or internal certificates issued using a self-managed public key infrastructure (PKI). Best practice is to use public certificates for the Edge Servers and internal certificates (that is, issued by a private CA) for the internal servers. Although this hybrid approach serves to meet the certificate requirements of Skype for Business and reduce the cost of the certificates, it does require that an internal PKI be deployed before the deployment of the Skype for Business infrastructure. Deploying an internal PKI is a project unto itself, and organizations that do not already manage an internal PKI deployment may choose to procure server certificates from a third-party CA for Skype for Business internal servers as well. The one exception is the OAuth certificate. This certificate does not need to be issued by a CA because it is a self-signed certificate generated by the Skype for Business internal servers.

Certificates expire and need to be renewed. If certificate expiration is not monitored and certificates are not renewed before they expire, your Skype for Business Server 2015 deployment will stop functioning unexpectedly and will result in a service outage. This can be catastrophic if Skype for Business Server 2015 is a mission-critical service in your organization. Best practice is to carefully monitor each server certificate used by Skype for Business Server 2015. The Certificate Expiration Alerting utility can aid you in this effort (https://blogs.technet.microsoft.com/nexthop/2011/11/17/certificate-expiration-alerting/).

The topic of how to plan and manage an internal PKI goes well beyond the scope of this chapter. However, the specifics of what types of certificates are required for Skype for Business are included here to allow for this aspect of a Skype for Business deployment to be planned appropriately.

Skype for Business Server Certificate Requirements

Following are the primary uses for certificates within Skype for Business:

- Communication between Skype for Business clients and Skype for Business servers is encrypted using TLS.
- Authentication between Skype for Business servers using MTLS uses the default server certificate. Authentication between Skype for Business Server and other server applications such as Exchange servers, SharePoint servers, and Office 365 uses OAuth certificates.
- Communications between Skype for Business servers is encrypted using MTLS.

- Automatic DNS discovery of partners for federation uses certificates for authentication.
- Remote or external user access for any Skype for Business functionality is encrypted, including IM, audio/video (A/V) sessions, application sharing, and conferencing.
- A mobile request using automatic discovery of web services is encrypted.

Following are the common requirements that apply to the SSL certificates issued for use with Skype for Business Server:

- All server certificates must support server authorization (Server EKU).
- All server certificates must contain a CRL distribution point (CDP).
- Auto-enrollment is supported for internal Skype for Business Servers, but is not supported for Edge Servers.
- Key lengths of 2048 and 4096 are supported.
- Supported hash algorithms include RSA (the default), ECDH_P256, ECDH_P384, and ECDH_P521.
- All certificates are standard web server certificates and must include the private key.

Following are the requirements that apply to the OAuth certificates issued for use by Skype for Business Server:

- The certificate issued for OAuth must be the same across all Skype for Business servers in the environment, and therefore the private key must be exportable for the certificate.
- A Web Server certificate that has the name of the SIP domain as the subject name (SN) can be used as an OAuth certificate. Additional SIP domains can be added in the subject alternative name (SAN) of the certificate.
- Generally, any Skype for Business Server SSL certificate can also be used as an OAuth certificate, provided that all other requirements are met. However, if the default Skype for Business Server certificate is used for both SSL and OAuth, it must be assigned twice, once for each certificate usage.

NOTE

Distribution of the OAuth certificate between Skype for Business Front End Servers is handled automatically via Central Management Store replication.

Installing Skype for Business Certificates

The number of certificates required for a Skype for Business deployment and the configuration of those certificates vary greatly depending on the topology chosen and the features deployed. Server certificates must be configured on all Skype for Business Servers. Internal Skype for Business Servers include Front End Server, Mediation Server, Director, and Persistent Chat Server. Certificates for those server roles can be issued from an internal CA. Directly external-facing Skype for Business Servers (that is, Edge Servers), reverse proxy, and the session border controller (SBC) must be assigned a combination of both public and internal certificates.

Skype for Business Server 2015 provides a wizard for requesting, installing, and assigning server certificates. For example, the following procedure is used to create an offline SSL certificate request to be sent to a third-party CA for a Front End Server:

1. Log on to the Front End Server and then launch the Skype for Business Server Deployment Wizard.
2. At the opening screen, click Install or Update Skype for Business Server System.
3. The Deployment Wizard determines the current state of the environment and provides links to various installation options as needed. Assuming that the Local Configuration Store is installed and at least one Skype for Business Server component has been installed, the link to run Step 3: Request, Install or Assign Certificates will be available. Click Run on Step 3 to begin the certificate request.
4. When the Certificate Request screen appears (see Figure 10.1), expand the arrow to the left of Default Certificate to display the certificate usage options. As shown in Figure 10.2, by default the certificate requested will be used as the default Skype for Business server certificate, and it will also be used for both the internal and external web services. If a separate certificate is planned for any of these, that usage can be deselected here. When finished, click Request.

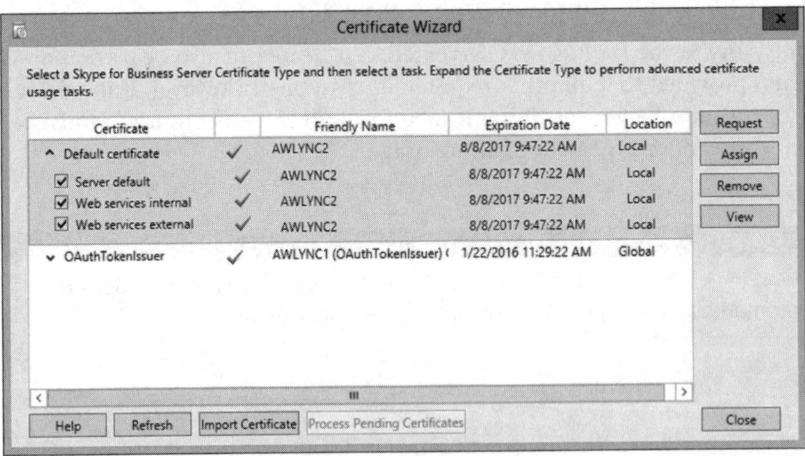

FIGURE 10.1 Skype for Business certificate request.

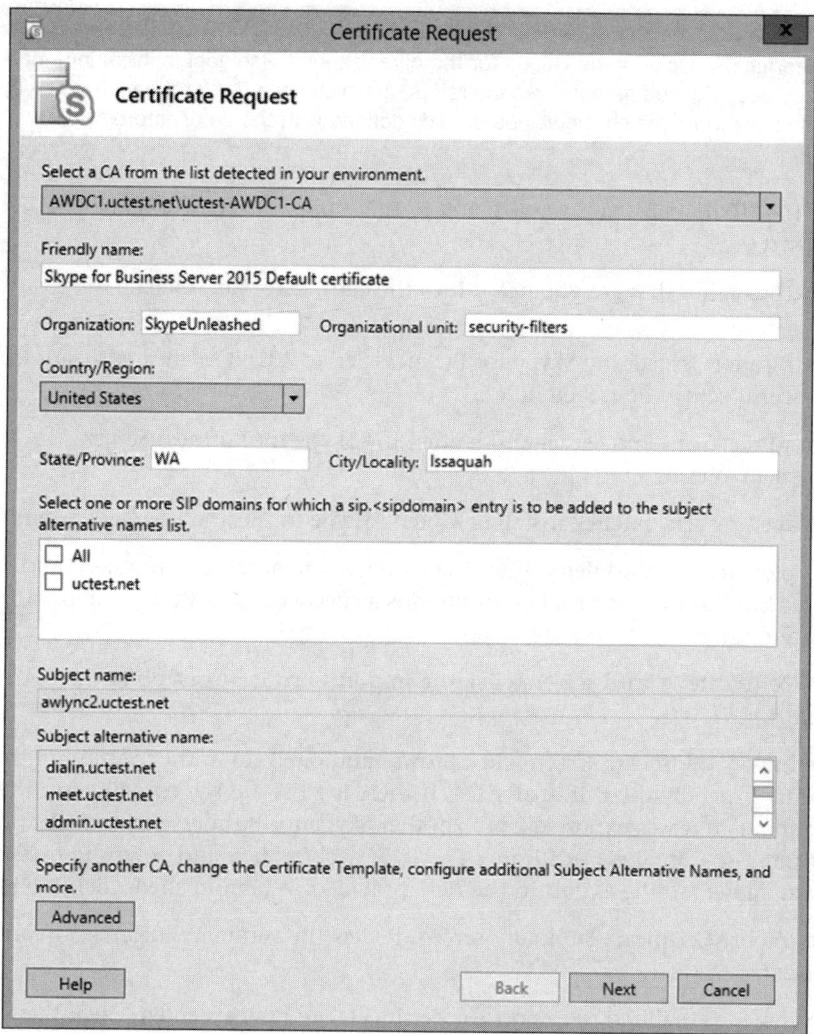

FIGURE 10.2 Skype for Business certificate usages.

5. The Certificate Request Wizard now launches. Click Next.
6. Specify a friendly name for the certificate, which makes it easier to identify later.
7. Specify your organization and organizational unit in the corresponding fields.
8. Specify your country from the drop-down menu and then enter the information into the State/Province and City/Locality fields.

TIP

With an external CA, typically the values for the organizational and geographical information have already been defined as naming constraints, in which case the information entered on these screens must match the values already defined with the certificate provider.

9. Check the SIP domains you want to add to the subject alternative name (SAN). Click Next.
10. Review the names that are populated into the certificate. Click Next.

After the certificate is issued, the Skype for Business Server 2015 Certificate Wizard is used to assign the certificate as described here:

1. Log on to the Front End Server and launch the Skype for Business Server Deployment Wizard.
2. At the opening screen, click Install or Update Skype for Business Server System.
3. The Deployment Wizard determines the current state of the environment and provides links to various installation options as needed. Click Run on Step 3 to install and assign the certificate.
4. At the Certificate Wizard screen, click the Import Certificate button at the bottom of the screen.
5. At the Import Certificate screen, click Browse and navigate to the location of the certificate issued by the third-party CA. If there is a private key contained in the file (for example, if it was exported from another Skype for Business server), select the Certificate File Contains Certificate's Private Key check box and enter the password that was applied to the export in the field provided. When finished, click Next.
6. At the Import Certificate Summary screen, review the summary information and click Next.
7. The commands required to import the certificate are now executed. Click View Log to determine whether any errors occurred during the certificate import process. When finished, click Finish to return to the Certificate Wizard.
8. At the Certificate Wizard screen, click Assign.
9. At the Certificate Assignment screen, click Next.
10. Select the newly issued certificate to assign to Skype for Business Server and then click Next.

TIP

If there are several certificates in the local certificate store of the server, at first glance it might be difficult to differentiate between these in order to make the right selection. If so, click the View Certificate Details button at the bottom of the screen. Typically, the Friendly Name field or the Subject Alternative Name field will make it evident as to which certificate is intended for Skype for Business.

11. At the Certificate Assignment Summary screen, review the summary information and then click Next.

12. The commands required to assign the certificate are now executed. Click View Log to determine whether any errors occurred during the certificate assignment process. When finished, click Finish to return to the Certificate Wizard.

13. The default certificate is now assigned to the server, as shown in Figure 10.3. Click Close to exit the Certificate Wizard.

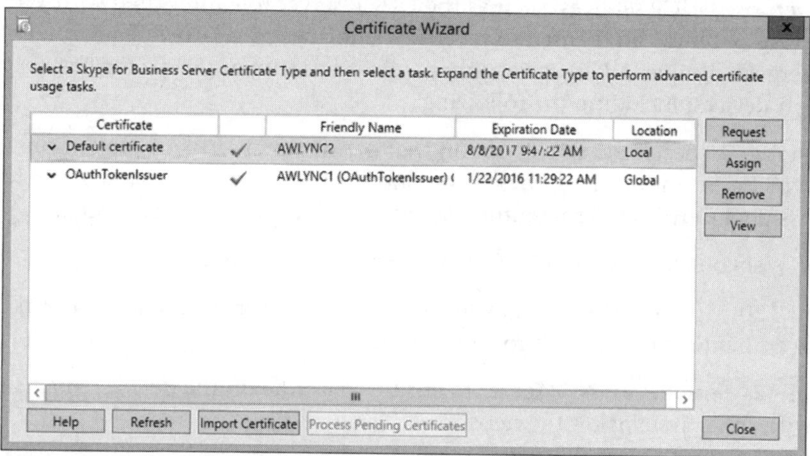

FIGURE 10.3 Assigning a certificate.

Network Dependencies

Skype for Business Server 2015, like any communications product, depends heavily on the network it is installed on to deliver the functionality and quality of service it is designed for. Whereas some network dependencies are obvious, such as connectivity and sufficient bandwidth, other dependencies might not be so evident, such as DHCP requirements, network site definitions, and configuration of specific features on network switches.

Best practice is to perform a network assessment before deploying Skype for Business Server 2015. Use the Skype for Business Bandwidth Calculator to assess how much network bandwidth capacity is needed versus what is available. You can find this calculator at https://www.microsoft.com/en-us/download/details.aspx?id=19011. Once your bandwidth capacity is calculated, set up quality of service (QoS) to control bandwidth utilization.

Skype for Business Server 2015 can bring to light issues with your internal network. It will likely uncover poor network configurations and network bandwidth constraints, and the first to experience these issues will be your users. As the Skype for Business administrator, the quality of your deployment will quickly be questioned. Being able to identify the root cause of dropped calls and poor audio/video quality as a Skype for Business or networking issue will become important.

Supporting Skype for Business Phone Edition with DHCP

Whereas Skype for Business clients inherit network connectivity from the host computer on which the client is installed, networking for specialized devices such as VoIP desk phones is typically managed centrally. Traditionally, these devices are configured via dynamic host configuration protocol (DHCP), not only for IP addressing assignments but also as a centralized method of informing the devices that updated firmware is available. To allow centralized management of Skype for Business Phone Edition devices, specific DHCP requirements must be met.

Standard enterprise DHCP services, such as the DHCP server role integrated with Windows Server operating systems, can be used to meet Skype for Business DHCP requirements. However, there are unique DHCP options that are used to support Skype for Business Phone Edition devices, including the following:

- **Option 43**—A specialized DHCP option that consists of a series of sub-options. For Skype for Business Server, these sub-options are used to specify the Skype for Business pool Certificate Provisioning Service URL in the following format:

  https://WebPoolDFQDN:443/CertProv/CertProvisioningService.svc

- **Option 120**—Specifies the list of Skype for Business servers (registrar) that can handle authentication requests for the device.

- **Option 42**—Specifies an NTP server to ensure that time on the device remains in sync with other systems on the network.

NOTE

Additional DHCP options might also be required for Skype for Business, depending on the network. For example, the preferred method of configuring phone devices with a dedicated voice VLAN is Link Layer Discovery Protocol–Media Endpoint Discovery (LLDP-MED), but not all Ethernet switches support this feature. Where LLDP-MED is not supported, additional DHCP vendor classes and associated options can instead be configured to supply the voice VLAN ID to the device.

Although several of the DHCP options previously listed are very straightforward for anyone familiar with DHCP, option 43 in particular can be challenging to configure correctly, due to the fact that numerous sub-options are used, each involving hex-encoded binary strings. Thankfully, Microsoft provides the DHCPUtil utility along with an associated script, which together can be used to generate and then apply the correct values for options 43 and 120 to a Microsoft DHCP server. For environments where a non-Microsoft DHCP server is used, these values will need to be configured manually in order to support Skype for Business Phone Edition devices.

NOTE

Each Skype for Business Front End Server also includes a built-in DHCP component, which is disabled by default. The built-in Skype for Business DHCP service cannot provide IP address leases, and is simply used to provide the values for DHCP options 43 and 120 for small Skype for Business deployments where IP addressing is handled manually.

The following procedure is used to configure DHCP options 43 and 120 using DHCPUtil:

1. Copy the DHCPUtil.exe and DHCPConfigScript.bat files from the following location on a Skype for Business Front End Server to a local subdirectory on the DHCP server:

   C:\Program Files\Common Files\Skype for Business Server 2015

2. If it is not already installed, install the Microsoft Visual C++ Redistributable Package on the DHCP server as a prerequisite for running DHCPUtil.exe (located in the Setup\amd64 directory on the Skype for Business Server 2015 media with a filename of vcredist_x64).

3. On the DHCP server, open an elevated command prompt. Navigate to the subdirectory where the files were copied previously in step 1, and execute the following command, in which the fully qualified name of the Skype for Business pool is labeled as `<Pool_FQDN>`:

   ```
   DHCPUtil.exe -SipServer <Pool_FQDN> -RunConfigScript
   ```

   A series of `netsh` commands executes, configuring the appropriate values for DHCP options 43 and 120 within the local DHCP instance.

TIP

Only a 64-bit version of DHCPUtil.exe is supplied with Skype for Business Server 2015, and this cannot be used to configure a 32-bit DHCP server. In this situation, the next best option is to run DHCPUtil.exe directly on the Skype for Business Front End Server, and then use the output from the command to manually supply the values that will be used with the DHCPConfigScript.bat script on the DHCP server.

Ethernet Switch Considerations

All Skype for Business Phone Edition devices have two important features that have an impact on the choice of Ethernet switch: LLDP-MED and PoE (Power over Ethernet). To leverage these features, the connected Ethernet switch ports must support these same features. Specifically, LLDP-MED requires support for the IEEE802.1AB and ANSI/TIA-1057 standards. To utilize PoE, the switch ports must support one of two PoE standards: either 802.3AF or 802.3at.

The configuration of LLDP-MED is specific to the Ethernet switch model. Often, this feature needs to be enabled globally within the switch, and typically the voice VLAN must be specified for use with LLDP-MED within the switch configuration.

Defining Networks

Skype for Business Server organizes the network into network regions and network sites. These network regions and sites are used to organize resources according to geography and bandwidth. Network regions consist of multiple network sites. Network sites are associated with IP subnets so that the Skype for Business Servers can identify the locations where endpoints are located. A correctly configured network site topology allows Front End Servers to determine how call setup and routing should be handled; therefore, this is an important aspect of the Skype for Business configuration. All subnets in a network should be defined and associated with a network site. Although this can be configured using the Skype for Business Server Control Panel, in an enterprise network it could take a considerable amount of time to input all IP subnets into the configuration. For larger networks, this task is more easily handled using a simple comma-separated value (CSV) file and the Skype for Business Management Shell. For example, a CSV file can be created including separate fields for network address, subnet mask bits, description, and network site ID, as shown here:

```
IPAddress, mask, description, NetworkSiteID
10.0.0.0, 24, "NA:SF subnet", SF
10.1.0.0, 24, "EMEA:Dublin subnet", Dublin
10.2.0.0, 24, "EMEA:London subnet", London
```

Using a sample CSV filename of subnet.csv, these values can then be easily imported into the Skype for Business Central Management Store by using the Skype for Business Management Shell to execute the following command:

```
import-csv subnet.csv | foreach {New-CSNCSSubnet $_.IPAddress -MaskBits
➥$_.mask -Description $_.description -NetworkSiteID $_.NetworkSiteID}
```

This command can then be scheduled to run regularly as a script, such that whenever new sites or subnets are added to the network, the CSV file is adjusted to reflect these and the script maintains the most current network topology.

NOTE

Although somewhat similar in purpose, Skype for Business network sites are not related to Active Directory sites. Both the Active Directory and the Skype for Business network site configurations allow resources to be grouped by geography and bandwidth such that related network traffic is routed appropriately; therefore, it is common to see a similar pattern of site definitions and associated subnets between these two technologies.

Office Web Apps Server Dependencies

Although not a Skype for Business Server role in itself, Skype for Business Server leverages Office Web Apps Server to offer PowerPoint sharing capabilities in Skype for Business meetings. Office Web Apps Server delivers browser-based versions of Microsoft Office applications. This web service is designed to work with products that support Web

Application Open Platform Interface protocol (WOPI). Office Web Apps Server is leveraged by Exchange, SharePoint, and Skype for Business.

System Requirements

Office Web Apps Server must be installed on a separate server, and this computer must be joined to Active Directory. High availability is also supported for Office Web Apps Server and can be implemented via the installation of multiple servers and the use of a hardware or software load-balancing solution. Whether a single server or multiple servers are deployed, each installation is referred to as an Office Web Apps Server farm. The following requirements and guidelines apply for servers used to run Office Web Apps Server:

- Supported operating systems are Windows Server 2008 R2 SP1 up to Windows Server 2012 R2.
- Minimum hardware requirements are 4 × 64-bit cores, 8GB RAM, 80GB system hard drive.
- Server virtualization is supported.
- No other applications can be installed on the system, including any Skype for Business roles, SQL Server, or server applications.
- For multiple server farms, any software or hardware load-balancing solution can be used.

Office Web Apps Server must be configured with a server certificate to interop with Skype for Business Server. The following requirements apply to the certificate that can be used:

- The certificate must be issued by a trusted CA (either internal or third party).
- For single-server installations, the FQDN of the Office Web Apps Server must be included in the SAN (subject alternative name) field of the certificate.
- For load-balanced server farms, the certificate must be imported into the load balancer.
- The certificate must have an exportable private key.
- The friendly name applied to the certificate must be unique within the Trusted Root Certificate Authorities store on the system running Office Web Apps Server. This allows the cmdlet to determine which certificate is being targeted.

NOTE

Standard procedures can be used to request and install the certificate used for the Office Web Apps Server using the IIS Management Console, Certificate Authority Web Enrollment, or another method. However, the certificate binding should not be performed using the IIS Management Console. Rather, the certificate binding for Office Web Apps Server is performed using the same PowerShell command used to create the farm (`New-OfficeWebAppsFarm`), as detailed later.

The following are prerequisites for the installation of Office Web Apps Server:

- .NET Framework 4.5 (included with Windows Server 2012)
- Windows PowerShell 3.0 (included with Windows Server 2012)
- Windows Update KB2592525 (Windows Server 2008 R2 only)
- The Web Server (IIS) server role, along with the following role services:
    - Static Content
    - Default Document
    - ASP.NET (Windows Server 2008 R2) or ASP.NET 4.5 (Windows Server 2012)
    - .NET Extensibility (Windows Server 2008 R2) or .NET Extensibility 4.5 (Windows Server 2012)
    - ISAPI Extensions
    - ISAPI Filters
    - Server Side Includes
    - Windows Authentication
    - Request Filtering
    - IIS Management Console
    - Static Content Compression (recommended)
    - Dynamic Content Compression (recommended)
- The Ink and Handwriting Services feature

Office Web Apps Server Installation

Download Office Web Apps Server from your volume licensing service center (VLSC). After the prerequisite software has been installed along with the server certificate, the following procedure is used to install and then configure the Office Web Apps Server:

1. From the Office Web App Server media, double-click the setup.exe file.
2. Read the licensing terms. If you agree, select I Accept the Terms of This Agreement and then click Continue.
3. At the File Location screen, either keep the default location for file installation on the C: volume or enter an alternative path if desired. When finished, click Install Now.
4. After the file installation is complete, click Close.
5. Open Windows PowerShell and execute the following command to import the Office Web Apps application into PowerShell:

```
Import-Module OfficeWebApps.
```

6. Execute the following PowerShell command to create a single-server Office Web Apps Server farm, with the fully qualified name of the Office Web Apps Server used as the `<servername>` value, and the friendly name of the certificate used as the `<CertFriendlyName>` value:

   ```
   New-OfficeWebAppsFarm -InternalURL https://<servername>
   ➥-CertificateName "<CertFriendlyName>"
   ```

   If the farm is successfully created, the attributes of the new farm are automatically displayed in PowerShell.

7. Verify that the Office Web Apps Server is installed and configured correctly by using a web browser to connect to the discovery URL at the following address, with the fully qualified name of the Office Web Apps Server used as the `<servername>` value: `https://<servername>/hosting/discovery`. If the installation is successful, a WOPI discovery XML file is displayed in the browser.

Follow these steps to configure your Skype for Business 2015 Front End Servers to use your Office Web Apps Server or farm:

1. Open Skype for Business Server Topology Builder.
2. Download the topology from your existing deployment.
3. Expand the Shared Components node.
4. Right-click Office Web Apps Servers node and then select New Office Web Apps Server.
5. Specify the FQDN of your Office Web Apps Server or farm (see step 7 in the previous list).
6. Specify the discovery URL of your Office Web Apps Server or farm (see step 7 in the previous list).
7. Click OK.
8. Expand the site where you want to assign your Office Web Apps Server to.
9. Expand Skype for Business Server 2015.
10. Expand Standard Edition Front End Servers or Enterprise Edition Front End pools.
11. Right-click the server or pool you want to assign your Office Web Apps Server.
12. Click Edit Properties.
13. Check the box labeled Associate Pool with an Office Web Apps Server.
14. Select the newly added Office Web Apps Server defined in steps 4–7. Alternatively, you can define the Office Web Apps Server by clicking New next to the drop-down box.
15. Click OK.

SQL Server Dependencies

Skype for Business Server, like many other Microsoft applications, depends on SQL Server as a storage platform. With Skype for Business Server, SQL databases are used to store topology, configuration, and application information. One of the primary differences between the Standard and Enterprise Editions of Skype for Business Server 2015 is the use of a back-end database. In the Standard Edition, a local SQL Express Edition database is automatically installed by the Deployment Wizard as part of the Skype for Business installation. Enterprise Edition, on the other hand, requires a dedicated SQL Server back-end system. This section covers installation of SQL as it pertains to a Skype for Business Server 2015, Enterprise Edition deployment, and introduces administrators to some basic SQL management tasks.

Skype for Business Database Requirements

The first SQL database required for a new Skype for Business Server 2015 installation is the Central Management Store (CMS), which is used to store the configuration data that is replicated to all the Skype for Business servers in the environment. Beyond the CMS, the Front End Servers also require databases for persistent and dynamic user data as well as address book information. Additional databases are also used depending on specific optional features that might be deployed, such as the Response Group, Call Park, and Archiving and Monitoring services. Collectively, these databases are referred to as the Skype for Business Back End databases, and the supported database platforms are SQL Server 2008 R2, 2012 and 2014.

TIP

Either the Enterprise or Standard Editions of SQL Server 2008 R2, 2012, and 2014 can be used for the Skype for Business Back End databases. For SQL Server high availability, two options are available: SQL mirroring and SQL AlwaysOn. SQL mirroring is supported in both editions, although SQL mirroring support is being deprecated. SQL AlwaysOn is the replacement for SQL mirroring and is only supported in the Enterprise Edition. SQL AlwaysOn is the recommended high-availability solution for the Enterprise Edition of Skype for Business back-end databases.

Depending on the topology, Skype for Business will collocate databases if Skype for Business Server roles are collocated as well. Database collocation options are only applicable to Enterprise Edition pools. Skype for Business Standard Edition uses SQL Express.

NOTE

Microsoft supports installation of the Back End, Monitoring, Archiving, and Persistent Chat databases on the same SQL Server, and these can use either the same SQL instance or separate instances. However, only one of each type of database is supported on any given SQL Server. For many Skype for Business deployments, only one of each type of database is actually required; however, there are circumstances in which more than one of a certain database might be needed. For example, the Monitoring Server role can only be associated with a single Front End pool.

SQL Backup Procedures

With the new added support for SQL AlwaysOn, which synchronizes the Skype for Business Back End databases between two SQL Servers (Enterprise Edition) in an Enterprise pool, the need to manually back up the Skype for Business Back End databases is substantially reduced, except in the Skype for Business Standard Edition case. Nevertheless, it's still a good idea to regularly back up the Central Management Store by running the Skype for Business Server 2015 PowerShell command `export-CsConfiguration`. It is recommended to perform a backup before performing major configuration changes.

There are actually a number of ways to back up the Skype for Business SQL databases, including backing up the VM (if the Skype for Business Server is virtualized), native Windows Server backup, SQL-based backup that outputs the data into a flat file, and third-party backup solutions that support SQL. In the following sections, two methods of backing up the Skype for Business Back End databases are detailed, including Windows Server native backup and SQL 2014 native backup.

Backing Up SQL Using Windows Server Native Backup

Windows Server provides a native backup application called Windows Server Backup. The sample backup procedure that follows is based on Windows Server 2012 R2. Because Windows Server Backup is not installed by default, it is necessary to add this feature by performing the following steps:

1. From the Server Manager console, select Local Server in the left pane.
2. From the Manage drop-down menu, click Add Roles and Features.
3. At the Select Installation Type screen, keep the default option of Role-Based or Feature-Based Installation and then click Next.
4. At the Select Destination Server screen, keep the default option of Select a Server from the Server Pool and verify that the Skype for Business Back End database server is selected in the Server Pool list at the bottom of the screen. Click Next.
5. At the Select Server Roles screen, click Next.
6. At the Select Features screen, scroll down to the bottom of the list of features and select Windows Server Backup. Click Next.
7. At the Confirm Installation Selections screen, click Install.
8. When the installation has completed, click Close.

Now that the Windows Server Backup feature is installed, it can be used to back up SQL using the following procedure:

1. From the Server Manager console, select Local Server in the left pane.
2. From the Tools drop-down menu, click Windows Server Backup.
3. In the Action pane at the far right, click Backup Once.

4. In the Backup Options Wizard, either select Scheduled Backup Options to use previously configured backup settings or select Different Options to make a backup with new options. Click Next.

NOTE

If this is the first time that Windows Server Backup is being used, the Scheduled Backup Options selection will not be available.

5. At the Select Backup Configuration screen, choose either Full Server or Custom Backup. If Custom Backup is selected, be sure that all volumes containing SQL program files and data are included in the backup item selections. For Skype for Business Server SQL backup purposes, Full Server backup is typically the best choice. After the selection is made, click Next.
6. At the Specify Destination Type screen, either select Local Drives to store the backup file locally or select Remote Shared Folder to store the backup file on the network. Click Next.

NOTE

Windows Server Backup will only allow backups to be targeted to drive volumes that are not selected as part of the backup job. Therefore, unless an external disk is attached to the system that can be used as a target, the Remote Shared Folder option is typically the best choice for destination type.

7. Depending on the selection made on the preceding screen, either the Select Backup Destination screen or the Specify Remote Folder screen is presented. For a local backup destination, choose an available drive volume from the drop-down menu and select whether backup verification will be enabled after the backup file is written. For a remote folder, specify the remote location using the UNC path format; then in the Access Control section select whether access to the backup file will require credentials. When finished, click Next, which will validate the backup destination.
8. After the backup destination is validated, review the backup job settings listed on the Confirmation screen, and then click Backup to begin the backup job.
9. After the backup job completes, click Close.

Backing Up SQL Using SQL Server Management Studio

Another way to back up SQL is by using the native backup function of SQL to create a flat file backup, which can then become the target for a separate backup application if necessary. This method is especially useful if an environment already has a centralized backup infrastructure that doesn't support SQL natively. The sample backup procedure that follows is based on SQL Server 2014.

To back up SQL through the SQL Server Management Studio, perform the following steps:

1. Log on to the SQL Server where Skype for Business Back End databases are installed using an account with SQL administrative rights and then open SQL Server Management Studio.
2. At the Connect to Server prompt, keep the default options of connecting to the local server with Windows Authentication and then click Connect.
3. Expand Databases in the left pane.
4. Right-click the database you want to back up, select Tasks, and click Back Up.
5. At the Back Up Database screen, the first set of options for the backup job appears. In the Source section, select a backup type of either Full or Differential, and select the Copy-Only Backup option if desired. In the Backup Set section, either keep the default name for the backup set or enter an alternative name, along with a description if desired. Also, you can choose a backup set expiration date if necessary. In the Destination section, either keep the default backup destination, which is the standard SQL Backup directory on the local system, or click Add and specify an alternative destination.
6. Click Options in the left pane to view a second set of options for the backup job. In the Overwrite Media section, several media set options are available that determine whether the backup data will append to or overwrite an existing backup set or whether a new media set will be created. In the Reliability section, options for backup verification, checksums, and error handling are available. In the Compression section, one of several compression options can be selected. After making the desired selections, click OK to start the backup job.
7. When the backup has completed, click OK.

Maintaining the Skype for Business SQL Databases

An important aspect of the health of any Skype for Business deployment is maintaining the SQL databases. To keep Skype for Business Server operating smoothly and with optimal performance, regular maintenance should be performed on each SQL Server database. Such maintenance tasks include rebuilding indexes, checking database integrity, updating index statistics, and performing internal consistency checks, and backups. Database maintenance tasks can be performed either by executing Transact-SQL commands or by running the Database Maintenance Wizard.

This section provides information and recommendations for maintaining the databases that store Skype for Business Server data and configurations. Also, details are provided on how to automate and schedule the major maintenance tasks by creating database maintenance plans through SQL Server Database Maintenance Wizard.

Checking and Repairing Database Integrity

`DBCC CHECKDB` is a Transact-SQL command that is frequently used for checking the logical and physical integrity of databases. Essentially, `DBCC CHECKDB` is a superset command that actually runs three checks (`CHECKALLOC`, `CHECKTABLE`, and `CHECKCATALOG`).

The following are some recommendations for using `DBCC CHECKDB` to check and repair SQL database integrity:

- Always ensure that recent backups are on hand before running the command.
- Generally it is better to run the `DBCC CHECKDB` superset command than to execute the individual operations, because this will serve to identify the majority of the errors and is generally safe to run in a production environment.
- After `DBCC CHECKDB` has been run, the command can be run again with the `REPAIR` argument to repair reported errors. However, consideration should also be given to restoring the database from backup instead, because the `REPAIR` options should be considered a last resort.
- `DBCC CHECKDB` can require a considerable amount of time to run against large databases, and it performs schema locks that prevent metadata changes. Therefore, it is highly recommended to run the command during nonproduction hours.
- For large databases, the command can be run with the `PHYSICAL_ONLY` option, which will limit checking to the integrity of the physical structure of the page and record headers, along with the allocation consistency of the database. For these larger databases, it is therefore recommended to run the command with the `PHYSICAL_ONLY` option on a more frequent basis and to perform a full run of `DBCC CHECKDB` only on a periodic basis.

Monitoring and Reducing Fragmentation

Although indexes can speed up the execution of queries, some overhead is also associated with them. Indexes consume extra disk space and require some time to be updated whenever any data is updated, deleted, or inserted in a table. When indexes are first built, little or no fragmentation is present. Over time, as data is inserted, updated, and deleted, fragmentation levels on the underlying indexes can begin to increase.

When a data page is completely full and further data must be added to it, a page split occurs. To make room for the new data, SQL Server creates another data page somewhere else in the database (not necessarily in a contiguous location) and moves some of the data from the full page to the newly created one.

The effect of this is that the blocks of data are logically linear but physically fragmented. Therefore, when searching for data, the database engine is forced to jump from one page to somewhere else in the database looking for the next page it needs, instead of just sequentially moving to the next physical page. The end result is performance degradation and inefficient space utilization.

The fragmentation level of an index is the percentage of blocks that are logically linear and physically nonlinear. The `sys.dm_db_index_physical_stats` transact-SQL command can be used to monitor this, with the `avg_fragmentation_in_percent` column showing the fragmentation level. The value for `avg_fragmentation_in_percent` should be as close to zero as possible for maximum performance. However, up to 10% might be acceptable without noticeable degradation.

Shrinking Data Files

Free space can be reclaimed from the end of data files to remove unused pages and recover disk space. However, shrinking data files is not recommended unless the database has lost at least half of its data. This typically occurs after an activity has been performed that creates whitespace in the database, such as moving a large amount of data from one database to another or deleting a large amount of data. Shrinking Skype for Business Server databases is generally not recommended because there are typically not enough deletions to cause a significant amount of free space.

Creating SQL Server Maintenance Plans

Maintaining the Skype for Business Server Back End databases is important to the overall health and performance of a Skype for Business deployment. Yet this is an aspect that frequently gets overlooked, primarily because administrators are kept busy caring for other aspects of the Skype for Business environment.

Fortunately, Microsoft has provided maintenance plans as a way to automate the tasks required to maintain SQL database health. A maintenance plan performs a comprehensive set of SQL Server jobs that run at scheduled intervals. For example, a maintenance plan can include tasks that ensure that databases are performing optimally, are regularly backed up, and are checked for anomalies.

TIP

SQL maintenance plans should be scheduled to run during off-peak hours to minimize the performance impact.

The example SQL Server maintenance plan configuration shown next is based on SQL Server 2014. The following steps are used to configure a SQL Server database maintenance plan:

1. Log on to the server where Skype for Business Back End databases are installed using an account with SQL administrative rights and then open SQL Server Management Studio.

2. At the Connect to Server prompt, keep the default options of connecting to the local server with Windows Authentication and then click Connect.

3. In the Object Explorer, expand Management and then right-click Maintenance Plans and select Maintenance Plan Wizard.

TIP

If the Maintenance Plan Wizard is initiated on a new instance of SQL Server, an error might occur stating that the command cannot be executed due to the security configuration for the server. If this is the case, the SQL Server Agent extended stored procedures need to be enabled. You can do this by executing the following statements in the SQL Query window:

```
sp_configure 'show advanced options', 1;
GO
RECONFIGURE;
GO
sp_configure 'Agent XPs', 1;
GO
RECONFIGURE
GO
```

4. At the SQL Maintenance Plan Wizard screen, click Next to begin the configuration.
5. At the Select Plan Properties screen, enter a name and description for the maintenance plan. Several options are also presented for the scheduling of the maintenance plan. To configure separate schedules for individual tasks within a single maintenance plan, select Separate Schedules for Each Task. To configure a single schedule for the entire plan, select Single Schedule for the Entire Plan or No Schedule. If this option is selected, the Change button is available to configure the scheduling for the plan.
6. Click Change to display the New Job Schedule dialog box. Select from the available scheduling options to configure the frequency and timing of the plan. When finished, click OK to save the schedule. Click Next to continue with the Maintenance Plan Wizard.
7. On the Select Maintenance Tasks screen, select the maintenance tasks to include in the plan and then click Next to continue.
8. At the Select Maintenance Task Order page, review the order in which the tasks will be executed. If necessary, change the order by selecting a task and then clicking either Move Up or Move Down as needed. When finished, click Next.
9. The wizard now provides options for each task that was selected.

TIP

From the list of available maintenance tasks, the Check Database Integrity and Maintenance Cleanup tasks should be selected for all Skype for Business Server databases. It is also recommended to *not* select the Shrink Database task, primarily because the automatic shrinking of databases on a routine basis leads to excessive fragmentation as well as excessive I/O, which can negatively impact the performance of Skype for Business Server.

10. Continue the configuration of each task that was selected as part of the maintenance plan on each successive screen, selecting the desired options.

11. At the Select Report Options page, keep the default option of Write a Report to a Text File and then change the report file location if necessary. If an email report is desired, select this option and enter the target email address. When finished, click Next.

12. At the Complete the Wizard screen, review the listed options for accuracy and then click Finish to complete the wizard.

Summary

Skype for Business Server 2015 depends on a number of external systems to provide needed functionality. Active Directory and DNS provide vital infrastructure services, and server certificates are used to secure communications between systems. There are various network dependencies that need to be considered and planned. Office Web Apps Server provides an enhanced meeting experience for sharing PowerPoint. SQL Server 2008 R2, 2012, and 2014 provide the database storage.

CHAPTER 11

Firewall, Reverse Proxy, and Security Requirements

IN THIS CHAPTER

- Firewall Requirements
- Ports Required for Internal and External Access
- Using Network Address Translation (NAT)
- Reverse Proxy Requirements
- File Share Permissions
- Securing Service Accounts
- Security Threats

Most companies deploy Skype for Business Server 2015 so that they can support IM and conferencing services with users who connect from outside the corporate network. To properly protect the Skype for Business Server 2015 systems from attack, apply a layered approach to security that's practical and addresses the security requirements for your organization. In the case of Skype for Business Server 2015, this means a combination of firewalls, Edge Servers, reverse proxies, an intrusion detection system (IDS) solution, and a vetted methodology for provisioning access to internal resources and services.

This chapter lays out approaches for applying layers of security onto Skype for Business Server 2015. Although securing an environment (preventing unauthorized access from the Internet) and enforcing secure practices (such as configuring accounts for least privilege) can be a fair amount of effort, the benefits reaped in terms of security greatly outweigh the efforts. The lack of strong security measures and policies to protect your organization's crown jewels (that is, intellectual property) as well as your customers' privacy often result in catastrophic consequences both in reputation and financially, as evidenced by hackings of Target, Sony, Ashley Madison, and many other organizations.

Firewall Requirements

Wikipedia defines a *firewall* as a part of a computer system or network that is designed to block unauthorized access while permitting authorized communications. It is a device or set of devices configured to permit or deny computer applications based on a set of rules and other criteria.

There are several types of firewall techniques, including the following:

- **Packet filtering**—Packet filtering inspects packets as they are passed through the network and rejects or accepts these packets based on defined rules. Typically, these rules will specify a source and destination address, a port, and either an allow or deny statement to define the behavior of the packet-filtering rule. Packet-filtering firewalls are generally fast but can be difficult to configure for applications that dynamically choose ports for communications after an initial handshake.
- **Application gateway**—Application gateways apply security enforcement to specific applications. In other words, the gateway understands the applications and can recognize their packets. It makes its decisions based on which applications are allowed to pass through the firewall. Application gateways can be relatively easy to configure but are generally processor intensive and therefore cannot handle as much throughput as a packet-filtering firewall.
- **Proxy/reverse proxy server**—A proxy server intercepts all messages entering and leaving the network. It inspects the packets and then continues the conversation on behalf of the protected system. In this way, packets never go directly from the source to the protected destination or from the protected source directly to the uncontrolled destination. Not unlike applications gateways, proxy servers are processor intensive.

Network-Based Firewalls

Most implementations of Skype for Business Server 2015 deploy the Edge Server and reverse proxy behind a network-based firewall, thus creating a buffer between the Internet and these servers, and deploy another network-based firewall between the internal network and Edge Server and reverse proxy. The network between these two sets of network-based firewalls is referred as the *network perimeter* or *demilitarized zone* (DMZ). The purpose of a firewall is to ensure that only the necessary Skype for Business services are available externally.

Dual firewalls are technically more secure because if an attacker compromises the firewall that's exposed externally, the attacker would still have to compromise the second (or internal) firewall before gaining access to the internal hosts.

The first step in implementing this type of firewall for Skype for Business Server 2015 is to understand what services you plan to expose externally, and then you need to determine exactly which ports and protocols need to be opened on the firewalls.

Microsoft does not recommend placing firewalls between internal users or internal users and Skype for Business pools because these internal firewalls can block or substantially limit optimal communication traffic that is dynamically established between these endpoints using the ICE protocol.

TIP

By default, Skype for Business clients send media using dynamic ports over the port range 1024–65535. If your organization has internal firewalls restricting access between users, you will need to coordinate with your firewall administrator to specify which port ranges Skype for Business clients are allowed to use. You can then restrict Skype for Business clients to use this limited media port range using the PowerShell command `Set-CsConferencingConfiguration`. This media port range configuration can be applied at the global, site, or server level.

Using Operating System Firewalls

In Windows Server 2003 SP1, Microsoft introduced an integrated firewall into the Windows operating system. As with most Microsoft products, it has improved with each iteration. Flash-forward to Windows Server 2012, and you find that the integrated firewall is quite good. Skype for Business Server 2015 does an excellent job of integrating into the Windows Server Firewall at the time of installation.

Layering an OS-layer firewall with a network-layer firewall is an excellent way to improve overall security of a system with minimal expense. With these two layered together, if the network firewall becomes compromised, the attacker has to pierce the OS-layer firewall to compromise the computer. Similarly, given that many attack vectors can come from within the company itself, the OS-layer firewall offers protection from trusted systems that might have become compromised.

When installing Skype for Business Server 2015 on Windows Server, it is not necessary to turn off Windows Firewall.

If the Windows Firewall is enabled and started at the time of installation of Skype for Business Server 2015 components, the necessary exceptions are created automatically.

CAUTION

Although many administrators are tempted to disable the Windows Firewall, it is certainly worth leaving it in place with the necessary rules configured.

TIP

If Windows Firewall was off during the first installation, you can simply turn on Windows Firewall and run step 2 in the Skype for Business Server 2015 Deployment Wizard to configure an exception in the Windows Firewall Rules for Skype for Business Server 2015.

Ports Required for Internal and External Access

The specific ports needed to open on a firewall vary depending on which services are placed in the DMZ and which services need to be accessible from the Internet.
This section summarizes commonly deployed DMZ server roles and the ports necessary to

support them. The description calls out the port, traffic type, type of firewall it applies to (internal or external), and purpose for the opening.

Table 11.1 describes, in detail, the port requirements for publishing Skype for Business through the reverse proxy.

TABLE 11.1 Reverse Proxy Port Requirements

Service	Protocol	Port	Direction	Description
External interface	HTTP	80	Inbound	(Optional) Redirects to HTTPS. This port is required to be opened inbound for Office Web Apps and autodiscover.
External interface	HTTPS	443	Inbound	This port must be opened inbound to allow web traffic for autodiscover, joining meetings, dial-in conferencing, address book downloads, address book web queries, client updates, Skype for Business Mobile clients, Skype for Business Web Apps, EWS, and Office Web Apps.
Internal interface	HTTP	8080	Inbound	External web traffic sent to port 80 on the external interface is routed internally to Skype for Business Web services over port 8080.
Internal interface	HTTPS	4443	Inbound	External web traffic sent to port 443 on the external interface is routed internally to Skype for Business Web services over port 4443.
Internal interface	HTTPS	443	Inbound	This port is used by Office Web Apps Server by Skype to do PowerPoint presentations by Business clients.

Table 11.2 describes, in detail, the port requirements for the Edge Server with three separate public-facing IP addresses. In the case where the Edge Server is NAT-ed and exposes a single public IP address externally, you cannot use the same port (443) for the Access Edge, A/V Edge, and Web Conferencing Edge. You will need to specify different ports. Only one of the Edges can be assigned port 443.

TABLE 11.2 Edge Server Port Requirements

Service	Protocol	Port	Direction	Description
A/V Edge	TCP	50000–59999	Inbound	These ports are required to be opened inbound only for A/V if federating with OCS 2007.
A/V Edge	TCP	50000–59999	Outbound	These ports should be opened outbound for federation, as well as for ensuring the optimal media path for internal-to-external communications for Desktop Sharing.

A/V Edge	UDP	50000–59999	Inbound/outbound	These ports are required for A/V only if federating with OCS 2007.
A/V Edge	UDP	3478	Inbound/outbound	You must open this port for media to flow among all internal and external participants, including federation.
A/V Edge	TCP	443	Inbound	You must open this port for media to flow among all internal and external participants, including federation.
Access Edge	TCP	80	Outbound	You must allow Certificate Revocation List check requests outbound from the Edge Server for federation.
Access Edge	TCP/UDP	53	Outbound	The Edge Server must be able to query external DNS.
Access Edge	TCP	443	Inbound	You must allow remote users to connect to the Access Edge over 443 using TLS.
Access Edge	TCP	5061	Inbound/outbound	This port must be opened inbound and outbound to allow for federation. These connections will use TLS.
Web Conferencing Edge	TCP	443	Inbound	This port must be open to allow for web conferencing traffic.
XMPP Service	TCP	5269	Inbound/outbound	If XMPP federation is enabled, you must allow this port for XMPP federation to work.
Internal Edge Service	TCP	5061	Inbound/outbound	You must open this port between the internal servers (Director, Front End, and so on) and the internal Edge interface.
Internal Edge Service	TCP	8057	Inbound	All Front End Servers must be able to communicate with the Edge Server on 8057 for Web Conferencing media traffic.
Internal Edge Service	UDP	3478	Inbound	You must open this port to allow internal clients to communicate with the internal Edge for media traversal.
Internal Edge Service	TCP	443	Inbound	You must open this port to allow internal clients to communicate with the internal Edge for media traversal.
Internal Edge Service	TCP	5062	Inbound	You must open this port to allow all Front End Servers to communicate with the Media Relay Authentication Service (MRAS).
Internal Edge Service	TCP	4443	Inbound	This port must be opened to the Edge Server to allow for CMS replication and Skype Directory Search.

(Continued)

TABLE 11.2 (*Continued*)

Service	Protocol	Port	Direction	Description
Internal Edge Service	TCP	50001–50003	Inbound	This port must be opened to the Edge Server to allow the Central Logging Server (CLS) to collect logs from the Edge Server.

NOTE

The terms *inbound* and *outbound* refer to the direction between the Internet or internal network and the specified Edge service. For example, if the service is A/V Edge, and the column in the table says "Inbound," you must open the port with the destination address of the A/V Edge service IP address.

Using Network Address Translation (NAT) with Skype for Business Server 2015

Firewall NAT-ing of the external network interfaces is supported for single Edge Server deployments or Edge pool deployments that use DNS load balancing. NAT is not supported on the internal network interface of the Edge Server or Edge pool. NAT effectively takes packets bound for the firewall and forwards them to hosts inside the firewall based on port rules. This enables a company with limited numbers of routable IP addresses to support multiple services with fewer public IP addresses. In addition, it enables protected systems to hide their IP information because they never appear to be the source of a packet on the Internet; the firewall always appears to be the source. The NAT address for the A/V Edge must be specified in Topology Builder.

TIP

If you enable NAT for the external firewall, configure firewall filters that are used for traffic from the Internet to the Edge Server with Destination Network Address Translation (DNAT). Similarly, configure and filter for traffic going from the Edge Server to the Internet with Source Network Address Translation (SNAT). Note that the inbound and outbound filters for this purpose must use the same internal and external addresses. If externally the Edge is reachable at 11.22.33.44 and is mapped to an Edge Server internally at 10.1.1.44, outbound traffic from the Edge Server, 10.1.1.44, out to the Internet needs to come from the external IP address, 11.22.33.44. Although this might seem obvious, there are many situations in which all internal hosts appear to come from the same IP address. This is called PAT, or Port Address Translation, or is sometimes called NAT overload.

CAUTION

NAT-ing is not supported for Edge pool configurations that are load balanced using a hardware load balancer (HLB) because this would result in NAT-ing the connection twice, which is not supported for audio/video traffic. Therefore, the external firewall cannot be configured for NAT.

Reverse Proxy Requirements

Using reverse proxies such as F5, NetScaler, and A10 is an excellent way to securely publish applications such as Skype for Business Server 2015 to the Internet. Reverse proxies provide an intermediary layer between internal web servers and the Internet. Web requests from the Internet cannot reach internal web servers directly; they are proxied by reverse proxies. This best practice is recommended for exposing Skype for Business web services to the Internet. The following sections discuss how to configure reverse proxies to work with Skype for Business Server 2015.

Why a Reverse Proxy Is Required

It is important to understand why a reverse proxy solution is required for Skype for Business Server 2015. A reverse proxy is required to publish Skype for Business web services to external users. These web services are responsible for the following:

- **Autodiscover**—`lyncdiscover.<SIP domain>` is the preferred DNS record for Skype for Business clients to discover the organization's Skype for Business Server.
- **Simple URL publishing**—Allows users to join a Skype for Business meeting or obtain meeting dial-in information.
- **Meeting Web Scheduler**—This web service allows users to schedule a Skype for Business meeting without using the Skype for Business plug-in for Microsoft Outlook.
- **Web conferencing content**—Allows users to share collaboration content (application, desktop, whiteboard) during a Skype for Business meeting.
- **Address book and distribution list (DL) expansion**—Used by Skype for Business clients to download the Address Book and perform group expansion of distribution lists (DL). This enables users to search other internal users and groups.
- **Windows authentication**—Remote users can sign in to Skype for Business Server using NTLM authentication. Kerberos authentication is not possible for remote users.
- **Certificate provisioning**—Skype for Business Server supports client certificate authentication (TLS-DSK) to authenticate remote users. This web service allows remote clients to obtain a certificate from Skype for Business web services. Once obtained, the Skype for Business client can authenticate the user using the certificate instead of prompting for the user's username and password (NTLM).
- **Passive authentication**—Skype for Business Server supports OAuth to authenticate remote users. Skype for Business Server 2015 can be configured to enforce passive authentication for mobile clients only if desired. Passive authentication enables multifactor authentication (MFA) when integrated with a third security token service (STS).
- **Web ticket**—Once the remote user is authenticated using NTLM, TLS-DSK, or passive authentication, Skype for Business Server 2015 issues a compact web ticket (CWT) to the client. This CWT, similar to a cookie, allows the user to remain

authenticated for 8 hours without the server challenging the user to re-authenticate with each subsequent request. The Skype for Business client refreshes the CWT by TLS-DSK authentication using the client certificate before it expires in order to remain authenticated to the server.

- **Device updates**—Skype for Business Phone Edition devices require access to the Skype for Business Web Services to obtain software updates.
- **RGS client access**—This web service allows Skype for Business users to participate in a response group service remotely.
- **Web App**—This Skype for Business web service allows participants to join a Skype for Business meeting from a browser for those users who do not have a Skype for Business client.
- **Mobility**—Skype for Business clients on the mobile platforms Windows Phone, Android, and Apple iOS connect through the Skype for Business UCWA web services.

In addition to these Skype for Business web services that a reverse proxy exposes to the Internet, remote Skype for Business clients need access to Exchange Web Services (EWS) to obtain calendar information and join meetings. If the reverse proxy does not publish Exchange Autodiscover and EWS to the Internet, the functionality of remote Skype for Business clients will be impaired.

To share PowerPoint presentations, Skype for Business Server 2015 leverages Office Web Apps Server to enable this functionality. To allow remote Skype for Business clients to share PowerPoint presentations, Office Web Apps server must be published through the reverse proxy; otherwise, remote users will not be able to present or view PowerPoint presentations.

Deploying a reverse proxy solution with Skype for Business Server 2015 is absolutely critical in order to enable external user access. To deploy Skype for Business Web services, the reverse proxy solution must meet the following requirements:

- **HTTPS publishing**—Devices must be capable of securely publishing application content. Devices that support this functionality will specifically call this out as a feature.
- **SSL bridging**—Skype for Business Server 2015 requires the reverse proxy to listen for connections on TCP port 443 and bridge those connections to the Front End Web services on TCP port 4443. This is required because the Skype for Business web services contain separate virtual web directories. The external Skype for Business web services directory listens on port 4443 and should be used when publishing to the Internet.
- **Authentication bypass**—The reverse proxy should allow user authentication to occur at the Skype for Business Servers, not be authenticated by the reverse proxy itself.

CAUTION

It is not recommended (or supported by Microsoft) to deploy external web services without a reverse proxy solution. Do not use NAT as a replacement for a reverse proxy solution.

TIP

As a low-cost alternative, you can use Microsoft Application Request Routing (ARR) as a software-based reverse proxy. ARR is installed on a Windows Server with IIS configured.

Certificate Requirements

Chapter 10, "Dependent Services," covers certificate requirements in detail. In general, the reverse proxy certificate requires a public certificate with the following entries:

- **Skype for Business web services external FQDN**—This is defined in the topology and should be configured as the Subject Name (SN) of the certificate.
- **Simple URL entries**—There should be a certificate entry in the subject alternative name (SAN) field for every meeting and dial-in URL. There is typically a single dial-in FQDN, and there is a meeting FQDN for each SIP domain your organization is authoritative for.
- **LyncDiscover**—Skype for Business clients discover your Skype for Business Servers by querying for the DNS entry `lyncdiscover.<sipdomain>`. The first authentication is against this URL over HTTPS. As such, the reverse proxy certificate requires an entry for each SIP domain in the SAN.

Reverse Proxy Configuration

This section outlines tasks for configuring a reverse proxy for Skype for Business Server 2015.

Creating DNS Records for Reverse Proxy

To enable clients on the Internet to find Skype for Business Server 2015, add an address (A) record to an external DNS that is authoritative for your organization's domain. This includes (A) records, as described in Chapter 10.

NOTE

The procedure for creating records depends on the domain name server used. In the case of an externally hosted DNS, it might be as simple as calling your service provider and requesting the records.

Keep in mind that it might take several minutes to as much as a few hours for the new records to propagate and become available to clients.

On most reverse proxies, it is possible to have all external Skype for Business web services DNS records point to the same IP address.

Verifying Access to Skype for Business Web Services

Assuming that the firewall rules are in place and that the necessary DNS records are published externally, use the test connectivity tool (https://testconnectivity.microsoft.com)

from Microsoft to verify that your Skype for Business web services are accessible through your reverse proxy. This web-based utility will validate whether your Exchange Server and Skype for Business Server are correctly published to the Internet.

File Share Permissions

Skype for Business Server 2015 utilizes a file share for each pool. You can use the same file share for multiple pools or a separate file share per pool. This file share is used to store conferencing, CMS configuration replication, and address book information. This file share has strict permission requirements, and Skype for Business Server 2015 will assign permissions to these file shares during the deployment of your pools. Do not change the file share security permissions.

When deploying any Skype for Business Server 2015 topology changes, you must make sure that you have read/write access to the file shares in the topology. When you publish a topology change, Topology Builder will validate permissions on the file shares.

TIP

If the file-share permissions are ever changed by accident, simply publish the Skype for Business Server 2015 topology again and these permissions will be re-created.

Securing Service Accounts

When you are deploying Edge Servers in the DMZ, these Windows Servers are not domain-joined to the internal Active Directory Domain Services to maintain separation of access between the DMZ and the internal network. The same is true if using a Windows Server-based reverse proxy. Resources in the DMZ should not have direct or permissive access to the internal network unless explicitly permitted.

By limiting access to internal resources from the systems in the DMZ, you reduce the opportunities an attacker can leverage to access the internal network. This includes service accounts. The service account used by Skype for Business Server 2015 to run the Edge services are local accounts and not domain accounts. The Edge services use the Network Service account. This way, should the Edge Server become compromised, this service account doesn't have any permissions to internal resources.

Security Threats

Any server product that exposes services to the Internet is at risk of being compromised and becoming a conduit for unauthorized access into the organization's internal network. Skype for Business Server 2015 is no different. The primary entry points into a corporate network's Skype for Business Servers are the Edge Servers, reverse proxies, and the Session Border Controller (SBC).

The Edge Server is used for federation and remote user access. It allows Internet access to the following protocols:

- **SIP**—Used for signaling and IM traffic
- **SRTP**—Used for audio/video traffic
- **PSOM**—Used for web conferencing traffic

The reverse proxy provides access to Skype for Business mobile clients and Web App and other web services. It allows Internet access to internal Skype for Business web services over HTTPS.

The SBC is used as a point of demarcation between your network and the ITSP when connecting Enterprise Voice to the PSTN. The SBC, though generally connected to the ITSP through a private network, can use the Internet as an interconnect.

Each of the entry points (that is, ports) used by Skype for Business Server 2015 may be susceptible to attack, and the protocols used through these ports can be exploited. It is no longer sufficient to restrict port access as a security measure. All web services use the same port (443, for example). Therefore, blocking external access to port 443 is not a practical solution. In order to control access at a more granular level, it is necessary to secure access at the protocol level. Table 11.3 outlines the ports and protocols for all the functionality used by Skype for Business clients.

TABLE 11.3 Ports and Protocols for External Access to Skype for Business Server 2015 from the Internet

Functionality	Product	External Entry Point	Protocol	Port
Remote access	Skype for Business	Edge Server – Access Edge	SIP	TCP:443
Federation	Skype for Business	Edge Server – Access Edge	SIP	TCP:5061
Audio/video	Skype for Business	Edge Server – A/V Edge	SRTP	TCP:443, UDP:3478
Web conferencing	Skype for Business	Edge Server – Conf Edge	PSOM	TCP:443
File transfer	Skype for Business	Edge Server – A/V Edge	ICE	TCP:443
XMPP interop	Skype for Business	Edge Server – Access Edge	XMPP	TCP:5269
Application sharing	Skype for Business	Edge Server – A/V Edge	RDP	TCP:443
Dial-in	Skype for Business	Reverse Proxy	HTTPS	TCP:443
Address book	Skype for Business	Reverse Proxy	HTTPS	TCP:443
Certificate provisioning	Skype for Business	Reverse Proxy	HTTPS	TCP:443

(Continued)

TABLE 11.3 *(Continued)*

Functionality	Product	External Entry Point	Protocol	Port
Lyncdiscover	Skype for Business	Reverse Proxy	HTTPS	TCP:443
Group expansion	Skype for Business	Reverse Proxy	HTTPS	TCP:443
Mobility	Skype for Business	Reverse Proxy	HTTPS	TCP:443
Meeting join	Skype for Business	Reverse Proxy	HTTPS	TCP:443
Passive authentication	Skype for Business	Reverse Proxy	HTTPS	TCP:443
Persistent chat website	Skype for Business	Reverse Proxy	HTTPS	TCP:443
Skype Web App	Skype for Business	Reverse Proxy	HTTPS	TCP:443
Request handler	Skype for Business	Reverse Proxy	HTTPS	TCP:443
Response group client access	Skype for Business	Reverse Proxy	HTTPS	TCP:443
Meeting Web scheduler	Skype for Business	Reverse Proxy	HTTPS	TCP:443
Storage	Skype for Business	Reverse Proxy	HTTPS	TCP:443
UCWA	Skype for Business	Reverse Proxy	HTTPS	TCP:443
Web ticket	Skype for Business	Reverse Proxy	HTTPS	TCP:443
Calendar and free busy information	Exchange	Reverse Proxy	HTTPS	TCP:443
PowerPoint sharing	Office Web Apps	Reverse Proxy	HTTPS	TCP:443

The first step in protecting your organization is studying the possible risks of attacks. Although the number of open ports necessary for Skype for Business Server 2015 is smaller than the number of protocols used, the number of different protocols to inspect is large.

For the most part, Skype for Business Server 2015, Exchange, and Office Web Apps servers require users to authenticate before their clients can access any resources. However, this still leaves open several opportunities for attack that many organizations that have deployed Skype for Business Server 2015 or Lync Server are not aware of. Attacks on Skype for Business Server 2015 can be categorized into the following main classes:

- Attacks on Skype for Business Servers
- Attacks on user accounts
- Attacks on the authentication protocol
- Attacks on clients

These categories of attacks are discussed in the context of Skype for Business Server 2015 in more details next.

Attacks on Skype for Business Servers

When your Skype for Business Server 2015 infrastructure is configured for federation, external access, or anonymous meeting joins, you must deploy an Edge Server and publish Skype for Business Server 2015 through a reverse proxy, or in most cases do both. This exposes your internal Skype for Business Servers to potential attacks, which you should be aware of and determine whether a countermeasure is a requirement for your organization.

Federation-Specific Attacks

In the case of federation, the Edge Server is the conduit into your internal network. You should determine whether any organization is permitted to connect to yours or whether access is restricted to specific organizations controlled by your organization. Are internal users permitted to communicate with consumers on the Skype network? This decision determines the type of federation and public IM connectivity (PIC) to configure.

Once you've determined the type of federation (see Chapter 32, "Planning to Deploy External Services") to use, your organization may require further restrictions such as the ability to restrict specific groups of internal users to federate with select partners. This type of ethical wall restriction may be a corporate policy requirement or government requirement for privacy or compliance reasons.

In Skype for Business Server 2015, it is possible to block federated users from seeing the presence or contacting internal users until the internal user adds the federated user to their contact list. This behavior is configurable in Skype for Business Server 2015 on a per-federated-SIP-domain basis. To configure this feature, change the parameter `VerificationLevel` to `AlwaysUnverifiable` for the desired federation domain. This setting is only configurable from PowerShell for Skype for Business Server 2015 (on-premises) by calling the cmdlet `Set-CsAllowedDomains`. Run the cmdlet `Get-CsAllowedDomains` to validate your configuration.

However, this feature may not be sufficient because it would only enforce this behavior on a federated SIP domain basis, and not be sufficient granularly to restrict only specific groups of people to communicate across corporate boundaries. Policy-driven requirements may further dictate which forms of communications (IM, audio, video, application sharing, file transfer) are permitted. The `AlwaysUnverifiable` option does not restrict the type of media that can be used between internal users and federated users.

Specific industries require auditing of communications and restricting certain types of information from crossing corporate boundaries to meet compliance regulations, such as preventing insider trading fraud or divulging confidential information. You should determine whether you might not be in compliance when enabling Skype for Business federation.

This level of granular control of federation is not available in Skype for Business Server and requires integration with third-party solutions (such as Lync-Solutions, Actiance, and MultiUX).

Attacks on Anonymous Meeting Joins

If internal users are permitted to schedule meetings that allow external users to participate as anonymous users, you are opening direct access to your Skype for Business Servers without requiring any authentication. Intruders can discover your users' meeting URL through brute force, or in the case of static meeting URLs, each internal user reuses the same URL assigned to them for every meeting. In this particular case, an intruder only needs to be invited to a meeting once by an internal user, and the assailant knows the internal user's meeting URL.

In either case, every attempt to join a Skype for Business meeting results in the internal Skype for Business Servers having to process the request, whether it's valid or not. With a sufficient number of such meeting join requests, valuable resources on the Skype for Business Server 2015 will be consumed, and potentially exhaust the server's resources, causing a denial-of-service attack. If your Skype for Business Server 2015 infrastructure is considered mission-critical, which it should when using Enterprise Voice, such DoS attacks could be catastrophic to your organization's business.

Attacks on User Accounts

If your Skype for Business Server 2015 infrastructure is configured to allow users to sign in remotely from outside your corporate network, then intruders can attack your user accounts. The simplest attack is locking out user accounts by attempting too many invalid sign-ins. If your AD Directory Services enforces an account lockout, then user accounts enabled for Skype for Business can easily be locked out. This disruption of service is a nuisance because it requires the legitimate users to contact the helpdesk to get their accounts unlocked.

In the worst case, an intruder can brute-force a user's account password, particularly if an account lockout policy isn't enforced. Once the intruder cracks the user's password, they'll have full access to internal resources that the user has permissions to, and it might be months before the intrusion is detected.

Attacks on user accounts can come through two paths. Attacks can target the Edge Server and reverse proxy because Skype for Business Server 2015 requires remote users to sign in through SIP and HTTPS.

Because Skype for Business clients also connect to Exchange Server to retrieve the users' calendar information and free busy information, attacks on users' account passwords are not limited to Skype for Business Server 2015, but can also target Exchange Server.

When planning your security response, it's important to think holistically. If remote users can authenticate and connect to several services (Skype for Business, Exchange, SharePoint, web services, and so on), you should consider enforcing a centralized audit trail of all login attempts, both successful and failed logins. If you can control login access at the DMZ by enforcing account lockout policy at the network perimeter, you protect users logged in internally from being locked out.

Attacks on Authentication Protocol

Skype for Business Server 2015 allows remote users to authenticate using the following authentication protocols: NTLM, TLS-DSK, and Passive Authentication.

NTLM relies on the user's Active Directory username and password to authenticate the user. This information can be stolen without the user's awareness. A user's account could be compromised for months before the organization may become aware of the breach. Therefore, it becomes critical that users only sign in from secured devices and not enter their credentials on unsecure devices where these credentials can be stolen (through keyloggers, for example). Also, if a user can authenticate to a network service with their NTLM credentials, an attacker can attempt to brute-force the user's credentials by attempting all possible combinations against the server. Therefore, it is important to secure your Edge Servers against denial-of-service (DoS) and password brute-force attacks.

TLS-DSK relies on a client certificate to authenticate the user. This protocol is more secure because it requires an intruder to steal the private key associated with that certificate. In theory, this is more secure because the private key is marked as non-exportable when stored in the user's Personal certificate store in Windows and tied to the specific device; however, it has been found that a private key can be stolen using a utility called mimikatz. Although the level of difficulty in stealing the client certificate private key is much higher, it isn't foolproof.

It becomes important to use additional security methods such as tracking every device from which users sign in to Skype for Business because each device will have obtained a client certificate allowing it to connect on behalf of the user.

Should a Skype for Business device get lost or stolen, you should revoke the user's client certificate issued to that device to prevent it from signing in to your Skype for Business Servers. Skype for Business Server 2015 issues the certificate to the user and not the user's device. However, a different user certificate is issued to each device, making the user certificate unique for each device. Therefore, you must revoke the user's certificate issued to the device that was stolen or lost. Alternatively, you can revoke all certificates issued to that user. The client certificate can be revoked using the PowerShell command `revoke-CsClientCertificate`.

CAUTION

Revoking the user's certificate does not immediately restrict the device's access to Skype for Business Server 2015. If the Skype for Business client on that device is still signed in, the device may remain connected up to 8 hours until its compact web ticket (CWT) expires. It will request a new user certificate from Skype for Business Server 2015. To prevent the device from requesting a new user certificate and remain connected, you must disable the user's account before revoking the user certificate assigned to the stolen device.

Here is the complete procedure:

1. Temporarily disable the user account in Skype for Business (see Figure 11.1). All the user's Skype for Business clients will get disconnected.
2. Wait a minimum of 15 minutes.
3. Revoke the device's user certificate.

4. Reset the user's account password or force the user to change their password; otherwise, the stolen device will be automatically signed in to Skype for Business if the user's password is saved and will request another user certificate.

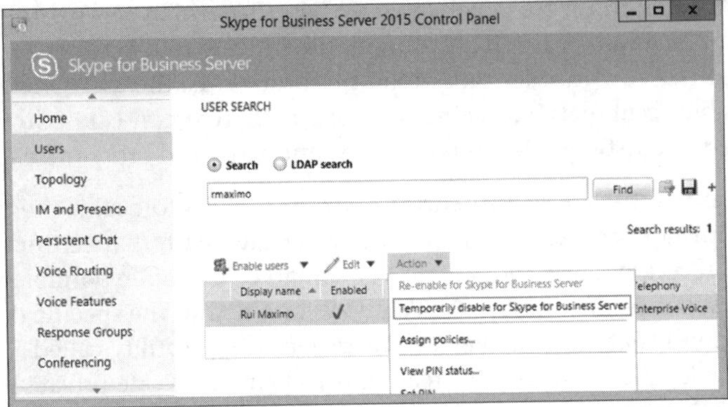

FIGURE 11.1 Temporarily disable user for Skype for Business.

Passive Authentication enables organizations to use an alternate authentication token than the user's Active Directory username and password. Passive Authentication allows Skype for Business Server 2015 to offload the authentication process to a different server, referred as the Security Token Service (STS). ADFS is Microsoft's STS, but still relies on Active Directory as the authoritative source of user identity. This means the user is still authenticated based on their Active Directory credentials, which essentially is equivalent to authenticating using NTLM. To authenticate using an alternate form of authentication, you must leverage a third-party STS to use a different source of user identity not tied to the user's credentials from Active Directory.

By using a different source of user authentication for Skype for Business, you enable the user's Active Directory credentials to remain uncompromised when potentially compromised devices are used. Passive Authentication is not an authentication method of itself, but allows alternate forms of authentication such as one-time passwords (OTPs) or other forms of authentication challenges enforced by the STS.

Attacks on Clients

Skype for Business clients are extensions of the corporate network because they have access to internal resources. By stealing a user's device, the intruder can gain access to the user's corporate data (contact list, conversation history, address book, meeting information) stored by the Skype for Business client. To protect the data stored by Skype for Business Mobile, all data at rest is encrypted. In addition to encrypting data stored by the Skype for Business Mobile client, you can enable a PIN lock that's separate from the device PIN lock as an added measure of security.

Summary

As shown in this chapter, properly securing a Skype for Business Server 2015 implementation is an important process because it protects the servers from potential exploitation. By utilizing existing technologies such as firewalls and reverse proxies, one can greatly reduce the attack surface of Skype for Business Server 2015. Through the use of limited rights and managed service accounts, one can greatly reduce the possibility of unauthorized users gaining access to the new system.

Configuring protective features in the operating system is a relatively painless process that can go a long way toward securing the overall implementation. Tasks as simple as limiting rights to shares and controlling services will also serve to reduce the surface area of attack of your Skype for Business Server 2015 deployment. This process of locking down systems is especially important if servers will be accessible from outside the organization.

Following defense-in-depth best practices, it is recommended that you harden the Windows Server running the Edge Server even if it's deployed behind an Internet-facing firewall. Microsoft has published a security whitepaper, Microsoft Lync Server 2010 Security Guide, with best practices that remains mostly applicable for Skype for Business Server 2015. You can download it from https://www.microsoft.com/en-us/download/details.aspx?id=2729.

CHAPTER 12

Monitoring Skype for Business Server 2015

IN THIS CHAPTER

- Understanding Key Areas to Monitor in Your Deployment
- Monitoring the Health and Performance of Skype for Business Server 2015

Organizations deploying Skype for Business Server 2015 all have unique requirements for monitoring the health, performance, and usage of the environment. At a minimum, all organizations should be concerned with the health and performance of the environment, and organizations in certain verticals will be required to retain usage data for regulatory purposes. Skype for Business Server 2015 includes many tools that enable organizations to meet monitoring and archiving needs of all types. In addition to built-in tools, a rich ecosystem exists with many third-party vendors catering to the needs of all organizations.

This chapter provides an understanding of key areas to monitor in Skype for Business Server 2015, as well as of the features and tools available to perform such monitoring.

Understanding Key Areas to Monitor in Your Deployment

When you are deploying Skype for Business Server 2015, it is important to identify all monitoring and archiving requirements for the organization deploying the solution. Every organization deploying Skype for Business Server 2015 should be encouraged to monitor the health and performance of the environment. Additionally, many organizations require communication data retention for legal compliance purposes.

Clearly, outlining requirements and strategies for monitoring and archiving will go a long way in ensuring a successful Skype for Business Server 2015 deployment. The sections that follow provide a definition of each common requirement and common examples of where each one would apply.

Health and Performance Requirements

Monitoring the health and performance of the environment should be a top priority for any Skype for Business Server 2015 deployment. Without the proper tools in place, guaranteeing service availability and troubleshooting service quality issues are nearly impossible. Skype for Business Server 2015 spans many different IT systems in order to provide services to end users. Monitoring the Skype for Business Server 2015 solution from end to end enables administrators to confidently support all Skype for Business Server 2015 modalities. At the same time, solutions that monitor the entire Skype for Business Server 2015 solution enable upper management to have insight into the health of the environment, and to have confidence in the system deployed.

Monitoring the health of the Skype for Business Server 2015 environment can be accomplished in various ways. The details of how to use these tools for health monitoring are described in later sections, but they include the following:

- Windows event logs
- Skype for Business Server 2015 synthetic transactions
- System Center Operations Manager (SCOM)
- Third-party (non-Microsoft) monitoring solutions
- Call Quality Dashboard (CQD)

In addition to monitoring the overall health of the environment, you should carefully monitor the performance of the system. When Skype for Business Server 2015 is being deployed, careful planning will ensure that capacity requirements are met. However, it is important to identify performance baselines and to monitor system performance for issues. There are many instances in which systems can malfunction or usage has simply increased, which can result in service degradation. Although performance is a contributing factor to the health of the environment, it is important to identify performance baselines as well as ongoing monitoring as separate tasks in the deployment and post-deployment phases.

Performance can be monitored using various tools. This chapter outlines how to use the following tools in later sections:

- Windows Performance Monitor (Perfmon)
- SCOM
- Third-party network monitoring tools

When planning to establish performance baselines and performance monitoring, do not forget the supporting infrastructure, such as the network, SQL Server, and, if virtualization is used, the virtual infrastructure.

Usage, Adoption, and Archiving Requirements

Nearly every organization is required to retain communications data for compliance purposes. Organizations across all common verticals must follow strict regulations, and these regulations will carry over to the Skype for Business Server 2015 infrastructure to retain data, such as instant messaging conversations and web conferencing content. Additionally, some organizations require audio recordings of all calls for certain users. There are many ways to meet these requirements, including Skype for Business Server 2015 built-in functionality as well as third-party solutions.

It is also important to track the usage and adoption of the Skype for Business Server 2015 system. Monitoring the usage and overall adoption of a Skype for Business Server 2015 service is critical in the deployment and post-deployment stages. During the deployment, identifying how users are adopting the solution will provide key metrics for success of the project, as well as the return on investment (ROI) of the solution. Post-deployment, identifying how users are utilizing the system can provide insight into cost analysis, as well as performance tweaking metrics. These are just some examples of why it is important to monitor the usage and adoption of the Skype for Business Server 2015 system. Many organizations have key performance indicators (KPIs) for their Skype for Business Server 2015 deployment, and monitoring these areas is critical in reporting on the status of those KPIs.

Monitoring the Health and Performance of Skype for Business Server 2015

For any Skype for Business Server 2015 deployment to be successful, a robust set of solutions should be deployed to monitor the health and performance of the service. Any organization that has designated an SLA to their Skype for Business Server 2015 system will require monitoring all components of Skype for Business Server 2015 to ensure availability of the environment. The end goal should be to provide the highest level of availability and the highest level of insight into the environment, with the least amount of effort for administrators. A combination of solutions can be utilized to enable administrators and management with the necessary confidence in the health of their Skype for Business Server 2015 deployment, and this section outlines common examples and considerations for deployment.

Using Performance Monitor to Establish Performance Baselines

The Windows operating system has included a performance monitoring utility for many releases. Over the years, this tool has become more powerful, and applications continue to allow critical performance monitoring through this tool. The tool, Performance Monitor (sometimes called Perfmon), enables administrators to view numerous metrics about the hardware and software on a Windows machine. In relation to Skype for Business Server 2015, key performance metrics related to CPU, disk, memory, and network can be monitored as part of the default OS configuration. Additionally, Skype for Business Server 2015 includes a vast library of counters that can be tracked in the Performance Monitor utility.

It is a best practice to establish a performance baseline when first enabling a Skype for Business Server 2015 deployment. A performance baseline enables administrators to have a record of how one or many Skype for Business Server 2015 systems are performing during normal operations. This baseline can then be referenced when issues are reported.

Establishing a performance baseline also enables administrators to confirm proper sizing of the deployed environment. Microsoft provides recommended topologies based on standard use cases and environmental variables. If an organization does not match all conditions of the Microsoft use cases, Performance Monitor can be used to validate sufficient system resources and load distribution for various Skype for Business Server 2015 services.

NOTE

When establishing a performance baseline, be sure to capture a sufficient amount of data. At least one week of data should be collected to identify all peak-hour and off-hour usage for all Skype for Business Server 2015 services.

If major changes to the Skype for Business Server 2015 service occur, such as adding users or functionality or adding or removing servers, a new baseline should be established.

Important Performance Monitor Counters

The Windows operating system and Skype for Business Server 2015 enable administrators to monitor a very large number of counters in Performance Monitor. This section outlines key Performance Monitor counters for a performance baseline with Skype for Business Server 2015. It is recommended to explore the Performance Monitor counters available on your servers to become familiar with the tools you will have available in any troubleshooting situation.

To explore the Performance Monitor counters available for Skype for Business Server 2015, do the following:

1. Open the Performance Monitor tool, located in the Administrative Tools on a Windows Server.
2. Select Performance Monitor and then click the green plus sign to add a new counter. See Figure 12.1 for an example.

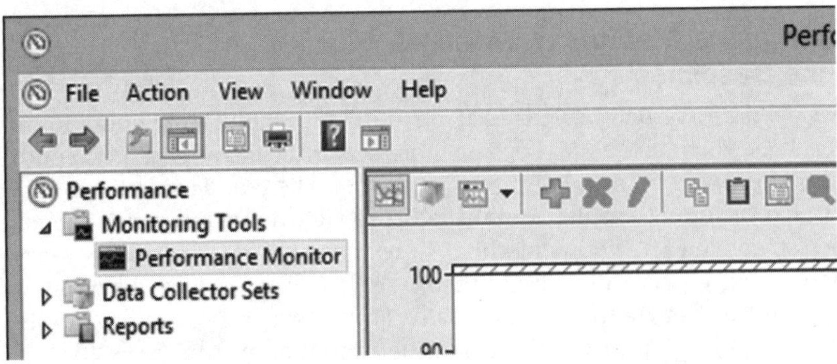

FIGURE 12.1 Add a performance counter.

3. All Skype for Business Server 2015 counters will start with "LS:"; check the box for Show Description, and each counter will display a description to help with identifying the counters. Figure 12.2 shows an example of the initial set of LS counters in Performance Monitor.

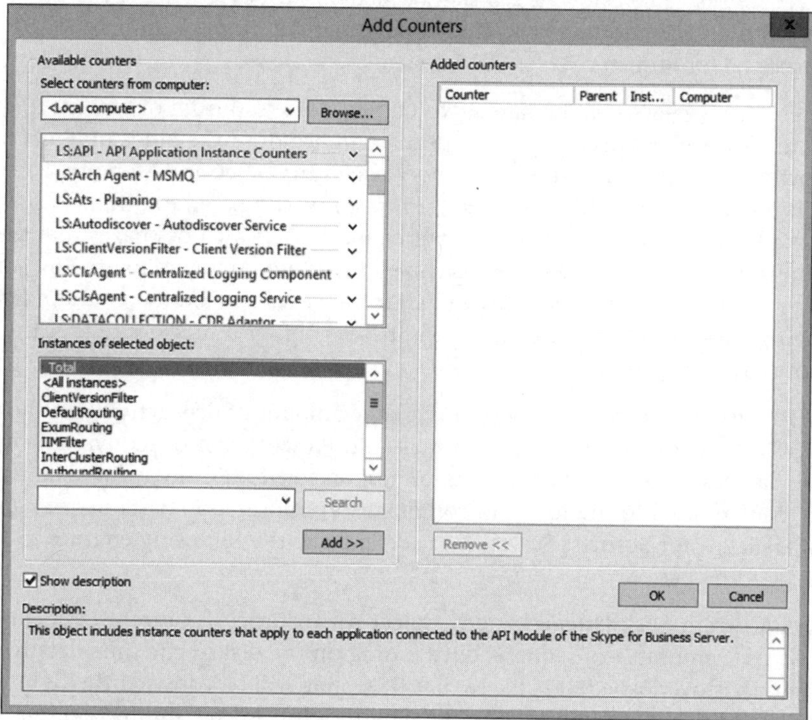

FIGURE 12.2 Skype for Business Server 2015 performance counters.

After you've explored the available performance counters for Skype for Business Server 2015, it should be evident that there are many different aspects of Skype for Business Server 2015 available for monitoring. However, establishing a performance baseline on your servers should involve only a few key counters. Use the sections that follow as a guide for counters to choose when establishing a performance baseline.

CPU Skype for Business Server 2015 media processing can apply a large CPU load on any server. Depending on how the Skype for Business Server 2015 deployment was designed, servers can have varying CPU utilization. Use the following counter to ensure that CPU usage is not too great on your Skype for Business Server 2015 servers.

Processor\% Processor Time: This counter is the percentage of time elapsed that the processor spends to execute a non-idle thread. This is the primary indicator of processor activity, and it displays the average percentage of busy time observed during the sample interval. If this value is above 80% consistently, a machine might be overutilized.

Memory Skype for Business Server 2015 services are heavy in memory utilization, especially conferencing servers. Use the following counters to ensure that memory utilization is not too high on your Skype for Business Server 2015 servers.

Memory\Available Mbytes: This counter simply keeps track of the available memory to the system. When this value is low, it is a sign of memory utilization being too high. This will also help with understanding the scaling impact that additional features and users have on your Skype for Business Server 2015 systems.

Memory\Pages/sec: Pages/sec is the rate at which pages are read from or written to disk to resolve hard page faults. This counter is a primary indicator of the kinds of faults that cause systemwide delays. It is the sum of Memory\Pages Input/sec and Memory\Pages Output/sec. It is counted in numbers of pages, so it can be compared to other counts of pages, such as Memory\Page Faults/sec, without conversion. It includes pages that are retrieved to satisfy faults in the file system cache and that are usually requested by applications using mapped memory files. A high rate for the Pages/sec counter could indicate excessive paging. Monitor the Memory\Page Faults/sec counter to make sure that the disk activity is not caused by paging.

Disk Skype for Business Server 2015 performs a large amount of disk activity on the Front End and Back End Servers. Front End Servers maintain Presence and other dynamic data in the local SQL database, and Back End Servers are responsible for all Skype for Business user information, conference information, and configuration information. Disk performance is critical on all Skype for Business Server 2015 servers. Use the following counter to keep track of disk performance.

Physical Disk\Current Disk Queue Length (select All Instances): Current Disk Queue length represents the number of requests outstanding on the disk at the time data is collected. If a disk is overloaded, it is likely that this value will be consistently high. Requests experience delays proportional to the length of this queue, minus the number of spindles on the disks. For good performance, the difference should average less than 2.

Network Modern hardware does not often allow for overutilizing server network interface cards (NICs). However, it is important to understand the amount of traffic your servers are sending and receiving for baseline performance. In some instances, this network traffic might increase without notice, and it might help identify issues.

Network Interface\Bytes Total/sec: Bytes Total/sec is the rate at which bytes are sent and received over each network adapter, including framing characters. Network Interface\Bytes Total/sec is a sum of Network Interface\Bytes Received/sec and Network Interface\Bytes Sent/sec. This counter should be lower than the maximum bandwidth that the current network link provides.

Skype for Business Server 2015 Skype for Business Server 2015 includes many counters that monitor the service activity, health, and performance. The following counters are important for baseline performance monitoring, as well as ongoing monitoring and troubleshooting.

LS:MEDIA—Operations\Global Health: This counter represents the overall health of the different Skype for Business Server Media components installed on a server. This can include the Application Sharing MCU (ASMCU), the A/V MCU (AVMCU), Call Park Service, Conferencing Announcement Service, Conferencing Attendant, Response Group Service, Reach Server (Web App), and the Mediation Server service. Every media component provides a numeric health indicator, the values of which follow:

0 = Disabled

1 = Normal

2 = Light Load

3 = Heavy Load

4 = Overload

LS:MEDIA—Planning\Number of Conferences with NORMAL Health State: This counter represents the number of currently active conferences across all media components. It provides an overview of what media or conferences are currently active, and how many are in a healthy state. This can include the ASMCU, the AVMCU, Call Park Service, Conferencing Announcement Service, Conferencing Attendant, Response Group Service, Reach Server (Web App), and the Mediation Server service.

LS:MEDIA—Planning\Number of Conferences with OVERLOADED Health State: This counter represents the number of currently active conferences across all media components. It provides an overview of what media or conferences are currently in an unhealthy state. This can include the ASMCU, the AVMCU, Call Park Service, Conferencing Announcement Service, Conferencing Attendant, Response Group Service, Reach Server (Web App), and the Mediation Server service.

LS:SIP—Load Management\Average Holding Time for Incoming Messages: This counter represents the average time that a server held incoming messages before processing. A healthy Skype for Business Server 2015 system should have a holding time of less than 3 seconds.

LS:SIP—Peers\Incoming Requests/sec: This counter represents the per-second rate of received SIP requests. Having a baseline of this counter enables administrators to identify problem areas in troubleshooting scenarios.

LS:SIP—Responses\Local 503 Responses/sec: This counter represents the per-second rate of 503 SIP responses that are generated by the server. A SIP 503 response indicates a service failure.

LS:USrv—DBStore\Queue Depth: This counter represents the number of requests waiting to be run by the Skype for Business Server user services to the SQL Server service. A healthy Skype for Business Front End Server should show a queue depth of less than 1000.

LS:USrv—DBStore\Queue Latency (msec): This counter represents the time a request spends in a Skype for Business Server queue waiting to be serviced by the SQL Server service. A healthy Skype for Business Server and SQL Server connection should show a value of less than 5000 msec.

LS:USrv—DBStore\SProc Latency (msec): This counter represents the time it takes for the SQL Server Service to service requests from the Skype for Business Server. This value should have an average of less than 80 msec during normal operations. A high value for this counter is a clear sign of SQL Server performance issues.

LS:USrv—Directory Search\Search Latency (ms): This counter represents the average time it takes to perform LDAP searches. This counter can be used to identify delays in queries to Global Catalog servers in AD.

LS:USrv—Pool Conference Statistics\Active Conference Count: This counter represents the number of active conferences of all types in the Front End Server pool. This can be used to show the true maximum concurrency of any conferencing pool. This can also be referenced when changes are made to the environment to see the effect those changes have had on usage.

LS:USrv—Pool Conference Statistics\Active Participant Count: This counter represents the number of active conferencing participants of all types in the Front End Server pool. This can be used to show the true maximum user concurrency of any conferencing pool. This can also be referenced when changes are made to the environment to see the effect those changes have had on usage.

LS:USrv—REGDBStore\Queue Depth: This counter represents the number of requests waiting to be run by the Skype for Business Registrar Service. A healthy Skype for Business Front End Server should show a queue depth of less than 500.

LS:USrv—REGDBStore\Queue Latency (msec): This counter represents the time a request spends in a Skype for Business Server queue waiting to be serviced by the SQL Server Service. A healthy Skype for Business Server and SQL Server connection should show a value of less than 5000 msec.

LS:USrv—REGDBStore\SProc Latency (msec): This counter represents the time it takes for the SQL Server service to service requests from the Skype for Business Server. This value should have an average of less than 80 msec during normal operations. A high value for this counter is a clear sign of SQL Server performance issues.

Collecting and Analyzing Performance Monitor Data

The Performance Monitor utility enables administrators to collect data and view it in real time, or to collect data over a period and report on that data when collection has been stopped. For collecting a performance baseline, the latter approach is more appropriate. This feature, called *data collection sets*, allows a number of counters and various other settings to be combined into a single collection activity. To create a data collector set for Skype for Business Server 2015, perform the following steps:

1. Open the Performance Monitor utility, located in the Administrative Tools on a Windows Server.
2. Expand Data Collector Sets and select User Defined. Right-click and choose New, and then choose Data Collector Set. See Figure 12.3 for an example.

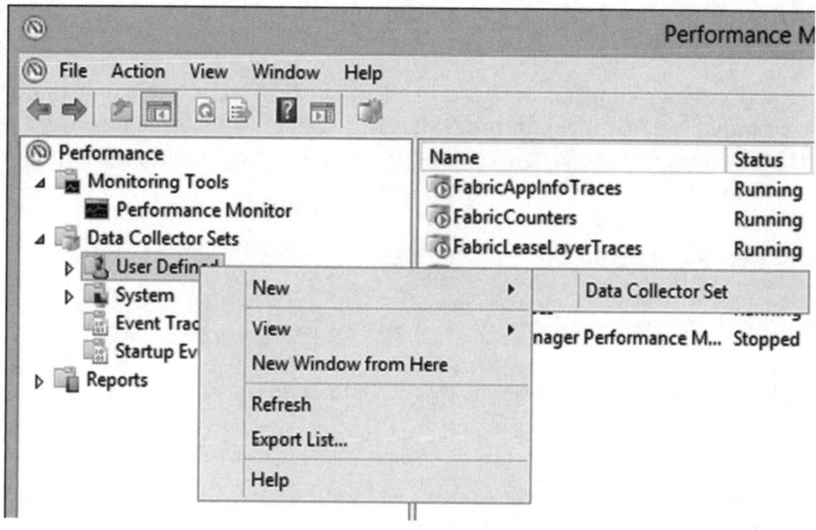

FIGURE 12.3 Creating a New Data Collector Set.

3. On the Create New Data Collector Set screen, enter a name, such as **Skype for Business Server Baseline**, and select the option labeled Create Manually (Advanced). Figure 12.4 shows an example of this process. Click Next to continue.

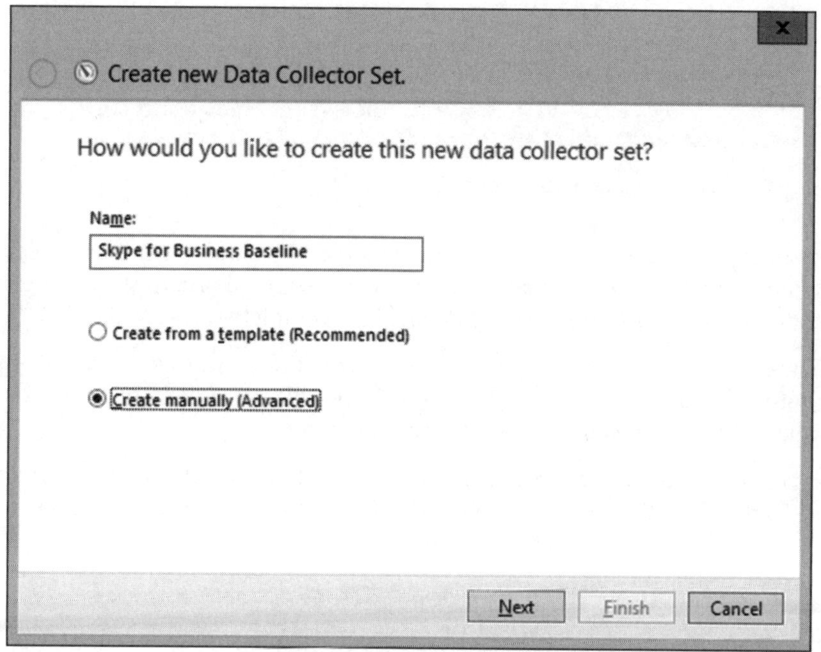

FIGURE 12.4 Naming the Data Collector Set.

4. Choose the option Create Data Logs and check the box for Performance Counter. Click Next to continue.

5. Add the performance counters outlined in the preceding section to the list and then choose a sample interval. Keep in mind that the smaller the sample interval, the larger the data logs will be. When you are finished, the list should look similar to that shown in Figure 12.5. Click Next to continue.

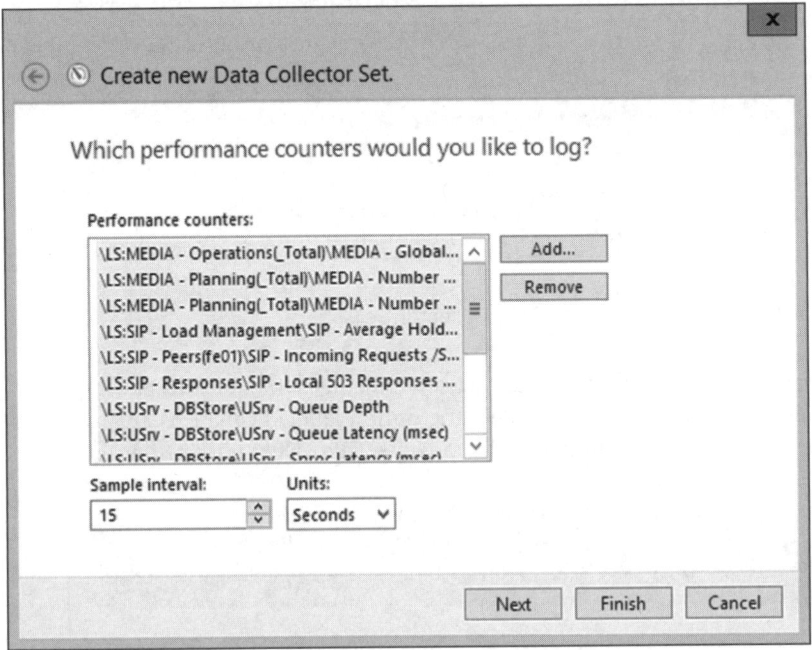

FIGURE 12.5 Data Collection Set counters selected.

6. On the next page, enter a path to save the data files. By default, these are stored on the system drive in a PerfLogs folder. If you have a separate disk to store these on, it is important to define this here. Click Finish to complete the wizard.

7. The new data collector set now shows in the user-defined list. If you want to apply other settings such as a schedule or stop conditions based on disk space or duration, right-click the collector set and choose Properties.

8. When you are ready to begin collecting data, right-click the data collector set and choose Start. When the set is running, it displays a running symbol over the icon (which is green), as shown in Figure 12.6.

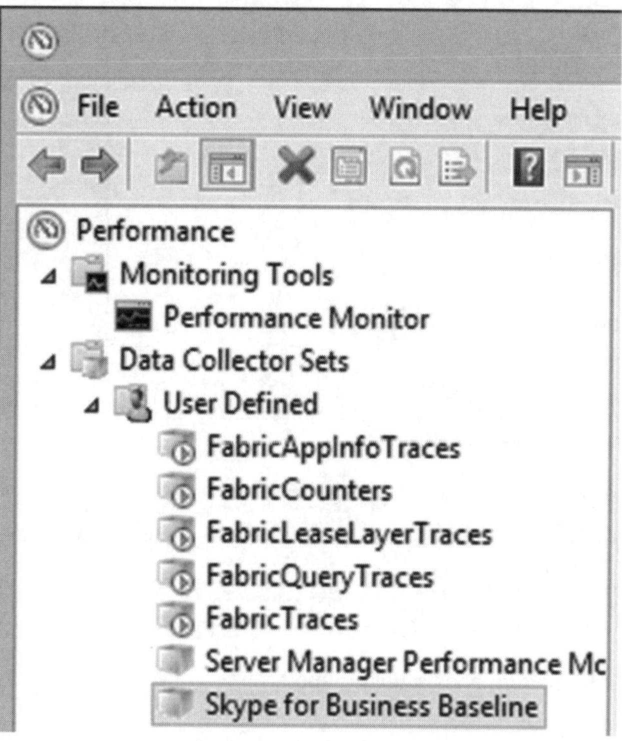

FIGURE 12.6 Example of a Data Collection Set running.

Analyzing Performance Monitor Data Logs Perform the following steps to analyze Performance Monitor data logs collected using the data collection set created in the preceding section:

1. Right-click the data collection set and choose Stop.
2. Right-click the data collection set and choose Latest Report. The report should automatically appear, enabling you to analyze the data collected. Use this screen to view a graph or a numeric representation of each value. When you select each value, you are presented with the Last, Average, Minimum, and Maximum values for each counter. Compare these numbers with the acceptable values described in earlier sections to determine the health of your environment. See Figure 12.7 for a sample report.

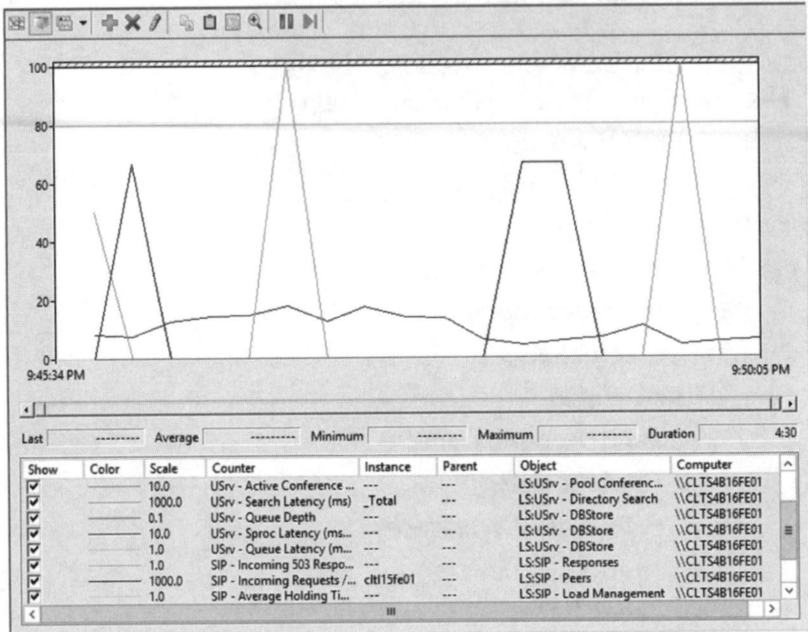

FIGURE 12.7 Example of a performance monitor report.

In addition to the reports built into Performance Monitor, a community tool is available to analyze Performance Monitor data logs and provide feedback based on known thresholds. The tool, named Performance Analysis of Logs (PAL), reads performance logs generated by Performance Monitor, analyzes them, and then outputs an HTML report that attempts to call out critical areas based on known thresholds. Although this is not built specifically for Skype for Business Server 2015, it does understand basic thresholds from Office Communications Server 2007 R2, as well as the Windows operating system thresholds. The goal of PAL is to automate the analysis work and provide administrators with a clear definition of counters that show a problem with a system. Also, you can edit and add threshold files for models that PAL does not support. To download PAL, see the following link: http://pal.codeplex.com/.

Performance Monitor is a powerful tool. Skype for Business administrators should be familiar with the counters available to them. Not only will this be helpful for planning purposes, but it has produced great results in troubleshooting scenarios as well.

Features Available in Skype for Business Server 2015 for Health Monitoring and Troubleshooting

In addition to identifying performance baselines and monitoring the performance of Skype for Business Server 2015 servers, there are many other critical components of Skype for Business Server 2015 that should actively be monitored to determine the health of the service. Skype for Business Server 2015 allows for various ways to monitor and test the health of the system, all of which are familiar to administrators of the Windows operating system.

This section provides an overview of how to use the Windows Event Viewer and synthetic transactions to monitor and troubleshoot the health of Skype for Business Server 2015 services.

Using Windows Event Logs to Identify Health Issues

Windows event logs are a critical resource for any administrator of a Windows-based application. In addition to the operating system writing all activity in these logs, many applications, including Skype for Business Server 2015, write activity to the Windows event logs. Skype for Business Server 2015 logs important informational, warning, and critical events to the Windows event log. These logs can be found in Event Viewer under Applications and Services Logs, under Lync Server. Figure 12.8 shows an example of these logs on a Skype for Business Server 2015.

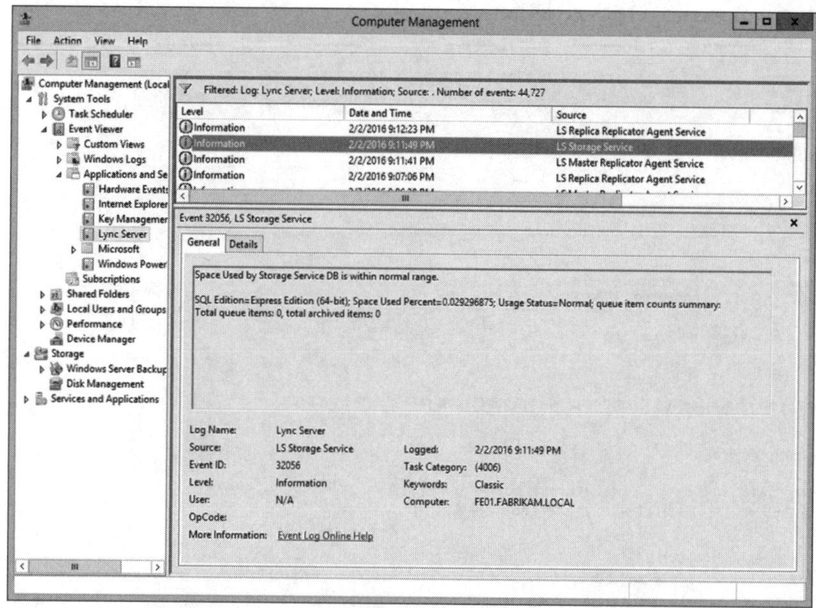

FIGURE 12.8 Skype for Business Server event logs in Event Viewer.

Because event logs are written in the order in which they occur, they often should be the first place to look when you are troubleshooting issues. Skype for Business Server 2015 writes all service activity as well as critical failures in the application, such as conference join failures or outbound call routing failures.

In Skype for Business Server 2015 deployments of all sizes, collecting event logs for each server can become a daunting task. In order to help with this, it is recommended to configure a server to receive event logs for all machines. This functionality requires the following:

- Windows Remote Management (WinRM) enabled on all Skype for Business Servers
- Visual C++ 2012 Redistribution Package on the receiving server
- Skype for Business Server 2015 core components on the receiving server

The Skype for Business Server 2015 core components allow the receiving machine to understand Skype for Business Server logs without any additional work from the administrator.

Perform the following tasks to create an Event Collector for Skype for Business Server 2015 event logs:

1. Open Event Viewer, located in the Administrative Tools on Windows Server.
2. Right-click the Subscriptions folder and choose Create Subscription. When prompted to configure the Event Collector Service, click Yes.
3. When in the Subscription Wizard, you should set a subscription name and choose the computers and events you will be collecting. Figure 12.9 shows an example of the basic subscription properties configuration.

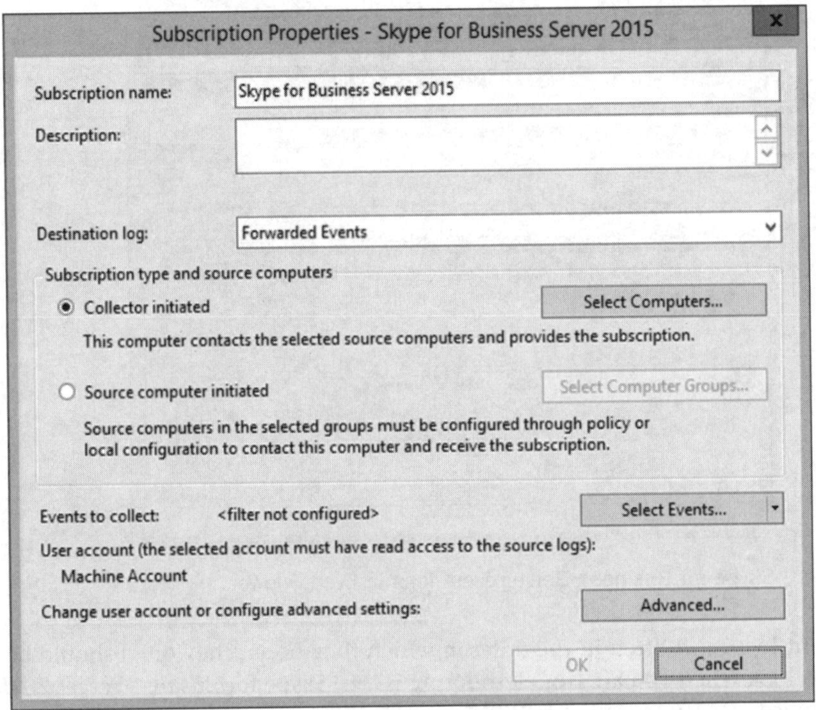

FIGURE 12.9 Skype for Business Server 2015 event subscription.

4. Choose Select Computers and add the appropriate servers for your environment. Figure 12.10 shows an example of a Persistent Chat and SQL Server being selected for the subscription.

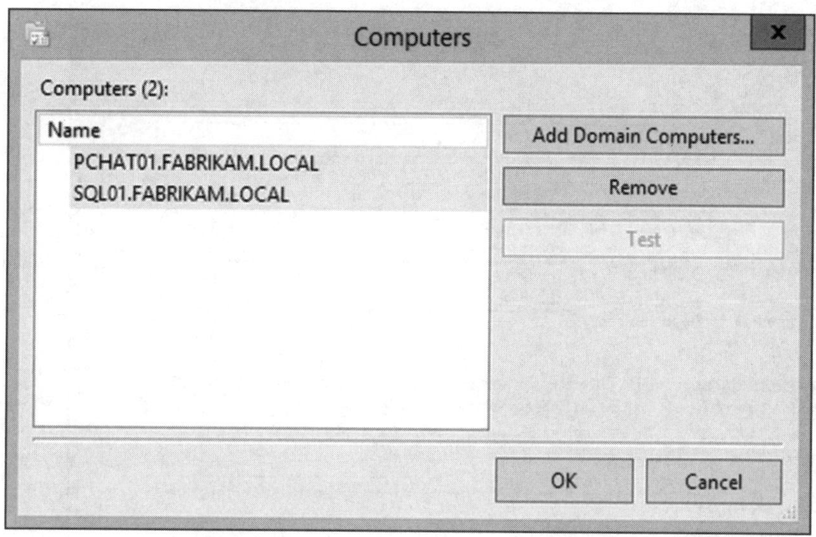

FIGURE 12.10 Adding Skype for Business Server 2015 servers to an event subscription.

5. Next, choose Select Events. This box enables you to filter the events you want to receive. Figure 12.11 shows an example of just Skype for Business Server events being selected for the subscription.

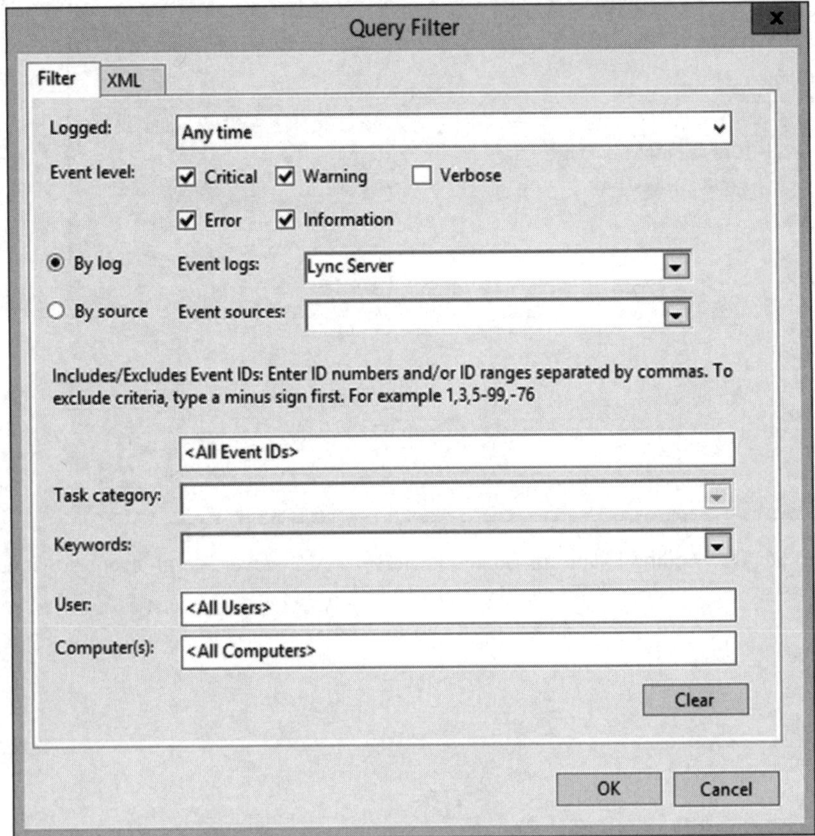

FIGURE 12.11 Choosing events for an event subscription.

6. Click OK to close the Select Events box. Then click OK to close the Subscription Wizard.
7. Events from this subscription now show under the Windows Logs\Forwarded Events folder in Event Viewer.

Windows Event Viewer can also be used on client machines to diagnose issues. By default, logging on Skype for Business clients is not enabled. However, enabling this feature is recommended and provides a great source of information in troubleshooting specific end-user scenarios. When this is turned on, the application event log on client machines is populated with Skype for Business client event logs. This can be used to troubleshoot sign-in and other critical issues. Turning on this feature can be done in two ways: on the Skype for Business client and through a Skype for Business Client Policy, controlled by the administrator.

To enable event logging in the Skype for Business Client Policy, do the following:

1. Open the Skype for Business Server Management Shell (PowerShell).
2. Run the following command. The command shown here enables the global client policy with event logging; if you have separate client policies, substitute the `Identity` value.

```
Set-CSClientPolicy -Identity Global -EnableEventLogging $True
```

To enable event logging on the Skype for Business client, do the following:

1. Open the Skype for Business Options menu by clicking the Options Wheel in the far upper-right corner of the Skype for Business client. See Figure 12.12 for an example.

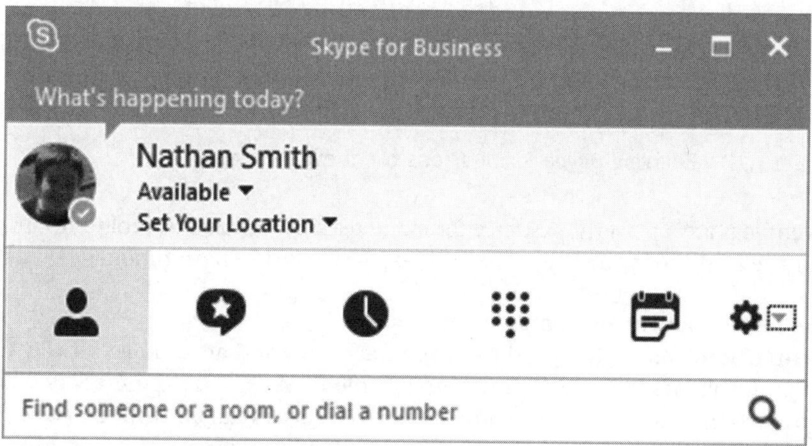

FIGURE 12.12 Opening the Skype for Business options menu.

2. When in the General options window, check the box Also Collect Troubleshooting Info Using Windows Event Logging. See Figure 12.13 for an example.

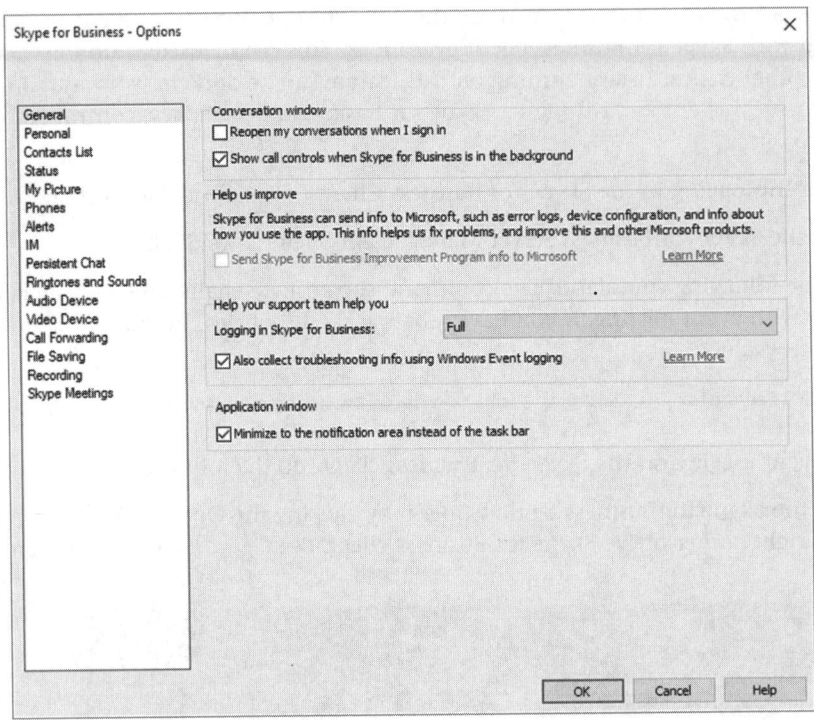

FIGURE 12.13 Enabling Skype for Business client event logging.

Windows event logs are a powerful resource for many reasons. Utilize this tool to troubleshoot and monitor the health of your Skype for Business Server 2015 environment.

Using Synthetic Transactions to Identify Health Issues

Synthetic transactions were introduced in Lync Server 2010 and are a powerful way for administrators to validate the health of the environment. Skype for Business Server 2015 synthetic transactions allow many different scenarios to be tested, all through PowerShell. These tasks are able to validate end-to-end scenarios such as making a call or joining a Skype for Business conference. This section provides an understanding of how synthetic transactions work and common transactions that can be used to identify health issues.

Creating Skype for Business Test Accounts for Synthetic Transactions Test user accounts are required for synthetic transactions to validate user functionality. Although it is possible to run synthetic transactions by providing the credentials for valid user accounts, it is not recommended. The `New-CSHealthMonitoringConfiguration` cmdlet is used to define test accounts for each pool. When administrators specify two valid test accounts for each pool, it makes running synthetic transactions much easier because administrators are not required to provide credentials for each test. Before running this command, you should create two test accounts and enable the accounts for Skype for Business Server 2015. Also, be sure to assign any appropriate policies to account for scenarios you want to test. If you want to test PSTN calling, make sure that these users are enabled for Enterprise Voice and configured properly.

The command shown next creates a new health-monitoring configuration for `FEPOOL01.fabrikm.local`. This pool will use `test1@skypeunleashed.com` and `test2@skypeunleashed.com` for synthetic transaction test accounts.


```
New-CSHealthMonitoringConfiguration -Identity FEPOOL01.fabrikam.local
➥-FirstTestUserSIPUri sip:test1@skypeunleashed.com
➥-SecondTestUserSipURI sip:test2@skypeunleashed.com.com
```

Using Synthetic Transactions After test accounts have been created, services can be tested using synthetic transactions. When performing synthetic transactions using preconfigured health accounts, the Skype for Business Server 2015 machine account will be used to impersonate those users. As such, the use of synthetic transactions can become very simple; see the following text for examples.

To test that a user can sign on to the pool, essentially proving that the Front End Server is healthy for registration, use this:

```
Test-CSRegistration -TargetFQDN fepool01.fabrikam.local
```

If it's successful, the output should look similar to this:

```
Target Fqdn        : fepool01.fabrikam.local
Result             : Success
Latency            : 00:00:07.6614315
Error Message      :
Diagnosis          :
```

To test that a user can make an outbound PSTN call, including testing registration, the dial plans, and routing policies assigned, as well as the signaling and media path to the PSTN endpoint, use this:

```
Test-CSPSTNOutboundCall -TargetPSTNPhoneNumber 6000
➥-TargetFQDN fepool01.fabrikam.local
```

If successful, the output should look similar to this:

```
Target Fqdn        : fepool01.fabrikam.local
Result             : Success
Latency            : 00:00:10.5099552
Error Message      :
Diagnosis          :
```

TIP

All Skype for Business synthetic transactions are PowerShell cmdlets that begin with `Test-`. To identify a full list of cmdlets available, you can type `Get-Command *test-cs*` into a PowerShell window, which will return a list of available cmdlets.

The previous examples are just a small taste of what is available as part of Skype for Business synthetic transactions. For a full list of synthetic transactions, navigate to the following URL and explore all cmdlets with `Test-CS` in the name: http://technet.microsoft.com/en-us/library/gg398867.aspx.

Enabling Rich Logging for Synthetic Transactions In Lync Server 2010, synthetic transactions were a great utility for identifying service issues. However, the information reported by a failed transaction test was often not enough to help users identify where the failure was occurring. At best, the verbose output of the cmdlets would provide a record of each step tested, and it might enable an administrator to narrow down the source of the issue.

Skype for Business Server 2015 introduces rich-logging capabilities in synthetic transactions. Each time a transaction is run, the following information is generated:

- The time started
- The time finished
- The action that was performed
- Messages generated by the activity (informational, verbose, warning, or error)
- SIP registration messages
- Exception records or diagnostic codes generated when the activity ran
- The result of the activity

Although this information is generated each time, a parameter must be added to a manually run synthetic transaction to output to a log file. This parameter is `OutLoggerVariable`. Use the following example to test logging in to Skype for Business Server 2015 using `Test-CSRegistration` and then to export the logging data to an HTML file for review.

Run the `Test-CSRegistration` cmdlet with the output parameter:

```
Test-CSRegistration -TargetFQDN fepool01.fabrikam.com -OutLoggerVariable
➥TestRegistration
```

Notice that the `OutLoggerVariable`, `TestRegistration`, is not preceded by a dollar sign ($), as we normally use in PowerShell. The logging data is then stored in the variable `$TestRegistration` as defined in the preceding cmdlet. Use the following command to export this data to HTML format:

```
$TestRegistration.ToHTML() | Out-File C:\logs\TestRegistration.Html
```

The report can then be opened in Internet Explorer to view the sequence of events and any errors, as appropriate. The info can be expanded to show all details of the synthetic test. The example in Figure 12.14 shows a successful registration test.

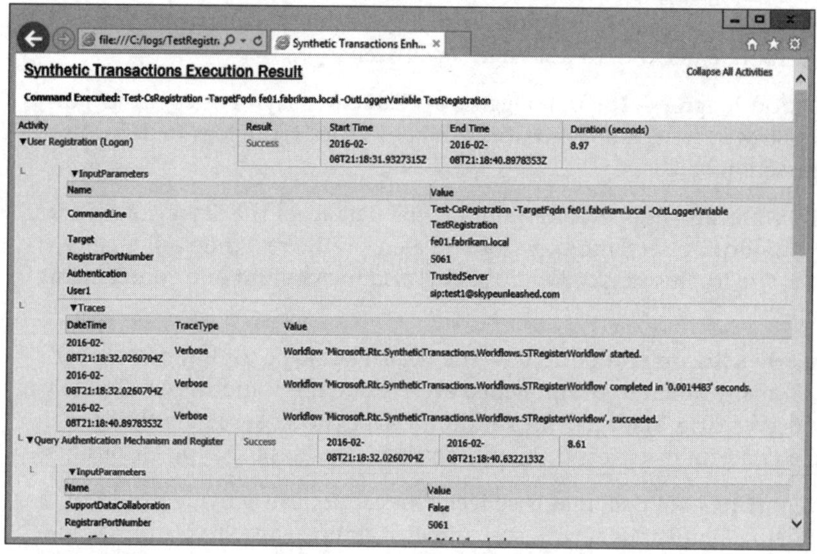

FIGURE 12.14 Viewing a Synthetic Transaction rich logging report.

Synthetic transactions should be a primary tool for administrators of all Skype for Business Server 2015 environments. With this utility, administrators have the ability to test and troubleshoot end-to-end user scenarios without requirements for end-user intervention.

Capabilities and Benefits of System Center Operations Manager with Skype for Business Server 2015

System Center Operations Manager is a comprehensive monitoring solution by Microsoft. SCOM is deployed at many organizations to monitor servers and networking equipment. SCOM operates on a model of management packs, which are collections of monitors, rules, and configuration criteria that define how to monitor a service. SCOM includes Windows Server and network equipment monitoring by default. Many organizations also use SCOM to monitor applications such as Exchange Server, Active Directory, SQL Server, and third-party applications.

Microsoft also provides a management pack for Skype for Business Server 2015. When deploying the Skype for Business Server 2015 Management Pack for SCOM, organizations can proactively monitor the end-to-end Skype for Business Server 2015 environment. Essentially, all topics discussed previously in this chapter, including Performance Monitor, event logs, and synthetic transactions, are wrapped into a monitoring package with the

Skype for Business Server 2015 Management Packs for SCOM. The benefits of using SCOM for Skype for Business Server 2015 monitoring are as listed here:

- **Scenario availability using synthetic transactions**—The Skype for Business Server 2015 Management Pack allows synthetic transactions to automatically be run for a number of scenarios. SCOM also supports running synthetic transactions from outside the corporate network to test Edge Server scenarios.
- **Rich transaction logging**—The rich logging available with synthetic transactions is available in SCOM as well. Administrators can access the HTML logs to determine why the transaction failed.
- **Call reliability monitoring**—SCOM monitors the data from the Skype for Business Server 2015 Monitoring Server to monitor and alert on the real-time call quality for users. In Skype for Business Server 2015 this also includes IM and conferencing scenarios.
- **Monitoring downstream components**—The health of Skype for Business Server 2015 relies on many different components, even inside the Windows OS. The Skype for Business Server 2015 Management Pack for SCOM checks several critical dependencies and alerts administrators on their impact as it relates to Skype for Business.
- **Historical reporting**—All data that is collected by SCOM can provide historical reports that help administrators with scenario availability, capacity planning, and the overall health of the environment.

SCOM combines the detailed Windows OS performance and health monitoring with enhanced Skype for Business 2015 functionality, such as synthetic transactions, call reliability alerts, media quality alerts, service and component health, and dependency health. Figure 12.15 shows an example of a monitoring view in SCOM, monitoring the critical services for Skype for Business Server 2015.

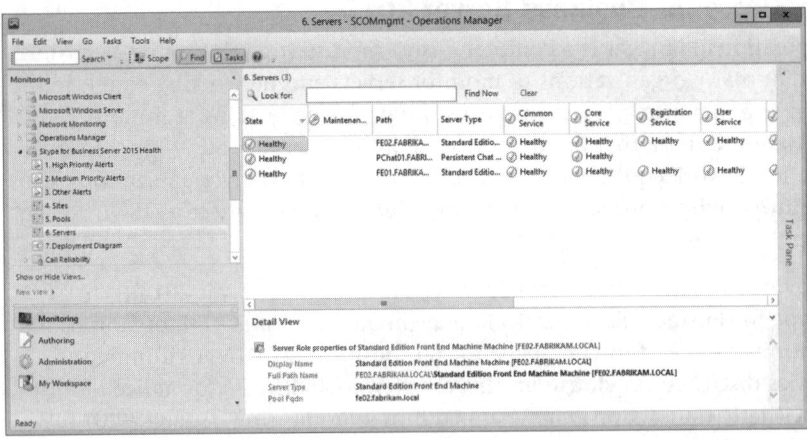

FIGURE 12.15 Example of the SCOM monitoring console for Skype for Business Server 2015.

Monitoring the Health of Skype for Business Server 2015 with SCOM

Deploying SCOM to monitor Skype for Business Server 2015 is a relatively simple task. The model of importing preconfigured managed packs allows administrators to enable Skype for Business Server 2015 monitoring with little effort. Skype for Business Server 2015 has two management pack offerings for SCOM:

- **Component and User Management Pack**—This management pack is responsible for tracking event logs, performance counters, and CDR/QoE data. This allows for an out-of-the-box monitoring experience for the service health and performance of Skype for Business Server 2015.
- **Active Monitoring Pack**—This management pack is responsible for running synthetic transactions through SCOM. This allows for a greater level of monitoring, but requires additional configuration.

Both management packs can be downloaded from the following URL:

> http://www. microsoft.com/en-us/download/details.aspx?id=35842&WT.mc_id=rss_alldownloads_all

The sections that follow outline basic configuration tasks required to monitor Skype for Business Server 2015 with SCOM.

Configure Component Monitoring by Importing the Component and User Management Pack The following tasks assume that a SCOM server has been deployed already. Additionally, all Skype for Business Server 2015 servers in the environment should already have a SCOM agent deployed to them.

1. Open the SCOM Operations Console and navigate to the Administration pane.
2. Right-click Management Packs and choose Import Management Pack.
3. In the Import Management Packs Wizard, choose Add and then Add from Disk.
4. Navigate to the location where you downloaded your Skype for Business Server 2015 management packs; by default, this location is `%SystemDrive%\Program Files\Skype for Business Server 2015\Management Packs\Management Packs`. Choose the `Microsoft.LS.2015.Monitoring.ComponentAndUser.mp` and `Microsoft.LS.2015.Monitoring.ActiveMonitoring.mp` files and click Open.
5. Click Install and wait for the import to be completed.
6. Every Skype for Business Server 2015 server must be configured as a System Center Agent Proxy. To do this, in the Administration panel click the Agent Managed section.
7. Right-click each Skype for Business Server 2015 computer and choose Properties.

8. Under the Security tab, check the box for Allow This Agent to Act as a Proxy and Discover Managed Objects on Other Computers. See Figure 12.16 for an example.

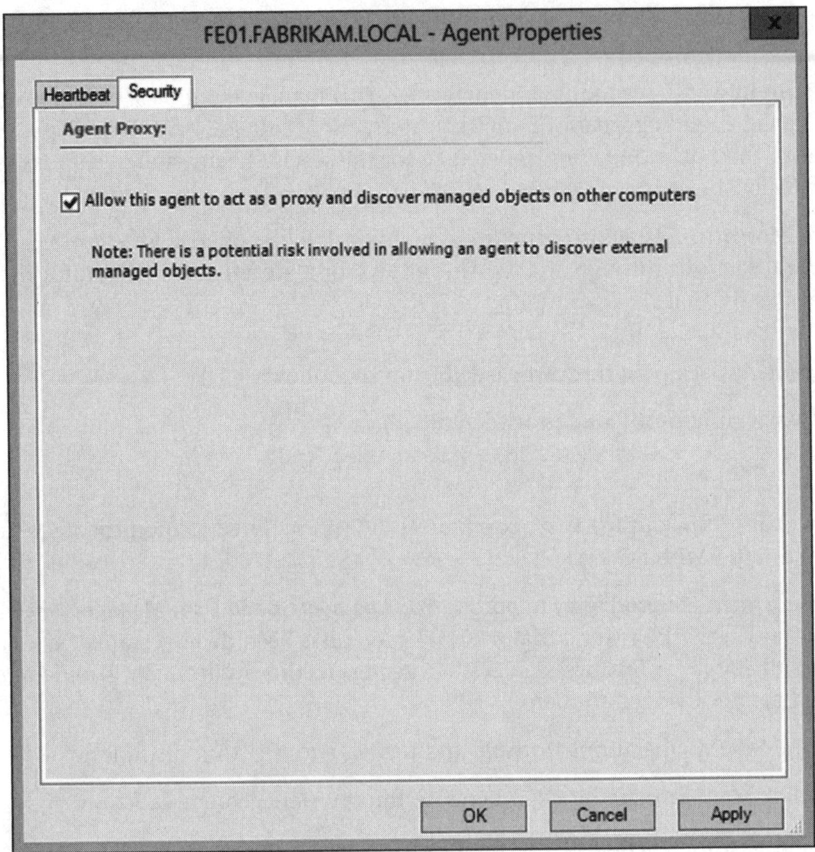

FIGURE 12.16 Agent proxy configuration.

The discovery process will happen over a random period. To validate proper discovery of your environment, expand the Microsoft Skype for Business Server 2015 folder under the Monitoring pane and validate that Skype for Business Server 2015 computers show under the Servers tab and that services are monitored.

It is recommended that you monitor the frequency of events in your environment to establish a proper notification configuration. Before configuring email alerts, consider analyzing the active alerts in the environment over a set period. After the environment has been stabilized and cleaned up, it is then appropriate to configure email alerting for critical issues in the environment.

Deploying Synthetic Transaction Monitoring with SCOM SCOM also allows for synthetic transactions to be automated through the SCOM service. Enabling this functionality requires the deployment of a watcher node. The watcher node acts as a trusted Skype for

Business Server 2015 computer that is running synthetic transactions on behalf of test users. This watcher node reports statuses to SCOM servers, resulting in real-time monitoring and alerting on real user scenarios.

The synthetic transactions available in the Skype for Business Server 2015 Management Pack test the scenarios given in Table 12.1.

TABLE 12.1 Synthetic Transactions Available in SCOM

Test Name	Scenario	Default/Nondefault
`Test-CsAddressBookService` (ABS)	Confirms that users are able to look up users who aren't in their contact list.	Default
`Test-CsAddressBookWebQuery` (ABWQ)	Confirms that users are able to look up users who aren't in their contact list via HTTP.	Default
`Test-CsAVConference` (AvConference)	Confirms that users are able to create and participate in an audio/video conference.	Default
`Test-CsGroupIM` (GroupIM)	Confirms that users are able to send instant messages in conferences and participate in instant message conversations with three or more people.	Default
`Test-CsIM` (P2P IM)	Confirms that users are able to send peer-to-peer instant messages.	Default
`Test-CsP2PAV` (P2PAV)	Confirms that users are able to place peer-to-peer audio calls (signaling only).	Default
`Test-CsPresence` (Presence)	Confirms that users are able to view other users' presence.	Default
`Test-CsRegistration` (Registration)	Confirms that users are able sign in to Skype for Business.	Default
`Test-CsPstnPeerToPeerCall` (PSTN)	Confirms that users are able to place and receive calls with people outside of the enterprise (PSTN numbers).	Nondefault, Extended

`Test-CsAVEdgeConnectivity` (AVEdgeConnectivity)	Confirms that the Audio/Video Edge servers are able to accept connections for peer-to-peer calls and conference calls.	Nondefault
`Test-CsDataConference` (DataConference)	Confirms that users can participate in a data collaboration conference (an online meeting that includes activities such as whiteboards and polls).	Nondefault
`Test-CsDialinConferencing` (DialinConferencing)	Confirms that users are able to dial phone numbers to join conferences.	Nondefault
`Test-CsExumConnectivity` (ExumConnectivity)	Confirms that a user can connect to Exchange Unified Messaging (UM).	Nondefault
`Test-CsGroupIM-TestJoinLauncher` (JoinLauncher)	Confirms that users are able to create and join scheduled meetings (by a web address link).	Nondefault
`Test-CsLyncSkypeIM` (LyncSkypeIM)	Confirms the health state of synthetic transactions that monitor Skype and Lync Federation IM.	Nondefault
`Test-CsLyncSkypeMedia` (LyncSkypeMedia)	Confirms the health state of synthetic transactions that monitor Skype and Lync federation media.	Nondefault
`Test-CsMCXP2PIM` (MCXP2PIM)	Confirms that mobile device users are able to register and send instant messages.	Nondefault
`Test-CsP2PVideoInteropServerSipTrunkAV` (P2PVideoInteropServerSipTrunkAV)	Confirms that Video Interop Server is up and can handle incoming connections over a video SIP trunk.	Nondefault
`Test-CsPersistentChatMessage` (PersistentChatMessage)	Confirms that users can exchange messages by using the Persistent Chat service.	Nondefault
`Test-CsTenantPowerShell`	Monitors the health state of synthetic transactions that monitor User Unified Contact Store.	Nondefault

`Test-CsUcwaConference` (UcwaConference)	Confirms that users can join conferences via the Web. Requires that UCWA be installed on the pool.	Nondefault
`Test-CsUnifiedContactStore` (UnifiedContactStore)	Confirms that a user's contacts can be accessed through the Unified Contact Store. The Unified Contact Store provides a way for users to maintain a single set of contacts that can be accessed by using Skype for Business, Microsoft Outlook messaging and collaboration client, and/or Microsoft Outlook Web Access.	Nondefault
`Test-CsXmppIM` (XmppIM)	Confirms that an instant message can be sent across the Extensible Messaging and Presence Protocol (XMPP) gateway.	Nondefault

Transactions in Table 12.1 marked as Default are transactions that are turned on by default when you configure a watcher node in SCOM. Transactions marked as Nondefault are not run by default, but can easily be enabled on the watcher node. Transactions marked as Extended are nondefault transactions that can also be run multiple times during each pass. Extended transactions are targeted at scenarios such as multiple voice routes for a pool.

The watcher node used for Skype for Business Server 2015 monitoring should be a dedicated server. Synthetic transactions can generate a large amount of traffic; as such, an existing production server should not be used. A server that will act as a watcher node must meet the following requirements:

- All Skype for Business Server 2015 prerequisites
- Full version of .NET Framework 4.5
- Windows Identity Foundation
- Windows PowerShell 3.0

The high-level steps required for deploying a watcher node are as listed here:

1. Install the Skype for Business Server 2015 core files on the watcher node computer. You can do this by running the Skype for Business 2015 Deployment Wizard and choosing to install administrative tools.
2. Install the SCOM agent files by deploying an agent to the watcher node computer using the SCOM console.
3. Run the `watchernode.msi` file included as part of the Skype for Business Server 2015 Management Pack on the watcher node computer.
4. Configure the watcher node settings in Skype for Business Server 2015 using Skype for Business Server 2015 Management Shell and `New-CSWatcherNodeConfiguration`.

A watcher node computer can authenticate with Skype for Business Server 2015 in two ways to run synthetic transactions. The authentication method will decide the configuration steps required. See Table 12.2 for an overview of these authentication methods.

TABLE 12.2 Authentication Methods Available to Watcher Nodes

Authentication Method	Description	Location Supported
Trusted Server	Uses a certificate to authenticate as a Skype for Business Server and bypass user authentication challenges. This is the recommended configuration and requires the least amount of operational overhead.	Inside the corporate network. The watcher node must be in the same domain as the servers being monitored.
Credential Authentication	Stores usernames and passwords securely in the Windows Credential Manager on the watcher node. This requires more operational overhead to manage passwords.	Outside the corporate network. Inside the corporate network.

If the watcher node will be used inside the corporate network, it should be deployed as a trusted server. To configure the watcher node computer as a trusted server, perform the following steps:

1. Open Skype for Business Server Management Shell (PowerShell).
2. Run a command similar to the following. This example shows creating `watcher01.fabrikam.local` as a watcher node:

```
New-CSTrustedApplicationPool -identity watcher01.fabrikam.local -Registrar
➥FEPOOL01.fabrikam.local -ThrottleAsServer $True -TreatAsAuthenticated $True
```

```
➥-OutboundOnly $false -RequiresReplication $True -ComputerFQDN
➥watcher01.fabrikam.local -site Redmond
```

3. After creating the trusted application pool, you must create a trusted application identity. Run the following command:

```
New-CSTrustedApplication -ApplicationID STWatcherNode
➥-TrustedApplicationPoolFQDN watcher01.fabrikam.local -Port 5061
```

4. Run `Enable-CSTopology` in the Skype for Business Server 2015 Management Shell. When it has completed, restart the watcher node computer.

12

After the watcher node computer has been configured as a trusted application server, run the Skype for Business Server 2015 Deployment Wizard and install a certificate using the Request, Install, or Assign Certificate Wizard.

After the previous steps are completed, the `watchernode.msi` file must be run on the watcher node computer. Perform the following steps on the watcher node computer:

1. Open a command prompt as Administrator.
2. Navigate to the folder where `watchernode.msi` is located.
3. Run the following command:

```
watchernode.msi Authentication=TrustedServer
```

TIP

The `watchernode.msi` syntax is case-sensitive. `TrustedServer` must be entered exactly as shown or the install will fail.

After the watcher node computer has had all files installed, the watcher node must be configured to run synthetic transactions. Before enabling synthetic transactions, health testing accounts should be created. For information on how to create test accounts, see the section "Creating Skype for Business Test Accounts for Synthetic Transactions," earlier in this chapter. To test all scenarios, you must enable three test accounts for use with the watcher node.

When test accounts have been created, perform the following steps to enable a new watcher node to run synthetic transactions:

1. Open the Skype for Business Server Management Shell (PowerShell).
2. Run the following command to deploy the default synthetic transactions:

```
New-CSWatcherNodeConfiguration -TargetFQDN fepool01.fabrikam.local
➥-PortNumber 5061 -TestUsers
➥@{add=sip:test1@skypeunleashed.com, sip:test2@skypeunleashed.com,
➥sip:test3@skypeunleashed.com}
```

This command will create a new watcher node using default settings. The target Front End pool will be `fepool01.fabrikam.local`. The watcher node will use the test accounts `test1@skypeunleashed.com`, `test2@skypeunleashed.com`, and `test3@skypeunleashed.com`.

At this point, the environment will be configured with basic activity monitoring. To validate the configuration of the watcher nodes in the environment, run the cmdlet `Test-CSWatcherNodeConfiguration`.

This section has provided a summary of the benefits of monitoring Skype for Business Server 2015 with SCOM and how to enable this functionality in a Skype for Business Server 2015 environment. This monitoring solution includes many more features than described here, and it is recommended that you explore all the available configuration options and capabilities of SCOM monitoring. For a complete guide on monitoring Skype for Business 2015 with SCOM, see the TechNet library located at http://technet.microsoft.com/en-us/library/jj205188.aspx.

Third-party Monitoring Solutions

Microsoft System Center components are not the only way to monitor a Skype for Business Server 2015 environment. Several third-party solutions have emerged in the last couple of years that provide for rich monitoring of an installation.

The first is UC Commander from Event Zero. UC Commander has many modules to choose from. Some are based around analytics and quality reporting, while others provide features such as key health indicator (KHI) reporting and watcher node-like monitoring. The UC Commander products use an extremely lightweight connector installed on each server and a web-based portal that is either installed on-premises or in a tenant hosted by Event Zero.

Operations: KHI provides for real-time monitoring of not just the key health monitoring that Microsoft has published, but others as well. Monitoring of KHI data is crucial because the performance of the servers on which Skype for Business Server 2015 is installed can adversely affect end-user experience, including whether communications are even established. Event Zero's web-based portal shows alerts for all KHI counters that exceed published thresholds. Warnings are broken down into the typical rings, as used in datacenter monitoring, with Ring 0 being system and hardware, including processor utilization, memory, and disk activity. Ring 1 warnings are those involving networking and queuing. Ring 2 warnings include those remaining health indicators within the Skype for Business Server 2015 application itself.

Operations: Monitoring is Event Zero's watcher node-like functionality. One key difference between the Event Zero offering and that built into System Center's watcher node is that a watcher node's synthetic tests only check signaling. There is no measuring of quality. Operations: Monitoring uses strategically placed connectors to initiate communications between themselves, measuring not just signaling, but quality. This is accomplished by the connectors placing an actual call between configured users and then playing a known audio file. Because the contents and quality of the audio file are known, the resulting quality at the receiving end can be determined with extreme accuracy. A perfect scenario to use this is between branch offices and datacenters. A connector can be configured on a receptionist's workstation and will work in the background. Test scenarios include peer to peer, workflow, and conferencing. In the conferencing scenario, one connector initiates a conference and invites another connector-configured user. Once the second connector joins the conference, the audio file is then played and metrics are gathered. This is much more informative than just the synthetic tests that measure signaling.

UC Commander's web-based dashboard can display results of recent tests. See Figure 12.17 for an example.

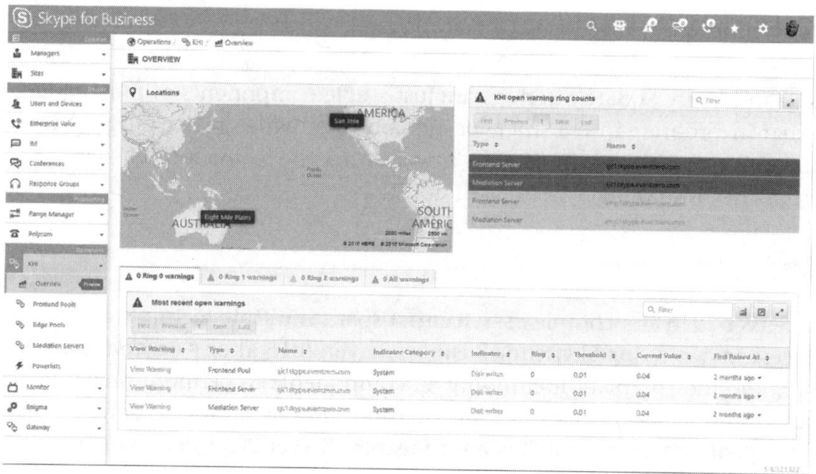

FIGURE 12.17 UC Commander KHI alerts.

For more information on the UC Commander platform, see http://www.eventzero.com.

NOTE

The UC Commander product was recently acquired by Microsoft, with the apparent intention to roll the functionality into Office 365.

Another company that provides a monitoring solution is Unify Square. Unify's cloud-based solution, called PowerSuite, also includes a monitoring component. Service Availability Monitoring uses a server-side agent and a cloud-based web dashboard to show both successful and failed states of Skype for Business-related components, including the status of services, root cause analysis, and queues and the result of synthetic tests. See Figure 12.18 for an example.

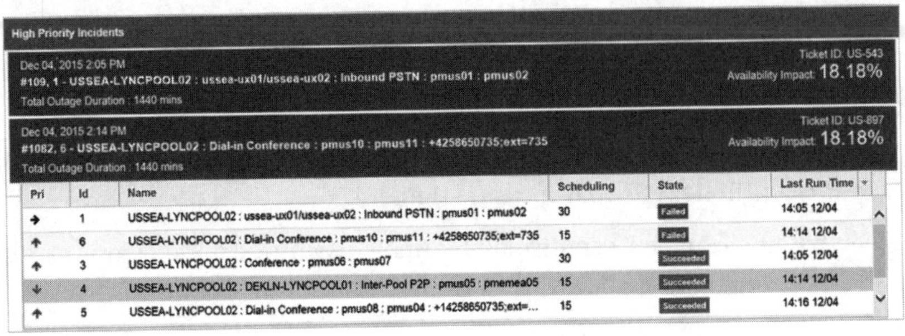

FIGURE 12.18 Service availability monitoring by Unify Square.

Both the Event Zero and Unify Square offerings are just single components of much larger product offerings that incorporate into a single dashboard to provide greater insight into the Skype for Business Server 2015 environments in ways that the Skype for Business Server 2015 Control Panel and Management Shell don't.

Summary

Skype for Business Server 2015 is a complex service that spans multiple technologies. A major key to success in deploying Skype for Business Server 2015 at any organization is establishing a proper monitoring plan. Identifying all components to be monitored, and implementing a solution that seamlessly monitors each solution, will move organizations one step closer to the goal of a successful Skype for Business Server 2015 deployment.

The Windows operating system includes tools available to monitor Skype for Business Server 2015, including Performance Monitor and event logs. Additionally, Skype for Business Server 2015 can provide end-user scenario testing and health validation using synthetic transactions. System Center Operations Manager is a utility that can be used to automate all monitoring tools available to Skype for Business Server 2015 under a single management interface. SCOM enables organizations to successfully monitor the availability and quality of the Skype for Business Server 2015 service deployed in their environment. Finally, the offerings from several vendors in the Skype for Business Server 2015 space provide additional features and functions to augment those already available.

CHAPTER 13

Administration of Skype for Business Server 2015

IN THIS CHAPTER

- Administration Overview
- Using the Skype for Business Topology Model
- Managing Servers and Users
- Configuring Quality of Service
- Troubleshooting
- Best Practices

Administration of Skype for Business Server 2015 is a welcome relief for those who ever spent time managing a Live Communications Server or Office Communications Server deployment. The older products were based on a Microsoft Management Console snap-in that was not intuitive and often required many clicks to perform simple tasks. This chapter covers some of the improvements found in Skype for Business Server 2015, such as the Skype for Business Server 2015 Control Panel and the Skype for Business Server Management Shell.

The Skype for Business Server Management Shell follows the precedent set by the Microsoft Exchange Server team, and the Skype for Business team has taken another cue by including role-based access control (RBAC) in this release, which was introduced in Lync Server. The Skype for Business RBAC differs slightly from Exchange RBAC and is compared in this chapter.

Also discussed is the topology model introduced in Lync Server 2010, in which all server planning and configuration is performed centrally. Building a topology using the Topology Builder and storing the configuration in the Central Management Store (CMS) are explained in this chapter. The scope-based policies are covered as well.

Common management tasks, such as draining servers or configuring quality of service (QoE) settings, are detailed in this chapter. Finally, common troubleshooting steps are described with examples, and how to use the new Centralized Logging Service (CLS) is covered.

Administration Overview

The life of a Skype for Business Server administrator varies depending on the role within the organization, and Skype for Business Server 2015 accommodates many different scenarios and administrator use cases. Instead of resorting to a complex and difficult management console or Visual Basic script files, Skype for Business Server 2015 continues with an improved user interface backed by a management shell based on Windows PowerShell, just as in Exchange Server since 2007 and most all server products currently available from Microsoft today. Combined with the role-based access control, administrators can tackle specific delegated tasks, either in the Skype for Business Server 2015 Control Panel or via the Skype for Business Server Management Shell command-line interface.

Skype for Business Server 2015 Control Panel

A fairly drastic shift that started with Lync Server 2010 was the initiative to completely remove the emphasis on managing servers using the Microsoft Management Console (MMC). As in Lync Server 2010 and 2013, the MMC is replaced with the Skype for Business Server Control Panel, which is a web-based management interface that uses the Microsoft Silverlight runtime for management tasks. Figure 13.1 shows the layout of the new interface.

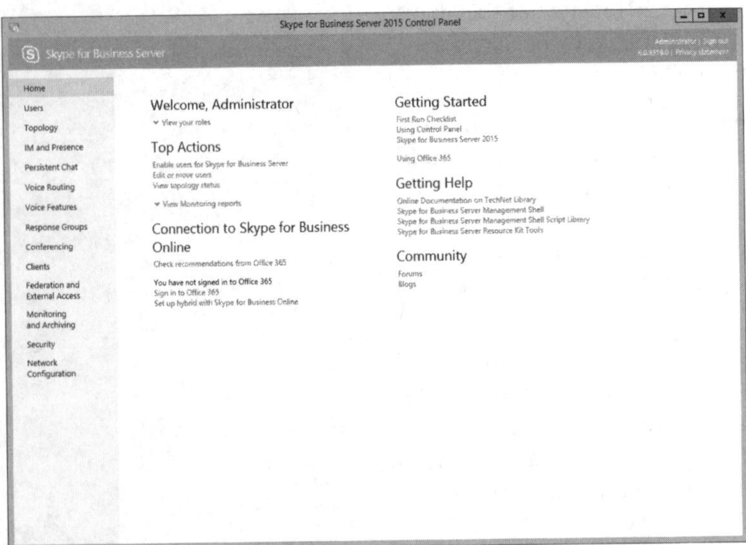

FIGURE 13.1 Skype for Business Server 2015 Control Panel interface.

This change has several benefits that are immediately visible to administrators familiar with installing the old management tools on a separate workstation. Installation of the administrative tools took manually going through four to five different installation package prerequisites before the OCS administrative tools could be installed. Instead, the requirement now is that the end user must have the latest Silverlight plug-in for the web browser.

From within the Skype for Business Server 2015 Control Panel, administrators have a centralized dashboard for all management activities. This includes managing user accounts and policies that control what features are available to users.

NOTE

Opening the Skype for Business Server 2015 Control Panel is similar to opening a web browser to the administrative web page. By default, Internet Explorer does not pass credentials to a site unless specifically allowed, so administrators are prompted for credentials each time. To prevent the prompt for credentials, add the Skype for Business administrative URL to the Local Intranet Zone in Internet Explorer. By default, this is https://<Pool FQDN or admin simple URL>.

The Skype for Business Server 2015 Control Panel is divided into several sections, and each section has subsections for specific actions or policies. Here is an overview of the options available within each section:

- **Users**—Enables or disables users for Skype for Business services, assigns policies to users, and moves users between pools.
- **Topology**—Provides a health overview of the deployment and reports on the status of all services. The different server applications and trusted applications are also displayed in this section.
- **IM and Presence**—Provides the file transfer and intelligent IM filter settings.
- **Persistent Chat**—Sets the configuration for Persistent Chat categories, policies, and global configuration.
- **Voice Routing**—Contains settings for dial plans, voice policies, routes, trunk configuration, and PSTN usages. This section also contains test cases for assessing whether dial plans and routing are working as expected.
- **Voice Features**—Contains settings for the voice applications such as Call Park and unassigned number routing.
- **Response Groups**—Provides links to the management interface for Response Group configuration. Queues and groups can be added or modified in this section as well.
- **Conferencing**—Configuration of conferencing policies, meetings, dial-in access numbers, and PIN policies.
- **Clients**—Controls Skype for Business client versioning and updates. Firmware updates and device configuration for Lync Phone Edition phones are managed in this section. Also included is some mobility and push notification policy configurations.
- **Federation and External Access**—Contains external access policies controlling federation and public IM connectivity. Federated domains and allowed public IM networks are configured within this section.

- **Monitoring and Archiving**—Configures settings for Call Detail Records, Quality of Experience monitoring, and instant message archiving.
- **Security**—Controls authentication methods for clients and PIN policies for Lync Phone Edition devices.
- **Network Configuration**—Configures the topology used for Call Admission Control, Media Bypass, and E-911. Location and bandwidth policies are also configured here.

NOTE

Although the Skype for Business Server 2015 Control Panel has its advantages over MMC management tasks, there are also some downsides, such as the fact that no right-click functionality is available. This might be an adjustment that helps drive more administrators to learn the Skype for Business Server Management Shell instead.

Skype for Business Server Management Shell

A big change first introduced in Lync Server 2010, and carried through Lync Server 2013 and into Skype for Business Server 2015, is the addition of the Management Shell. The Skype for Business Server Management Shell is built on Microsoft's PowerShell command and scripting environment and is really the core of what drives Skype for Business Server 2015 management. Many administrators will use the Skype for Business Server 2015 Control Panel by default because they are more familiar with a graphical user interface, but as time goes on, it should become apparent that all of Skype for Business server management can be done in a more efficient manner through the Skype for Business Server Management Shell.

Many organizations that use Microsoft Exchange Server are already familiar with how the Management Shell operates. When Microsoft first introduced the Exchange Management Shell as part of Exchange Server 2007, many administrators were frustrated and even intimidated by having some functionality available only in a command-line interface. The same is now true with the Skype for Business Server Management Shell for previous administrators of LCS and OCS. Often, the same team within an organization who manages Exchange is responsible for managing Skype for Business. If administrators have experience with the Exchange Management Shell, the change might not seem quite as drastic. For those entirely new to a command-line interface, it might take some time to feel comfortable. Microsoft has now incorporated PowerShell components into all of its server products, including Exchange, Skype for Business, SharePoint, Windows Server, and more.

Benefits of the Management Shell

For administrators primarily familiar with using graphical user interface (GUI) tools to manage systems, the Skype for Business Server Management Shell might seem a bit intimidating at first, but Skype for Business Server administrators new to PowerShell should spend some time getting acquainted with the new command-line-based toolset for several reasons. One reason for using Skype for Business Server Management Shell is that some tasks and actions simply do not exist within the Skype for Business Server 2015

Control Panel, so for these types of features, administrators must resort to using the Skype for Business Server Management Shell. For example, in Live Communications Server and Office Communications Server, changing the port that a Front End Server used for SIP communication involved just a few check boxes within the management console. With Skype for Business Server, the only way to modify the port or add a port is to use the Skype for Business Server Management Shell.

Another major benefit of the Skype for Business Server Management Shell is that bulk tasks are much easier to accomplish. With the older products, a task such as moving users between pools or modifying assigned policies was typically done through the management consoles and involved running through multiple pages of a wizard. Selecting the correct users to modify was also somewhat difficult because there was no breakdown of groups or divisions within the GUI. In the end, it was apparent that performing bulk tasks needed some attention from the product group. With the Skype for Business Server Management Shell, administrators have an incredible degree of flexibility in how to perform certain tasks. It is easy for administrators to select a group of users based on an attribute and modify all policies or move users quickly.

CAUTION

Although bulk changes are easy to make with the Skype for Business Server Management Shell, that also means it can be easy to make a mistake and have it affect many user accounts. Be sure to always test bulk changes on a smaller subset of users. If possible, have a test or development environment where bulk changes can be verified before they run against the production systems.

Some organizations familiar with PowerShell use custom scripts to provision new user accounts. Scripting these kinds of operations greatly reduces the chance for a human error to affect the account creation.

Just imagine how many times the wrong dial plan, voice policy, or conferencing policy can be applied to a new account when left as a manual process. For small organizations this isn't typically an issue, but for larger companies having a standardized, automated method is a necessity.

This kind of PowerShell-based provisioning has been fairly typical for Exchange mailboxes since Exchange 2007. Because OCS did not have any native PowerShell support, organizations were forced to continue using VBScript or some other method to automatically enable new accounts for OCS. Starting with Lync Server Management Shell in Lync Server 2010, and now with the Skype for Business Server Management Shell, an entire workflow script can be used to create new accounts. When a new user joins the company, a PowerShell script is used to automatically create the new user account, place it in the correct organizational unit, provision a home folder, create an Exchange mailbox on the correct database, enable the user for Skype for Business, and assign the correct voice and conferencing policies. Not only is the chance for error reduced, but consider how much time is saved by not requiring extra work or extra training.

Management Shell Basics

Tasks are performed in PowerShell through commands called cmdlets. Cmdlets each have a specific function, and their names begin with a verb, such as `Get` or `Set`, indicating what action will be taken. The remainder of the cmdlet name determines what specific object will be viewed or acted on. The Skype for Business Server Management Shell is built on top of the Windows PowerShell engine, meaning that everything you can do within Windows PowerShell can also be done within the Skype for Business Server Management Shell. The opposite, however, is not true.

When the Skype for Business Server Management Shell is loading, an extensive list of more than 800 custom cmdlets is loaded on top of the base PowerShell cmdlets available. These new cmdlets are specific to Skype for Business Server and enable administrators to manage Skype for Business components through the Management Shell. Updates for Skype for Business Server 2015, called Cumulative Updates, sometimes include updated versions of cmdlets, or even new cmdlets altogether.

Most of the cmdlets within the Skype for Business Server Management Shell are consistent in their naming approach because they follow a format consisting of a verb, a hyphen, the letters *Cs*, and, lastly, an item.

NOTE

All the cmdlets in Skype for Business Server 2015 include the `Cs` designator, which stands for Communications Server. The history here is that the actual name change from Communications Server 2010 to Lync Server 2010 happened fairly late in the product life cycle, and the cmdlet naming was never, and probably never will be, updated.

This might seem long, but it makes sense when you view the actual cmdlets. Commands to view the configuration or properties of an item all begin with `Get`, and when changing or assigning new properties, the cmdlet begins with `Set`. For example, to view the properties of a particular Skype for Business user account, the cmdlet `Get-CsUser` can be used. To set one of the properties for a user account, such as a phone number, the `Set-CsUser` cmdlet can be used.

The first parameter in any cmdlet is referred to as the identity, which signifies what object will be acted on. Not all `Get` cmdlets require an identity to be provided, and when it is omitted, a list of all the matching objects is returned. For example, running `Get-CsUser -Identity sip:crichard@skypeunleashed.com` returns the properties of only a single user, but simply running `Get-CsUser` with no identity specified returns a list of all users and their properties.

When a `Set` command is used, though, an identity must be specified so that the Management Shell knows which object should be modified. Additionally, the attribute of the object being modified must be specified. Only the attribute being changed must be included, so if other attributes are staying the same there is no need to include them.

For example, if a user needs to be enabled for Enterprise Voice and assigned a Line URI, the command looks like the following string:

```
Set-CsUser -Identity sip:crichard@skypeunleashed.com -EnterpriseVoiceEnabled $true
➥-LineUri tel:+12223334444
```

Commands can also be strung together, or "piped" to one another. When piped to another cmdlet, the results from the first cmdlet are passed to the second cmdlet. Continuing the preceding example, an equivalent command to the `Set-CsUser` example is the following string:

```
Get-CsUser -Identity sip:crichard@skypeunleashed.com | Set-CsUser
➥-EnterpriseVoiceEnabled $true -LineUri tel:+12223334444
```

13

This might not seem beneficial when a single user is involved, but when multiple objects are piped to another cmdlet, they will each run through the destination cmdlet. Consider a scenario in which an organization wants to enable all users who have a display name starting with the letter *T* for Enterprise Voice. First, the `Get-CsUser` cmdlet is used, but to return only the users whose display name begins with *T*, a `Filter` parameter is used. For those familiar with filtering using the `Where-Object` cmdlet, the `Filter` parameter uses the same syntax and operators. The `Where-Object` cmdlet can also be used here, but the built-in `Filter` parameter is more straightforward:

```
Get-CsUser -Filter {DisplayName -like "T*"}
```

The `Filter` option is more efficient because the cmdlet only retrieves the objects that meet the filter, whereas the `Where-Object` method returns all objects and then filters out the objects that don't apply.

This can be built on even further by piping the results to a `Set-CsUser` cmdlet where the users can be enabled for Enterprise Voice:

```
Get-CsUser -Filter {DisplayName -like "T*"} | Set-CsUser
➥-EnterpriseVoiceEnabled $true
```

This short string of cmdlets can enable thousands of users for Enterprise Voice in a much faster method than using the Skype for Business Server 2015 Control Panel.

Tips and Tricks

Quite a few shortcuts and tricks can be used within the Skype for Business Server Management Shell to save time. This section discusses a few tips that might make using the Management Shell a bit easier and more efficient.

Use the Tab Key

Instead of typing a full cmdlet name, begin by typing the first few letters after the action verb and press the Tab key. The Management Shell automatically cycles through the cmdlets that match the string already entered. For example, typing `Get-CsP` and then pressing Tab automatically changes the string to `Get-CsPartnerApplication`. Pressing Tab again changes it to `Get-CsPersistentChatActiveServer`. Use Tab to go forward through the list and press Shift+Tab to cycle backward. The Tab key can also autocomplete parameters inside the cmdlet, so it is handy when recalling the exact parameter name. If the Tab complete feature is not working, it probably means the command is already misspelled and no match can be found, or the user is assigned an RBAC role that does not allow the desired cmdlet.

Skip the Identity

Although the identity specifies an object and is a required parameter when changing an object, it's not required to type the entire `Identity` parameter. If the identity is not explicitly referenced, the first string after the cmdlet is assumed to be the identity. For example, the following two commands are equivalent in functionality, but one requires fewer characters:

```
Get-CsVoicePolicy -Identity Executives
Get-CsVoicePolicy Executives
```

Surround Spaces with Quotation Marks

When referencing objects, names, or any values that have spaces or special characters, make sure that the entire text string is enclosed in quotation marks or single quotation marks. When PowerShell detects a space, it assumes that the next character will be the beginning of a new parameter. When the text string is not within quotation marks, commands might fail. Both single and double quotation marks are acceptable. For example, if you are trying to retrieve the user Claudia Richard, this command generates an error:

```
Get-CsUser Claudia Richard
```

To successfully return the correct user, use the following command:

```
Get-CsUser "Claudia Richard"
```

Integrated Scripting Environment (ISE)

Windows also includes the PowerShell Integrated Scripting Environment, or ISE. With the ISE, you can run commands and write, test, and debug scripts in a single Windows graphic user interface with multiline editing, tab completion, syntax coloring, selective execution, and context-sensitive help. The PowerShell ISE is available from the Start Menu.

Leverage `Get-Help`

Included within all the Skype for Business Server Management Shell cmdlets is a built-in help reference. To retrieve assistance with any cmdlet, simply type `Get-Help` followed by the name of the cmdlet. For example, to get assistance with the `Set-CsDialPlan` cmdlet, type

```
Get-Help Set-CsDialPlan
```

This help request returns a description of the cmdlet's purpose, the full syntax and parameters available in the cmdlet, and a summary of what the cmdlet does. More information can also be requested using the `-Examples`, `-Detailed`, and `-Full` flags at the end of the command. `-Examples` returns sample commands with the correct syntax, `-Detailed` returns a description of each parameter, and `-Full` returns the complete documentation available. Using the `-Online` flag will open a web browser to the TechNet page for the specified cmdlet.

13

Having this help reference available without manually searching through documentation is incredibly useful. It can also come in handy when you're having trouble remembering a specific cmdlet name. In these cases, wildcards can be used to search through the documentation for a match. For example, the following command returns a list that displays `Set-CsBandwidthPolicyServiceConfiguration` and `Set-CsBlockedDomain`:

```
Get-Help Set-CsB*
```

Microsoft routinely updates help information for various cmdlets. An administrator can update the local help information by utilizing the `Update-Help` cmdlet. PowerShell will then download all new help data.

Role-Based Access Control

As originally introduced in Lync Server 2010, Skype for Business Server 2015 has the concept of role-based access control. RBAC allows for a degree of flexibility in the management of the infrastructure that's simply not possible with a traditional approach to administration control. In prior versions of the product, an administrator typically had full control of the environment and was able to modify any part of a deployment. With RBAC, permissions can be defined in a more granular method so that different levels of administrators can be delegated specific settings to manage. Users will only have access to specific features and options, whether using the Skype for Business Server 2015 Control Panel or the Management Shell.

Skype for Business Versus Exchange RBAC

The basis for role-based access control is to provide a specific set of permissions and actions allowed to a group. For those familiar with Exchange RBAC, it should be apparent that the Skype for Business version is not nearly as flexible. Exchange 2010 administrators can define the exact cmdlets and attributes allowed for each management role. With Skype for Business Server 2015, administrators can only base new roles on an existing template, but individual cmdlets can be added or removed from specific roles. Assignment of a management role can be done only by placing user accounts within a security group.

Default Roles

Skype for Business Server 2015 ships with several predefined RBAC roles. These roles exist in any deployment after the preparation steps have been completed and have a global scope. The default RBAC roles in Skype for Business Server 2015 include the following:

- **`CsAdministrator`**—This is the equivalent of `RTCUniversalServerAdmins` from OCS 2007. Users assigned this role have complete control over any part of the system. They can modify the topology, manage user accounts, and create additional RBAC roles. The CS Administrators group in Active Directory is assigned this role.
- **`CsArchivingAdministrator`**—Allows for modifying the archiving policies and configuration within the organization. This role is intended for compliance or legal department users who are responsible for archiving policies. The CS Archiving Administrators group in Active Directory is assigned to this role.
- **`CsHelpDesk`**—This role is slightly more advanced than `CsViewOnlyAdministrator` and includes the capability to perform basic troubleshooting. This role cannot modify any user properties or assign policies as `CsUserAdministrator` can. The CS Help Desk group in Active Directory is assigned to this role.
- **`CsLocationAdministrator`**—This role has the capability to modify and associate the locations and network subnets involved in E911. The CS Location Administrators group in Active Directory is assigned to this role.
- **`CsPersistentChatAdministrator`**—This role has the capability to manage the Persistent Chat global settings, categories, and chat rooms. The CS Persistent Chat Administrators group in Active Directory is assigned to this role.
- **`CsResponseGroupAdministrator`**—This role permits modification of Response Group queues, agent groups, and workflows. It is intended for users who are responsible for a small call center or the Interactive Voice Response (IVR) systems in the organization. The CS Response Group Administrators in Active Directory is assigned to this role.
- **`CsResponseGroupManager`**—This role allows members the ability to manage limited configuration of assigned Response Groups.
- **`CsServerAdministrator`**—This role can manage individual Skype for Business Servers. It is geared toward users who manage, monitor, and troubleshoot Skype for Business Servers. It is slightly a step below the `CsAdministrator` role because no changes that globally affect the deployment, such as topology modifications, are permitted. This role typically is assigned to users who are responsible for day-to-day operations and management of Skype for Business Servers. The CS Server Administrators group in Active Directory is assigned to this role.

- **CsUserAdministrator**—This role relates to the RTCUniversalUserAdmins group from OCS 2007. This role is geared toward helpdesk administrators and allows for enabling or disabling users for Skype for Business. This role can also move users between pools and assign policies to accounts. The CS User Administrators group in Active Directory is assigned this role.
- **CsViewOnlyAdministrator**—Permits read-only access to the Skype for Business Server deployment. This includes topology, pool, server, and user configuration, but no changes can be made. The CS View-Only Administrators group in Active Directory is assigned to this role.
- **CsVoiceAdministrator**—Users assigned to this role can manage any of the voice features found in Skype for Business Server 2015. This includes creation and modification of dial plans, routes, voice policies, and PSTN usages. Typically this is assigned to telephony or voice team users. The CS Voice Administrators group in Active Directory is assigned to this role.

NOTE

You cannot modify the default RBAC roles. Instead, create new roles to suit the needs of each organization.

Creating New Roles

Organizations can build on the default RBAC roles by creating their own custom roles. To create a new role, use the following steps:

1. Create a security group with the same name as what the role will be named.
2. Identify a preexisting RBAC role that contains most of the cmdlets required for the new role. It will serve as a template for the new role.
3. Decide on a Skype for Business Server scope for the new role. This can be a global site, a single site, or multiple sites.
4. (Optional) Decide on an organization scope for the new role. A role can be limited to affect only user accounts within a specific OU in Active Directory.

To create a new RBAC role, use the following syntax within the Skype for Business Management Shell:

```
New-CsAdminRole -Identity <AD Security Group Name> -Template
➥<Preexisting Role Name> -ConfigScopes <Skype for Business Configuration Scope>
➥-UserScopes <Organizational Units>
```

For example, to create a new role called `SanFranciscoUserAdmins` scoped to the SF site and the SF OU, use the following syntax:

```
New-CsAdminRole -Identity SanFranciscoUserAdmins -Template CsUserAdministrators
➥-ConfigScopes "site:Redmond"
➥-UserScopes "OU=Redmond Users,OU=Company,DC=fabrikam,DC=local"
```

NOTE

Users logged on locally to a Skype for Business Server and executing the commands in the Skype for Business Management Shell are not affected by RBAC. RBAC roles are enforced only when using the Skype for Business Server 2015 Control Panel or PowerShell Remoting.

Using the Skype for Business Topology Model

Starting with Lync Server 2010, some significant changes to how the deployment is managed have been made. Instead of individually installing and configuring servers, the deployment is managed centrally through a tool called Topology Builder. This shift in management helps make administration easier for organizations and limits the potential for mistakes.

For those familiar with Office Communications Server 2007 R2, administrators had to log on to each server in the topology and manually configure options such as next hops, monitoring associations, and service ports. With Skype for Business Server 2015, the configuration is completed in advance and then published to the Central Management Store (CMS).

When a server is deployed, it installs SQL Server Express. A local copy of the CMS is then replicated to this SQL instance so that the server can reference the entire topology. When the administrator begins installation, the server reads the topology and installs any roles within the topology that match the fully qualified domain name of itself.

NOTE

The only configuration required to link or associate servers with each other is performed automatically during the installation process. This helps reduce the chance for incorrect settings that cause unpredictable or problematic behavior for the servers.

To review, the deployment model with Skype for Business Server 2015 follows the following high-level steps:

1. The administrator creates the topology by defining all sites, servers, and gateways in the deployment.
2. The topology is then published to the Central Management Store.

3. A Skype for Business Server installs the SQL Express engine and creates a local replica of the CMS.

4. The Skype for Business Server reads the local CMS replica and installs the roles matching its FQDN.

Central Management Store

The preceding section referenced the Central Management Store. To understand the responsibility of the CMS, it is important to understand how prior versions of the product operated such that server and service configuration was stored within Active Directory. Live Communications Server and Office Communications Server both stored configuration information within the System partition of the forest root domain. In many cases, this was acceptable, but it caused performance problems in scenarios in which a remote office had poor connectivity to a domain controller in the forest root domain.

This was because the System container is not replicated to all domain controllers in the forest, so servers could be required to leverage WAN links to read settings even if a domain controller existed locally.

To mitigate these problems, Office Communications Server 2007 R2 recommended migrating the settings to the Configuration container instead, which is replicated to all domain controllers in the forest. This solved the problem, but organizations had a confusing manual migration path to move settings to the new container and often skipped this step. Furthermore, organizations could not move the settings after installing OCS 2007 R2, so they were stuck in this state with performance problems.

Starting with Lync Server 2010, the settings for the deployment have moved from Active Directory to the CMS, which is just an additional SQL database. The CMS must be populated before the first pool is created, and this is done automatically if the first pool is a Standard Edition server. The CMS is often stored on the same SQL server and instance acting as a Back End Server for a pool, and after installation the CMS can be moved to another server at any time.

As indicated earlier, when a server is prepared for a Skype for Business Server 2015 installation, the first action it takes is to install a local replica of the CMS. As changes occur in the CMS, they are synchronized out to all members of the topology, which removes the need for servers to maintain a constant connection to a centralized configuration store. Servers synchronize the changes regularly and use the information stored locally instead of contacting a central point for settings, which improves performance and stability.

Topology Builder

Included with Skype for Business Server 2015 is the Topology Builder application, shown in Figure 13.2. The Topology Builder is a centralized configuration point for adding servers to the deployment or changing configuration, and it includes information from Lync Server 2010 and Lync Server 2013 resources, if any are deployed. All naming, IP addressing, and association of servers is performed through the Topology Builder so that administrators do not need to individually configure servers. This helps reduce the number of errors made during the configuration of pools with multiple members.

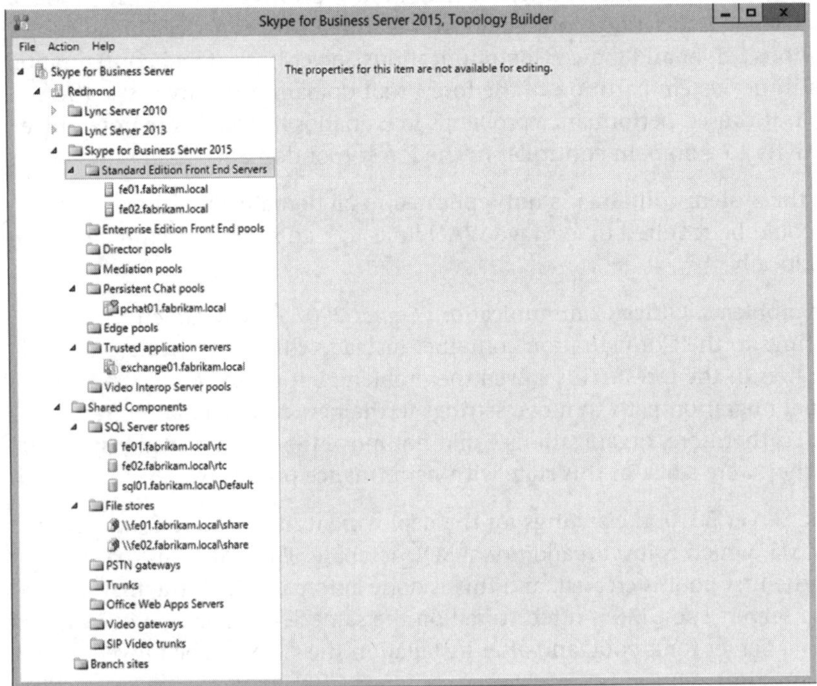

FIGURE 13.2 The Topology Builder tool.

Each server site is defined within the Topology Builder, and then each specific server role is defined and associated with a site. When completed, administrators can publish the topology to the CMS, where it can be read by servers.

Scopes

Scopes in Skype for Business Server 2015 are available to help define the boundary of a policy. Scopes are applied based on the topology built within the Topology Builder. The highest level that exists is the Global level. Within the Global level are sites, which represent physical locations where pools exist. Sites typically are datacenters where the Front End pool servers reside. Each site then contains the pools that make up the deployment. A site can have one pool or multiple pools. This arrangement is depicted in Figure 13.3.

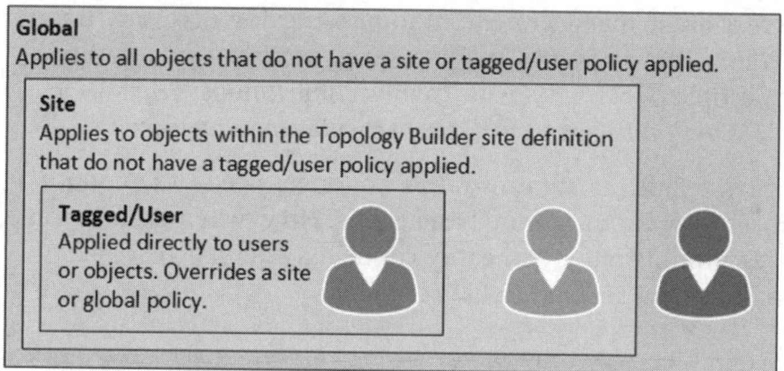

FIGURE 13.3 Scope priority.

After the topology is defined, default policies for many aspects of Skype for Business Server 2015 are created. For example, global policies are created for Voice Policies, Conferencing Policies, and External Access Policies.

Global policies apply to all sites, pools, and users by default. Additional policies can be created at any of the other scopes as well, giving flexibility on overriding the defaults. The benefit of applying policies to a site or pool scope is that the additional task of assigning a policy directly to the users is no longer required. Instead, policies defined at a higher level are automatically applied to all scopes below as long as the lower scope does not have a policy already defined.

Administrators can still create new policies and assign them directly to a user account to override any global or site policies. This might be necessary to grant executives or VIP users a higher level of access than the default for everyone else in the site.

NOTE

In terms of priority, the policy assigned closest to the user account takes precedence. User policies override pool policies, pool policies override site policies, and site policies override the global policy. Policies automatically trickle down from the global level unless a policy exists closer to the user, similar to Group Policy Objects.

Managing Servers and Users

There are some tasks that most administrators of Skype for Business Server 2015 will manage at some point. This section covers some of these items that don't occur on a daily basis but might be required at some point.

Skype for Business Server Logging Tool

When all else fails and the problem cannot be diagnosed, perform a diagnostic trace of the server traffic. Logging in Skype for Business Server 2015 has changed quite a bit from prior versions in which a GUI logging tool was available to collect traces. Logging in Skype for Business Server 2015 uses the Centralized Logging Service, which is collecting logs by default, and is intended to give a single management point for retrieving necessary traces. In Lync 2010 and earlier, an administrator had to enable logging individually on every single server in a pool, even multiple pools if the issue involved a few hops. This was a very tedious process and made it very difficult to locate a particular message flow.

The CLS is constantly logging by default, so administrators no longer need to reproduce an issue after enabling the traces in order to capture basic traffic. Now, when users report an issue, the Skype for Business administrators can easily conduct a search across all servers involved in a user's message and see that traffic centrally.

NOTE

Traditional tools such as Microsoft Network Monitor and Wireshark are unable to display Skype for Business traffic by default because it is TLS-encrypted. Although it is possible to decrypt the traffic after loading certificates and private keys, it is far easier to use the native tools and CLS to log Skype for Business SIP traffic.

The `ClsController.exe` tool is now used manage the logging and searches. It can be found on any system with the Skype for Business administration tools installed in `C:\Program Files\Common Files\ Skype for Business Server 2015ClsAgent`, but it is actually managed using PowerShell cmdlets native to Skype for Business. Another change is that the tool now logs based on specific scenarios instead of requiring an administrator to select specific trace components. A Windows GUI tool is also available, as detailed later in this chapter.

You can retrieve the current logging configuration using

```
Get-CsCsClsConfiguration
```

The logs are stored on each server in the `%TEMP%\Tracing` folder by default, and will allow only up to 80% of available disk space.

Searching the Log Files

Because most cases will be covered by the default AlwaysOn scenario, administrators can begin troubleshooting by searching for a specific pool or user with the `Search-CsLogging` cmdlet.

For example, to search for a specific user's traffic on a single pool during a known time frame, use this:

```
Search-CsClsLogging -Pools LYNCPOOL01.fabrikam.com -Uri
➥"crichard@skypeunleashed.com" -StartTime "12/9/2015 10:00AM" -EndTime
➥"12/9/2015 1:00 PM" -MatchAll
```

By default, any parameter included in the search is considered an acceptable match. That is to say that the `-MatchAny` parameter is always assumed unless the administrator specifies `-MatchAll` within the search. The preceding example would have returned all traffic on `LYNCPOOL10.fabrikam.com`, all traffic from the user `crichard@skypeunleashed.com`, and all traffic in the organization between 10:00 a.m. and 1:00 p.m. on 12/9/2015 if `-MatchAll` had not been specified.

Alternatively, use the following syntax to search for a single user's traffic across all pools in the organization, which is the really powerful part of the new service:

```
Search-CsClsLogging -Uri "crichard@skypeunleashed.com"
```

Viewing Log Files

`Search-CsClsLogging` generates log files that can be read using the same Snooper tool found in the Resource Kit download package. Open the resulting file in Snooper to inspect the traffic.

A message-by-message view of the conversation is located on the left side. Clicking any of the lines changes the view in the right-side pane to display the entire SIP message selected. Error messages are highlighted in red for easy identification. A search bar, where keywords such as a username or phone number are entered, is located at the top of the window. After you've entered a search string and pressed Enter, the view is filtered to display only messages with that string. This kind of filtering can be useful when searching for problems with a single user because it removes all the other traffic through the server.

Figure 13.4 displays a sample SIP trace using the Snooper tool.

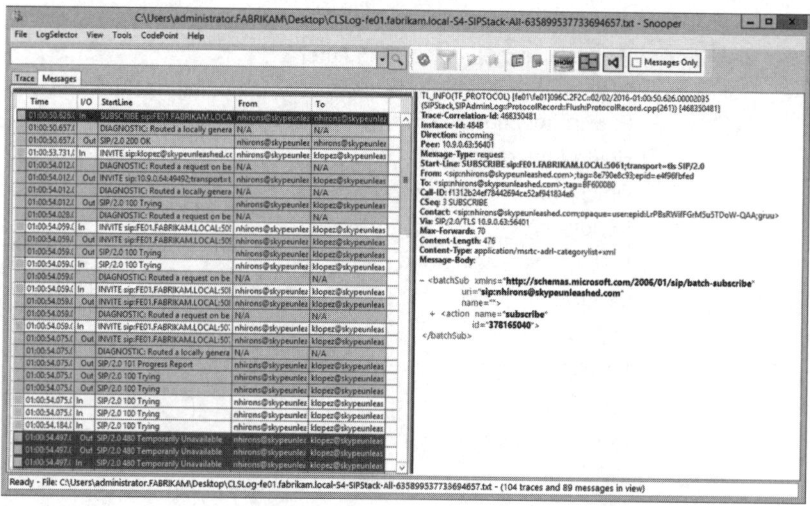

FIGURE 13.4 Using Snooper to view a SIP trace.

Starting and Stopping Logging

As mentioned previously, most scenarios are going to be covered by AlwaysOn being enabled by default. If administrators do need to log on different components, the following syntax can be used with a specific scenario:

```
Start-CsClsLogging -Scenario <Scenario Name> -Duration <Time in Days:Hours:Minutes>
➥-Pools <Comma-Separated List of Pool Names>
```

Use the `Stop-CsClsLogging` cmdlet to manually stop a scenario, but keep in mind that any started logging scenarios will stop automatically after the specified duration expires. Whereas Lync Server 2013 has two dozen logging scenarios, Skype for Business Server 2015 increases that to 43. The different scenarios available include those listed in Table 13.1.

TABLE 13.1 Available Centralized Logging Scenarios

Scenario	Description
ACPMCU	
AddressBook	Address book generation and distribution group expansion
AlwaysOn	Default
ApplicationSharing	Desktop and application sharing
AudioVideoConferencingIssue	Audio and video conferencing
Authentication	
CAA	Conferencing Auto Attendant
CLS	Centralized Logging Service
CmdletDebug	PowerShell cmdlet debugging
CPS	Call Park Service
Data Collection	
DeviceUpdate	Device update service
Dialin	Dialin Conferencing
FilterApps	IM Filter and Client Version Filter
HADR	High Availability/Disaster Recovery, including backup service, PowerShell, database sync agent, and user services
HostedMigration	Hosted migration
Hybrid Voice	Office 365 hybrid voice
IISLog	IIS logging
IMAndPresence	Instant messaging and Presence
IncomingAndOutgoingCall	Call routing
LILRLegacy	Log retention
LILRLYSS	Log retention for Lync Storage Service
LYSSaAndUCS	Lync Storage Service
LyssFabric	Lync Storage Service Fabric Service
ManagementCore	CMS
MediaConnectivity	Media connections
MeetingJoin	Meeting join experience
MonitoringAndArchiving	Monitoring and Archiving Service
NonTopologyAlwaysOn	
OnlineDialinConferencing	Skype for Business Online conferencing
PowerShell	PowerShell
PresenceAndRouting	User Presence and routing

Scenario	Description
Provisioning	Provisioning
RGS	Response Group Service
SP	Support Portal
UserReplicator	User Replicator Service
Telemetry	
TraceTest	
UcsProtocol	Unified Contact Store protocol
UCWA	Unified Communications Web API
VoiceMail	Exchange voice mail integration
WAC	Office Web Apps integration
XMPP	XMPP Service

CLS Logging Tool

In Lync Server 2013, there was a logging tool called Lync Logger. It was run on a local Lync Server to start and stop logging. Once logging was finished, Lync Logger could span Snooper to display the log file.

In Skype for Business Server 2015, there is a new tool called CLS Logger. This tool combines some of the graphical user interface features of Lync Logger with some of the features of Centralized Logging Service. This provides a means of starting and stopping logging scenarios across entire pools (or a group of pools) in an easy to navigate interface. In addition to starting and stopping scenarios, scenarios can be created, edited, or deleted, as well as CLS logs searched. Once search results are output to a file, Snooper can be used to view the log file.

The CLS Logger tool is part of the Skype for Business Debugging Tools, which is a separate download from Microsoft. Once installed, CLS Logger is available at `C:\Program Files\Skype for Business Server 2015\Debugging Tools\ClsLogger.exe`.

Figure 13.5 displays a sample the Skype for Business Logging Tool.

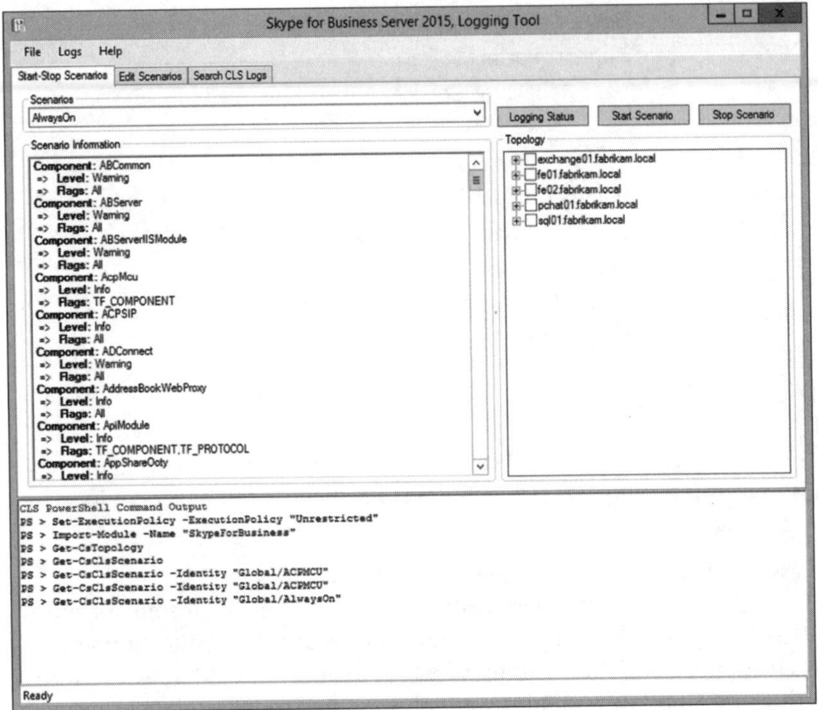

FIGURE 13.5 The Skype for Business Logging Tool.

Server Draining

A useful feature in Skype for Business Server 2015 is the concept of draining a server when preparing it for maintenance. This enables an administrator to prepare a server for maintenance without immediately affecting users. Existing sessions on the server are ended immediately and users are transferred to a different server within the pool.

To prepare a server for maintenance, follow these steps:

1. Open the Skype for Business Server Control Panel.
2. Click Topology.
3. Highlight the server to be modified.
4. Click Action and select Prevent New Connections for All Services.
5. Alternatively, double-click the server to drill down further and manage the individual services.

The server can also be drained using Skype for Business Management Shell:

```
Stop-CsWindowsService -Graceful
```

This will achieve the same result as the previous method. After the command completes, the `Get-CsWindowsService` cmdlet will show any services that are still running.

NOTE

Preventing new connections is a feature that only works with DNS load balancing and has no effect on whether a hardware load balancer continues to send traffic to a server. If you're using a hardware load balancer, perform the draining steps there instead.

This feature also does not cover load balancing of the web component services. The hardware load balancer used to distribute traffic to these services must also be drained to prevent new connections to the server prepared for maintenance.

Database Import/Export

A tool familiar to many LCS, OCS, and Lync Server administrators is the database import/export tool called `dmbimpexp.exe`. This tool enables administrators to import or export user contact lists using XML files. Typically a SQL server backup captures the rtc database that contains the user contact lists, but having the XML version available can be useful when restoring from a backup that is slow or unavailable.

Starting with Lync Server 2013, this tool was removed and replaced with a series of native cmdlets providing similar functionality. The `Export-CsUserData`, `Import-CsUserData`, `Update-CsUserData`, and `Convert-CsUserData` cmdlets provide these same features and offer a solution native to the Skype for Business Server Management Shell.

There are many options when running `dbimpexp`, but the basic functionality is fairly straightforward. For a full list of the options available, see the `dbimpexp-readme.html` file included in the same folder as the executable.

To export all user contact lists from an Enterprise or Standard Edition pool, the same syntax can now be used:

```
Export-CsUserData -PoolFQDN "<Pool FQDN>" -FileName "<Path and Filename>.zip"
```

After the contact lists are exported to XML and safe, they can be applied back to the users at any time. A scheduled task can easily perform this action on a nightly or weekly basis. Importing the contact lists is just as simple as the export procedure. By default, the contents of the XML file are merged with a user's existing contacts, but the `/delete` option can be used to empty the contact list before an import is performed.

To import all user contact lists from an Enterprise or Standard Edition pool, use the following syntax:

```
Import-CsUserData -PoolFQDN "<Pool FQDN>" -FileName "<Path and Filename>.zip"
```

CAUTION

In Skype for Business Server 2015, the Front End Service must be restarted on all pool members before the imports are visible. Use the `Update-CsUserData` cmdlet instead to skip the restart requirement.

These cmdlets are very powerful tools and can have a visible impact on user accounts if used incorrectly, so run some test scenarios before doing these changes in bulk. The export and import procedures can be targeted to only a single user via the `-UserFilter` parameter.

Configuring Quality of Service

Quality of service (QoS) can be used in networks where the media traffic used by Skype for Business Server 2015 servers and clients should have a higher priority than other traffic using the same infrastructure. This is done by having the Skype for Business Servers and endpoints tag their media traffic packets with a specific Differentiated Services Code Point (DSCP) value. Routers within the network are then configured to prioritize traffic based on the DSCP values included with packets.

DSCP marking in Skype for Business Server 2015 is done by using the policy-based QoS first introduced with Windows Server 2008 and Windows Vista. These policies are controlled through Windows Group Policy and can mark traffic with DSCP codes based on application names and port ranges. Because these policies can be centrally managed and controlled by the organization, it should be acceptable to trust the markings sent from client endpoints. Using a separate port range for each type of traffic enables the policy-based QoS to tag the traffic appropriately. For example, audio traffic using one port range can be assigned a DSCP code with higher priority than the port range used for video or application sharing.

CAUTION

Network equipment is typically configured to ignore or not trust DSCP markings from computers on the regular data network. Because Skype for Business is a softphone and operates using the same VLAN as PCs, the markings from machines on the data VLAN must be trusted to use QoS with Skype for Business.

Server Configuration

Skype for Business servers operate similarly to clients and tag media traffic through the use of policy-based QoS in Group Policy. Each media type has one of the following default port ranges assigned:

- Audio (49,152–57,500)
- Video (57,501–65,535)
- Application sharing (49,152–65,535)

These port ranges can then be matched through policy-based QoS and assigned a DSCP marking. The default port range for application sharing overlaps with both audio and video. If application sharing is tagged differently than either traffic, a separate port range must be configured. Port ranges for each media type can be configured using the `Set-CsConferenceServer` and `Set-CsMediationServer` cmdlets.

Unfortunately, the Skype for Business product team uses overlapping port ranges by default, so administrators cannot determine whether traffic is application sharing or audio or video. To effectively implement QoS, the port ranges should be nonoverlapping. For example, to separate application sharing into its own port range, run the following command:


```
Set-CsConferenceServer -AppSharingPortStart 40803
```

This changes application sharing to use ports 40,803–57,185 while keeping the same number of ports available. The latest Skype for Business documentation actually recommends also adjusting the `AppSharingPortCount` to 8348 as part of the QoS configuration.

Using the same port ranges on each conferencing, application, and Mediation Server will help simplify configuration. Use the `Set-CsConferenceServer`, `Set-CsApplicationServer`, and `Set-CsMediationServer` cmdlets to configure these ranges.

Client Configuration

QoS tagging of the media is performed by the Skype for Business client itself, so it must be provisioned in a way that it understands what ports to use for each type of traffic. By default, no tagging is done and all traffic uses the port range 5350–5389. The Skype for Business client supports using different port ranges for the following types of traffic and recommends using a minimum of 20 ports per modality. This roughly translates to 20 concurrent calls per modality, which should be more than enough for any single endpoint.

First, to enable separate port ranges for each media type, run the following command:

```
Set-CsConferencingConfiguration -ClientMediaPortRangeEnabled $true
```

Next, define a unique port range for each type of traffic. As an example, the ports used on the client side can be the same as those on the server. The sample numbers used here are well beyond the minimum number of ports required and are used only to show how the default port ranges can be moved. The port ranges used should be limited to the recommended sizes for ease of management and troubleshooting.

```
Set-CsConferencingConfiguration -ClientAudioPort 500020 -ClientAudioPortRange 20
➥-ClientVideoPort 58000-58019 -ClientVideoPortRange 20 -ClientAppSharingPort 40803
➥-ClientAppSharingPortRange 20 -ClientFileTransferPort 40783
➥-ClientFileTransferPortRange 20
```

NOTE

The suggested port range from TechNet as of this writing uses overlapping ranges for application sharing and file transfer. The preceding example breaks File Transfer into a separate range so it is not accidentally tagged as application-sharing traffic.

Creating a Client QoS Policy

After modifying the Skype for Business clients and servers to use specific port ranges, you must create QoS policies for the servers and clients to add the appropriate DSCP value to traffic originating from each port range. The steps required to use policy-based QoS through Group Policy are similar, but the port ranges used for servers and clients will likely differ. Create at least two separate policies: one for servers and one for clients. To create a new policy, perform the following steps:

1. Open a new Group Policy object.
2. Expand Computer Configuration, Windows Settings, and then click Policy-Based QoS.
3. Right-click Policy-Based QoS and select Create New Policy.
4. Enter a name for the policy, such as **Skype for Business Audio**.
5. Enter a DSCP value, such as **46**, and click Next.
6. For the client policy, limit the tagging only to Skype for Business clients by selecting Only Applications with This Executable Name, and enter **lync.exe**. (The executable name for the client did not change in Skype for Business.) Do not specify an executable for the server policies. Click Next.
7. Allow the policy to apply to Any Source IP Address and Any Destination IP Address.
8. In the Select the Protocol This QoS Policy Applies To area, select TCP and UDP.
9. In the Specify the Source Port Number section, select From This Source Port Number or Range and then enter the range used for audio traffic, such as **50020:50039**.
10. Click Finish to complete the policy.
11. Repeat these steps for each type of media using a unique port range, which should be tagged differently. Figure 13.6 demonstrates what a policy with separate audio and video settings looks like.

NOTE

The A/V Edge Service behaves a bit differently. First, because it typically is not part of the domain, it might be necessary to create the policies locally on each server. Second, the port range used to define each service should be specified as a *destination* port instead of source port. This ensures that traffic passed between the Edge Server and the Front End pool is marked correctly. The defined port range used for the Front End or clients will always be a destination port range from the Edge Server's perspective.

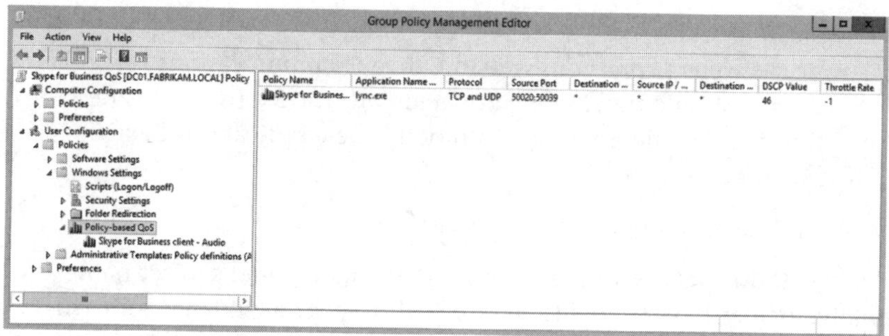

FIGURE 13.6 Policy-based QoS.

13

Non-Windows-Based Devices

Because QoS policies can be created only on Windows Vista or later operating systems, the process for enabling QoS on third-party devices is slightly different. These devices receive instructions to enable QoS through the following command:

```
Set-CsMediaConfiguration Global -EnableQoS $true
```

Lync Phone Edition QoS

The final client type that can use QoS settings is the Lync Phone Edition client, which can run on third-party partner hardware. Lync Phone Edition settings are determined through in-band signaling to the devices. In addition to a DSCP value for audio traffic, the Lync Phone Edition clients also support 802.1p.

To set the Lync Phone Edition QoS settings, use the following command on a Skype for Business server:

```
Set-CsUcPhoneConfiguration -VoiceDiffServTag 46
```

`Set-CsUcPhoneConfiguration` still includes the `Voice8021p` parameter used to define a 802.1p class, but it has no effect on devices in Skype for Business Server 2015. Instead, use DSCP values for providing QoS markings.

It can be difficult to determine all areas where QoS policies and settings apply, and their correct values. Skype for Business MVP Pat Richard has developed a QoS calculator that streamlines the process; it provides not only the correct values, but PowerShell commands that can be copied and pasted into Skype for Business Server 2015 to configure those policies as well as automatically create and configure the required Group Policy Objects. That calculator can be found at http://www.ehloworld.com/2821.

Troubleshooting

Troubleshooting a Skype for Business Server 2015 installation might become necessary in the event that users are unable to sign in or features seem to not work correctly. This section discusses the key components to check when issues arise. Common troubleshooting tools and tips are also provided, which should resolve many issues.

Certificates

Incorrectly issued certificates were a common issue in Office Communications Server deployments, but these issues should mostly be mitigated with the Skype for Business Server wizards. The option to manually request and modify the certificate still exists, which might lead to some problems.

Follow these guidelines to rule out any certificate issues:

- **Subject and subject alternative names**—Ensure that the required subject name and subject alternative names have been entered for each role. The guidance for each role varies, so verify the names required when deploying a new server. Always use the Certificate Wizard's suggested names if possible. Wildcard certificates are still technically supported for certain scenarios, but the recommendation is still to avoid these due to a number of caveats.
- **Key bit length**—The certificate bit length must be 1024, 2048, or 4096 to be supported by Skype for Business Server 2015.
- **Template**—The template used to issue the certificate should be based on the web server template. If the Skype for Business Server 2015 Certificate Wizard is used, the correct template will automatically be applied.
- **Private key**—The server certificate must have the private key associated to be used by Skype for Business Server 2015. In situations in which certificates are exported or copied between servers, export the private key with the certificate.
- **Certificate chain**—The server must be able to verify each certificate up to a Trusted Root Certification Authority. Additionally, because the server is presenting the certificate to clients, it must contain each intermediate certificate in the certificate chain.
- **Certificate store**—All certificates used by a server must be located in the Personal section of the local computer certificate store. A common mistake is to place certificates in the Personal section of the user account certificate store.
- **Certificate trust**—Be sure that the clients and servers communicating with the server all contain a copy of the top-level Certificate Authority of the chain in their Trusted Root Certification Authority local computer store. When the Certificate Authority is integrated with Active Directory, this is generally not an issue, but when an offline or nonintegrated Certificate Authority is used, it might be necessary to install root certificates on clients and servers.

DNS Records

Successful operation of Skype for Business Server 2015 is heavily dependent on correctly configuring DNS. All necessary DNS records should exist and resolve to the correct locations. Verify that all servers have a host record configured in DNS. Separate web component URLs and simple URLs are not automatically entered and must be manually created by an administrator.

Use the following sample `nslookup` sequence within a command prompt to check the host record of the pool:

```
Nslook_up
set type=a
lyncpool01.fabrikam.com
```

A successful query returns a name and an IP address. Verify that the IP returned matches the IP addresses assigned to the servers or load balancer and that no extra, or surprise, IP addresses are returned.

To verify the SRV record required for automatic client sign-in internally, the syntax is slightly different. The following is another sample `nslookup` sequence:

```
nslookup
set type=srv
_sipinternaltls.tcp.fabrikam.com
```

A successful query returns a priority, weight, port, and server hostname. Verify that the server name matches the pool name and that the correct port is returned.

Event Logs

A good source of information in troubleshooting any server issue is the event logs. Skype for Business Server 2015 creates a dedicated event log for informational activities, warnings, and errors within the standard Windows Server Event Viewer console. To view this event log, following these steps:

1. Click Start.
2. Type **eventvwr.msc** and click OK to open the Event Viewer Microsoft Management Console.
3. Expand the Applications and Services Logs folder.
4. Click the Lync Server log.
5. Examine the log for warning or error events, which might provide additional insight into any issues.

Skype for Business Server Management Shell

The Skype for Business Server 2015 Management Shell provides several cmdlets, which are used to test various functions of a server. A useful cmdlet for verifying the overall health of a server is `Test-CSComputer`, which verifies that all services are running, the local computer group membership is correctly populated with the necessary Skype for Business Server Active Directory groups, and the required Windows Firewall ports have been opened. The `Test-CSComputer` cmdlet must run from the local computer and uses the following syntax:

```
Test-CSComputer -Report "C:\Test-CSComputer Results.xml"
```

After running the cmdlet, open the generated XML file to view a detailed analysis of each check.

Synthetic Transactions

A feature in Skype for Business Server 2015 is the introduction of synthetic transactions, which are sets of PowerShell cmdlets used to simulate actions taken by servers or users in the environment. These synthetic transactions enable an administrator to conduct realistic tests against a service. In the case of a Director, the most useful synthetic transaction is the `Test-CSRegistration` cmdlet, which simulates a user signing in to the specified server. Synthetic tests only test signaling. They do not test call quality.

The `Test-CSRegistration` cmdlet requires providing a target server, user credential, and SIP address. A registrar port can optionally be included. The user credential parameter's username and password must be collected by an authentication dialog box and saved to a variable as in the following command:

```
$Credential = Get-Credential "fabrikam\crichard"
```

After the credentials are collected, the cmdlet can be run with the user credential variable previously saved:

```
Test-CSRegistration -TargetFQDN lyncpool01.fabrikam.com -UserCredential $Credential
➥-UserSipAddress "sip:crichard@skypeunleashed.com" -RegistrarPort 5061 -Verbose
```

As you can see in the results of this command, shown below, the value of the Result parameter is Success.

```
TargetFQDN      : lyncpool01.fabrikam.com
Result          : Success
Latency         : 00:00:10.9506726
Error           :
Diagnosis       :
```

As seen in the output, the registration test was successful.

Telnet

Telnet is a simple method of checking whether a specific TCP port is available from a client machine. From a machine that is having trouble contacting a server, use the following steps to verify connectivity to the Registrar service:

1. Open a command prompt.
2. Type the following command:

```
telnet <Front End pool FQDN> 5061
```

If the window goes blank and only a flashing cursor is seen, it means the connection was successful and the port can be contacted without issue. If the connection fails, an error is returned. Check that the services are running on the Director and that no firewalls are blocking the traffic.

TIP

The Telnet client has not installed by default since Windows Vista and Windows Server 2008. On a desktop operating system, it must be installed using the Turn Windows Features On or Off option found in Programs and Features. On a server operating system, it can be installed through the Features section of Server Manager.

Time

A key component of any service running successfully in Skype for Business Server 2015 is the computer time. Verify that the clocks on the Skype for Business Server 2015 servers are correctly set and have the appropriate time zones configured. If the clocks between a server and a client are off by more than 5 minutes, authentication will begin to fail, which might prevent users from logging on successfully.

Services

Basic troubleshooting always begins with making sure that the Skype for Business Server 2015 services are all running. When services are in a stopped state, users will see many issues such as being unable to sign in or connect to the server. Verify that the following services are configured to start automatically and are running. Verification of the services can be done either through the traditional Services MMC or through the Skype for Business Server Management Shell.

To verify that the services are running, open the Skype for Business Server Management Shell and run the `Get-CsWindowsService` cmdlet. As shown here, this cmdlet returns both the service status and how many active connections exist, which can be valuable information when a server is being drained for maintenance.

```
PS C:\> Get-CsWindowsService

    Status Name          Activity Level
    Running W3SVC

    Running REPLICA

    Running RTCCLSAGT

    Running
    FabricHostSvc
    Running RTCSRV       Incoming requests per second=0
    Running RTCCAA       Concurrent Calls=0
    Running RTCCAS       Concurrent Conferences=0
    Running RTCRGS       Current Active Calls=0
    Running RTCCPS       Total Parked Calls=0
    Running RTCATS       Current Active Calls=0
    Running RTCIMMCU     Active Conferences=0
    Running RTCDATAMCU   Active Conferences=0
    Running RTCAVMCU     Number of Conferences=0
    Running RTCASMCU     Active Conferences=0
    Running RTCMEDSRV

    Running RTCXMPPTGW

    Running RTCHA        Current Outbound Calls=0
```

The following command quickly identifies nonrunning services by skipping the activity check:

```
Get-CsWindowsService -ExcludeActivityLevel | Where-Object {$_.Status -ne "Running"}
```

Third-party Tools

With the advent of PowerShell, and more specifically Skype for Business Management Shell, comes a plethora of simple and free tools to help streamline installation, configuration, and administration of Skype for Business. PowerShell's simple syntax makes it easy to customize these tools as well.

Microsoft maintains the Gallery, which lists many tools available for free. The Gallery is available at https://gallery.technet.microsoft.com/office.

Some of the other more popular third-party tools available from the community are listed in Table 13.2. Most of the authors are recognized experts in the Skype for Business space and have been awarded the Microsoft MVP Award for Skype for Business.

TABLE 13.2 Third-party PowerShell Tools

Author(s)	URL
Lasse Nordvik Wedoø	http://uc.lawedo.net/
Alessio Giombini	http://blog.giombini.com/
Paul Bloem	https://ucscripts.wordpress.com/
Richard Brynteson and Michael LaMontagne	http://www.skypevalidator.com/
James Cussen	http://www.myskypelab.com/
Greig Sheridan	http://greiginsydney.com/
Pat Richard	http://www.ehloworld.com
C. Anthony Caragol	http://www.lyncfix.com/

Best Practices

The following are best practices from this chapter:

- Use the new Skype for Business Server Management Shell for bulk administration tasks or to perform tasks more quickly than possible within the Skype for Business Server Control Panel.
- Create RBAC roles, which are scoped appropriately for administrators within the organization. Different sets of users can be managed by different administrators easily with this new flexibility.
- Use quality of service (QoS) on Skype for Business servers and clients to help improve media quality on unreliable or oversaturated networks.
- Use synthetic transactions to test Skype for Business Server services easily. These PowerShell cmdlets do not require a test workstation, but can simulate user activities against the server.
- Become familiar with the Skype for Business Server Logging Tool and how to diagnose issues with SIP tracing. This greatly improves the speed and accuracy in resolving problems.

Summary

It should be apparent that the administration model is going to make lives easier within many organizations. Although the Skype for Business Server Control Panel certainly has its nuances, such as no right-click functionality, the layout and organization are welcome changes. For the tasks that are tedious to perform in a user interface, administrators now have the full power of the Skype for Business Server Management Shell at their disposal. This automates batch tasks or enables organizations to develop scripts to create new users based on PowerShell.

The topology model also helps to reduce the number of errors or anomalies created by requiring administrators to configure servers individually in prior versions. This centralized approach to setup ensures that all pool members are identical and that the topology should work before ever being placed into production. Scope-based policies enable organizations to standardize on global or site policies easily, ensuring that users are not assigned different policies.

A good portion of any Skype for Business Server administrator's life includes some troubleshooting, so becoming familiar with the most common issues and tools is highly recommended. The new synthetic transactions can help administrators stay on top of problems before they become major issues, and the Skype for Business Server Logging Tool is a valuable resource for diagnosing errors.

CHAPTER 14

High Availability and Disaster Recovery

IN THIS CHAPTER

- Defining Business Requirements for High Availability and Disaster Recovery
- Designing for High Availability
- Designing for Disaster Recovery
- Configuring Skype for Business Server 2015 for High Availability
- Executing Disaster Recovery Procedures

Planning for availability and recovery of business-critical applications is a process that must be carried out in every IT organization. As organizations shift real-time communications to Skype for Business Server 2015, there are many important considerations for ensuring service-level agreements (SLAs) and service uptime. This chapter provides best practices for deploying Skype for Business Server 2015 as a highly available, business-critical application in any organization.

Defining Business Requirements for High Availability and Disaster Recovery

For a Skype for Business Server 2015 deployment of any type to be successful, the integrator deploying the technology must first understand the business requirements for the solution. Not only is this important for defining functional requirements, but the business must also be consulted on the SLA requirements for the environment. Organizations must plan and document the availability requirements of the Skype for Business infrastructure as well as the disaster recovery requirements. For disaster recovery, two key requirements must be identified: recovery point objective (RPO) and recovery time objective (RTO). This section should help you understand what is required to properly identify what level of availability is required, as well as identify the RPO and RTO for organizations.

Identifying Availability Requirements

Many organizations have predefined service levels for IT applications and services. Skype for Business Server 2015 often falls into many different service-level definitions, depending on the workloads deployed. Table 14.1 provides an example of service levels in a typical enterprise organization.

TABLE 14.1 Skype for Business Service Levels

Skype for Business Functionality	Service Level	Description
IM and Presence	Medium	IM and Presence are often classified as requiring medium or even high service levels at organizations. Many businesses rely on IM and Presence for business-critical communications.
Conferencing	High	When conferencing is moved to Skype for Business Server 2015 from a previous provider, the service level should be considered high. This functionality is critical for internal and external collaboration and communications. Audio bridges are often used as the primary tool for communicating with customers and partners.
Enterprise Voice	High	When Skype for Business Server 2015 is being used to replace a legacy telephony system, the Skype for Business service is classified as a high service level.

The service levels described in Table 14.1 represent a generic overview of common Skype for Business service levels. These levels also translate to detailed requirements for availability. Availability is presented based on the percentage of downtime throughout the entire year. Services with a high service level are often targeting 99.999% availability. However, it is important to understand what those percentages actually translate to in order to guide businesses down the right path for a highly available Skype for Business Server 2015 system.

What Do Service Levels Really Mean?

Availability is defined as the level of redundancy applied to a system for ensuring an absolute degree of operational continuity during planned and unplanned outages. Many organizations will require that Skype for Business Server 2015 systems are available without service interruption at all times. However, many people forget to consider the impact that regular maintenance on the Skype for Business systems, as well as contributing components such as the network and directory services, can have on the availability of Skype for Business. When an organization states that they want to have "five 9's" of availability for Skype for Business, it would mean that the Skype for Business service can have no more than 5.256 minutes of downtime for the entire year! SLA percentages are often misunderstood, and they can have a major impact on the design of the infrastructure a well as the surrounding operations. Table 14.2 outlines the most common SLA definitions and the associated downtime.

TABLE 14.2 SLA Definitions and Associated Downtime

Nines	Availability	Downtime Per Year
One nine	90%	36.5 days
Three nines	99.9%	8.76 hours
Four nines	99.99%	52.56 minutes
Five nines	99.999%	5.256 minutes
Six nines	99.9999%	31.536 seconds

It is important to be familiar with common SLA definitions when you are defining business requirements for any organization. Because planned outages such as maintenance and upgrades are often counted toward the overall downtime of a system, it is critical to design the Skype for Business system to accommodate that requirement. A Skype for Business system with an SLA of four nines would allow only 52.56 minutes of downtime for the entire year. Even this will require maintenance to happen without any service interruption to end users.

Understanding the Business Impact of High Availability and Disaster Recovery

The availability required of a Skype for Business Server 2015 system can have a major financial impact. It is important to work with the business owners to understand the appropriate balance of availability and cost. As the availability of a system is increased, cost rises in the areas covered in the following subsections.

Server Hardware and Software The most obvious area where an organization will see increased costs is in server costs. When a Skype for Business service is being scaled to match high service levels, additional servers and software for those servers are required. In a typical case, each server can come with additional costs, such as the following:

- Physical hardware
- Hardware warranty/service
- Datacenter space (if physical)
- Windows operating system license
- SQL Server license (if backend or witness for failover)
- Skype for Business Server license
- Antivirus license
- System management software license (such as Microsoft SCOM or other management software)

As can be seen in the preceding list, adding more systems to the environment can introduce lots of new costs. In many organizations, the cost to deploy additional servers is worth the investment for providing service availability. However, it is important to consider these costs when designing for availability.

Networking Major network investments must be made to support any highly available Unified Communications (UC) service. In addition to often having to increase bandwidth and deploy additional circuits for redundancy, the network configuration will become much more complex. Consider the following areas when planning for network costs related to availability:

- Network bandwidth
- Additional network circuits
- Network hardware (routers, switches, firewalls, hardware load balancers, and so on)
- Licensing for advanced features (many systems require additional licensing to support high-availability scenarios)

The network often requires a major investment when deploying UC. A major portion of the network investment might be related to capacity and quality increases to support usage, but a large portion should also be considered for supporting the availability of the entire UC service.

System Operations Complexity To support the additional servers and network equipment and configurations that are deployed, highly skilled engineers are required to follow very well-defined procedures. Keep in mind that in order to ensure the service availability for Skype for Business Server 2015, end-to-end management of the infrastructure must be streamlined. This includes everything from server management, client deployment, and support, to network management and facilities management.

The processes deployed to support a highly available service increase the complexity of the environment, and as a result the service is more expensive to run. This cost is associated with the staff to manage the environment. Consider the time that must be spent supporting the complex systems, as well as following procedures to ensure proper availability. This will result in additional head count as well as more advanced resources. In some instances, this may also result in third-party support contracts. Although a third-party support service might be required to ensure service availability, it often is not accounted for in initial financial planning.

Designing for High Availability

With an understanding of the business requirements for high availability, you can now properly design for providing that level of service availability. This section outlines how to properly design for high availability. It also provides detailed high-availability options for Skype for Business Server 2015 components.

Understanding High Availability

Availability describes the redundancy that has been applied to Skype for Business Server to keep the service up and running for users. The secondary focus of high availability is to reduce the end-user impact in the event of a system failure. To make a Skype for Business Server 2015 system highly available, it often means deploying redundant quantities of every component. The simplest example of this is to deploy at least two of each server type; in theory, this provides the system with high availability. However, it is not always that simple and there are other considerations that affect the design. Skype for Business 2015 has many components, as well as shared systems, that must be accounted for.

High-Availability Options in Skype for Business Server 2015

Skype for Business Server 2015 was designed by Microsoft to enable organizations to support even the most stringent of high-availability service requirements. The next sections outline how each system component can be made highly available.

Table 14.3 outlines the failure scenarios and the capabilities to provide high-availability in earlier versions of Lync Server and Skype for Business Server 2015.

TABLE 14.3 Skype for Business Server 2015 High-Availability Capabilities

Scenario	Lync Server 2010	Lync Server 2013	Skype for Business Server 2015
Server failure	Server pool via HLB and DNS load balancing	Same as Lync Server 2010	Same as Lync Server 2010 and 2013
Backend (SQL) failure	SQL clustering and SAN-based shared storage	SQL clustering and SAN-based shared storage OR SQL mirroring without the need for shared storage Support for auto-failover and failback with a witness Integrated configuration with Planning Tool, Topology Builder, and Control Panel	SQL AlwaysOn clustering and SAN-based shared storage OR SQL mirroring without the need for shared storage Support for auto-failover and failback with a witness Integrated configuration with Planning Tool, Topology Builder, and Control Panel OR SQL AlwaysOn Availability Groups (Active/Passive only) Support for auto-failover and failback Integrated configuration with Planning Tool, Topology Builder, and Control Panel

What Services Are Supported for Skype for Business Server 2015 High Availability?

First, let's cover what services are able to be made highly available. The following list of services outlines the highly available components in Skype for Business Server 2015:

- Peer-to-peer (all modalities)
- Presence

- Conferencing (all modalities)
- UC Web App
- Archiving
- CDR/QOE
- Federation
- PIC federation
- Unified Contact Store
- Skype for Business Server 2015 Control Panel
- Persistent Chat
- PSTN Voice
- Voice applications (CAA, CAS, PVA, and GVA)
- RGS, Call Park, E911
- Call Admission Control
- XMPP

As shown in the list, Skype for Business Server 2015 allows all components to be made highly available.

SQL Server Backend High Availability

Skype for Business Server 2015 Enterprise Edition pools rely on a SQL Server backend to support the environment. Skype for Business Server 2015 introduces support for SQL Server AlwaysOn Availability Groups, and this is the preferred high-availability backend architecture. SQL AlwaysOn Failover Cluster Instances, SQL failover clustering, and SQL Database Mirroring are also fully supported.

The concept of Availability Groups exists in other Microsoft platforms, with the common goal being that of database redundancy without requiring shared infrastructure. For a SQL AlwaysOn Availability Group, you can provide failover capabilities for a subset of databases on the server or instance that all fail over to a common secondary node. In order to maintain data synchronization, the primary database replica sends transaction logs for each of the databases in the Availability Group to each of the secondary databases. Each secondary database then applies the transaction logs to the appropriate database, keeping all copies up to date.

In the event of a SQL Server failure, the secondary replica server takes over. This failover can be invoked by an administrator, or it can happen automatically. Unlike SQL Database Mirroring, automatic failover of an Availability Group does not require an additional SQL server witness role.

To deploy this functionality, the minimum supported SQL version is SQL Server 2012; you must also deploy all SQL servers in the Availability Group on the same SQL version.

NOTE

Although it is possible to configure a SQL AlwaysOn Availability Group to include a node in a datacenter geographically separated from your Front End pool, this is not recommended. As in Lync Server 2013, Skype for Business Server 2015 does not support "stretched" Front End pool components.

The actual configuration of a SQL AlwaysOn Availability Group is covered in the "Configuring an Enterprise Edition Front End Server Pool with a SQL AlwaysOn Availability Group" section. For an overview of how SQL AlwaysOn Availability Groups provide high availability, see Figure 14.1.

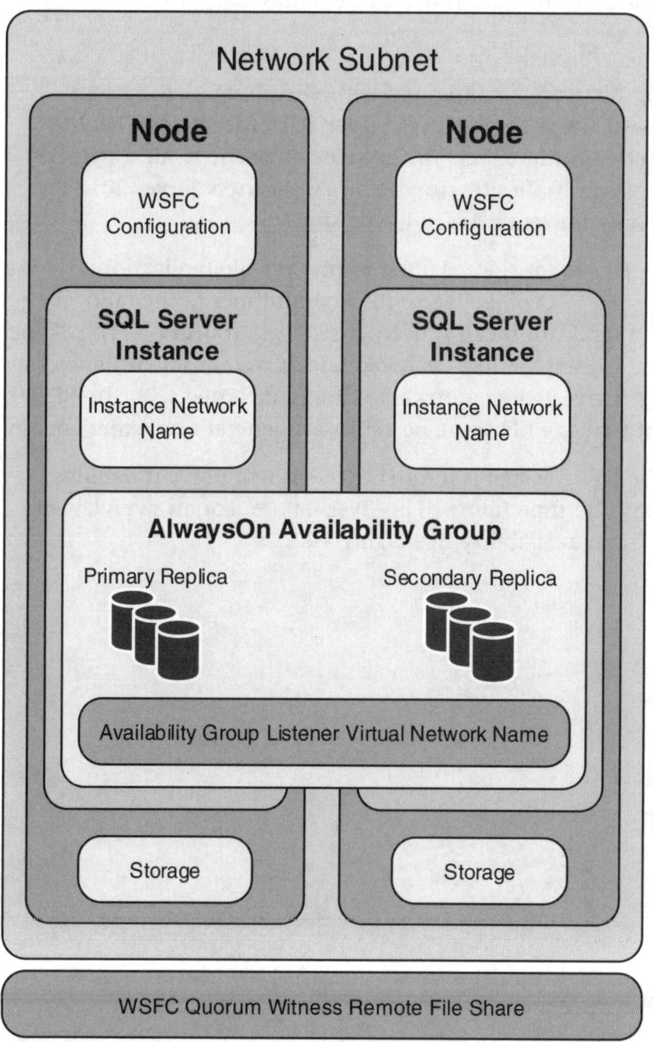

FIGURE 14.1 SQL AlwaysOn Availability Groups high-level architecture.

RTO and RPO for SQL AlwaysOn Availability Groups With SQL AlwaysOn Availability Groups, the RTO and RPO are based on several variables that are dependent on the performance of your specific SQL environment. In general, the RTO and RPO for a properly performing AlwaysOn Availability Group should be significantly less than the 5 minutes stated for SQL mirroring. This means that the service can be brought back online in less than 5 minutes, and less than 5 minutes of data could be lost.

User Impact During Failover In the event of a SQL Server failure, very little use impact is expected. Assuming one of the previously mentioned SQL high-availability solutions has been deployed, the failover will happen so quickly that users are not likely to notice a change. If SQL high availability has not configured, users will enter resiliency mode. This provides a notification that the system is down, and some features will not be available to the users until the administrator has initiated the failover.

File Share High Availability

Microsoft recommends deploying file servers configured with Distributed File System (DFS) to provide high-availability of Skype for Business Server 2015 file shares. DFS has been tested to support failover between file servers in the same datacenter. Although DFS itself can support replication across multiple sites, for Skype for Business Server 2015 it is recommended that DFS be used only for redundancy in the site.

RTO and RPO for File Share DFS DFS is considered "best effort" for file replication. Because of this, there is no published RTO objective or RPO commitment. The failover tends to happen quickly, but data replication can prevent a seamless transition. The Skype for Business Server 2015 file share is used for address-book data as well as for conferencing data that is uploaded. Therefore, many organizations are not as concerned with the RPO of the system, but it is important that the file share be active for general user experience.

It is recommended to back up the DFS file shares frequently. This will prevent data loss if replication has not completed in the time frame of a server failure. For an overview of how DFS can be used to provide high availability, see Figure 14.2.

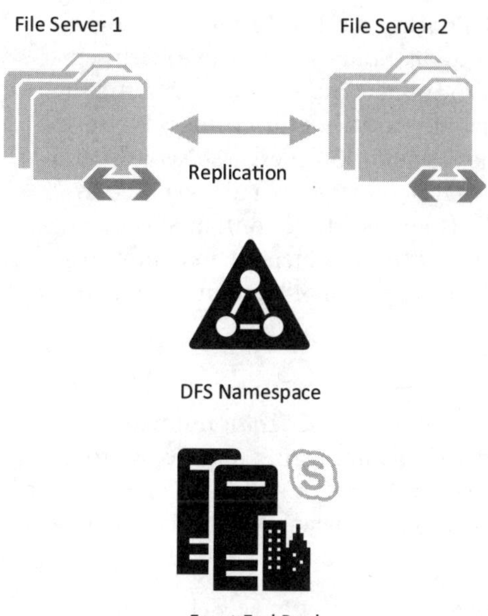

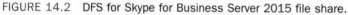

FIGURE 14.2 DFS for Skype for Business Server 2015 file share.

Skype for Business Front End Server High Availability

Providing high availability to Skype for Business Front End Servers is the core of a Skype for Business Server 2015 high-availability design. Front End Servers run nearly every critical service in a Skype for Business Server 2015 deployment, and without access to a Front End Server, users cannot even sign in. Skype for Business Front End Servers can be configured in the topology as pools. These pools can contain up to 12 servers, allowing for increased scale and redundancy.

Skype for Business Server 2015 allows for load balancing Front End Server pools using two methods: DNS load balancing and hardware load balancing.

DNS Load Balancing DNS load balancing is the primary, and preferred, method for providing high availability to Skype for Business Front End Server pools. DNS load balancing leverages application-aware DNS round-robin functionality to provide users the IP addresses of all Front End Servers in the Front End Server Pool. DNS load balancing in Skype for Business Server 2015 is a combination of DNS round-robin and application-level load-balancing intelligence that is used to dynamically manage registration and conferencing load on the Front End Servers. DNS load balancing provides the simplest method of delivering high availability to Front End pools. However, even when you are using DNS load balancing, a hardware load balancer (HLB) is still required for providing high availability to Skype for Business web services. Configuration of DNS load balancing is covered in Chapter 10, “Dependent Services.”

Hardware Load Balancing (HLB) Hardware load balancing has been around for some time. However, these devices were originally used to distribute web traffic to web servers. As applications have evolved, HLBs have evolved to support more advanced traffic such as SIP traffic. HLBs are used to provide high availability to Skype for Business Front End Server pools by providing a virtual IP (VIP) for the Skype for Business web services and directing traffic to available Front End Servers in that pool. HLBs can also be used to distribute SIP traffic across Front End Server pools. However, these configurations are often complicated and provide little or no benefit to offset the increase in complexity. It is highly recommended that you use DNS load balancing for SIP and other pool-based traffic.

Skype for Business Edge Server High Availability

The Skype for Business Edge Server provides remote access and federation functionality to users. The Edge Server allows for the same high-availability configurations as Front End Servers. Skype for Business Edge Servers can be configured as a pool of servers in the topology, and they can be load-balanced through DNS load balancing or a hardware load balancer.

Unlike Skype for Business Front End Servers, Edge Servers do not have web services that must be load balanced. In many organizations, this allows for a simple DNS load-balancing configuration to provide redundancy to Edge Server pools. However, it is important to note that OCS 2007 R2 and earlier do not support connecting to servers using DNS load balancing. Although this scenario is much less common today than it was in previous versions, it is still an important consideration when you are federating with partners running OCS 2007 R2 and earlier versions. If your organization will be federated with these earlier server versions, it is important to plan your redundancy approach appropriately.

Skype for Business Mediation Server High Availability

Skype for Business Mediation Servers provide connectivity to the PSTN and legacy telephony systems. Mediation Servers can also be configured as a pool in Topology Builder. Mediation Server pools are load balanced using DNS load balancing for inbound calls, and for outbound calls Skype for Business Server 2015 dynamically routes calls to maintain an even load across servers.

Persistent Chat High Availability

Skype for Business Server Persistent Chat contains two key components: a backend and a frontend. The backend component is SQL based and follows the same rules for redundancy as described in the "SQL Server Backend High Availability" section. When deploying Persistent Chat, you can use the same SQL Servers used for your Front End pools, or you can deploy new SQL Servers for Persistent Chat.

Persistent Chat Front End Servers act much like Skype for Business Front End Servers. These servers can be configured in a pool, with up to eight servers in each pool. However, only four servers may ever be active in a pool at a time. DNS load balancing is used to distribute traffic among the four active servers. Hardware load balancing is not supported for distributing traffic to Persistent Chat servers.

Stretched Persistent Chat pools are covered in the "Persistent Chat Disaster Recovery" section, later in this chapter.

Shared Components High Availability

Skype for Business Server 2015 relies on many commonly shared services to provide Skype for Business services. This includes Active Directory, Office Web Apps Server, Exchange Server, and various network components such as firewalls and hardware load balancers.

Active Directory It is important to ensure that Active Directory is configured in a redundant fashion. Active Directory topologies vary across every organization; however, a general rule of thumb is to make sure that each site where Active Directory components are deployed always contains a redundant server configuration. It is more important to take Active Directory availability into consideration when planning for the availability of your Skype for Business infrastructure and to identify any gaps in redundancy before deployment.

Office Web Apps Server In the context of providing high availability to Office Web Apps Server, it is best classified as a simple web application. Office Web Apps Server can be configured as a farm with multiple servers in the farm. Office Web Apps Server requires the use of a hardware load balancer to distribute traffic to all servers in the farm, providing redundancy and increased scale.

Exchange Server Exchange Server redundancy has had many books written about it, so it is not outlined in detail here. However, much as with Active Directory, it is important to consider the availability of Exchange Server in your Skype for Business Server 2015 service availability planning. Remember, the availability of your Skype for Business Server 2015 solution is only as high as the weakest link; if voicemail goes down, your SLA may be compromised.

Network Equipment, Firewalls, Reverse Proxies, and Hardware Load Balancers Network switches, routers, firewalls, reverse proxies, and hardware load balancers of all types support redundant configurations. In many cases, these devices support being configured as a redundant pool or pair. This allows for a seamless failover of one node while retaining services on the failover node. Regardless of how the devices are configured for redundancy, it is important to make sure that all equipment supporting your Skype for Business users and servers is deployed with high availability in mind.

Designing for Disaster Recovery

The preceding section discussed how to provide redundancy and high availability to Skype for Business Server 2015 components. This section outlines how to design for disaster recovery and explains why that sometimes differs from high availability.

Defining Disaster Recovery

By definition, recovery is the restoration or continuation of a technology infrastructure critical to an organization after a natural or human-induced disaster. Disaster recovery assumes that a major event has occurred, resulting in the loss of an entire site or a large section of infrastructure.

Disaster recovery is measured on recovery point objective and recovery time objective—two measurements that were discussed earlier in this chapter. Designing for disaster recovery differs from that of high availability because the two goals, though they might seem relatively similar, are actually different. Designing for disaster recovery requires planning for redundant resources end to end, even across multiple sites. Additionally, disaster recovery planning involves defining a recovery playbook, which outlines exact steps for performing a recovery in the event of a disaster.

In its simplest form, disaster recovery for Skype for Business Server 2015 implies deploying a secondary infrastructure that can support users in the event that the primary infrastructure is not available. However, the operational considerations for the recovery procedure often become much more complicated.

As the RPO and RTO objectives get closer to zero, the cost of the infrastructure and the operations will become much more expensive. This is why disaster recovery should be considered outside of the scope of high availability and redundancy. High availability should refer to the level of redundancy inside the pool of servers or inside the Skype for Business Server 2015 site. Disaster recovery should refer to how users will be provided services in the event of a total pool or total site loss.

Disaster Recovery Options in Skype for Business Server 2015

Skype for Business Server 2015 has come a long way in providing disaster recovery options in a simplified manner. In Lync Server 2010, there were three options for disaster recovery:

- **Backup registrar**—Backup registrar functionality was introduced in Lync Server 2010. This feature allowed pools to be configured as a backup for the registrar service only. In the event of a pool failure, users would register against the backup pool in limited functionality mode, essentially enabling users to make and receive calls. This was critical in providing the level of availability required for Enterprise Voice.
- **Metropolitan site resiliency**—This solution split pools between two physical servers. Geographically dispersed clusters were deployed to support SQL and file servers. Synchronous data replication was then deployed between the geographically dispersed clusters. This solution introduced unnecessary complexity to environments, requiring high-speed, high-latency WAN connectivity across physical sites using stretched VLANs. Although this solution worked for a unique set of enterprise customers, it did not provide an acceptable disaster recovery solution for the general population.

- **Forced failover**—This solution resulted in deploying a secondary pool and all supporting servers in the second physical site. The administrator would configure backups of all primary data and copy that data to the secondary site. In the event of a disaster, the data could be restored using `DBIMPEXP.EXE`, and users could be force-moved to the secondary site. This solution was an acceptable option, although it did result in a high RTO. Importing data and moving a large number of users could often take hours and had a heavy dependency on custom scripts and resource kit tools.

Similar to Lync Server 2013, Skype for Business Server 2015 combines the best of Backup Registrar and Metropolitan Site Resiliency functionality into an integrated disaster recovery model. Skype for Business Server 2015 continues to use the concept of pool pairing, which allows for Skype for Business Server 2015 to constantly replicate critical data between two server pools. Exactly how pool pairing works is described in a later section.

Skype for Business Server 2015 pool pairing is the only supported disaster recovery method; previous methods are not supported and are not recommended.

Table 14.4 outlines the disaster recovery capabilities in earlier versions of Lync as well as Skype for Business Server 2015.

TABLE 14.4 Skype for Business Server Disaster Recovery Capabilities

Scenario	Lync Server 2010	Lync Server 2013	Skype for Business Server 2015
Pool failure	Voice resiliency through backup registrar.	Maintain voice resiliency in Lync 2013 through pool pairing and voice routing.	Maintain voice resiliency in Skype for Business Server 2015 through pool pairing and voice routing.
	Metropolitan site stretched pool for Presence and conferencing resiliency.	PSTN trunks can be configured for auto-failover and failback.	PSTN trunks can be configured for auto-failover and failback.
		Support for Presence and conferencing resiliency via pool pairing through manual failover and failback.	Support Presence and conferencing resiliency via pool pairing through manual failover and failback.
		Integrate with Planning Tool, Topology Builder, and Control Panel.	Integrate with Planning Tool, Topology Builder, and Control Panel.
		Does not cover RGS/CPS/E911/CAC.	Does not cover RGS/CPS/E911/CAC.
Site failure	Metropolitan site stretched pool.	Same as above.	Same as above.

What Services Are Supported for Skype for Business Server 2015 Disaster Recovery?

First, let's cover what services are available in a disaster recovery scenario. Table 14.5 provides an outline of these services.

TABLE 14.5 Skype for Business Server 2015 Services Available During Disaster Recovery

Feature	Supports Disaster Recovery
Peer-to-peer (all modalities)	Yes
Presence	Yes
Conferencing (all modalities)	Yes
UC Web App	Yes
Archiving	Yes
CDR/QOE	No
Federation	Yes
PIC federation	Yes
Unified Contact Store	Yes
Skype for Business Server 2015 Control Panel	Yes
Persistent Chat	Yes
PSTN Voice	Yes
Voice Applications (CAA, CAS, PVA, and GVA)	Yes
RGS, Call Park, and E911	No
Call Admission Control	No
XMPP	Yes

As shown in Table 14.5, applications that often have a unique site configuration, such as E911, Call Park, Response Group, and Call Admission Control, are not supported in a disaster recovery scenario. In the event of a disaster, this functionality will not be available to users until connectivity to the primary pool is restored. Additionally, CDR and QOE information will not be submitted from users who are in recovery mode.

SQL Server Backend Disaster Recovery

Providing disaster recovery to the SQL backend services in Skype for Business Server 2015 does not require admin intervention. Data that is stored in the SQL Server database will instead be replicated through the Skype for Business Server 2015 pool pairing functionality and imported to the secondary site SQL database.

SQL high availability, regardless of the method chosen, should be deployed only in a single site and should not be considered for cross-site configurations to provide some level of disaster recovery.

Skype for Business Front End Server Disaster Recovery

Skype for Business Front End Server disaster recovery is at the core of disaster recovery in Skype for Business Server 2015. As mentioned earlier, Skype for Business Front End Servers provide disaster recovery first through backup registrar functionality. This enables users to immediately fail over to a secondary pool for basic registration and inbound and outbound voice routing.

In the event of a prolonged outage, administrators can leverage pool pairing to provide Presence and conferencing services to users. Skype for Business Server pool pairing uses Windows Fabric to synchronize data across two Skype for Business Front End pools. In the event of a failure, the administrator can invoke a pool failover, which will result in the import of presence and conferencing data to the secondary pool database.

Backup Registrar Relationship Details Skype for Business Server 2015 backup registrar relationships must always be a 1:1 configuration and will always be reciprocal. This means that if Pool 1 is the backup for Pool 2, then Pool 2 must be the backup for Pool 1. Additionally, neither can be the backup for any other Front End pool. The exception to this rule is that each Front End pool can also be the backup registrar for any number of survivable branch appliances or survivable branch servers.

Pool Pairing Relationship Details When planning for pool pairing, the following items should be considered:

- **Consider the distance between the datacenters**—Although there is no limit on the distance between two datacenters that contain paired pools, keep in mind that depending on the connectivity between sites, data replication might take longer, resulting in a longer RPO. Additionally, it is important to not have two datacenters in close proximity to each other in the event of a natural disaster.
- **Pool types must match**—Enterprise Edition pools can be paired only with other Enterprise Edition pools. Similarly, Standard Edition pools must be paired only with other Standard Edition pools.
- **Physical and virtual must match**—Physical pools can be paired only with other physical pools. Similarly, virtual pools can be paired only with other virtual pools.
- **Consider capacity**—Each pool in the pair should have the capacity to serve all users from both pools in the event of a disaster. This is very important when planning server capacity in a multisite scenario.

These best practices are recommended to avoid providing an insufficient disaster recovery design.

NOTE

Topology Builder will not prevent an administrator from configuring two pools in an unsupported matter. However, it is absolutely critical to deploy solutions in a supported configuration, and as such, Microsoft's recommendations should always be followed.

RTO and RPO for Skype for Business Server 2015 Pool Pairing Microsoft has engineered Skype for Business Server 2015 pool pairing to provide a recovery time objective of 15 minutes. Administrators must manually initiate the failover as part of a disaster recovery procedure. Fifteen minutes is the time it takes for the procedure to complete—it does not account for the time it takes to identify the disaster and make a decision for failover. When an administrator initiates a pool failover, the data must be imported to the new pool. The time it takes for the failover to complete results in the engineered RTO of 15 minutes.

For Skype for Business Server 2015 pool pairing, the recovery point objective is 5 minutes. This means that up to 5 minutes' worth of data could be lost due to replication latency of the Skype for Business Backup Service.

The RTO and RPO numbers are based off of a pool with 40,000 concurrent users and 200,000 users enabled on the pool.

Central Management Store Recovery The Central Management Store (CMS) is responsible for all configuration data in the Skype for Business Server 2015 environment. The CMS runs on one active Front End pool in the environment, and subsequently one active SQL backend. When pool pairing is configured on a pool that is hosting the CMS, a backup CMS database is configured on the backup pool, and the CMS services are also installed on that pool. CMS data is also replicated by the Skype for Business Server Backup Service to the standby pool. When initiating a pool failover involving the CMS, the administrator must first execute a CMS failover.

The engineering target for RPO and RTO of the CMS is 5 minutes. CMS data is not as large as Presence and conferencing data; as such, the replication latency and import time are reduced when compared to Front End pool RPO/RTO.

Skype for Business Edge Server Disaster Recovery

Skype for Business Edge Servers do not provide a native disaster recovery solution. In the event of a disaster scenario, manual steps must be taken to direct services through the secondary Edge Server pool. However, proper planning can reduce the amount of effort required for these tasks. When planning for Edge Server disaster recovery, consider the strategies discussed in the following subsections.

Weighted DNS Records for Access Edge Services It is possible to deploy the DNS SRV records required for Skype for Business remote access and federation with a priority and weight. This configuration essentially allows for a primary and secondary DNS A record to be configured. Clients will always use the DNS record with the lowest-numbered priority value first and fall back to other records if the connection to the host fails. The weight value on SRV records should be used only for providing load balancing between services.

Example for Access Edge sign-on services:

```
_sip._tls.skypeunleashed.com 86400 IN SRV 10 10 443 sip.skypeunleashed.com
_sip._tls.skypeunleashed.com 86400 IN SRV 20 10 443 sip2.skypeunleashed.com
```

In the preceding configuration, the first record has a priority of 10, and as a result, clients would attempt to connect to the server `sip.skypeunleashed.com`. If the client cannot connect to that server, the second record, with a priority of 20, would be used, and users would attempt to connect to `sip2.skypeunleashed.com`.

This configuration can provide an automatic failover for inbound Access Edge services. However, failover will not be immediate. Keep in mind that the Skype for Business client will cache records of servers to connect to, and it will attempt to connect to servers in that cache first. This can result in a slight sign-on delay in disaster scenarios while the client discovers the secondary DNS record.

Example for Access Edge federation services:

```
_sipfederationtls._tcp.skypeunleashed.com 86400 IN SRV 10 10 5061 sip.
skypeunleashed.com
_sipfederationtls._tcp.skypeunleashed.com 86400 IN SRV 20 10 5061 sip2.
skypeunleashed.com
```

In the preceding configuration, the first record has a priority of 10, and as a result, federated partner Edge Servers would attempt to connect to the server `sip.skypeunleashed.com`. If the server cannot connect to `sip.skypeunleashed.com`, the second record, with a priority of 20, would be used, and the server would attempt to connect to `sip2.skypeunleashed.com`.

This configuration can provide an automatic failover for inbound federation requests; however, it does not account for enhanced federation configurations. Enhanced federation is when organizations define Access Edge server records for a federated partner. In this configuration, federation requests do not query the SRV record for connectivity options. If your organization is deploying enhanced federation, keep this in mind.

Outbound Federation Route Every Skype for Business Server 2015 Topology may have only a single outbound federation route defined. These routes may be defined per site; however, they are defined to a single Edge Server pool. In the event of a failure, this configuration must be manually updated to point to the secondary pool. The steps to perform this are covered in the "Executing Disaster Recovery Procedures" section.

A/V Edge Failover The A/V Edge services on each Edge Server are statically associated with a Front End pool. No intervention is required in the event of a failure. When users are connected to the secondary pool, they will use the Edge Server pool in the secondary site for media traversal capabilities.

Skype for Business Mediation Server Disaster Recovery

Providing disaster recovery to Skype for Business Mediation Servers is not done through a Mediation Server configuration. Instead, voice routes should be configured to contain multiple Mediation Server pools for failover purposes. When you are planning for voice resiliency, it is important to identify all inbound and outbound routing policies, and to make sure that cross-pool policies are configured where necessary. Pool 1 users should be able to route calls through the Pool 2 Mediation Servers to the PSTN as a last resort. Additionally, inbound PSTN should be configured to have redundancy to Pool 2 in the event that Pool 1 is not available. The details of designing Skype for Business Enterprise Voice, including resiliency, are given in Chapter 33, "Planning for Voice Deployment."

Persistent Chat Disaster Recovery

With Skype for Business Server 2015, the disaster recovery mechanism for Persistent Chat is more in line with the rest of the product when compared to Lync Server 2010. Unlike Skype for Business Server Front End pools, Persistent Chat pools cannot be paired to provide disaster recovery. Persistent Chat pools require introducing a stretched pool configuration to provide disaster recovery.

Providing disaster recovery to Persistent Chat pools will require the following configurations:

- **Primary SQL Servers**—Persistent Chat will rely on a stretched pool configuration. SQL Servers should be located in the same physical datacenter as the Persistent Chat Front Ends to provide normal operations. For high-availability purposes, it is recommended that this be a SQL mirror, with a third SQL Server configured as a witness for automatic failover.
- **SQL Log Shipping**—Providing disaster recovery to the Persistent Chat backend is done through SQL Log Shipping. This must be manually configured by administrators, and will perform transaction backups to the secondary datacenter.
- **Primary file share**—SQL Log Shipping requires a file share to be created and designated for SQL transaction logs. The share must have read and write privileges to all SQL Server services that are running Persistent Chat services in both datacenters.
- **Secondary file share**—A secondary file share must be designated to receive SQL transaction logs. This can be located on the secondary SQL Server.
- **Secondary SQL Server**—In the datacenter designated for disaster recovery, a secondary SQL Server should be designated. SQL log shipping will be used to back up all SQL data to the secondary datacenter.

The configuration options covered in the following subsections are available when Persistent Chat is being deployed with disaster recovery available.

Stretched Persistent Chat Pool in Low-Bandwidth and High-Latency Scenarios Persistent Chat pools can contain up to eight servers. However, only four servers can be active at once. In a scenario in which the connectivity between two datacenters is not efficient, placing four servers in each datacenter in an active/standby configuration is ideal. The requirements outlined in the preceding section, "Persistent Chat Disaster Recovery," detail the resources required to complete this configuration. See Figure 14.3 for an example of this design.

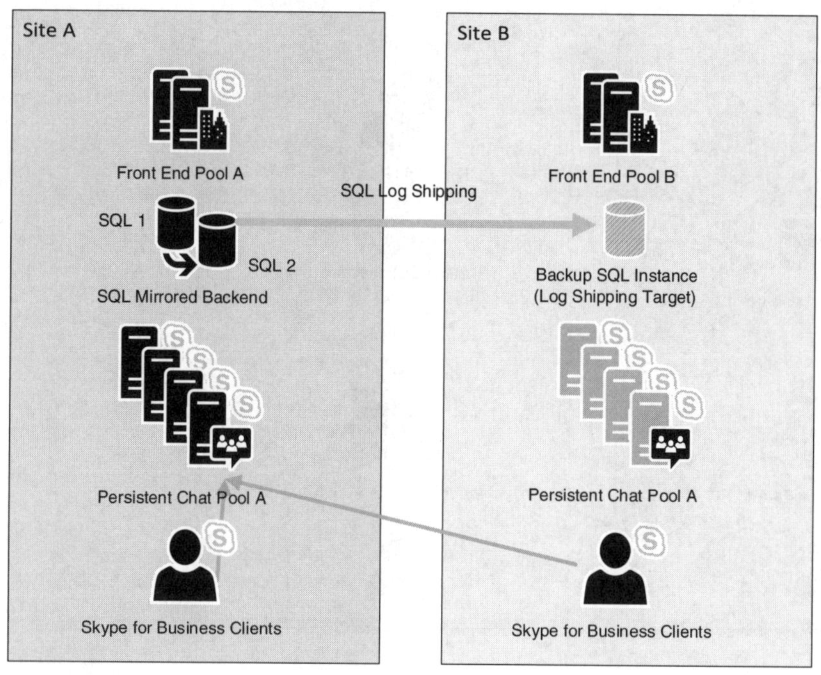

FIGURE 14.3 Stretched Persistent Chat pool in low-bandwidth and high-latency scenarios.

The following statements are true in this configuration:

- Site A and Site B both contain a Front End Server pool, servicing a subset of users. Each site shares Persistent Chat Pool A for Persistent Chat.
- Site A contains four active Persistent Chat servers; all users in Site A and Site B will connect to those servers for access to Persistent Chat Pool A.
- SQL Log Shipping is configured between SQL1 and SQL3. Every transaction will be shipped to SQL3, and in the event of a disaster, data can be restored.
- Site B contains four standby Persistent Chat servers. In the event of a disaster, these servers can be marked as active and serve users from Site A and Site B.

Stretched Persistent Chat Pool in High-Bandwidth and Low-Latency Scenarios When bandwidth and latency are efficient, it is possible to split the Persistent Chat pool in an active/active configuration across two datacenters. Requirements discussed in earlier sections apply. However, in this configuration, two servers in each datacenter are designated as active. See Figure 14.4 for an example of this design.

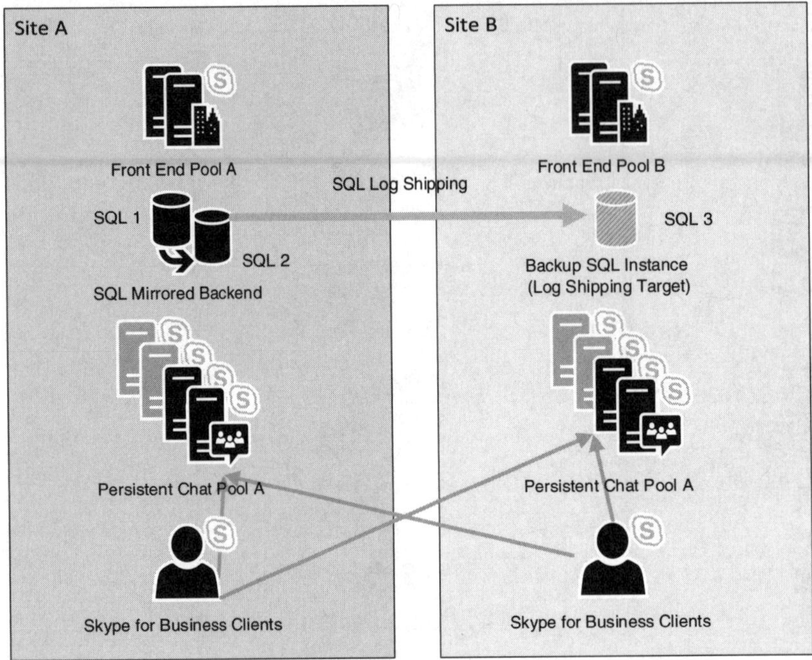

FIGURE 14.4 Stretched Persistent Chat pool in high-bandwidth and low-latency scenarios.

The following statements are true in this configuration:

- Site A and Site B both contain a Front End Server pool, servicing a subset of users. Each site shares Persistent Chat Pool A for Persistent Chat.
- Site A and Site B both contain two active Persistent Chat Front End Servers. DNS load balancing will be used to distribute traffic across the pool to all four active servers. Users in Site A and Site B will connect to any active server, including in the other datacenter.
- SQL Log Shipping is configured between SQL1 and SQL3. Every transaction will be shipped to SQL3, and in the event of a disaster, data can be restored.
- Site A and Site B will contain two standby Persistent Chat Servers each. In the event of a disaster, the standby servers can be activated to maintain capacity. All users will connect to the active datacenter in that scenario.

The process for configuring Persistent Chat disaster recovery, as well as initiating a failover, are covered in the "Executing Disaster Recovery Procedures" section.

Shared Components Disaster Recovery

Skype for Business Server 2015 relies on several shared services to provide various functionality. It is important when planning for disaster recovery scenarios that all shared components are accounted for. This includes Active Directory, Exchange Server, Office

Web Apps Server, and Network Equipment. It is critical to ensure a seamless transition to the second datacenter in a disaster scenario. When developing a disaster recovery strategy, make certain to document all dependencies and ensure that those dependencies will be available in the secondary environment.

Configuring Skype for Business Server 2015 for High Availability

This section acts as a guide for configuring Skype for Business Server 2015 for high availability. Step-by-step instructions for configuring the SQL Servers, Skype for Business Servers, and other shared components for high availability are covered.

Configuring an Enterprise Edition Front End Server Pool with a SQL AlwaysOn Availability Group

In Skype for Business Server 2015, Microsoft has included support for SQL Server AlwaysOn Availability Groups for backend high availability. Unlike SQL mirroring, the configuration of the AlwaysOn Availability Group is a standalone process that mostly occurs outside of Skype for Business Server 2015 Administrative Tools. However, when deploying a Front End Server pool in Topology Builder, administrators can specify that an AlwaysOn Availability Group will host the backend databases. The following steps outline the process for building an AlwaysOn Availability Group and configuring integration with Skype for Business Server 2015.

NOTE

The following instructions outline the steps required to configure an AlwaysOn Availability Group on Windows Server 2012 R2 running SQL 2014. The steps for other supported operating systems and SQL versions may vary slightly. It is also assumed that SQL Server has already been installed.

Creating the Windows Server Failover Cluster to Support the SQL AlwaysOn Availability Group

Prior to any Skype for Business Server 2015 installation, the first step in the deployment process is configuring a SQL AlwaysOn Availability Group. First, we will configure the Windows Server Failover Clustering (WSFC) within the operating system. Follow these steps to configure WSFC.

1. On each SQL Server that will participate in the Availability Group, launch Server Manager.
2. Within Server Manager, click Add Roles and Features.
3. At the Add Roles and Features and Features Wizard, click Next.
4. Ensure Role-based or Feature-based installation is selected. Click Next.

5. Verify the destination server is the local server. Click Next.
6. On the Select server roles page, click Next.
7. On the Select features page, select Failover Clustering and then click Next.
8. When prompted to add features that are required for failover clustering, click Add Features. Click Next.
9. At the Confirm Installation Selections screen, click Install.
10. Once installation has completed successfully, click Close.
11. Repeat Steps 1 through 10 on the server that will host the Secondary Replica.
12. On the server that will host the Primary Replica, launch Server Manager. Click Tools and then click Failover Cluster Manager.
13. In the Failover Cluster Manager, right-click Failover Cluster Manager and then click Validate Configuration, as shown in Figure 14.5.

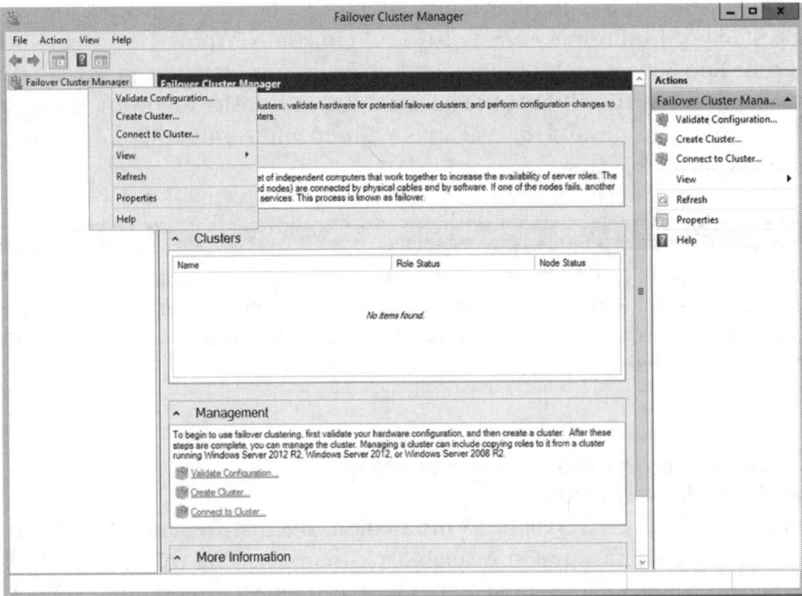

FIGURE 14.5 Validate the cluster configuration.

14. At the initial screen, click Next.
15. On the Select Servers or a Cluster page, enter the names of your SQL Servers that will participate in the Availability Group and then click Add, as shown in Figure 14.6. Once both servers have been added, click Next.

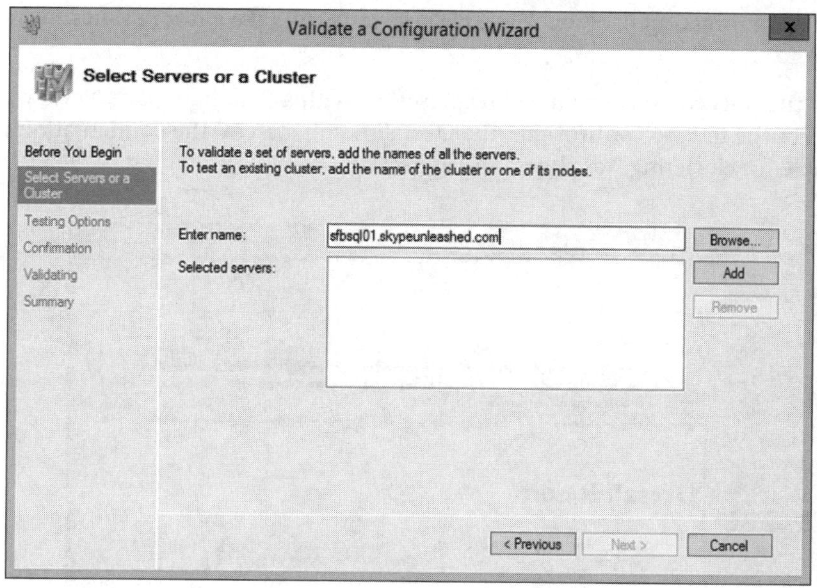

FIGURE 14.6 Adding servers to the failover cluster.

16. On the Testing Options screen, make sure Run All Tests (Recommended) is selected, as shown in Figure 14.7. Click Next.

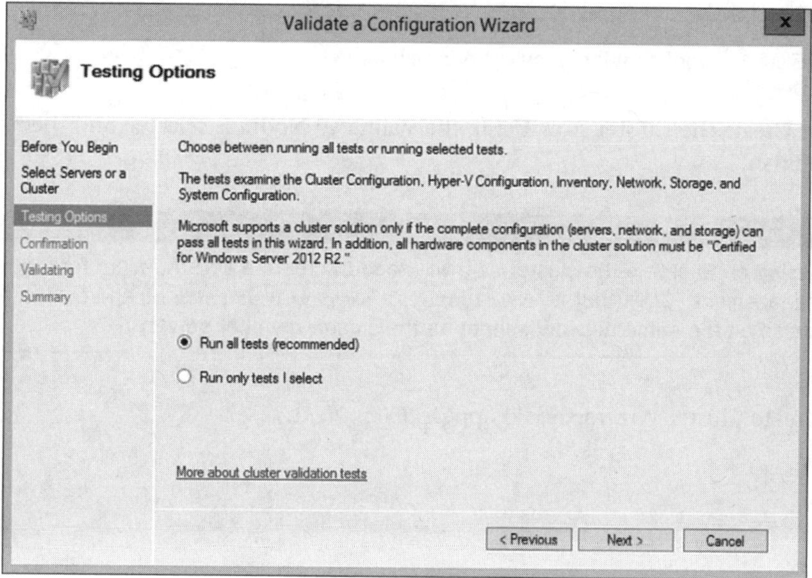

FIGURE 14.7 Validation test selection.

17. On the Confirmation page, click Next. These tests will take a few minutes to complete.

18. When the tests complete, you will be presented with a Summary page. Review the results of the tests to confirm that the Overall Result state of the configuration is "suitable for clustering," as shown in Figure 14.8.

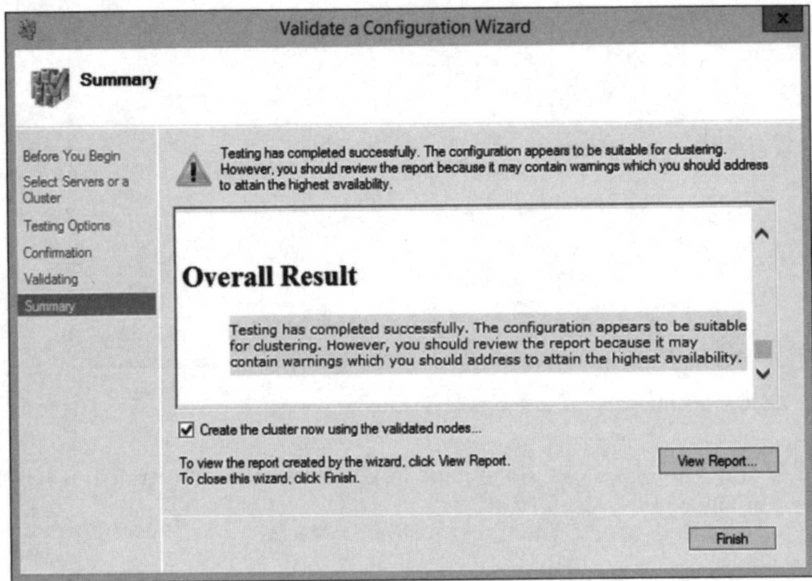

FIGURE 14.8 Configuration is suitable for clustering.

19. Ensure Create the Cluster Now Using the Validated Nodes is selected and then click Finish.

NOTE

Before moving on to create the cluster, you will need to create a DNS A record for the cluster management FQDN (that is, `sqlcluster01.skypeunleashed.com`) and point it to an IP address on the same network subnet as the cluster member server.

20. The Create Cluster Wizard should appear. Click Next.

21. On the Access Point for Administering the Cluster page, enter the cluster name and IP address, as shown in Figure 14.9. Click Next.

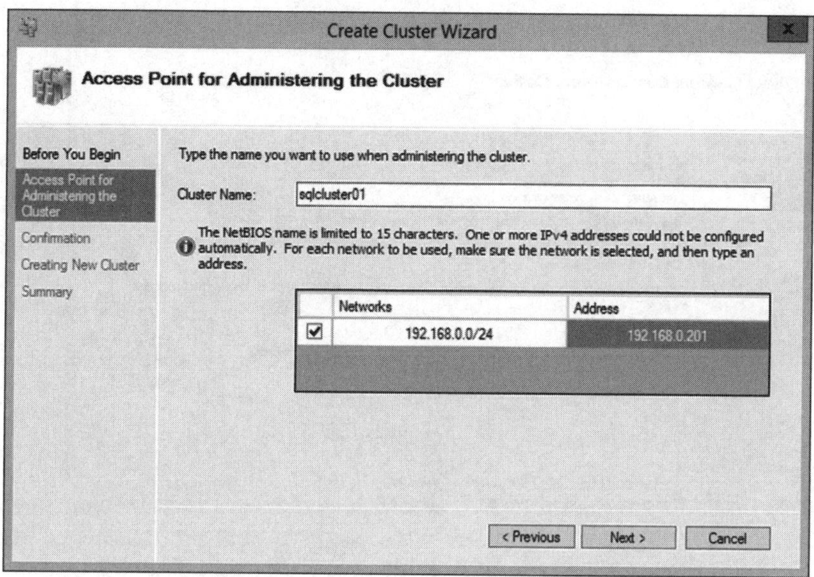

FIGURE 14.9 Create the cluster access point for administration.

22. At the Confirmation page, verify configuration and click Next.
23. Verify successful completion of the Create Cluster Wizard and then click Finish.
24. On the SQL Server that will host the Primary Replica, launch the Failover Cluster Manager if it is not already open.
25. Right-click your failover cluster (that is, `sqlcluster01.skypeunleashed.com`), click More Actions, and then click Configure Cluster Quorum Settings.
26. At the initial Configure Cluster Quorum Wizard screen, click Next.

27. Select the radio button for Select the Quorum Witness, as shown in Figure 14.10. Click Next.

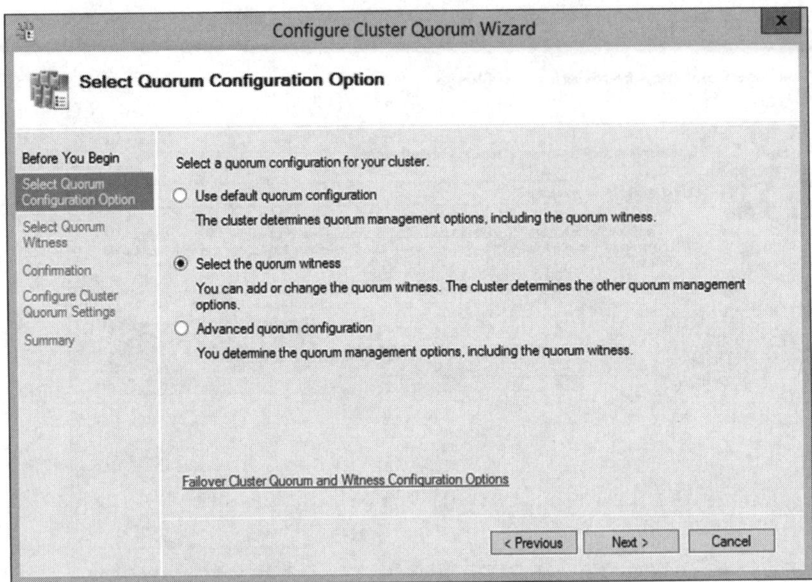

FIGURE 14.10 The Select Quorum Configuration Option screen.

28. On the Select Quorum Witness screen, select Configure a File Share Witness, as shown in Figure 14.11. Click Next.

NOTE

The file share used for the File Share Witness should be created and shared before you complete the Create Cluster Wizard.

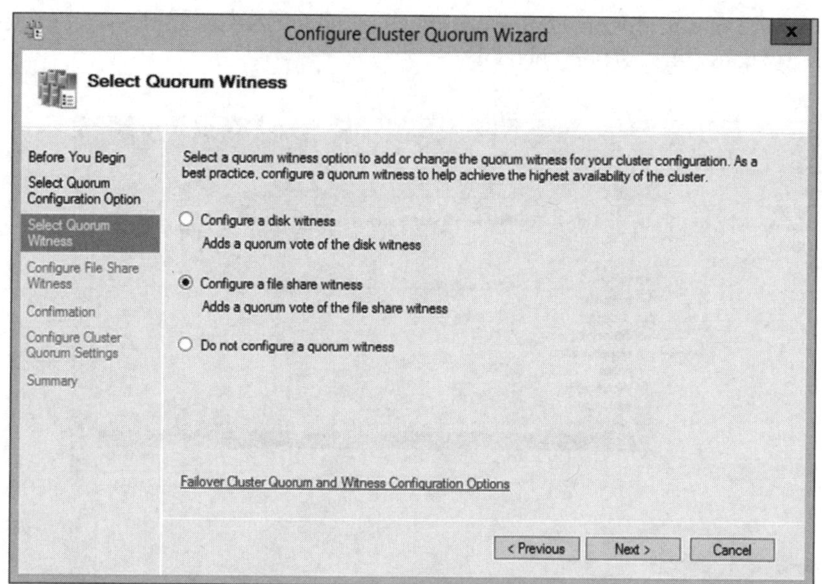

FIGURE 14.11 Configure the File Share Witness.

29. Provide a path to the file share that will be used for the File Share Witness. Click Next.

30. At the Confirmation page, verify the settings and then click Next.

31. When the Configure Cluster Quorum Wizard completes successfully, click Finish.

32. Close the Failover Cluster Manager.

33. We will now need to configure the login server roles on each of the cluster member servers. Launch SQL Server Management Studio on the Primary Replica server and connect to the SQL instance where the Skype for Business databases will be installed. Ensure the account being used has administrative permissions to the instance.

34. In Object Explorer, expand Security, expand Logins, and right-click the login for the Secondary Replica SQL Server (that is, `SKYPEUNLEASHED\sfbsql02$`). Then click Properties.

35. Click Server Roles in the navigation window on the left. Select all the server roles, as shown in Figure 14.12. Then click OK.

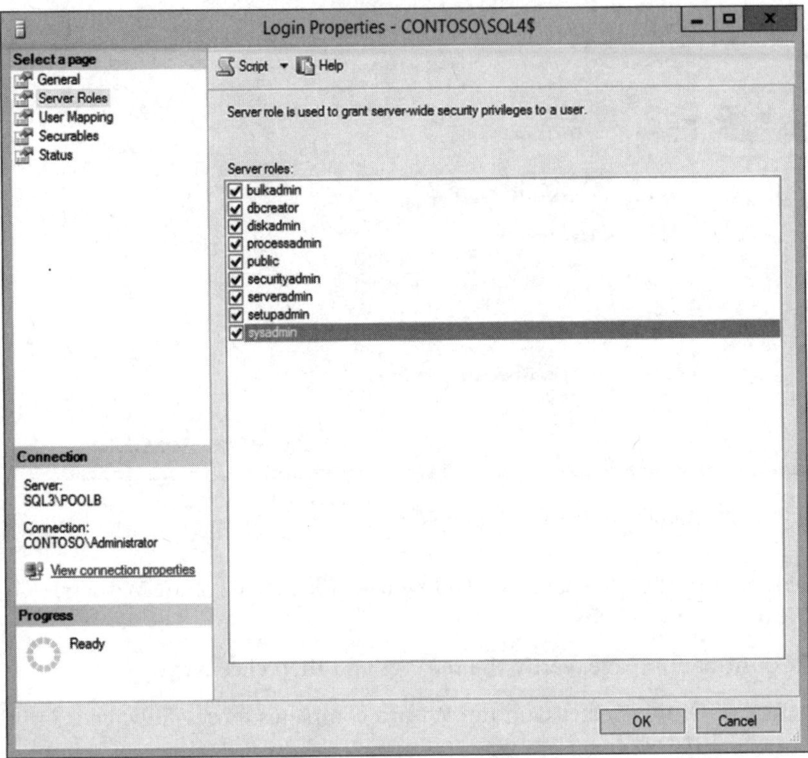

FIGURE 14.12 SQL Server login server role permissions.

36. Leave SQL Server Management Studio open.

37. Repeat Steps 32 through 35 on the server where the Secondary Replicas will reside. Ensure you are modifying the permissions of the login for the Primary Replica server (that is, `SKYPEUNLEASHED\sfbsql01$`).

Configuring a Front End Server Enterprise Edition Pool and Installing the Backend Databases

Providing Skype for Business Server Front Ends with high availability involves creating a pool of servers that will service all users assigned to that pool. The following section outlines how to configure a pool of servers in the Topology Builder, the configuration of DNS load balancing for proper availability, as well as the integration with a SQL AlwaysOn Availability Group.

Enterprise Edition pools can contain up to 12 Front End Servers to provide scaling and high availability to Skype for Business Server 2015 services. The steps that follow outline how to configure these pools in Topology Builder:

1. Open Skype for Business Server 2015 Topology Builder.
2. Download the topology from the existing deployment, or create a new topology if this is a brand-new infrastructure.
3. Expand Skype for Business Server 2015, expand the site where this pool will be located, and expand Skype for Business Server 2015.
4. Right-click the Enterprise Edition Front End Pools and select New Front End Pool.
5. Click Next and continue with the Define New Front End Pool Wizard (see Figure 14.13). Specify a Pool FQDN such as `sfbpool01.skypeunleashed.com` and click Next.

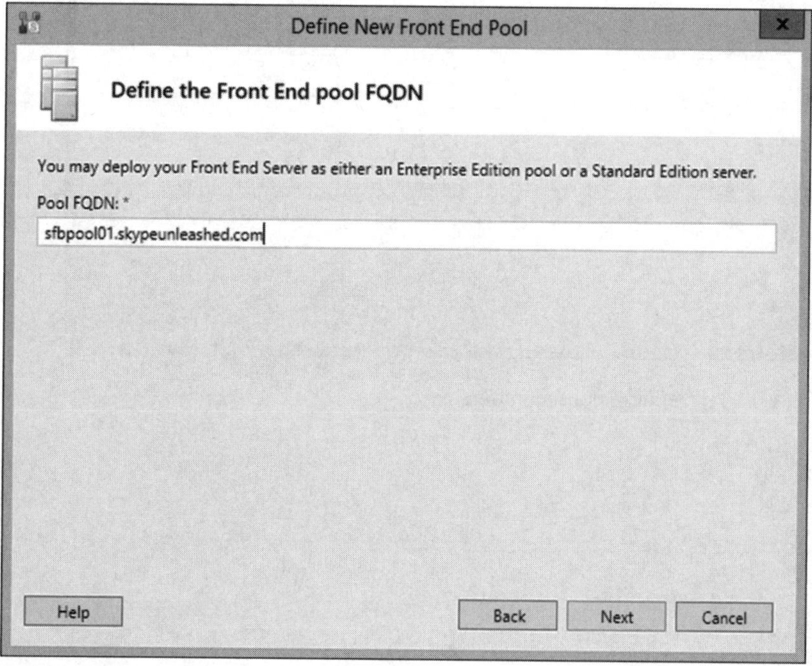

FIGURE 14.13 Specify a pool FQDN.

6. Next, you must define the computers in the pool. These names should be the computer FQDN of all Skype for Business Front End Servers currently part of this pool. Specify the computer FQDN and click Add for each server in the pool. When you are finished, click Next. Figure 14.14 provides an example of how the pool members configuration should look in Topology Builder.

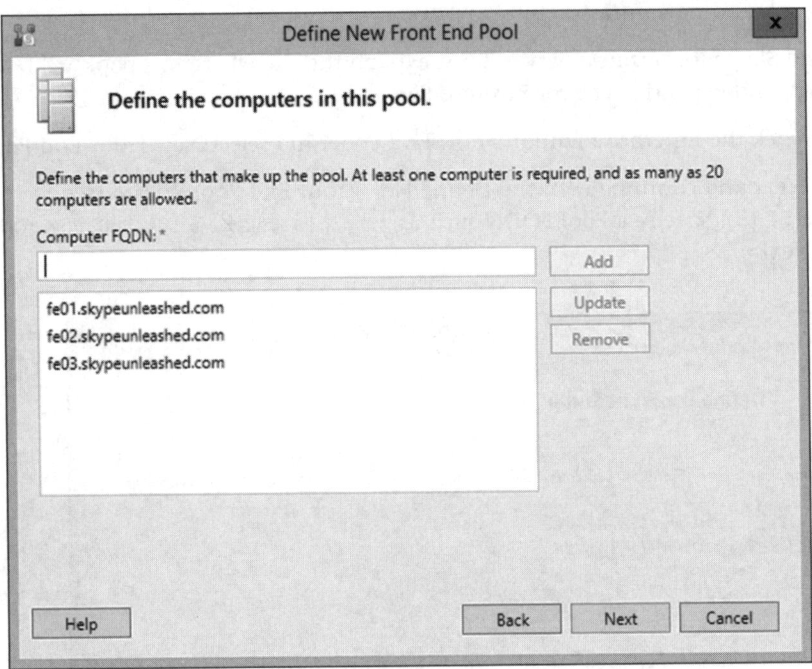

FIGURE 14.14 Defining pool members.

7. Specify the services the pool will offer (see Figure 14.15). This can include Conferencing, PSTN Conferencing, Enterprise Voice, Call Admission Control (only one pool per site is allowed to be enabled for CAC), Archiving, and Monitoring. Select all boxes that apply to this pool and click Next.

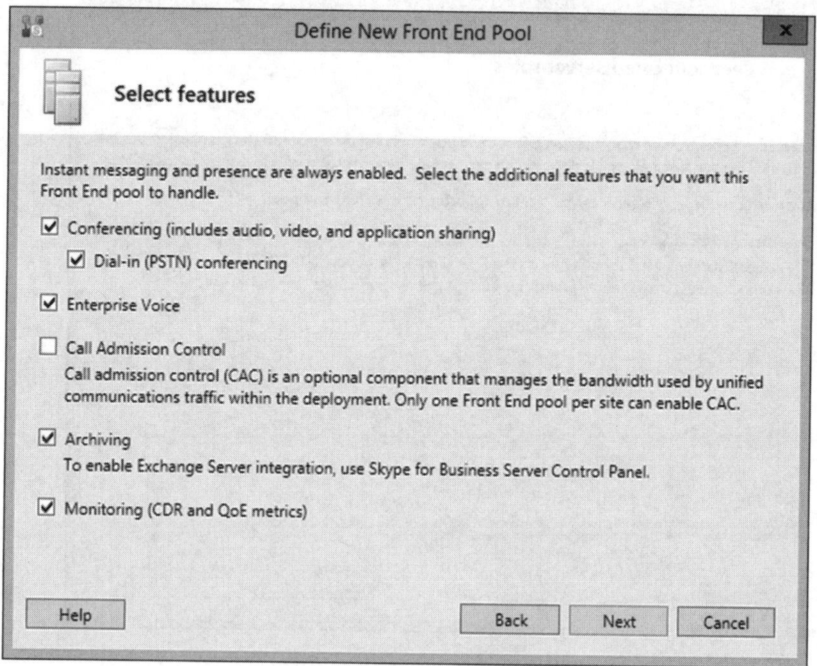

FIGURE 14.15 Choose services offered by the pool.

8. If you plan to collocate the Mediation Server role on the Front Ends, make sure the Collocate Mediation Server box is checked (see Figure 14.16). Otherwise, uncheck this box. Click Next.

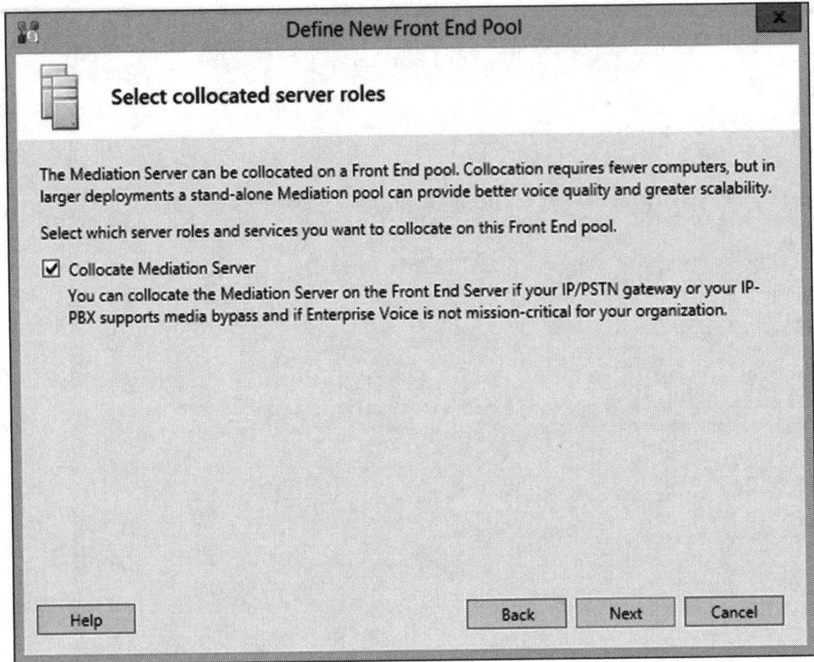
Define New Front End Pool
Select collocated server roles
The Mediation Server can be collocated on a Front End pool. Collocation requires fewer computers, but in larger deployments a stand-alone Mediation pool can provide better voice quality and greater scalability.
Select which server roles and services you want to collocate on this Front End pool.
Collocate Mediation Server
You can collocate the Mediation Server on the Front End Server if your IP/PSTN gateway or your IP-PBX supports media bypass and if Enterprise Voice is not mission-critical for your organization.
Help
Back
Next
Cancel

FIGURE 14.16 Collocation of the Mediation Server role.

9. On the Associate Server Roles with This Front End Pool screen (see Figure 14.17), click Next.

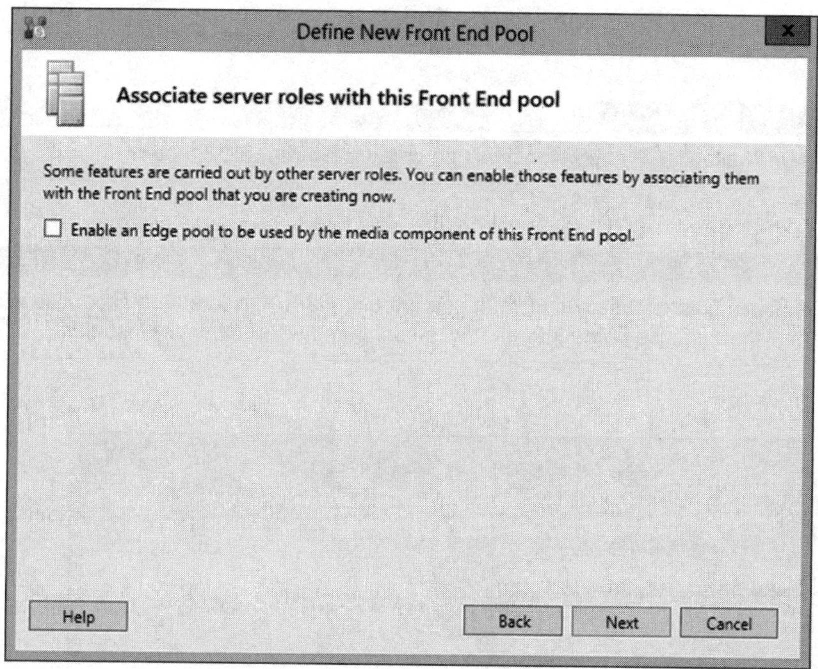

FIGURE 14.17 Association of the Edge pool with the Front End pool.

10. At the Define SQL Server Store screen, click New.

11. On the Define New SQL Server Store page, enter the SQL Server Availability Group listener FQDN, select the appropriate SQL Instance option, check the High Availability Settings box, choose SQL AlwaysOn Availability Groups, and then enter the SQL Server FQDN for your Primary Replica server, as shown in Figure 14.18. Click OK.

NOTE

The AlwaysOn Availability Group listener will be created later in this chapter.

NOTE

The SQL Instance field is case-sensitive. If you are using a SQL Named Instance, you will need to enter the instance name just as it was configured when originally installed.

FIGURE 14.18 The Define New SQL Server Store page.

12. Back at the Define SQL Server store page, click Next.
13. Complete the remaining wizard tasks to deploy your Enterprise Edition pool. For complete details on this process, see Chapter 4, "Skype for Business Server 2015 Front End Server."
14. Once the Front End Wizard has been completed, publish the topology.
15. On the initial Publish Topology screen, click Next.
16. At the Select Databases page, verify that the box is checked for your SQL Server, as shown in Figure 14.19, and then click Next.

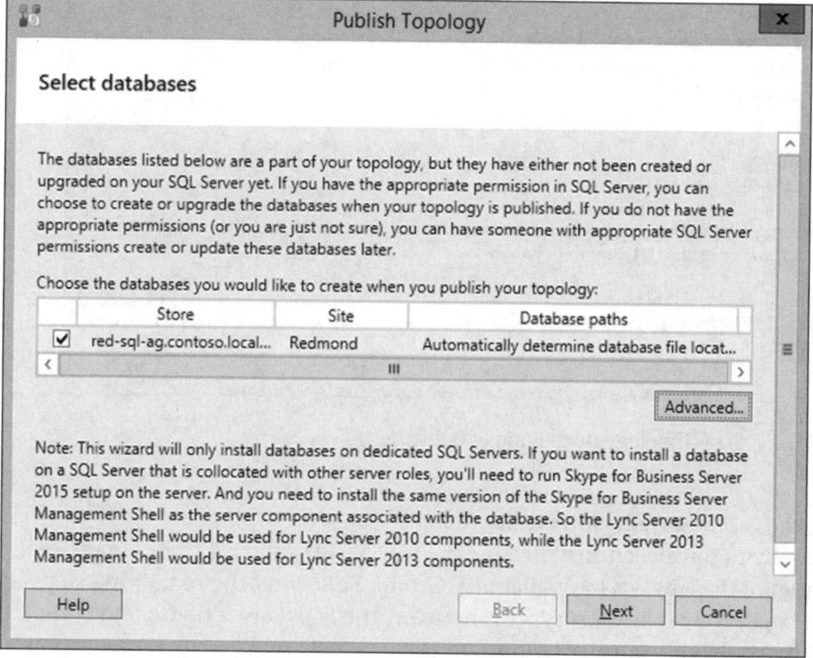

FIGURE 14.19 Select the databases to install.

17. Verify the topology was successfully published, as shown in Figure 14.20, and then click Finish. If there are any errors, resolve them before moving on.

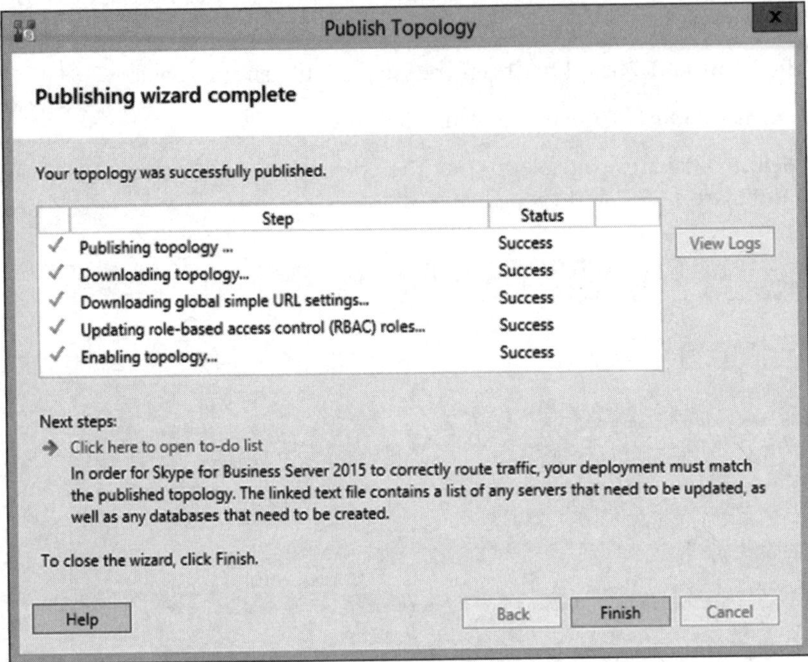

FIGURE 14.20 Topology successfully published.

Configuring the SQL AlwaysOn Availability Group

After the databases have been installed on the SQL Server used for the Primary Replicas, we can configure the AlwaysOn Availability Group. Following the remaining steps in this section will begin the replication process between the SQL Server nodes and complete the database high availability configuration.

1. First, we must re-create the database folder structure on the Secondary Replica server to ensure that the databases exist in the same location on both servers. Unless you specified the folder path during database installation, the databases were placed in a folder called CsData on the volume with the most available free disk space. Log on to one of the SQL Servers and run the following command from an elevated command prompt:

```
xcopy \\sfbsql01\c$\CsData \\sfbsql02\c$\CsData /t /e
```

   When prompted, type **d** and press Enter. When this is complete, close the Command Prompt window.

2. On the Primary Replica SQL Server, launch SQL Server Configuration Manager.

3. In the left navigation pane, click SQL Server Services.

4. In the right pane, right-click SQL Server (Instance Name) and click Properties.
5. Go to the AlwaysOn High Availability tab and then check the box for Enable AlwaysOn Availability Groups, as shown in Figure 14.21. Click OK.

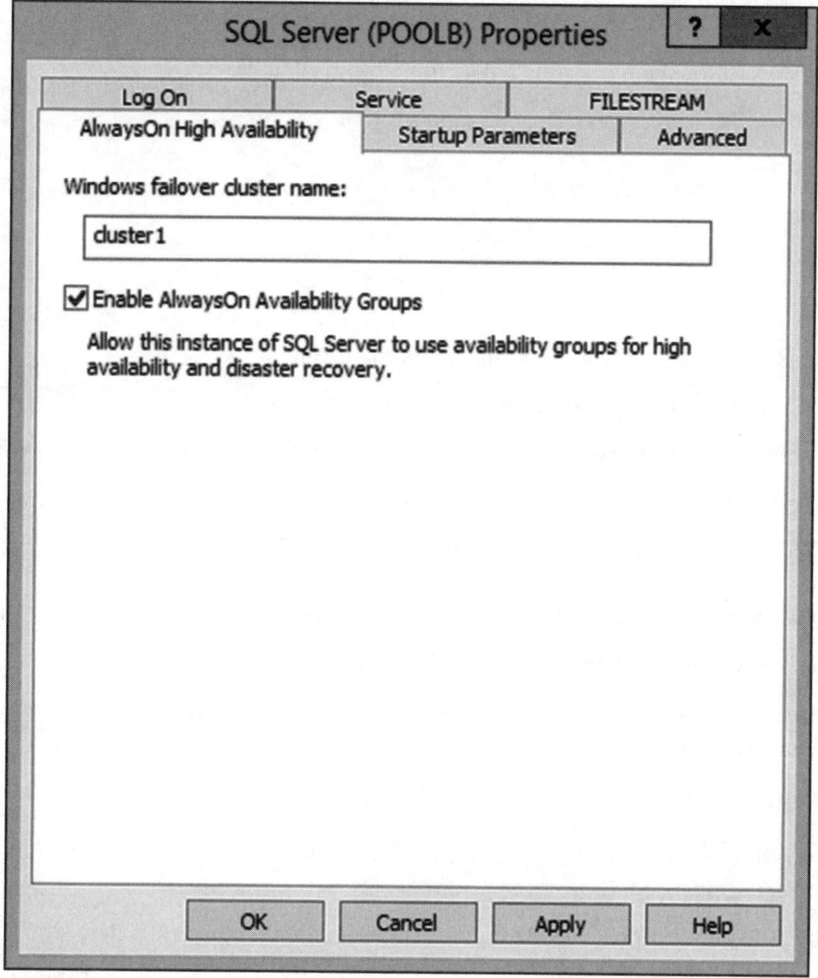

FIGURE 14.21 Check the Enable AlwaysOn Availability Groups box.

6. At the warning prompt, click OK.
7. Back in the main SQL Server Configuration Manager window, right-click the SQL Server (Instance Name) and then click Restart.
8. Repeat steps 2 through 7 on the Secondary Replica SQL Server. Once this is complete, close the SQL Server Configuration Manager on both servers.
9. On the Primary Replica SQL Server, open SQL Server Management Studio.

10. In Object Explorer, expand Databases. Right-click the cpsdyn database and click Properties. Under Options, change the Recovery model to Full and then click OK. Alternatively, a PowerShell command can be run:

```
Invoke-Sqlcmd -Query "ALTER DATABASE cpsdyn SET RECOVERY FULL WITH NO_WAIT;"
➥-ServerInstance "SQLServer\InstanceName"
```

11. Repeat step 10 for the remaining Skype for Business databases:

    - rgsconfig
    - rgsdyn
    - rtcab
    - rtcshared
    - rtcxds
    - xds (only exists in the pool that hosts the CMS)
    - lis (only exists in the pool that hosts the CMS)
    - LcsCDR (only exists when Monitoring is deployed)
    - LcsLog (only exists when Archiving is deployed)
    - QoEMetrics (only exists when Monitoring is deployed)

12. In Object Explorer, right-click the SQLServer\InstanceName and then click Restart.
13. At the SQL Server Management Studio confirmation prompt, click Yes.
14. Back up all the databases outlined in steps 10 and 11 using the following command, run once per database:

```
Backup-SqlDatabase -ServerInstance "SQLServer\InstanceName" -Database cpsdyn
```

15. After backing up all the Skype for Business Server 2015 databases, return to SQL Server Management Studio.
16. In Object Explorer, right-click AlwaysOn High Availability and click Refresh.
17. Expand AlwaysOn High Availability, right-click Availability Groups, and then click Refresh.

18. Right-click Availability Groups once more and then click New Availability Group Wizard, as shown in Figure 14.22.

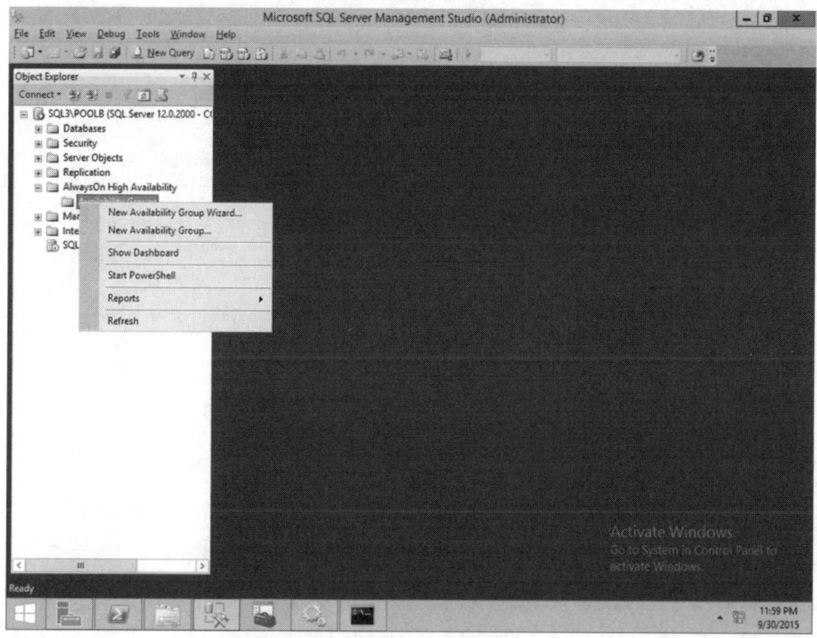

FIGURE 14.22 Create a new Availability Group.

19. At the initial Introduction page, click Next.

20. Enter a name for the Availability Group, as shown in Figure 14.23. Click Next.

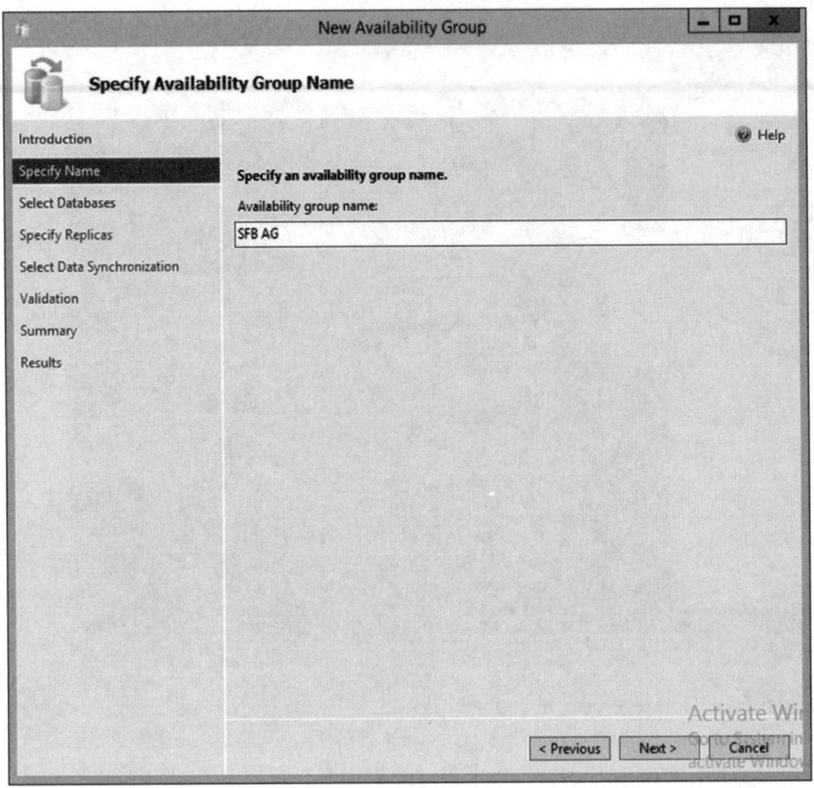

FIGURE 14.23 Enter Availability Group name.

21. In the Select User Databases for the Availability Group window, select all the Skype for Business Server 2015 databases, as shown in Figure 14.24. Click Next.

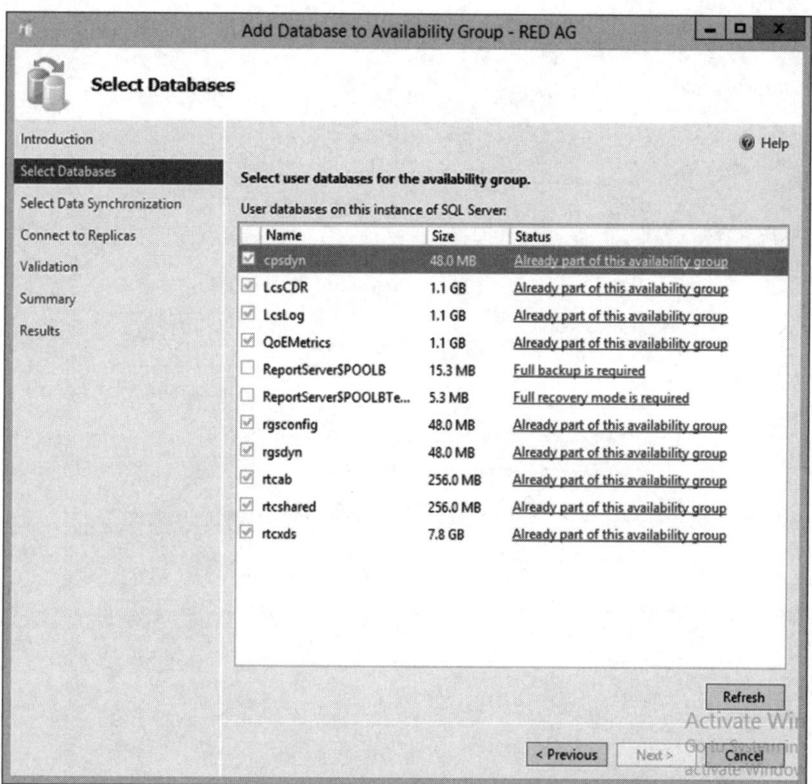

FIGURE 14.24 Database selection for the Availability Group.

22. On the Specify Replicas page, check the boxes for Automatic Failover and Synchronous Commit for the Primary. Then click Add Replica.

23. In the Connection window, enter the SQL Server name and Instance name for the Secondary Replica and then click Connect.

24. Back on the Specify Replicas page, check the boxes for Automatic Failover and Synchronous Commit for the Secondary role, as shown in Figure 14.25. Click Next.

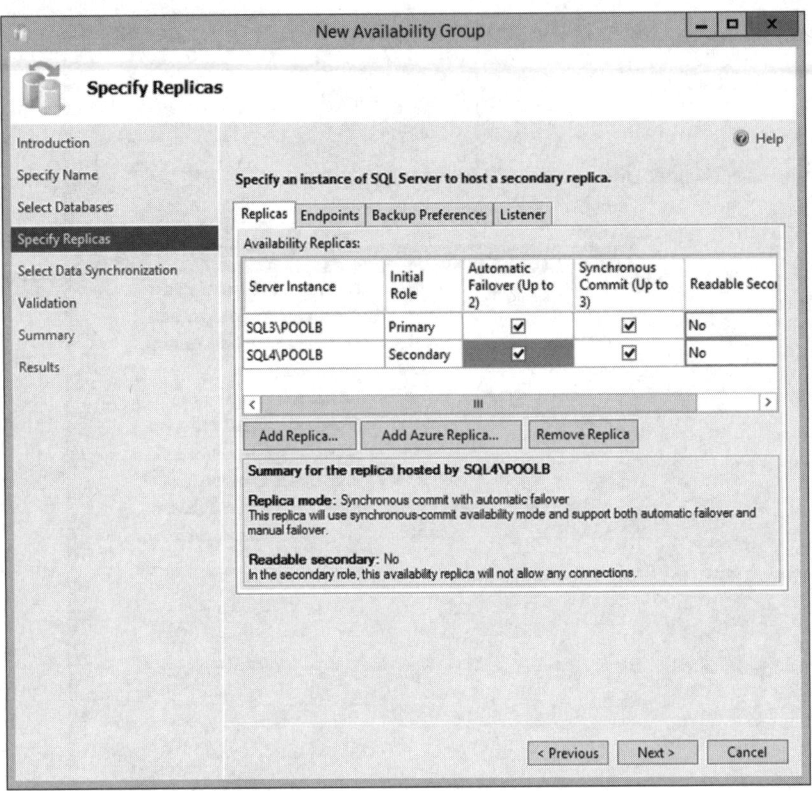

FIGURE 14.25 Specify replicas for the Availability Group.

25. On the Select Initial Data Synchronization page, ensure Full is selected and then provide a path to a network share to be used for the initial synchronization (see Figure 14.26). This folder must be created and shared prior to moving past this screen. Click Next.

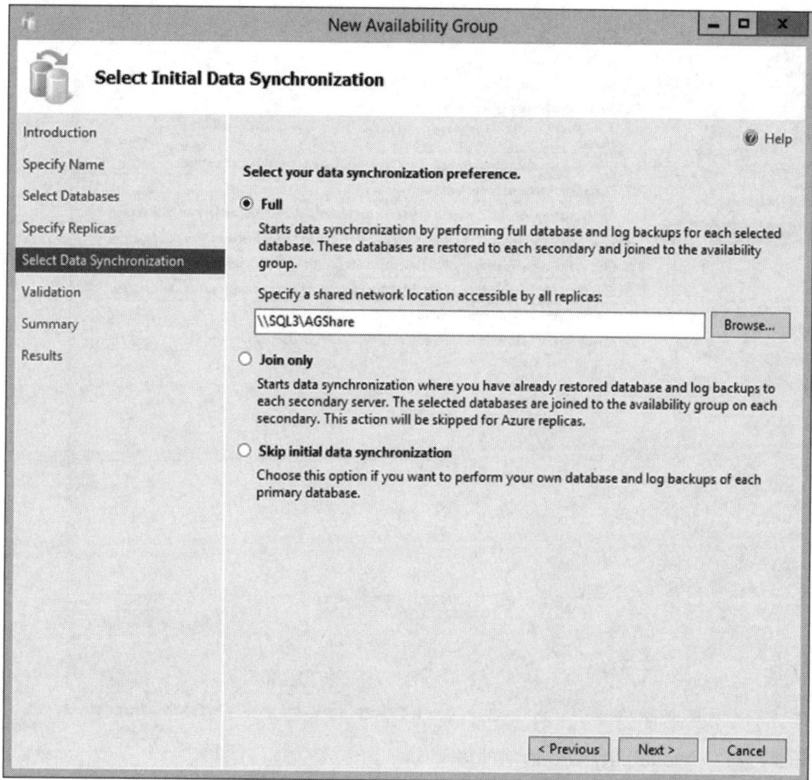

FIGURE 14.26 Specify initial synchronization and share path.

26. At the Validation page, click Next. The warning about the listener configuration can be safely ignored, as shown in Figure 14.27.

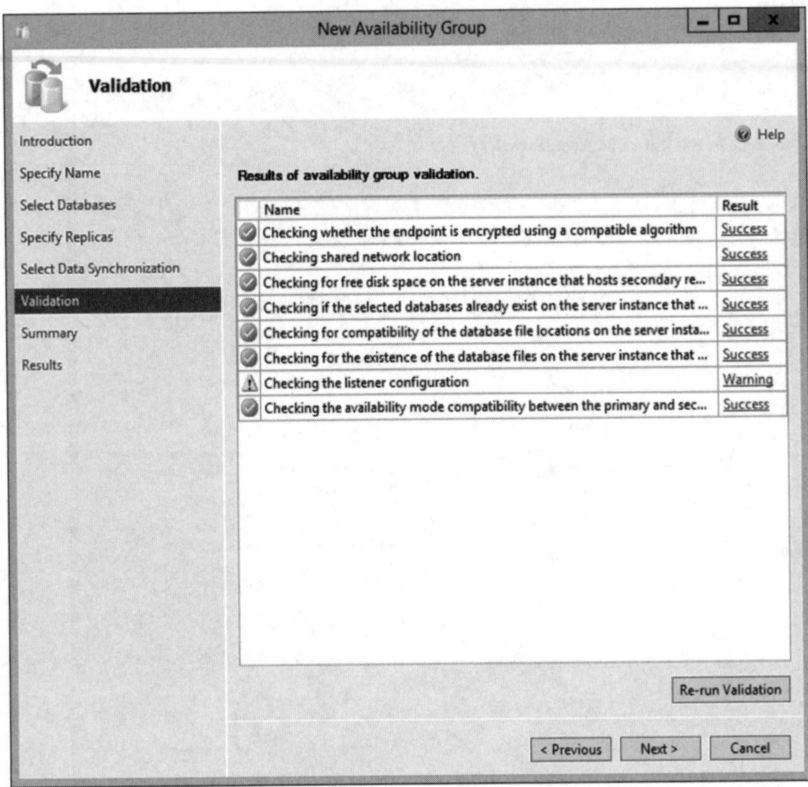

FIGURE 14.27 Availability Group validation.

27. On the Summary screen, click Finish. The configuration of the Availability Group may take a couple minutes, as shown in Figure 14.28.

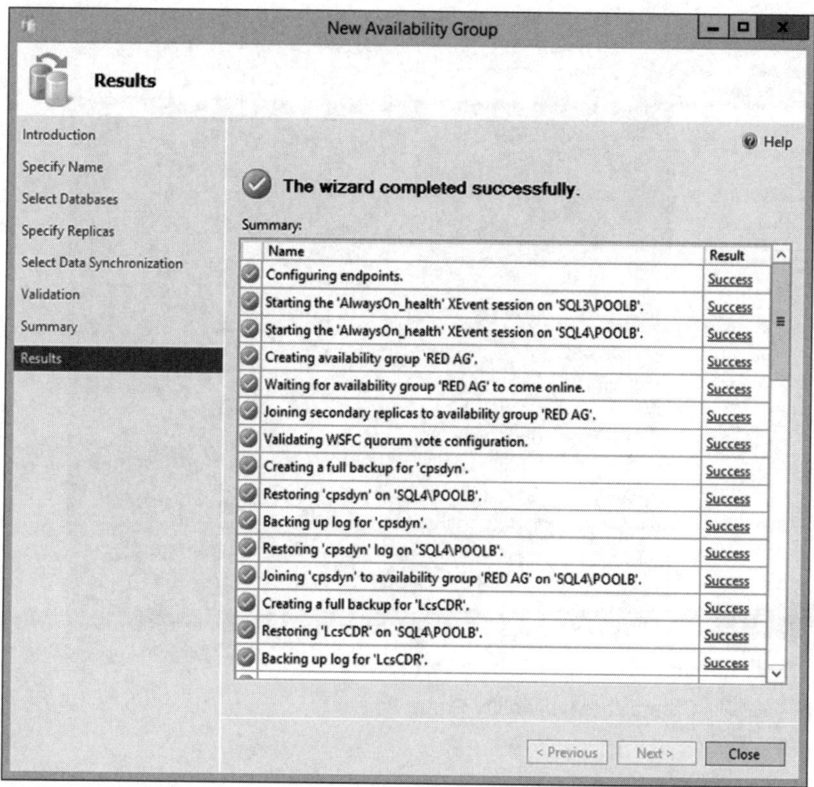

FIGURE 14.28 Availability Group creation.

28. Once this is completed, click Close.

29. Back in SQL Server Management Studio Object Explorer, expand Availability Groups, right-click the newly created Availability Group, and click Add Listener, as shown in Figure 14.29.

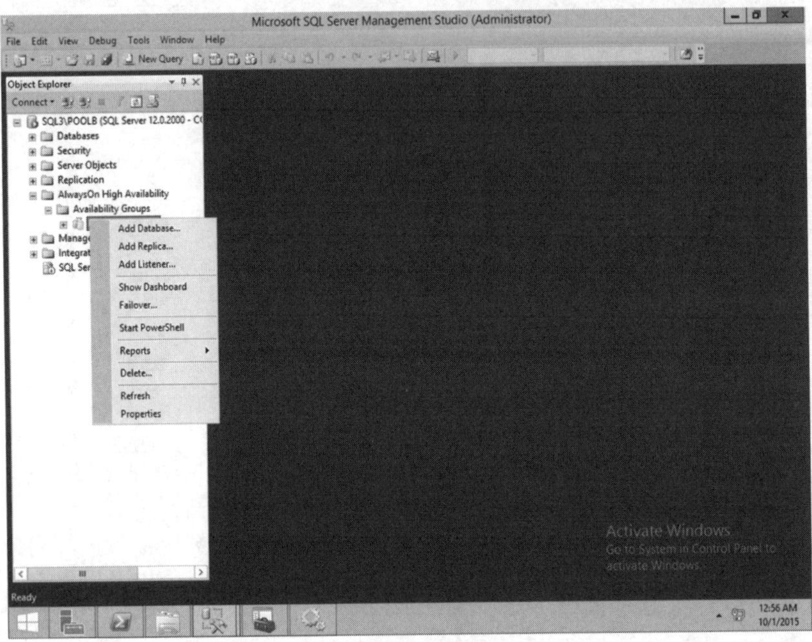

FIGURE 14.29 Create the Availability Group listener.

30. In the Listener DNS Name page, enter the name that was provided when configuring the SQL Store in Topology Builder, enter port 1433, and set the Network Mode field to Static IP and add an available IP address, as shown in Figure 14.30. Click OK.

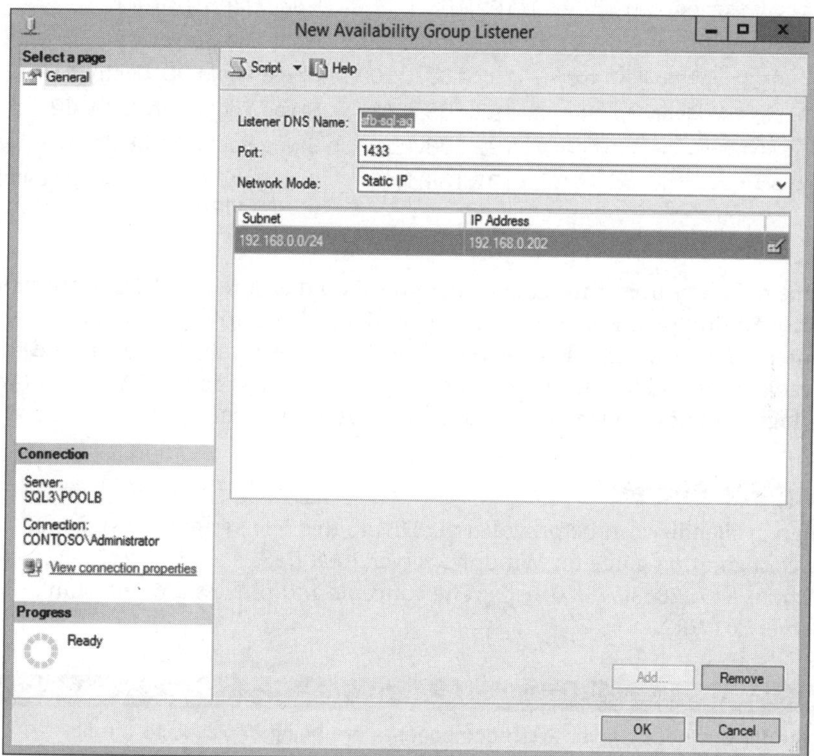

FIGURE 14.30 Configure the Availability Group listener.

31. Once the Availability Group listener is created, you can confirm that the databases exist on both SQL Servers by viewing them under the corresponding Availability Group in SQL Server Management Studio.

Configuring DNS Load Balancing for Enterprise Edition Pools

DNS load balancing is the preferred load-balancing method for all Skype for Business Server 2015 components, excluding the Skype for Business Web Services, which still require a hardware load balancer (HLB). Table 14.6 outlines the DNS records that would be required to provide DNS load balancing for a single Enterprise Edition pool.

TABLE 14.6 DNS Records for DNS Load Balancing a Front End Server Pool

Hostname	IP Address	Description
`Fe01.skypeunleashed.com`	192.168.1.10	Front End Server #1
`Fe02.skypeunleashed.com`	192.168.1.11	Front End Server #2
`Fe03.skypeunleashed.com`	192.168.1.12	Front End Server #3
`sfbpool01.skypeunleashed.com`	192.168.1.10	Skype Pool FQDN Entry #1
`sfbpool01.skypeunleashed.com`	192.168.1.11	Skype Pool FQDN Entry #2
`sfbpool01.skypeunleashed.com`	192.168.1.12	Skype Pool FQDN Entry #3
`sfbweb.skypeunleashed.com`	192.168.1.13	Web Services FQDN, should point to HLB VIP

The important takeaway from this table is that you should ensure that DNS entries for your Enterprise Edition pool FQDN are properly defined. A record for the pool FQDN should be entered for each Front End Server in the pool. This results in DNS round-robin requests to each Front End Server in the pool. Skype for Business Server 2015's built-in distribution logic handles the load distribution after users connect.

Configuring File Shares

File share high availability can be provided via Distributed File System (DFS). For a step-by-step configuration guide for Windows Server 2008 DFS, see http://technet.microsoft.com/en-us/library/cc732863(WS.10).aspx. The concepts and process are very similar for Windows Server 2012/R2.

TIP

When Skype for Business Server 2015 components are being deployed to the file share, Topology Builder requires that the administrator deploying the topology have full Administrator access to the file share. The Skype for Business Server 2015 Topology Builder uses NTFS file permissions to provide ACLs to the folders. Make sure that the account being used to deploy the topology has these permissions. Using a Network File System (NFS) share is not supported or recommended.

Configuring Persistent Chat Server Pools

When Persistent Chat is being configured for high availability or disaster recovery, a single pool is created regardless of the physical location of the servers. Defining a Persistent Chat pool is a simple process and is completed in the Topology Builder. Here are the steps to follow:

1. While in Topology Builder, expand Skype for Business Server 2015. Right-click the Persistent Chat Pools node and choose New Persistent Chat Pool.

2. Select Multiple Computer Pool and specify the pool FQDN, such as `pchatpool01.skypeunleashed.com`. Click Next. See Figure 14.31 for an example of how this configuration should look in Topology Builder.

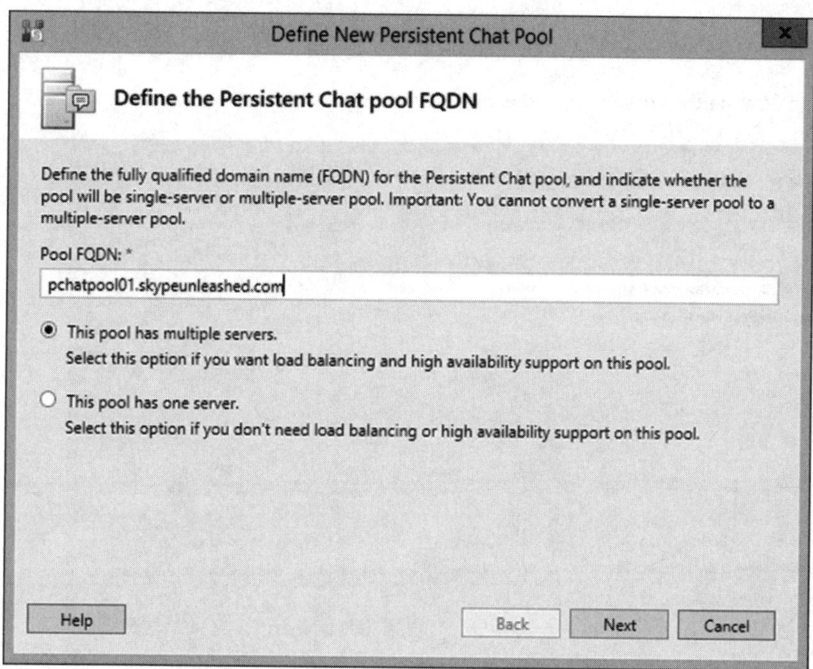

FIGURE 14.31 Defining a new Persistent Chat pool.

3. On the Define the Computers in This Pool page, specify the FQDN of each computer in the pool and click Add. Click Next. Figure 14.32 provides an example of how the defining members' configuration should look in Topology Builder.

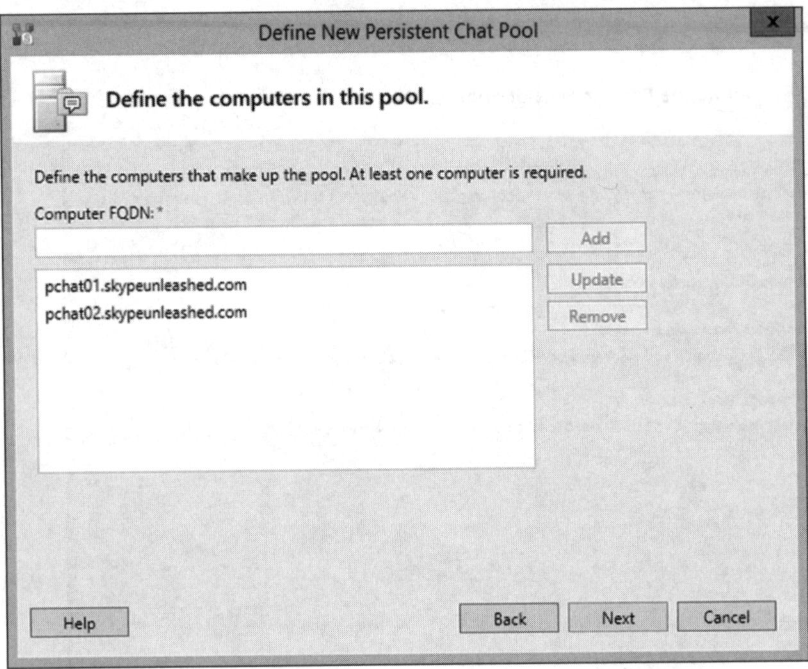

FIGURE 14.32 Defining the computers in a Persistent Chat pool.

4. On the Define Properties of the Persistent Chat Pool page, specify a display name. This name can be anything and is mainly used for administrative purposes.

5. Specify a Persistent Chat port (the default is 5041). There should be no reason to change this port number.

6. If compliance is required, check the box to enable compliance on the pool.

7. If you plan to provide disaster recovery through a backup SQL Server store using SQL Log Shipping, check the box Use Backup SQL Server Stores to Enable Disaster Recovery.

8. If you want to make this Persistent Chat pool the default for any or all sites, check the remaining boxes as they apply. Figure 14.33 provides an overview of the Persistent Chat properties configuration in Topology Builder.

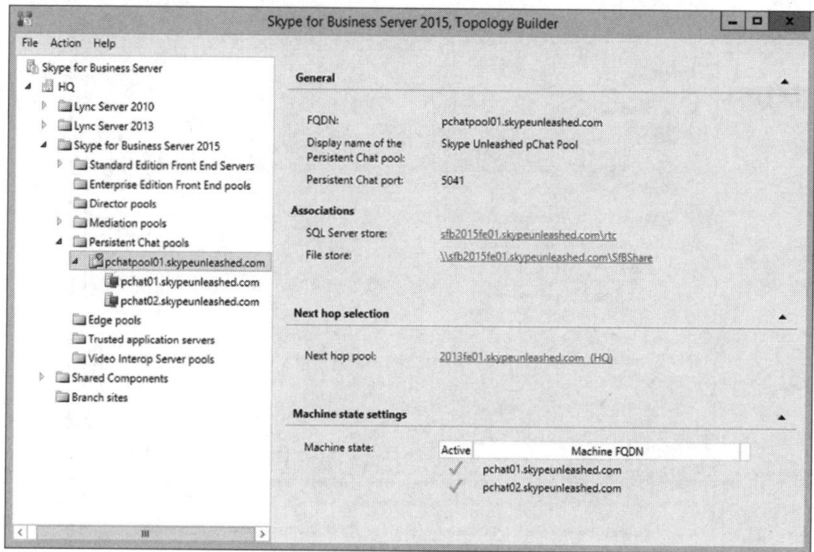

FIGURE 14.33 Summary of Persistent Chat properties.

9. Complete the remaining steps for the Persistent Chat pool and publish the topology. For complete details on this process, see Chapter 8, "Persistent Chat."

Executing Disaster Recovery Procedures

A detailed document should be developed to outline all procedures in the event of a disaster recovery scenario. Think of this as the disaster recovery "playbook," and it is absolutely critical to being successful in disaster recovery scenarios. The following section covers common disaster recovery procedures.

Configuring Front End Server Pairing

To provide disaster recovery to Front End Server pools, each pool must be paired for failover. Follow these steps to configure Front End Server pool pairing:

1. Open the Topology Builder.

2. If the two pools you want to pair are not yet defined, use Topology Builder to create these pools.

3. In Topology Builder, navigate to the Front End Server pool you want to configure pairing on. Right-click one of the two pools and then choose Edit Properties.

4. Select Resiliency and then check the Associated Backup Pool box.

5. Specify the pool you want to configure as a pair. This is for voice resiliency and for pool failover. Figure 14.34 provides an example of how this configuration should look in Topology Builder.

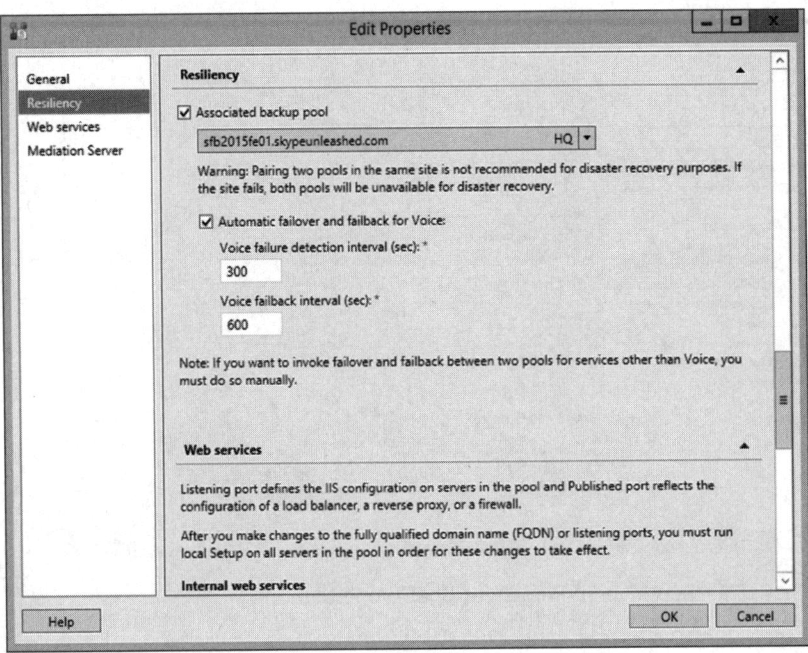

FIGURE 14.34 Specifying a backup Front End Server pool.

6. If you want to provide automatic failover for voice services (this is recommended), check the box Automatic Failover and Failback for Voice.

TIP

Consider the timing for your failover and failback intervals. Be sure not to set these values too low; however, you should note that by default failure detection is 300 seconds, or 5 minutes. If you want to provide failover more quickly than that, adjust that timer. Setting these values too low can result in failover and failback occurring too quickly in scenarios in which pool availability is fluctuating for whatever reason.

7. This configuration will set resiliency options on the other pool as well. When you are finished, use Topology Builder to publish the topology.

8. The Skype for Business Server 2015 Deployment Wizard must now be run on all Front End Servers in the pools where you configured pairing. Specifically, Step 2 (Setup or Remove Skype for Business Server Components) should be re-run. This is required to install the Skype for Business Server Backup Service, which will be responsible for replicating pool data.

9. After running the Deployment Wizard on each server, run the following command in the Skype for Business Server 2015 Management Shell on each server to start the Skype for Business Backup Service:

```
Start-CSWindowsService -Name LyncBackup
```

10. After the service has been installed and started on all servers, you can now force a synchronization of the pool data. To do this, run the following commands on Skype for Business Server 2015 Management Shell from any server in the pools (you need to run this only once):

```
Invoke-CSBackupServiceSync -PoolFQDN <FQDN of the First Skype for Business Pool>
Invoke-CSBackupServiceSync -PoolFQDN <FQDN of the Second Skype for Business Pool>
```

11. To check on the status of the synchronization, run the following commands in Skype for Business Server 2015 Management Shell:

```
Get-CSBackupServiceStatus -PoolFQDN <FQDN of the First Skype for Business Pool>
Get-CSBackupServiceStatus -PoolFQDN <FQDN of the Second Skype for Business Pool>
```


When synchronization is complete, your Front End Server pools will automatically maintain synchronization without any administrator intervention. At this point, your pools are configured for disaster recovery.

Failing Over the Central Management Store

In the event of a pool or site failure, the first consideration must be of the Central Management Store (CMS). The CMS must be functional in order to provide failover of any other services. If a Front End Server pool has failed, or the site hosting that pool has failed and it was running the CMS, the CMS first must be failed over to the secondary pool. The CMS is backed up as part of the pool pairing configured in earlier steps. Figure 14.35 provides an overview of the configuration to be used in the examples that follow. Pool A is currently running the CMS, and it will be the failing pool.

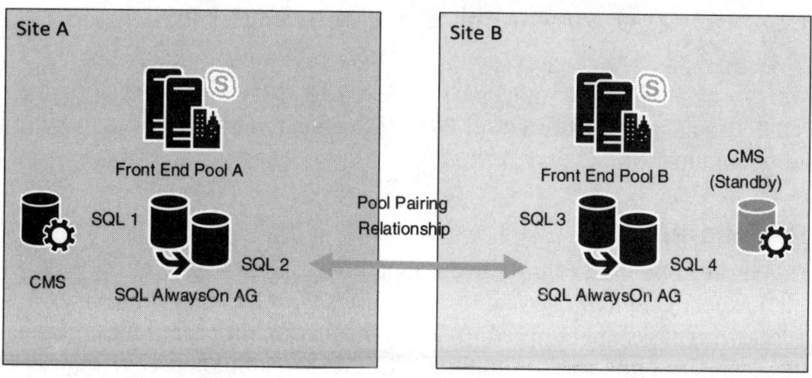

FIGURE 14.35 Skype for Business Server 2015 disaster recovery example.

1. To find out which pool is hosting the CMS, run the following command from the Skype for Business Server 2015 Management Shell:

   ```
   Invoke-CSManagementServerFailover -WhatIf
   ```

2. The following example assumes the CMS is hosted on Front End Pool A in Figure 14.35. Next, identify the backup pool relationship for Pool A. You can complete this by opening Topology Builder and reviewing resiliency settings, or by running the following command:

   ```
   Get-CsPoolBackupRelationship -PoolFQDN SkypePoolA.skypeunleashed.com
   ```

3. Before initiating the CMS failover, ensure that the secondary pool has been configured to host the CMS in the event of a failover. To do this, check the database state for the existence of a CMS mirror. Run the following command:

   ```
   Get-CsManagementStoreReplicationStatus -CentralManagementStoreStatus
   ```

   This command should show the `ActiveMasterFQDN` and `ActiveFileTransferAgents` referring to the Front End pool that hosts the active CMS. If these values are empty, the CMS is unavailable and you should begin the failover process.

4. Begin the failover of the CMS by issuing the following command:

   ```
   Invoke-CsManagementServerFailover
   ➥ -BackupSQLServerFQDN sfb-sqldr-ag.skypeunleashed.com
   ```

5. When this command has completed, you can validate that the CMS has failed over by running the following command. The `ActiveMasterFQDN` and `ActiveFileTransferAgents` attributes should point to the FQDN of Pool B.

   ```
   Get-CSManagementStoreReplicationStatus -CentralManagementStoreStatus
   ```

6. After you have validated that the secondary pool is now hosting the CMS, run the following command to validate CMS replication across all servers. When all replicas have a value of `True`, you can continue with your disaster recovery procedures.

   ```
   Get-CsManagementStoreReplicationStatus
   ```

At this point, the CMS should now be hosted on Pool B. The next section outlines how to initiate a Front End pool failover.

Initiating a Pool Failover

The following procedures can be used to initiate a pool failover for full feature recovery. Voice resiliency will automatically fail over and provide users with basic registration and voice routing. The following tasks are required to fail over functionality that relies on the SQL backend to the secondary pool, such as contact lists, Presence, and conferencing. Figure 14.35 provides an overview of the sample configuration used in this scenario.

CAUTION

Before failing over your Front End pool, check whether the Edge Server is still active in that site. If only the Front End pool is down, but the Edge Server is up and accepting requests, you should adjust the next-hop destination for that Edge Server. Adjust this setting in Topology Builder and publish the topology, or run the `Set-CSEdgeServer` command in the Skype for Business Server 2015 Management Shell.

1. Failing over a Front End Server pool can be done only via the Skype for Business Server 2015 Management Shell and is done using a single command. Run the following command to fail over Pool A to Pool B:

```
Invoke-CsPoolFailover -PoolFQDN SkypePoolA.skypeunleashed.com
➥-DisasterMode -Verbose
```

2. When Pool A has been restored, initiating a pool failback is also completed in Skype for Business Server 2015 Management Shell using a single command. Run the following command to fail back Pool A:

```
Invoke-CsPoolFailback -PoolFQDN SkypePoolA.skypeunleashed.com -Verbose
```

Initiating Persistent Chat Failover

Persistent Chat failover for disaster recovery relies on SQL Log Shipping as well as setting active Persistent Chat servers. Reference the earlier section "Persistent Chat Disaster Recovery" for possible scenarios. This section outlines the steps required to fail over the Persistent Chat database to the secondary server using SQL Log Shipping, as well as how to configure active Persistent Chat servers for the stretched pool.

The following procedures must be completed from the secondary Persistent Chat Server database. This server will have been the destination for Log Shipping.

1. Disable SQL Log Shipping. Open SQL Server Management Studio and connect to the database instance where the secondary Persistent Chat server database is located.
2. Open a SQL query window on the Master database and use the following command to disable Log Shipping:

```
exec sp_delete_log_shipping_secondary_database mgc
```

3. Bring the backup Persistent Chat database (MGC is the database name) back online. In the same SQL query window that was used before, run the following command:

```
\restore database MGC with recovery
```

14

If there are existing connections on the MGC database, you must end these connections by running the following command:

```
\exec sp_who2
```

Based on the connections previously identified, run the following command to end the connection:

```
\kill <SPID of Connection>
```

4. At this point, the SQL configuration is complete and the database will be brought online with the latest data available.

5. Skype for Business Server 2015 must be configured to recognize the SQL Server change for failover. On a Skype for Business Server 2015, run the following command in Skype for Business Server 2015 Management Shell:

   ```
   Set-CsPersistentChatState service:<Persistent Chat Pool FQDN>
   ➥-PoolState FailedOver
   ```

   This command allows Skype for Business Server 2015 to use the backup SQL Server as the SQL database for Persistent Chat.

6. Because Persistent Chat relies on stretched pools, and these pools will have a subset of servers that are not active, a failover scenario requires activating these servers for the Persistent Chat service. Reference the disaster recovery design in place and use the `Set-CSPersistentChatActiveServer` command to set these servers online. The example that follows assumes a stretched Persistent Chat pool with four active and four passive servers. CHAT1 and CHAT2 are located in Site A, which is the failed site, and CHAT3 and CHAT4 are located in Site B, which is the secondary site being activated.

   ```
   Set-CSPersistentChatActiveServer -Identity
   ➥<Persistent Chat Pool Display Name or FQDN> -ActiveServers $null
   Set-CSPersistentChatActiveServer -Identity
   ➥<Persistent Chat Pool Display Name or FQDN> -ActiveServers
   ➥@{Add="CHAT3.skypeunleashed.com","CHAT4.skypeunleashed.com"}
   ```

The first command will remove all active servers from the configuration; this is the quickest way to adjust those servers in a failover scenario. The second command will add CHAT3 and CHAT4 to the active server configuration.

At this point, the failover for Persistent Chat is complete.

Summary

Skype for Business Server 2015 continues many of the efficient high-availability and disaster recovery scenarios introduced in Lync Server 2013 to organizations deploying Skype for Business Server 2015. Proper planning is critical for the success of a Skype for

Business Server 2015 deployment—and even more critical because it relates to the recovery and survivability of the environment. As part of the design process in Skype for Business Server 2015, the business requirements must be understood first and foremost. Business requirements for recovery and availability will drive key decisions in the design process. After all requirements have been identified, a clear path to a final Skype for Business Server 2015 design that meets business expectations will be defined.

As part of the high-availability and disaster recovery design, it is critical to establish clear documentation with step-by-step instructions on executing all related tasks. The tasks outlined in this chapter have been greatly simplified as compared to Lync Server 2010 and other legacy versions, but they still require preparedness and a detailed disaster recovery playbook to be successful.

CHAPTER 15

Migrating from Lync Server 2010/2013

IN THIS CHAPTER

- Overview of the Migration Process
- Migration Steps: Side-by-Side Method
- Migration Steps: In-place Upgrade Method
- Troubleshooting
- Migration Best Practices

With Skype for Business Server 2015, there are a couple methods to perform the upgrade or migration. The approach taken for the upgrade process depends heavily on the legacy version of Lync that currently exists in the environment.

The first migration method involves building Skype for Business Server in parallel to the existing environment on separate servers. This is commonly referred to as a side-by-side migration, and it's the required migration method for environments moving directly from Lync Server 2010 to Skype for Business Server 2015. The process is fairly straightforward, with only a few challenging areas. The seasoned Lync or Skype for Business architect will be very familiar with this approach.

The second migration method is new in Skype for Business Server 2015, and only available for those environments upgrading from Lync Server 2013. Microsoft has finally heard the masses and has provided a way to perform a true "upgrade" to Skype for Business Server 2015 on existing hardware. Because there have not been any major architectural changes between Lync Server 2013 and Skype for Business Server 2015, an upgrade may be performed "in place" on existing Lync Server 2013 servers. Keep in mind that in Lync Server 2013 to Skype for Business Server 2015 upgrade scenarios, a side-by-side migration is still supported as well.

If your organization is still using Office Communications Server 2007 or 2007 R2, you've got your work cut out for you. An upgrade to at least Lync 2010 will be required as an interim step before moving on to Skype for Business Server 2015.

As with any migration, planning will be the key to success. When planning to upgrade from Lync Server 2010, become familiar with the changes in architecture for Skype for Business Server 2015. Assuming that Lync Server 2010 is already in place, the Skype for Business architect will want to plan the architecture, starting with deploying a Skype for Business Server 2015 Front End pool and then an Edge Server. The Skype for Business Server 2015 Edge Server can proxy connections for users in both Skype for Business Server 2015 pools and legacy Lync Server 2010 or 2013 pools. This means there is no need to maintain separate Edge Servers during the coexistence period. This chapter goes into more detail in the "Edge Migration to Skype for Business Server 2015" section coming up. If you have completed a migration from Lync Server 2010 to Lync Server 2013, the process will be very familiar to you. The migration sequence is always site-by-site and side-by-side, starting with the first site deploying the Skype for Business Server 2015 Front End pool, Edge, and Director (if required), and then migrating the pools side-by-side. For Skype for Business server roles where the "migration" is a simple "rip and replace," like the Archiving Server role and Monitoring Server role, the topic isn't covered in great detail.

For those planning to use the "in-place upgrade" process from Lync Server 2013 to Skype for Business Server 2015, a different type of planning is required. The Skype for Business architect will need to understand the impact of this approach to the existing infrastructure. Because services will need to be updated on upgraded servers, the decision must be made on how to handle the service outage. If you are upgrading "paired" Lync Server 2013 pools, users may be moved temporarily to a secondary pool during the upgrade. If only a single Lync Server 2013 pool exists, then a larger service outage should be planned. Similar to the side-by-side method, you will want to upgrade the environment from the "inside out," starting with the Front End pool and followed by the Edge Servers.

This chapter highlights the full lifecycle of the migration processes. Both methods for upgrading to Skype for Business Server 2015 are covered in detail. Finally, the chapter concludes with troubleshooting and best practices.

Migration Steps: Side-by-Side Method

If you have previously migrated from Lync Server 2010 to Lync Server 2013, then the migration process covered in this section will be all too familiar. When you are upgrading from Lync Server 2010, this is the supported migration path because the "in-place" upgrade is only available if your servers are running Lync 2013. In some scenarios, you may want to use the side-by-side method even if you are currently running Lync Server 2013. Common reasons for using the side-by-side process to upgrade from Lync Server 2013 may include a server hardware refresh, an operating system refresh, and migration of single-pool deployments that require minimal downtime.

As in the previous versions, the Front End Server migration is where you will start the migration process to Skype for Business Server 2015. The first step is to prepare Active Directory for Skype for Business Server 2015. In fact, all the necessary steps to build a Skype for Business Front End are covered in Chapter 4, "Skype for Business Server 2015 Front End Server."

NOTE

After a Skype for Business Server 2015 pilot pool is deployed, you cannot use Lync Server 2010/2013 Topology Builder or Lync Server 2010/2013 Control Panel to manage any Skype for Business Server 2015 resources. You must use Skype for Business Server 2015 tools to manage Skype for Business Server 2015 and Lync Server 2010/2013 resources. In general, you should use the administrative tools for the latest version of the product that is installed within the environment. Skype for Business Server 2015 and Lync Server 2010/2013 administrative tools cannot be installed together on the same computer.

Before you begin the migration process, it is important to ensure that you have the latest Lync Server 2010 or Lync Server 2013 updates applied to the environment. As with any major migration, it is also prudent to back up the Lync Server 2010 or Lync Server 2013 environment. You should back up the SQL databases as well as export user configuration and content using the `dbimpexp.exe` tool or the `Export-CsUserData` command. Exporting a copy of the CMS from the Lync Server 2010 or Lync Server 2013 pool using the `Export-CsConfiguration` command is also highly suggested. Configuration of the legacy Lync Server clients should be considered as well. It is recommended that you use a Client Version Filter to only allow clients with the most current updates to connect. The Client Version Filter is found in the Skype for Business Control Panel under the main heading "Clients" and the subheading "Client Version Policy."

Any experienced architect will understand that if the existing environment is having problems, those problems should be resolved before migration. A migration is not going to fix things that were not working correctly to begin with. Here is a high-level overview of items to check:

- Verify that the Lync Server 2010 or Lync Server 2013 services are started.
- Verify the federation and Edge Server settings.
- Verify XMPP services and federated partners.

Front End and User Migration to Skype for Business Server 2015

After the forest and domain have been prepared, you need to download the existing topology using the Skype for Business Topology Builder from the Lync Server 2010 or Lync Server 2013 homed Central Management Server (CMS). After this has been completed, you will be able to define the new Skype for Business Server 2015 servers. This is shown in Figure 15.1.

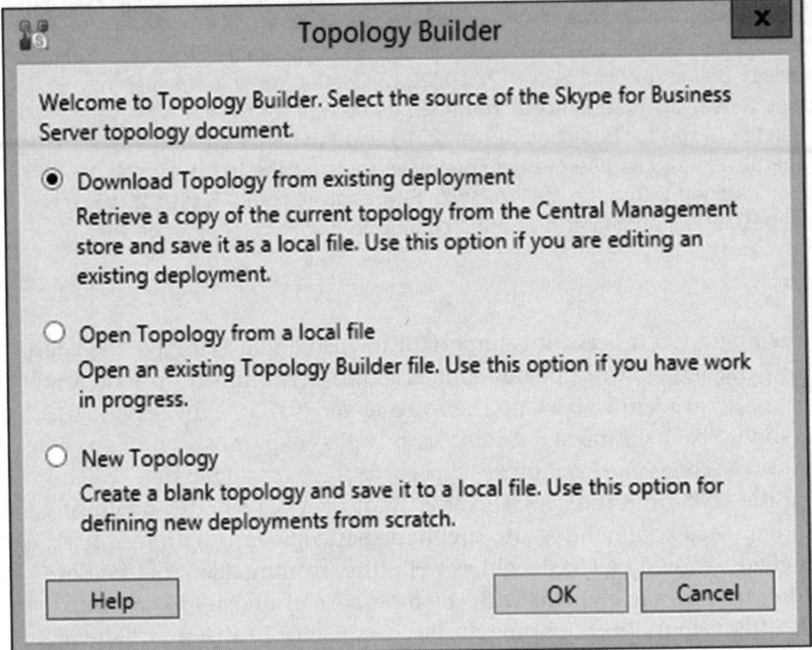

FIGURE 15.1 Download the Topology from an existing Lync Server 2010 or 2013 environment.

The CMS was introduced in Lync Server 2010 to hold important configuration information related to the entire Lync environment. Because Skype for Business Server 2015 also uses the CMS architecture, there is no need to import any configuration from the Lync Server 2010 or Lync Server 2013 environment. When you open Topology Builder, you will see your legacy Lync environment and right below you will see the Skype for Business Server 2015 node, as shown in Figure 15.2. You add servers to the topology the same way you did with the legacy Lync Topology Builder.

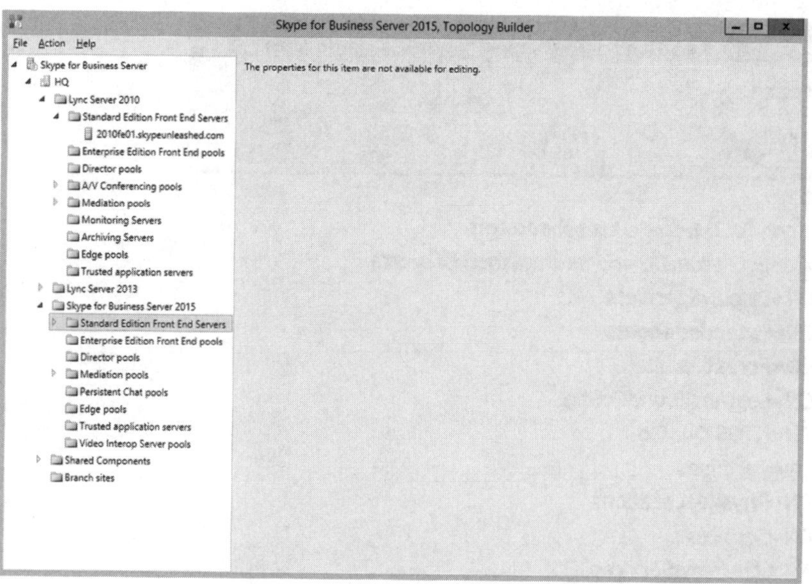

FIGURE 15.2 Skype for Business Server 2015 Topology with Lync Server 2010 and Lync Server 2013.

NOTE

You might see references to the Central Management Server and Central Management Store. The main difference is that the Central Management Server is the Front End responsible for the read/write copy of the Central Management Store, which is the actual data in the database. The master database location is referenced by a service connection point (SCP) in Active Directory Domain Services (AD DS). Connect to the correct context, whether Configuration or System. To see the configuration context, expand C=Services, CN=RTC Service, CN=Topology Settings. The location in Active Directory is shown in Figure 15.3.

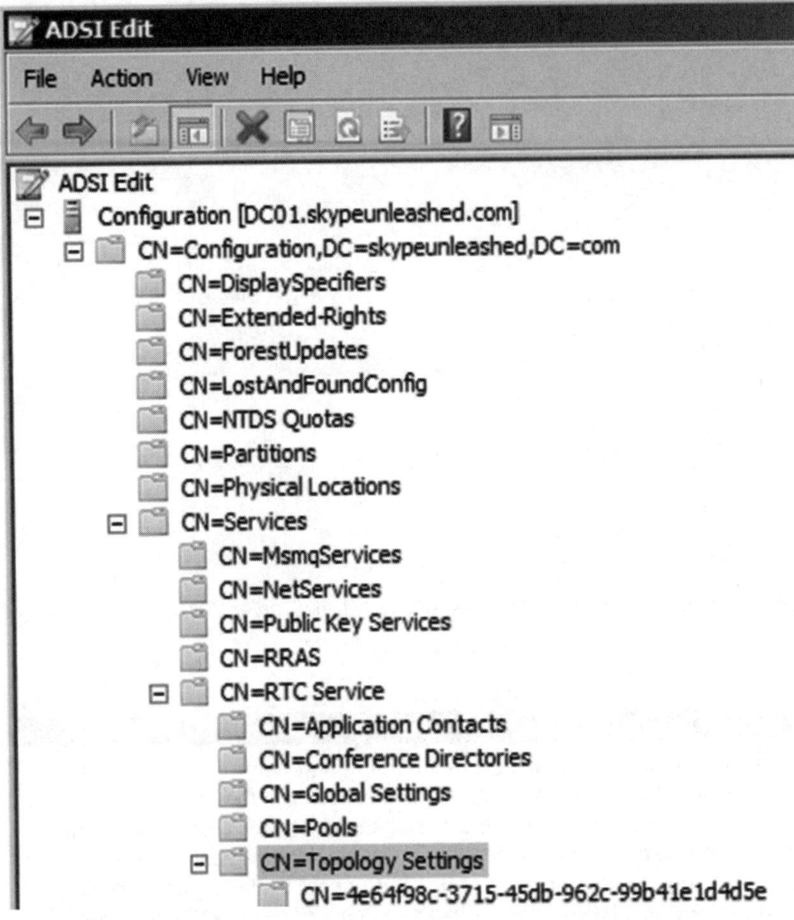

FIGURE 15.3 Skype for Business Server SCP location in Active Directory.

After you have deployed the Skype for Business Server 2015 pool, it is important to verify coexistence with the legacy Lync Server 2010 or Lync Server 2013 pool. Here are the tasks that should be completed:

- Verify that the Skype for Business Servers have started, navigate to the Administrative Tools\Services applet, and verify that all services that begin with "Skype for Business Server" are in the started state.
- Open the Skype for Business Server 2015 Control Panel. Open the Control Panel from the Front End Server in your Skype for Business Server 2015 deployment. Select the Skype for Business Server 2015 pool for a Standard Edition deployment, or the Internal Web Services FQDN for an Enterprise Edition deployment.

NOTE

On Skype for Business Server 2015, Silverlight version 5 needs to be installed before the Skype for Business Server Control Panel is used.

- In the Topology section of the Skype for Business Control Panel, the topology now includes the Lync Server 2010 or Lync Server 2013 and Skype for Business Server 2015 roles.

After a successful Skype for Business Server 2015 pool installation, the next step is to set the Skype for Business Server 2015 pool to use the legacy Lync Edge Server. This allows a period of coexistence, which is necessary so that you can maintain full external functionality while you are in coexistence mode. Later you will transition to the Skype for Business Server 2015 Edge for external connectivity. To finish this process, you need to complete the following steps:

1. Open Topology Builder and select your site, which is directly below the Skype for Business Server node.
2. Under the Action menu, select Edit Properties.
3. In the left pane, select Federation Route.
4. Under Site Federation Route Assignment, select Enable SIP Federation, as shown in Figure 15.4, and then select the Lync Server 2010 or Lync Server 2013 Edge Server (this can be a Lync Server 2010 or Lync Server 2013 Director if a Director exists in the legacy environment).

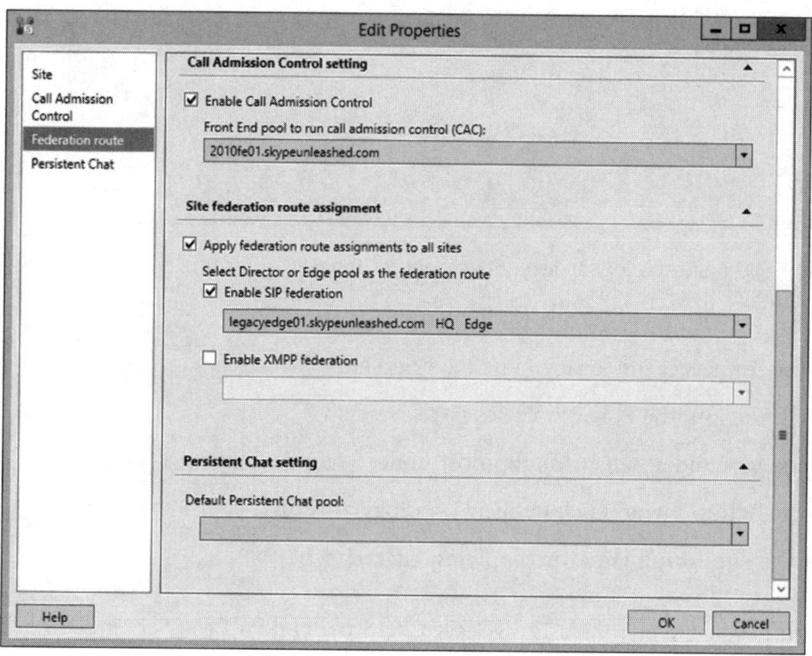

FIGURE 15.4 Site federation route assignment association.

5. Click OK to close the Edit Properties page.
6. In Topology Builder, under the Skype for Business Server 2015 node, navigate to the Standard Edition Server or Enterprise Edition Front End pools, right-click the Skype for Business Server 2015 pool, and then click Edit Properties.
7. Under Associations, select the check box next to Associate Edge Pool (For Media Components). This is shown in Figure 15.5.

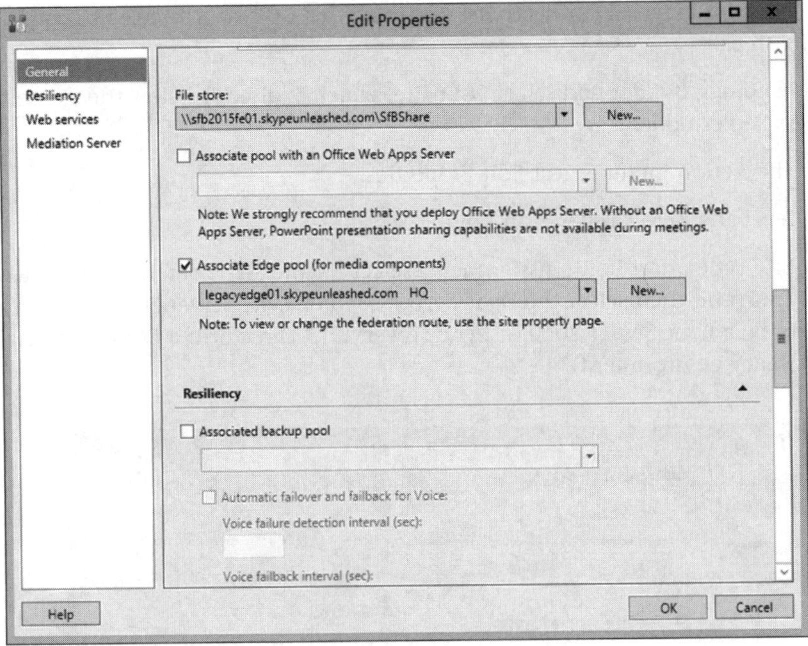

FIGURE 15.5 Set the legacy Lync Edge pool for the Skype for Business Edge pool media route.

8. From the list, select the legacy Lync Edge Server.
9. Click OK to close the Edit Properties page.
10. In Topology Builder, select the topmost node, Skype for Business Server.
11. From the Action menu, click Publish Topology and then click Next.
12. When the Publishing Wizard completes, click Finish.

Now that you have a Skype for Business Server 2015 pool and a Lync Server 2010 or Lync Server 2013 pool, you can move pilot users to the new Skype for Business Server 2015 pool to verify functionality between pools. To move a user between pools, you can use the Skype for Business Control Panel or Skype for Business Management Shell. Let's go over using the Skype for Business Control Panel first.

1. From the Skype for Business Server 2015 Front End, open the Skype for Business Control Panel. Click Users, click Search, and then click Find.
2. Select the user you want to move to Skype for Business Server 2015.
3. On the Action menu, select Move Selected Users to Pool.
4. From the drop-down list, select the Skype for Business Server 2015 pool. Click OK.

CAUTION

When moving users or data from a legacy Lync Server pool to Skype for Business Server 2015, *always* use the Skype for Business Server Management Shell or Control Panel. Using legacy admin tools to move data from a legacy Lync Server pool to a Skype for Business Server 2015 pool can result in data loss.

TIP

A Force option is present in the Move Users dialog box. Checking this box will move the user account to the new pool, but will delete user data associated with the account (such as conferences that have been scheduled). Force should be used only in a failure scenario, and only if you are confident that you have no other option.

Verify that the Registrar Pool column for the user now contains the Skype for Business Server 2015 pool. If you see the Skype for Business Server 2015 pool, the move was successful.

Now that you know how to move a user in the Skype for Business Control Panel, let's take a look at moving a user using the Skype for Business Management Shell. Use the following commands to move a user using the Skype for Business Server Management Shell:

1. Open the Skype for Business Management Shell.
2. At the command line, type the following:

```
Move-CsUser -Identity "User1" -Target "sfb2015fe01.skypeunleashed.com"
```

3. To verify that the move was successful, type the following:

```
Get-CsUser -Identity "User1"
```

4. The `RegistrarPool` identity now reflects the Skype for Business Server 2015 pool.

NOTE

At this point in the migration process, you are in a coexistence configuration. You have a Lync Server 2010 or Lync Server 2013 pool and a Skype for Business Server 2015 pool configured. For external Edge services you are using the legacy Lync Edge Server. In the next section you will complete the migration process to Skype for Business Server 2015 for the Edge services.

It is recommended that you test functionality between users in both the legacy Lync Server 2010 or Lync Server 2013 pool and the Skype for Business Server 2015 pool before moving all users and services. Run the following tests:

- Test users from at least one federated domain, an internal user on Skype for Business Server 2015, and a user on Lync Server 2010/2013. Test instant messaging (IM), Presence, audio/video (A/V), and desktop sharing.
- Test users of each public IM service provider that your organization supports (and for which provisioning has been completed) by communicating with a user on Skype for Business Server 2015 and a user on Lync Server 2010/2013.
- Verify that anonymous users are able to join conferences.
- Test a user hosted on Lync Server 2010/2013 using remote user access (logging in to Lync Server 2010/2013 from outside the intranet but without VPN) with a user on Skype for Business Server 2015 and then a user on Lync Server 2010/2013. Test IM, Presence, A/V, and desktop sharing.
- Test a user hosted on Skype for Business Server 2015 using remote user access (logging in to Skype for Business Server 2015 from outside the intranet but without VPN) with a user on Skype for Business Server 2015 then and a user on Lync Server 2010/2013. Test IM, Presence, A/V, and desktop sharing.

So that's it for the Front End pool. The next section covers legacy Lync Edge to Skype for Business Server 2015 Edge migration.

Edge Migration to Skype for Business Server 2015

The Edge Server migration process is actually the easiest part of the overall migration process because it's a direct replacement. A Skype for Business Server 2015 Edge Server can proxy connections for Lync Server 2010 or Lync Server 2013 Front End pools, meaning there is no need to run both versions of Edge in parallel during the coexistence period. This section covers the migration aspect of the Skype for Business Server 2015 Edge Server; a full review of the Edge Server design process is covered in Chapter 32, "Planning to Deploy External Services." In addition, the Edge Server build process is covered in detail in Chapter 5, "Skype for Business Server 2015 Edge Server." This section covers the changes that need to be made for migrating from the Lync Server 2010 or Lync Server 2013 Edge Server to a Skype for Business Server 2015 Edge Server.

This section covers adding a Skype for Business Server 2015 Edge Server to the Skype for Business Server 2015 pool and migrating legacy Lync Server external Edge functions to the Skype for Business Server 2015 Edge Server.

The first step in the Edge Server migration process is to update the federation routes. The federation route needs to be updated to use the Skype for Business Server 2015 Edge Server. Federation is a trust relationship between two or more SIP domains that permits users in separate organizations to communicate across network boundaries. At this point in the migration, you are using the legacy Lync Edge Server as your federation route for the Skype for Business Server 2015 Front End pool. You need to update this configuration so that you can begin to move Lync Edge functions from the legacy Lync Edge Server to the new Skype for Business Server 2015 Edge Server.

Finally, you must repoint the appropriate DNS records to the new Edge Server[md]that is, `sip.skypeunleashed.com`. In addition to the new DNS records listed in Chapter 5, the existing SRV records need to be modified as well. Here are the SRV records required and what they should be changed to:

- For remote user access:
  - `_sip._tls.skypeunleashed.com` points to port 443 for the FQDN of the Access Edge Service on the Edge Server.
- For federation:
  - `_sipfederationtls._tcp.skypeunleashed.com` points to port 5061 for the FQDN of the Access Edge Service on the Edge Server.
  - `_xmpp-server._tcp.skypeunleashed.com` points to port 5269 for the FQDN of the Access Edge service on the Edge Server.

NOTE

If your organization has any partners who do not use open federation, they will need to update their Edge Server federation settings with the name of the new Skype for Business Server 2015 Edge Server.

NOTE

Changing the federation and media traffic route requires that you schedule maintenance downtime for the Skype for Business Server 2015 and legacy Lync Edge Servers. During the transition, federated access will be unavailable for the duration of the outage. There are several reasons why downtime is required. You might have decided to use new IP addresses on the Skype for Business Server 2015 Edge Server. This means that external DNS entries would need to be updated to reflect the new IP addresses. DNS propagation can take a while depending on TTL values and other external DNS servers updating records. Downtime can also be caused by the decision to use the same IP addresses on the Skype for Business Server 2015 Edge Server that were used on the legacy Lync Edge Server. In that case, you will have to be really quick and swap an Ethernet cable (I can picture an engineer in the datacenter, hand on the Ethernet cable, waiting for the word "Go!" and then quickly moving the cable to the new server hoping there is no outage) or else disable the NIC on the legacy Lync Edge Server and enable the NIC on the Skype for Business Server 2015 Edge Server. That, of course, would mean that you had preconfigured the NIC(s) on the Skype for Business Server 2015 Edge Server before the downtime.

To transition the federation and media route from the legacy Lync Edge Server to the Skype for Business Server 2015 Edge Server, you need to make a few configuration changes. First, you need to remove the legacy federation association from Skype for Business Server 2015 sites. To do that, you must complete the following steps:

1. Open Topology Builder on the Skype for Business Server 2015 Front End Server.
2. In the left pane, navigate to the site node, which is located directly below Skype for Business Server.
3. Right-click the site and then click Edit Properties.
4. In the left pane, select Federation Route.
5. Under Site Federation Route Assignment, clear the Enable SIP Federation check box to disable the federation route through the legacy Lync Server environment, as shown in Figure 15.6.

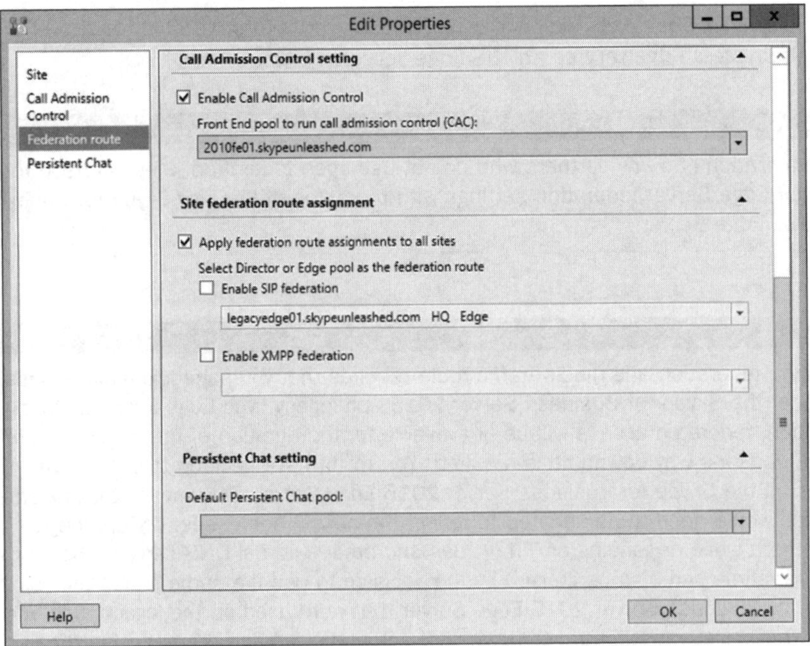

FIGURE 15.6 Federation disabled at the site level.

6. Click OK to close the Edit Properties page.
7. From Topology Builder, select the top node, Skype for Business Server.
8. From the Action menu, click Publish Topology.
9. Click Next to complete the publish process and then click Finish.

The next step is to configure the legacy Lync Edge Server as a nonfederating Edge Server. This is in preparation for the Skype for Business Server 2015 Edge Server to take over this function. Here are the steps to follow:

1. In the left pane, navigate to the legacy Lync Server 2010 or Lync Server 2013 node and then expand the Edge Pools node.
2. Right-click the Edge Server and then click Edit Properties.
3. Select General in the left pane.
4. Clear the Enable Federation for This Edge Pool (Port 5061) check box entry, as shown in Figure 15.7, and then click OK to close the page.

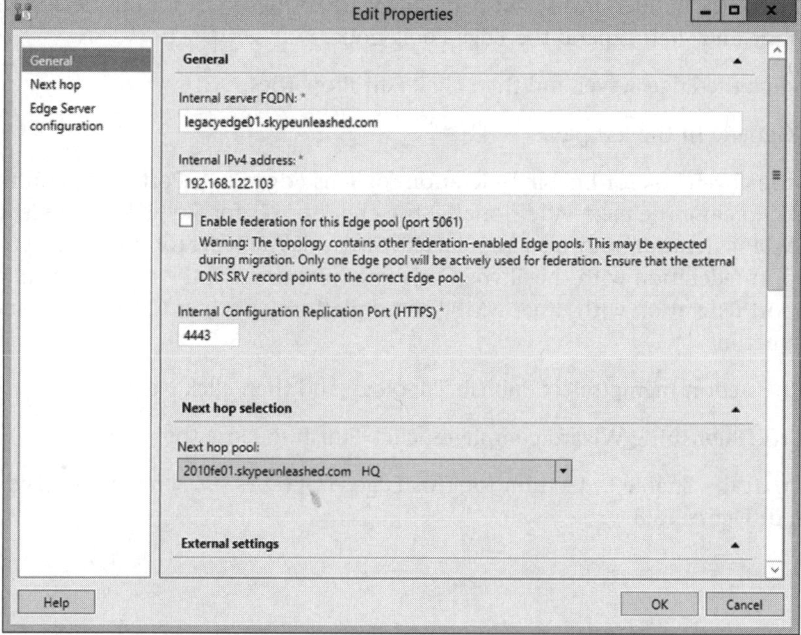

FIGURE 15.7 Federation disabled at the Edge pool level.

5. From the Action menu, select Publish Topology and then click Next.
6. When the Publishing Wizard completes, click Finish to close the wizard.
7. Verify that federation for the legacy Edge Server is disabled in the legacy Edge Server properties.

You now need to enable federation on the Skype for Business Server 2015 Edge Server and then change the federation route to use the Skype for Business Server 2015 Edge Server.

15

NOTE

At this point it is important to remind you of the certificate requirements of the Skype for Business Server 2015 Edge. It is assumed that the Skype for Business Server 2015 Edge Server has all the correct IP addresses assigned and external SSL certificates assigned to the Access Edge service, Web Conferencing Edge service, and A/V Edge External service (also referred to as the A/V Authentication service). It is also important in an Edge pool configuration where there are multiple Lync Server Edge Servers that the same SSL certificate with private key be assigned to the A/V Edge service (A/V Authentication service) of each Edge Server in the pool.

Here are the steps to complete:

1. From Topology Builder, in the left pane, navigate to the Skype for Business Server 2015 node and then expand the Edge Pools node.
2. Right-click the Edge Server and then click Edit Properties.
3. Select General in the left pane.
4. Select the check box for Enable Federation for This Edge Pool (Port 5061) and then click OK to close the page. Additionally, the check boxes for Skype-Skype federation and XMPP federation may also be selected. Skype-Skype federation must be enabled to support federation with the Skype Consumer platform. XMPP must be enabled to support federation with other XMPP-based platforms such as Cisco Jabber and IBM Sametime.
5. From the Action menu, select Publish Topology and then click Next.
6. When the Publishing Wizard completes, click Finish to close the wizard.
7. Verify that the Enable Federation for This Edge Pool (Port 5061) box is checked, as shown in Figure 15.8.

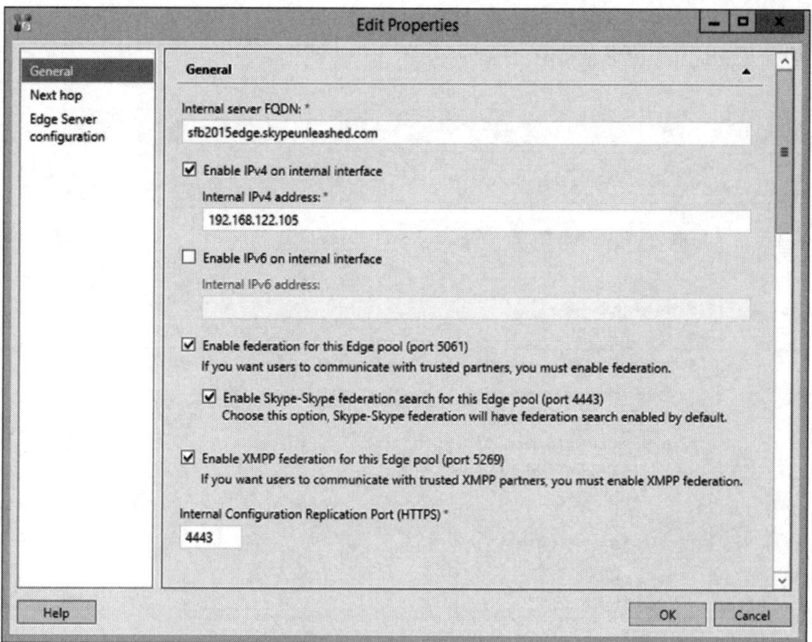

FIGURE 15.8 Federation enabled at the pool level.

Next you need to configure the Skype for Business Server 2015 Edge Server next hop to point to the Skype for Business Server 2015 pool:

1. From Topology Builder, in the left pane, navigate to the Skype for Business Server 2015 node and then to the Edge Pools node.
2. Expand the node, right-click the Edge Server listed, and then click Edit Properties.

15

3. On the General page, under Next Hop Selection, select the Skype for Business Server 2015 pool from the drop-down list, as shown in Figure 15.9.

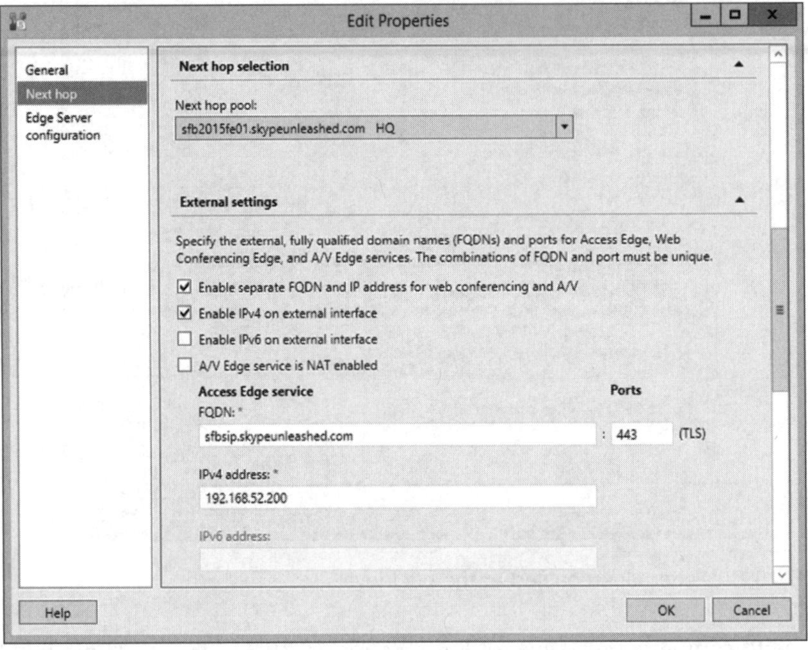

FIGURE 15.9 Edge pool next hop updated.

4. Click OK to close the Edit Properties page.
5. From Topology Builder, select the top-node Skype for Business Server.
6. Right-click and then click Publish Topology and complete the wizard.

Next you need to configure the Skype for Business Server 2015 pool to use the Skype for Business Server 2015 Edge Server as the outbound media path:

1. From Topology Builder, in the left pane, navigate to the Skype for Business Server 2015 node and then to the pool below Standard Edition Front End Servers or Enterprise Edition Front End pools.
2. Right-click the appropriate Front End pool and then click Edit Properties.
3. In the Associations section, select the Associate Edge Pool (for Media Components) check box.

4. From the drop-down box, select the Skype for Business Server 2015 Edge Server, as shown in Figure 15.10.

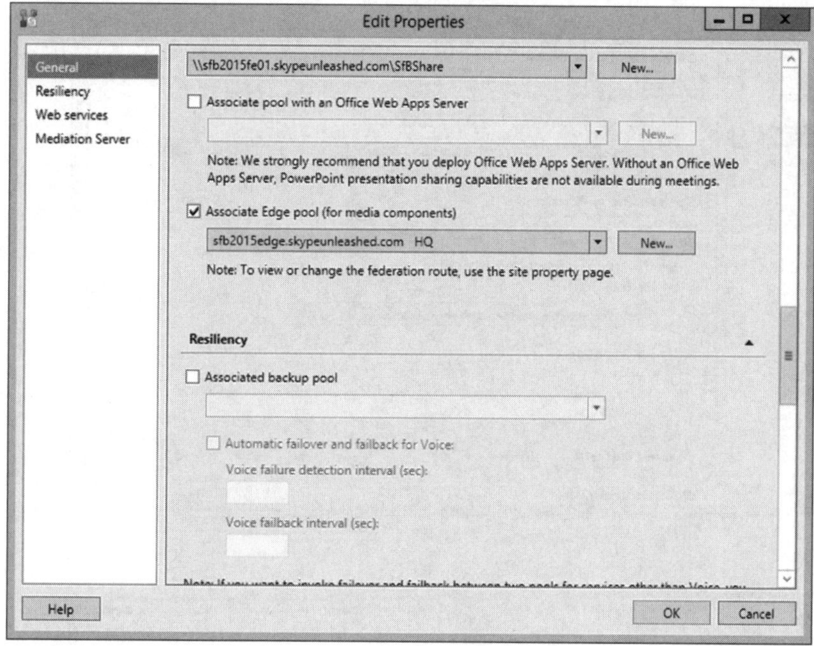

FIGURE 15.10 Skype for Business Server 2015 Edge Server associated for media.

5. Click OK to close the Edit Properties page.

To enable the Skype for Business Server 2015 Edge Server for federation, follow these steps:

1. From Topology Builder, in the left pane, navigate to the Skype for Business Server 2015 node and then to the Edge Pools node.
2. Expand the node, right-click the Edge Server listed, and then click Edit Properties.
3. On the General page, verify that the Enable Federation for This Edge Pool (Port 5061) setting is checked.
4. Click OK to close the Edit Properties page.
5. Navigate to the site node.
6. Right-click the site and then click Edit Properties.
7. In the left pane, click Federation Route.

15

8. Under Site Federation Route Assignment, select Enable SIP Federation. Then from the list, select the Skype for Business Server 2015 Edge Server, as shown in Figure 15.11.

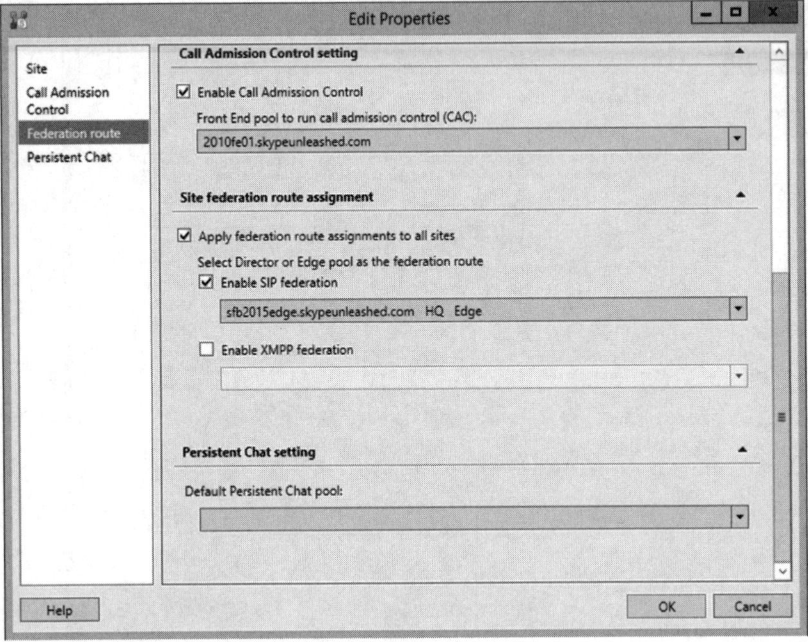

FIGURE 15.11 Skype for Business Server 2015 Edge pool enabled for federation route.

9. Click OK to close the Edit Properties page.

Next you need to configure the legacy Lync Server Front End pool to use the Skype for Business Server 2015 Edge Server for outbound media. This is required so that the users who are homed on the legacy Lync Server Front End pool will be able to use the Skype for Business Server 2015 Edge Server for external Edge features. If all users and services have been moved to Skype for Business Server 2015, this step is not required.

1. From Topology Builder, in the left pane, navigate to the legacy Lync Server 2010 or Lync Server 2013 node and then to the pool below Standard Edition Front End Servers or Enterprise Edition Front End pools.
2. Right-click the pool and then click Edit Properties.
3. In the Associations section, select the Associate Edge Pool (for Media Components) check box.

4. From the drop-down box, select the Skype for Business Server 2015 Edge Server, as shown in Figure 15.12.

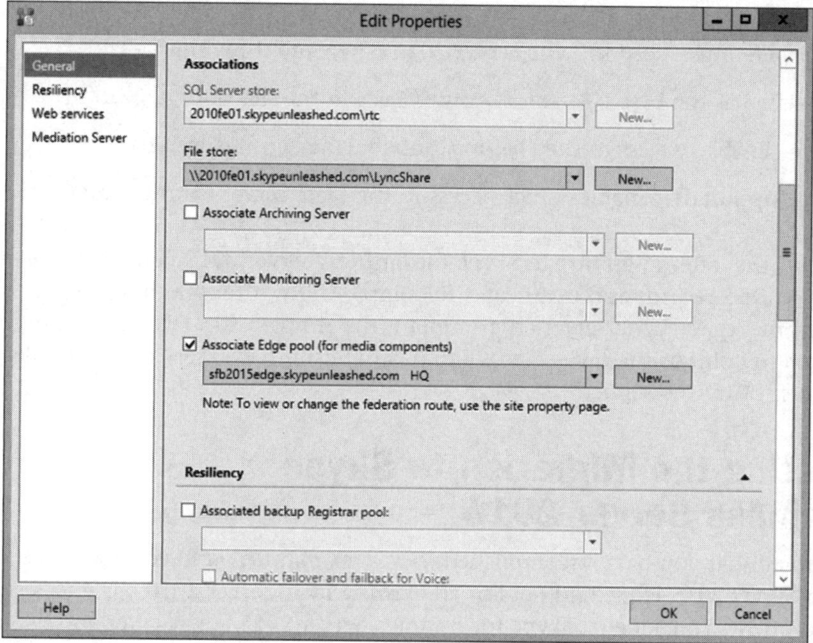

FIGURE 15.12 Skype for Business Server 2015 Edge pool associated for media.

5. Click OK to close the Edit Properties page.

The last step is to publish the Edge Server configuration changes:

1. From Topology Builder, select the top node, Skype for Business Server.
2. Right-click and then select Publish Topology and complete the wizard.
3. Wait for topology replication to occur in all pools in the deployment.

NOTE

You might see the following message:

"Warning: The topology contains more than one Federated Edge Server. This can occur during migration to a more recent version of the product. In that case, only one Edge Server would be actively used for federation. Verify that the external DNS SRV record points to the correct Edge Server. If you want to deploy multiple federation Edge Servers to be active concurrently (that is, not a migration scenario), verify that all federated partners are using Lync Server. Verify that the external DNS SRV record lists all federation-enabled Edge Servers."

This warning is expected and can be safely ignored. This is because there is more than one Edge Server pool defined in the topology enabled for federation, and only one pool can be used for the federation route.

Simple URLs were introduced in Lync Server 2010. There are three simple URLs:

- **Meet**—Used as the base URL for all conferences in the site or organization
- **Dial-in**—Enables access to the Dial-in Conferencing Settings web page
- **Admin (optional)**—Enables quick access to the Lync Server Control Panel

It is important that after migrating to Skype for Business Server 2015 you are aware of the impacts to DNS records and certificates for simple URLs. After you have migrated all services from the legacy Lync Server environment, the Simple URLs DNS records need to be updated to point to the reverse proxy that is publishing web services to the Skype for Business Server 2015 web service.

Completing the Migration to Skype for Business Server 2015

So let's recap all that you have accomplished up to this point. You have deployed a Skype for Business Server 2015 Front End pool in an existing Lync Server 2010 or Lync Server 2013 environment. You added a Skype for Business Server 2015 Edge Server and moved all Edge functionality to the new Skype for Business Server 2015 Edge Server. There are only a few items left to finish before the migration process is complete.

At this point the remaining users on the legacy Lync Server Front End pool should be moved to the Skype for Business Server 2015 pool. This is completed in a way similar to the process discussed earlier when we moved a single user using the Skype for Business Control Panel and the Skype for Business Management Shell. The only difference is that instead of selecting a single user in the Skype for Business Control Panel, you would select multiple users by pressing Ctrl or Shift on the keyboard while selecting the users you would like to move to the Skype for Business Server 2015 pool.

CAUTION

When issuing commands related to the migration of data from a legacy Lync Server version to Skype for Business Server 2015, be sure to use the Skype for Business Server management tools to do so. Migrating data to Skype for Business Server 2015 using Lync Server 2010 or 2013 Management Shell and Control Panel can result in data loss.

If you are completing this process in the Skype for Business Management Shell, you would follow these steps:

1. Open the Skype for Business Management Shell.
2. At the command line, type the following:

```
Get-CsUser -OnLyncServer | Move-CsUser -Target "sfb2015fe01.skypeunleashed.com"
```

CAUTION

This command will move *all* users to the new Skype for Business pool. If you have deployed multiple Skype for Business pools, you may want to scope the `Get-CsUser` command to a specific pool using the `-Filter` parameter. Here's an example:

```
Get-CsUser -Filter {RegistrarPool -eq "2010fe01.skypeunleashed.com"}
```

3. To verify that the move was successful, use the following command. It should not return any users.

   ```
   Get-CsUser -Filter {RegistrarPool -eq "2010fe01.skypeunleashed.com"}
   ```

4. The `RegistrarPool` identity now points to the Skype for Business Server 2015 pool.

CAUTION

In addition to migrating users, several other items need to be migrated, as detailed in the subsections that follow.

Dial-in Access Numbers

Dial-in access numbers need to be migrated from the legacy Lync Server to Skype for Business Server 2015 before the legacy pool is decommissioned.

NOTE

Dial-in access numbers that you created in Lync Server 2010 or Lync Server 2013 but moved to Skype for Business Server 2015, or that you created in Skype for Business Server 2015 before, during, or after migration have the following characteristics:

- They appear on Lync Server 2010 or Lync server 2013 meeting invitations and the dial-in access number page.
- They appear on Skype for Business Server 2015 meeting invitations and the dial-in access number page.
- They can be viewed and modified in the Lync Server 2010/2013 Control Panel and in Lync Server 2010/2013 Management Shell.
- They can be viewed and modified in the Skype for Business Server 2015 Control Panel and in Skype for Business Server 2015 Management Shell.
- They can be resequenced within the region by using the `Set-CsDialinConferencingAccessNumber` cmdlet with the `Priority` parameter.

To identify and move dial-in access numbers, complete the following steps:

1. Start the Skype for Business Server Management Shell: Click Start, All Programs, Skype for Business Server 2015, and then select Skype for Business Server Management Shell. To identify the existing dial-in access numbers, run the following command:

   ```
   Get-CsDialInConferencingAccessNumber
   ```

2. To move each dial-in access number to a Skype for Business Server 2015 pool, from the command line run this:

```
Move-CsApplicationEndpoint -Identity "+14255551212@skypeunleashed.com" -Target
➥"sfb2015fe01.skypeunleashed.com"
```

3. Open Skype for Business Server Control Panel.
4. In the left navigation bar, click Conferencing.
5. Select the Dial-in Access Number tab.
6. Verify that no dial-in access numbers remain for the legacy Lync Server pool from which you are migrating.

Call Park Application Settings

The Call Park configuration includes the Call Park orbit range, the pickup timeout threshold, the maximum call pickup attempts, the timeout request, and music-on-hold files. It is important to note that the process of configuring the Call Park application does not move the configuration or music-on-hold files that the service might be using. Those files are stored on the legacy Lync Server Front End pool file store. A file copy utility such as Xcopy would need to be used to copy the files from the legacy Lync Server Front End pool file store to the Skype for Business Server 2015 file store. An example of an `Xcopy` command is shown here:

```
Xcopy "<Lync Server 2010 Filestore Path>\LyncFileStore\X-ApplicationServer-
➥X\AppServerFiles\CPS\"    "<Skype for Business Server 2015
➥Filestore Path>\SfBFileStore\X-ApplicationServer-X\AppServerFiles\CPS\"
```

To reconfigure the Call Park service settings, you need to follow the procedure listed here:

NOTE

You are just configuring the Call Park service for the Skype for Business Server 2015 pool at this point. All the values being entered would be obtained by referencing the legacy Lync Server Call Park configuration.

1. From the Skype for Business Server 2015 Front End Server, open the Skype for Business Server Management Shell.
2. At the command line, type the following:

```
Set-CsCpsConfiguration -Identity "<SfB2015 Call Park Service ID>"
➥-CallPickupTimeoutThreshold
"<LS2010 CPS TimeSpan>" -EnableMusicOnHold "<LS2010 CPS value>"
➥-MaxCallPickupAttempts "<LS2010
CPS pickup attempts>" -OnTimeoutURI "<LS2010 CPS timeout URI>"
```

The next step would be to reassign all Call Park orbit ranges from the legacy Lync Server pool to the Skype for Business Server 2015 pool. This can be completed in either the Skype for Business Server Control Panel or the Skype for Business Server Management Shell. Let's go through the Skype for Business Server 2015 Control Panel first:

1. Open Skype for Business Server Control Panel.
2. In the left pane, select Voice Features.
3. Select the Call Park tab.
4. For each Call Park orbit range assigned to a legacy Lync Server pool, edit the FQDN of the destination server setting and select the Skype for Business Server 2015 pool that will process the Call Park requests.
5. Click Commit to save the changes.

To reassign all Call Park orbit ranges using the Lync Server Management Shell, follow this process:

1. Open the Skype for Business Server Management Shell.
2. At the command line, type the following:

```
Get-CsCallParkOrbit
```


This cmdlet lists all the Call Park orbit ranges in the deployment. All Call Park orbits that have the `CallParkServiceId` and `CallParkServerFqdn` parameters set as the legacy Lync Server pool must be reassigned.

To reassign the legacy Lync Server Call Park orbit ranges to the Skype for Business Server 2015 pool, at the command line type the following:

```
Set-CsCallParkOrbit -Identity "<Call Park Orbit Identity>" -CallParkService
➥"service:ApplicationServer:<Skype for Business Server 2015 Pool FQDN>"
```

Response Groups

The Response Group move process is an all-or-nothing procedure. You can move either all the legacy Lync Server Response Group configuration or none at all. It is also a 1:1 move process between pools. You cannot move individual Response Groups from one pool between different pools. To move the Response Group applications, complete the following steps:

1. Log on to the computer with an account that is a member of the `RTCUniversalServerAdmins` group or has equivalent administrator rights and permissions.
2. Start the Skype for Business Server Management Shell: Click Start, All Programs, Skype for Business Server 2015, and then select Skype for Business Server Management Shell.

3. Run the following:

```
Move-CsRgsConfiguration -Source 2010fe01.skypeunleashed.com -Destination
➥sfb2015fe01.skypeunleashed.com
```

4. After you migrate Response Groups and agents to the Skype for Business Server 2015 pool, the URL that agents use to sign in and sign out is a Skype for Business Server 2015 web service URL and is available from the Tools menu in the Skype for Business client. Remind agents to update any references, such as bookmarks, to the new URL.

Address Book

The Address Book can be an important item that most of the time is left to be forgotten on the legacy Lync Server pool. This file is important if there are any customized rules for the organization, such as normalizing Active Directory telephone numbers or normalizing telephone numbers in RCC environments. It is important to replicate this configuration in the Skype for Business Server 2015 environment. Here are the steps to take:

1. Find the `Company_Phone_Number_Normalization_Rules.txt` file in the root of the Address Book shared folder and copy it to a server running the Skype for Business Server 2015 management tools.

NOTE

In the past, we needed to place the `Company_Phone_Number_Normalization_Rules.txt` file into the Address Book shared folder's root directory. Having to manage a text file on every Lync file share was a bit cumbersome. Thankfully, in Skype for Business Server 2015, the `Company_Phone_Number_Normalization_Rules.txt` file has been replaced with several `*-CsAddressBookNormalizationRule` commands that store the related Address Book normalization rules in the Central Management Store. A default set of rules is created, which can be reviewed by issuing the `Get-CsAddressBookNormalizationRule` command. Existing rules that reside in the text file can be imported using the `Import-CsCompanyAddressBookNormalizationRule` command, as you will see in the following steps.

2. Launch the Skype for Business Server Management Shell: Click Start, All Programs, Skype for Business Server 2015, and then select Skype for Business Server Management Shell.

3. Run the following:

```
Import-CsCompanyAddressBookNormalizationRule -Filename "C:\Data\
➥Company_Phone_Number_Normalization_Rules.txt" -Identity Global
```

4. To verify that all of the Address Book normalization rules have been imported into the Skype for Business Server 2015 pool, from the Skype for Business Server Management Shell type the following:

```
Get-CsAddressBookNormalizationRule -Identity "Global"
```

Common Area Phones

Common area phones have a contact object that is associated with the pool where they were originally created. In a migration scenario, it is important to move all common area phone contact objects to the Skype for Business Server 2015 pool. Here is the process:

1. From the Skype for Business Server 2015 Front End Server, open Skype for Business Server Management Shell.
2. From the command line, type the following:

```
Get-CsCommonAreaPhone -Filter {RegistrarPool
➥-eq "2010fe01.skypeunleashed.com"} |
Move-CsCommonAreaPhone -Target sfb2015fe01.skypeunleashed.com
```

3. To verify that all contact objects have been moved to the Skype for Business Server 2015 pool, from the Skype for Business Server Management Shell type the following:

```
Get-CsCommonAreaPhone -Filter {RegistrarPool
➥-eq "sfb2015fe01.skypeunleashed.com"}
```


Analog Devices

Analog devices are similar to common area phones in the sense that they are also contact objects associated with the legacy Lync Server pool. These objects need to be moved. The process is pretty much the same as moving common area phones, but using a slightly different command. Here are the steps to follow:

1. Start the Skype for Business Server Management Shell: Click Start, All Programs, Skype for Business Server 2015, and then select Skype for Business Server Management Shell.
2. At the command line, type this:

```
Get-CsAnalogDevice -Filter {RegistrarPool -eq "2010fe01.skypeunleashed.com"} |
➥Move-CsAnalogDevice -Target sfb2015fe01.skypeunleashed.com
```

3. Verify that all contact objects have been moved to the Skype for Business Server 2015 pool. At the command line, type this:

```
Get-CsAnalogDevice -Filter {RegistrarPool
➥-eq "sfb2015fe01.skypeunleashed.com"}
```

Voice Routing

Voice routes and how they are impacted during a migration to Skype for Business Server 2015 is an important item to cover. When you are in a period of coexistence with a legacy Lync Server pool that includes Lync Server Mediation Servers, you probably have gateways and/or SBCs associated with the Lync Server Mediation Server or Mediation Server pool. Voice routing interoperability between Lync Server 2010 or Lync Server 2013 and

Skype for Business Server 2015 is fully supported, meaning that you can have users homed on a legacy Lync Server pool and use a Lync Server or a Skype for Business Server 2015 Mediation Server/pool, or have users homed on Skype for Business Server 2015 and use a Lync Server 2013 or Lync Server 2010 Mediation Server/pool. The point here is that before decommissioning the legacy Lync Server environment, you will need to configure Skype for Business Server 2015 Mediation Servers or pools with the gateways and/or SBCs and also configure the Voice over IP gateways and/or SBCs to direct inbound traffic to the Skype for Business Server 2015 Mediation Servers.

Another important note here is that a Lync Server 2013 SBA (survivable branch appliance) is supported in a Skype for Business Server 2015 pool.

Internal DNS for Client Auto-Configuration

Before you decommission the legacy Lync Server environment, a few configuration changes need to be made before you can call the migration task complete. This first is to update internal DNS SRV records for every SIP domain that is supported by your environment. The process that follows describes how to complete this task. Complete this task from a server that has the DNS administrative tools installed:

1. On the DNS server, click Start, Administrative Tools, DNS.
2. In the console tree for your SIP domain, expand Forward Lookup Zones, expand the SIP domain in which Skype for Business Server 2015 is installed, and navigate to the _tcp setting.
3. In the right pane, right-click _sipinternaltls and select Properties.
4. In Host Offering This Service, update the host FQDN to point to the Skype for Business Server 2015 pool (if the pool is a Standard Edition Server, enter the server FQDN). This is shown in Figure 15.13.

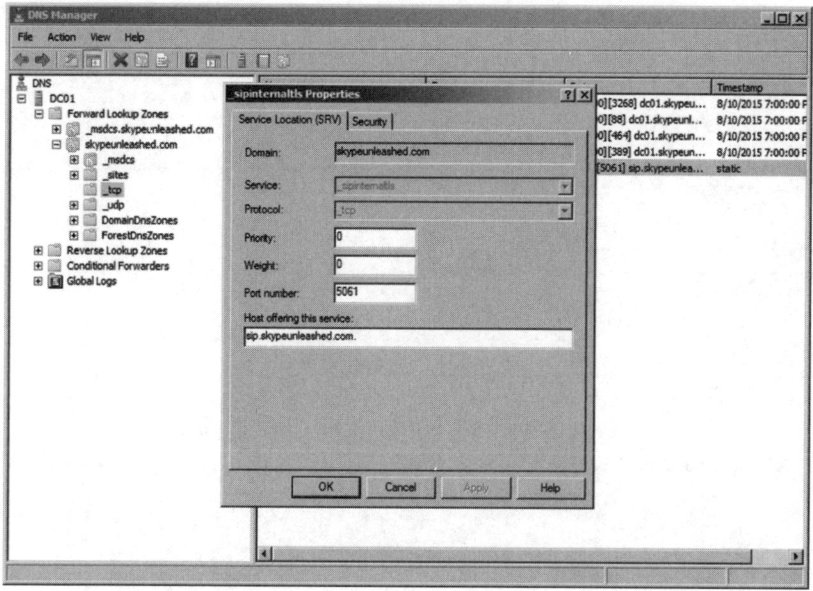

FIGURE 15.13 Update the SRV record for all SIP domains supported.

5. Click OK.
6. Navigate back to the root of the Forward Lookup Zone.
7. In the right pane, right-click the lyncdiscoverinternal record and select Properties.
8. In IP Address, update the address to point to the Skype for Business Server 2015 internal web services IP address (if the pool is a Standard Edition Server, enter the server IP address; if the pool is an Enterprise Edition pool, enter the internal web services load balancer IP address). This is shown in Figure 15.14.

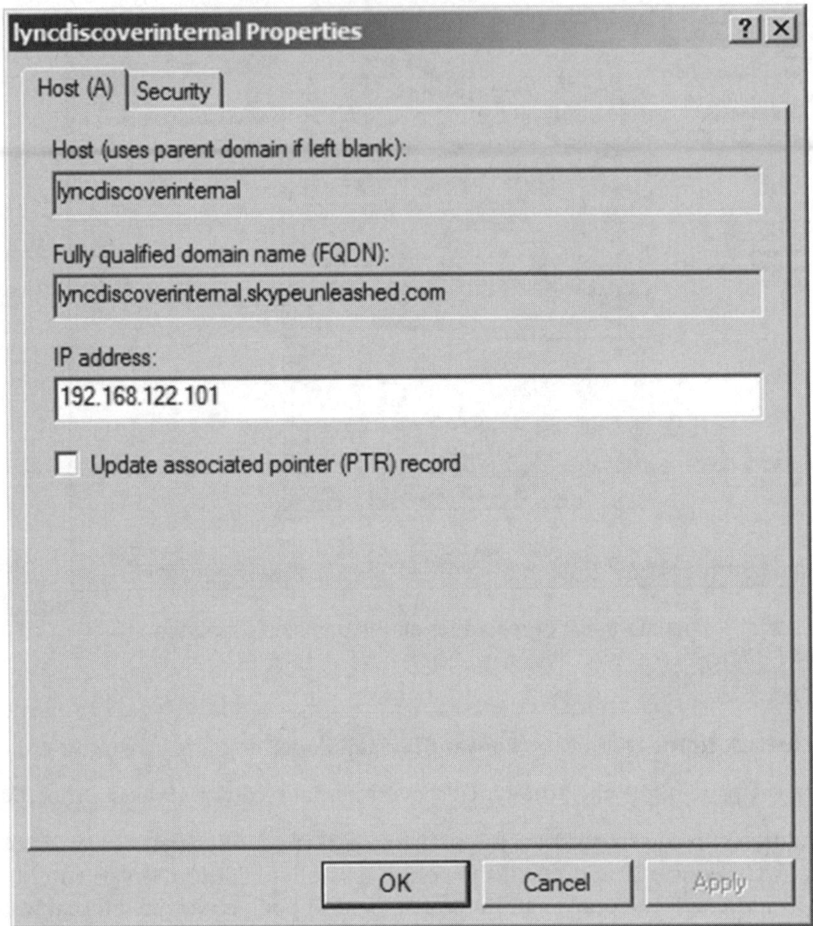

FIGURE 15.14 Update the lyncdiscoverinternal record for all SIP domains supported.

Central Management Store

Earlier you read about the Central Management Store. If you recall, the Central Management Store is still associated with the legacy Lync Server pool. You need to move the Central Management Store to the Skype for Business Server 2015 pool. This process is outlined next.

If you deployed Skype for Business Server 2015 Standard Edition, here are the steps for preparing the environment:

1. On the Skype for Business Server 2015 Standard Edition Front End Server where you want to relocate the Central Management Store, log on to the computer where the Skype for Business Server Management Shell is installed, as a member of the `RTCUniversalServerAdmins` group.

2. Open the Skype for Business Server Deployment Wizard.

3. In the wizard, click Prepare First Standard Edition Server.

4. On the Executing Commands page, SQL Server Express is installed as the Central Management Store. Necessary firewall rules are created. When the installation of the database and prerequisite software is completed, click Finish.

5. To create the Central Management Store, you need to complete this process from the Skype for Business Server Management Shell. Type the following:

```
Install-CsDatabase -CentralManagementDatabase
➥-SQLServerFQDN "sfb2015fe01.skypeunleashed.com"
➥-SQLInstanceName RTC
```

6. Confirm that the status of the Skype for Business Server Front End service is Started.

If you deployed Skype for Business Server 2015 in an enterprise pool configuration, here are the steps for preparing the environment:

1. On the Skype for Business Server 2015 Enterprise Edition Front End Server where you want to relocate the Central Management Store, log on to the computer where the Skype for Business Server Management Shell is installed, as a member of the `RTCUniversalServerAdmins` group.

2. Open the Skype for Business Management Shell.

3. To create the new Central Management store in the Skype for Business SQL Server database, in the Skype for Business Server Management Shell, type this:

```
Install-CsDatabase -CentralManagementDatabase -SQLServerFQDN
➥"SQL01.skypeunleashed.com" -SQLInstanceName LYNC
```

4. Confirm that the status of the Skype for Business Server Front End service is Started.

Now that you have prepared the environment and created a blank XDS and LIS database, you can move the Central Management Store to the Skype for Business Server 2015 pool. To do that, you have a few more commands to run:

1. On the Skype for Business Server 2015 server that will be the Central Management Server, log on to the computer where the Skype for Business Server Management Shell is installed, as a member of the `RTCUniversalServerAdmins` group. You must also have the SQL Server database administrator user rights and permissions.

2. Open Skype for Business Server Management Shell.

3. In the Skype for Business Server Management Shell, type this:

   ```
   Enable-CsTopology
   ```

4. On the Skype for Business Server 2015 Front End Server or from one of the Front End pool servers in an Enterprise pool, in the Lync Server Management Shell, type this:

   ```
   Move-CsManagementServer
   ```

5. Skype for Business Server Management Shell displays the servers, file stores, database stores, and service connection points of the current state and the proposed state. Read the information carefully and confirm that this is the intended source and destination. Type **Y** to continue or **N** to stop the move.

6. Review any warnings or errors generated by the `Move-CsManagementServer` command and resolve them.

7. On the Skype for Business Server 2015 server, open the Skype for Business Server Deployment Wizard.

8. In the wizard, click Install or Update Skype for Business Server System. Click Step 2: Setup or Remove Skype for Business Server Components. Then click Next, review the summary, and click Finish.

9. On the legacy Lync Server that previously hosted the Central Management Store, open the Lync Server Deployment Wizard.

10. In the wizard, click Install or Update Lync Server System. Click Step 2: Setup or Remove Lync Server Components. Then click Next, review the summary, and click Finish.

11. To confirm the new location of the Central Management Store, run the following command:

    ```
    Get-CsManagementConnection
    ```

12. Additionally, verify that replication with the new Central Management Store is occurring. In the Skype for Business Server Management Shell, type this:

    ```
    Get-CsManagementStoreReplicationStatus
    ```

NOTE

The replication may take some time to update all replicas.

Conference Directories

The conference directories store important information about conferences scheduled by users. Migration of these to the new environment is a critical step in this process. You will not be able to remove the legacy pool if conference directories are still associated with it. Additionally, if you simply remove the conference directories rather than migrate them to the Skype for Business Server 2015 pool, users will need to open their previously scheduled Lync/Skype for Business meetings and update them. Needless to say, this is a situation that should be avoided. The process for moving the conference directories is as follows:

1. Start the Skype for Business Server Management Shell: Click Start, All Programs, Skype for Business Server 2015, and then select Skype for Business Server Management Shell.
2. At the command line, type the following to migrate all of the conference directories on the legacy Lync Server pool to the Skype for Business Server 2015 pool:

```
Get-CsConferenceDirectory | Where-Object {$_.ServiceID
➥-match "2010fe01.skypeunleashed.com"} | Move-CsConferenceDirectory
➥-TargetPool "sfb2015fe01.skypeunleashed.com"
```

3. Verify that all conference directories have been moved to the Skype for Business Server 2015 pool. At the command line, type this:

```
Get-CsConferenceDirectory
```


Miscellaneous

If you had Lync Server 2010/2013 Archiving or Monitoring roles installed and associated with the Lync Server 2010/2013 pool, those associations will need to be removed before the decommissioning of the Lync Server 2010/2013 environment. Details on that process are not given here.

Okay, you are in the home stretch. Migration from Lync Server 2010/2013 to Skype for Business Server 2015 involves quite a few components, as you might have been able to tell. You have a few more items left, and then you can go grab a cup of coffee (or a well-deserved cocktail)!

Call Admission Control (CAC) has a component called PDP (Policy Decision Point). This component is responsible for making CAC decisions and adhering to the policies defined. That service is hosted on a single pool in each site. You need to move this configuration to the Skype for Business Server 2015 environment. The following is the process:

1. Open Topology Builder.
2. Right-click the site node and then click Edit Properties.
3. Under Call Admission Control setting, make sure that Enable Call Admission Control is selected.

4. Under Front End Pool to Run Call Admission Control (CAC), select the Skype for Business Server 2015 pool that is to host CAC, as shown in Figure 15.15. Click OK.

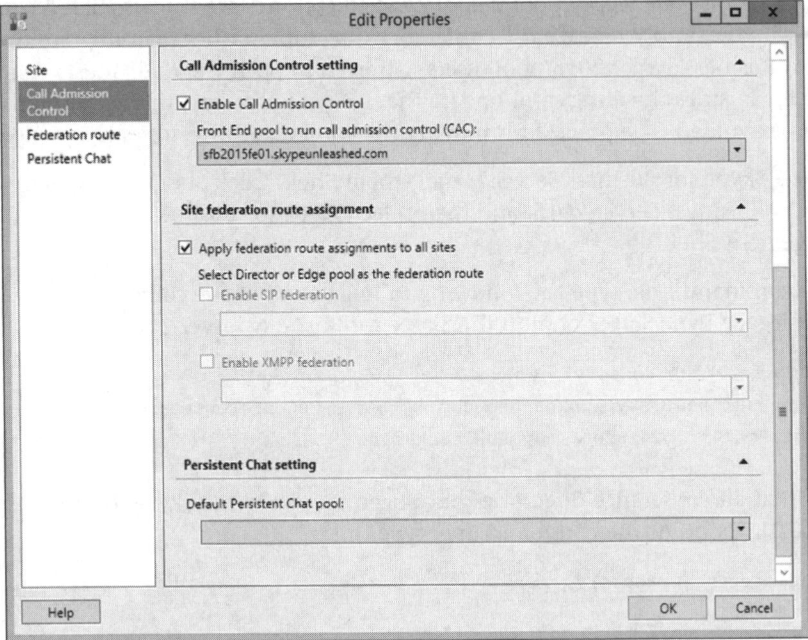

FIGURE 15.15 Update the PDP and Call Admission Control configuration.

5. Publish the topology.

After the topology has been published, it is important to update the legacy Lync Server and Skype for Business Server 2015 pools so that the CAC services are removed and added correctly. To do that, complete the following steps on each pool:

1. In the Skype for Business Server Deployment Wizard, click Install or Update Skype for Business Server System. Click Step 2: Setup or Remove Skype for Business Server Components. Then click Next, review the summary, and click Finish.

2. On the legacy Lync Server, open the Lync Server Deployment Wizard.

3. In the wizard, click Install or Update Lync Server System. Click Step 2: Setup or Remove Lync Server Components. Then click Next, review the summary, and click Finish.

Now that all dependent services have been moved to the Skype for Business Server 2015 environment, it is time to remove the legacy Lync Server configuration.

The first thing you need to do is stop services and prevent new sessions to the legacy Lync Server pool:

1. From each server in the pool, run the following command:

```
Stop-CsWindowsService
```

Lync Server Enterprise Edition does not exist as a standalone computer. At least from a Lync Server topology perspective, you always need to define a pool, and in that pool you define the Enterprise Edition Servers. The process that follows guides you through removing an individual Front End Server from an existing environment:

1. Open the Skype for Business Server 2015 Front End Server and then open Topology Builder.
2. Navigate to the legacy Lync Server node.
3. Expand Enterprise Edition Front End Pools, expand the Front End pool with the Front End Server that you want to remove, right-click the Front End Server that you want to remove, and then click Delete.

The final step is removing the actual Lync Server Standard Edition or Enterprise Edition pools from the topology.

To remove an Enterprise Edition Front End Server pool, follow this procedure:

1. Open Topology Builder.
2. Navigate to the legacy Lync Server node.
3. Expand Enterprise Edition Front End pools, expand the Front End pool, right-click the Front End pool that you want to remove, and then click Delete.
4. Publish the topology, check the replication status, and then run the Lync Server Deployment Wizard as needed.

To remove a Standard Edition Front End Server, follow this procedure:

1. Open Topology Builder.
2. Navigate to the legacy Lync Server node.
3. Expand Standard Edition Front End Servers, right-click the Front End Server that you want to remove, and then click Delete.
4. Expand SQL stores, right-click the SQL Server database that is associated with the Standard Edition Front End Server, and then click Delete.

NOTE

You must remove the collocated SQL Server databases from the Standard Edition Front End Server.

5. Publish the topology, check the replication status, and then run the Lync Server Deployment Wizard as needed.

So that's it—if you are reading this, you survived a Lync Server to Skype for Business Server 2015 side-by-side migration. If you followed the steps in this chapter, you should have great success with your migration efforts.

Migration Steps: In-place Upgrade Method

Finally! Microsoft has delivered a method of migrating to the latest release of its Unified Communications platform that does not require a complete new environment to be established. As previously mentioned, if you are currently running Lync Server 2013, you now have a supported path to perform an "in-place upgrade" to Skype for Business Server 2015. This is especially desirable for organizations that leverage or plan to leverage Skype for Business as a telephony platform. In most cases, a software upgrade can be achieved much more easily than a side-by-side migration that also requires additional hardware. Reduced time to implement, reduced administrative effort, and increased cost savings are all compelling reasons to use the "in-place upgrade" method.

There are other considerations and prerequisites required to ensure that the process goes off without a hitch. For instance, if your organization was an early adopter of Lync Server 2013, the underlying operating system may be Windows Server 2008 R2. Even though you may be able to upgrade the Lync Server application, there is no method to upgrade the operating system, which would require a side-by-side migration to do so. Additionally, if your organization only has a single Lync Server 2013 Front End pool, the only way to perform the "in-place upgrade" process is to take your Front End pool completely offline. For some environments, even a couple of hours may be too long of an outage to endure. Environments that are running Windows Server 2012 or greater, and where multiple pools exist (paired or unpaired), are prime candidates for this migration method. Having multiple pools allows the architect to migrate users to another pool while the upgrade is taking place, thus creating a "near-zero" downtime situation. Taking all of the aforementioned into consideration, the following sections will guide you through the in-place upgrade process.

In-place Upgrade Prerequisites

As you begin planning the upgrade process for your environment, there are several things to note before you dive right into installing Skype for Business Server 2015. In fact, the upgrade process requires many of the same initial work that is performed in the side-by-side migration process. The following items should be performed or verified before you initiate the upgrade process on any Lync Server 2013 role:

- Back up user and topology data that exists on the Lync Server 2013 pool to be upgraded.
- Verify that the latest Lync Server 2013 Cumulative Updates have been applied.
- Verify that the local installation of SQL Server Express 2012 is running the latest service pack on each Lync Server 2013 server. SQL Server Express 2012 SP1 is the minimum required.

- Verify that the latest Windows operating system updates have been applied.
- Verify there is at least 32GB of free space on the volume where Skype for Business Server 2015 will be installed.
- Uninstall the Lync Room System Admin Tool for Lync Server 2013.
- Verify that the Lync Server 2013 services are running on the pool to be upgraded.
- Verify the following updates specific to the operating system indicated have been applied:
  - **Windows 2008 R2**—Microsoft KB2533623, "Microsoft Security Advisory: Insecure library loading could allow remote code execution."
  - **Windows 2012**—Microsoft KB2858668, "PLA data collector sets stop after 72 hours on a Windows Server 2012-based computer."
  - **Windows 2012 R2**—Microsoft KB2982006, "IIS crashes occasionally when a request is sent to a default document in Windows 8.1 or Windows Server 2012 R2." (KB2919355 and KB2969339 must be installed prior to KB2982006 being installed.)

CAUTION

We should pause here for a moment and point out some important tips to observe during the upgrade process. Following these guidelines will ensure the upgrade process goes smoothly:

- If you use Kerberos authentication for Web Services, you will need to reassign the Kerberos accounts and reset the passwords after completing the in-place upgrade.
- Once the upgrade process has started for a pool, you must complete the upgrade process for all servers in the pool. Running a partially upgrade pool is unsupported.
- If paired Front End pools exist, do not "unpair" them prior to beginning the upgrade process.
- If upgrading a paired set of Front End pools, you should plan to upgrade both pools within a short timeframe. Running paired pools in extended coexistence is not recommended. The reason for this is because it is unsupported to issue the `Invoke-CsPoolFailover` command when one pool is running Lync Server 2013 and the other is running Skype for Business Server 2015. Doing so may result in data loss.
- Only perform the in-place upgrade process if the environment consists of only Lync Server 2013. If Lync Server 2010 still exists in the topology, complete the upgrade to Lync 2013 or decommission the Lync Server 2010 servers prior to proceeding.

Installation of Skype for Business Server 2015 Administrative Tools

Because you will need the Skype for Business Server 2015 Topology Builder to initiate the upgrade process, the first step will be the install the Skype for Business Server Administrative Tools. It is important to note that the tools will need to be installed onto a PC or server that does not already have any other legacy Lync Server 2010 or 2013 Administrative Tools installed. This means you have to automatically exclude any existing Lync Server 2013 servers as an option. Outlined here are the prerequisites and steps to install Skype for Business Server 2015 Administrative Tools:

- 64-bit edition of one of the following:
    - Windows Server 2008 R2
    - Windows Server 2012
    - Windows Server 2012 R2
    - Windows 7
    - Windows 8/8.1
    - Window 10
- .NET Framework 4.5
- Microsoft Visual C++ 2013 Redistributable x64 12.0.21005. The Deployment Wizard will automatically install this package if it is not already installed.

After the prerequisites are installed, the actual installation of the Topology Builder tool can begin.

1. Run `setup.exe` from the Skype for Business Server 2015 installation media. It is located at `\setup\amd64\setup.exe`.
2. If the installer prompts you to install the Microsoft Visual C++ 2013 Redistributable, click Yes and follow the Installation Wizard.
3. Click Install Administrative Tools from the right-column menu of the Deployment Wizard. This installs all the tools, including Topology Builder.
4. After installation is complete, there should be a green check mark next to the Install Administrative Tools link, grayed out, as shown in Figure 15.16.

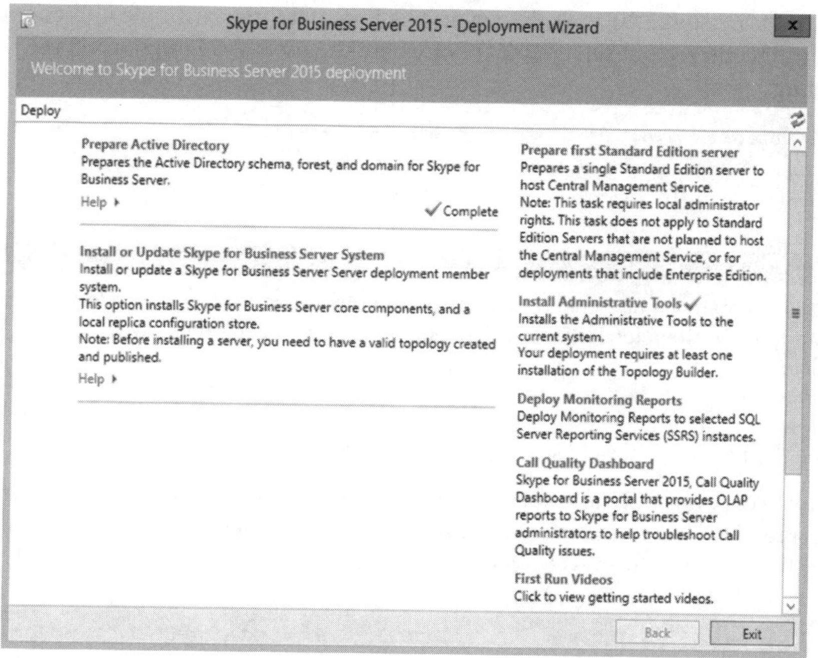

FIGURE 15.16 Completed Topology Builder installation.

As indicated at the start of this section, there are two proven methods for how to handle the in-place upgrade process. The first is the "Move User" method, where users and their related data will be moved to a different Front End pool while their primary pool is undergoing the upgrade process. This can only be achieved if your environment has multiple Front End pools. Second is the "Offline" method. In the Offline method, users and their data are kept on the primary and you simply take the services offline to upgrade the pool. Note that in the Offline method that users will be unable to use Lync or Skype for Business Server 2015 services for the duration of the upgrade.

Both of the upgrade methods follow the same core steps. Because the "Move User" method has some additional steps, both in advance and after the upgrade process, we will take a look at that first.

Move User In-place Upgrade Method

The "Move User" method enables the architect to perform the upgrade to Skype for Business Server 2015 without downtime. Using this method requires multiple Lync Server 2013 pools, but allows access to Lync and Skype for Business Services for the duration of the upgrade. The steps required to perform this upgrade are as follows:

1. From a server where the Lync Server 2013 Management Shell is installed, migrate from the Lync Server 2013 pool to be upgraded to another pool in the environment. To do so, type the following:

```
Move-CsUser -Identity "User1" -Target "2013fe02.skypeunleashed.com"
```

2. From the Lync Server 2013 Management Shell, migrate the existing conference directories to the same Lync Server 2013 pool where the users were migrated. Type the following:

```
Get-CsConferenceDirectory | Where-Object {$_.ServiceID
➥-match "2013fe01.skypeunleashed.com"} | Move-CsConferenceDirectory
➥-TargetPool "2013fe02.skypeunleashed.com"
```

NOTE

Migrating the conference directories to another pool during the in-place upgrade process will ensure that the Conference ID for scheduled conferences can be resolved and will be available.

3. Follow the in-place upgrade steps in the next section.
4. Upon successful completion of the pool upgrade process, run the same commands to migrate the users and conference directories back to their original, upgraded pool using the Skype for Business Server Management Shell.

CAUTION

When moving users or data from a legacy Lync Server pool to Skype for Business Server 2015, *always* use the Skype for Business Server Management Shell or Control Panel. Using legacy admin tools to move data from a legacy Lync Server pool to a Skype for Business Server 2015 pool can result in data loss.

Offline In-place Upgrade Method

Hopefully if you're reading this, you have already migrated the users and conference directories off of the pool using the steps outlined in the "Move User In-place Upgrade Method" section of this chapter, or have planned a maintenance window for your Lync Server 2013 pool. The following procedure will walk through the process of upgrading to Skype for Business Server 2015 and can be applied to all Lync Server 2013 server roles in your environment.

NOTE

Although we say this process can be applied to all server roles in the environment, an in-place upgrade of a Lync Server 2010 or 2013 survivable branch appliance (SBA) or survivable branch server (SBS) is not supported. Coexistence between a legacy SBA/SBS and Skype for Business Server 2015 Front End pool is supported. However, during the upgrade process, you will want to move the users homed to the SBA/SBS to another pool.

To begin the in-place upgrade process on the designated Lync Server 2013 pool, complete the following steps:

1. Connect to a PC or server where the Skype for Business Server 2015 Administrative Tools have been installed. Open Skype for Business Server Topology Builder.
2. Select Download Topology from Existing Deployment and click OK, as shown in figure 15.17

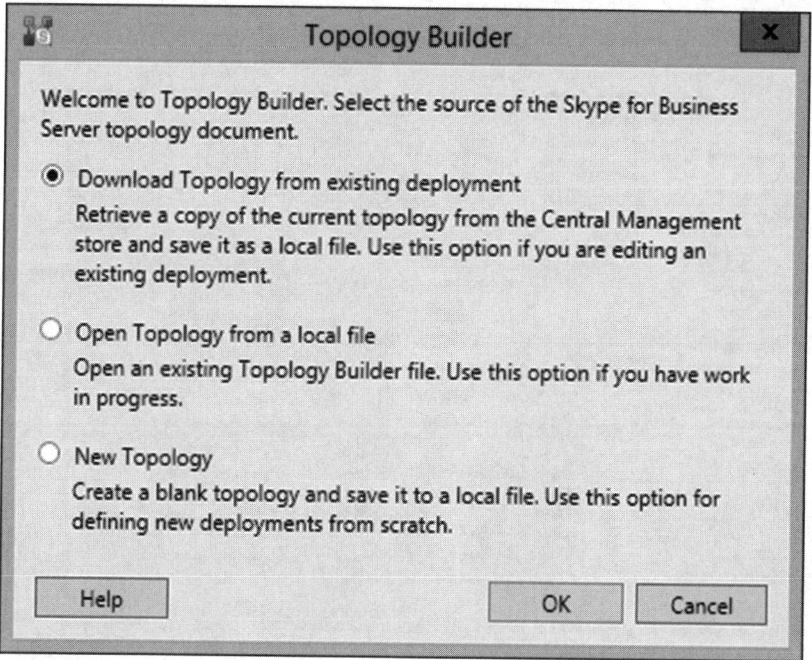

FIGURE 15.17 Download Topology from Existing Deployment.

3. In the left pane, expand the Lync Server 2013 node and navigate to the Lync Server 2013 pool that will be upgraded.

4. Right-click the Lync Server 2013 pool and select Upgrade to Skype for Business Server 2015, as shown in Figure 15.18. When you're upgrading a pool of servers, this action will be performed on the pool-level node. When you're upgrading a standalone server, this action will be performed on the server-level node.

NOTE

If you do not want your Archiving or Monitoring databases upgraded, remove the association with the Front End pool prior to completing step 4.

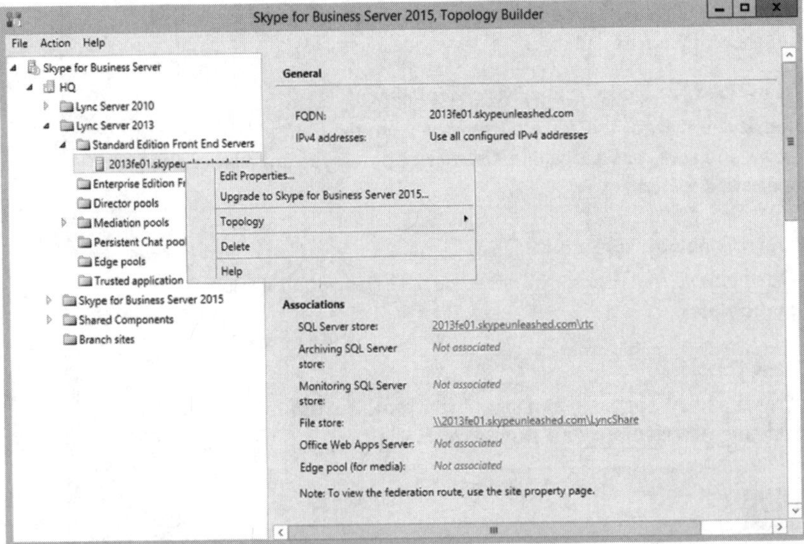

FIGURE 15.18 Upgrade the Lync Server 2013 pool to Skype for Business Server 2015 in Topology Builder.

5. You will receive an upgrade confirmation with the opportunity to cancel the upgrade, as shown in figure 15.19. Click Yes.

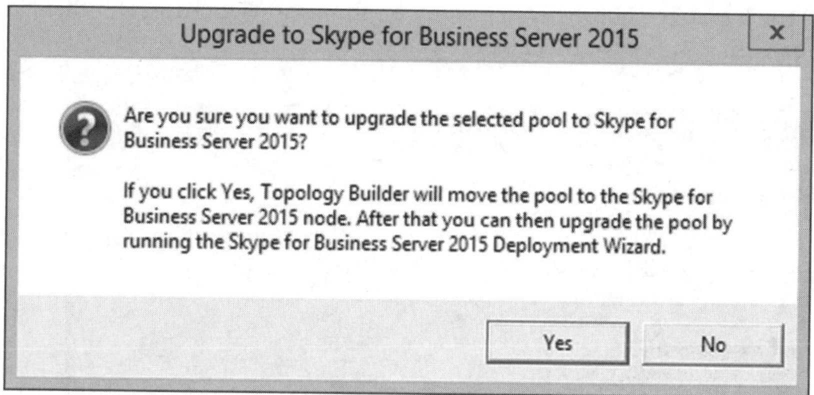

FIGURE 15.19 Upgrade to Skype for Business Server 2015 confirmation in Topology Builder.

6. Note that after you click Yes in the previous step, the server or pool will be moved to the appropriate place in the Skype for Business Server 2015 node in Topology Builder, as shown in Figure 15.20.

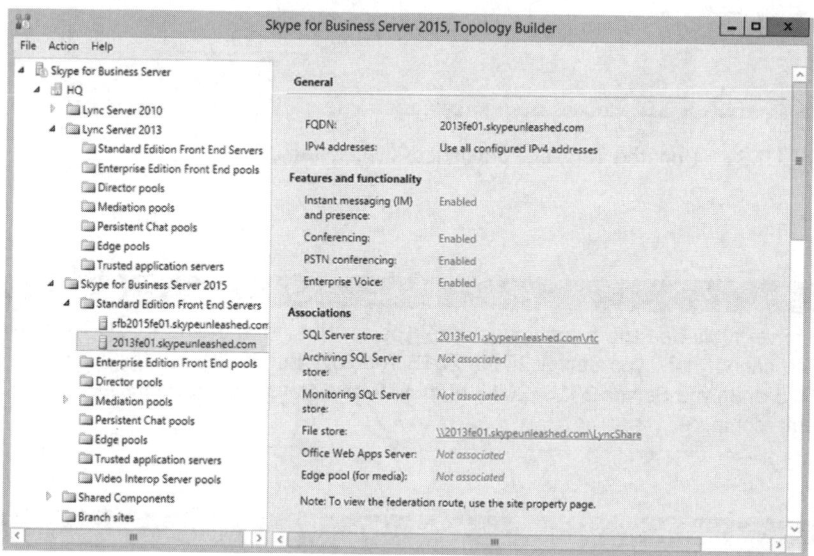

FIGURE 15.20 Target pool is moved to the corresponding Skype for Business Server 2015 node.

7. Right-click the top Skype for Business Server node and then select Publish Topology.
8. Click Next.
9. Ensure the topology publishes successfully, as shown in Figure 15.21. If there are any errors or warnings, resolve them before you continue.

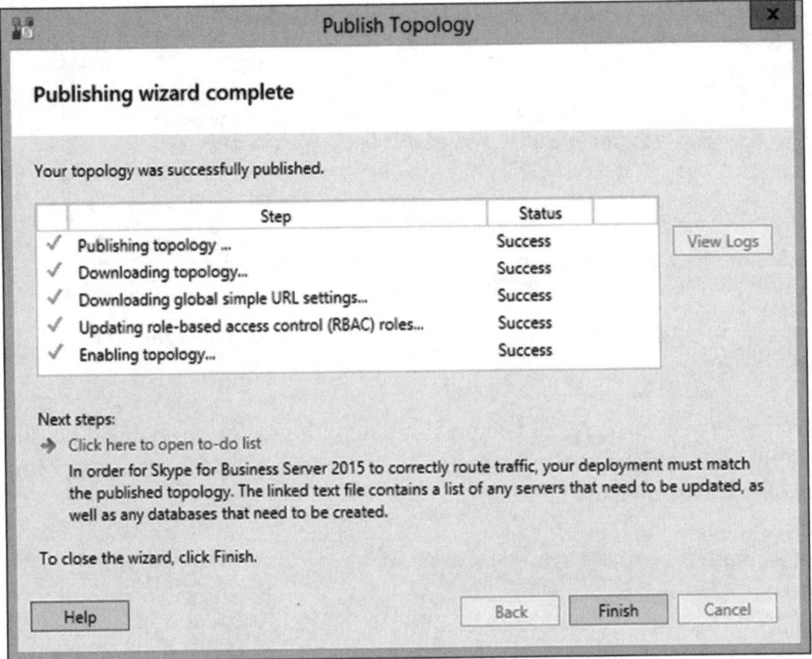

FIGURE 15.21 Updated Topology published successfully.

10. Click Finish.

NOTE

After you have published the topology using Skype for Business Server 2015 Topology Builder, you cannot use Lync Server 2010/2013 Topology Builder. Skype for Business Server 2015 and Lync Server 2010/2013 administrative tools cannot be installed together on the same computer.

CAUTION

Before continuing, make sure the services are running on the pool you will be upgrading. Be sure to verify the changes have replicated throughout the environment by running the `Get-CsManagementStoreReplicationStatus` command.

11. Connect to the Lync Server 2013 server that will be upgraded and then launch the Lync Server 2013 Management Shell with elevated privileges.

12. Stop and disable the Lync Server 2013 services using the following command:

```
Disable-CsComputer -Scorch
```

13. When prompted to confirm execution of the command, type **Y** and press Enter.

14. After the command completes successfully, close all open OS or Lync Server 2013 management tools. Be sure to check for other open or disconnected sessions.

15. With the Skype for Business Server 2015 media loaded, run `setup.exe`. It is located at `\setup\amd64\setup.exe`.

16. When prompted to check for updates, select Connect to the Internet to Check for Updates, as shown in Figure 15.22. If the server doesn't have Internet access, select Don't Check for Updates Right Now. Click Next.

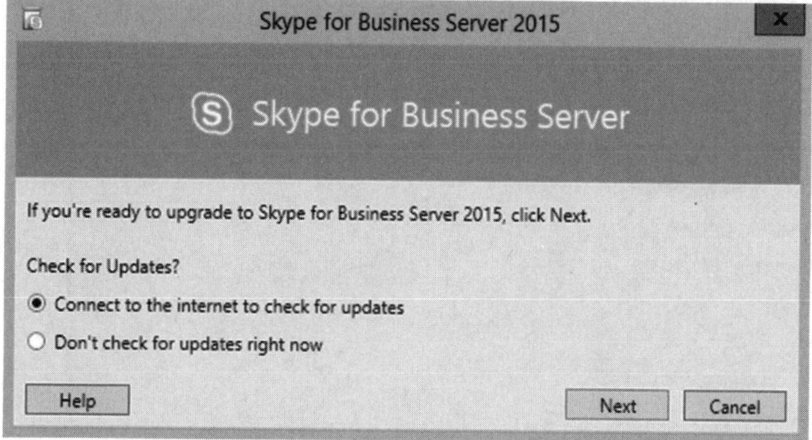

FIGURE 15.22 Skype for Business Server 2015 installer prompt to check for updates.

17. If prompted for the license agreement, click I Accept Terms in the License Agreement and then click OK.

18. After the installer checks for updates, click Next.

19. At this point, the upgrade installer will launch and begin the upgrade process, as shown in Figure 15.23. It will take some time to complete this process. If you're upgrading a multiserver pool, now would be a good time to start the upgrade process on the next server in the pool. If you're upgrading a single server pool, now would be a good time to go get some coffee.

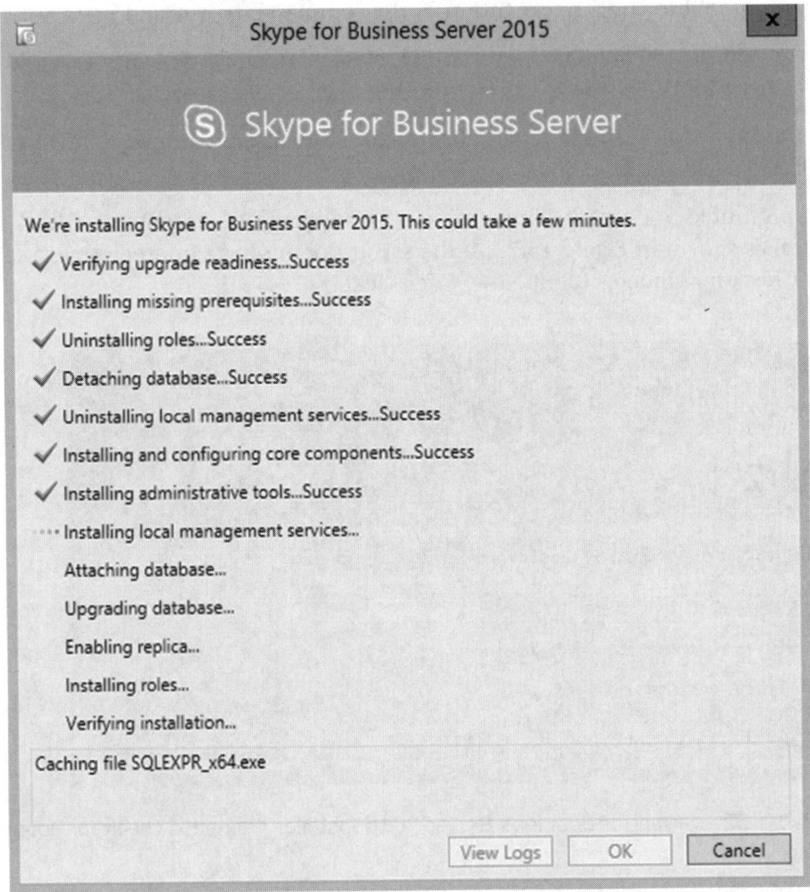

FIGURE 15.23 Skype for Business Server 2015 update installer running.

20. Once the installation completes, as shown in Figure 15.24, click OK.

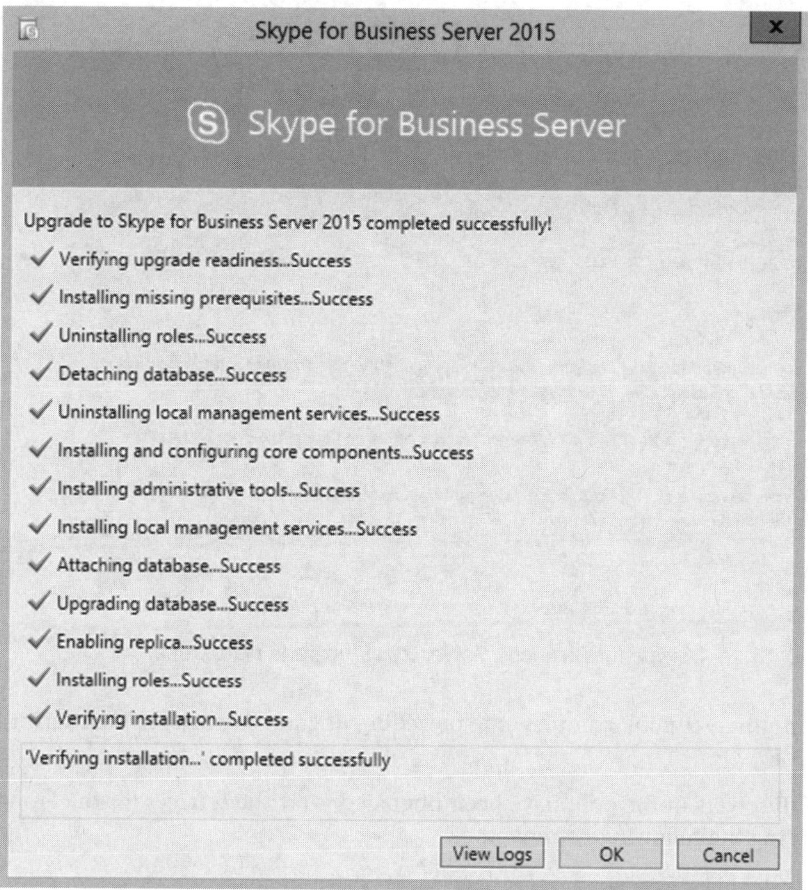

FIGURE 15.24 Skype for Business Server 2015 upgrade completed successfully.

21. A prompt that outlines the next steps will appear, as shown in Figure 15.25. Review these steps and then click OK.

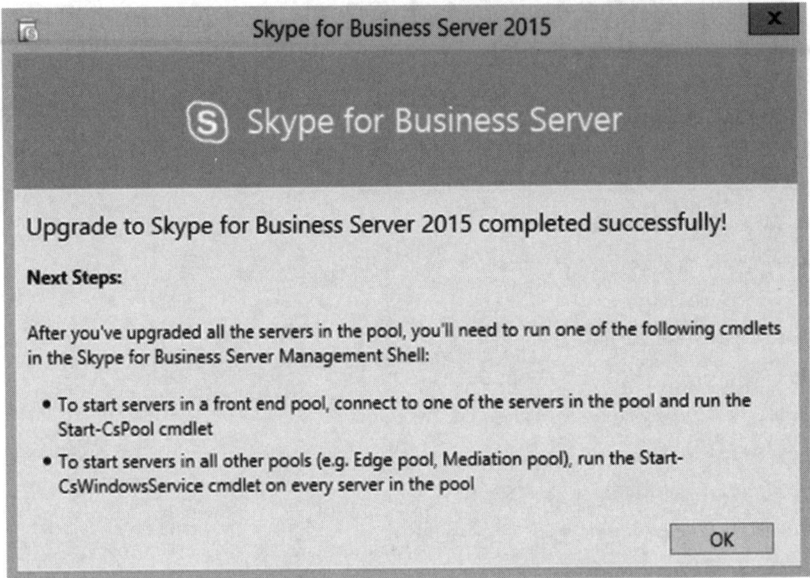

FIGURE 15.25 Skype for Business Server 2015 upgrade next steps.

22. For a multiserver pool, complete the preceding upgrade process for each server in the pool.
23. Once all servers in the pool have been upgraded, start the services for the Front End pool using the following command:

```
Start-CsPool -PoolFqdn "2013fe01.skypeunleahsed.com"
```

For non–Front End pools, you will need to connect to each server and issue the following command:

```
Start-CsWindowsService
```

24. If prompted for confirmation of pool startup, type **Y** then press Enter.
25. Verify the services have started successfully on all servers in the pool. If there are additional pools to upgrade, keep going. Otherwise, your upgrade is complete!

NOTE

The in-place upgrade process also upgrades the local databases (and Central Management Store, if applicable), so many of the additional migration tasks required in the side-by-side method are not required!

So by now you have successfully completed your first Skype for Business upgrade. There is no doubt that the new "in-place" upgrade process will streamline the migration path moving forward and beyond Skype for Business Server 2015. If you followed the processes outlined in this chapter, you should have continued success with your migration efforts.

Troubleshooting

As with any migration, there's a lot that can go wrong regardless of how well you've planned. The biggest item to check is ensuring that Active Directory is healthy and functioning properly. A close second is ensuring that all the required manual DNS changes have been made and that DNS is working flawlessly. Of course, there are the firewall ACLs that need to be in place for the new Skype for Business Server 2015 Edge Server as well. The added convenience of the Deployment Wizard doesn't lessen the importance of certificates. They are still core to all server and server-client communications.

If you run into an issue, be sure to check the various log files that are created. It's great news that nearly every action, whether done in the Skype for Business Control Panel or the Skype for Business Management Shell, creates a detailed log file in the Windows `%userprofile%\AppData\Local\Temp` directory. Administrators should review these files regularly to gain insight into their deployment and understand any errors that occur. The Lync Server event log is also a good place to check for errors. From the Start Menu, select Administrative Tools and then Event Viewer. Expand the Applications and Services Logs item and select Lync Server. All events related to Skype for Business Server 2015 functions reside here. Often the error description is enough to identify the problem and make a clear the resolution. Finally, Microsoft has invested a significant amount of effort to include checks and balances in the new "in-place" upgrade process. Those items, coupled with the guidelines and insight provided throughout this chapter, you should be well on your way to completing your migration to Skype for Business Server 2015!

Best Practices

The following are the best practices from this chapter:

- Perform an Active Directory health check before beginning the upgrade and migration process. Resolve any issues before starting the process.
- Although the Skype for Business Server Control Panel might seem more familiar at first, there are many functions that can be accomplished only in the Skype for Business Server Management Shell.
- Publish the topology often and after each significant configuration change.
- Ensure that all users and other objects, such as Exchange Unified Messaging (UM) auto-attendant accounts, are migrated to Skype for Business Server 2015 before beginning the Lync Server decommission process.
- Make sure that firewalls do not exist between internal Lync and Skype for Business servers.

- Regardless of the migration path taken, the order of upgrades is the same. Upgrade the environment from the "inside out," starting with the Front End pool, followed by the Edge servers. If you have multiple Front End pools to upgrade, save the pool that hosts the CMS for last.
- Before starting migration planning for Skype for Business Server 2015, be sure that your existing environment consists of a single legacy version. So-called "tri-existence" of Lync Server 2010, 2013, and Skype for Business Server 2015 is not supported.

Summary

Skype for Business Server 2015 includes a new migration option, depending on the version of Lync Server currently installed in the environment. When you are migrating from Lync Server 2010, the only applicable migration method is the "side-by-side" migration. For seasoned Lync architects, this methodology will be familiar because it was previously the only supported migration path for Office Communications Server and Lync. Environments running Lync Server 2013 may choose to perform a "side-by-side" migration as well. However, organizations running Lync Server 2013 now also have the option to perform a Skype for Business Server upgrade "in-place" using their existing Lync Server 2013 infrastructure. Regardless of the migration path chosen, be sure to carefully plan the execution. Factors such as organization size, Lync server topology, maintenance windows, and rollback processes are all critical to a migration to Skype for Business Server 2015. Planning accordingly and following the recommended best practices will ensure a successful upgrade.

CHAPTER 16

Skype for Business Server 2015 Telephony and Voice Integration

IN THIS CHAPTER

- Understanding Telephony Fundamentals
- Integration Methods
- End-User Scenarios
- Analog Devices
- Skype for Business Voice Routing

In the days of Office Communications Server 2007 when Microsoft first dipped into the voice integration features, there was a lot of discussion about whether it could actually function as a real PBX replacement. Over the next few years there was a lot of debate comparing its shortcomings to more mature systems, but with Lync Server 2010, Lync Server 2013, and now Skype for Business Server 2015, Microsoft has an incredibly strong story with the product. It's no longer considered an add-on or supplemental service to existing PBXs—Skype for Business Server 2015 can hold its own in the most demanding of enterprise telephony environments.

This chapter is intended to provide a foundation for some of the concepts found in later chapters covering Enterprise Voice and planning for voice services. A high-level overview of telephony concepts is discussed to provide a foundation for future concepts. Afterward, the various integration methods used to provide coexistence or migration paths to Skype for Business Server 2015 are covered, and the same is done from the perspective of an end user in each of those scenarios.

Analog device connectivity for phones and fax machines was introduced in Lync Server 2010 and remains unchanged in Skype for Business Server 2015, but the overall call-flow concepts are reviewed. The final section of this chapter is an absolute must-read for any Skype for Business voice administrator; it covers each of the components used within Skype for Business voice routing and provides examples of how they interact to allow users to place a phone call.

Understanding Telephony Fundamentals

To understand the options for integrating Skype for Business Server 2015 with an existing voice infrastructure, it is important to understand some fundamentals of telephony. This section discusses some basic concepts in telephony and how they apply to Skype for Business Server 2015.

Public Switched Telephone Network (PSTN)

The Public Switched Telephone Network is the common network of telephony systems across the world. For those with more of a computer systems administration background, consider it similar to the Internet, like a cloud through which phone systems (as opposed to computers) are connected. The PSTN is composed of circuit switched analog lines, digital trunks such as T1s or E1s, cellular connections, and satellite transmissions, all of which can call each other through connected switching centers around the world. There is an incredible number of varying protocols and standards between different vendors and regions of the world to the point where it's remarkable how well the system works. Figure 16.1 shows a logical representation of the PSTN.

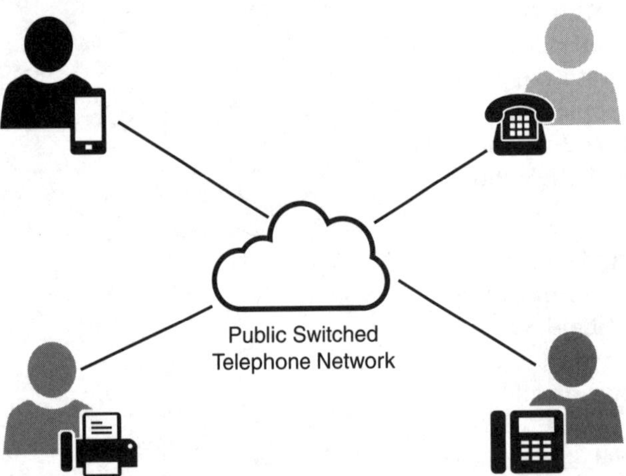

FIGURE 16.1 The Public Switched Telephone Network.

Private Branch Exchange

A private branch exchange (PBX) is a device that organizations install in their environment that enables internal connectivity for phones or fax machines. PBXs were historically expensive to purchase or required long lease agreements, but were considered an investment that could be utilized for a period as long as 10 to 30 years, and sometimes more.

The PBX on-premises allows for users within the organization to call each other without traversing the PSTN and incurring any charges. A PBX also usually has trunk lines that connect to the PSTN so that internal users can make and receive calls with other PSTN users outside of the office, as shown in Figure 16.2.

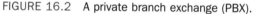

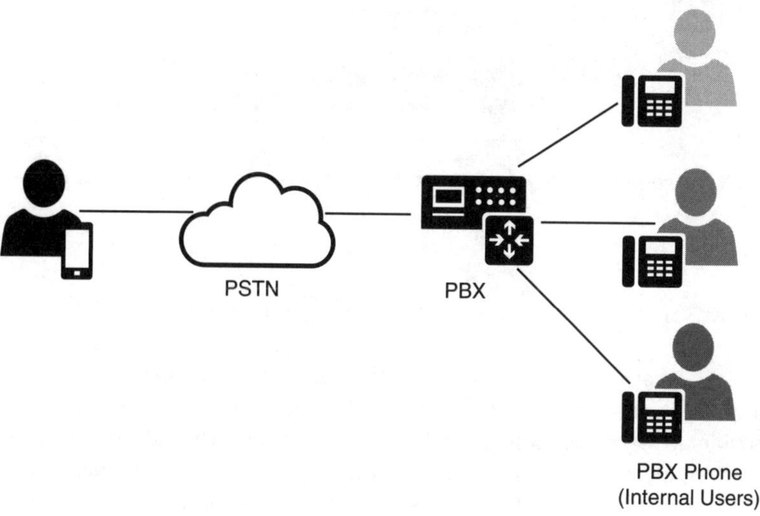

FIGURE 16.2 A private branch exchange (PBX).

As telephony has evolved over the years, so too have the different types of PBXs available on the market. Usually they fall into one of three categories:

- **Traditional PBX**—A traditional PBX is one that does not have any IP capabilities. These are generally older or low-end systems with limited feature sets. These systems are usually entirely based on analog or digital handsets for end users.
- **IP PBX**—An IP PBX is a system that is entirely based on Voice over IP (VoIP). It does not.support any analog devices natively, and all endpoints are IP-based network devices.
- **Hybrid PBX**—Most current PBXs have the capability to function both as a traditional PBX with analog endpoints and as an IP PBX through the purchase of expansion modules and software upgrades, like shown in Figure 16.3. These PBXs offer the most flexibility for an organization because they can connect many types of devices as the business transitions to IP telephony.

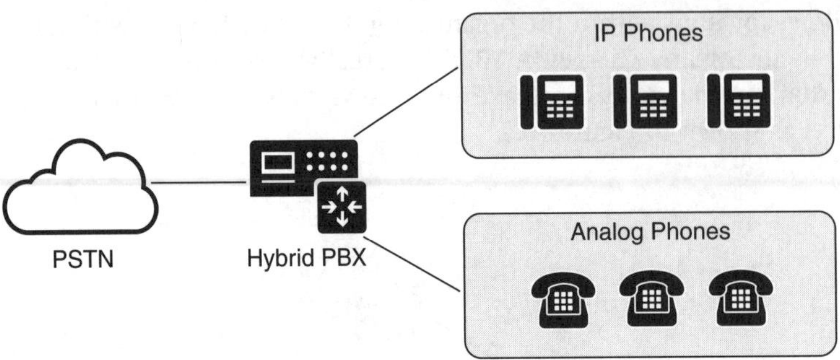

FIGURE 16.3 Hybrid PBX connecting analog and IP phones.

Signaling

In the world of telephony, some information must be exchanged between the PBX and the end users, such as the phone number of the caller and the phone number of the callee, in order to place a call. This is referred to as the signaling information, and it usually contains much more than just phone numbers; for the sake of this section, however, it can be considered what controls the calls. The signaling information is how a call is placed, transferred, or ended. The actual voice traffic, or the audio a user speaks and hears, is considered the media. In any call there is signaling information to control the call as well as a media stream that is the actual audio heard. Keep in mind that the path taken by these two items does not have to be identical.

Signaling information can come in the form of in-band or out-of-band information. In-band means the information shares the same channel or line as the media. The most common form of in-band signaling is Dual-Tone Multi-Frequency signaling (DTMF), which is what is sent when keys are pressed on a phone. Each key transmits a unique tone, indicating a different piece of information to the PBX.

Signaling can also be carried "out of band," which is typical for PBX trunk lines to the PSTN or when connecting directly to another PBX. Out-of-band signaling usually uses a dedicated channel for the signaling information while the media or actual voice traffic is carried in different channels. Take a North American T1 connection as an example: There are 24 channels each, with 64Kbps of bandwidth available. For a primary rate interface (PRI), the first 23 channels will each carry voice traffic, with a single call consuming one of these 23 channels, for a total of 23 simultaneous calls supported. The 24th channel carries all signaling information for the first 23 channels concurrently. This is considered "out of band" because the signaling and media are in separate channels on the connection. An example of this is shown in Figure 16.4.

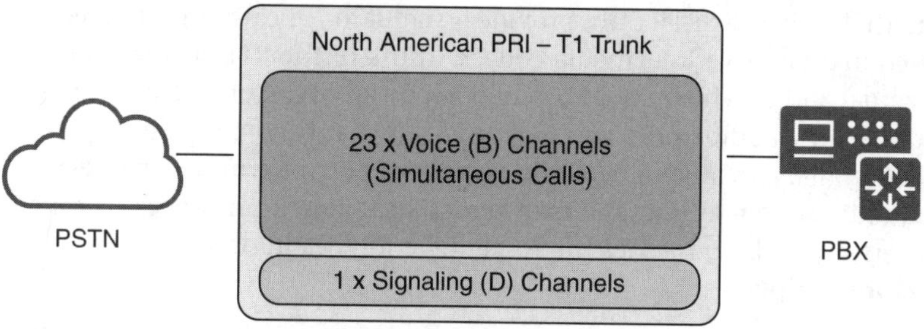

FIGURE 16.4 Out-of-band signaling.

Voice Over IP (VoIP)

As internal networks began to grow, it paved the way for Voice over IP (VoIP) based PBXs to emerge. Instead of using traditional analog lines to provide connections between internal users, the VoIP handsets connected to the PBX over the IP, just like a computer or any other device on the network. This allowed voice and data traffic to share a common, converged infrastructure, which cuts down on wiring and management overhead. The disadvantage to VoIP in early implementations was that it relied on shared networks where there were few controls in place and no quality of service (QoS) deployed for the voice traffic. As networks and IP PBX systems matured in later years, more businesses attracted by the lower total cost of ownership and advanced feature sets offered by IP PBX systems began to migrate away from legacy PBXs. Just as with traditional PBXs, VoIP requires some form of signaling to control the calls. An early form of signaling used for VoIP was H.323, and the Media Gateway Control Protocol (MGCP) also has gained widespread adoption.

The Session Initiation Protocol, or SIP, has also emerged as a standard that many IP PBXs use for signaling, including Lync and Skype for Business Server 2015. Skype for Business Server 2015 and all previous versions of the product use SIP for the internal signaling and for integrations with other PBX vendors because it provides a common framework for controlling calls. Vendors can also implement extensions on top of SIP to provide additional signaling capabilities. That's not to say that because two systems both use SIP that they will be compatible. Often there are differences in the SIP message flow, protocols used, or extensions used that prevent systems from direct integration. Still, the basic concepts of SIP messaging should be understood by any Skype for Business administrator.

Media and Codecs

Although SIP meets the needs for signaling information in calls, VoIP PBXs still require a method to transmit the actual media stream, whether it is audio or video. The Realtime Transport Protocol (RTP) is used in almost every VoIP implementation and was developed specifically for transmitting audio and video traffic across networks. Encryption of the media traffic was later added in the form of Secure Realtime Transport Protocol (SRTP), which is what Skype for Business Server 2015 uses by default to ensure that the media cannot be intercepted and played back.

It's important to note that RTP and SRTP only provide a standard for carrying the media traffic, which can be composed of various media codecs. Think of the RTP stream as a wrapper around the actual audio, which could be encoded by any type of codec. Media codecs are a way of translating audio and video data into bits that can be transmitted across a network. A codec analyzes an analog audio waveform and determines the best way to represent that audio stream as digital bits of zeroes and ones. That process is called encoding, and the reverse, decoding, is what the receiving end does in order to reconstruct the audio waveform for playback.

For two users to have an audio conversation, the codec used by both parties must match in order to correctly encode and decode the traffic. Figure 16.5 shows that while SRTP carries the real-time media, the parties must agree on a codec to use in order to actually have a conversation.

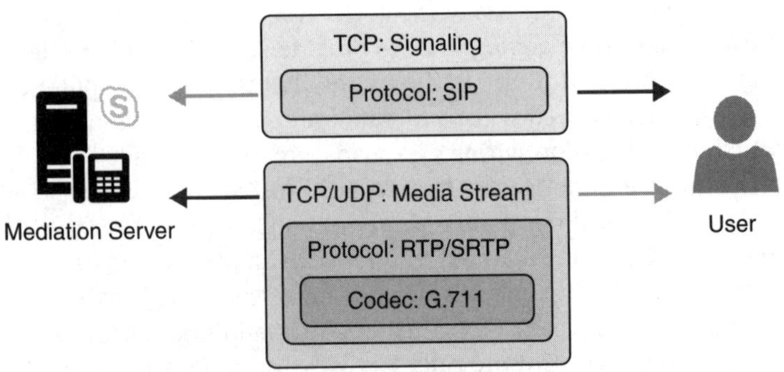

FIGURE 16.5 SIP signaling and SRTP media.

Skype for Business Audio Codecs

Skype for Business endpoints use various codecs within the RTP streams but select the appropriate one for each situation. This codec selection is mostly based on the type of call being placed, but endpoint type, server policies, or Call Admission Control settings can force alternative behaviors. These are the types of codecs used:

- **SILK Wideband**—The default codec used between two Skype for Business endpoints in a peer-to-peer call. This codec produces a high-fidelity audio call using minimal bandwidth and offers several bit rates to accommodate varying network conditions. This codec has been adopted from the Skype consumer platform to enable interoperability and is the successor to the RTAudio Wideband codec.

- **SILK Narrowband**—The lowest bit rate SILK codec available. This is used in peer-to-peer Skype for Business calls when bandwidth is restricted. Just as with the Wideband version, this version has been adopted from the Skype consumer platform to enable interoperability and is the successor to the RTAudio Narrowband codec.

- **RTAudio Wideband**—The default codec used between a Skype for Business and legacy Lync endpoint in a peer-to-peer call. It produces a high-fidelity audio call using minimal bandwidth.

- **RTAudio Narrowband**—Used between a Skype for Business endpoint and a Mediation Server when a PSTN call is placed. The PSTN user cannot hear the wideband audio fidelity, so there is no need to send a higher-quality stream between the Skype for Business endpoint and the Mediation Server. This can also be used in peer-to-peer calls between Skype for Business and legacy Lync endpoints when bandwidth is restricted.
- **G.711**—Used between the Mediation Server and a media gateway. The Mediation Server transcodes a Skype for Business endpoint's RTAudio Narrowband stream and sends it as G.711 to the gateway. If the Media Bypass feature is enabled, a Skype for Business endpoint can send G.711 audio directly to the media gateway, bypassing the Mediation Server transcoding operation.
- **G.722**—Used for conference calls when the round-trip latency to the A/V conferencing server is less than 25ms. This is a high-quality wideband audio codec.
- **Siren**—Used for conference calls when the round-trip latency to the A/V conferencing server exceeds 25ms. It is typically used by users joining a conference across a WAN connection or through the A/V Edge server.

The SILK and RTAudio codecs are Microsoft proprietary technology, which means they can be used only by endpoints that license the technology. IP PBX and media gateway vendors typically do not want to incur this additional cost or complexity, so they instead support more common codecs such as G.711. This is why the Mediation Server role exists; it handles the conversion, or transcoding, process by translating a SILK/RTAudio stream to G.711, and vice versa, allowing for integration through the media gateways covered in the next section. Another unique feature of the Microsoft media stack is the ability to switch between many of these codecs mid-call to accommodate changing network conditions.

Integration Methods

There are various ways to integrate Skype for Business Server 2015 with an existing PBX, whether it is a legacy or IP PBX. The methods discussed in this section can be used to support a period of coexistence with the existing telephony infrastructure, which allows businesses to evaluate and test Skype for Business Enterprise Voice without performing a full migration. A brand-new "greenfield" deployment is rare to come across, so many deployments will require an extended coexistence situation to be supported for some time. The following methods allow for a coexistence period during which the feature sets of Skype for Business are evaluated and users are gradually migrated.

Direct SIP

The easiest and generally most cost-effective way of integrating Skype for Business Server 2015 with an existing PBX is if the PBX supports SIP trunking. Many IP PBXs support this functionality natively, and many other hybrid PBXs support SIP trunking through minor hardware or software upgrades. This type of integration generally requires no additional hardware because the link between systems is purely a logical trunk that exists between two IP endpoints.

In Direct SIP scenarios the Mediation Server role serves as the conversion point between the two systems. The signaling on both sides of a SIP trunk is SIP, but the Mediation role translates the media stream between G.711 on the PBX side and SILK/RTAudio on the Skype for Business Server 2015 side, as shown in Figure 16.6.

Direct SIP integration allows for various end-user scenarios, which are discussed later in this chapter. Generally, specific extensions, or a range of extensions, will be configured to be "owned" by Skype for Business Server 2015 instead of the PBX. These extensions will be then configured on the old PBX to route across the SIP trunk to let Skype for Business handle the call. It is the PBX's way of saying it is not responsible for those numbers, but it knows where they can be reached. This type of routing is similar to tie-lines or trunks that can exist between multiple legacy PBXs.

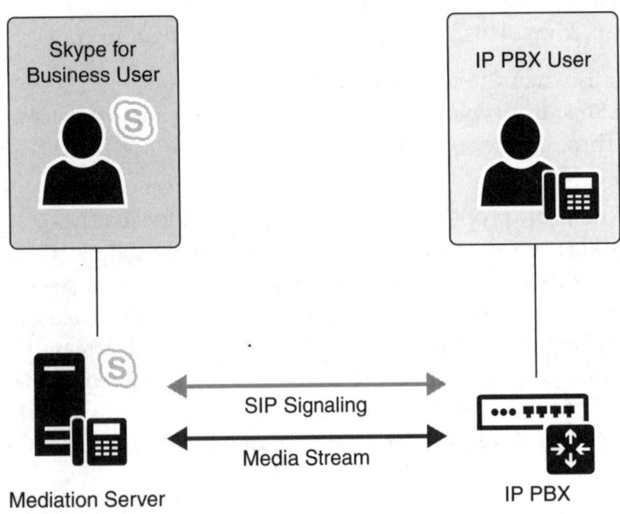

FIGURE 16.6 Direct SIP integration.

A very compelling feature in Skype for Business Server 2015 that was previously available in Lync Server 2013 is the ability to route calls between two SIP trunks associated with Mediation Servers called inter-trunk routing. Prior to Lync Server 2013, all calls had to either start or end with a Lync endpoint, but the voice routing can now be configured to send calls between two different trunks that are potentially attached to two different PBXs. This allows an organization to place the Skype for Business servers "in front" of legacy systems, and handle the core routing logic within Skype for Business, which can help simplify migration or consolidation of platforms.

Media Gateways

If Direct SIP is not an option because the PBX does not support the feature or has no IP PBX capabilities, a third-party device called a media gateway can be used to complete the integration. Media gateways act as an intermediary between the PBX and Skype for Business Server 2015 to help translate traditional PBX protocols to SIP traffic that Skype for Business Server 2015 can understand. In some cases it may be preferable to use a media gateway instead of Direct SIP, even if the legacy PBX is IP capable. This allows for greater control over phone number translation and increases transcoding capabilities. Media gateways are produced by many vendors today and provide a wide array of integration options for businesses looking to implement the voice features of Skype for Business Server 2015. They typically have traditional telephony ports for T1/E1 digital trunks or FXS/FXO ports, along with network adapters to communicate with Skype for Business Server. Media gateways can be used to provide interoperability with an existing PBX or connect directly to the PSTN, or both simultaneously. Figure 16.7 shows a logical layout of how a media gateway fits in the topology.

Also, when a Direct SIP trunk link is being configured, some reconfiguration of the PBX is necessary so that it knows to route calls for specific extensions to the media gateway, which will then deliver the calls to Skype for Business Server. An additional layer of complexity is involved because the media gateway must also be configured to route calls appropriately, but on the other hand, the media gateway provides a degree of flexibility in call manipulation that sometimes is not possible natively with a PBX or Skype for Business Server.

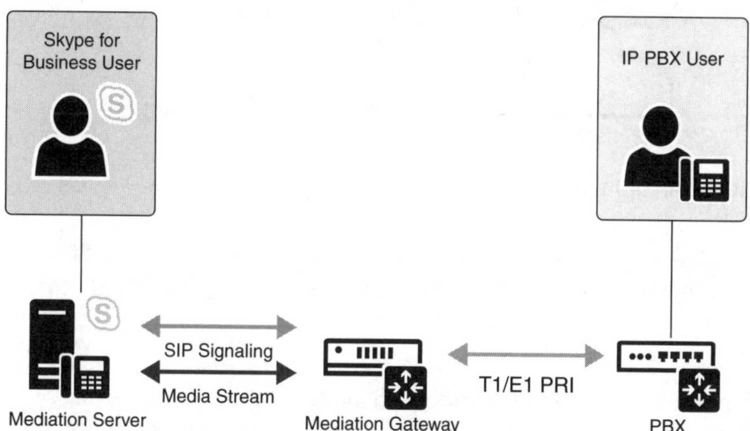

FIGURE 16.7 PBX Integration with media gateway.

Depending on the media gateway and business requirements, it might make sense to terminate existing trunks at the media gateway and place it in front of an old PBX, as shown in Figure 16.8. This could potentially have a bigger impact on the organization, but can greatly simplify some of the routing configuration during a large migration. Some gateway vendors have software that can detect whether a user's extension is Enterprise Voice or whether they have a legacy phone by reading specific Active Directory attributes. This might not seem like a big advantage up front during a pilot phase, but as users are migrated to Enterprise Voice it becomes advantageous not to have to constantly change routing rules on the PBX itself to indicate where an extension exists.

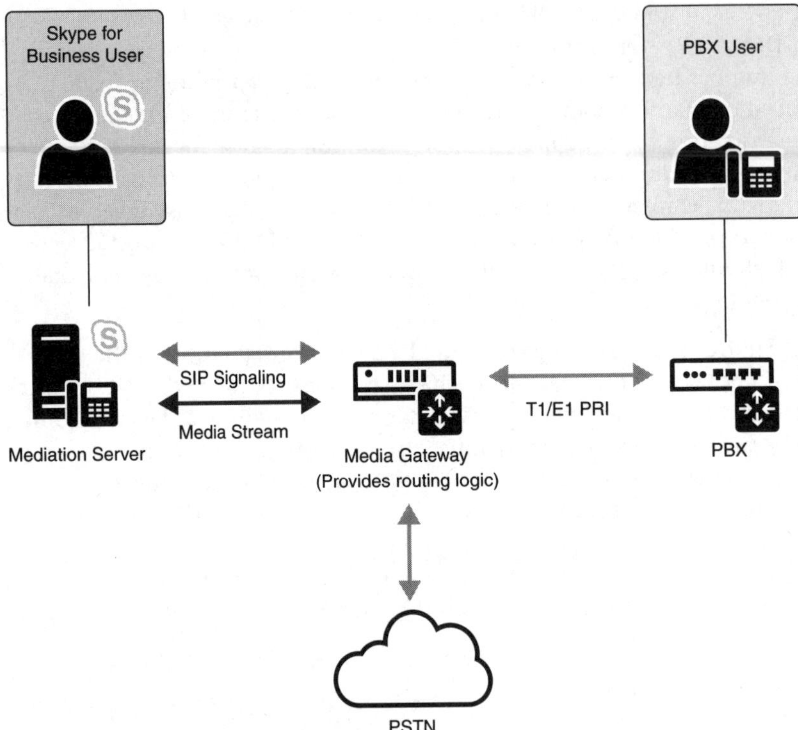

FIGURE 16.8 Media Gateway in front of PBX.

Regardless of the media gateway placement, it can provide a great deal of flexibility for organizations looking to move to or test Skype for Business Server Enterprise Voice.

Call via Work

Call via Work is a concept that was originally introduced along with the Lync Server 2010 Mobile client. On the 2010 Mobile client, this feature offered an innovative way to provide telephony calling capabilities without having to natively support the audio stack and capabilities of the full desktop Lync client. In Skype for Business Server 2015, the Call via Work capability is being leveraged in a different way to approach a similar challenge during legacy PBX interoperability. Call via Work is an extension of the Enterprise Voice feature set, which enables users to make outbound calls and leverage their legacy PBX handset to do so.

As shown in Figure 16.9, the user initiates the call from their Skype for Business client. However, in this scenario, rather than using a headset and a PC, the Skype for Business client tells Skype for Business Server 2015 to initiate a call to the user's configured "call-back" number. Once the initial call is established to the call-back endpoint, Skype for Business Server 2015 initiates an outbound call to the destination number. Finally, once the destination call is answered, the two calls are bridged so that the conversation can take place.

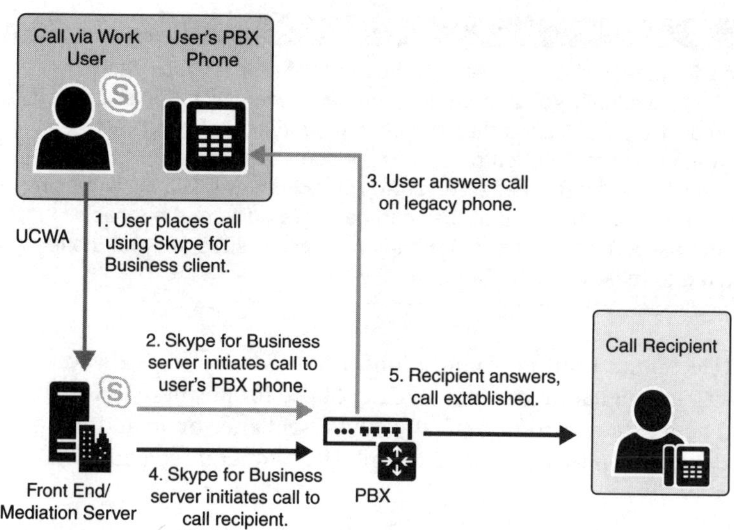

FIGURE 16.9 Call via Work for outbound calls.

A major benefit of Call via Work over Remote Call Control is that Call via Work is universally applicable, regardless of the legacy PBX platform used during interoperability. Remote Call Control was historically only available when integrating with certain PBX platforms. Additionally, Call via Work removes the requirement for a separate Computer Supported Telecommunications Applications (CSTA) gateway or server. Another distinct advantage of Call via Work is the ability to use it when working remotely. Working from home but forgot your headset? No problem. Simply set the call-back number as your home/hotel phone so that you don't have to deal with the headaches of using your PC's mic and speakers. That said, even with all of the advantages offered through the Call via Work integration, it is not a direct replacement for Remote Call Control. If Remote Call Control is currently deployed, you will want to carefully plan the transition to Call via Work.

Remote Call Control

Remote Call Control is mentioned here only for posterity and is no longer a recommended integration method in Skype for Business Server 2015. Furthermore, the client-side Remote Call Control feature set has been removed from the Skype for Business 2016 client. Remote Call Control was the original form of Lync Server PBX integration introduced with Live Communications Server 2005. It enables users to control their legacy desk phone from their Lync or Skype for Business client. Users can click to dial a contact in their buddy list, which actually instructs the legacy PBX desk phone to place the call. It also allows for their Presence to be automatically updated to "In a call" when they are using the legacy phone. In this case, the media stream and codec negotiation is not handled by Lync or Skype for Business Server 2015 at all. Instead, SIP signaling between the Mediation Server and the PBX enables only call control of the legacy endpoint.

NOTE

Be wary of deploying new Remote Call Control setups. Support for new Remote Call Control implementations was originally going to be dropped back when Lync Server 2010 was released, but the product team adjusted that stance and continued support. With the introduction of Call via Work, Remote Call Control has finally been deprecated in Skype for Business Server 2015. The Skype for Business Server 2015 backend will still allow a user to be configured for Remote Call Control so that they can be migrated from the legacy Lync version. However, the Skype for Business 2016 client no longer supports the Phone Integration options required to make Remote Call Control work.

A Computer Supported Telecommunications Applications (CSTA) gateway was always required to translate the SIP call signaling between Lync or Skype for Business Server 2015 and the integrated PBX. These gateways were generally a PBX appliance or an additional server component from the PBX vendor that added complexity and required additional configuration.

Remote Call Control does not provide users any Enterprise Voice features for controlling calls, assigning delegates, or configuring call forwarding settings. It does not work when connected via the Lync or Skype for Business Server 2015 Edge, so a user must be on the corporate network, which limits its usefulness for remote workers. Remote Call Control is considered an inferior option, and organizations should avoid new deployments of this scenario.

SIP Provider Trunking

The final integration method isn't so much integration with an existing PBX as it is a way to provide voice services between the end users without one of the other methods. SIP provider trunking uses an ITSP (Internet Telephony Service Provider) to deliver voice services across TCP/IP networks to an organization with Skype for Business Server 2015, similar to how a service provider provisions Internet access.

The advantages to SIP trunking come in the form of flexibility, redundancy, and capacity. Failover of Direct Inward Dial (DID) numbers between geographic regions using TDM infrastructure is usually impossible or incredibly expensive, but because SIP trunks are simply a TCP/IP connection, they can point at multiple locations for primary and backup delivery points. Depending on the provider, the trunk capacity can also be adjusted very quickly without having to install or remove a physical circuit connection. This helps to cut down on the lead time to deploy new services.

If integration with an existing PBX is not possible with any of the other means, or if an organization wants to move away from the legacy PBX, an ITSP can replace those services. In this situation Enterprise Voice users can communicate with users still hosted on the PBX, but only by traversing the PSTN. Figure 16.10 shows how this is not an optimal call path for users who might be physically sitting next to each other on different systems, but does provide a connectivity option if no others exist. After users are migrated to Skype for Business, an organization's PBX and existing TDM contracts can be deactivated, allowing for all voice services to be delivered via the ITSP.

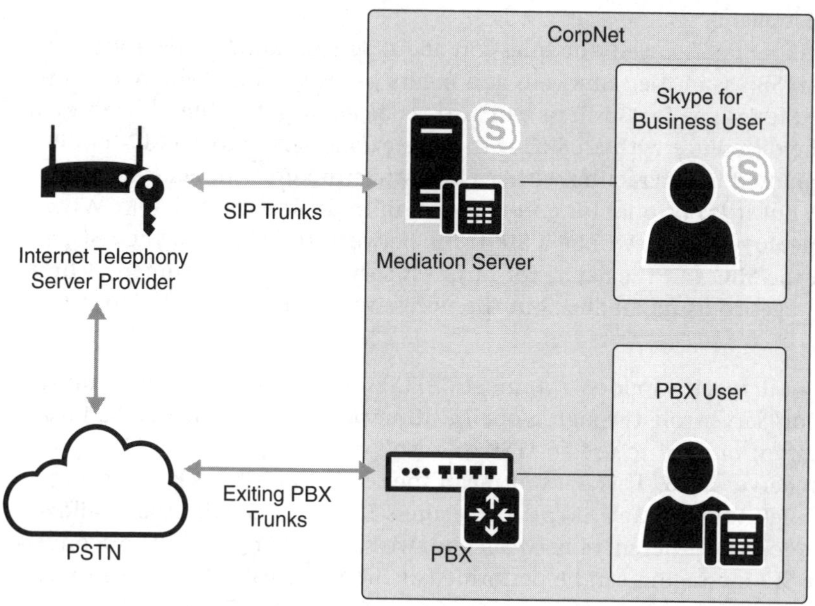

FIGURE 16.10 SIP trunking.

SIP trunks can be delivered to an organization via a few different methods:

- **Internet**—Organizations create the SIP trunk between the ITSP's public IP address and a public IP address owned by them. This generally requires a firewall that is SIP aware and can modify the content inside the incoming and outgoing SIP messages dynamically. A traditional firewall NAT is not sufficient for SIP trunking. The primary disadvantage of this method is that traffic is subject to the Internet, which has no quality of service (QoS) and which a business has no control over. Audio packets also might not be encrypted, which could allow an attacker to capture and replay a sensitive phone conversation or even collect transmitted signaling information such as account numbers.

- **Encrypted over the Internet**—Instead of using an unencrypted connection across the Internet, this method relies on certificates and Secure RTP (SRTP) to protect traffic between the ITSP and a business. This can help secure the calls through encryption, but adds additional overhead to each packet and does nothing to solve the QoS issue.

- **MPLS**—The most reliable method for an ITSP connection is to connect to the provider's MPLS network. In this scenario the SIP trunk appears as a logical connection across a private WAN circuit. Quality of service can be enabled on the connection, and there is no need for firewall traversal and NAT inspection for SIP. This is the best of both worlds, but also usually comes at the highest price. Organizations should strive to leverage this method for the least complex and highest quality connection.

Session Border Controllers

Any time SIP trunking is discussed, the question about Session Border Controllers (SBCs) appears. An SBC is in the same vein as a media gateway, and in many cases the gateways qualified for Skype for Business can also act as an SBC, but their purposes are very different. The difference with an SBC is that it's exclusively used for SIP-to-SIP connections as opposed to interacting with a TDM infrastructure. These devices are used by the ITSP, but it is optional for an organization to deploy its own SBC. When an SBC is being deployed, there will be a SIP trunk between the ITSP and the SBC, and another between the SBC and the Skype for Business Server 2015 environment. There are several advantages to using an SBC, but the necessity of using one will depend on the situation.

- **Flexibility**—Microsoft supports a number of ITSPs with Direct SIP connections to the Mediation Server role through a qualification process. In some cases a business might want or need to use an ITSP that isn't directly qualified with Skype for Business Server 2015. This doesn't mean the service won't work, but using an SBC between the ITSP and Skype for Business Server 2015 will usually allow remediation for any differences between the two sides. Manipulations or conversions in the SIP messaging can be performed at the SBC to allow for the service to function properly.
- **Security**—SBCs can perform the NAT and SIP message inspection for firewalls that cannot handle the conversion themselves. This allows an organization to hide any internal server names or IP addresses from being sent to the ITSP.
- **Transcoding**—In some cases a provider cannot deliver a G.711 audio stream to the business, or a different codec mighty be desired for bandwidth reasons. An SBC can act similarly to the Mediation Server role and transcode audio streams between differing codecs.
- **Authentication**—Some ITSPs offer the capability for authentication on the SIP trunk in the form of a username/password or shared secret. The Mediation Server role cannot perform this function, so an SBC can be used for terminating the SIP trunk and authenticating the business.

End-User Scenarios

This section discusses the different types of PBX integrations from the perspective of an end user. Organizations can deploy a mix of these scenarios to meet the needs of different users and don't have to pick just one path. For example, some users might be completely migrated to Enterprise Voice, but others might want to retain a legacy phone for use with audio conferencing. While users transition to Enterprise Voice, they might even configure call forwarding settings to simultaneously ring their legacy PBX phone. Presenting more options to end users makes managing the solution more difficult, but might be necessary during a coexistence period. What scenarios are possible is very dependent on the integration methods referenced earlier.

Enterprise Voice

In this scenario, end users have full Enterprise Voice functionality and use only Skype for Business endpoints as their phones. These endpoints can be a mix of Skype for Business PC or Mac clients, Lync Phone Edition or third-party IP phone (3PIP) devices, and Skype for Business mobile applications. Enterprise Voice for all users is the long-term goal for voice deployments and also provides the most flexibility to the end users. This is the state Enterprise Voice users are in for a brand-new deployment with no existing PBX, or when a migration has been completed.

Enterprise Voice with Legacy Phone

In this scenario, end users have full Enterprise Voice functionality, but also retain a legacy PBX phone on their desks, like shown in Figure 16.11. This scenario is typical for migrations from a legacy PBX in which a period of coexistence is required while users become accustomed to the new Skype for Business endpoints. Users have the choice of which system to use when placing or receiving calls through the use of simultaneous ring. As the users grow more familiar Skype for Business, they will rely less and less on the legacy phone until it becomes unnecessary and can be removed. As the migration ends and legacy devices are retired, the organization actually ends in the pure Enterprise Voice state. Although the idea of simultaneous ring sounds attractive and it generally works well for basic calls, it's important to work through all the possible use cases required to maintain two systems. For example, consider boss/admin scenarios, voicemail-forwarding features, and any directory search attendants.

Most implementations require a user to have two extensions during this period of coexistence. One extension is the user's primary, or publicly known, extension that other users dial and that is associated with the user's Skype for Business account. The other is a secondary, or unpublished, extension that is associated only with the legacy phone.

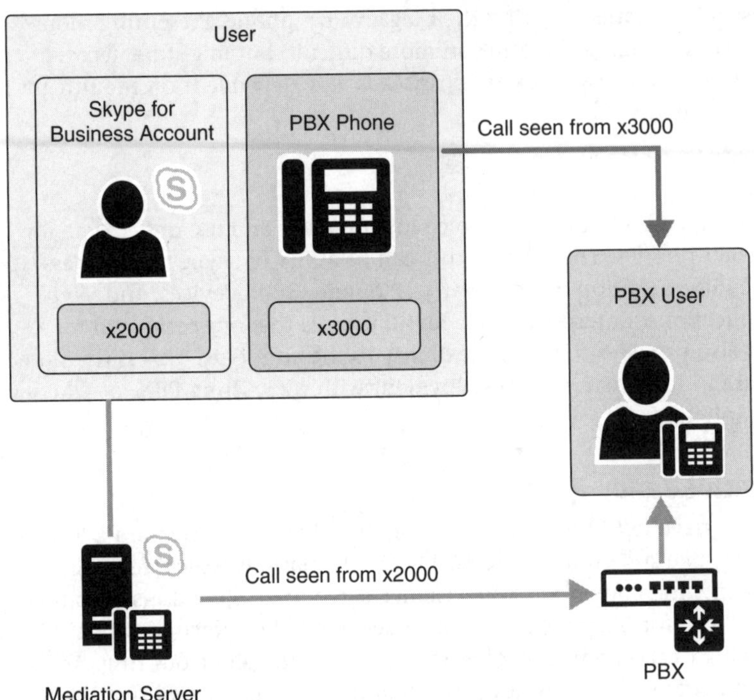

FIGURE 16.11 Enterprise Voice with a legacy phone.

When placing calls, users can choose whether to use Skype for Business or the legacy phone. One caveat shown here in Figure 16.12 is that, when calling from Skype for Business, the callee will see the call from the user's primary, published number in the organization, but calls coming from the legacy phone will show as coming from the unpublished number. This can be mitigated slightly with PBXs that support sending a display name, but the extension might still appear as unrecognized to the callee. Again, as users begin to leverage Skype for Business more and more, this becomes less of an issue.

Receiving calls on both devices in this scenario can be accomplished by the users configuring simultaneous ring within Skype for Business. Inbound calls will be routed first to the Skype for Business account, which determines what should happen to the call. Users generally set their Skype for Business call-forwarding options to simultaneously ring the secondary extension associated with their legacy PBX phone. This allows them to answer incoming calls either with a Skype for Business endpoint or on the legacy phone without the caller's noticing where the call was picked up. As the migration period goes on, users can adjust their simultaneous ring to stop ringing the legacy phone altogether. The downside to this approach is that users won't be able to use simultaneous ring with a mobile number because Skype for Business allows only a single number to be targeted for simultaneous ring. This concern is mitigated by allowing the mobile client to handle VoIP calls rather than simultaneous ring.

Something to keep in mind is that, depending on the current PBX, the simultaneous ring might not scale well. Consider when a media gateway device is used to bridge a legacy PBX and Skype for Business Server 2015. If inbound calls still flow through the PBX initially and then are directed through the media gateway to Skype for Business Server 2015, each call requires one channel on the media gateway. If a user configures simultaneous ring to a legacy phone, then yet another channel is required on the media gateway and PBX to support the call.

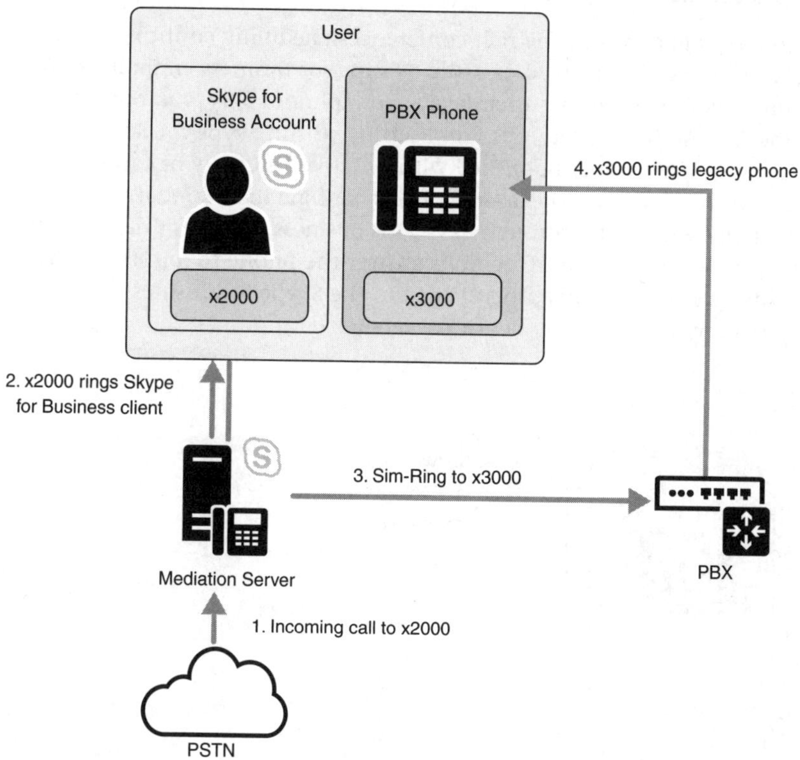

FIGURE 16.12 Simultaneous ring.

16

NOTE

Analyze peak capacity of the PBX and media gateways when planning for simultaneous ring. As an example, a media gateway with two T1s configured to a legacy PBX might support an initial pilot integration with Skype for Business Server 2015. Now when users start all using simultaneous ring, it might be necessary to use up to twice the number of channels, so four T1s might be required to support the coexistence. The simultaneous ringing feature is intended to be used with a mobile or alternate phone number instead of for migration purposes.

Legacy Phone for Conferencing

Another scenario that can be attractive to organizations not looking to fully implement Enterprise Voice features or replace existing handsets is to leverage the conferencing features of Skype for Business Server 2015 with their existing investments. This allows an organization to migrate away from a legacy or hosted conferencing system without changing the fundamental way users function. Organizations can save a significant amount of monthly fees for hosted conferencing services just by switching to Skype for Business Server 2015 as the dial-in conferencing solution with existing handsets.

Users in this scenario have full access to the rich conference-scheduling controls within Outlook and Skype for Business, but instead of using a Skype for Business endpoint to participate in audio conferences, they can use their legacy desk phone. This is accomplished through the use of the Join Audio Conferences From setting within Skype for Business. Users can elect to be called at a number published within Active Directory or can enter a number manually. Figure 16.13 shows an example of this configuration so that when a user is joining a conference with audio through Skype for Business, the user's desk phone will ring automatically, so all the user needs to do is answer the phone to join the audio conference. Because the user has already authenticated to the Skype for Business client, there is no need to enter any participant codes or conference IDs.

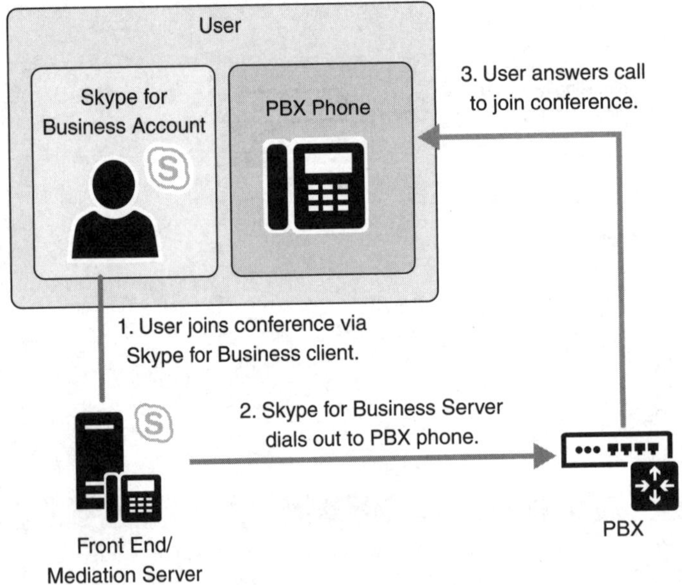

FIGURE 16.13 Legacy phone for conferencing.

Legacy Phone Presence and Click-to-Call

A more limited set of features can be deployed to users that gives the "click-to-call" functionality, or Call via Work functionality. This allows the end users to click a contact's phone number within their Skype for Business contact list and have that contact's number connected from their legacy PBX phone. Additionally, when a user initiates an outbound call through Call via Work, the user's Presence in Skype for Business will show as "In a Call." However, for inbound calls to the user's phone number, their Presence will not be updated because the call is delivered directly to the legacy PBX phone.

Although Call via Work provides great flexibility for interoperability with other PBX platforms, it generally provides only the most basic integration options; calls placed through Call via Work can limit the call control features and capabilities to the end user. When Call via Work is configured, the delegation of calls, participation in response groups, and advanced call control features are not available.

PBX Software Plugin

The final end-user scenario is one in which the PBX vendor uses the Skype for Business client APIs to develop add-on software for the desktop to integrate with Skype for Business. Examples of this are Cisco's UC Integration for Microsoft Lync (CUCILYNC) and Avaya's Application Enablement Server (AES) products, which must be installed and managed separately from the Lync or Skype for Business client.

These solutions might seem appealing to organizations with an existing investment in telephony platforms that offer these options, but these plugins can introduce a layer of complexity in troubleshooting any voice issues. These actually remove the Enterprise Voice functionality and instead use their own software shims to control the voice features. Call signaling flows through the PBX, and the client's audio or video traffic uses the PBX's configuration and not Skype for Business's dynamic media stack, as shown in Figure 16.14. Instead of seeing the native call controls provided by Skype for Business, users will see a UI developed by the PBX vendor, which could be a point of confusion for end users. These solutions also don't work through the Skype for Business Edge Server and require a user to connect a VPN client before signing in through Skype for Business remotely.

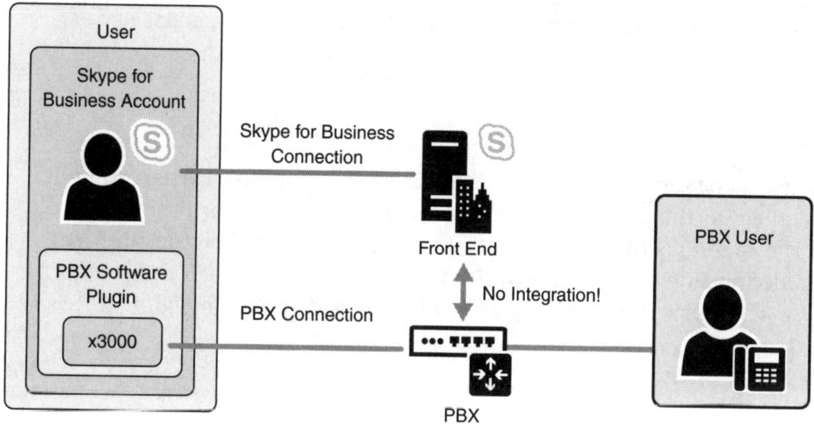

FIGURE 16.14 Skype for Business software plugin traffic flow.

The main difference with these solutions over Remote Call Control or Call via Work is that the Presence and phone control features are on the client side as opposed to the server side. Instead of Skype for Business Server integrating with a PBX for Presence updates and phone control, the software plugin handles the call control and updating the user's Presence, meaning no CSTA gateway is required. The confusing end-user experience and reduced Skype for Business client functionality are the biggest downsides, but also keep in mind that organizations using this approach are now at the mercy of a PBX vendor for approving any upgrades to both Lync and Skype for Business clients and the plugin software. The last point here is to consider how many resources and how much time a PBX vendor really wants to invest in working on improving integration with a competitor's product.

Analog Devices

Support for analog device connectivity, a feature added in Lync Server 2010, remains largely unchanged in Skype for Business Server 2015. Because Skype for Business Server 2015 is entirely TCP/IP based, FXS/FXO ports must be provided by some kind of media gateway, similar to how connectivity to digital T1/E1 trunks is achieved. This kind of setup allows Skype for Business Server 2015 to support analog phones, fax machines, paging systems, door buzzers, or any other kind of analog telephony device.

The Skype for Business Server 2015 configuration for an analog device consists of creating a contact object via the `New-CsAnalogDevice` cmdlet and assigning a Line URI, dial plan, and voice policy just as with a user account. The main difference with an analog device contact is that it also specifies a gateway parameter so Skype for Business Server 2015 knows exactly which gateway to route the call toward in order to reach the analog device.

NOTE

Any trunk configuration manipulations still apply to calls destined for analog devices through the gateway. Be sure that the gateway configuration of the analog endpoint number accounts for this change.

Inbound Routing

Calls destined for an analog device from a Skype for Business endpoint are sent straight to the gateway specified on the contact object. In this case, the Skype for Business user experience is that the call looks like it was placed to a PSTN number. The trickier part is how calls from a caller outside of Skype for Business Server 2015 will reach the analog device. The call flow resembles the following sequence and is depicted in Figure 16.15:

1. The PSTN or PBX caller dials the analog device DID.

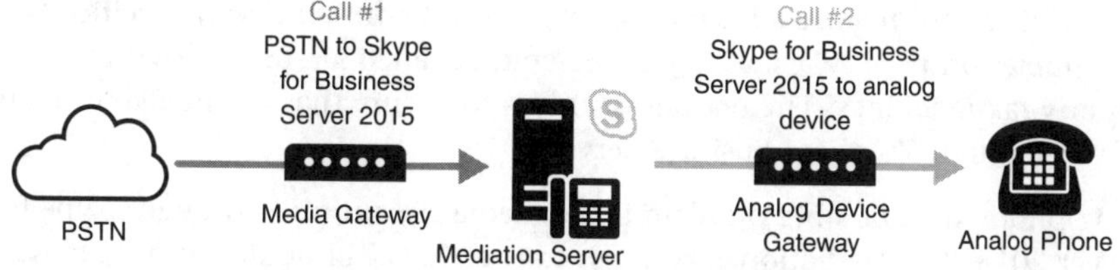

FIGURE 16.15 Inbound call to an analog device.

2. The call is routed through the media gateway and to Skype for Business Server 2015.
3. Skype for Business Server 2015 determines that the DID belongs to an analog device.
4. Skype for Business Server 2015 places a new, outbound call to the analog device with the calling party set to the PSTN or PBX phone number.
5. The call is routed to the media gateway associated with the analog device.
6. Gateway configuration associates the destination number with a specific analog port and then rings the device.

The takeaway here is that there are really two legs to this call. The first is between the PSTN or PBX caller and the Skype for Business Server 2015, and the second is between the Skype for Business Server 2015 and the analog device.

Outbound Routing

Calls placed from an analog device follow a process similar to that for inbound routing, but in a reverse order. Additionally, the dial plan and voice policy assigned to the analog device are applied at the server before the call is placed. This is the process:

1. The analog device dials a DID.
2. Gateway configuration routes all calls from the associated analog device port to Skype for Business Server 2015.
3. Skype for Business Server 2015 determines that the call is from a specific analog device based on the calling party ID matching the Line URI configured on the analog device contact object.
4. Skype for Business Server 2015 applies the dial plan assigned to the analog device contact.
5. The call is routed to a media gateway based on the voice policy assigned to the analog device contact.
6. The call routes through the media gateway and rings the PSTN or PBX user.

Fax Machines

Fax machines are supported in a similar manner to other analog devices in Skype for Business Server 2015, but require a bit more planning and configuration. Specifically, there is a parameter on the `New-CsAnalogDevice` cmdlet called `AnalogFax` that must be set to `$true` for any fax machines. The reason for this is to ensure that the media for a fax call is never routed through Skype for Business Server 2015.

For an analog phone it's not a big problem if the media stream runs through Skype for Business Server 2015. The Mediation Server can transcode G.711 audio from a gateway to RTAudio and back again if needed, but the issue is that the Mediation Server cannot handle the T.38 fax tones properly. So the point of identifying fax machines is to indicate to Skype for Business Server 2015 that it must remain out of the media path and allow the analog device to leverage media bypass.

The media problem isn't an issue if the fax machine is connected to the same media gateway from which the call came in, but in order to support calls from one gateway reaching a fax machine attached to a second gateway, the two gateways must be configured to route calls between one another. Assuming a call comes in through a media gateway and the fax machine is connected to a device referred to as the fax machine gateway, the call flow resembles the following process shown in Figure 16.16:

1. The PSTN or PBX caller dials a fax machine.

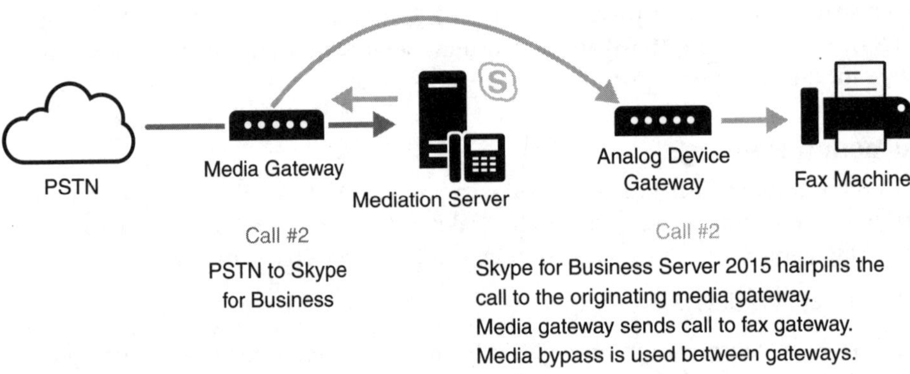

FIGURE 16.16 Fax call.

2. The call is routed through the media gateway and to Skype for Business Server 2015.
3. Skype for Business Server 2015 determines that the DID belongs to an analog fax device.
4. Skype for Business Server 2015 places a new, outbound call to the analog device with the calling party set to the PSTN or PBX phone number. The call is always sent directly back to the same gateway that originally sent the call, not the fax machine gateway.

5. Media gateway is now responsible for routing the new call from the Skype for Business Server 2015 to the fax machine gateway.
6. The call is placed from the media gateway to the fax machine gateway, and media bypass is enabled.
7. The two gateways use the G.711 codec between them for the fax transmission.

The takeaway in this scenario is that the Mediation Server is out of the media path, and a fax machine behaves like a Skype for Business media bypass client. The difference is that the fax machine gateway is taking the place of the Skype for Business client, but the concept is the same. This requires media bypass to be enabled on the trunk configuration for both gateways. It is also possible for a single physical gateway to have both T1 and FXS ports so that a dedicated analog gateway is not required.

The Routing Choice

Although analog device support exists in Skype for Business Server 2015, it's all done via the media gateways and there is a fair bit of configuration involved, especially when fax machines are included. An alternative method is to simply configure the analog device routing directly on the gateways and bypass the Skype for Business Server 2015 configuration. In this scenario, the gateways hold the routing logic of where to send calls destined for analog phones or fax machines, which can help simplify the deployment. It might even reduce the overhead costs involved because many gateway vendors charge extra for IP-to-IP connectivity between two gateways required for fax machines. The biggest disadvantage to this method is the loss of call detail record (CDR) data. Skype for Business Server 2015 creates CDR reports for all calls to or from analog devices, which can be tracked through the Monitoring Server reports, but this data is lost when the routing is being configured directly on gateways. Organizations can make these decisions on a case-by-case basis to determine whether CDR data for analog devices is a requirement.

Skype for Business Voice Routing

Configuration of voice routing in Skype for Business Server 2015 involves a combination of what Microsoft refers to as dial plans, voice policies, PSTN usages, routes, and trunks. This section covers the fundamental concepts of these objects and how they all interact so that users can make phone calls from Skype for Business. Any Skype for Business voice administrator should have a solid understanding of these items in order to properly configure Skype for Business Enterprise Voice.

All voice routing in Skype for Business Server 2015 is based on the international standard E.164 format for phone numbers. E.164-formatted numbers start with a + sign and are followed by a country code, and the remainder of the number varies depending on the country. For example, an E.164-formatted number in the United States consists of the + sign followed by the North American prefix, 1, a three-digit area code, and seven additional digits. A fictional sample number usually written as (234) 567-8901 within the United States formatted for E.164 is written as +12345678901.

Skype for Business Server 2015 dial plans, routes, and trunk translation rules use regular expression patterns to offer a degree of flexibility rarely found in PBX systems. Regular expressions, or regex for short, are a special text syntax that can be used to identify a pattern. There are entire books on regular expressions, but for Skype for Business's purpose it allows admins to easily identify specific number patterns. Skype for Business voice administrators should become familiar with basic regular expression syntax before configuring Enterprise Voice.

Dial Plans

The dial-plan object in Skype for Business Server 2015 is responsible for normalization of numbers, which is the process of taking a set of numbers that a user enters and converting the numbers to some other format. The dial plan does not control what numbers a user can call or dictate where a call is sent. Each user enabled for Enterprise Voice is assigned a dial plan, which contains an ordered list of normalization rules that are processed from top to bottom looking for a matching rule.

The first step in placing a Skype for Business call is to normalize the digits a user has entered to the E.164 format. Because regions and countries all dial numbers differently, this ensures that all numbers are in an equivalent format before any decisions on how the call is to be routed are attempted. Skype for Business Server 2015 dial plans must contain rules to normalize the different types of calls users will make. For example, users in the United States are used to dialing seven-digit numbers for local calls from legacy systems, so the dial plan needs logic to convert the seven digits a user enters to E.164 by prepending the + sign, the North America region code, and an appropriate three-digit area code.

Each normalization rule in a dial plan consists of a pattern to match as well as a translation pattern. The pattern to match is a regular expression pattern that searches against the number a user entered. If the dialed number matches the pattern, the rule is selected and the corresponding translation pattern applied. The translation pattern uses some part or all of the dialed number and manipulates it to the point where it matches the E.164 format. In the previous example, the pattern to match would look for seven dialed digits, and the translation pattern would add the +1 and a three-digit area code. The originally dialed seven digits would be placed at the end of the string.

NOTE

Skype for Business users can bypass the normalization rules by entering a + sign in front of any number. Skype for Business assumes that any number prefixed with a + has already been normalized to the E.164 format.

United States users also dial 10 digits for national calls, but can optionally dial 11 digits when including the North America region code, so the dial plan needs to allow for both of these options. Dialing an international number in North America is done by entering the digits 011 followed by the country code and the remainder of the number. In this case, a normalization rule needs to add the + sign and then remove the 011 prefix in order to convert the number to the E.164 format. These examples are specific to the United States, but each country or region has its own standards or habits that normalization rules should accommodate. The end result is that any number a user dials should be converted to E.164 through the dial plan.

Organizations migrating to Skype for Business Enterprise Voice will also need to configure rules for PBX extensions within the Skype for Business dial plan. For example, many businesses use some shortened form of internal dialing, such as a three- to six-digit extension that identifies each user. This cuts down on the number of digits users need to dial when calling each other, and even allows users to memorize the extensions for each other.

This form of shortened dialing can be accommodated in Skype for Business through the use of normalization rules within the dial plans. Just as with local, national, or international calls, the rules should search for a matching pattern and apply a translation pattern. For example, one rule might search for four digits and then apply a translation to prepend the + sign, a 1, a three-digit area code, and the three-digit local exchange. In this case, a four-digit number entered by a user has been converted to a full E.164-formatted number. It's very common for different internal extension ranges to correspond to different Direct Inward Dial ranges as well, so the pattern 5xxx might need to normalize differently from the pattern 6xxx. Two separate normalization rules are required to handle the differing translation patterns for those scenarios. The number of normalization rules required in each dial plan will be driven by the number of DID ranges a company owns.

The preceding section described how to configure normalization for DID numbers, but some organizations do not allow DID calls and instead use extensions that are not reachable directly from the PSTN. Outside callers typically route through a single main listed number, which goes to a receptionist or an automated attendant that can transfer callers to the internal user. Skype for Business Server 2015 can accommodate these scenarios as well, by use of a format within the translation rule that specifies an extension. The translation pattern prepends an E.164-formatted main-line number, followed by the string ";ext=" and the user's extension. For example, assuming that the main line is +12345678900, the normalization rule would convert the extension 5555 to +12345678900;ext=5555. The Skype for Business client displays the number in a much cleaner format to the users, so to them the dialed number appears as +1 (234) 567-8900 (X5555).

NOTE

Be careful when basing the Line URIs and normalization rules around a published main line or attendant number. This generally prevents Skype for Business users from calling the main line without the use of additional normalization rules. It might be easier to select a new "main" number for the Skype for Business internal-only extensions.

Service Codes

The E.164 format is intended to provide a standard for calls between multiple countries, but each country will usually have its own form of service codes, such as directory assistance, emergency services, or automated systems that simply speak the date and time.

These systems are not dialed internationally, but still need support within Skype for Business for users within those regions. It is acceptable for these services to provide only normalization rules that simply prepend a + sign and no additional information. For example, dial plans within the United States will have a normalization rule that looks for any digit in the range 2 through 9 followed by two 1s, and prepends only the + sign. This covers services such as 411, 611, and 911. At this point, Skype for Business considers the number normalized and it can be included within the voice routes.

Voice Policies

The voice policy in Skype for Business Server 2015 is used to control the class of service, or calling capabilities, and is the only other voice-routing object assigned directly to users. Voice policies have two pieces of configuration. The first is a set of true or false values indicating which features a user has available. This includes capabilities such as call forwarding, simultaneous ring, PSTN reroute, and delegate access. The second facet of the voice policy dictates which numbers a user can call, and what route the call should use.

Voice policies are discussed in more detail after PSTN usages and routes are covered. It is important to know the purpose of all three of these objects in order to understand how they work together to place a call. For right now, know that the voice policy holds an ordered list of PSTN usages.

PSTN Usages

The PSTN usage object in Skype for Business Server 2015 often seems confusing because it has no settings or configuration options other than a name. There are no user options or policies configured on a usage, and it cannot even be created by itself. PSTN usages can be considered the glue between a voice policy and a route in Skype for Business Server 2015.

PSTN usages are usually named based on a particular type of call and a destination, or an egress point. For example, a usage called US-CA-SFO-National might be used to identify national calls leaving through a gateway in the San Francisco, California office. Another example could be a usage called US-IL-CHI-Local, which identifies calls considered local to a gateway in the Chicago, Illinois office.

Remember, though, a PSTN usage is simply a name. Nothing more, nothing less. It is, however, associated with both a voice policy and a route, which is why it is considered the glue between the two.

NOTE

The obvious question here is why bother with PSTN usages if all they do is tie two other objects together? Wouldn't it make more sense to just put routes inside a voice policy? The answer is, because a single usage can be associated with multiple routes.

Routes

Routes in Skype for Business Server 2015 consist of a pattern to match and a list of trunks to use, which ultimately determines which gateway or SIP trunk is used to place a call. The patterns on routes again use regular expressions to search for a match against the E.164-formatted number after it has been processed by the dial plan. There are no translation rules on routes—the pattern is only evaluated to see whether a match exists. If the pattern matches, the route can be used and the call will be sent to one of the trunks listed on the route.

Each route is also associated with one or many PSTN usages. The fact that the associated PSTN usages are included in a voice policy is what allows a particular route to be used for a call. The specific pattern a route is searching for is typically described by the name of both the PSTN usage and the route.

Voice Policies Redux

After covering the voice policies, PSTN usages, and routes separately, you can begin to understand how they all work together. The starting point is the E.164-formatted number that has been normalized by a user's dial plan. The next step is to review the user's voice policy to see whether the user is allowed to call the number.

The first PSTN usage in the voice policy is selected, and any routes associated with that PSTN usage are reviewed. The normalized number is compared to the match patterns on each returned route. If there is a match, the route is selected and the call is placed through one of the trunks.

If there is no match pattern for any of the associated routes, the process repeats. The next PSTN usage in the voice policy is selected, and any routes associated with that usage are reviewed for a possible match. Again, if there is a match, the route is selected and the call is placed through one of the trunks.

This process continues as each PSTN usage and associated routes in the voice policy are reviewed. If the end of the list is reached and no match has been made, it is determined that the user is unable to place that call. Figure 16.17 depicts a simplified version of the call-routing logic.

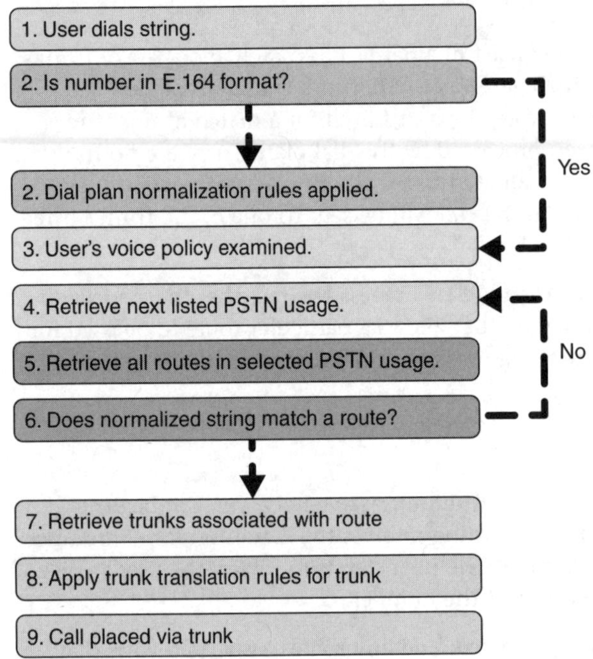

FIGURE 16.17 Call routing process.

For example, assume that a user's voice policy contains only two PSTN usages, such as US-CA-SFO-Local and US-CA-SFO-National. The Local PSTN usage is associated with a route that has a pattern matching a +1 followed by area codes local to San Francisco, such as 415, 510, and 650. The National PSTN usage is associated with a route with a pattern that matches a +1 followed by 10 digits.

If the user dials a number matching either of those patterns, the call will route successfully. But if the user tries to dial a hotel in England that starts with the country code +44, the call will fail. In that example, the +44 is first compared against the US-CA-SFO-Local PSTN usage and any associated routes. There is no match, so the next PSTN usage, US-CA-SFO-National, is evaluated. Again, there is no match. Because there are no more PSTN usages to evaluate, the call fails and the user is informed that they are not allowed to dial that particular number.

Trunks

Trunks are just a logical representation between Skype for Business Server 2015 and some form of PSTN or PBX connectivity. The end of a trunk might be a media gateway, another PBX, or an ITSP providing a SIP trunk. A Skype for Business trunk consists of an IP/PSTN gateway name or IP, a listening port on the IP/PSTN gateway, a Mediation Server, and a listening port on the Mediation Server. Routes include a list of trunks that can be used to place a call after a route is selected.

Trunk configuration in Skype for Business Server 2015 is used to apply additional logic to a call after a voice route and trunk have been selected. At this point the server knows which trunk the call will be sent to, but trunks can all have different settings. This allows Skype for Business Server 2015 to accommodate many gateway vendors and PBX integrations with different support for features such as media bypass, SIP refer messages, and the Real-Time Control Protocol (RTCP).

The other main use for trunk configuration settings is to provide manipulation for the called and calling party numbers. While numbers and routing decisions within Skype for Business Server 2015 are based on E.164, a significant number of PBXs and telephony providers don't support the format. The trunk configuration allows Skype for Business Server 2015 to manipulate the numbers into a format that will be supported on the other end of the trunk immediately before delivering the call.

Each trunk configuration contains an ordered list of trunk translation rules that evaluated in a top-to-bottom order. These trunk translation rules are very similar to dial plan rules in that they are composed of a pattern to match and a translation rule. This allows Skype for Business administrators to search for specific patterns on numbers and manipulate the format before sending the call to a PBX or gateway. If there are no trunk translation rules, or if the number dialed does not match any patterns, then the call is placed in the E.164 format.

An example of a trunk translation rule might be to prepend a leading external-access prefix used by the PBX such as a 9 to PSTN calls. Another example would be to prepend the 011 string to any international calls.

As in Lync Server 2013, Skype for Business Server 2015 has the capability to manipulate the calling party (caller's) number. Lync Server 2010 allowed manipulation of the called party (dialed) number, but any source-number manipulation had to be done at the PBX or gateway. The addition of the calling party manipulation per trunk is a great addition that should make life much easier on Skype for Business administrators.

Best Practices

The following are best practices from this chapter:

- Identify whether an existing IP PBX supports SIP for a Direct SIP integration path.
- Evaluate the media gateway vendors and devices to find a feature set that meets the needs of the organization.
- Ensure that media gateways have enough channels to handle peak capacity, especially when using simultaneous ring or Call via Work.
- Identify which features end users will be provisioned with before determining hardware requirements.
- Spend time training users on the integration and how to use the systems during a period of coexistence.
- Avoid new deployments involving Remote Call Control or PBX software plugins.

Summary

Skype for Business Server 2015 provides a robust platform that organizations can use to provide highly reliable and resilient voice services. The platform is also extremely flexible and offers various integration methods so that businesses can quickly establish coexistence as well as work toward migrating users incrementally if needed.

The voice routing engine also offers a high degree of customization and granularity over any call decisions. This allows administrators to provide various classes of service, depending on the user, while accommodating all local dialing habits across varying regions and geographies.

CHAPTER 17

Advanced Skype for Business Server 2015 Voice Configuration

IN THIS CHAPTER

- Building the Skype for Business Server 2015 Topology
- Telephony Voice Routing
- Telephony Voice Features
- Advanced Enterprise Voice Features
- External Dial-in Conferencing
- Response Groups

Building on the success of Lync Server 2013, the Skype for Business Server 2015 platform is now regarded as one of the industry standards for Enterprise Voice telephony with many organizations replacing their incumbent private branch exchange (PBX) for the more feature-rich solution. As with many software-based telephony platforms, it offers an exceptional amount of flexibility and control, and becomes a very attractive telephony platform for nearly any business, both large and small.

With each release of the Microsoft unified communications (UC) collaboration tool, Microsoft has made great strides in addressing the shortcomings of previous versions and improving the overall stability of the product. Skype for Business Server 2015 is no different and builds on the already solid foundation of Lync Server 2013, bolstered by many years of Microsoft development in the UC space.

This chapter discusses the configuration of Enterprise Voice components found in Skype for Business Server 2015—from dial plans to trunk configurations, and on to more advanced concepts such as Call Admission Control (CAC) and the emergency U.S. stipulation of E911. It also covers supporting features such as external dial-in conferencing, Response Groups, and how to configure analog devices.

TIP

This chapter focuses on the administrative steps required to configure each of the voice features. For a more detailed discussion about planning for each of these scenarios, see Chapter 33, "Planning for Voice Deployment."

Building the Skype for Business Topology

Many components make up a Skype for Business topology, and in this section we go through and define the components required to provide a successful enterprise voice solution. As with all processes and procedures within the Skype for Business configuration, there is an element of order to achieve the desired result; for example, with Enterprise Voice (EV), its necessary to have one or many of the following components: a Mediation pool, the possibility of survivable branch appliances (SBAs) or servers (SBSs), third-party PSTN gateways, and trunk routing. In order for any telephony traversal in the Skype for business environment, there is a mandatory step to publish the topology before any voice routing can be configured.

Defining the Mediation Pool Options

The simplest way to deploy a Mediation pool is to collocate the Mediation Server role onto the Skype for Business Front End pool. Perform the steps outlined in Chapter 4, "Skype for Business Server 2015 Front End Server," and simply check the box labeled Collocate Mediation Server on the Select Collocated Server Roles page while defining the Front End pool, as shown in Figure 17.1.

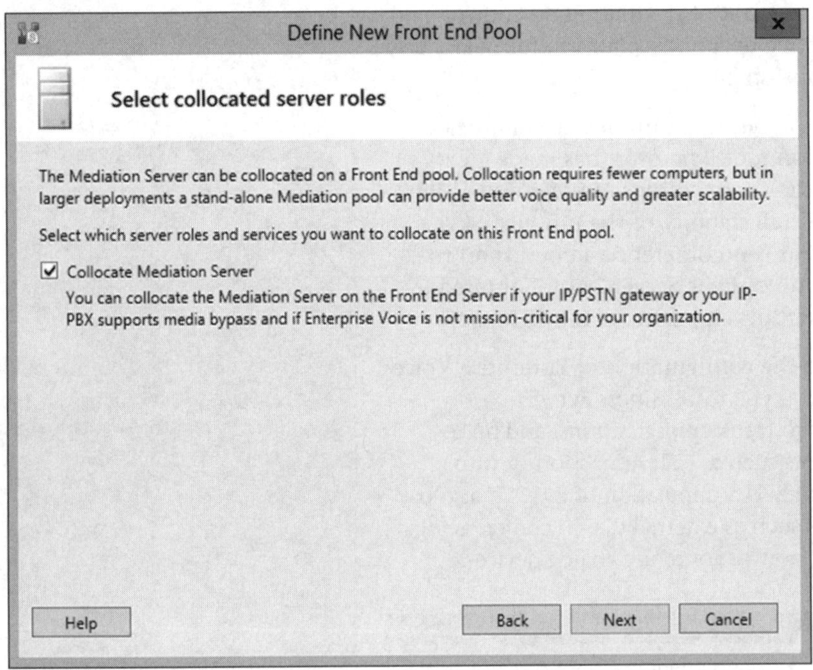
Define New Front End Pool
Select collocated server roles
The Mediation Server can be collocated on a Front End pool. Collocation requires fewer computers, but in larger deployments a stand-alone Mediation pool can provide better voice quality and greater scalability.
Select which server roles and services you want to collocate on this Front End pool.
Collocate Mediation Server
You can collocate the Mediation Server on the Front End Server if your IP/PSTN gateway or your IP-PBX supports media bypass and if Enterprise Voice is not mission-critical for your organization.
Help
Back
Next
Cancel

FIGURE 17.1 Collocating the Mediation Server role onto a Skype for Business Front End pool.

NOTE

Collocating the Mediation Server role onto a Front End pool is a supported Microsoft topology. However, if you are a company with heavy user requirements for Enterprise Voice, it might be prudent to create a dedicated Mediation pool to service your full Enterprise Voice needs, as shown in Figure 17.2. Heavy telephony usage is generally defined as requiring more than 150 concurrent calls per Mediation Server.

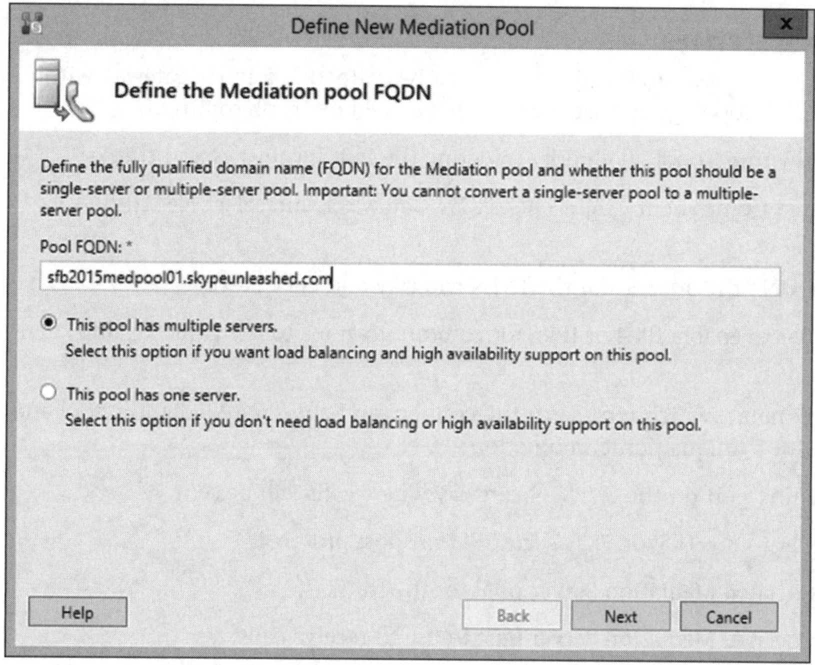

FIGURE 17.2 Creating a dedicated Mediation pool for high usage telephony.

To deploy a standalone Mediation Server pool, within the Skype for Business Server 2015 Topology Builder, follow these steps:

1. Right-click Mediation Pools and select New Mediation Pool.
2. Enter a Pool FQDN, select either Multiple Computer Pool or Single Computer Pool, and click Next.
3. If deploying a multiple-computer pool, enter the Computer FQDN of each server and click Add. Click Next when all servers have been added, and then click Next again.
4. Select a Front End pool as the next-hop pool for the Mediation pool and click Next.
5. If necessary, select an Edge pool to be used for media traversal by the Mediation pool and click Next.
6. Click Finish.

17

If the Mediation pool needs to listen for unsecured TCP SIP connections, follow these additional steps:

1. Right-click the pool and select Edit Properties.
2. Select Enable TCP Port and enter a TCP port range.
3. Click OK.

Defining PSTN Gateways

Each media gateway, IP PBX, or ITSP SIP trunk must be defined as a PSTN gateway within the Skype for Business topology so that it can be referenced by trunk routing.

Follow these steps within Topology Builder to define the PSTN gateways and trunks:

1. Expand Shared Components, right-click PSTN Gateways, and select New IP/PSTN Gateway.
2. Enter the FQDN or IP address for the PSTN gateway and click Next.
3. Select whether to enable IPv4 or IPv6 for communications to the gateway, and then click Next.
4. Enter a trunk name, which represents the connection between a Mediation pool and a gateway with a unique port combination.
5. Enter a listening port on the IP/PSTN gateway where calls will be sent.
6. Select whether to use TCP or TLS as the SIP transport protocol.
7. Select an associated Mediation Server pool for the trunk.
8. Select an associated Mediation Server port to use to receive calls.
9. Click Finish when complete.

Repeat these steps for any additional PSTN gateways in the environment.

Defining Additional Trunk Associations

A single trunk is created when a new PSTN gateway is being defined, but administrators can always create additional trunks to the same PSTN gateway later with the M:N trunk routing support. To create a new trunk to an existing PSTN gateway, follow these steps within Topology Builder:

1. Expand Shared Components, right-click Trunks, and select New Trunk.
2. Enter a trunk name, which represents the connection between a Mediation pool and a gateway with a unique port combination.
3. Select an associated PSTN gateway.
4. Enter a listening port on the IP/PSTN gateway where calls will be sent.

5. Select whether to use TCP or TLS as the SIP transport protocol.
6. Select an associated Mediation Server pool for the trunk.
7. Select an associated Mediation Server port to use to receive calls.
8. Click OK when complete.

A sample configuration is shown in Figure 17.3.

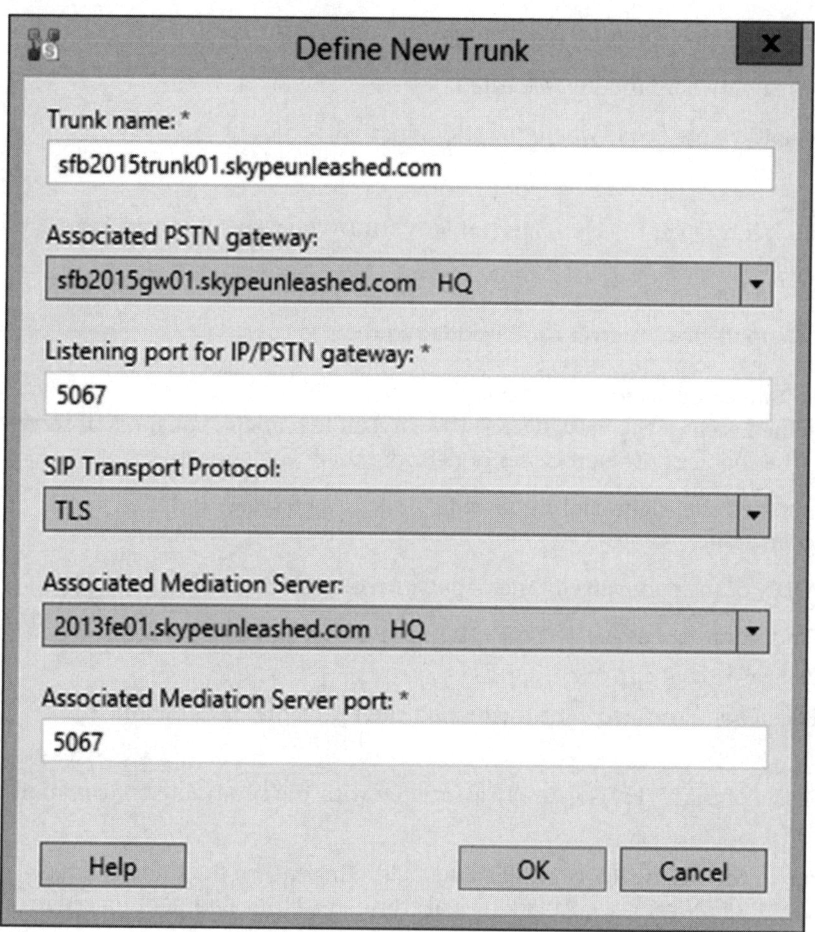

FIGURE 17.3 Defining a trunk.

Repeat these steps for any additional trunks that need to be created.

Defining Branch Sites

The first step, whether deploying a survivable branch appliance or a survivable branch server, is to define each branch site within the Skype for Business Server topology. Within Topology Builder, follow these steps:

1. Right-click Branch Sites and select New Branch Site.
2. Enter a name for the site and, optionally, a description.
3. Click Next.
4. Enter the city where the site is located.
5. Enter a state/region where the site is located.
6. Enter a two-digit country code where the site is located.
7. Click Next.
8. Clear the check box Open the New Survivable Wizard When This Wizard Closes. Then click Finish.

A survivable branch appliance or server can be added to the site later.

Defining Survivable Branch Appliances and Servers

After you have defined each of the branch sites, the survivable branch appliances or server must be added to the topology. The processes of defining them is identical:

1. Expand the branch site, right-click Survivable Branch Appliances, and then select New Survivable Branch Appliance.
2. Enter the FQDN of the survivable branch appliance or server, and then click Next.
3. Select the Front End pool associated with the survivable branch appliance or server, and then click Next.
4. Select the Edge Pool associated with the branch site for media traversal and click Next.
5. Enter the FQDN of the IP/PSTN gateway associated with the survivable branch appliance or server.
6. Enter a name in the Define Root Trunk Name field. This will be the primary trunk used with the IP/PSTN gateway. An additional trunk to a Front End pool for redundancy can be created later.
7. Click Gateway FQDN or IP Address and enter the name or IP address of the gateway used for routing inbound and outbound calls with the branch site.
8. Enter a listening port for the IP/PSTN gateway.
9. Select either TCP or TLS for the SIP transport protocol.
10. Click listening port and enter the correct port.
11. Click Finish.

Be sure to publish the topology after all Mediation pools, PSTN gateways, branch sites, and survivable branch appliances or servers have been defined. Failure to do so, or if you receive any warnings when publishing the topology, could result in a failure in Enterprise Voice routing.

Deploying a Survivable Branch Appliance

The exact procedures for each survivable branch appliance will vary depending on the vendor, but there are generally some steps common to each deployment. These are outlined in the following sections.

NOTE

Use the same procedures as a Front End Server when deploying a survivable branch server to prepare the local configuration store, install server components, and issue certificates. The following sections are specific to survivable branch appliances and should not be performed for survivable branch servers.

Adding the Survivable Branch Appliance to Active Directory

Each survivable branch appliance deployed needs to have a computer account in Active Directory defined before being placed in operation. The intent of this step is that the technician in a branch site will not have rights to join a server to the Active Directory domain.

Follow these when deploying only a survivable branch appliance:

1. Log on to a computer with the Active Directory Domain Services role's administration tools installed.
2. Open Active Directory Users and Computers.
3. Right-click an organizational unit, select New, and select Computer.
4. Enter a computer name for the survivable branch appliance. This is just the hostname, not the fully qualified domain name.
5. Under User or Group, click the Change button.
6. Enter `RTCUniversalSBATechnicians`, and then click OK.
7. Click OK.

Defining the Service Principal Name

After a computer account has been staged for the survivable branch appliance, a service principal name (SPN) must be added to the computer account.

Follow these steps to add the SPN:

1. Open ADSI Edit.
2. Right-click the ADSI Edit root node and select Connect To.
3. Leave the default options selected and click OK.

4. Expand the Default Naming Context and locate the survivable branch appliance's computer account.
5. Right-click the account and select Properties.
6. Highlight `servicePrincipalName` and click Edit.
7. Enter `HOST/<Survivable Branch Appliance FQDN>` and click Add.
8. Click OK twice.

NOTE

Normally, using the `SETSPN` command is the preferred way to manage SPNs associated with domain accounts. Because the survivable branch appliance has not joined the domain yet, the `SETSPN` commands do not work properly. Instead, use ADSI Edit to configure the appropriate SPN.

Installing a Survivable Branch Appliance

Installation and configuration varies widely depending on the survivable branch appliance vendor and software. Most of the installations include the following tasks:

1. Physically cable and rack the survivable branch appliance.
2. Configure IP addresses. (One IP address is typically required for the Media Gateway element and a second IP address is required for the survivable branch appliance element.)
3. Join the domain.
4. Enable a replica of configuration.
5. Request and assign certificates.
6. Start services.
7. Test connectivity.
8. Move user accounts.
9. Complete voice testing and sign off.

NOTE

The user account used to join the SBA to the domain must be a member of the `RTCUniversalSBATechnicians` group. This is the group selected to join the computer to the domain when the computer account is created in Active Directory.

Voice Routing

Voice routing in Skype for Business Server 2015 is determined by the association of various components such as policies, routes, and trunks. A quick overview of the key pieces is given here:

- **Dial plan**—A dial plan contains a set of normalization rules to convert digits entered by a user into a routable format.
- **Normalization rules**—Normalization rules are associated with a dial plan and convert the digits a user might enter into the Skype for Business client in a localized standard, but the expected format would be E.164. Using what's known as RegEx, the entered number would be reformatted into the correct expected format.
- **Voice policies**—Voice policies determine what voice features users are allowed to use, such as call forwarding, simultaneous ring, call transfer, and call park. They also define which PSTN usages can be accessed by a user. For example, you might have a policy where only certain people are only allowed to ring inner-city (local) rate numbers, or maybe you might create a policy where certain higher profile users can call internationally.
- **PSTN usages**—Usages are a class of call that is then associated with voice policies. If a user's voice policy does not contain a specific PSTN usage, the user is not allowed to place the call.
- **Routes**—Routes are used in Skype for Business Server 2015 to direct calls through a specified trunk or set of trunks.
- **Trunks**—Routes deliver calls to specified trunks, which can be a media gateway, direct SIP trunk, or a legacy PBX solution via direct SIP trunking.
- **Trunk configuration**—Each trunk might require unique settings or translation rules, so a trunk configuration defines those parameters per trunk; for example, you might have a contact center team where you want the outbound calling presentation to always display the main company telephony number. To achieve this, you would set it within the trunk configuration.
- **Translation rules**—Translation rules are associated with a trunk configuration to manipulate dial strings before being delivered to the trunk. These rules can manipulate the dial string sent across the trunk if the opposite end is not capable of handling E.164 numbers.

Configuring a Dial Plan

A dial plan in Skype for Business Server 2015 is associated with users and contains a set of normalization rules. Normalization rules are used to convert dial strings entered by users into a format routable by Skype for Business Server 2015. Dial plans can differ based on region or site depending on how users are used to dialing digits. Additional dial plans are usually created to accommodate different dialing habits based on sites or users. A dial plan can be scoped to apply at the site level, to a specific pool, or even just to a specific set of users.

TIP

Global, site, or pool dial plans cut down on administrative steps when enabling users, but tagged, or user, dial plans offer the most flexibility because they can be assigned directly to individual users.

Skype for Business Server 2015 dial plans have the following options available:

- **Simple Name**—A name used by the system for the dial plan that includes no spaces or special characters. Leaving the default, suggested simple name is usually sufficient.
- **Dial-in Conferencing Region**—The dial-in region name associated to users assigned this dial plan. This name appears in Online Meeting invitations. It also worth noting that setting the Dial-in Conferencing Region to a user will expose the external dial-in numbers associated with that region ID.
- **External Access Prefix**—A leading digit used to indicate that a call is trying to dial an external number. Many organizations use the digit 8 or 9 for this functionality.
- **Associated Normalization Rules**—An ordered list of normalization rules that will be applied to calls coming from users assigned to this dial plan.

To create a new dial plan, follow these steps:

1. Open the Skype for Business Server 2015 Control Panel.
2. Click Voice Routing.
3. Click Dial Plan.
4. Click New, and then select Site Dial Plan, Pool Dial Plan, or User Dial Plan.
5. Leave the suggested simple name for the dial plan.
6. Enter a description for the dial plan.
7. If the dial plan is associated with a dial-in conferencing region, enter the name of that region.
8. Enter an external access prefix, if used.
9. Select any normalization rules to be included in the dial plan.
10. Click OK to save the dial plan.

Alternatively, the `New-CsDialPlan` cmdlet can be used to create a new dial plan using the Skype for Business Server 2015 Management Shell. One parameter is not available in the Skype for Business Server 2015 Control Panel interface:

- **`OptimizeDeviceDialing`**—A `true` or `false` value that determines whether the external access prefix will be applied for calls placed to numbers external to the company.

Creating Normalization Rules

Normalization rules are associated with a dial plan and provide a way for administrators to translate dial strings that users enter into full E.164 format. For instance, a country code and local area code might be automatically appended when a user tries to dial only seven digits. Many organizations use four-digit or five-digit internal extensions, and normalization rules can convert those dial patterns to a full E.164 number, which in turn would match the internal user's `LineURI` and therefore make an internal call as opposed to an external bridged call.

Administrators can define the normalization rules either using regular expressions or using the Normalization Rule tool. To create a new normalization rule, follow these steps:

1. On the Edit Dial Plan screen, click the New button in the Associated Normalization Rules section.
2. Provide a name for the rule and a description for the rule.

> **NOTE**
>
> This example uses the Normalization Rule tool, but for more advanced pattern matching, click the Edit button at the bottom of the screen to manually enter the matching pattern and translation rule using regular expressions.

3. In the Starting Digits field, enter the beginning digits of the string to be matched.
4. Specify a length for the string to be matched. Options include matching at least a specific number of digits, exactly a certain number of digits, or any number of digits.
5. Specify a number of digits to remove after a string matches the starting digits and length. These digits will be removed from the left side of the number.
6. Specify digits to add after the selected number of digits have been removed.
7. If the pattern matches numbers that are internal to the organization, check the box Internal Extension.
8. Click OK to save the translation rule and click OK again to save the trunk configuration.

> **NOTE**
>
> The Internal Extension check box works in conjunction with the external access prefix specified on the dial plan and is specific to off-hook dialing from Lync Phone Edition (LPE) clients. (Note: At the time of writing this chapter, the Skype for Business LPE has not been released from Microsoft.) Off-hook dialing refers to when a user either lifts the receiver or presses the speakerphone button before dialing. If an LPE client enters the external access prefix as the first digit during an off-hook dial, the client will skip all the rules flagged as an internal extension. This helps ensure that the user does not accidentally dial an internal extension because they entered digits too slowly.

The `New-CsVoiceNormalizationRule` cmdlet can also be used to create rules using the Skype for Business Server 2015 Management Shell.

Configuring Voice Policies

Voice policies in Skype for Business Server 2015 are a way of controlling the features and calling capabilities of users. Voice policies are assigned to user accounts through a global, site, or direct method. The following options are available when a voice policy is being created:

- **Enable Call Forwarding**—Enables users to forward calls to other users or devices.
- **Enable Delegation**—Enables users to specify other users to answer and place calls on their behalf, or to schedule Online Meetings for another user.
- **Enable Call Transfer**—Enables users to transfer calls to other users.
- **Enable Call Park**—Enables users to place a call on hold and pick it up from another phone or location by dialing a call park orbit number.
- **Enable Simultaneous Ringing of Phones**—Enables users to simultaneously ring another user or phone number such as a mobile phone.
- **Enable Team Call**—Enables users to answer calls on behalf of another team member.
- **Enable PSTN Reroute**—Enables users to place calls to be rerouted to the PSTN network when the wide area network (WAN) is congested or unavailable.
- **Enable Bandwidth Policy Override**—Enables users to avoid limitations imposed by Call Admission Control policies. This applies only for inbound calls to a user.
- **Enable Malicious Call Tracing**—Enables users to report malicious calls, which are viewable in the Skype for Business monitoring reports.
- **Associated PSTN Usages**—Allows specific PSTN usage to be accessed by users assigned to this voice policy.
- **Call Forwarding and Simultaneous Ringing PSTN Usages**—Defines which PSTN usages can be accessed during a call-forwarding or simultaneous-ringing situation. Administrators can enforce calls only to internal users or a custom set of PSTN usages.

To create a new voice policy, complete the following steps:

1. Open the Skype for Business Server 2015 Control Panel.
2. Click Voice Routing.
3. Click Voice Policy.
4. A voice policy can be scoped to apply at the site level or pool level. Click New and then select either Site Policy or User Policy.

5. Enter a name and description for the policy.

6. Select or deselect the various calling features discussed previously.

7. Click Select to choose any PSTN usages that should be associated with the voice policy. Highlight any desired PSTN usages and click OK.

8. In the Call Forwarding and Simultaneous Ringing PSTN Usages selection, either leave the default option to use the voice policy's PSTN usages or else choose to route to internal Skype for Business users only or route using custom PSTN usages. After selecting Route Using Custom PSTN Usages, click Select again to choose any PSTN usages that should be associated with the voice policy for forwarding. Highlight any desired PSTN usages and click OK.

9. Click OK to save the voice policy. Figure 17.4 shows an example of a voice policy.

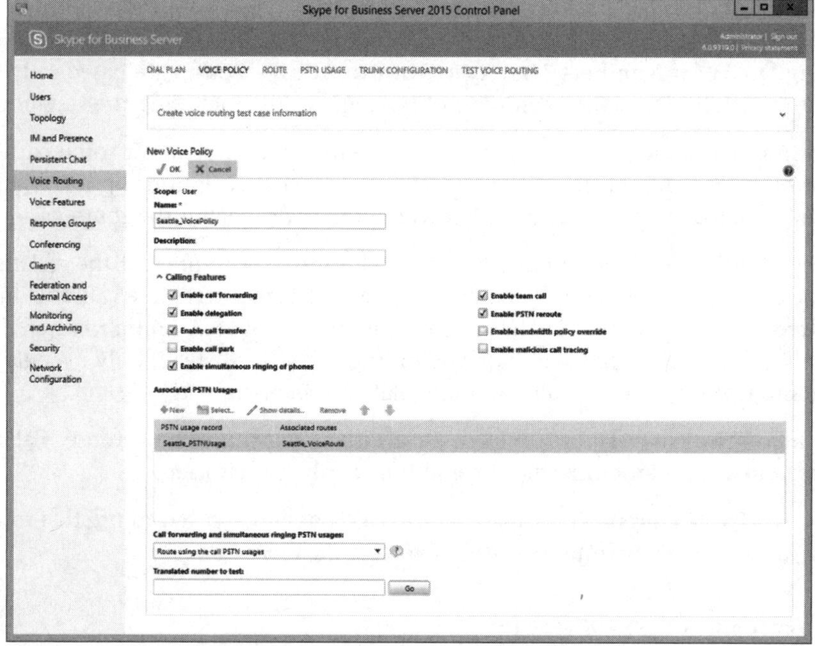

FIGURE 17.4 Voice policy options.

Alternatively, the Skype for Business Server 2015 Management Shell can be used to create a new voice policy through the `New-CsVoicePolicy` cmdlet. Several parameters are not available in the Skype for Business Server 2015 Control Panel interface:

- **`EnableVoicemailEscapeTimer`**—Has a `true` or `false` value that helps ensure that calls to a mobile device that is turned off or out of cellular service do not end up in the mobile device's voicemail.

- `PSTNVoicemailEscapeTimer`—Specifies the amount of time in milliseconds that a call is answered too quickly and is assumed to be the mobile device voicemail. Setting this timer correctly will ensure bypassing of the mobile device's voicemail system and continue to ring the Skype for Business client/endpoint.
- `PreventPSTNTollBypass`—Forces calls between branch sites to leverage the PSTN network instead of WAN connections.
- `VoiceDeploymentMode`—Indicates that the voice policy is for OnPrem, Online, OnlineBasic, or OnPremOnlineHybrid.

Creating Voice Routes

Routes are used in Skype for Business Server 2015 to direct calls through a specified gateway or a set of gateways. Routes are processed after numbers are normalized based on a dial plan, and they determine which gateway will place a call. Creating a new route has the following options:

- **Starting Digits for Numbers That You Want to Allow**—Routes are based only on a matching pattern. Enter the beginning of the digit string, including the + symbol.
- **Exceptions**—In some cases, using route priority might be difficult or some patterns should be excluded from traversing a specific trunk. The Exceptions option enables an administrator to exclude strings that would otherwise match the route pattern.
- **Suppress Caller ID**—This option enables an administrator to prevent the caller's actual caller ID from being passed along on the route. An alternative caller ID must be entered that is typically a main or generic phone number. A limitation here is that this cannot be variable based on the calling party ID. Instead, only a single phone number displayed for all outbound calls can be used.
- **Associated Trunks**—A list of trunks that calls matching this route can use. Calls will be placed in a round-robin fashion if multiple trunks are associated.
- **Associated PSTN Usages**—This specifies the PSTN usages allowed to use this route. Usages are associated with users through voice policies.

To create a new route, follow these steps:

1. Open the Skype for Business Server 2015 Control Panel.
2. Click Voice Routing.
3. Click Route.
4. Click New to create a new route.
5. Enter a name for the route.
6. Enter a description for the route.
7. In the Starting Digits for Numbers That You Want to Allow field, enter the beginning digits that this route should match, and then click Add.

8. Repeat this step for any additional patterns this route should handle.
9. If any numbers that might match this pattern should be excluded, click the Exceptions button and enter those numbers.
10. If the outbound caller ID should be altered for this route, check the box Suppress Caller ID and enter an alternative caller ID.
11. In the Associated Trunks section, click the Add button, select the outbound trunks, and click OK.
12. In the Associated PSTN Usages field, click Select, choose any PSTN usages, and click OK.
13. Click OK to save the route.

The Skype for Business Server 2015 Management Shell can also be used to create new voice routes via the `New-CsVoiceRoute` cmdlet. A Priority parameter is available that can be used to order the listing of voice routes *displayed*, but it should not be used to try to control the order of route *selection*. That should instead be done by ordering PSTN usages within the voice policies.

Creating PSTN Usages

PSTN usage records are associated with routes and voice policies to provide a way to control which users are allowed to use specific routes. Voice policies are applied to users, containing a list of PSTN usages. If a user dials a number that matches a route with one of those PSTN usages, the call is placed. If not, the user is unable to make the call.

To create a new PSTN usage record, follow these steps:

1. On the Edit Voice Policy screen, click the New button in the Associated PSTN Usages section.
2. Enter a name for the PSTN usage.
3. Click the Select button in the Associated Routes section to associate the usage with an existing route. Alternatively, click New to create a new route for the usage.
4. Select a route and click OK.
5. Click OK to save the PSTN usage record.

Creating a Trunk Configuration

A trunk is a logical connection between the Mediation Server role and a PBX, PSTN gateway, or Internet telephony service provider (SIP trunk provider). Trunk configurations can be scoped so that they apply globally, to a Skype for Business Server 2015 site, or to a specific trunk. If these settings vary across devices connected via trunks, a new trunk configuration might be required.

NOTE

These settings are specific to the signaling and features available across a SIP trunk. Use Topology Builder to create the actual SIP trunk definitions.

A new trunk configuration has the following options:

- **Maximum Early Dialogs Supported**—This is the number of forked responses the device on the opposite side of the trunk can support for a single SIP invite that is sent to the Mediation Server.
- **Encryption Support Level**—Required means that Secure Realtime Transport Protocol (SRTP) must be used to encrypt the media traffic on the trunk, Optional means that the Mediation Server attempts to use encryption if the gateway supports it, and Not Supported means that the media traffic is not encrypted on the trunk.
- **Refer Support**—This indicates whether the trunk supports Skype for Business sending the SIP REFER method for call transfers. Third-party call control (3PCC support) on the trunk is another available choice that can be useful for E911 or operator-based SIP services.
- **Enable Media Bypass**—Use this option if Skype for Business endpoints should be allowed to send G.711 streams to the opposite side of the trunk. This configuration is highly recommended to reduce processing on the Mediation Server as the media flow would be carried out directly between the two endpoints in the call.
- **Centralized Media Processing**—Use this option if the signaling and media traffic for this trunk terminate at the same IP address. If Media Bypass is enabled, this option must also be selected.
- **Enable RTP Latching**—RTP latching is an alternative option used to support NAT traversal on a SIP trunk when an SBC or a firewall is incapable of properly fixing the SDP messages for specifying the media IP address.
- **Enable Forward Call History**—Use this to include any forwarded call history across the trunk. This might be required by SIP trunk providers in forwarding or simultaneous ring situations to validate that the call was originally destined to a number associated with the organization.
- **Enable Forward P-Asserted-Identity Data**—Use this if the P-Asserted-Identity (PAI) SIP header should be forwarded across the SIP trunk.
- **Enable Outbound Routing Failover Timer**—This flag places a 10-second limit on responses from the opposite end of the trunk. If the trunk device takes longer than 10 seconds to respond, Skype for Business Server 2015 will try the next available route, or end the call if no more routes are available.
- **Associated PSTN Usages**—This is used for inter-trunk routing in Skype for Business Server 2015. This parameter specifies which usages are allowed to be called through this trunk.

- **Calling Number Translation Rules**—This is used to manipulate the calling party of numbers dialed through this trunk.
- **Called Number Translation Rules**—This is used to manipulate the called party of numbers dialed through this trunk.

To create a new trunk, complete the following steps:

1. Open the Skype for Business Server 2015 Control Panel.
2. Click Voice Routing.
3. Click Trunk Configuration.
4. Click New, and then select either Site or Pool scope.
5. Enter a value for the Maximum Early Dialogs Supported field.
6. Select an encryption support level.
7. Select an option for Refer Support.
8. Optionally, check the box for Enable Media Bypass.
9. Optionally, check the box for Centralized Media Processing.
10. Optionally, check the box for Enable RTP Latching.
11. Optionally, check the box for Enable Forward Call History.
12. Optionally, check the box for Enable Forward P-Asserted-Identity Data.
13. Optionally, check the box for Enable Outbound Routing Failover Timer.
14. Click Select and choose any PSTN usages that can be accessed through this trunk via inter-trunk routing.
15. Select any calling number translation rules and called number translation rules to be associated with the trunk.
16. Click OK to save the trunk configuration.

Alternatively, the Skype for Business Server 2015 Management Shell can be used to create a trunk configuration via the `New-CsTrunkConfiguration` cmdlet. Several parameters are available only through the Skype for Business Server 2015 Management Shell:

- **`EnableMobileTrunkSupport`**—A `true` or `false` value to indicate whether the trunk is a mobile carrier.
- **`EnableSessionTimer`**—A `true` or `false` value to indicate whether each session is timed to determine whether it is currently active. Calls exceeding the session timer without a keep-alive response are dropped.

- `EnableSignalBoost`—A `true` or `false` value to indicate whether the opposite end of the SIP trunk should boost the audio volume of packets sent to Skype for Business. This works only if the opposite end of the SIP trunk supports the feature.
- `RemovePlusFromUri`—A `true` or `false` value to indicate whether Skype for Business Server 2015 should remove the plus prefix (+) from any URIs before sending them across this SIP trunk.
- `RTCPActiveCalls`—A `true` or `false` value to indicate whether the trunk sends RTP Control Protocol packets for active calls.
- `RTCPCallsOnHold`—A `true` or `false` value to indicate whether the trunk sends RTP Control Protocol packets for calls placed on hold.
- `EnableOnlineVoice`—A `true` or `false` value to indicate whether the trunk supports Office 365 hosted voicemail for on-premises Skype for Business users.
- `EnablePIDFLOSupport`—A `true` or `false` value to indicate whether the trunk supports the PIDF-LO location information sent by a Skype for Business client for E911 purposes.

Configuring Inter-Trunk Routing

Inter-trunk routing is a feature introduced in Lync Server 2013 that allows calls to route through the Lync or Skype for Business environment to another platform. This enables administrators to place Skype for Business Server 2015 "in front of" a PBX or another system and still be able to route calls to the downstream, legacy PBX.

Inter-trunk routing is configured by assigning a collection of PSTN usages to a specific trunk configuration. As calls come in to Skype for Business Server 2015 through that trunk, they will be evaluated against the PSTN usage list and potentially routed out another trunk. From an outbound routing perspective, treat the trunk the call was received on as the Skype for Business voice user. Similar to how a user's voice policy processes PSTN usages to select an outbound route, the PSTN usages assigned to that trunk will be processed and look for a matching route.

Creating Translation Rules

Translation rules are a powerful feature first introduced in Lync Server 2013 that enables digit manipulation to a PBX or media gateway. Skype for Business Server 2015 recommends that all numbers be in the E.164 format, but a PBX or gateway might be configured for local dialing or might require special access codes before accepting dial strings. Skype for Business Server 2015 has expanded on the initial functionality and now includes the capability to manipulate the calling party of numbers on a trunk.

Trunk translation rules are assigned to trunk configurations and behave identically to dial plan normalization rules. Administrators can define the translation rules either by using regular expressions or by using the Translation Rule tool.

To create a new translation rule, complete the following steps:

1. On the Edit Trunk Configuration screen, click the New button in the Associated Translation Rules section.
2. Provide a name for the rule and a description for the rule.

NOTE

This example uses the Translation Rule tool, but for more advanced pattern matching, click the Edit button at the bottom of the screen to manually enter the matching pattern and translation rule using regular expressions.

3. In the Starting Digits field, enter the beginning digits of the string to be matched.
4. Specify the length of the string to be matched. Options include matching at least a specific number of digits, matching exactly a certain number of digits, or matching any number of digits.
5. Specify a number of digits to remove after a string matches the starting digits and length.
6. Specify digits to add after the selected number of digits have been removed.
7. Click OK to save the translation rule, and click OK again to save the trunk configuration.

TIP

The Trunk Configuration page now includes a Phone Number to Test field, similar to the Dial Plan page. Use this to validate calling and called number manipulations without resorting to SIP traces.

The `New-CsOutboundCallingNumberTranslationRule` and `New-CsOutboundTranslationRule` cmdlets can also be used to create new rules through the Skype for Business Server 2015 Management Shell.

Publishing Voice Configuration Changes

Changes made through the Skype for Business Server 2015 Control Panel are always entered in a pending state and are not actively used until the changes are committed by selecting Commit All in the Commit drop-down submenu. This enables administrators to fully configure all aspects of voice routing before pushing a single change to the end users.

To publish the uncommitted changes, follow these steps:

1. Open the Skype for Business Server 2015 Control Panel.
2. Click Voice Routing.
3. From any submenu, click the Commit button and then select Commit All.
4. The uncommitted changes are displayed again on this screen. Review the modifications and then click Commit to save the changes.

NOTE

Navigating away from the Voice Routing page before committing changes will cause pending changes to be lost.

Export and Import Voice Configuration

Skype for Business Server 2015 enables administrators to easily export and import the entire voice-routing configuration.

TIP

Always export the voice configuration before making any modifications. This enables an administrator to easily roll back any changes that might have introduced an issue to the environment. This is especially important in organizations with multiple voice administrators because the last administrator to commit a change will overwrite any previous ones.

To export a configuration, follow these steps:

1. Open the Skype for Business Server 2015 Control Panel.
2. Click Voice Routing.
3. From any of the submenu selections, click Actions and then click Export Configuration.
4. Select a location and filename for the configuration file and then click Save.

To import a previously saved configuration file, follow these steps:

1. Open the Skype for Business Server 2015 Control Panel.
2. Click Voice Routing.
3. From any of the submenu selections, click Actions and then click Import Configuration.
4. Locate the configuration file and click Open.
5. Commit the changes using the steps discussed previously.

Creating Test Cases

Test cases enable administrators to verify that the voice configuration works as expected without resorting to testing using a client or SIP traces. Within each test case an administrator can define a source dialed number, a dial plan, a voice policy, and the expected number translation, PSTN usage, and route. To create a new voice routing test case, follow these steps:

1. Open the Skype for Business Server 2015 Control Panel.
2. Click Voice Routing.
3. Click Test Voice Routing.

4. Click the New button to create a new test case.
5. Enter a name for the case.
6. Enter a dialed number to test. This is the number a user enters into the Skype for Business client and is normalized based on the dial plan selected next.
7. Select a dial plan.
8. Select a voice policy.
9. Enter an expected translation. This is the string that the dialed-number-to-test string is expected to be translated to, including the leading + sign. If a normalization rule in the dial plan does not convert the dialed number to this string, the test is recorded as a failure.
10. Select an expected PSTN usage for the test case. This field is optional. If the test case matches a PSTN usage other than the one selected here, the test is recorded as a failure.
11. Select an expected route for the test case. This field is optional. If the voice test matches a route other than the one selected here, the test is recorded as a failure.
12. Click the Run button to begin the test, as shown in Figure 17.5.

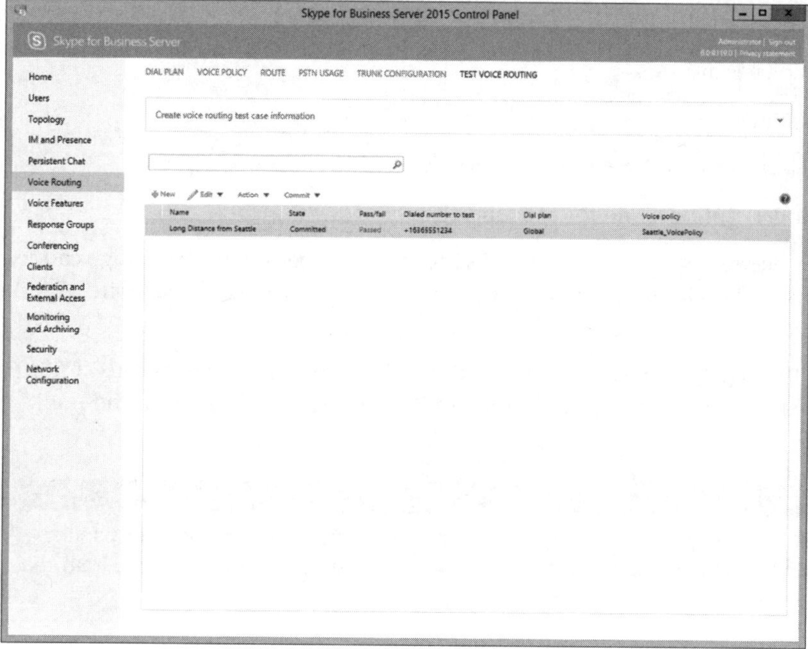

FIGURE 17.5 Creating a voice routing test case.

13. To save the test case, click the OK button.

After each voice routing change, the test case can be run to ensure that call routing is still working as expected. The test case does have some limitations because it will not account for failover routing, but it does provide a simple way to validate basic functionality.

Voice Features

The voice-features section of Skype for Business Server 2015 contains two additions carried over from Lync Server 2013. The first feature, Call Park, enables users to place a call on hold and pick it up from another extension or endpoint. The second feature, Unassigned Numbers, enables the organization to route calls to numbers not associated with a specific user to some other location. Configuration of analog devices is also covered in this section.

Call Park

The Call Park service, first introduced in Lync Server 2010, enables users to place a call on hold and then pick up that same call at another endpoint or location or endpoint extension. To enable a call park, administrators must first configure a call park orbit table or a group of pseudo extension numbers to be used for parking calls. As users park calls, an extension is randomly selected from the orbit table and assigned to the call.

To create a new range for parking calls, follow these steps:

1. Open the Skype for Business Server 2015 Control Panel.
2. Click Voice Features.
3. Click Call Park.
4. Click New to create a new number range.
5. Enter a descriptive name for the range.
6. Enter a beginning and ending number for the number range. The range can use up to nine total digits and can begin with a # or * so as not to overlap with existing extensions.
7. Select the FQDN name of the destination server from the selection box. Calls parked to the specified extension range are handled by the specified Front End pool.

NOTE

If your call park range is associated with a Front End pool to which the user parking/picking up the call isn't associated, the call will traverse the Front End pools from the user to the call park service for routing.

TIP

Numbers in the call park orbit ranges should not be manipulated by normalization rules, or the number might not route to the call park service. An advantage to using the # or * prefix is that it won't overlap with any existing extensions or normalization rules.

Alternatively, the Skype for Business Server 2015 Management Shell can be used to configure a new call park orbit through the `New-CsCallParkOrbit` cmdlet.

Configuration of the following additional call park settings can be performed only in the Skype for Business Server 2015 Management Shell through the `Set-CsCpsConfiguration` cmdlet:

- **`CallPickupTimeoutThreshold`**—The amount of time a call that has been parked waits without answer before it rings back to the endpoint that originally answered. This is to ensure that a call is not parked and then forgotten.
- **`EnableMusicOnHold`**—A `true` or `false` value that determines whether on-hold music is played to the caller while parked.
- **`MaxCallPickupAttempts`**—The number of times a call rings back to the phone that originally answered before it times out and is forwarded to a specified SIP URI.
- **`OnTimeoutURI`**—A SIP URI where calls that are not picked up are forwarded. This is typically an operator or a main line.

Configuring Call Park Music on Hold

Whether on-hold music is played is determined by the `EnableMusicOnHold` parameter, but the actual Music on Hold file is configured using the `Set-CsCallParkMusicOnHoldFile` cmdlet.

First, the `CsCallParkMusicOnHoldFile` cmdlet requires the `AudioFile` parameter in byte format. To make the transfer easy, store the file in a variable, and then pass that variable to the `Content` parameter. Storing the audio file correctly looks like the following example:

```
$AudioFile = Get-Content -ReadCount 0 -Encoding byte <Path and File Name>
```

Then use the `Set-CsCallParkMusicOnHoldFile` cmdlet to assign the audio file:

```
Set-CsCallParkMusicOnHoldFile -Service ApplicationServer:<FQDN of
➥Front End Pool with music file> -Content <Byte[]>
```

Unassigned Numbers

Similar to Call Park, the Unassigned Numbers feature was first introduced in Lync Server 2010 and will be a welcome addition for organizations deploying Skype for Business Server 2015. The Unassigned Numbers range enables companies to send calls that don't match a user to an operator or attendant instead of returning a user-not-found message to the caller.

NOTE

The ranges defined for unassigned numbers can actually contain numbers that *are* assigned to users. Skype for Business prioritizes a user matching the number over the unassigned number range so that it does not interfere with call routing. A best practice is to include each number range used by an organization.

Calls that match an unassigned number range can be routed in only one of two ways: Either an announcement can be played to the caller or the caller can be transferred to an Exchange Unified Messaging auto-attendant extension.

To create a new unassigned number range, follow these steps:

1. Open the Skype for Business Server 2015 Control Panel.
2. Click Voice Features.
3. Click Unassigned Number.
4. Click New.
5. Enter a name identifying this range of numbers.
6. In the first Number Range field, enter the first number in the range.
7. In the second Number Range field, enter the last number in the range.
8. In the Announcement Service field, select either Announcement or Exchange UM. Refer to the appropriate section for each option in the following text to continue the necessary steps.

Playing an Announcement

Before you can use a prerecorded audio file as an announcement, it must be imported using the Skype for Business Server 2015 Management Shell. To import a file, first store the content in a temporary variable:

```
$MyAudioFile = Get-Content <File path and name> -ReadCount 0 -Encoding Byte
```

Then import the announcement file to the file share using the variable:

```
Import-CsAnnouncementFile -Parent service:ApplicationServer:<Front End
➥FQDN> -Content $MyAudioFile
```

Finally, complete the remaining steps:

1. Click Announcement Service.
2. Click Select.
3. Choose an application server in the organization with an audio announcement configured and then click OK.
4. Select an announcement to be played and then click OK.
5. Click OK again to save the range definition.

Transferring to an Exchange UM Auto Attendant

Another option for handling calls destined for unassigned numbers is to route them to an Exchange Unified Messaging auto attendant. To route calls to the auto attendant, follow these steps:

1. Click the auto-attendant phone number.
2. Click Select.
3. Choose a phone number to transfer callers to and then click OK.
4. Click OK again to save the range definition.

> **TIP**
>
> These two options are mutually exclusive within the Unassigned Number configuration, but keep in mind you can always use the custom greetings on an Exchange Unified Messaging auto attendant to also play an announcement for callers.

Configuring Call via Work

In Skype for Business Server 2015, Microsoft have deprecated Remote Call Control (RCC), which was present in Lync Server 2010 and Lync Server 2013, in favor of a new user friendly feature called Call via Work (CvW). Essentially, Call via Work enables the integration of the Skype for Business platform with that of an incumbent private branch exchange (PBX). The Call via Work integration works by bridging two calls together into one seamless call.

For example, suppose User A has a legacy PBX phone and has been enabled for Call via Work on Skype for Business Server 2015. User A places a call for the Skype for Business client to an external callee, User B.

The Skype for Business Server 2015 Mediation Server will be prompted to initiate a call to User A's legacy PBX phone. The caller ID for this leg of the call will display a special number, referred to as the "Admin Callback Number." Once User A answers the call, the Skype for Business Server 2015 Mediation Server will then initiate the call to the external caller, User B. When User B answers, the Skype for Business Server 2015 Mediation Server merges both legs of the call into one.

The Call via Work feature is configured through commands in the Skype for Business Server 2015 Management Shell, as detailed in the following sections.

Create the Call Via Work Global Phone Number

You create the Call Via Work global phone number via the Skype for Business Server 2015 Management Shell's `Set-CsRoutingConfiguration` cmdlet:

```
Set-CsRoutingConfiguration -CallViaWorkCallerId +<PhoneNumber>
```

Here, `CallViaWorkCallerId` is the command parameter for setting the global phone number. Here's an example:

```
Set-CsRoutingConfiguration -CallViaWorkCallerId +123456789
```

Create a Call Via Work Policy

You create a Call Via Work policy via the Skype for Business Server 2015 Management Shell's `New-CsCallViaWorkPolicy` cmdlet:

```
New-CsCallViaWorkPolicy [-Identity] <XdsIdentity>
➥[-Tenant <guid>]
➥[-Enabled <bool>]
➥[-UseAdminCallbackNumber<bool>]
➥[-AdminCallbackNumber <string>]
➥[-InMemory]
➥[-Force]
➥[-WhatIf]
➥[-Confirm]
➥[<CommonParameters>]
```

For example, the following cmdlet creates a Call Via Work policy called `SkypeUnleashed-CvWP` that requires the user to use an admin callback number and sets that callback number to 1-234-567-8901:

```
New-CsCallViaWorkPolicy -Identity Tag:SkypeUnleashedCvWP -Enabled $true
➥-UseAdminCallbackNumber $true -AdminCallbackNumber +12345678901
```

Assign the Call Via Work Policy to a User

You assign the Call Via Work policy to a user via the Skype for Business Server 2015 Management Shell's `Grant-CsCallViaWorkPolicy` cmdlet:

```
Grant-CsCallViaWorkPolicy
➥[-Identity <UserName>]
➥[-PolicyName Tag:<PolicyName>]
```

For example, the following cmdlet assigns the Call Via Work policy `SkypeUnleashedCvWP` to the user named `SkypeUnleashedUser1`:

```
Grant-CsCallViaWorkPolicy -Identity SkypeUnleashedUser1 -PolicyName
➥Tag:SkypeUnleashedCvWP
```

TIP

Because this feature is new in Skype for Business Server 2015, you must be aware of some limitations before proceeding with it:

- If a call is initiated via Call Via Work, it can be only a person-to-person call with no capability to invite others into the conversation.

- If the user has voicemail as part of their desk phone configuration, there is no capability to call the PBX desk phone VM from the Skype for Business client via the Call via Work function.
- For the U.S. user base, E911 call identification is not available through Call via Work.
- Using Call Via Work, users are unable to use Delegation, Team Call, and Response Groups features.

Configuring Analog Devices

Analog devices in Skype for Business Server 2015 are configured using only the Skype for Business Server 2015 Management Shell and are represented as an Active Directory contact object that is SIP enabled. Each contact is explicitly assigned a gateway parameter so Skype for Business Server 2015 will route all calls destined for that analog device to the gateway it is physically attached to.

To create a new analog device and contact object, use the `New-CsAnalogDevice` cmdlet:

```
New-CsAnalogDevice -Gateway <FQDN or IP of IP/PSTN Gateway>
➥-LineUri <String> -OU <Organizational Unit>
➥-RegistrarPool <FQDN of Primary Registrar> -DisplayName
➥<Active Directory Contact Display Name>
➥-DisplayNumber "<Phone Number Display Format>" -AnalogFax <$True | $False>
```

The only difference when configuring a fax device is to set the `AnalogFax` parameter to `$true`. This ensures the media for calls to those devices will never traverse a Skype for Business Mediation Server. Set the `AnalogFax` parameter to `$false` for all other types of analog devices.

Dial plans and voice policies will not be applied locally by an analog device, but can still be assigned so that the server will enforce these policies.

To grant a dial plan to an analog device, use the `Grant-CsDialPlan` cmdlet:

```
Grant-CsDialPlan -Identity <Analog Device Account Name>
➥-PolicyName <Dial Plan Policy Name>
```

To grant a voice policy to an analog device, use the `Grant-CsVoicePolicy` cmdlet:

```
Grant-CsVoicePolicy -Identity <Analog Device Account Name>
➥-PolicyName <Voice Policy Name>
```

Advanced Enterprise Voice Features

This section covers topics that might not be applicable to all deployments and are considered more advanced configuration options. These features include Call Admission Control, Media Bypass, and E911.

Defining the Network Configuration

The first step in configuring the three advanced Enterprise Voice features—Call Admission Control, Media Bypass, and E911—is to define the network configuration. Each of these features relies on the network configuration to work correctly. The following sections explain how to create the necessary network objects before configuring any of the advanced features.

Creating Network Regions

A network region in Skype for Business Server 2015 is generally a large area that encompasses a number of network sites. These are the hubs or backbones of the network. Each region is associated with a central site where a Skype for Business Server 2015 Front End pool exists.

> **TIP**
>
> For a typical MPLS WAN architecture, define the network region as the MPLS cloud and create a network site for each site with an MPLS connection.

A primary driver for creating multiple network regions is to have multiple policy decision points (PDPs) so that the failure of a central site in one region does not impact the capability of a central site in another region to enforce Call Admission Control locally.

Follow these steps to create a new network region:

1. Open the Skype for Business Server 2015 Control Panel.
2. Click Network Configuration.
3. Click Region.
4. Click the New button.
5. Enter a name for the region.
6. Select a central site for the region. This is a site in the topology containing Skype for Business Servers.
7. Select Enable Audio Alternate Path if this region allows audio traffic to use alternative routes. This must be selected for calls to Internet users to succeed.
8. Select Enable Video Alternate Path if this region allows video traffic to use alternative routes. This must be selected for calls to Internet users to succeed.
9. Click Commit. Network sites can be associated later.

Alternatively, a new network region can be created with the Skype for Business Server 2015 Management Shell through the `New-CsNetworkRegion` cmdlet.

Creating Network Sites

A network site represents a particular office location that can be a main headquarters, a branch office, or a collection of buildings in a campus. Although not required, network sites typically have similar bandwidth, and each site is then associated with a network region. The network site serving as the central site defined for the region must also be created because it is not done automatically.

Follow these steps to create a new network site:

1. Open the Skype for Business Server 2015 Control Panel.
2. Click Network Configuration.
3. Click Site.
4. Click the New button.
5. Enter a name for the site.
6. Enter a description for the site.
7. Select a region to associate the site with from the drop-down menu.
8. Bandwidth policy, location policy, and associated subnets can be added later after those objects exist.
9. Click the Commit button.

Alternatively, a new network site can be created with the Skype for Business Server 2015 Management Shell through the `New-CsNetworkSite` cmdlet.

Creating Network Subnets

Network subnets in Skype for Business Server 2015 are the bond that binds a client connection to a specific network site and region. When a Skype for Business client signs in, its network address is delivered to the server, which then associates the client to a network site and region based on the subnet.

Follow these steps to create a new network site:

1. Open the Skype for Business Server 2015 Control Panel.
2. Click Network Configuration.
3. Click Subnet.
4. Click the New button.
5. Enter a subnet ID that is the actual network IP address.
6. Enter a mask for the subnet. This value is the number of bits used for the subnet mask. For example, if the subnet uses a 255.255.255.0 mask, enter **24** for this value.
7. Select a network site ID to associate with the subnet.
8. Enter a description for the subnet.
9. Click Commit.

Alternatively, a new network site can be created with the Skype for Business Server 2015 Management Shell through the `New-CsNetworkSubnet` cmdlet.

TIP

Do not summarize network subnets in this section. Instead, enter the network address for each individual subnet at a particular site. Call Admission Control supports summarization, but Media Bypass does not. To support both features, the subnet ID entered on this screen should always be the network address of the subnet. This is because the Skype for Business client will apply its own local subnet mask to its IP address before sending its network address to the server.

Configuring Call Admission Control

After network regions, sites, and subnets have been created, Call Admission Control can be configured and enabled. Be sure to create all the necessary objects before proceeding with the Call Admission Control configuration. Call Admission Control enables clients to determine whether an audio or video call can actually be established based on available network bandwidth.

Defining Bandwidth Policy

After the required network objects have been created, the next step in configuring Call Admission Control is to create bandwidth policies. Each bandwidth policy defines the total bandwidth limit for a site or region as well as the bandwidth limit per session for both audio and video. The per-session limits refer to one-way traffic.

Follow these steps to create a new bandwidth policy profile:

1. Open the Skype for Business Server 2015 Control Panel.
2. Click Network Configuration.
3. Click Policy Profile.
4. Click the New button.
5. Enter a name for the profile. Usually this is indicative of the link speed of the network to which it is applied, or it matches a network site name.
6. Enter an audio limit in Kbps. This is the collective limit of all audio sessions.
7. Enter an audio session limit in Kbps. This is the limit applied to an individual audio session.
8. Enter a video limit in Kbps. This is the collective limit of all video sessions.
9. Enter a video session limit in Kbps. This is the limit applied to an individual video session.
10. Enter a description for the bandwidth policy profile.
11. Click Commit.

Alternatively, a new bandwidth policy profile can be created using the Skype for Business Server 2015 Management Shell with the `New-CsBandwidthPolicyProfile` cmdlet.

Associate Bandwidth Policy Profile

The next step is to associate the bandwidth policies to network sites. To use the Skype for Business Server 2015 Control Panel to perform this task, follow these steps:

1. Open the Skype for Business Server 2015 Control Panel.
2. Click Network Configuration.
3. Click Site.
4. Highlight an existing site, click the Edit button, and select Show Details.
5. Select a bandwidth policy from the selection box.
6. Click Commit, as shown in Figure 17.6.

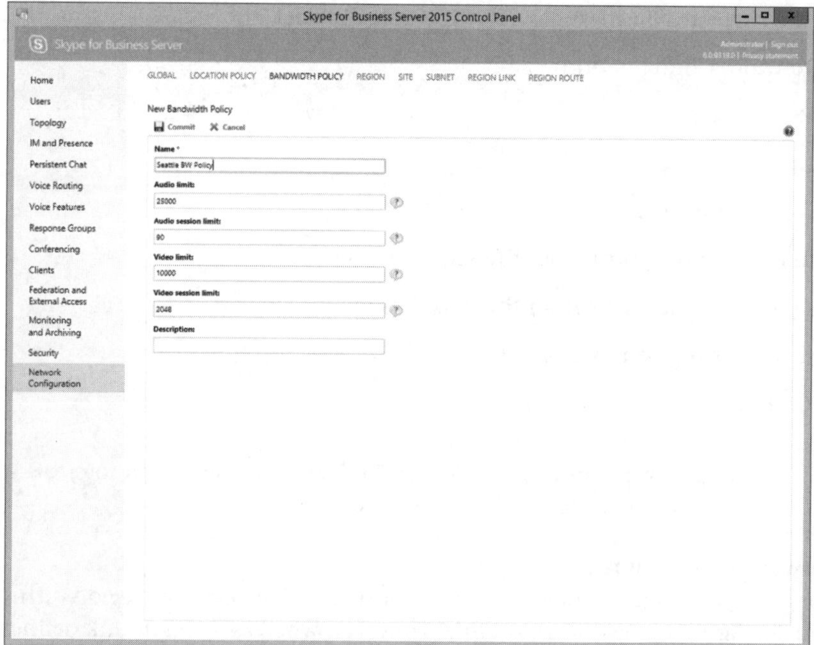

FIGURE 17.6 Creating a bandwidth policy.

7. Repeat these steps to associate each site with a bandwidth policy profile.

Alternatively, to use the Skype for Business Server 2015 Management Shell to associate a bandwidth policy profile with a site, use the `Set-CsNetworkSite` cmdlet.

17

TIP

If a deployment has a single central site, there is no need to define the network region links or network region routes discussed next. Skip to the "Creating Network Inter-Site Policies" section.

Network Region Links

Network region links in Skype for Business Server 2015 represent a bandwidth constraint between two network regions or central sites. Because network regions are generally geographically large, these links apply to a number of sites when communicating across regions. For example, a region link might be defined between North America and Europe for an organization. Region links are created between only two regions and can have a bandwidth policy profile associated. The bandwidth policy can be an existing policy, or an administrator can create a new policy specifically for the region link.

To create a new network region link, follow these steps:

1. Open the Skype for Business Server 2015 Control Panel.
2. Click Network Configuration.
3. Click Region Link.
4. Click the New button.
5. Enter a name for the link.
6. Choose network region #1 from the selection menu.
7. Choose network region #2 from the selection menu.
8. Choose an existing bandwidth policy.
9. Click Commit.

Alternatively, to use the Skype for Business Server 2015 Management Shell to create a network region link, use the `New-CsNetworkRegionLink` cmdlet.

Creating Network Region Routes

A network region route object represents the network path between two regions. This might sound similar to a network region link. However, whereas a region link defines bandwidth on a direct link, a route defines only the network path between regions.

In many cases, such as a direct connection, there is a 1:1 ratio between region links and region routes, but this might differ when direct links between regions do not exist. For example, consider a scenario in which North America and Europe have direct connectivity, and Europe and Asia also have direct connectivity, each with network region links defined. Because North America and Asia do not have direct connectivity, a network region route must be created to indicate that calls between those two regions must traverse through Europe.

In simple terms, a region route is a list of the region links traversed when communication is taking place between two regions. When a call traverses multiple region links, the bandwidth policy of each link is applied.

To create a new network region route, follow these steps:

1. Open the Skype for Business Server 2015 Control Panel.
2. Click Network Configuration.
3. Click Region Route.
4. Click the New button.
5. Enter a name for the route.
6. Choose network region #1 from the selection menu.
7. Choose network region #2 from the selection menu.
8. Click the Add button, select a region link, and click OK.
9. Repeat for any additional region links that will be traversed by this path.
10. Click Commit.

Alternatively, to use the Skype for Business Server 2015 Management Shell to create a network region route, use the `New-CsNetworkInterRegionRoute` cmdlet.

Creating Network Inter-Site Policies

Network inter-site policies are used to define a bandwidth policy between two sites that are connected to the same region, but that also have a direct link to each other. In some cases this link might have additional WAN bandwidth that can be leveraged for calls, or that might even be preferred over a call traversing through the central site. Similar to a region link, two sites are defined and a bandwidth policy profile is associated with the link. It's very possible that no network inter-site policies need to be created. Network inter-site policies can be created only using the Skype for Business Server 2015 Management Shell.

For each inter-site policy required, use the following syntax:

```
New-CSNetworkInterSitePolicy -InterNetworkSitePolicyID <Inter-Site Policy Name>
➥-NetworkSiteID1 <Network Site 1 ID> -NetworkSiteID2 <Network Site 2 ID>
➥-BWPolicyProfileID <Bandwidth Policy Profile ID>
```

Enabling Call Admission Control

After all the required objects and links are configured, the final step in the process is to actually enable Call Admission Control.

To enable the feature, follow these steps:

1. Open the Skype for Business Server 2015 Control Panel.
2. Click Network Configuration.
3. Click Global.
4. Highlight the global policy, click Edit, and then select Show Details.
5. Check the box Enable Call Admission Control.
6. Click Commit.

Alternatively, the Skype for Business Server 2015 Management Shell cmdlet `Set-CsNetworkConfiguration` can be used to enable Call Admission Control.

Media Bypass

Media Bypass is a feature that allows Skype for Business endpoints to send a G.711 audio stream directly to a device on the opposite side of a trunk, as opposed to sending the media through a Mediation Server. For Media Bypass to work, the following requirements must be met:

- Media Bypass must be enabled on the SIP trunk configuration. The centralized media processing option must also be enabled on the trunk.
- Media Bypass must be enabled at a global level.

Enabling Media Bypass

Media Bypass must be enabled at a global level before clients attempt to use the bypass features. An administrator has two options to choose from when enabling Media Bypass:

- **Always Bypass**—This choice instructs clients to always bypass the Mediation Server role, but works only if a trunk configuration also has the Enable Media Bypass option selected. All Skype for Business clients must have good network connectivity to the other end of every single SIP trunk for this option to be effective. This option might make sense in very small deployments or for multiple global Skype for Business pools.
- **Use Sites and Region Configuration**—This choice is a better option when Skype for Business endpoints might not have good network connectivity to each SIP trunk; it enables the network region and site configuration to limit when Media Bypass is actually used. Enable Bypass for Non-Mapped Sites can be selected only if Use Sites and Region Configuration is selected first. This allows for sites and subnets not explicitly configured to still use Media Bypass.

NOTE

If Call Admission Control is enabled, the only available option for Media Bypass is to use the network site and region configuration.

To select a choice in enabling Media Bypass, follow these steps:

1. Open the Skype for Business Server 2015 Control Panel.
2. Click Network Configuration.
3. Click Global.
4. Highlight the global policy, click Edit, and then select Show Details.
5. Check the box Enable Media Bypass.
6. Select either Always Bypass or Use Sites and Region Configuration.
7. If selecting Use Sites and Region Configuration, optionally check the box Enable Bypass for Non-Mapped Sites.
8. Click Commit.

Creating Bypass IDs

All Skype for Business network sites have a Bypass ID parameter assigned that is used to determine whether a client can use Media Bypass between itself and a trunk. This determination is based on comparing the Bypass ID of the trunk with the Bypass ID of the Skype for Business endpoint.

In a new environment, all network sites share the same Bypass ID, which means Media Bypass can be used between any site. After a site has a bandwidth policy applied, it is assigned a unique Bypass ID, but the other sites all retain the same, shared Bypass ID.

Media Bypass is blocked only if there is a bandwidth constraint between the two sites, so to prevent Media Bypass from being used between two sites, an administrator must associate a bandwidth policy to either network site. The actual values of the bandwidth policy don't matter, but as long as a bandwidth policy is applied, a unique Bypass ID is generated for the site.

If the Bypass IDs of the client and trunk match, Media Bypass can be used. If they are different, Skype for Business assumes that there is bandwidth constraint between the sites and will not use Media Bypass for the call to help preserve bandwidth.

Configuring E911

Enhanced 911 (E911) is a feature that provides the caller's telephone number and street address to a emergency services dispatcher automatically. This is an advantage over a very basic 911 service that requires the caller to provide an address where assistance is required.

Skype for Business Server 2015 maintains a Location Information Service (LIS) database for an organization that associates specific gateways, subnets, and wireless SSIDs with physical location addresses. Skype for Business Server 2015 supports E911 with support from a certified emergency services provider or through an ELIN certified media gateway. Emergency calls are routed through these options to the emergency services provider.

Configuring Site Locations

Skype for Business Server 2015 enables clients to detect their locations on a network automatically, but a database of locations in the organization must be defined in advance for this automation to work correctly. Skype for Business can match clients to a street address location based on the following network objects:

- **Wireless Access Point**—Matches a wireless access point based on the Basic Service Set Identifier (BSSID) of the wireless access point.
- **Subnet**—Matches a site based on the subnet network address of the Skype for Business endpoint.
- **Switch and Port**—Matches a unique port on a switch based on the switch's MAC address and the port ID. This requires the switch to support LLDP-MED and works only with Lync Phone Edition devices and Skype for Business clients running on Windows 8.
- **Switch**—Matches a switch based on the chassis ID MAC address. The Skype for Business endpoint sends its own IP and MAC address to the Skype for Business Server, which then leverages a third-party service to perform a lookup and determine which switch that device is attached to. The MAC address of the switch in the response is then matched to the MAC defined for a specific switch and location in the LIS.

When defining each of the previous objects, they can be associated with an address. The address parameters configurable are listed here:

- **`City`**—The location city; for example, `Seattle`.
- **`CompanyName`**—The name of the company at this location; for example, `Company ABC`.
- **`Country`**—The two-character location country; for example, `US`.
- **`HouseNumber`**—The location address number; for example, `123`.
- **`HouseNumberSuffix`**—Additional information after the address number; for example, **B**.
- **`Location`**—A more detailed location after the street number, such as a suite or specific floor; for example, `Suite 456`.
- **`PostalCode`**—The location postal code; for example, `12345`.
- **`PostDirectional`**—Any directional information after the street address; for example, `NE`.
- **`PreDirectional`**—Any directional information before the street address; for example, `SW`.
- **`State`**—The location state; for example, `CA`.
- **`StreetName`**—The location street name; for example, `Market`.
- **`StreetSuffix`**—The location street suffix; for example, `Street` or `Avenue`.

TIP

The Skype for Business client displays the text for a matching location and city in the Location field. Using the previous example, a client would show that its own location is "Suite 456 Seattle."

All the location information must be entered through the Skype for Business Server 2015 Management Shell. Creating each object is done through the following cmdlets:

- `Set-CsLisWirelessAccessPoint`
- `Set-CsLisSubnet`
- `Set-CsLisPort`
- `Set-CsLisSwitch`

For example, to create a new subnet and location definition, use this:

```
Set-CsLisSubnet -Subnet 192.168.22.0 -Description "Client Subnet"
➥-CompanyName "Company ABC" -HouseNumber 123 -Location "
➥Suite 456" -StreetName "Fake" -StreetSuffix "Avenue"
➥-City "Seattle" -State CA -PostalCode 12345 -Country US
```

Because importing every single wireless access point, subnet, port, or switch manually would be a tedious task, defining all the required objects in advance through a CSV file can help speed up the process of building the LIS database. The CSV file can then be used with the Skype for Business Server 2015 Management Shell for a bulk-import process.

After all the Location Information Service objects have been created, the configuration must be published before becoming active. To publish the location database, run the following cmdlet from the Skype for Business Server 2015 Management Shell:

```
Publish-CsLisConfiguration
```

Validating Civic Addresses

Skype for Business Server 2015 cannot route emergency calls with location information directly by itself and instead relies on an E911 service provider to route the calls appropriately. To bypass the step of an E911 operator validating an address, all address information can be validated in advance. This validation is done through a web service URL supplied by the service provider.

To configure a service provider, use the following cmdlet:

```
Set-CsLisServiceProvider -ServiceProviderName <Name> -ValidationServiceUrl
➥<URL from Provider> -CertFileName <Certificate path and filename issued
➥by provider> -Password <Password issued by provider>
```

After a provider has been assigned, each address in the location database should be validated with the provider. To run a test against all existing addresses, use the following cmdlet:

```
Get-CsLisCivicAddress | Test-CsLisCivicAddress -UpdateValidationStatus
```

`UpdateValidationStatus` also stamps each address with an attribute indicating that it has been verified successfully.

Create Location Policy

For Skype for Business Server 2015 to support location information objects, users must be associated with a location policy that allows these features. Location policies can exist at the global, site, or user level. When creating a location policy, an administrator has the following options:

- **Enable Enhanced Emergency Services**—This setting enables the client for E911.
- **Location**—This setting takes effect only if the Enable Enhanced Emergency Services setting is enabled, and it is used when a Skype for Business client cannot determine a location automatically. Setting this value to No means the user is not prompted for a location. A value of Yes means the user sees a visible red error in the location field, so they enter the information. Disclaimer means the user is prompted for a location and cannot dismiss the prompt until a location is entered. Users cannot place any calls except to emergency services unless entering a location with this setting.
- **Use Location for Emergency Services Only**—Location information gathered from Skype for Business clients can also be shared with team members. Selecting this option prevents Skype for Business from sharing location information between users.
- **PSTN Usage**—This is the PSTN usage associated with placing emergency calls. This determines which voice routes are used for emergency calls associated with this location policy. This usage must already exist, so be sure to define a new emergency services usage before configuring a location policy.
- **Emergency Dial Number**—This is the number sent by Skype for Business to match a route within the emergency services PSTN usage. Do not include the leading + sign.
- **Emergency Dial Mask**—This is a list of semicolon-separated dial strings that users might use to dial emergency services. This can include an external access prefix or additional codes sometimes used to call emergency services.
- **Notification URI**—This is the SIP URI that receives an instant message notification when an emergency call is placed. It should contain the "sip:" prefix. This can be useful for security teams to receive notification that a user has called emergency services.

- **Conference URI**—This is the SIP URI that should be conferenced into the call when an emergency call is placed. It should contain the "sip:" prefix and can also be a phone number.
- **Conference Mode**—This specifies whether the conference URI contact can be included in the call using one-way or two-way communication. One-way means the conference URI can only listen to the call as it occurs, and two-way means the contact can participate.

To create a new location policy, follow these steps:

1. Open the Skype for Business Server 2015 Control Panel.
2. Click Network Configuration.
3. Click Location Policy.
4. Click New and select either Site Policy or User Policy.
5. Check the box Enable Enhanced Emergency Services to enable the feature.
6. Select a location specification requirement policy.
7. Select whether to use location for emergency services only.
8. Enter an emergency dial number.
9. Enter any emergency dial masks, separated by semicolons.
10. Enter a notification URI, if necessary.
11. Enter a conference URI, if necessary.

12. Select a conference mode.
13. Click Commit, as shown in Figure 17.7.

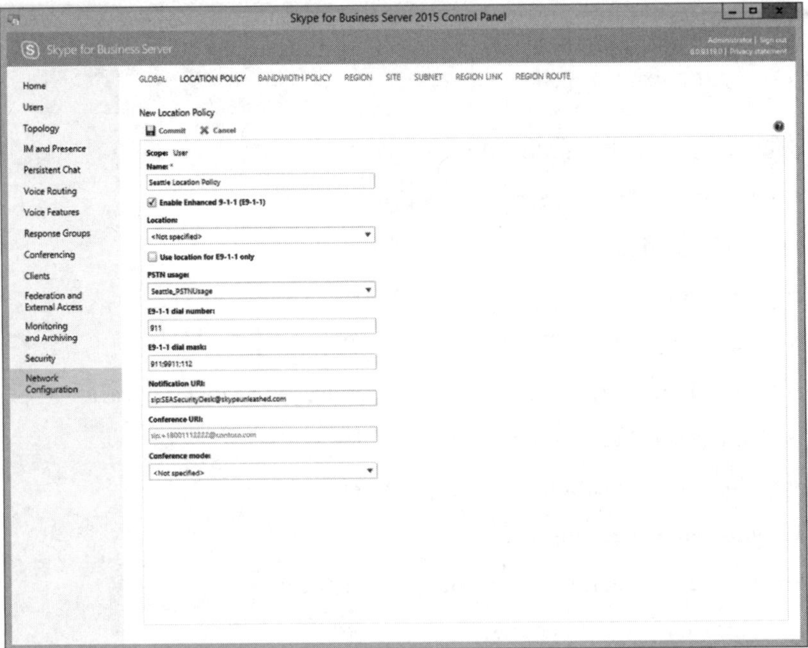

FIGURE 17.7 Creating a location policy.

Alternatively, the Skype for Business Server 2015 Management Shell can be used to create a location policy through the `New-CsLocationPolicy` cmdlet.

Dial-in Conferencing

Leveraging the Skype for Business Server 2015 dial-in conferencing features depends greatly on the voice routing and trunk configuration already in place. The actual steps for adding dial-in conferencing to a functional voice infrastructure is not difficult and can be provisioned quickly. This section covers the different aspects of the configuration process.

Creating Dial-in Conferencing Regions

Each dial plan created can be associated with a dial-in conferencing region, which is what determines the access numbers displayed for Online Meeting invitations. Despite the identical and overused terminology, regions are not actually tied to the network region definitions used for the Call Admission Control and Media Bypass features. Dial-in conferencing regions can be defined and created only through a dial plan object in the voice routing section, as described earlier in this chapter.

Creating Dial-in Access Numbers

Dial-in access numbers are the phone numbers users dial to reach the audio conferencing service. For each access number, a SIP-enabled contact object is created within Active Directory.

Each dial-in access number has a dial-in conferencing region associated that ties it to a particular dial plan. The following options are available when you are creating a dial-in access number:

- **Display Number**—The text format of the number as it is displayed to users in the Online Meeting invitation.
- **Display Name**—The name of the Active Directory contact created for the access number.
- **Line URI**—The phone number assigned to the dial-in access contact. This should be specified in E.164 format with the "tel:" prefix.
- **SIP URI**—The SIP URI assigned to the contact object. It must be unique within the organization and use a "sip:" prefix.
- **Pool**—The pool where the contact object is homed.
- **Primary Language**—The primary language used to make conferencing announcements.
- **Secondary Languages**—Any secondary language choices for conferencing announcements. Up to four secondary languages can be specified.
- **Associated Regions**—Dial plan regions that are associated with the dial-in access number. Multiple regions can be associated to a single number, or a region can be associated to multiple dial-in access numbers.

Perform the following steps to create a new dial-in access number:

1. Open the Skype for Business Server 2015 Control Panel.
2. Click Conferencing.
3. Click Dial-in Access Number.
4. Click New.
5. Enter a display number for the contact.
6. Enter a display name for the contact.
7. Enter a line URI in E.164 format using a "tel:" prefix.
8. Enter a SIP URI using a "sip:" prefix and select a SIP domain internal to the organization.
9. Select a pool where the object will be homed.
10. Select a primary language for the conference announcements.

11. Click the Add button and select up to four secondary languages.
12. Click the Add button and select associated regions for the dial-in access number.
13. Click Commit when finished.

To use the Skype for Business Server 2015 Management Shell to create the dial-in access number, use the `New-CsDialInConferencingAccessNumber` cmdlet.

Modifying a Dial-in Access Number Ordering

If you are an organization with many dial-in access numbers associated within your regions, based on the automatic ID numbering used by Skype for Business Server 2015, you might have a requirement to reorder the dial-in conferencing numbers presented within the meeting scheduling.

To perform the steps to reorder the dial-in access numbers, it is required to use the Skype for Business Server 2015 Management Shell cmdlet `Get-CSDialinConferencingAccessNumber`:

```
Get-CSDialinConferencingAccessNumber -Region "Seattle" | format-list *
```

For example, if you had three dial-in conference numbers associated with the Seattle regions, you would run the following set of commands and specify the priority order (with 0 being the highest priority):

```
Set-CsDialInConferencingAccessNumber -Identity sip:SEA1dialin@skypeunleashed.com
➥-Priority 0 -ReorderedRegion "Seattle"
Set-CsDialInConferencingAccessNumber -Identity sip:SEA2dialin@skypeunleashed.com
➥-Priority 1 -ReorderedRegion "Seattle"
Set-CsDialInConferencingAccessNumber -Identity sip:SEA3dialin@skypeunleashed.com
➥-Priority 2 -ReorderedRegion "Seattle"
```

Modifying a Conferencing Policy

After a dial-in access number is configured, it does not appear in Online Meeting invitations unless the conference organizer's conferencing policy allows PSTN dial-in. The key settings in the conferencing policy that should be reviewed include the following:

- **Allow Participants to Invite Anonymous Users**—Controls whether anonymous, unauthenticated users from outside the organization can participate in conferences. Although this setting is not required to be enabled, if it is not selected, it limits the use of audio conferencing to only users inside the organization.
- **Enable PSTN Dial-in Conferencing**—Must be enabled for dial-in conferencing to function. It controls whether dial-in conferencing is allowed for meetings scheduled by users assigned this policy.

- **Allow Anonymous Participants to Dial Out**—Controls whether anonymous, unauthenticated users from outside the organization can join an audio conference and be called at a PSTN number by the conferencing service. Users may still dial in to the conferencing service if this option is not selected, but may not request the conferencing service call them.
- **Allow Participants Not Enabled for Enterprise Voice to Dial Out**—Controls whether authenticated users without Enterprise Voice can request that the conferencing service call them to join the conference.

To verify whether these settings are configured correctly, perform the following steps:

1. Open the Skype for Business Server 2015 Control Panel.
2. Click Conferencing.
3. Click Conferencing Policy.
4. Highlight an existing conferencing policy, click Edit, and select Show Details.
5. Verify that the Allow Participants to Invite Anonymous Users option is set.
6. Verify that the Enable PSTN Dial-in Conferencing option is set.
7. Verify that the Allow Anonymous Users to Dial Out option is set.
8. Verify that the Allow Participants Not Enabled for Enterprise Voice to Dial Out option is set.
9. Click Commit.

The Skype for Business Server 2015 Management Shell can also be used to configure these settings with the `Set-CsConferencingPolicy` cmdlet.

Modifying PIN Policies

Skype for Business Server 2015 enables users to join audio conferences through a plethora of devices and options, such as the Skype for Business client, Skype for Business Web application, Skype for Business smartphone application, or by simply dialing in from a traditional terrestrial phone. When dialing from a phone, the users are unauthenticated until they enter an extension and matching PIN. This is required because when joining conferences from a Skype for Business client, users are already authenticated after passing Active Directory credentials to log in to Skype for Business. When the user is dialing in from a phone, the PIN and extension provide a method for Skype for Business Server 2015 to still validate the user as internal to the organization. Administrators can define PIN policies that apply globally to all users, only to a specific site, or to assigned user accounts.

NOTE

The PIN policy discussed here is separate from an organization's PIN for Exchange Unified Messaging. The PINs between the two systems are not synchronized in any way, and users must maintain them separately. For that reason, strong end-user communication is encouraged so that the users understand the difference and the need to change PINs in both locations. Like Lync Server 2013, Skype for Business Server 2015 doesn't have a mechanism to synchronize the users' PIN or policy between Skype for Business Server 2015 dial-in conferencing and Exchange Server Unified Messaging policies.

When configuring a PIN policy, administrators have the following options:

- **Minimum PIN Length**—The minimum number of digits a user may use for a PIN. Only a minimum value can be specified, so users may choose any number of digits for their PIN equal to or more than this value.
- **Maximum Logon Attempts**—The number of times a user may attempt to authenticate with a PIN before the PIN is locked out and must be reset by an administrator. If a user successfully authenticates with a PIN, this counter is reset to zero.
- **PIN Expiration**—A setting that determines whether a PIN will expire. The PIN expiration value is set in days. Using a value of 0 for PIN expiration means the user PINs will never expire.
- **PIN History Count**—The number of PINs the system remembers before a user is allowed to reuse a PIN.
- **Allow Common Patterns**—A setting that determines whether commonly used patterns are allowed for a PIN. Examples of common patterns are repeating digits, four consecutive digits, and PINs that match a user's phone number or extension.

To create a new PIN policy, perform the following steps:

1. Open the Skype for Business Server 2015 Control Panel.
2. Click Conferencing.
3. Click PIN Policy.
4. Click New and select either Site Policy or User Policy.
5. Select a minimum PIN length.
6. Select whether to specify maximum logon attempts and enter a maximum number of attempts.
7. Select whether to enable the PIN Expiration option and enter a number of days.
8. Select whether to enable the Allow Common Patterns option.
9. Click Commit when complete.

To create a new PIN policy using the Skype for Business Server 2015 Management Shell, use the `New-CsPinPolicy` cmdlet.

Modifying Meeting Configuration

The meeting configuration commands in Skype for Business Server 2015 are provided to give organizations more control over what types of meetings are allowed to occur. When a meeting configuration is being modified, the following options are available:

- **PSTN Callers Bypass Lobby**—Controls whether users who dial in to the conference from a PSTN phone are automatically entered into the meeting. If this option is not enabled, a presenter must admit all users in the lobby before they can participate in the conference. This generally is not an obstacle when the presenter is using Skype for Business and can visibly see that users are waiting in a lobby, but consider a scenario in which presenters dial in from a PSTN number and do not have this visual clue. Presenters can use DTMF controls to admit users in the lobby, but not all users know this feature or find it easy to use.
- **Designate as Presenter**—Controls which users can be promoted as presenters throughout the meeting. This can be set to no one, people from inside the organization, or everyone.
- **Assigned Conference Type by Default**—Controls whether meetings are created with unique meeting IDs. An assigned conference in Skype for Business is a static, persistent URL and conference ID that each user has. If set to `true`, each scheduled meeting has the same ID by default. If set to `false`, each meeting generates a unique ID. Using a unique ID can be helpful so that if a user has back-to-back meetings, attendees from the second meeting do not accidentally join the first meeting.
- **Admit Anonymous Users by Default**—Controls whether anonymous, unauthenticated users are admitted into meetings by default.
- **Logo URL**—Provides a custom image that is inserted in Online Meeting invitations.
- **Help URL**—Provides a custom URL users can access to receive assistance with Online Meetings.
- **Legal Text URL**—Provides a custom URL users can access to read legal disclaimer information.
- **Custom Footer Text**—Adds text to the end of Online Meeting invitations.

To configure the meeting configuration, perform the following steps:

1. Open the Skype for Business Server 2015 Control Panel.
2. Click Conferencing.
3. Click Meeting Configuration.
4. Highlight an existing configuration, click Edit, and select Show Details.
5. Select whether PSTN callers can bypass lobby.
6. Select a group to designate as the presenter.
7. Select whether to use the assigned conference type by default.

8. Select whether to admit anonymous users by default.
9. Optionally, enter custom URLs for Logo URL, Help URL, and Legal Text URL.
10. Optionally, enter any custom footer text.
11. Click Commit when complete.

Two parameters for the meeting configuration are available only through the `Set-CsMeetingConfiguration` cmdlet:

- **`RequireRoomSystemsAuthorization`**—A `true` or `false` value indicating whether all users must authenticate before joining a meeting using a Skype for Business room system video endpoint.
- **`EnableAssignedConferenceType`**—A `true` or `false` value indicating whether the persistent, static conference IDs are allowed to be used.

Modifying Conference Announcements

Conference announcement settings in Skype for Business Server 2015 control what occurs when participants join or leave a meeting. These settings can be configured at a global level or assigned to a specific site.

NOTE

Enabling or disabling the announcements is a default preference that can be passed to users. However, users can change this default as they desire.

When you are configuring conferencing announcements, the following options are available:

- **Enable Name Recording**—Controls whether users are prompted to record their name before joining the conference. Internal users are not prompted to record a name, and their name is played through the text-to-speech engine instead.
- **Entry and Exit Announcements Type**—Defines the type of announcement played when attendees join or leave the meeting. The options are to use the person's name or to simply play a tone.
- **Entry and Exit Announcements Enabled by Default**—Controls whether announcements are enabled or disabled by default for new Skype for Business user accounts. This is simply a default setting passed to users that they might change.

The conference announcement settings can be configured only through the Skype for Business Server 2015 Management Shell using the following syntax:

```
Set-CsDialInConferencingConfiguration -Identity <Identity>
➥-EnableNameRecording <$True | $False> -EntryExitAnnouncementsEnabledByDefault
➥<$True | $False> -EntryExitAnnouncementsType <UseNames | ToneOnly >
```

Customizing DTMF Commands

Skype for Business Server 2015 enables attendees to use DTMF commands when in a conference to control certain features normally visible within a Skype for Business client. For example, users can send DTMF tones that might mute their microphone, play an attendee roll call, or lock the conference. Usually these features can be accessed through a Skype for Business client, but without a visible user interface, DTMF tones must be used. By default, a global configuration of the key mappings is assigned to all users. If required, administrators can modify the global configuration or modify the key mappings on a per-site basis.

The following DTMF commands are available to assign to phone keys:

- **`AdmitAll`**—Enables users waiting in the lobby to join the meeting. This key is not enabled by default. Assign a value to enable this feature.
- **`AudienceMuteCommand`**—Mutes all microphones except the presenter. This key is 4 by default.
- **`CommandCharacter`**—Designates the key pressed before entering any other DTMF command digits. This key is * by default.
- **`EnableDisableAnnouncementsCommand`**—Toggles whether entry and exit announcements are played during the meeting. This key is 9 by default.
- **`HelpCommand`**—Plays a summary of the DTMF commands available to a user. This key is 1 by default.
- **`LockUnlockConferenceCommand`**—Toggles whether the audio conference is locked or unlocked to allow new participants to join. This key is 7 by default.
- **`MuteUnmuteCommand`**—Toggles whether the participant's audio microphone is muted or unmuted. This key is 6 by default.
- **`PrivateRollCallCommand`**—Plays a roll call of participants only to the user issuing the command. This key is 3 by default.

To set the DTMF values, an administrator must use the following Skype for Business Server 2015 Management Shell syntax:

```
Set-CsDialInConferencingDtmfConfiguration -Identity <Global or site:<Site Name>
➥-AdmitAll <Digit> -AudienceMuteCommand <Digit> -CommandCharacter <Digit>
➥-EnableDisableAnnouncementsCommand <Digit> -HelpCommand <Digit>
➥-LockUnlockConferenceCommand <Digit> -MuteUnmuteCommand <Digit>
➥-PrivateRollCallCommand <Digit>
```

Response Groups

The Response Groups feature was first introduced in Office Communications Server 2007 R2 and was enhanced in Lync Server 2010 and remains largely unchanged in Skype for Business Server 2015. A Response Group is a method to route calls to a specific queue or set of agents. Some consider Response Groups to be on a similar level as hunt groups from traditional telephony, but an administrator typically has much greater control over a Response Group than a PBX hunt group. Many PBXs call this feature Automatic Call Distribution (ACD).

Response Groups in Skype for Business Server 2015 are composed of the following components:

- **Agent groups**—Agent groups contain a specified set of user accounts that belong to a Response Group. How calls are routed in the group and what options a member has are configured at the agent group level.
- **Queues**—A queue is an object that holds callers as they dial in to the Response Group. A queue can contain multiple agent groups, or sometimes just a single agent group is included. Settings such as timeouts and call capacity are configured at the queue level.
- **Workflows**—Workflows are the glue that ties together the agent groups and the queues. The workflow settings determine how a caller reaches a specific queue depending on question responses, time of day, or holidays.

The following sections explain each of these components in more detail and discuss how to configure a complete Response Group.

Configuring Agent Groups

An agent group is a collection of users, which can be distribution groups or individual user accounts. The following options are available during the creation of an agent group:

- **Participation Policy**—Determines whether agents need to sign in or out of the group manually. Selecting Formal here means users have to manually enter and leave the agent group through a web page. Informal means the agents are automatically included in the group as long as they are signed in to Skype for Business.
- **Alert Time**—Sets the number of seconds for which a call rings an agent before attempting to ring the next agent.
- **Routing Method**—Specifies how the calls are routed among agents in the group. Options include Longest Idle, Parallel, Round Robin, Serial, and Attendant.
- **Agents**—Specifies the user accounts or a distribution group used for the agent group membership. Keep in mind that distribution groups do not recognize nested groups and that only one distribution group can be specified.

NOTE

Response Group agents must be Enterprise Voice users. Users enabled for Skype for Business services but not Enterprise Voice cannot be selected to participate in an agent group.

Understanding Routing Methods in Agent Groups

The routing methods are a key part of defining how agents take calls. These options are separated here for some additional clarity on behavior:

- **Longest Idle**—The call is routed to the agent who has had a Presence status of Available the longest without taking a call. For example, if three agents are part of the agent group and one agent is "Busy" while two are "Available," the call is routed to the user who has had the Available presence the longest.
- **Parallel**—This rings all agents at the same time. The agent who accepts the call first is placed in a conversation with the caller.
- **Round Robin**—Call requests are evenly sent to agents. Assuming that three agents exist, the first call goes to Agent A, the second to Agent B, and the third to Agent C. The fourth call rings Agent A again.
- **Serial**—Calls are sent to agents in the order defined in the agent list. Assuming that three agents exist, the first call goes to Agent A. The next call again attempts to ring Agent A, and if Agent A is unavailable, the call then goes to Agent B. The difference from round-robin distribution is that the next call follows the same order, starting with Agent A again.
- **Attendant**—Calls are routed to all agents just as in parallel fashion, but this option includes agents who are busy or currently in a call. Calls are not routed to agents with a status of Do Not Disturb.

Creating an Agent Group

To create a new agent group, follow these steps:

1. Open the Skype for Business Server 2015 Control Panel.
2. Click Response Groups.
3. Click Group.
4. Click New.
5. Select an application server and click OK.
6. Enter a name for the group.
7. Enter a description for the group.
8. Select a participation policy for the agents.
9. Specify the alert time (in seconds) for how long a call will ring an agent.
10. Select a routing method for the group.
11. If using a distribution list for the agent list, select the Use an Existing Email Distribution List option and then enter the distribution list address.
12. If manually adding agents to the group, select Define a Custom Group of Agents and click the Select button.

13. Enter a search for users and click Find.
14. Highlight the selected user and click OK.
15. Repeat for any additional users who will be part of the agent group.
16. Click Commit after all agents have been added.

Alternatively, the Skype for Business Server 2015 Management Shell can be used to create a new agent group through the `New-CsRgsAgentGroup` cmdlet.

Configuring Queues

A Response Group queue is used to hold calls while waiting for an agent to answer. A queue can contain a single agent group, or administrators can add multiple agent groups to a queue. The following options are available during the creation of a queue:

- **Groups**—The agent groups responsible for answering calls in this queue. The groups can be ordered so that certain groups are attempted before others.
- **Enable Queue Time-out**—A determination of whether a time limit is enforced when callers wait for an agent.
- **Time-out Period**—The number of seconds a caller can remain in the queue before timing out.
- **Enable Queue Overflow**—A determination of whether the queue supports a maximum number of calls.
- **Maximum Number of Calls**—The number of calls that can be in the queue at any given time.
- **Forward the Call**—A determination of whether the call is forwarded when the queue reaches a maximum number of calls. Administrators can choose to forward either the oldest call in the queue or the newest call.
- **Call Action**—The action taken when a call reaches the timeout period. The options for call targets are discussed in greater detail later in this section.

In a situation in which either the time period elapses or the maximum number of calls is reached, an administrator has several choices for how to route the call:

- **Disconnect**—Drops the call.
- **Forward to Voice Mail**—Forwards the call to an Exchange UM voicemail address, which must be a SIP URI.
- **Forward to Telephone Number**—Forwards the call to a telephone number in the `sip:<number>@<domain>` format.
- **Forward to SIP Address**—Forwards the call to another user account in the `sip:<username>@<domain>` format.
- **Forward to Another Queue**—Forwards the call to another Response Group queue.

Creating a Queue

To create a new queue, follow these steps:

1. Open the Skype for Business Server 2015 Control Panel.
2. Click Response Groups.
3. Click Queue.
4. Click New.
5. Select an application server and click OK.
6. Enter a name for the queue.
7. Enter a description for the queue.
8. Click Select to choose existing agent groups that belong to the queue.
9. Highlight any groups to add and click OK.
10. Check the box Enable Queue Time-out, if required.
11. After selecting the queue timeout, enter a timeout period.
12. After selecting the queue timeout, select a call action and enter an appropriate SIP URI if required.
13. Check the box Enable Queue Overflow, if required.
14. After selecting Enable Queue Overflow, enter a maximum number of calls.
15. After selecting Enable Queue Overflow, click Forward the Call and select an option.
16. After selecting Enable Queue Overflow, select a call action and enter an appropriate SIP URI if required.
17. Click Commit when completed.

Alternatively, the Skype for Business Server 2015 Management Shell can be used to create a new queue through the `New-CsRgsAgentGroup` and `New-CsRgsCallAction` cmdlets.

Configuring Workflows

The Response Group workflow is what ties together the agent groups and workflows along with how calls should be routed. Two types of workflows can be created:

- **Hunt Group**—A simple workflow that routes callers to queues based on time of day and agent availability.
- **Interactive**—Allows the user to be prompted with questions and then routed to queues based on the responses.

The two types of workflows share many configuration options:

- **Activate the Workflow**—If this is selected, the workflow immediately begins to accept calls. This parameter can be changed later if the workflow should not immediately be active.
- **Enable for Federation**—The workflow can be contacted by federated contacts if this option is selected.
- **Agent Anonymity**—Selecting this option hides the identity of the agent after the call is established. There are some feature limitations imposed during the call if this is enabled. For example, conferencing, application and desktop sharing, file transfer, and call recording are not available.
- **Group Address**—This is the SIP URI assigned to the workflow. This should be a unique URI in the organization.
- **Display Name**—This is the name visible to clients when calling the workflow.
- **Telephone Number**—This is the line URI for the workflow.
- **Display Number**—This is the number visible to clients when calling the workflow. This can be in any format.
- **Description**—This is a description for the workflow.
- **Workflow Type**—This controls whether the workflow can be left unmanaged, or managed by designated Response Group managers.
- **Language**—This determines the language used for speech recognition or text-to-speech conversion.
- **Welcome Message**—A configurable audio message can be played to callers as they enter the workflow. This can be accomplished either through text-to-speech or by uploading an existing audio recording.
- **Time Zone**—This is the time zone that the opening and closing times are based around.
- **Business Hours Schedule**—The schedule for the workflow can be based on an existing schedule created separately, or it can be a custom schedule defined directly within the workflow.
- **Outside Business Hours Message**—A configurable audio message can be played to callers if they dial the workflow outside of the defined business hours. This can be done through text-to-speech or by uploading an existing audio recording.
- **Outside Business Hours Action**—If callers reach the workflow outside of the defined open hours, the call can be disconnected, forwarded to a voicemail box, forwarded to another SIP URI, or forwarded to a telephone number. This action occurs after the message is played, if it is defined.
- **Holiday Lists**—This is a collection of days that are defined as holidays. A separate action can be taken on these days.

- **Holidays Message**—A configurable audio message can be played to callers if they dial the workflow on a defined holiday. This can be done through text-to-speech or by uploading an existing audio recording.
- **Holidays Action**—If callers reach the workflow during a defined holiday, the call can be disconnected, forwarded to a voicemail box, forwarded to another SIP URI, or forwarded to a telephone number. This action occurs after the message is played, if it is defined.
- **Queue**—The queue selected here receives calls for this workflow.
- **Music on Hold**—The default Music on Hold can be selected or administrators can configure a custom Music on Hold file.

Creating Workflows

To create a new Response Group workflow, follow these steps:

1. Open the Skype for Business Server 2015 Control Panel.
2. Click Response Groups.
3. Click Workflow.
4. Click Create or Edit a Workflow.
5. Select an application server to host the Response Group, and then click OK.

The Response Group Configuration Tool opens in a web browser. Unlike the rest of the Response Group setup, workflow creation is done using an interface separate from the Skype for Business Server 2015 Control Panel. What type of workflow is created depends on the administrator. Steps for creating each type of workflow can be found in the next section.

Creating a Hunt Group Workflow

To create a new hunt group workflow, follow these steps after launching the Response Group Configuration Tool:

1. Under Hunt Group, click the Create button.
2. Select whether to activate the workflow.
3. Select an option for Enable for Federation.
4. Select an option for Enable Agent Anonymity.
5. Enter a SIP address for the workflow. The "sip:" prefix is automatically prepended.
6. Enter a display name for the workflow.
7. Enter a telephone number to associate with the workflow. The "tel:" prefix is automatically included, so just the E.164 format is required with the + sign prefix.
8. Enter a display number for the telephone number.

9. Enter a description for the workflow.
10. Select whether the Workflow Type setting is Unmanaged or Managed, and then specify any managers.
11. Select a language.
12. Choose whether to play a welcome message, and then select the message type.
13. Specify the time zone.
14. Select a business hours schedule by choosing Use a Preset Schedule or by choosing Use a Custom Schedule and defining the schedule.
15. Select whether to play a message when the response group is outside business hours, and then select a message type.
16. Select an action to take for Outside of Business Hours, Process Call as Follows.
17. Select a standard holiday list if one has been created.
18. Select whether to play a message during holidays, and then select a message type.
19. Select an action to take for During Holidays, Process Call as Follows.
20. Configure a queue to receive the calls.
21. Select an option to configure Music on Hold.
22. Click Deploy to complete the workflow creation.

Creating an Interactive Workflow

To create an interactive workflow, follow these steps after launching the Response Group Configuration Tool:

1. Under Hunt Group, click the Create button.
2. Select whether to activate the workflow.
3. Select an option for Enable for Federation.
4. Select an option for Enable Agent Anonymity.
5. Enter a SIP address for the workflow. The "sip:" prefix is automatically prepended.
6. Enter a display name for the workflow.
7. Enter a telephone number to associate with the workflow. The "tel:" prefix is automatically included, so just the E.164 format is required with the plus prefix.
8. Enter a display number for the telephone number.
9. Enter a description for the workflow.
10. Select whether the Workflow Type setting is Unmanaged or Managed, and then specify any managers.

11. Select a language.
12. Choose whether to play a welcome message, and then select the message type.
13. Specify the time zone.
14. Set the Business Hours Schedule option to Use a Preset Schedule or Use a Custom Schedule, and then define the schedule.
15. Select whether to play a message when the response group is outside business hours, and then select a message type.
16. Select an action to take for Outside of Business Hours, Process Call as Follows.
17. Select a standard holiday list if one has been created.
18. Select whether to play a message during holidays, and then select a message type.
19. Select an action to take for During Holidays, Process Call as Follows.
20. Select an option to configure Music on Hold.
21. Select whether to use text-to-speech or select a recording to use for the first interactive question.
22. Enter a voice response text phrase and select a digit to assign a keypad response.
23. Select a queue the caller is placed in when matching the voice or keypad response.
24. Repeat the previous steps for any additional valid responses or questions that should be asked.
25. Click Deploy to complete the workflow creation.

Configuring Business-Hour Collections

Business-hour schedules can be created in advance and then reused across multiple workflows. Defining business-hour collections is a task that can be performed only via the Skype for Business Server 2015 Management Shell. Use the `New-CsRgsTimeRange` cmdlet to create each unique new time range, and store it in a variable that can be passed to a business-hours collection object later. Times should be defined using a 24-hour format.

```
$Weekdays = New-CsRgsTimeRange -Name <Name of Time Range> -OpenTime
➥<Time when business hours start> -CloseTime <Time when business hours end>
```

After a unique variable has been created for each different set of hours, the business hours collection object can be created with the `New-CsRgsHoursOfBusiness` cmdlet:

```
New-CsRgsHoursOfBusiness -Parent ApplicationServer:<Front End Pool FQDN> -Name
➥<Business Hours Collection Name> -MondayHours1 <Time Range Object>
➥-TuesdayHours1 <Time Range Object> -WednesdayHours1 <Time Range Object>
➥-ThursdayHours1 <Time Range Object> -FridayHours1 <Time Range Object>
➥-SaturdayHours1 <Time Range Object> -SundayHours1 <Time Range Object>
```

This cmdlet accepts two values for each day of the week. If the business stays open with no break, only `Hours1` parameters need to be specified. If the business hours include a break, such as from 12:00 to 13:00, the `Hours1` parameter should be from business open to 12:00, and the `Hours2` parameter should be from 13:00 to business close.

Configuring Holiday Sets

Much as with business-hour collections, Skype for Business administrators can create a holiday set to define the appropriate holiday schedule for a business. A holiday set can also only be created using the Skype for Business Server 2015 Management Shell.

The first step in defining a holiday set is to create a unique variable for each holiday that defines a name, a start date, and an end date. After all the holidays are stored in variables, they can be added to a holiday set. To create a holiday and store it in a variable, follow this syntax:

```
$Christmas = New-CsRgsHoliday -Name <Holiday Name> -StartDate <Date formatted as
➥dd/mm/yyyy> -EndDate <Date formatted as dd/mm/yyyy>
```

After repeating the previous step to create each of the holiday objects, use the following syntax to create the holiday set. Naming the object based on the year usually makes the most sense because some holidays fall on different days depending on the year. To configure a new holiday set, use the following cmdlet:

```
New-CsRgsHolidaySet -Parent ApplicationServer:<Front End Pool FQDN> -Name
➥<Holiday Set Name> -HolidayList (<Comma-separated list of each variable
➥representing a holiday>)
```

Creating Workflows Using the Skype for Business Server 2015 Management Shell

Creating a Response Group workflow entirely in the Skype for Business Server 2015 Management Shell gives some added flexibility to configuration. Specifically, interactive workflows have no limit to the number of questions or responses, unlike the Response Group Configuration Tool, which limits both items.

TIP

Take care not to make interactive workflows with too many menu levels because callers can quickly become frustrated and end the call if they have to navigate through too many levels. Also, always provide a “break out” option to the workflow for users who become confused and need to speak with an operator.

NOTE

Much of the Response Group configuration done using the Management Shell relies heavily on storing objects as variables. Being descriptive with variable names can reduce the complexity involved when trying to tie all the pieces together.

A basic hunt group workflow can be created easily. All workflows need a default action defined, so the first step in creating a workflow within the Management Shell is to store a default action in a variable. The `New-CsRgsCallAction` cmdlet creates an action stored in memory that can be used in another command. A simple example that stores the action and sends calls to a specific queue is displayed here:

```
$TransferToCustomerServiceQueue = New-CsRgsCallAction -Action TransferToQueue
➥-QueueID CustomerService
```

After an action has been created, a workflow object can be created. The actual workflow setup is flexible and can become extremely complicated. Building off the previous example and stored `$TransferToCustomerService` variable, here is a simple hunt group workflow example:

```
New-CsRgsWorkflow -Name MyWorkflow -Parent
➥service:ApplicationServer:Skype For Businesspool.companyabc.com -PrimaryUri
➥CustomerService@companyabc.com -DefaultAction $TransferToCustomerServiceQueue
➥-Description "Routes callers dialing customer support" -DisplayNumber "
➥+1 (234) 456-7890" -LineURI "tel:+1234567890"
```

NOTE

An interactive workflow requires more upfront preparation and object configuration before creation of the workflow object. Each prompt, question, and answer object must be defined in *advance* of the Response Group configuration because much of using the Management Shell relies heavily on storing objects as variables. Being descriptive with variable names can reduce the complexity involved when trying to tie all the pieces together.

To get started, a new prompt must be created and saved using the `New-CsRgsPrompt` cmdlet. The `New-CsRgsPrompt` cmdlet accepts an audio file as input if one has been stored in a separate variable; the alternative is to enter a text string that reads as text-to-speech. For example, to store the prompt in a variable using an audio file saved earlier as `$MyAudioFile`, use the following:

```
$PromptDoYouNeedHelp= New-CsRgsPrompt -AudioFilePrompt $MyAudioFile
```

After a prompt has been created to be played to calls, a question must be posed in an interactive workflow. What might seem a little backward is that an answer list must be formed before a question can be created when the shell is used. For example, to store an answer option if the caller says "yes" or presses 1 on the keypad, use this:

```
$AnswerYesMaybe = New-CsRgsAnswer -Action $TransferToCustomerServiceQueue
➥-DtmfResponse 1 -VoiceResponseList "Yes"
```

Because there is more than one option, assume that another Response Group answer object exists called `$AnswerNo` and that it disconnects the call if the user says "no" or presses 2 on the keypad.

After all the possible answers have been defined, a Response Group question object can be created. Continuing with the previous example, assume that the custom prompt asks the caller if they actually need help. So far, a response of "yes" has an action that transfers the caller to the Customer Service queue. If the user says "no," the call ends. The following example ties the two responses into a question and stores it in yet another variable:

```
$DoesCustomerNeedHelpQuestion = New-CsRgsQuestion -Prompt $DoYouNeedHelp -AnswerList
➥$YesMaybe,$No -Name "Do you need help" -NoAnswerPrompt $AreYouStillThere
```

This example shows creating just one question with only two responses. Be sure to thoroughly plan a workflow before continuing with the setup because it does require quite a bit of scripting. Repeat the previous steps for any additional prompts, questions, and answers that will be part of the workflow.

Before the workflow can be created, the initial prompt must be assigned to a default action object:

```
$AskIfHelpNeeded = New-CsRgsCallAction -Action TransferToQuestion -Question
➥$DoesCustomerNeedHelpQuestion
```

Now that a question and call action have been created, an entire interactive workflow can be initiated. To finish the example, the following commands create the workflow that asks the caller whether they need help:

```
New-CsRgsWorkflow -Name "Customer Service Workflow" -Parent
➥service:ApplicationServer:Skype For Businesspool.companyabc.com -PrimaryUri
➥CustomerService@companyabc.com - -DefaultAction $AskIfHelpNeeded
➥-Description "Asks user if they need help and routes to Customer Service if yes"
➥-DisplayNumber "+1 (234) 456-7890" -LineURI tel:+1234567890
```

Best Practices

The following are the best practices from this chapter:

- Collocate Mediation Servers with a Front End Server when possible to reduce the hardware requirements for each deployment.
- Create multiple trunk associations between different pools to the same gateway for additional resiliency.
- Carefully follow the steps provided by a survivable branch appliance (SBA) vendor before placing the SBA in service.
- Use a unique dial plan for each location that has different dialing habits.

- Use translation rules on a trunk configuration only if the opposite end of the trunk is not manipulating digits.
- Configure the required network objects before attempting Call Admission Control, Media Bypass, or E911 setup.
- Use test cases to verify an Enterprise Voice configuration before publishing changes.
- Use a survivable branch appliance or survivable branch server in each remote office without a resilient WAN connection to the central site.
- Plan a Response Group workflow with diagram tools before attempting to create the workflow.

Summary

Skype for Business Server 2015 is an extremely flexible and feature-rich platform that organizations can use to provide voice services throughout the enterprise. The platform is equipped with features that are expected of a true enterprise-ready telephony solution. Beyond core telephony capabilities, Skype for Business Server 2015 also provides native conferencing features that also lead to cost savings for many organizations.

The voice-routing engine also offers a high degree of customization and granularity over all call decisions. This allows administrators to provide various classes of service and features depending on the user, while accommodating all local dialing habits across varying regions and geographies.

CHAPTER 18

Skype for Business Native Video and Data Conferencing

IN THIS CHAPTER

- Skype for Business 2015 Peer-to-Peer Video
- Skype for Business Server 2015 Video Conferencing
- Skype for Business Server 2015 Data Conferencing

Although video and data conferencing technology is not new to Microsoft UC, Skype for Business Server 2015 continues to leverage many enhancements to this functionality. This includes the ability for more endpoints to participate in high-definition video conferences, while at the same time allowing administrators greater control over video conferencing usage. The Skype for Business 2016 client also expands on the existing application-sharing and desktop-sharing functionality by introducing Video-based Screen Sharing (VbSS). This enhancement to screen and application sharing will over time replace the existing Remote Desktop Protocol (RDP). This new protocol leverages the existing H.264 SVC video for a higher frame rate at lower bandwidth consumption. Currently this VbSS desktop sharing capability is only available within the Office 2016 Skype for Business client and for peer-to-peer calling, but is expected to be extended to multiparty calling in the near future.

Multiparty H.264 SVC video conferencing was introduced with Lync 2013 and allows users to have a more immersive UC experience, while at the same time introducing new administrative and planning challenges for IT administrators. This section provides details on what this new functionality is, what is required to implement it, and how to properly manage it.

Skype for Business Peer-to-Peer Video

Skype for Business allows users to participate in immersive HD video calls with other Skype for Business users. Peer-to-peer (P2P) video has been available in the Microsoft UC Suite since LCS and has seen many evolutions over the years. In Lync 2013, Microsoft placed a major focus on video. This continues with Skype for Business: Microsoft introduced the H.264 SVC codec to the Lync 2013 platform, and HD video can now be extended to almost all users. This is a major end-use enhancement over the switched video conferencing offered prior to Lync 2013, but organizations must plan carefully and make sure that their environment can support HD video. This section outlines what the new video features in Skype for Business are, including details on the H.264 codec. This section also covers important bandwidth and hardware requirements for video as well as covers common configuration options for P2P video.

Video Features

Skype for Business Server 2015 includes key peer-to-peer and conferencing video features. At the core of these changes is a default video codec, H.264 SVC. The use of this codec allows for higher-quality video, with fewer server and client resources. The following features are available within Skype for Business and affect P2P video functionality:

- **H.264 video codec**—The H.264 video codec supports a greater range of resolutions and frame rates, as well as improving video scalability.
- **1080p video**—HD 1080p video is now available in two-party and multiparty conferences.

H.264 Video

The H.264 video codec has been adopted today for everything from video conferencing to Blu-ray. In Skype for Business Server 2015, Microsoft leverages H.264 SVC as the default codec for peer-to-peer video calls and conferences. SVC stands for Scalable Video Coding, and this extension to H.264 adds new profiles and scalability capabilities, which provide major advantages for real-time video communications.

The term *scalability* can be used to describe many audio and video codecs in the industry. However, the scalability that H.264 SVC provides is complementary to one of the goals of Microsoft Skype for Business: to provide end users with full functionality on any device, and on any network connection. H.264 SVC allows Skype for Business Server 2015 to provide a rich conferencing experience to all endpoints by allowing users to view different levels of video quality on demand, and it does not require real-time decoding or encoding of video streams by the Multipoint Control Units (MCUs; in the case of Skype for Business Server 2015, the A/V Conferencing Server). H.264 SVC leverages the endpoints (PCs, tablets, phones, cameras) to perform the processing of the video streams. This allows Skype for Business endpoints to dynamically send and receive a video resolution and frame rate that best suits them. As a result, the Skype for Business Server 2015 A/V Conferencing Server is now able to act as a simple video relay mechanism, sending video streams to endpoints that they request on demand, and without requiring an increased processing load. The introduction of this functionality is what has allowed Microsoft to include HD resolutions in video conferences and at the same time to remove the need for a dedicated A/V Conferencing Server role.

How Does H.264 SVC Work?

H.264 SVC provides the scalability described previously by building video streams out of individual, complementary layers. This all starts with the base layer, which has the lowest resolution and frame rate that can be displayed. Enhancement layers are then provided as needed, which will deliver higher quality to endpoints that request it. Again, these enhancement layers are complementary, so when combined with the base layer, the video resolution and frame rate are increased. This is best described in the form of a diagram, as shown in Figure 18.1.

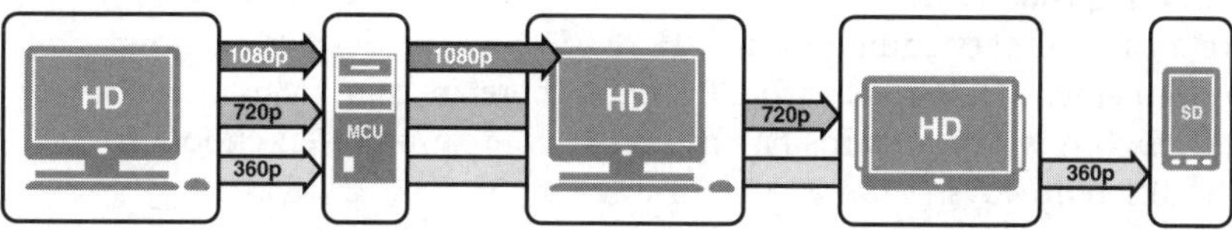

FIGURE 18.1 H.264 SVC layering example.

In this example, a PC endpoint is able to send up to 1080p HD video and is connected to a conference. That conference is run by an MCU (Skype for Business Server 2015 A/V Conferencing Server), and there are three other participants in the call. In versions prior to Lync Server 2013, the video resolution would be dropped to the lowest common denominator. For example, if the phone that supported only 360p video joined the video conference, everyone would send and receive 360p video. With Skype for Business Server 2015 and H.264 SVC, that limitation no longer exists.

In this scenario, the base layer is built on 360p video, which is the lowest resolution needed for participants in the conference. The endpoint knows how to build its layers based on what each endpoint asks the MCU for when joining the conference. The sending endpoint then adds additional layers, for additional resolutions all the way up to 1080p, because another participant has asked for that resolution.

The sending endpoint sends all layers to the MCU, and the MCU then sends each layer that is requested to the other participants. Because the mobile phone is limited to 360p, it is sent only the base layer. The tablet, on the other hand, can support 720p video, so it is sent two layers to make up the 720p video stream. The third participant can also support 1080p video, so it is sent all three layers. It is important to remember that these layers are additive, so there is no duplicate data sent, only the delta. Because only the delta data is sent in the enhancement layers, the bandwidth used by H.264 SVC calls is similar to that of other codecs. Another great feature introduced with this codec is that everything is dynamic. Participants in the conference notify the MCU of any changes to its capabilities. A great example of this happening would be if the second PC that is capable of 1080p video did not have the video in full-screen mode. If that user is not requesting to view a 1080p video stream, there is no reason for the other party to encode and transmit a 1080p stream. If that user then decided to expand to full-screen mode, however, the MCU would dynamically change the stream resolutions. This allows for efficient processing and bandwidth utilization on the MCU and the endpoints.

The largest benefit to this technology is seen by the A/V Conferencing Server. Although this role has never encoded or transcoded media, only with the introduction of H.264 SVC Skype for Business Server 2015 is able to provide more functionality without increasing processing requirements. This does, however, increase the processing load on endpoints. Microsoft has always leveraged endpoints for encoding and decoding media streams, for both audio and video. In Lync 2013, this processing load was increased for HD video scenarios, and the details of those requirements are covered in the "Peer-to-Peer Video Endpoint Requirements" section.

Microsoft's H.264 SVC Implementation

Now that you have a basic understanding of how H.264 SVC works, let's cover how Microsoft chose to implement H.264. As with all codecs, there are many variations of H.264 SVC, and although it is a "standards-based" codec, companies often choose to implement them in different ways.

Microsoft partnered with Polycom, HP, and LifeSize to form the Unified Communications Interoperability Forum (UCIF), which is focused on creating specifications and guidelines for common UC protocols. From this partnership, Microsoft also announced it would be adopting the H.264 SVC codec that Polycom developed. The version of H.264 SVC that Microsoft has adopted supports many different configuration modes; however, Microsoft has chosen to implement only two of these configuration modes in Skype for Business Server 2015:

- **UCConfig Mode 0**—Non-Scalable Single Layer AVC BitStream
- **UCConfig Mode 1**—SVC Temporal Scalability with Hierarchical P

The additional modes are the following:

- **UCConfig Mode 2q**—SVC Temporal Scalability + Quality/SNR Scalability
- **UCConfig Mode 2s**—SVC Temporal Scalability + Spatial Scalability
- **UCConfig Mode 3**—Full SVC Scalability (Temporal + SNR + Spatial)

With each mode, a new level of scalability is introduced. Each mode is additive, and in the end you are left with full SVC scalability.

Mode 0 essentially means that no scalability is supported. This mode should be supported by all systems that support this type of H.264 SVC codec. This mode will most likely be important in interoperability scenarios in the future. This mode does allow for multiple streams to be sent, but not multiple frame rates per resolution. Table 18.1 shows an example of the Mode 0 layers that would be available.

TABLE 18.1 H.264 SVC Mode 0 Sample Layers

Stream	Layer
1	1080p 30fps
2	720p 30fps
3	360p 30fps

Mode 1 introduces temporal scaling. This level of scalability starts to introduce some of the "cool" stuff that H.264 SVC can do. With Mode 1, the endpoint can send a single video stream per resolution for multiple frame rates. The receiving endpoint can then decide whether it wants to display that resolution at 30fps, 15fps, or 7.5fps by dropping entire frames of the video sequence. For example, if the highest frame rate sent is 30fps, the receiving endpoint could scale down to 15fps by dropping every other frame it receives. Table 18.2 shows an example of the H.264 SVC Mode 1 layers.

TABLE 18.2 H.264 SVC Mode 1 Sample Layers

Stream	Layers		
1	1080p 30fps	1080p 15fps	1080p 7.5fps
2	720p 30fps	720p 15fps	720p 7.5fps
3	360p 30fps	360p 15fps	360p 7.5fps

NOTE

Although Lync 2013 and Skype for Business clients can support multiple frame rates within a single stream, this is capped at up to two layers. Typically this is two layers of 15fps, which can satisfy the requirement of either 15 or 30fps.

Skype for Business Server 2015 leverages H.264 SVC UCConfig Mode 1 for video conferencing functionality. Three more UCConfig modes are included in the spec published by Microsoft and Polycom; therefore, one would assume that this functionality will be introduced in later releases.

In addition to the flexibility that H.264 SVC provides, Microsoft has also added dynamic Forward Error Correction (FEC). If you are not familiar with FEC, in short, it allows for media streams to be dynamically rebuilt in packet-loss scenarios. This functionality, combined with H.264 SVC, provides room for impressive video quality on any type of network connection.

As you can see, H.264 SVC includes the flexibility required for many of the video features within Skype for Business Server 2015. H.264 SVC allows Skype for Business Server 2015 to deliver the video conferencing quality, and functionality, without increasing the load on the A/V Conferencing Server. By including H.264 SVC as the default video codec in Skype for Business Server 2015, Microsoft has also opened the door for many new interoperability scenarios. Because H.264 is the base for many standard video codecs, integration with systems that use a compatible version of H.264 will allow for higher quality and simplified video interoperability scenarios. This is demonstrated by Microsoft's new Video Interoperability Server (VIS) introduced with Skype for Business Server 2015.

Peer-to-Peer Video Bandwidth Requirements

As mentioned before, this functionality in Skype for Business Server 2015 does not come without a price. It's true to say that many organizations are not using HD video today due to network impact. Many organizations are moving toward adopting and supporting this technology, but for the majority of organizations it is not widely deployed yet. Table 18.3 lists some bandwidth examples for Skype for Business that are provided by Microsoft.

TABLE 18.3 Skype for Business Bandwidth Requirements

Quality	P2P or Single View	
	Bandwidth (Max)	Resolution
Minimum	250Kbps	320×180
Okay	350Kbps	424×240
Good	2,500Kbps	1280×720
Optimum	4,000Kbps	1920×1080

When comparing the bandwidth numbers to those for Lync 2010, you can see that there is not much of a difference. There is essentially the introduction of 1080p video, which, as you can see, comes with a much larger bandwidth utilization. For organizations currently exploring 1080p video on other platforms, these numbers should be similar to those in the rest of the industry.

One area that Microsoft can improve on is to introduce more bandwidth compression. The H.264 codec does allow for more compression than Microsoft is currently using, with bandwidth reductions up to 50% of what is displayed in Table 18.3. When and whether Microsoft will choose to introduce this technology is unknown. A major caveat of introducing that bandwidth reduction is an even greater processing load on the endpoints.

When organizations are planning for peer-to-peer bandwidth, it is recommended that they consider the max possible bandwidth used in a media stream, which is what is shown in Table 18.3. However, there is the concept of an average bandwidth usage to be considered as well. In video calls, only data that is changed is sent. For example, less bandwidth is used with less movement. If I am sitting still in my office chair, and none of my background is changing, technically less data is being transmitted, and you will see reduced bandwidth utilization. Additionally, the capability to dynamically reduce the frame rate allows for less bandwidth utilization as well.

Peer-to-Peer Video Endpoint Requirements

In the "H.264 Video" section, it was mentioned that Skype for Business video requires more processing power on the endpoints for HD video. Although this is true, Microsoft has also introduced the capability for hardware-accelerated encoding and decoding.

Hardware acceleration is the use of a graphical processing unit (GPU) for encoding and decoding of video. Rather than using the software and the primary CPU, this processing load can be offloaded to the GPU chip. Hardware-accelerated video encoding and decoding is available on many modern platforms. This can be included in processors, graphics cards, and even USB webcams. Microsoft supports the following types of hardware acceleration in Skype for Business:

- H.264 encoding, with support for Intel HD Graphics accelerating processing units (APUs) on second- or third-generation SandyBridge and IvyBridge CPUs.
- Second-generation Advanced Micro Devices (ARM) Fusion APUs.
- H.264 HW encoding based on the USB Video Class v1.5 standard. It should be noted that the Skype for Business client prioritizes encoding on the GPU, and it is unlikely to offload this capability to a UVC 1.5-based camera. In fact, receiving uncompressed video via a USB camera when paired with a modern-day CPU produces better results with overall lower CPU overhead.

Because of hardware acceleration, Skype for Business supports HD video on endpoints with dual-core CPUs, removing the previous requirement for quad-core CPUs. Table 18.4 outlines the hardware requirements that are provided from Microsoft for video. It is important to note that, in addition to CPU requirements, Microsoft is also leveraging WinSAT scores to determine capabilities. For encoding, VideoEncodeScore is leveraged and for decoding GraphicsScore is used. Hardware accelerated decoding is also available using DirectX Video Acceleration (DXVA).

TABLE 18.4 Lync 2013 Video Endpoint Requirements

Capable Encode Resolution	Capable Decode Resolution	Requirement	Notes
424×240	424×240	One core and VideoEncodeScore > 4.0	No DXVA and no hardware acceleration
640×360	640×360	Two cores and VideoEncodeScore > 4.5	
640×360	1280×720	Two cores and VideoEncodeScore > 4.5	
640×360	1920×1080	Four cores and VideoEncodeScore > 4.5	
1280×720	1280×720	Four cores and VideoEncodeScore > 7.3	
1280×720	1920×1080	Four cores and VideoEncodeScore > 7.3	
1920×1080	1920×1080	N/A	
424×240	1920×1080	One core and VideoEncodeScore > 3.0	DXVA but no hardware acceleration

(Continued)

TABLE 18.4 *(Continued)*

Capable Encode Resolution	Capable Decode Resolution	Requirement	Notes
640×360	1920×1080	Two cores and VideoEncodeScore > 4.5	
960×540	1920×1080	Two cores and VideoEncodeScore > 6.0	
1280×720	1920×1080	Four cores and VideoEncodeScore > 6.7	
1920×1080	1920×1080	Four cores and VideoEncodeScore > 8.2	
1280×720	1920×1080	All 2nd- and 3rd-generation Intel HD graphics	DXVA and Intel HD graphics hardware acceleration
1920×1080	1920×1080	All 2nd- and 3rd-generation Intel HD graphics and GraphicsScore > 5.0	

NOTE

Windows 7 has a maximum WinSAT score of 7.9. Therefore, the encoding capability without hardware acceleration can only be achieved on Windows 8 where the maximum WinSAT score is 9.9.

The adoption of H.264 SVC expands the endpoints that can participate in HD video conferences. Additionally, ARM-powered tablet devices will be able to encode and decode HD H.264 video.

Organizations deploying Skype for Business should carefully consider the impact that video will have on existing machines. Even with Lync 2010, some customers would experience issues in which older PCs would be negatively impacted by the Lync client during audio and video calls. This not only can cause a poor user experience for Skype for Business, but also impact other business applications. Before you upgrade to Skype for Business, it is important to perform an audit on the PCs that will be used by end users. If it is known that machines are not capable of supporting high-quality video, the video quality should be restricted using in-band provisioning.

The next section outlines common configuration tasks for peer-to-peer video in Skype for Business.

Configuring Peer-to-Peer Video Options

In Skype for Business Server 2015, administrators are able to have control over Skype for Business video functionality through in-band provisioning.

In Lync 2010, video bandwidth could be controlled through two key policies: the conferencing policy assigned to users, and the media configuration. In addition to these policies, Call Admission Control (CAC) could be used to control video bandwidth across sites.

In Skype for Business Server 2015, the conferencing policy and CAC configurations remain, but the media configuration policy is no longer used by Skype for Business Server 2015 servers and users.

NOTE

Lync 2010 clients will still use the media configuration value `MaxVideoRateAllowed`. This should be considered in coexistence scenarios where Lync 2010 clients may be connecting to Skype for Business Server 2015.

Although it is called a conferencing policy, in Skype for Business Server 2015 the conferencing policy still is the place where administrators control video bandwidth for peer-to-peer and conference calls. The Skype for Business Server 2015 conferencing policy includes attributes that relate to peer-to-peer video and conferencing calls. These settings can be managed using the following:

- `Get-CSConferencingPolicy`
- `Set-CSConferencingPolicy`
- `New-CSConferencingPolicy`

The attributes introduced with Lync Server 2013 are listed here:

- **`VideoBitRateKb`**—This setting specifies the maximum video bit rate in Kbps for video that is sent by a user.
- **`TotalReceiveVideoBitRateKb`**—This setting specifies the maximum allowed bit rate in Kbps for all the video streams that the client receives. It specifies a combined total of all video streams, except for any panoramic video streams.

NOTE

If you enable Gallery View video in Skype for Business conferences, `TotalReceiveVideoBitRateKb` must not be set below 420Kbps, or a Gallery View experience will not be delivered.

- **`MaxVideoConferencingResolution`**—This setting is for legacy clients only, but it does apply to Skype for Business Server 2015 conferences. In scenarios with coexistence with Lync 2010 or older clients, administrators should consider configuring this setting as well.

The listed features are used in parallel with CAC, if both are deployed. The conferencing policy will specify how much bandwidth can be used for video irrespective of the path, whereas CAC will set a bandwidth limit specifically on the media path. Consider the following examples:

- If `VideoBitRateKb` is set to 500Kbps, and the CAC policy for the media path is set to 250Kbps, the limit will be set to 250Kbps.
- If `VideoBitRateKb` is set to 250Kbps, and the CAC policy for the media path is set to 500Kbps, the limit will bet set to 250Kbps.

These examples are pretty straightforward; the lowest limit will always take effect, which should be the desired behavior. It is important to carefully plan your conferencing policies and CAC configuration together.

A common question asked is how Skype for Business enforces the bandwidth limits for media streams. Skype for Business does not buffer packets because it can cause issues with the real-time media stream. However, Skype for Business does dynamically adjust attributes of the codec to keep in line with the bandwidth rate that is enforced. This can also happen irrespective of any policies or CAC configuration. With video, there are much fewer tweaks that can happen when compared to audio streams; however, it is common for the frame rate and resolution of a video stream to dynamically adjust to respect policy enforcement, or real-time bandwidth congestion.

The following section explains how these policies can impact conferencing scenarios.

Skype for Business Server 2015 Video Conferencing

Skype for Business Server 2015 video conferencing benefits from the H.264 SVC codec introduced with Lync Server 2013. This codec allows for more video capabilities in conferences, with much fewer server resources. This section covers these features as well as some key requirements for these features.

Video Conferencing Features

Skype for Business Server 2015 offers the capability to have HD video in conferences, as well as the capability to view up to five active speaker video streams:

- **Gallery View**—In video conferences, users can see video of up to five participants at once. If the conference has more than five users, video of the most active five users is shown, and a photo appears for the rest of the users.
- **HD video**—In video conferences, users can now send and receive HD video streams.

- **Face detection**—In video conferences, Skype for Business automatically tracks and frames the participants' faces. This helps users stay focused on the center of the video stream being sent by other users. Additionally, these framed video streams are used in the Gallery View to provide a consistent video experience in conferences. When multiple participants are detected from the same video source, the Skype for Business client automatically removes this framing. Alternatively, this framing can be disabled by an end user within the Skype for Business client video settings.
- **Split audio and video**—With Skype for Business Server 2015, participants can add their video stream to a conference but join audio through another endpoint.
- **Video spotlight**—Presenters are able to "pin" the video spotlight on a participant during a conference. When this is done, every participant sees that video stream in the main window, and this stream will be a full frame and resolution of the video stream, up to HD quality.

Gallery View

A great feature in many video conferencing systems is the capability to view multiple active speaker video streams at once. Some people have referred to this as the "Brady Bunch" view or "Hollywood Squares." Many video conferencing systems provide the capability to view multiple squares of live video from participants. If you think back to the two classic TV shows just mentioned, this reference should be clear.

Before Lync Server 2013, this was a major feature that Microsoft lacked. With the introduction of H.264 SVC, Microsoft has enabled this functionality in Skype for Business Server 2015. This video codec allows the Skype for Business Server 2015 A/V Conferencing Server to provide multiple video streams with very little processing power. If you remember from the earlier sections, H.264 SVC has intelligence that allows for the MCU to act as a simple video switch, while leveraging the endpoints to facilitate which level of video quality it is capable of sending and receiving. Some traditional video conferencing systems leverage very powerful MCUs to actively build the multiple-video-stream view and deliver that view to endpoints as a single video stream. This approach requires much more processing power in the central MCU, and this would not work well in a Skype for Business Server 2015 environment.

As you can see in Figure 18.2, Microsoft has implemented this functionality in an elegant way, focused on the end-user experience.

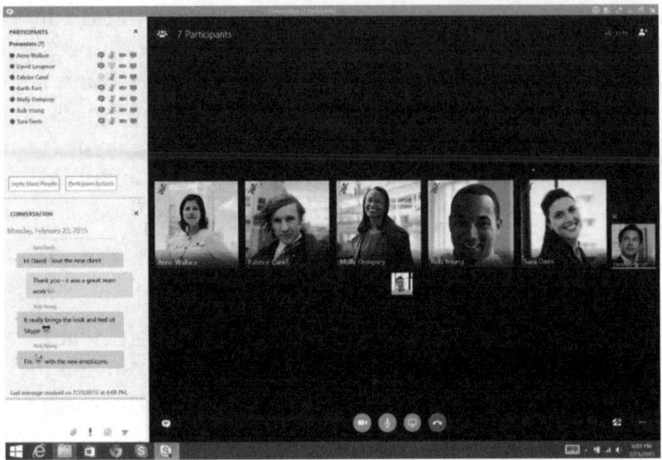

FIGURE 18.2 Skype for Business 2015 Gallery View.

How Does Gallery View Work?

Skype for Business Server 2015 Gallery View delivers a great user experience, but how does it work? This functionality includes a level of intelligence within the Skype for Business Server 2015 A/V Conferencing Server. The A/V Conferencing Server in Lync Server 2010 would actively manage all video streams from participants, but it still was just a video switch and would not encode or decode media. The easiest way to think of this was in the form of a simple on or off switch. Lync Server 2010 was limited to a single active speaker, and there were only two active video streams in a conference at one time. The current active speaker video stream would be sent to all participants in the video conference, and the previous active speaker video stream would be sent to the new active speaker. Although all participants were sharing their video, they would not be actively sending a video stream until they were designated the active speaker. This helped to reduce the bandwidth requirements and processing load on the A/V Conferencing Server. This is also why there was a slight delay in the video switching to the active speaker.

Lync Server 2013 introduced the intelligence to include not only up to five different video streams, but also multiple resolutions and frame rates. The H.264 SVC codec handles most of this functionality. Each video endpoint is responsible for providing the A/V Conferencing Server what it is capable of sending and receiving four video streams. The A/V Conferencing Server is capable of dynamic optimization during a conference, including the following situations:

- **New participants joining**—When a new participant joins the conference, the A/V Conferencing Server will automatically adjust video streams that are sent and received based on participants who enter and leave the meeting.
- **Bandwidth changes**—For each participant, if the network conditions change at all, the A/V Conferencing Server dynamically adjusts video streams to accommodate.

- **Video window size changes**—Each participant has the capability to view video streams in different sizes. The A/V Conferencing Server dynamically adjusts the video streams that are sent and received by each participant however they want to see it. For example, if Adam has his video full-screen, but Alex has his video smaller as part of the presentation window, Pat's video stream will be sent to the A/V Conferencing Server as a full-screen (HD) stream, but Alex will receive only the reduced video size. If Adam was to shrink his video window and HD video was no longer needed from Pat, then Pat would stop sending HD video to the Conferencing Server.
- **Forward Error Correction**—Forward Error Correction is built in to the Skype for Business Server 2015 and Skype for Business Client media codecs. This is the capability to rebuild media streams in packet-loss scenarios. Essentially, if packet loss is detected, FEC will kick in and endpoints will start sending redundant packets. The receiving endpoint then has the intelligence to rebuild the media stream with the packets it receives. The A/V Conferencing Server is also able to use FEC for video conferencing scenarios.

Skype for Business Server 2015 video conferencing utilizes much of the same intelligence described previously for non-Gallery View conferences. The only difference between regular video conferences and Gallery View conferences is that there are more than two streams to manage for a conference; other than that, the way the A/V Conferencing Server functions is the same.

Server Requirements for Video Conferencing

In Skype for Business Server 2015, the dedicated A/V Conferencing Server role that was introduced with Lync Server 2010 is not available; however, dedicated VIS Servers can be deployed for scaling deployments of standards-based video teleconference devices (VTCs). This will be covered in more detail in Chapter 19. The ability to collocate the A/V Conferencing Server role might come as a surprise, especially considering the 1080p video delivered as a part of Skype for Business Server 2015 video conferences. However, it shows how powerful the H.264 SVC codec is, and how much it permits Microsoft to deliver a more interactive video conferencing technology with little processing requirement on the servers.

With that said, the A/V Conferencing Server role will live within the Skype for Business Front End Server. This can be part of an Enterprise Edition pool or a Standard Edition Server. Table 18.5 outlines the requirements for each.

TABLE 18.5 Skype for Business Server 2015 Video Conferencing Server Requirements

Hardware Component	Recommended
CPU	64-bit dual processor, hex-core, 2.26 gigahertz (GHz) or higher. Intel Itanium processors are not supported for Skype for Business Server 2015 roles.
Memory	32GB.
Disk	Eight or more 10,000rpm hard disk drives with at least 72GB free disk space (two of the disks using RAID 1 and 6 using RAID 10). OR Solid state drives (SSDs) able to provide the same free space and similar performance as eight 10,000rpm mechanical disk drives.
Network	One dual-port network adapter, 1Gbps or higher (two network adapters can be used, but they need to be teamed with a single MAC address and a single IP address).

As you can see, this information is the same as the requirements for any Skype for Business Front End Server. It is more important to understand that the A/V Conferencing Server role is now always collocated with the Skype for Business Front End Server.

Video Conferencing Bandwidth Requirements

Many organizations that look to deploy video conferencing might be worried about the bandwidth requirements, a perfectly reasonable concern. Skype for Business Server 2015 includes the video for up to five active video streams and can have an impact on the network. Additionally, the support for 1080p video in conferences must carefully be planned for. When planning for conferences without Gallery View, organizations should reference Table 18.3, which is valid for conferencing scenarios without Gallery View. Table 18.6 outlines the bandwidth requirements for Skype for Business Server 2015 video conferencing with Gallery View.

TABLE 18.6 Skype for Business Server 2015 Bandwidth Requirements

	Two Participants	Three Participants	Four Participants	Five Participants	Six Participants
Max resolutions received	1920×1080	1280×720	640×360	640×360 320×240	640×360 320×240
Total average bit rate (Kbps)	2128	4050	1304	1224	1565
Total Maximum bit rate (Kbps)	4063	5890	2860	2699	3017

Although five Gallery View video streams can require a large amount of bandwidth, it is probably not as much as many people would originally estimate. The reason for this is that it is not possible for a single endpoint to receive multiple high-resolution video streams. Screen real estate will always be limited, and therefore it is not possible for a single endpoint to receive five 1280×720 video streams (which would require 7500Kbps of bandwidth). If you consider a modern PC display that can handle 1920×1280 resolution, it would be possible to fit only a single full 1280×720 video stream and then one-half of a second video stream at that same resolution. Another consideration is that when content is being leveraged within a meeting, additional screen real estate is used and a switched video experience becomes the default behavior, also driving down bandwidth utilization.

NOTE

Although it appears that each Skype for Business client is sending cropped squares of video for each participant, in actual fact more often a full uncropped 16:9 stream is sent along with coordinates that map to Microsoft's "Smart Framing" facial detection technology.

Configuring Video Conferencing Options

Many of the configuration policies used for peer-to-peer video sessions are also used for video conferences in Skype for Business Server 2015. This is where the use of the conferencing policy actually makes sense, in conferencing scenarios. Administrators can manage video conferencing settings and bandwidth through conferencing policies in addition to Call Admission Control. These settings can be managed using the following:

- `Get-CSConferencingPolicy`
- `Set-CSConferencingPolicy`
- `New-CSConferencingPolicy`

As a reminder, attributes introduced with Lync Server 2013 are as shown here:

- **`VideoBitRateKb`**—This setting specifies the maximum video bit rate in Kbps for video that is sent by a user.
- **`TotalReceiveVideoBitRateKb`**—This setting specifies the maximum allowed bit rate in Kbps for all the video streams that the client receives. It specifies a combined total of all video streams, except for any panoramic video streams. This is important for conferencing scenarios, specifically with Gallery View.
- **`AllowMultiView`**—This setting specifies whether users can schedule conferences that allow the Skype for Business Server 2015 Gallery View, showing up to five active video streams. This setting applies to the organizer of the conference, not to the attendees.

- `EnableMultiViewJoin`—This setting specifies whether users can join conferences that allow the Skype for Business Server 2015 Gallery View. This setting is applied at the per-user level, meaning you could have a conference with users who can see the Gallery View as well as users who are not allowed to see the Gallery View.

NOTE

If you enable Gallery View video in Skype for Business conferences, `TotalReceiveVideoBitRateKb` must not be set below 420Kbps, or Gallery View will not work.

- `MaxVideoConferencingResolution`—This setting is for legacy clients only, but it does apply to Skype for Business Server 2015 conferences. In scenarios with coexistence with Lync 2010 or older clients, administrators should consider configuring this setting as well.

For more details on how these configuration options coexist with Call Admission Control, see the earlier section "Configuring Peer to-Peer Video Options."

Skype for Business Server 2015 Data Conferencing

The term *data conferencing* is a generic term used to describe sessions among two or more participants that involve sharing computer data in real time. In the UC world, this is often referred to as *web conferencing* and can include the sharing of applications, desktops, and other content through a UC desktop application or a web browser. Web conferencing is at the core of enhanced collaboration across organizations. In Lync Server 2010, Microsoft collapsed all web conferencing functionality into the Lync 2010 client, providing enhanced conferencing functionality all in a single UI. With Skype for Business Server 2015, Microsoft includes the following features

- **Join Launcher**—When a client of any type attempts to join a meeting, the web service will validate each meeting before launching a client. This allows for a better user experience if there is an error contacting the meeting. In Lync Server 2010, meeting join failures on mobile and desktop clients were not very informative for end users. The Join Launcher helps to provide users with more information on the meeting join process. Additionally, this consolidates the meeting join functionality for all clients on computers and mobile devices.
- **PowerPoint sharing with Office Web Apps**—Skype for Business Server 2015 requires Office Web Apps Server to handle PowerPoint presentations. The use of this server allows for higher-resolution display of PowerPoint presentations and better support for enhanced PowerPoint capabilities, multiway control, and whiteboarding.
- **Archiving**—When organizations configure integrated archiving with Exchange Server 2013 or 2016, any documents that are shared in meetings will also be placed into the Exchange Archiving Store. This includes PowerPoint presentations, attachments, whiteboards, and polls.

Skype for Business Server 2015 data conferencing is made up of three content sharing types: desktop sharing, collaboration content, and PowerPoint sharing. These next few sections outline exactly what functionality is included in each content sharing type, and provide a technical overview of how Skype for Business Server 2015 makes all of this work.

Desktop Sharing

Desktop sharing in Skype for Business Server 2015 is the capability to broadcast a Skype for Business user's desktop to another Skype for Business client in peer-to-peer and conferencing scenarios. Skype for Business Server 2015 utilizes both the Remote Desktop Protocol (RDP) over RTP and H.264 SVC to deliver the desktop media stream between Skype for Business users. Presenters can share any number of monitors that are used on the PC, as well as specify a single application to be shared.

Skype for Business Server 2015 includes performance-tuning RDP (8fps versus a default of 2.5fps) for desktop sharing in the Skype for Business client, which comes at a cost of up to 10Mbps network utilization. The Office 2016 Skype for Business client introduces the capability of VbSS. This H.264 SVC-based protocol allows higher fidelity content sharing to be set up in half the time with up to 1080p 15 content at 2Mbps bandwidth. This VbSS functionality is currently available for peer-to-peer desktop sharing only, although an update is expected that will include this for multiparty scenarios.

How Does Desktop Sharing Work?

In Skype for Business Server 2015, the Application Sharing Conferencing Server service is responsible for desktop and application sharing in conferences. This role is installed on all Skype for Business Front End Servers and is one of the many MCUs in Skype for Business Server 2015. Because each Skype for Business Server handles all conferencing modalities, the boundaries for each MCU are often mixed up. The following list describes the MCUs in Skype for Business Server 2015 and what they are used for:

- **Web conferencing**—Manages conferencing data collaboration. (See the section "Collaboration Content" for more information.)
- **A/V conferencing**—Manages audio and video media streams in conferences.
- **IM conferencing**—Manages instant messaging (IM) conferencing in conferences.
- **Application sharing conferencing**—Manages desktop and application sharing media streams in conferences.

18

NOTE

In Lync Server 2010, a Legacy Web Conferencing MCU was installed on each Front End Server, providing access to legacy conferencing scenarios involving the Live Meeting 2007 client. This role is not included in Skype for Business Server 2015, which must be considered for migration scenarios from OCS 2007 R2 to Skype for Business Server 2015.

The App Sharing MCU was introduced in Lync Server 2010, and in Skype for Business Server 2015 the functionality remains the same. The key functionality that this MCU allows for is the capability to present and share control of specific applications. This MCU uses the following protocols:

- **C3P/HTTP**—The C3P protocol is used to communicate conferencing control commands. C3P over HTTP is used by the conferencing servers to communicate with each other.
- **C3P/SIP**—Skype for Business clients also communicate with the conferencing server using C3P to create conferences and to communicate changes to the conference. For Skype for Business clients, this is done securely over SIP.
- **SIP/SDP**—Application and desktop sharing traffic is delivered over RTP, and because of this, Session Description Protocol (SDP) is used to establish the RDP over RTP media stream. Skype for Business clients communicate with the App Sharing MCU over SIP to perform this negotiation and establish a media stream.
- **RDP/RTP**—Lastly, the desktop and application sharing media stream uses the RDP codec, and it is delivered over an RTP media stream.

Application and desktop sharing is also available in peer-to-peer sessions between two users. These sessions do not interact with the App Sharing Conferencing Server because they are only between two participants. These sessions do use the same protocols currently with the exception of VbSS; otherwise, the functionality is much the same as in conferences.

It is important not to overlook the bandwidth requirements for desktop sharing. The Microsoft RDP codec can provide very high-quality desktop sharing capabilities; however, this can come at a huge cost in bandwidth utilization. Bandwidth utilization for desktop sharing is dynamic and can fluctuate depending on many variables, such as the following:

- Resolution of the shared desktop
- Application that is shared
- Amount of movement in the shared desktop
- Number of monitors shared
- RDP frame rate configuration

These factors can cause Skype for Business desktop sharing to use up to 10Mbps of bandwidth. On average, desktop sharing in peer-to-peer and conferencing scenarios uses between 70Kbps and 2Mbps. Administrators should consider controlling this functionality, while still considering the end-user experience. Limiting the bandwidth available for desktop sharing will limit the quality of the sharing experience. Skype for Business Server 2015 allows administrators to control the bandwidth used by application sharing in the Skype for Business conferencing policy. See the "Configuring Data Conferencing Options" section for more information on how to configure these polices. When you are controlling the bandwidth used by Skype for Business desktop sharing, it is important to understand that reducing the bandwidth used will only degrade the sharing frame rate. At this time, it is not possible to adjust color depth, resolution, or other quality factors in Skype for Business Server 2015. If bandwidth is limited for Skype for Business desktop sharing, users will have a negative experience, but this might be required to maintain network capacity in certain scenarios.

Although Skype for Business Server 2015 application and desktop sharing can use up to 10Mbps of bandwidth, more realistic numbers are provided in Table 18.7. These numbers are provided by Microsoft as guidance for network scaling, assuming common usage scenarios.

TABLE 18.7 Skype for Business Server 2015 Desktop Sharing Bandwidth Requirements

Modality	Bandwidth	
	Average (Kbps)	Max (Kbps)
Application sharing using RDP	434 sent per sharer	938 sent per sharer

It is a best practice for organizations to use the bandwidth estimates referenced in Table 18.6 when planning to implement Skype for Business Server 2015 desktop sharing.

As mentioned previously, VbSS is capable of delivering higher fidelity video-based content, up to 30fps, by leveraging the same H.264 SVC video codec at approximately 25% more bandwidth than RDP performing at 3fps.

Collaboration Content

Skype for Business Server 2015 allows users to collaborate in real time during conferences by sharing whiteboards and polls. Virtual whiteboard functionality was introduced in Lync Server 2010 and is one of the most commonly used collaboration features in Skype for Business Server. Whiteboards allow users in a Skype for Business Server conference to collaborate in real time on drawings, pictures, tables, and more. Polling functionality is often used in web conferences to collect participant feedback. Many presenters utilize this functionality either to understand the audience they have in front of them or to collect feedback after a presentation. The polling functionality in Skype for Business Server 2015 allows presenters to collect feedback that can either be kept private or shared with the audience. Additionally, the results of the polls can be exported by the presenter.

How Does Collaboration Content Sharing Work?

The Web Conferencing Conference Service is responsible for managing collaboration content sharing in conferences. This service is installed on all Skype for Business Front End Servers. When whiteboards and polls are shared during a meeting, the content is created and stored in the Skype for Business Server File Store defined for the pool of the conference organizer. This content is then distributed to conference participants over HTTPS. Internal and external users connect to the web service URLs defined in the topology. For external users, this traffic is relayed through the reverse proxy solution deployed.

When a presenter decides to share a whiteboard or poll, the presenter uploads the content to the conference using the Persistent Shared Object Model (PSOM) protocol.

This protocol is a Microsoft proprietary protocol that has been used in web conferencing since OCS 2007 and the Live Meeting products. In addition to the initial content upload, any modifications of a whiteboard are submitted using the PSOM protocol. See the diagram in Figure 18.3 for the content upload and download process in a web conferencing scenario.

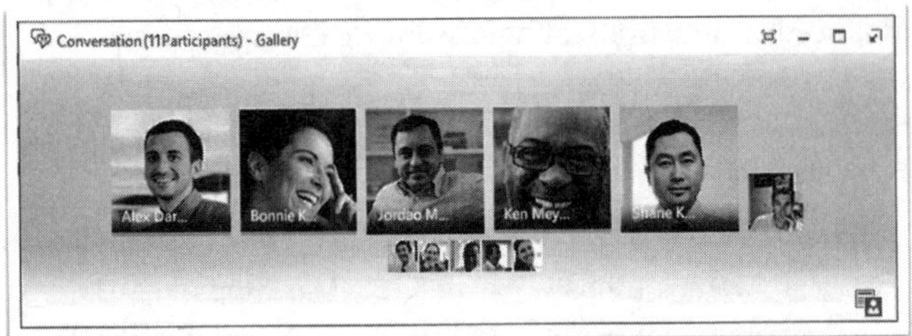

FIGURE 18.3 Content upload over PSOM and download over HTTPS.

In Figure 18.3, Client 1 is a presenter in the conference who is sharing a whiteboard. The process for whiteboard sharing is described here:

1. Client 1 sends a PSOM upload request to the web conferencing service.
2. After the conferencing service validates the request, the client sends the actual whiteboard content to the service.
3. The Web Conferencing Service saves the content to the Skype for Business file store defined for that pool. This content is created in a subfolder specific to the organizer and the conference.
4. The Web Conferencing Service then sends the presenter and participants a download URL and key to be used when making the HTTPS download request. This request is sent to the Skype for Business clients over PSOM.
5. Each client then sends an HTTPS request to the Skype for Business Web Services for the content.
6. The Skype for Business Web Services requests the content from the file store and then delivers this to each user over HTTPS.

In Skype for Business Server 2015, if archiving is enabled, any content including whiteboards and polls that is uploaded to a meeting will be archived. If Exchange Server integration is enabled, this content will be archived in to the Exchange Server data store.

Skype for Business Server 2015 collaboration content sharing does not have a major network bandwidth impact on many organizations. The data that is sent and received during meetings is often very small. However, organizations that are expecting a heavy usage of this functionality should consider the read and write impact on the file servers that will be maintaining the Skype for Business file store. Table 18.8 is provided by Microsoft for file activity capacity planning for Content Collaboration sessions.

TABLE 18.8 Skype for Business Server 2015 Content Collaboration Upload and Download Rates

Modality	Usage in Bytes per 10,000 Users	
	Average Usage	Max Usage
Web Conferencing Service content upload and download	Received: 706,655 bytes Sent: 860,224 bytes	Received: 17,803,480 bytes Sent: 19,668,079 bytes

PowerPoint Sharing with Office Web Apps

Since Lync Server 2013, PowerPoint received a complete overhaul to the sharing experience in conferences. In Lync Server 2010, PowerPoint content was delivered using the Web Conferencing Service. Although this worked, it provided limited functionality. PowerPoint presentations were often delivered at low quality, and given the Silverlight requirements in Lync 2010, the content was not viewable on a wide range of devices. In Skype for Business Server 2015, Office Web Apps Server is used to provide PowerPoint sharing in conferences.

Office Web Apps Server is a product designed to deliver browser-based versions of Microsoft Office applications. This server is required in any Skype for Business Server 2015 deployment using conferencing. Without this server role, users will not be able to share PowerPoint presentations.

Using Office Web Apps Server for PowerPoint sharing in Skype for Business Server 2015 has the following benefits:

- **Support for more devices**—Because Office Web Apps Server is designed to work with products that support the Web Application Open Platform Interface protocol (WOPI), nearly any device with a web browser can now view PowerPoint sharing in Skype for Business Server 2015. The HTML5-based Skype for Business Web App supports this functionality and is natively integrated into that experience, which allows for conferencing support on many endpoints.
- **More PowerPoint functionality**—Skype for Business Server 2015 allows users to share high-resolution PowerPoint presentations that include slide transitions and animations. The transitions and animations play during the presentation; this functionality was not available in Lync Server 2010. In conferences, users with appropriate privileges are able to scroll through a PowerPoint presentation independent of the presentation itself. Additionally, if videos are embedded in a PowerPoint presentation, Skype for Business conferences support synchronous playback of videos to participants.

The Office Web Apps Server or Server Farm used by Skype for Business Server 2015 does not have to be a dedicated deployment. Organizations can leverage a shared infrastructure to support their SharePoint, Exchange, and Skype for Business deployments that require Office Web Apps.

Supported Office Web Apps Server Topologies

The actual process of integrating Office Web Apps Server and Skype for Business Server 2015 is covered in Chapter 10, "Dependent Services and SQL." This section provides a brief overview of how to plan for integration of your Office Web Apps Server installation with Skype for Business Server 2015.

Option 1: Office Web Apps Server Installed On-premises in the Same Network Zone as Skype for Business Server 2015

In this configuration, the Office Web Apps Server farm is installed on the organization's network and ideally in the same network zone as the Skype for Business Server 2015 server. It is not a requirement for the server to be installed in the same network zone; however, this does reduce the administration overhead of configuring firewall rules and routing. With this topology, internal Skype for Business clients connect to the Office Web Apps Server using an internally defined URL, and any external clients connect through the reverse proxy solution to an externally defined URL. This topology works best for organizations that are deploying a dedicated Office Web Apps Server farm for Skype for Business Server 2015. Figure 18.4 shows how the topology would look.

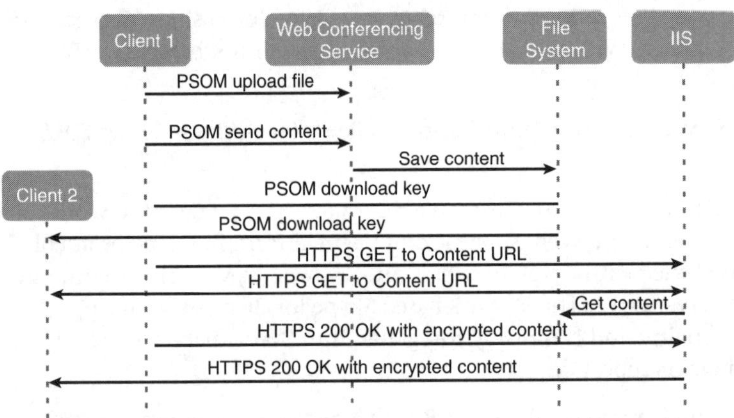

FIGURE 18.4 Office Web Apps Server on-premises on an internal network.

Option 2: Office Web Apps Server Installed On-premises in the DMZ

Because Office Web Apps Server is able to provide services to Skype for Business, Exchange, and SharePoint, some organizations might also choose to deploy this server in the DMZ. In this configuration, both internal and external clients are routed through the reverse proxy server to access the Office Web Apps Server. This topology is ideal for organizations that are looking to deploy a shared Office Web Apps Server Farm for multiple server technologies. Figure 18.5 shows how this topology would look.

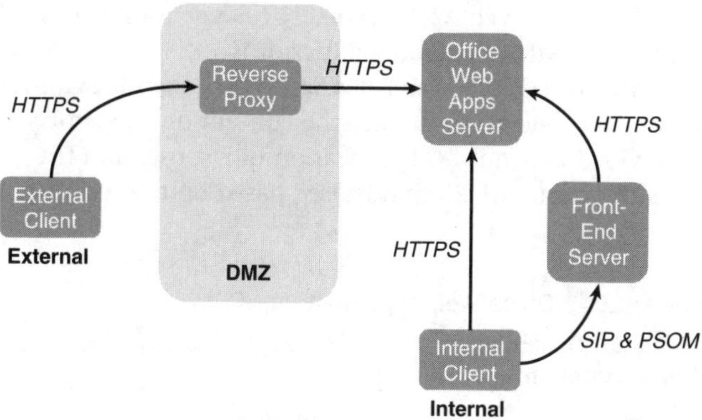

FIGURE 18.5 Office Web Apps Server on-premises in the DMZ.

Option 3: Office Web Apps Server as a Hosted Service Outside the Internal Network

Office Web Apps Server can also be provided as a third-party hosted service. In this topology, Skype for Business Server 2015 is deployed on-premises but uses an externally hosted Office Web Apps Server. Figure 18.6 shows how this topology would look.

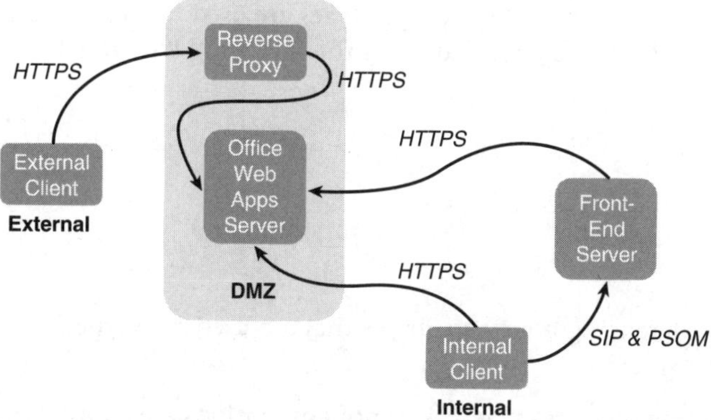

FIGURE 18.6 Office Web Apps Server hosted on an external network.

Firewall requirements for all of these scenarios are outlined in Chapter 11, "Firewall, Reverse Proxy and Security Requirements." However, it is important for organizations that are planning an Office Web Apps Server deployment to take note that not only the Skype for Business clients but also the Skype for Business Front End Server must be able to communicate with the Office Web Apps Server farm.

Topology Impacts

Each Skype for Business Front End pool will establish connections with the configured Office Web Apps Server farm in order to establish PowerPoint sharing sessions for conferences. The PowerPoint file is stored within the corresponding Skype for Business Server file store, but the delivery mechanism is the Office Web Apps Server. The Skype for Business Front End server acts as a facilitator for all conferencing modalities; it is responsible for establishing a session with the Office Web Apps Server and then providing each Skype for Business client with a URL to view and modify the content on the Office Web Apps Server. The URL that is provided depends on the location of the user and the topology defined. Table 18.9 outlines the content URL that is used based on the topology and client location.

TABLE 18.9 Skype for Business Server 2015 Office Web Apps Content URLs

Web Apps Server Configuration	Skype for Business Client Location	Content Download URL
Internal	Internal	Internal URL
Internal	External	External URL
External	Internal	External URL
External	External	External URL

Configuring Data Conferencing Options

As with Skype for Business Server 2015 video conferencing, administrators can control data conferencing functionality through a set of policies that are delivered in-band by the Skype for Business Server. Skype for Business conferencing policies are used to control data conferencing functionality. These policies are managed using the following PowerShell commands:

- `Get-CSConferencingPolicy`
- `Set-CSConferencingPolicy`
- `New-CSConferencingPolicy`

This section explains common conferencing policy attributes that are used for Skype for Business Server 2015 data conferencing:

- **`AllowAnnotations`**—This setting indicates whether or not annotations are allowed on any content shared during a meeting. Additionally, this setting determines whether or not whiteboard sharing is allowed in a conference. This setting applies to the organizer of the conference.
- **`AllowParticipantControl`**—This setting controls whether or not meeting participants are able to take control of desktops or applications that are shared during a meeting. This setting applies to the organizer of the conference.
- **`AllowPolls`**—This setting controls whether or not users are allowed to create polls during online meetings. This is also a setting applied based on the organizer of the conference.

- **AppSharingBitRateKb**—This setting can be used to define the maximum bit rate in kilobits that can be used for application sharing. Administrators should use this to control the bandwidth used by each application and desktop sharing session. This setting will apply to peer-to-peer and conferencing sessions.
- **AllowUserToScheduleMeetingsWithAppSharing**—This setting specifies whether an organizer can schedule a meeting with application and desktop sharing. This setting applies to the organizer of the conference. If this is set to false, any conference the organizer schedules will not allow app sharing of any type. If this is set to true, and administrators want to limit what certain users can share in meetings, they should set the `EnableAppDesktopSharing` attribute.
- **EnableAppDesktopSharing**—This setting controls what type of applications are able to be shared in a conference. Administrators can specify the following options:
  - **Desktop**—Users are able to share their entire desktop.
  - **SingleApplication**—Users are allowed to share only a single application.
  - **None**—Users are not allowed to share any applications or their desktop.

  Administrators also have the ability to enable higher frame rate desktop sharing by creating a new conferencing policy tagged with `HighSharingBitRateKb`. The maximum value of 13,000 will increase the frame rate to 10fps. For this to take effect within conferences, a client policy needs to also be enabled (see `EnableHighPerformanceP2PAppSharing` in the following list).

  This setting is enforced at the per-user level. For example, some users in the conference might be allowed to share their desktop, some might be allowed to share an application, and some might be allowed to share nothing.
- **EnableDataCollaboration**—This setting controls whether users can organize meetings that allow the sharing of whiteboards and annotations.
- **DisablePowerPointAnnotations**—This setting applies specifically to PowerPoint sharing in Skype for Business Server 2015. If this is set to `true`, users cannot annotate PowerPoint presentations. However, if `AllowAnnotations` is set to `true`, users have access to whiteboard functionality.
- **EnableHighPerformanceP2PAppSharing**—This setting applies specifically to desktop sharing in Skype for Business. If this is set to `true`, users can take advantage of higher frame rate desktop sharing. However, this is likely to consume a much higher level of bandwidth. For P2P sharing, leveraging VbSS instead is recommended.

Skype for Business Server 2015 provides administrators with the ability to enable and disable functionality for data conferencing scenarios at the organizer and participant levels. This is important because some participants may require restrictions on content that they can share, but they should be able to join meetings that include application or desktop sharing sessions.

Summary

Skype for Business Server 2015 provides video and data conferencing functionality that empowers users to efficiently collaborate from anywhere. Skype for Business Server 2015 continues to deliver on investments made by Microsoft with Lync Server 2013 with an emphasis on providing high-definition video to as many endpoints as possible, and in conferencing scenarios. Skype for Business Server 2015 also introduces the capability for participants to share high-fidelity video-based content within peer-to-peer calls.

This video and data conferencing functionality in Skype for Business Server 2015 enables organizations to collaborate through unified communications without any sacrifices. The Skype for Business Server 2015 platform is also extremely flexible, allowing organizations to configure policies that adapt Skype for Business Server 2015 functionality to their technical and business requirements.

CHAPTER 19

Skype for Business Video Integration with Third-Party Products and Services

IN THIS CHAPTER

- ▶ Microsoft Video Interoperability Server
- ▶ Third-Party Video Integration Basics
- ▶ Gateways
- ▶ Native Registration
- ▶ Media Transcoding Gateways
- ▶ Multipoint Control Units
- ▶ Software Plugins
- ▶ Summary and Comparison

Microsoft Lync Server has been capable of integrating with third-party video systems for some time now. This has also been carried forward into Skype for Business Server 2015. However, standards-based video interoperability still requires planning and use case study. Although Microsoft introduced its Video Interoperability Server (VIS) within Skype for Business Server 2015, there continues to be a number of vendors who offer a greater set of capabilities than VIS. These will be further explained within this chapter. It is also worth noting that previously Microsoft offered video certification programs for partners; these have since been deprecated as a part of Skype for Business Server 2015, given the inclusion of VIS. Therefore, *most* are supported directly by their respective vendor.

Starting with Lync Server 2013, Microsoft moved to using the industry-standard H.264 codec. This in turn reduced the barrier for entry for existing H.264 VTCs; however, there are still differences in the signaling layers and profiles used within the Microsoft implementation of this codec. The real benefit here is that embedded VTC processors can be leveraged for H.264 encoding, as with desktop GPUs. This could not be said for Microsoft's RTVideo codec. As a consequence, we now see third parties integrate their solutions in certain cases, taking advantage of what SVC has to offer—specifically a more interactive experience, where up to five participants can be seen within conferences in up to HD 1080p versus active speaker switched video.

Microsoft Video Interoperability Server (VIS)

During Lync Conference 2013, Microsoft announced its plans to facilitate a direct integration with Cisco VTCs. This was welcomed by the industry because enterprises generally require that their existing investments in standards-based video endpoints be integrated within their chosen UC platform. It is also in many cases an important consideration within Cisco environments. Although VIS does provide a basic integration, in many cases it does not address all customer needs. Major differences are called out in Table 19.1.

TABLE 19.1 Comparison of VIS and Third-Party Video Interoperability

Requirement	VIS	Third Party
Calling from Skype for Business to VTC	Yes	Yes
Calling from VTC to Skype for Business	No	Yes
Support for multiple VTC vendors (in addition to Cisco)	No	Yes
Support for RTVideo	No	Yes
Scheduled meeting join via CAA	Yes	Yes
Scheduled meeting join via calendar "Click-to-Join"	No	Yes
"Hollywood Squares" experience	No	Yes
Bi-directional content sharing	No	Yes
Scalable architecture	Yes	Yes
Support for federated dialing and conference join	No	Yes
Support for Skype for Business Online	No	Yes
Direct Skype for Business VTC registration	No	N/A
VTC Presence	No	Yes

VIS, unlike other server roles, cannot be collocated within Front Ends. This is largely due to the increased processing requirements. Each H.264 video stream has a need for video translation and, when configured, encoding for additional lower-resolution simulcast streams. As such, each VIS server is able to facilitate up to 16 concurrent VTCs. Additional VIS servers can be deployed with DNS load balancing being leveraged for load distribution.

Another consideration, as stated within Table 19.1, is that customers are unable to decommission their existing Cisco infrastructure due to Microsoft only supporting a "VIS to Cisco Call Manager" SIP trunk. Each VIS server shares the same hardware requirements as a fully loaded Front End, and deployment is carried out within Skype for Business Server 2015 Topology Builder.

Third-Party Video Integration Basics

Third-party video integration with Skype for Business Server 2015 has only gotten easier over the years. However, there are many tradeoffs based on the chosen technology and method. This chapter covers the process and the pros and cons of each.

Trusted Applications

Integration with any third-party solution is achieved by first defining the third-party systems as trusted applications within the Skype for Business Server 2015 topology. The definition as a trusted application is what allows the Skype for Business Server 2015 systems to establish a connection to other servers or endpoints that are not actually Skype for Business Server 2015 systems.

Before a trusted application can be created, administrators must first define a trusted application pool in the topology. After the trusted application pool is created, the trusted application representing the third-party system can be created.

Static Routes

Next, a static route must be created for a particular matching SIP URI and then pointed to the trusted application pool as a next hop. In many cases, an organization may choose to leverage an existing SIP namespace. However, this is *not recommended* because it will cause routing issues for hybrid online topologies and often flood the third-party infrastructure with SIP subscription events.

Although trusted application and static route configuration has not changed since the prior server version, additional TLS validation is now performed against the trusted application pool name. To ensure this additional security validation is passed, your third-party video system requires that a SAN certificate be created that includes the FQDN for both the static route domain and the trusted application pool name.

Figure 19.1 demonstrates the logical structure of this integration.

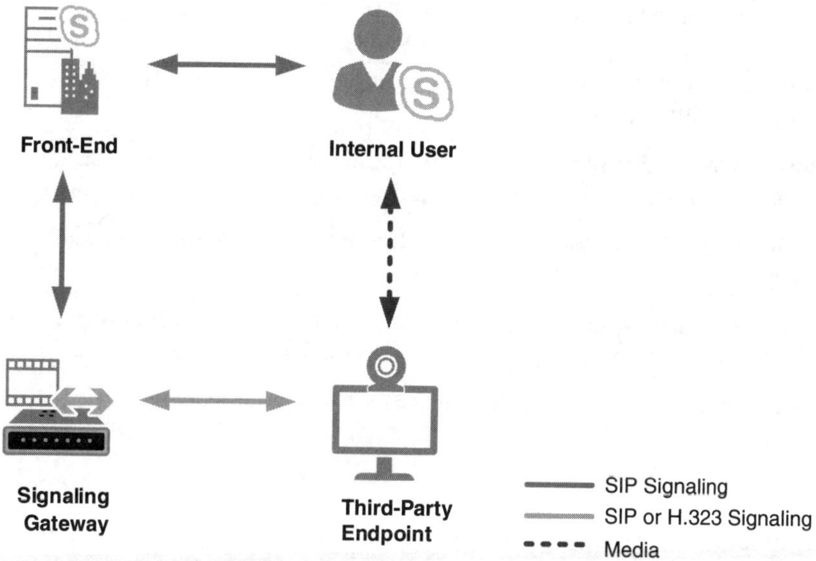

FIGURE 19.1 Trusted application.

19

Skype for Business Server 2015 operates similarly to Exchange's Internal Relay method for an accepted domain with respect to a shared SIP domain. It first attempts to resolve a URI internally, and only if no match is found does it route the call to the third-party system.

The end result is that Skype for Business Server 2015 will send audio or video calls for a matching URI to the trusted application pool as a next hop, which is the third-party system.

The overall process can be simplified with this logical summary and is depicted in Figure 19.2:

1. Skype for Business user `adam@skypeunleashed.com` places a video call to `alex@video.companyabc.com`.

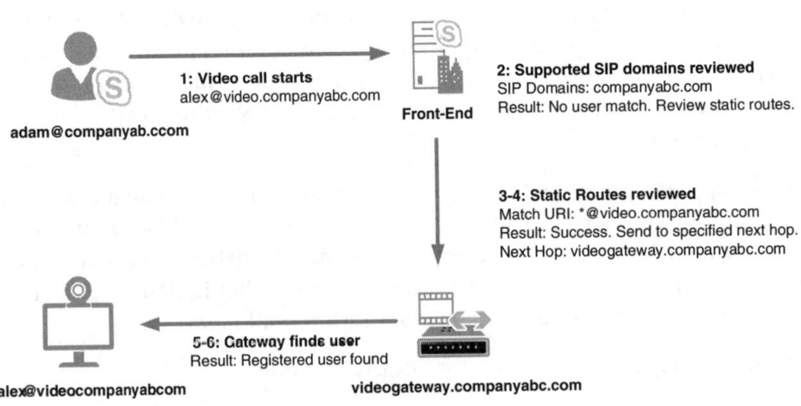

FIGURE 19.2 Static route to a third-party system.

2. Skype for Business Server 2015 determines `video.skypeunleashed.com` is not an internally supported SIP domain.
3. Skype for Business Server 2015 locates the static route for `video.skypeunleashed.com`, which points to a next hop defined as `videogateway.skypeunleashed.com`.
4. Skype for Business Server 2015 forwards the SIP Invite message to `videogateway.skypeunleashed.com`.
5. The `videogateway.skypeunleashed.com.com` device determines that it is authoritative for the video and rings anything registered as `alex@video.skypeunleashed.com`.
6. The third-party user `alex@video.skypeunleashed.com` receives the incoming video call.

The third-party endpoint can be registered to the signaling gateway via SIP or H.323, depending on the product. The signaling gateway may accept a mixture of the two protocols among endpoints.

Namespace Considerations

With any third-party video integration, it is very important to spend time planning the namespaces and to determine whether any overlap exists. Although with Skype for Business Server 2015 it is possible to use the same SIP namespace within Skype for Business Server 2015 and the third-party system, this is not recommended, as mentioned previously. Organizations should use separate domains or subdomains for the video infrastructure to logically separate components, such as using `companyabc.com` for Skype for Business users and `video.companyabc.com` for standards-based video.

The use of a single domain will produce a large amount of SIP traffic between the two systems. This is because each system must first attempt to resolve a user internally whenever a Presence request is made, and then forward that request to the opposite system if there is no internal match. The large amount of unnecessary traffic being passed back and forth can cause issues depending on the signaling gateway's hardware specifications.

If separate namespaces are used, Presence requests will be forwarded only for contacts belonging to the opposite system's namespace. This also helps uniquely identify where the traffic will ultimately terminate.

Another scenario that is impacted by a single domain is the ability to leverage a hybrid topology because the static route takes precedence over the hosting provider shared address space configuration that is required for "Split-Domain" with Skype for Business Online.

NOTE

Even if a separate namespace is used for the video endpoints, it might still be of some value to configure the additional namespace support within Skype for Business Server 2015. Although it should not be assigned to any users as a SIP domain, it will allow federation requests to flow through the Skype for Business Server 2015 infrastructure and reach the video endpoints.

Gateways

There are many different types of gateways. Some manage only the signaling portion of the connection, whereas others can also transcode the media stream. A description of each gateway type is included in this section.

Signaling-Only Gateways

The first type of video integration that ever existed between Lync, or OCS, and third-party systems was achieved using a signaling gateway. In this scenario, a SIP trunk exists between the Skype for Business Server 2015 pool and the third-party system's control unit. This is not the same type of SIP trunk used with Mediation Servers for voice calls, nor is it defined and managed the same way. A Mediation Server does not proxy video as part of its back-to-back user agent (B2BUA) model, so video calls to other systems must be managed differently.

This approach, given the reliance on codec parity between both Skype for Business and the VTC, is no longer of much value. This is due to the deprecation of H.263 support within Lync 2013 and Skype for Business.

When supported, this form of integration was very basic. The signaling gateway and Skype for Business Server 2015 Front End pool communicate via SIP to provide the signaling traffic, but the Microsoft user's endpoint and the third-party system's user endpoint must have direct IP connectivity to send the media stream between each other. This kind of integration was limited to H.263 CIF quality video using a 352×288 resolution. Even with H.264 support, introduced within Lync 2013, media needs to be translated, which requires processing capabilities that are not present within a signaling only gateway.

Transcoding Gateways

In the past, video gateways would often be distinguished from, for example, a video bridge (MCU), but more recently this capability is embedded within the third-party MCU. Gateway calling is not only available for peer-to-peer calling, but also AVMCU conferences. When Polycom's RealConnect feature spearheaded the ability to join conferences scheduled within Skype for Business Server 2015, other vendors followed suit, including Acano, Pexip, and even Microsoft within its VIS solution.

These gateway solutions perform video and signaling translation and therefore require more processing power, which is why they are usually more expensive than signaling-only gateways.

Peer-to-peer gateway solutions often include presence proxy solutions and the ability to route dynamically between Skype for Business clients and VTCs by configuring just a few matching rules.

Cisco also has a video gateway solution: the Video Communication Server (VCS) product. This is in addition to its recent Acano acquisition, which already had its own solution (this is covered in the next section). It should be noted that although the Cisco VCS supports Skype for Business clients, it cannot be directly integrated with a Skype for Business Server 2015 backend.

Back-to-Back User Agents

The use of back-to-back user agents (B2BUAs)—the process of mediating two legs of a SIP call while maintaining call flow between two endpoints—is often an integral part to any video gateway.

Cisco introduced the back-to-back user agent starting in version 7 of its VCS platform, which is no longer supported when directly integrated with a Skype for Business Server 2015 backend. To start with, the static route is completely gone from the equation and should actually be removed as part of the upgrade process if it previously existed.

The B2BUA serves a similar purpose as the VIS role and effectively serves as what the Skype for Business Mediation Server does for audio calls, and it terminates two independent calls. The difference from a static route configuration is that the endpoints no longer relay media directly to each other. Instead, the Cisco video endpoint sends a stream to the B2BUA, and the Skype for Business endpoint does the same on the opposite side. The B2BUA does not do any kind of media transcoding or scaling, so the two endpoints still need to support the same codec as if they were still relaying traffic directly. In VCS 8.1, Cisco added support for Microsoft's SVC codec, which in turn means there is no longer a requirement for a Cisco Advanced Media Gateway (AMG).

Although this approach simplifies the integration, it does introduce a bottleneck in the deployment because all video between the two systems must now pass through the B2BUA; the same scenario is also true for peer-to-peer video gateway calls. This can be an issue for calls between two internal systems, which must now traverse the WAN to pass through the B2BUA.

The B2BUA also enables a feature called FindMe by Cisco, which enables the B2BUA to synchronize Skype for Business Presence with a user's Cisco endpoint and fork calls between the systems. The idea here is that if a user receives a call on their Cisco endpoint, their Skype for Business client will ring and be answered at either endpoint. The same is true for calls to the user's Skype for Business endpoint.

Edge Traversal

With the exception of VIS, all third-party standards-based video solutions support Microsoft ICE. For example, Polycom's RMX can be configured to communicate with the Skype for Business Edge Server in order to relay traffic for remote users.

Edge traversal is achieved in a number of ways—for example, by providing a username and password that is already provisioned for Skype for Business, by terminating to a federation SRV with a media relay, and via the deployment of a trusted application endpoint. The pros and cons of each are shown in table 19.2.

TABLE 19.2 Pros and Cons of Edge Traversal Mechanisms

Edge Traversal Mechanism	Pros	Cons
Federation SRV record	No on-premises Skype for Business infrastructure required.	Only facilitates direct-dial virtual meeting room dialing; no support for gateway scenarios.
Skype for Business account	Easy to deploy; facilitates gateway functions.	Limited number of concurrent connections (12); requires on-premises Skype for Business infrastructure.
Trusted application endpoint	No connection restrictions; facilitates gateway functions.	Requires on-premises Skype for Business infrastructure.

Acano, for example, leverages a username to register to Skype for Business Server 2015. It then receives Media Relay Authentication Service (MRAS) credentials, which in turn will be used to support calls between Skype for Business users and internal or remote endpoints. In the case of Polycom RMX, it leverages a trusted application endpoint. This is recommended because, unlike the user account approach, it is not limited to 12 concurrent connections.

Native Registration

Another type of integration used by third-party systems is native registration to Skype for Business Server 2015 Front End pools, where the third-party system's video endpoint registers to Skype for Business Server 2015 just like any other endpoint. In many cases, the third-party endpoint supports dual-registration so that it can maintain a connection to its traditional control system and simultaneously stay registered to Skype for Business Server 2015, as depicted in Figure 19.3.

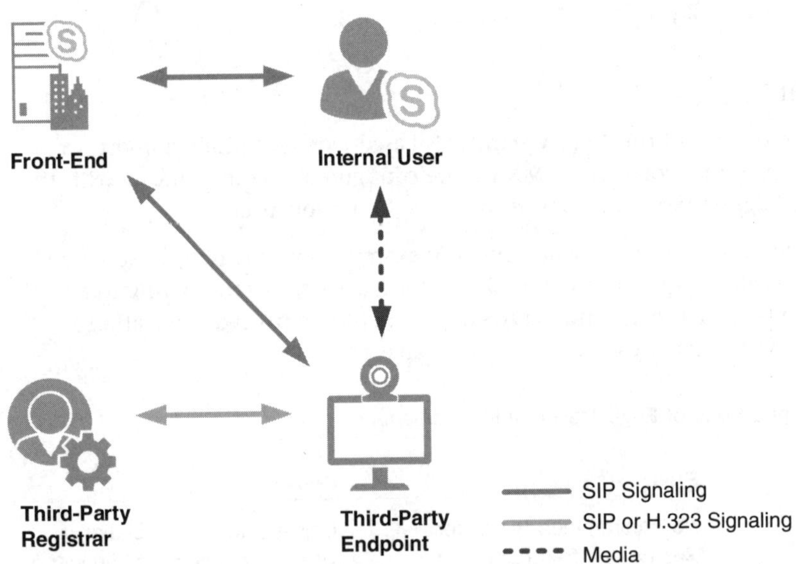

FIGURE 19.3 Native Skype for Business Server 2015 registration.

The process for this is usually much more straightforward and involves minimal server configuration. A user account is created to represent the third-party endpoint, and the endpoint is then configured with those credentials. The endpoint then uses NTLM authentication to authenticate to the Front End pool; then it behaves like another Skype for Business user.

NOTE

The fact that NTLM authentication is required is an important point. If an organization disables NTLM authentication for security reasons, third-party endpoints will be unable to register to the Skype for Business Server 2015 server.

The advantage to this method is that it provides Presence for the endpoint so that other Skype for Business users can tell whether the signed-in user is available, away, or currently in a call. This solves a number of problems and results in a much more refined user experience. Seeing "Presence Unknown" for every third-party endpoint is confusing to end users because there is no notification that this is expected, so it appears there is an error with Skype for Business. Having the Presence reflected even unidirectionally is a big step forward.

Video Codec Support

Just as is the case with using a signaling gateway, this form of integration relies on the third-party endpoint and the Skype for Business endpoint sharing a common codec within their media stack. Backward compatibility support for RTVideo is also a consideration, because without this capability any Lync 2010 clients would not be able to send video to the VTC.

Polycom is the only vendor to add native support for RTVideo and Microsoft H.264 SVC, which was introduced as a Microsoft video interoperability license for its Group Series endpoints. Cisco added support for Microsoft H.264 also, but only for peer-to-peer calls and not without the presence of VCS within the deployment. The Polycom Group Series systems are able to take advantage of SVC when participating within an AVMCU conference call, providing a Polycom equivalent Gallery View–style experience.

Conferencing

The same Polycom feature key provides the ability to schedule Skype for Business meetings and invite the Group Series mailbox, thus facilitating a "Click-to-Join" experience. Also, as with any Skype for Business client, the Group Series endpoint understands Microsoft's Conference Control Protocol (CCCP), which allows the Polycom system to participate in a Skype for Business conference. Users are also able to drag and drop a Group Series into an existing Skype for Business conference.

Although Polycom's previous generation of VTCs (the HDX) was unable to provide any content support, the Group Series has the ability to receive Remote Desktop Protocol (RDP) content when shared as either an application or desktop. The expectation is that additional capabilities will be possible when Microsoft's VbSS protocol is available for all types of calling scenarios because this leverages H.264 versus RDP, which is more difficult to encode. Sharing modalities such as PowerPoint, whiteboards, and polls continue to be unavailable when Group Series endpoints are participating within a Skype for Business meeting.

LifeSize and Polycom HDX systems are no longer supported with Skype for Business.

Edge Traversal and More

Native registration to Skype for Business Server 2015 also allows for additional features to be used, such as STUN/TURN and secure RTP media encryption.

With native registration, the third-party endpoint will receive MRAS credentials from the Skype for Business Edge Server and present remote and relay candidates when participating in Skype for Business calls, enabling remote users to seamlessly connect without VPN.

Additionally, native registration will support secure RTP transport of the media stream.

Another advantage to this native registration is that Polycom supports Skype for Business Call Admission Control policies. No other vendor supports this functionality today.

These Polycom VTCs currently do not support registration to Skype for Business Online; however, given customer adoption within Office 365, support for this is expected in the future.

Multipoint Control Units

Multipoint Control Units, or MCUs as they are more commonly called, allow for multiple participants to interact in a conference. The MCU is in control of the conference and determines what codecs are used, who the presenter is, and which video to show, and it also mixes the audio. It is a complicated and critical component in conferences.

The Skype for Business Server 2015 A/V MCU service is a software-based MCU that provides this functionality for Skype for Business endpoints, but traditional video conferencing has used a hardware-based MCU (leveraging DSPs). More recently these could be deployed in software also, but often with less resources or ports being available. Polycom has a product called the RMX, and Cisco has its own MCU, previously called the Codian devices while under the Tandberg name. The shortcoming of a hardware-based MCU is that it has a fixed hardware specification and can handle a limited number of total participants. Cisco recently acquired Acano, which can, like Polycom, be deployed in both software or hardware configurations. Popular MCUs from Polycom, Acano, and Pexip also have embedded video gateway functions that facilitate peer-to-peer and conference join capabilities. Gateway calling between VTCs that do not natively support Skype for Business Server 2015 integration has become more popular than directly dialing Virtual Meeting Rooms (VMRs) because it provides a richer, more integrated user experience. In the past, video gateways were considered a separate category of solution. Today, this is often bundled into the same third-party infrastructure.

Layout Control

Third-party MCUs, as with Skype for Business Server 2015, are capable of showing multiple video streams in a single conference, which is referred to as continuous Presence. Many products also include the capability to customize the layout of the video streams in a conference, or overlay text to identify specific users or locations. Since Lync Server 2013,

Microsoft also provides a similar experience, allowing for up to five concurrent video streams to be displayed. Microsoft added the capability to pin specific video streams for viewing, but this still falls short of the flexibility provided by third-party MCUs, which can display more concurrent participants (typically 16+ persons). For the vast majority of use cases, the native Skype for Business Server 2015 functionality should be sufficient, but there might be cases in which it's still advantageous to use a third-party MCU.

Interoperability

One specific use case that Skype for Business Server 2015 does not solve on its own is the capability to conduct a conference using many types of endpoints. VIS adds support for a Cisco endpoint running TC 7.0 or greater, but as per the previous section, has a number of limitations. The Skype for Business Server 2015 MCU can host a meeting with Skype for Business endpoints and third-party endpoints using native Skype for Business Server 2015 registration, but for any other third-party systems, the ability to join a Skype for Business meeting is brokered by a conference gateway.

By using a third-party MCU, an automated VMR can be used to dial in to the meeting, allowing Skype for Business endpoints and traditional video endpoints to participate in a single meeting. These meetings can provide audio, video, and bidirectional application and desktop sharing, which is achieved by transcoding standards-based H.239 or BFCP content into RDP, and vice versa.

When this intelligent VMR automatically joins the conference, vendors are able to receive all H.264 SVC streams relayed by the Skype for Business Server 2015 AVMCU and create a composition that delivers a similar experience to dialing a VMR on the VTC.

As mentioned previously, this technology was pioneered by Polycom with RealConnect; then Acano followed suit with Dual Home, and more recently Pexip introduced Fusion.

Virtual Meeting Rooms

Virtual Meeting Rooms is the more traditional way to enable interoperability between almost any type of standards-based endpoint and Skype for Business Server 2015, with many organizations allocating personal VMR numbers to users when provisioned within Active Directory. But, as mentioned previously, this approach is becoming less common within Microsoft environments because it forces everyone to follow a different join process for meetings that include VTCs. The problem with this approach is that although meeting organizers know who they are inviting, they are unaware of the type of endpoint being used to join the meeting. It is also often true that leveraging MCU resources is more expensive, unless the organization has completely moved from AVC to SVC-based endpoints, which is rarely the case. However, some organizations have applications or meeting scenarios whereby specific conference layouts are required, which may also include the need to see more than five concurrent participants.

Deployment of these third-party MCUs follows the same approach as illustrated within the "signaling gateway" discussion of this chapter; more specifically, the creation of a trusted application within a trusted application pool. This process also facilitates the ability for vendors to publish Presence for VMRs, with some MCUs also updating this Presence status when participants join the meeting. A VMR is a virtual conference that exists on an MCU either persistently or for a period of time. It is a configured meeting space where conferences can be conducted and third-party endpoints or Skype for Business endpoints can join the conference at any time. These rooms will only leverage resources when being used. These resources are often referred to as "ports," with hardware-based models typically providing a greater count. However, most vendors will offer the ability to scale these deployments by adding additional MCUs and therefore greater resource capabilities.

Edge Traversal

Another advantage when vendors integrate their MCUs as a trusted application is the capability to register with the Skype for Business Front End Server and receive MRAS credentials. This enables the MCU VMR to provide remote and relay candidates for media relay during the ICE negotiation process, so remote Skype for Business users can seamlessly join meetings hosted on the MCU.

NOTE

Keep in mind that the Edge traversal discussed here is specific to enabling remote Skype for Business endpoints to join a conference and that remote third-party endpoints are not capable of joining the meeting through a Skype for Business Edge Server. Third-party vendors usually provide a similar border element to facilitate remote standards-based endpoints joining a meeting, such as Polycom RealPresence Access Director (RPAD) or Cisco's VCS Expressway (VCSe).

Hardware Versus Software

Media transcoding video solutions can be either hardware based or software based, which generally determines the price point. The Cisco Advanced Media Gateway is an example of a hardware-based transcoding device that is typically deployed to provide HD video integration with legacy Cisco/Tandberg systems. This system comes at a fairly significant price point that puts it out of reach for many organizations.

Polycom, Acano, and Pexip have both hardware and software variants of their solutions, providing a software-based media transcoding device as part of their platform. Vendors typically provide preconfigured virtual machines, typically for VMware, but in some cases Hyper-V also. These can then be deployed on a virtual infrastructure, so performance is limited by the hardware an organization runs the application on rather than what a vendor bundles and ships. An example of a transcoding gateway is shown in Figure 19.4.

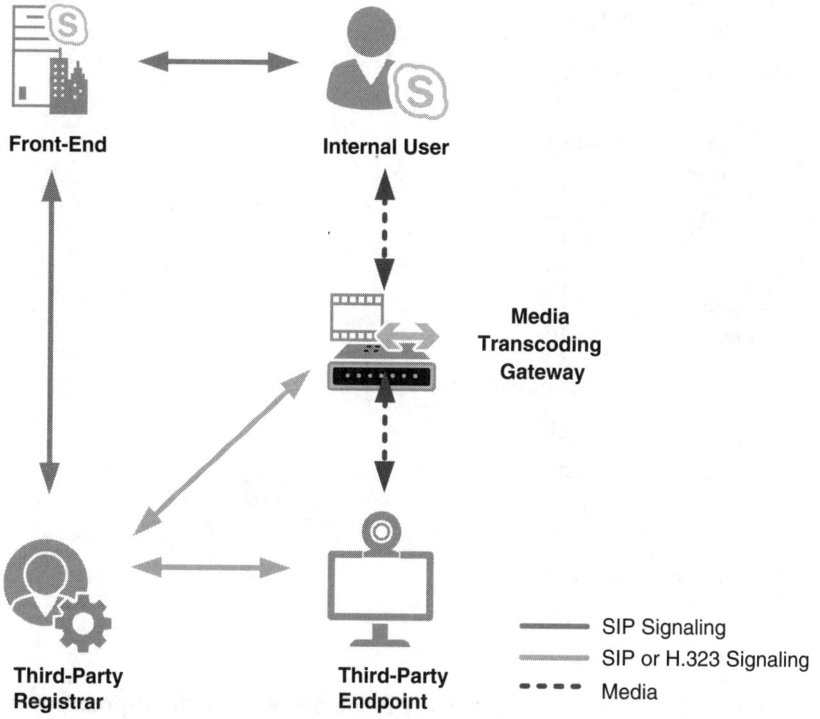

FIGURE 19.4 Media transcoding gateway.

Any kind of transcoding gateway requires a significant amount of processing power, so these types of products generally can handle only a handful of simultaneous calls.

Media Flow

It is important to understand that all media must pass through this gateway to be converted when a media transcoding gateway is being used. This is not an issue for SIP signaling traffic, but it can have a significant impact on the user experience when the media transcoding gateway is located across a WAN connection.

Consider a scenario in which a Skype for Business endpoint and third-party endpoint are in the same office, but the media-transcoding device is in a datacenter geographically far from the office. Instead of the traffic being relayed between the two endpoints in a peer-to-peer sense, both endpoints must submit their media stream across the WAN connection to the media-transcoding gateway, as shown in Figure 19.5. The voice and video quality might suffer, depending on the latency between the office and the datacenter.

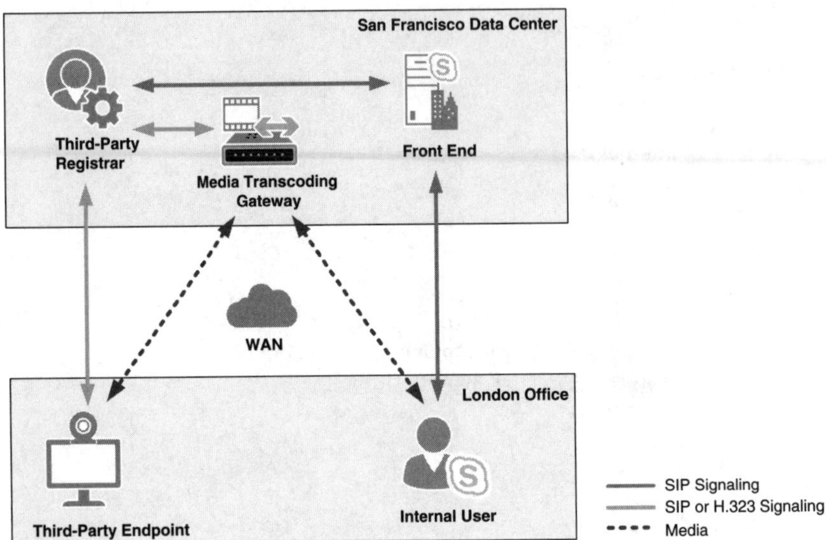

FIGURE 19.5 Media transcoding gateway WAN.

Cloud MCUs

An emerging trend in the video conferencing industry is the move from an on-premises hardware- or software-based MCU to a cloud-hosted MCU. Companies such as Blue Jeans and Polycom have already started to introduce services with these features. The advantage to this approach is that an organization can limit its on-premises investment in MCUs, which was sometimes very cost-prohibitive in the case of a hardware-based MCUs. Software-based MCUs generally came at a lower price point, but a hosted subscription model in the cloud is becoming a very popular concept.

The shift to these cloud MCUs has also sparked new possibilities for interoperability that were previously not considered with traditional MCUs. For example, Blue Jeans supports nearly any type of endpoint joining the same meeting through their service, including Skype for Business, Skype, Google, Polycom, Cisco, LifeSize, traditional H.323 systems, and even clients through a web browser. The frustrating days of trying to configure a meeting between two partners using different video vendors are addressed by using a cloud service that supports nearly any type of system.

Cloud MCUs might sound very attractive, and they certainly do have their advantages, but there is a level of control that is lost, as is the case with any cloud service. There are options to customize and control meetings, but a traditional on-premises MCU typically has many more options available to administrators.

The other consideration with a cloud MCU is that all video traffic is going out to the Internet and back, even for calls that only involve the organization, as shown in Figure 19.6. A call that might have typically traversed the WAN or stayed on the internal network now requires a significant amount of Internet bandwidth. Whether a cloud MCU makes sense depends on the organization's network architecture and Internet service.

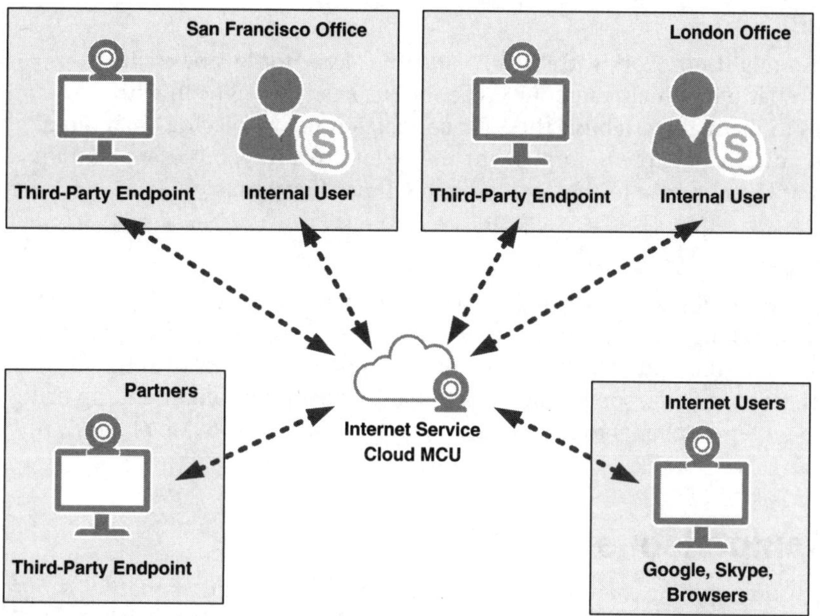

FIGURE 19.6 Cloud MCU interoperability.

Software Plugins

Some organizations are providing video interoperability to Skype for Business through the use of software plugins on the desktop clients. These plugins effectively replace the capability to make Skype for Business video calls using the Microsoft platform; instead, calls are placed through the plugin while still being presented on the user's desktop as if the user made a Skype for Business call. Examples of this include Cisco's CUCILYNC plugin and Avaya's Aura product. The pitch with these products is generally along the lines of selling the organization on managing the video in a single system that the business has already invested heavily in. The disadvantage is that these products typically require additional licensing, limit the great features within Skype for Business Server 2015, and result in a really poor, and confusing, end-user experience. Plug-ins from multiple vendors are often frowned upon by IT departments because deployment and maintenance is difficult to manage.

End User and Client Confusion

These aforementioned products bolt onto the Skype for Business user interface and provide contextual menus for launching a video call using their backend system rather than Skype for Business video. It's important for IT administrators to carefully plan the deployment and ensure that the appropriate Skype for Business options are disabled so that users don't see two different video call options that might work differently.

Edge Traversal

These products also might not work without VPN like the Skype for Business client. Consider a basic scenario in which a remote Skype for Business user signs in without VPN, but then has to manually establish the VPN connection before placing an audio or video call. It is technically possible to implement the system this way, but user adoption typically suffers and the response to the deployment will not be favorable.

Software Updates

Organizations deploying these software plugins become dependent on the plugin vendor to certify and approve all updates to Skype for Business servers and clients going forward. It's conceivable that a future update will change how the plugin interacts with the Skype for Business client, or even break some other functionality. Businesses might end up being unable to upgrade servers or clients to fix one issue just because the software plugin is no longer compatible.

Solution Comparisons

This section covers some specific examples of products developed by vendors that fit into each of the categories discussed in this chapter. This is not meant to be an exhaustive list of every product available, but is meant to provide an overview of typical solutions used.

Signaling Gateway Vendor Examples

At time of writing, there are no signaling-only gateways that support the ability to be directly integrated to a Skype for Business Server 2015 server.

Native Registration Vendor Examples

The following highlights the single vendor that supports native registration to a Skype for Business Server 2015:

- **Polycom Group Series**—The Polycom Group Series codec series supports native Skype for Business Server 2015 registration out of the box. The Microsoft interoperability license key can be added to any of these devices.

Media Transcoding Gateway Vendor Examples

This list highlights the vendors that handle media transcoding between Skype for Business Server 2015 and third-party endpoints:

- **Acano MCU**—The Acano MCU allows for layout flexibility and virtual rooms; federated VMRs without the need for an on-premises Skype for Business Server 2015 deployment; and peer-to-peer and conference gateway services.
- **Pexip MCU**—The Pexip MCU allows for layout flexibility and virtual rooms; federated VMRs without the need for an on-premises Skype for Business Server 2015 deployment; and peer-to-peer and conference gateway services.

- **Polycom RMX**—The Polycom RMX platform is a scalable system that also provides advanced conferencing services for standards-based endpoints as well as peer-to-peer and conference gateway services.

MCU Vendor Examples

The following devices support conferencing for Skype for Business endpoints:

- **Polycom RMX**—The Polycom RMX platform is a scalable system that also provides advanced conferencing services for standards-based endpoints; peer-to-peer and conference gateway services; and support for scheduled Skype for Business online conferences via their RealConnect conference gateway.
- **Acano MCU**—The Acano MCU allows for layout flexibility and virtual rooms; federated VMRs without the need for an on-premises Skype for Business Server 2015 deployment; peer-to-peer and conference gateway services; and support for scheduled Skype for Business online conferences via their Dual Home conference gateway.
- **Pexip MCU**—The Pexip MCU allows for layout flexibility and virtual rooms; federated VMRs without the need for an on-premises Skype for Business deployment; peer-to-peer and conference gateway services; and support for scheduled Skype for Business online conferences via their Fusion conference gateway.

Cloud MCU Vendor Examples

The following cloud-based video services support some form of Skype for Business integration:

- **Blue Jeans**—Currently supports the highest number of video platforms, including Skype for Business, Skype, Google, H.323, and browsers.
- **Polycom RealPresence Cloud**—Integrates with other systems for address-book functionality and allows browser-based conferencing.
- **WebEx Meeting Center with Collaboration Meeting Rooms (CMR)**—Supports direct dial for multiple video endpoint types, with voice, video, and content.
- **Zoom**—Zoom previously only offered a plugin-based solution; the ability to dial in to a Zoom meeting via federation is also now possible without additional client-side software.
- **Office 365 Cloud Interoperability Service**—At Enterprise Connect 2016, Microsoft and Polycom announced a joint hosted video interoperability service. This new service, due to launch in the second half 2016, is expected to deliver a hosted Polycom RealConnect solution and be easily provisioned via the existing Office 365 tenant portal.

Software Plugin Vendor Examples

The following products can be considered a software plugin method for providing third-party video:

- **Zoom (Zoom Lync Plugin)**—Zoom's cloud conferencing solution integrates with Lync and Skype for Business clients by offering a contextual "Start Zoom Meeting" menu once their client-side plugin is installed.
- **Cisco UC Integration for Microsoft Lync (CUCILYNC)**—Cisco's product that integrates with VCS and Cisco Unified Communications Manager. All the media is done through Cisco's plugin rather than the Lync client.
- **Avaya Microsoft Lync Integration**—Previously called Microsoft ACE, this product behaves similarly to CUCILYNC and ensures that all the media occurs within the Avaya infrastructure.

Summary

The video integration story is constantly changing, and always improving, as vendors find new methods for providing interoperability. Microsoft's adoption of H.264 and the introduction of its Video Interoperability Server have helped third-party vendors with their respective on-premises VTC integrations. Microsoft Cloud customers, however, are still presented with limited options. The expectation is that as we see Office 365 adoption, online video interoperability options will start to become more prevalent.

CHAPTER 20

Unified Contact Store, Exchange, and SharePoint Integration

IN THIS CHAPTER

- Server-to-Server Authentication
- Exchange Integration Features
- SharePoint Integration Features

Previous versions of Lync Server have featured some useful integrations with Microsoft Exchange and SharePoint, and these have proven to extend the value of all three of the products. With Skype for Business Server 2015, Microsoft continues to support these same hooks into Exchange and SharePoint. This chapter focuses on the details behind these integration features that will no doubt provide additional value for many organizations that deploy these applications together. Although Microsoft has recently released Exchange Server 2016, the steps and features listed here apply to both Exchange Server 2013 and 2016. As such, this chapter will refer to both as Exchange Server for simplicity.

Server-to-Server Authentication

To allow Skype for Business Server 2015, Exchange Server, and SharePoint 2013 systems to communicate securely with each other, the OAuth (OpenAuthentication) protocol is used. OAuth certificates allow the exchange of security tokens that grant access to resources for a time. Server-to-server authentication and authorization using OAuth is required for any of the integration features described in this chapter. For a full description of the process used to request and install an OAuth certificate for Skype for Business Server 2015, see Chapter 10, "Dependent Services."

After an OAuth certificate is installed on the first Skype for Business Server 2015 Front End Server in the environment, the certificate is automatically replicated to other Skype for Business Servers via Central Management Store replication, thereby establishing the required trust relationship between

Skype for Business Servers. Similarly, Exchange Server and SharePoint 2013 use certificates to establish trust with other servers running the same software. However, for Skype for Business Server 2015 to establish trust with Exchange Server and SharePoint 2013, the certificates on both sides must first be exchanged, and then the applications must also be configured as partner applications on both sides. A partner application is any application that Skype for Business Server 2015 can exchange security tokens with directly, without the need for a third-party security token server.

To facilitate the certificate exchange between systems, each application features an authentication metadata document, which contains the certificates and other authentication information required to establish trust. The metadata documents are then exposed to the other application using a web service, as described in the sections that follow.

Exchange Server Autodiscover Configuration

An initial prerequisite that must be met to allow integration between Skype for Business, Exchange, and SharePoint is the configuration of the Exchange Server Autodiscover service. The Exchange Server Autodiscover service is used by both Skype for Business and SharePoint to find and read the Exchange authentication metadata document; therefore, Autodiscover must be configured and operational before these applications are configured as partner applications for Exchange. In mixed Exchange environments that include both Exchange 2010 and Exchange 2013/2016, Skype for Business and SharePoint should be configured to connect to the Exchange Server Autodiscover service.

Exchange Autodiscover can be configured using the `Set-ClientAccessServer` cmdlet. Here's an example:

```
Set-ClientAccessServer -Identity exchange01.fabrikam.local
➥-AutoDiscoverServiceInternalUri https://autodiscover.skypeunleashed.com/
➥autodiscover/autodiscover.xml
```

Additional tasks that are required for Autodiscover to function include the configuration of a DNS host record for the service, as well as the installation of a server certificate assigned to IIS that includes the Autodiscover name as a subject alternative name.

TIP

As part of the Exchange Server installation, a self-signed certificate named Microsoft Exchange Server Auth Certificate is created and placed in the local certificate store of each system. This default server authentication certificate is automatically associated with the server authentication configuration, and is suitable for this purpose. On Client Access Server systems, however, an additional self-signed certificate is created and assigned to IIS and other Exchange services; this certificate must be replaced with a server certificate from an internal or third-party Certificate Authority before integration with Skype for Business is established. The reason for this is that Skype for Business will attempt to connect to the Exchange Server Autodiscover service hosted on IIS to read the Exchange authentication metadata document, and the certificate must be trusted for this connection to succeed. At a minimum, the certificate must include the Autodiscover FQDN as a subject alternative name to enable Skype for Business to successfully connect to the Exchange authentication metadata document.

The following sections provide details on the procedures required to establish server-to-server authentication between these systems.

Configuring Skype for Business and Exchange as Partner Applications

After Autodiscover is configured, Skype for Business and Exchange can be configured as partner applications by exchanging certificates using the authentication metadata documents exposed on each side. On the Exchange Server side, a PowerShell script named `Configure-EnterprisePartnerApplication.ps1` is provided and is used to connect to the URL of the Skype for Business Server 2015 metadata document and retrieve the required information from it. The default URL for the Skype for Business Server 2015 authentication metadata document is https://<Skype4BFqdn>/metadata/json/1, where <Skype4BFqdn> is the fully qualified domain name of a Skype for Business Server 2015 Front End Server. For example, the following procedure would be used to configure Skype for Business Server 2015 as a partner application for the `skypeunleashed.com` Exchange Server deployment:

1. Log on to a system where the Exchange Server administrative tools are installed using an account that has administrative rights to Exchange.
2. Open the Exchange Management Shell and navigate to the Exchange scripts directory, which is by default `C:\Program Files\Microsoft\Exchange Server\V15\Scripts`.
3. Execute the following command:

```
.\Configure-EnterprisePartnerApplication.ps1 -AuthMetadataUrl
➥https://fe01.fabrikam.local/metadata/json/1 -ApplicationType Lync
```

4. If the command is successful, the script creates a disabled user account linked to the partner application and assigns several Exchange management roles to the account to grant the required permissions, as shown in Figure 20.1.

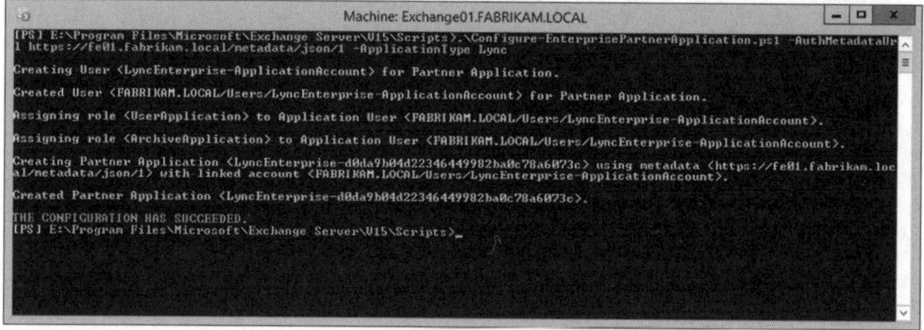

FIGURE 20.1 Configuring Skype for Business Server 2015 as a partner application in Exchange.

5. To prepare the system for new OAuth connections, execute the `iisreset` command on both the Client Access and the Mailbox Servers in the site.

20

On the Skype for Business Server 2015 side, the `New-CsPartnerApplication` cmdlet is used to configure Exchange Server as a partner application for Skype for Business Server 2015. The default URL for the Exchange authentication metadata document is https://autodiscover.<domain>/autodiscover/metadata/json/1, where <domain> is the DNS domain of the Exchange systems. For example, follow these steps to configure Exchange as a partner application for the `skypeunleashed.com` Skype for Business Server 2015 deployment:

1. Log on to a system where the Skype for Business Server 2015 administrative tools are installed using an account that is a member of the `CsAdministrator` group and has administrative rights on the local system.
2. Open the Skype for Business Server Management Shell and execute the following command:

```
New-CsPartnerApplication -Identity exchange01 -ApplicationTrustLevel full
➥-MetadataUrl "https://autodiscover.skypeunleashed.com/
➥autodiscover/metadata/json/1"
```

3. If the command is successful, the properties of the new partner application are displayed, as shown in Figure 20.2.

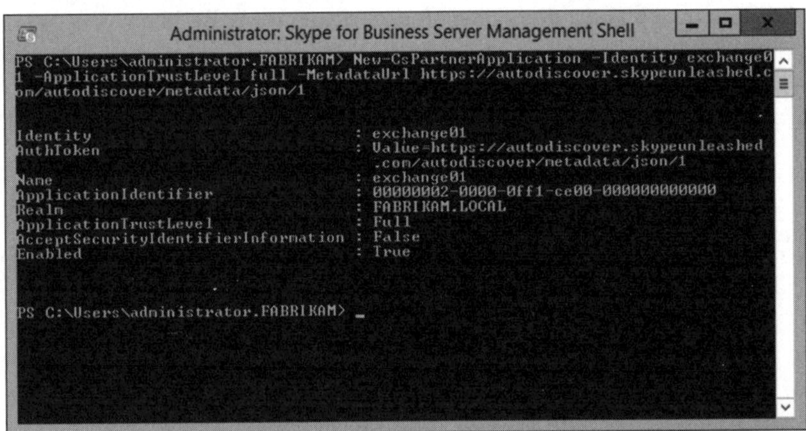

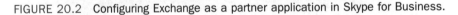

FIGURE 20.2 Configuring Exchange as a partner application in Skype for Business.

After Skype for Business Server 2015 and Exchange have been configured as partner applications, server-to-server authentication between the systems can be tested by using the Skype for Business Server Management Shell to execute a synthetic transaction. The `Test-CsExStorageConnectivity` cmdlet has been provided for this purpose. This synthetic transaction uses OAuth to write an item into the conversation history folder of an Exchange Server mailbox, and then it optionally deletes the item. For example, the following command is used to test server-to-server authentication between Skype for Business Server 2015 and Exchange for `skypeunleashed.com`, specifying the SIP URI of a Skype for Business user who has an Exchange Server mailbox:

```
Test-CsExStorageConnectivity -SipUri jrossen@skypeunleashed.com -Binding NetTCP
➥-DeleteItem -HostNameStorageService fe01.fabrikam.local
```

Configuring Skype for Business Server 2015 and SharePoint as Partner Applications

Before Skype for Business Server 2015 and SharePoint are configured as partner applications, certificates must be installed for each application. For Skype for Business Server 2015, server authentication certificates are installed as part of the Skype for Business Server 2015 deployment process. For SharePoint, certificates are not installed by default as part of the deployment process; therefore, at least one server certificate must be installed and mapped to a SharePoint site before server-to-server authentication with Skype for Business Server 2015 is configured.

After the certificates are installed on both sides, Skype for Business Server 2015 and SharePoint can be configured as partner applications by exchanging the certificates using the authentication metadata documents exposed on each side. On the SharePoint 2013 side, the `New-SPTrustedSecurityTokenIssuer` cmdlet is used to connect to the URL of the Skype for Business Server 2015 metadata document and retrieve the required information from it. The default URL for the Skype for Business Server 2015 authentication metadata document is https://<LyncFqdn>/metadata/json/1, where <LyncFqdn> is the fully qualified domain name of a Skype for Business Server 2015 Front End Server. For example, the following procedure would be used to configure Skype for Business Server 2015 as a partner application for the `skypeunleashed.com` SharePoint 2013 deployment:

1. Log on to a system where the SharePoint 2013 administrative tools are installed using an account with local administrative rights on the system and that has been assigned the `securityadmin` fixed server role on the SharePoint SQL instance, as well as the `db_owner` fixed database role on the SharePoint SQL databases.

2. Open the SharePoint Management Shell and execute the following command:

```
New-SPTrustedSecurityTokenIssuer -MetadataEndpoint
➥https://fe01.fabrikam.local/metadata/json/1 -IsTrustBroker
➥-Name "Skype for Business trust"
```

3. If the command is successful, the Management Shell displays details regarding the Skype for Business Server 2015 certificate and the new partner relationship.

On the Skype for Business Server 2015 side, the `New-CsPartnerApplication` cmdlet is used to configure SharePoint 2013 as a partner application for Skype for Business Server 2015. The default URL for the SharePoint authentication metadata document is https://<SPfqdn>/_layouts/15/metadata/json/1, where <SPfqdn> is the fully qualified domain name of any SSL-enabled web application on the SharePoint 2013 farm. For example, the following procedure would be used to configure SharePoint as a partner application for the `skypeunleashed.com` Skype for Business Server 2015 deployment:

1. Log on to a system where the Skype for Business Server 2015 administrative tools are installed using an account that is a member of the `CsAdministrator` group and has administrative rights on the local system.

2. Open the Skype for Business Server Management Shell and execute the following command:

```
New-CsPartnerApplication -Identity sharepoint -ApplicationTrustLevel full
➥-MetadataUrl https://abcsite.fabrikam.local/_layouts/15/metadata/json/1
```

3. If the command is successful, the properties of the new partner application are displayed, as shown in Figure 20.3.

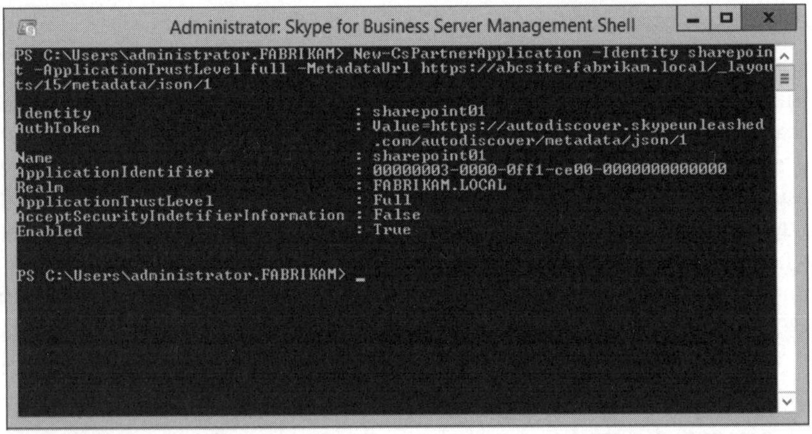

```
Administrator: Skype for Business Server Management Shell
PS C:\Users\administrator.FABRIKAM> New-CsPartnerApplication -Identity sharepoin
t -ApplicationTrustLevel full -MetadataUrl https://abcsite.fabrikam.local/_layou
ts/15/metadata/json/1

Identity                              : sharepoint01
AuthToken                             : Value=https://autodiscover.skypeunleashed
                                        .com/autodiscover/metadata/json/1
Name                                  : sharepoint01
ApplicationIdentifier                 : 00000003-0000-0ff1-ce00-000000000000
Realm                                 : FABRIKAM.LOCAL
ApplicationTrustLevel                 : Full
AcceptSecurityIndetifierInformation   : False
Enabled                               : True

PS C:\Users\administrator.FABRIKAM> _
```

FIGURE 20.3 Configuring SharePoint as a partner application in Skype for Business Server 2015.

Configuring SharePoint and Exchange as Partner Applications

To enable SharePoint eDiscovery of Skype for Business archive data, SharePoint 2013 must be configured as a partner application to Exchange Server as opposed to Skype for Business Server 2015. The reason for this is that Skype for Business Server 2015 must first be configured to archive content to Exchange Server before SharePoint eDiscovery can be used to search that data. Similar to the configuration of Skype for Business Server 2015 and Exchange as partner applications, the Exchange Server Autodiscover service must be configured and operational as a prerequisite before SharePoint and Exchange can be configured as partner applications.

After Autodiscover is configured, SharePoint and Exchange can be configured as partner applications by exchanging the certificates using the authentication metadata documents exposed on each side. On the Exchange Server side, a PowerShell script named `Configure-EnterprisePartnerApplication.ps1` is provided and is used to connect to the URL of the SharePoint 2013 metadata document and retrieve the required information from it. The default URL for the SharePoint authentication metadata document is https://<SPfqdn>/_layouts/15/metadata/json/1, where <SPfqdn> is the fully qualified domain name of any SSL-enabled web application on the SharePoint 2013 farm.

For example, the following procedure would be used to configure SharePoint as a partner application for the `skypeunleashed.com` Exchange Server deployment:

1. Log on to a system where the Exchange Server administrative tools are installed using an account that has administrative rights to Exchange.
2. Open the Exchange Management Shell and navigate to the Exchange scripts directory, which is by default `C:\Program Files\Microsoft\Exchange Server\V15\Scripts`.
3. Execute the following command:

```
.\Configure-EnterprisePartnerApplication.ps1 -AuthMetadataUrl
➥https://abcsite.companyabc.com/_layouts/15/metadata/json/1
➥-ApplicationType sharepoint
```

4. If the command is successful, the script creates a disabled user account linked to the partner application, and it assigns several Exchange management roles to the account to grant the required permissions.

On the SharePoint 2013 side, the Exchange Web Services Managed API v2.0 must first be installed, and then the `New-SPTrustedSecurityTokenIssuer` cmdlet is used to configure Exchange Server as a partner application for SharePoint. The default URL for the Exchange authentication metadata document is https://autodiscover.<domain>/autodiscover/metadata/json/1, where <domain> is the DNS domain of the Exchange systems. For example, the following procedure would be used to configure Exchange as a partner application for the `skypeunleashed.com` SharePoint deployment:

1. Log on to a system where the SharePoint administrative tools are installed using an account that has SharePoint administrative rights.
2. Download Exchange Web Services Managed API v2.0 from the Microsoft Download Center, and then install the software using the default installation options.
3. Open the SharePoint Management Shell and execute the following series of commands:

```
New-SPTrustedSecurityTokenIssuer -name "Exchange" -MetadataEndPoint
➥https://autodiscover.skypeunleashed.com/autodiscover/metadata/json/1
$sts = Get-SPSecurityTokenServiceConfig
$sts.HybridStsSelectionEnabled = $true
$sts.AllowMetadataOverHttp = $false
$sts.AllowOAuthOverHttp = $false
$sts.Update()
$exchange = Get-SPTrustedSecurityTokenIssuer "Exchange"
```

```
$app = Get-SPAppPrincipal -Site https://abcsite.skypeunleashed.com
➥-NameIdentifier $exchange.NameId
$site = Get-SPSite https://abcsite.skypeunleashed.com
Set-SPAppPrincipalPermission -AppPrincipal $app -Site $site.RootWeb
➥-Scope sitesubscription -Right fullcontrol -EnableAppOnlyPolicy
```

Exchange Integration Features

With Skype for Business Server 2015, the integrations with Exchange that existed in previous versions will continue to be featured, and several additional integrations are introduced as well. Skype for Business Server 2015 integrations for Exchange include the following:

- Unified Contact Store
- Skype for Business Server 2015 archiving integration
- High-resolution photo storage
- Outlook Web App integration
- Unified Messaging voicemail integration

NOTE

The Exchange integration features previously listed require both Skype for Business Server 2015 and Exchange 2013/2016. Therefore, an organization must upgrade both products to those versions in order to take advantage of all the Exchange integration features built in to Skype for Business Server 2015.

Unified Contact Store

An existing integration feature that is available with Skype for Business Server 2015 and Exchange Server is Unified Contact Store, which presents a common repository for user contacts that is shared between the Skype for Business and Outlook clients. When this feature is enabled, the Skype for Business client connects to Exchange Web Services (EWS) to read and maintain contacts instead of using SIP to connect the Skype for Business Front End Server for contacts, as in previous versions.

Migrating Users to Unified Contact Store

There are no adjustments to the Skype for Business Server 2015 topology that are required to enable Unified Contact Store. After the prerequisites for Skype for Business and Exchange integration have been met, Unified Contact Store is automatically enabled. There are three conditions that must be met for a user's contacts to be migrated to Unified Contact Store:

- The user is assigned a user services policy where the `UcsAllowed` property is set to `True` (the default).
- The user is provisioned with an Exchange Server mailbox and has logged in to that mailbox at least once.
- The user logs in to Skype for Business using the Skype for Business client.

If these three conditions are met, the user's contacts are automatically migrated from the Skype for Business Server database to Exchange Server. The user can then manage their contacts using Skype for Business, Outlook 2013, or Outlook Web App.

TIP

If a user logs in to Skype for Business using the Lync 2010 or earlier client, and the user's contacts have not already been migrated to Unified Contact Store, the user services policy applied to the user will have no effect, and the user's Skype for Business contacts will remain stored in the Skype for Business Server 2015 database. This is also true if the user is not provisioned with an Exchange Server mailbox or has never logged on to the mailbox. If a user logs in to Lync using the Lync 2010 or earlier client after the user's contacts have been migrated to Unified Contact Store, the contacts will be available and up to date. However, the user will not be able to manage those contacts using the legacy client.

The first time the user logs in to Skype for Business after being enabled for Unified Contact Store, in-band provisioning will cause the user's contacts to be migrated to a new folder in the Exchange Server mailbox named Skype for Business Contacts. After the migration is complete, the user is prompted to sign out of Skype for Business and sign back in to access his contacts, as shown in Figure 20.4.

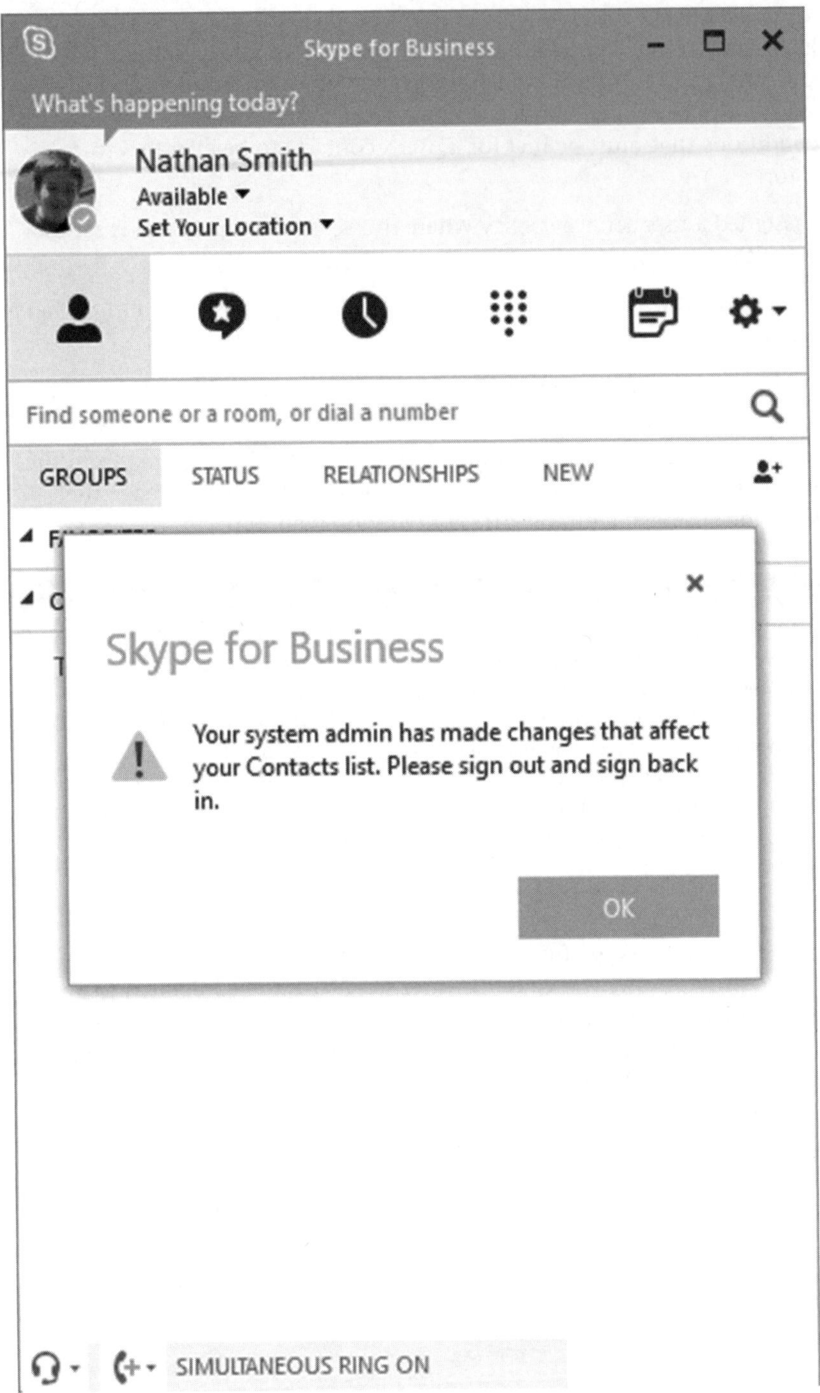

FIGURE 20.4 User notification after a migration of contacts to Exchange.

There are several ways to determine whether a user's contacts have been successfully migrated to Unified Contact Store. From the client computer, the Skype for Business client configuration settings can be viewed to determine the source of the user's contacts. To access the Skype for Business client configuration settings, hold down the Ctrl key and right-click on the Skype for Business system tray icon in the lower-right corner of the desktop; then select Configuration Information from the menu. Included in the resulting Skype for Business Configuration Information screen is the Contact List Provider, which displays either Skype for Business Server, if the contacts have not been migrated, or UCS, if the contacts have been migrated, as shown in Figure 20.5.

Another way to determine whether the contacts have been migrated from the client side is the registry key

```
HKEY_CURRENT_USER\Software\Microsoft\Office\15.0\Lync\<SIP URL>\UCS
```

where `<SIP URL>` is the user's SIP address. The version number of 15.0 in that path may also be different if a later version of the client is used, such as the Office 2016 client. If the user's contacts have been migrated, this key will contain a property named `InUCSMode`, and the value of the property will be `2165`. From the Skype for Business Server 2015 side, the Skype for Business Server Management Shell can be used to determine whether a user's contacts have been migrated to Unified Contact Store using the `Test-CsUnifiedContactStore` cmdlet. The user's credentials must first be supplied as a parameter, and these are obtained via the `Get-Credential` cmdlet. The following example shows the commands used to determine the contact migration status for a user:

```
$cred = Get-Credential "fabrikam\jrossen"
Test-CsUnifiedContactStore -TargetFqdn fe01.fabrikam.local
➥-UserSipAddress sip:jrossen@skypeunleashed.com -UserCredential $cred
```

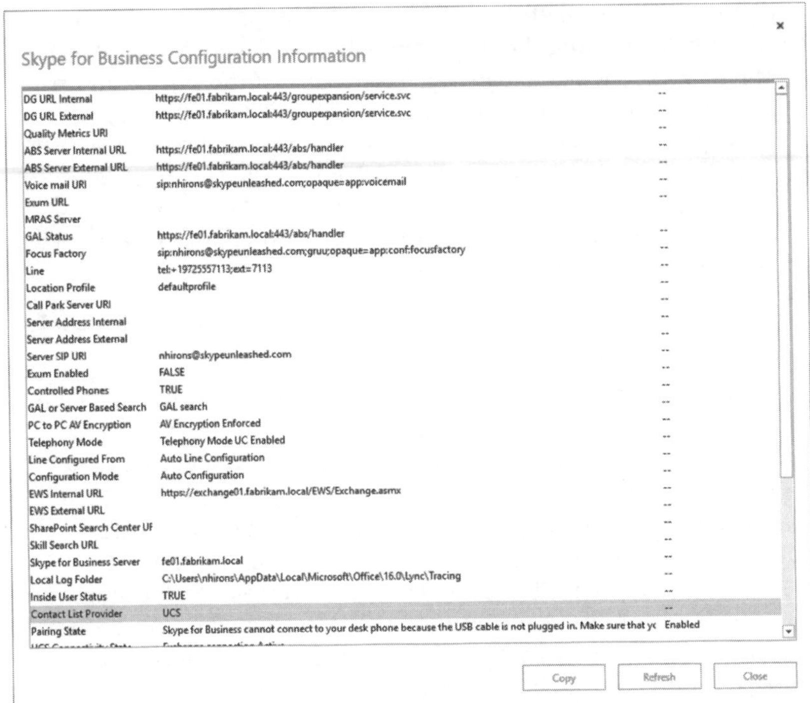

Skype for Business Configuration Information
DG URL Internal https://fe01.fabrikam.local:443/groupexpansion/service.svc
DG URL External https://fe01.fabrikam.local:443/groupexpansion/service.svc
Quality Metrics URI
ABS Server Internal URL https://fe01.fabrikam.local:443/abs/handler
ABS Server External URL https://fe01.fabrikam.local:443/abs/handler
Voice mail URI sip:nhirons@skypeunleashed.com;opaque=app:voicemail
Exum URL
MRAS Server
GAL Status https://fe01.fabrikam.local:443/abs/handler
Focus Factory sip:nhirons@skypeunleashed.com;gruu;opaque=app:conf:focusfactory
Line tel:+19725557113;ext=7113
Location Profile defaultprofile
Call Park Server URI
Server Address Internal
Server Address External
Server SIP URI nhirons@skypeunleashed.com
Exum Enabled FALSE
Controlled Phones TRUE
GAL or Server Based Search GAL search
PC to PC AV Encryption AV Encryption Enforced
Telephony Mode Telephony Mode UC Enabled
Line Configured From Auto Line Configuration
Configuration Mode Auto Configuration
EWS Internal URL https://exchange01.fabrikam.local/EWS/Exchange.asmx
EWS External URL
SharePoint Search Center UF
Skill Search URL
Skype for Business Server fe01.fabrikam.local
Local Log Folder C:\Users\nhirons\AppData\Local\Microsoft\Office\16.0\Lync\Tracing
Inside User Status TRUE
Contact List Provider UCS
Pairing State Skype for Business cannot connect to your desk phone because the USB cable is not plugged in. Make sure that yc Enabled
Copy
Refresh
Close

FIGURE 20.5 Using the Skype for Business Client to view the Unified Contact Store status for a user.

The first command causes an interactive prompt for the password user. After the credentials are entered, they are stored in the variable that is referenced in the second command. The end result is then displayed as success or failure. If a failure occurs, error messages can also be displayed to facilitate troubleshooting the issue further.

Selectively Enabling Users for Unified Contact Store

As noted previously, Unified Contact Store automatically becomes available and is enabled when the environmental and systems prerequisites are met. However, in some network environments it might be advantageous for a Skype for Business administrator to selectively enable users for Unified Contact Store. This can be accomplished using several Skype for Business Server Management Shell cmdlets that were created for this purpose. Using these cmdlets, users can be enabled globally, by site, by individual user, or by distribution group.

Since Unified Contact Store is enabled by default, if selectivity will be used, it is first necessary to disable the feature globally. The following procedure would be used to globally disable the users for Unified Contact Store using the Skype for Business Server Management Shell:

1. Log on to a system where the Skype for Business administrative tools are installed using an account that is a member of the `CsAdministrator` group and has administrative rights on the local system.

2. Open the Skype for Business Server Management Shell and execute the following cmdlet to disable Unified Contact Store for all users:

```
Set-CsUserServicesPolicy -Identity global -UcsAllowed $False
```

After unified contact store has been disabled globally, it can be enabled selectively. For example, the following command would be used to enable the feature for a specific site, in this example, the site named SF:

```
New-CsUserServicesPolicy -Identity SF -UcsAllowed $True
```

To selectively enable individual users for Unified Contact Store, the user policy must first be created and then applied to the user accounts. For example, the following two commands would be used to create a policy for enabling the users and then to apply the policy to an individual user:

```
New-CsUserServicesPolicy -Identity "Enable Users for UCS" -UcsAllowed $True
Grant-CsUserServicesPolicy -Identity "Julie Rossen"
➥-PolicyName "Enable Users for UCS"
```

Unified Contact Store Rollback Procedure

At times, it might be necessary to roll back a user's contacts from Exchange to Skype for Business. For example, in a mixed environment, if the user's mailbox is moved from Exchange 2013/2016 back to Exchange 2010 or to Office 365, or if the user account is moved from a Skype for Business pool back to Lync 2010, the user's contacts will first need to be rolled back to Skype for Business. This can be accommodated using the `Invoke-CsUcsRollback` cmdlet.

The `Invoke-CsUcsRollback` cmdlet can be executed against a single user by simply including the identity of the user in the command. However, at times it might be necessary to roll back a group of users (for example, an entire pool). This can be accomplished by using the `Get-CsUser` cmdlet to retrieve a specific list of users filtered by the required criteria, and then piping the output to the `Invoke-CsUcsRollback` command. For example, the following command could be used to roll back contacts for an entire pool of users:

```
Get-CsUser -Filter {RegistrarPool -eq "fe01.fabrikam.local"} |
➥Invoke-CsUcsRollback -Confirm:$False
```

Once a user is rolled back, the "Skype for Business Contacts" contacts folder in the Exchange Server mailbox remains (this folder is created when a user is migrated to UCS). It does not get deleted by the rollback process.

20

TIP

If a user's contacts are rolled back from Exchange to Skype for Business because the user's mailbox will be moved to Exchange 2010, and then the user's mailbox is subsequently moved back to Exchange 2013/2016, the user's contacts will migrate back to Exchange in 7 days. This behavior is due to the user services policy remaining enabled for Unified Contact Store. If the intention is to prevent the user's contacts from being moved to Unified Contact Store for whatever reason, the user services policy must be adjusted to prevent this.

Skype for Business Server 2015 Archiving Integration

Another integration feature available with Skype for Business Server 2015 and Exchange Server is archiving integration. With archiving integration, Skype for Business Server 2015 archive data is written to a user's Exchange Server mailbox instead of the Skype for Business Server 2015 archiving database. The end result is a common repository of archival data that simplifies compliance and eDiscovery tasks across the two communications platforms. Coexistence between the archiving platforms is also supported, such that archive data for some users can be maintained in Skype for Business Server 2015, while archive data for other users is stored in Exchange. This is particularly beneficial for mixed environments that include both Exchange 2010 and 2013. For example, if an organization is gradually transitioning mailboxes from Exchange 2010 to Exchange 2013/2016, archiving to Exchange is supported for the users with Exchange 2013/2016 mailboxes, and archiving to the Skype for Business Archiving database can be used for users with Exchange 2010 mailboxes.

When archiving integration is enabled for a user, the archive data is written to the `Purges` folder in the user's mailbox. This folder is hidden from the user's normal view but is indexed by the Exchange Server search engine, and can therefore be viewed using either the `MailboxSearch` function or SharePoint 2013 Discovery Center. This same folder is also used as the target for the Exchange Server in-place hold feature; therefore, all user archive data becomes searchable using a single centralized location.

Archiving Policies in Skype for Business Server 2015 and Exchange

Several levels of polices come into play to determine whether archiving integration will be enabled for a user. First, there is the Skype for Business Server 2015 archiving configuration, which can be used to enable or disable archiving integration at the global, site, and pool levels. If archiving to Exchange is enabled at one of these levels, several other policies come into play at an individual user level, depending on whether Skype for Business Server 2015 and Exchange are installed in the same Active Directory forest or in separate forests.

When Skype for Business Server 2015 and Exchange are installed in the same forest, and archiving to Exchange has been enabled within Skype for Business Server 2015, Exchange Server in-place hold policies determine whether archive data will be stored in Exchange. In-place hold policies are used to preserve mailbox items indefinitely, for a specific period, or based on a match of query parameters. Authorized users can place a mailbox user on an in-place hold to allow eDiscovery searches to be performed, either to satisfy litigation requirements or for other purposes. When archiving to Exchange is enabled within Skype for Business Server 2015, and an in-place hold has been placed on a user's mailbox, the Skype for Business Server 2015 User Replicator will detect this and will enable the user for archiving to Exchange.

When Skype for Business Server 2015 and Exchange are installed in separate forests, and archiving to Exchange has been enabled within Skype for Business Server 2015, the `ExchangeArchivingPolicy` parameter applied to the Skype for Business user determines whether archiving to Exchange will be enabled. Four possible values can be configured for the `ExchangeArchivingPolicy` parameter:

- **`Uninitialized`**—Allows the Exchange Server in-place hold settings to determine whether archiving to Exchange is enabled.
- **`UseLyncArchivingPolicy`**—Specifies that archiving to Skype for Business Server 2015 should be used rather than Exchange.
- **`NoArchiving`**—Disables archiving for the user, overriding any Skype for Business Server 2015 archiving polices assigned to the user.
- **`ArchivingToExchange`**—Enables archiving to Exchange Server, regardless of whether in-place hold settings are assigned to the user's mailbox.

Archiving Configuration

The first step in configuring archiving integration is enabling this feature using a Skype for Business Server 2015 archiving configuration at the global, site, or pool level. This is accomplished via the Skype for Business Server Control Panel or via the Management Shell using the `Set-CsArchivingConfiguration` cmdlet. There is only one global archiving configuration, which is automatically created when Skype for Business Server 2015 is deployed, and it is simply named Global. This Global archiving configuration contains default settings that can be changed as needed, but the Global configuration itself cannot be deleted. If additional archiving configurations are created at the pool or site level, these override the same settings that are configured at the global level for the affected users.

In addition to enabling archiving for Exchange, the archiving configuration is used to determine the type of content to archive: IM sessions, web conference sessions, or both. For example, the following procedure is used to enable archiving of IM and web conference sessions to Exchange on a global level, and to purge all archiving data after 120 days:

1. Log on to a system where the Skype for Business Server 2015 administrative tools are installed using an account that is a member of the `CsAdministrator` group. Then open the Skype for Business Server 2015 Control Panel.
2. In the left pane, select Monitoring and Archiving and then click the Archiving Configuration tab at the top.
3. Select the Global archiving policy. Then, from the Edit drop-down menu, select Show Details.
4. At the Edit Archiving Setting–Global screen, use the drop-down menu under the Archiving setting to select Archive IM and Web Conferencing Sessions.
5. Select the options for Exchange Server Integration and Enable Purging of Archiving Data.

6. Keep the default radio button option of Purge Exported Archiving Data and Stored Archiving Data After Maximum Duration (Days), and then change the number of days to 120.
7. When you are finished, the configuration should appear as shown in Figure 20.6. Click Commit to save the changes to the Global archiving configuration.

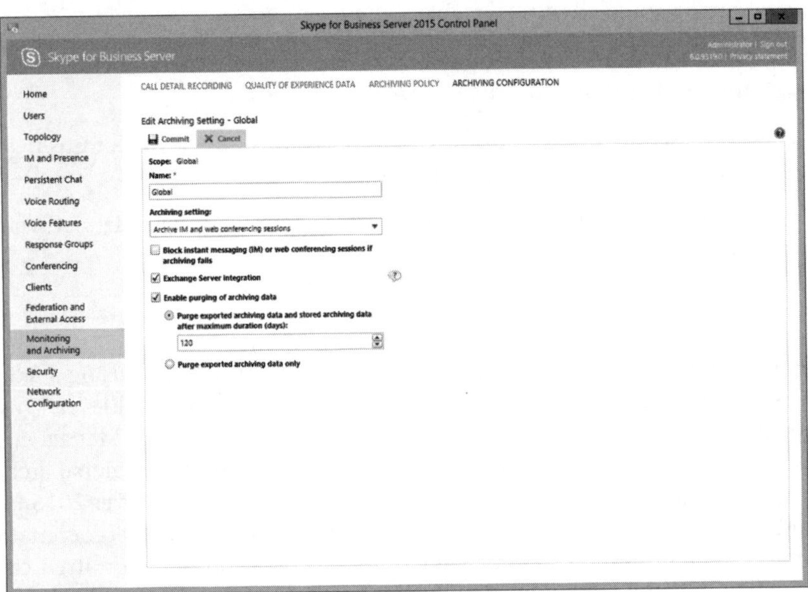

FIGURE 20.6 Archiving to Exchange enabled at a Global level.

After archiving is enabled within Skype for Business Server 2015, the next step is dependent on whether the Skype for Business Server 2015 and Exchange systems are installed in the same Active Directory forest or separate forests. If Skype for Business Server 2015 and Exchange are part of the same forest, Exchange in-place hold polices can be configured against user mailboxes to enable the archiving of Skype for Business Server 2015 data to Exchange. For example, the following command is used in the Exchange Management Shell to create a mailbox search with an in-place hold against a user with an Exchange Server mailbox:

```
New-MailboxSearch -Description "klopez in-place hold" -Name klopez
➥-InPlaceHoldEnabled $true -SourceMailboxes klopez
```

After this command is executed, within a few minutes the Skype for Business Server 2015 User Replicator detects this change and configures Skype for Business to begin archiving to the user's mailbox.

If Skype for Business Server 2015 and Exchange are in separate forests, the `ArchivingToExchange` parameter can be configured for each Skype for Business user to determine whether archiving to Exchange will be enabled. The `ArchivingToExchange` parameter can be configured only from the Management Shell, using the `Set-CsUser` cmdlet. The following example shows the command that is used to configure a user for archiving all data to Exchange:

```
Set-CsUser klopez -ExchangeArchivingPolicy ArchivingToExchange
```

After this is executed, all Skype for Business Server 2015 archive data is stored in the user's Exchange Server mailbox.

High-Resolution Photos

The capability to use photos with Skype for Business contacts was introduced in Lync 2010, with the source of those photos limited to either the Active Directory user object (using the `thumbnailPhoto` attribute) or a URL reference to a public website. Although Active Directory was naturally the better choice for organizations seeking to standardize this feature, many Skype for Business Server 2015 administrators held back from implementing photos in Skype for Business due to concerns with how Active Directory replication would be impacted. For this very reason, limitations were also placed on the resolution of photos that could be used with Lync 2010.

In an effort to circumvent these limitations, Skype for Business Server 2015 offers additional options for the use of photos by way of integration with Exchange Server. Although the storage of limited-resolution photos (up to 48 × 48) using the Active Directory `thumbnailPhoto` attribute is still supported, for organizations that use both Skype for Business Server 2015 and Exchange, the use of high-resolution photos stored in Exchange is a much more attractive option. When Skype for Business Server 2015 and Exchange Server are configured for integration, photos of up to 648 × 648 resolution can be stored as a hidden item at the root of a user's Exchange Server mailbox. The photos can be uploaded to the mailbox by the user using Outlook Web App, or by an Exchange administrator using the `Set-UserPhoto` cmdlet in the Exchange Management Shell.

An additional benefit of this new feature is that the upload process stores the photo in an internal format that supports different resolutions for different platforms. For example, uploading a high-resolution photo using the Exchange Management Shell automatically updates the `thumbnailPhoto` attribute of the user's Active Directory account with a 48 × 48 version of the photo.

NOTE

Only the newer methods of uploading photos into Exchange result in an update to the Active Directory `thumbnailPhoto` attribute. If any other method is used to update the AD `thumbnailPhoto` attribute directly, this does not cause the photo in the Exchange Server mailbox to be updated.

Uploading Photos Using the Exchange Management Shell

To upload a photo using the Exchange Management Shell, place a copy of the photo in a local subdirectory that is accessible to the Management Shell. The filename of the photo can then be referenced in a variable within the shell and used to apply the photo to the user account. For example, the following series of Exchange Management Shell commands would be used to upload a photo with a filename of `klopez.jpg` to the corresponding user account:

```
$photostring = "c:\temp\klopez.jpg"
$pic = ([Byte[]] $(Get-Content -Path $photostring -Encoding Byte -ReadCount 0))
Set-UserPhoto -Identity klopez -PictureData $pic -confirm:$false
Set-UserPhoto -Identity klopez -save -confirm:$false
```

Uploading Photos Using Outlook Web App

To upload photos as a user, Outlook Web App (OWA) is used. The following procedure would be used by the end user to upload the same photo to the mailbox using OWA:

1. Open a web browser and connect to the OWA URL, which by default is the fully qualified name of the Exchange Server Client Access Server, followed by /owa (for example, https://exchange01.fabrikam.local/owa).
2. At the Outlook Web App screen, enter the credentials for the user whose photo will be uploaded, and then click Sign In.
3. If this is the first time the user is logging on to OWA on this system, an additional screen is presented allowing preferred display language and home time zone settings to be changed. Make any changes if necessary, and then click Save.
4. When the mailbox is displayed, click the user's name in the upper-right section of the OWA window. The first item that appears in the resulting drop-down menu is the photo section; click the Change link.
5. At the Change Photo screen, click Browse, and then navigate to the location of the photo for the user. After the photo is selected, click Open.
6. The photo is now uploaded to the mailbox and is displayed in the Change Photo screen, as shown in Figure 20.7. Click Save.

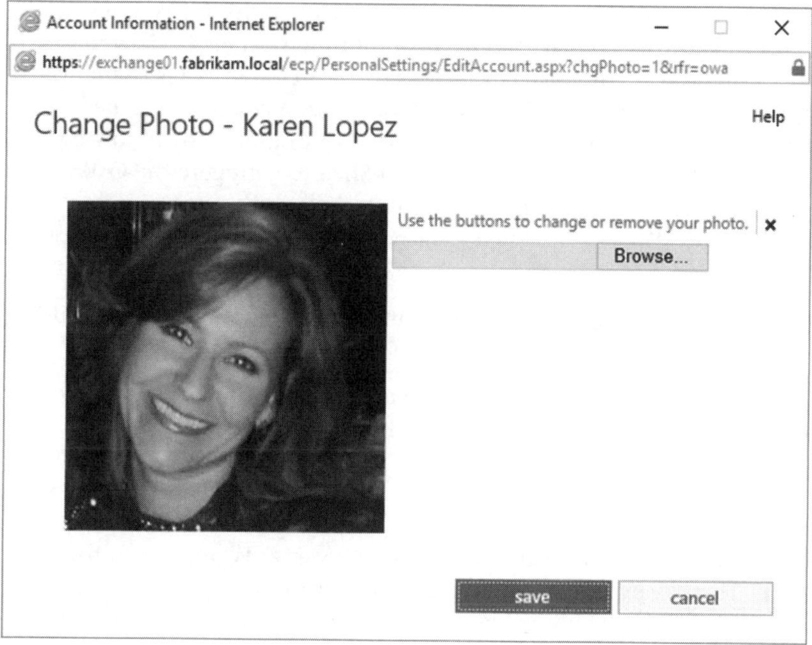

FIGURE 20.7 Uploading a photo using OWA.

Outlook Web App Integration

Outlook Web App integration is a feature that provides a nice convenience for Skype for Business users who frequently use OWA to connect to their Exchange mailbox. Skype for Business Server 2015 integration with OWA allows Presence and IM capabilities to be extended to an OWA session and also includes the following useful features:

- Presence for internal and federated Skype for Business Server 2015 contacts
- The capability to start and maintain chat sessions directly from OWA
- Skype for Business Server 2015 contact list integration, including adding and removing contacts and groups
- The capability to control Skype for Business Presence states from OWA

20

NOTE

OWA integration is possible using either Exchange 2010 or 2013. However, depending on the version of Exchange and the topology, it may be necessary to configure OWA as a trusted application within Skype for Business Server 2015. Also, if Exchange Server is used, then the Unified Communications Managed API 4.0 Runtime must be installed on the Exchange backend server.

Depending on whether Exchange UM is configured, the systems running OWA may need to be added to the list of known servers within Skype for Business Server 2015, which can be accomplished using the `New-CsTrustedApplicationPool` cmdlet. After Exchange is trusted by Skype for Business Server 2015, the OWA integration can be performed by adjusting the properties of the OWA virtual directories. For example, the following commands would be used in the Exchange Management Shell to configure the OWA virtual directories for Skype for Business Server 2015 integration, with a combination frontend/backend Exchange 2013 server named `exchange01` and the Skype for Business Server 2015 pool named `fe01.fabrikam.local`:

1. Log on to a system where the Exchange 2013 administrative tools are installed using an account that has administrative rights to Exchange.

2. Open the Exchange Management Shell, and execute the following command to view the certificates that are available to be used with Exchange:

```
Get-ExchangeCertificate
```

3. From the list of certificates presented, identify the certificate that has been assigned to IIS, which will be the first certificate listed where the letter *W* appears in the Services column. Then, copy the thumbprint for this certificate to the Windows Clipboard and use it to add the following two lines to the <AppSettings> section of the Web.config file in the C:\Program Files\Microsoft\Exchange Server\V15\ClientAccess\Owa directory:

```
<add key="IMCertificateThumbprint"
➥value="03554BB4BF96AC1081BDA4878997C7FE52D43127"/>
<add key="IMServerName" value="fe01.fabrikam.local"/>
```

4. Using a single command, execute the `Get-OwaVirtualDirectory` cmdlet to retrieve the OWA virtual directory, and then pipe the results to the `Set-OwaVirtualDirectory` cmdlet to adjust the properties of the OWA virtual directory. For example, the following command would be used to enable OWA integration for a server named exchange01:

```
Get-OwaVirtualDirectory | Set-OwaVirtualDirectory
➥-InstantMessagingEnabled $True -InstantMessagingType OCS
```

5. Execute the following command to enable Skype for Business Server 2015 integration for the default OWA mailbox policy:

```
Set-OwaMailboxPolicy -Identity Default
➥-InstantMessagingEnabled $true -InstantMessagingType OCS
```

After OWA integration has been enabled, the users will see the results the next time they log in to OWA. The first indication that OWA integration has been enabled is that the Presence states are listed in the drop-down menu that appears when a user clicks the display name in the upper-right section of the OWA window, as shown in Figure 20.8.

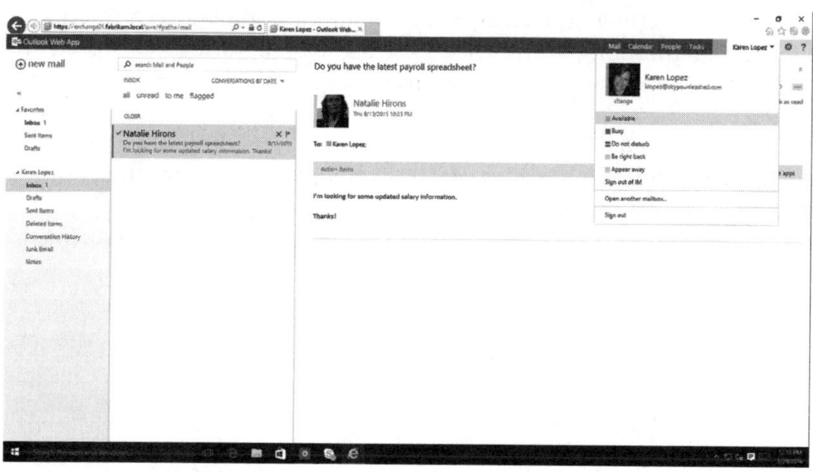

FIGURE 20.8 Skype for Business Presence states within OWA.

Integration with Exchange Online

Some organizations may elect to use Exchange Online for email but an on-premises installation of Skype for Business Server 2015. Such a configuration requires, among other things, Microsoft's DirSync to synchronize account info between the on-premises Active Directory domain and that in Office 365. Configuration of DirSync between an on-premises domain and Office 365 can be complex, and is outside the scope for this book. Microsoft does have plenty of articles and guides on setting it up, including using a virtual machine in Azure to manage the directory sync. Ensure that DirSync is working correctly in the environment before attempting to integrate Skype for Business Server 2015 and Office 365.

If you haven't yet installed the Microsoft Online Services cmdlets, two steps are required before proceeding. First, download and install the 64-bit version of the Microsoft Online Services Sign-in Assistant. Next, download and install the 64-bit version of the Microsoft Online Services Module for PowerShell. Detailed information for installing and using the Microsoft Online Services Module can be found on the Office 365 website. These instructions also describe how to configure single sign-on, federation, and synchronization between Office 365 and Active Directory.

Integration requires several simple steps, as detailed in the following sections.

Configuring a Shared SIP Address Space

In order for Skype for Business Server 2015 to integrate with Exchange Online, a shared SIP address space must be configured. Both Exchange Online and Skype for Business Server 2015 support this configuration.

On a server with the Skype for Business Management Server Shell, use the `Set-CsAccessEdgeConfiguration` cmdlet to allow federated users:

```
Set-CsAccessEdgeConfiguration -AllowFederatedUsers $true
```

While it may appear that this setting only enables the communication between internal users and those in other organizations, it also allows users to communicate in a shared SIP address space with Exchange Online and Skype for Business.

Configuring a Hosting Provider on an Edge Server

The next step is configuring a hosting provider. Hosting providers are organizations that provide hosted SIP services for other organization. A hosting provider is also used in shared SIP address space scenarios. From the Skype for Business Management Server Shell, use the `New-CsHostingProvider` cmdlet:

```
New-CsHostingProvider -Identity "Exchange Online" -Enabled $True
➥-EnabledSharedAddressSpace $True -HostsOCSUsers $False
➥-ProxyFqdn "exap.um.outlook.com" -IsLocal $False
➥-VerificationLevel UseSourceVerification
```

This configures a hosting provider called "Exchange Online" and allows for the shared SIP address space using the `exap.um.outlook.com` proxy. It's important to note that the `HostsOcsUsers` parameter be set to `false`.

Verification of Replication of the Updated Central Management Store

The two previous steps enabled the configuration for shared SIP address space. The last step is to ensure that the configuration replicates correctly. This is verified in two steps.

The first step is ensuring that the configuration has replicated throughout the topology. From Skype for Business Management Server Shell, verify the results of the `Get-CsManagementStoreReplicationStatus` cmdlet. And, finally, confirm that the Edge Servers have applied the changes by using the cmdlet `Get-CsHostingProvider -LocalStore`.

When users have mailboxes in Exchange Online, but they are homed on an on-premises instance of Skype for Business Server 2015, there are some additional steps to ensure that users can schedule Skype for Business meetings from a browser within Office 365. This requires many manual steps. Some, but not all, of these tasks can be done with existing administrative tools, but they can all be done using PowerShell. Here, the Skype for Business community has risen to the challenge. Aaron Marks has written a PowerShell script that automates most of the tasks, including the following:

- Locates the Office 365 TenantID
- Cleans up any legacy entries
- Creates a new OAuth server
- Creates a new partner application
- Uploads the OAuth certificate to Office 365
- Adds the external web services name

Because the manual method is full of potential for error and confusion, using Aaron's `Configure-OAuth_ExOn_SfB_Server.ps1` script is recommended. It is available at https://gallery.technet.microsoft.com/office/Configure-OAuth-between-5705f1ac. Whichever method used, there are some prerequisites. The first is that the Microsoft Online Service Sign-In Assistant needs to be installed on the machine where you'll run the script. This can be any computer with the Skype for Business Server 2015 Shell installed. The Sign-In Assistant is available at http://go.microsoft.com/fwlink/?LinkID=286152. Next, the Microsoft Azure Active Directory PowerShell module is needed and is available at http://go.microsoft.com/fwlink/p/?linkid=236297.

The next requirement is to note the external web services URL for Skype for Business Server 2015. This is easily found in the Topology Builder.

And, finally, the OAuth certificate from Skype for Business Server 2015 needs to be exported to a file. This can be accomplished in three lines of PowerShell. Simply open PowerShell and enter the following:

```
$Thumbprint = (Get-CsCertificate -Type OAuthTokenIssuer).Thumbprint
$OAuthCert = Get-ChildItem -Path Cert:\LocalMachine\My\$Thumbprint
Export-Certificate -Cert $OAuthCert -FilePath c:\oauth.cer -Type CERT
```

Note the `FilePath`, as it is needed when calling Aaron's script. The script can be as follows:

```
.\Configure-OAuth_ExOn_SfB_Server.ps1 -CertPath
➥c:\oauth.cer -WebExt web.skypeunleashed.com
```

When this is completed, the "Skype Meeting" option should be visible in the toolbar at the top of meeting requests for users using Outlook Web App, as shown in Figure 20.9.

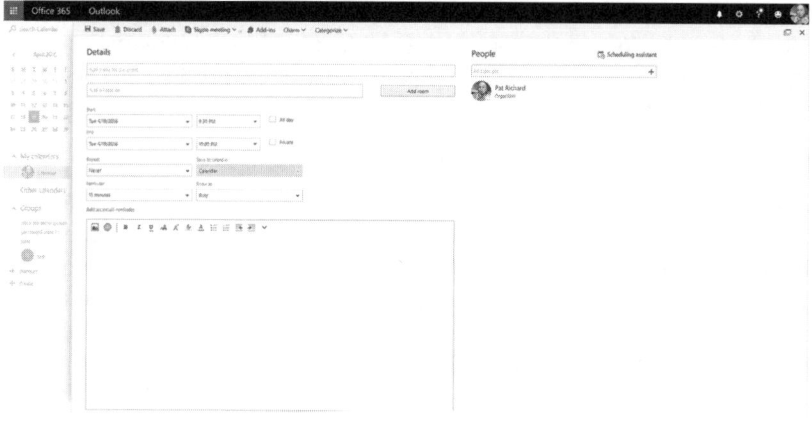

FIGURE 20.9 Skype Meeting option in Outlook Web App.

Unified Messaging Voicemail Integration

Exchange Unified Messaging (UM) is an optional Exchange Server component that serves as an integrated voicemail system for Exchange mailbox users. Exchange UM allows voicemail, email, and fax messages to be consolidated into a user's inbox, and provides additional features to enhance the UC experience, such as Outlook Voice Access and automated attendants. Although Exchange UM certainly adds to the UC experience for users of Microsoft Exchange, it provides even more value when configured for integration with Skype for Business Server 2015. The integration of Skype for Business Server 2015 with Exchange UM enables users to view and manage voicemails directly from the Skype for Business client, providing additional flexibility and efficiency in terms of how the various forms of communication are handled.

NOTE

Microsoft has made several architectural changes to Unified Messaging in Exchange 2013, and those continue in Exchange 2016. With previous versions of the product, UM was a unique server role requiring dedicated hardware. With Exchange 2013, the UM components are split between the Client Access Server and the Mailbox Server roles. Essentially, the Client Access Server acts as a proxy for incoming calls using the Unified Messaging Call Router service, whereas the Mailbox Server handles the majority of the voice load by way of the Unified Messaging service. However, these server roles can also be collocated, such that both the frontend and backend UM services are hosted on a single system.

Exchange UM Components

The deployment of Exchange Unified Messaging involves the configuration of several internal components, and these must be configured in a specific way to allow for integration with Skype for Business Server 2015. This section includes a description of these components to provide background on Exchange UM, as well as an explanation as to how the Exchange UM components fit into the picture with Skype for Business Server 2015 and Exchange UM integration.

Following are the components included in an Exchange Server UM deployment:

- **UM dial plan**—UM dial plans are the central component of the Exchange Unified Messaging architecture. A UM dial plan logically corresponds to the set of extensions that are planned and assigned using a PBX. Some additional important purposes of the UM dial plan are that it associates the extension for subscriber access, and it establishes a common set of policies for a group of users, such as number of digits in an extension. Even in an environment where Skype for Business Server 2015 is used for Enterprise Voice and is therefore used to establish the dial plan for the organization, one UM dial plan is still required for Skype for Business Server 2015 to integrate with Exchange UM.
- **UM mailbox policy**—Unified Messaging mailbox policies are used to apply and standardize configuration settings for UM-enabled users. Some of the more

important policy settings applied by a Unified Messaging mailbox policy include PIN policies, dialing restrictions, and maximum greeting duration. By default, a single UM mailbox policy is created every time a UM dial plan is created, and is named after the dial plan. The new UM mailbox policy is also automatically associated with the UM dial plan. Although only a single UM mailbox policy is required to enable users for Unified Messaging, additional UM mailbox policies can be created in order to apply a common set of mailbox policy settings for groups of users. The mailbox of each UM-enabled user must be linked to a single UM mailbox policy when the mailbox is enabled for Unified Messaging.

- **UM IP gateway**—A Unified Messaging IP gateway object is a container object that logically represents a physical IP gateway hardware device, an IP-PBX, or another SIP server that can interoperate with Exchange Unified Messaging. Before the IP gateway can be used to process UM calls, it must be represented by an object in Active Directory. The combination of the IP Gateway object and a UM hunt group object establishes a logical link between an IP gateway hardware device and a UM dial plan. There can be only one UM IP gateway for each physical IP/VoIP gateway, and this is enforced through IP addresses.
- **UM hunt group**—With Exchange UM, hunt groups are used to act as a link between the UM IP gateway and the UM dial plan. UM hunt groups are used to locate the PBX hunt group from which the incoming call was received. A pilot number that is defined for a hunt group in the PBX must also be defined within the UM Hunt group, and it's used to match the information presented for incoming calls through the SIP signaling information on the message. The pilot number enables the Unified Messaging service to interpret the call together with the correct dial plan so that the call can be routed correctly.
- **UM auto attendant**—Unified Messaging auto attendants are used to help internal and external callers locate users or departments that exist in an organization and transfer calls to them. The UM auto attendant is a series of voice prompts or .wav files that callers hear when dialing the organization.

Exchange UM Configuration for Skype for Business Server 2015

Because the Exchange UM components are included in the Client Access Server and Mailbox Server roles with Exchange Server, the installation of Exchange UM is much more streamlined than with previous versions. However, the configuration of Exchange UM involves several steps, and these need to be completed before integration between Skype for Business Server 2015 and Exchange UM can be configured. Although the full details of the planning and deployment process for Exchange UM are outside the scope of this chapter, the steps required to configure Exchange UM in preparation for Skype for Business Server 2015 integration are included in the text that follows. This will serve to provide a background on the Exchange UM configuration process, as well as the details on how the Exchange UM configuration is affected when integration with Skype for Business Server 2015 is planned.

Following is a summary of the steps involved in configuring Unified Messaging for integration with Skype for Business Server 2015:

- **Create the UM dial plan**—The UM dial plan is created manually using either the Exchange Administrative Center or the Exchange Management Shell. For integration with Skype for Business Server 2015, the number of digits configured for the UM dial plan should match the number of digits used in the PBX or Skype for Business Server 2015 dial plan. Additional important choices include the URI type, which should be specified as `SipName` to cause the calling and called party information from Skype for Business Server 2015 to use the standard SIP addressing format. The VoIP security mode chosen must also be compatible with the encryption level configured for the Skype for Business client; setting the VoIP security mode to Secured will cause SIP signaling and media traffic to be encrypted as a requirement. Following is a sample command that would be used to create a UM dial plan using the Exchange Management Shell:

```
New-UMDialPlan -Name "Redmond_UM_Dial_Plan" -VoIPSecurity secured
➥-NumberOfDigitsInExtension 3 -URIType sipname -CountryOrRegionCode 1
```

- **Assign a subscriber access number**—A subscriber access number is used to specify the extension that is used by subscribers to access the voicemail system. When the UM dial plan is created, no subscriber access number is assigned, and therefore it must be assigned manually using the Exchange Management Shell. For example, the following command would be used to assign a three-digit extension as the subscriber access number for an existing UM dial plan:

```
Set-UMDialPlan -Identity "Redmond_UM_Dial_Plan" -AccessTelephoneNumbers 123
```

- **Configure the UM mailbox policy (optional)**—A UM mailbox policy is automatically created whenever a UM dial plan is created. However, the default settings in the policy might need to be adjusted to meet the requirements of the organization. If desired, additional UM mailbox policies can also be manually created using the Exchange Administrative Center or the Exchange Management Shell and then assigned to individual users when they are enabled for UM as needed. The following sample Management Shell command would be used to adjust an existing UM mailbox policy to change the minimum pin length to 4:

```
Set-UMMailboxPolicy -Identity "Redmond_UM_Dial_Plan Default Policy"
➥-MinPINLength 4
```

- **Create the UM IP gateway and UM hunt group**—For integration with Skype for Business Server 2015, a UM IP gateway and UM hunt group are automatically created to represent the Skype for Business Server 2015 pool by executing the `exchucutil.ps1` PowerShell script, which is located in the C:\Program Files\Microsoft\Exchange Server\V15\Scripts folder on an Exchange server. In addition to creating the UM IP gateway and IP hunt group objects, the script grants permissions to Skype for Business Server 2015 to read the required UM-related objects in Active Directory. The name applied to the gateway object is by default the same as the name of the Skype for Business Server 2015 pool. Figure 20.10 shows an example of a UM IP gateway object that is automatically created as a result of the `exchucutil.ps1` script being run.

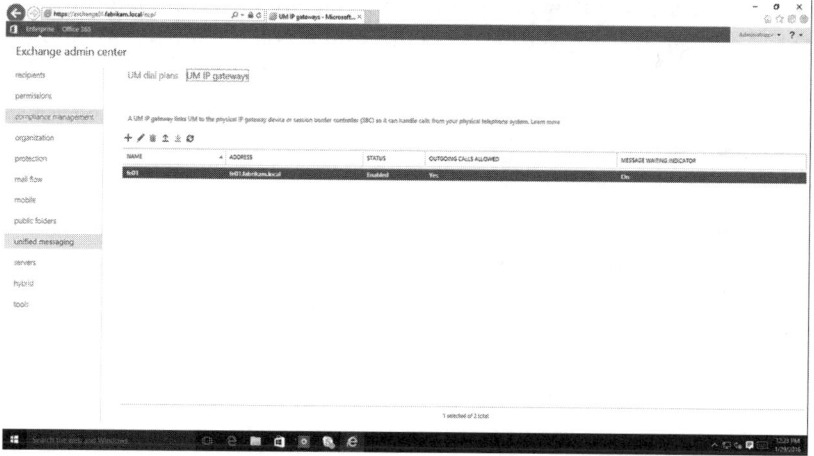

FIGURE 20.10 Exchange UM IP gateway automatically created for the Skype for Business Server 2015 pool.

- `Create auto attendants (optional)`—If Exchange UM will be used to handle incoming calls and direct these to the appropriate mailbox, one or more auto attendants need to be configured. Each auto attendant is created as part of a UM dial plan and is assigned a unique access number that will be used to handle incoming calls. Auto attendants can be created as part of the UM dial plan configuration in the Exchange Administrative Center, or using the Exchange Management Shell. The following sample Management Shell command would be used to create an auto attendant, assign it to a dial plan, and assign a pilot number to handle inbound calls:

```
New-UMAutoAttendant -Name "Redmond_AutoAttendant"
➥-UMDialPlan "Redmond_UM_Dial_Plan"
➥-Status Enabled -SpeechEnabled $true -PilotIdentifierList +14151234567
```

- **Change the UM Service startup mode**—By default, the UM service is configured to start up in TCP mode, which is not compatible if encryption is being used. The startup mode of the UM service must therefore be changed to dual mode to support encryption that is required for Skype for Business Server 2015 integration. The following sample Management Shell command would be used to add the dial plan to the server and change the UM startup mode to dual:

```
Set-UmService -Identity exchange01 -DialPlans "Redmond_UM_Dial_Plan"
➥-UMStartupMode dual
```

- **Assign a certificate to the Unified Messaging service**—By default, no certificates are assigned to the Unified Messaging service within the Exchange configuration. To allow Exchange UM to communicate securely with clients and with Skype for Business Server 2015, a server certificate must be assigned to the service. This can be accomplished using either the Exchange Administrative Center or the Exchange

Management Shell. The following sample Management Shell commands would be used to assign an existing certificate to the Unified Messaging service and then restart the service:

```
Enable-ExchangeCertificate -Thumbprint 03554BB4BF96AC1081BDA4878997C7FE52D43127
➥-Services UM
restart-service MsExchangeUM
```

- **Enable mailboxes for UM**—Each user must also be associated with a UM mailbox policy at the time that the user is enabled for UM. Users can be enabled for UM using the Exchange Administrative Center or the Exchange Management Shell. The following sample Management Shell command would be used to enable a user for UM and assign a mailbox policy:

```
Enable-UMMailbox -Identity jrossen
➥-UMMailboxPolicy "Redmond_UM_Dial_Plan Default Policy"
➥-Extensions 812 -PIN 13579
➥-SIPResourceIdentifier "jrossen@skypeunleashed.com" -PINExpired $true
```

- **Integrate the UM Call Router with Skype for Business Server 2015**—The Exchange UM Call Router must be prepared for integration with Skype for Business Server 2015, which requires several Exchange Management Shell commands. The following sample Management Shell commands would be used to prepare an Exchange 2013 Client Access Server named `exchange01` and a dial plan named `SF_DP` for integration with Skype for Business Server 2015, followed by a restart of the UM Call Router service:

```
Set-UmCallRouterSettings -UMStartupMode dual -DialPlans
➥"Redmond_UM_Dial_Plan" -server exchange01
Enable-ExchangeCertificate -server exchange01 -Thumbprint
➥03554BB4BF96AC1081BDA4878997C7FE52D43127 -Services iis,umcallrouter
restart-service MsExchangeUMCR
```

Skype for Business Server 2015 Configuration for Exchange UM

With the Exchange UM configuration in place, Skype for Business Server 2015 can be configured to integrate with Exchange UM as the final step in the process. If Skype for Business Server 2015 dial plans have not already been configured at this point, the dial plans would need to be configured to allow call routing between the various components. For details on the process for configuring Skype for Business Server 2015 dial plans and voice routing, see Chapter 16, "Skype for Business Server 2015 Telephony and Voice Integration." After a dial plan is in place, the remaining task is to create the AD contact objects that are required to resolve and locate the Exchange UM subscriber access and auto-attendant services. To facilitate creating these contact objects, Microsoft provides the Exchange UM Integration Utility, which has an executable filename of `OcsUmUtil.exe` and is located in the subdirectory C:\Program Files\Common Files\Skype for Business Server 2015\Support on each Skype for Business Server 2015 Front End Server. The following procedure is used to configure the subscriber access and auto-attendant contact objects using the Exchange UM Integration Utility:

1. Log on to the Skype for Business Server 2015 Front End Server using an account with permissions to create Active Directory objects in the domain, and then use Windows Explorer to navigate to the C:\Program Files\Common Files\Skype for Business Server 2015\Support directory and double-click `OcsUmUtil.exe`.

2. The Exchange UM Integration Utility dialog box appears. Click Load Data, which causes the Exchange UM Dial Plan Forest field to automatically populate the AD forest name, as shown in Figure 20.11. Any UM dial plans that have been created in Exchange also appear in the SIP Dial Plans column.

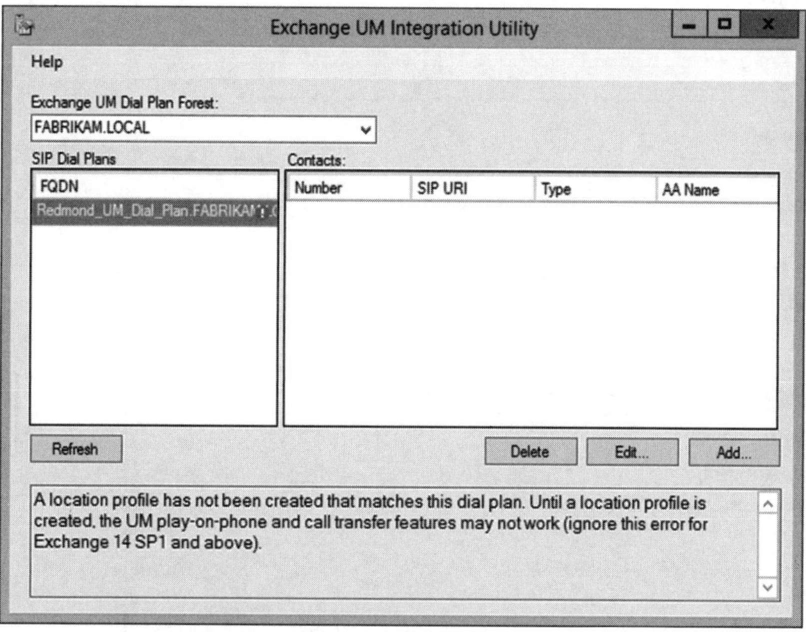

FIGURE 20.11 Exchange UM integration utility.

3. Click Add, and then at the Contact dialog box click Browse. Use the OU Picker to browse Active Directory and select the organizational unit that will be used as the location for the contact objects. It is also possible to create a new OU for this purpose by clicking the Make New OU button. After the OU has been specified, click OK to return to the Contact dialog box.

4. Review the default setting and make adjustments where necessary. For example, default values are displayed for the contact name and SIP address, but these can be edited if necessary. In the Phone Number section, verify that the phone extension specified as the subscriber access number in Exchange UM is automatically populated, as shown in Figure 20.12.

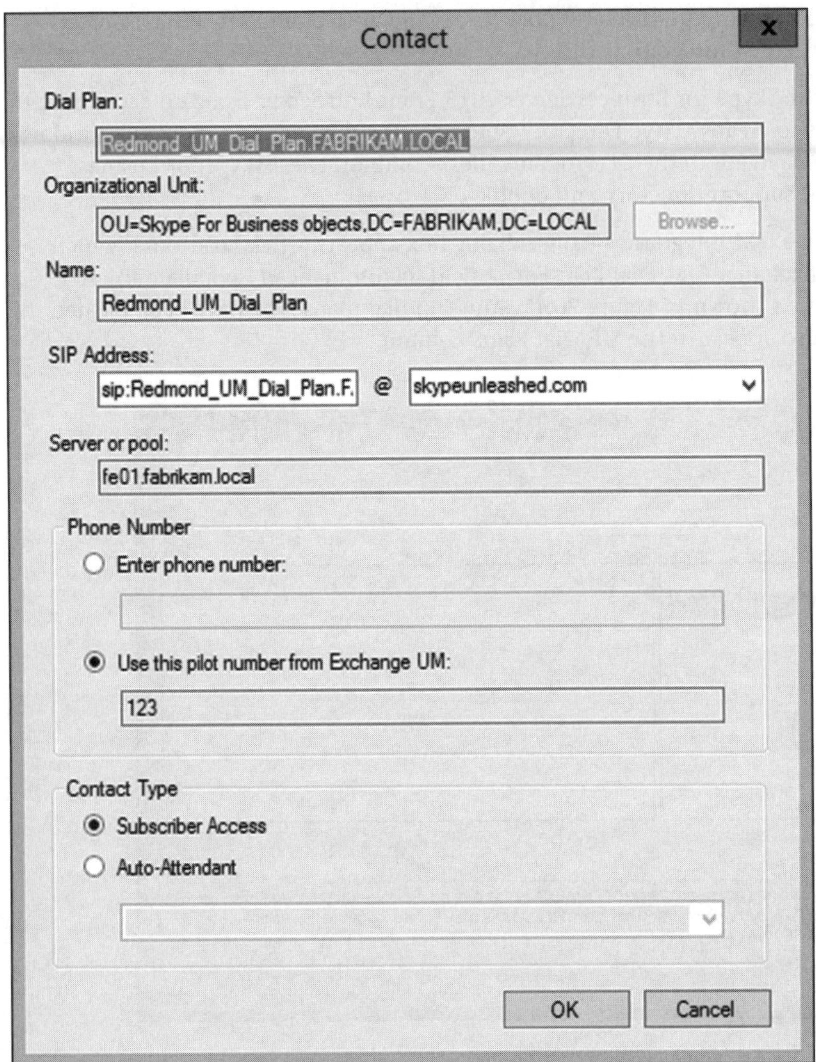

FIGURE 20.12 Creating a subscriber access contact object.

5. Keep the default Contact Type of Subscriber Access, and then click OK to create the subscriber access contact object.
6. To create an auto-attendant object, click Add; then at the Contact dialog box, in the Contact Type section select Auto-Attendant.
7. If several auto attendants have been created in Exchange UM, use the drop-down menu at the bottom of the dialog box to select the auto attendant for which a contact object will be created.

8. Review the remainder of the fields that are automatically populated for accuracy, and make any adjustments if necessary. When finished, click OK to create the auto-attendant object.
9. If additional auto-attendant contact objects are needed, repeat steps 6 to 8 to create additional contact objects for these.
10. When finished, exit the Exchange UM Integration Utility.

Testing the UM Integration

Microsoft provides two synthetic transactions that can be used to test the UM integration feature. The `Test-CsExUmConnectivity` cmdlet tests whether Skype for Business Server 2015 can connect to Exchange Server UM for a given user, and the `Test-CsExUmVoiceMail` cmdlet deposits a voicemail into the user's inbox.

The following Skype for Business Management Server Shell commands would be used to test the Exchange UM integration for a user:

```
$credential = Get-Credential -UserName fabrikam\nhirons
Test-CsExUMConnectivity -TargetFqdn fe01.fabrikam.local
➥-UserSipAddress nhirons@skypeunleashed.com -UserCredential $credential
```

The following series of commands would be used to deposit a voicemail for the same user, using a sample .wma file that is included as part of the Skype for Business Audio Test Service:

```
$credential = Get-Credential -UserName fabrikam\klopez
Test-CsExUMVoiceMail -SenderSipAddress klopez@skypeunleashed.com
➥-ReceiverSipAddress nhirons@skypeunleashe.com -SenderCredential $credential
➥-WaveFile "C:\Program Files\Skype for Business Server 2015\Application Host\
➥Applications\Audio Test Service\Media\en-US\Welcome.wma"
```

After Skype for Business Server 2015 has been successfully configured for Exchange UM integration, and the user has been enabled for UM, a voicemail icon will automatically appear within the Skype for Business client, as shown in Figure 20.13.

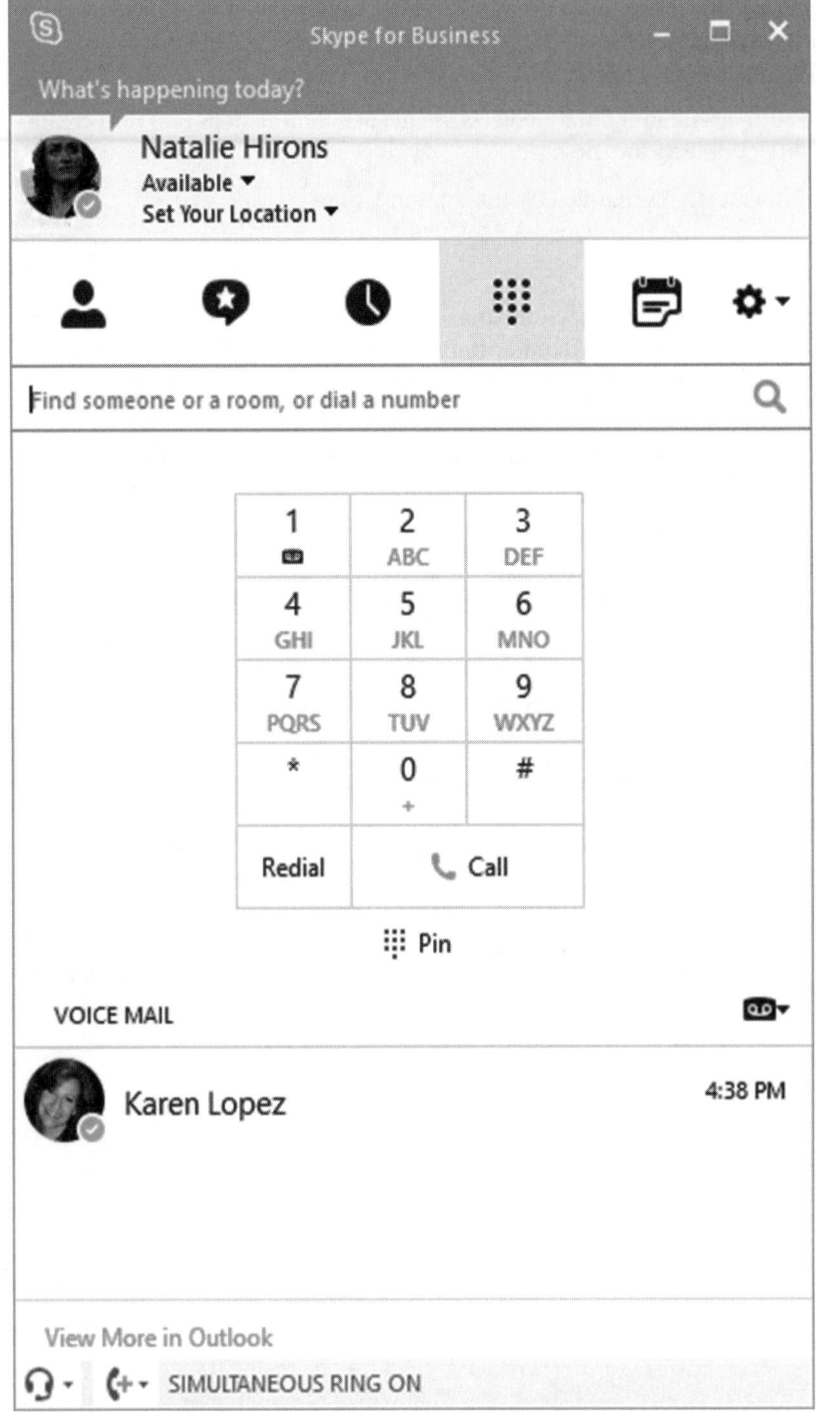

FIGURE 20.13 Exchange UM voicemail in the Skype for Business client.

Configuring Voicemail for Skype for Business Server 2015 Users Who Have Mailboxes in Exchange Online

The configuration of voicemail for hybrid users is straightforward but does involve quite a few steps. Components that need to be configured include DNS, federation, hosting providers, dial plans, routing numbers, and Active Directory contact objects. When these steps are completed, users can be configured for voicemail in Exchange Online. The steps outlined here should be followed in the order in which they are listed.

Create a DNS SRV Record

This record is no different from the record required for federation. In the external DNS zone of the SIP domain, such as `skypeunleashed.com`, create a Service Location (SRV) record using the values found in Table 20.1.

TABLE 20.1 Service Location (SRV) DNS Record Parameters

Parameter	Value
Domain	This should be the public SIP domain, such as `skypeunleashed.com`.
Service	_sipfederationtls
Protocol	_tcp
Priority	0
Weight	0
Port number	5061
Host offering this service	Public name of the Skype for Business Server 2015 Edge pool that will provide access.

An example of the DNS record can be seen in Figure 20.14.

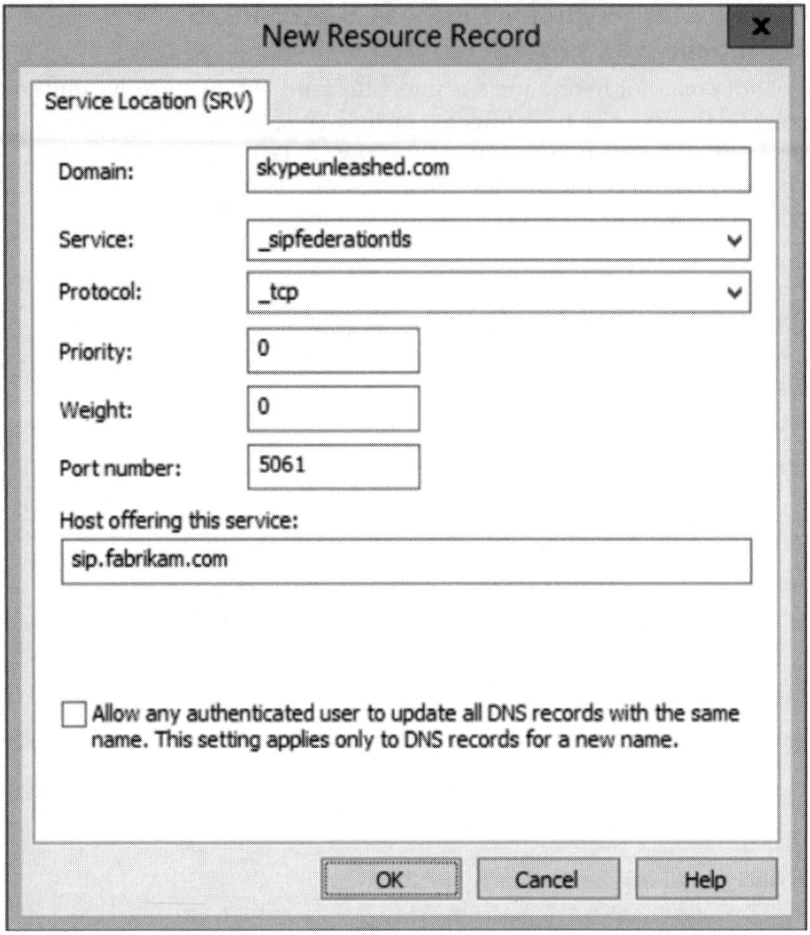

FIGURE 20.14 Federation DNS record.

Configure an Edge Server for Federation

The next step entails configuring the Edge Server for federation. On a server with the Skype for Business Management Server Shell, use the `Set-CsAccessEdgeConfiguration` cmdlet to allow federated users:

```
Set-CsAccessEdgeConfiguration -AllowFederatedUsers $true -UseDnsSrvRouting
```

Create a Hosted Provider on the Edge Server

Setting up connectivity with Exchange Online was already discussed previously in this chapter, in the section "Configuring a Hosting Provider on an Edge Server." Refer to that section and the `New-CsHostingProvider` command to run from within the Skype for Business Server 2015 Management Shell.

Create or Edit Hosted Voicemail Policies

Depending on requirements, a single hosted voicemail policy may be all that is needed. By default, a single global hosted voicemail policy is created by Skype for Business Server 2015. It can be configured easily by supplying two values to the `Set-CsHostedVoicemailPolicy` cmdlet. Those two are `Destination`, which is where the voicemail resides, and `Organization`, the tenant. `Destination` should always be `exap.um.outlook.com`, whereas `Organization` is the Exchange tenant FQDN containing users who are configured for on-premises Skype for Business Server 2015 server. This is usually something similar to `fabrikam.onmicrosoft.com`. You can set those both using the following command in the Skype for Business Server 2015 Management Shell:

```
Set-CsHostedVoicemailPolicy -Identity Global -Destination exap.um.outlook.com
➥-Organization fabrikam.onmicrosoft.com
```

Create a UM Dial Plan

Select Admin, Exchange, Unified Messaging. Click UM Dial Plans and then the "+" symbol to create a dial plan. Give the dial plan a name and specify the extension length. This should match the number of digits in a user's LineURI extension. Next, set the dial plan type to be SIP URI, and leave the VoIP security mode set at Unsecured. Pick the audio language and enter the country/region code. For the U.S., that's 1. An example of what the dialog box should look like is shown in Figure 20.15.

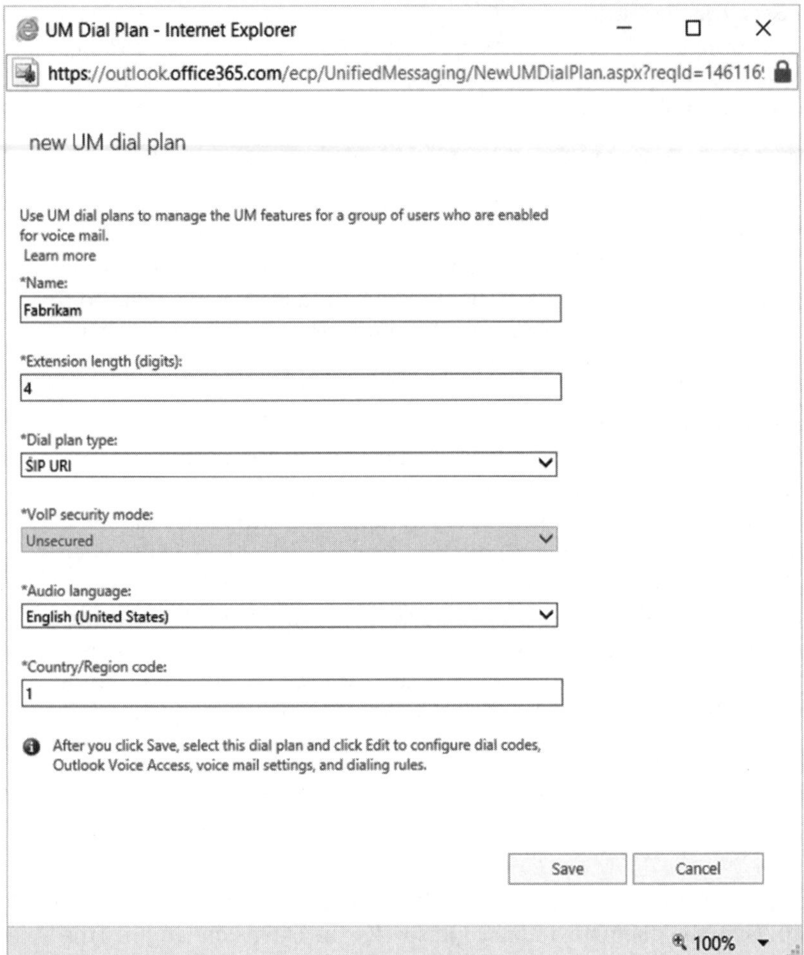

FIGURE 20.15 Creating a dial plan in Office 365.

Create a Routing Number

Once the dial plan is created, click the pencil icon to edit the new dial plan. Click the Configure box to configure dial codes, Outlook Voice Access, voicemail settings, and so on. Click Outlook Voice Access on the left side. Under E.164 Routing Numbers for Your SIP Server, enter a valid number in E.164 format that users can call to access Outlook Voice Access. Then click the "+" to add it to the list. In the next section down, enter the same number, but in a more human readable format, and again, click the "+" to add it to the list. This is the number that is shown in the email sent to users when they are enabled for voicemail. An example of configuration is shown in Figure 20.16.

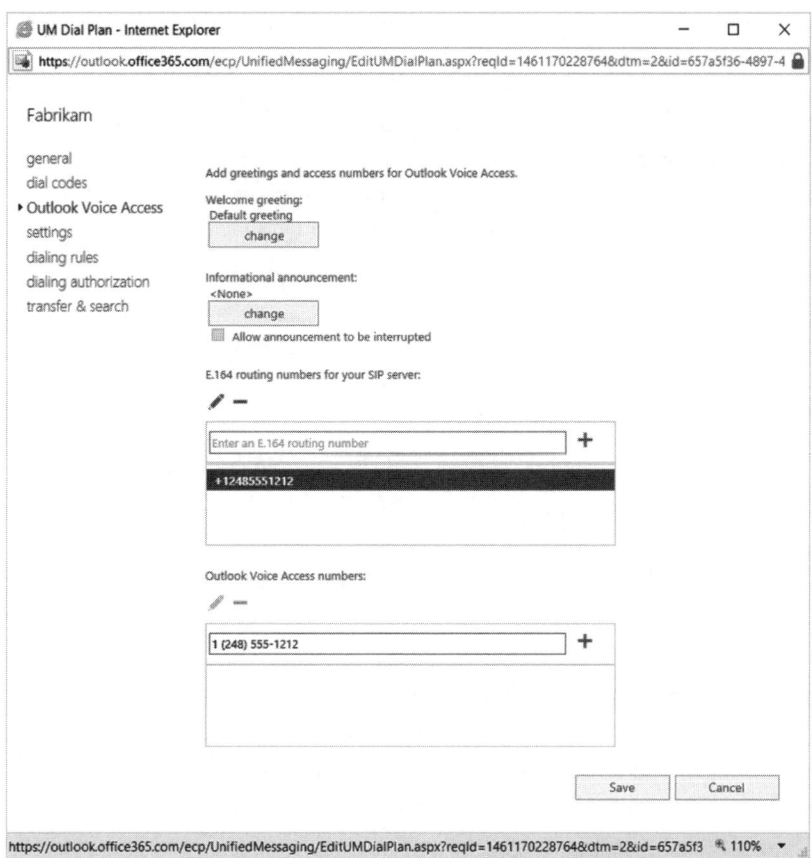

FIGURE 20.16 Assigning routing and Outlook Voice Access numbers.

Create a Contact Object for the Dial Plan

Back on-premises, you need to create a contact object in Active Directory to represent the newly created dial plan. This is easily accomplished in Skype for Business Server 2015 Management Shell using the `New-CsExUmContact` cmdlet. Four values are needed. The first is the `DisplayNumber`, which is the phone number you used. Second is a SIP address for the contact. It can be anything. Next is the registrar pool, and, finally, the OU where the contact will reside. Here is an example of the syntax:

```
New-CsExUmContact -DisplayNumber +12485551212 -SipAddress
➥sip:EX-UM @skypeunleashed.com -RegistrarPool
➥fepool01.fabrikam.local -OU "OU=EXUMContacts,DC=fabrikam,DC=local"
```

20

Assign the Hosted Voicemail Policy to the Contact

Finally, you assign a policy to the newly created contact. This is straightforward in the Skype for Business Server 2015 Management Shell. As with all policy-related commands, if the Global policy is used, the `PolicyName` parameter isn't required, but can be included. It is included here to show the syntax:

```
Grant-CSHostedVoiceMailPolicy -Identity "ex-um" -PolicyName Global
```

Enable Users for Hosted Voicemail

Enabling users for hosted voicemail is a pretty simple two-step process using the Management Shell. The Skype for Business Server 2015 Control Panel cannot be used because those options are not exposed in the GUI.

First, you grant the hosted voicemail policy to the user using

```
Grant-CSHostedVoiceMailPolicy -Identity "Nathan Smith" - PolicyName Global
```

Obviously, you would adjust the identity accordingly.

Next, you set the same user to use hosted voicemail. This is a simple command as well:

```
Set-CsUser -Identity "Nathan Smith" -HostedVoiceMail $True
```

Once this is completed, users with mailboxes in Office 365 and Skype for Business Server 2015 on-premises will be able to use voicemail.

SharePoint Integration Features

With Skype for Business Server 2015, the integrations with SharePoint that existed in previous versions will continue to be supported, and some added integration features are introduced as well. Skype for Business Server 2015 integrations for SharePoint include the following:

- eDiscovery of Skype for Business Server 2015 archive data
- IM and presence integration
- Skill search

eDiscovery of Skype for Business Server 2015 Archive Data

An integration feature introduced in Lync Server 2013 and continued with Skype for Business Server 2015 and SharePoint 2013 is the use of SharePoint eDiscovery to search Skype for Business Server 2015 archive data. eDiscovery describes the process of searching through electronic content, which could include documents, websites, email messages, and other electronic sources, and then collecting and acting on the content that meets some particular criteria, such as that which might be needed for a legal case. Typically, eDiscovery is a task that is performed by records managers and litigators, and SharePoint 2013 facilitates the eDiscovery process for content that is stored in SharePoint through the use of eDiscovery Centers. An eDiscovery Center is a central SharePoint site that is used to manage perseveration, search, and export of content stored in SharePoint and Exchange across multiple servers and server farms. For example, the in-place hold feature can be used to preserve data within SharePoint sites or Exchange mailboxes, but still allow users to continue editing and deleting preserved content.

Although eDiscovery of Skype for Business Server 2015 archive data can correctly be called an integration feature for Skype for Business Server 2015 and SharePoint 2013, in reality this feature involves integration of both products with Exchange Server as well. The reason for this is that Skype for Business Server 2015 must first be configured to archive content to Exchange Server before SharePoint eDiscovery can be used to search that data. In reality then, the first task involved in configuring eDiscovery of Skype for Business archive data is the integration of Skype for Business Server 2015 archiving to Exchange, as detailed in the "Skype for Business Server 2015 Archiving Integration" section earlier in this chapter.

NOTE

To enable discovery of Skype for Business Server 2015 content through SharePoint, all three of the products involved must be running the 2013 or later version of the software: Skype for Business 2015, Exchange Server, SharePoint 2013, and so on.

After Skype for Business Server 2015, Exchange Server, and SharePoint 2013 have been configured as partner applications as described in the "Server-to-Server Authentication" section earlier in this chapter, and after Skype for Business Server 2015 archiving integration has also been configured, SharePoint eDiscovery can be configured to search Skype for Business Server 2015 data that has been archived to Exchange. The following example shows the steps involved in using SharePoint eDiscovery to search Skype for Business Server 2015 archive data:

1. To begin the eDiscovery process, the user who will be performing the discovery must be assigned to the Discovery Management role group in Exchange. The following Exchange Management Shell command would be used to assign a user to the role:

   ```
   Add-RoleGroupMember "Discovery Management" -member jrosen
   ```

2. The next step is to create an eDiscovery site. For example, the following two commands would be used in the SharePoint Management Shell to create an eDiscovery site under an existing SharePoint site named `abcsite.fabrikam.local`, with the user who will be performing the discovery being specified as the owner:

   ```
   $template = Get-SPWebTemplate | Where-Object {$_.title -eq "eDiscovery Center"}
   New-SPSite -Url http://abcsite.fabrikam.local/sites/Discovery
   ➥-OwnerAlias jrosen -Template $template -Name "Discovery Center"
   ```

3. To generate Skype for Business Server 2015 archive data to be searched using eDiscovery, the Skype for Business Server 2015 archiving policy needs to be enabled for archiving to Exchange for at least one user. For a detailed description of the Skype for Business Server 2015 archiving integration feature, see the "Skype for Business Server 2015 Archiving Integration" section earlier in this chapter. The following sample command would be used to enable archiving to Exchange for an individual user:

   ```
   Set-CsUser crichard -ExchangeArchivingPolicy ArchivingToExchange
   ```

4. After Skype for Business Server 2015 data has been archived to Exchange, Exchange Server needs to be added as a content source in SharePoint. The SharePoint 2013

Central Administration site can be used for this. Start by clicking Manage Service Applications and then Search Service Application.

5. Add a new result source named Exchange, with the protocol also specified as Exchange. For Exchange Source URL, enter https://<ExchangeFQDN>/ews/exchange.asmx, with <ExchangeFQDN> being the fully qualified domain name of the target Exchange Server, as shown in Figure 20.17. Also, ensure that Autodiscover is not selected.

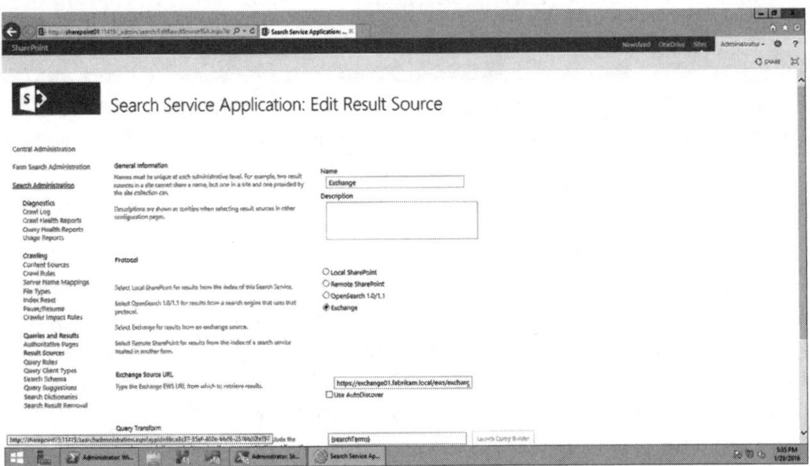

FIGURE 20.17 Exchange configured as a content source in SharePoint.

6. The user who has been granted Discovery Management rights now logs on to the Discovery site created previously and uses it to create an eDiscovery case. The URL to connect to is https://<SharePointSite>/sites/discovery, or for this example http://abcsite.fabrikam.local/sites/discovery. When a title and website address are specified for the case, these should be named in a descriptive manner so that the case can be easily found; for example, the name of the user whose mailbox will be searched can be included in both.

7. After the case has been created, the final task is to create an eDiscovery set using the eDiscovery case created in the preceding step. Within the properties of the eDiscovery set, specify the user who has been configured for archiving to Exchange. Start and end dates for the discovery can also be specified, and in-place hold can be enabled as well.

8. SharePoint now initiates a search against the specified mailbox and displays the results in a preview window. The eDiscovery can be saved at this point so that the same discovery criteria can be used later.

IM and Presence Integration

Presence within SharePoint does not require any additional modifications to either SharePoint or Skype for Business Server 2015. Presence is displayed via an ActiveX control and Skype for Business Server 2015 APIs. On the client side, the only requirement is that a version of Microsoft Office be installed on the client computer where Presence will be displayed.

Skill Search

An interesting integration feature that was introduced with Lync 2010 and continues to be available with on-premises Skype for Business Server 2015 is skill search. Skill search enables Skype for Business users to search skills, expertise, and organizational information from SharePoint My Sites. If users populate expertise information into fields in their SharePoint My Site, Skype for Business users will be able to discover this information based on the content of these fields. For example, an IT Manager user might have a need to track down an internal resource with skills in a particular development platform. To find someone with these skills, the manager simply enters the search criteria in Skype for Business, and a list of internal contacts who have flagged themselves as experts in that development language are listed. This integration feature can therefore result in a real-time savings, especially for a large organization, because it is no longer necessary to manually build a list of whom to contact for specific subjects. Users can instead build a dynamic searchable database of skills and organizational information right from the Skype for Business client, which makes it much easier to find the right personnel to collaborate with.

To enable skill search, users must have a SharePoint deployment that includes My Sites. The full version of SharePoint must also be used, because Windows SharePoint Services is not compatible with skill search. The SharePoint search center URL is made available to Skype for Business clients through in-band provisioning, which also means that SharePoint must be published to the Internet for remote users to take advantage of this feature.

To configure skill search, a Skype for Business Server 2015 client policy must be configured and applied to the Skype for Business clients specifying the SharePoint URLs. A single policy can be used to configure both the SPSearchInternalURL and the SPSearchExternalURL values. Via the Skype for Business Server Management Shell, use the following command, where <SPserver> is the name of the SharePoint Server:

```
Set-CSClientPolicy -SPSearchInternalURL "http://<SPserver>/
➥_vti_bin/search.asmx" -SPSearchExternalURL
➥"http://<SPserver>/_vti_bin/search.asmx"
```

Optionally, the Search Center URL can also be configured to display at the bottom of the search results when users run a skill search query. To configure the URL to be displayed, you would use the following additional Management Shell command:

```
Set-CSClientPolicy -SPSearchCenterInternalURL
http://<SPserver>/SearchCenter/Pages/PeopleResults.aspx -SPSearchCenterExternalURL
➥http://<SPserver>/SearchCenter/Pages/PeopleResults.aspx
```


After these commands are run, a Skype for Business client will pick up the change through in-band provisioning the next time the client is started. There are two ways to determine whether the skill search settings have been applied. First, as shown in Figure 20.18, when a user is searching a contact in the Skype for Business client, two additional options are now listed: Name and Skill.

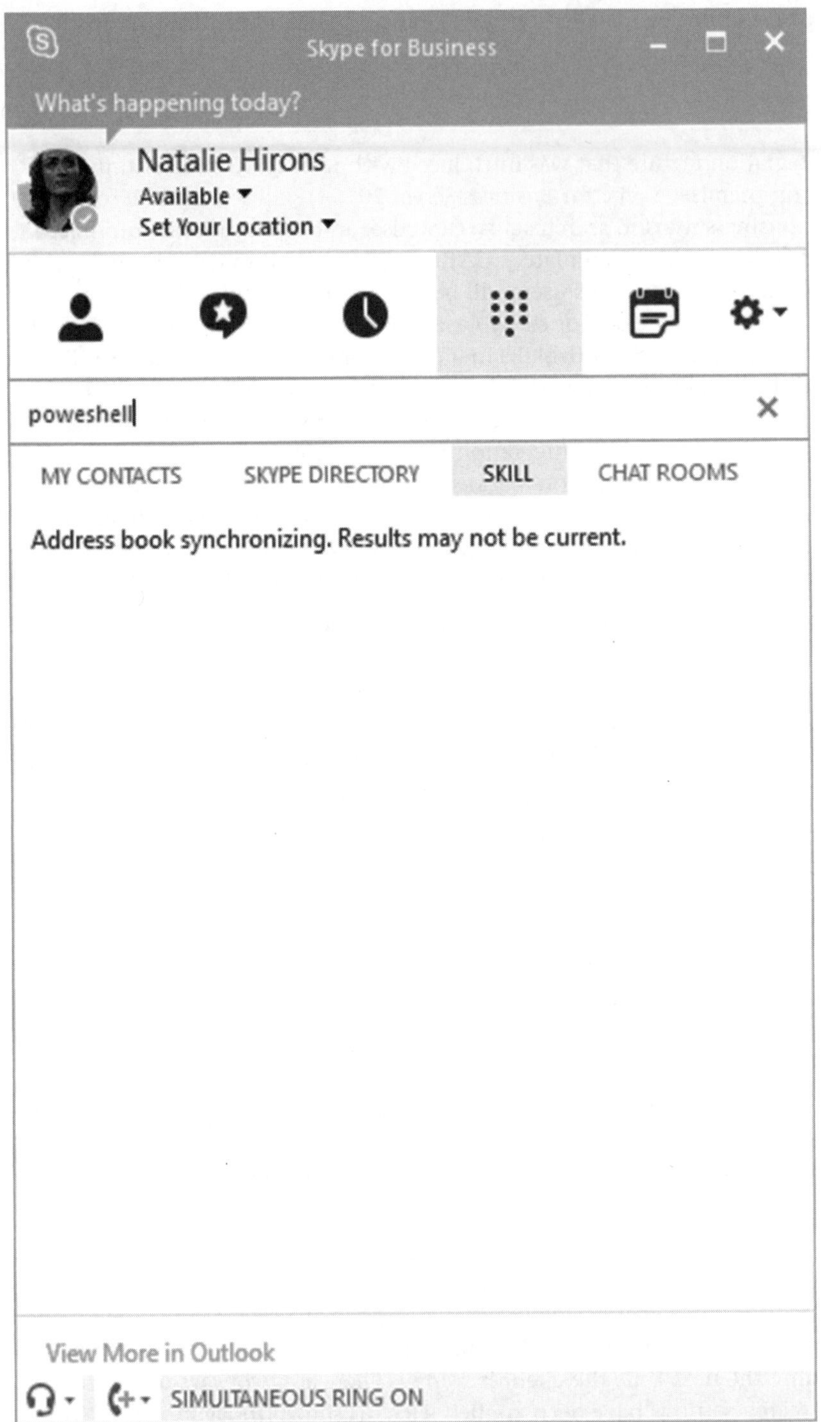

FIGURE 20.18 Skill search options in the Skype for Business client.

The other way to determine whether skill search has been applied is by viewing the Skype for Business client configuration settings. To access the Skype for Business client configuration settings, hold down the Ctrl key and right-click the Skype for Business system tray icon in the lower-right corner of the desktop; then select Configuration Information from the menu. Included in the resulting Skype for Business Configuration Information screen is the skill search URL, as shown in Figure 20.19.

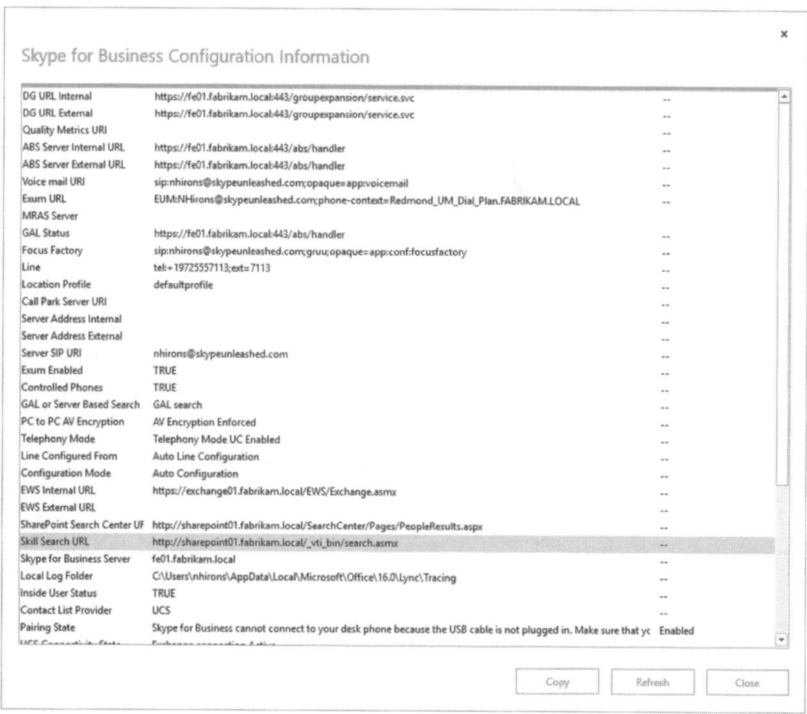

FIGURE 20.19 Skill search URL in the Skype for Business client configuration settings.

If results are found, at the bottom of the client an option is presented to view the results in SharePoint. This connects the user to the full SharePoint interface to display more detailed information about the results.

Summary

As with previous versions, Microsoft continues to put significant development efforts into the integration features of Skype for Business Server 2015, Exchange, and SharePoint. With the 2013 and later versions of these applications, there are many ways for organizations to leverage features across these three applications. The integrations that became popular with previous versions of Skype for Business Server 2015, such as Unified Contact Store and eDiscovery archive data, continue to be supported and allow even greater efficiencies and cost savings for organizations that deploy these products together.

CHAPTER 21

Developing Skype for Business Solutions

IN THIS CHAPTER

- Overview of Skype for Business Applications
- Choosing a Skype for Business SDK
- Skype for Business Application Scenarios
- Debugging Skype for Business Applications

Skype for Business Server 2015 provides an end-to-end unified communications solution, but it's also more than that. It is a development platform. Specialized solutions and features can be added to Skype for Business Server 2015, such as communications recording (voice, video, application sharing), compliance enforcement (scanning IM conversations and blocking violating messages), interactive voice response (IVR), call center applications, security enhancements, and many more applications. Another area of development is to enable existing business applications for communications, commonly referred as CEBP (communication-enabled business process). By enhancing existing business applications, corporate organizations can improve productivity by increasing the speed of communications between applications and users. We'll explore the different APIs that Skype for Business Server 2015 offers for you to consider how you can build on top of your Skype for Business Server 2015 environment to amplify the effect of unified communications.

Developers can add Skype for Business communication functionality into line of business (LOB) applications. By integrating communication into business applications and business process flows, the full benefit of unified communications can be truly realized.

The Skype for Business client and mobile clients are not the only ways users can interact with Skype for Business Server 2015. If businesses have specialized requirements, then an application with a custom user interface may be required, and may be more effective. Users don't even need to know they are using Skype for Business Server 2015 to make their video calls (because they're using a completely customized application), and that's okay. It's more important to focus on streamlining the user experience and have the technology stay out of the way of the user experience.

Skype for Business Server 2015 is a distributed client-server communications platform that sends, routes, redirects, and receives data in discrete TCP and UDP packets across the IP network. The Skype for Business APIs abstract the low-level packetization of this network traffic as well as the details of the various protocols (SIP, SIMPLE, SRTP, PSOM, HTTPS) used by Skype for Business Server 2015. The protocol details are accessible through methods and events. This makes it easier for developers to build applications that are communications enabled without the need to become an expert in the protocols used by Skype for Business Server 2015.

This chapter provides a snapshot of what is possible today. However, the only certain fact about the future of Skype for Business Server 2015 development is that it will change and evolve. As more and more people move toward working on mobile devices and connecting to cloud services, expect to see more and different tools that empower developers to continue to make their applications communications enabled.

Overview of Skype for Business Applications

One of the most confusing things when starting out developing with Skype for Business is how many different APIs, SDKs, controls, and libraries there are. Choice is good and in some ways necessary to cover all the different areas where developers may want to write code (desktops, servers, and so on), but it can be overwhelming for anyone starting out. Figure 21.1 illustrates the different types of applications that can be developed for Skype for Business Server 2015.

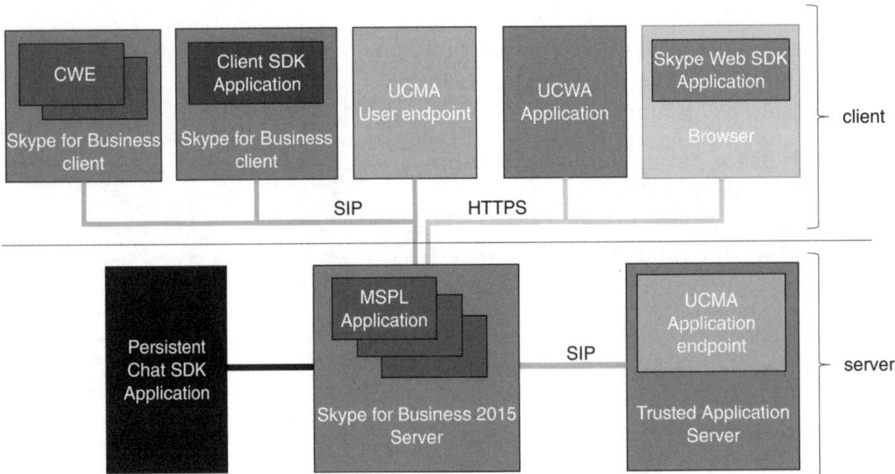

FIGURE 21.1 Unified communications types of applications.

Building Client Applications

This category describes the tools available to developers who want to build client-side applications designed to run on users' computers. These types of applications require the Skype for Business client to be installed and running on the users' computers. This requirement constrains the rollout of such applications and therefore limits their reach. These applications will only run on Microsoft Windows with the Skype for Business client installed. Their value is in either automating functionality from the client or exposing parts of the client in other applications. Because these tools are really just exposing existing Skype for Business client functionality, these APIs will work with on-premises Skype for Business Server 2015 deployments, hybrid deployments, and Office 365 accounts.

Client SDK

The Client SDK for Skype for Business is a .NET library that gives developers a programmatic way to control the Skype for Business client. Nearly everything that can be done in the client can be achieved using the Client SDK in code. This includes signing in, making and receiving calls, sending instant messages, updating contact information, and more. The Client SDK exposes events, allowing developers to write applications that can react to actions in Skype for Business, such as receiving an incoming call. The Client SDK doesn't, however, allow developers to modify the look and feel of the native Skype for Business client, which remains visible at all times and can still be operated by the user. Developers use the Client SDK by referencing the Microsoft .Lync.Model.dll in their applications. The Client SDK can be downloaded from https://www.microsoft.com/en-gb/download/details.aspx?id=36824.

UI Suppression Mode

Not technically a separate control but a special mode of invoking the Client SDK, UI Suppression Mode is a technique where the Skype for Business client is hidden from the user, although the Skype for Business client process continues to run in the background. The visible components of the Client SDK are not available, except for the video window. This allows developers to write their own user interface for Skype for Business—in fact, it is required because the user won't have access to the native client. Toggling UI Suppression Mode on and off is done via the following registry setting:

```
[HKEY_CURRENT_USER]\Software\Microsoft\Office\15.0\Lync\UISuppressionMode
```

(Note that the version number, 15.0, may differ based on client version.) If this setting has a DWORD value of 1, UI suppression is enabled. UI Suppression Mode is mainly used in dedicated scenarios, such as information kiosks where a dedicated, full-screen interface is required. UI Suppression Mode does, however, provide the developer with capabilities to create a completely custom Skype for Business client with as much functionality as required. Because every part of the experience must be coded (including signing in, signing out, showing contact lists, and receiving incoming calls), creating a client application using the Client SDK in UI Suppression Mode requires considerably more effort than augmenting the native client with some additional functionality using the Client SDK normally, but it is the only way to produce an entirely customized user interface.

There are limitations when using the Skype for Business client in UI Suppression Mode. The `Microsoft.Lync.Model.Extensibility` namespace is not available to start conversations or meetings. Components such as the Microsoft Skype for Business Controls for Silverlight browser, WPF applications, and the meeting content and resource sharing modalities cannot be used in your application.

Conversation Window Extension (CWE)

A Conversation Window Extension is an extensible part of the standard conversation window in the Skype for Business client. In the same way that a desktop-sharing session opens an extra area to the right of an instant message conversation to display the sharing content, a Conversation Window Extension is an extra area that can be used to display a web page. The web page is hosted by an Internet Explorer engine. Therefore, it can be a fully featured, rich website that users can navigate (although there is no chrome, no forward and back buttons, and no favorites).

Each CWE must be added to a user's registry with the name, two URLs, and one of three pre-fixed sizes. An internal URL is accessible from the internal network, as well as from an external URL for when the Skype for Business client connects outside the corporate network. The CWE is listed in the ellipses button shown in the bottom right of a Skype for Business conversation. When the user chooses the menu item, the web page is opened and displayed within the Skype for Business client frame. These CWEs can also be automatically opened by UCMA applications (see the following section), which greatly increases their usefulness because it means they can be triggered on certain actions. It is also possible to host Silverlight applications in CWEs, and if this is done, a dedicated Silverlight DLL is provided as part of the Client SDK download that allows Silverlight applications to interact with the client.

Building Server Applications

Server-side development refers to applications that interact directly with Skype for Business Servers to enhance the standard Skype for Business logic and functionality in some way. Rather than applications that run on client computers, these applications are designed to be run constantly and to be installed on servers. They typically either automate common features, provide additional services to users, or modify the way that Skype for Business works.

Unified Communications Managed API (UCMA)

The Unified Communications Managed API (UCMA) is a .NET library like the Client SDK. Where the similarity ends, however, is that whereas the Client SDK is a code abstraction of the client, UCMA is an API for interacting directly with Skype for Business Servers.

UCMA functionality divides broadly into being able to create one of two types of Skype for Business endpoints: user endpoints and application endpoints. User endpoints (as the name suggests) are created using the credentials of a user enabled for Skype for Business, and are limited in their functionality to whatever that user would normally be able to achieve with a standard Skype for Business client. Applications that leverage a user endpoint connect to Skype for Business Servers, but their connections are throttled by the server to prevent denial-of-service attacks. The difference with UCMA compared to the Client SDK is that the Skype for Business client is not required, so developers can write a custom end-user application independent of the Skype for Business client.

Application endpoints, however, are much more powerful. They are not tied to any specific user. In fact, they can impersonate any user in the Skype for Business environment and perform any actions as that user, such as changing Presence or sending instant messages. In addition, application endpoints can perform administrative-level functions such as joining conferences invisibly and manipulating the audio routing (control who hears what). Optionally, application endpoints can be assigned specific SIP URIs and line URIs (that is, phone numbers) with which users can interact. These SIP URIs are exposed in users' Skype for Business contact lists and can be added to client contact lists like regular users. Finally, UCMA applications support advanced functions such as the sending and receiving DTMF tones, text-to-speech capabilities, and some basic speech recognition. Applications that use an application endpoint are trusted by Skype for Business Servers. Therefore, connections are not throttled by Skype for Business Servers. If these applications are poorly designed, they can compromise the performance of your Skype for Business Servers.

Because application endpoints are so powerful, there are restrictions on how they can be run. Such applications can technically be run on Front End servers; however, the recommendation is to run such applications on a dedicated server operating system, called a trusted application server. This is a specific server type in the Skype for Business Server 2015 topology. When an application is run, unless it is running on a trusted server, an exception will be thrown. This provides a level of security to UCMA applications—the assumption being that if an application has been installed on a server that is a trusted application server in the Skype for Business topology, then implicitly it can be trusted.

To get started, download UCMA from https://www.microsoft.com/en-us/download/details.aspx?id=47345.

Microsoft SIP Processing Language (MSPL)

If you imagine all the SIP messages that flow through a Front End Server as a giant firehose of data, then Microsoft SIP Processing Language (MSPL) is a way of sifting through this flow of data. MSPL is a small domain-specific scripting language with a few important functions. It allows developers to identify specific SIP messages and take various actions on them, such as modifying them or blocking them to prevent SIP messages from travelling further through the system and to their intended destination.

There are two ways to use MSPL. The first is as a pure scripting language. Developers write an MSPL script in a manifest file (this file has an extension of ".am"). This manifest must be registered with a Skype for Business Server 2015 pool in order to run. MSPL scripts can modify the SIP message at different stages as the message flows through the SIP stack. Skype for Business Server 2015 maintains a strict ordering system for running MSPL scripts. Therefore, developers should specify the priority level in which their script should run. Once enabled, the script will process every qualifying SIP message. Colima provides a free tool, SimpleRoute, to help you write simple MSPL scripts.

The second way is to use MSPL for the manifest file to dispatch SIP messages for processing to a .NET application or Windows service. This approach is recommended for developing more complex routing logic that's not possible or easily done in MSPL scripting. By dispatching the processing of SIP messages, it offers a lot more flexibility that is not confined by the MSPL scripting language, which is more restrictive in the functionality it offers. It's important to streamline the routing logic in your MSPL applications so it doesn't impact the performance of your Skype for Business Server 2015.

Persistent Chat SDK

A separate SDK covers Persistent Chat functionality. It is structured somewhat similarly to UCMA but is focused purely on working with Persistent Chat. Using this SDK, developers can write applications that write message to chat rooms or react to messages being posted to a chat room. Persistent Chat maintains a history of every message posted to every chat room. The Persistent Chat SDK provides access to this information. Developers can write applications that can mine this information. The Persistent Chat SDK can also automate the administration of creating and maintaining chat rooms as well as adding and removing users to and from chat rooms.

Building Web Applications

Web-based applications target users who don't have a Skype for Business client but still need access to their organization's communications infrastructure. Typically, this is when an organization wants to expose some communication functionality to its users, such as Presence information, IM experience, and more from a web browser embedded as part of web-based applications.

Unified Communications Web API (UCWA)

The Unified Communication Web API (UCWA) is a HTTP REST API for communication with Skype for Business Server 2015. Think of it as the SIP and SIMPLE protocols translated into REST calls encapsulated in HTTPS. This has both advantages and disadvantages. Because UCWA is uses HTTP request and response calls, it is possible to write applications that communicate with Skype for Business Server 2015 anywhere without needing a full SIP stack implementation, such as embedded devices, Linux/Unix machines, and Internet of Things (IoT) appliances. However, using UCWA to communicate with Skype for Business Server 2015 is fairly complex to achieve, even for the most basic tasks such as signing in. UCWA offers the same functionality as the SIP protocols (signaling, Presence, contact lists, and so on) and SIMPLE protocols (sending and receiving IMs). However, UCWA does not provide the equivalent of the SRTP protocol. This implies that you cannot use UCWA to make or receive audio or video calls.

Skype Web SDK

The Skype Web SDK is Microsoft's newest SDK for Skype for Business Server 2015. It leverages UCWA to communicate with Skype for Business Server 2015. The Skype Web SDK is a JavaScript library with concepts familiar to JavaScript developers, such as Promises/A+, observable properties, and lazy collections. Its aim is to abstract the complexities of Skype for Business Server 2015 as much as possible and present an abstraction to developers so that they can incorporate communication features into their sites.

Developers can speed up their software development efforts of integrating communications functionality into their web-based applications by leveraging this JavaScript library without needing to know the details of UCWA.

In order to use the Skype Web SDK, the domain hosting the SDK code needs to be added as a trusted domain to the Cross Domain Authorization List, which is done with the `Set-CsWebServiceConfiguration` PowerShell command. Every domain that the SDK might be run on needs to be added to this list, including development machines. It is possible to add *localhost* to this list for development environments, although this represents an unacceptable security risk for production environments as it effectively allows anyone to connect by running code locally. Trusted domains need to be added to every Front End and Edge Server in the Skype for Business Server 2015 topology.

The Skype Web SDK requires sign-in credentials of a Skype for Business user to be useful. There is an anonymous sign-in capability, but this limits functionality to only joining Skype meetings as an anonymous user. Once the developer is signed in, the Skype Web SDK allows the developer to modify a user's contact list, update their presence as well as subscribe to other user's presence, make and receive IMs, create and join Skype meetings, and establish audio and video calls. To take advantage of the audio/video capabilities requires a browser plug-in to be installed, called the Skype for Business Web App Plug-in. This is available for both Windows and Mac computers and is supported on newer versions of Internet Explorer, Firefox, Chrome, and Safari on OS X (full supportability matrix can be found at https://technet.microsoft.com/en-us/library/gg425820.aspx). Microsoft has stated intentions to support WebRTC in the near future and to upgrade the Skype Web SDK so that it does not require a plug-in.

Choosing a Skype for Business SDK

The different Skype for Business SDKs target different problem spaces, and selecting the most appropriate SDK can be difficult when there are several options. However, once you identify the functionality you need from Skype for Business Server 2015, the selection process becomes easier. There is not much overlap between the different Skype for Business SDKs, so the problem is more of an issue of choosing the SDK that can meet your requirements rather than choosing from a number of different options, each of which can meet your requirement to a certain degree. When selecting the right Skype for Business SDK to develop your applications, you should ask yourself the following questions:

Is my code visual/interactive, or is it autonomous?

If the code modifies the Skype for Business experience for a single person from a user-experience perspective and can depend on the Skype for Business client being installed on the end user's computer, then the Client SDK might be best option. If, however, the application performs an autonomous task on behalf of the user (such as ensuring that a specific set of contacts are always shown in a user's favorites list) and shouldn't run on the user's computer, then UCMA would be a better fit because it can run as a Windows service on a server where it can be scheduled and monitored more easily than an application running on an end-user's computer.

Does my code affect a single user or multiple users?

Taking the preceding example further, if you need to populate a set of contacts on multiple users' contact lists, then UCMA would be a better choice than deploying a Client SDK application to every user's computer. A UCMA application runs on a server and can impersonate every user and manipulate their contact list accordingly.

How will users interact with my application?

If users will be interacting via a web page, this narrows your choices to either the Skype Web SDK or UCWA—most likely Skype Web SDK, unless there is a compelling reason not to use it. If users will be interacting with a contact in their contact list, such as a bot, then UCMA is your only option. If they will be interacting with a system tray application or running a program, then the Client SDK is the most appropriate choice.

What is my specific use case?

The Skype for Business SDKs are designed with some common use cases in mind. Therefore, it's worth reviewing this list of common use cases to determine if your use case matches one of them. For instance, if you want to present contextual information alongside a conversation, then Conversation Window Extensions are a natural fit. If you want to develop a full-screen kiosk-style application, then you should investigate UI Suppression Mode. If you want to work with Persistent Chat data, then your only real choice is to use the Persistent Chat SDK.

Will my application modify how SIP messages are sent and received?

If your application needs to modify the Skype for Business SIP routing logic, such as preventing some messages from being delivered or rerouting messages intended for one person to another, then you need a Skype for Business SDK that allows you to intercept those messages before they reach the client. A Client SDK solution to prevent certain messages from being received or to modify how they appear will never work as elegantly and effectively as an MSPL solution, which is able to intercept the messages on the server.

Sometimes there are multiple ways to solve the same problem. In that case, it's worth carefully considering the advantages and disadvantages of each SDK within the larger context of an application and not just the choice of SDK. If a problem could be done in either the Client SDK or UCMA, which is preferable? It depends on whether the application needs to run on every user's computer and must remain running to be useful. With many computers (for instance, on a large corporate network), that can become an IT headache. However, a centralized UCMA application only needs a server instance running, which is a lot easier to manage. That server instance is more easily monitored than hundreds or thousands of user computers. On the other hand, a UCMA application requires a trusted application server, which represents an investment in money and time for an organization if they don't already have one.

Regarding Office 365, most of these Skype for Business SDKs were developed before Office 365, and consequently do not work against Office 365. All the SDKs covered in this chapter assume an on-premises deployment of Skype for Business Server 2015. Only the

UCWA, Client SDK, UI Controls, and UI Suppression Mode will work equally well with Office 365. Expect this situation to change over time as new APIs are released in response to a shift to cloud-first computing.

Skype for Business Application Scenarios

The list of applications that can be developed using the Skype for Business development tools is practically limitless, and is bounded only by the requirements and constraints of your organization as well as your imagination. What follows are some examples of common applications that have been built.

Auxiliary Call Notifications

An organization that runs several factories has rolled out Skype for Business Server 2015 to meet their communication needs. However, they found that in the factories, workers couldn't hear the incoming sounds played by the Skype for Business client, due to the standard computer speakers in use. Their solution was to use a USB flashing light and a simple application that uses the Client SDK to trigger the USB light for incoming messages and calls.

An organization federates with several suppliers to enable communication between organizations. The organization developed a Conversation Window Extension (CWE) that staff can open when communicating with a supplier. The CWE application dynamically shows information about the supplier, which can be determined by examining the SIP domain of the federated user's SIP address. The CWE displays information such as materials supplied, any outstanding purchase orders, invoices, and so on.

Pausing Music on Incoming Call

If you listen to music, you'll notice that the Skype for Business client reduces the volume of the music when you receive an incoming call. However, having music play at a low volume can still be distracting. A Client SDK system tray application can be written to be notified for incoming calls and automatically pause any playing music. The application can also listen for when the call ends and automatically resume playback. This is relatively easy to do using the Client SDK and could be achieved in a few ways: For example, you could subscribe to the `ConversationAdded` event raised by the `ConversationManager`, which will notify you of every new conversation (including ones you make as well as incoming ones) and then monitor the state of the conversation to see if it becomes active and includes the `AudioVideo` modality. The application can mute playing music as a result of this event. Another approach is for the application to monitor your own Presence state. The Skype for Business client automatically changes your Presence state to Busy with an activity of "In a call" when you accept an audio call. The application can use the `ContactInformationChanged` event to subscribe to contact status changes including the signed-in user. By monitoring this event, the application can pause playing music.

A GitHub example showing how this could be done is available at https://github.com/tomorgan/LyncPauseMusicOnCall.

Contextual Information on Incoming Calls

Another good use for the Client SDK is to retrieve and display contextual information to the user about the caller or subject of the call. Consider the example of a school receptionist who receives an incoming call. The Client SDK application running on the receptionist's computer analyzes the incoming number and matches it against a database of students and their parents/guardians' numbers. Upon finding a match, it displays the name of the student, the names of the parents or guardians, and provides a one-click button to jump to the student's record in the school's database application to display more information. This functionality facilitates the receptionist in answering calls with relevant information about the caller's student within easy access. The receptionist has contextual information within the Skype for Business client conversation immediately. This avoids the customary list of questions the receptionist needs to ask in order to establish which student the caller is calling about.

Order Lookup via IM

An organization has a legacy order-tracking system, written in-house. The application is old but gets the job done. There is no integration with any communications solutions at all. The data used by this legacy application is stored in a database. Orders are tracked daily using this application to determine the current status of orders and customers. The mobile sales force complains that they can't access the system when they are at client sites because it only works when they are in the office and isn't supported on their mobile devices. A UCMA application can expose a bot as a contact on the mobile user's contact lists in the Skype for Business Mobile client (or any Skype for Business client). When an order or customer number is sent as an IM to the bot, the application receives the message, queries the relevant information from the database, and returns a summary of the relevant information as an IM. As a result, the legacy order-tracking system becomes accessible to users with a Skype for Business client on desktop computers, browsers (using Skype Web App), and mobile devices.

UCMA Interactive Voice Response

UCMA can also be used to create an Interactive Voice Response (IVR) system. PSTN numbers can be assigned to UCMA endpoints so that incoming calls are routed to the UCMA trusted server application. The UCMA trusted server application answers the calls and processes them. UCMA can play WMA files, which means that prerecorded announcements can be played to users. The text-to-speech capabilities built in to UCMA provide a dynamic interactive voice interface. DTMF tones can also be processed by UCMA. This allows users to navigate through a tree structure of options (press 1 for technical support, press 2 for sales, press 3 for helpdesk, and so on). Finally, UCMA can forward calls to users, voicemail boxes, or response groups (RGs). These features combined can be used to create a fully featured IVR system to complement a Skype for Business Server 2015 environment.

A GitHub example showing how this could be done is available at https://github.com/tomorgan/UCMA-IVR-Demo.

Granular Federation

An organization wants to federate with organizations but needs to maintain tight control over which users are permitted to communicate outside the company over Skype for Business. To enable this scenario, an MSPL server application running on the Edge Server can control the flow of messages between the organization and its federated partners according to dynamic security rules. Users who are whitelisted by the MSPL server application are allowed to communicate with federated users using Skype for Business client. Users not authorized by the server application will be blocked from contacting federated partners.

Web Chat

An organization with a customer services team answers customer questions on their products over the phone. To respond to customers who prefer to get help via the Internet, the organization wants a web-based chat interface on the company's website. Because the organization already uses Skype for Business Server 2015, they want to leverage it to route IM inquiries directly to their customer services team using the Skype for Business client. The Skype Web SDK can enable this scenario by allowing customers to start an IM conversation with members of the customer services team directly from the company's website by developers embedding this functionality into the web pages.

A GitHub example showing how this could be done is available at https://github.com/tomorgan/SkypeWebSDKSamples/tree/gh-pages/SkypeWebSDKSimpleWebpageChatExample.

Debugging Skype for Business Applications

The complexity in developing your application stems from properly understanding the behavior and proper usage of the Skype for Business APIs. Once you have a solid grasp of how the Skype for Business APIs work, your development process will speed up. Depending on the type of application you're developing for Skype for Business, your approach to debugging your application will differ. Some recommendations are provided in this section.

Client Applications

A big advantage of the Client SDK over UCMA is that the code can run locally on a developer's workstation, which means that the full debugging capabilities of Visual Studio can be used. This makes debugging Client SDK applications relatively easy, especially because the SDK does a good job of exposing useful errors in many cases. Problems usually come down to not respecting the asynchronous pattern (such as querying a contact before sign-in has finished executing) or doing something unsupported (such as sending an instant message to a conversation that's been terminated).

One area to be aware of, though, is writing Client SDK applications that will be used by Office 365 users. When the Client SDK was first released, the concept of running Lync in

Office 365 was not established and the SDK was not developed with this use case in mind. Because the low-level Lync traffic between on-premises and online is the same, the Client SDK mostly runs just fine, but there are some differences in behavior. These differences stem from the fact that things in Office 365 take longer, relatively, than they do online because of the differences in network and the distance between the two paradigms. When you're writing Client SDK code for on-premises users, it's perfectly okay to sign in using `Begin..EndSignin` and then proceed to work with the signed-in user, perhaps listing favorite contacts by using the `FavoriteContacts` group in the `ContactManager`. However, if you try and do this with an Office 365 user, you'll likely get errors. Even though the SDK returns at the end of the asynchronous sign-in method, the sign-in is still taking place. You'll also find that the `FavoriteContacts` group isn't fully populated immediately, but will populate over the course of a few seconds. This delay isn't well catered for by the SDK, which really has no knowledge of it, and can cause significant and nasty troubleshooting problems. The workaround is to rely solely on `StateChanged` events to tell you what's happening and not to make any assumptions. In the preceding example, wait for the `StateChanged` event of the `LyncClient` object to notify that the client is signed in, and then use the `ContactAdded` event of the `FavoriteContacts` group to notify you as each contact is added to the `FavoriteContacts` group. In this way, your code will be able to work even on very slow networks because it will be reacting to the data as it is being received, not assuming that the data has already arrived by the time it is read.

Web Applications

If you come across problems running your Skype Web SDK or UCWA application, first make sure you have fulfilled the minimum requirements for server architecture and added the domain where your application is running to the Cross Domain Authorization list. Be specific about the protocol and subdomain. Next, analyze the console output of your browser to see if the problem is being reported there—many common errors are caught and presented back to you by both Skype Web SDK and UCWA.

If that still doesn't work, then use an HTTP traffic analyzer such as Fiddler to monitor the HTTP calls being made and received between your web application and the reverse proxy. This will expose problems with firewalls. Looking at the Fiddler traffic of a functioning web application is also a great way to understand what the expected HTTP traffic should be when you invoke a Skype Web SDK method, such as subscribing to a user's Presence or even just signing in to Skype for Business.

Server Applications

Debugging server applications, whether UCMA or MSPL applications, is more difficult because it's unpractical to run these types of applications from within Visual Studio and debug them locally. For MSPL applications (not scripts), you would need to install Visual Studio on the Skype for Business Server 2015. For UCMA applications, Visual Studio would have to be installed on the trusted application server.

In certain cases, you might be able to debug your application remotely using Visual Studio Remote Debugging. This avoids having to install Visual Studio on the trusted application server for UCMA applications or the Skype for Business Server 2015 for MSPL applications. Only Visual Studio Remote Debugging needs to be installed. Breakpoints, step-in, and other debugging commands are all supported, and the experience is similar to debugging a local application.

These two options might be fine in a Skype for Business development environment; however, this is not likely an acceptable option for production environments. Therefore, the only other option for debugging is to instrument your application to provide verbose logging, preferably via a configuration switch. This logging will make it possible to determine root case analysis. Exceptions thrown by UCMA are descriptive in identifying the problem and should be logged for analysis. Exceptions in asynchronous methods will be thrown on the `End..` method, so be sure to wrap both the `Begin..` and `End..` methods in `try..catch` blocks. The logging solution you employ should identify the thread ID executing the code; otherwise, a UCMA application under heavy load will generate unintelligible logging output.

If All Else Fails...

If the Skype for Business API you are calling isn't returning the expected behavior, no need to get frustrated. Ultimately all the Skype for Business APIs must communicate with a Skype for Business Server 2015 over SIP. Therefore, you can intercept the SIP traffic on the server and analyze exactly what's being sent to and received from the server. This approach requires a working knowledge of the protocols used by Skype for Business.

The Skype for Business Server 2015 Debugging Tools provides valuable tools that allow you to trace SIP traffic. It can be run on both servers and clients. Isolate the Skype for Business Server 2015 traffic by reproducing just the scenario you are troubleshooting as much as possible. This will reduce the amount of noise you have to sift through in the SIP logs.

If you are troubleshooting a UCMA application, you should capture SIP traffic on the trusted application server where your application is installed. If you capture SIP traffic on servers running Skype for Business Server 2015, your SIP logs will include all the SIP traffic handled by the server. You will see a lot of SIP traffic that is not relevant to your application.

If you are troubleshooting an MSPL application, you should capture SIP traffic on the Skype for Business Server 2015 server where your application is installed instead of a different Skype for Business Server 2015 server. This way, you'll only capture SIP traffic that your MSPL application will be exposed to.

SIP logs generated by CLSLogger.exe can get very large very quickly. This makes it difficult to copy the log files off the server to examine offline, and more importantly large log files become very difficult for manual inspection. If you're troubleshooting an issue on a Skype for Business Server 2015 production server, try to collect the SIP logs during off-hours when there is less SIP traffic that is not relevant to your application that will be captured. Leverage snooper.exe to examine client-side and server-side SIP logs.

Summary

Skype for Business Server 2015 is more than just a unified communications solution. It provides a rich development platform that developers can leverage to build vertical solutions and organizations can use to enable their line of business applications with communications capabilities. The benefits to an organization are often significant.

This chapter provided an overview of the different types of application scenarios that can be built using Skype for Business Server 2015. Depending on the type of scenario you are developing, you will leverage the client, server, or Web SDK (or a combination of them), depending on the complexity of the solution you're building.

Understanding which SDK to use is important. The functionality provided by the SDK selected will dictate the architecture of your application. The complexity of the different Skype for Business SDKs makes it more difficult for software developers to ramp up and learn the behavior of these APIs. This translates to longer development cycles compared to other types of software projects (such as Web applications). Depending on the type of application, troubleshooting and resolving issues related to the interaction between your application and the Skype for Business SDK used often requires a detailed understanding of the underlying protocols (SIP, RDP, STUN/TURN, PSOM, and so on) used by Skype for Business Server 2015. Finding or developing this talent can be expensive. The net result is higher development costs.

CHAPTER 22

Skype for Business Online and Hybrid Deployments

IN THIS CHAPTER

- Overview of Skype for Business Online and Office 365
- System Requirements
- Experiencing Skype for Business Online
- Deploying Skype for Business Online
- AD FS Deployment for SSO
- Configuring Directory Synchronization
- Skype for Business Hybrid Deployment

In an effort to keep pace with the movement toward cloud-based IT services, in recent years Microsoft has been heavily focused on developing the online versions of popular applications, including Lync and Skype for Business. With the initial release of Lync Online, for the first time organizations had a choice between implementing Lync 2010 on-premises and using the online version of the product, either as a standalone service or as part of the Office 365 online suite. With the 2015 release of Skype for Business, Microsoft continues to develop and invest in the online version as well, and has rebranded Lync Online to Skype for Business Online. This new online release not only improves the features that are offered, but further illustrates Microsoft's dedication to the Office 365 platform through hybrid and cloud-based Skype for Business telephony support. This chapter provides a description of the updated version of Skype for Business Online, along with the deployment steps for both cloud-only and hybrid installations.

Overview of Skype for Business Online and Office 365

Skype for Business Online is a service offering that can be purchased either separately or as part of Office 365 Enterprise, Microsoft's cloud collaboration and productivity suite, which also includes Exchange Online, SharePoint Online, Office Professional Plus, Office Web Apps, and Yammer. Skype for Business Online offers features that are very similar to Skype for Business Server 2015, including IM and Presence, sharing and collaboration, peer-to-peer voice and video calls, and online meetings. With the purchase of Cloud PBX and PSTN Conferencing licenses, hosted voice and dial-in conferencing are also included as part of the feature set.

With the current release of Office 365, Microsoft is seeking to close the gap by offering additional features, as well as support for hybrid deployments involving both on-premises and cloud services for the same SIP domain. Microsoft offers a standard set of features for all cloud services, including Skype for Business Online. Following is a summary of the standard Microsoft cloud service features:

- **Secure access**—All traffic is secured using 128-bit SSL or TLS encryption.
- **Intrusion monitoring**—Microsoft continuously monitors all online systems for unusual or suspicious activity, and notifies customers of issues as needed.
- **Security audits**—Microsoft regularly assesses the infrastructure of online systems to ensure that antivirus signatures are updated and security updates are installed.
- **High availability**—There is a 99.9% scheduled uptime for online systems, with SLA guarantees in place.
- **Service continuity**—Redundant systems are located in geographically dispersed data centers to handle unscheduled service outages.
- **Directory synchronization**—Synchronization of directory information between the local Active Directory and Office 365 is made available using the free Azure Active Directory Connect tool.
- **Single sign-on**—Single sign-on is achieved by deploying an instance of Active Directory Federated Services on-premises and using it to federate with the cloud tenant.

System Requirements

As a cloud service, there are not many system requirements that need to be met to use Skype for Business Online. However, there are some prerequisites that need to be met to ensure compatibility, or in the very least to allow for the best user experience. The following sections provide details on the specific requirements.

Operating System and Browser Requirements

Skype for Business Online and Office 365 are compatible with specific combinations of operating systems and web browsers, as shown in Table 22.1.

TABLE 22.1 Operating System and Browser Requirements for Skype for Business Online

Operating System	Supported Browsers
Windows 10	Edge
	Internet Explorer 11 and later (32-bit and 64-bit)
	Firefox 12 and later (32-bit)
	Chrome 18 and later (32-bit)
Windows 8.1	Internet Explorer 10 and later (32-bit and 64-bit)
	Firefox 12 and later (32-bit)
	Chrome 18 and later (32-bit)
Windows 8	Internet Explorer 10 and later (32-bit and 64-bit)
	Firefox 12 and later (32-bit)
	Chrome 18 and later (32-bit)
Windows 7 with SP1	Internet Explorer 9 and later (32-bit and 64-bit)
	Firefox 12 and later (32-bit)
	Chrome 18 and later (32-bit)
Windows Server 2008 R2 with SP1	Internet Explorer 9 and later (32-bit and 64-bit)
	Firefox 12 and later (32-bit)
	Chrome 18 and later (32-bit)
Windows Server 2008 with SP2	Internet Explorer 9 and later (32-bit only)
	Firefox 12 and later (32-bit)
	Chrome 18 and later (32-bit)
Mac OS X 10.8 and later	Safari 5 and later (64-bit)
	Firefox 12 and later (32-bit)
	Chrome 18 and later (32-bit)

Client Software Requirements for Skype for Business Online

To fully leverage the capabilities of Skype for Business Online, the Skype for Business 2016 client, the Skype for Business 2015 client, the Lync 2013 client, the Lync 2010 client with cumulative update 2 or higher, and the Lync for Mac 2011 client are all supported. For the current release of Skype for Business Online/Office 365, no additional client-side software is required.

Experiencing Skype for Business Online

Skype for Business Online offers many, but not all, of the features included in an on-premises deployment. The following sections provide a summary of the features that are available to a Skype for Business Online user compared with those that are available only with an on-premises Skype for Business deployment.

Skype for Business Online Clients

The same Skype for Business client software is used for Skype for Business Online and Skype for Business Server 2015 on-premises. All the basic features of Skype for Business are available to Skype for Business Online users, including IM and Presence, peer-to-peer and multiparty audio and video calls, online meetings (both scheduled and ad hoc), and content sharing. In addition to the Skype for Business client software, Skype for Business Web App client software is available for external users for attending online meetings. Lync Phone Edition devices and supported third-party IP phones (3PIP) are supported for use with the Skype for Business Online Cloud PBX features. The mobile device clients that are supported for use with Skype for Business Server 2015 on-premises are also supported for use with Skype for Business Online, including Windows Phone, Apple iPhone, Apple iPad, and Android.

NOTE

Although multiparty video is supported, Skype for Business Online does not yet support interoperability with third-party, room-based conferencing systems.

Scheduling Skype for Business Meetings Without the Outlook Client Plugin

For users who do not have Outlook installed on their client system, and therefore cannot benefit from the Online Meeting add-in that enables meetings to be scheduled from within Outlook, there are two options. Because these users will typically access their Exchange mailbox through Outlook Web App (OWA), they can leverage the same interface for scheduling Skype for Business Meetings as well. The native integration between Exchange Online and Skype for Business Online allows users of OWA to enhance any meeting by clicking the Online Meeting button when creating a new meeting invitation. Alternatively, Microsoft provides a standalone web interface for scheduling Skype for Business Meetings, called the Skype for Business Web Scheduler. The Skype for Business Web Scheduler, accessed using the URL https://sched.lync.com, provides Skype for Business Online users with a simple web interface for managing meetings, as shown in Figure 22.1. After meetings have been created, they can be exported from the Web Scheduler as an iCalendar event and then sent to meeting attendees.

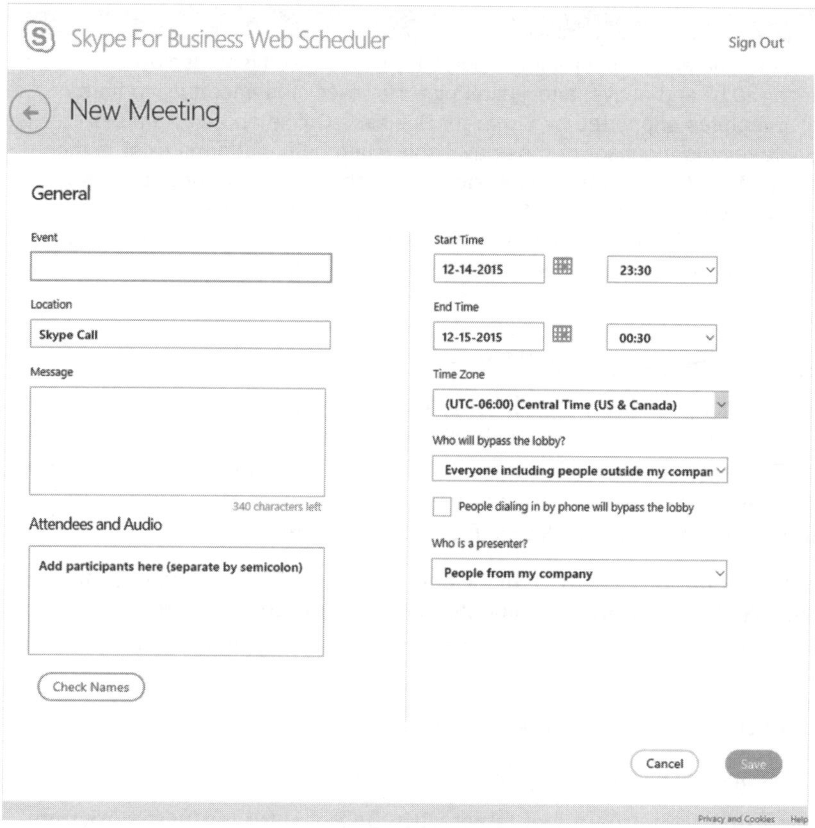

FIGURE 22.1 Skype for Business Online Web Scheduler.

Integration Features

Skype for Business Online offers client software integration features that are similar to Skype for Business Server 2015 on-premises. Skype for Business Presence information is embedded into other applications included in Office 2007 and above. Single-click scheduling of online meetings is available in Outlook. If Exchange Online is also used, Presence status is automatically updated based on Exchange calendar information, and IM and Presence are made available from Outlook Web App. If SharePoint Online is also used, Presence indicators are also displayed in SharePoint. However, the Lync/Skype for Business Skill Search feature is not available with Skype for Business Online.

NOTE

Skype for Business Online also supports interoperability with on-premises deployments of Exchange (2010 and above) and SharePoint. However, it is important to note that the number of features supported by Skype for Business Online and on-premises Exchange and SharePoint is a subset of those available when both platforms exist in the same architecture (both online or both on-premises). For instance, Skype for Business Online does not support Exchange Unified Messaging on-premises, and Skill Search in SharePoint on-premises is also unavailable. Presence indicators in SharePoint Online and Outlook are available only on systems where the Skype for Business client is installed.

Skype for Business Online Cloud PBX

Cloud PBX is a feature that provides a "single work number" experience for Skype for Business Online users, and is available as an add-on license for organizations using Skype for Business Online (Plan 2) or Office 365 "E" plans (E1, E3). To enable Cloud PBX, simply purchase and assign the license to a user. After the service is purchased and configured, the following features are available with Skype for Business Online Cloud PBX:

- ▶ Capability for PSTN phone calls to be made and received using the Skype for Business client on multiple devices, using a single phone number provided by the calling service. Laptops, smartphones, and tablet devices with the Skype for Business client are all supported.
- ▶ Click-to-call functionality from Outlook and other office applications.
- ▶ Simultaneous ring and call forwarding to a mobile phone.
- ▶ Initiating calls using a smartphone or tablet with the Skype for Business work number displayed to outside parties.
- ▶ Mid-call transfer from a PC to a mobile phone or to another number.
- ▶ The ability to drag and drop contacts into an existing Skype for Business call or meeting.
- ▶ Delegation, enabling an assistant to make or receive calls on a user's behalf.
- ▶ Team call, in which several users can be grouped to pick up incoming calls.
- ▶ Voicemail delivered to an Exchange inbox.

Skype for Business Federation and Public IM

Skype for Business Online supports federation with other organizations that use either Skype for Business Online or Lync/Skype for Business on-premises. Federated contacts can see each other's Presence and can use IM, peer-to-peer audio, and video to communicate. As with an on-premise deployment, federation needs to be configured by both parties, and public DNS configuration is required. Whitelists and blacklists are also available to control which domains are available for federation. One difference between the federation features of Skype for Business Online and Skype for Business Server 2015 on-premises is that file transfer is not available with Skype for Business Online federated connections.

In addition to Skype for Business federation, Skype for Business Online users can communicate with contacts that use the Skype consumer platform. However, federation with other public IM platforms, as well as federation with XMPP networks, is not available for Skype for Business Online.

NOTE

Federation with the Skype consumer platform is disabled by default, but can be enabled by a Skype for Business Online service administrator.

Dial-in Audio Conferencing

In December of 2015, Microsoft released native dial-in functionality in Skype for Business Online, called "PSTN Conferencing." This capability can be added through an incremental license to any existing Skype for Business Online Plan 2 or Office 365 "E" plans (E1, E3), and is included with the Office 365 E5 plan. Additionally, the option to leverage a third-party Audio Conference Provider (ACP) is still available through the same Skype for Business Online and Office 365 plans. Both services allow for scheduling from within the Outlook email client, joining a Skype for Business meeting from any phone, as well as initiating a call to an external number from within a Skype for Business meeting. Microsoft maintains an up-to-date list of approved audio conferencing partners that can be used for this service on the Office 365 Marketplace site.

Deploying Skype for Business Online

Several steps are involved in starting a new deployment of Skype for Business Online for an organization. The following sections provide details on the procedures required to get Skype for Business Online up and running once a subscription to Skype for Business Online has been purchased.

Adding Domains to Skype for Business Online/Office 365

The first task involved in getting Skype for Business Online up and running is adding the SIP domains that will be used with the service. When you are signing up for a Skype for Business Online or Office 365 subscription, a single DNS domain is assigned. This initial domain is referred to as the tenant domain, and it always has a suffix of `.onmicrosoft.com`. This tenant domain is meant only for administration of the Skype for Business Online organization and is not intended to be used as a SIP domain.

To add a new domain to Skype for Business Online/Office 365, follow these steps:

1. Log on to the Office 365 Portal and go to the Admin app.
2. On the left side of the main page, click Domains.
3. At the Domains page, click the link for Add Domain.
4. At the Add a Domain in Office 365 page, click Let's Get Started.

5. At the Which Domain Do You Want to Use? page, enter the fully qualified name of the domain owned by the organization that will be used for Skype for Business Online, and then click Next.

6. At the Confirm Ownership page, read the instructions presented regarding the requirement for adding a DNS record to verify ownership of the domain. The drop-down menu offers a choice of common DNS providers; select one of these to view instructions for adding the required DNS record using that DNS provider. If the DNS registrar for the SIP domain being added does not appear in this drop-down list, select General Instructions to view the generic steps for adding the required DNS record, as shown in Figure 22.2.

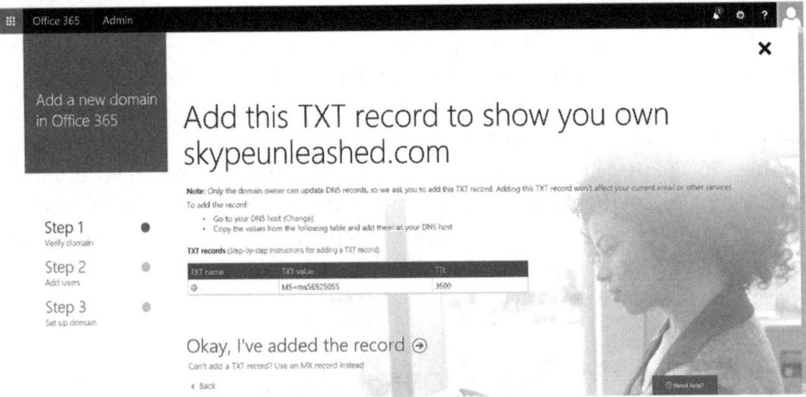

FIGURE 22.2 Office 365 domain verification instructions.

7. Follow through with the instructions to add either the TXT or the MX record to the public DNS zone, and then wait for the change to take effect. The amount of time required will depend on DNS propagation delay, as well as the DNS provider being used.

NOTE

Although either the TXT or the MX record can be used for validation with Office 365, the TXT record is the preferred method of validation. The reason for this is that the MX record required for validation specifies an address value ending in `.invalid`, and not all DNS providers support this record. The TXT record, on the other hand, is much more commonly supported.

8. Click Next to complete the verification process. If the domain verification is not successful, it might be necessary to wait some additional time and continue clicking this button until the verification succeeds.

9. After the verification is successful, the next screen offers to configure users with the new domain suffix. If necessary, update the user accounts; otherwise, click Skip This Step.

10. If new users will be added to the domain right away, do so through the Add New Users screen that appears next. Otherwise, click the link for Skip This Step, and then follow the instructions in the "Adding Skype for Business Online User Accounts" section later in this chapter to add the new users.

11. At the Get Ready to Update DNS Records to Work with Office 365 page, click Next.

12. At the Do You Want Us to Set Up DNS Records for Office 365 for You? page, select "No, I have an existing website or prefer to manage my own DNS records." Click Next.

13. The next page is Which Services Do You Want to Use with <SIPdomain>? Select the check boxes for the services that will be deployed. Click Next. Once the DNS records are in place, click the "Done, go check" button to complete the DNS record verification process. If the domain verification is not successful, it might be necessary to wait some additional time and continue clicking this button until the verification succeeds.

14. After the services are selected, the Now We'll Add Your DNS Records page will appear. For some DNS providers, the DNS records can be created automatically. Click the link View the DNS Records We'll Add. Alternatively, the DNS records may have to be added manually. If the DNS records required for Skype for Business Online have not already been configured based on the information in Chapter 29, "Planning for Skype for Business Online and Hybrid Deployments," then these DNS records will need to be added.

15. Once the records have been manually added, click Okay, I've Added the Records. DNS verification will continue. After the DNS record verification is successful, the next screen confirms that the required DNS records were found. Click Finish to complete the procedure. The new domain now appears in the list of verified domains.

Adding Skype for Business Online User Accounts

Several methods can be used to add user accounts to Skype for Business Online/Office 365. User accounts can be added manually using either the online portal or Windows PowerShell. It is also possible to create user accounts in bulk using an import process. User accounts can also be automatically created using directory synchronization, which is described in detail in the "Configuring Directory Synchronization" section later in this chapter.

Adding User Accounts Using the Online Portal

Use the following procedure for creating a new user account using the Online Portal:

1. Log on to the Office 365 Portal and go to the Admin app.

2. On the left side of the main page, expand Users and select Active Users.

3. At the Active Users page, click the plus symbol just above the user list.

4. At the Details page, mandatory fields for the new account are displayed, as shown in Figure 22.3. Enter the first name, last name, display name, user name, and alternate email address for password delivery for the new user account.

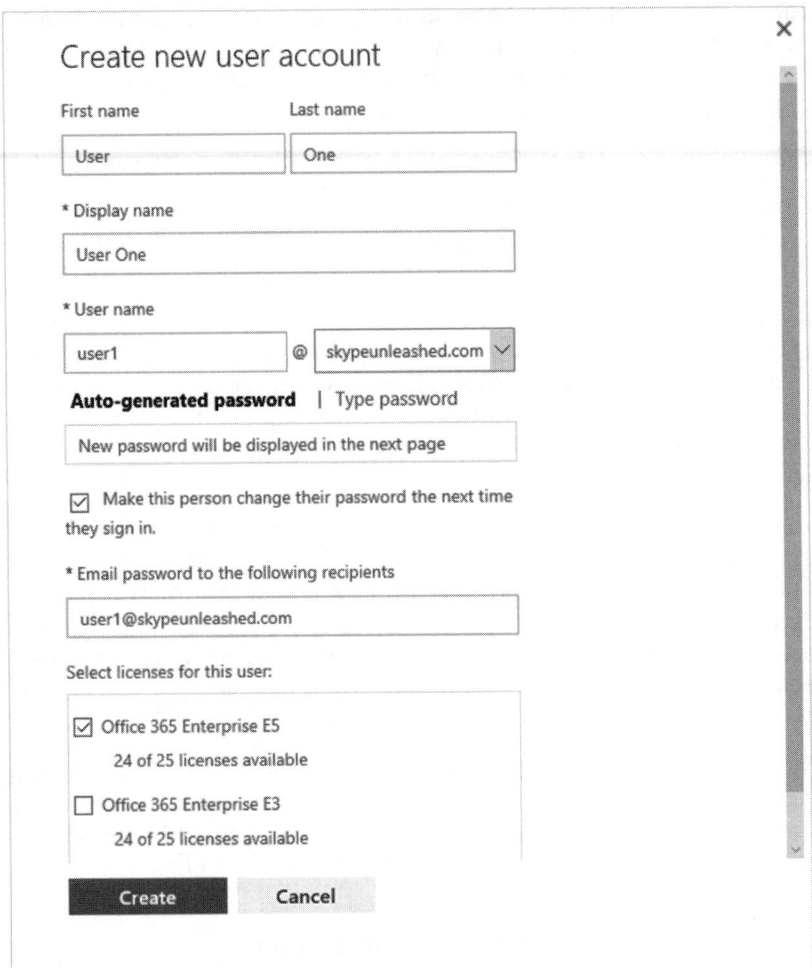

FIGURE 22.3 Creating a new user account using the Office 365 Portal.

5. Use the drop-down menu at the end of the User Name field to select from among the available domains for this user account. This list is automatically populated with domains that have already been verified for this Skype for Business Online/Office 365 account.

6. Click Create, and a confirmation page will appear.

7. At the confirmation page, verify that the user account has been successfully created and make note of the temporary password automatically generated. Click Close to complete the procedure and return to the Active Users page.

Adding User Accounts Using PowerShell

User accounts can be added to Skype for Business Online/Office 365 using Windows PowerShell in conjunction with the Microsoft Azure Active Directory Module.

The installation steps and system requirements for the Microsoft Azure Active Directory Module are detailed later in this chapter in the section "Establishing Trust with Office 365 for SSO." After the Microsoft Azure Active Directory Module is installed on a system with PowerShell, use the following steps to create a new user account using PowerShell:

1. Log on to the system where Windows PowerShell and the Microsoft Azure Active Directory Module are installed.
2. Open Windows PowerShell and import the Microsoft Azure Active Directory Module using the following command:

```
Import-Module MSOnline
```

3. Execute the following command, and then at the prompt enter the credentials of an Office 365 administrative account.

```
$cred=Get-Credential
```

4. Execute the following command, which creates a connection to Office 365, as required to run the remaining cmdlets:

```
Connect-MsolService -Credential $cred
```

5. Execute the `New-MsolUser` cmdlet to create the new user account. For example, the following command would be used to create a new account named Test User in the `skypeunleashed.onmicrosoft.com` organization:

```
New-MsolUser -UserPrincipalName "TestUser@skypeunleashed.onmicrosoft.com"
➥-DisplayName "Test User" -FirstName "Test" -LastName "User"
```

6. If the command completes successfully, the new user account properties will display, including the temporary password assigned to the account.

TIP

The `New-MsolUser` command creates the user account; however, it does not apply licensing to the user. The licenses can be assigned after the user account is created using the online portal.

Adding User Accounts in Bulk

User accounts can be added to Skype for Business Online/Office 365 using a comma-separated values (CSV) file. The CSV file must be specifically formatted with the correct column headings to be successfully imported. To facilitate this process, Microsoft provides a sample CSV file with the appropriate column headings that can be downloaded from the Online Portal and then adjusted using a text editor.

The following steps describe the process for downloading the sample CSV file, editing the file, and then importing it into Skype for Business Online/Office 365:

1. Log on to the Office 365 Portal and go to the Admin app.
2. On the left side of the main page, expand Users and click Active Users.

3. At the Active Users page, click the Bulk Add symbol, which is just to the right of the plus symbol above the user list.
4. At the Select a CSV file page, click the option Download a Blank CSV File.
5. At the File Download prompt, click Save and then choose a local subdirectory to save the file to.
6. Use Excel or a text editor such as Notepad to navigate to the location where the file was saved, and then open the file named `Import_User_Template_en.csv`.
7. Edit the file, entering the user data into the appropriate fields for the users who will be imported into Skype for Business Online.
8. When you are finished, save the file and then return to the Select a CSV File page in the Online Portal. Click Browse, navigate to and select the import file, and then click Next.
9. At the Verification Results screen, the results of the import process are displayed. If there are errors, click the View link to display the log file and determine the cause of the errors. For example, in Figure 22.4, the log file reveals a spelling error in the domain name of one of the user accounts, whereas the other accounts were verified. At this point, it is possible to correct any errors in the CSV file, click the Back button, and then reimport the file.

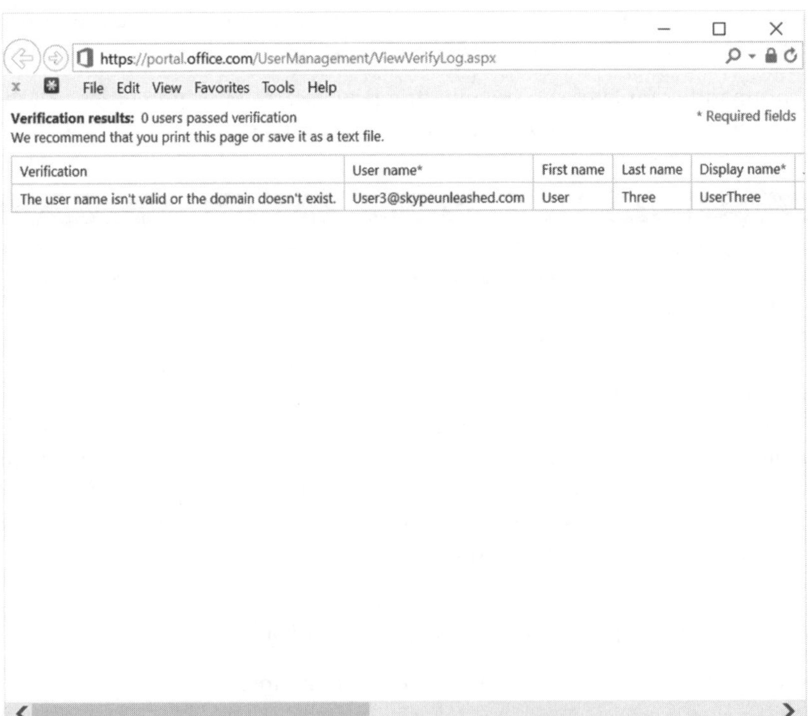

FIGURE 22.4 Log file from the bulk user import process.

10. After all user accounts have been verified, click Next at the Verification results screen.
11. At the Settings screen, under Set Sign-in Status, select either Allowed or Blocked to set the initial status of the users when the accounts are created.
12. In the Set User Location section, use the drop-down menu to select the user's location and then click Next.
13. At the Assign Licenses screen, select the check box for the Skype for Business Online plan that the user will be licensed for, along with any other Office 365 services and plans that the organization has a subscription for. Click Next.
14. At the Send Results in Email page, keep the default selection of "Send email if the username and temporary password for the new account should be sent to an administrator via email," and then enter up to five recipient email addresses separated by semicolons. When finished, click Create.
15. At the Results page, verify that the user accounts have been successfully created and make note of the temporary passwords automatically generated. Click Close to complete the procedure.

Preparing Client Systems for Skype for Business Online

The preparation of client systems for Skype for Business Online is largely a matter of installing the Skype for Business client on each system. The client is included in the Click-to-Run version of the Office client platform, which is included in the Office 365 "E" plans. For customers who do not own the Office client software, either licensed or through an Office 365 subscription, a standalone Lync/Skype for Business Basic client is available for download from the Microsoft site.

Configuring Federation and Public IM

For each new instance of Skype for Business Online, federation with other organizations and with public IM providers is by default disabled for the organization. The following steps are used to enable federation and public IM:

1. Log on to the Office 365 Portal and go to the Admin app.
2. On the left side, expand Admin and then select Skype for Business. This will launch the Skype for Business Admin page in a new window.
3. On the left side, click Organization and then click the link for External Communications at the top.
4. At the External Communications page, under External Access, use the drop-down menu to select the domain federation option that meets the organization's policy for communication with external organizations. If the organization will manage a blacklist of SIP domains for which communication is not allowed, select the option On Except for Blocked Domains. If the organization will instead manage a whitelist of SIP domains for which communication is allowed, select the option On Only for Allowed Domains.

5. To enable communication with public IM providers, click the check box under Public IM Connectivity.
6. Depending on the domain federation mode option chosen in the previous step, the SIP domain list displayed under the Blocked or Allowed Domains section will be used as either a whitelist or a blacklist. To add a SIP domain to the list, click the plus symbol that appears above the list.
7. At the Add a Domain box, enter the name of the domain that will be allowed or blocked in the Domain Name field, and then click Add to save the setting. The domain is then listed as an allowed or blocked domain, as shown in Figure 22.5.

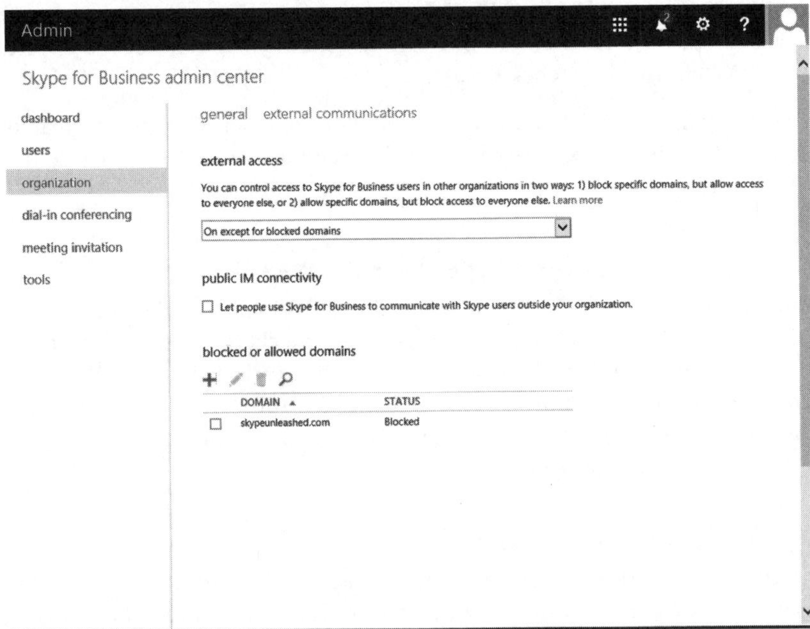

FIGURE 22.5 Federation and public IM settings in the online portal.

8. Repeat steps 6 and 7 to add any additional SIP domains that will be blocked or allowed, as needed.

TIP

Turning on federation or public IM for a Skype for Business Online organization, along with the configuration of a SIP domain whitelist or blacklist, can require up to a day to activate due to replication requirements within the Microsoft data center infrastructure. With that in mind, it is recommended that you enable these features and immediately configure the whitelist or blacklist at least several days before the users need to begin communicating with external organizations.

Configuring Microsoft PSTN Conferencing

If a PSTN Conferencing license has been purchased, dial-in conferencing can be enabled for each user by configuration of the dial-in conferencing properties of the user accounts.

The following steps are used to configure Microsoft PSTN Conferencing for Skype for Business Online users through the Online Portal:

1. Log on to the Office 365 Portal and go to the Admin app.
2. On the left side, expand Admin and then select Skype for Business. This will launch the Skype for Business Admin page in a new window.
3. On the left side, click Dial-in Conferencing and then click Microsoft Bridge at the top.
4. A list of available dial-in phone numbers will be presented. This is the list of global dial-in numbers available through the Microsoft PSTN Conferencing service, and numbers cannot be added or removed. If desired, the default dial-in phone number and the supported languages for each number can be changed, but in most cases the default language will be appropriate.
5. At the top, click Microsoft Bridge Settings.
6. At the Meeting Join Experience screen, a list of available organization-wide configuration defaults are available, including meeting entry and exit notifications, a prompt for users to record their name when joining the meeting, the required PIN length, and email notifications to users if their PSTN dial-in configuration changes. Configure these options as required. When finished, click Save.

NOTE

Just as with an on-premises Skype for Business deployment, the organization-wide configuration defines the defaults for meetings scheduled by users. The user still has the option to customize conference settings through Outlook's Skype for Business Meeting plug-in on the client side.

7. For any user assigned a PSTN Conferencing license, Microsoft will be the default dial-in conferencing provider assigned.
8. Click Dial-in Users at the top to view the newly applied conferencing properties for the users, as shown in Figure 22.6.

22

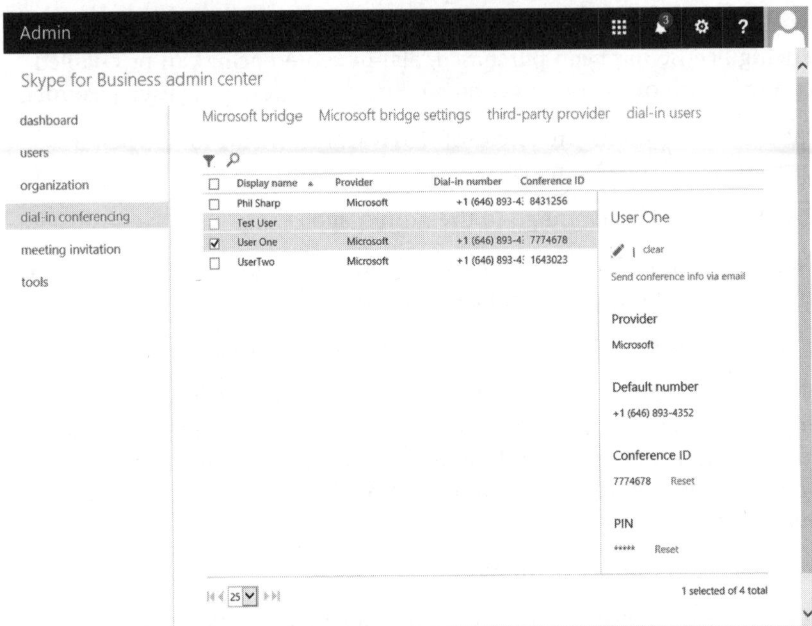

FIGURE 22.6 Dial-in conferencing properties applied to Skype for Business Online user accounts.

Configuring Third-Party Dial-in Conferencing

If a dial-in conferencing service has been purchased from an approved Microsoft partner, dial-in conferencing can be enabled for each user through configuration of the dial-in conferencing properties of the user accounts. Although this can be performed manually, if there are many accounts to be configured, then this would require a lot of administrative effort. To ease this process, it is possible to import a file supplied by the audio conferencing provider containing the phone numbers and passcodes for the user accounts. To start the process, a file containing the list of users to be enabled for dial-in conferencing must be exported using the online portal. This list is then used by the provider to generate a file that can be used to import the settings for the user accounts.

The following steps are used to configure dial-in conferencing for Skype for Business Online users in bulk using the export and import method:

1. Log on to the Office 365 Portal and go to the Admin app.
2. On the left side, expand Admin and then select Skype for Business. This will launch the Skype for Business Admin page in a new window.

3. On the left side, click Dial-in Conferencing and then click Third-Party Provider at the top.
4. Under Import and Export users, click the link for Export Wizard.
5. At the Export Users Wizard Getting Started screen, click Next.
6. At the initial Select Users screen, in the drop-down list, select which users should be exported. The options are as follows:
   - Export all users
   - Export users with dial-in conferencing
   - Export users without dial-in conferencing
   - Export selected users

   After choosing the applicable option, click Next.
7. At the File Download prompt, click Save and then choose a local subdirectory to save the file to.
8. Click Finish to complete the Export Users Wizard and return to the Dial-in Conferencing Provider page.
9. Send the downloaded file, named `AcpUsers.csv`, to the audio conferencing provider so that the appropriate dial-in conferencing properties can be filled in.
10. After the file has been returned by the audio conferencing provider, save the file to a local subdirectory and then return to the Dial-in conferencing Provider page in the Skype for Business Admin Center.
11. Under Import and Export users, click the link for Import Wizard.
12. At the Import Users Wizard Getting Started screen, click Next.
13. At the Select File screen, click Browse. Navigate to and select the import file that was sent by the audio conferencing provider and then click Next.
14. At the Results screen, the results of the import process are displayed. If the import was successful, click Finish to complete the Import Wizard. If errors are contained in the file, the option to download the error log file is automatically selected. If this is the case, click Finish; then at the File Download prompt, click Save and choose a local subdirectory to save the error log file to.
15. If necessary, send the downloaded error log file named `ErrorUsers.csv` to the audio provider to make any needed corrections.
16. After the adjusted file has been returned, repeat steps 12 to 15 to import the adjusted file and confirm that the import is now successful.

17. After the file from the audio provider is successfully imported, click Dial-in Users in the Skype for Business Admin Center to view the newly applied conferencing properties for the users, as shown in Figure 22.7.

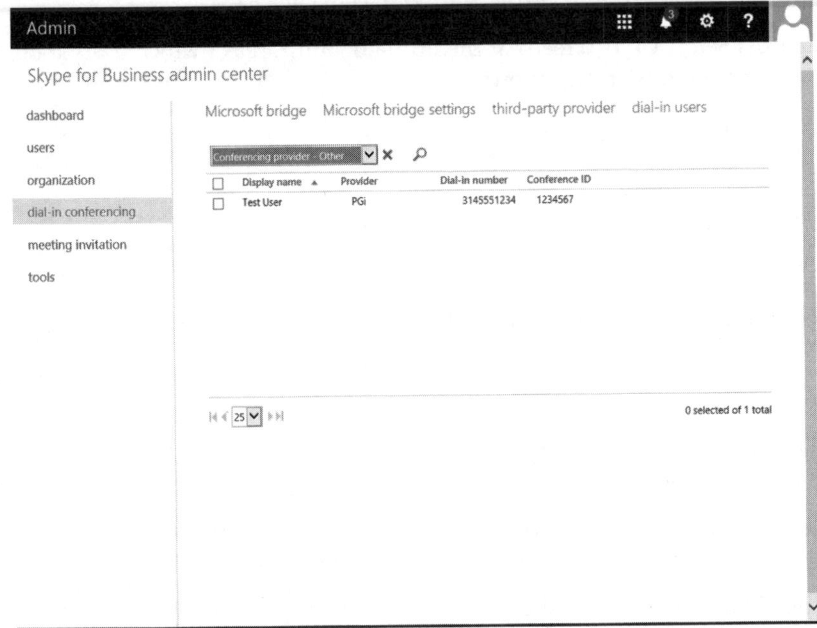

FIGURE 22.7 ACP dial-in conferencing properties applied to Skype for Business Online user accounts.

Configuring Skype for Business Meeting Broadcast

To leverage the new Skype for Business Meeting Broadcast features, the service must be enabled for the Skype for Business Online/Office 365 tenant. Additionally, each user who plans to use Skype for Business Meeting Broadcast must exist in the online tenant and be assigned a Skype for Business Online Plan 2 or Office 365 "E" plan (E1, E3, or E5) license.

The following steps are used to configure the Skype for Business Online/Office 365 tenant for Skype for Business Meeting Broadcast through PowerShell:

1. Log on to the system where Windows PowerShell and the Skype for Business Online Modules are installed.

2. Execute the following command; then, at the prompt, enter the credentials of an Office 365 administrative account:

```
$cred=Get-Credential
```

3. Execute the following command:

```
$O365Session=New-CsOnlineSession -Credential $cred
```

4. Execute the following command to connect to Skype for Business Online, as required to run the remaining cmdlets:

```
Import-PSSession $O365Session
```

5. Execute the following command to enable Skype for Business Broadcast Meeting for the tenant:

```
Set-CsBroadcastMeetingConfiguration -EnableBroadcastMeeting $true
```


Next, verify whether external access for Skype for Business Online is configured to support communication with the Skype for Business Meeting Broadcast service:

1. Log on to the Office 365 Portal and go to the Admin app.
2. On the left side, expand Admin and then select Skype for Business. This will launch the Skype for Business Admin page in a new window.
3. On the left side, click Organization and then click the link for External Communications at the top.
4. At the External Communications page, under External access, confirm which domain federation configuration option is selected. If "On except blocked domains" is selected, then no action is required. If "On except for allowed domains" is selected, then add the following list of domains to the allowed list:
   - noammeetings.lync.com
   - emeameetings.lync.com
   - apacmeetings.lync.com
   - resources.lync.com
5. To enable communication with the Skype consumer platform, click the check box for "Let people use Skype for Business to communicate with Skype users outside your organization."
6. Click Save.

No further configuration is required at this point if only Skype for Business Online is deployed. However, to support Skype for Business Meeting Broadcast in a hybrid deployment with Lync Server 2010, Lync Server 2013, or Skype for Business Server 2015 on-premises, some additional steps are required:

1. Log in to an on-premises Front End server within the organization and launch the Lync or Skype for Business Server Management Shell.
2. Execute the following command to configure the Hosting Provider for Skype for Business Online resources:

```
New-CsHostingProvider -Identity LyncOnlineResources
➥-ProxyFqdn sipfed.resources.lync.com -VerificationLevel AlwaysVerifiable
➥-Enabled $True -EnabledSharedAddressSpace $True -HostsOCSUsers $True
➥-IsLocal $False
```

3. Execute the following commands to ensure the on-premises Edge servers are configured to allow communication to the Skype for Business Online resources federated domains:

```
New-CsAllowedDomain -Identity "noammeetings.lync.com"
New-CsAllowedDomain -Identity "emeammeetings.lync.com"
New-CsAllowedDomain -Identity "apacmeetings.lync.com"
New-CsAllowedDomain -Identity "resources.lync.com"
```

4. After completing the preceding steps according to organizational requirements, point a browser to https://broadcast.skype.com and authenticate as a licensed Skype for Business Online (Plan 2) or Office 365 "E" plan user.

5. Click New Meeting at the top, and then enter the details of the Skype for Business Broadcast Meeting to validate the configuration was successful, as shown in Figure 22.8.

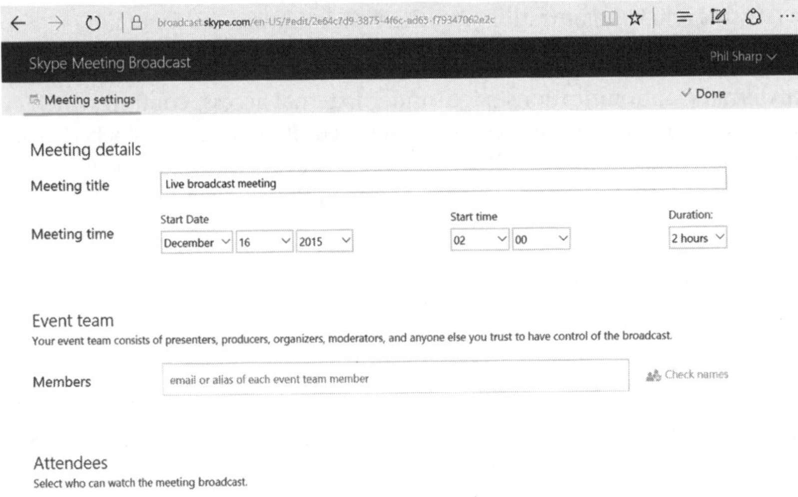

FIGURE 22.8 Set up a Skype for Business Meeting Broadcast.

Configuring Skype for Business Properties for User Accounts

After user accounts have been added to Skype for Business Online, the Skype for Business properties of the user accounts can be configured using the Online Portal. Use the following procedure to adjust the Skype for Business properties for a user:

1. Log on to the Office 365 Portal and go to the Admin app.
2. On the left side of the main page, expand Users and select Active Users.
3. At the Active Users page, select the check box for the user account to be edited; then, under Quick Steps on the right side of the screen, click Edit Skype for Business Properties.

4. At the Options screen, options are presented for various basic Skype for Business features, as shown in Figure 22.9. Select or deselect the check boxes to enable or disable individual features.

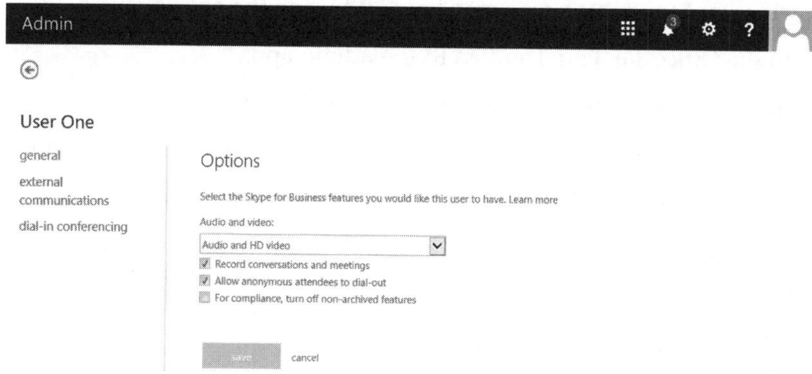

FIGURE 22.9 Editing the Skype for Business properties of a user account.

5. On the left side, click External Communications to view options for federation and public IM. Select or deselect the check boxes to enable or disable individual features.
6. On the left side, click Voice. If a Cloud PBX license has been purchased and configured for this user, the phone number assigned will be displayed.
7. On the left side, click Dial-in Conferencing. If Microsoft PSTN Conferencing or a third-party dial-in conferencing service has been purchased, select the provider from the drop-down menu. For the Microsoft PSTN Conferencing service, the default number can be changed, the Conference ID and PIN can be reset, and meeting options can be updated. For a third-party dial-in conferencing service provider, the values for toll number, toll-free number, and passcode can then be assigned using the appropriate fields.
8. When finished, click Save.

TIP

With an approved third-party Audio Conference Provider (ACP), the dial-in conferencing settings can also be applied to user accounts in bulk, instead of configuring each user account manually. For details, see the "Configuring Third-Party Dial-in Conferencing" section of this chapter.

Configuring Cloud PBX

If a hosted voice service has been purchased through Microsoft Cloud PBX licensing, you can also purchase a PSTN calling plan to enable inbound and outbound calling to external phone numbers. Once the Skype for Business Online/Office 365 tenant has been configured with the corresponding subscriptions, the service for each user can be set up and a phone number can be provisioned.

Use the following steps to enable a user for Cloud PBX using the online portal:

1. Log on to the Office 365 Portal and go to the Admin app.
2. On the left side of the main page, expand Users and select Active Users.
3. At the Active Users page, click the name of the user to be enabled for Cloud PBX.
4. On the right side, in the Quick Steps window, under Assigned License click Edit.
5. For users with a Skype for Business Online Plan 2 or Office 365 E3 license assigned, check the boxes for Cloud PBX and Skype for Business PSTN Calling (National or International). For users with an Office 365 E5 license, only the PSTN calling plan needs to be selected. Once you are finished, click Save.
6. On the left side of the main page, expand Admin and select Skype for Business to launch the Skype for Business Online Admin portal.
7. On the left side, click Voice.
8. If this is the first time Cloud PBX has been configured, select Emergency Locations at the top.
9. Click the plus sign just above the location list to define a new location.
10. Enter the information for the physical address of the Cloud PBX user. When you are finished, click Validate to confirm the address. After the address is validated, click Save. At least one validated address is required to be able to assign a phone number to a user.

NOTE

The initial release of Skype for Business Online only supports "static" Enhanced 911 service. This means that the phone number is associated with a physical address and can only be updated by a Skype for Business Online/Office 365 administrator. However, when a call is placed to 911 by a Cloud PBX user, each call is routed through the Microsoft service provider's certified Public Safety Answering Point (PSAP), who will attempt to verify the address of the caller before routing to the local PSAP that services the caller's location.

11. At the top, click Voice Users.
12. In the user list, select the user to which a phone number will be assigned. On the right side, click the Assign Number link.

13. On the Assign number screen, as shown in Figure 22.10, click the drop-down to select a phone number to assign to the user. Under Find City, type the name of the city where the user will reside. Results will only be returned for addresses that have been entered and validated in the Emergency Locations list. Click Save to complete the Cloud PBX user configuration.

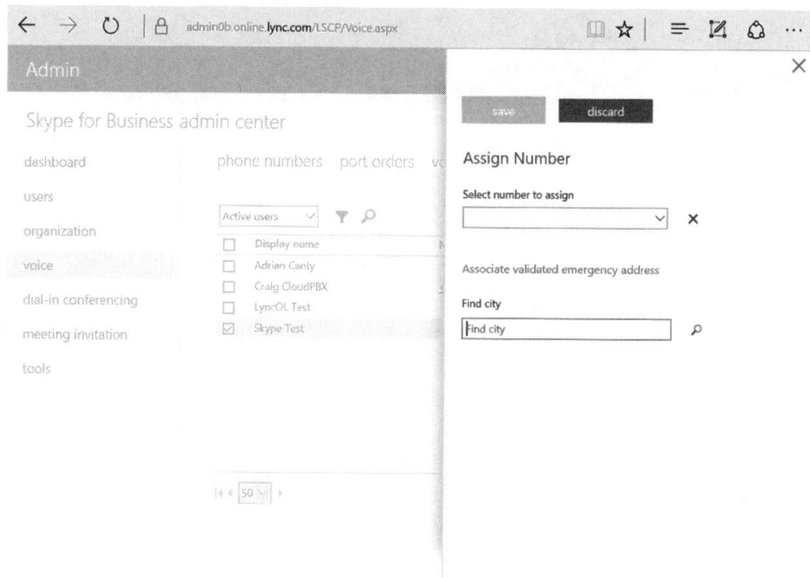

FIGURE 22.10 Assigning a Cloud PBX phone number to a user account.

Acquiring New Phone Numbers for Cloud PBX

An appealing aspect of using Skype for Business Online as a telephony platform is the ease of deployment and management. It should come as no surprise that Microsoft has taken steps to simplify the acquisition of new phone numbers through the Skype for Business Online/Office 365 portal.

The following steps can be used to procure new PSTN phone numbers from Microsoft for use with the PSTN Calling service:

1. Log on to the Office 365 Portal and go to the Admin app.
2. On the left side of the main page, expand Admin and select Skype for Business to launch the Skype for Business Online Admin portal.
3. On the left side, click Voice.
4. At the top, click Phone Numbers. A list of phone numbers, along with their assignment status, is presented.

5. Click the plus sign just above the phone number list to request a new set of phone numbers.
6. On the New Numbers screen, select the state and city for which new numbers will be requested. Enter the quantity of numbers that will be reserved. When you are finished, click Add, as shown in Figure 22.11.

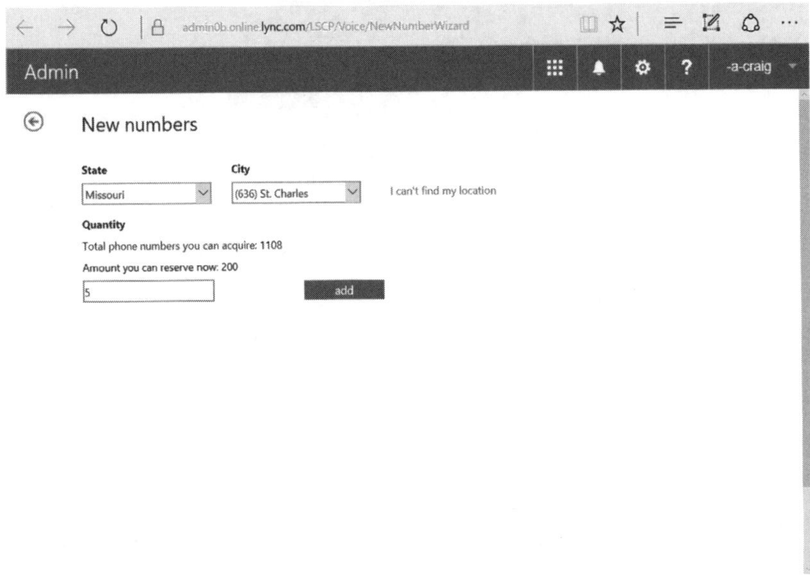

FIGURE 22.11 Acquiring new phone numbers through Skype for Business Online portal.

7. To see the phone numbers, click Show Numbers.
8. Select the phone numbers that will be kept, and then click Acquire Numbers.
9. Back on the Phone Numbers screen, you will see the list of newly acquired phone numbers in the list. Although the numbers can be immediately assigned to users, the service may take up to 1 hour to activate.
10. Assign the newly acquired phone numbers to users as outlined in the preceding steps in the section "Configuring Cloud PBX".

Porting Phone Numbers to Cloud PBX

For many established organizations, the prospect of changing existing phone numbers would be a roadblock to migrating telephony services to the cloud. Fortunately, Microsoft understands that providing customers the option to port existing phone numbers to the Cloud PBX service is critical to adoption of the platform. Just as with the number-acquisition process, Microsoft has taken great strides to simplify the number-porting process. Before beginning the number-porting process, the following information will need to be provided to Microsoft:

- Carrier account number(s)
- Carrier service address
- Carrier billing telephone number (BTN)
- List of phone numbers to transfer
- Signature authority on the account (Letter of Authorization)

Once all that information has been collected, you will be ready to begin the porting process. Assuming all of the required information for the port request is correct and no rejections occur on the port order, Microsoft estimates that the actual phone number transfer can occur according to timelines outlined in Table 22.2.

TABLE 22.2 Estimated Phone Number Porting Timeframes for Skype for Business Online Cloud PBX

Quantity of Numbers to Be Ported	Estimated Timeframe
< 100	Within 7 days
100 to 999	Approximately 3–4 weeks
> 999	Approximately 3–4 weeks

To initiate the port request, use the following procedure:

1. Log on to the Office 365 Portal and go to the Admin app.
2. On the left side of the main page, expand Admin and select Skype for Business to launch the Skype for Business Online Admin portal.
3. On the left side, click Voice.
4. At the top, click Port Orders. Review the options for transferring numbers. Under Take the Helm, click the link for "I'm ready to create a port order."
5. At the New Local Number Port Order Overview screen, click Let's Get Started.

NOTE

If 1000 or more phone numbers will be ported, the process is different than described here. In this scenario, due to the large quantity of numbers, the carrier will treat the number port as a project. Microsoft support will need to work directly with the carrier and the organization requesting the port to ensure all of the requirements are met and the port can be completed successfully.

6. On the Account Information screen, enter all the required fields. Failure to accurately enter information exactly as the carrier has it on file will result in a rejection of the order. Click Next.

7. At the Numbers screen, enter the numbers that will be ported. Individual numbers, ranges of numbers, or all numbers may be ported. Once these are entered, click Check Number Portability.
8. On the Transfer Date screen, select the date and time that the number port should start. Click Next.
9. On the Letter of Authorization screen, read the terms of the agreement; if the terms are acceptable, complete the required fields. Click Next.
10. At the Submit screen, note that the Skype for Business Online/Office 365 administrator will be notified of progress on the request. Additional people can also be notified. Review the order details on the right side, and click Submit Port Order when done.
11. After submission, the confirmation page will appear and the port request will be initiated.

Configuring Voicemail for Cloud PBX

If Cloud PBX has been purchased and configured as part of the Skype for Business Online subscription, then all Cloud PBX–enabled users will be automatically configured with Cloud PBX voicemail. Unlike Exchange Unified Messaging, Cloud PBX voicemail leverages the Azure Media Network to receive and record voicemail messages. Voicemail messages are still delivered to the users' inbox, and they behave similarly to native Exchange Unified Messaging voicemail messages. This is true regardless of whether the PSTN ingress and egress are provided via Office 365 or through on-premises PSTN connectivity. For the initial release of Cloud PBX, minimal customization can be made to the user voicemail box, and there is no option to configure Exchange Online Unified Messaging as the voicemail platform.

AD FS Deployment for SSO

After Skype for Business Online is up and running, Active Directory Federated Services (AD FS) can be deployed to enable single sign-on (SSO) functionality. For an introduction on using AD FS to achieve SSO with Office 365, as well as detailed information on systems requirements for the AD FS deployment, see Chapter 29. The following sections provide details on the AD FS software deployment and subsequent configuration for use with Skype for Business Online.

Preparing Systems for AD FS

Systems that are planned for the federation server role should be fully patched and joined to the domain before AD FS installation. Systems that are planned for the federation server proxy role should be patched and then connected to a DMZ subnet as a workgroup member. If multiple servers will be used for resiliency, the load-balancing configuration should also be completed before AD FS installation on both federation server and federation server proxy systems. Although a dedicated load-balancing solution should be used with AD FS, this section provides guidelines for the configuration of Windows NLB for use with AD FS.

Following are some guidelines regarding the installation of NLB in preparation for AD FS:

- The NLB feature is integrated with both the Standard and Enterprise Editions of Windows Server 2012 and Windows Server 2012 R2; therefore, it simply needs to be installed from the list of available Windows features, and typically Standard Edition is fine for this purpose.
- Two network adapters are typically recommended for each NLB node, although this is not required. The second adapter allows for one adapter to be dedicated for NLB functions, while the other adapter can be used for other network functions.
- NLB is not supported for use with DHCP; therefore, a static IP address must be applied to a system before NLB is installed.
- A cluster IP address must be selected as the virtual IP that is shared by every member of the NLB cluster. The IP address must be unique within the environment and will be used to receive traffic destined for the federation service.
- The cluster operation mode can be specified as either unicast or multicast. While either mode can work, multicast is often recommended when NLB is installed on virtual machines, because it tends to reduce the complexity involved in ensuring that traffic flows properly through the virtualization environment.
- The default port rules configuration specifies load balancing for all ports. For a federation server cluster, the default port rule can be modified to configure load balancing for only ports 80 and 443, because these are the only ports that will be used by the federation service. For a federation server proxy cluster, only port 443 is required.

An additional requirement before running the AD FS Configuration Wizard is the installation of a wildcard or standard SSL certificate that will be used as the Server Authentication Certificate. The certificate must be purchased from a public CA that is trusted by all the client systems that will be connecting to AD FS, and it must use the federation service FQDN as the subject name.

TIP

If a Skype for Business hybrid deployment is planned, the subject name of the server authentication certificate will instead need to be sts.<SIPdomain>, where <SIPdomain> is the DNS domain that will be split across the Skype for Business Online and Skype for Business on-premises deployments. For details, see Chapter 29.

Preparing the Network for AD FS

After the NLB cluster has been created, several DNS records need to be manually created, and several firewall ports might need to be opened, depending on whether AD FS will be available externally. For specifics on which DNS records and firewall port openings are required for a given scenario, see Chapter 29.

If a dedicated service account will be used for AD FS, as required for a multiple-server deployment, the account must be created before the initial configuration of AD FS. The service account does not require any particular rights to the AD domain; however, it must be a member of the local Administrators group on each federation server.

Installing AD FS

In Windows Server 2012, AD FS is now a native role included within the operating system. Installation of the AD FS software can be performed either via the Add Roles and Features Wizard or via PowerShell. Use the following procedure to install AD FS using the wizard:

1. Log on to the server using an account with local administrator rights.
2. Launch Server Manager.
3. In Server Manager, on the Dashboard, click Configure This Local Server and then click Add Roles and Features.
4. On the Select Installation Type screen, ensure that Role-based or feature-based installation is selected and then click Next.
5. On the Select Destination Server screen, in the Server Pool list, verify that the local server is selected and then click Next.
6. At the Select Server Roles screen, under Roles, select the Active Directory Federation Services check box and then click Next.
7. On the Features screen, click Next.
8. On the Active Directory Federation Services screen, review the information and click Next.
9. At the Confirm Installation Selections screen, click Install.
10. Wait for the installation to complete. Once the installation finishes, click Close.

After the installation is complete, the AD FS server will need to be configured, as outlined in the next section. The latest updates for the AD FS should also be applied by running Windows Update at this point.

Configuring the First Federation Server in the Farm

To complete the configuration of AD FS, the Active Directory Federation Services Configuration Wizard will need to be run. The wizard is used to configure the first federation server in a farm, using the following procedure:

1. In Server Manager, on the toolbar, click the notifications flag and then click Configure the Federation Service on This Server.
2. In the Welcome screen of the Active Directory Federation Services Configuration Wizard window, verify that Create the First Federation Server in a Federation Server Farm is selected and then click Next.

3. On the Connect to AD DS screen, accept the default and then click Next.
4. On the Specify Service Properties screen, click the SSL Certificate menu and then select the certificate you installed on the server at the beginning of this section.
5. Click the Federation Service Name menu and then click the appropriate service name (that is, `sts.skypeunleashed.com`).
6. In the Federation Service Display Name field, type the name you would like displayed on the AD FS landing page and then click Next.
7. At the Specify Service Account screen, select Create a Group Managed Service Account.
8. In the Account Name field, type **`ADFSservice`** and then click Next.
9. On the Specify Database screen, accept the default (Create a Database on This Server Using Windows Internal Database) and then click Next.
10. On the Review Options screen, click Next.
11. At the Pre-requisite Checks screen, review the details and then click Configure.
12. On the Results page, click Close.

Adding Federation Servers to the Farm

After the first federation server has been configured, the AD FS role can be installed to additional servers. The same SSL certificate installed on the primary federation server should be imported to any additional servers before AD FS is configured. To add an additional server to the federation service farm, use the following procedure:

1. Follow the steps under the "Installing AD FS" section earlier in this chapter.
2. In Server Manager, on the toolbar, click the notifications flag, and then click Configure the federation service on this server.
3. In the Welcome screen of the Active Directory Federation Services Configuration Wizard window, select Add a Federation Server to a Federation Farm and then click Next.
4. On the Connect to AD DS screen, accept the default and then click Next.
5. On the Specify Service Properties screen, click the SSL Certificate menu and then select the certificate you installed on the server at the beginning of this section.
6. On the Specify Farm screen, enter the name of the primary federation server.
7. On the Specify SSL Certificate screen, select the SSL certificate that was imported earlier. This should be a copy of the certificate from the primary federation server.
8. At the Specify Service Account screen, enter the name of the service account that was used to configure the primary federation server.

9. On the Review Options screen, click Next.
10. At the Pre-requisite Checks screen, review the details and then click Configure.
11. On the Results page, click Close.

Verifying That the Federation Service Is Operational

After the federation service has been configured, verify that the service is operational:

1. On a client computer that is a member of the same AD forest as the federation service, open a web browser and connect to the following URL, where <fedservFQDN> is the fully qualified domain name of the federation service: https://<fedservFQDN>/adfs/ls/idpinitiatedsignon.htm.
2. At the sign in screen, click Sign In. Depending on how the site is configured within the browser, you may be prompted to provide credentials, or you may be signed in using SSO.

Federation Server Proxy Configuration

After the federation service is up and running, the AD FS configuration can be performed on the systems that will be used as federation proxies. The same SSL certificate installed on the federation servers should be imported to each server that will be used as a federation server proxy. There are several ways to provide proxy services to the AD FS servers, including the use of a dedicated load-balancing solution and the installation of the Web Application Proxy (WAP) role in Windows Server 2012 R2. To configure WAP as the federation server proxy role, use the following procedure:

1. Log on to the server using an account with local administrator rights.
2. Launch Server Manager.
3. In Server Manager, on the Dashboard, click Configure This Local Server and then click Add Roles and Features.
4. On the Select Installation Type screen, ensure that role-based or feature-based installation is selected and then click Next.
5. On the Select destination server screen, in the Server Pool list, verify that the local server is selected and then click Next.
6. At the Select Server Roles screen, under Roles, select the Remote Access check box and then click Next.
7. On the Features screen, click Next.
8. On the Remote Access screen, review the information and click Next.
9. On the Select Role Services screen, select the Web Application Proxy check box and click Next.
10. At the Confirm Installation Selections screen, click Install.

11. Wait for the installation to complete. Once the installation finishes, click Open the Web Application Proxy Wizard.
12. In the Welcome screen of the Web Application Proxy Configuration Wizard window, click Next.
13. On the Federation Server screen, enter the FQDN for the federation services name (that is, `sts.skypunleashed.com`), along with an account that has local admin permissions on the AD FS servers.
14. At the AD FS Proxy Certificate screen, select the previously imported certificate from the AD FS server(s).
15. At the Confirmation screen, review the PowerShell command and then click Configure.
16. Wait for the configuration of the AD FS proxy to complete successfully and then click Close.

Verifying That the Federation Proxy Is Operational

After the federation proxy service has been configured, use the following procedure to verify that the service is operational:

1. Log on to the federation server proxy system using an account with local administrator rights.
2. Open the Event Viewer; then, under Applications and Service Logs, expand AD FS and click Admin.
3. In the Event ID column, search for an event with ID 245. If event ID 245 is shown, this indicates that the federation server proxy service was started successfully and is now communicating with the AD FS server farm.

Establishing Trust with Office 365 for SSO

After the federation service is fully operational, the next step is to configure the trust between AD FS and Azure Active Directory (Office 365). This is accomplished using the Microsoft Azure Active Directory Module for Windows PowerShell, which installs a set of Windows PowerShell cmdlets that can be used to configure the trust and enable SSO for a domain, as described in the following sections.

Installing the Microsoft Azure Active Directory Module

The Microsoft Azure Active Directory Module can be downloaded directly from the Office 365 site and is available in a 64-bit version only. Following are the requirements for a system to run the Microsoft Azure Active Directory Module:

- Supported operating systems are Windows 8, Windows 8.1, Windows Server 2012, and Windows Server 2012 R2.
- .NET Framework must be enabled as a Windows feature.

The Microsoft Azure Active Directory Module also requires administrative access to AD FS for the cmdlets to execute successfully. If the module will not be installed and run directly on a federation server, remote access to AD FS must be enabled. You can accomplish this by opening Windows PowerShell as an administrator on the federation server and executing the cmdlet `enable-psremoting`.

Adding or Converting a Domain for SSO

Each domain that will be used for SSO with Skype for Business Online/Office 365 must either be added as an SSO domain or be converted from a standard domain to SSO. The Microsoft Azure Active Directory Module is used to add or convert the domain, which sets up a trust between the internal AD FS deployment and Office 365.

Use the following procedure to add a new domain for SSO:

1. Open the Microsoft Azure Active Directory Module.

2. Execute the following command, and then at the prompt enter the credentials of an Office 365 administrative account:

   ```
   $cred=Get-Credential
   ```

3. Execute the following command, which creates a connection to Office 365, as required to run the remaining cmdlets:

   ```
   Connect-MsolService -Credential $cred
   ```

4. Execute the following command, where `<ADFSprimary>` is the fully qualified domain name of the primary federation server. This cmdlet creates a connection to the internal federation service.

   ```
   Set-MsolAdfscontext -Computer <ADFSprimary>
   ```

NOTE

If the Microsoft Azure Active Directory Module is installed on the federation server, the `Set-MsolAdfscontext` cmdlet is not required.

5. Execute the following command, where `<Domain>` is the domain to be added and enabled for SSO:

   ```
   New-MsolFederatedDomain -DomainName <Domain>
   ```

6. The results of the `New-MsolFederatedDomain` cmdlet include information that must be used to verify ownership of the new domain. Specifically, a new DNS record (either a TXT record or an MX record) must be created within the zone that will be enabled for SSO, and this DNS record is used by Office 365 to confirm domain ownership. Follow through with the instructions to add either the TXT or the MX record to the public DNS zone, and then wait for the change to take effect. The amount of time required will depend on DNS propagation delay, as well as the DNS provider being used.

NOTE

Although either the TXT or the MX record can be tested for validation for Office 365, the TXT record is the preferred method of validation. The reason for this is that the MX record required for validation specifies an address value ending in `.invalid`, and not all DNS providers support this record. The TXT record, on the other hand, is much more commonly supported.

7. After the DNS verification record has propagated, the `New-MsolFederatedDomain` cmdlet is executed a second time, specifying the same domain name to finalize the addition of the new SSO domain.

The following procedure would be used to convert a domain that has already been added to Office 365 from a standard domain to SSO:

1. Open the Microsoft Azure Active Directory Module.
2. Execute the following command, and then at the prompt enter the credentials of an Office 365 administrative account:

```
$cred=Get-Credential
```

3. Execute the following command, which creates a connection to Office 365, as required to run the remaining cmdlets:

```
Connect-MsolService -Credential $cred
```

4. Execute the following command, where `<ADFSprimary>` is the fully qualified domain name of the primary federation server. This cmdlet creates a connection to the internal federation service.

```
Set-MsolAdfscontext -Computer <ADFSprimary>
```

NOTE

If the Microsoft Azure Active Directory Module is installed on the federation server, the `Set-MsolAdfscontext` cmdlet is not required.

5. Execute the following command, where `<Domain>` is the domain to be converted to SSO:

```
Convert-MsolDomainToFederated -DomainName <Domain>
```

NOTE

When a domain that has already been added to Office 365 is converted to SSO, every licensed user automatically becomes federated for SSO.

Configuring Directory Synchronization

For most organizations that deploy SSO, directory synchronization is the next step, because the combination of SSO and directory synchronization offers a seamless experience for Skype for Business Online users. The first step with directory synchronization is to validate that the Active Directory environment has been prepared for synchronization, with the help of the Microsoft Office 365 Support Assistant. For details on preparing AD for directory synchronization with the use of this tool, see Chapter 29. After the environment has been fully prepared, the information in the following sections can be used to configure synchronization with Active Directory.

Activating Directory Synchronization

Before installing Azure Active Directory Connect, you must first activate the feature using the Office 365 Portal. Use the following procedure to activate directory synchronization using the online portal:

1. Log on to the Office 365 Portal and go to the Admin app.
2. On the left side of the main page, expand Users, click Active Users, and then click the Set Up link next to Active Directory Synchronization.
3. At the top of the Active Users page, click the Set Up link next to Active Directory Synchronization.
4. At the Set Up and Manage Single Sign-On page, under Activate Active Directory Synchronization, click the Activate button.

NOTE

The activation process can require up to 24 hours to complete. Skype for Business Online administrators should plan ahead and activate AD synchronization several days before the AD user accounts need to be populated into the online directory.

Installing the Directory Synchronization Tool and Synchronizing the Directories

Azure Active Directory Connect can be downloaded directly from the Microsoft site. Several sets of administrative permissions are required for the user account that runs the tool:

- Local administrator permissions on the system where Azure Active Directory Connect will be installed
- Enterprise Administrator permissions in the Active Directory forest of which the system running Azure Active Directory Connect is a member
- Administrative permissions to the Skype for Business Online/Office 365 tenant

Use the following procedure to download and install Azure Active Directory Connect on a system that has been prepared for this purpose:

1. Log on to the system using an account with local administrator permissions.
2. After the file has been downloaded, double-click the `dirsync.exe` file to begin the installation.
3. At the Welcome to Azure AD Connect screen, review the information; then, if you agree to the license terms, select the I Accept radio button and click Continue.
4. On the Express Settings screen, review the information and then click Use Express Settings.
5. On the Connect to Azure AD screen, type your Office 365 tenant administrator username and password and then click Next.
6. At the Connect to AD DS screen, enter the credentials for the Enterprise Administrator account.
7. At the Ready to Configure screen, if the directory synchronization configuration will be performed right away, select the check box for "Start the synchronization process as soon as the configuration completes." If the synchronization will be performed later, deselect this check box. Click Install to complete the installation.
8. On the Configuration complete screen, click Exit to complete the installation.

NOTE

When configured, the directory synchronization service automatically creates a service account named MSOL_AD_SYNC or AAD_xxxxxxxxxxxx in the Users container at the root of Active Directory, and it applies a randomly generated password that never expires. This service account is used by the Directory Synchronization tool to read the local Active Directory and write to Office 365, using the credentials provided in the Microsoft Online Services Credentials page of the Configuration Wizard. This service account should never be moved or removed, and the password on the account should never be manually reset; otherwise, synchronization failures will occur.

After directory synchronization has been configured, it will run every 3 hours automatically. If there are changes that need to be synchronized more urgently, synchronization can be forced. To force directory synchronization without the need to enter credentials, Windows PowerShell can be used. Use the following procedure to force directory synchronization using a Windows PowerShell cmdlet:

1. Log on to the system where Azure Active Directory Connect is installed using an account with local administrator permissions.
2. Open Windows PowerShell.

3. Enter the following command to navigate to the directory where Azure Active Directory Connect is installed (by default, `%programfiles%\Microsoft Azure AD Sync\Bin`).

```
CD "C:\Program Files\Microsoft Azure AD Sync\Bin"
```

4. Execute the following command to force directory synchronization.

```
.\DirectorySyncClientCmd.exe initial
```

Activating Synchronized Users

After the initial synchronization is complete, AD users and groups will appear in the Skype for Business Online/Office 365 directory with a status of "Synced with Active Directory," as shown in Figure 22.12. Although the users are now part of the directory, they are not enabled for Skype for Business Online until they are activated. To activate newly synchronized user accounts, use the follow these steps:

1. Log on to the Office 365 Portal and go to the Admin app.

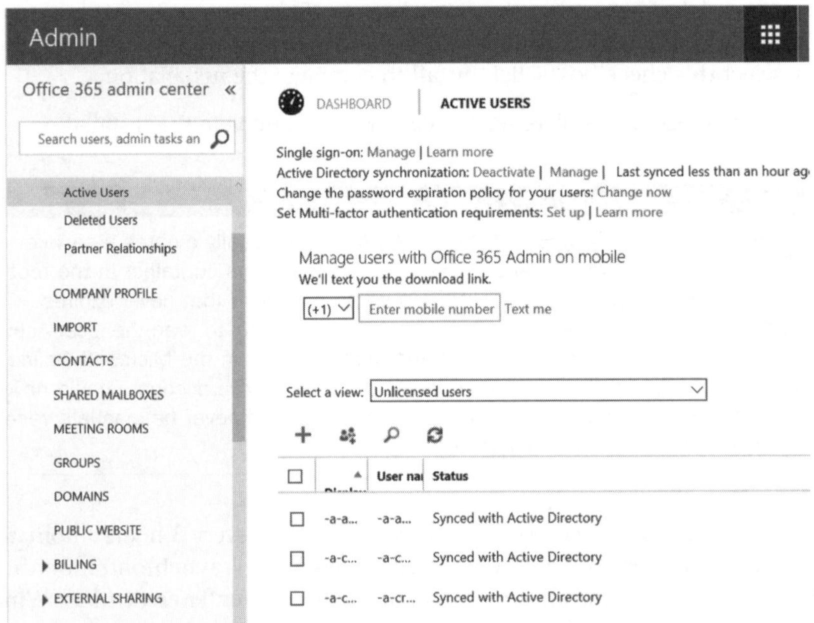

FIGURE 22.12 Newly synchronized users in the Skype for Business Online/Office 365 directory.

2. On the left side of the main page, expand Users and then click Active Users.
3. Use the Select a View drop-down menu to select Unlicensed Users.
4. From the list of unlicensed users, either click the check box next to individual user accounts or click the check box at the top of the list to select all user accounts.

5. From the Quick Steps menu at the right, click Activate Synced Users.
6. At the Assign Licenses screen, select the check box for the Skype for Business Online plan that the user will be licensed for, along with any other Office 365 services and plans that the organization has a subscription for.
7. At the Send Results in Email page, keep the default selection of "Send email if the username and temporary password for the new account should be sent to an administrator via email," and then enter up to five recipient email addresses separated by semicolons. When finished, click Activate.
8. At the Results page, verify that the user account has been successfully activated, and make note of the temporary password automatically generated. Click Finish to complete the procedure.

Skype for Business Hybrid Deployment

The procedures for building a Skype for Business hybrid deployment can be significant, depending on whether there is an existing Lync or OCS installation in place or whether the entire environment will be built from scratch. Many of the tasks involved in building a hybrid deployment are found either in other sections of this chapter or in other chapters of this book. Although these other sections will be referred to for the appropriate guidance, there are also some deployment tasks that are specific to the hybrid environment, and these are detailed in the following sections.

Installing the On-Premises Systems

A Skype for Business hybrid deployment starts with the installation of the on-premises Skype for Business Server 2015 infrastructure, if there is no existing Skype for Business Server 2015 environment in place. At a minimum, the on-premises deployment requires one Front End pool and one Edge pool, with the Edge pool enabled for federation. Although a Lync Server 2010 Front End pool and Edge pool can be used for this, at least one Lync Server 2013 or Skype for Business Server 2015 Edge and Mediation Server needs to be installed to support voice features. For further details on the on-premises topology options supported for a hybrid deployment, see Chapter 29. Although it's not required, consideration should be given to building high availability into the solution, leveraging the built-in resilience features of Skype for Business Server 2015. For details regarding the planning process for the Skype for Business Server 2015 on-premises systems, see Chapters 30 to 33.

After the Skype for Business Server 2015 on-premises installation is in place and functional, and the Skype for Business Online or Office 365 subscription is active, the next steps are required to prepare the on-premises systems for a hybrid deployment:

- If it has not already been added, the SIP domain that will be split between the on-premise and cloud deployment will need to be added to Skype for Business Online/Office 365, with the ownership verified. For details on this procedure, see the "Adding Domains to Skype for Business Online/Office 365" section of this chapter.

- Install Active Directory Federated Services to enable SSO for the hybrid deployment, using a minimum of one federation server. If users will be connecting remotely, at least one AD FS proxy should also be included, and should be installed in a DMZ subnet. As part of the deployment, request an SSL certificate from a public Certificate Authority with the `sts.<SIPdomain>` name specified as the subject name, and apply the certificate to the default website on both the federation server and the federation proxy server systems.
- After the internal federation service is operational, a trust relationship must be established with the Skype for Business Online/Office 365 deployment. For details on planning AD FS for use with Skype for Business Online, see Chapter 29. For details on installing AD FS and configuring it for SSO with Skype for Business Online, see the "AD FS Deployment for SSO" section of this chapter.
- Activate the online tenant for AD synchronization; then configure directory synchronization between the on-premises Active Directory and the Skype for Business Online/Office 365 directory, and synchronize the on-premises users and groups to Skype for Business Online. For details on planning directory synchronization between AD and Skype for Business Online/Office 365, see Chapter 29. For details on installing and configuring directory synchronization, see the "Configuring Directory Synchronization" section of this chapter.

Preparing the Network for a Skype for Business Hybrid Deployment

The network requirements for a Skype for Business hybrid deployment are similar to the requirements for a cloud-only deployment. However, there are several additional firewall port requirements compared to a cloud-only deployment, and there is at least one additional DNS requirement for the hybrid deployment, depending on the configuration. For specifics on which DNS records and firewall port openings are required for a given scenario, see Chapter 29.

Configuring Federation with Skype for Business Online

To establish interoperability between the on-premises deployment and Skype for Business Online, the on-premises Edge pool must be configured for federation with the Skype for Business Online tenant. The following steps are used to configure federation between an on-premises Edge pool and a Skype for Business Online tenant:

1. Log on to a system where the Skype for Business Server 2015 management tools are installed and open the Skype for Business Server 2015 Management Shell.
2. Execute the following command to enable federation and set basic parameters:

```
Set-CSAccessEdgeConfiguration -AllowOutsideUsers 1
➥-AllowFederatedUsers 1 -UseDnsSrvRouting
```

3. Execute the following command to establish federation with Skype for Business Online:

```
New-CSHostingProvider -Identity LyncOnline -ProxyFqdn "sipfed.online.lync.com"
➥-Enabled $true -EnabledSharedAddressSpace $true -HostsOCSUsers $true
➥-VerificationLevel UseSourceVerification -IsLocal $false
➥-AutodiscoverUrl
➥https://webdir.online.lync.com/Autodiscover/AutodiscoverService.svc/root
```


Configuring Skype for Business Online for Shared SIP Address Space

To establish interoperability between the on-premises deployment and Skype for Business Online, the Skype for Business Online/Office 365 tenant must be configured to support a shared SIP address space. The following steps are used to configure the Skype for Business Online tenant:

1. Log on to the system where Windows PowerShell and the Skype for Business Online Modules are installed.

2. Execute the following command; then, at the prompt, enter the credentials of an Office 365 administrative account:

   ```
   $cred=Get-Credential
   ```

3. Execute the following command:

   ```
   $O365Session=New-CsOnlineSession -Credential $cred
   ```

4. Execute the following command to connect to Skype for Business Online, as required to run the remaining cmdlets:

   ```
   Import-PSSession $O365Session
   ```

5. Execute the following command to enable the Skype for Business tenant for shared SIP address space:

   ```
   Set-CsTenantFederationConfiguration -SharedSipAddressSpace $true
   ```

Moving Users Between Skype for Business On-Premises and Skype for Business Online

After both environments have been fully deployed and the relationship between them has been established, users can be moved from an on-premises pool to the Skype for Business Online tenant using a PowerShell cmdlet. Before you can move users to Skype for Business Online, the pool FQDN of the Skype for Business Online tenant must first be determined, because it must be entered as one of the parameters for the PowerShell cmdlet. The following steps can be used to determine the pool FQDN of the Skype for Business Online tenant:

1. Log on to the Office 365 Portal and go to the Admin app.

2. On the left side of the main page, expand Admin and select Skype for Business to launch the Skype for Business Online Admin portal.

3. In the browser address bar, copy the first portion of the address listed, up to the `lync.com` string. For example, a typical Skype for Business Online pool FQDN

would be https://webdir0a.online.lync.com. Replace webdir with admin. Then, append the following string to the URL just copied: /HostedMigration/hostedmigrationservice.svc. These two strings combine to form the HostedMigrationOverrideUrl value, which will be specified in the PowerShell cmdlet used to move users to the online tenant. Using the preceding example, the resulting URL value would be https://admin0a.online.lync.com/HostedMigration/hostedmigrationservice.svc.

After the HostedMigrationOverrideUrl value is identified, use PowerShell to move an on-premises user to the online tenant, using the following steps:

1. Log on to a system where the Skype for Business Server 2015 management tools are installed and then open the Skype for Business Server 2015 Management Shell.
2. Execute the following command to establish credentials for the session:

```
$cred=Get-Credentials
```

3. At the prompt, enter the credentials of a Skype for Business Online/Office 365 administrative account.
4. Execute the following command to move the user to the online tenant, where <SIPaddress> is the SIP URI of the user account, and <URL> is the value previously identified as the HostedMigrationOverrideUrl for the online tenant:

```
Move-CsUser -Identity <SIPaddress> -Target sipfed.lync.online.com
➥-Credentials $cred -HostedMigrationOverrideUrl <URL>
```

To move a user from the online tenant back to an on-premises Skype for Business pool, use the following procedure:

1. Log on to a system where the Skype for Business Server 2015 management tools are installed and then open the Skype for Business Server 2015 Management Shell.
2. Execute the following command to establish credentials for the session:

```
$cred=Get-Credentials
```

3. At the prompt, enter the credentials of a Skype for Business Online/Office 365 administrative account.
4. Execute the following command to move the user to the on-premises Skype for Business pool, where <SIPaddress> is the SIP URI of the user account and <PoolFQDN> is the fully qualified domain name of the on-premises Skype for Business pool:

```
Move-CsUser -Identity <SIPaddress> -Target <PoolFQDN> -Credentials $cred
```

Configuring Users for Skype for Business Online Cloud PBX with On-Premises PSTN Connectivity

Organizations that are looking to transition to a cloud-based telephony platform but have existing carrier contracts or other specific requirements related to their on-premises telephony integration might look to Microsoft's hybrid voice solution. If you have followed all the preceding sections and steps for Skype for Business hybrid configuration, then most all of the prerequisites have been met to support Cloud PBX with On-Premises PSTN Connectivity. As the name implies, the on-premises Skype for Business deployment can provide access to PSTN calling services for Cloud PBX users. For information regarding planning the on-premises deployment to support telephony services, refer to Chapters 30–33. The following steps are required to configure a Cloud PBX user with hybrid voice capabilities, assuming that the required Skype for Business on-premises infrastructure and voice configuration exist:

1. Identify the users who will be migrated to Skype for Business Online and enabled for Cloud PBX. These users must be enabled in the on-premises infrastructure.
   If they are currently enabled in Skype for Business Online, follow the instructions in the previous section, "Moving Users Between Skype for Business On-Premises and Skype for Business Online," and migrate the accounts to the on-premises Skype for Business pool.

2. Log on to a system where the Skype for Business Server 2015 management tools are installed and then open the Skype for Business Server 2015 Management Shell.

3. Ensure each user to be configured for hybrid voice is enabled for Enterprise Voice and has a Line URI assigned. The following command should be run against each user, where `<SIPaddress>` is the SIP URI of the user account, and `LineURI` includes their phone number in E.164 format:

   ```
   Set-CsUser -Identity <SipAddress> -EnterpriseVoiceEnabled $true
   ➥-LineURI "tel:+14025551234"
   ```

4. Configure a new Voice Routing Policy that will be assigned to the user and then define the call routing once they are migrated to Skype for Business Online. Execute the following command to create the on-premises Voice Routing Policy, which assumes the "Local" and "Long Distance" PSTN Usages have already been created with routes assigned:

   ```
   New-CsVoiceRoutingPolicy -Identity HybridVoice -Name HybridVoice
   ➥-PSTNUsages "Local", "Long Distance"
   ```

NOTE

After a user has been migrated to Skype for Business Online and is configured to use Cloud PBX with On-Premises PSTN Connectivity, they will have two voice policies applied. The first is the on-premises Voice Routing Policy, which defines the path their calls will take. The second is the Skype for Business Online Voice Policy, which defines which calling features are available to the user. The Skype for Business Online Voice Policy is controlled by Microsoft and is applied to all Cloud PBX with On-Premises PSTN Connectivity users.

5. Apply the newly created Voice Routing Policy to the users with the following command:

```
Grant-CsVoiceRoutingPolicy -Identity <SipAddress> -PolicyName HybridVoice
```

6. Verify that the users have been synchronized to the Skype for Business Online/Office 365 tenant. If necessary, invoke a manual synchronization with Azure AD Connect, using the following command run from the AD Connect server:

```
.\DirectorySyncClientCmd.exe delta
```

7. Assign the designated users a Skype for Business Online Plan 2 or Office 365 "E" plan license, plus the Cloud PBX license as outlined in the "Configuring Cloud PBX" section of this chapter.

8. Execute the following command to move the user to the online tenant, where `<SIPaddress>` is the SIP URI of the user account, and `<URL>` is the value previously identified as the `HostedMigrationOverrideUrl` for the online tenant:

```
Move-CsUser -Identity <SIPaddress> -Target sipfed.lync.online.com
➥-Credentials $cred -HostedMigrationOverrideUrl <URL>
```

The final steps in the process are to enable the newly migrated Skype for Business Online users for Cloud PBX and voicemail, like so:

1. Log on to the system where Windows PowerShell and the Skype for Business Online Modules are installed.

2. Execute the following command; then, at the prompt, enter the credentials of an Office 365 administrative account:

```
$cred=Get-Credential
```

3. Execute the following command:

```
$O365Session=New-CsOnlineSession -Credential $cred
```

4. Execute the following command to connect to Skype for Business Online, as required to run the remaining cmdlets:

```
Import-PSSession $O365Session
```

5. Execute the following command to enable the Skype for Business tenant for shared SIP address space:

```
Set-CsUser -Identity <SIPaddress> -EnterpriseVoiceEnabled $true
➥-HostedVoiceMail $true
```

Summary

As Microsoft continues to develop its portfolio of cloud services, Skype for Business Online will no doubt continue to gain momentum, because it provides an attractive alternative for rolling out UC features at a reasonable cost. The additional Skype for Business Online and hybrid deployment options will provide unprecedented flexibility for meeting the varied UC needs of many organizations. Several unique steps are involved in the deployment of any Skype for Business Online solution, whether it's a cloud-only or a hybrid solution. In addition to providing an overview of Skype for Business Online and a description of the user experience, this chapter includes detailed guidance on the steps involved in provisioning Skype for Business Online for all topology options, and it serves as a comprehensive build reference for any Skype for Business Online initiative.

CHAPTER 23

Skype Integration

IN THIS CHAPTER

- Skype Connectivity Features
- Configuring Skype Connectivity for Skype for Business Server 2015
- Configuring Skype Connectivity for Office 365
- Troubleshooting Skype Connectivity

Skype for Business Server 2015 is the first release since the acquisition of Skype by Microsoft. Skype for Business Server 2015 tightens the integration with Skype Connectivity that started with Lync Server 2013. Lync Server 2013 introduced federation with Skype as a Public IM Connectivity (PIC) provider. This allowed IM and Presence integration for person-to-person conversations. Skype for Business Server 2015 builds on this integration with support for audio and video. AOL federation and Yahoo! federation are no longer supported.

This chapter provides an overview of the integration of Skype Connectivity with Skype for Business Server 2015 and explains how to configure Skype Connectivity in Skype for Business Server 2015, step by step.

Skype Connectivity Features

Skype Connectivity offers IM and Presence integration between Skype consumer users and Skype for Business users. Figure 23.1 illustrates an IM conversation between a Skype client and Skype for Business client.

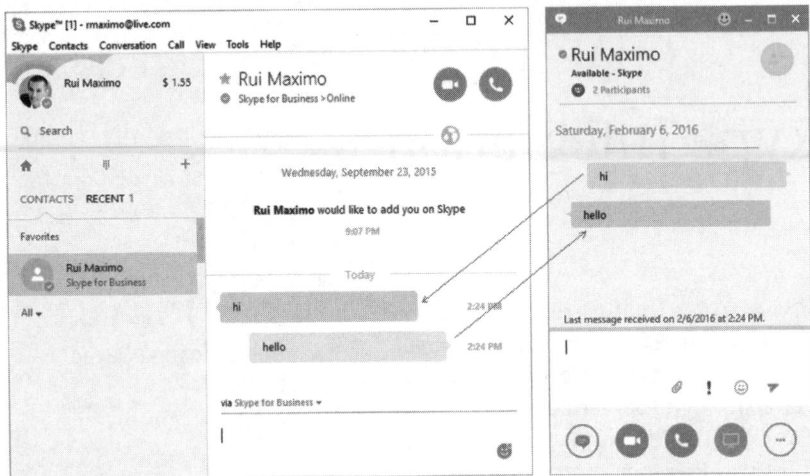

FIGURE 23.1 IM and Presence integration.

This feature was already introduced in Lync Server 2013. This integration was the first step in making the Skype network a digital version of the PSTN, where business-to-consumer (B2C) real-time communication is not only possible, but at Internet scale. Enterprise users using Skype for Business Server 2015 or Lync Server 2013 can communicate with over 300 million users on Skype without making a PSTN call.

Skype for Business Server 2015 builds on this integration by making it possible to make audio and video calls between Skype users and Skype for Business users. Figure 23.2 illustrates this deeper integration with both clients on the same computer using two different cameras.

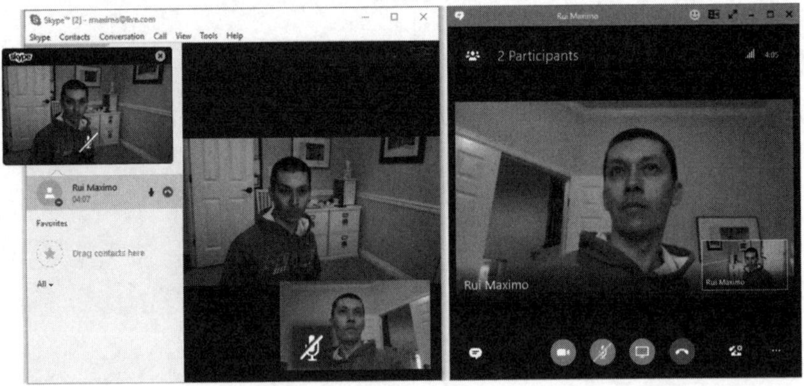

FIGURE 23.2 Audio and video integration.

Unfortunately, application sharing, desktop sharing, and screen sharing integration is still not available, but it's only a matter of time.

Now that you've seen the type of modalities possible between Skype and Skype for Business, let's examine how communication is initiated. Before a Skype for Business user can communicate with a Skype user, the Skype for Business user must add the Skype user to their contact list. This is done by clicking the Add icon, selecting Add a Contact Not in My Organization, and then clicking Skype. This is shown in Figure 23.3.

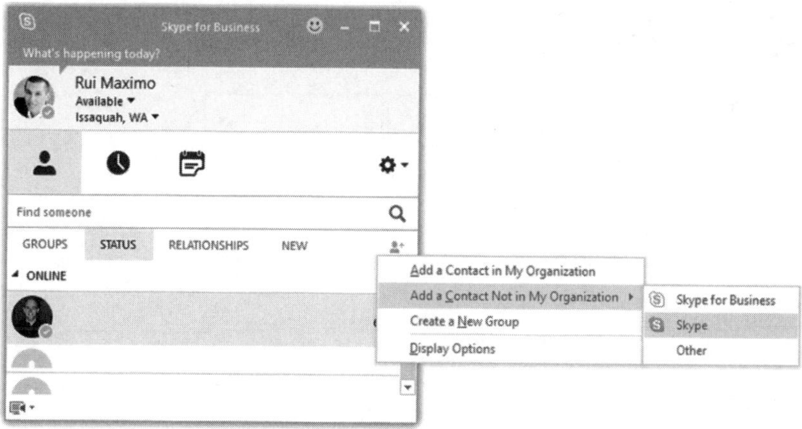

FIGURE 23.3 Adding a Skype user to a Skype for Business contact list.

This brings up the Skype Directory tab, where Skype users can be searched for and added to the Skype for Business user's contact list. You can search by Skype ID as shown in Figure 23.4.

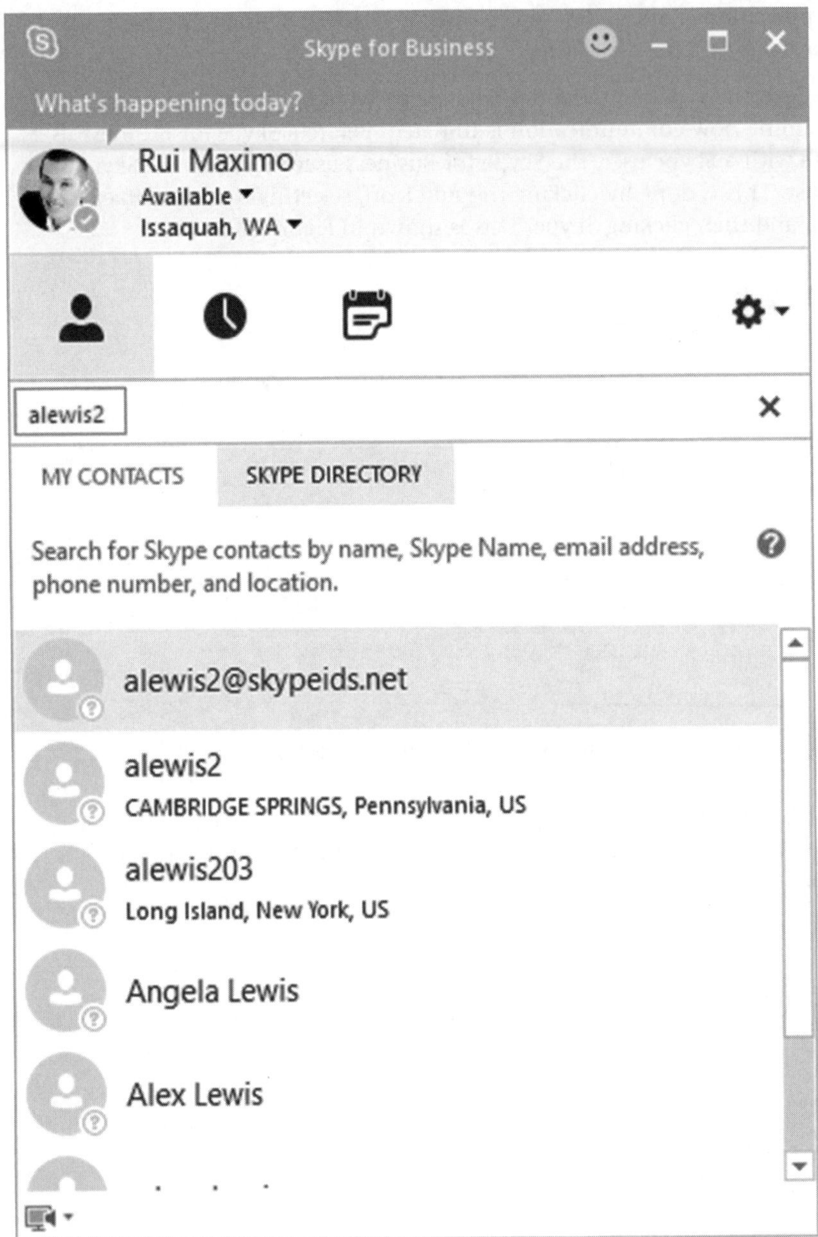

FIGURE 23.4 Search by Skype ID.

Skype users can be discovered by their phone number if configured by the Skype user. This is illustrated in Figure 23.5.

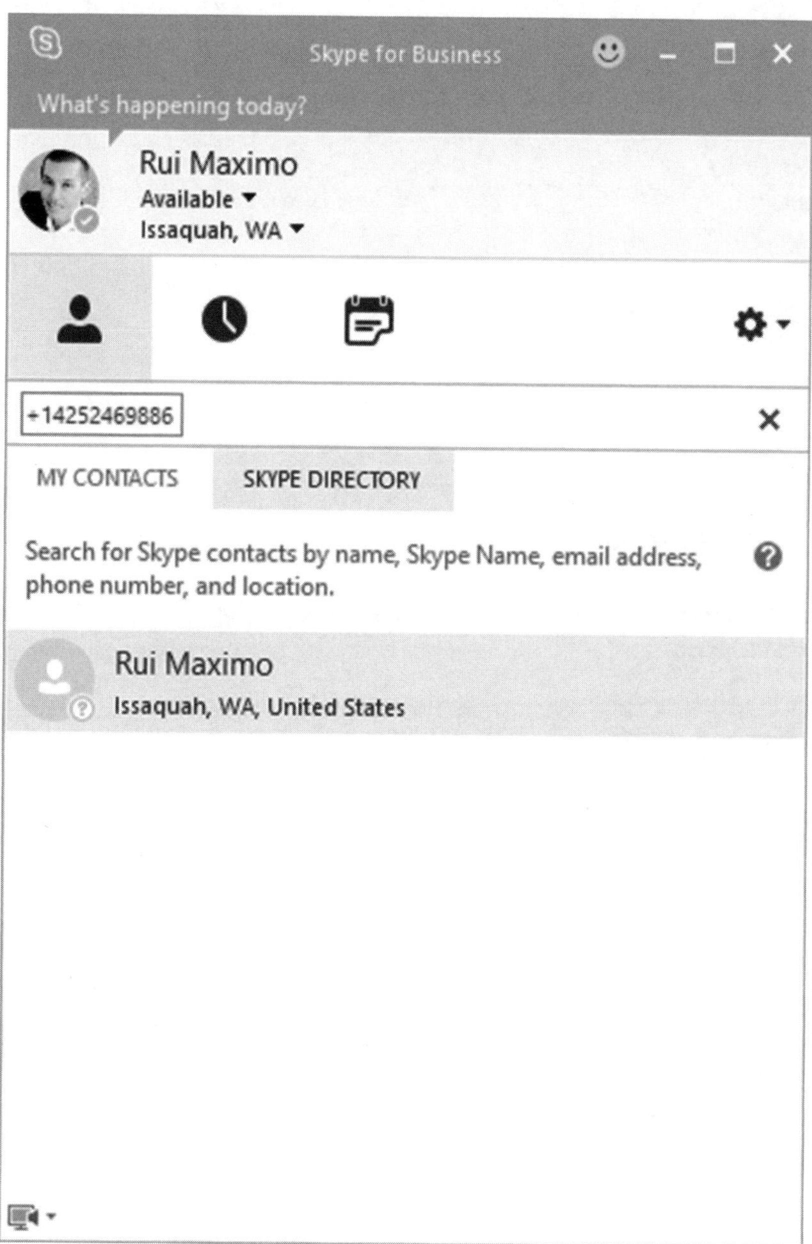

FIGURE 23.5 Search by phone number.

Skype users can be searched for by their email address, as shown in Figure 23.6.

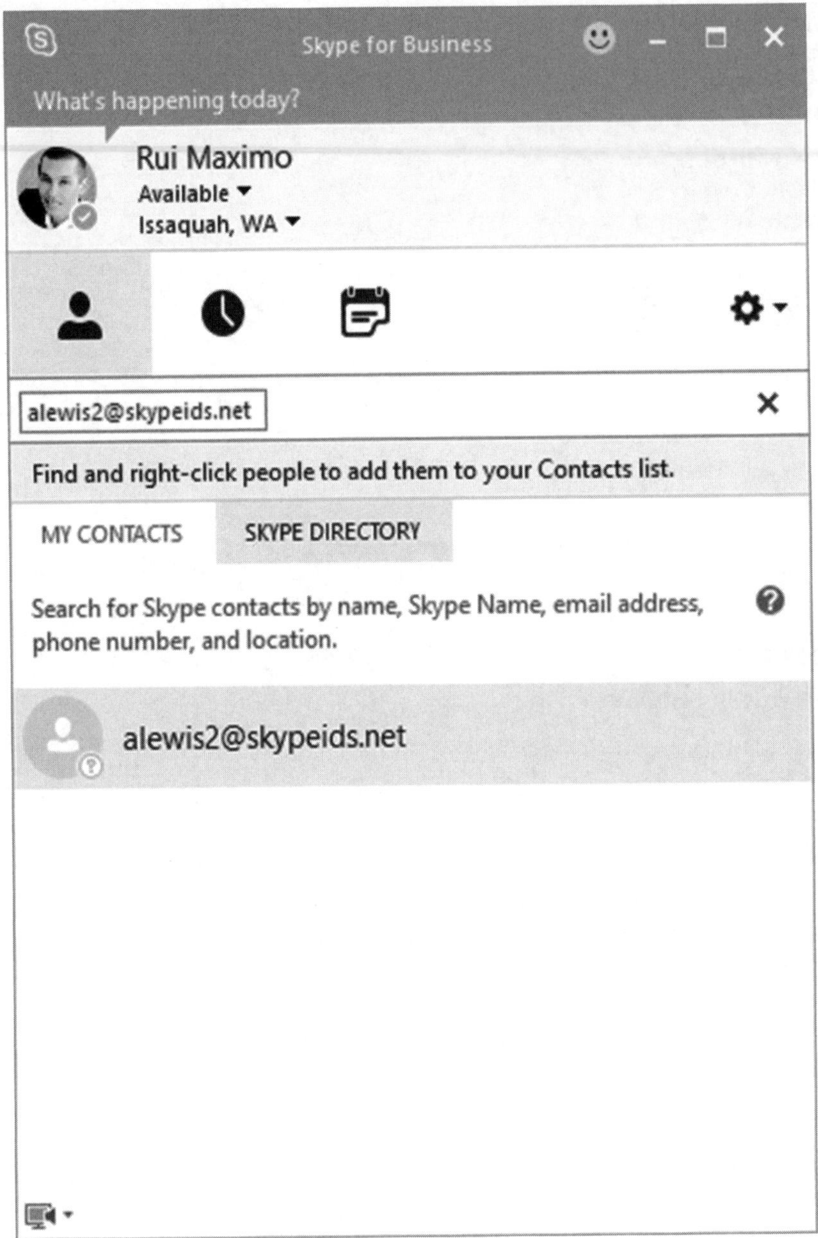

FIGURE 23.6 Search by email address.

If you only know the Skype user's name, you can search for them by display name (see Figure 23.7). Of course, you're likely to get a large result set, so being as specific as possible is advisable. If the user you're searching for has a common name, searching by display name is not likely to yield the Skype user you're looking for.

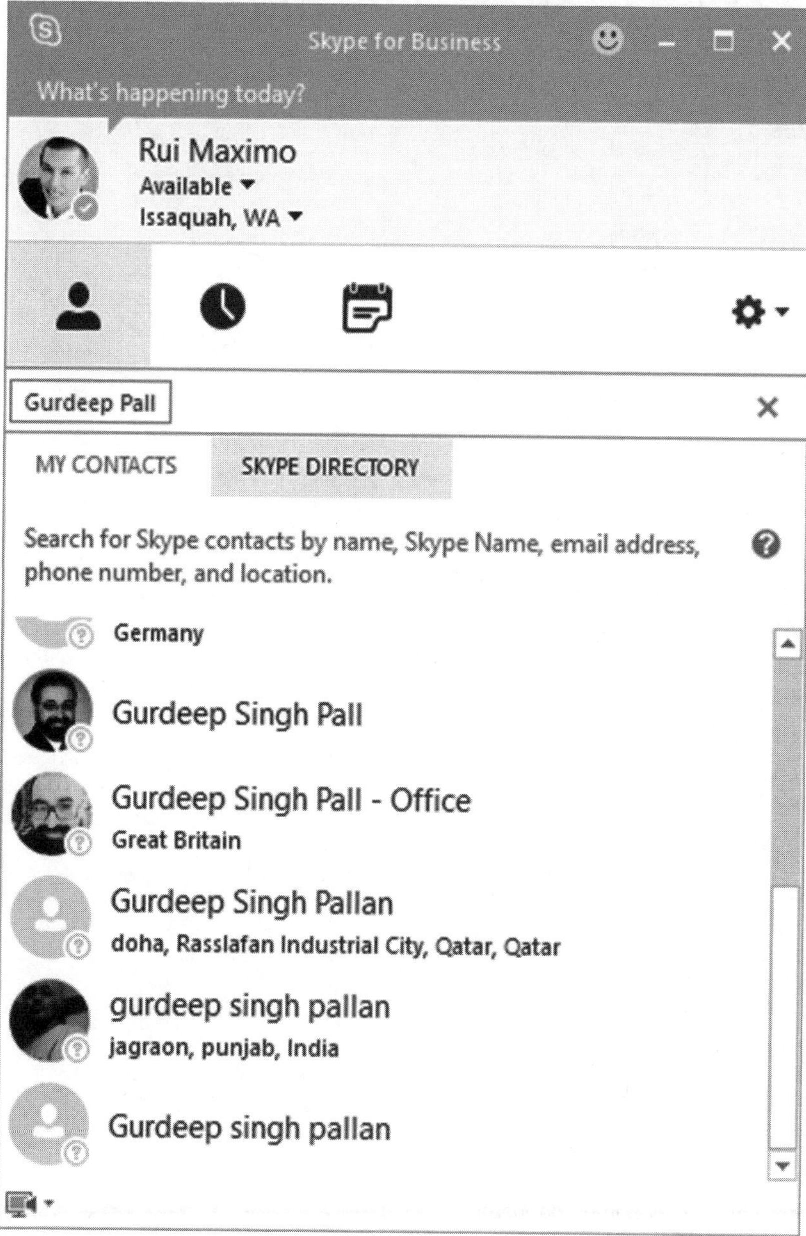

FIGURE 23.7 Search by display name.

If searching by display name is too broad, you can narrow down the search by specifying the Skype user's general location such as city, state, or country (see Figure 23.8).

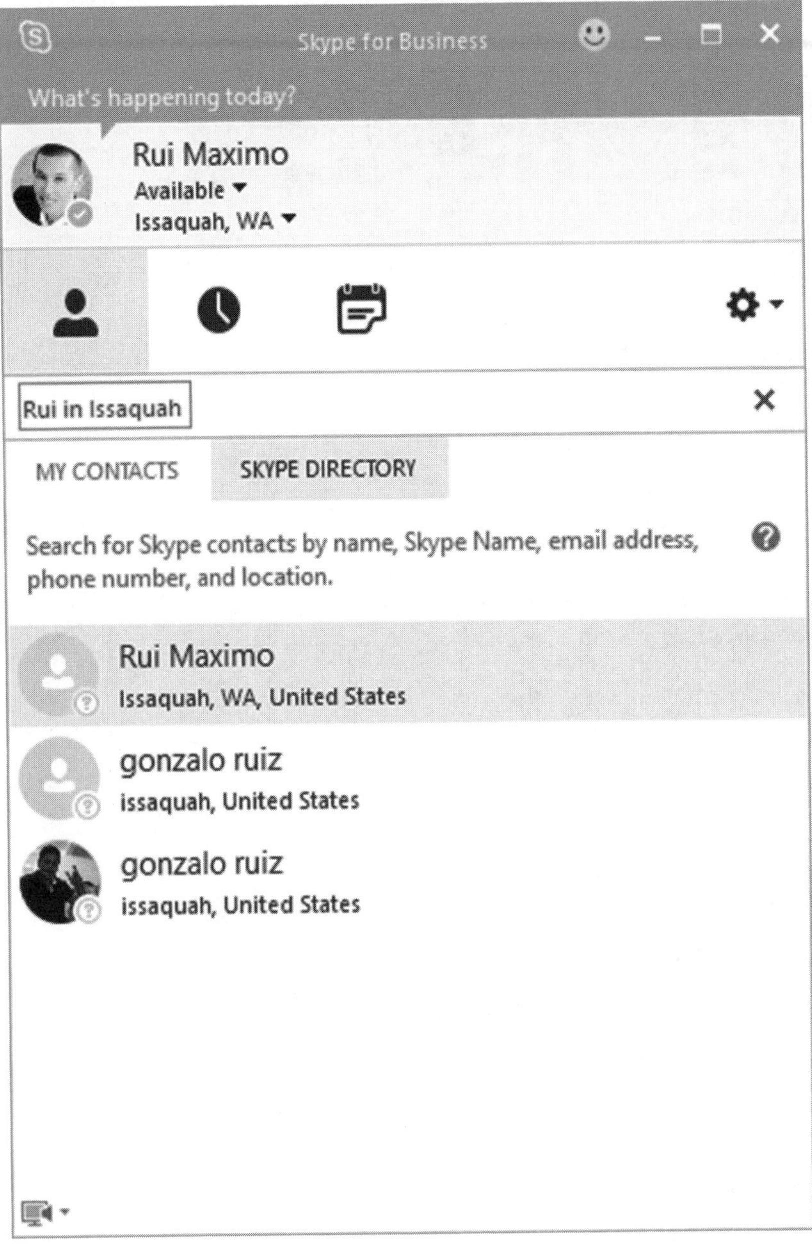

FIGURE 23.8 Search by display name and location.

Once you've located the Skype user and added them to your contact list, a request will appear in the Skype client. The request doesn't propagate to the Skype user immediately. This is illustrated in Figure 23.9. The Skype user must accept the request before the Skype for Business user can communicate with them.

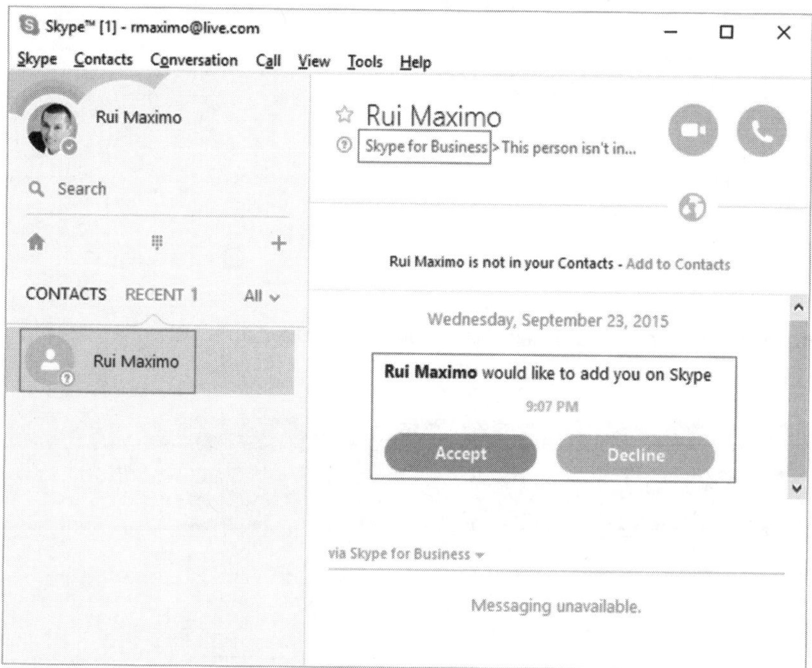

FIGURE 23.9 Skype request.

Once the request is accepted, the Skype user can view the Presence of the Skype for Business user, as shown in Figure 23.10, and the Skype for Business user can view the Skype user's Presence (see Figure 23.11). Notice the indicator that the user is a Skype user when the user's Presence is listed.

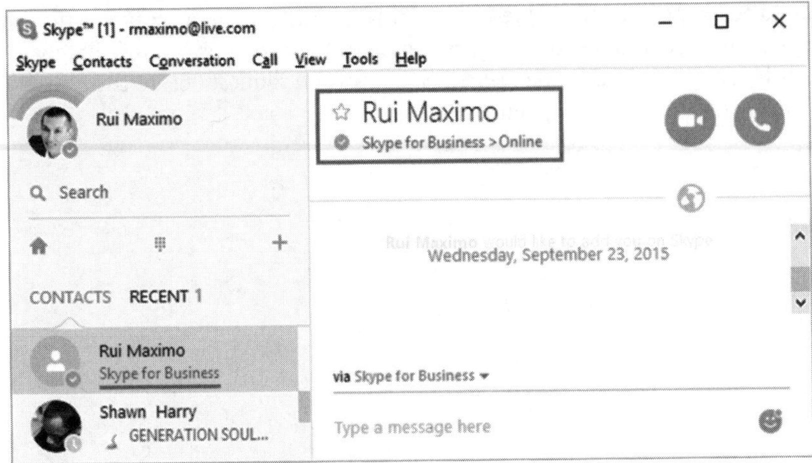

FIGURE 23.10 Presence of Skype for Business user from Skype client.

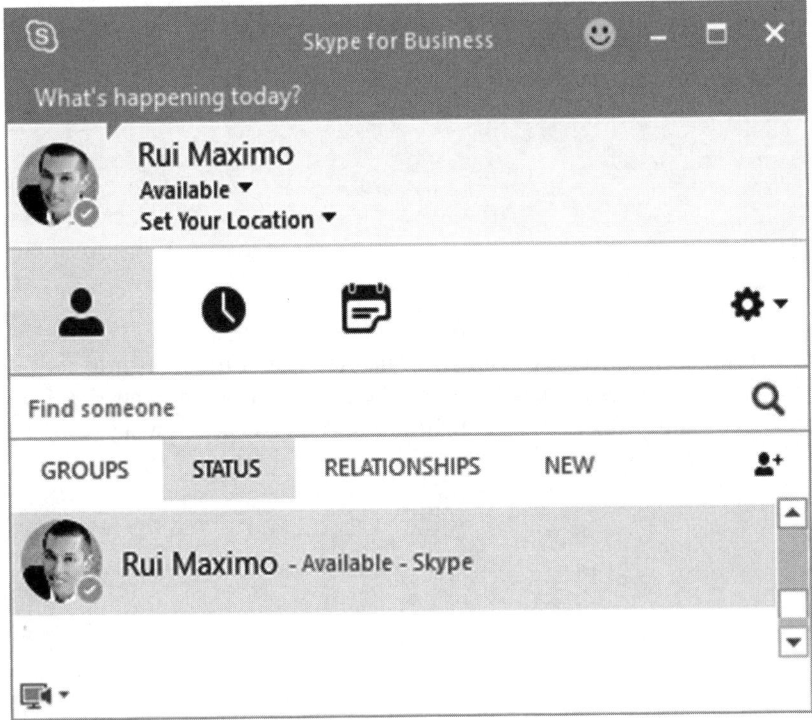

FIGURE 23.11 Presence of Skype user from Skype for Business client.

We've examined the user experience from the perspective of both the Skype for Business client and Skype client. Let's now examine what's involved in configuring Skype Connectivity.

Configuring Skype Connectivity for Skype for Business Server 2015

Configuring Skype Connectivity requires setting up federation between your organization and Microsoft Skype. This implies your organization must deploy an Edge Server and configure it for federation. This chapter focuses on configuring Skype Connectivity and assumes an Edge Server or Edge pool is already deployed.

Configuring Skype Connectivity involves the following four steps:

- Requesting Skype Connectivity from Microsoft
- Configuring the Edge Server
- Enabling the external access policy
- Configuring Skype as a federated provider

The following sections dive into the details of each of these steps.

Requesting Skype Connectivity

To configure Skype Connectivity with your organization, you need to request Microsoft to set up Skype federation with your organization. This is a painless process that Microsoft has made easy to complete. You will need the following information to complete this process:

- Your Microsoft agreement number or partner ID
- Your Access Edge Server/pool fully qualified domain name (FQDN)
- Your SIP domain(s)
- Additional Access Edge FQDNs (if any)
- Your corporate contact information

Navigate to https://pic.lync.com and sign in with your Microsoft account, as shown in Figure 23.12.

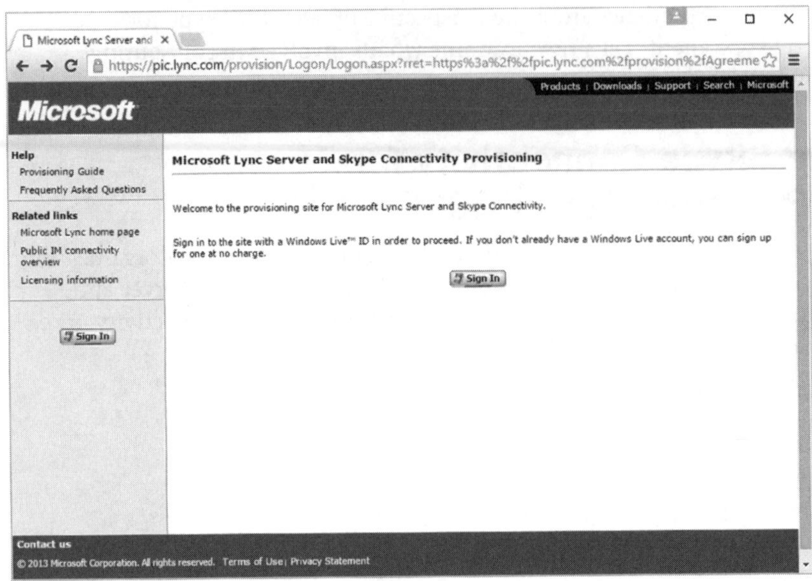

FIGURE 23.12 https://pic.lync.com.

Next, select the type of agreement you have with Microsoft. This is shown in Figure 23.13.

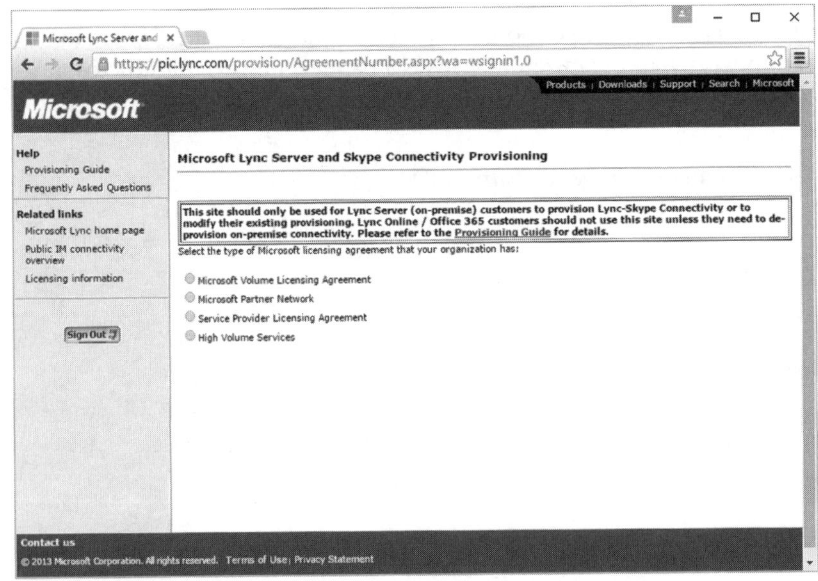

FIGURE 23.13 Microsoft agreement type.

After selecting the type of Microsoft agreement your organization has, you'll need to acknowledge the terms and conditions by checking the box. Depending on the type of agreement selected, you'll specify your Microsoft agreement number (see Figure 23.14) or partner ID (see Figure 23.15).

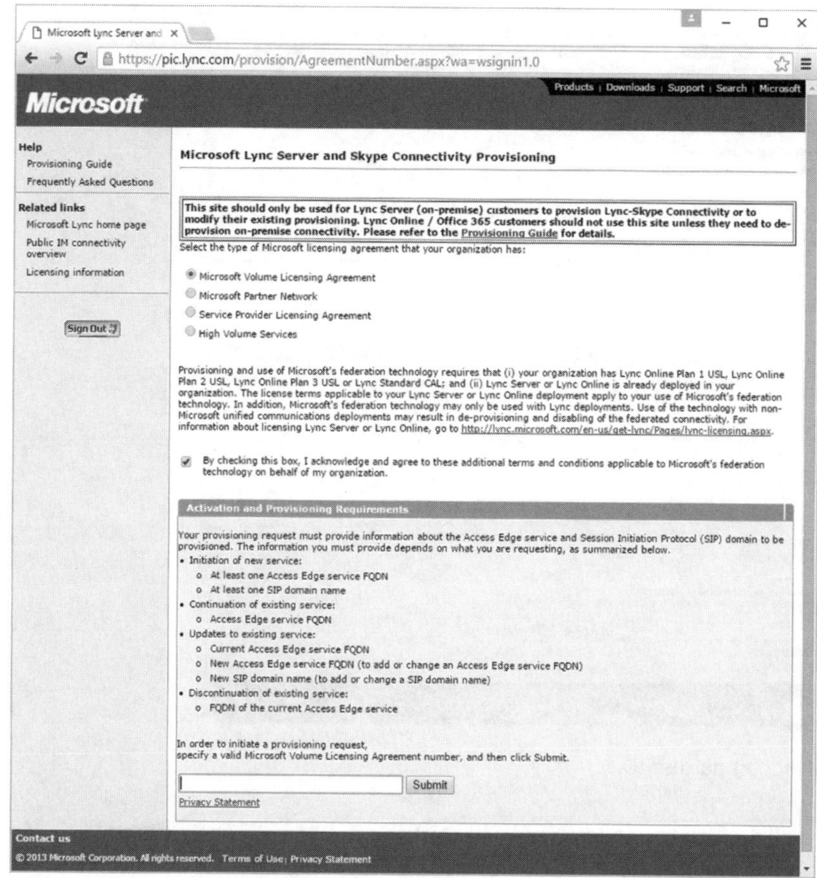

FIGURE 23.14 Microsoft agreement number.

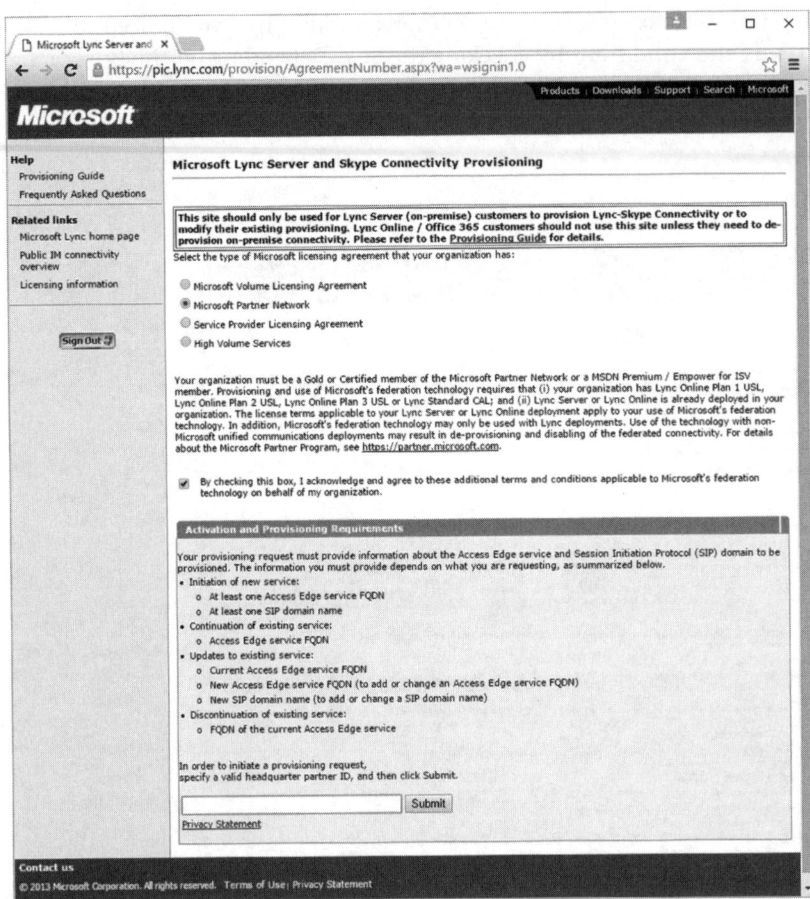

FIGURE 23.15 Microsoft partner ID.

The next step is to click Initiate Service. This will start the process of configuring Skype Connectivity with your organization. Don't worry. You can make updates and stop the service at any time, as shown in Figure 23.16. You can also setup multiple federation with Skype for multiple SIP domains such as subsidiaries.

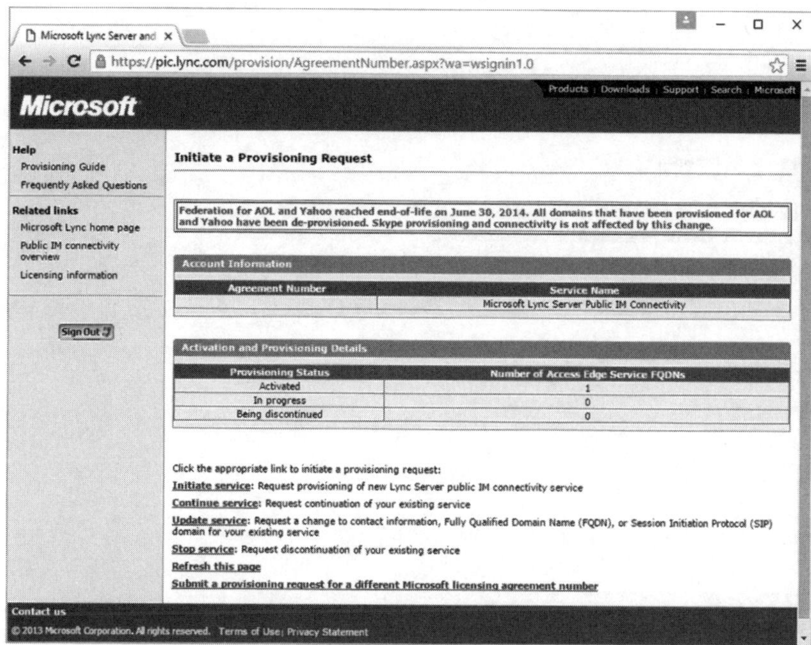

FIGURE 23.16 The Initiate a Provisioning Request page.

You'll need to enter your organization's contact information (see Figure 23.17). Click Next when done.

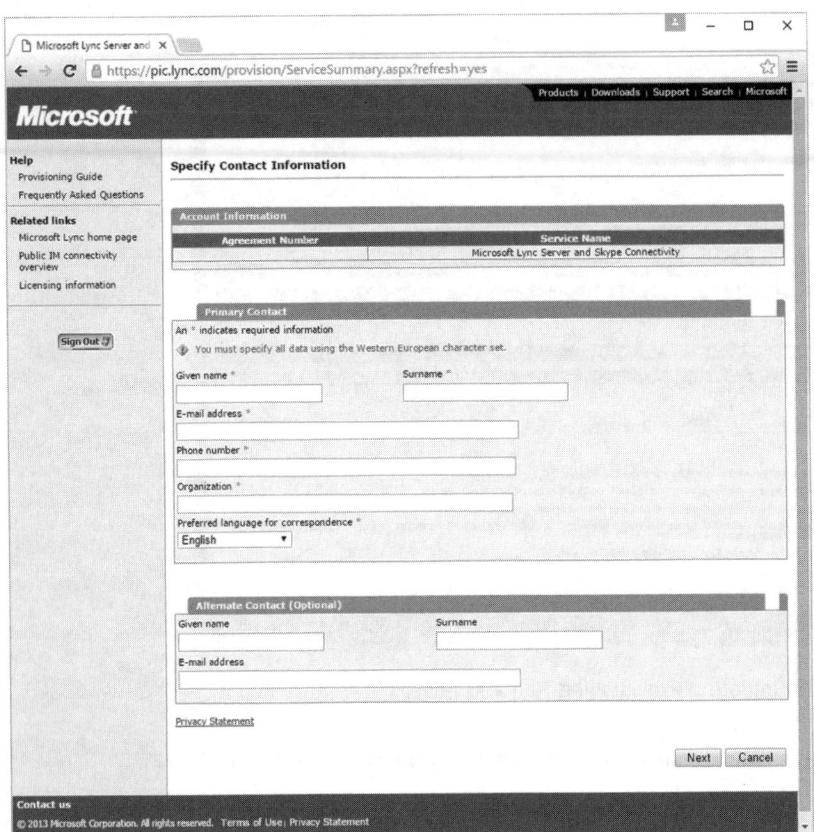

FIGURE 23.17 Contact information.

Specify your Access Edge FQDN and SIP domains serviced by this Access Edge. If necessary, you can specify additional Access Edge FQDNs in the case you have multiple datacenters, each with its own Edge pools. This is illustrated in Figure 23.18. Click Next when done.

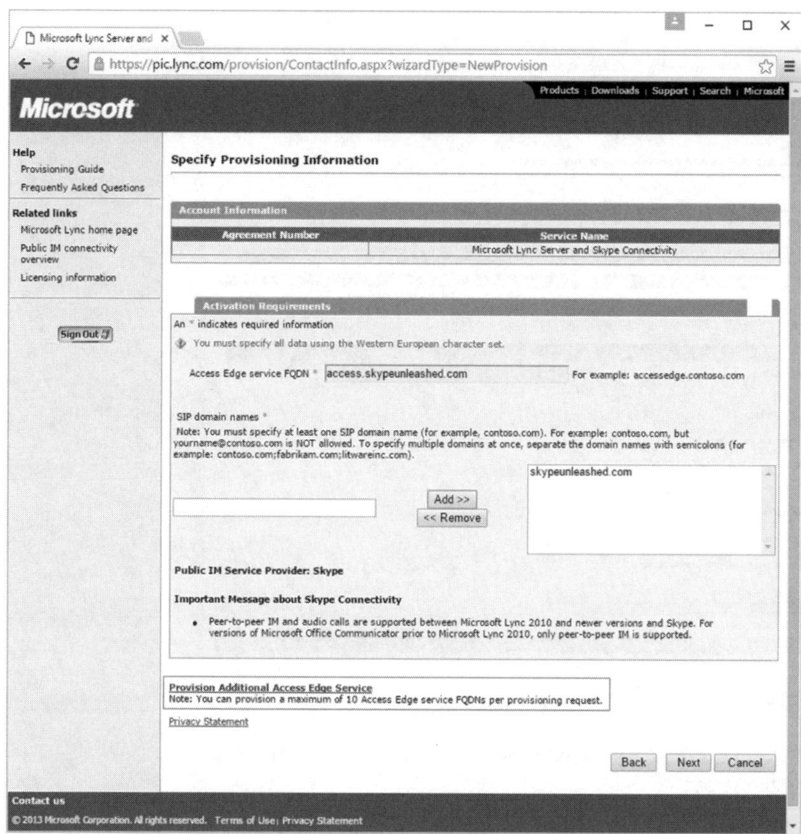

FIGURE 23.18 Provisioning information.

Finally, review your settings before clicking Next to finalize your Skype Connectivity provisioning request to Microsoft, as shown in Figure 23.19.

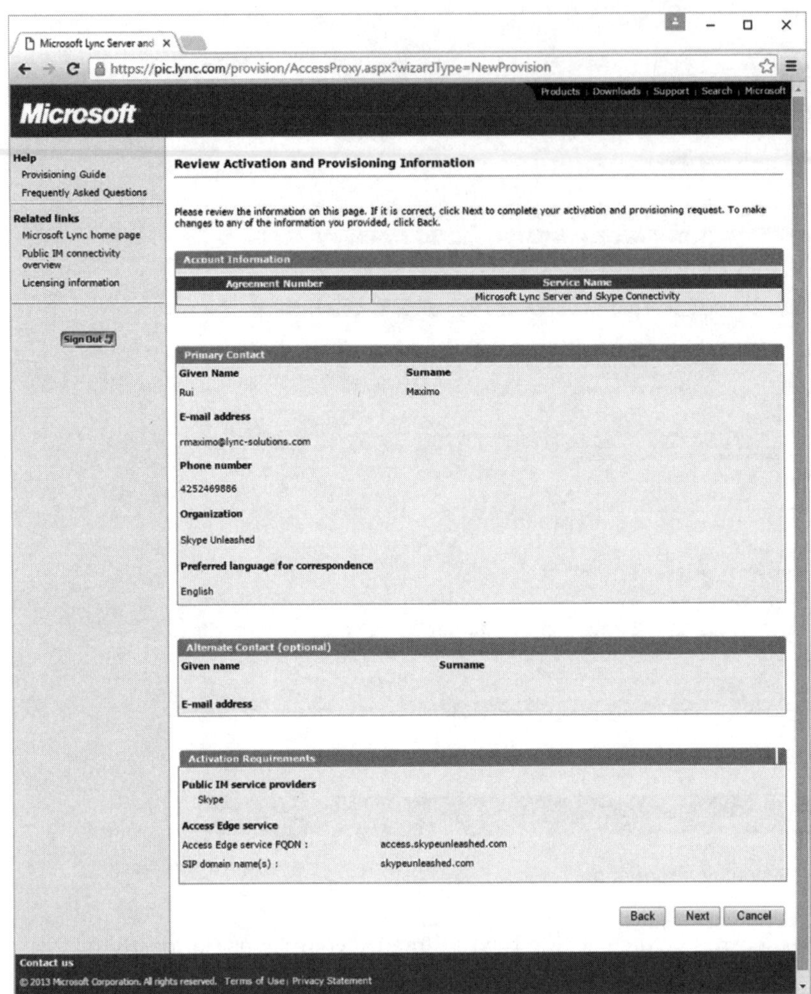

FIGURE 23.19 Review the contact and provisioning information.

This complete the process of requesting Skype Connectivity from Microsoft. Microsoft's response time is surprisingly fast, and the process is often completed within an hour, even though the SLA (service-level agreement) is 24 hours.

Configuring Edge Server

The next step is to configure your Edge Server for federation if it hasn't been already. To enable Skype federation discovery, which is the ability to search Skype for users, as illustrated previously, you must configure your Edge Server for Skype-Skype federation search. This configuration is performed from the Topology Builder.

Open the Skype for Business Server 2015, Topology Builder. If you're setting up a new Edge Server for Skype Connectivity, right-click Edge Pools and click New Edge Pool, as shown in Figure 23.20.

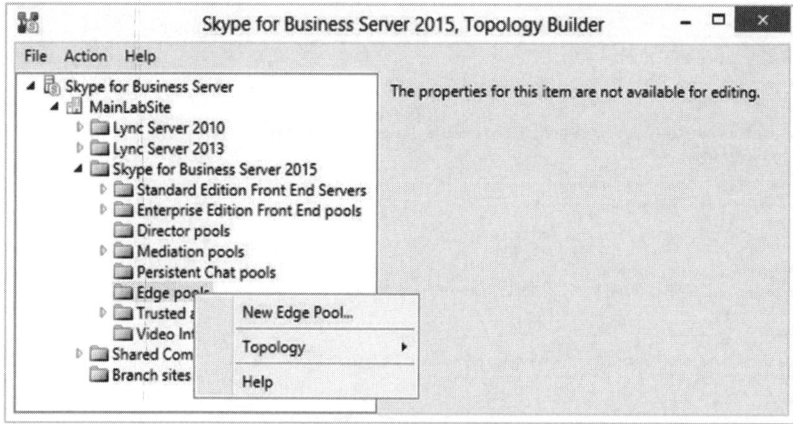

FIGURE 23.20 Skype for Business Server 2015, Topology Builder.

Click Next to start the wizard (see Figure 23.21).

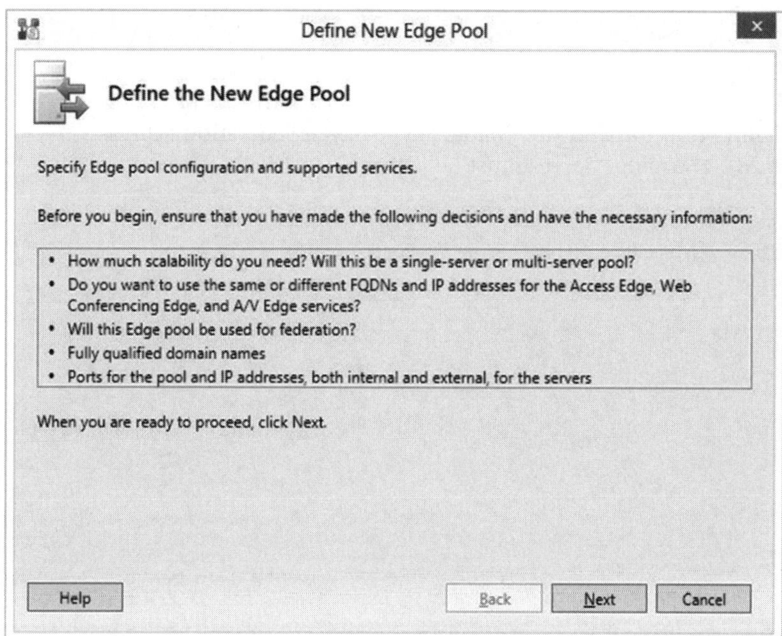

FIGURE 23.21 The Define New Edge Pool Wizard.

Specify the fully qualified domain name (FQDN) of your Edge Server and type of Edge pool and then click Next, as illustrated in Figure 23.22.

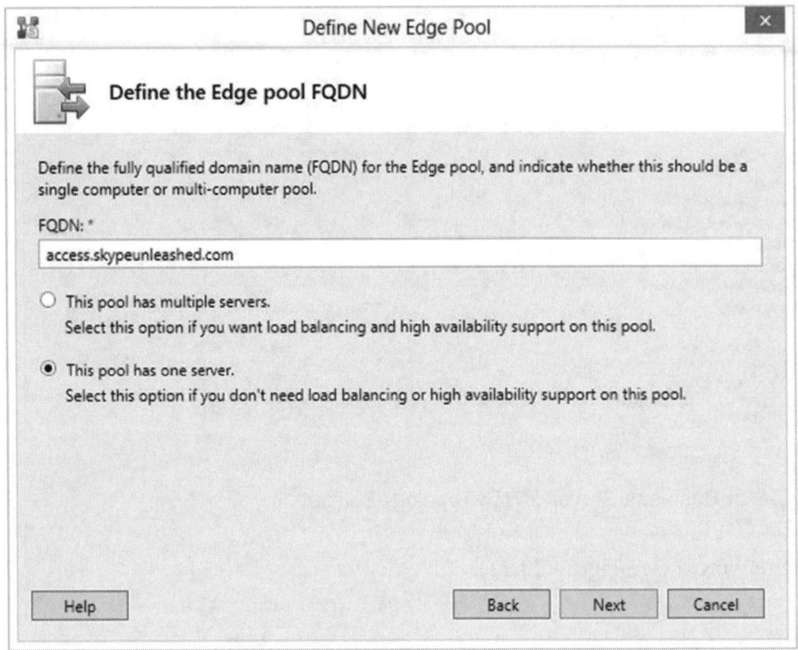

FIGURE 23.22 Edge Pool FQDN.

Click the Enable Federation option and the Enable Skype-Skype Federation Search option (see Figure 23.23). Your Edge Server must be externally accessible over ports 5061 and 4443.

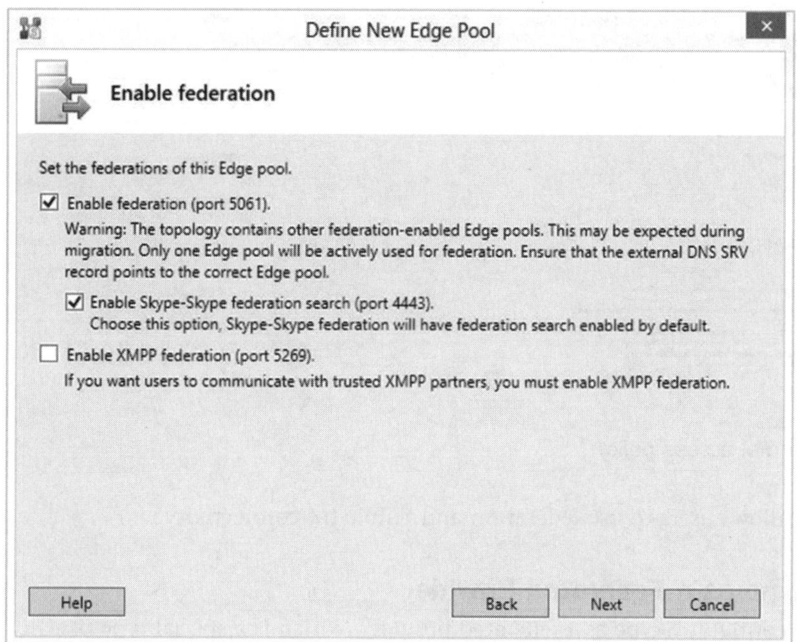

FIGURE 23.23 Enable federation and Skype federation search.

Complete the remainder of configuration process, as required.

To configure an existing Edge Server, right-click your Edge Server in Skype for Business Server 2015, Topology Builder and select Edit Properties. Then check the Enable Federation option and the Enable Skype-Skype Federation Search option.

Enabling External Access Policy

Once your Skype for Business Server 2015 infrastructure is configured for federation, users must be permitted to connect to Skype. This is configured in an external access policy from the Skype for Business Server 2015 Control Panel under Federation and External Access and External Access Policy. It can be configured in the default global policy or a user or site policy defined for your organization. As shown in Figure 23.24, the following options must be selected: Enable Communications with Federated Users and Enable Communications with Public Users.

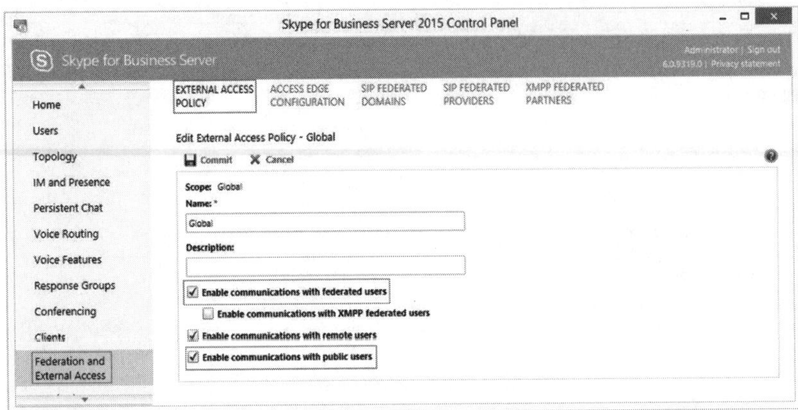

FIGURE 23.24 External access policy.

This configuration allows users to use federation and public IM connectivity.

Configuring Skype as a Federated Provider

The final step is to configure Skype as a federated provider, which is a special type of federation. From the Skype for Business Server 2015 Control Panel, under Federation and External Access, click the Sip Federated Providers tab. Verify that the LyncOnline hosted provider is enabled. This hosted provider specifies the following Edge Server FQDN: sipfed .online.lync.com. You may need to change the default verification level based on your organization's security policy. Figure 23.25 shows a federated provider configuration.

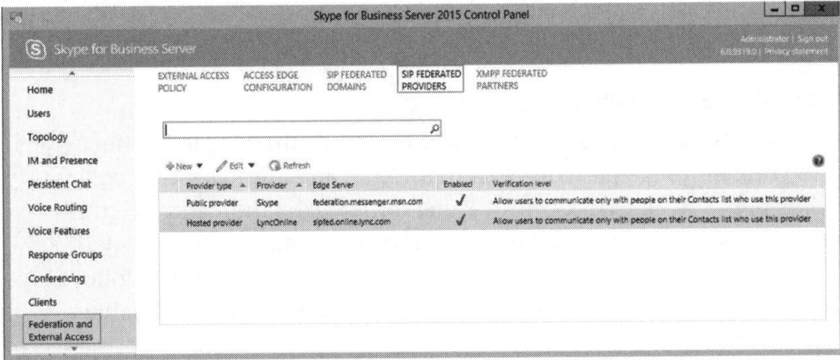

FIGURE 23.25 Federated provider.

This completes the configuration of Skype Connectivity with your on-premises Skype for Business Server 2015 infrastructure. Your users should be able to start communicating with Skype users; however, it's recommended that you test out the connectivity before broadcasting this functionality to your organization.

Configuring Skype Connectivity for Office 365

If your organization uses Skype Online in Office 365, configuring Skype Connectivity is very simple for your cloud users. You'll need to connect to your Office 365 portal as a tenant administrator. Go into the Admin section, as shown in Figure 23.26.

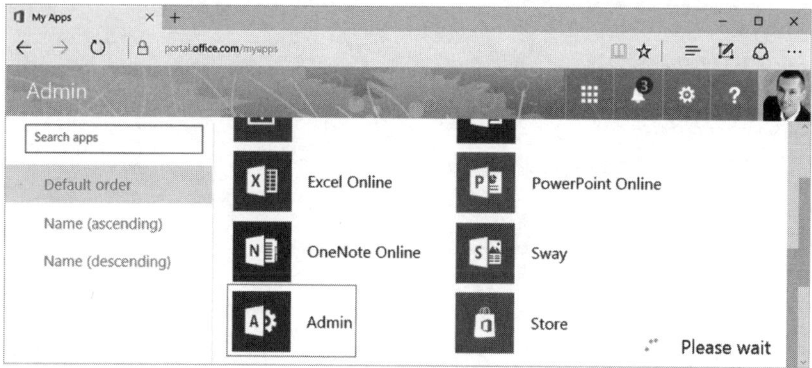

FIGURE 23.26 Office 365 Admin.

From the Office 365 admin center, select Skype for Business. This is shown in the left menu in Figure 23.27.

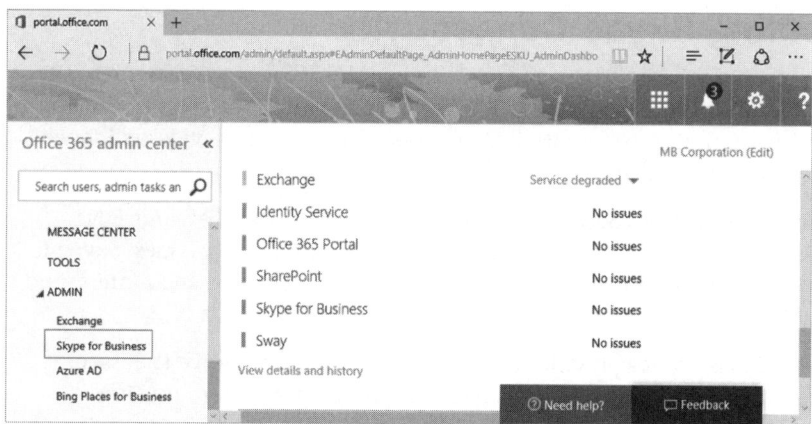

FIGURE 23.27 Office 365 Skype for Business.

From the left menu, click Organization and then click External Communications in the top menu, as illustrated in Figure 23.28. To configure Skype Connectivity for your online users, check the option Let People Use Skype for Business to Communicate with Skype Users Outside Your Organization.

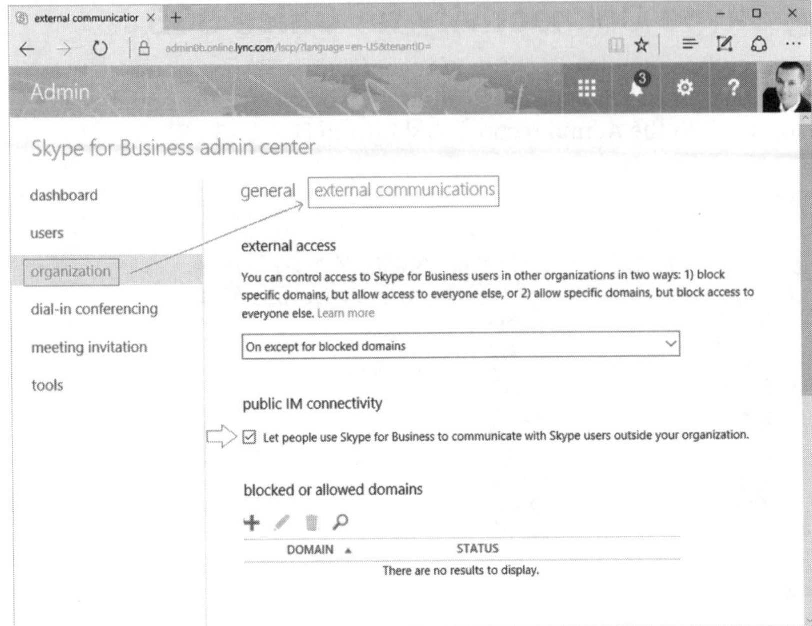

FIGURE 23.28 Enable communication with Skype users.

Troubleshooting Skype Connectivity

If you run into connectivity issues with your on-premises Skype for Business Server 2015 environment, which should be apparent if you're not able to search for users in the Skype Directory or establish communication with a Skype user, this section provides guidance on how to troubleshoot these issues.

First, check the Skype for Business Server 2015 logs in the Event Viewer of your Edge Server. This should be your default reaction when troubleshooting server issues. Skype for Business Server 2015 generally provides detailed information on errors it encounters, and can help you troubleshoot issues.

If, however, the event logs do not provide sufficient information to resolve the issue, capture a SIP trace using clslogger.exe or ocslogger.exe, and open the output using snooper.exe. Select the Messages tab to more easily examine the SIP traffic. Any errors will be highlighted in red. Select an error and evaluate the error message embedded in the SIP message. This should provide you a definite understanding of the root cause.

One possible root cause is DNS, especially if the FQDN of the Access Edge of your Edge Server was not published in the public DNS.

Firewalls can often be blamed. Either the port was not opened on the external firewall or all the firewalls in the SIP federation traffic path. If users cannot search for users in the Skype Directory, examine whether port 4443 is opened externally because your Edge Server connects to Skype on this port. If IM and Presence aren't working, make sure your

Edge Server is reachable externally on port 5061. If audio/video doesn't work, it's likely the default media port range 50,000–59,999 has not been opened on the external firewall.

Certificates can also be the culprit. If you see an error message stating that the connection was actively rejected, it's possible that the certificate configured on the Access Edge of your Edge Server doesn't have a subject alternative name (SAN) matching the Edge Server's public FQDN or the certificate has expired or is not trusted because it wasn't issued by a publicly trusted Certificate Authority. There are many other reasons why your Edge Server's public certificate was rejected.

In general, these are the most common causes of Edge Server external connectivity problems.

Summary

Skype Connectivity provides federation integration between Skype and your on-premises Skype for Business Server 2015 infrastructure or Office 365 tenant. With over 300 million users on Skype, it's likely that the external party you're trying to reach has a Skype account. This integration gives your users the ability communicate with users on the consumer Skype network (B2C). The ramification of this functionality allows users in your organization to have a richer communication experience than is possible with a PSTN call, which was often the only option, or using an alternate consumer platform such as WhatsApp. The richness of this communication with Skype users will continue to increase. The convenience of using a single communications client, Skype for Business 2015, for all your communications and collaboration needs can't be understated, and is a major selling feature.

We're moving past the era of having to use separate clients for Presence, IM, xweb conferencing, audio, video, and application sharing, which has always been very confusing for users and more costly. It's likely that the communications platform with the best integration and reach will be the option chosen by most organizations.

CHAPTER 24

Microsoft Lync for Mac Client

IN THIS CHAPTER

- Installing the Client
- Feature Comparison
- Navigation and Layout
- Managing Contacts
- Managing Groups
- IM Features
- Audio/Video Calls and Conferencing
- Making a Video Call
- Web Conferencing
- Client Integrations with Other Applications
- Tuning Hardware for the Lync:Mac Client
- Troubleshooting

Microsoft has moved to a more "open" stance as of late, providing clients for its major application servers for many platforms. Skype for Business is a great example of this. There currently are clients for all major desktop and mobile platforms. Despite the overwhelming use of Microsoft Windows in the enterprise when compared to the Macintosh (Mac) operating system, Mac usage is slowly increasing in these environments. In addition, in many enterprises, it is the senior-level executives who are using Macs, so support for the Mac with regard to Skype for Business is critical. The current client is the Microsoft Lync for Mac 2011 release. The Mac client supports these core capabilities:

- Instant messaging
- Presence
- PC-to-PC calls
- Enterprise Voice functions
- Video conferencing
- Web conferencing
- Desktop sharing

The Lync:Mac 2011 client has many similarities with the Windows client, but is still missing a few key features. In this chapter, we compare the feature and functionality differences between the Lync:Mac client and the Skype for Business PC desktop client and provide honest guidance where applicable.

Note that the Microsoft Lync:Mac client is a separate client from the Microsoft Messenger client, which is part if the Office:Mac 2011 installer. Microsoft Messenger cannot connect to Lync and is meant for the pubic IM services provided by Microsoft. Microsoft Lync:Mac is an add-on to Office 2011 that allows for connectivity to Lync Server 2010 through Skype for Business Server 2015 and offers additional integration into Office 2011 and Office 2016 applications.

Installing the Client

The Lync:Mac 2011 client is considered an "Enterprise" client and as such is not available as a consumer download; it is available as part of the Microsoft Volume Licensing Center, Software Assurance, and through an Office 365 subscription.

The following link provides more information on obtaining the Lync:Mac 2011 client:

> https://support.office.com/en-us/article/Set-up-Skype-for-Business-Lync-for-Mac-2011-for-Office-365-ae3ebd0e-a1a7-48cf-9350-36b144dc5f88

To install Office 2011, perform the following steps:

1. Download the Lync:Mac 2011 installer; typically this will be a file with a .DMG extension.
2. Double-click the .DMG file.
3. Double-click the Lync Installer icon, shown in Figure 24.1.

FIGURE 24.1 Running the Lync Installer.

4. The first screen is the Welcome to the Microsoft Lync for Mac Installer screen. The installer will guide you through the installation process. Click Continue.
5. On the Software License Agreement screen, read the licensing agreement if you are looking for some fun. Click Continue.

6. Click Agree to accept the license agreement.
7. On the Change Install Location screen, you may choose which hard drive will be used for the installation. Click Change Install Location if you want to change installation location, or click Install to accept the recommended location.
8. When prompted, enter your Mac user password to authorize the installation. Click Install Software.
9. The Mac client installer will continue. You can view the progress through the progress indicator.
10. You will be prompted when the installation is successful. Click Close.

There should now be a Blue "L" icon in the Dock, as shown in Figure 24.2. Click it to launch the Lync:Mac 2011 client.

FIGURE 24.2 Lync:Mac running in the Dock.

When the Microsoft Lync:Mac client launches, you may be asked again to accept the license agreement. Click Accept. Lync:Mac now offers to make itself the default application for the following functions:

- Presence
- Telephone calls
- Conferences

For each offer, check the box marked Do Not Show This Message Again and then click Use Lync.

The Lync:Mac 2011 client will load and prompt you for an email address (SIP URI). It also provides an option to sign in using a certain status (such as Busy or Do Not Disturb), as shown in Figure 24.3.

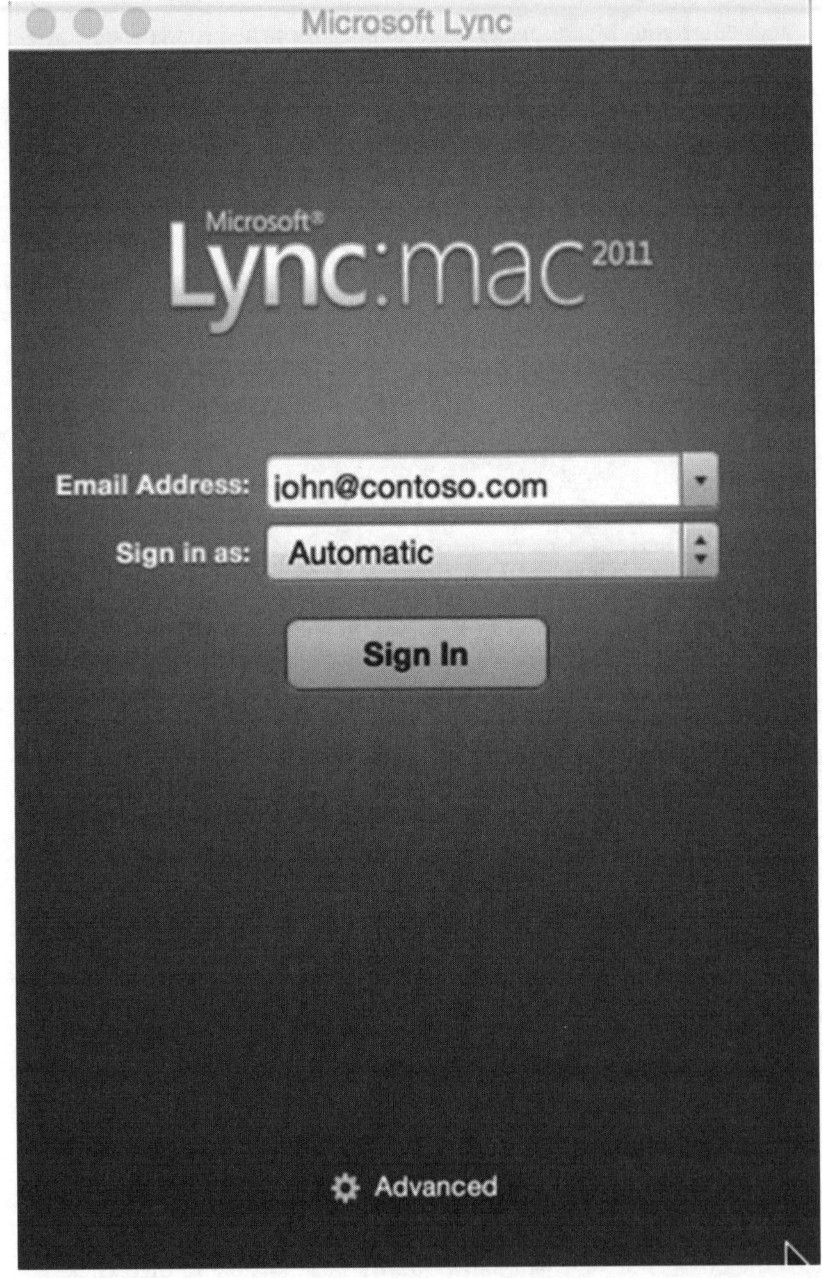

FIGURE 24.3 Lync:Mac login screen.

NOTE

The client looks for the user's SIP URI, not the user's email address, which in some environments may not match.

After you are signed in, the client populates with any contacts added to the list and any user-created groups, as shown in Figure 24.4.

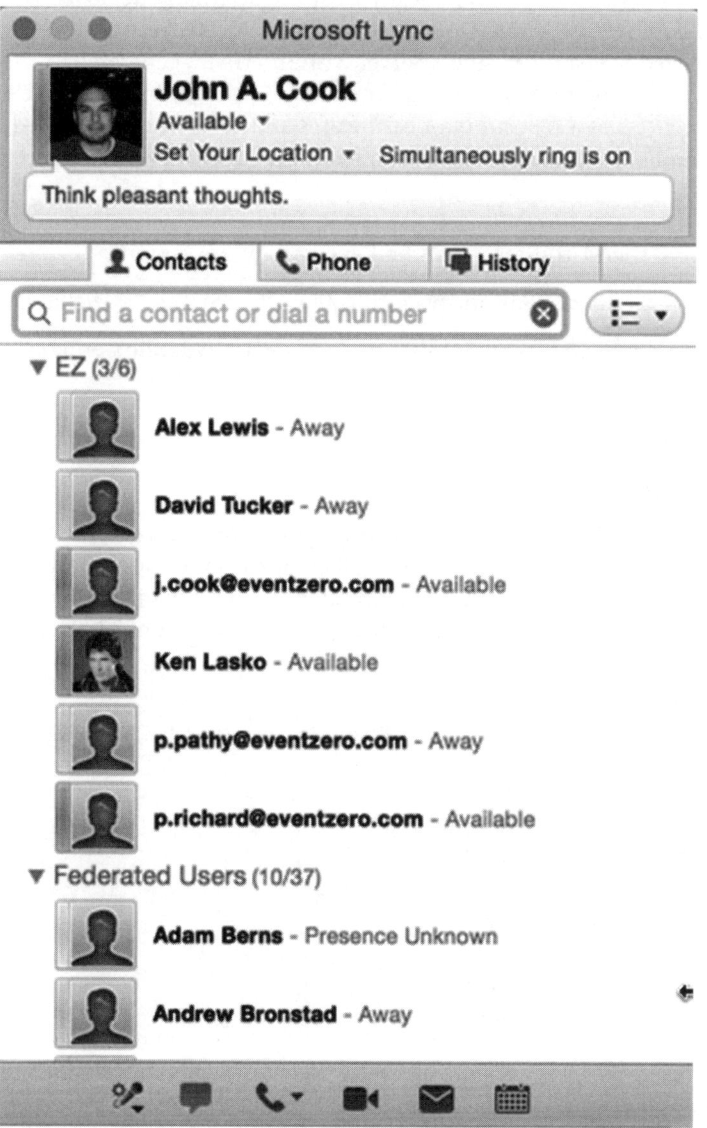

FIGURE 24.4 Lync:Mac contact list.

In the same manner as the Windows client, the Mac client will attempt to use the SRV lookup process to locate the Skype for Business pool or server. If the necessary SRV records are not available or configured in the Skype for Business deployment, the Lync:Mac client also has the option to manually configure the connection endpoint; however, using the correct SRV records is the preferred. This process is covered in detail in Chapter 10, "Dependent Services."

Dealing with Certificates

Whereas domain-joined Windows PCs will automatically trust the internally deployed Certificate Authority, Macs do not trust Active Directory–based Certificate Authorities by default. If you have deployed Skype for Business Server with internally generated certificates, you will need to have the root and any intermediates imported into the Mac's Keychain. The Keychain functions as a repository of certificates and other security-related items. This is a relatively simple process and can be completed with the following steps:

1. Open Finder.
2. Expand Applications and then Utilities. Select the Keychain Access option.
3. Drag the applicable Root Certificate Authority certificate to the "System" Keychain.
4. When prompted, type a name and password that has administrative rights on your Mac and then click Modify Keychain.

Feature Comparison

The Lync:Mac 2011 client improves on many previous features and introduces some new ones as well, as detailed in Table 24.1. In addition, an overall comparison to the Windows Skype for Business client is included. Feature support is indicated by check marks in the table. For more information, see https://technet.microsoft.com/en-us/library/dn933896.aspx.

TABLE 24.1 Client Comparison

Feature/Capability	Skype for Business	Lync for Mac 2011
Enhanced Presence Support		
Publish and view status	✓	✓
View status based on calendar free/busy information	✓	✓
View status notes and Out of Office messages	✓	✓
Add a custom location	✓	
Add a custom note	✓	✓
Use a photo from any public site for My Picture	✓[1]	
Contacts and Contact Groups Support		
View Contacts list	✓	✓
Modify Contacts list	✓	✓

Tag contacts for status change alerts	✓	
Control privacy relationships	✓	
Search the corporate address book	✓	✓
Search Microsoft Outlook contacts	✓	✓
Manage contact groups	✓	✓
Expand distribution groups	✓	
Search for Response Groups	✓[2]	
Display recent contacts group	✓	
Display current conversations group	✓	
Display alternate contact views (for example, tile)	✓	✓
Sort contacts by Group, Relationship, or New (people who've added you to their Contacts list)	✓	
Sort contacts by Status (availability)	✓	✓
IM Support		
Initiate IM with a contact	✓	✓
Navigate among multiple IM conversations/track multiple conversations in a single tabbed window	✓	✓
Log IM conversations in Outlook	✓	Saved in Lync for Mac
Initiate an email to a contact	✓	✓
Use prepared conversation templates		
Spelling checker	✓	✓
Skill search (with SharePoint Server integration)	✓[3]	
Persistent Chat (Group Chat) integration	✓[4]	
Escalate a Persistent Chat room to a Lync Meeting with one click	✓[4]	
Inline pictures of sender and receiver in IM window	✓	
Send ink messages		
Receive ink messages	✓	
Conferencing Support		
Add computer audio	✓	✓
Add video	✓	✓
View multiparty video (gallery view)	✓	
Use in-meeting presenter controls	✓	✓
Access detailed meeting roster	✓	✓
Participate in multiparty IM	✓	✓
Share the desktop (if enabled)	✓	✓[5]

(Continued)

TABLE 24.1 (*Continued*)

Feature/Capability	Skype for Business	Lync for Mac 2011
Share a program (if enabled)	✓	View only
Add anonymous participants (if enabled)	✓	✓
Use dial-in audio conferencing	✓[6]	✓
Initiate a Meet Now meeting	✓	✓
Add and present Microsoft PowerPoint files	✓	View only; annotations not available[7]
Navigate Microsoft PowerPoint files	✓	✓
Add and edit OneNote meeting notes	✓	
Use a whiteboard	✓	
Conduct polls	✓	
Upload files to share with others	✓	✓
Schedule a meeting or conference	Outlook or Lync Web Scheduler	Outlook
Create public meetings with static meeting IDs from Outlook	✓	
Q&A Manager	✓	
Telephony Support		
Initiate a voice call	✓[8]	✓
Click to call a contact	✓[8]	✓
Transfer a call	✓[8]	✓
Manage call forwarding	✓[9]	✓
Manage team call settings	✓[9]	
Manage delegates	✓[9]	✓
Initiate a call to a Response Group	✓[9]	
Support emergency services (E911)	✓[9]	
Connect to voice mail, set up or change greeting	✓[9]	
Make calls on behalf of another contact (manager/delegate scenario)	✓[9]	
Handle another's calls if configured as a delegate	✓[9]	
Manage a high volume of calls		
Call park	✓[9]	
Group call pickup	✓[9]	
External Users Support		
Initiate IM with a public contact	✓	✓
Initiate IM with a federated contact	✓	✓
Conduct two-party or multiparty calls with external users	✓[10]	✓

Recording Support		
Client-side recording of audio, video, application sharing, desktop sharing, and uploaded content	✓[11]	
Client-side recording of file transfers, shared OneNote pages, and PowerPoint annotations	✓[12]	
Select preferred recording resolution	✓	
Archiving, Compliance, and Logging Support		
Archiving of IM conversations in Outlook Conversation History	✓[13]	Saved in Lync for Mac
Client-side archiving of audio, video, application sharing, desktop sharing, and uploaded content	✓[13]	
Client-side archiving of file transfers, shared OneNote pages, and PowerPoint annotations	✓[14]	
Access sign-in logs from Lync icon in the taskbar	✓	

[1]*This feature is not available in Skype for Business Online and Office 365.*

[2]*This feature is not available in Skype for Business Online and Office 365.*

[3]*On-premises Skype for Business Server and on-premises SharePoint 2013 are required for skill search.*

[4]*Persistent Chat is not available for Skype for Business Online and Office 365.*

[5]*Participants cannot control desktops that are shared by Lync for Mac 2011 or Communicator for Mac 2011 users. Lync for Mac 2011 and Communicator for Mac 2011 users can control desktops shared by Windows users.*

[6]*This feature requires an audio conferencing provider for Skype for Business Online and Office 365.*

[7]*The Lync for Mac 2011 client cannot view Microsoft Office 2013 PowerPoint presentations when they have been shared in a conference by the Skype for Business Web App.*

[8]*This feature is available for PC-to-PC calls only in Skype for Business Online and Office 365.*

[9]*This feature is not available in Skype for Business Online and Office 365.*

[10]*This feature is not available in Skype for Business Online and Office 365.*

[11]*Recording is unavailable in certain Skype for Business Online and Office 365 standalone plans. Recording requires full Skype for Business client rights.*

[12]*Recording of file transfers, shared OneNote pages, and PowerPoint annotations is unavailable in Skype for Business Online and Office 365.*

[13]*For Skype for Business Online and Office 365 users, this feature requires Exchange Online and is controlled by the user's Exchange mailbox In-Place Hold attribute.*

[14]*Archiving of file transfers, shared OneNote pages, and PowerPoint annotations is unavailable in Skype for Business Online and Office 365.*

Navigation and Layout

For users not familiar with the OS X operating system, options that are normally found in the client interface on a PC are typically accessed through the menu bar at the top of the screen. The menu bar displayed is for the application that is currently in focus. In the case of Lync:Mac 2011, the options across the top of the application include the following:

- Lync
- Edit
- View
- Status
- Contact
- Conversation
- Window
- Help

The options for the more salient of these menu items are outlined in the following sections.

Lync

The Lync menu includes basic program commands for the Lync:Mac application, including the following:

- **About Lync**—Gives version information and a summary of the end-user license agreement.
- **Preferences**—Enables you to set general application preferences for Lync:Mac 2011. It includes the submenus Appearance, General, Phone Calls, Account, Alerts, Audio, Video, History, and Photos.
- **Quit Lync**—Quits and exits the Lync:Mac 2011 application.

Edit

The following typical editing commands are located in the Edit menu:

- **Undo**—Undoes the previous action, if possible.
- **Cut**—Cuts the selected text.
- **Copy**—Copies the selected text.
- **Paste**—Pastes from the clipboard.
- **Clear**—Clears the selected area.
- **Select all**—Selects everything in the active window.

- **Spelling**—Offers, via a submenu, the options Show Spelling and Grammar as well as Check Spelling While Typing.
- **Special Characters–Emoji and Symbols**—If emoji are your thing, and you can't live without them, selecting this option will bring up a separate window where you can select from many different images.

View

The View menu enables you to change the way the client appears and how contacts are organized. Here are the options available in the View menu:

- **View by Name**—Organizes contacts by name. Note that there is no apparent order to the names; it's not alphabetical.
- **View by Group**—Organizes contacts into user-created groups.
- **Use Compact View**—Removes user photos and displays only the Presence icon for users. Also does not show status messages or out-of-office updates.
- **Show Status Text**—Shows your status in text to the right of your name, if this option is checked.
- **Show Friendly Name**—Shows the display name if this option is checked; otherwise, shows your SIP URI.
- **Show Offline Contacts**—Includes contacts who are offline in the your contact list. If this is option is unselected, offline contacts are hidden from the contact list.
- **Collapse All Groups**—Collapses all expanded groups. Great for cleaning up the user interface in a hurry.
- **Show All Fields**—Shows any currently hidden fields.
- **Show Message Timestamp**—Shows the timestamp when each IM message is sent or received.

Status

The Status menu allows for another way, apart from within the application itself, to change your Presence status as well as sign out of Lync:Mac 2011. The available status settings are Available, Busy, Do Not Disturb, Off Work, Be Right Back, Appear Away, and Reset Status.

Contact

The Contact menu lists several ways of contacting a user when their contact is selected in the Lync:Mac application as well as manipulating the contact list. The options include the following:

- **Send an Instant Message**—Sends an IM to the selected contact.
- **Call**—Calls the selected contact. The submenu allows you to choose to call a user's published number via PSTN or a Lync call.

- **Send an Email Message**—Opens the default email client and sends an email addressed to the selected contact.
- **Schedule a Meeting**—Opens a Lync meeting invite via email and adds the selected user to the To field.
- **Move Contact To**—A submenu expands with a list of contact groups you have created within your Skype for Business address book in order to move the contact to a different group.
- **Copy Contact To**—Opens a submenu with all the contact groups you have created. It enables you to copy the contact to a different group.
- **Block**—Blocks all interaction to or from the selected contact.
- **Remove from Group**—Removes the selected contact from the group that is currently expanded.
- **Create New Group**—Creates a new contact group in the Lync:Mac 2011 client. After clicking this option, you are asked to create a name for the new group.
- **Rename Group**—While a contact group is selected, this option enables you to rename an existing contact group. (Available only when a group is selected.)
- **Delete Group**—While a contact group is selected, this option enables you to delete an existing contact group. (Available only when a group is selected.)
- **Tag for Status Change Alerts**—Similar to the Windows client, choosing this option for a contact will "tag" that contact so when that contact comes online or changes status, Lync:Mac will notify you of this change with an additional "toast" pop-up.
- **View Past Conversations**—Choosing this option will launch a separate window showing all previous conversations with the selected contact. This is only available if the Save Conversations to Outlook option is also checked.
- **View Contact Card**—Displays the contact card for the selected contact.

Conversation

This menu outlines the options related to conversations.

- **Invite By Name or Phone Number**—This option will become available during an open conversation with a contact. Choosing this option launches a separate dialog box where you can invite other users via their contact or dial out to a phone number if you are "Enterprise Voice enabled" and your Skype for Business Deployment is connected to the PSTN.
- **Meet Now**—Enables you to start an ad hoc conference with audio, video, or desktop sharing through the expanded menu bar options. This is similar to a scheduled conference, and you will be able to provide a meeting link URL and dial-in info if configured.

- **Join Online Meeting by URL**—Why this feature is missing in the Windows client is unclear. This option allows you to join a Lync meeting by typing or pasting a meeting link URL.
- **Save**—Saves the content of the current conversation.
- **Save as Web Page**—Saves the content of the current conversation as HTML.
- **Print**—Prints the content of the current conversation.

Window

The Window menu contains the following options for window management:

- **Minimize**—Minimizes the current window.
- **Zoom**—Zooms in on the current window.
- **Close**—Closes the current window. (Note that this does not exit the client if the main Lync:Mac application is the current window.)
- **Contact List**—Shows the main Lync:Mac application with the contact list in focus.
- **Conversation History**—Shows the conversation history. (Note that this includes only conversations on this Mac. There is no integration with the conversation history folder in Exchange/Outlook.)
- **Bring All to Front**—Brings all Lync windows to the front.

Help

The Help menu allows you to search for help by topic and also be directed to a link on Microsoft.com for additional Lync:Mac help. It also enables you to manually check for updates for the Lync:Mac client and other Microsoft Office applications.

Managing Contacts

Contact discovery in Microsoft Outlook is typically done by searching the address book for a user by name in a new message or the address book to select to send a message to that contact. The Microsoft Lync:Mac client follows this paradigm by allowing you to search for a contact by name.

Locate the search bar by looking for the magnifying glass in the Lync:Mac client. Type the user's name, and the contacts stored in the address book will be searched for a match as you type. Right-clicking the desired contact object gives you several options to add the contact object to any contact groups you have created. Once added, the user will receive a notification that you have added their contact, and they can confirm or deny the request. If the request is confirmed, you will begin to see Presence information for the contact.

Once a contact is added to your contact list, you can move the contact from one group to another group by clicking and dragging the contact. In addition, by hovering over the name of the contact, you can see any notes as well as the user's contact photo, as shown in Figure 24.5.

FIGURE 24.5 Lync:Mac contact details.

Managing Groups

The Microsoft Lync:Mac client enables users to organize contacts by placing them inside contact groups. By default, the group is Other Contacts.

Groups show a status of how many contacts there are in that group and how many are currently online. You can expand the group by clicking the triangle to the left of the name to expand the contact group. Right-clicking the group itself will bring up some additional options, such as Call, which will call all contacts within the group from the Lync:Mac client.

IM Features

The Lync:Mac instant messaging (IM) functionality behaves similarly to any other IM client. The Presence state of the user you are trying to contact via IM is displayed. Users have access to the typical features, such as altering the font, color, and size of the text, as well as a menu of emoticons. Starting an IM conversation is as simple as double-clicking a contact. Doing so launches the IM window, as shown in Figure 24.6.

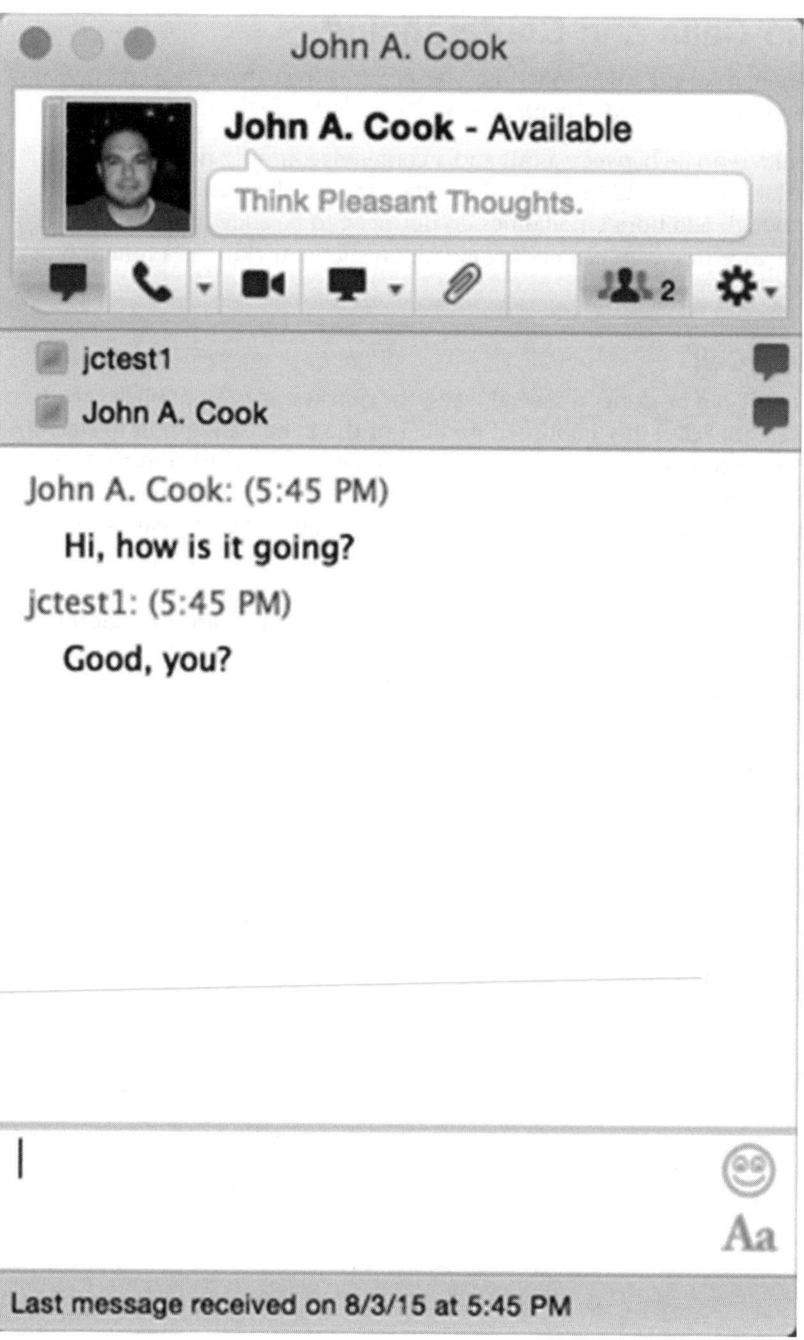

FIGURE 24.6 Instant Messaging conversation.

Audio/Video Calls and Conferencing

Another core component of the Microsoft Lync:Mac client is the capability to participate in Skype for Business audio and video conferences.

It is important to differentiate between a call and a conference; if only two parties are involved, it is considered a call. Adding any additional users escalates that call to a conference. Even though additional modalities do not need to be added for a call to be escalated to a conference (for example, adding a desktop share), it really is a function of the number of users.

Making an Audio Call

Initiating an audio call can be done in several ways; the quickest is to right-click the contact and choose Call. Select any published number or the Lync Call option to start the call. Clicking the user's contact object will also bring up the contact card, and clicking the microphone icon, as shown in Figure 24.7, will initiate a Skype for Business call. Clicking any of the published numbers will also dial that number. When a call is initiated, the contact receives a pop-up and an audio notification and has the option to answer, decline, or redirect the call. Answer and Decline, not surprisingly, answer and decline the call, respectively, whereas Redirect gives the option to reply via IM, redirect to another number such as a mobile number or to voicemail, or to set one's status to Do Not Disturb. Accepting the call updates both users' status to In a Call.

24

(a)

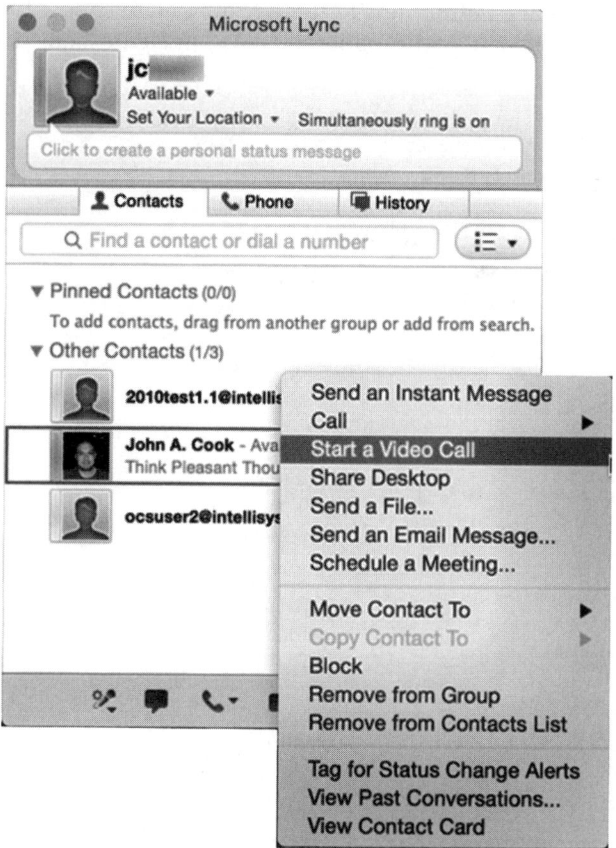

(b)

FIGURE 24.7 Initiating a call.

If you are already in an IM conversation, you can initiate a Skype for Business call by clicking the telephone icon or the drop-down button next to the microphone to choose to call additional published numbers—over the PSTN. This option is shown in Figure 24.8.

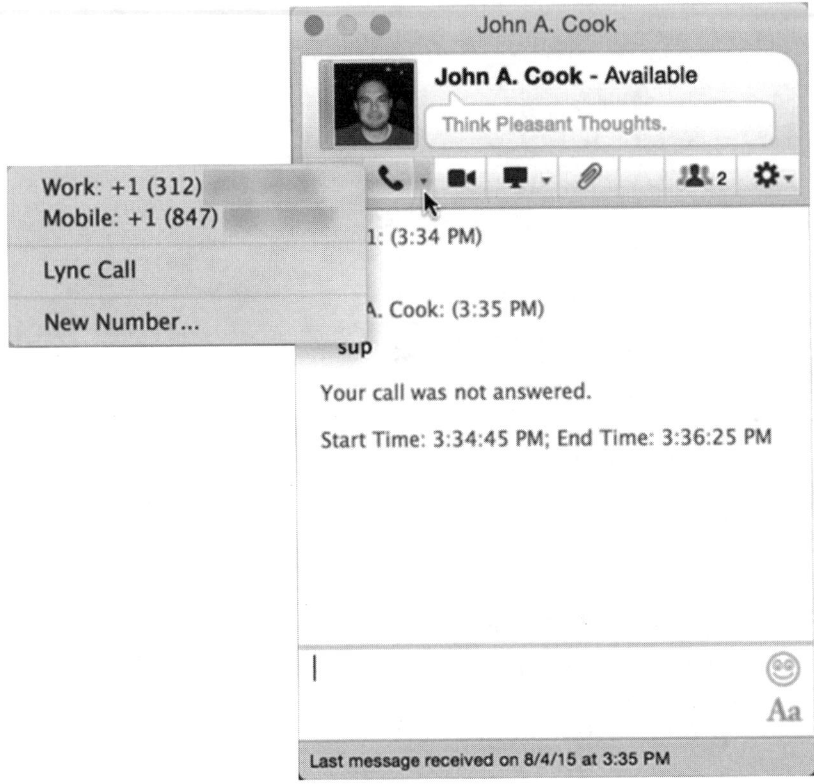

FIGURE 24.8 Calling a Lync contact.

Making a Video Call

Initiating a video call can be done in several ways; the quickest is to right click the contact and choose Start a Video Call. Select any published number or the Lync Call option to start the call. Clicking the user's contact object will also bring up the contact card, and clicking the camera icon will initiate a Skype for Business video call. When a call is initiated, the contact receives a pop-up and an audio notification and has the option to accept, decline, or redirect the call. Answer and Decline, not surprisingly, answer and decline the call, respectively, whereas Redirect gives the option to reply via IM, redirect to another number such as a mobile number or voicemail, or to set one's status to Do Not Disturb.

When the video call is connected, the caller will automatically send their video, but the recipient will need to click the arrow on the video preview box located in the video window in order to start sending their video to the caller. The video preview box can be moved anywhere within the video window. Right-clicking anywhere in the video window shows two options: Show My Video Preview, which turns on or off the video preview box, and Start My Video, which starts and stops the local video, the same as clicking the arrow.

Inside the video window are several buttons, including the following:

- Hang Up
- Put Call on Hold
- Show Keypad
- Transfer Call
- Enter Full Screen
- Click to Mute
- Change the Audio Device for This Call

Enter Full Screen expands the video windows to encompass the entire screen, and the row of control buttons becomes a floating toolbar that defaults to the lower left of the screen.

Clicking Hang Up ends the call and closes the window on the recipient side or returns to an IM window if the call was initiated from an IM conversation.

Web Conferencing

The Lync:Mac client can be used to participate in the full range of Skype for Business web conferencing modalities—voice, video and desktop sharing. Additional notes on integration with Microsoft Outlook are provided in this section.

Joining a Conference

In most corporate environments, Skype for Business meeting invites tend to be sent via email as meeting requests from Microsoft Exchange or Office 365. Microsoft Outlook for Mac can be used to schedule a Skype for Business meeting request. This is shown as an "Online Meeting" in Outlook for Mac. When a user creates a new Online Meeting request, a conference is defined within in Skype for Business and a web URL for the meeting is placed in the body of the meeting invite. Recipients will click to join the meeting, which will launch each user's default web browser. The user will be presented with the option of joining via web browser or the Lync:Mac client, if it is installed. The Outlook for Mac meeting request is shown in Figure 24.9.

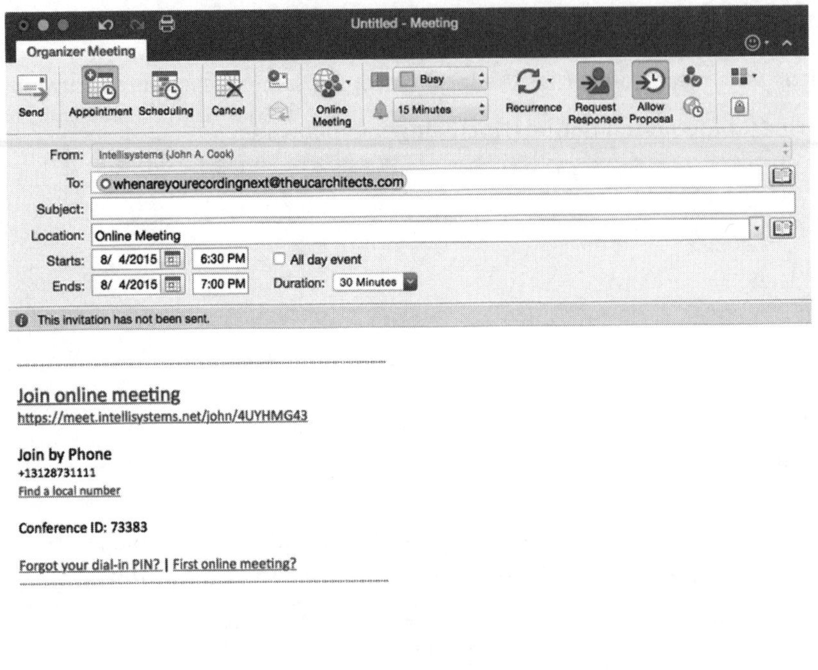

FIGURE 24.9 Invitation to join a Lync web conference with Outlook for Mac.

Client Integration with Other Applications

Like its Windows counterpart, the Lync:Mac client will share the logged-in user's Presence via an API to other applications, including Microsoft Outlook for Mac. These integration capabilities are discussed in the following sections.

Integration with Outlook

As stated earlier, when Office for Mac is installed along with the Lync:Mac client, the Lync:Mac client will share Presence information with other applications, including Outlook for Mac. For example, when an email is received in Outlook for Mac, you will see Presence information for any Skype for Business users who are listed in the To, CC, and From fields. By clicking a name within Outlook Mac that has Presence information, you will be shown the user's contact card, as shown in Figure 24.10.

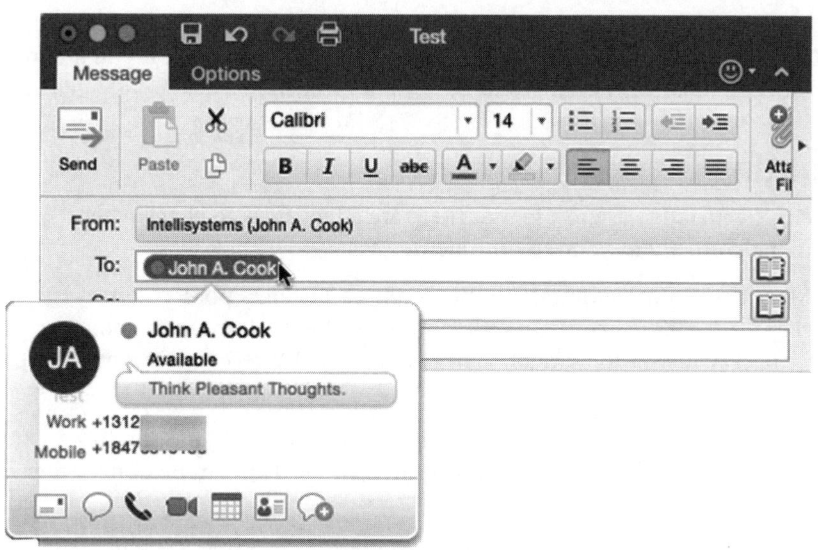

FIGURE 24.10 Office contact card.

Shown in the contact card is the user's display name, title, Presence, calendar information, status message, and any published phone numbers. The available options include the following:

- Send Mail
- Send an Instant Message
- Call Contact
- Start a Video Call
- Schedule a Meeting
- Open Outlook Contact
- Add Contact to Instant Messaging Contact List

Send an Instant Message is self-explanatory; this will start an IM session with a user. Clicking Call Contact results in the contact getting a pop-up indicating that the other person is requesting a Skype for Business audio call.

Clicking Start a Video Call results in the contact getting a pop-up indicating that the other person is requesting a video connection. Schedule a Meeting will launch an Outlook for Mac meeting request and add the user to the To: field. Finally, clicking Add Contact to Instant Messenger Contact List adds contacts that are not currently in your contact list.

The Lync:Mac client will also access your calendar information if your mailbox is hosted on Exchange or Office 365 and update your status accordingly. For example, if you are in a meeting, your status automatically changes to Busy (In a Meeting).

Troubleshooting

The Lync:Mac client is generally easy to use, but there are a few areas to check when things are not working correctly in your environment:

- If the Lync:Mac client cannot connect to the Skype for Business pool or server, try setting the client to a manual configuration and enter the pool or server name. If you can connect while set to manual, verify your DNS SRV records are configured properly.
- If you cannot connect, you can verify basic port availability by attempting to connect to TCP Port 5061 on your Skype for Business pool. This can be done using the OS X Terminal, for example.
- Another excellent way to check on the network connection to Skype for Business Server 2015 is the `netstat` command, also available through the Terminal app. If a connection on TCP 5061 is in a `Syn_sent` state, it means the Skype for Business Server is unavailable. If the connection is sitting at `Time_Wait`, odds are that the application is having issues. It means that the connection was acknowledged, but the application is not sending data.
- If you are using certificates from your own CA and external users are having issues connecting, they might not trust your root CA. The public certificate from the Root CA needs to be imported into the Trusted Root store in Keychain. If external systems trust the Root CA but are not able to reach the Certificate Revocation List for the CA, they will fail to connect.
- Similar to the Windows client, from Lync through Skype for Business, there is a local log file that records the entire SIP conversation and is extremely useful for troubleshooting issues from the client's perspective. To enable the log, open the Lync:Mac Preferences pane by selecting Preferences from the Lync:Mac menu bar. Select the General tab and under Logging ensure the Turn on Logging for Troubleshooting option is selected. This is shown in Figure 24.11.

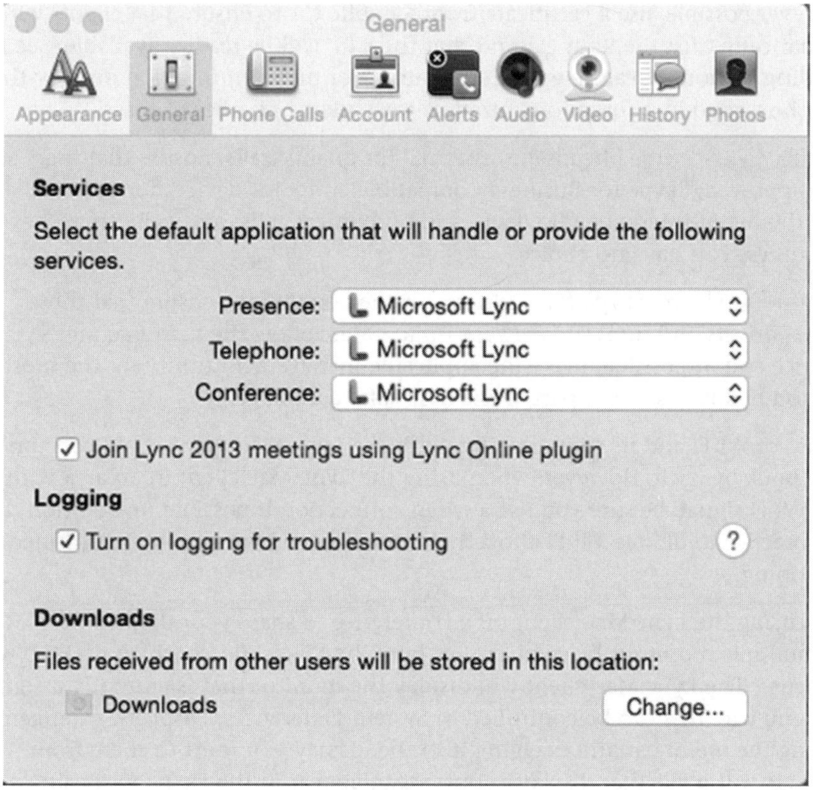

FIGURE 24.11 Turn on logging for troubleshooting.

Once this option is selected, log out and log back into the Lync:Mac client. The log will then be created and data will be written to it. The location of the log file is

```
users/username/Library/Logs.Microsoft-Lync-0.log
```

The raw text file can be opened with any text editor, but the best way to look at the contents is with the Snooper utility on a PC. You may be familiar with this utility, which is part of the Lync Server 2013 and Skype for Business Server Debugging Tools application. This application can also be installed on a Windows workstation to get access to the Snooper utility. Using Snooper, open the log file from your Lync:Mac client and, behold!, all the secrets are yours.

Best Practices

By following a few best practices, you can optimize the Microsoft Lync:Mac experience for your users. Ensuring an overall quality Skype for Business experience is dependent on many factors:

- Whenever possible, use a certificate from a public CA to ensure that clients will automatically trust the Root CA and that the CRL will be readily available. See the preceding section, "Dealing with Certificates," for more information on why this might be a good idea for an organization with a large number of Macs.
- A quality Lync-certified headset is essential for quality calls. Ensure that users are using approved, Skype for Business–compatible endpoint devices for any media calls. Limit the use of internal audio devices to noncritical calls, but really try to never use them unless you have no choice.
- In addition to using Skype for Business–certified endpoints, ensure that these devices' drivers and firmware are kept up to date. Follow the manufacturer's guidance and, if possible, make the applicable management utility for the most common endpoints in use part of the base software image.
- The use of Wi-Fi and its supportability with the Lync:Mac client could consume an entire book by itself. However, when using the Lync:Mac client in an area with a weak Wi-Fi signal, be sure you use a wired connection if possible. In addition, it is a good practice to disable Wi-Fi altogether once a wired connection is confirmed to be functioning.
- When using the Lync:Mac client on a conference to share your desktop on a Mac with multiple monitors, be cognizant of how the Mac chooses which desktop will be in "focus." The Lync:Mac client will display the monitor that is currently assigned the menu bar. This can be controlled in System Preferences, Displays, Arrangement. Clicking the menu bar and dragging it to the display you want to share from Lync:Mac will make that display's contents to appear in the Skype for Business conference.
- Finish your meetings with the Remove Everyone and End the Meeting function from the People menu.
- Consider using Managed Preferences to block specific features or functions of the Lync:Mac client. This is essentially the equivalent of the options that are set on a Skype for Business Windows client through in-band policy. These policies apply local settings to enable or disable features within the Lync:Mac client. Think of it as the registry for the Lync:Mac client.

Summary

As with other platforms, such as Windows and web browsers, Microsoft provides a client for Mac users. Although it does not have complete feature parity with the Windows client, it does allow for users to communicate via instant message and Enterprise Voice, using an interface that is easy to navigate and use by those familiar with the Mac platform. Additionally, troubleshooting the client is straightforward, with many of the same steps used with other client platforms.

CHAPTER 25

Mobile Clients

IN THIS CHAPTER

Microsoft introduced mobile client support with Office Communications Server on the Windows Mobile Platform. In Lync Server 2010 this mobile experience was enhanced and introduced to all major smartphone platforms. This includes Windows Phone, Android, and Apple iOS.

This chapter provides an overview of the new mobile features introduced in Skype for Business Server 2015, technical overview of the mobility architecture, and deployment details to be mindful of.

Introducing New Mobile Features

Skype for Business Server 2015 introduces a number of improvements that make the mobile client experience almost comparable to the desktop client experience, and much needed. These improvements include the following:

- ▶ Skype interface
- ▶ Contact list management
- ▶ Server-side conversation history
- ▶ Auto-accept incoming IMs
- ▶ Content viewing for Android clients
- ▶ PowerPoint uploading and presenting for iPad clients
- ▶ Notification of upcoming Skype meetings
- ▶ Call back on poor network connections
- ▶ Enhanced security

Similar to the desktop client, the mobile client has adopted the Skype look and feel, a reduced number of clicks to find commonly used features, and a better dialing experience.

Skype for Business 2015 Mobile introduces several new features, such as the ability to view upcoming Skype meetings. To make it easier to view upcoming Skype meetings and join them, the new mobile client displays Skype meetings directly within Skype for Business 2015 Mobile without having to switch to a calendar application.

Joining Skype meetings as a guest is now possible from the Android version. Skype for Business Mobile Android reaches parity with the mobile client of iOS. Android users can now view content shared in a Skype meeting. Management of meetings by adding or removing participants is also available, bringing the meeting experience on the mobile client closer on par to the desktop meeting experience.

Lync Mobile 2013 didn't allow you to update your contact list. This forced users to add and remove users in their contact list, including favorites. This was very annoying because it forced you to make these updates from a desktop Lync client. Fortunately, with Skype for Business Server 2015 and Skype for Business Online, users can add users to their contact list from Skype for Business Mobile.

With server-side conversation history introduced in Skype for Business Server 2015, users will be able to retrieve all conversations they've had from any device, including mobile. They can start a conversation from their desktop client and continue it from their mobile client. Skype for Business Server stores the conversation on Exchange Server. Exchange Server 2013 is the minimum version required to provide server-side conversation history. Mobile clients retrieve the user's conversation history using UCWA, which is a web-based protocol over HTTPS.

To enable server-side conversation history, OAuth must be configured on Skype for Business. This is done using the following PowerShell command:

```
Get-CsCertificate -type OAuthTokenIssuer
```

Verify that Exchange Server 2013 is configured for OAuth:

```
Get-PartnerApplication
```

Finally, enable server-side conversation history:

```
Set-CsConversationHistoryConfiguration -EnableServerConversationHistory $true
```

Organizations that are concerned with having confidential information available on mobile devices can disable this feature by using the following PowerShell command:

```
Set-CsConversationHistoryConfiguration -EnableServerConversationHistory $false
```

The handling of incoming IMs on Skype for Business Mobile clients is now in parity with the desktop client. Skype for Business Mobile clients automatically accept incoming IMs using the same logic as desktop clients. This avoids the spinning donut, where the sender waits until the mobile user accepts the message. Another problem that is avoided is lost IMs. In Lync 2013 Mobile, if the user didn't accept the incoming message in time, it would disappear.

In Skype meetings, Skype for Business Mobile Android monitors the active call in the dashboard and will prompt to call back the mobile user over PSTN when the media quality becomes poor over Wi-Fi. Anonymous Skype meeting join is now supported in Skype for Business Android.

When in a call that has poor Wi-Fi connectivity, the Skype for Business Mobile client provides the capability to call back the user from the cellular network to achieve a better call quality. This is much better than suffering through a bad call.

Skype for Business 2015 Mobile enhances the security supported in Lync 2013 Mobile with the following new features:

- Data-at-rest encryption
- Passive Authentication support
- ADAL support

Administrators can enforce Skype for Business Mobile to encrypt data stored on the mobile device through policy using in-band provisioning on all three mobile platforms. Both iOS and Windows Phone devices will encrypt just the application's data. For Android devices, the entire device is encrypted.

Lync Server 2013 introduced a new authentication method called Passive Authentication, in addition to NTLM, Kerberos, and TLS-DSK authentication. Passive Authentication made it possible to integrate third-party Security Token Services (STSs). These STSs could provide alternative methods of authentication besides Active Directory credentials (username/password), such as OTP (One-Time Password) and certificate-based authentication. Although in principle the intent was valuable and met customer needs, the implementation was unfortunately flawed. Customers wanting to use Passive Authentication for mobile clients required administrators to configure all users homed on a pool to use Passive Authentication exclusively, which made for a different authentication experience on the desktop for those users. Administrators couldn't configure an alternative authentication mechanism for mobile clients only with Passive Authentication. Also, users authenticating using Passive Authentication could no longer connect to their Exchange Server from their Lync Mobile clients. This meant users couldn't access their calendar, for example, from their Lync Mobile because Exchange Server doesn't support Passive Authentication (SAML authentication). Exchange Server 2013 supports OAuth authentication instead. This made for a broken user experience.

ADAL (Azure AD Authentication Library) remedies these two primary issues with Passive Authentication. ADAL is an API library that abstracts away the different authentication protocols (NTLM, Kerberos, TLS-DSK, SAML, OAuth, and so on) from the application. This means applications that leverage ADAL, such as Skype for Business and Exchange Server, no longer need to implement specific authentication protocols. Lync Server 2013 only supports NTLM, Kerberos, TLS-DSK, and SAML (that is, Passive Authentication). By using ADAL, Skype for Business gets support for OAuth authentication automatically without additional development effort.

Because ADAL supports the OAuth 2.0 protocol, which is supported by Exchange Server, users no longer get a broken experience. To use ADAL requires ADFS (Active Directory Federation Services) on Windows Server 2012 R2 and above. Additionally, with Skype for Business, administrators can configure a different authentication mechanism for mobile clients only. This allows organizations to enforce Skype for Business Mobile clients to use a different authentication protocol than desktop clients.

ADAL is the recommended path for customers wanting to use alternative credentials or to enhance user authentication using multifactor authentication (MFA), such as validation of a code sent to the user's phone (something the user has in possession). MFA using ADAL is supported for users homed in Microsoft's cloud, Office 365. It is currently not supported for on-premises deployments of Skype for Business Server 2015 or Exchange Server 2013, or Skype for Business Server 2015 with March 2016 Cumulative Update. A Security Token Service from a third-party provider is necessary to provide MFA for your on-premises deployment.

We've covered the major feature enhancements in Skype for Business 2015 Mobile. However, there are many more features introduced in Skype for Business 2015 Mobile that haven't been covered, and more enhancements and bug fixes are being developed by Microsoft.

Understanding Skype for Business Mobility

Because Skype for Business Mobile is a mobile app available for Windows Phone, iOS, and Android, these devices connect to your corporate Skype for Business Server 2015 server over the Internet or through the Wi-Fi. Unlike the desktop client, Skype for Business Mobile clients do not connect to the Front End Servers through the Edge Server for SIP traffic. Mobile clients only connect to the Edge Server for media traffic (audio, video, application sharing, and so on). Skype for Business Mobile clients connect to the Front End Web services through an external-facing reverse proxy using HTTPS.

This allows a lighter-weight protocol to be used on these devices that doesn't require constant network connectivity and can traverse NATs and firewalls. This results in greater battery life, a seamless experience across device platforms, and the capability to maintain connection state on unreliable cellular networks.

The Mobility architecture is composed of the following components:

- Unified Communications Web API (UCWA)
- Mobility service (MCX)
- LyncDiscover service

These components are installed on the Front End Servers.

Figure 25.1 provides a simplistic overview of how a Skype for Business Mobile client connects to Skype for Business Server 2105. The reverse proxy proxies the Skype for

Business mobility traffic to pool2; however, the Skype for Business Mobile user is homed on pool1. The point is to illustrate that the Skype for Business Mobile client authenticates twice: once with pool1 when performing the LyncDiscover process, and a second time when connecting to the user's home pool.

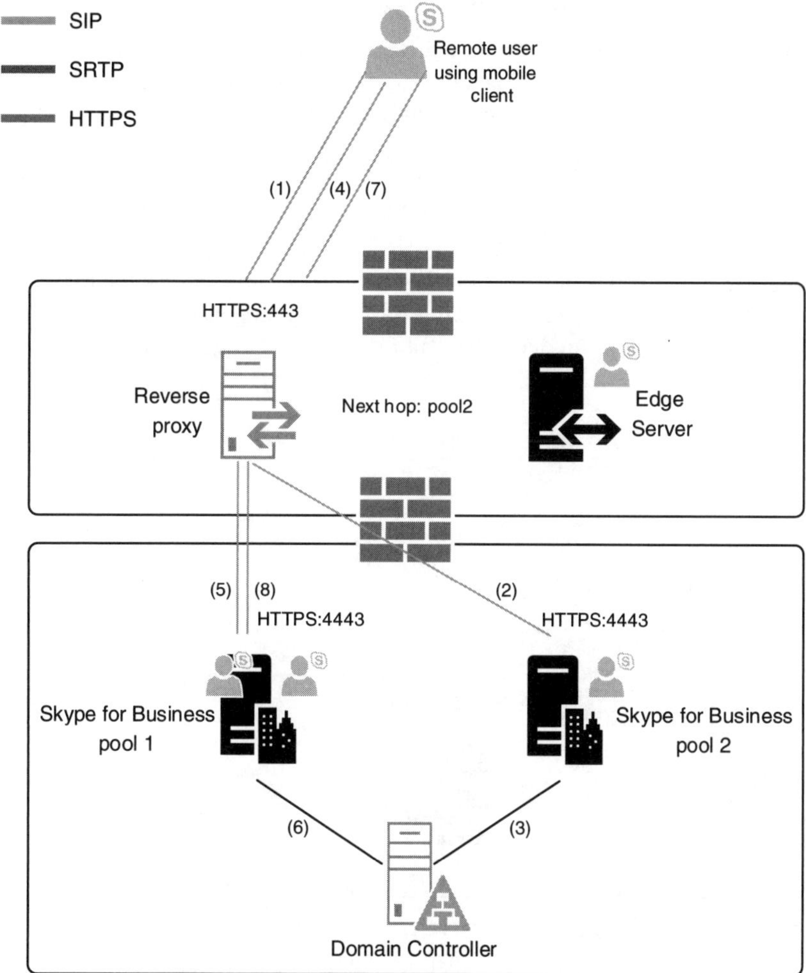

FIGURE 25.1 Skype for Business Mobile initial connection overview.

When a Skype for Business Mobile client connects to the user's home pool, it performs the following steps:

1. The Skype for Business Mobile client connects to the `lyncdiscover.<domain>` URI, which resolves to the reverse proxy.
2. The reverse proxy proxies the request to the next-hop Skype for Business Server's External Web Service (in this example, pool2).

3. Pool2 authenticates the remote user, returns a compact web ticket (CWT) authentication token, discovers the user's home pool (that is, pool1), and redirects the mobile client to the user's home pool External Web Service.
4. The mobile client connects to pool1's External Web Service via the reverse proxy.
5. The reverse proxy proxies the authentication request to pool1.
6. Pool1 authenticates the remote user. Pool1 signs in the user to Skype for Business and returns a CWT token to the mobile client via the reverse proxy. The mobile client uses the CWT to validate subsequent requests send to pool1.
7. The mobile client requests a client certificate from pool1.
8. Pool1 returns a self-signed certificate to the mobile client.

Figure 25.2 illustrates a Skype for Business Mobile client calling an internal Skype for Business user. Note that the media traverses the Edge Server (A/V Edge). Skype for Business Mobile only uses the Edge Server for media (SRTP) traffic, not signaling (SIP) traffic.

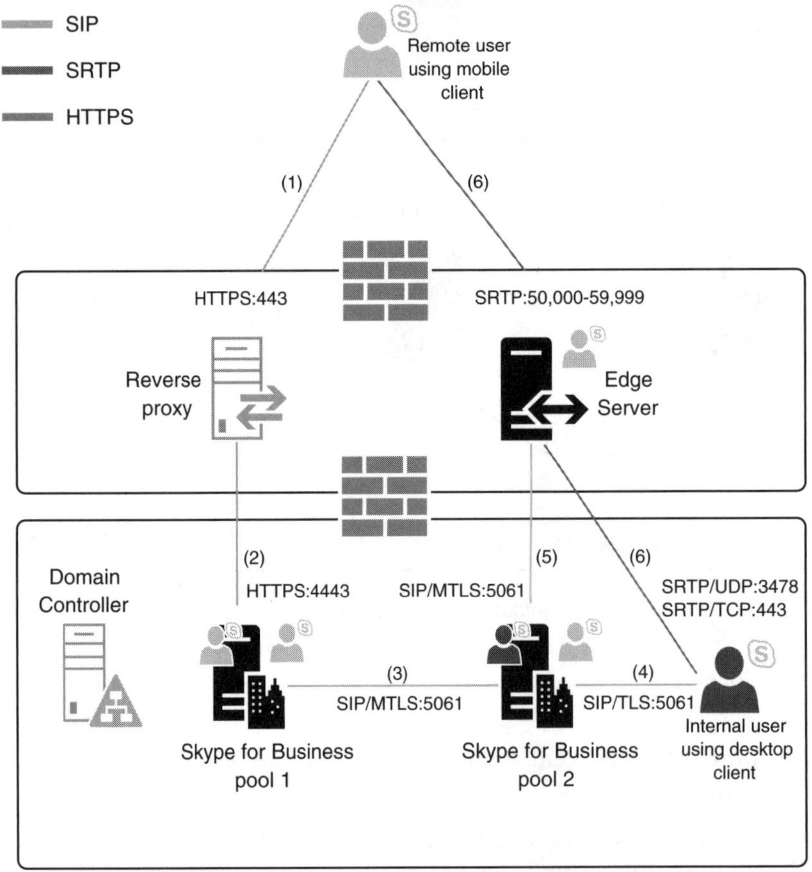

FIGURE 25.2 Skype for Business Mobile call overview.

When a Skype for Business Mobile client initiates a call with an internal Skype for Business user, it performs the following steps:

1. The Skype for Business Mobile client is signed in to user's home pool (that is, pool1) through reverse proxy. The user calls an internal user.
2. Reverse proxy forwards call signaling to pool1.
3. Pool1 initiates the SIP call to the internal user's pool (pool2).
4. Pool2 rings the internal user's active endpoints.
5. Pool2 requests the Edge Server to generate authentication credentials for a dynamically selected port on the external AV Edge to allow the remote client to establish a media path to the internal user.
6. The internal user connects to the internal Edge of the Edge Server. The Edge Server bridges the external media traffic and internal media traffic.

This section outlines the architecture and services of Skype for Business mobility.

LyncDiscover Service

The LyncDiscover service was introduced in Lync Server 2010 to provide autodiscovery of Lync services to Lync Mobile clients. This method for discovering Skype for Business Servers expanded to desktop clients. The Skype for Business Server 2015 LyncDiscover service is similar to the Exchange Server Autodiscover service. The simple principle is that users connect to a web address, authenticate, and then request the next server (that is, the user's home pool) to connect to that can service their request. By standardizing on this method, all Skype for Business clients can discover the user's home pool without having to use different methods, depending on the client used.

There is an added benefit to using the LyncDiscover (DNS A record) method versus the Service (DNS SRV record) method. An organization may need to deploy multiple pools across geographic regions to optimize communications for users in each region. By using the LyncDiscover method, the organization can use GeoDNS internally to direct the Skype for Business client to the closest Skype for Business web service to them, which is likely their home pool. Similarly, the organization can use GeoDNS externally to direct the client to the closest reverse proxy to them. This enables organizations to simplify the deployment of Skype for Business clients.

The LyncDiscover service runs as a web service on all Skype for Business Front End and Director Servers.

Requests to LyncDiscover are authenticated before service information is delivered. When the Skype for Business Mobile client signs in the user, the client prompts the user for their SIP URI and credentials. The client extracts the SIP domain from the user's SIP URI and appends it to LyncDiscover to perform the DNS query for `lyncDiscover.<sipdomain>`. All clients will try to connect to `LyncDiscover.<sipdomain>` and `LyncDiscoverinternal.<sipdomain>`. For a user in the `skypeunleashed.com` SIP domain, this FQDN would be `LyncDiscover.skypeunleashed.com`.

The external DNS query for `LyncDiscover.<sipdomain>` resolves to the public IP address of the reverse proxy, which proxies the connection to the internal Skype for Business web service. LyncDiscover returns the following information to the client:

- Web service URL to connect to Mobility Services
- Front End Server FQDN for SIP connectivity
- FQDN and port of the Access Edge Service associated with the Front End Server pool for remote SIP client connectivity

The Skype for Business web service challenges the client for credentials and authenticates the user using NTLM, TLS-DSK, or OAuth, whichever is configured. Once the user is authenticated, the Skype for Business web service issues a compact web ticket (CWT). This CWT is valid up to 8 hours. If the Skype for Business web service is not the user's home pool, the web service looks up the user's home pool FQDN and redirects the client to it. If the Skype for Business web service is the user's home pool, the mobile client requests a certificate from the server. The Skype for Business web service issues a self-signed user certificate that is specific to the user's device. Every device the user uses gets a separate self-signed certificate. This certificate allows the Skype for Business client to authenticate using TLS-DSK the next time the user signs in from the same device.

Later in this chapter you learn details about the messages exchanged between the client and the server for LyncDiscover.

CAUTION

Mobile devices and desktops clients located on the internal corporate network can connect to the `LyncDiscoverinternal` URL for server discovery. Because of this, it is important to identify a certificate strategy for those clients that might not trust a private Certificate Authority by default, such as mobile phones. The "Certificate and DNS Requirements" section covers this topic in greater detail.

Mobility Service

Skype for Business Server 2015 uses the Unified Communications Web API (UCWA) to convert the SIP protocol into a Web API, making it possible for HTTPS-based clients to connect to Skype for Business Server 2015 on-premises or in the cloud (Office 365). UCWA is a REST-based API that sends XML messages encapsulated using HTTPS that are then translated into SIP messages over TLS (encrypted TCP) by the Front End Server. UCWA was introduced in Lync Server 2013. UCWA supersedes MCX, which was the first mobility service introduced in Lync Server 2010. MCX is used for Lync Mobile 2010 clients, which use cookies for persistence. However, Lync Mobile 2013 and Skype for Business Mobile 2015 clients use UCWA. Cookie-based persistence is no longer used in UCWA. UCWA uses a token, called a compact web ticket (CWT), to track each signed-in client. This CWT is generated by the server upon positive authentication, and it remains valid for up to 8 hours. It is automatically renewed using the client's self-signed certificate issued by the server. This certificate is requested by the client after obtaining the CWT. This certificate is issued to the user and is unique per client (that is, device) the user is signed in to. It is valid for a default period of 6 months and is automatically renewed by the client.

Clients without a SIP stack that can communicate to Skype for Business Server 2015 using SIP/TLS can use UCWA/HTTPS to connect to Skype for Business Server 2015. It is used to facilitate communications from all HTTPS-based clients. This service is open to developers and is also responsible for providing Skype Web App connectivity.

SIP traffic is often referred to as being "chatty"—chatty traffic can consume a lot of bandwidth and power. When a mobile client is being deployed, it is critical that this client does not decrease the increasingly precious battery life of mobile devices. By implementing an HTTPS/XML-based client, Microsoft is able to achieve the following:

- Standardize and simplify the clients across multiple platforms.
- Decrease the frequency and size of traffic used when compared with SIP.
- Decrease the battery drain of the mobile clients.
- Increase session resiliency and session recovery time for mobile clients, which are often changing connection state frequently.

The Skype for Business Mobility services act under a simple concept: Translate mobile XML messages to SIP messages that Front End Servers can understand. This service acts much like a back-to-back user agent (B2BUA), receiving a request from a mobile device and then initiating another request over SIP and maintaining the state of the two separate connections. The Mobility services will perform functionality such as updating Presence and initiating calls.

The Skype for Business UCWA and MCX services are deployed on all Front End Servers in the environment, and details on the actual messages exchanged between clients and servers is shown in later in this chapter.

Security Risks

Skype for Business mobility requires organizations to publish their Skype for Business external web services in the public DNS because mobile clients can only connect from the Internet. Publishing the external web services is done through a reverse proxy. This exposes your Skype for Business environment to security risks, many of which have been identified in Chapter 11, "Firewall, Reverse Proxy, and Security Requirements." The following list covers security risks that are applicable to Skype for Business Mobile:

- **Multifactor authentication (MFA)**—Mobile platforms are often not considered to have as strong security as their desktop and server counterparts' operating systems. As a result, many organizations do not want their users to enter their Active Directory credentials on mobile devices.
- **Mobile device protection**—Users enabled for remote access can download the Skype for Business or Lync client on any device and sign in. Administrators need the ability to identify and track such devices if they get lost or stolen, and then disable their access to the corporate Skype for Business infrastructure.

- **IP network mapping**—Internal IP addresses are easily discoverable when establishing a call with an internal user. Skype for Business uses ICE (STUN/TURN protocols) to negotiate a network path through NAT and firewalls to establish a media call. In this negotiation, internal IP addresses are sent to the external party in the candidate list of the SIP traffic. Mapping the internal IP network helps hackers infiltrate the corporate network by knowing which computers to target.

Skype for Business Server 2015 provides a lot of built-in security; however, these security concerns aren't addressed out of the box in Skype for Business. Many customers mistakenly think a Mobile Device Management (MDM) solution from a third-party MDM vendor such as MobileIron, AirWatch, or Good will address these security concerns, but they do not because Microsoft does not allow Skype for Business Mobile to be containerized by an MDM. Microsoft does not make the IPA (iOS) and IPK (Android) available to be code-signed by third-party MDM solutions.

Therefore, organizations must leverage security solutions from third-party vendors such as Lync-Solutions and PointSharp to fill these security gaps.

Skype for Business Mobile Sign-in Process

The sign-in process involves DNS resolutions and authentication to the LyncDiscover service before getting redirected to the user's home pool. The following list provides each step of the LyncDiscover process. Figure 25.3 provides an overview of the LyncDiscover process. The Lync Connectivity Analyzer can help you troubleshoot issues with LyncDiscover. It's a free download from Microsoft and installs on a desktop computer.

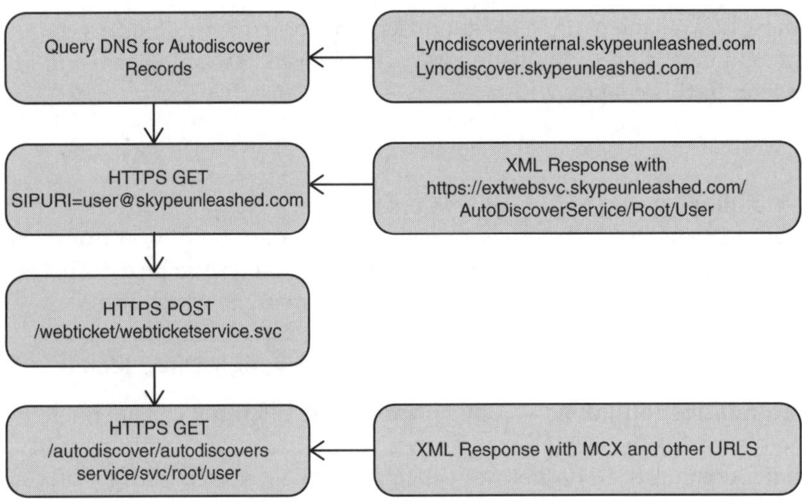

FIGURE 25.3 LyncDiscover process.

The following steps describe the LyncDiscover process:

1. The client queries the DNS records for `LyncDiscoverinternal` first and then for `LyncDiscover`.
2. The client connects to the appropriate URL, including the SIP URI of the user as part of the URL.
3. The LyncDiscover service responds with the full LyncDiscover service URL and web ticket service URL for users to request server information.
4. The LyncDiscover service requires the client to authenticate and receive a valid web ticket. The client performs authentication with the web ticket service before attempting to interact with the LyncDiscover service again.
5. When the client has a valid web ticket, it sends a full request to the LyncDiscover service. If the message is valid, the LyncDiscover service returns connectivity information for that client and user.

At this stage, a client will have authenticated with the web ticket service, essentially authenticating with Active Directory. Also, the client is redirected to the Skype for Business external web services of the user's home pool. The home pool's external web services will challenge the client for user authentication, at which point the client authenticates the user a second time to the user's home pool web ticket service before being allowed to connect.

Deploying Skype for Business Mobility

Skype for Business Mobility relies on various services and must be carefully planned for to ensure a successful deployment. The LyncDiscover, UCWA, and MCX services are all installed by default on all Front End Servers. Even though the MCX service is now a legacy service to support Lync Mobile 2010, it is available in Skype for Business Server 2015 by default. No additional configuration is required to install these services. However, configuration is required for DNS, certificates, reverse proxy, hardware load balancers (HLBs), and mobile policies. This section outlines the prerequisites to support Skype for Business Mobile.

Certificate and DNS Requirements

The LyncDiscover service requires a static DNS entry that is dedicated to this service. The DNS requirements for Skype for Business are given in Table 25.1.

TABLE 25.1 LyncDiscover DNS Requirements

DNS Record	Points To
`LyncDiscoverinternal.skypeunleashed.com`	Internal IP address of the Front End Server or Front End web services VIP
`LyncDiscover.skypeunleashed.com`	External IP address of the reverse proxy for external web services

The LyncDiscover service is used by Skype for Business devices and desktop clients to discover the user's Skype for Business Server 2015 home pool. To properly support devices that are connected to either the internal corporate network or public network, both the `LyncDiscoverinternal` and the `LyncDiscover` records must be created and must point to the appropriate IP addresses.

The certificate implications for the previous requirements become increasingly important in Skype for Business Server 2015. In the past, a single, privately issued certificate was common for all Front End Services. When certificates are being configured for a Front End Server, there is an option to assign a certificate for default, internal web services and for external web services. This essentially enables administrators to assign a certificate for each of the web service directories and then all other Skype for Business services.

With Skype for Business Mobile, these devices connect via the Wi-Fi or the cellular network. Because the large majority of organizations follow INFOSEC best practices, Wi-Fi is considered insecure and therefore external. Wi-Fi is not directly connected to their internal network. The cellular network, which is managed by wireless carriers, is always considered external. Therefore, as external clients, mobile devices connect through the organization's reverse proxy to the Skype for Business external web services.

Table 25.2 outlines a possible certificate configuration to provide Autodiscover Services to all endpoints.

TABLE 25.2 LyncDiscover Certificate Requirements

Friendly Name	Server Certificate	Web Services Certificate
Issued By	Private CA	Public CA
Usages	Server default	Web server internal Web server external

Common Name	`Nypool.skypeunleashed.local`
	`Sip. skypeunleashed.local`
		`Nypoolwebsvc.skypeunleashed.com`
		`Nypoolwebsvc.skypeunleashed.com`
		`Nypoolwebsvcexternal.skypeunleashed.com`
		`LyncDiscoverinternal.skypeunleashed.com`
		`LyncDiscover.skypeunleashed.com`
		`Meet.skypeunleashed.com`
		`Dialin.skypeunleashed.com`

In the configuration outlined in Table 25.2, the web services certificate could be applied to the Front End Server web services as well as the public interface of the reverse proxy. This would allow for internal clients that are connecting to the internal LyncDiscover service to connect seamlessly, as well as external clients.

The preceding example is just one way to work with the certificate requirements for LyncDiscover. There are many ways to meet the requirements of an organization. The key is that the LyncDiscover records must be present on a certificate, and the clients must trust that certificate as well as its certificate chain.

Reverse Proxy and Hardware Load Balancer Considerations for Mobility

All Skype for Business mobile traffic will go through a reverse proxy regardless of the client location. Given the roaming nature of mobile clients, connection affinity is better controlled when the client connects through the same service. In the case of Skype for Business Mobile, that service will always be the external web services directory, which is published through a reverse proxy. When external Skype for Business services are being deployed, a reverse proxy must be configured to publish the Front End pool external web services to the Internet. The mobility service will run on the same URL as the Front End pool web services. However, the LyncDiscover service, although it will point to the same Front End Server web service, will require a unique FQDN defined, and the reverse proxy will require an entry to support that FQDN.

Reverse Proxy Certificate Requirements

When the LyncDiscover service is published through a reverse proxy, there are two possible solutions:

- Include `LyncDiscover.<sipdomain>` as a subject alternative name (SAN) entry on the web services public certificate. This can become costly when there are many SIP domains supported in the environment.
- Publish the LyncDiscover service over HTTP. When the service allows connections on port 80, the initial request will not be over TLS; clients are then redirected to the external web services FQDN of the Front End pool, resulting in no requirement for a LyncDiscover entry on the certificate.

Initial requests to the LyncDiscover service, whether they are over HTTPS or HTTP, are not authenticated; as such, there is not a great security risk with publishing this service over HTTP. The initial connection will simply be used to identify the full URL to connect to for the LyncDiscover service, and this information is given to connecting clients whether they connect over HTTP or HTTPS.

For details on configuring a reverse proxy for Skype for Business Server 2015, see Chapter 11.

Hardware Load Balancer Requirements

Skype for Business Server 2015 Front End pools require a hardware load balancer (HLB) to be deployed to provide high availability for the web services. Lync Server 2010 introduced Lync Mobility, which required cookie-based persistence to be configured on the HLB to provide session affinity to Lync Mobile clients. Because the session for each connected client was maintained only on the Front End Server it connected to, the client would always be required to connect to that same server. As such, cookie-based persistence was required to provide this affinity. In Skype for Business Server 2015, the requirements for cookie-based persistence have been removed, including for Lync 2010 Mobile clients connecting to Skype for Business servers. Front End Servers will maintain session affinity for mobile clients; as such, source address affinity should be configured on the HLB instead of cookie-based persistence.

Firewall Rules Required for Skype for Business Mobile

Mobile clients connect through the Skype for Business external web services, which should be published on port TCP:443. This requirement is fairly standard and should be implemented with all Skype for Business deployments involving external users.

Steps to Enable Mobility

Deploying mobile services in Skype for Business Server 2015 is relatively simple. Based on the guidance in previous sections, follow these high-level steps to enable mobility in a Skype for Business environment.

DNS Configuration

DNS records will be required for the LyncDiscover service for both internal and external users.

Create an internal DNS A record for `LyncDiscoverinternal.<sipdomain>` that points to the internal web services IP address or VIP of the hardware load balancer.

Create an external DNS A record for `LyncDiscover.<sipdomain>` that points to the external interface of your reverse proxy for the external web services.

Certificate Configuration

If LyncDiscover services are being deployed over HTTPS, a SAN must be created on all web service certificates for the LyncDiscover URLs.

Mobile Enable Users

Finally, enable users for mobility functionality by running the `Set-CSMobilityPolicy` cmdlet. Here is an example:

```
Set-CSMobilityPolicy -EnableMobility $True
```

Controlling Functionality with Mobility Policies

Skype for Business Mobile functionality can be controlled using policies. The following are mobility-related policies configurable through the PowerShell cmdlet `*-CsMobilityPolicy`, where `*` can be `New`, `Set`, or `Get`.

Configure audio/video for mobile users:

- **`EnableIPAudioVideo`**—Used to allow audio and video communication in the Mobile Client.
- **`EnableOutsideVoice`**—Used to enable the user for Call via Work. The user must be assigned a voice policy with Enable Simultaneous Ringing of Phones enabled.

Limit data usage:

- `RequireWiFiForIpAudio`
- `RequireWiFiForIpVideo`
- `RequireWiFiForSharing`

Configure saving conversation history on mobile devices:

- `EnableIMAutoArchiving`
- `EnableCallLogAutoArchiving`

Control local caching on mobile clients:

- **`AllowSaveCredentials`**—Controls whether user credentials are stored on the device
- **`AllowSaveIMHistory`**—Controls whether conversation history is stored on the device
- **`AllowSaveCallLogs`**—Controls whether call logs are stored on the device

Summary

Mobile functionality is key to providing a true unified communications solution, and Skype for Business Server 2015 brings more functional parity to mobile clients compared to what is currently available on the desktop client. Skype for Business Server 2015 provides users mobile access across all major platforms with a consistent user experience. New web services were introduced to support mobile devices, including the MCX service for Lync 2010 clients and the Unified Communications Web API (UCWA) service for Lync 2013 and Skype for Business clients. These business external web services act as intermediary points between the Skype for Business mobile clients that communicate using XML over the HTTPS protocol and Skype for Business Servers that communicate using SIP over the TLS protocol. The LyncDiscover service enables mobile devices to automatically discover Skype for Business web services, resulting in a seamless automatic configuration of clients.

Deploying Skype for Business Mobility to a Skype for Business Server 2015 deployment introduces unique DNS and certificate requirements, and must be carefully planned for. After these requirements have been identified and met, the actual deployment of the services is a relatively simple process. Also, controlling the Skype for Business Mobile services and functionality available to end users is available using provisioning policies, all controllable through the Skype for Business Server 2015 Management Shell and the Skype for Business Server 2015 Control Panel.

CHAPTER 26

Windows and Browser Clients

IN THIS CHAPTER

- Installing the Windows Client
- Navigating in the Windows Client
- Peer-to-Peer Conversations
- Conferencing
- Persistent Chat
- Integration with Other Applications
- Skype for Business Browser Capabilities
- Skype for Business Server 2015 Web App Technical Review
- Requirements to Deploy Skype for Business Browser Functionality

Although Skype for Business Server 2015 is an impressive application by itself, most users experience Skype for Business Server 2015 only through one of its many clients. The most common client is likely Skype for Business in most environments. Skype for Business is the Windows-based client that enables users to access the client-side functionality of Skype for Business Server 2015. This includes functions such as the following:

- Instant messaging
- Presence
- PC-to-PC calls
- Enterprise Voice functions
- Video conferencing
- Web conferencing
- Desktop and application sharing

Skype for Business Server 2015 provides enhanced cross-platform support for all communication modalities. Skype for Business Server 2015 Web App enables users to join conferences from a browser and participate in full-featured conferencing without the need to install a client. This chapter also provides an overview of the browser capabilities across all operating systems, as well as a technical review of how Skype for Business Web App is deployed and provides services to users. Lastly, the requirements to deploy Skype for Business Server browser capabilities are reviewed.

This chapter covers the more commonly used functions of the Skype for Business clients and should act as the basis of end-user training that most administrators want to provide to their user community to ensure successful adoption of Skype for Business Server 2015.

NOTE

For those upgrading from Office Communications Server 2007 R2, Skype for Business, like the Lync 2010 and 2013 packages, is a single installation package, so there is no longer a need to install Communicator, Live Meeting, and the Conferencing plugin separately.

In older versions of Office Communications Server, there were multiple clients for instant messaging, web conferencing, and group chat. Skype for Business combines all these features into a single client to make it even more seamless for users to participate in multiple types of collaborative communications.

NOTE

Both the Skype for Business 2015 client (which is an upgrade for the Lync 2013 client) and the Skype for Business 2016 client, provided in Office 2016, offer full features when connecting to Skype for Business Server 2015. This chapter refers to both as the Skype for Business client.

Installing the Client

The Skype for Business client for Windows now comes as part of the Microsoft Office 2013 setup package.

Installation of Skype for Business occurs automatically when Office Professional Plus is installed. In fact, there is no option for a custom installation. Installation is simple:

1. Launch the Office 2013 installation package.
2. Click Customize.
3. Click each product and select Not Available, as shown in Figure 26.1.

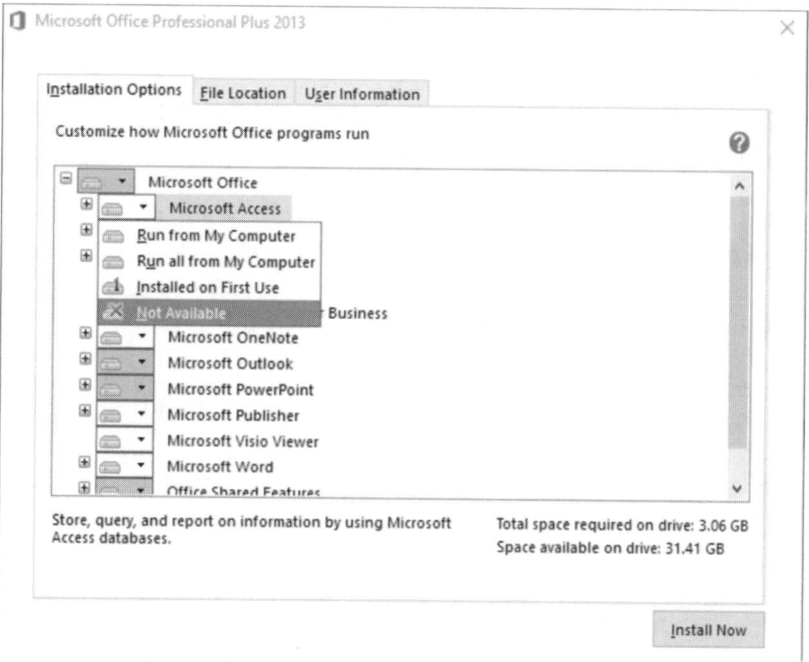

FIGURE 26.1 Skype for Business client installation.

4. Click Microsoft Lync and select Run from My Computer.
5. Click Install Now.
6. Install the latest Windows Updates to update the Lync Client in Office 2013 to the Skype for Business client.

The installation of the Skype for Business 2015 client is not as flexible. You must install Office in its entirety; there is no option to select which components are installed.

A free standalone client called Microsoft Skype for Business Basic can be downloaded from https://www.microsoft.com/en-us/download/details.aspx?id=49440. The Basic client, however, does not include every feature that the rich desktop client does. The following features are not available in the Basic client:

- ▶ The ability to use a picture from a URL
- ▶ Searching for Response Groups
- ▶ Skill Search
- ▶ OneNote integration
- ▶ Conferencing Q&A options
- ▶ Ink messages
- ▶ Managing Call Forwarding
- ▶ Managing Team Call settings

- Managing delegates
- Initiating a call to a Response Group
- Connecting to voicemail and setting up or changing the greeting
- The ability to answer another's calls if configured as a delegate
- Call Park
- Group Call pickup

With the Skype for Business 2015 client installed, two different GUI versions are available. The first is the legacy Lync 2013 client, and the second is the new Skype for Business client. This is controlled by a client policy, and is a great option during migrations and upgrades. The new client can be rolled out, but retain the legacy client look and feel until all clients are upgraded, or until end-user training takes place. To keep the Lync 2013 GUI, open Skype for Business Shell on a Skype for Business server, and type the following:

```
Set-CsClientPolicy -Identity Global -EnableSkypeUI $False
```

The client picks up policy settings when it logs in, or every 8 hours, whichever comes first. However, the Skype for Business client will open the first time with the Skype for Business GUI, until it receives the policy. At that time, the user will be prompted to restart the client, which will then have the Lync 2013 interface.

For more information on Administration, see Chapter 13, "Administration of Skype for Business Server 2015."

NOTE

The Skype for Business client can actually coexist on the same system with Communicator 2007 R2 or Lync 2010. The legacy versions are not automatically removed during the installation.

Signing In

After the client is installed, a user can try to sign in. In a typical corporate environment, the user's SIP address is automatically detected from Active Directory, and credentials are passed to Skype for Business transparently, so no action is required.

In some cases, the user might need to enter a SIP address and password. If the user's SIP address is not the same as the user principal name (UPN) within Active Directory, the user will also be challenged for the NetBIOS domain name and username.

If automatic sign-in cannot be used, the server settings can be manually configured through the Skype for Business options. Click the Options icon on the right side of the screen, click Personal, and then click the Advanced button. Select Manual configuration and then enter an internal and external server name. The format for these entries should be `<Skype for Business Pool FQDN>:<Port Number>`. The internal server port will typically be 5061, while the external server port is usually 443.

Navigating in the Client

The Skype for Business client is broken into a few sections, as shown in Figure 26.2, starting with the user's personal area at the very top. This is where a user can enter a status update in the What's Happening Today? field, change their Presence, or define a location they are currently working from.

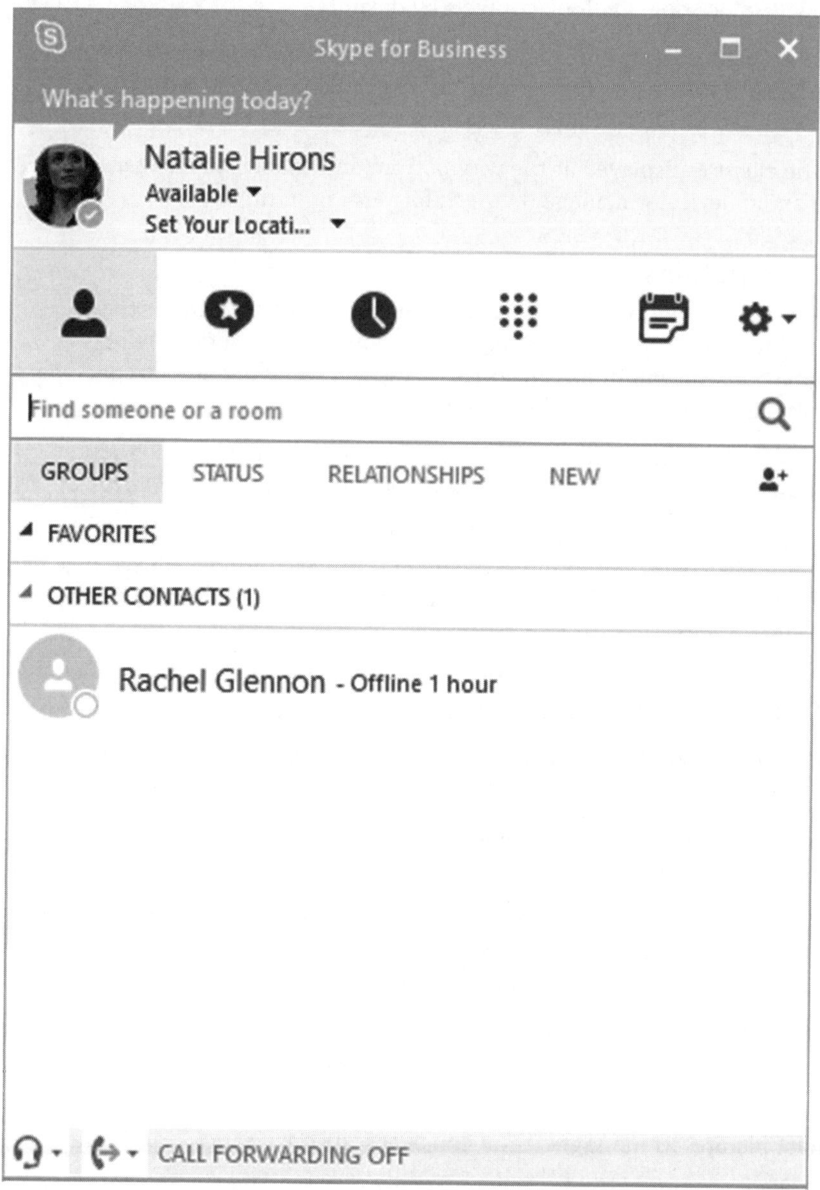

FIGURE 26.2 The Skype for Business client interface.

The next section of the client is a tabbed navigation area that enables the user to jump between their contact list, Persistent Chat rooms, conversation history, telephony features, and meeting information. Some of the tabs may not be visible if a user is not enabled for a particular function, such as Persistent Chat or Enterprise Voice.

Continuing toward the bottom is a search field where users can enter names or phone numbers when trying to locate a contact. This search happens across the user's Skype for Business contact list and personal Outlook contacts by default.

The main area of the client is next. It displays content for each of the tabbed areas discussed previously, so it will switch between the user's contact list, Persistent Chat rooms, previous conversations, telephony, and calendar features.

The final area of the client is displayed at the very bottom and enables the user to easily switch a preferred audio device or manage their call forwarding settings.

Configuring Basic Options

You can reach the personal options by clicking the gear icon at the far right of the navigation tabs and then clicking Tools and, finally, Options. In the Options windows, the options are broken up into multiple categories. These categories are organized in the left pane for easy access and include the following:

- **General**—This is where users can turn on or off emoticons, modify background colors for messages, turn logging on or off, and configure tabbed conversations.
- **Personal**—This is where users can alter their logon information, determine Skype for Business's startup behavior, opt to integrate Presence information with Exchange or Outlook, configure Skype for Business conversation archiving to Outlook, and opt to show photos for contacts.
- **Contacts List**—This is where users can adjust how contacts are displayed, how they are ordered, and how much information is shown.
- **Status**—This section contains options for how Presence is automatically updated and viewable.
- **My Picture**—This is where users can determine whether to present a photo with their contact information.
- **Phones**—This is where users can modify phone number information, as well as opt to integrate Skype for Business client with the phone system, enable functions such as TTY, or configure behavior for joining conference calls.
- **Alerts**—This is where users can choose to be notified if someone else adds them to the contact list or configure the behavior of their Do Not Disturb status.
- **IM**—This section controls various settings for instant messaging, including spell check, contact pictures in messages, emoticons, tabbed conversations, and font settings.

- **Persistent Chat**—This is where the user can customize notifications they receive for new messages in subscribed chat rooms.
- **Ringtones and Sounds**—This is where the user can choose the incoming-call ringtone or configure sounds on specific events.
- **Audio Device**—This is where users can choose which audio devices will be used by the Skype for Business client. They can also change the volume associated with the speakers and ringer, as well as modify the microphone sensitivity. These settings are useful for optimizing the user experience. When adjusting the microphone, simply slide the bar all the way to the right and then speak into the microphone a bit louder than normal. If the resulting signal is deemed too high, the slider automatically moves left after you finish speaking.
- **Video Device**—This is where users can choose the video source and access that device's settings. These settings include exposure, focus, brightness, contrast, hue, sharpness, gamma, and backlight compensation. The user can also access advanced and extended settings to include zoom, white balance, and even face tracking, if the device supports it.
- **Call Forwarding**—This is where users can view and change call forwarding, simultaneous ring, and voicemail settings. Team-call group and delegate members can also be defined on this screen.
- **File Saving**—This is where users determine where file transfers and Skype for Business recordings will be saved.
- **Recording**—This is where users can view and change the settings related to meeting recordings. Settings include the folder to save recordings into and the image resolution options for video recordings.
- **Skype Meetings**—This is where users can configure the user interface for meetings. Settings include whether IM and participant lists are visible, which client to use when joining meetings, and how to handle audio.

Managing Contacts

Most people are accustomed to the behaviors in Outlook, where you can quickly look up a user in the contacts or find the user by starting to type that person's name. The Skype for Business client follows this model by organizing contacts by groups and by enabling users to quickly search for contacts by simply typing the person's name.

For example, on the Find Someone or a Room line or the Dial a Number line, if you type a name, the client suggests names based on the contacts. From here, right-click the contact, select Add to Contacts List, and select a group for the user. When this occurs, the person you've added receives a notification of the addition and has the option to add you as well. After being added, the contacts appear in the group you selected, and you are able to see their Presence information at any time.

NOTE

The Skype for Business client downloads the address book on a random interval after the first sign-in. It might take up to an hour before corporate search results appear. For the Skype for Business 2015 client, creating a DWORD called `GalDownloadInitialDelay` with a value of `0` in the Windows registry at `HKLM\Software\Policies\Microsoft\Office\15.0\Lync` will force the address book to download immediately for all users on that workstation. For the Skype for Business 2016 client, the location is `HKLM\Software\Policies\Microsoft\Office\16.0\Lync`.

After a contact is added, you can move the contact from one contact group to another by simply left-clicking and dragging the contact from one group to another. You can also right-click and select Move to another group, or you can select Copy to if you wish to have the user listed in multiple groups.

Managing Groups

The Skype for Business client enables users to organize their contacts by placing them inside groups. The first tab in the Skype for Business defaults to a view where contacts are organized by groups. By default, these are the following groups:

- Favorites
- All Contacts

The Favorites group is automatically populated by the client based on how often particular contacts are used, or the user can manually pin certain contacts to the group. The All Contacts group becomes the Other Contacts group as soon as a user creates the first custom group. Groups can be deleted or renamed by way of the right-click function.

NOTE

Contacts can exist within multiple groups at a time. Right-click any contact and select Copy Contact To in order to create a duplicate contact entry within another group.

A convenient use of groups is to organize members of a project or department. By right-clicking the group name, you can choose to launch a conference call that invites all members of that group. You can achieve similar functionality by selecting multiple contacts by Ctrl-clicking them and then right-clicking to choose Start a Conference Call. This call can use Skype for Business's PC-to-PC call features or the PSTN/PBX gateway.

You can organize groups within the client either by using the right-click-accessed Move Group Up and Move Group Down functions or by simply dragging them from one position to another. Right-click any existing group and select Create New Group to manually build a new group.

Status View

The default view of the contact list is to organize the user's contacts by groups, but users can also sort based on the current status of each contact. In this view, their group membership is irrelevant and only their current status affects where their contact appears. Statuses include the following:

- Online
- Away
- Unknown
- Unavailable

The status view is a quick and easy way to determine which of your contacts are available at any time.

Relationship View

The third view available in the Skype for Business client is the relationship view. This view is a bit more interesting because the relationships actually enforce behaviors on the contacts that are members of them. The relationships include the following:

- **Friends and Family**—Contacts in this relationship can view all your contact information except meeting details.
- **Workgroup**—Contacts in this relationship can view all your contact information except Home and Other Phone; they can interrupt the Do Not Disturb status.
- **Colleagues**—Contacts in this relationship can view all your contact information except Home, Other Phone and Mobile Phone, and meeting details.
- **External Contacts**—Contacts in this relationship can view only your name, title, email address, company, and picture.
- **Blocked Contacts**—Contacts in this relationship can view only your name, email address, office, and picture; they can't reach you through Skype for Business.

Beyond these permissions, the relationship view operates the same way as the other two views in terms of initiating IMs with contacts.

Chat Rooms

The second tab visible in the client is for the Persistent Chat feature. Only users enabled for Persistent Chat will have this tab visible. Available subtabs in this tab allow a user to see chat rooms they are currently following, those which they are a member of, and new chat rooms that are now available. On the far right is a + symbol that allows users to follow a room, create a room, create a feed for following, search for a room, and configure chat room options. Clicking that last option takes the user to the same dialog page as if they chose the Tools, Options route. Double-clicking a chat room in either the Followed list or Member Of list opens the chat interface for that room and shows all historical conversations in that room.

Recent Conversations

The third tab displayed in the client shows conversation history. All instant message conversations, phone calls, and Skype for Business meetings are displayed in this section for reference. Users can also filter for conversations that include audio or filter by missed conversations within the navigation filters at the top of the screen. Right-click any conversation and select Continue Conversation to rejoin.

Telephony

The fourth tab visible in the Skype for Business client is specific to telephony features and is displayed only when a user is enabled for Enterprise Voice. A dial pad is displayed, and a button to initiate an audio quality test call is available. The user's voicemail is also displayed on this page and can be played back or managed via the Skype for Business client. This helps users' productivity because they don't have to jump between Skype for Business and Outlook to manage voicemail messages. The voicemail options on the right side of the client provide entry hooks to call voicemail, change personal greetings, and run through the initial voicemail setup.

Meetings

The final tab available in the client is for meeting information. When it is selected, a user can view upcoming meeting information. Double-clicking any meeting listed here will automatically join the meeting.

Useful Skype for Business Client Shortcuts

Microsoft has gone out of its way to improve functionality and accessibility in the Skype for Business client, and one of the ways is the ability to create hotkeys for commonly used tasks. This sort of information makes a great cheat sheet for new users of the Skype for Business client because it not only simplifies accessing certain functions, but also serves to highlight what functions are available. Some of those commonly used tasks are highlighted in Tables 26.1–26.3.

TABLE 26.1 Global Hotkeys

Shortcut Key	Description
Windows key+A	Accept an incoming toast invitation
Windows key+Esc	Decline a toast invitation
Windows key+Y	Bring the Skype for Business main window to the foreground
Windows key+F4	Mute or unmute audio
Windows key+F5	Turn the camera on or off
Ctrl+Shift+spacebar	Focus on the application-sharing toolbar
Ctrl+Alt+spacebar	Take back control during screen sharing
Ctrl+Shift+S	Stop screen sharing

TABLE 26.2 Main Window Shortcuts

Shortcut Key	Description
Ctrl+1	Go to the Contact List tab
Ctrl+2	Go to the Persistent Chat tab
Ctrl+3	Go to the Conversation List tab
Ctrl+4	Go to the Phone tab
Ctrl+1 or Ctrl+Shift+1	As a delegate, transfers a call to another user's work number
Alt+M	Start Meet Now

TABLE 26.3 Conversation Window Shortcuts

Shortcut Key	Description
Escape	Exit full-screen view if present, or close the conversation window only if it has no audio, video, or sharing.
Alt+C	Accept invite notifications, including audio, video, call, and sharing requests.
Alt+F4	Close the conversation window.
Alt+I	Ignore invite notifications.
Alt+R	Rejoin audio.
Alt+S	Open the Save As dialog box.
Alt+V	Invite a contact to a conversation.
Ctrl+S	Save a conversation to IM history.
Ctrl+W	Show/hide IM area.
Ctrl+F	Send a file in peer-to-peer calls; add an attachment in a conference.
Ctrl+N	Take notes using OneNote.
Ctrl+R	Show/hide the participant list.
Ctrl+Shift+Enter	Add or end video.
Ctrl+Shift+H	Hold or resume an ongoing audio conversation.
Ctrl+Shift+I	Mark a conversation as high importance.
Ctrl+Shift+Y	Show or hide the sharing stage.
Ctrl+Shift+P	Use Compact View.
Ctrl+Shift+K	Use the content-only view.
Ctrl+Enter	Add or end audio.

26

Peer-to-Peer Conversations

Many of the conversations performed within Skype for Business are between only two users in a peer-to-peer fashion. This section covers the different modalities available for two-party interactions. This can include instant messaging, audio or video calls, and content sharing.

Instant Messaging

For most environments, the most commonly used feature in the Skype for Business client is instant messaging. This function enables users to stop cluttering mailboxes with messages such as "Where do you want to go for lunch?" and enables users to limit their messages to only people who are likely to respond quickly. This is where accurate Presence information really comes in handy.

Starting an IM conversation is as simple as double-clicking a contact. Doing so launches the IM window that defaults to the IM.

The IM client works like any other IM client. You can see the status information for the person with whom you are communicating, and there are two areas in the window: one to type in and one to display the conversation. Users have access to the usual features, such as altering the font, color, and size of the text, as well as a menu of emoticons. You can access emoticons with the usual combinations of characters.

Using Tabbed Conversations

Added in the Lync 2013 client was the capability to use tabbed conversations. This is continued in the Skype for Business client and is enabled by default. After starting one IM, simply double-click another contact to start a separate conversation, and the windows will be automatically grouped together with tabs, as shown in Figure 26.3.

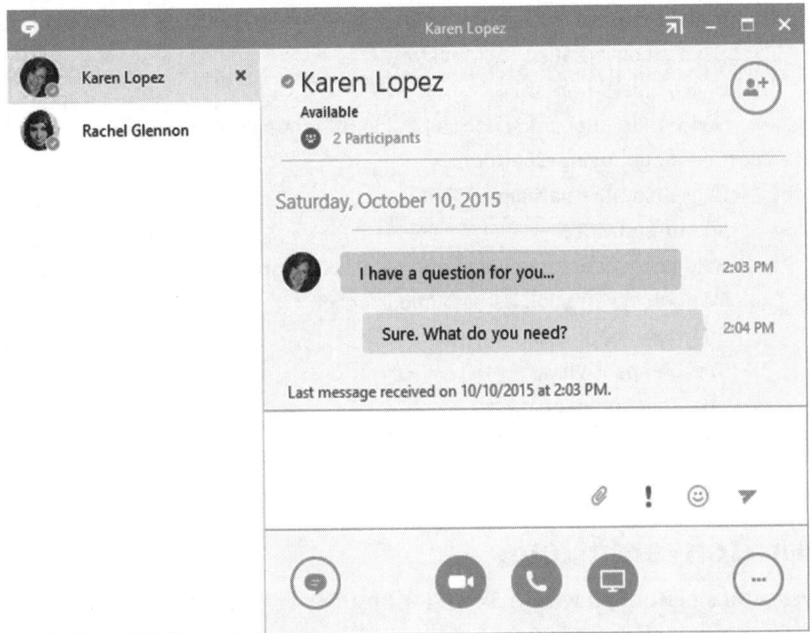

FIGURE 26.3 Tabbed conversations.

NOTE

Tabbed windows apply only to IM and Persistent Chat conversations. When a user makes an audio call or joins a meeting, that conversation is opened in a separate window.

Users can adjust the order of the conversations by left-clicking a conversation and dragging the tab up or down. Tabbed conversations can also be closed with a click of the X that appears on the right side of each tab.

Users can manually pop out a tab by right-clicking it and selecting Pop Out Conversation. This can be useful when the user needs to separate the windows for reference.

Archiving IM Conversations

IM conversations can be archived in several ways. One way is for an administrator to implement an archiving policy to archive conversations either on an archiving server that utilizes SQL Server or via integration with Exchange Server. However, this data is not accessible by the users. The other way is to archive messages into Outlook so that users can reference previous conversations easily. Either one method, or both, can be utilized. For a review on implementing archiving policies on an archiving server, refer to Chapter 6, "Microsoft Skype for Business Server 2015 Monitoring and Archiving Best Practices."

In the Options area, under the Personal tab, is the option Save Instant Message Conversations in My Email Conversation History Folder. This is enabled by default, and it ensures that each conversation is saved into this email folder at the time the IM window is closed. This is a useful way to access old conversations, and this folder's contents are indexed for easy searches.

Participating in Audio and Video Calls

One of the most interesting features in the Skype for Business client is the capability to participate in audio or video conferences with other users in the Skype for Business Server 2015 environment. Before their first participation in an audio or video conference, users should configure their audio and video devices as described in the "Configuring Basic Options" section earlier in this chapter. After these devices are configured, users are ready to start their first conference.

Making Audio Calls

Initiating an audio call is as simple as right-clicking a contact, choosing Call, and specifying that it should be a Skype for Business call. Then, the contact receives a pop-up and an audio notification and has the option to answer, decline, or redirect. Answer and Decline should be fairly obvious as to what they do. Redirect gives the option to reply through IM or to set one's status to Do Not Disturb. Accepting the call updates both users' status to In a Call.

Users can easily escalate an existing IM conversation to audio by clicking the phone icon at the bottom of the conversation window. This pops the conversation out into its own window, similar to what happens when a brand-new call is placed.

When the call connects, a new window displays that looks similar to the IM window. In fact, it is the same window, but now has the audio portion joined.

The call window enables the user to easily mute the device by clicking the microphone icon, which shows a microphone during an active call. Muting the microphone alters the icon on the client that muted their microphone. A connection signal strength and call timer are displayed in the upper-right corner of the conversation.

Users can access additional call-management options by clicking the phone icon in the lower right (not to be confused with the handset icon). After that, the following options are displayed:

- **Dial Pad**—Used to enter DTMF tones when in a call. Users can also start pressing digits on the keyboard without first using the mouse to expose this menu.
- **Mute**—Mutes the user's local microphone. The phone icon changes to indicate that the user is muted and cannot be heard by the other party.
- **Volume**—This adjusts the volume for the call.
- **Hold**—Places the call on hold. A notification bar appears with a Resume button to pick up the call again.
- **Transfer**—Enables the user to transfer the call to a mobile device, or to someone else. The call can also be parked through this option if the Call Park feature is enabled.
- **Devices**—Allows the user to fine-tune the speaker volume, or switch to another audio device while in a call.

The call can be ended with a click of the red phone icon in the upper-right corner of the conversation window. This ends only the audio portion of the call, and keeps the conversation active if IM or sharing is being used. Clicking the standard Windows close icon would end the entire conversation.

If Conversation History is enabled, the call is logged in the user's Outlook folder. The call itself is neither recorded nor stored, but the list of participants and the duration of the call are captured.

Additional meeting options are available by clicking the ellipsis button (three horizontal dots) in the lower-right corner. Options here include recording controls, font style and size, high priority, merging calls together, and help.

Network Connectivity Icon

One of the other icons visible in the window is the Network Connectivity status, which is displayed in the upper-left corner of the call. This indicates the quality of the network connection and is useful in troubleshooting issues with voice quality on a call.

Making Video Calls

Initiating a video call is as simple as right-clicking a contact and choosing Start a Video Call. Much as with the audio call, the recipient has the option to accept, decline, or redirect. Redirect gives the option to reply with an IM or to mark the recipient as Do Not Disturb.

When the call is accepted, the usual client window opens and is located on the Video tab. The recipient initially sees the caller, but the caller doesn't see the recipient until after the recipient clicks Start My Video in the window.

While in an active conversation, users can leverage the new Video Preview feature to check what their video will look like before initiating the call. Hover over the video icon to see a preview, and then click Start My Video to initiate the call.

By default, participants in a two-way call see themselves in a picture-in-picture window inside the main video window. You can hide this preview by hovering over the video and clicking the downward-facing arrow. Click the upward-facing arrow to restore the video preview.

The same audio controls for mute, hold, and devices discussed previously are still available within a video call. Clicking the video icon again stops the user from sending video, and another click resumes it.

Users can also detach the video content from the conversation window by hovering over the main video and clicking the arrow in the upper-right corner. This can be useful for users with multiple monitors, enabling them to maximize the video on one screen while continuing to use the other monitor for another purpose.

NOTE

If you expect widespread adoption of video conferencing and calls in your environment, don't skimp on the video cameras. Modern webcams have rather nice lenses, and modern processors can easily keep up with the load of high-definition video conferencing.

Sharing Content

Using Skype for Business to collaborate is a favorite feature of end users because of how simple it is to quickly share a desktop or an application. While in an active conversation, click the presenter icon, which looks like a monitor, as shown in Figure 26.4. From here a user can share the following types of content:

- **All Monitors**—Shares all the screens currently connected. Depending on the resolution of each user, the other end might need to zoom and pan to be able to read the content.

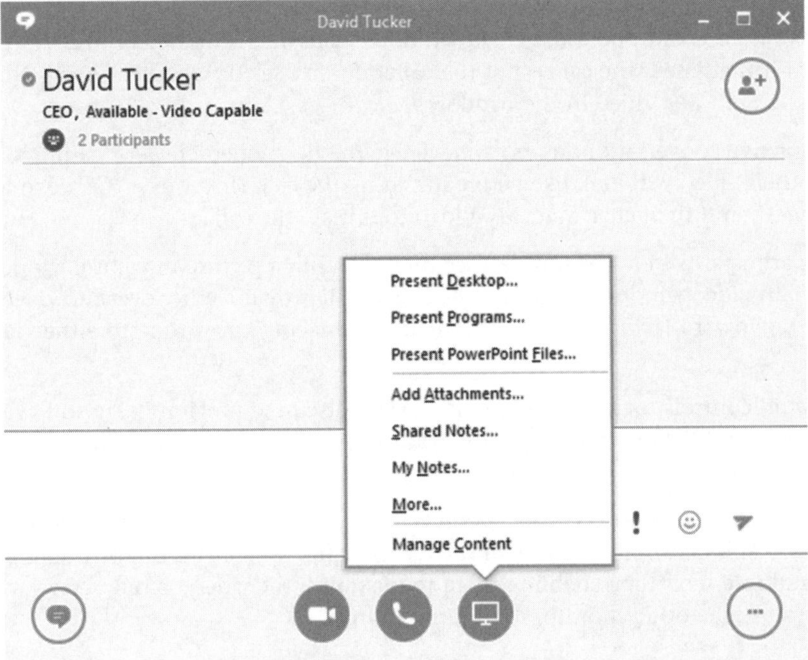

FIGURE 26.4 Skype for Business content sharing.

- **Specific Monitor**—Shares only a specific screen if multiple monitors are attached. As the user hovers over the monitor options, a yellow border is displayed on the monitor about to be shared. This way, the user knows exactly what content will be shown to the other user.
- **Program**—Shares only a specific application. This is usually the best experience for users because it is more efficient and uses less bandwidth. It can also be useful for keeping private information hidden from the opposite party.
- **PowerPoint**—Escalates the conversation to a Skype for Business meeting and begins sharing a PowerPoint deck. The user is prompted to select a PowerPoint file to present.

- **Whiteboard**—Escalates the conversation to a Skype for Business meeting and begins sharing a new whiteboard. This option is accessible via the More option.
- **Poll**—Escalates the conversation to a Skype for Business meeting and presents a poll for the other person to select. The poll can be given a name, a question, and up to seven possible choices. Like the Whiteboard, this option is accessible via the More option.

Sending and Receiving Files

The IM interface enables one person to send a file to the other participant of the IM conversation. The easiest way to send a file is to just drag it from the desktop onto the current conversation window.

Alternatively, at the bottom of the conversation window is an icon with a monitor in it for sharing. Click that icon and then click Attachments at the top. Clicking Add Attachment launches a window that enables the user to select a file to transfer.

The person set to receive the file receives a notification and has the option to Accept, Save As, or Decline the file. Accepting the file triggers a warning window to warn the user that the file might contain harmful malware and that they should accept file from only someone they know. After it is accepted, it downloads and a link displays to access the file. The sender of the file receives a notification that the transfer was successful.

Conferencing

Probably the biggest driving force behind companies implementing Skype for Business Server 2015 is replacing outsourced web conferencing services. Many companies spend tens of thousands of dollars a month on services, such as WebEx or GoToMeeting. Although there might be situations in which a company running Skype for Business Server 2015 needs to create a conference so large that its infrastructure isn't sufficient, the other 95% of the time it can use a platform it owns rather than pay an external company for these services.

Conferences in Skype for Business can be generated in a few ways, but the meeting experience is identical in each case. The most dynamic way to create a meeting is by presenting a PowerPoint, a whiteboard, or a poll within an existing peer-to-peer conversation. Sharing any of those items immediately escalates the conversation to a conference. Similarly, adding a third participant by simply dragging another contact into an existing conversation also escalates it to a conference.

NOTE

There is no distinction within Skype for Business about what is an IM conference versus a video conference versus a PowerPoint-sharing session. From the client's perspective a conference exists, and any of the modalities are available within that conference.

Using the Meet Now Function

Users sometimes think they need to schedule a conference or reserve resources because of how they interacted with a legacy system. The Skype for Business client can dynamically generate a conference if the user clicks the drop-down arrow next to the Options icon and selects Meet Now. This is equivalent to dragging participants into an existing conversation, but it creates an empty conference that the organizer can then set up before inviting participants.

Click the participants icon in the upper-right area of the window and select participants to add. The organizer can also just drag and drop contacts from the main Skype for Business contact list window into the meeting window to add participants.

When contacts are being invited by name or phone number, Skype for Business displays the existing contacts to simplify adding an attendee who is already known to the meeting organizer. Highlighting the contact and clicking OK sends an invite to the contact. The person is notified by a pop-up box and can opt to either join the conference or ignore the invitation.

Controlling a Meeting

Presenter can sometimes find it useful to have a bit more control over the meeting experience. Skype for Business offers meeting organizers some excellent tools for managing a meeting. For example, right-click attendees to mute their audio, remove them from the conference, or modify their meeting privileges as presenter or attendee. The mute tool is especially useful when a participant is making a lot of background noise that is impacting the meeting experience.

Clicking the Participant Actions button while in a conference reveals a number of additional controls:

- **Mute Audience**—Mutes the entire audience, which can be useful in presentation mode.
- **No Meeting IM**—Disables the instant messaging feature for all attendees. Attendees will see a notification that a presenter has turned off the meeting IM, and the IM section of the client in the lower left will turn gray.
- **No Attendee Video**—Prevents attendees from sending any video to the meeting. Again, this is useful in a presentation or broadcast mode in which only presenter video should be shown.
- **Hide Names**—Hides names of participants on their photos or video stream.
- **Everyone an Attendee**—Forces all meeting participants to be an attendee. This helps ensure that only specified presenters can share content or control the meeting.
- **Invite by Email**—Generates an email invitation with the meeting information. This can be sent to participants who should join the conference.

Managing Meeting Content

With the web conference up and running, participants who were allowed to become presenters based on the meeting options can use the presenter button in the Skype for Business client to add resources to the conference. These options include the same features discussed in the "Sharing Content" section earlier in this chapter.

Sharing a whiteboard reveals several tools on the far-right side so users can collaborate easily. There are pointers, text, shapes, pens, highlighters, erasers, stamps, line art, and a tool for inserting an existing image. The ellipsis icon reveals a few additional options, including the capability to save to OneNote or an image file.

PowerPoint decks can also be uploaded and shared out, and optionally made available for download. After the deck is uploaded, presenters can click Thumbnails or Notes to view the slide previews and any presenter notes. These features are not available to meeting attendees. The upper-right corner displays a pen icon that offers the use of the same whiteboard markup tools.

TIP

Always use the PowerPoint feature instead of doing a desktop or application share. This ensures that the slides are scaled and formatted to fit the various-size screens that might be used for viewing the presentation. It also ensures that content is sent using HTTPS, a more bandwidth-efficient protocol. Sharing the application uses the more bandwidth heavy Remote Desktop Protocol.

After a poll is created, the presenters can choose to show the results to attendees or hide them from attendees, open or close the poll, clear the votes, or save the poll for reference later.

After content has been shared, it stays available within the meeting for reuse or distribution. Clicking the presenter icon and selecting Manage Content displays all the shared content. Presenters can switch between different pieces of content, assign permissions to each piece so that attendees can download it, or remove a component from the meeting.

Changing the Layout

Within each conference is a Layout icon, which is in the toolbar at the very top right of the client window. This enables the users to modify their view of the meeting experience. Depending on the meeting, one of the following layout options might make more sense than others:

- **Gallery View**—This view uses a mixture of video or photos along the top of the screen, and then shows the shared content below. Gallery view is only available when there are at least three participants.
- **Speaker View**—This view focuses on the active speaker. The current speaker's video is displayed next to the shared content.
- **Content View**—This view removes the video from the display and focuses on only the shared content. This option is only available when content is being shared.

While in the Gallery View, right-click any user's photo or video feed and select Pin to Gallery to always show that content. The Gallery View is displayed in Figure 26.5.

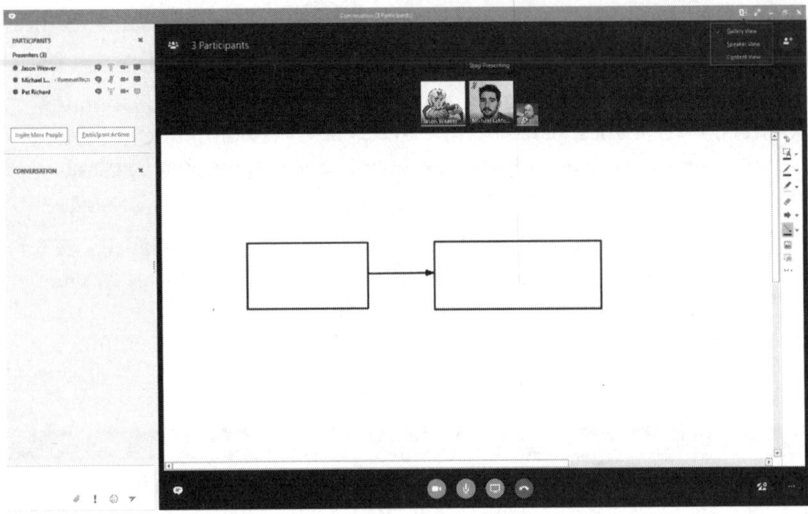

FIGURE 26.5 Skype for Business Gallery View.

Customizing Meeting Options

Within any existing Skype for Business meeting is the capability for organizers to adjust the meeting settings. Clicking the ellipsis icon at the lower-right corner of the conversation window and selecting Skype Meeting Options reveals the various options available:

- **Lobby**—Controls who gets access to the meeting automatically. This can be set to Anyone (no restrictions), Anyone from My Organization, People I Invite, or Only The Meeting Organizer. PSTN callers can optionally bypass the lobby.
- **Announcements**—Controls whether an announcement is played as users enter and exit the meetings. Whether names or tones are used is controlled by a server policy. Users cannot customize that choice.
- **Presenters**—Controls who is allowed to share content and let participants into the meeting.
- **Annotations**—Dictates who can mark up and annotate PowerPoint presentations.
- **Content Viewing**—Controls who can view content at their own pace, such as flipping between different PowerPoint slides without affecting the presenter's view.

Meeting Information

While in a meeting, there can sometimes be a need for participants to view the meeting URL or conference ID so that it can be distributed to someone else. Clicking the ellipsis icon at the lower-right corner of the conversation window and selecting Meeting Entry Info displays details about the current meeting. There is a Copy All Info button on this screen that copies the information to the Clipboard so that it can be pasted into an email or instant message or stored in personal notes.

Recording

If administrators have enabled recordings for conferences or peer-to-peer conversations, users will be able to save conversation IMs, audio, video, and shared content. Within an active conversation, click the ellipsis icon and select Start Recording. This alerts all participants that a recording has started so that they are not caught off guard.

The recorder sees controls to pause or stop the recording at any time. After the recording has stopped, the Skype for Business Recording Manager application begins converting the recorded content and stores it as a saved MP4 video file. This file can then be distributed to users who might have missed a meeting or training session.

Scheduling a Meeting

Dynamically creating an ad hoc meeting has been discussed previously in this chapter, but many users will need to schedule Skype for Business meetings in advance. This can be done through Outlook with the plugin that's installed with the Skype for Business client.

NOTE

Users must be signed in to Skype for Business in order to schedule Skype for Business Meetings through Outlook.

Within Outlook, click the New Items menu and select Skype Meeting. The meeting URL and dial-in bridge information are automatically populated into the meeting notes section. Proceed with adding attendees the same way any other Outlook meeting would be created.

The Skype for Business Meeting button also appears within the ribbon when a regular Outlook meeting is being scheduled. Users can then just click the Skype for Business Meeting button to populate the notes field with the meeting URL and dial-in information, as shown in Figure 26.6.

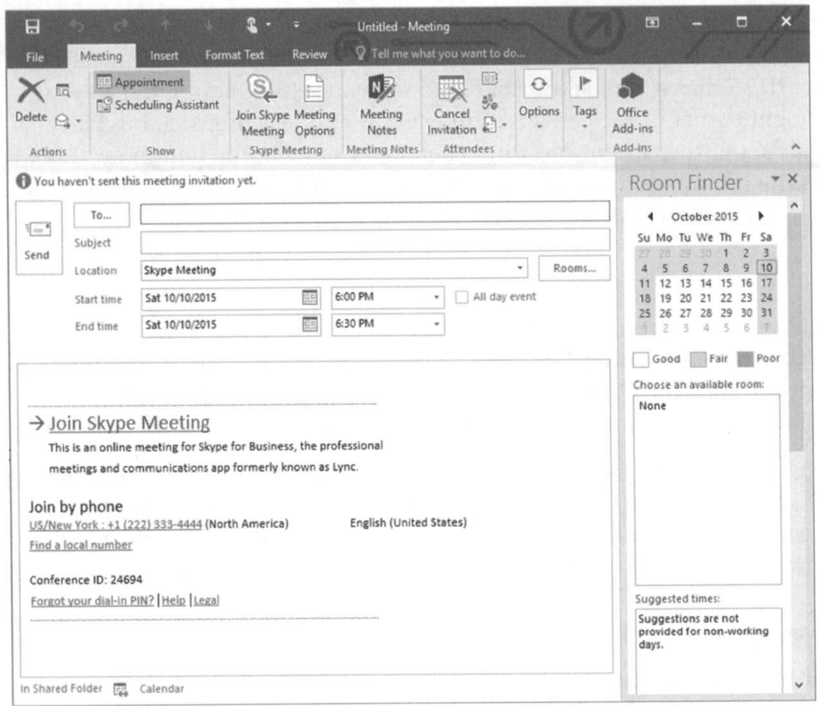

FIGURE 26.6 Skype for Business meeting invitation.

The Meeting Options button also appears within the Outlook ribbon so an organizer can customize the meeting experience before the invitation is sent to users. Clicking the Meeting Options button reveals the screen where an organizer can use the dedicated meeting space, or create a new space for the meeting with a unique conference ID, as shown in Figure 26.7. The PSTN dial-in numbers displayed can also be changed through the Phone section within the Meeting Options.

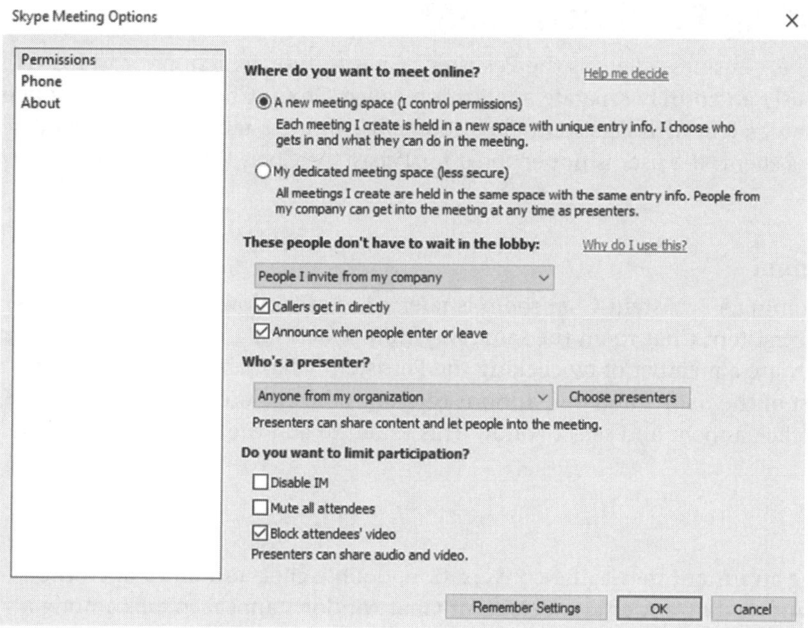

FIGURE 26.7 Skype for Business meeting options.

Joining Meetings

Joining meetings with the Skype for Business client is a simple experience for users. Clicking the Join Skype Meeting hyperlink found within any Skype for Business Meeting automatically launches the conference.

The other easy way to join Skype for Business Meetings is to leverage the Outlook meeting reminder that pops up before a meeting. When Outlook detects that the meeting is a Skype for Business Meeting, it displays a Join Online button to the user. The user does not even need to open the calendar invite but can instead click the Join Online button and immediately enter the meeting.

Users can also dial in to the conference bridge through the Skype for Business client, or have another participant drag them into an existing meeting. This can sometimes be faster than trying to hunt for a calendar invite, especially if Outlook is not already open. There is also no requirement to use both the web conferencing and dial-in bridge. The web conferencing components can be used even if no audio is required in a meeting.

By default, Skype for Business joins the user's PC audio to a conference, but if a user has selected the option Before I Join Meetings, Ask Me Which Audio Device I Want to Use, they are prompted by Skype for Business for an audio source. This enables the user to not join audio at all, which can be useful on a PC with no audio device. Users can also specify a number, such as a mobile phone, for Skype for Business to call them at when they're joining the conference.

Understanding Persistent Chat

New to the Skype for Business client is the Persistent Chat feature, which, prior to Lync 2013, was previously an entirely separate application called Group Chat. The two products are now tightly integrated, with Persistent Chat rooms becoming a tab within the main Skype for Business client. If a user is not enabled for Persistent Chat, that user does not see the tab.

Following Rooms

The concept of joining a Persistent Chat room is referred to as "following a room." Users can search for a Persistent Chat room the same way they search for a user, or they can see which rooms they are a member of by clicking the Persistent Chat tab and then clicking Member Of. A list of the names and descriptions of each room the user belongs to is then displayed. Right-click a room and select Follow This Room to add the room to the user's Followed list.

Using Rooms

Similar to starting an instant messaging conversation, double-click a room to open the contents and begin sending a message. Persistent Chat windows appear in tabs among a user's other IM windows, and they can also be arranged or popped out if necessary.

Type a message and press Enter to deliver the text. The difference with Persistent Chat is that the message will still be there the next time the user or any other user visits the room.

Persistent chats sometimes involve longer posts, referred to as stories. To enter a large portion of text that doesn't cause the room to scroll very far, right-click in the text window and select Post as a Long Message. Then enter a message title and post the longer text. Other users see the longer message as a collapsible hyperlink that helps keep the room organized.

Users within the same room are displayed along the top in a Gallery View, but for larger rooms it can be useful to see a bigger roster. Click the participants icon at the bottom of the room to view an expanded roster.

Using Topic Feeds

Topic feeds in Persistent Chat can be used to receive notifications when a particular keyword is posted in a room. This feature is useful for monitoring specific phrases such as a customer, project, or product name and then being alerted to the discussion in real time.

To create a new topic feed, click the + sign in the upper-right corner of the Persistent Chat section and select Create a New Topic Feed. Enter a name for the feed, select people whom the feed pertains to, and enter keywords to search on. A user can also override the default Persistent Chat settings for a particular feed.

Ego Feed

A single-topic feed called the Ego Feed is enabled for all users when they first sign in, which alerts them if their name is mentioned by anyone. This feed can be deleted by an end user and is intended to just provide a feed example.

Searching Group Chat Rooms

Users can also conduct searches against rooms they follow. Each room presents a search button at the bottom of the conversation window that enables searching that specific room for content. Users can also create a new search across all rooms by clicking the + sign in the upper-right corner of the Persistent Chat section and selecting Search Room History. This enables the user to search across any rooms they follow or belong to, and specify specific date ranges or users that should be searched.

Managing Rooms

Management of Persistent Chat rooms is actually done through a web interface. There are various integration points for Persistent Chat moderators to be redirected to that web interface when they're trying to create or modify an existing room. The steps for creating and managing rooms are covered in much more detail in Chapter 8, "Persistent Chat."

Integration with Other Applications

As is typical with many Microsoft back-office applications, one of the key value propositions is integration with other Microsoft applications. Microsoft touts its concept of "better together" when selling its products, and Skype for Business Server 2015 is no different. After the client is installed, there are hooks into several other Microsoft applications, which are discussed in this section.

Outlook

One of the strongest areas of integration for the Skype for Business client is with Outlook. When the Skype for Business client is installed, it adds several buttons to the Respond area of the Outlook toolbar with the capability to reply via IM or initiate a call.

Instead of being locked into responding to an email with another email, you can choose to start up an IM conversation, initiate a voice call, or initiate a web conference. This offers tremendous flexibility in how to collaborate with co-workers.

This integration extends to the contacts managed by Outlook. By looking at an email received from a co-worker and double-clicking that person's name, you can see the integrated Skype for Business functionality on the contact card. Figure 26.8 shows how you can trigger an IM or a call, or immediately start a shared desktop conference, with the other user. You can also see the Presence information for the other user, which often influences how you respond.

FIGURE 26.8 Outlook contact card.

The last area of integration is Presence information. When looking at email messages from other Skype for Business Server 2015 users, you can see their current status. Hovering the mouse over the Presence icon gives additional information and exposes the menus to enable you to immediately send an IM, place an audio or video call, schedule a meeting, or start sharing resources.

OneNote

Skype for Business has a new level of integration with OneNote for taking notes during Skype for Business Meetings. Just as in previous versions of the product, users can initiate a new note from an existing conversation. Click the Presentation icon and select My Notes. This prompts the user to select a notebook for the note and then automatically populates the subject, date, time, and participants.

New to Skype for Business is the capability to select Shared Notes, which again prompts the user for a notebook to store the notes in. The difference with Shared Notes is that all meeting participants can simultaneously edit the notes, which helps ensure that no information is missed. This feature is dependent on all meeting participants having access to a shared notebook on SharePoint or Windows OneDrive. Skype for Business provides the integration point, but does not provision or provide access to the shared notebook. This functionality can be tested in advance of a meeting to ensure it works properly.

Office Applications

Skype for Business offers some integration with Microsoft Office that can make it easier to collaborate with other users. For example, in Microsoft Word, you can go into the File area of the ribbon and look at the info page. The name of the person who authored the file and the name of the person who last edited the file are located on the far right. Notice that the Presence "jelly bean" is shown next to each of the names with accurate Presence information. If you have a question about the last set of edits made to a document, simply hover over the Last Modified By name to get the option to IM or call that person through Skype for Business. This level of integration makes collaborative communications easy, and quickly becomes second nature for most users.

Skype for Business integration with Office also adds two share options in the Review ribbon.

You can send the document to a contact through the Send by IM button, or you can click Share Now and choose a contact to open a screen-sharing session with that user. This enables two people to share the document and make changes to it collaboratively.

Skype for Business Server Browser Capabilities

Lync Server 2010 introduced basic browser capabilities. Users who joined meetings through a web browser were able to view and present content, as well as initiate a dial-out to a PSTN phone number to join through audio. Skype for Business Server 2015 introduces a new experience for users in the web browser. Skype for Business Web App provides web-based conferencing functionality to users, including audio and video, without a requirement for a Skype for Business client to be installed. Refer to Table 26.4 for Skype for Business Web App capabilities.

TABLE 26.4 Skype for Business Web App Browser Capabilities

OS	Meeting Join	View Content	Full Audio and Video
Windows 7 SP1	X	X	X
Windows Server 2008 R2 SP1	X	X	X
Windows 8	X	X	X
Windows 8.1	X	X	X
Windows 10	X	X	X
Mac OS-X	X	X	X
Windows XP SP3	X	X	
Windows Vista SP2	X	X	
Windows Server 2008 SP2	X	X	

Microsoft's goal was to enable a seamless experience between Skype for Business Web App and the Skype for Business client. Short of a few supportability gaps in older operating systems or web browsers, users can experience full functionality in the browser.

Joining Meetings from the Browser Client

Skype for Business Web App enables guests and authenticated Skype for Business Users to join Skype for Business meetings with a single click. To join with audio and video, a plugin is required. This plugin is designed to be a rapid install with user-level dependencies, and Silverlight is no longer required. Skype for Business Web App users cannot, however, initiate meetings.

Content Collaboration

Skype for Business Web App users are able to participate in a full collaboration experience. This includes desktop sharing, application sharing, control of desktop, real-time note taking, PowerPoint sharing, whiteboards, and polls.

Voice and Video

Skype for Business Web App users who install the browser plugin are able to participate in IP audio and video. Multiparty HD video is also available to users who join through Skype for Business Web App. Additionally, dial-out functionality is still available to users who want to join from a PSTN device.

Meeting Management

Skype for Business Web App users also can manage the meeting from the browser. Meeting presenters can manage the participant list and basic meeting control. However, meeting options such as allowed functionality and locking of the meeting cannot be adjusted in Skype for Business Web App.

Figure 26.9 provides an example of Skype for Business Web App being used to present video in a Skype for Business meeting.

FIGURE 26.9 Skype for Business Web App functionality.

Skype for Business Server 2015 Web App Technical Review

Skype for Business Server 2015 Web App is an HTML-based user interface. This is a drastic change from previous versions that leveraged Silverlight for client rendering. Understanding this new architecture will go a long way in deploying and troubleshooting conferencing deployments with Skype for Business Web App functionality.

Architecture Overview

Skype for Business Web App is built around two core components:

- **JavaScript-powered HTML user interface**—This interface is responsible for rendering most of the UI. It was designed to work on many platforms.
- **Native UI**—The Native UI is responsible for rendering audio, video, and screen sharing during meetings.

Figure 26.10 outlines the logical separation of these components.

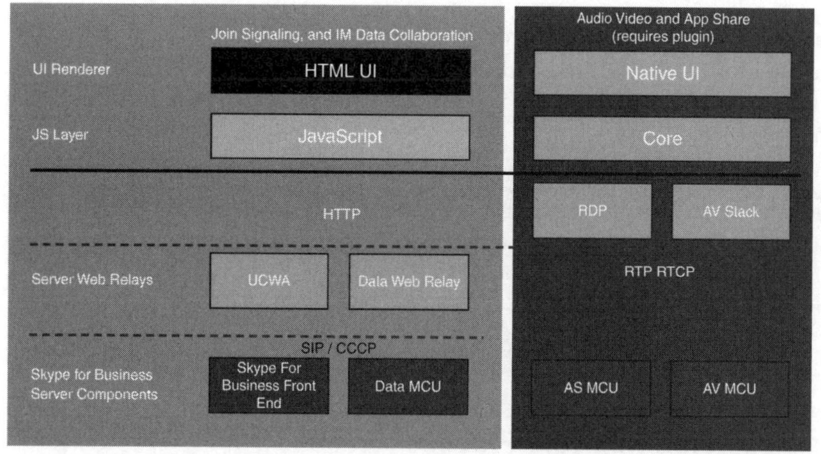

FIGURE 26.10 Skype for Business Mobile architecture.

Skype for Business Web App communicates directly with Unified Communications Web API (UCWA), which is a new API introduced with Skype for Business Server 2015, enabling applications to leverage Skype for Business functionality in a web browser. UCWA will communicate to the Skype for Business Conferencing Servers to establish signaling sessions. The Skype for Business Native UI, which is the plugin-based UI, will talk to the media stack on the Skype for Business Servers for audio, video, and application/desktop-sharing functionality.

Skype for Business Web App Websites

Skype for Business Web App is provided through internal and external websites. Similar to all Skype for Business Web Services, Skype for Business Web App is deployed on each Front End Server; the logical separation of internal and external web directories provides additional security, while enabling internal users to have a seamless join experience.

Authentication Methods Supported

Skype for Business Web App supports standard authentication methods. On-premises users are able to authenticate through forms-based authentication, through Integrated Windows Authentication, or through multifactor authentication that is powered by ADFS. For Skype for Business Online users, OrgID authentication is supported, which is the primary authentication method for all Microsoft Online services. Lastly, guests or unauthenticated users can join if the conferencing policy permits.

Skype for Business Web App Proxy Support

Skype for Business Web App enables users who are configured with an HTTP proxy to use Skype for Business Web App for all functionality. If an HTTP proxy is configured for Basic Authentication, media traffic does not work. For media to pass through the HTTP proxy, the proxy must be configured for Kerberos, NTLM, or Digest authentication.

Skype for Business Web App Port Requirements

Skype for Business Web App is a web application that communicates over HTTPS. By default, this traffic is over port 443 TCP and is secured with certificates. Administrators can adjust this port if desired.

TIP

Although Skype for Business Web App communicates only over 443 TCP for web traffic, the A/V plugin communicates directly with the Conferencing Server or Edge Server using standard media ports. Keep this in mind when planning your Skype for Business Web App deployment.

Skype for Business Web App Join Process

This section provides an overview of the join process in Skype for Business Web App. Understanding how clients connect to these services will greatly help in deploying and troubleshooting Skype for Business Server 2015 conferencing. Figure 26.11 and the list that follows outlines the join process.

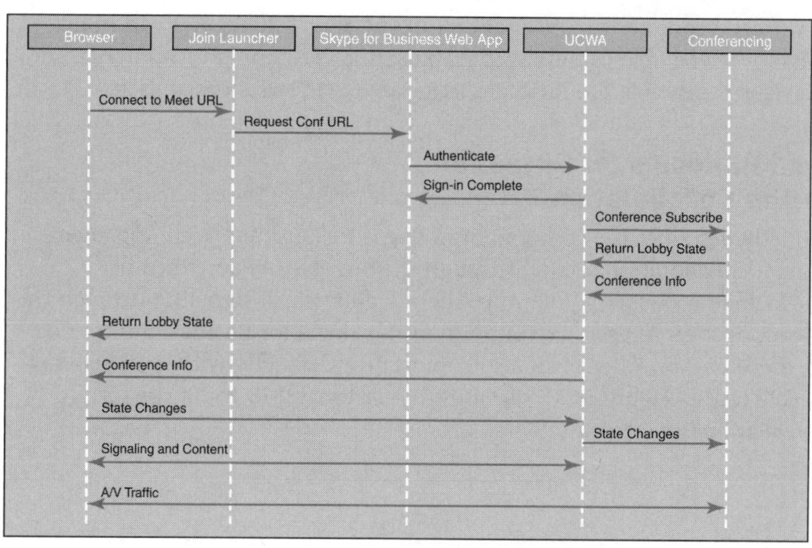

FIGURE 26.11 Skype for Business Web App join process.

1. When a client clicks the meeting URL in the meeting invite, they are connected to the Skype for Business Web Services. The Join Launcher component identifies the client type that is connecting and either launches the installed Skype for Business client or launches Skype for Business Web App.

2. The Join Launcher connects to Skype for Business Web App and requests the conferencing URLs to be used.

3. Skype for Business Web App communicates with UCWA to authenticate the user. This can happen over various methods, but ultimately the connecting user must be issued a web ticket to securely connect to Skype for Business Web App and UCWA.

4. When initiated, UCWA initiates requests to the Conferencing Focus to join the user to the conference.

5. The user is placed in the meeting lobby and joins when admitted.

6. Going forward, all communications with the Conferencing Focus happen through UCWA. These communications include state changes for the user and the conference.

7. The user receives conference join information in-band to connect to the A/V portions of the conference. Going forward, the browser client communicates directly with the Conferencing Server for media, or through the Edge Server if the user is remote.

For those familiar with the conference join process in Lync Server 2013, you will notice that the join process for Skype for Business Web App users is very similar. An important note: UCWA will always be involved to facilitate signaling for browser-based users.

Components and Protocols for Skype for Business Web App Collaboration

This next section briefly describes the components a Skype for Business Web App client interacts with during a collaboration session through the browser. As described in earlier sections, the Skype for Business Web App Client facilitates all signaling through the Unified Communications Web API service running on the Skype for Business Front End Services. However, the Web App Client will also communicate directly with conferencing components for media traffic. Figure 26.12 outlines the protocol flow for Skype for Business Web App collaboration sessions.

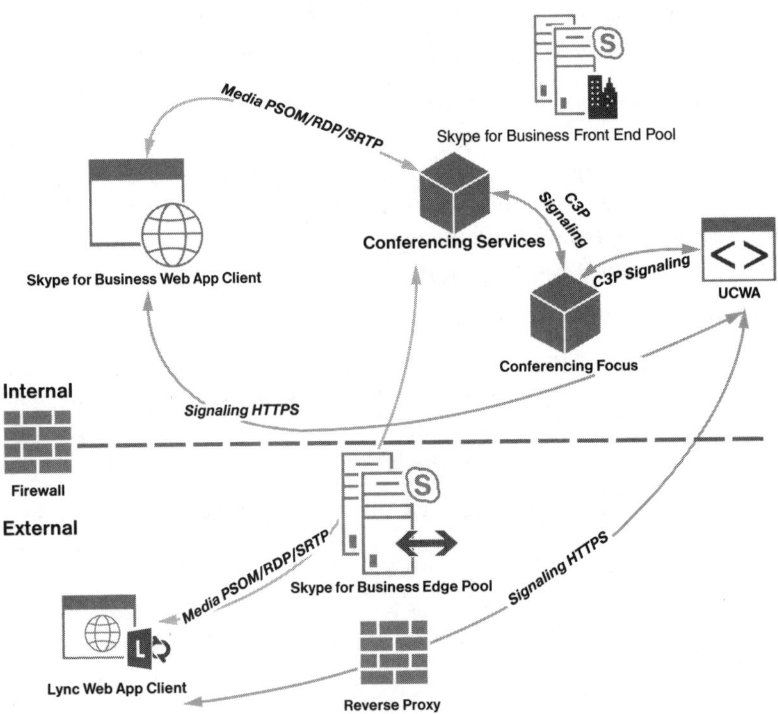

FIGURE 26.12 Skype for Business Web App protocol flow.

The following information is outlined in Figure 26.12:

- The Conferencing Services and Conferencing Focus are logical services located on Skype for Business Front End Servers. The Conferencing Focus is responsible for coordinating conferencing resources and the conferencing join process for clients. The Conferencing Services would include the Audio/Video Conferencing

Service, Application Sharing Conferencing Service, Data Conferencing Service, and IM Conferencing Service. The services have been combined in the diagram for simplicity.

- Skype for Business Web App clients send all signaling traffic to the Front End pool and through the UCWA service. If the user is external (see the bottom of the diagram), this traffic must be securely published through a reverse proxy solution.
- Skype for Business Web App clients send media traffic through the appropriate conferencing service. If the user is external, the traffic is securely relayed through the Skype for Business Edge Server.

Summary of the Browser Client Architecture and Components

In Skype for Business Server 2015, the browser-based capabilities have been enhanced. With the changes in functionality, architectural changes were introduced. At the core of the architecture is the Unified Communications Web API. This API enables web-based clients to communicate over open standards and perform full Skype for Business functionality. The UCWA service acts as a communication proxy between web-based clients and the other Skype for Business services. UCWA is also at the core of mobility scenarios, and it's an API that can be developed on to enhance Skype for Business functionality even further.

After the Skype for Business Web App client has connected to the UCWA service for signaling, it acts much like any other Skype for Business client for collaboration scenarios. The Skype for Business Web App client communicates over HTTPS to receive collaboration content such as PowerPoint presentations and whiteboards, while the ActiveX plugin enables the client to communicate with the media conferencing services over secure RTP.

Requirements to Deploy Skype for Business Browser Functionality

Deploying Skype for Business Web App is a relatively simple process. However, this section outlines the client and server requirements for a successful implementation.

Installing Skype for Business Web App Server

Skype for Business Web App functionality is installed on all Front End Servers in the environment. No extra steps are required to install these services. When Skype for Business Front End Servers are configured, all services, certificates, and DNS requirements for Skype for Business Web App Server are completed as well.

Configuring Skype for Business Web App

Although Skype for Business Web App components are installed by default, there are several common configurations to control Skype for Business Web App functionality and access.

Enabling Skype for Business Web App Access for Anonymous Users

For anonymous users (users not enabled for Skype for Business) to join meetings through Skype for Business Web App, you must configure the web service for your Skype for Business topology to allow this. This is done using the `Set-CSWebServiceConfiguration` PowerShell cmdlet. An example of how to perform this configuration is shown here:

1. Open the Skype for Business Server Management Shell.
2. Run the following command to see the existing web service configuration:

```
Get-CSWebServiceConfiguration
```

Here is the sample output:

```
Identity                                  :Global
TrustedCACerts                            :{}
CrossDomainAuthorizationList
MaxGroupSizeToExpand                      :100
EnableGroupExpansion                      :True
UseWindowsAuth                            :Negotiate
UseCertificateAuth                        :True
UsePinAuth                                :True
UseDomainAuthInLWA                        :True
EnableMediaBasicAuth                      :False
AllowAnonymousAccessToLWAConference       :False
EnableCertChainDownload                   :True
InferCertChainFromSSL                     :True
CASigningKeyLength                        :2048
MaxCSRKeySize                             :16384
MinCSRKeySize                             :1024
MaxValidityPeriodHours                    :8760
MinValidityPeriodHours                    :8
DefaultValidityPeriodHours                :4320
MACResolverUrl                            :
SecondaryLocationSourceUrl                :
ShowJoinUsingLegacyClientLink             :True
UseWebClientLegacyUI                      :False
ShowDownloadCommunicatorAttendeeLink      :True
AutoLaunchLyncWebAccess                   :True
ShowAlternateJoinOptionsExpanded          :False
UseWsFedPassiveAuth                       :False
WsFedPassiveMetadataUri                   :
AllowExternalAuthentication               :True
MobilePreferredAuthType                   :None
EnableStatisticsInResponse                :False
HstsMaxAgeInSeconds                       :31536000
```

By default, there is only a Global web service configuration. However, if you have previously made site- or pool-specific configurations, you can access them through the following command:

```
Get-CSWebServiceConfiguration -Identity <XDS Identity>
```

`<XDS Identity>` refers to the name of the service; for a site this is `site:<site name>`.

3. If `AllowAnonymousAccesstoLWAConference` is set to `false`, run the following command to enable this functionality:

```
Set-CSWebServiceConfiguration -AllowAnonymousAccesstoLWAConference $true
```

4. Running `Get-CSWebServiceConfiguration` again should return the following results:

```
Identity                                  :Global
TrustedCACerts                            :{}
CrossDomainAuthorizationList
MaxGroupSizeToExpand                      :100
EnableGroupExpansion                      :True
UseWindowsAuth                            :Negotiate
UseCertificateAuth                        :True
UsePinAuth                                :True
UseDomainAuthInLWA                        :True
EnableMediaBasicAuth                      :False
AllowAnonymousAccessToLWAConference       :True
EnableCertChainDownload                   :True
InferCertChainFromSSL                     :True
CASigningKeyLength                        :2048
MaxCSRKeySize                             :16384
MinCSRKeySize                             :1024
MaxValidityPeriodHours                    :8760
MinValidityPeriodHours                    :8
DefaultValidityPeriodHours                :4320
MACResolverUrl                            :
SecondaryLocationSourceUrl                :
ShowJoinUsingLegacyClientLink             :True
UseWebClientLegacyUI                      :False
ShowDownloadCommunicatorAttendeeLink      :True
AutoLaunchLyncWebAccess                   :True
ShowAlternateJoinOptionsExpanded          :False
UseWsFedPassiveAuth                       :False
WsFedPassiveMetadataUri                   :
AllowExternalAuthentication               :True
MobilePreferredAuthType                   :None
EnableStatisticsInResponse                :False
HstsMaxAgeInSeconds                       :31536000
```

Skype for Business Web App Conferencing Policies

Users who join a conference through Skype for Business Web App will honor all conferencing policies associated with that conference, and their own conferencing policy if applicable. It is important to treat the Skype for Business Web App Client as another Skype for Business client; if conferencing functionality is enabled for regular Skype for Business users, it is also available in the Skype for Business Web App client.

Publishing Skype for Business Web App Service to External Clients

External users access Skype for Business Web App through the Skype for Business Web Services. Skype for Business Web Services are published for several critical Skype for Business client services, including Meeting Join, Dial-in Conferencing information page, Address Book Service, Collaboration Services, and Skype for Business Web App. Skype for Business Web Services, and as a result, Skype for Business Web App, must be securely published through a reverse-proxy solution to provide access to external users. For information on deploying Skype for Business Web Services through a reverse proxy, see Chapter 11, "Firewall, Reverse Proxy, and Security Requirements."

Operating System Requirements for Skype for Business Web App Client

The following operating systems are supported for the Skype for Business Web App client:

- Windows 10 (Intel based)
- Windows 8.1 (Intel based)
- Windows 8 (Intel based)
- Windows 7 with SP1
- Windows Vista with SP2
- Windows XP with SP3
- Windows Server 2008 R2 with SP1
- Windows Server 2008 R1 with SP2
- Windows Server 2012
- Windows Server 2012 R2
- Mac OS-X (Intel based)

Windows 10, Windows 8/8.1, Windows 7, Windows 2008 R2/2012/2012 R2, and Mac OS X systems that meet the preceding operating system requirements can perform full collaboration sessions, including audio and video through the web browser. Windows XP, Windows Vista, and Windows Server 2008 R1 systems that meet the requirements do not have audio and video available; these clients can still perform application viewing and sharing through Skype for Business Web App.

Browser Requirements for Skype for Business Web App Client

The following web browsers are supported for the Skype for Business Web App Client:

- Edge browser in Windows 10
- 32-bit Internet Explorer 11
- 64-bit Internet Explorer 11
- 32-bit Internet Explorer 10
- 64-bit Internet Explorer 10
- 32-bit Internet Explorer 9
- 64-bit Internet Explorer 9
- 32-bit Firefox 12.x
- 64-bit Safari 5.x
- 32-bit Chrome 18.x

A Microsoft ActiveX browser plugin is required for participating in audio and video sessions through the web browser.

Summary

In this chapter, we covered the primary clients for Windows users to connect to Microsoft Skype for Business Server 2015. You saw what features are available in terms of IM, audio/video conferencing, and application sharing. As users become more and more familiar with the application, this chapter will serve as a guide for how they can access various functions within the system and should help ease the transition to this application.

Administrators should take advantage of the troubleshooting and best practices offered in this chapter to try to provide for the best end-user experience possible. Ultimately, the success of a Microsoft Skype for Business Server 2015 deployment will be measured by the end users, and taking advantage of the information in this chapter will help increase the odds of having happy end users.

It is useful for administrators to understand the limitations of the various clients so that users can be trained and informed about the different features available. This can be especially useful when external users who attach via the web-based clients are involved. By knowing when to use various client options, administrators and helpdesk staff can guide users toward the best decisions on how to meet their needs.

Skype for Business enables browser-based users to experience full-featured conferencing functionality. This service can be provided across both Windows and Macintosh operating systems as well as through various popular web browsers. The architecture changes introduced to the server platform to support this functionality are built-in standard applications and codecs. Understanding the components and architecture for Skype for Business Web App will enable an administrator to deploy and support Skype for Business Web App functionality with confidence.

CHAPTER 27

VDI

IN THIS CHAPTER

Many companies and service providers today use a virtual desktop infrastructure for easy management of end-user desktops. For service providers, the advantage is being able to offer a centrally managed desktop on unmanaged devices. The business case for companies using virtual desktops is being able to offer a desktop across a wide range of hardware, including thin clients. The challenge in the virtual desktop approach is being able to offer good audio and video experience for Lync and Skype for Business. This specifically is crucial for end users who want to consume telephony features without having an extra IP phone at their desk. Here is where the Lync VDI plugin comes in to play. This chapter provides some background on VDI technology and then presents details on the Lync VDI plugin that Microsoft has developed to optimize the performance of Lync and Skype for Business in a VDI environment.

NOTE

The VDI plugin was first introduced in Lync 2013 and is still supported in Skype for Business with the same features and limitations. For Skype for Business, you will still install the Lync VDI plugin and patch it with the latest Skype for Business update to align the version match with the Skype for Business build in the remote desktop.

VDI Basics

Although there are certainly different approaches used and different technologies implemented by VDI vendors, the idea behind VDI is consistent. It is a technology that enables users to connect remotely to a desktop environment that is stored, executed, and managed centrally, with the presentation of the desktop being delivered to the user via a remote desktop protocol. VDI is also powered by virtualization technology in the datacenter, which enables the desktop to be separated from the underlying hardware. The end result is a flexible desktop environment that increases management control compared to the physical desktop environment, which can potentially decrease desktop costs. There are also potential security benefits with VDI, because it can be used to gain tighter control of corporate resources that are typically distributed on desktop systems throughout an organization, sometimes in a rather haphazard manner.

Following are the components commonly included in the majority of the VDI solutions on the market:

- **Hypervisor**—The software layer used to manage the hardware allocation of a server host as well as handle the creation and management of virtual desktops on that host.
- **Connection broker**—Software used to handle the provisioning of virtual desktops to users, typically based on user credentials.
- **Application presentation**—A system that centrally manages the distribution of applications to the virtual desktop environment, typically allowing a centralized repository of standard applications and on-demand delivery.
- **Virtual desktop**—The virtual machine that is accessed remotely by the user, providing an isolated desktop environment that can be either customizable or restricted.
- **Remote desktop presentation protocol**—A technology used to present the desktop interface to the client device, which can either be installed as client software or integrated with the client hardware. The most common remote desktop presentation protocols are Remote Desktop Protocol (RDP), Independent Computing Architecture (ICA), and PC-over-IP (PCoIP).
- **Endpoint device (or access device)**—The hardware device used to access the virtual desktop.

VDI Vendors

As the interest in VDI has increased, so has the number of vendors providing VDI solutions. Although many firms offer VDI products, two vendors stand out in the crowd as providing enterprise-ready end-to-end VDI solutions: Citrix, with the XenDesktop product, and VMware, which offers View. Microsoft has also invested heavily in VDI technology and includes a VDI offering with the Windows operating system as part of the Remote Desktop Services portfolio. However, for enterprise-level VDI, Microsoft has largely partnered with Citrix to offer a complete solution. There are numerous other players in the VDI market as well, some offering alternatives to the mainstream VDI approach, and others marketing a specific part of the solution, such as application packaging and deployment or performance monitoring for the VDI environment.

Challenges to VDI Adoption

Even with the benefits noted previously, VDI is still a relatively new technology, and with practically any new technology there are challenges to overcome before widespread adoption can be achieved. One of the primary challenges for VDI has been that, although many applications are very well suited for the VDI environment, some applications do not function nearly as well with VDI as they do in a native desktop environment. Most often this is due to performance characteristics of the application or hardware dependencies. With Microsoft Lync, Skype for Business, and other unified communications software, performance-related challenges come into play when real-time media workloads are virtualized. Because of this, Microsoft has focused on directly addressing these issues in an effort to allow near-native performance for the Lync and Skype for Business client when running in the VDI environment. The end result of Microsoft's efforts is the VDI plugin introduced with Lync 2013, which is explored in detail in the following sections.

The Lync VDI Plugin

The Lync VDI plugin was introduced with Lync 2013 and is supported for Skype for Business. It was created to provide an audio and video experience for a Lync client in a VDI session that is close to the experience of a locally installed client. To support this, the VDI plugin uses media redirection, in which the encoding and decoding of media are offloaded from the datacenter and handled directly by the thin client or access device, using the client's local resources. Other non-media features of Lync, such as IM, Presence, and desktop sharing, are still executed from within the virtual desktop.

Historically, using Lync 2010 when the VDI plugin was not available had several inherent limitations that where presented when the Lync 2010 media workloads were virtualized. For example, note the peer-to-peer audio communication scenario depicted in Figure 27.1, in which one user is using Lync 2010 locally on a desktop, and the second user is running Lync 2010 within a VDI client without the possibility of the VDI plugin. Unlike in a standard peer-to-peer audio session using two locally installed clients, the media stream for the VDI desktop user is sent and received from the datacenter, as opposed to the user's location. This results in higher bandwidth usage at the datacenter, limits audio and video conferencing capabilities, and reduces the scalability of the server. This frequently results in a poor media experience for the user because media has to go through the remote desktop presentation protocols, which are not optimized for UDP media traffic. The same challenges are present today when running Skype for Business without the Lync VDI plugin.

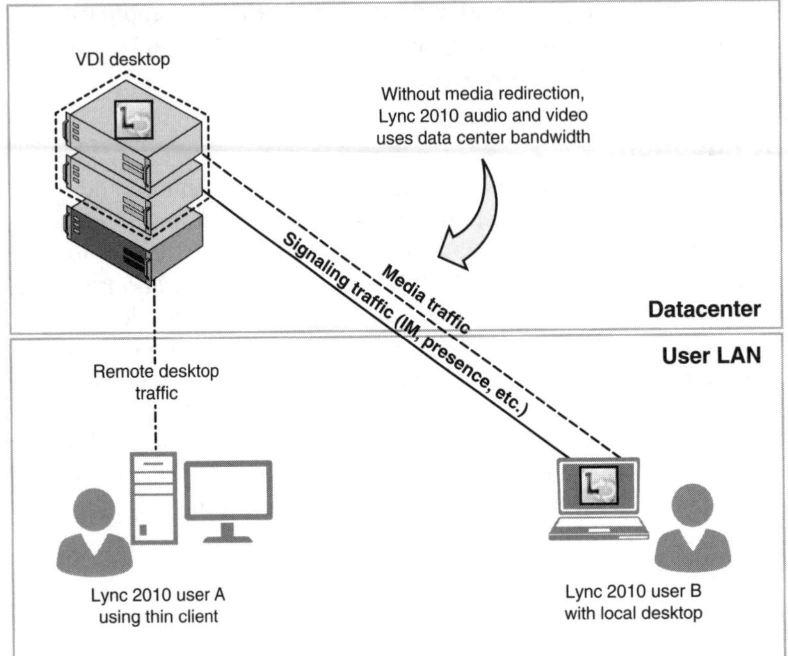

FIGURE 27.1 Peer-to-peer communication with VDI using Lync 2010.

In contrast, Figure 27.2 shows the same peer-to-peer communication, but this time using Lync 2013 along with the VDI plugin. With this set of components, audio and video originate and terminate at the plugin running on the thin client using native codecs and UDP for transport, while the signaling traffic continues to use the VDI desktop in the datacenter. This results in minimal bandwidth consumption between the end device and the datacenter, enables all conferencing capabilities, and provides a significantly better media experience for the user. An additional benefit that results from this media redirection is that Lync and Skype for Business server scalability improves, as the CPU-intensive media processing is offloaded to the client for each VDI user.

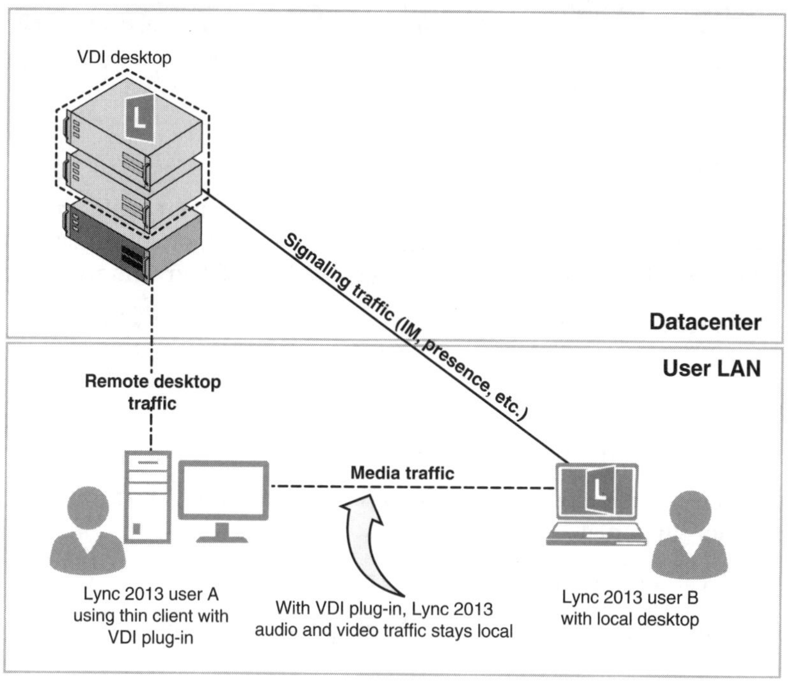

FIGURE 27.2 Peer-to-peer communication with VDI using Lync 2013 and the VDI plugin.

Lync VDI Plugin Device Support

For use with the VDI plugin, Microsoft supports any audio and video devices that are qualified for Lync and Skype for Business, such as headsets and cameras. The following features are supported when these devices are used in combination with the VDI plugin:

- Call controls from a device
- Presence integration on a device
- Multiple HID (human interface device) support
- Location and emergency services support
- Support for all modalities, including IM, audio, video, desktop and application sharing, file transfer, and so on
- Audio and video support for peer-to-peer and conference calls

NOTE

Office 365/Skype for Business Online does not support the Lync VDI plugin.

Lync VDI Plugin Limitations

Although the majority of the functionality included in a standard Lync client deployment is also available in a VDI session, there are some features that are not supported. Following are the known limitations for using Lync and Skype for Business in a VDI environment:

- Integrated audio and video device-tuning pages are not available (device selection and tuning can be adjusted using the access device).
- Multiview video is not supported.
- Recording of conversations is not supported.
- Joining meetings anonymously (specifically meetings hosted by an organization that is not federated) is not supported.
- Customized ringtones and music on-hold features are not supported.
- The Call Delegation and Response Group Agent Anonymization features are not supported.
- Lync Phone Edition devices are not supported in combination with the VDI plugin.
- Call continuity in the event of a network outage is not supported.
- Office 365/Skype for Business Online does not support the Lync VDI plugin.
- The Lync VDI plugin cannot be installed on computers where the full Lync and Skype for Business client is installed. Users with laptops need to choose between the experience of a local client or a VDI plugin client.

Deploying the Lync VDI Plugin

The Lync VDI plugin is a standalone application that is available in 32-bit and 64-bit versions, and it can be freely downloaded from the Microsoft download site. For Skype for Business, you can install the Lync VDI plugin and patch it with the latest Skype for Business update to align the version match with the Skype for Business build in the remote desktop. The plugin must be installed on the endpoint device that will be used to access the VDI desktop, which is typically a repurposed desktop or a thin client device. To use the plugin, certain systems prerequisites must first be met, as detailed in the following section.

TIP

The full Skype for Business client does not need to be installed on the endpoint device used to access the VDI desktop; only the Lync VDI plugin software is required. It is not supported or possible to have both the full Skype for Business client and the Lync VDI plugin installed on the same machine. Users with laptops need to choose between the experience of a local client or a VDI plugin client.

System Requirements

Before the VDI plugin is used, certain prerequisites must be met for both the virtual machine and the access device used for the VDI session:

- The VDI desktop must be running one of the following operating systems: Windows 7, Windows 8, Windows 10, or Windows Server 2008 R2 with the latest service pack.
- The access device must be running one of the following operating systems: Windows Embedded Standard 7 with SP1, Windows 7 with SP1, Windows 8, Windows 8.1 Embedded, Windows 10 Embedded, or Windows 10.
- Minimum hardware specs for installing the VDI plugin on an access device include a 1.5GHz processor, 2GB RAM, and either 700MB hard drive space (for the 32-bit plugin) or 900MB hard drive space (for the 64-bit plugin).
- If Remote Desktop Services will be used to host the virtual desktops, the bitness of the Lync VDI plugin must match the bitness of the OS on the access device (either 32-bit or 64-bit accordingly). However, the bitness of the OS on the access device does not need to match the bitness of the OS on the virtual machine. If a different virtualization solution is used to host the VDI desktops, different bitness requirements might apply and will depend on the virtualization solution used.
- If Remote Desktop Services will be used to host the virtual desktops, and the access device is running Windows 7 with SP1 or Windows Server 2008 R2, the Windows 8 version of the Remote Desktop Services client should be installed. Before the Windows 8 version of the Remote Desktop Services client is installed, the Windows update described in Microsoft Knowledge Base article #2574819 must first be installed as a prerequisite. After the prerequisite update is installed, the following link can be used to download the Remote Desktop Protocol update for Windows 7 SP1 and Windows Server 2008 R2 SP1: http://support.microsoft.com/kb/2592687.

Remote Desktop Connection Settings

If Remote Desktop Services will be used to host the virtual desktops, the remote desktop client settings must be configured so that audio plays on the local system, and remote recording must be disabled. The following procedure is used to configure the Remote Desktop Connections settings on the local system in preparation for deploying the Lync VDI plugin:

1. Log on to the local system and open the Remote Desktop Services client by selecting Start, All Programs, Accessories, Remote Desktop Conncction.
2. Click Options to expand the dialog box, and then select the Local Resources tab.
3. In the Remote Audio section, click Settings to display the remote audio settings, as shown in Figure 27.3.

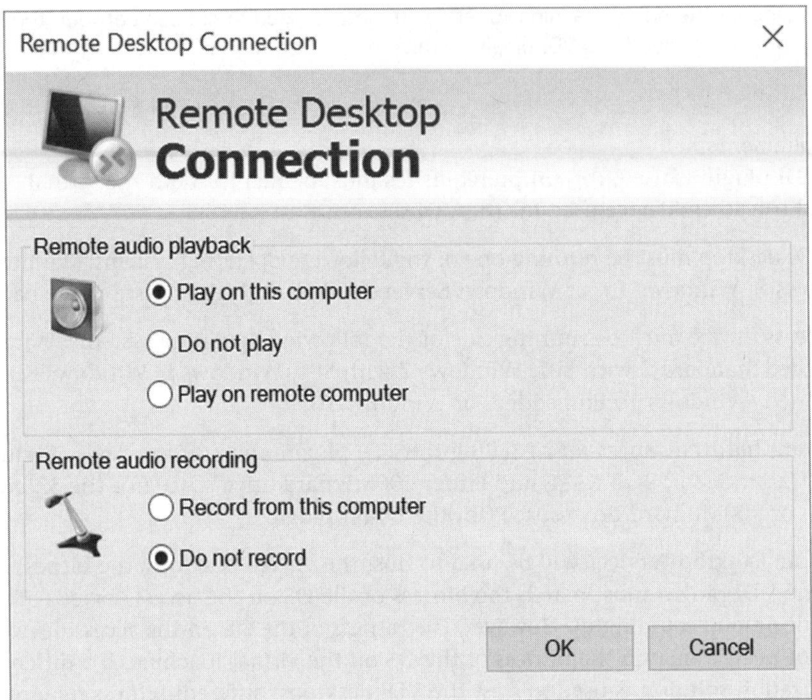

FIGURE 27.3 Remote audio settings used with the Lync VDI plugin.

4. Under Remote Audio Playback, select Play on This Computer.
5. Under Remote Audio Recording, select Do Not Record and then click OK.
6. Select the Experience tab.
7. In the Performance section, clear the option for Persistent Bitmap Caching.
8. Select the General tab and then click Save As. At the Save As dialog box, choose a location where the RDP file will be saved.

Lync Client Policy Configuration for VDI

Skype for Business client policies are used to determine the features of Skype for Business Server that are made available to users. Client policies can be configured at the global, site, and user levels; a policy at the user level has the highest priority, and a policy configured at the site level overrides the policy at the global level for any users in that site. For Skype for Business, a client policy is automatically created at the global level, and is simply named Global.

TIP

It is easy to confuse client policy with client version policy based on the similar names, but these two policies have very different purposes in Skype for Business. Client version policy is used to control the specific applications that can be used to log on to Skype for Business Server. Client policy, on the other hand, is used to control the specific Skype for Business features that will be available to users.

In Lync Server 2013, a new client policy setting was created to allow administrators to be selective regarding which users are enabled for the media redirection feature. By default, media redirection is disabled within the default client policy at the global level. This means that before users can leverage the Lync VDI plugin, either media redirection must be enabled in the global client policy or a new client policy must be created with the setting enabled and then applied at either the site or user level. To create a new Skype for Business client policy, or to adjust an existing one, the Skype for Business 2015 Server Management Shell is used.

The following example outlines the procedure for using the Skype for Business Server 2015 Management Shell to create a new client policy named `VDI_Policy` with media redirection enabled, and then applying the policy to all users in the IT department:

1. Log on to a system where the Skype for Business Server 2015 Administrative Tools are installed using an account that is a member of the `CsAdministrator` or `CsServerAdministrator` group in AD and that has administrative rights on the local system.
2. Open the Skype for Business Server 2015 Management Shell and execute the following command to create a new client policy named `VDI_policy` with media redirection enabled:

```
New-CsClientPolicy -Identity VDI_Policy -EnableMediaRedirection $true
```

3. If the command is successful, the client policy is created and the properties of the policy are displayed, as shown in Figure 27.4.

FIGURE 27.4 Creating a new client policy with media redirection enabled.

4. Execute the following command to apply the new client policy to each user in the IT department that is enabled for Skype for Business:

```
(Get-ADUser -Filter {msRTCSIP-UserEnabled -eq $True -and Department -eq
➥"IT"}).DistinguishedName | Grant-CsClientPolicy -PolicyName VDI_Policy
```

In the first portion of the PowerShell command executed previously in step 4, the `Get-ADUser` cmdlet, is used with filter parameters to return a collection of users who are enabled for Skype for Business and whose `Department` attribute in Active Directory is configured as `IT`. Then we pick the `DistinguishedName` attribute and pipe that to the second portion of the command. Using `Get-ADUser` requires the Active Directory PowerShell module to be installed. This will give you the best flexibility to choose attributes to filter because you can call all attributes present on the user object Active Directory.

The second portion of the command is where the `Grant-CsClientPolicy` cmdlet is used to apply the client policy to the IT users. Many different combinations of these cmdlets can be used to selectively apply client policies to users across the organization, granting the ability to use media redirection along with a host of other features, many of which are displayed in Figure 27.4. After the client policy has been applied, the `Get-CsUser` cmdlet can be used to verify that the client policy has been correctly applied to the user, as shown in Figure 27.5.

TIP

The only policy settings that are displayed when the `Get-CsUser` cmdlet is used are those that are applied at the user level. However, for each Skype for Business policy, a user-, site-, or global-level policy setting is applied for each user. If some policy values display as null with the `Get-CsUser` cmdlet (such as shown in Figure 27.5), this means that either a site-level policy is applied (if it exists) or a global policy is applied. You can verify this by first retrieving the user's site identity and then determining whether a particular policy is applied at the site level. If not, the global policy settings are applied to the user for that particular policy.

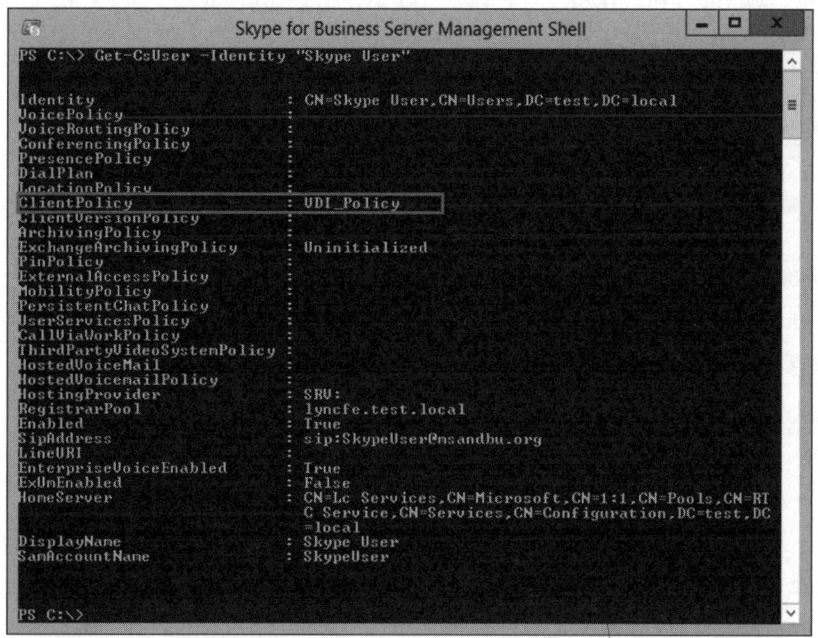
Skype for Business Server Management Shell
PS C:\> Get-CsUser -Identity "Skype User"
Identity : CN=Skype User,CN=Users,DC=test,DC=local
VoicePolicy :
VoiceRoutingPolicy :
ConferencingPolicy :
PresencePolicy :
DialPlan :
LocationPolicy :
ClientPolicy : VDI_Policy
ClientVersionPolicy :
ArchivingPolicy :
ExchangeArchivingPolicy : Uninitialized
PinPolicy :
ExternalAccessPolicy :
MobilityPolicy :
PersistentChatPolicy :
UserServicesPolicy :
CallViaWorkPolicy :
ThirdPartyVideoSystemPolicy :
HostedVoiceMail :
HostedVoicemailPolicy :
HostingProvider : SRV:
RegistrarPool : lyncfe.test.local
Enabled : True
SipAddress : sip:SkypeUser@msandbu.org
LineURI :
EnterpriseVoiceEnabled : True
ExUmEnabled : False
HomeServer : CN=Lc Services,CN=Microsoft,CN=1:1,CN=Pools,CN=RT
C Service,CN=Services,CN=Configuration,DC=test,DC
=local
DisplayName : Skype User
SamAccountName : SkypeUser
PS C:\>

FIGURE 27.5 Verifying the client policy setting for a user in the Management Shell.

The Installation of the VDI Plugin

At the time of writing this chapter, there has not been a new release of the Lync VDI plugin, but you can use it, patch it with the latest Lync client patch, and get the Skype for Business client UI. The Lync VDI plugin can be downloaded from the Microsoft download site and is available in 32-bit and 64-bit versions. Use the following procedure to install the VDI plugin on a system that will be used to access VDI desktop sessions with Skype for Business:

1. Log on to the system where the plugin will be installed using an account with local administrator rights.

2. From the Microsoft download site, download the version of the VDI plugin that matches the local hardware, either 32-bit or 64-bit, and save the file to a local subdirectory on the system.
3. Double-click the downloaded file, named `Lyncvdi.exe`.
4. At the Read the Microsoft Software License Terms screen, read the software license terms. Click the I Accept the Terms of This Agreement option if you agree to the terms and then click Continue.
5. At the Choose the Installation You Want screen, either click Install Now to install the software using the default settings or click Customize to choose specific installation options.
6. If you chose to customize the installation in the preceding step, three tabs offering several options for customization are displayed, as shown in Figure 27.6. If there are specific features that will not be installed, this can be configured on the Installation Options tab; click the drop-down menu next to the feature and select Not Available. If a customized installation path for the plugin files is needed, this can be configured on the File Location tab; enter the new path or browse to the desired location. If the user information needs to be adjusted from the default values, this can be configured on the User Information tab. When finished, click Install Now.

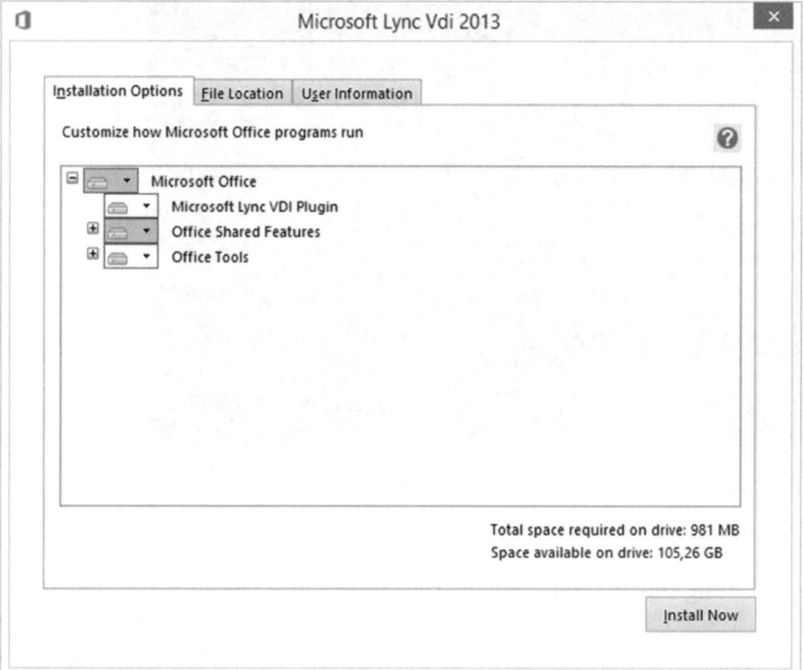

FIGURE 27.6 Customization options for the Lync VDI plugin.

7. After the software is installed, click Close.
8. If prompted, click Yes to reboot the system and complete the installation.
9. After the reboot, you can log on using remote desktop. It is important that it is a new session and that you can verify the connection.
10. The VDI plugin will pair with a Skype for Business client unpatched, but getting the latest fixes and updates is recommended.
11. The Lync VDI plugin uses the regular Lync 2013 client cumulative update. You can find the latest cumulative update at the following location:

    https://technet.microsoft.com/en-us/office/dn788954.aspx

    Remember to install the required updates first, such as the Office 2013 SP1 update and the April 2015 update, as described on the download page.

TIP

After the plugin is installed, two files (LyncVdiPlugin.dll and UcVdi.dll) should be present in the C:\Program Files (x86)\Microsoft Office\Office15 directory (for 32-bit installations) or the C:\Program Files\Microsoft Office\Office15 directory (for 64-bit installations).

User Experience with the Lync VDI Plugin

As noted previously, the primary goal for developing the VDI plugin is for Lync and Skype for Business users to have the same experience, regardless of whether the client is running on a physical desktop or as part of a VDI session. As such, there is practically no noticeable difference in the user experience between a local Skype for Business installation and a VDI installation, with the exception of the initial login process. When the user signs in to the Lync client from a VDI desktop, the client detects the presence of the plugin. At that point, the user is prompted to reenter credentials, as shown in Figure 27.7. This additional credential prompt is necessary to confirm the pairing of the plugin with the client because the plugin is installed only on the local hardware. After the Skype for Business client and the plugin have been paired, the user is not prompted again during the session, and the Skype for Business client looks and performs exactly the same as it would on a local desktop. Additionally, the user can select the Save My Password check box displayed in Figure 27.7 to prevent being prompted to reenter credentials when signing in to Skype for Business from the VDI desktop in the future.

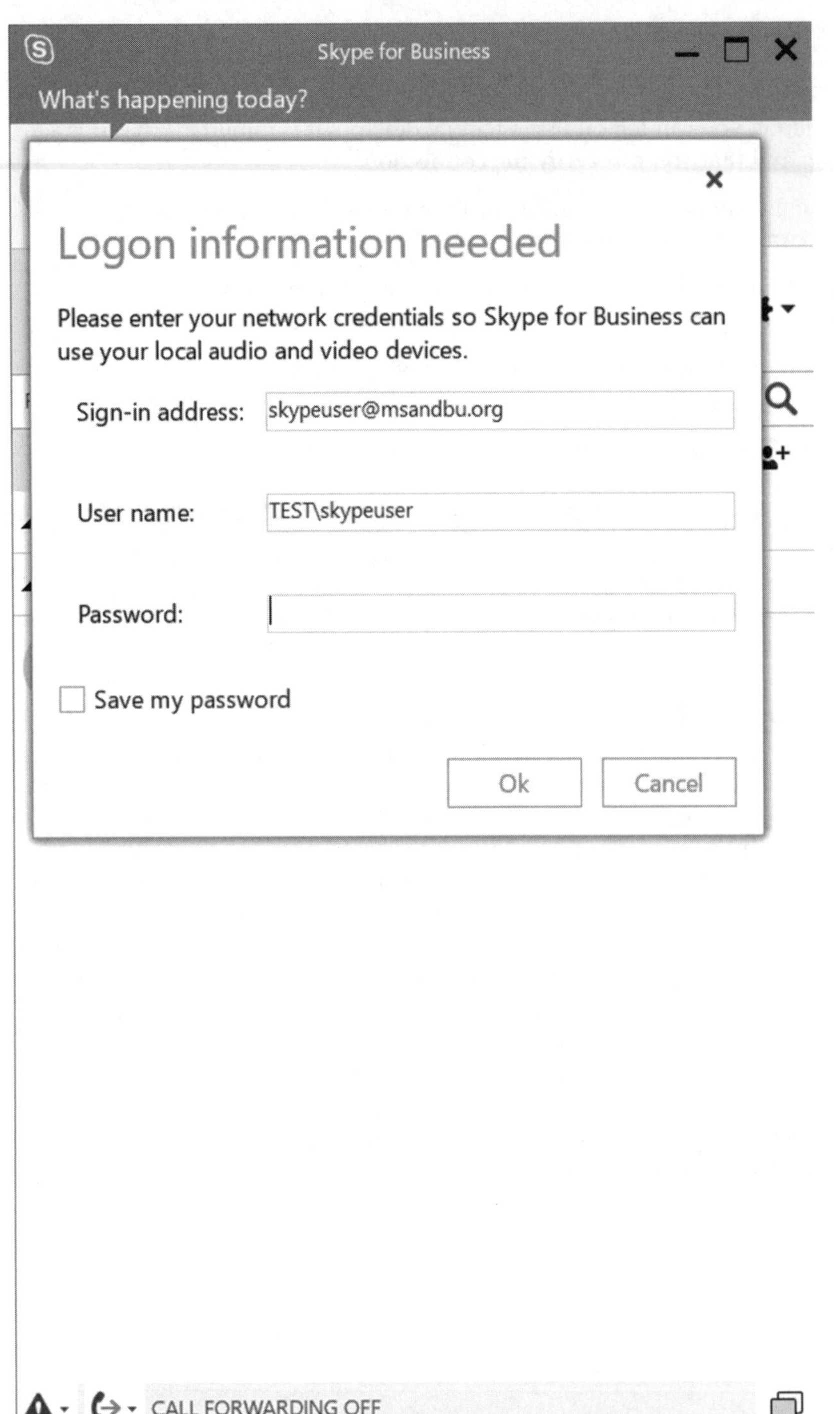

FIGURE 27.7 User prompted for credentials to confirm pairing of the Skype for Business client with the VDI plugin.

Also, visual cues appear within the VDI session that indicate the status of the Skype for Business plugin. While the Skype for Business client is in the process of pairing with the plugin, the status bar at the bottom of the Skype for Business client displays two icons. As shown in Figure 27.8, the icon on the left indicates that no audio devices are yet available, and the icon on the right blinks to indicate that the VDI pairing is in progress.

FIGURE 27.8 Skype for Business client status bar indicating that pairing with the VDI plugin is in progress.

After the pairing process is complete, the left icon indicates which audio device will be used for Skype for Business calls, and the right icon indicates that pairing with the VDI plugin is complete, as shown in Figure 27.9. The user can now answer and place calls using the audio device shown, and Presence will be displayed on all compatible devices.

FIGURE 27.9 Skype for Business client status bar indicating that pairing with the VDI plugin is successful.

Validating the Media Path When Using the Lync VDI Plugin

When the pairing process is complete and you are ready to place a call, it could be useful to validate the media path of the audio and video in the call. The fastest way to do so is to download and use the Microsoft Message Analyzer. Message Analyzer enables you to capture, display, and analyze protocol messaging traffic, as well as to trace and assess system events and other messages from Windows components. Use the following procedure to validate that the source of the media traffic is local and the destination is to an endpoint on the same subnet or the Edge server if you are remote:

1. Log on to the system where the plugin is installed using an account with local administrator rights.
2. Download and install Microsoft Message Analyzer.
3. Make sure you run the application using Administrator privileges.
4. Start a capture on the local network card.
5. Log on to the VDI session, make sure the pairing process completes successfully, and place a call to a user on the same network as the client computer.
6. In the Message Analyzer, stop the capture and filter the view using the filter box at the top-right corner. Filter on the RTP protocol, which is the media protocol for voice over IP systems.
7. You will then see that the source and destination are the computers on the local network and not the remote desktop, which means that media was local using the native media path for Skype for Business.

8. Now do the same as an external user, if possible, where the remote desktop is in the local server network in the datacenter and the client is remote from an external location.
9. In the Skype for Business client, press the Alt key on your keyboard and choose Meet Now, and then join the meeting using Skype for Business audio. Talk to yourself or the meeting participants.
10. In the Message Analyzer, stop the capture, filter for RTP traffic, and look at the last packets captured. There you can verify that the media path was between the Edge server and the local computer and not through the remote desktop session.

Troubleshooting the Lync VDI Plugin

In a locked-down environment, it could be difficult to get the Lync VDI plugin to work, and to resolve connection issues you must understand the sign-in process, pairing process, and the different media path possibilities for the Lync VDI plugin environment. We will not go into details in this chapter, but we can recommend a recorded session from the Lync Conference 2014 called "Understanding and Troubleshooting VDI Scenarios." You can find the session on Channel 9 using this link:

https://channel9.msdn.com/Events/Lync-Conference/Lync-Conference-2014/CLNT401

Protocol Partner Solutions for the Lync VDI Plugin

Out of the package, the downloadable Lync VDI plugin software supports only a native Windows environment, using Remote Desktop Protocol. However, Microsoft also has a goal of achieving platform independence with this new technology. To allow for this, the plugin was built to leverage Dynamic Virtual Channels (DVCs), which is a standard set of APIs that are platform independent. Other Remote Desktop Protocol vendors can then take advantage of DVCs to deliver their own solutions, which combine the Lync VDI plugin with their own software. VDI vendors that are developing solutions with Microsoft based on the Lync VDI plugin are referred to as "protocol partners."

NOTE

The Dynamic Virtual Channel APIs have already been implemented in Microsoft Remote Desktop Protocol version 8, which is the reason that RDP is natively supported with the Lync VDI plugin.

For the initial release of the VDI plugin, Microsoft has been working with two of the leading VDI vendors to develop third-party solutions based on the VDI plugin: Citrix and VMware. The following sections provide a description of the Lync VDI solutions available for each of these partners.

Citrix Receiver with Integrated Lync VDI Plugin

Citrix has been a steady player in the virtualization business for many years, starting with the XenApp product line, which has long been used to extend the application presentation functionality of Microsoft's Terminal Services and Remote Desktop Services components. In more recent years, Citrix has developed the XenDesktop product line into one of the most popular VDI products on the market. XenApp and XenDesktop are often used together as complementary products to create a comprehensive VDI solution, with Citrix Receiver used as the client component to provide access to the VDI desktop. Citrix has developed versions of Citrix Receiver for Windows, Mac, Linux, and more, making it a truly multiplatform VDI solution.

To optimize Lync 2010 with XenApp and XenDesktop solutions, Citrix released the Citrix HDX Optimization Pack for Lync 2010. The concept behind the Citrix HDX Optimization Pack for Lync 2010 was very similar to that of the VDI plugin developed by Microsoft for Lync 2013, in which the media processing bypasses the Citrix server environment and is instead handled by the client device. It is no surprise, then, that Microsoft and Citrix worked together to provide the same optimized architecture for running Lync 2013 and now Skype for Business in a XenDesktop VDI environment. The end result of this effort is that the Citrix Receiver includes the Lync VDI plugin functionality and with HDX RealTime Optimization Pack 2.0 Citrix and Microsoft now offers a joint support statement. The same presentation protocol used with most all XenApp and XenDesktop solutions, Independent Computing Architecture, is used to present the desktop interface to the user.

Because the Lync VDI plugin functionality is included in Citrix Receiver through their RealTime Media Engine, XenDesktop and XenApp users are able to use USB-connected audio and video devices that are certified for Lync and Skype for Business within a VDI session, along with other standard features of Citrix Receiver.

There are four ways to combine Citrix with Skype for Business:

Lync VDI Plugin

- Same experience and limitations apply, but you access the remote desktop through Citrix Receiver.

Citrix Generic HDX

- Works with most endpoints, but will run media through the Citrix protocol and process media locally on the virtual desktop back end.
- There is no server offloading, and quality is not on par with the VDI plugin experience.
- Supports MAC and Linux devices.

Local App Access

- The local full version of the Skype for Business client will be dragged into the receiver session.
- Requires Citrix platinum licenses on the Citrix platform and is limited to Windows endpoints.

Citrix HDX RealTime Optimization Pack 2.0

- Will do media offloading like the VDI plugin does with Citrix RealTime Media Engine.
- Office 365 and Skype for Business Online is supported along with Lync Server 2013 and Skype for Business Server 2015.
- Supports Windows, MAC, Linux, and ThinOS 8.2 clients.
- Supports XenDesktop 7 and newer and XenApp 6.0 and newer.
- Requires a Citrix platinum license.
- Media will go through ICA protocol if client loses connection to Skype for Business Edge or Front-End.
- Will revert to the VDI plugin on computers where it is installed.

VMware View with Lync VDI Plugin

VMware is widely considered to be the market leader in virtualization technology, primarily due to the popularity of the vSphere product line for server virtualization. VMware has also been able to capitalize on their market share by developing VMware View as one of the more popular enterprise-level VDI products offered. View leverages vSphere to host virtual desktops for a VDI deployment, with the VMware View agent installed as part of the virtual desktop build to allow connections from client systems. The VMware View client is then installed on user desktops or thin client systems to connect to the View VDI desktops.

The presentation protocol used by VMware View is "PC over IP," more commonly referred to as PCoIP. PCoIP compresses, encrypts, and encodes the user desktop experience at a datacenter and transmits the associated pixels to a VMware View client with PCoIP integrated.

VMware currently supports Microsoft Lync 2013 and Skype for Business with VMware Horizon 6.2. It has the same capabilities as Lync VDI plugin with Windows Remote Desktop, such as media redirection. Environments supported are those running Windows 7 SP1 or newer. Windows 10 is supported.

Thin Client Hardware Optimized for Skype for Business

Because a large percentage of VDI implementations make use of thin client hardware as an endpoint device, Microsoft has worked with some of the leading thin client manufacturers to test and validate the functionality of the Lync VDI plugin on thin client devices. Although the opportunity to test and validate endpoint devices for Skype for Business optimization is available to any thin client OEM partner, for the initial release of the plugin, Microsoft has chosen to partner with two market leaders in this area: Dell Wyse and HP.

Both Wyse and HP have been leading manufacturers of thin client devices for several years, including units that are specifically designed to work with Microsoft and Citrix VDI environments. Wyse was recently acquired by Dell, giving Dell a significant footprint in the desktop virtualization space, which includes not only the thin client hardware portfolio, but also enterprise device management and cloud computing software.

There is a rich diversity among the thin client hardware products in the Dell Wyse and HP portfolios. For example, there are low-cost "zero client" models with no operating system, flexible thin clients that provide expansion options, and mobile thin clients that resemble laptop systems, with built-in LED screens and keyboards.

Microsoft partnering with Dell Wyse and HP has resulted in the Lync VDI plugin being used to enable media redirection and other optimizations for VDI sessions that use Dell Wyse and HP thin clients. With certain models, the Lync VDI plugin is being combined with additional VDI optimization technologies, such as Microsoft RemoteFX, to further enhance the UC experience when these devices are used. With any of the Dell Wyse and HP thin clients that are validated for Lync 2013 and therefore work with Skype for Business, any Lync- and Skype for Business–certified USB audio and video devices can be connected to the device and accessed from the VDI session, with the media being redirected locally.

NOTE

For organizations that routinely deploy thin clients, it is a standard practice to develop an image that administrators can use to deploy the devices quickly with all required software and configuration settings, because this reduces the amount of management required and helps ensure consistency for the builds. If Skype for Business will be among the standard applications accessed using thin clients, it is important for administrators to include the Lync VDI plugin as part of the packaged image.

For the initial testing and validation of the Lync VDI plugin with Dell Wyse hardware, the following thin client models were validated:

- **Z90D7**—Thin client device with dual-core AMD processor running Windows Embedded Standard 7
- **R90LE7**—Thin client device with AMD Sempron processor running Windows Embedded Standard 7

- **X90m7**—Mobile thin client device with dual-core AMD processor and built-in LED backlit display, running Windows Embedded Standard 7 (see Figure 27.10)

FIGURE 27.10 Dell Wyse X90m7 mobile thin client.

For the initial testing and validation of the Lync VDI plugin with HP hardware, the following thin client models were validated:

- **t610**—Thin client device offering flexible configuration options, with a dual-core AMD processor running HP ThinPro, Windows 7e Embedded, or Windows Embedded Standard 2009 (see Figure 27.11).
- **t5740e**—Thin client device with an Intel Atom processor running Windows Embedded Standard 7.

FIGURE 27.11 HP t610 thin client.

Additional Dell Wyse and HP thin client models are being tested and validated with the goal of providing customers with additional VDI endpoint options that are optimized for use with Skype for Business.

Summary

As VDI continues to gain popularity in the enterprise, the importance of ensuring a quality UC experience for VDI users will also increase. Although many efforts have already been made by different vendors to improve the media experience for VDI, developing the Lync VDI plugin was an important step in the right direction for Microsoft. Not only does the VDI plugin enable Skype for Business to be optimized for Microsoft native remote desktop technologies, but it was developed as an extensible solution, such that other VDI vendors can leverage the plugin to develop their own Lync- and Skype for Business–optimized VDI solutions. As a result, the Skype for Business user experience can be virtually the same, whether a local desktop or a remote VDI desktop is used, with various remote desktop protocols and endpoint devices to choose from.

CHAPTER 28

UC Endpoints

IN THIS CHAPTER

- ▶ Standalone IP Phones
- ▶ USB Headsets, Speakerphones, and Handsets
- ▶ Webcams
- ▶ Conferencing Devices
- ▶ Best Practices

Although many administrators might pass over this chapter in the book, it is likely one of the most important. The concept of "user experience" is an oft-overlooked idea and yet vital to a successful unified communications (UC) deployment. IT success is often measured by metrics and numbers, but they rarely tell the whole story. UC adoption can be viral, but only if the right tools are in place and end users have a quality experience. The backend infrastructure is certainly important; however, end users never see any of it. What they use everyday is a UC endpoint.

UC endpoints encompass a wide range of devices. Although some people argue that PCs should be included, my personal experience suggests that they provide a poor experience. Instead, a dedicated, purpose-built device such as a headset or an IP/USB phone should be used for an optimal experience. For that reason, we'll leave laptops and PCs out of the discussion in this chapter.

Microsoft ensures that specific devices meet set user-experience quality levels through a third-party test and evaluation process. Without getting into a sales pitch over what's the best, the key point here is to recognize that devices certified to work with Skype for Business are sure to provide a quality end-user experience. In addition, the Skype for Business client will always prefer "Optimized" devices over standard devices. At the writing of this book, Microsoft lists well over 100 optimized devices, ranging from wired and wireless headsets to webcams, IP phones, and conference devices. Skype for Business–optimized devices are literally plug-and-play. The Skype for Business client finds the device automatically as soon as it is plugged in and can start using the device immediately. This chapter covers a wide range of devices:

- ▶ Standalone IP phones
- ▶ USB headsets, speakerphones, and handsets

- Webcams
- Conferencing devices

Finally, the chapter concludes with best practices for choosing and deploying UC endpoints for various scenarios.

Standalone IP Phones

There are two types of standalone IP phones for Microsoft Skype for Business: ones that run Lync Phone edition and compatible phones, often called 3PIP (for Third-Party Interoperability Program) certified.

The Lync phone edition (LPE) phones include the following models and provide a consistent experience for users requiring a handset. They are currently deprecated and being phased out; however, there are still some valid use cases for these native LPE devices:

- Polycom CX700
- Polycom CX600
- Aastra 6725ip
- HP 4120

These phones enable a user to sign in and, if desired, connect the phone to a PC via USB to use it as a USB audio device for the Skype for Business Client. This is called "USB tethering" or the "better together experience." The phones offer a full-color LCD screen, and some models have a touchscreen as well. Per the Microsoft reference design, all phones in this category must also have a speakerphone and support wideband audio or a supported variant of HD voice. They also offer integration features such as calendar view from the on-phone screen.

The Third-Party Interoperability Program (3PIP) is largely dominated by the Polycom VVX series; however, some other manufacturers are jumping into the fray as well. The feature set often varies between manufacturers, and even between devices from the same manufacturer. Although Microsoft specifies a specific matrix of minimum requirements, there is a lot of room for vendors to differentiate and offer additional functionality beyond the minimum requirements. Here's a list of the devices in the 3PIP:

- Polycom VVX series
- Polycom SoundPoint IP series
- SpectraLink wireless phones, with the appropriate controller
- Yealink T48G and T22p phones
- AudioCodes "HD" series

USB Headsets, Speakerphones, and Handsets

USB headsets and their bulkier counterparts, handsets, are the most common UC endpoints available, with USB speakerphones having a niche market. The Skype for Business client functions as a softphone, eliminating the need for a dedicated desk phone for most users.

USB Headsets

The best thing about headsets is they're portable! And they provide a superior experience over a traditional handset in nearly every way. However, they do take a little bit of getting used to. A wide variety of headsets are available from various manufacturers. In fact, there are too many individual headset models to discuss all of them here, so I will highlight just one from each category (wired, wireless, and hybrid).

A good example of a USB wired headset is the Plantronics Blackwire 725, shown in Figure 28.1. This is great solution designed for desktop users. It provides binaural audio with an adjustable noise-cancelling boom microphone.

FIGURE 28.1 Plantronics Blackwire 725.

Other solutions include monaural audio, which might be better for some deployments where workers still need to hear the environment around them.

Wireless headsets often have a dongle plugged in to the user's PC but need no other connections. The headset enables users to roam freely up to 300 feet (and sometimes farther) from their PC while continuing their conversation. Many also have controls on the headset for redial, answer, hang up, and volume control. Most wireless solutions have docking stations used for recharging, whereas others come with just a USB charging cable. The latter solutions are better for users who travel often or don't have a permanent office. The Logitech H820e shown in Figure 28.2 is a great example of an office wireless headset.

FIGURE 28.2 Logitech H820e.

Then, finally, there are hybrid devices, such as the Plantronics Voyager Focus UC, shown in Figure 28.3. This headset can connect to a PC via USB and to a mobile phone via Bluetooth at the same time. It's truly the best of both worlds. It also supports A2DP for users who want to stream music to their headset while they work.

FIGURE 28.3 Plantronics Voyager Focus UC.

Speakerphones

Speakerphones become more and more important as "huddle rooms" take the place of classic conference rooms. These devices are great for impromptu meetings or group conversations in locations without a dedicated conferencing device.

The Logitech P710e, shown in Figure 28.4, works with PCs, Macs, and mobile devices over Bluetooth. That makes it very flexible as a travel device.

FIGURE 28.4 Logitech P710e.

Another option is the Jabra Speak 510. It transports in a form-fitting neoprene case and has good sound quality.

USB Handsets

Sometimes there's no need for a desk phone, but a user insists on having a handset form factor. These devices connect to a user's PC via USB but provide the familiar user interface and look and feel of a traditional phone handset. From the PC's perspective, the handset is just another audio device for the Skype for Business client. However, for the user, the handset is a familiar tool that works the same way as the legacy phone they're used to. This can be a great tool to begin the process of empowering nontechnical users with UC.

Webcams

It's hard to say that anything is more revolutionary than desktop video. Even better is high-definition desktop video. Add integration with popular video conferencing solutions from Logitech and Polycom and you have a complete solution. Adding video to a conversation has a profound impact. Although most newer laptops are equipped with webcams, USB-connected webcams are ideal for users with desktop systems or external monitors. USB webcams also usually offer far superior image quality as compared to webcams built in to laptops.

Users with a webcam can share video with one user or multiple users at the same time. The receiving user sees a request bar asking to share video for the current conversation. The industry standard is the Logitech C930e, shown in Figure 28.5. It was chosen to be the video portion of the Skype Room System and is available as a standalone device for laptops and desktops.

FIGURE 28.5 Logitech C930e.

Conferencing Devices

The Polycom RealPresence Trio conference phone is a true conference room solution. It just needs power (AC or PoE) and an Ethernet cable; no PC required! It also allows for Outlook contacts searching and requires just one click to join Skype for Business conference calls.

The Polycom Group Series room systems natively support the Microsoft-specific H.264 SVC codecs, making them an easy choice for companies requiring integration between room devices and desktop video conferencing.

Microsoft's Skype Room Systems offer a proven and certified combination of devices ideally suited for outfitting a small-to-mid-sized conference room.

For smaller rooms, sometimes a large or expensive solution isn't ideal. The Logitech ConferenceCam Connect, shown in Figure 28.6, makes a great office or huddle room device for audio, video, and even screen sharing over Miracast.

FIGURE 28.6 Logitech ConferenceCam Connect.

Best Practices

- ▶ Although some users will demand desk phones, in general headsets provide a better and more mobile overall solution.
- ▶ Replace legacy conferencing devices with Skype-enabled devices such as the Polycom RealPresence Trio.
- ▶ Wherever possible, deploy webcams to users. The addition of video adds a lot of value to communication and collaboration.
- ▶ Deploy headsets to new employees as part of their laptop/desktop system, and teach them to use the unified communications (UC) solution during orientation. Training is key, especially for nontechnical users.
- ▶ Encourage use by letting users choose from various devices, depending on their situation.

Summary

The difference between certified devices and "any old headset" is vast. Tools such as Event Zero's UC Commander run voice quality reports on certified versus noncertified devices, and the difference in quality is dramatic. Prepare your users for the best Skype for Business experience by outfitting them with certified devices.

CHAPTER 29

Planning for Skype for Business Online and Hybrid Deployments

IN THIS CHAPTER

- Comparing Topology Options
- Skype for Business Online and Office 365 Subscription Plans
- Planning for Single Sign-On with AD FS
- Planning for Directory Synchronization
- Planning for Skype for Business Online
- Planning for a Hybrid Deployment

Whether Skype for Business Online was purchased as a separate service or as part of the Office 365 suite, the planning process for a Skype for Business Online deployment is very different from that of an on-premises deployment and includes some unique requirements. Microsoft continues to evolve the Office 365 offerings as "evergreen" services, which enables customers to take advantage of the latest platform releases and features as they become available. The transition from "Lync Online" to "Skype for Business Online" highlights this approach, as existing Office 365 and Lync Online tenants were upgraded shortly after the public release of Skype for Business Server 2015. With this version of Skype for Business Online/Office 365, hybrid deployments that blend the Skype for Business cloud offering with an on-premises deployment will continue and are expected to become more common, even when the majority of an organization's user population resides in the on-premises environment. Compelling features are being released by Microsoft as "cloud-only" services, which include Skype for Business Online Cloud PBX, PSTN Conferencing, and Meeting Broadcast. These features were released publicly in December 2015 and are available to customers who subscribe to Skype for Business Online/Office 365 services. Microsoft's continued expansion of Skype for Business Online services should be an indicator that the hybrid scenario is here to stay. However, a hybrid deployment has its own unique requirements and will involve additional upfront planning to ensure a seamless unified communications experience for Skype for Business users, regardless of whether they are homed online or on-premises. This chapter provides a preview of the steps involved in planning for both cloud-only and hybrid installations.

Comparing Topology Options

One of the biggest planning considerations with regard to Skype for Business Online is whether a cloud-based Skype for Business deployment is the right choice, and if so, which cloud deployment option best meets the needs of the organization. With the new cloud-centric features available, this decision requires more thought than ever before. As we continue to see the shift away from traditional, fully on-premises deployments, keep in mind the Skype for Business topology options to choose from: cloud-only topology, on-premises topology, and hybrid topology. The following sections present some comparisons and considerations that can be used to help a Skype for Business architect guide their organization in determining which Skype for Business topology best meets their unique requirements.

Skype for Business Online Versus Skype for Business On-Premises

The desire of Microsoft to close the feature gap between the on-premises and online Skype for Business offerings has never been more evident than in the current releases. As the platform evolves, expect to see these two deployment scenarios begin to reach feature parity. However, at the present time, Skype for Business Online offers many, but not all, of the features that are included with an on-premises deployment. This means that although a cloud-based UC platform will provide a cost savings for many organizations, an on-premises deployment might still be a more appropriate solution for some organizations, depending on which UC features are critical to deploy. As part of the overall Skype for Business planning process, it is therefore important to consider the feature differences between the two platforms. At the time of publication, the following list summarizes some key features that are available with an on-premises Skype for Business Server 2015 deployment but are not included in any of Skype for Business Online service plans:

- Skill Search in SharePoint
- Persistent Chat
- Privacy mode
- Federation with XMPP networks
- Interoperability with on-premises video conferencing systems
- Outgoing Direct Inward Dialing (DID) manipulation
- Customized dial plans and policies

- Survivable branch appliance
- Call Admission Control (CAC)
- Support for analog devices and endpoints
- Response groups
- Call park
- Private line
- Malicious call trace
- Unassigned number
- Integration with call-center solutions

If none of these features is considered a requirement, a cloud-only Skype for Business Online deployment is a valid option. However, many of the features that are not included with a cloud-only topology are available with a hybrid topology.

From a cost perspective, it is important to note that each Skype for Business Online subscription includes the Client Access Licenses (CALs) that are required to use the features included with that subscription. Therefore, any budgeting exercise that compares the cost of a cloud topology with that of an on-premises topology should take into account the cost of both licensing and hardware that would be required for an on-premises deployment. The planning topics outlined in this chapter should also be compared with the information in Chapters 30 through 33 to determine the true cost of an on-premises deployment versus that of a Skype for Business Online deployment. This comparison will allow an organization take into account not only the feature sets included with each topology option, but also the hardware, software, licensing requirements, and effort involved in building and maintaining each type of deployment.

Skype for Business Hybrid Deployment Considerations

Building upon the success of the Lync Server 2013 and Lync Online hybrid capabilities, Microsoft has expanded the capabilities and functionality when Lync and Skype for Business are deployed in a hybrid topology. A Skype for Business hybrid deployment involves an on-premises deployment of Lync Server 2013 or Skype for Business Server 2015, which is federated with a Skype for Business Online tenant, enabling the same SIP domain to be applied and shared between both on-premises and online users. The end result is that Skype for Business users within an organization can be moved between the on-premises deployment and the cloud, and can use the Lync or Skype for Business Server on-premises infrastructure, including PSTN connectivity, regardless of the location of their account.

NOTE

With the first release of Office 365 and Lync Online, it was possible for an organization to deploy Lync Server 2010 for some users on-premises, and simultaneously provision the Lync Online cloud-based service for other users, with Lync federation configured between the two deployments. However, this configuration required separate SIP domains to be used for the on-premises Lync organization versus the cloud-based Lync organization. Due to this restriction, very few organizations deployed Lync Online in tandem with Lync on-premises with the first version of the cloud service.

The value proposition for Skype for Business hybrid depends on the overall UC goals for an organization. For example, some organizations have a goal of moving all enterprise services to the cloud, but are forced to do so in a gradual fashion due to business or technical constraints. The Skype for Business hybrid deployment would allow such an organization to perform a phased transition of UC services to the cloud, and continue to provide a full UC feature set and a seamless experience for users throughout the transition period. For other organizations, moving to a cloud UC service has good potential, but a period of time is needed to test-drive the Skype for Business Online offering and compare it to the Skype for Business on-premises deployment. The Skype for Business hybrid deployment provides the opportunity to test out Skype for Business Online functionality without making a full commitment. Finally, still other organizations might desire to provide different levels of UC service for various types of users, and this might include having certain user profiles hosted in the cloud, with other user profiles hosted on-premises. This enables an organization to continue to leverage existing investments in an on-premises PBX, carrier contracts, and other dedicated telephony systems for the users who require these services, yet provide a basic set of functionality for cloud users who do not require them. The Skype for Business hybrid deployment easily allows for such a configuration and makes it easy to move user accounts back and forth as needed.

Comparing Voice Options Between Topologies

For many organizations, Enterprise Voice capabilities have the largest impact on the choice of which platform to use. Microsoft recognizes this, of course, and as a result has moved to ensure that there are several voice options to choose from within the available Skype for Business topologies. For organizations that rely heavily on voice, it is important to understand the differences between the voice features offered with the various platforms. With that in mind, Table 29.1 presents a list of important Skype for Business voice features, and shows which of these features are offered across the various Skype for Business topologies. After the specific voice requirements of an organization are well understood, these requirements can be compared with the information in Table 29.1 to determine which platform presents the right voice feature set.

TABLE 29.1 Skype for Business Voice Options Per Topology

Skype for Business Voice Features	On-Premises Enterprise Voice	Skype for Business Online Hosted Voice (Cloud PBX with PSTN Calling Plan)	Skype for Business Hybrid Voice (Cloud PBX with on-premises PSTN connectivity)
Call Hold/Retrieve	X	X	X
Call Transfer	X	X	X
Call Forwarding	X	X	X
Voicemail	X	X	X
USB peripherals	X	X	X
Outside voice—mobile	X	X	X
Delegation, Team Call	X	X	X
Integration with on-premises PBX	X		X
Call via Work	X		
Private line	X		
Voice resiliency	X	X	X
Enhanced 911	X	X	X
IP telephony Handsets	X	X	X
Response Group Service (RGS)/Call Park Service (CPS)	X		
Analog devices, Common Area Phones	X		
Integration with on-premises call-center solutions	X		
Media bypass	X		

Skype for Business Online and Office 365 Subscription Plans

An important part of the initial planning for Skype for Business Online is determining which of the subscription plans represents the best fit for an organization. Skype for Business Online can be purchased as a standalone service, or it can be included as part of a more comprehensive Office 365 subscription. The details on each of these options are provided in the following sections.

Skype for Business Online Subscription Plans

Skype for Business Online offers two separate plans and pricing tiers, with each successive plan offering additional Skype for Business services. The lowest tier is Plan 1, which is the least expensive and offers the following basic set of Skype for Business features:

- User authentication
- IM and Presence
- Online meeting attendance
- PC-to-PC audio and video calling
- Federation with other organizations that use Lync or Skype for Business

The next tier is Plan 2, which offers all the features included with Plan 1, and adds the following:

- Initiation of online meetings with up to 250 attendees, both ad hoc and scheduled
- Initiation of multiparty audio/video sessions
- File transfer using the Skype for Business client
- Content sharing within online presentations (screen sharing, whiteboard, PowerPoint upload)
- Interoperability with certified partners for dial-in audio conferencing
- Client-side API support

The new features and capabilities provided by Cloud PBX and PSTN Conferencing can be applied incrementally to Skype for Business Plan 2. Adding these licenses also grant the rights to their corresponding features:

- **Cloud PBX**—Inbound/outbound calling using either on-premises PSTN connectivity or a Microsoft PSTN calling plan with the features outlined in the previous section.
- **PSTN Conferencing**—Not to be confused with Audio Conference Provider (ACP) integration with Skype for Business Online. Microsoft PSTN Conferencing is a first-party-provided toll-based PSTN dial-in capability for Skype for Business Online meetings.

NOTE

Each Skype for Business Online subscription plan includes the rights to Skype for Business Server Client Access Licenses with the plan. Plan 1 includes a Lync/Skype for Business Standard CAL for each user, and Plan 2 includes the Enterprise CAL. There was previously a Lync Online Plan 3, which included the Lync/Skype for Business Plus CAL, but this plan has since been retired.

Office 365 Subscription Plans

It is also possible to purchase Skype for Business Online by way of a more comprehensive Office 365 Suite subscription plan. Several of the Office 365 "E" plans include Skype for Business Online Plan 2, and the highest-level subscription plan (E5) also includes Skype for Business Online Plan 2, Cloud PBX, PSTN Conferencing, as well as dual-access rights for all on-premises Skype for Business Server 2015 workloads. With the licensing included in the Plans E1 and E3, an organization also has the option of purchasing Skype for Business Plus CALs for users of an on-premises Lync or Skype for Business deployment, while granting those same users access to the other Office 365 applications in the cloud. For some organizations, this may be a cost-effective way to provide users with full Enterprise Voice features via an on-premises Skype for Business deployment, but use the cloud for the other Office 365 applications. Table 29.2 shows the components that are included in the Office 365 "E" subscription plans at the time of writing.

TABLE 29.2 Office 365 Subscription Plans

Office 365 Plan E1	Office 365 Plan E3	Office 365 Plan E5
Exchange Online (Plan 1)	Exchange Online (Plan 2)	Exchange Online (Plan 2)
SharePoint Online (Plan 1)	SharePoint Online (Plan 2)	SharePoint Online (Plan 2)
Skype for Business Online (Plan 2)	Skype for Business Online (Plan 2)	Skype for Business Online (Plan 2)
		Skype for Business Cloud PBX
		Skype for Business PSTN Conferencing
		Power BI Pro
		Delve Analytics
		Customer Lockbox
		Advanced Threat Protection
		Enhanced eDiscovery
Yammer	Yammer	Yammer
Office Web Apps	Office Web Apps	Office Web Apps
	Office Professional Plus	Office Professional Plus

Deciding on a Subscription Plan

The decision of whether to pursue a standalone Skype for Business Online subscription or a full Office 365 subscription of course depends on whether cloud services are desired for the other Office applications outside of Skype for Business. Also, as shown in Table 29.2, Skype for Business Online Plan 1 is available only as a standalone subscription, because it is not included in any of the Office 365 subscription plans. This means that for organizations that are looking for only the most basic UC functionality and are not pursuing cloud services for Exchange, SharePoint, or Office, Skype for Business Online

Plan 1 is likely the right option. Following are some additional key points that can be taken into account in comparing the two Skype for Business Online subscription plans:

- For organizations seeking to supplement an existing VoIP system with additional functionality such as IM and Presence, Skype for Business Online Plan 1 would be a good option and would be the lowest cost. Currently, Plan 1 is priced at $2 per user per month.
- If online meetings are a requirement but PSTN connectivity is not, Skype for Business Online Plan 2 would be a good fit. Interoperability with third-party dial-in conferencing partners is also included in Plan 2, and can be used to extend conferencing to PSTN users. Additionally, the new Microsoft PSTN Conferencing may be added for an additional flat fee of $4 per license per month, with no additional per minute charges. Currently, Plan 2 is priced at $5.50 per user per month standalone, or it can be purchased as part of Office 365 "E" plans.
- If all the features offered with Skype for Business Online need to be leveraged, including Cloud PBX and PSTN Conferencing services, then these licenses can be added to an existing Skype for Business Online Plan 2 subscription on a per-seat basis. The Cloud PBX and PSTN Conferencing licenses can be purchased for $8 and $4 per seat, respectively. In order to take advantage of Cloud PBX as a "pure" cloud offering, a Microsoft PSTN calling plan can be added for $12 for U.S. national calling or $24 for U.S. international calling. Note that at initial release, Cloud PBX with PSTN calling plans are only available in the U.S., but Microsoft plans to quickly expand this feature to other regions. Alternatively, the whole suite of Skype for Business Online capabilities, with the exception of PSTN calling plans, can be purchased as part of the all-inclusive Office 365 Plan E5.

Planning for Single Sign-On with AD FS

For organizations that maintain an internal Active Directory deployment, implementing single sign-on (SSO) is typically a high priority, because this provides the most seamless experience for Skype for Business Online users. SSO enables each user to log on to a client system one time with Active Directory credentials and then access both Skype for Business Online and on-premises resources without being prompted for additional credentials. To allow this functionality, Active Directory must first be prepared for SSO, and Active Directory Federation Services must also be installed on-premises and configured for federation with the Skype for Business Online organization.

Specifically, the deployment of SSO for Skype for Business Online requires the following components:

- Active Directory must be deployed on-premises using Windows 2003 native mode or higher.
- An AD FS 2.0 or greater instance involving at least one federation server must be deployed on-premises, using Windows Server 2008 or higher. If users will be connecting to Skype for Business Online from outside the network, at least one AD FS proxy is also required and should be installed in a DMZ network.

- The Microsoft Online Services Module for Windows PowerShell must be installed and configured to establish a trust with Skype for Business Online.
- All required updates for Office 365 must be installed on client systems.

The following sections take a closer look at these requirements as part of the planning process for SSO.

Preparing Active Directory for SSO

Aside from the Active Directory functional level requirements previously mentioned, the user principal name (UPN) configuration might also need to be adjusted in preparation for SSO. Following are the requirements for a UPN to be used with SSO:

- The UPN suffix configured for each Skype for Business Online user must be identical to the domain that will be enabled for SSO with Skype for Business Online.
- The UPN suffix must be a publicly registered domain.
- A UPN used with SSO can contain only letters, numbers, periods, dashes, and underscores.

TIP

With many Active Directory deployments, the UPN suffix for users matches the Active Directory DNS domain, and for this reason it is typically a private domain name that's registered only on internal DNS servers, such as `companyabc.local`. For SSO to function properly with Skype for Business Online, a publicly registered name must instead be configured for each Skype for Business Online user. Typically, it makes the most sense to use the organization's primary SMTP domain as the UPN value because this usually is also specified as the SIP domain for Skype for Business Online purposes.

Planning Active Directory Federation Services for SSO

The primary component that drives SSO for Skype for Business Online is Active Directory Federation Services (AD FS). AD FS is a claims-based authentication platform that runs on Windows and is used to simplify access to applications and services using secure tokens. In the case of Skype for Business Online, AD FS is used to establish federation between the on-premises Active Directory deployment and the Skype for Business Online tenant. After the appropriate trusts are configured, a secure channel is created over which authentication tokens are passed, allowing users to log on seamlessly to Skype for Business Online using their AD credentials. Although prior versions of AD FS are included with the Windows Server OS, the minimum AD FS version required for Skype for Business Online SSO is version 2.0, which is included natively on Windows Server 2012 (v2.1) and Windows Server 2012 R2 (v3.0).

NOTE

Although this chapter is focused on Skype for Business Online, SSO is also leveraged with the other applications included in the Office 365 suite. If a full Office 365 subscription is used as opposed to just Skype for Business Online, the same AD FS instance would be sufficient to enable SSO for all applications, and the SSO planning process described in this chapter would also remain the same.

Planning the AD FS Topology

The first consideration in the AD FS planning process is the number of federation servers to be deployed as well as the sizing of those servers. In the AD FS section of the TechNet site, Microsoft provides detailed capacity planning guidance along with a sizing calculator that can be used to determine how many federation servers are needed, along with the sizing recommendations for each server. However, the reality is that for a new Skype for Business Online deployment, most organizations will not have the data that must be input to make use of the sizing tools provided. For this reason, and also because the resource requirements for a federation server are not significant, Microsoft also provides separate guidance for AD FS deployments that are planned for Office 365. This information can be used to estimate the number of federation servers and federation server proxies that should be deployed based on the number of users who will be accessing Office 365. For example, Table 29.3 provides guidelines on the number of servers recommended based on the Skype for Business Online user count.

TABLE 29.3 Recommended Number of AD FS Servers Based on User Count

Number of Skype for Business Online Users	Minimum Number of Servers to Deploy
Fewer than 1,000 users	Two load-balanced, collocated, or dedicated federation servers (must be Windows Server 2008 or greater).
1,000 to 15,000 users	Two load-balanced, dedicated federation servers.
15,000 to 60,000 users	Between three and five load-balanced, dedicated federation servers. (Five servers is the maximum when WID is used as the database platform).

TIP

As shown in Table 29.3, for small environments with fewer than 1,000 users, it is acceptable to install the federation server role on nondedicated systems and still expect good performance. For example, the federation server role can be installed on domain controller systems. However, the federation server software is compatible only with Windows Server 2008 or greater; therefore, with a Windows Server 2003-based Active Directory environment, it might still be necessary to use dedicated federation server systems. Also, if the federation server role is installed on domain controller systems, another system needs to be used for the load-balancing function to provide redundancy.

Note from Table 29.3 that a minimum of two servers is recommended for all scenarios, regardless of user count. The reason for this is that, although a single federation server can handle many user connections, this configuration would represent a single point of failure for a relatively critical service. Two federation servers is therefore the minimum recommendation to allow resiliency for SSO. Connections to multiple federation servers in a farm must be load balanced, which can be accomplished using Microsoft's built-in network load balancing (NLB) feature, but using a dedicated load balancing solution is recommended.

Regardless of the number of servers involved, each deployment of AD FS constitutes a single instance of a federation service, and each federation service is represented by a fully qualified domain name that is unique within the organization. If the federation service will provide connections from external systems, a public DNS name is required. If split-brain DNS is used, a DNS host record for the federation service needs to be configured for both the internal and the external zones.

One service account is also used to run AD FS across all servers within a federated service instance. With a standalone AD FS deployment, a dedicated service account is not required, and the NETWORK SERVICE account is automatically specified by the AD FS installer to serve this purpose. However, a dedicated service account is still recommended for standalone deployments to reduce the attack surface of the federation server. A user account should therefore be created for this purpose in Active Directory before the installation of AD FS, and then configured as a dedicated service account for AD FS during the initial configuration. The service account does not require any particular rights to the AD domain; however, it must be a member of the local Administrators group on each federation server.

Choosing the AD FS Database Platform

After it is determined how many servers will be needed, the next important consideration is the database platform. The configuration data for AD FS is stored in the AD FS configuration database. For database platforms, AD FS 2.0 or newer supports either a full installation of SQL Server (2005 or newer) or the Windows Internal Database (WID) feature that is included with Windows Server 2008 and up. From a performance perspective, there is not much difference between the two database platforms, and the AD FS functionality is also nearly equal between the two.

For use with Office 365 or Skype for Business Online, Microsoft recommends using the WID database platform for the AD FS topology, because this provides data resiliency, is simple to deploy, and also saves on licensing costs compared to SQL. When the first federation server is installed, this server becomes the primary federation server, and a read/write copy of the configuration database based on WID is installed locally. Any additional federation servers added to the farm are secondary federation servers, and they replicate changes to the configuration database from the primary federation server to a local read-only copy.

NOTE

WID supports a maximum of five federation servers. Each dedicated federation server can support approximately 15,000 user connections; therefore, WID can be used to support very large Skype for Business Online and Office 365 implementations. If more than five federation servers will be needed, SQL Server should be used as the database platform for AD FS.

Planning for External Access to AD FS

External access to the federation service is granted by means of a federation server proxy. A federation server proxy acts as an intermediary proxy service between client systems on the Internet and a federation service that is located behind a firewall on the corporate network. To enable Skype for Business Online users to log on using SSO from outside the corporate network, a minimum of one AD FS proxy server is needed. However, if remote access to Skype for Business Online is considered critical to the organization, then more than one proxy must be installed, and connections to the proxy systems would be load balanced using either a hardware load balancer or the Microsoft NLB feature.

The federation server proxy system (or cluster, if more than one system is used) must be accessible from the Internet using a public IP address. The DNS name assigned to the federation server proxy must also match the DNS name that is assigned to the internal federation server farm. The public server certificate that is applied to the internal federation server systems is also applied to each of the federation server proxy systems. Federation server proxy systems are typically installed in a DMZ subnet and are configured as members of a workgroup to reduce the firewall port requirements between the federation proxies and the internal federation servers.

Figure 29.1 shows an example of a fully redundant AD FS topology that can be used to support SSO for Skype for Business Online, using a pair of load-balanced federation proxies and a pair of load-balanced federation servers.

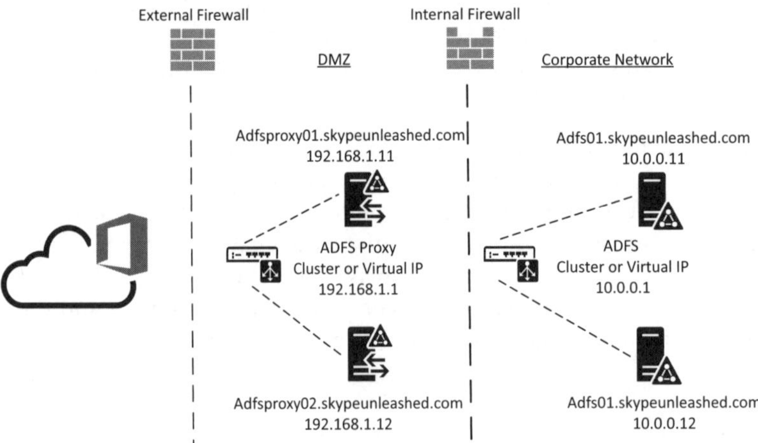

FIGURE 29.1 Example of redundant AD FS topology for Skype for Business Online.

Planning AD FS Hardware

Server virtualization platforms are supported for both the federation server and the federation server proxy roles. The hardware and software requirements for federation server and federation server proxy systems are the same. For either type of system, the following hardware minimums apply:

- **Operating system**—Windows Server 2008
- **CPU speed**—Single-core 1.4GHz
- **RAM**—512MB
- **Disk space**—32GB

These minimum specifications should be used only as a starting point for resource allocation. To increase capacity, additional RAM and CPU can be added, or the number of servers can be increased. For example, the capacity planning guidelines listed in Table 29.3 are based on the following hardware specifications:

- **Operating system**—Windows Server 2012 R2
- **CPU speed**—Quad-core 2GHz CPU
- **RAM**—4GB
- **Disk space**—100GB

Planning AD FS Certificates

Several certificates are used with the federation service. The first of these is referred to as the server authentication certificate, which is a standard SSL certificate used to secure communications between federation servers, clients, and federation server proxy computers. The server authentication certificate must be purchased from a public Certificate Authority using the federation service FQDN as the subject name. The certificate is then applied to each of the federation servers in the AD FS topology.

TIP

If a Skype for Business hybrid deployment is planned, the subject name of the server authentication certificate instead needs to be `sts.<SIPdomain>`, where `<SIPdomain>` is the DNS domain that will be split across the Skype for Business Online and Skype for Business on-premises deployments. For details, see the "Planning for a Hybrid Deployment" section of this chapter.

29

The second type of certificate required is the token-signing certificate, which is a standard x.509 certificate used to digitally sign all security tokens that are created. This certificate is not public facing; however, the public key associated with the cert must be supplied to Skype for Business Online/Office 365 as part of a trust configuration. By default, AD FS automatically generates a self-signed certificate for token-signing every year and automatically rolls it over before the certificate expires.

TIP

When the token-signing certificate is rolled over, the online tenant needs to be notified about this change; otherwise, requests to the online tenant will fail. To avoid this situation, Microsoft provides a utility named the Microsoft Office 365 Federation Metadata Update Automation Administration Tool, which can be downloaded for free. When installed, the tool automatically monitors and updates the Office 365 federation metadata on a regular basis, so that any changes made to the token-signing certificate are replicated to the online tenant automatically, preventing an outage.

The federation server proxy systems also require a standard SSL certificate to secure communications with client systems on the Internet, as well as the internal federation servers. However, the same public FQDN should be assigned to both the federation service and the federation proxy cluster. For this reason, the same SSL certificate assigned as the server authentication certificate on the federation servers can also be used on the federation server proxy systems.

Planning the Network for AD FS

Other than standard TCP/IP connectivity, network requirements for AD FS consist of DNS entries that must be configured to direct traffic to the AD FS systems as well as firewall ports that need to be opened. Following are the specific DNS requirements for AD FS:

- For internal connectivity to AD FS, a single host record can be added to the internal DNS zone, mapping the fully qualified name of the federation service to either the IP address of the federation server (for single-server installations) or the virtual IP address of the load-balancing cluster (for multiple-server installations).
- For external connectivity to AD FS, a single host record can be added to the external DNS zone, mapping the fully qualified name of the federation service to either the public IP address assigned to the federation server proxy (for single-server federation proxy installations) or the public virtual IP address of the load-balancing cluster (for multiple-server federation proxy installations).
- If the federation server proxy systems in the DMZ are configured to connect to internal DNS servers for DNS resolution, no additional DNS configuration is required to enable the proxy systems to connect to the internal federation servers. However, for security purposes, the DMZ servers might not be configured to connect to internal systems for DNS resolution. If there are DNS servers hosted in the DMZ segment for this purpose, a single host record can be added to the DNS zone on the DNS DMZ servers, mapping the fully qualified name of the federation service to either the IP address of the federation server (for single-server installations) or the virtual IP address of the load-balancing cluster (for multiple-server installations). As an alternative, the `HOSTS` file can instead be edited on each of the federation proxy servers to include the required mapping.

TIP

If a Skype for Business hybrid deployment is planned, additional DNS records will be required to support AD FS with the hybrid configuration. For details, see the "Planning for a Hybrid Deployment" section of this chapter.

Firewall ports that need to be opened for AD FS connectivity include the following:

- For external connectivity to the federation server proxy systems in the DMZ, TCP port 443 needs to be opened inbound.
- For connectivity between the federation server proxies in the DMZ and the internal federation servers, TCP ports 80 and 443 need to be opened between the systems in both directions.
- For connectivity between the internal federation service and Office 365, TCP port 443 needs to be opened outbound.

Planning Browser Support for AD FS

Skype for Business Online and Office 365 are compatible with most modern web browsers, including Internet Explorer, Firefox, Chrome, and Safari. However, by default, the use of SSO with Skype for Business Online/Office 365 is dependent on a browser's support for Extended Protection for Authentication, a feature that helps protect against man-in-the-middle attacks. If a browser does not support Extended Protection for Authentication, users will likely receive logon prompts on a regular basis when accessing Skype for Business Online and other Office 365 services.

At the time of writing, several versions of Firefox, Chrome, and Safari did not support Extended Protection for Authentication; therefore, if these browsers are planned for Skype for Business Online, some adjustments to the default configuration might be required. Following are two adjustments that can potentially be used to avoid logon problems for Skype for Business Online users connecting with a browser that does not support Extended Protection for Authentication:

- The Extended Protection for Authentication setting can be disabled on AD FS 2.0 systems. To adjust this setting on a federation server, log in using an account with local administrator permissions, open Windows PowerShell, and execute the following command:

  ```
  Set-ADFSProperties -ExtendedProtectionTokenCheck None
  ```

  If multiple federation servers are used, the command must be executed on each federation server in the farm.

- The AD FS 2.0 web page on each federation server can be reconfigured to use forms-based authentication instead of integrated Windows authentication. The implications of such a change should be carefully considered before this adjustment is made, because this will affect all Skype for Business Online/Office 365 users, regardless of the browser being used. If it is determined that this change will be made, the AD FS documentation on TechNet should be consulted for specific procedures to be used.

Planning for Directory Synchronization

Directory synchronization is an important feature for organizations that use Active Directory, because it enables Active Directory user and group accounts to be synchronized to Office 365. For most organizations, it makes sense to use directory synchronization in tandem with SSO, because the combination of SSO and directory synchronization creates a seamless experience for Skype for Business Online users. Although it is possible to configure directory synchronization without SSO, this would result in two sets of credentials to manage, and it's therefore recommended only for small organizations.

Directory synchronization with Office 365 is made possible using Azure Active Directory Connect, the successor to Microsoft Online Services Directory Synchronization Tool. The following sections provide the necessary planning details to ensure that directory synchronization with Skype for Business Online/Office 365 functions smoothly.

NOTE

Directory synchronization with Office 365 should be considered a long-term commitment, particularly since the synchronized objects can be edited only with the on-premises tools.

Activating the AD Synchronization Feature

Before directory synchronization with Skype for Business Online/Office 365 is used, this feature must be activated within the online tenant. Activating the feature is a one-time process and is as simple as clicking a button within the online portal. However, the activation process can require up to 24 hours to complete. With that in mind, Skype for Business Online administrators should plan ahead and activate AD synchronization several days before the AD user accounts need to be populated into the online directory.

Preparing Active Directory for Synchronization

To ensure that the on-premises Active Directory is prepared for synchronization with the online directory, the Microsoft Office 365 Support Assistant is used. The Microsoft Office 365 Support Assistant inspects the local Active Directory environment and provides a report that includes a prerequisite check and an attribute assessment, as shown in Figure 29.2. If changes are required, these are listed so that they can be handled before directory synchronization is enabled.

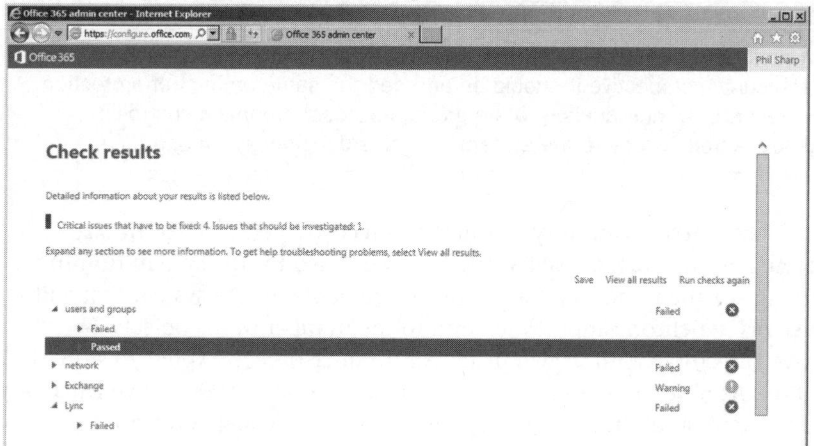

FIGURE 29.2 Report from the Microsoft Office 365 Support Assistant.

The Microsoft Office 365 Support Assistant can be accessed from the Office 365 portal, and it can be executed on any domain-joined system by any domain user. After the tool is run and the report is generated, any changes that are listed should be made to prepare the environment for directory synchronization. The report can then be rerun as many times as needed to ensure that all required changes have been completed. After the environment is fully prepared, the directory synchronization feature can be enabled by a Skype for Business Online/Office 365 administrator using the online portal.

Preparing a System for the Azure Active Directory Connect

Microsoft Azure Active Directory Connect can be downloaded directly from the Office 365 portal or the Microsoft Download site. Before the tool is installed, there are specific requirements for the network as well as the system that will be used to run the tool.

The following requirements apply to the system that will be used to run Azure Active Directory Connect:

- Supported operating systems are Windows Server 2008 and greater.
- If using the "Express Settings," the system must be a member of an Active Directory domain, and the domain must be within the same forest as the domain that will be synchronized to Skype for Business Online/Office 365.
- The system cannot be running Active Directory Federation Services.
- .NET Framework 4.5.1 or later must be installed.
- Windows PowerShell 3.0 or later must be installed.

NOTE

The system that runs directory synchronization contains sensitive information, and therefore from a security perspective it should be afforded the same amount of protection as a domain controller. Only individuals who are granted access to domain controller systems should be granted access to the system that runs directory synchronization.

The performance of Azure Active Directory Connect is directly dependent on the size and complexity of Active Directory, as well as the hardware used for the system running the tool. Table 29.4 shows the minimum hardware requirements for the system that will be used to run directory synchronization in relation to the number of AD objects. By default, Azure Active Directory Connect will install an instance of SQL Express to store the directory information. As noted in the table, if there are more than 50,000 Active Directory objects to be synchronized, a full instance of SQL Server 2012 or greater is required.

TABLE 29.4 Minimum Hardware Requirements for the System Running Azure Active Directory Connect

Number of AD objects	CPU	Memory	Hard Disk
Fewer than 50,000	1.6GHz	4GB	70GB
50,000–100,000	1.6GHz	16GB	100GB
100,000–300,000 (requires full SQL Server)	1.6GHz	32GB	300GB
300,000–600,000 (requires full SQL Server)	1.6GHz	32GB	450GB
More than 600,000 (requires full SQL Server)	1.6GHz	32GB	500GB

Planning for Skype for Business Online

After it has been determined that a cloud UC deployment meets the needs of the business, the planning process for Skype for Business Online can begin. At the start of the planning phase, it is important to identify the business goals that the organization seeks to achieve as a result of the deployment. For example, the desired Skype for Business Online user experience should be defined, and the organization's plan for administering the online tenant should also be well understood. Identifying these business goals will help the organization make the first important decision regarding the Skype for Business Online service: determining which Skype for Business Online identity scenario will allow the organization to achieve these goals.

Skype for Business Online Identity Scenarios

Skype for Business Online and Office 365 offer several identity scenarios that should be evaluated to determine which of these meet the specific business goals of the organization. The following sections describe the characteristics, advantages, and disadvantages of each of these identity scenarios.

Cloud Identity

The cloud identity scenario is ideal for smaller organizations, including those that do not maintain an on-premises Active Directory. Each Skype for Business Online user's identity is maintained only in the cloud, resulting in a simple deployment and minimal management. However, if password-protected systems are maintained on-premises, users will need to manage several sets of credentials. An additional consideration is that cloud identity does not allow for two-factor authentication options. For these reasons, the cloud identity scenario is not likely to be used by organizations that use Active Directory.

Cloud Identity + Directory Synchronization

Cloud identity + directory synchronization is similar to the cloud identity scenario already described, but is a more attractive option for organizations that maintain Active Directory on-premises. The directory synchronization features enable local AD user and group accounts to be synchronized to Skype for Business Online/Office 365, allowing coexistence. With Azure AD Connect and recent versions of the Microsoft Active Directory Synchronization tool, Microsoft introduced the capability to synchronize the user passwords in addition to the other Active Directory attributes. There are security implications in taking this approach, so make sure those are considered before turning this feature on. Some smaller organizations that use AD might find that cloud identity + directory synchronization is a good fit due to the simplicity of the deployment and limited management, because directory synchronization does not require much in the way of administration after it has been deployed. However, medium-to-large organizations will not likely choose this scenario due to more complex security requirements.

Federated Identity

Federated identity involves the configuration of single sign-on (SSO) using Active Directory Federation Services (AD FS), as well as directory synchronization. The combination of these two technologies creates the most seamless experience for Skype for Business Online users, because only a single set of credentials is required. However, federated identity is clearly the most complex option in terms of both implementation and ongoing management. Federated identity is also the only identity scenario that allows the use of two-factor authentication. Small organizations will likely find federated identity to be too complex, whereas for medium-to-large organizations this will be the most attractive option.

Planning Skype for Business Online Administration

An important aspect of planning for Skype for Business Online is determining how the cloud deployment will be administered. Much like an on-premises Skype for Business deployment, Skype for Business Online and Office 365 follow a role-based access control (RBAC) model, in which permissions and capabilities are defined by management roles. When an organization signs up for a Skype for Business Online or Office 365 subscription, the individual who handles the sign-up process automatically becomes a global administrator, or top-level administrator for the cloud deployment. Additional administrators can then be added as needed to handle various aspects of the online tenant. There are a total of five administrator roles within Office 365, as shown in

Table 29.5. Each user account that is added to the cloud organization is automatically assigned the user role, which has no administrative permissions. Individual user accounts can then be assigned to one of the administrative roles to delegate permissions to the online tenant.

TABLE 29.5 Skype for Business Online/Office 365 Administrator Roles

Office 365 Admin Role	Description
Global administrator	Includes full permissions to the online organization. This role is assigned to the initial user account created for the subscription and is used to assign admin permissions to other users.
Billing administrator	Includes full permissions for billing tasks only and read-only permissions for other objects. A user assigned to this role receives notifications for billing events.
Password administrator	Includes read-only access to all objects and has password-reset privileges. However, a user assigned to this role cannot reset the password of a global administrator, billing administrator, or user management administrator.
Service administrator	Includes read-only access to all objects but can manage individual services.
User management administrator	Includes read-only access to all objects and administrator permissions for user accounts. However, a user assigned to this role cannot make changes to the account of a global administrator or billing administrator.

NOTE

For each administrator account added to Skype for Business Online/Office 365, an alternative email address can be assigned to the account, which is used to reset the account password in the event that the password is lost or forgotten.

Planning the SIP Namespace

A key decision in the Skype for Business Online planning process is the SIP namespace that will be used for Skype for Business Online users. The deciding factor in this decision, however, is typically very simple: To provide a seamless UC experience for users, the SIP namespace used for Skype for Business Online must match the primary SMTP namespace used with the organization's messaging system. Because most organizations that sign up for Skype for Business Online already have an established primary SMTP namespace for use with their existing messaging system, this same namespace is also specified as the Skype for Business Online SIP domain. Multiple domains can also be added and used with Skype for Business Online if this is necessary.

TIP

A good example of the importance of matching the namespace between Skype for Business Online and the messaging system is seen in the interaction between the Skype for Business client and the Outlook email client when a new online meeting is created. When Skype for Business is installed on a system where Outlook is installed, the Online Meeting Add-in for Skype for Business is automatically enabled and is used to allow quick scheduling of online meetings from the Outlook client. When the user creates a new meeting request, the Outlook client attempts to redirect to Skype for Business Online using the user's SMTP address to create the meeting request. If the SMTP address does not match the SIP address, the online meeting request fails. In a circumstance in which it is not possible to match the SIP and SMTP namespaces, users are forced to use the Skype for Business Web Scheduler to create online meetings instead of Outlook.

After the SIP namespace has been determined, the SIP domain name is entered into the Office 365 portal as part of the initial setup process.

Planning the Network for Skype for Business Online

One key area that could easily be overlooked during the planning of a Skype for Business Online deployment is network planning. The following sections provide details on the various network elements that can be affected by a Skype for Business Online deployment so that these can be planned appropriately.

Planning Internet Connection Bandwidth for Skype for Business Online

With Skype for Business Online, the media experience for users is directly tied to the amount of Internet bandwidth available for use with Skype for Business. Particularly if an organization has been using the Internet only for web browsing, consideration needs to be given to adding bandwidth to accommodate the network requirements for Skype for Business audio and video.

To assist organizations with this aspect of planning for Skype for Business Online, Microsoft provides the Office 365 Fast Track Network Analysis tool. This is a tool that tests an Internet connection for connectivity to a Skype for Business Online service data center, and it helps an organization to determine whether adjustments might need to be made to an Internet connection that will potentially be used for Skype for Business Online. The tool specifically tests for response times, bandwidth, allowed ports, routes, and connection quality with respect to real-time media. The feedback provided by the tool can be quite detailed and useful for proper planning of the network for Skype for Business Online. For example, Figure 29.3 shows the summary of the VoIP test performed using the Office 365 Fast Track Network Analysis tool, which helps identify the expected audio quality of Skype for Business Online audio if used with this Internet circuit. The Office 365 Fast Track Network Analysis tool is available at several URLs published on the Microsoft support site, which allows the user to select the URL closest to their physical location. Java Runtime Environment is a prerequisite for running the tool.

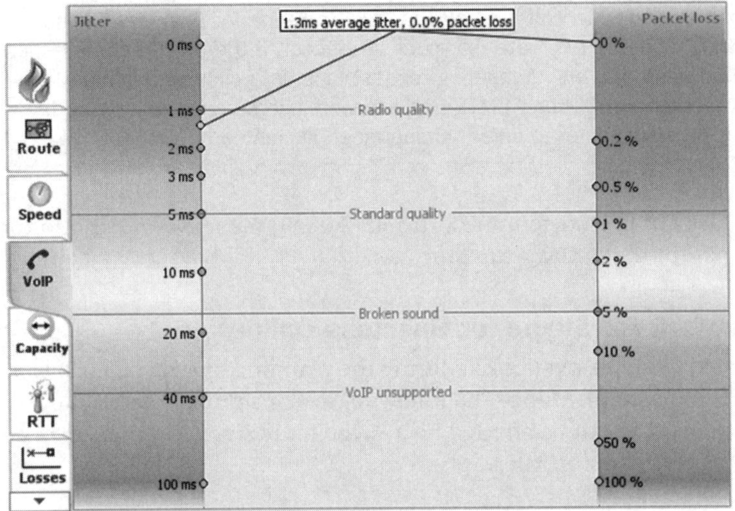

FIGURE 29.3 Office 365 Fast Track Network Analysis tool VoIP results.

NOTE

If you are considering deploying Skype for Business Online Cloud PBX, it is highly recommended that you also deploy Azure ExpressRoute for Office 365. ExpressRoute for Office 365, simply put, is a way to connect to the Office 365 backbone network as another destination on an organization's corporate WAN. This is important when considering using a cloud-based service to provide real-time communications for a couple reasons. First, the ExpressRoute circuit has a service-level agreement (SLA) of 99.9% uptime, which aligns with the Office 365 SLA. Second, any traffic prioritization performed on media packets within the corporate network are honored and maintained through the ExpressRoute Multiprotocol Label Switching (MPLS) circuit and the Office 365 network. Ultimately, this means that connectivity to Skype for Business Online becomes more predictable and behaves like an extension of the corporate network.

Firewall Port Requirements for Skype for Business Online

Another important consideration with regard to planning the network for Skype for Business Online is firewall port requirements. Skype for Business Online does not have any port requirements for inbound traffic; however, many organizations use outbound filters or proxy servers to control the type of traffic that is permitted outbound. If outbound filtering is used, specific ports need to be opened on the firewall or proxy server to allow Skype for Business outbound traffic, as shown in Table 29.6.

TABLE 29.6 Firewall Port Requirements for Skype for Business Online

Source Port	Destination Port	Protocol	Usage
Ephemeral ports TCP	443/TCP	SIP/TLS	Client registration and signaling
Ephemeral ports TCP	443/TCP	HTTPS	HTTPS downloads
Ephemeral ports TCP	443/TCP	PSOM/TLS	Data sharing sessions
Ephemeral ports TCP	5223/TCP	TCP	Lync Mobile 2010 push notifications on iOS and Windows Phone 7.5
50000–50019/TCP and UDP	443/TCP, 3478/UDP, 50000–59999/TCP and UDP	RTP/UDP	Audio sessions
50020–50039/TCP and UDP	443/TCP, 3478/UDP, 50000–59999/TCP and UDP	RTP/UDP	Video sessions
50040–50059/TCP and UDP	443/TCP, 3478/UDP, 50000–59999/TCP and UDP	RTP/UDP	Desktop sharing sessions

As for individual client systems, when the Skype for Business client is installed, the required adjustments are automatically made to the Windows Firewall to enable Skype for Business Online traffic to flow. Therefore, no additional adjustments to the Windows Firewall should be needed.

DNS Requirements for Skype for Business Online

For each DNS domain that will be used with Skype for Business Online, several external DNS CNAME records need to be added to support the client Autodiscover service. Table 29.7 shows the external DNS CNAME records that are needed, where `<DomainName>` is the external DNS domain that will be used with Skype for Business Online.

TABLE 29.7 External DNS CNAME Records Used to Support Autodiscover with Skype for Business Online

Client Type	Host Name	Destination	TTL
Desktop	`sip.<DomainName>.com`	`sipdir.online.lync.com`	1 hour
Mobile	`lyncdiscover.<DomainName>.com`	`webdir.online.lync.com`	1 hour

In addition to the CNAME records used for authenticated clients, several external SRV records might be required to support additional scenarios. Specifically, one external SRV record is needed to allow Autodiscover for anonymous (unauthenticated) users, and one external SRV record is needed to support federation and public IM connectivity if these will be used. Table 29.8 shows the external SRV records that are required to support these scenarios, where `<DomainName>` is the external DNS domain that will be used with

29

Skype for Business Online. The first entry would be used to support Autodiscover for anonymous users, whereas the second entry would be used to support federation and public IM.

TABLE 29.8 External DNS SRV Records Used for Anonymous Autodiscover and Federation

Service	Protocol	Port	Weight	Priority	TTL	Name	Target
_sip	_tls	443	1	100	1 hr	`<DomainName>.com`	`sipdir.online.lync.com`
_sipfederationtls	_tcp	5061	1	100	1 hr	`<DomainName>.com`	`sipfed.online.lync.com`

TIP

For most organizations, the DNS records detailed in this section are required for external DNS zones only. Although this approach is not typical, some organizations support split-brain DNS or filter outbound DNS queries using firewalls or Internet proxies. If this is the case, it is necessary to add the same DNS records to internal DNS zones to support these same Skype for Business Online functions from inside the network. If this is not possible, Autodiscover does not function, and the Skype for Business client needs to be manually configured to connect to the following server name for both internal and external connections: `sipdir.online.lync.com:443`.

Planning for Federation and Public IM

Skype for Business Online enables users to communicate with other users from external organizations that also use Skype for Business, Lync, or Office Communications Server by way of federation. In addition, Skype for Business Online users can communicate with consumer Skype users via public federation. By default, both of these services are turned off for new Skype for Business Online deployments. However, making use of these services is as simple as logging on to the Office 365 portal and enabling the features. Up to a day is required before activation after these services are enabled, so Skype for Business Online administrators should plan ahead and enable the services several days before the Skype for Business Online users need to begin using them.

From a planning perspective, one additional consideration is the policy the organization will adopt with regard to communication with external organizations. Skype for Business Online provides support for maintaining either a whitelist of organizations that the users will be allowed to communicate with or a blacklist of organizations that the users will not be allowed to communicate with. These lists are configured by entering the SIP domains of the organizations that will be either allowed or blocked; therefore, this configuration will dictate the level of maintenance that will be required on the part of the Skype for Business Online administrators to support the federation policy of the organization.

Using a blacklist results in a more open policy that should be adopted by organizations that are less concerned about which external organizations their users are communicating with, and it requires less maintenance for that very reason. On the other hand, organizations that prefer to maintain tight control of communication with external organizations should use the whitelist approach. This of course results in a higher level of maintenance to uphold the policy, particularly if there are many SIP domains with which the organization would like to communicate. This is because the Skype for Business administrators need to first determine the SIP domain for any organization that will be allowed for federation, and then add each SIP domain to the whitelist. Further, the external organization also needs to be configured for federation with the Skype for Business Online organization, and depending on whether that organization has an open or closed federation policy, it might be necessary for the Skype for Business administrators on both sides to communicate the required information before configuring federation.

NOTE

A Skype for Business Online tenant can federate not only with other Skype for Business Online tenants, but also with organizations that use Skype for Business, Lync, or Office Communications Server on-premises. The blacklist or whitelist settings configured in the Office 365 portal apply to either type of Skype for Business organization.

Planning for Dial-in Audio Conferencing

Skype for Business Online Plan 2 natively supports online conferences that can be initiated and attended by any user with one of the Skype for Business conferencing clients (including the full Skype for Business Client and Skype for Business Web App). However, dial-in conferencing, which enables attendees to dial in to the audio portion of a Skype for Business meeting, requires licensing for the Microsoft PSTN Conferencing service, or the purchase of a dial-in audio conferencing service from an approved Microsoft Audio Conference Provider partner. This latter service requires some planning before it can be made available to Skype for Business Online users.

In December 2015, Microsoft released its native Dial-in Conferencing capabilities within Skype for Business Online/Office 365, simply referred to as "PSTN Conferencing." Licensed as an add-on to existing Skype for Business Plan 2 and Office 365 "E" plans, this feature enables customers to provide dial-in capabilities into native Skype for Business Online Meetings without having to acquire service through a third-party provider. Planning for this capability is rather straightforward—once the user is licensed, it is simply a matter of turning it on or off. At launch, PSTN Conferencing will support toll-based dial-in capabilities in 15 countries. Support for additional countries and toll-free dial-in access are expected to be released and are listed on the official Microsoft roadmap. The dial-in numbers provided by Microsoft are part of a fixed list, and custom phone numbers are not supported. If local or toll-free dial-in access is required in a country where it is not yet provided by Microsoft, you will need to consider service from one of the certified Audio Conference Providers (ACPs).

Microsoft maintains a list of partners that are approved for providing dial-in audio conferencing in the Skype for Business section of the Office 365 Marketplace site, as shown in Figure 29.4. The first step in the planning process is therefore to visit the site, gather information on the available conferencing providers, and use it to evaluate and determine which service will best meet the conferencing needs of the organization.

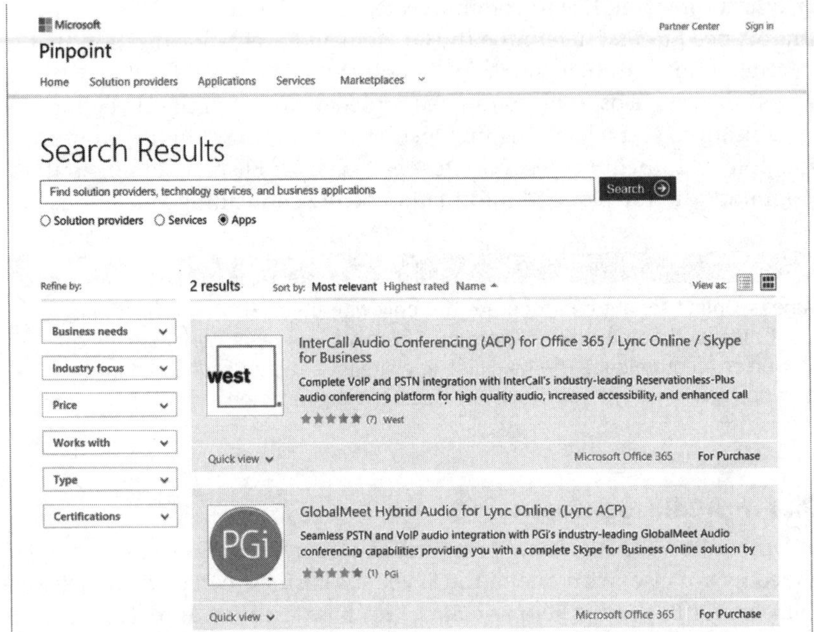

FIGURE 29.4 Approved Skype for Business Online conferencing providers.

NOTE

Organizations that already use dial-in conferencing might be tempted to pursue the use of an existing conferencing provider with Skype for Business Online, even though the service is not from an approved Microsoft partner. However, the use of a non-approved conferencing service with Skype for Business Online is discouraged for several reasons. For example, the integration of a dial-in conferencing service that has not been approved for Skype for Business Online is complex and troublesome to set up, because unlike with the approved conferencing services, no preconfigured connection is available for use. Also, if a nonintegrated audio conferencing service is used alongside Skype for Business Online, this results in separate audio streams for the online users versus the dial-in users. This configuration presents additional challenges; for example, the recording of a Skype for Business conference with two separate audio streams will not capture any of the audio that is transmitted using the conferencing provider.

After a dial-in conferencing provider has been selected and the service has been provisioned, the organization is assigned a block of toll-free numbers and passcodes for use with the service. These toll-free numbers and passcodes need to then be assigned to the Skype for Business Online users to enable this feature. If there are many users to be enabled for dial-in conferencing, it can be a significant administrative burden to manually configure these values for all of these users. Thankfully, Microsoft provides import/export functions into the Office 365 portal, and these can be used to quickly assign the dial-in conferencing values for the user accounts by direct editing of an XML file.

After the dial-in conferencing values have been configured for a Skype for Business Online user, the phone numbers for dial-in along with passcodes automatically appear on new meeting invites, in much the same fashion as with dial-in conferencing configured for an on-premises Skype for Business deployment.

Planning for Skype for Business Meeting Broadcast

Over the past few releases of Lync Server 2010/2013 and now Skype for Business Server 2015, there have been several options for leveraging Lync Server 2010/2013 or Skype for Business Server 2015 as a large-format meeting tool. These options consisted of expanded Front End pools with a standalone A/V Conferencing pool in Lync Server 2010, a dedicated Lync Front End pool specifically used to host conferences in Lync Server 2013, and other third-party solutions that offered their own solutions to this scenario. The capabilities, features, and end-user experience varied significantly depending on which path was chosen. Fortunately, Microsoft has recognized the need to provide a solution that can support more than 250 participants and has released Skype for Business Meeting Broadcast alongside the many other new features in Skype for Business Online.

Skype for Business Meeting Broadcast has been designed to provide an improved alternative for the few-to-many and one-to-many meetings. Leveraging the Azure Media Network, Skype for Business Meeting Broadcast, as the name implies, enables presenters to broadcast a Skype for Business meeting across the Internet to up to 10,000 people. Presenters leverage the Skype for Business client interface to manage and control the meeting, while the participants attend the meeting via web browser from virtually any device. The target use case for Meeting Broadcast is large virtual webinars or Town Hall–style meetings.

Because Meeting Broadcast is exclusively a Skype for Business Online–delivered service, in most cases the meetings are broadcast from the Internet, and the majority of the load of this service is handled by Microsoft. For this reason, an important consideration is corporate Internet throughput and load. If there is a significant number of users in a single site who are expected to attend a Meeting Broadcast, there is potential to overwhelm the Internet circuit. To reduce impact in this scenario, Microsoft is actively working with third-party vendors who specialize in enterprise video distribution. The technology from these partners will enable peer-to-peer redistribution of the Meeting Broadcast from behind corporate firewalls to help reduce the Internet bandwidth requirements and optimize the media flow.

Requirements for Meeting Broadcast are surprisingly simple. Skype for Meeting Broadcast is available to any user who is assigned a Skype for Business Online Plan 2 license, or Office 365 E1, E3, or E5 license. Meeting Broadcast may also be used by on-premises homed users. To do so, they must be assigned one of the previously mentioned licenses in

Office 365 as well as have Office 365 authentication, account synchronization, and hybrid connectivity between the on-premises infrastructure and the online tenant established.

Planning for Hosted Voice Using Cloud PBX

Previously, Microsoft had a cloud-based telephony solution called Lync-to-phone. In many ways, this offering was ahead of its time. The Lync-to-phone offering, although good in theory, did not pan out as expected. The approach from Microsoft at the time was to provide the core platform in Lync Online, but to allow customers to select a SIP telephony provider from a list of certified, integrated service providers, much like ACP works for dial-in access. From launch until deprecation, there was only a single telephony provider available, so the Lync-to-phone offering never really gained enough subscribers to make it a viable offering.

Learning from past experience, Microsoft has re-entered the realm of cloud telephony solution providers with a more complete offering than what was available previously. Skype for Business Online Cloud PBX is a new offering from Microsoft that enables customers to once again leverage Skype for Business Online, not only as their collaboration platform but also as their telephony platform.

Unlike Lync-to-phone, Microsoft directly provides PSTN connectivity to subscribers of the Cloud PBX solution. As with other services provided through Skype for Business Online, Cloud PBX aims to get Microsoft UC into the hands of an organization's users more quickly and with less administrative overhead than a comparable on-premises solution. Additionally, Cloud PBX enables an organization to expand or extend its telephony capabilities without having to further invest in an on-premises, legacy PBX.

Since initial release in December 2015, Cloud PBX has been made available worldwide, but the features of Cloud PBX consist of a subset of those available currently to an on-premises deployment. The list of features available at initial release include mostly client-side functions:

- Inbound/outbound calling
- Call hold
- Call delegation
- Call transfer
- Call forwarding and simultaneous ring
- Music on Hold (client side)
- Team calling
- Voicemail
- Enhanced 911 (static)

It is important to note that Cloud PBX comes in two flavors. The first is a "pure cloud" version, where the user is homed to Skype for Business Online and Microsoft provides all inbound and outbound calling capabilities. In this scenario, a PSTN calling plan is bundled with the Cloud PBX license to provide in-country calling, or optionally international calling. The second is a "hybrid" solution that leverages an organization's existing on-premises telephony carrier service while the rest of the user's services are provided by Skype for Business Online. This hybrid scenario is covered in more detail later in this chapter. Regardless of which scenario you choose, the features are limited by the capabilities of Cloud PBX.

In both scenarios, the carrier providing telephony service will also be responsible for routing calls to emergency services. When using a Microsoft PSTN calling plan, you must define the physical address of each office location where Cloud PBX users will reside. When the users are enabled, you will then be prompted to associate them with an address. In the United States, every 911 call placed by a Cloud PBX user with a PSTN calling plan will route through and be intercepted by a certified PSAP in order to validate the address of the caller.

For Cloud PBX, Microsoft has also gone to great lengths to reduce the amount of complexity involved in what are two of the most time-consuming processes in PBX management. First is the phone number porting process, which is especially painful because in most every situation it involves a change in telephony carrier. Microsoft has distilled the phone number porting process down and estimates completion of number porting within 7 days for fewer than 100 phone numbers and 3–4 weeks for ports of more than 100 numbers. Second, for customers who would like to acquire new phone numbers, Microsoft has built this capability into the Office 365 administrative tools and made it as simple as many of the other administrative aspects of Cloud PBX when coupled with a PSTN calling plan.

Planning for Voicemail Integration

In conjunction with Cloud PBX, Azure-powered Cloud Voicemail is available as the voicemail solution for Skype for Business Online users. Unlike the integration of Skype for Business and Exchange on-premises or even Skype for Business on-premises and Exchange Online, the initial feature set of Cloud Voicemail is much more limited. The initial feature set for Cloud Voicemail consists of basic unified messaging capabilities. This means that upon reaching an individual's voice mailbox, it will accept the message and deliver it into the recipient's email inbox. Because it is built upon a completely new architecture, Cloud Voicemail does not have many of the advanced features that Exchange Unified Messaging does, including personal auto-attendant and Find Me/ Follow Me. The upside to this approach is that there is virtually zero administrative overhead or complexity to manage. Cloud Voicemail is included whenever a user is licensed for Cloud PBX. After the licensing is in place, the integration between Skype for Business Online and Cloud Voicemail occurs automatically.

Planning for a Hybrid Deployment

Planning for a Skype for Business hybrid deployment involves a blend of planning for Skype for Business Online, as described in this chapter, and planning for an on-premises deployment, as described in Chapters 30 to 33. Depending on the services that will be included in the hybrid deployment, there are additional requirements and considerations unique to a hybrid deployment, and these will be detailed in the following sections.

Using On-Premises Systems with a Hybrid Deployment

The on-premises requirements for a hybrid deployment depend on whether hybrid voice will be included in the deployment. If there is an existing Lync Server 2010 pool, then a Lync Server 2013 or Skype for Business Server 2015 Mediation pool and Edge pool will need to be installed to support telephony integration.

If there is an existing Lync Server 2010 Front End pool and Edge pool, the Lync Server 2010 Edge pool can be federated with Skype for Business Online/Office 365 to create a hybrid deployment that offers basic hybrid features. Basic hybrid features are defined as shared SIP address space as well as direct migration of user accounts from on-premises to Skype for Business Online. To support hybrid telephony capabilities, either Lync Server 2013 Mediation and Edge Server pools or the upcoming Skype for Business Cloud Connector Edition are required to facilitate on-premises PSTN connectivity integration with Skype for Business Online. Regardless of the fact that PSTN connectivity resides on-premises, the features available to users are defined by Cloud PBX. These features currently include the following:

- Inbound/outbound calling
- Call hold
- Call delegation
- Call transfer
- Call forwarding and simultaneous ring
- Music on Hold (client side)
- Team calling
- Voicemail
- Enhanced 911 (static)

Figure 29.5 shows a sample hybrid topology with Skype for Business Server 2015 on-premises, which can be used to provide hybrid PSTN connectivity for Cloud PBX users.

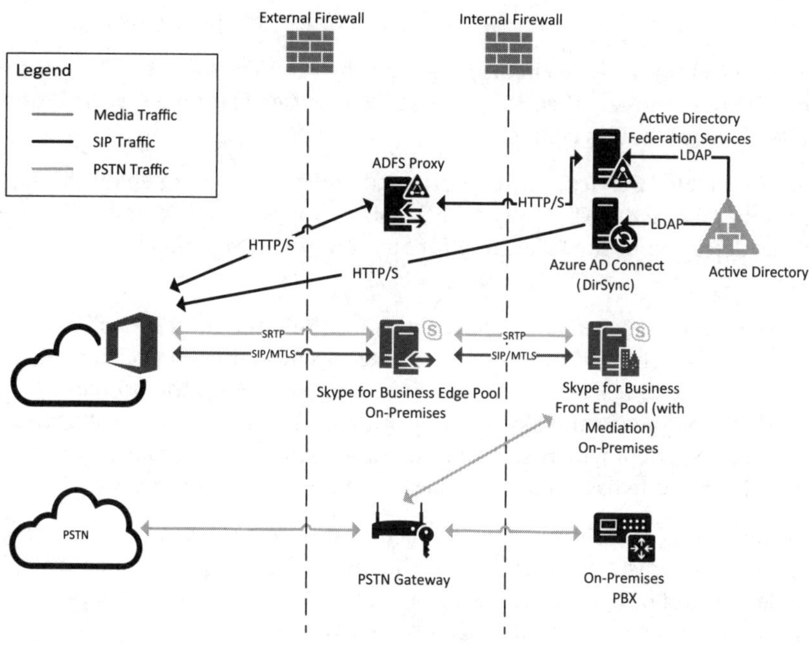

FIGURE 29.5 Hybrid topology with Skype for Business Server 2015 on-premises, supporting hybrid voice features.

For a new on-premises deployment of Skype for Business Server 2015, one Front End pool is required, using either the Standard Edition or the Enterprise Edition. As would be true of any on-premises deployment, voice functionality requires that the Mediation Server role be installed, along with the PSTN infrastructure. The Mediation Server role can either be collocated with the Front End pool or installed in a separate pool.

With any Skype for Business hybrid deployment, regardless of whether the on-premises installation includes earlier versions of Lync Server 2010/2013 or Skype for Business Server 2015, an Edge pool consisting of at least one Edge Server is required. The Edge pool must also be enabled for federation, including the external DNS records that are required for federation.

NOTE

An Edge pool used with a hybrid deployment takes on additional functions beyond those that are typical for a standard on-premises deployment. In addition to the standard Edge services of remote access and federation, the Skype for Business Edge pool in a hybrid deployment is used for federating with Skype for Business Online/Office 365, routing of SIP signaling traffic between the on-premises deployment and the cloud, and in some circumstances routing of media traffic for Skype for Business Online users who connect via the Internet.

Additional on-premises requirements for a hybrid deployment include the following:

- Directory synchronization must be enabled between the on-premises Active Directory and Skype for Business Online/Office 365, as described in the "Planning for Directory Synchronization" section of this chapter.
- Active Directory Federated Services must be installed and configured to enable SSO between the on-premise Active Directory and the Skype for Business Online/Office 365 directory, as described in the "Planning for Single Sign-On with AD FS" section of this chapter.
- In addition to the standard certificate requirements for the on-premises AD FS deployment, the public SSL certificate used as the server authentication certificate must use a subject name of `sts.<SIPdomain>`, where `<SIPdomain>` is the primary SIP domain that will be split across the Skype for Business Online and Skype for Business Server 2015 on-premises deployments. If additional, secondary SIP domains will be used, these can also be added as subject alternative names on the certificate.
- The Skype for Business 2015 administrative tools installed on a server that has access to connect to the on-premises environment. If the on-premises Front End pool is running an older version of Lync Server 2010/2013, the Skype for Business Server 2015 administrative tools should be installed on a separate server.
- To access Skype for Business Online, the Skype for Business client, Lync 2013 client, or the Lync 2010 client running cumulative update 2 and above can be used.

Network Considerations for a Hybrid Deployment

The network planning steps needed for a cloud-only deployment, as described in the "Planning the Network for Skype for Business Online" section of this chapter, are also applicable to a Skype for Business hybrid deployment. This includes bandwidth planning, as well as planning for firewall port and DNS requirements. However, with a hybrid deployment there are several additional firewall port requirements, as well as additional DNS requirements, depending on the configuration.

For a hybrid deployment, the external DNS host record that allows outside connectivity to AD FS is different from that of a standard Skype for Business Online deployment. Specifically, this record must use `sts.<SIPdomain>` as the target, where `<SIPdomain>` is the primary SIP domain that will be split across the Skype for Business Online and Skype for Business Server 2015 on-premises deployments. If additional, secondary SIP domains are used, one external DNS host record is also needed for each of these, using the same destination name format of `sts.<SIPdomain>`.

Edge Federation with a Hybrid Deployment

To support a hybrid deployment, the federation configuration for the on-premises Edge pool must match the federation settings configured in the Skype for Business Online tenant. For example, if the on-premises Edge pool is configured for partner discovery, also referred to as "open federation," then Skype for Business Online must be configured for open federation as well. If the on-premises Edge pool is configured with an allowed domains list, also known as "closed federation," then Skype for Business Online must be configured for closed federation as well. Also, the allowed domains and blocked domains lists configured in the on-premises Edge pool must exactly match the corresponding lists in the Skype for Business Online tenant configuration.

User Management with a Hybrid Deployment

The procedures used to create and manage user accounts with a hybrid deployment are different from a cloud-only deployment in several ways, and should therefore be taken into account when planning the hybrid deployment. After directory synchronization is enabled for a domain, updates and changes to the user accounts must be made using the on-premises tools only. This means that for any new user account that will be a Skype for Business Online user, the account must first be created in the on-premises Active Directory and then synchronized to Skype for Business Online/Office 365. If a user account is instead created in Skype for Business Online/Office 365 using the online portal, the account will not be synchronized with the on-premises Active Directory. After the account is created, the user can be moved from the on-premises Skype for Business Server 2015 pool to the Skype for Business Online/Office 365 tenant, and vice versa.

The following limitations and considerations should also be taken into account for user accounts that are moved from the on-premises pool to Skype for Business Online:

- User contact lists, groups, and ACLs are migrated with the user account when an on-premises user is moved to Skype for Business Online. However, the limit for user contacts in Skype for Business Online is 250. When an on-premises user is moved to Skype for Business Online, any contacts beyond 250 are removed from the user's contact list.
- Conferencing data, meeting content, and scheduled meetings are not migrated with the user account when moved to Skype for Business Online. Users must update previously scheduled meetings after their accounts are migrated to Skype for Business Online.
- Users can be enabled for IM, voice, and meetings either on-premises or in Skype for Business Online, but not both simultaneously.

Summary

Cloud-based computing continues to generate much interest in the business world, and this is likely to increase over time. With many of the new capabilities that have been introduced in Skype for Business Online, the planning aspect of a cloud-based UC deployment is very different from that of an on-premises deployment, and is often not well understood. A hybrid Skype for Business deployment holds promise for nicely bridging the gap between the on-premises and cloud-only options, providing a truly seamless UC environment. However, a hybrid deployment presents even more unique planning considerations that must be taken into account. The information presented in this chapter should be of great assistance to organizations considering a cloud-based Skype for Business solution, not only for determining which deployment option meets the needs of the business, but also for ensuring that important details are taken into account ahead of the deployment, thus ensuring a successful outcome.

CHAPTER 30

Virtualization Support

IN THIS CHAPTER

- Virtualization Overview
- Lync Virtualization Support Guidelines
- Skype for Business Server 2015 Virtual Machine Recommendations
- Host Server Hardware Recommendations
- Skype for Business Server 2015 Sample Virtual Topologies
- Sample Topology Considerations
- Client and Desktop Virtualization

The majority of organizations today, big and small, take advantage of the cost savings and flexibility of server virtualization in one form or another. Many now operate a "virtualize first" policy for new server deployments and are moving to a "private cloud" model for their internal IT. Lync Server 2010 was the first release to support virtualizing every workload, from IM and Presence to A/V conferencing and Enterprise Voice. Skype for Business Server 2015 continues to support virtualization of all workloads.

This chapter begins with a basic overview of what virtualization is and of the benefits a company can realize by leveraging virtualization. It also discusses some of the common virtualization platform features and the different names of these features in competing products, such as Microsoft Hyper-V, Citrix XenServer, and VMware vSphere.

Although virtualization of each role is possible, there are requirements around what is and is not supported and how Skype for Business Server 2015 is deployed in a virtualized environment. This chapter covers the configuration of Skype for Business Server 2015 when considering the use of a hypervisor. This includes processor, memory, disk, live migrations, high availability, and network considerations for each type of server. Sample topologies of some different virtual deployment models are also included. This should give you a good understanding of the support boundaries and overall virtualization best practices.

Virtualization Configuration

Virtualization is a technology that has been around for many years in different forms, but has made a significant impact over the past decade. Most organizations already leverage the technology for new flexibility and cost savings.

This section covers some of the basic concepts for those unfamiliar with virtualization so that the remainder of the chapter can be understood.

What Is Virtualization?

Virtualization enables a physical server to run multiple virtual instances of an operating system. In a traditional physical server deployment, every server has its own dedicated physical hardware, with a single operating system, and the server performs a specific function. When it is time to add a new server to the environment, companies purchase a new piece of hardware, install the operating system, and then configure any applications or services.

With virtualization, the physical hardware with its resources, such as processing power, memory, networking, and disk space, are referred to as the "host." Software called a hypervisor enables the physical host's resources to be shared among many virtual machines. The virtual machines residing in the hypervisor are often referred to as "guests." Guests have to share the resources from the physical server. For example, if a host machine has 64GB of RAM, only 64GB of RAM is available to be allocated among the virtual machine guests running on that host at any one time.

NOTE

Many virtualization products offer the capability to do some form of dynamic memory management so that overallocating or dynamically shifting physical memory between guests is possible, but the bottom line here is that guest machines use the physical resources installed in the host.

With virtualization, companies no longer require new physical hardware for every new server because virtual machines can share a common set of physical resources (typically multiple virtualization host servers).

Hypervisor Types

The key to virtualization is the concept of a hypervisor, which is a software layer that sits between the host physical hardware and the guest virtual machines. It is an abstraction layer between the guest operating system and the resources on the host. The hypervisor facilitates and manages access of the virtual machines to the physical hardware resources.

Virtualization hypervisors come in two distinct types. The first, Type 1 (also known as bare-metal, embedded, or native hypervisor), enables virtualization to occur directly within the existing operating system. Good examples of a Type 1 hypervisor are the Hyper-V, VMware vSphere, and ESXi. These hypervisors are their own operating system, as depicted in Figure 30.1.

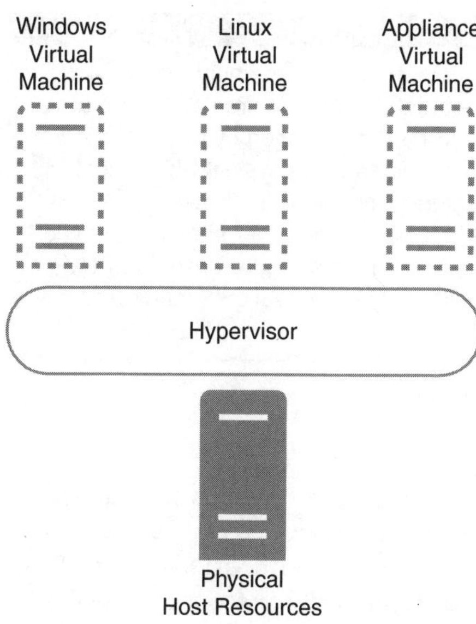

FIGURE 30.1 Type 1 hypervisor.

The second type of hypervisor, Type 2, is less efficient than Type 1 because it is installed on top of an existing operating system, as shown in Figure 30.2. This means that the guest machines must pass through the host operating system before access the hardware. This also means that anything running on the machine OS will interfere with the performance of the guest OS. These are typically best used for labs or running software that is not supported by the current operating system.

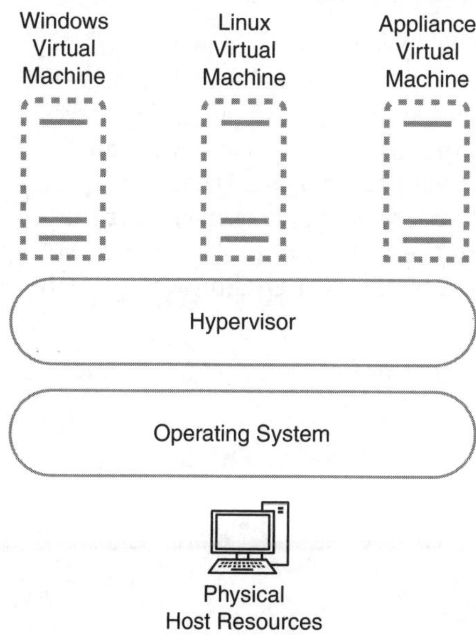

FIGURE 30.2 Type 2 hypervisor.

NOTE

The hypervisor manages more than just the physical resources (CPU, memory, and disk); it also manages the networking and storage. When a virtual machine is created, it has a virtual NIC as well. That NIC connects to a virtual switch that is managed by the hypervisor and manages the network traffic, and the switch then connects to a physical NIC. A host may have one switch or multiple switches that all the guests connect to. The virtual switch could be for assigning a VLAN tag or managing iSCSI data. Another shared managed resource is a virtual disk, which is where a machine typically stores the "C drive" of a system. A virtual disk could be a DAS or SAN disk. Typically, a single virtual disk may contain the "C drive" for multiple machines.

Benefits of Virtualization

It should be apparent from the previous few pages that virtualization offers companies a new level of flexibility in server deployment and management not possible using only physical hardware. The return on investment is greatly increased with virtualization. Take into account each server's requirement in a datacenter. Commonly a server is defined as the rack space it utilizes. If you think in terms of a highly available Skype for Business Server 2015 infrastructure, this could be up to eight servers between Front End pools and supporting services, anywhere from 8–20 rack units of space. That also includes two power supplies for servers, two or three network cables per server, including IPMI (Dell iDRAC or HP iLO, for example). The network cables have to go to a switch, so that is an equal number of ports on a network switch. Then there are the not-so-obvious costs, such as the heat and power consumption of each server. By using virtualization, you can reduce the networking down to two 10GB Ethernet adapters. With fiber channel or iSCSI for your storage, you reduce even more cables by utilizing a bladed infrastructure; you can add more capacity by simply adding a new blade, and no additional cabling is required.

The licensing for virtualization has also changed. In the past few years, and as more companies virtualize their environments, Microsoft has had to change their licensing. In previous versions of the Windows Server operating system, you had to purchase a server license for each server, virtualized or not. Now with the Datacenter version, you can deploy as many virtual machines as you want, as long as you have one Datacenter edition per physical server. For example, if you have three Hyper-V or vSphere servers and you have three instances of Datacenter installed (either as the hypervisor itself or as a guest), you can deploy as many versions of Datacenter as you require. For Enterprise edition, this is limited to four virtual machines, and Standard is one.

This section summaries some of the benefits that organizations can realize from hardware virtualization:

- **Optimized Hardware Resources**—Many bare-metal servers use a fraction of the resources they have available. This means that you may have excess capacity that is not being utilized. By using virtualization, you can use the maximum amount of resources available on each server while supplying each guest with the resources required.

- **Fewer physical servers**—By virtualizing servers, an organization requires fewer physical servers. Modern physical servers support multiple physical processors—in some cases more than 128 logical processors and 1TB of memory or more.
- **Infrastructure flexibility**—As physical servers begin to demand hardware upgrades, the traditional model requires organizations to purchase new servers, or more memory or processing power. In a virtual environment, administrators can easily shut down a virtual machine and add more virtual memory or processors or even move the virtual machine to a new host with more hardware resources. Some hypervisors and operating systems even allow these configuration changes to happen without shutting down the virtual machine. Additionally, expanding the infrastructure to accommodate new virtual machines can become a simple matter of adding a new physical host to the cluster. This adds an entirely new level of flexibility to managing server resources.
- **Increased availability**—In physical environments, servers were often built to be as redundant as possible with multiple hard drives and power supplies. These additional expenses are still useful for a host server but do not apply to virtual machines. As long as a virtual machine image is made highly available, it can be easily restarted on a different host if a physical host fails. It is still best practice to design the hosts to be fault tolerant. Organizations can achieve a higher level of service and availability for servers by abstracting the hardware layer through virtualization. However, it is important to remember that if you only have one physical machine and three guests that are part of a Skype for Business Front End Enterprise pool, although you will have availability at the guest level, there is none at the physical. Building a high availability cluster is as equally important as the guest applications.
- **Application isolation**—A significant challenge in the days of using only physical servers was that each new server required its own physical hardware. Best practice is to isolate each application to a specific server. Typically, this was difficult because of the additional expense involved in purchasing and installing a new dedicated server for each application. To work around budget issues, administrators began to collocate different applications on the same physical server, but because application vendors usually only test and expect their applications to have their own dedicated environment, this could cause performance or configuration issues that were difficult to troubleshoot. With virtualization, each application can have its own dedicated server virtual machine.
- **Legacy application support**—An unfortunate reality for many organizations is a need to support legacy applications that run on only legacy operating systems. As the hardware these systems run on begins to fail or needs replacement, without virtualization, organizations must redeploy these applications on new hardware or operating systems not certified for the product and incur the expense and complexity of redeploying the legacy application. Using virtualization, however, companies can create a new virtual machine running a legacy operating system very easily. They can also perform a physical-to-virtual (P2V) migration of the existing physical server to copy it as-is from a physical to a virtual machine.

- **Rapid deployment**—By building golden images using sysprep, you can rapidly deploy a system in a matter of minutes. It is simply how long it takes to copy the template file. By having your images ready, you can greatly decrease the time it takes to build your entire infrastructure.

TIP

When making your golden image, you should keep the size on disk as small as possible. This is a good use of thin provisioning of virtual machines. The smaller the image, the faster it will be deployed. Some hypervisors give you an option to shrink the disk when it is powered off. This is a good idea before you sysprep the guest.

Virtualization Vendors

Several vendors produce virtualization technologies today. Some of the most commonly used products are Microsoft Hyper-V, VMware vSphere, and Citrix XenServer. All these vendors offer a fairly similar base feature set with some unique features on top. In relation to Skype for Business Server 2015, Microsoft will fully support virtualized environments as long as Microsoft's published guidelines are followed.

Advanced Virtualization Features

As these enterprise-class virtualization products have grown, more features have been added, enabling organizations to cluster physical host machines, move virtual machines seamlessly between hosts while still online, and manage virtual machines from a single console. Most of these features are similar between VMware and Hyper-V products, but have different names. This section covers those naming differences and describes the various features because they are referenced later and have a direct effect on support in Skype for Business Server 2015.

- **Failover clustering/high availability**—This refers to the capability to join multiple physical hosts into a cluster where shared storage from a storage area network (SAN) is provisioned. When running on a clustered set of physical hosts, a virtual machine can be made highly available. If a physical host fails or restarts at some point, the highly available virtual machines running on that host can be automatically restarted on a different host. The virtual machine is also restarted during this process, similar to the power being turned off and then back on. Remember that if a host has a power failure, any guests on that system will powered off as though their power was disconnected and then powered back on in a new physical host.
- **Live migration/vMotion**—This provides the capability to move virtual machines between different hosts in a cluster without any disruption of service or perceived downtime. For example, a virtual machine that is online and running can be migrated to another host while users remain connected to the virtual machine. This is accomplished by the host machines transferring the memory state of the guest over the network and then simultaneously bringing the machine online on the new host while the previous host removes its copy. Both host machines must remain online during this process, and the virtual machine remains available to

users during the process. Be careful when migrating machines with large amounts of memory or under heavy load. Depending on your network and server hardware, you may have to shut down a machine under heavy workload before migrating it.

CAUTION

Live migration of an active Skype for Business server is not supported. This is due to the nature of real-time communications. If a server within the topology needs to move between hosts, it must first be shut down and then moved.

- **SR-IOV (single root input/output virtualization)**—With SR-IOV, the control and management of a physical network adapter can be assigned directly to a virtual machine. This reduces I/O (input/output) overhead and increases performance. SR-IOV is supported in Windows Server 2012 Hyper-V.
- **Dynamic memory/memory overcommit**—This involves the capability to dynamically change the level of physical and virtual memory allocated to a virtual machine. This enables the hypervisor to dynamically allocate resources to best meet the guest virtual machines' requirements.

CAUTION

All resources, including memory and CPU, must be dedicated. If your Front End Server requires 16GB of memory, and your Edge Server requires 8GB, you must have at least 24GB, plus additional memory for the hypervisor and system resources. You can find out more about these requirements later in this chapter.

- **Quality of service (QoS)**—QoS at the hypervisor level enables the provisioned virtual network to have an attached service-level agreement (SLA), enabling the physical network connection often shared between virtual machines to be configured to ensure that each virtual machine gets appropriate bandwidth.
- **System Center Virtual Machine Manager/VMware vCenter**—These two products are Microsoft and VMware's respective centralized management suites. When a single hypervisor is used, management of the host and guest virtual machines can be done individually, but as more hosts and guests are added to an environment, managing each host separately can become tedious. These management products offer a centralized view and configuration store of all the hosts and guests within the virtualization environment.
- **Backup and restore**—An additional advantage to virtualization is the ability for backups and restores. Most storage vendors have special APIs that when backing up a guest OS will also back up databases and put the proper truncation and backup markings as well. And using technologies like Hyper-V replication, you can replicate an entire VM between sites. For simple services, such as the file share, a virtual machine backup can be very useful in case the file share becomes unavailable; you can easily restore a backup with the complexity of using other technologies with just a minimum amount of data loss.

TIP

When designing your volumes for hosting the virtual disks of each system, take into account backup. Because many hypervisors allow for backup at a virtual disk level, as well as the guest level, creating large volumes could increase the time it takes to back up and restore a virtual disk. Making a virtual disk for each guest is also not advised because that will waste space due to how virtual disks are created and managed. A balance should be made. This can be done through roles, such as all your Front End Servers on a VMDK, or through grouping of functions. For example, one volume may contain the Front End Server, Edge Server, and web applications. SQL databases should always be on their own volume for performance and snapshot backups.

Skype for Business Server Virtualization Support Guidelines

In Skype for Business Server 2015, all roles are supported in a virtualized environment. With today's servers, any of the roles can be virtualized. However, it is important to remember that in some cases the amount of guest processing power is decreased because of shared memory and CPU. In order to best understand how your virtualization platform will support Skype for Business Server 2015, you will need to look at the existing utilization over an extended time frame.

Many vendors make a virtualized Session Border Controller. The virtual appliance is managed the exact same way as the physical server. The advantage to having a virtual SBC is that you can meet the same highly available requirements as your Skype for Business Server 2015 deployment without adding additional rack space, and you don't have to wait for it to be built and shipped; you can download it immediately.

The reverse proxy and load balancer are two other services that are now commonly virtualized; for example, Kemp Technologies and Citrix both have load balancers that can be virtualized. These usually require special configurations on your hypervisor to meet the networking requirements. And just like with their physical counterparts, you can reach the same performance requirements.

It should be understood that although virtualization of all the Skype for Business Server 2015 roles is supported, there are some very specific support limitations and recommendations:

- **Windows Server 2008 R2 and later, or VMware vSphere 5**—These are the only supported hypervisors at this time. This includes the Hyper-V 2008 R2 and Hyper-V 2012 standalone free server products and both the ESX and the ESXi products from VMware. This means that older versions such as Microsoft Virtual Server 2005, Microsoft Windows Server 2008 Hyper-V, and VMware ESX 4.0 are not supported for use with Skype for Business Server 2015.
- **No live migration**—Live migration or vMotion of Skype for Business Server 2015 virtual servers is not a supported feature. Because media traffic heavily depends on low latency and CPU processing, moving a Skype for Business Server 2015

VM between hosts can lead to a poor experience for users by either degrading or completely disconnecting a media stream. This means a single Skype for Business Server 2015 server cannot be considered "highly available" by virtue of being hosted on a virtualization platform that supports high availability at the virtualization layer.

NOTE

Even though live migration is not supported while the services are running, you can stop the Windows services by running `stop-cswindowsservice -graceful`. Once the services have stopped, you can then migrate the server to a new physical host and restart the services. You should also shut down the server before you migrate to it. Live migration or vMotion should not be considered part of your HA strategy; instead use the native method of HA in Skype for Business Server 2015.

- **Mixing virtual and physical servers within the same pool is not supported**—There are some additional guidelines when mixing physical and virtual servers for Skype for Business Server 2015, but the most basic one is that a pool cannot contain a mix of physical and virtual servers. All servers in a single Front End, Edge, Director, or Mediation pool must be either physical or virtual to be supported. The performance of each virtual machine in a pool should be equivalent (users will be balanced over each server equally regardless of each machine's performance characteristics).
- **Mix and match physical and virtual servers**—In previous versions of Lync Server, it was required that all components in a single site match platforms, meaning if your Front End pool was virtualized, the rest of the servers had to be as well (for example, the Edge Servers). This is no longer a requirement, so a virtualized Front End Server can be paired with a physical Edge Server. However, the same services should share the same platform; therefore, if one Front End Server in an Enterprise Pool is virtualized, all the other servers in the enterprise pool should be virtualized.
- **Call quality**—Call quality is a key component of Skype for Business Server 2015 at both the physical and virtual levels. Call quality relies on the availability of CPU and memory for the transcoding and networking to support the media. Adding video to this results in even more overhead. If you have a host that has a Front End Server and a SQL server, and the SQL server has a spike in I/O, that can have a performance hit on voice and video, especially during a meeting.

Virtualizing Servers That Work Alongside Skype for Business Server 2015

This section gives some brief guidance on the supportability of virtualizing server roles that work alongside Skype for Business Server 2015.

Office Web Apps Server 2013

Skype for Business Server 2015 has a dependency on Office Web Apps Server 2013 being available in the environment for PowerPoint sharing. This server is also supported in a virtualized environment. Detailed virtualization requirements are beyond the scope of this chapter; see the Office Web Apps Server 2013 documentation for detailed requirements.

Exchange Unified Messaging

Exchange Unified Messaging is required in a Skype for Business Server 2015 deployment to provide Unified Messaging voicemail and attendant functionality for Skype for Business users. In Exchange 2010 SP1 and later, Unified Messaging can be virtualized. Detailed virtualization requirements are beyond the scope of this chapter; see the Exchange documentation for detailed requirements.

Reverse Proxy

An often-overlooked component of a deployment can be the requirement for a reverse proxy server when enabling remote access. Microsoft's Web Application Proxy, part of routing and remote access, is a commonly used reverse proxy. There are many other vendors that have reverse proxies and load balancers that are supported in a virtualized environment. These include F5, Kemp, Citrix, A10, and others. Most companies that have a physical load balancer now have a virtualized version that will run on many hypervisors.

NOTE

The use of Web Application Proxy requires Active Directory Federation Services 3.0 to be deployed.

Again, if these virtual appliances are to be collocated on a host with Skype for Business Server 2015, their virtual hardware requirements should be considered. Be aware of any limitations in scalability of virtual load balancers in comparison to their hardware equivalents.

Understanding the Limits of Virtualization

One of the benefits of virtualization that has led the technology to be so popular is the capability to consolidate many physical servers onto a single virtual host. This is possible because most physical servers rarely utilize all their physical processor, memory and storage capacity, and I/O. So, for example, if you have four physical servers each using 20% of their CPU, you could consolidate them onto one physical server of the same CPU specification and not expect to impact performance perceivably (assuming that storage, network, and memory are also specified appropriately).

Real-time Media and Virtualization

It is the hypervisor that shares the physical resources between the virtual servers; if the virtual servers are processing non-time-sensitive data (for example, serving a web page or forwarding an email), a slight delay in processing might not matter. Skype for Business Server 2015 deals with real-time audio and video, and the fact that it is "real time" is key. Without consistent performance from the server, the audio or video could glitch or freeze. Therefore, a virtual Skype for Business Server 2015 server must perform consistently.

The physical hardware recommendations laid out by Microsoft give us an indication of the processing, memory, storage, and network performance required to deliver good Skype for Business Server 2015 performance. Their hardware recommendations are scaled for 6,600 users per Front End Server based on their user model data. It is important to understand that virtualization is not going to magically reduce this processing, memory, and storage requirement. In fact, virtualization is actually adding overhead in comparison to deploying directly onto physical hardware. Depending on your server hardware, the actual number of users could be less than the equivalent of bare metal. This is because of the shared resources in virtualization.

Reducing the amount of hardware required or costs is not a primary goal of virtualizing Skype for Business Server 2015.

Skype for Business Server 2015 Virtual Machine Recommendations

This section details the virtual hardware requirements for Skype for Business Server 2015 virtual guest machines. At the time of writing, Microsoft's guidance for Skype for Business Server 2015 is that virtual hardware should match physical hardware recommendations. All other variables being equal, you can expect around a 10% performance impact (so at least 10% reduction in supported users) on a virtual deployment.

Many hypervisors have a method for creating a pool or group of virtual guests. These pools can be used to manage the guaranteed amount of CPU and memory, for example. It is recommended that if possible you create a pool for each Skype for Business Server 2015 service you are deploying. A pool is a way to manage resources. It can be configured as a shared resource or dedicated to each resource in the pool. Pools allow for a more manageable methodology than working with each individual server. By making a change at a pool level, you change all guests in that pool so that ally systems are equal.

A policy should be created within the management tools to prevent certain virtual servers to be collocated on the same physical server. For example, if you have four physical servers and three Enterprise Front End Servers in a pool, a policy should be put in place to prevent any two of the Front End Servers to be on the same physical host unless specifically required.

Processor Recommendations

In Lync Server 2010 there was a support limitation of four vCPUs per virtual Lync Server, even though eight cores were recommended for a physical Lync 2010 Server. This limitation stemmed from Windows Server 2008 R2 Hyper-V supporting only four vCPUs per guest machine (and therefore Microsoft tested for support only to this level). This was the primary reason for virtualized Lync Server 2010 being specified to support approximately half the number of users of a physical server.

With Windows Server 2012, this Hyper-V limitation is removed and guests can now support up to 64 virtual CPUs, and as such the four-vCPU supportability limitation on Skype for Business Server 2015 is also removed.

Skype for Business Server 2015 Front End Servers, Backend SQL Servers, Standard Edition Servers, and Persistent Chat Servers are recommended to have two six core processors. Edge Servers, standalone Mediation Servers, and Directors should have two four-core processors. If your virtualization platform is already under a heavy load, additional processors may be required.

The high core count is because processing media requires many CPU cycles. Microsoft recommends dedicating logical cores to each virtual machine, and not overcommitting the cores assigned to Skype for Business Server 2015 Servers. Where possible, use of media bypass will reduce the processing load on Front End Servers with collocated Mediation Servers.

Memory Recommendations

Skype for Business Server 2015 Front End Servers, Backend SQL Servers, Standard Edition Servers, and Persistent Chat Servers are recommended to have 32GB of RAM. Edge Servers, Standalone Mediation Servers, and Directors are recommended to have 16GB of RAM.

Skype for Business Server 2015 memory requirements do not scale in a linear way. Servers can operate with less RAM, but you are at the risk of falling outside the support boundary.

The use of dynamic memory for virtual machines that run a Skype for Business 2015 Server is not supported. If the server does not have full control of the memory allocated to the physical or virtual machines on which it is running, degraded system performance and a poor client experience can result.

Other hypervisors have dynamic memory capabilities. Memory must not be overprovisioned at the hypervisor layer. Some hypervisors do not have the capability to provide dedicated resource segmentation/resource isolation for all four physical components: processor, memory, storage I/O, and network I/O. As a result, a guest on a hypervisor platform may consume resources that would then be unavailable or in limit availability for other guests on the same physical host, and degrade the user experience as a result.

Storage Recommendations

With today's storage, SSD disks are becoming more common. SSD offers better performance, but at a higher cost. While SSD may be suitable for SQL servers, that performance is not required for other services. Most Skype for Business 2015 servers are not heavily disk intensive. It may be a better option to use 105,000rpm drives for the rest of your servers, depending on the type of storage you are using.

When it comes to sizing the disks, especially capacity, you want to emulate what the physical server is requiring (see Chapters 4 through 8 for more details on actual storage requirements). The performance you receive on the virtual machine is based on the type of disk (SAN or Direct Attached), throughput (Fiber Channel, converged networking, or internal I/O), and RAID level.

Do not use checkpoints for the virtual machines in a Skype for Business Server 2015 production environment. When you create a checkpoint, Hyper-V creates a new secondary drive for the virtual machines. Write operations occur on the new drive, and read operations occur on both drives, resulting in reduced performance.

Virtual Disk Types: Fixed, Dynamic, and Pass Through

When you are creating a virtual machine, you have the option to create a hard disk for the VM as a fixed size or dynamically expanding. In VMware, the dynamically expanding disk is referred to as "thin provisioning." The difference is that with a fixed-size disk, the space allocated to a virtual machine is immediately accounted for on the host operating system disk volume. For instance, if the host has 500GB of free disk space and a 100GB fixed-size disk is created, the host reflects 400GB of free space. Dynamically expanding disks differ in that a maximum size is specified that the disk can grow to, but the space is not immediately consumed. Continuing the previous example, the virtual machine still believes it has a 100GB hard disk, but space on the host physical disk is consumed only as the virtual machine begins to write data to the disk. The virtual disk is negligible at first, but it might consume 10GB of space after an operating system is installed, and even more when applications and data are added.

Using a dynamic disk can have an impact on the performance of a machine. Take, for example, your disk that you have 500GB allocated to, but are really only using 100GB of. When that disk is creating, a continuous block is allocated; however, when it expands, the next set of storage may be on an entirely different shelf. Although this may be fine for the file share, it can have an impact on a database.

A third option in disk configuration for virtual machines is to use pass-through disks. Pass-through disks present a physical hard disk directly to a virtual machine. This configuration is not as typical for small environments, but where performance must be guaranteed, and resources are not shared with other virtual machines, pass-through disks are an attractive option.

For Skype for Business Server 2015 and SQL Servers, Microsoft recommends using either fixed-size disks or pass-through disks, and not using dynamic disks, due to the potential performance overhead in production.

Network Recommendations

Each virtual machine running a Skype for Business Server 2015 role should have at least one virtual network adapter added. Edge Servers require at least two virtual adapters (as with a physical installation). It is recommended that physical adapters be dedicated to the virtual machines, to avoid the impact of sharing network interface cards.

Synthetic Device Drivers

Both the Hyper-V and the VMware virtualization products contain emulated and synthetic device drivers. Emulated drivers were the original approach to virtualization; in this approach, each hard disk or network adapter assigned to a virtual machine is emulated in software. The advantage of emulated drivers is that almost all operating systems contain support for these drivers because the network adapter driver emulates a baseline set of capabilities. Synthetic drivers are used to provide an additional level of performance and capabilities within a virtual machine, such as jumbo frames or TCP offloading features.

With Skype for Business Server 2015, deployments always use a synthetic network adapter to achieve the best possible performance.

Virtual Machine Queue

Virtual Machine Queue (VMQ) is a network adapter feature that provides some performance benefit in a virtualized environment. VMQ enables the physical network adapter to provide virtual queues for each virtual machine running on the host. This enables the hypervisor to pass external traffic directly to each virtual machine without routing through the management operating system first. This feature should not be confused with Virtual Machine Chimney, which is a separate function that provides TCP offloading features from the guest virtual CPU to the physical network adapter.

If the adapters used on a host machine allow this feature, it should be enabled for optimal performance in Skype for Business Server 2015. Because media traffic is extremely sensitive to latency or delays, any optimizations at the network layer can lead to increased virtual machine performance. Adapters do not support an unlimited number of virtual machine queues, so VMQ should be enabled only for virtual machines that receive a heavy amount of traffic.

NOTE

Early versions of driver software that supported VMQ automatically disabled VMQ if an adapter used for virtual machines was placed in a network team. If you run an older version of the driver, be sure to update to the latest release to enable both teaming and VMQ to function.

SR-IOV

With SR-IOV, the control and management of a physical network adapter can be assigned directly to a virtual machine. This reduces I/O overhead and increases performance. SR-IOV is recommended.

VMware includes a feature called VMDirectPath, which gives a virtual machine direct access to the physical adapters.

Send/Receive Buffers

Microsoft recommends adjusting the send and receive buffers on any network adapter dedicated to virtual machines to be a value of at least 1024. This helps to improve network performance and reduces the number of dropped packets.

MPIO (Multipath I/O)

MPIO provides increased performance and fault tolerance by allowing more than one path between servers and storage. If nondirect attached storage is used, MPIO is recommended.

Guest Virtual Machine Operating System Requirements

Only Windows Server 2012 and 2012 R2 are supported as the guest operating system for new Skype for Business Server 2015 guests. It is strongly recommended to have Windows Server 2012 R2 as the guest operating system, because it has several performance benefits for a virtualized environment.

As with a physical host server, the Skype for Business Server 2015 virtual machines should not run any additional applications or services, because these can impact performance. Any antivirus applications should be configured to exclude the location of any Skype for Business Server 2015 binary files, database files, and the Skype for Business Server 2015 service executables.

When the virtual machines are being deployed, a policy should be set up to manage the order in which services should be powered back on when a physical machine is powered down. For example, you would not want your Front End Servers to come online before the SQL server services are available. The same is true for shutting a physical server down: You want to make sure that a domain controller is the last item to be shut down.

Host Server Hardware Recommendations

When virtualization of Skype for Business Server 2015 is being planned, the virtual host server hardware and configuration have a direct effect on how well the virtual machine guests can perform. You have seen from the Skype for Business Server 2015 guest specifications that there are some pretty specific requirements in terms of hardware and performance. This section summarizes some of the support requirements and performance recommendations to follow when you are specifying a host server. Most of these requirements are based around treating each Skype for Business Server 2015 virtual machine as if it were a physical server with its own dedicated processor, memory, disk, and network adapter. In many deployments it will make sense to have dedicated hardware for the virtual deployment to meet the specific hardware requirements.

There are two ways you would virtualize Skype for Business 2015 servers. The first is to use an environment already in production, and the other is to acquire new hardware to deploy Skype for Business Server 2015.

Sizing Using the Existing Virtual Infrastructure

If you already have an existing environment, you need to pay special attention to where each server is placed. You don't want to put a Front End Server on the same physical host as a highly utilized SQL server, nor do you want to put all of your Front End Servers on a single physical server in a pool. Different hypervisors have different counters, but in general here is a short list of performance counters to monitor. The statistics should be taken over several days. By just monitoring a single day, you could miss an important statistic (for example, network performance during a backup window).

- **CPU utilization**—If you have a physical server with heavy CPU usage, this would not be ideal for Front End or Mediation, but perhaps for the file share.
- **Memory usage**—If a physical machine has a high level of memory usage, the ability of the virtual machine to do real-time media will be impacted.
- **Network utilization**—In most modern servers, both 1GB and 10GB are very common, and usually not at capacity. Not only should the health be monitored at the server level, but at the network level as well. You may also experience bad

packets at the network switch level. Any problems at the network level will show up in audio and video quality. This can usually be remediated with QoS.

- **Disk I/O**—Disk performance has one of the largest impacts on a system. If a backup is running during a large meeting, this requires CPU processing as well. This can also have an effect on the QoE database.
- **Number of virtual machines migrated**—If there is a physical server that continually activates live migrations based off a policy or resource constraint, this would not be an ideal candidate for a service.
- **Disk capacity**—A constant change in disk space availability could be related to snapshot backups and where they are located on a volume. This constant change could have an impact on the performance of your databases.

Processor Recommendations

Any host used for Skype for Business Server 2015 virtual machines should have a modern Enterprise-class CPU. From a planning perspective, the number of cores on the processor determines the maximum number of virtual machines that can run on the host. Therefore, the more cores you have available, the more Skype for Business 2015 Servers you can place on a single host.

The number of cores is the important value here, not the number of physical processors. For example, two quad-core processors are equivalent to four dual-core processors. Both yield eight physical cores that can be used by virtual machines. Typically, a host will have at least two physical CPU sockets.

NOTE

When you bind a guest to an actual CPU core, most hypervisors will not allow a live migration to another server.

NOTE

When deploying virtualization, it is important to enable the virtualization bit on the system processor in the BIOS settings. Most vendors require this setting to be enabled on the BIOS before the hypervisor can be installed. By enabling this setting, it allows for the hypervisor to interact more efficiently at the hardware level. This is especially important when it comes to live migrations.

When configuring your system for virtualization you should make the following changes to how your processors are configured:

- Disable hyperthreading on all hosts.
- Do not use processor oversubscription; maintain a 1:1 ratio of virtual CPU to physical CPU.

- Make sure your host servers support nested page tables (NPT) and extended page tables (EPT).
- Disable non-uniform memory access (NUMA) spanning on the hypervisor because this can reduce guest performance.

Memory Recommendations

You can see from the virtual guest requirements that a reasonable amount of memory is required to meet the needs of Skype for Business Server 2015. This memory should be allocated exclusively for each Skype for Business Server 2015 virtual machine. This means that if you have 64GB of memory on a system, it is shared among all the guests. While you can use memory reservations, these are not commonly applied. Fortunately, memory is relatively cheap these days. It is recommended that you assume the host OS will occupy around 8GB.

Microsoft does not list the recommended memory for a host machine, but look at your number of cores and virtual machine memory requirements to determine the amount of memory per host server. The "sweet spot" for amount of memory for the money is ever changing, but as with all hardware, more is always better—and particularly with database and real-time communications-intensive applications such as Skype for Business Server 2015.

Dynamic Memory/Memory Overcommit

Windows Server 2008 R2 Hyper-V Service Pack 1 and above has a new feature called dynamic memory that allows defining startup and maximum RAM values for a virtual machine. This feature should not be used with Skype for Business Server 2015. Likewise, virtual machines that run on VMware should not be overcommitted on memory. These features cannot be used with Skype for Business Server 2015 and have a negative impact on performance. Basically, you should have all the memory required on the virtual machine to run Skype for Business Server 2015. This is especially true for SQL, Front End, and Mediation.

Storage Requirements

The actual space consumed by Skype for Business Server 2015 virtual machines varies by role and by business requirements. Backend database servers hosting a Monitoring or Archiving database are going to consume much more space than a Front End or Edge Server.

Both direct attached storage (DAS) and storage area network (SAN) disks are supported to hold Skype for Business Server 2015 virtual machines. Which option is used depends greatly on the infrastructure that an organization already has in place. SAN provisioning is generally more flexible, but there is a significant upfront financial cost to these types of systems. DAS storage can be more affordable and yield acceptable performance for virtual machines.

Because Skype for Business Server 2015 now uses SQL Mirroring or AlwaysOn, there is no shared storage requirement for the backend SQL.

Another consideration for organizations is whether to use a single RAID volume for all virtual machines or to separate each virtual machine disk onto its own physical hard disk. There is no requirement for separate disk spindles. The downside to dedicated disks is that unless the disk count is doubled, there is no redundancy at the physical disk level. Many organizations find that placing virtual hard disks on RAID 1+0 or RAID 6 volumes meets the disk requirements of most virtual machines.

Storage I/O performance will be key for virtual hosts. Consider the server roles you have and their combined I/O requirements. The general rule of thumb is that the more spindles there are, and the faster the disks, the better.

NOTE

Most storage systems now are configured with RAID 1+0 or RAID 6. The closer a piece of data is to the center of the disk, the faster the read/write is. This means that ideally you would place your log files closest to the center, then the database, and so on. Some vendors allow the storage admin to manually set this up; in some cases, the first volume created is in the middle, and with some vendors it is scattered so all volumes perform the same.

Network Requirements

Depending on your specific needs, you may need six or more network ports per physical host. Take into account the following general port requirements:

- One port for management
- One port for live migration or vMotion
- One port for end-user communications (internal)
- One port for end-user communications (edge)
- One port for storage (either iSCSI or Fiber Channel)
- One port for IPMI

Double that if you want high availability. However, by using a converged network with 10GB throughput, you can achieve the same I/O performance using VLAN tagging. This means that by using two 10GB plus the IPMI, there are only two cables. The cost is greatly increased for deploying 10GB, but the performance and long-term cost is decreased as your I/O demands increase.

In a traditional virtualization environment, most virtual machines share traffic through a single or teamed set of physical network adapters. Virtual machines compete for network bandwidth resources through the same physical links and can be subject to delays or queues when other virtual machines have heavy bursts of traffic. If shared network cards must be used, a level of hypervisor QoS should be utilized to ensure that Skype for Business Server 2015 roles are provided with adequate bandwidth at all times.

Hypervisor Requirements

Currently there is a wide range of virtualized platforms available for Windows Server 2012 R2—from Hyper-V to VMware. You can find a list of the hypervisors supported for Windows Server 2012 R2 by going to the Windows Server Catalog. It is safe to say, however, that if you are currently running real-time communications software on your existing platform, such as Lync 2010 Server or Lync 2013 Server, it will run Skype for Business Server 2015.

CAUTION

You should never run a production Skype for Business Server 2015 server on a Type 2 hypervisor because the overhead of other applications and networking will decrease the performance of your actual environment. This includes running a domain controller, DHCP, DNS, or any other Windows service on a Hyper-V server.

Skype for Business Server 2015 Sample Virtual Topologies

There are various ways you can deploy a virtual Skype for Business Server 2015 infrastructure. This section gives some examples of a single-host lab configuration, a Standard Edition, and an Enterprise pool. These topologies are no different from what you would configure for a bare-metal system deployment of their counterparts. The memory, CPU, and disk requirements are all the same. The object is to demonstrate how you would lay out the locations of your guests, the networking, memory, and other physical requirements. This also includes virtualizing the reverse proxy, session border controller, and load balancer. The idea is to show the scalability and options. There are endless combinations of how to deploy Skype for Business Server 2015 in a virtual environment, and these are suggestions of typical deployments. By referring to the server requirements in Chapters 4 through 7, you can determine the virtual machine requirements. Remember, just because these environments are virtualized does not mean they need fewer physical resources.

Single-Host Server Deployment

This topology provides a simple pilot or very small deployment. This topology is primarily geared toward smaller deployments with no need for redundancy or for a proof-of-concept scenario in which rapid deployment is a priority. There is no high availability or backup pool. A single Skype for Business Server 2015 Standard Edition server, SharePoint Office Web Apps server, Edge Server, reverse proxy, SBC, and QoE database are deployed. Persistent Chat is deployed on the Front End Server. The entire configuration is built on a single server, as shown in Figure 30.3. There are three VLANs configured: DMZ, DMZ Internal, and Internal. This means that one of the physical network ports will have two VLANs assigned. Typically this would be the internal DMZ, and internal networks would be on the same physical port because most servers have at least two. All of the storage is based on DAS, so all of the disk IOPS are shared among all the systems.

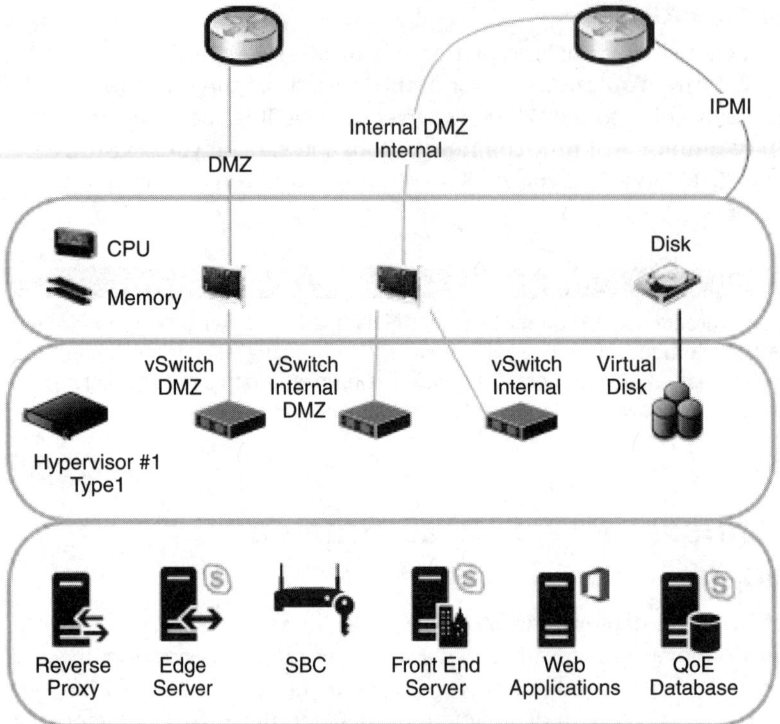

FIGURE 30.3 Single-host server deployment.

NOTE

Skype for Business Server 2015 supports SQL Mirroring and AlwaysOn. SAN storage is no longer a requirement for your QoE database, or your CMS database if using an enterprise pool. However, the cost of AlwaysOn may be prohibitive because that requires SQL Enterprise Edition. SQL Mirroring can be achieved with using SQL Standard Edition.

Here are the host server configuration requirements:

- Two 1GB Ethernet adapters
- 96GB of memory + hypervisor requirements + 10% for additional overhead (for example, backup services)
- Twelve 2.26 processor cores
- Four 500GB disks, hardware RAID 1+0 + hypervisor + backups

Small Business Deployment

This topology provides a great value deployment (see Figure 30.4). In this topology we have increased the number of network adapters required on the physical host and added a SAN storage array. By building two hosts with the same configuration, you can easily configure pool paring and build an infrastructure that can be quickly recovered in case of an outage. There are also additional vSwitches to allow for live migration, SAN storage, an internal DMZ, and a dedicated NIC for system management. Although this design offers resiliency at the Front End level with paring, it relies on hypervisor migration technologies to offer resiliency of other services.

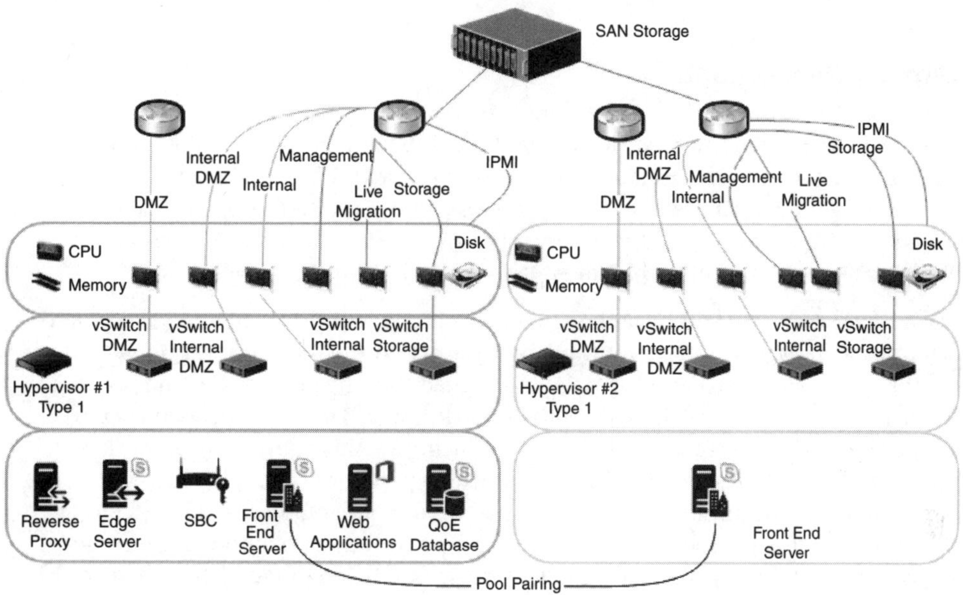

FIGURE 30.4 Small-business deployment.

The resources for this infrastructure are similar to the single-server configuration. Plus, there are additional network adapters, and the memory is increased to support the SAN storage requirements and additional network resources.

Here are the host configuration requirements:

- Six 1GB Ethernet adapters.
- 96GB of memory + hypervisor requirements + 20% for additional overhead for the SAN, network cards, and backup services.
- Twelve 2.26 processor cores.

- Two 500GB disks; hardware RAID 1.
- SAN storage with 2TB of storage available. (This assumes that there are two hypervisors that contain Skype for Business Server 2015 configured for pool pairing.)

NOTE

Even though all of the storage is configured on a single SAN storage device, external storage is designed for a highly available infrastructure, including multiple controllers and network interfaces and a more robust disk subsystem than what is found on most on-board server controllers.

Enterprise Deployment

This topology moves us to Skype for Business Server 2015 Enterprise Edition. This means you can scale to a higher number of users and get true high availability. You now require a load balancer for web services and Office Web Apps. With Enterprise Edition and backend SQL Mirroring or AlwaysOn, you can lose a host and have high availability for user services with no administrative intervention. With SQL Mirror or AlwaysOn in Skype for Business Server 2015, this deployment can work with direct attached storage.

For each hypervisor, you still have the same core components: disk, memory, CPU, and virtual disks. However, you have multiple hypervisors. In this scenario, it is more about where the guests are placed and the policies assigned to it, live migration, and resource pools. Figure 30.5 shows the changes to the infrastructure. The network adapters have been upgraded to a converged 10GB network utilizing VLAN tagging and network teaming. The disk at the server level is just for the hypervisor (although you could boot from the SAN). All the guests are held on virtual disks from volumes in the SAN storage. Because the SAN storage is key, there are multiple paths to it throughout the system; that way, if any one component has a failure, there will be no outage. The SQL database uses a pass-through disk so that the database files are connecting directly to the storage without the use of a virtual disk. This allows for the guest to manage the storage directly for expansion as well as backups.

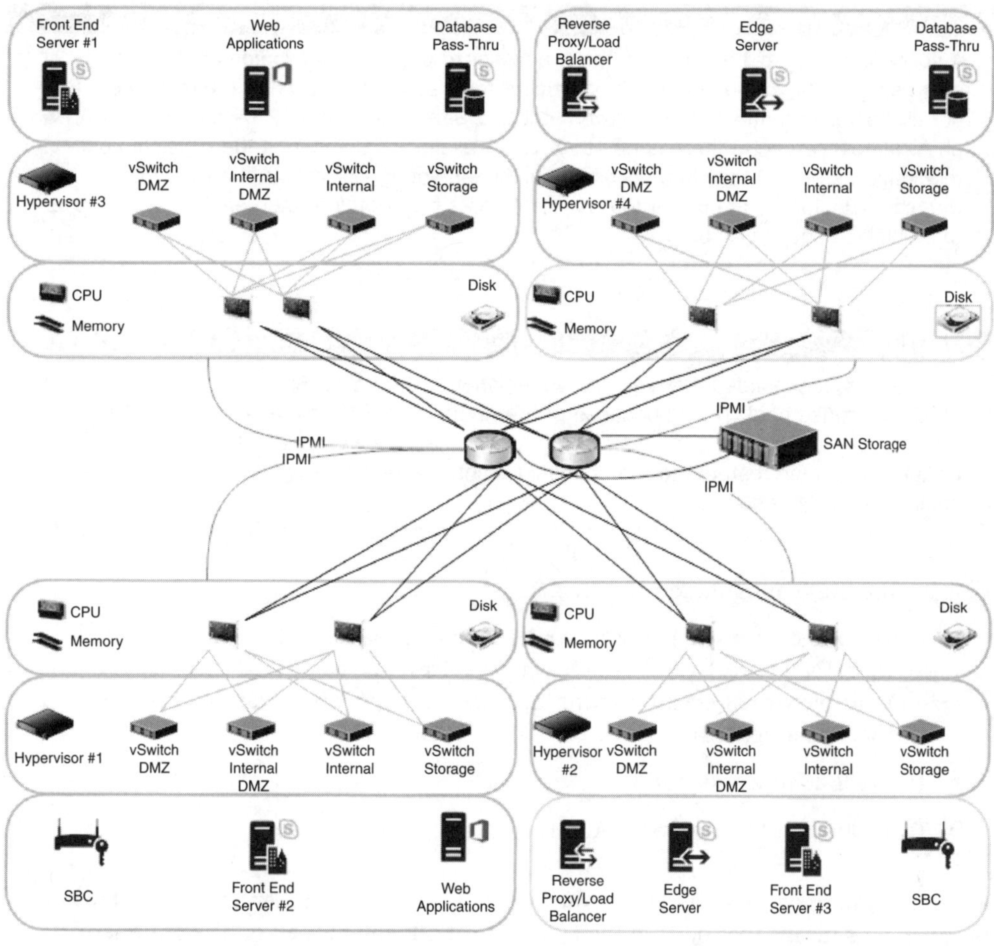

FIGURE 30.5 SAN Storage with 2TB of storage available. This assumes that there are two hypervisors that contain Skype for Business Server 2015 configured for pool pairing.

If a physical server has an outage, all guests on the virtual machine will be powered off and could result in a brief outage. If there is a call on one of those servers in progress, the connection will be dropped. Also, if a Front End Server is shut down, you have to look into how the fabric is affected as well.

This layout is based on using an equal load on each server to maintain the same performance. The physical resources are built so that if two of the four servers go offline, the services will still run at optimal capacity. By adding more memory and CPU, you could even lose three of the physical hosts. This is a true case where planning and budget can give you a highly available infrastructure.

TIP

A policy should be put in place on the hypervisor to prevent any two components from ever being on the same physical host, except for a server failure when the resources are not available. This means that no two Front End Servers should ever be on the same physical host, except if there is no other server available. Computing the physical host requirements should take into account your SLA. If you design a virtual environment that can withstand three out of four physical hosts being offline, then each host will have to be built to support all the roles.

CAUTION

It is never recommended that you use a snapshot backup for a Skype for Business Server 2015 Enterprise pool. This is because of the nature of real-time media and how the resource pools are managed within Skype for Business Server 2015. If a snapshot was to be taken and then restored to the snapshot point, the resource pools could end up in a split-brain configuration.

Here are the host configuration requirements:

- 162GB of memory + hypervisor requirements + 20% for additional overhead for the SAN, network cards, and backup services. The additional memory is to allow for multiple virtual machines running on a single host (for example, two Front End Servers if needed).
- Twelve 2.26 processor cores.
- Two 500GB disks, hardware RAID 1.

When placing the guests on a host, you want to balance out the services as much as possible. This means that putting the QoE, Front End, and SBC all on the same server may cause performance problems. Figure 30.6 shows an example of how to lay out each service using four hosts. If you only have three hosts, it becomes more complex to lay out the services. If you only have two hosts, running an Enterprise pool may not be the best option because two of the minimum required three servers will reside on the same physical host. In that scenario, you may be better off with Standard Edition pool pairing.

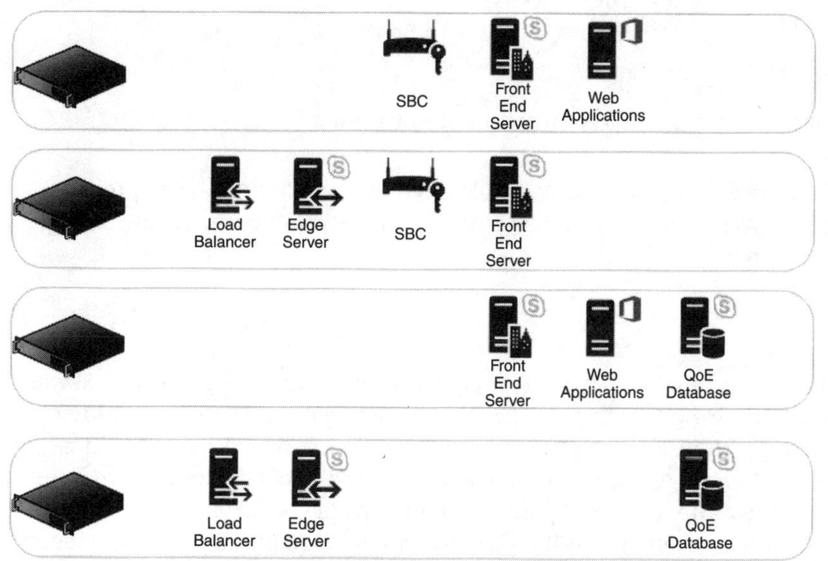

FIGURE 30.6 Example of each service using four hosts.

TIP

It is recommended to have three Front End Servers in a pool in Skype for Business Server 2015, so ideally one of the two hosts would be specified to have two Front End Servers. However, if you lose the host with two Front End Servers, the third server will stop its services due to quorum loss. In this scenario, you can use two Front End Servers per physical host, and the active SQL node will provide the final quorum vote. This is all due to the fact an Enterprise Front End pool uses Windows Fabric.

Best Practices

The following are the best practices from this chapter:

- Use a supported hypervisor for Skype for Business Server 2015 virtual machines such as Windows Server 2012 R2 Hyper-V or VMware vSphere 6.0.
- Use Windows Server 2012 R2 as the guest operating system for any Skype for Business Server 2015 virtual machine.
- Allocate an equal number of cores, memory, and physical network adapter(s) that you would use for the physical counterpart.
- Stress-test the virtual environment and monitor the Skype for Business Server 2015 performance counters before placing the system in production.
- Do not use live migration or vMotion/DRS for Skype for Business Server 2015 virtual machines.

- Use the VMQ feature if available.
- Use single-root I/O virtualization if available.
- Continue to monitor performance when in production.

Make sure that if you are using an existing virtual environment that it has the proper resources available. If you are building a new environment, ensure that there are enough resources for expansion.

Summary

There is little doubt that virtualized deployments will continue to be popular with Skype for Business Server 2015. However, it is important to remember that Skype for Business Server 2015 is dealing with real-time traffic and some intense workloads and should be carefully architected to ensure good performance. You should also keep in mind that just because virtualization is currently popular and supported by Skype for Business Server 2015, this does not automatically mean it is the correct deployment model. Requirements such as dedicated logical processors and network adapters are not typical in virtual environments, so companies might find themselves having to deploy new hardware specifically for Skype for Business Server 2015 even in a virtual deployment.

Although there are some restrictions and many considerations, using the information in this chapter should enable an organization to effectively plan for and successfully deploy Skype for Business Server 2015 in a virtualized topology.

CHAPTER 31

Planning for Basic Skype for Business Server 2015 Services

IN THIS CHAPTER

- Determining the Scope of the Deployment
- Determining Your Infrastructure Needs
- Planning for Capacity
- Planning for IM
- Planning for Conferencing
- Planning for Clients and Devices
- Planning for Archiving
- Defining Your Archiving Requirements
- Planning for Management
- Documenting the Plan
- Best Practices

When you are deploying a potentially complex application like Microsoft's Skype for Business Server 2015, it is critical to plan the deployment before the build in order to optimize the chances for a successful deployment. By planning the features to deploy and by determining the capacity needed and what hardware and software are necessary to support that capacity, you can avoid the pitfalls of deploying off the cuff and potentially having to make major changes to the architecture midway through a build—or, worse yet, midway through a deployment to the users.

Before reading this chapter, you should be familiar with the various roles and tools involved in Skype for Business Server 2015. You should understand the basics of Skype for Business on-premises and hybrid topologies, sites, and server pools. If you are not yet familiar with these items, review those sections of this book before proceeding with the upcoming planning chapters.

Determining the Scope of the Deployment

Skype for Business contains such a wealth of features that planning a deployment, even a limited one, can seem quite daunting at first. This section provides some guidance to assist with the process and assist administrators in creating a well-thought-out and well-structured implementation plan.

Rather than forging ahead with no plan or goals and simply building new servers, loading application software, and inserting them into an existing network environment, you should implement a more organized process to control the risks involved and define in detail what the end state will look like.

The first steps involve getting a better sense of the scope of the project—in essence, writing the executive summary of the design document. The scope should define from a high level what the project consists of and why the organization is devoting time, energy, and resources to its completion.

Creating this scope of work requires an understanding of the different goals of the organization, as well as the pieces of the puzzle that need to fit together to meet the company's stated goals for the project. For Skype for Business, this means understanding how the various parts of the business will use the new functionality to improve collaboration and real-time communication. Different groups will focus on different aspects, such as IM with federated partners, or on leveraging video conferencing for departmental meetings. Understanding the needs of the various groups is key to a successful deployment. This chapter focuses solely on on-premises deployment planning. Other chapters in this book are devoted to hybrid and online deployments.

Identifying the Business Goals and Objectives to Implement Skype for Business Server 2015

It is important to establish a thorough understanding of the company's goals and objectives that guide and direct the efforts of the different components of the company to help ensure the success of the Skype for Business Server 2015 project.

NOTE

It might seem counterintuitive to start at such a high level and keep away from the bits-and-bytes-level details; however, time spent in this area will clarify the purposes of the project and start to generate productive discussions.

As an example of the value of setting high-level business goals and objectives, an organization can identify the desire for zero downtime on IM and conferencing services. Starting with the broad goals and objectives creates an outline for a technical solution that will meet all the organization's criteria, at a lower cost and with a more easily managed solution.

In every organization, various goals and objectives need to be identified and met for a project to be considered successful. These goals and objectives represent a snapshot of the end state that the company or organization is seeking to create. For a smaller company, this process might be completed in a few brainstorming sessions, whereas a larger company might require more extensive discussions and assistance from external resources or firms.

High-Level Business Goals

To start the organizational process, it is helpful to break up business goals and objectives into different levels, or vantage points. Most organizations have high-level business goals, often referred to as the "vision of the company," which is typically shaped by the key decision makers in the organization (the CEO, CFO, CIO, and so on); these goals are commonly called the 50,000-foot view. Business unit or departmental goals, or the 10,000-foot view, are typically shaped by the key executives and managers in the organization (the VP of sales, director of human resources, site facilities manager, and so on). Most organizations also have well-defined 1,000-foot-view goals that typically are tactical in nature and are implemented by IT staff and technical specialists.

It is well worth the time to perform research and ask the right questions to help ensure that the Skype for Business Server 2015 implementation will be successful. To get specific information and clarification of the objectives of the different business units, make sure that the goals of a technology implementation or upgrade are in line with the business goals.

Although most organizations have stated company visions and goals—and a quick visit to the company's website or intranet can provide this information—it is worth taking the time to gather more information on what the key stakeholders feel to be their primary objectives. Often, this task starts with asking the right questions of the right people and then opening discussion groups on the topic. Of course, it also matters who asks the questions because the answers will vary accordingly, and employees might be more forthcoming when speaking with external consultants as opposed to coworkers. Often, the publicly stated vision and goals are the tip of the iceberg and might even be in contrast to internal company goals, ambitions, or initiatives.

High-level business goals and visions can vary greatly among different organizations, but generally they bracket and guide the goals of the units that make up the company. For example, a corporation might be interested in offering the best product in its class, and this requires corresponding goals for the sales, engineering, marketing, finance, and manufacturing departments. Additional concepts include whether the highest-level goals embrace change and new ideas and processes or instead refine the existing practices and methods.

High-level business goals of a company can also change rapidly, whether in response to changing economic conditions or as affected by a new key stakeholder or leader in the company. Therefore, it is also important to get a sense of the timeline involved for meeting these high-level goals.

NOTE

Examples of some high-level business goals include a desire to have zero downtime, access to the communications infrastructure from anywhere in the world, and secure communications when accessed inside or outside the office.

Business Unit or Departmental Goals

When the vision (or 50,000-foot view) is defined, additional discussions should reveal the goals of the different departments and the executives who run them. Theoretically, they should add up to the highest-level goals, but the findings might be surprising. Whatever the case turns out to be, the results will start to reveal the complexity of the organization and the primary concerns of the different stakeholders.

The high-level goals of the organization also paint a picture of which departments carry the most weight in the organization and will most likely get their budgets approved, which will assist in the design process. Logically, the goals of the IT department play an important role in a Skype for Business Server 2015 deployment project, but the other key departments shouldn't be forgotten.

NOTE

As an example of the business unit or departmental goals for an organization, an HR department might typically influence the decision for right-to-privacy access to core personnel records or drive HIPAA-compliance requirements. A legal department might influence security access on information storage rights and storage retention. These groups will prove invaluable when discussing topics such as archiving and whether to allow integration with public IM infrastructures.

If the department's goals are not aligned with the overall vision of the company, or don't take into account the needs of the key stakeholders, the result of the project might not be appreciated or fully adopted by the organization. Technology for technology's sake does not always fulfill the needs of the organization and in the long run is viewed as a wasteful expenditure of organizational funds.

In the process of clarifying the goals, the features of the collaboration system and network applications that are most important to the different departments and executives should be apparent. It is safe to assume that access to collaboration and presentation tools as well as the capability to rapidly communicate with one another will affect the company's ability to meet its various business goals.

The sales department most likely has goals that require a specific type of communication to be supported and will likely push hard for an optimal conferencing experience. The IT department has its key technologies that support the applications in use, store and maintain the company's data, and manage key servers and network devices, and these need to be taken into consideration to ensure that Skype for Business Server 2015 follows practices similar to those of existing systems.

It is also worth looking for gaps in the goals and objectives presented. Some of the less-glamorous objectives, such as a stable network, data-recovery capabilities, and protection from the hostile outside world, are often neglected.

A byproduct of these discussions will ideally be a sense of excitement over the possibilities presented by the new technologies that will be introduced, and this will convey to the executives and key stakeholders that they are involved in helping to define and craft a solution that takes into account the varied needs of the company. Many executives look for this high-level strategy, thinking, and discussions to reveal the maturity of the planning and implementation process in action.

NOTE

Examples of some departmental goals include a desire to have an integrated address book that enables departments to quickly add contacts for partner companies, the capability to add web-based conferencing to meeting requests, and the capability to participate in video conferences from home.

Determining Your Infrastructure Needs

To build a successful Skype for Business Server 2015 infrastructure to support basic functions such as instant messaging, web conferencing, and group chat, these services need to be built on a stable infrastructure. In other words, the services outside of Skype for Business Server 2015 need to be healthy, available, and of sufficient performance to take on the added load of Skype for Business Server 2015. It is also important to plan the hardware that will be used to support Skype for Business Server 2015 and ensure that it is capable of supporting the new environment.

Planning for Hardware and Software

Although many basic implementations of Skype for Business Server 2015 will be virtualized, both physical and virtual servers used for Skype for Business Server 2015 must meet a few standards. Keep these in mind when planning a Skype for Business Server 2015 deployment.

From a hardware perspective, the following specifications are recommended as a minimum for Skype for Business Server 2015. It is important to note that this specification holds true for all Skype for Business server roles except the backend database. Anecdotally, Skype for Business Server 2015 places a higher load on a server than Lync Server 2013 previously did. This is due to some changes in the conferencing MCU and the additional CPU required for transcoding the SILK codec.

- **CPU**—64-bit, dual hex core, 2.26GHz or higher
- **Memory**—32GB
- **Disk**—Eight or more 10,000rpm hard disk drives with at least 100GB usable space
- **Network**—A 1Gbps network adapter, except for the Edge Server role, for which four 1Gbps network adapters are recommended

From an operating system perspective, plan to use one of the following operating systems to support Skype for Business Server 2015:

- Windows Server 2012 (or R2) Standard
- Windows Server 2012 Enterprise
- Windows Server 2012 (or R2) Datacenter

Note that Skype for Business Server 2015 is *not* supported on the following platforms:

- The Server Core installation option of Windows Server 2012
- Windows Server 2012 HPC Edition

Also, plan for a somewhat standardized build for the operating system for Skype for Business Server 2015 systems. By planning what software and features will and won't be present on the system, you'll find it easier to understand the security posture of the systems, and they become easier to support because their configuration is well known and consistent to the group supporting them.

NOTE

The individual role chapters in this book (Chapters 4 through 8) go into detail on which roles need which features and services, and these should be accounted for in the planning of the deployment.

Planning for Network Infrastructure Requirements

When planning a basic Skype for Business Server 2015 deployment, don't forget to take into account the needs you will have of the network. Take into consideration plans for how servers will be logically deployed when determining their physical deployment. For example, if multiple Front End Servers are load balanced for redundancy, consider placing them into different physical racks and connecting them to independent power circuits.

CAUTION

Placing all the load-balanced systems into a single rack highly increases the possibility of a single event taking down all the systems, thus negating many of the benefits of load balancing for redundancy.

When planning the requirements for the local area network (LAN) or wide area network (WAN), you might notice some deviation between predicted loads and actual observed loads. Take this under consideration when evaluating whether existing network connections will handle the added load of Skype for Business Server 2015.

Use the following rules of thumb for Skype for Business Server 2015 when planning network usage:

- Plan for 65Kbps per audio stream and 1.5Mbps per video stream as peak values.
- Bidirectional audio and video sessions count as two streams.
- Skype for Business Server 2015 media endpoints can adapt to varying network conditions and can usually handle oversubscriptions of up to three times. Although an audio stream peaks its usage at 65Kbps, you can typically run three audio streams in the same 65Kbps without users noticing a drop in quality.

- If a site lacks the capacity to comfortably run video streams, consider using Call Access Control to limit video for that site.
- Expect degraded audio and video performance between endpoints separated by more than 150ms of latency.

While Skype for Business supports QoS through DSCP tagging, it is designed to work well in environments without QoS, such as the Internet. By default, Skype for Business Server 2015 assigns a DSCP value of 40 for voice and video traffic.

Planning for Active Directory Dependencies

Like most Microsoft applications, Skype for Business Server 2015 depends heavily on Active Directory to authenticate users, find server pools, and generally keep data flowing. As such, it is critical to account for this when planning a Skype for Business Server 2015 deployment of any kind. Plan to upgrade legacy domain controllers and be aware that Windows Server 2003 mixed mode is not supported by Skype for Business Server 2015.

One of the best things you can do before a large deployment into Active Directory is to perform an Active Directory health check. This involves reviewing event logs, running tools such as DCDiag and NetDiag, and checking replication health to ensure that the directory itself is healthy and operating correctly.

CAUTION

Failure to realize that the directory itself is unstable or unhealthy greatly increases the chances of running into problems during a deployment of an application such as Skype for Business Server 2015.

Although performing an Active Directory health check is beyond the scope of this chapter, many references are available on the Internet. In addition, Sams offers an e-book on this topic: *Performing an Active Directory Health Check* (ISBN: 0768668425).

Planning for Certificates

One of the more difficult decisions when using public key infrastructure (PKI) enabled applications such as Skype for Business Server 2015 is the decision to use internal or public certificates. In this context, *internal* is defined as coming from a Certificate Authority that is not automatically trusted by the operating system, whereas *public* means one coming from a Certificate Authority that is already present in the Trusted Root store of operating systems.

Skype for Business Server 2015 uses certificates for the following purposes:

- External or remote user access to audio/video sessions, as well as conferencing and application sharing
- Remote user access for instant messaging

- Federation using automatic DNS discovery of partners
- Mutual Transport Layer Security (MTLS) connections between servers
- Transport Layer Security (TLS) connections between client and server

Regardless of whether internal or public certificates are used, the following requirements must be met:

- All server certificates must support server authentication (Server EKU [1.3.6.1.5.5.7.3.1])
- All server certificates must contain a valid and reachable Certificate Revocation List (CRL) Distribution Point (CDP)
- Key lengths must be either 1024, 2048, or 4096. Note that 1024-bit keys are not considered secure, so using them is not considered a best practice.
- All server certificates must use one of the following hashes:
  - ECDH_P256
  - ECDH_P384
  - ECDH_P512
  - RSA

Various Skype for Business Server 2015 roles have specific needs around the names contained in the certificates. Luckily for administrators, the Certificate Wizard builds the certificate request automatically and accounts for pool names, fully qualified domain names of hosts, and simple URLs (such as meet and dial-in) that are created as a result of roles and features. The Skype for Business Server 2015 administrator should ensure that the Certificate Authority to be used, whether internal or public, supports subject alternative names.

NOTE

In general, subject alternative name (SAN) certificates are more expensive than traditional single-name certificates. Many public certificate providers charge the same price per name as they do a normal single-name certificate. Other providers offer a flat rate for a SAN certificate and allow the purchaser to insert as many names as will fit into the SAN certificate because there is a fixed amount of space available to fit names. Some providers place arbitrary limits on the number of SAN entries that can go into the certificate.

Planning for Capacity

One of the challenges that faces the new Skype for Business Server 2015 administrator is the eternal question of "How big do I build it?" Luckily, Microsoft offers some guidance, as detailed in the following sections, around sizing servers to provide sufficient capacity for various types of deployments.

General Sizing

Microsoft provides some general sizing guidelines, which are summarized in Table 30.1.

TABLE 30.1 General Sizing of Servers

Server Role	Maximum Number of Users Supported
One Standard Edition server	6,600
Front End pool with 12 Front End Servers and one Back End Server	80,000 unique users, plus 50% Multiple Point of Presence (MPOP), for a total of 120,000 endpoints
One Edge Server	12,000 remote users
One Director	12,000 remote users
One Monitoring Server	250,000 users if not collocated with Archiving Server; 100,000 if collocated
One Archiving Server	500,000 users if not collocated with Monitoring Server; 100,000 if collocated

A dual hex core, 2.26GHz, 32GB server supports 6,600 users as a Front End Server, whereas the same server supports up to 80,000 users as a Back End Server. That said, it is generally a good idea to account for an *n*+1 design when populating Front End Servers. If you were to plan for 30,000 users, take that number and divide it by the 6,600 users per Front End Server and add 1 for a total of six Front End Servers. This places a normal load of 5,000 users per server with the capability to redistribute to 6,000 users per server should a Front End Server suffer a failure or should it need to be brought down for maintenance.

For basic deployments that support external users, the typical rule of thumb is one Edge Server for every 12,000 remote users. It is recommended to always deploy at least two Edge Servers to provide for redundancy.

Capacity Planning for Collaboration and Application Sharing

One of the more common uses for Skype for Business Server 2015 conferences is to present a common document or application to multiple users. Sometimes this is a one-sided presentation and other times it might be a collaborative back and forth in which users share control and modify a single document or presentation. As such, it's useful to understand bandwidth and disk usage for application sharing and conferencing collaboration. Microsoft offers the information included in Tables 30.2 through 30.5 to help plan for the impact of this feature.

Note that Skype for Business broadcast meeting support is only available in hybrid and online deployments of Skype for Business Server 2015.

TABLE 30.2 Application Sharing Capacity Planning

Modality	Average Bandwidth (Kbps)	Maximum Bandwidth (Kbps)
Application sharing using Remote Desktop Protocol (RDP)	434 sent per sharer	938 sent per sharer
Application sharing using compatibility conferencing server	713 sent per sharer 552 received per viewer	566 sent per sharer 730 sent per sharer

TABLE 30.3 Application Sharing Capacity Planning for Persistent Shared Object Model (PSOM) Applications

Application Sharing Usage	Sent and Received (Kbps)	Processor Time	Average Bandwidth Usage per User (Kbps)
15 conferences, 90 users	Received: 1,370 (2,728 peak)	Average: 8.5	Sent per sharer: 713.57
	Sent: 6,370 (12,315 peak)	Peak: 24.4	Received per viewer: 552.92

TABLE 30.4 Content Collaboration Capacity Planning

Content Type	Average Size	Number of Instances per Conference
PowerPoint	40MB	4
Handouts	10MB	3
Total default share per meeting	250MB	N/A

TABLE 30.5 Content Collaboration Upload and Download Rate

Category	Peak Usage in Bytes per Read and Write, 10,000 Provisioned Users	Average Usage in Bytes per Read and Write, 10,000 Provisioned Users
Data Conferencing Server content upload and download	Received: 17,803,480 bytes/read Sent: 19,668,079 bytes/write	Received: 706,655 bytes/read Sent: 860,224

These values serve as a starting point for administrators and can be scaled up or down if the profile isn't a good match for a specific environment.

Planning for the Address Book

One area that is often overlooked when planning a Skype for Business Server 2015 deployment is the impact of the Address Book on the network. Depending on how well populated the Address Book is and whether all users have pictures in the Address Book, it has the potential to become quite large. Because each user will download the Address Book in its entirety when they first attach to Skype for Business Server 2015, a wide-scale deployment of clients can have a large impact on bandwidth usage. Microsoft offers the information in Tables 30.6 through 30.8 to estimate space and bandwidth around Address Book planning.

TABLE 30.6 Address Book Bandwidth

Modality	Number of Users	Average Bandwidth (Kbps)	Maximum Bandwidth (Kbps)
Initial Address Book Server download	80,000	99,000	332,000 (fresh deployment with 2,000 users onboarding every hour)
Overall Address Book Web Query service	80,000	40,000	60,000
Bandwidth utilization per query	1	160	240

TABLE 30.7 Storage Rate for Address Book Server Download

Storage	Size for 1 Day	Size for 30 Days
File-share size for Address Book Server, per user	1GB	26GB

TABLE 30.8 Database Storage Rate for Address Book Server and Address Book Web Query Service

Storage	Database Size
Address Book Server database size	3GB

These numbers are based on a large 80,000-user rollout and can be scaled appropriately for smaller deployments.

Planning for Instant Messaging

Although instant messaging (IM) is one of the simplest features offered by Skype for Business Server 2015, it is nonetheless important to plan for the implications of supporting this feature. Decisions around remote users, public users, and federated users influence how the environment is architected and deployed.

Considerations for Internal Users

When planning a deployment including IM, you have a few items to take into consideration when there will be internal users on the system. Although areas such as server capacity are accounted for with the capacity planning of the Front End Server, it is important to consider the following impacts:

- Compliance and regulatory requirements
- Impacts on supporting systems
- End-user training
- Appropriate usage policies

When planning a deployment, always be aware of laws and regulations that might affect your users and your implementation. For example, find out whether there are requirements around archiving IM traffic for particular departments such as legal, finance, or executives. If there are, be sure to account for the Archive role in the deployment and determine how much space is required to archive the data for the period specified by company policy or specific applicable regulations.

For general users, determine whether there will be integration between the Skype for Business client and applications such as Outlook. By default, Skype for Business wants to store conversations in Exchange so that they can be recalled later by the user. If this will be enabled, account for the added storage usage in Exchange. If storage quotas are already enforced in Exchange, this might not be an issue, but users should be made aware that their usage within Exchange might increase and that they might end up with a shorter window of messages in their mailbox in order to stay within their quota.

TIP

Consider creating archive rules within Outlook to manage the Conversation History folder.

One area often missed by deployments of enterprisewide applications, such as Skype for Business Server 2015, is the creation of appropriate end-user training. Although administrators spend a lot of their time researching and learning technologies, most end users do not. As such, it is the responsibility of the team deploying the application to develop training for end users. This typically should consist of cheat sheets explaining how to perform basic tasks and, when possible, should include screenshots to make it clear to users where to click and what to do.

The last thing to consider when planning a basic deployment of Skype for Business Server 2015 is the creation of an appropriate use policy. This is where you can set the rules around the usage of IM and define behaviors that are to be avoided. For example, although it might seem common sense to some, you should set a policy stating that instant messaging is not to be used to send sensitive materials outside the company.

TIP

By setting guidelines ahead of time, you greatly reduce the chances of the new tool being used to circumvent other protective measures that have already been put in place in the enterprise. The main point is to make sure that IM is seen as another potential source for a data leak.

Consideration for Remote Users

One of the big strengths of Skype for Business Server 2015 is the capability to communicate with users who are outside the corporate environment. This might include partner companies or random users on the Internet who need to participate in the occasional conversation and usually includes internal users who are in remote locations.

When planning for Skype for Business Server 2015, be mindful of which scenarios need to be supported. Typically, account for the following three major groups of external users:

- Remote users
- Federated users
- Public users

A remote user in this context refers to one who belongs to the organization but needs to connect from outside the organization. This might include situations in which the user travels or otherwise connects to Skype for Business Server 2015 without the need for a virtual private network (VPN) connection into the network.

The primary consideration for remote users includes planning for availability of the Edge Server role to ensure that they can always get a connection into the Skype for Business Server 2015 environment and planning for integration of certificates for Transport Layer Security (TLS) connections.

If the Skype for Business Server 2015 deployment uses public certificates, this will likely not be a problem because the majority of public Certificate Authorities are already trusted by the operating systems supported by the Skype for Business client and client OS. If, on the other hand, you plan to use an internal Certificate Authority, not only should you plan the deployment of the root certificate into the certificate trust store of the clients, but also ensure that the Certificate Revocation List of the Certificate Authorities involved are reachable by users when they are connecting remotely.

Because most Skype for Business Server 2015 deployments using internal PKI use Active Directory–integrated Certificate Authorities, typically you can depend on the directory to present the CRL to clients. Because domain controllers are almost never exposed to a demilitarized zone (DMZ) or the Internet, you must depend on the HTTP publishing of the CRL. Because this needs to be reached by remote clients who aren't connected to the internal LAN, the CRL path in the CRL distribution point should reference a web server that is reachable through the Internet. This ensures that systems can access a valid CRL to ensure that the certificates are good and thus enable successful connections over TLS.

The other value of an HTTP-published CRL is for the support of clients that aren't bound to Active Directory. In many environments, Macintosh computers, which can run the Lync:Mac client to connect to Skype for Business Server 2015, aren't bound to Active Directory. As such, they can't access the CRL through the LDAP path, so they'll end up using the HTTP path for CRL checking.

Federated users refers to those users from companies that also run Skype for Business Server 2015 or older versions of Lync or Office Communications Server. Federating is the creation of a formal relationship between the two environments that gives each the capability to share contact lists and Presence information with one another. The primary items to plan for are the creation of an external access policy and the establishment of a list of federated domains.

Skype for Business Server 2015 users may communicate with users on the consumer Skype service, assuming federation is configured. This allows your corporate users to communicate with customers, partners, and even family who may not use Skype for Business.

Planning for Conferencing

Conferencing in Skype for Business Server 2015 describes any type of audio or video communication that involves three or more people. Although this chapter focuses on basic deployments of Skype for Business Server 2015, this section also takes into consideration PC-to-PC conferences as part of an audio conference. Because both scheduled conferences and ad hoc conferences can be initiated by users, it is important to take both into account.

TIP

Don't underestimate the popularity of conferencing. After users know it's available, it will become extremely popular. Management will love the potential of reducing costs around external conferencing services, too.

Defining Your Requirements

The first big step in planning a deployment is determining which features you plan to support. This greatly influences the overall design, has a big impact on the server roles deployed, and affects infrastructure services such as the LAN and WAN.

If you plan to enable web conferencing, which includes both document and application sharing, account for the following:

- Enable conferencing for the Front End pool in the Topology Builder.
- Account for increased network usage for application sharing. The default throttling is 1.5KBps for each session and can be modified as needed.
- Build custom meeting policies if there is a need to enable either application sharing or document collaboration but a desire to prevent the other.

To enable audio and video conferencing, which in this type of deployment includes PC-to-PC conferences but not PBX integration, plan for the following tasks:

- Enable conferencing for the Front End pool in the Topology Builder.
- Account for increased network usage, typically 50Kbps for audio and 350Kbps for video. Note that increased bandwidth is required for high-definition (HD) video.

If requirements include supporting external users connecting to internally hosted conferences, consider the following tasks:

- Deploy Edge Servers in the topology.
- Properly protect access to the Edge Servers.
- Deploy reverse proxy for Skype for Business Server 2015 web services.
- Properly resolve the meeting URLs externally.
- Be sure users trust the certificates used on the Edge Servers to establish TLS connections.
- Decide whether federation will be supported.

Another decision that must be accounted for is whether it is necessary to support legacy clients on Skype for Business Server 2015. Each time a client connects, its version is checked and compared against policies to determine whether it can be used. Web-based connections attempt to detect a local client and always offer the option of the web-based client. This is an important decision because there are compatibility limitations between various clients and back ends. In general, a newer client is not supported talking to an older server version, and it is a best practice to avoid this situation.

Planning Your Conferencing Topology

Conferencing can be deployed in either the Standard Edition of Skype for Business Server 2015 or the Enterprise Edition.

Note that the Office Web Application server role is required for a full conferencing experience. Although this server is not explicitly part of Skype for Business Server 2015 and is in fact based more closely on Microsoft SharePoint, Skype for Business Web Conferencing does have a dependency on it for sharing PowerPoint files. A detailed description of the Office Web Apps Server is covered in Chapter 10, "Dependent Services."

Planning for Clients and Devices

You'll need to plan for several types of clients with Skype for Business Server 2015. Administrators have the ability to limit which clients can connect so that users can use only a client that is currently supported. This simplifies troubleshooting because it's possible to prevent unexpected clients from connecting. The current list of clients includes these:

- **Skype for Business**—The primary Windows client
- **Skype for Business Web App**—The web-based client that provides the primary features
- **Skype for Business Mobile**—The client for smartphones and tablets
- **Lync Phone Edition**—The client running on traditional handsets
- **Skype for Business–compatible phones (3PIP devices)**—This includes compatible phones from third parties such as Polycom, AudioCodes, and Yealink.

Another item to plan for on the topic of clients is the deployment of clients to end users. There are substantial differences between the MSI client downloaded from your Volume Licensing Portal and the Click-to-Run client available in the Office 365 portal. The differences and gaps between these clients change and grow regularly. You should speak with your Microsoft Technical Account Manager or a consultant before deciding which is the right version for your organization.

Planning for Archiving

When planning a basic deployment of Skype for Business Server 2015, determine whether archiving is required in the environment. Archiving, from the perspective of Skype for Business Server 2015, is the behavior of capturing IM conversations and conference attachments and storing them in a dedicated database for long-term storage. This enables administrators to review IM conversations and to see attachments that were part of conferences. Specifically, the following types of content are archived by the Archive Server:

- Peer-to-peer instant messages
- Multiparty IMs
- Uploaded conference content
- Conference events, such as joining, leaving, and uploading
- Conferencing annotations, whiteboard content, and polls

NOTE

Archiving data can also be stored in Exchange 2013 or higher, if deployed. For the sake of this example, the assumption is that a dedicated separate SQL database is used.

The primary driver behind archiving in Skype for Business Server 2015 is regulatory compliance. Some industries must archive all communications between users and potentially between internal users and external parties. Skype for Business Server 2015 allows for flexible archiving policies to be deployed to address these needs.

Defining Your Archiving Requirements

The first step in planning for archiving in a Skype for Business Server 2015 deployment is determining the requirements. Start by answering the following questions about the environment:

- Which sites and users in the organization require archiving support?
- Will archiving be needed for internal communications, external communications, or both?
- Should archiving include IM, conferencing, or both?

- Is archiving critical enough that IMs and conferences shouldn't be allowed to occur if archiving is unavailable?
- How long should archived materials be retained?

Answering these questions enables you to determine how the archiving policies should be created.

Archiving policies are used by Skype for Business Server 2015 to make decisions around what content should be archived, for whom it should be archived, and for how long it should remain in the archive. When planning the archiving policies, keep in mind that there are three types of archiving policies, each with a different intended purpose:

- **Global archiving policy**—This default policy applies to all users and sites in the deployment. The available options include the archiving of internal communications, external communications, or both. This policy cannot be deleted.
- **Site archiving policy**—This policy enables or disables archiving for a specific site within Skype for Business Server 2015. Typically when deploying site archiving policies, you should disable archiving in the global policy; otherwise, all sites effectively process the global policy.
- **User archiving policy**—This policy enables or disables archiving for a specific user within Skype for Business Server 2015, regardless of the sites with which the user is associated. This type of policy is typically used in environments where only a specific class of users requires archiving.

NOTE

If you use Microsoft Exchange 2013 (or higher) integration to store archived data, your Exchange settings control whether Skype for Business Server 2015 communications are archived. Controlling archiving for internal or external communications is available only for Skype for Business policy. For Exchange-integrated archiving, both of them will be either archived or not archived.

In each of the Skype for Business Server 2015 archiving policies, you can choose to archive IM only, conferences only, or both. If both site and user policies are implemented, user policies will override site policies.

The other decision that must be made when planning archiving policies is whether to implement critical-mode archiving. Critical mode enforces a behavior such that if archiving isn't available, the system prevents IM and conferencing from occurring. Critical mode is configured in the Archiving Configuration tab within the Skype for Business Server 2015 Control Panel.

Finally, when planning the archiving requirements, determine how long archived data should remain in the archive. By default, purging archives is not enabled. The purge period can be set to as low as 1 day or as high as 2,562 days (just over 7 years). You can also choose to purge only exported archiving data. This option purges records that have been exported and marked as safe to delete by the session export tool.

Planning Your Archiving Topology

In Skype for Business Server 2015, archiving consists of two components:

- **Unified data collection agents**—These agents are automatically installed on every Front End pool and Standard Edition server. The agent captures messages for archiving and sends them to a local file store and to the Archiving database.
- **Archiving Server backend database**—This is the SQL server that stores the archived messages. This database is recommended to be on a dedicated instance and is recommended to be on a dedicated server in larger deployments.

There are some common requirements that should be planned. In addition to the normal requirements for Skype for Business Server 2015 in terms of supported versions of Windows, also ensure that a valid version of SQL is used. The Archiving Server is compatible with the following versions of SQL:

- Microsoft SQL Server 2008 R2 Enterprise
- Microsoft SQL Server 2008 R2 Standard
- Microsoft SQL Server 2012 Enterprise
- Microsoft SQL Server 2012 Standard
- Microsoft SQL Server 2014 Enterprise
- Microsoft SQL Server 2014 Standard

From a scaling perspective, the Archiving Server will easily support all the users supported by the Front End Servers it is running on.

TIP

Be sure not to skimp on disks for Front End Servers when running Skype for Business Server 2015 archiving. The load increase is significant and requires the servers to meet the hardware specification noted earlier in this chapter.

Based on the typical Skype for Business Server 2015 user model, anticipate around 100KB of data per day per user. Based on this, database sizing can be approximated as the following:

$$\text{DB size} = (\text{DB growth per day per user}) \times (\text{number of users}) \times (\text{number of days})$$

For example, with a deployment to 10,000 users who will archive data for 60 days, the anticipated database size is the following for a DB size of 60GB:

$$\text{DB size} = (100\text{KB}) \times (10{,}000) \times (60)$$

If your organization varies significantly from the average Skype for Business Server 2015 user model, adjust the growth estimate accordingly.

Planning for Management

Skype for Business Server 2015 follows the currently popular model of role-based access control (RBAC). The concept is that one defines a role, typically based around common tasks, and then delegates the performance of these tasks to the role group. Existing security groups or individuals are then populated into that role group to grant them the necessary rights to perform the tasks.

Skype for Business Server 2015 has 11 RBAC groups that cover most of the commonly delegated tasks within Skype for Business Server 2015. These groups and their allowed tasks are as listed here:

- **CsAdministrator**—Members of this group can perform all administrative tasks and modify all settings within Skype for Business Server 2015. This includes creating and assigning roles, and modification or creation of new sites, pools, and services.
- **CsUserAdministrator**—Members of this group can enable or disable users for Skype for Business Server 2015. They can also move users and assign existing policies to users. They can neither create new policies nor modify existing policies.
- **CsVoiceAdministrator**—Members of this group can manage, monitor, and troubleshoot servers and services. They can prevent new connections to servers, apply software updates, and start and stop services. They cannot, however, make changes that affect global configuration.
- **CsServerAdministrator**—Members of this group can manage and troubleshoot servers and services, including preventing new connections, starting and stopping services, and applying software updates.
- **CsViewOnlyAdministrator**—Members of this group can view the deployment, including server and user information, in order to monitor deployment health.
- **CsHelpDesk**—Members of this group can view the deployment, including users' properties and policies. They can also run specific troubleshooting tasks. They can change neither user properties and policies nor server configuration and services.
- **CsArchivingAdministrator**—Members of this group can modify archiving configuration and policies.
- **CsResponseGroupAdministrator**—Members of this group can manage the configuration of the Response Group application within a site.
- **CsLocationAdministrator**—This group offers the lowest level of rights for Enhanced 911 (E911) management. This includes creating E911 locations and network identifiers and enables associating these with each other. This role is assigned with a global scope as opposed to a site-specific scope.
- **CsPersistentChatAdministrator**—Members of this group can manage Persistent Chat features and rooms.
- **CsResponseGroupAdministrator**—Members of this group can manage response groups. It can be scoped to specific response groups on a granular level.

To comply with RBAC best practices, do not assign users to roles with global scope if they are supposed to administer only a limited set of servers or users. This means creating additional role-based groups with similar rights to previous groups, but applied to a more limited scope because all default role groups in Skype for Business Server 2015 have a global scope. That is to say, the rights apply to all users and to servers in all sites.

These scoped role groups can be created through the PowerShell cmdlets provided with Skype for Business Server 2015 by using an existing global group as a template and by assigning the rights to a pre-created group in Active Directory. Here's an example:

```
New-CsAdminRole -Identity "Site01 Server Administrators" -Template
➥CsServerAdministrator
-ConfigScopes "site:Site01"
```

This cmdlet gives the Site01 Server Administrators group the same rights as the predefined CsServerAdministrator role, but rather than the rights being given globally, the rights apply only to servers in Site01.

A similar process can be used to create a role that is scoped based on users rather than on sites:

```
New-CsAdminRole -Identity "Finance Users Administrators" -Template
➥CsUserAdministrator
-UserScopes "OU:OU=Finance, OU=Corporate Users, DC=CompanyABC, DC=com"
```

This grants a group called Finance Users Administrators rights similar to the predefined CsUserAdministrator group, but rather than getting the rights across all user objects, they will be limited to user objects in the Finance OU as defined in the cmdlet.

After the necessary role groups have been defined, simply add users or other groups to the role groups through Active Directory Users and Computers.

NOTE

When users are placed into either a new security group or a role group, they need to log out and then log on for the Kerberos ticket to be updated with the new group membership. Without this process, they will not be able to use the new rights that they are granted.

For users who are given any level of administrative rights within Skype for Business Server 2015, carefully consider which tasks they need to perform and then assign them to the roles with the least privilege and scope necessary to perform the tasks.

For administrators interested in what rights are available to each of the predefined groups, Microsoft has published a fairly exhaustive list at the following URL:

http://technet.microsoft.com/en-us/library/gg425917(v=ocs.15).aspx

Note the RBAC groups are unchanged from Lync Server 2013.

Documenting the Plan

After all the various requirements have been determined and the options thought out and decided on, put these decisions and requirements into a design document. The complexity of the project affects the size of the document and the effort required to create it. The intention is that this design document summarizes the goals and objectives that were gathered in the initial discovery phase and describes how the project's result will meet them. It should represent a detailed picture of the end state when the new technologies and clients are implemented. The amount of detail can vary, but it should include key design decisions made in the discovery process and collaboration sessions.

The following list gives a sample table of contents and brief description of the design document:

- **Executive Summary**—Provides a brief discussion of the scope of the Skype for Business Server 2015 implementation. It should also include a high-level overview of the business value.
- **Goals and Objectives**—Includes the 50,000-foot-view business objectives, down to the 1,000-foot-view staff-level tasks that will be met by the project.
- **Background**—Provides a high-level summary of the current state of the network, focusing on problem areas, as clarified in the discovery process, as well as summary decisions made in the collaboration sessions.
- **Approach**—Outlines the high-level phases and tasks required to implement the solution (the details of each task are determined in the migration document).
- **End State**—Defines the details of the new technology configurations. For example, this section describes the number, placement, and functions of Skype for Business Server 2015.
- **Budget Estimate**—Provides an estimate of basic costs involved in the project. Whereas a detailed cost estimate requires the creation of the migration document, experienced estimators can provide order-of-magnitude numbers at this point. Also, it should be clear what software and hardware are needed, so budgetary numbers can be provided.

When developing the document further, one will want to add details in various sections to lay out the costs and benefits, as well as provide a long-term vision to the project. Consider including these details in the various sections of the document:

- **Executive Summary**—The executive summary should set the stage and prepare the audience for what the document will contain, and it should be concise. It should outline, at the highest level, the scope of the work. Ideally, the executive summary also positions the document in the decision-making process and clarifies that approvals of the design are required to move forward.
- **Goals and Objectives**—The goals and objectives section should cover the high-level goals of the project and include the pertinent departmental goals. It's easy to go too

far in the goals and objectives sections and get down to the 1,000-foot-view level, but this can end up becoming confusing; therefore, it might be better to record this information in the migration document and the detailed project plan for the project.

- **Background**—The background section should summarize the results of the discovery process and the collaboration sessions, and it can list specific design decisions that were made during the collaboration sessions. Additionally, decisions made about what technologies or features not to include can be summarized here. This information should stay at a relatively high level as well, and more details can be provided in the end state section of the design document. This information is useful as a reference later in the project when the infamous question "Who made that decision?" comes up.
- **Approach**—The approach section should document the implementation strategy agreed upon to this point, and it should also serve to record decisions made in the discovery and design process about the timeline (end to end and for each phase) and the team members participating in the different phases. This section should avoid going into too much detail because in many cases the end design might not yet be approved and might change after review. Also, the migration document should provide the details of the process that will be followed.
- **End State**—In the end state section, the specifics of the Skype for Business Server 2015 implementation should be spelled out in detail, and the high-level decisions that were summarized in the background section should be fleshed out. Essentially, the software to be installed on each server and the roles that will be installed on each server are spelled out here, along with the future roles of existing legacy servers. Information on the clients that will be supported, policies that will be enforced, and so on should be in this section. Diagrams and tables can help explain the new concepts and show what the solution will look like, where the key systems will be located, and how the overall topology of the implementation will look. Often, besides a standard physical diagram of what goes where, a logical diagram illustrating how devices communicate is needed.
- **Budget Estimate**—The budget section is not exact but should provide order-of-magnitude prices for the different phases of the project. If an outside consulting firm is assisting with this document, it can draw from experience with similar projects of like-sized companies. Because no two projects are ever the same, there needs to be some flexibility in these estimates. Typically, ranges for each phase should be provided. The goal is for the audience of the document to understand what the project will cost and what they are getting for that money. This is also a great place to point out anticipated returns on investment (ROI) because these often act as the primary justification for a Skype for Business Server 2015 implementation. See Chapter 3, "Business Case for Skype for Business Server 2015," for a full list of business cases and value propositions for Skype for Business Server 2015.

Best Practices

Several items recommended in this chapter should be taken into account when you are planning a basic deployment of Skype for Business Server 2015. By following these recommendations, you can be better prepared for the deployment and can avoid the common pitfalls associated with planning a topology and deployment of a complex technology. The following is a summary of recommended best practices from this chapter:

- Start the deployment planning with a comprehensive design document. This ensures that decisions have been made, and it gives an excellent opportunity to shop the design around to other groups to get buy-in and to ensure that other groups know how they'll be affected by the upcoming deployment.
- Treat your deployment like a formal project. Produce a project plan that includes anticipated tasks and anticipated durations as well as calls out the required resources. This makes it easier to get support from management to dedicate the appropriate resources and time to the deployment.
- Make sure that any constraints are understood before the completion of the design. Things such as regulator compliances have a major impact on decisions made in the design.
- Make sure that the deployment can handle the anticipated load. Use the Microsoft sizing guidelines to ensure that the design can support the load you expect to place on it.
- If possible, go overboard on RAM and disk speed/spindles. This is where smart administrators will squeeze out the best performance from their Skype for Business Server 2015 deployment.
- Start the deployment with a pilot. This gives an excellent opportunity to validate the impact of users on the system and gives administrators an opportunity to get familiar with the infrastructure while supporting only a limited number of users. Be sure to include users from multiple job functions, not just IT users. This will give the administrators insight into how Skype for Business Server 2015 will be used in their organization.
- Involve the networking group when designing a basic deployment. The features offered by Skype for Business Server 2015 will greatly impact a WAN, and the networking group will have bandwidth and latency information that might affect the design.
- Make decisions about how external users will be supported early in the process. Designs for internal-only versus external support will be significantly different. These decisions affect several other decisions, so the earlier this can be decided, the less impact it has on the overall effort.

- If possible, use public certificates that use subject alternative names. This greatly reduces the impact on end users and on external users because the certificates will already be trusted by the operating system.
- Use modern hardware. Current-generation processors can provide a much larger capacity than processors from only one generation ago. The Microsoft sizing guides are based on current-generation processors. Deviating from that practice renders the sizing guides inaccurate and puts the project at risk of being underpowered. This results in a poor user experience when loads increase.
- Train the end users on how to use the new system. Ensure that the users understand the limitations of various clients because they do not all provide the same features. Consider an online FAQ (frequently asked questions) or knowledge base for users to refer to.
- Define an acceptable use policy for the Skype for Business Server 2015 system. This reduces the exposure of the end users because they will know what behaviors can potentially put them at risk. It also enables administrators to more easily block risky behaviors because there will be a written policy to back up the configuration.
- Make sure that the archive is designed with enough storage to hold the anticipated volume of data.
- Regularly test the recovery of data from the archive. This helps ensure that the data will be available and readable when the time comes that it's needed for something important. Consider a monthly test.
- Plan carefully when using virtualization and understand what other services are provided by the virtualization farm. Most virtualization farms are oversubscribed because virtualization is a popular form of consolidation for servers. Be aware that not having dedicated resources reduces the potential capacity and performance of the systems.
- Whenever possible, use a system of role-based access control. Roles should be well defined and administrators should be given only the minimum of rights needed to perform their jobs. If their jobs change, their role-based group memberships should change. Don't forget that this goes both ways: Add them to new groups when they need additional rights, but don't forget to remove them from groups if there are tasks they longer perform.
- Don't forget to monitor the Skype for Business Server 2015 environment with an application such as SCOM, Event Zero UC Commander, or another IT Pro Tools–certified solution to ensure that the systems are available. Leverage the monitoring software to trend the loads on the system to be able to predict when extra capacity will need to be added to maintain an acceptable load on each server.

By following these best practices, administrators can maximize their chances for a successful Skype for Business Server 2015 deployment and can keep their end users happy and productive.

Summary

As you've seen in this chapter, there's a lot more to preparing for a deployment than merely gathering up the software and installing it. Often the most important items are the so-called "soft decisions" and the proper presentation of the project to the decision makers. This includes not only those who make the technical decisions but those who make the financial decisions as well. It's critical to understand the needs of the business and to determine how Skype for Business Server 2015 can address those needs in the best manner. By aligning the technology solutions with the business drivers, one can greatly increase the chances of getting the project approved and of implementing it successfully.

The goal in the preparation phase should be to build an architecture as simple as possible that still meets all the requirements of the environment. By the time the installation occurs, all questions should have already been answered and the answers accepted by all the project stakeholders. In this manner, there won't be any surprises because everyone will already know exactly what to expect from the project.

Always take the opportunity to look beyond the design and implementation and to ask questions such as "Who is going to manage this environment?" and "How will we make sure that the helpdesk can do their jobs without enabling them to break the application?" and plan for those events. When you've accounted for them in the preparation phase, it's easier to avoid situations in which one has to make suboptimal decisions at the last minute. With Skype for Business Server 2015, it's especially true that an ounce of prevention is worth a pound of cure.

CHAPTER 32

Planning to Deploy External Services

IN THIS CHAPTER

- Determining Feature Requirements
- Edge Server Planning
- Planning for High Availability
- Reverse Proxy Planning
- Planning for Certificates
- Network Planning
- Preparing for Edge Servers

The Edge Server role is a key part of why Skype for Business Server 2015 is such a compelling solution for businesses, but along with that power and flexibility comes a good deal of configuration work and upfront planning. Networking, firewalls, certificates, and load balancing mean the Edge Server touches practically every part of the network and, consequently, involves almost every team, from server administrators to network engineers.

This chapter discusses what details to consider when planning for an Edge Server and how to properly prepare an Edge Server's network adapters. It also details the firewall requirements and different topologies that can be used to support an Edge Server. Certificate requirements and planning guidance for the reverse proxy are also discussed. Lastly, some sample scenarios are presented for various deployment sizes with a full diagram, a list of certificate requirements, and DNS entries.

Determining Feature Requirements

The first step in planning for Edge services is to determine what the business requirements are, which features need to be deployed, and what kind of topology to use. For instance, a small business that wants to communicate with public IM networks might deploy a single Edge Server (consolidated Edge), whereas a larger business that wants to replace a hosted virtual conferencing solution might deploy multiple load-balanced Edge Servers with full support for A/V conferencing. This section discusses the different forms of remote access and considerations for each feature.

Providing Remote Access

The primary functionality that an Edge Server provides is remote access to the entire Skype for Business Server 2015 environment. One of the most compelling Skype for Business Server 2015 features is the fact that a client seamlessly operates identically whether the user is in the office or is working remotely without a VPN, and that functionality is possible via the Edge Server. The Edge Server provides a secure channel for users to sign in remotely, leverage web conferencing, conduct audio/video calls, and even make and receive PSTN phone calls using the Skype for Business client. Deploying an Edge Server to support this functionality is a common part of nearly every Skype for Business Server deployment because of the flexibility it provides to an organization's workforce.

Remote access can be configured at a policy level and then granted to specific groups of users if an organization needs to control who can sign in remotely. The sign-in process takes place over an SSL channel on TCP port 443 or possibly 5061 before any credentials are exchanged, and all subsequent traffic is encrypted.

Using Multifactor Authentication

Skype for Business Server 2015 can support multifactor authentication when configured for Passive Authentication with ADFS (ADFS 2.0 for SAML support or ADFS 3.0 for OAuth support) or a third-party security token service (STS). ADFS is Microsoft's security token service. Skype for Business relegates the task of authenticating the user to the STS. The STS dictates what form of authentication the user is required to provide (smart card, security token, one-time password, and more). Once the user is authenticated, the STS returns a token, which the client then presents to the Skype for Business Server. The Skype for Business Server accepts the token and signs in the client on behalf of the user. Passive Authentication can be configured for all users (both internal and remote) or just remote users only. Multifactor authentication (MFA) is possible with Passive Authentication in Skype for Business Server 2015 by using a third-party STS that supports MFA.

Skype for Business Server 2015 resolves a drawback when Passive Authentication was first introduced in Lync Server 2013. When configured, Passive Authentication broke integration with Exchange Server because Exchange Server doesn't support the SAML authentication protocol used by Lync Server 2013. Skype for Business Server 2015 switched to the OAuth authentication protocol, which is more commonly used, including by Exchange Server. Also, Skype for Business Server 2015 Passive Authentication can be configured for mobile clients only or for all clients (desktop and mobile).

By default, multifactor authentication is not enabled. Instead, remote Skype for Business clients provide the user's NTLM credentials over a secure channel (SSL) during the initial sign-in, and then use a certificate created by the Front End Servers for subsequent sign-ins. The certificate is specific to the remote endpoint and is stored locally on the client to expedite the sign-in process for future logins. This also means that any home user with Skype for Business installed on a personal PC can enter their Active Directory credentials to sign in to Skype for Business remotely.

With the increasing number of high-profile cases of hacking incidents, more and more customers are reevaluating their security policies, particularly when it comes to remote access. Many organizations have security mandates that require two-factor authentication or at a minimum one-factor authentication that doesn't use Active Directory credentials for any form of remote access. The remote user is required to use alternative credentials that are more secure against theft than their Active Directory password when connecting outside the corporate network.

Using ADFS, Skype for Business Server 2015 can provide multifactor authentication for desktop clients. However, a common misconception many customers have is that Skype for Business Server 2015 provides two-factor authentication using Passive Authentication and ADFS for mobile clients. This is not correct. ADFS serves as a security token service (STS) taking on the responsibility of authenticating users instead of Skype for Business Server 2015; however, ADFS still requires the remote user to authenticate using their AD credentials. Although the authentication protocol is different, this is no different from authenticating users using NTLM. Users are still required to enter their AD credentials to authenticate. This solution does not meet either of the preceding two requirements.

Luckily, it is possible to enforce two-factor authentication or the use of an alternative form of authentication other than AD credentials. This is possible by configuring Passive Authentication in Skype for Business Server 2015 and using a third-party solution that provides two-factor authentication or an alternative authentication solution other than Active Directory credentials. This third-party solution can be a separate security token service (STS) such as offered by Lync-Solutions or an extension to ADFS, where ADFS is the STS. The security token service takes over the responsibility of authenticating the user. Once the user is authenticated by the STS, it passes back a token to the client, which then presents it to Skype for Business Server 2015 for validation and access.

To meet these requirements, a business can still deploy Edge Servers to support federation or SIP providers (such as Skype) but disallow remote access for Skype for Business users through a policy. This forces a user to first establish a VPN connection that requires two-factor authentication, and then Skype for Business can connect to the internal Front End Servers. There are some serious disadvantages to this approach with regard to the media quality discussed later in this chapter.

When discussing remote access, organizations should follow these guidelines:

- Determine whether remote access will provide additional value to the Skype for Business deployment.
- Identify which users should be configured for remote access, and then create appropriate access policies to assign to end users.
- Determine whether two-factor authentication is a security requirement; if so, identify the maturity of the deployed solution and any current issues.

Allowing Anonymous Access

Whether an organization supports anonymous access to Skype for Business Server 2015 meetings is a decision the business must make when considering an Edge Server deployment. Anonymous users are external users who do not have Skype for Business 2015 in their own internal organization and therefore cannot federate with your own organization. Allowing anonymous access provides the capability for internal users to invite participants from outside of the organization to web and A/V conferences. This capability can often replace hosted or subscription-based conferencing services for most users, providing immediate cost savings. Skype for Business Server 2015 now supports larger meetings up from 250 to 1000 participants with the deployment of a dedicated Front End pool. For even larger meetings, customers can extend their Skype for Business meetings to the Office 365 cloud. This service is called "Skype Meeting Broadcast." Participants join the meeting broadcast using a web browser. For more information, refer to https://technet.microsoft.com/en-us/library/mt297718.aspx.

Another option is that only specific users, groups, or locations can be allowed to communicate with anonymous users. These restrictions can be configured through conferencing policies. This gives administrators the flexibility of allowing all authenticated users to use web conferencing while allowing only a select few to host conferences with anonymous participants.

When discussing remote access, organizations should follow these guidelines:

- Determine whether anonymous participants are permitted to join Skype for Business meetings for outside vendors or partners.
- Identify which users should be allowed to invite anonymous participants.
- Create the appropriate conferencing policies to control anonymous access and the features available within meetings containing anonymous participants.

Configuring Federation Types

A consideration for organizations when deploying Skype for Business Server 2015 is to determine whether to configure federation with external partners. Federation requires an Edge Server role. Even if remote access will not be allowed for employees, an Edge Server must still be deployed to provide federation or public IM connectivity capabilities.

Federation allows organizations that have deployed Skype for Business Server 2015 to communicate securely with partners, and users can see the Presence of partners they work with frequently. Additionally, all communication modalities are available through federation, so users have a consistent experience when escalating an IM to audio, video, or web conferencing.

There are three types of federation models Skype for Business Server 2015 provides: Discovered Partner Domain, Allowed Partner Domain, and Allowed Partner Server.

Discovered Partner Domain

Discovered Partner Domain (formerly known as Open Enhanced or Dynamic Federation) allows users in different organizations to simply type each other's SIP addresses in the Skype for Business client and start communicating immediately. This works well if both organizations have deployed Edge Servers, published the necessary SRV records in public DNS, and used public certificates that are trusted by the partner's Edge Server. In many cases, this just works and requires no administrator intervention. The user experience is similar to sending an email because users don't have to ask their administrators for permission to contact a third party. Organizations can enable Discovered Partner Domain federation by publishing the necessary SRV records in public DNS and enabling partner domain discovery within the Skype for Business Server 2015 Control Panel.

Allowed Partner Domain

Allowed Partner Domain (formerly known as Enhanced federation) lifts a security limit imposed with Discovered Partner Domain federation in which an Edge Server will accept only up to 20 SIP messages each second from a partner's Edge Server. This is a reasonable limit for many organizations, and it helps prevent a partner's Edge Server from overwhelming your own Edge Servers and possibly impacting other services such as remote access.

Enabling Allowed Partner Domain federation for a domain removes this "20 messages per second" limit for the specified partner's SIP domain, but this obviously requires some form of administrator configuration. Organizations should identify partners they will federate with and plan to enable Allowed Partner Domain federation with those partners. Edge Servers will log events indicating which partner SIP domains are using Discovered Partner Domain federation so that administrators can proactively monitor those lists and enable Allowed Partner Domain federation for those partners that are hitting this limit as required. In terms of configuration, enabling Allowed Partner Domain federation for a domain is a matter of simply specifying the partner's SIP domain name but leaving the Access Edge field empty.

Specifying the Access Edge FQDN is required only for Allowed Partner Server, discussed in the next section. The SRV records published to public DNS for a SIP domain are instead used to locate the partner's Access Edge FQDN.

Allowed Partner Server

Allowed Partner Server (formerly known as Direct Federation) is really the legacy version that was introduced back in Live Communications Server 2005. Allowed Partner Server federation requires each partner to specify the SIP domain name *and* the Access Edge FQDN of the partner they wish to federate with. Allowed Partner Server federation operates the same way as Allowed Partner Domain federation in that it doesn't allow any more messages per second, and it requires greater administrator overhead. Not only do users need to request federation with a specific partner's SIP domain, but the Skype for Business administrators from both parties must exchange information about each other's Edge Server.

The main use case for Allowed Partner Server federation is when the Edge Server's FQDN does not match the partner's SIP domain. For example, partners trying to reach tom@skypeunleashed.com must locate an Edge Server also in the skypeunleashed.com DNS namespace, or they will drop the connection because the namespace does not match. Allowed Partner Server federation overrides the check that the Access Edge FQDN must match the SIP domain, and it tells the Edge Server to ignore the name mismatch by connecting to the specified Access Edge FQDN. The disadvantages to Allowed Partner Server federation are in the administration overhead, and the fact that this can easily break if one organization changes an Access Edge FQDN.

A good analogy here when considering whether to enable federation, and allow dynamic discovery, is to think of federation in terms of email. Imagine if email operated like Allowed Partner Server federation such that users in different domains could not send mail to each other without administrators on both sides first manually configuring a connection to each other's domain. If that were the case, email probably would not have become the universal communication modality that it is today. Instead, any user can generally send mail to any domain without administrators making server configuration changes. Discovered Partner Domain and Allowed Partner Domain federation are the Skype for Business Server equivalent of that capability; users have full access to Presence, instant messaging, web conferencing, and A/V conferencing with any other user across the world without any additional configuration.

When discussing federation, organizations should follow these guidelines:

- Identify whether federation to partners or Office 365 for mobile push notifications is a business requirement. This is recommended.
- Discuss whether dynamic federation and partner discovery will be enabled.
- Prepare a list of federated partners by involving end users or monitoring existing Edge Server logs, and add those domains for enhanced federation.
- Identify which partners will require direct federation and collect the Access Edge FQDN of these partners.

Enabling SIP Provider Connectivity

Skype for Business Server 2015 public SIP provider connectivity enables users to communicate with the Skype network. It operates in a similar fashion to federation in that it uses the same ports and topology, but it has a slightly different set of steps to configure. The main difference is that public IM connectivity must be configured through Microsoft.

Administrators can choose to allow only specific SIP domains to communicate with the Skype network, and each SIP domain supported for public IM connectivity must be provisioned through the licensing site, https://pic.lync.com. After the public IM connectivity is provisioned, it can take up to 30 days, though it is usually much faster before each provider activates the change.

Skype, which is the only public SIP provider supported, has a more limited feature set than federation does. Skype does not support multiparty IM or conferencing, so all conversations are limited to a maximum of two participants.

When discussing SIP provider connectivity, organizations should do the following:

- Identify whether connectivity to the Skype network and consumers in general is a business requirement.
- Plan to enable Skype within remote access policies only for users who require these features.
- Evaluate the security risks by connecting their network and users to Skype.

Configuring XMPP Proxy

Skype for Business Server 2015 Edge Server allows federation with XMPP servers. The XMPP interoperability allows Skype for Business users and XMPP users to exchange instant messages and Presence information between each other. There are no audio/video capabilities between Skype for Business Server 2015 and other XMPP partners today.

When discussing the XMPP proxy, organizations should do the following:

- Identify any needs to federate with partners that currently leverage XMPP Presence and IM services.
- Collect the XMPP partner domains and proxy FQDN if the DNS SRV records are not published in public DNS.

Planning Edge Server Architecture

When you are planning a Skype for Business Server 2015 environment, any remote access or federation features require significant planning to ensure that the features work correctly and to properly secure the infrastructure. Because the Edge Servers and reverse proxy components are typically deployed in a perimeter network, an extra level of coordination is required between the security teams that manage the firewall, load balancers, or reverse proxy, and the team responsible for deploying Skype for Business Server 2015.

Organizations might have a dedicated network security team that is different from the team responsible for implementing and managing Skype for Business Server 2015.

Because the deployment planning typically crosses different teams, it is important for all parties to meet early in the planning stages to discuss the deployment requirements. Much of the work and troubleshooting with Edge Server firewall configuration is a collaborative effort between multiple teams to ensure that each component is configured correctly.

The following section discusses the various topologies that can be used for the Edge Server and key considerations for each design.

Edge Server Placement

Edge Server placement is critical in a deployment to optimize media paths. The SIP signaling used for Presence and IM is more tolerant of slight delays, but web conferencing and A/V traffic are sensitive to latency, so it is important to properly plan Edge Server placement.

TIP

As a rule of thumb, Edge Servers are generally deployed in any location with a Front End pool that supports remote web and A/V conferencing. This isn't a mandate, and there are many other factors at play, but Edge Servers are typically deployed near a Front End pool.

For example, consider a small deployment for company SkypeUnleashed.com, as shown in Figure 32.1, where a single Front End Server in San Francisco exists. In this deployment, only a single Edge Server is necessary to support all the remote features. Media paths are all local to San Francisco.

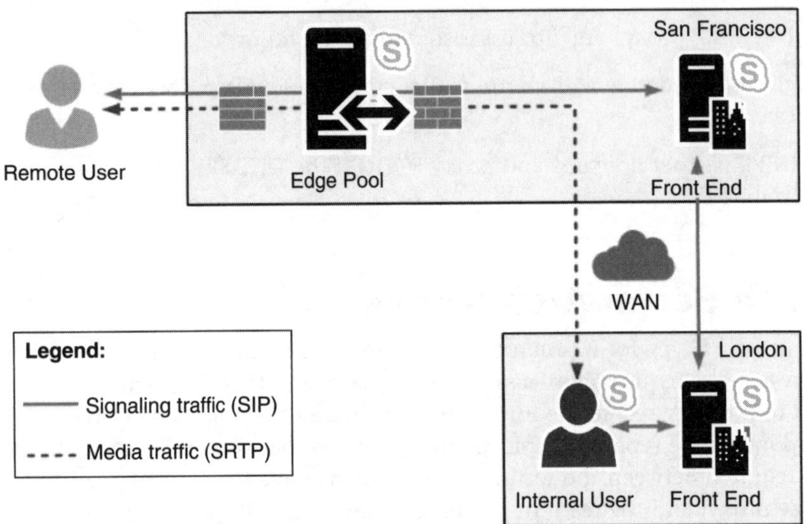

FIGURE 32.1 Single Edge Server with multiple sites.

Imagine that company SkypeUnleashed.com expands with a new office in London with a WAN link back to San Francisco and adds a new Front End pool for the London users. When London users sign in remotely and try to IM with a London user in the office, they will communicate with the Edge Server in San Francisco, which sends traffic to the Front End in San Francisco, which ultimately proxies the SIP traffic to the London user's Front End pool in London, and finally arrives at the London office user. Although this seems like a lot of hops, it's not going to cause an issue for the remote London users as long there's no web or A/V traffic. If the users get a Presence update or an IM half a second late, they're not going to notice.

Now consider if a London user goes home for the day and tries to place an audio call to another London user still in the office. The traffic flow for the audio stream is from the remote user to the San Francisco Edge Server and then straight to the user in the London office. The media stream skips the San Francisco and London Front End hops, but the result is probably still a poor-sounding audio call. Even though the two London users are physically close in proximity, the call is "hairpinning" through the San Francisco Edge Server and possibly creating a lot of latency, or delay, on the call.

The solution in this scenario is to also deploy an Edge Server in London, which would allow for the London office user to have a more direct path to the remote London user. If company SkypeUnleashed.com deploys an Edge Server in London, the traffic flow shown in Figure 32.1 changes to the traffic flow shown in Figure 32.2. In this case, remote users can exchange media traffic with London users directly across the Internet with a lesser amount of latency.

TIP

It isn't necessary to deploy Edge Servers in every location with a Front End pool, but it generally results in an improved experience for the end users. Many deployments try to distribute Edge Servers to service distinct geographical boundaries such as opposite coasts or continents to limit traversing long WAN links. For example, using separate Edge Servers per continent, or on each side of a continent in North America, Europe, and Asia, is a common deployment model.

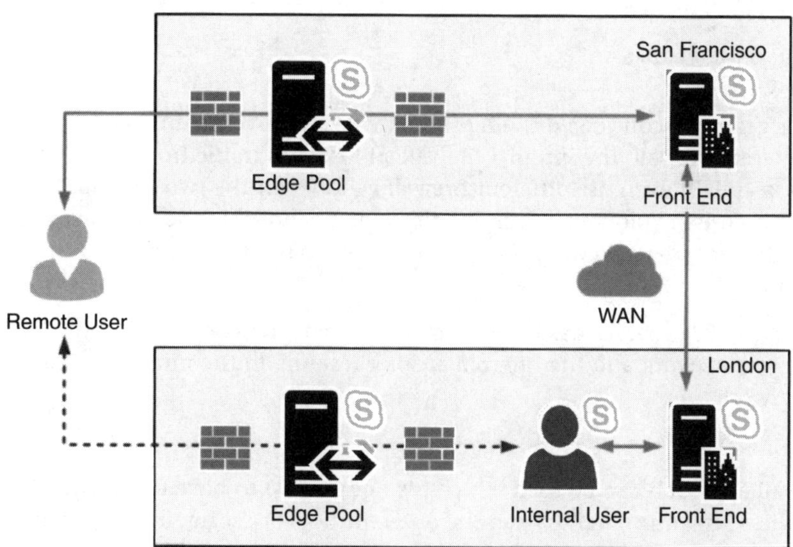

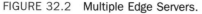

FIGURE 32.2 Multiple Edge Servers.

Perimeter Network Models

A potentially confusing point for organizations trying to deploy Skype for Business Server 2015 is how the Edge Server fits into a network from a logical and physical perspective. Various methods can be used, as discussed in this section.

The key point to keep in mind is that the Edge Server requires two network adapters. One is "internal facing" and communicates with the internal Front End Servers, Directors, and clients, and the second adapter is "external facing" and communicates with the external traffic from the Internet. The two network adapters must also be in distinct networks, or VLANs (virtual LANs), to be officially supported by Microsoft.

Back-to-Back Firewalls

The ideal approach to any perimeter network or DMZ is to utilize two different security devices such that one provides a layer of defense from the Internet to the perimeter network and the other provides another layer of defense by filtering traffic between the perimeter network and the internal network. The Edge Servers are situated between the two firewalls in the perimeter network. This approach is illustrated in Figure 32.3.

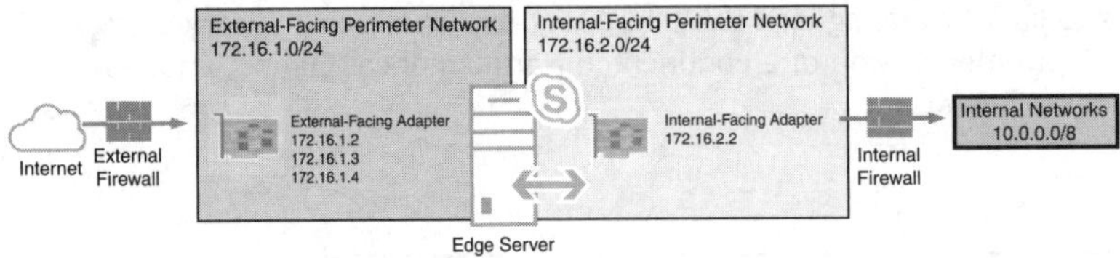

FIGURE 32.3 Back-to-back firewalls.

This configuration is generally considered the most secure because even if an attack compromises the external firewall, the internal firewall still isolates traffic from the attacker. Organizations might even use different firewall vendors for the two firewalls. This ensures that if a security exploit exists for one firewall, it is unlikely the same exploit can be used against the secondary firewall, thus keeping malicious attacks contained to the perimeter network.

In this configuration, the Edge Server has the external-facing adapter connected to the more external perimeter network and the internal adapter residing in the internal or more trusted perimeter network.

Three-Legged Firewall

A three-legged firewall approach can be used when it is not feasible to have two physically separate firewall devices separating traffic from the different network segments. Typically, a smaller organization does not have or want to manage a back-to-back firewall, so a single device is used instead to logically construct the same functionality as a back-to-back firewall provides. This single firewall device generally has at least three physical network interfaces or "legs" that are all connected to different networks: one to the public Internet, one to the perimeter network, and one to the internal network.

In this scenario, the Edge Server has two network adapters connected within the perimeter network, but these should still be two separate VLANs. Even though both VLANs exist within the perimeter network zone of the firewall, they are still separate network segments. Figure 32.4 shows the logical layout of a three-legged firewall design.

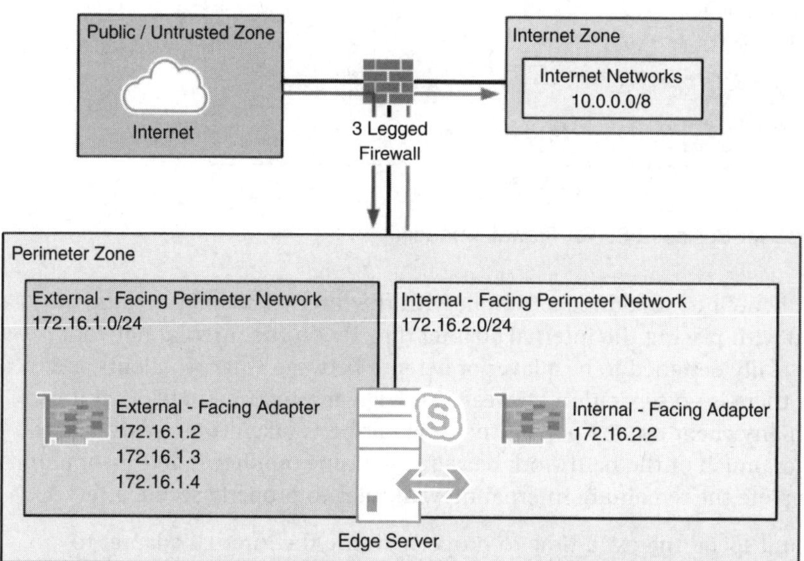

FIGURE 32.4 Three-legged firewall.

Firewall rules can still be used to control the flow of traffic between each segment as in a back-to-back scenario, but the primary difference here is that all traffic is run through the same physical device. Whether it is external traffic destined for the perimeter network or perimeter network traffic destined for the internal network, it all flows through the same device.

The primary advantage of a three-legged firewall is that it is generally less expensive because only a single device is required. The disadvantage is that although a three-legged firewall can be used to simulate a back-to-back configuration, the rules can be more difficult to configure, manage, and troubleshoot. It can be easy to mistakenly associate a rule with the wrong source or destination interface.

Another downside compared to a back-to-back firewall design is that if an attacker compromises the firewall, access to all network segments is achieved. Instead of having to infiltrate both firewall devices, simply using one exploit grants access to all networks. That said, a three-legged firewall design is a very popular one for small and medium-sized businesses.

Straddling the Internal Firewall

Another firewall topology that, unfortunately, is used too often is where the internal interface of the Edge Server does not pass through any firewall. Instead, it straddles the firewall by being connected directly to the internal network. Administrators still secure the external adapter in this scenario. However, instead of creating the appropriate rules for the internal adapter, they just place it on the internal network, as shown in Figure 32.5.

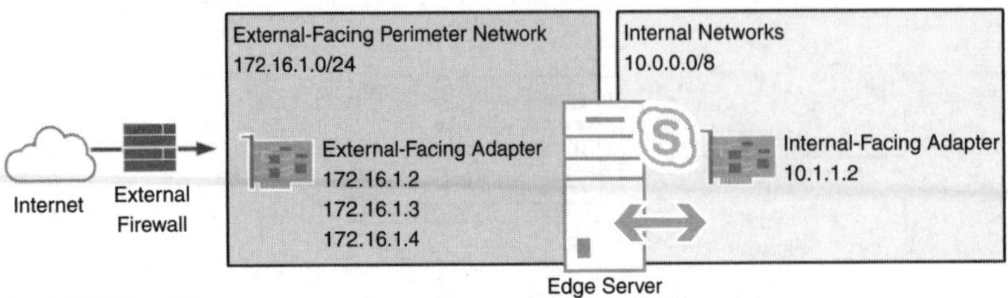

FIGURE 32.5 Skype for Business Server firewall straddling.

There is not much benefit to straddling a firewall with the internal adapter because of the risks associated with placing the internal adapter directly on the internal network. The Edge Server is really designed to be a layer of defense between Internet clients and internal users, but there is no separation between the Edge and internal network if it can communicate with any client on any port. If the time has been taken to properly secure the external adapter, much of the hard work has already been completed, and it shouldn't be difficult to complete the remaining internal firewall rules to properly secure a server.

Organizations should spend the extra time to properly secure the internal adapter to protect the rest of the Skype for Business Server 2015 infrastructure. If a second perimeter network VLAN does not exist, a business should spend time planning to add one to place each Edge network adapter in a separate physical network or VLAN.

TIP

Microsoft has designed the Edge Server to be secured properly on both the internal- and external-facing interfaces. Therefore, always avoid placing the internal adapter directly on the internal network whenever possible.

No Perimeter Network

Organizations without a perimeter network today should take the time to properly plan and design one before deploying Edge Servers. An Edge Server should never be deployed on an internal network.

Publicly Routable IP Addresses

One consideration when planning for Edge services is that each Edge Server should use three separate publicly routable IP addresses: one for the Access Edge service, one for the Web Conferencing Edge service, and one for the A/V Edge service. All three of these services run on TCP 443, so Skype for Business Server 2015 requires a separate IP address for each unique service. It is possible to run all three services on a single IP address and use nondefault ports for some services, but this approach is not recommended.

A decision point for organizations is to determine whether they will assign publicly routable IP addresses directly to the Edge Server adapters, or whether Network Address Translation (NAT) will be used. The deciding factor in that discussion will usually be whether an organization already has a perimeter network segment that uses publicly accessible IP addresses for servers or devices.

Using publicly routable IP addresses on the Edge Server network adapters is a perfectly valid design choice, but this suggestion is typically met with a negative reaction from network security teams that are accustomed to using NAT to allow external access to any service. It is important to note that NAT is not a method of security. Instead, it is designed to accommodate a shortage of IPv4 addresses, and although it might mask a server's internal IP address, as long as the external ports are publicly accessible, NAT does not provide any extra security in protecting those externally accessible ports.

This is not to suggest that an Edge Server external interface should be directly exposed to the Internet. Even though publicly routable IP addresses can be bound to the network adapter, the servers are still logically behind a firewall device that limits the ports and protocols allowed to reach the Edge Server. The only difference is that the IP addressing used is part of the public address space instead of a privately addressable space.

The reason for the publicly routable network interface requirement is because of how the A/V Edge uses Interactive Connectivity Establishment (ICE), Session Traversal Utilities for NAT (STUN), and Traversal Using Relay NAT (TURN) to facilitate media traffic between endpoints that might be masked by NAT, such as two users at home behind their own routers. Without delving into too many of the technical details, this requirement comes from the fact that in order for two remote users to communicate, they must be able to send media directly to each other, or both relay their traffic through some common server such as the Edge Server.

Network Address Translation

The Access Edge and Web Conferencing Edge services have always worked fine with NAT, but when Office Communications Server 2007 was released, it was a requirement to have a publicly routable address space for the external A/V Edge Server interface. In Office Communications Server 2007 R2, support was added for using NAT on the A/V Edge Server interface, but only if a single Edge Server existed in that location. If Edge Server redundancy was required, each A/V Edge interface required a publicly routable address on the adapter.

Lync Server 2010 introduced the capability to use NAT for all three services, including the A/V Edge interface for pools with multiple Edge Servers. Skype for Business Server 2015 continues to support this feature by allowing administrators to specify the public IP address associated with each private A/V Edge address in Topology Builder so that the server will still hand out the correct public IP to clients.

There are some caveats to using NAT, particularly around firewall rules and load balancing.

Hardware Load Balancing

NAT can be used for the Edge Servers only if an organization uses Skype for Business Server 2015's built-in DNS load-balancing feature. Organizations that prefer to use hardware load balancers for the Edge pool still require publicly routable IP addresses for the AV Edge of each Edge Server in the Edge pool. There is a VIP for each edge—Access Edge, Web Conf Edge, and A/V Edge—but the A/V Edge of each Edge Server must still be publicly routable. This is required because of ICE negotiation (STUN/TURN protocols), which, in turn, also requires separate public address. The remote client initially connects via the A/V Edge VIP, but then the media flows directly between the remote client and the Edge Server's A/V Edge.

Internal Network NAT

When discussing NAT, the conversation usually centers around the external-facing network adapters of an Edge Server. It's important to keep in mind that the internal-facing network adapter of the Edge Server must be *routable* from the internal network. Unlike the external interfaces, it cannot be translated by NAT through a firewall under *any* circumstance. It can be a private address, but it must be completely routable from all server and client subnets without address translation. All clients on the internal network are allowed to communicate directly with an Edge Server's internal-facing network interface, and those connections cannot be translated. Using NAT between the internal-facing Edge network adapter and the internal network will result in problematic audio/video calls.

The 50,000–59,999 Port Range

The final NAT caveat centers around the use of the TCP/UDP 50,000–59,999 port range that was required to be open for the A/V Edge in Office Communications Server 2007. This requirement was removed in Office Communications Server 2007 R2, which introduced the capability for Edge Servers to relay media between each other. However, because it was not possible to use NAT with multiple Edge Servers back then, it did not cause any issues.

Because Lync Server 2010 and 2013 both support NAT for Edge pools with multiple servers, there is an additional wrinkle to the inbound firewall rules that must be considered. Imagine a scenario in which an organization has two Edge Servers in a single Edge pool, both using NAT for the A/V Edge service. If a remote user has media relay IP addresses allocated for them on Edge Server A, and an internal user has media relay IP addresses allocated for them on Edge Server B, the users might be unable to establish a connection.

Normally, in this scenario Edge Server A and Edge Server B would communicate using each other's public IP address, and the connection would work. When the Edge Servers are each hidden by NAT, though, they might be unable to communicate with each other's public IP because of firewall restrictions. Most modern firewalls prevent "hairpinning," shown in Figure 32.6, or the capability for a server in one security zone to reach a public IP that has a NAT to another server in the same zone.

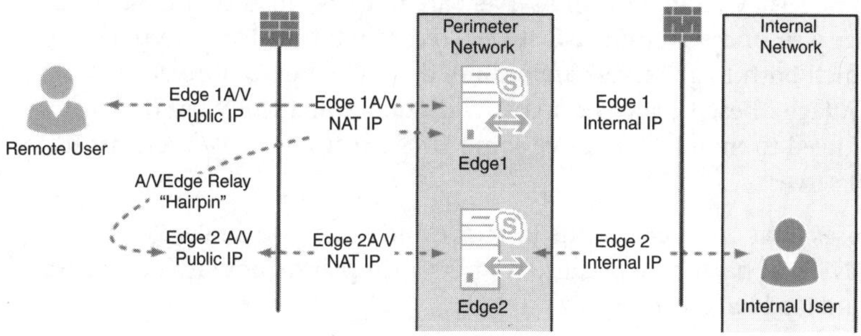

FIGURE 32.6 Edge Server NAT and hairpin.

Because the Edge Servers will relay media only through their public IP addresses, the call will fail when the firewall drops the connection due to a hairpinning attempt. There are two possible solutions to this issue if an organization insists on using NAT:

- Configure static NAT rules at the firewall to allow the Edge Servers to use hairpinning between each other's A/V Edge public IP address.
- Open TCP and UDP 50,000–59,999 inbound to each A/V Edge public IP address.

Planning for High Availability

When adding high availability to an Edge Server deployment, an organization must make a decision about how it will provide load-balancing features. The only options available for load-balancing Edge Servers are to use DNS load balancing or to leverage a hardware load balancer.

CAUTION

Windows Network Load Balancing (NLB) is not supported for load balancing any of the Skype for Business Server 2015 roles, including Edge Servers.

DNS load balancing seems like an attractive feature at first because it requires very little configuration, but it does have some minor limitations. Organizations should review these limitations and then make a decision whether a hardware load balancer is preferred. The main limitation of DNS load balancing is that it does provide automatic failover for some features or legacy endpoints, including these:

- Endpoints running previous versions of the Office Communicator client
- Federated organizations running Office Communications Server 2007 R2 or previous
- XMPP-based providers and servers
- Exchange Server 2007 Unified Messaging

This simply means these legacy endpoints and servers are not DNS load balancing aware, and they could leverage a second server if the first DNS record returned is not responding. So in a scenario in which both Edge Servers are online, there will be no difference. However, during an outage, these legacy endpoints will not automatically fail over. Administrators might need to manually remove some DNS entries to prevent clients from connecting to a failed server.

If your organization uses Lync 2010 endpoints or above and Exchange Server 2010 SP1 or higher, then use DNS load balancing because it offers a simpler deployment and cost savings over a hardware load balancer.

Requirements for Hardware Load Balancing

Using a hardware load balancer comes at a greater cost than DNS load balancing, but adds some flexibility and backward compatibility that an organization might require. Planning the hardware load balancer deployment is typically more difficult than the implementation in an Edge Server deployment simply because most vendors provide templates for rapid configuration of their hardware load balancer (F5, KEMP, JetNexus, and more).

Some basic guidelines must be followed when using a hardware load balancer for Edge Servers:

- Each external-facing Edge needs a publicly routable virtual IP address.
- Each Edge Server needs a publicly routable IP address assigned to the A/V Edge.

This logical configuration is depicted for an Edge pool composed of two Edge Servers in Figure 32.7.

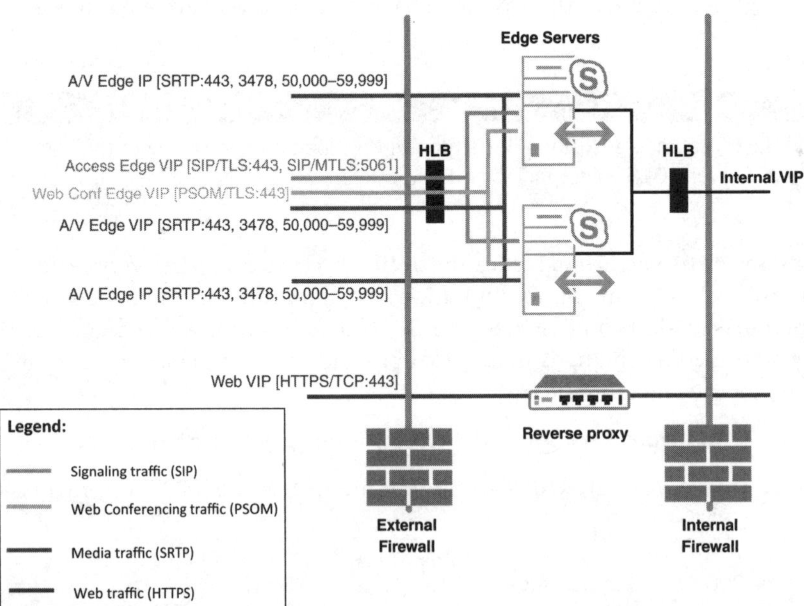

FIGURE 32.7 Hardware load balancer VIPs and Edge Server real IPs.

In addition to the public IP addressing requirements, there are some stipulations about what type of Network Address Translation must be configured on the load balancer. For traffic from the Internet to the Edge Server, the hardware load balancer must use Destination Network Address Translation (DNAT).

This means that as a packet is received from the Internet to the virtual IP address (VIP) of the hardware load balancer, the hardware load balancer rewrites the packet to change the destination IP address to one of the IP addresses assigned to an Edge Server network interface.

CAUTION

The fact that the term NAT is used here does not imply that the Edge Server uses private IP addresses. Even though the Edge Server has a public IP address, the load balancer must somehow still translate requests sent to the VIP address into an IP address actually assigned to an Edge Server.

For traffic from the Edge Server to the Internet, the hardware load balancer must be configured for Source Network Address Translation (SNAT). This means that network packets sent outbound from the Edge Servers are translated by the hardware load balancer back to the VIP address of the hardware load balancer, which external clients expect to receive communications from.

Hardware Load Balancer Configuration

This section discusses the hardware load balancer configuration for an Edge pool. There are two perspectives to look at for load balancing Edge Servers because the external-facing adapter and the internal-facing adapter have different requirements. An Edge Server must be load balanced on both sides to function properly, but each side has slightly different requirements, as shown in Figure 32.8.

CAUTION

Many hardware load balancers have the option to balance "all ports" for a given pool. Avoid this configuration, no matter how tempting and easy it seems. Instead, load balance only the ports found in the tables that follow. This allows the load balancer to properly monitor the health of a particular service and use different persistence methods for each type of traffic.

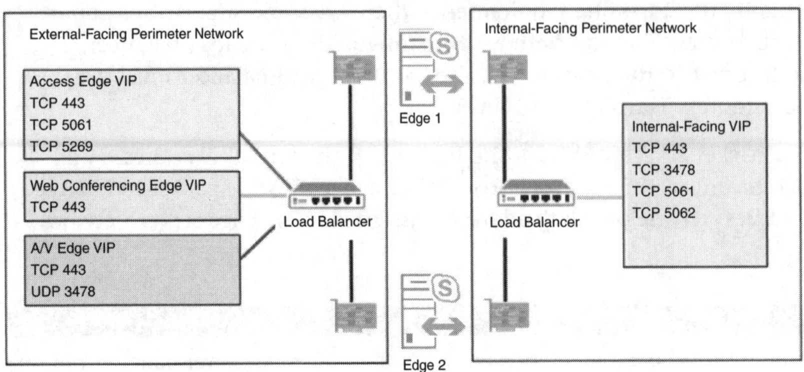

FIGURE 32.8 Edge pool load-balanced ports.

Table 32.1 outlines which ports must be load balanced for each VIP address.

TABLE 32.1 External Edge Interface Load Balancing

Virtual IP Address	Port	Function
Access Edge	TCP 443	Remote access
Access Edge	TCP 5061	Federation and public IM
Access Edge	TCP 5269	XMPP federation
Web Conferencing Edge	TCP 443	Remote web conferencing
A/V Edge	TCP 443	STUN
A/V Edge	UDP 3478	STUN

After the external interface load balancing has been configured, the internal adapter configuration must be completed. Unlike the external adapter that uses three VIP addresses, only a single VIP address is required for the internal network adapter because each Edge Server has only a single IP address for its internal network adapter.

Table 32.2 outlines which ports must be load balanced to each virtual IP address.

TABLE 32.2 Internal Edge Interface Load Balancing

Virtual IP Address	Port	Function
Edge Internal interface	TCP 5061	Signaling
Edge Internal interface	TCP 5062	A/V authentication
Edge Internal interface	TCP 443	STUN
Edge Internal interface	UDP 3478	STUN

CAUTION

There is no entry here for load balancing the internal Web Conferencing Edge interface. That is not an omission or error; port 8057 on the internal interface should not be load balanced by the hardware load balancer. The Front End pools automatically distribute requests to multiple Web Conferencing Edge Servers if configured. Don't forget to include TCP 8057 in the firewall rules, though, because even though it's not load balanced, the Front End Servers need to be able to reach that port on Edge Servers.

Requirements for DNS Load Balancing

If the limitations of DNS load balancing described earlier don't pose any issues to an organization's Skype for Business Server 2015 deployment, the organization can proceed with that method instead of purchasing a hardware load balancer. There are actually some advantages to using DNS load balancing: mainly the simplicity involved in configuration that just involves using multiple A records for the same name in public DNS. Table 32.3 shows the DNS records required to achieve DNS load balancing.

TABLE 32.3 DNS Load-Balancing Entries

Host Record	IP Address
sip.skypeunleashed.com	Access Edge Server A IP address
sip.skypeunleashed.com	Access Edge Server B IP address
webconf.skypeunleashed.com	Web Conferencing Edge Server A IP address
webconf.skypeunleashed.com	Web Conferencing Edge Server B IP address
av.skypeunleashed.com	A/V Edge Server A IP address
av.skypeunleashed.com	A/V Edge Server B IP address

When DNS load balancing is used, the Edge Server can use private IP addresses that are translated by NAT for all three roles, including the A/V Edge. This is a big advantage for organizations that might not have many public IP addresses available, or an existing perimeter network with publicly routable addresses.

DNS load balancing also requires three fewer IP addresses than a hardware load-balancing solution. Each Edge Server IP still needs to be mapped to a unique public IP address if it is being translated by NAT, but there is no concept or need for a VIP. Instead, Skype for Business endpoints have logic built in to the client to recognize that there are multiple servers with separate IP addresses to which it could connect.

Another advantage of DNS load balancing is that the native server-draining feature in Skype for Business Server 2015 is available. This enables administrators to prepare a server by maintenance through the Skype for Business Server 2015 Control Panel the same way as the other roles.

In some organizations, the team responsible for Skype for Business Server 2015 might not be the same team that manages the network and hardware load balancers, which can make it difficult to coordinate preparing a server for maintenance. Instead of the Skype for

Business Server 2015 administrators quickly draining a server's connections, they might need to submit a request to have the network team drain the load balancer connections for a particular node and then check back later to determine whether the connections have cleared. Sometimes this separation of teams can be just as efficient as one person having complete control, but often it slows down the maintenance process.

NOTE

Although DNS load balancing is available for Edge Servers, keep in mind that the reverse proxy for web component services is a critical piece of remote access. Load balancing for a reverse proxy must be addressed separately and can be done either with a hardware load balancer or possibly through Windows Network Load Balancing (NLB).

Reverse Proxy Planning

A critical piece in planning for Edge services is the reverse proxy. Unfortunately, this tends to be overlooked or considered a secondary task, even though it provides some important functionality to a deployment. Without a reverse proxy, the following features will not be available to remote users:

- Skype for Business Mobile clients
- Address book download
- Distribution group expansion
- Web conferencing content such as whiteboards, uploaded presentations, and document sharing
- Device updates
- Dial-in conferencing page
- Simple meet conferencing pages

The first item might be a bit of a surprise, but the mobile clients for Skype for Business use HTTPS web services to encapsulate the SIP signaling information into REST-based APIs called Unified Communications Web APIs (UCWA). Organizations that neglect planning for a reverse proxy are effectively preventing their users from accessing Skype for Business web services or allowing connectivity from Skype for Business Mobile clients.

The concept of a reverse proxy is simple to understand when considering it as an extra hop or barrier between external clients and an internal resource. In the overall scheme of external services, the reverse proxy fits in as depicted in Figure 32.9.

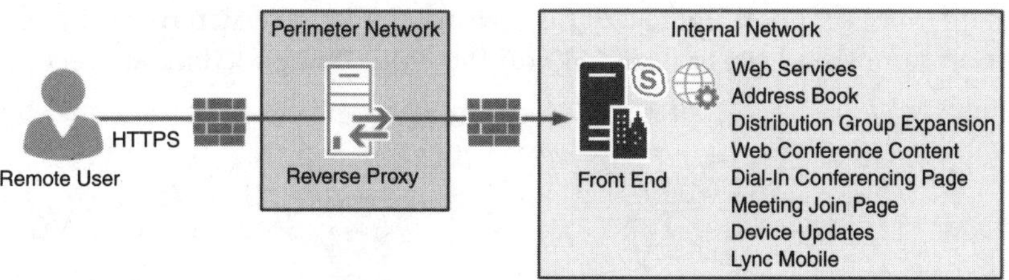

FIGURE 32.9 Reverse proxy for web services.

Reverse Proxy Methodologies

After understanding the functionality of a reverse proxy, it's important to comprehend the different methods a reverse proxy can use to publish internal services. Three main methods are used, and not all of them are available depending on the reverse proxy used.

SSL Pass-Through

The most basic method is SSL pass-through. This means that the traffic from Internet clients runs through the reverse proxy, but the SSL connection exists from the client all the way to the internal resource, as shown in Figure 32.9. This is the most basic form of reverse proxy.

SSL Offloading

Another common methodology in reverse proxy scenarios is to use SSL offloading. In this scenario, the client's SSL tunnel terminates at the reverse proxy, which then initiates a clear-text HTTP request to the internal resource. In this scenario, the SSL tunnel is terminated at the reverse proxy, which then communicates over port 80 to the Front End pool, leaving an unencrypted component. Many hardware load balancers offer this functionality and advertise that they can improve the performance of servers by "offloading" the SSL encryption and decryption duties from the internal server.

This is a valuable feature when a server is CPU constrained, but with modern hardware, this is rarely necessary. Any hardware used for Skype for Business Server 2015 probably far exceeds the CPU capabilities of most load-balancing devices. Furthermore, Skype for Business Server 2015 is designed to operate in a secure manner from end to end and does not actually support SSL offloading.

SSL Bridging

The final methodology, which is the preferred scenario, is to use SSL bridging. In this case, the client's SSL tunnels to the reverse proxy, as in an offloading scenario, but the reverse proxy then opens a second HTTPS connection back to the internal resource. This ensures that the entire transmission is encrypted from end to end.

There is also some added flexibility in this case, in that a reverse proxy can redirect that second connection to a port other than 443 back on the internal resource without the client's knowledge. As far as the client knows, it still has a connection on port 443 to the internal resource, even though the reverse proxy might bridge this connection to port

4443 on the internal Front End pool. Figure 32.10 shows where the reverse proxy bridges a port 443 connection from the client to port 4443 on the Front End pool, but still secures the traffic.

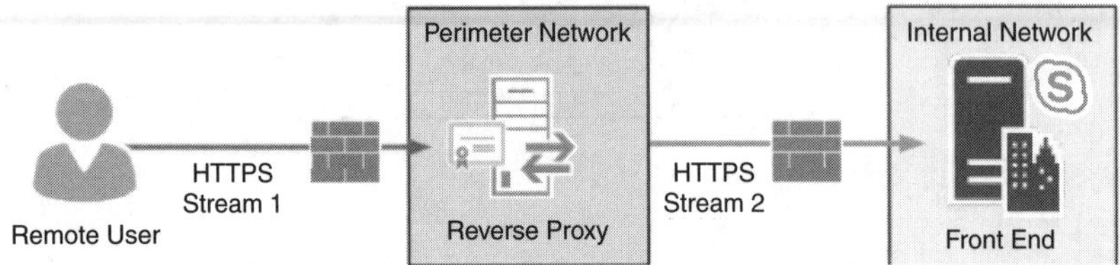

FIGURE 32.10 SSL bridging.

To summarize the options, the preferred method for Skype for Business Server is SSL bridging to ensure an end-to-end encryption of the traffic with the most flexibility. SSL offloading is not supported, so if bridging is not an option, the reverse proxy should be configured for SSL pass-through.

NOTE

A common question to ask is whether a reverse proxy is actually needed, or whether an organization can simply perform a port translation at the firewall to a Front End pool. Though technically possible, this scenario is entirely unsupported by Microsoft and should be avoided. Not using a reverse proxy also means that public certificates might need to be placed on the Front End Servers because they will communicate directly with Internet users, and unsecure traffic through port 80 is open by default, unless restricted.

Placement and Configuration

Placement of the reverse proxy follows the same concept as the Edge Server. So wherever an Edge Server is deployed, a reverse proxy should be deployed in that same location. Even if the client connects through the reverse proxy, media traffic (A/V, application sharing, file transfer) will still flow through the Edge Server. Matching the traffic path of the reverse proxy to that of the Edge Server will make it easier to troubleshoot issues, and can be optimized for both.

Setting up the reverse proxy is similar to setting up an Edge Server. Generally, the reverse proxy is placed in a perimeter network and has two network adapters: one internal facing and one external facing. To reach the internal subnets, static routes must also be configured. Some products also have the ability to use a single network adapter while acting as a reverse proxy.

Reverse Proxy Products

With the discontinuation of Microsoft Threat Management Gateway (TMG), customers must choose a vendor to provide a reverse proxy solution for Microsoft Skype for Business Server 2015 or Exchange deployments such as F5's BIG-IP, KEMP Technologies'

LoadMaster, Citrix's NetScaler, or A10's Thunder ADC. Most of these vendors offer a hardware- or software-based reverse proxy solution. The list of qualified reverse proxy vendors can be found https://technet.microsoft.com/en-us/office/dn788945. Microsoft also provides two options—IIS Application Request Routing (ARR) and Web Application Proxy (WAP)—as a reverse proxy for Skype for Business Server 2015. Microsoft's Web Application Proxy requires deploying ADFS.

Reverse Proxy Load Balancing

Each reverse proxy product will handle load balancing differently, but planning for redundancy will generally involve using multiple reverse proxies and load balancing the services. The only port required for load balancing the reverse proxy is TCP 443, but organizations might also want to load balance TCP 80 and redirect that traffic automatically to TCP 443 instead. This ensures that a request is still routed if a user manually types in a simple URL for meetings or dial-in information but forgets to specify HTTPS.

Exchange Services Publishing

Many components of Skype for Business Server 2015 rely on connections to Exchange Web Services (EWS), a web-based component of Exchange Server. Though EWS is preferred, the Skype for Business client itself is fairly resilient, and can fail back to MAPI calls to Outlook for information, but clients like Skype for Business Phone Edition and Skype for Business Mobile heavily depend on Exchange Web Services being published remotely.

Exchange Web Services are typically published through the same reverse proxy Skype for Business Server 2015 uses, but in some cases organizations might restrict access to Outlook or Exchange Web Services from remote clients. It's important to discuss Exchange Web Services early on when planning to provide remote Skype for Business services because it can greatly affect the user experience. For example, Skype for Business Mobile cannot view any calendar data or join online meetings if EWS is not accessible.

TIP

Advanced scripting engines in some reverse proxy products or third-party Security Web Filters can be used to restrict Exchange Web Services access to specific application host headers. This can be useful for organizations that want to allow Skype for Business Mobile or Skype for Business Phone Edition clients to access Exchange Web Services, but prevent other applications such as Outlook for PCs and Macs from connecting.

Skype for Business endpoints leverage many components of Exchange. It is important to ensure that Exchange services are also properly published through a reverse proxy when planning a Skype for Business Server 2015 deployment.

Office Web Apps Server

Skype for Business Server 2015 uses Office Web Apps Server to share PowerPoint presentations. It is necessary to publish the Office Web Apps Server to the Internet to provide this functionality also for external users. The Office Web Apps Server is typically published through the same reverse proxy used by Skype for Business Server 2015.

Planning for Certificates

Provisioning certificates for Edge Servers was a sore subject back in the Office Communications Server days, but the process has been greatly simplified in the latest releases. This section discusses the certificate requirements and considerations for organizations deciding between public certificates and privately issued certificates.

An Edge Server requires certificates for the following network interfaces:

- Internal Edge
- Access Edge
- Web Conferencing Edge
- A/V Edge

TIP

Although the A/V Edge Media Relay service also runs on TCP 443, it does not have a certificate assigned. Instead, a key used to encrypt and decrypt the media flowing through this port is first exchanged through the Access Edge FQDN. There is no need to include the A/V Edge FQDN in the Edge Server certificate request. The recommendation is to use the Skype for Business Server 2015 Certificate Wizard.

Public Versus Private Certificate Authorities

A common misconception is that all of these certificates should be purchased from a public Certificate Authority, which is only partly true. Only certificates used for the external-facing Edge interfaces should come from a public Certificate Authority. Best practice is for internal certificates, including the Edge Server's internal interface certificate, to be issued from the organization's PKI (internal Certificate Authority).

External Edge Server Interface

This certificate should be issued by a public Certificate Authority. The specific requirements for subject names and subject alternative names for the certificate on the external interface of an Edge Server pool are outlined next. The same certificate and private key should be exported and installed on each member of the same Edge pool.

- **Access Edge**—The subject name should match the published name of the Access Edge FQDN in the public DNS. If a hardware load balancer is used, this is the name of the virtual IP address that clients resolve. The subject alternative name field should contain any supported SIP domains in the `sip.<SIP Domain>` format.
- **Web Conferencing Edge**—The subject name should match the published name of the Web Conferencing Edge FQDN in the public DNS. If a hardware load balancer

is used, this is the name of the virtual IP address that clients resolve. No subject alternative names are required.

- **A/V Edge**—This service is associated with a certificate, but it is included here to provide clarity that the A/V Edge FQDN should *not* be included in a certificate request.

Skype for Business Server 2015 uses subject alternative name (SAN) certificates in many locations, including the external-facing Edge Server certificate. Organizations typically include the Access Edge, Web Conferencing Edge, and any supported SIP domains on a single certificate to reduce maintenance costs and overhead.

Internal Edge Server Interface

This certificate should be issued by an internal, private Certificate Authority. The specific requirements for subject names and subject alternative names for the certificate on the internal interface of an Edge Server in an Edge pool are outlined next. The same certificate and private key should be exported and installed on each member of the same Edge pool.

- **Internal Edge**—The subject name should match the published name (that is, FQDN) of the internal network interface of the Edge pool. If a hardware load balancer is used, the subject name must resolves to the virtual IP address load balancing the internal Edge of the Edge Servers. No subject alternative names should be included in this request.

Reverse Proxy Interface

The certificate for the public-facing (that is, Internet-facing) network interface of the reverse proxy should be issued by a public Certificate Authority. The specific requirements for subject names and subject alternative names for the certificate on a reverse proxy are outlined next.

- **Reverse Proxy**—The subject name should match the published name of the external web services FQDN. The subject alternative name should contain any simple URLs for dial-in, online meetings, and an entry for `lyncdiscover.<SIP Domain>` for each supported SIP domain.

TIP

Organizations can reduce the number of certificates from a public Certificate Authority by simply including the reverse proxy naming requirements as additional subject alternative names used for the external network interface of the Edge Server. The same public certificate can then be deployed to the Edge Servers and reverse proxy.

In addition, organizations with many SIP domains can reduce the amount of required subject alternative names if they use the following simple URL model for meeting URLs:

https://uc.contoso.com/SIPdomain1/meet

https://uc.contoso.com/SIPdomain2/meet

https://uc.contoso.com/SIPdomain3/meet

Wildcard Certificates

Wildcard certificates in the format of `*.<domain>` have become increasingly popular because they provide a way to secure a large number of websites at a low cost by using only a single certificate. Using a wildcard certificate for the reverse proxy works perfectly fine, but it is not supported for Skype for Business Server 2015, including the Edge Server.

Network Planning

Deploying a Skype for Business Server 2015 Edge Server will always invoke discussions around alternative remote access technologies such as VPN and Microsoft's DirectAccess. There are some additional considerations with network equipment such as firewalls and WAN accelerators that should be discussed when deploying an Edge Server.

VPN Connectivity to Skype for Business

Virtual private network (VPN) is a concept many users and organizations have been familiar with for years. The concept is that a remote user establishes a VPN connection to the office and has full access to all internal resources, which raises the question of why Edge Server is required at all.

VPN works by encapsulating all traffic within a secured tunnel, but that tunnel generally includes a lot of overhead and additional latency. Skype for Business's signaling traffic (SIP) and A/V media traffic (SRTP) are already securely encrypted. So the additional VPN tunnel encapsulating the traffic is really redundant. This isn't a huge problem for SIP signaling, but when two users try to establish an A/V call, that overhead, shown in Figure 32.11, can significantly impact the call quality.

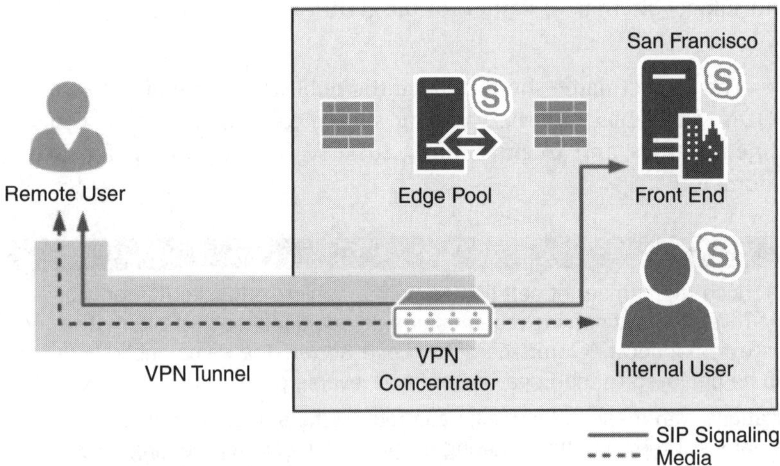

FIGURE 32.11 VPN double encryption.

The Edge Server provides the most optimal path for A/V calls for remote users. Any deployment leveraging audio or video features of Skype for Business should not be relying on VPN to provide a way to connect calls for remote users.

Blocking Media over VPN

In fact, organizations deploying Edge Servers should be going out of their way to avoid the possibility of clients connecting a media stream over the VPN tunnel. Skype for Business clients always prefer a direct peer-to-peer connection when negotiating a call, but they don't have any logic to determine whether they are on a VPN connection. So when a user establishes a VPN and then tries to call a user on the internal network, the two clients will think they should connect "peer to peer" instead of relaying their traffic through the Edge Server.

Depending on the VPN technology, organizations can use a combination of defined port ranges, IP address ranges, and source executable names to effectively block Skype for Business clients from connecting over VPN. These blocks need to be put in place between VPN clients and internal network users, and between the VPN users and Skype for Business Front End Servers and Mediation Servers.

After these restrictions are established, a user's Skype for Business client will use the Edge Server for all signaling and media, as depicted in Figure 32.12, regardless of whether a user has a VPN connected. This does require split-tunnel access to the Edge Server's public addresses so that the Skype for Business client resolves the public IP addresses of the Edge Server and reverse proxy instead of the internal IP addresses of the Skype for Business servers. This is achieved by using pinpoint zones in the internal DNS that resolve public IP addresses in response to queries from clients connecting through the VPN.

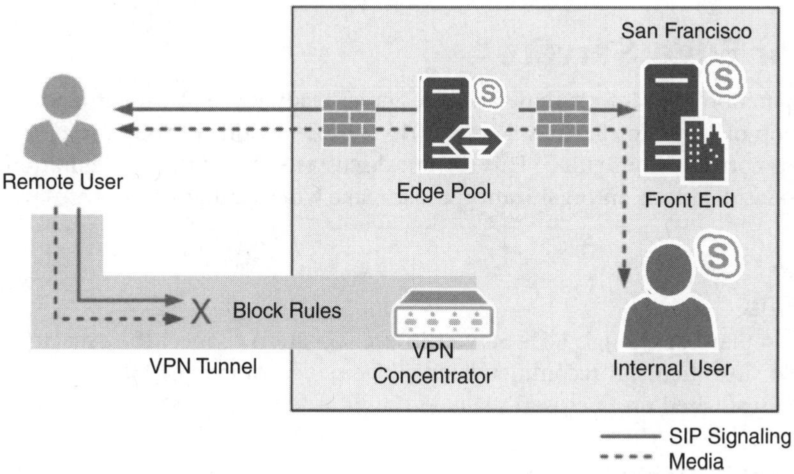

FIGURE 32.12 VPN deny rules.

Blocking Media over DirectAccess

Microsoft's DirectAccess technology is another form of remote connectivity that has gained popularity over the past few years. DirectAccess maintains a persistent IPv4 connection to the corporate network's IPv6 resources using tunneling, which then allows remote users to transparently access internal servers. Skype for Business Server 2015 does not support DirectAccess for remote connectivity to Front End pools due to the same limitations as any VPN solution (that is, redundant encapsulation of media traffic).

Administrators can block remote users from connecting to Skype for Business internal servers over DirectAccess by implementing exceptions in the Name Resolution Policy Table (NRPT) on the DirectAccess servers. DirectAccess is based on FQDNs instead of IP addresses like a traditional VPN technology, so these exclusions prevent remote users from resolving internal Skype for Business resources to their tunneled IPv6 address.

Avoiding WAN Acceleration

Many organizations deploy multiple sites that are separated by wide area network (WAN) connectivity with limited bandwidth, and they work to deploy WAN accelerator devices that help optimize the network traffic by compressing it. WAN accelerators work only if both sides of a network contain the same device that can compress and then unpack the traffic identically.

Unfortunately, the connections used by Skype for Business servers and clients are completely encrypted, so the WAN accelerators are unable to efficiently compress the traffic. WAN accelerators can even negatively affect an audio stream or persistent TLS connections between servers in different sites. A best practice is to exclude all Skype for Business Server IP addresses from any form of traffic optimization devices.

Preparing for Edge Servers

A good deal of preparation goes into making an Edge Server ready for deployment, and the actual installation of Skype for Business Server 2015 is probably one of the easiest parts after a server is correctly configured. This section discusses some of the configuration requirements and considerations an organization must make when preparing an Edge Server.

Capacity Planning

Organizations should plan for enough Edge Servers in each location to meet the capacity requirements of that site. Microsoft recommends one Edge server for every 12,000 concurrent remote users based on Microsoft's standard user model.

Domain Membership Considerations

Edge Servers do not store any directory information or user data, and they shouldn't be joined to an internal Active Directory domain. Edge Servers are typically deployed in workgroup mode, which can create some additional issues, such as security policy enforcement and patching. Administrators must manually account for patching these servers and changing local security policies instead of using Group Policy and Windows Server Update Services (WSUS). By not being part of the domain, these servers can potentially be left unpatched with security vulnerabilities.

There are workarounds to these issues, such as using SCOM with a Skype for Business management pack, using registry keys to point servers at an internal WSUS server, and allowing Edge Servers to automatically update patches. However, organizations might block the ports required for WSUS to a perimeter network or might not want servers to apply patches without being tested first.

Another option is to join Edge Servers to a separate Active Directory forest that has been deployed within the perimeter network. Some businesses deploy a separate forest to work around the management and maintenance issues previously discussed.

If the Edge Server is part of a workgroup configuration, be sure to define a primary DNS suffix for the machine, and use that FQDN within Topology Builder and for any certificates (see the section "Configure Networking" in Chapter 5, "Skype for Business Server 2015 Edge Server").

Network Adapter Configuration

Setting up IP addresses, DNS servers, and gateways on the Edge Server adapters can be a point of confusion in a deployment because of the requirement for dual network adapters. To begin with, an Edge Server must have two separate network adapters: one that is internal facing and one that is external (or public) facing.

The internal adapter should have a single IP address, and the external adapter should have three separate IP addresses associated—one for each Edge service.

TIP

It always helps to name the network connections descriptively instead of leaving the "Local Area Connection <Connection Number>" name on the adapter. Naming the interfaces "Internal" and "External" makes a clear distinction about what function each adapter serves.

Default Gateways and Routing

Another point of confusion when one is configuring the network adapters is where to place the default gateway. Many administrators try to place gateways on both network adapters, which causes extremely unreliable traffic flows. It does not matter whether the adapters are all on the same or different subnets; only one adapter should have a default gateway assigned.

For an Edge Server, always place the default gateway on the external-facing network adapter of the Access Edge. This applies whether a single network adapter is used for all three Edge services or whether multiple network adapters are used. This ensures that all requests the Edge Server does not know how to route are passed through the external network adapter.

The tricky part of configuring an Edge Server is to make sure that it always uses the internal-facing network adapter to communicate with any internal servers or clients. Administrators can accomplish this by creating persistent static routes on each Edge Server. Routing is something generally associated with network devices, but in the case of a multihomed server, an administrator must configure the routing table to act appropriately. For an Edge Server, the administrator must manually enter route statements to use that internal adapter for internal subnets. Figure 32.13 shows how the external network adapter has a default gateway associated but route statements for internal networks make use of the internal network adapter.

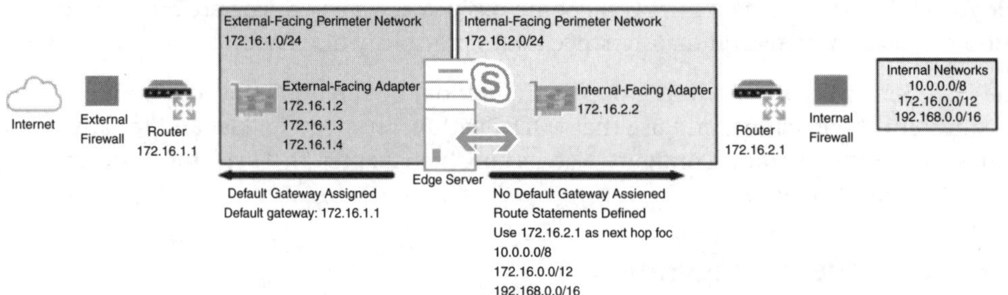

FIGURE 32.13 Edge Server gateways and routing.

Summary

Spending a good deal of time planning for Edge services makes any deployment much easier. Admittedly, there are so many moving pieces to an Edge Server deployment that it is easy to miss something, but Microsoft has made great strides to improve the installation and configuration process with Skype for Business Server 2015. Planning the Edge names, IP addressing, routing, and firewall configuration in advance of any installation streamlines the deployment process.

CHAPTER 33

Planning for Voice Deployment

IN THIS CHAPTER

One of the most exciting and useful aspects of Skype for Business Server 2015 is its telephony features, known collectively as Enterprise Voice. Enterprise Voice turns any Skype for Business desk phone, PC/Mac client, or Windows/Android/iOS mobile device into a very capable replacement for a traditional PBX. With careful planning and implementation, it can easily scale to global enterprise levels and provide truly unified communications to the entire company.

Once a user is enabled for Skype for Business IM and Presence, it only takes a few more clicks to enable them for Enterprise Voice, but to get to that point, a large amount of planning and work needs to be completed. At minimum, for Enterprise Voice to work for a user, the following items need to be defined and set properly:

- **Skype for Business Mediation Servers**—These servers need to be installed and configured.
- **PSTN integration**—This is how Skype for Business Server 2015 connects to the telephone network.
- **Line URI definition**—This is a unique phone number assigned to the user that's formatted to acceptable standards.
- **Dial plan**—The dial plan controls how the user dials phone numbers.
- **Voice policy**—The voice policy defines what rights a user has in the Enterprise Voice environment and how their calls are routed.

This chapter discusses the details that administrators need to consider when designing a Skype for Business Enterprise Voice solution.

Enterprise Voice Overview

Enterprise Voice relies on the Mediation Server role in order to send and receive calls from the PSTN. The primary purpose of the Mediation Server role is to act as an intermediary between the PSTN and the Skype for Business Server 2015 environment. It transcodes media to the format required by the next hop (usually G.711) and encrypts/decrypts media as required.

The Mediation Server role can be collocated with the Front End Server, or it can be deployed separately in a Mediation pool of one or more servers. Dedicated Mediation Servers can handle many more simultaneous calls than collocated Mediation Servers. For example, according to Microsoft's capacity planning document, a collocated Mediation Server can handle roughly 150 simultaneous calls (assuming the server was built to recommended specifications). A dedicated Mediation Server with the same server specifications can potentially handle 1,500 simultaneous calls.

At a high level, there are two components to a voice conversation:

- **Signaling**—Deals with call setup, negotiation, and call control
- **Media**—The actual audio transmission

In Skype for Business Server 2015, signaling is done via Session Initiation Protocol (SIP) and media uses one of a variety of codecs, depending on client/server capabilities, modality, and network conditions.

The next hop from the Mediation Server may be either directly to the Public Switched Telephone Network (PSTN) or it could be to an internal office private branch exchange (PBX). The connection type could be one or more digital lines (that is, Integrated Services Digital Network, or ISDN) or analog telephone lines (FXS/FXO or POTS—Plain Old Telephone System) over dedicated purpose-built networks, or it could use some flavor of SIP over TCP/IP.

If the connection point is a certified Skype for Business SIP solution, then the Mediation Server can connect directly to it using native SIP over TCP/IP without any intervening hardware. This is called a Direct SIP connection. As the name suggests, a Direct SIP connection is done entirely in software using native SIP signaling and media. Because it's done in software and requires no additional hardware, Direct SIP is often the least expensive solution.

Skype for Business Server 2015 can connect via Direct SIP to a certified third-party SIP provider that is reachable via the Internet. The SIP provider accepts SIP and translates it into the required format to connect to the PSTN, as in Figure 33.1.

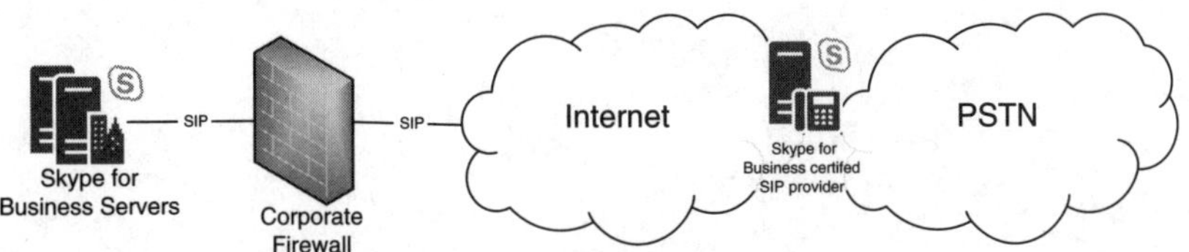

FIGURE 33.1 Direct SIP to external supported SIP provider.

Conceptually, connecting to a certified IP-PBX is very similar to connecting to a Direct SIP provider, except the connection point is in the internal network, as in Figure 33.2.

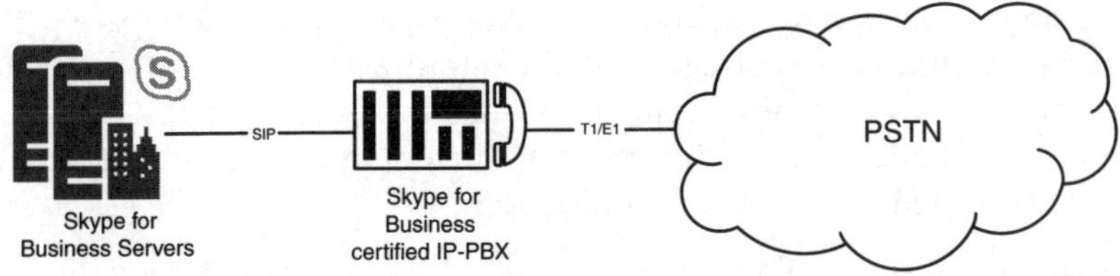

FIGURE 33.2 Direct SIP to supported IP-PBX.

If the SIP provider or IP-PBX is not Skype for Business certified, then an intermediary gateway known as a Session Border Controller (SBC) may be required. The SBC is responsible for translating Microsoft's specific flavor of SIP to the flavor of SIP used by the SIP provider or IP-PBX. Typically, the biggest issue for non-Microsoft-certified SIP providers is that Skype for Business Server 2015 uses TCP for SIP signaling, whereas most SIP providers use UDP. Without an SBC, call setup cannot happen because neither end is listening for SIP messages on the network protocol they expect. A Session Border Controller is also beneficial for connecting to certified SIP providers because it provides an element of security, so the Skype for Business Servers are not directly exposed to the Internet, as in Figure 33.3.

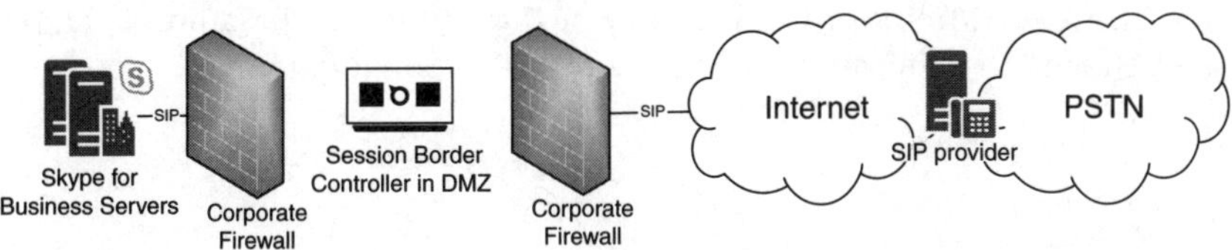

FIGURE 33.3 SBC to external SIP provider.

In many cases, the PSTN connection is done over traditional digital interfaces such as ISDN or analog lines. For most companies, connections use ISDN PRI interfaces (often incorrectly referred to as T1s or E1s, depending on location), which use the same RJ-45 connector as a typical Ethernet cable (but not the same wiring layout). For these connections, a PSTN gateway is required. A PSTN gateway has both Ethernet and T1/E1 interfaces (and possibly others) and translates SIP signaling and media into the format required for the particular PSTN interface in use. This is shown in Figure 33.4.

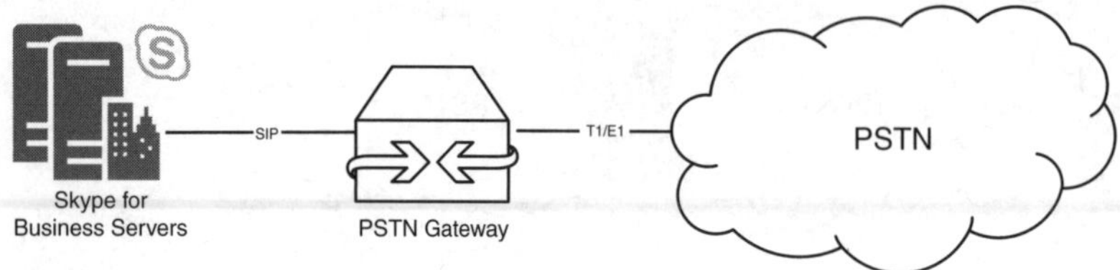

FIGURE 33.4 PSTN gateway connection.

Integration Scenarios

One of the earliest decisions in the Enterprise Voice planning stage is how to integrate Skype for Business Server 2015 into the existing telephony infrastructure. There are several integration scenarios available to a company deploying Skype for Business Enterprise Voice. The best integration scenario could be different for different offices within the same company and should be evaluated on an office-by-office basis.

Unless the site is new, most will already have an existing telephony solution. Integrating Skype for Business Server 2015 into an existing telephony deployment depends on the capabilities of the existing PBX, costs, and the overall goals of the integration project.

High-level Integration Options

There are three different PBX/PSTN connection options for Skype for Business Server 2015 at an office with an existing PBX: behind the PBX, in front of the PBX, and beside the PBX.

Skype for Business Behind the PBX

In the first scenario, Skype for Business Server 2015 is placed behind the PBX, so that calls to the PSTN originating from Skype for Business Server 2015 have to traverse the PBX, as shown in Figure 33.5. This option has the least impact on the existing infrastructure, but can often require a fair bit of routing configuration on the PBX to allow calls from Skype for Business Server 2015 to exit to the PSTN. This may be difficult if the PBX administrators are not experienced enough to perform the required advanced configuration.

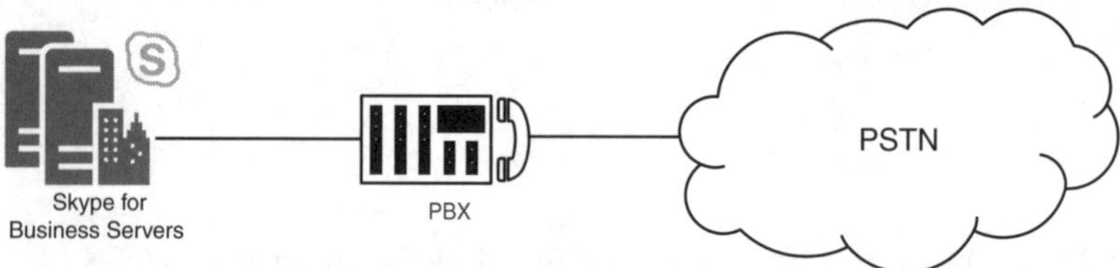

FIGURE 33.5 Skype for Business behind the PBX.

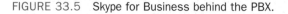

The specific method of connecting Skype for Business Server 2015 to the PBX depends on several factors. If the PBX is of a relatively recent vintage, it is likely known as an IP-PBX, and Skype for Business Server 2015 may be able to connect directly to it via a

Direct SIP connection. Some IP-PBX vendors may require extra licenses for a Direct SIP connection, and costs can vary widely depending on the agreement between the vendor and the company.

For this option to work, the IP-PBX should be on the Supported Infrastructure for Microsoft Skype for Business IP-PBX list (available on Microsoft TechNet). Certain features may not work as expected, and will likely be called out on any available integration documentation provided either by Microsoft or the IP-PBX vendor.

If the IP-PBX vendor is not on the supported list, this does not necessarily mean that Direct SIP integration won't work. In many cases, Direct SIP integration will work, but features that do not work may not become apparent until late in the integration process. Much time may also be wasted on discussions with the IP-PBX vendor trying to fix issues. If a satisfactory solution is not available, this may mean a return to the drawing board.

If Direct SIP isn't an option, then a Skype for Business qualified PSTN gateway will be required between the PBX and the Skype for Business Server 2015 infrastructure. The PSTN gateway will require telephony interfaces that match up with the available interfaces on the PBX and will translate the call format into the format required for Skype for Business Server 2015. Additional licenses or physical connection cards may also be required, which may not be available or have a high associated cost, and they may be a hard sell due to the limited life expectancy of what is likely to be an aging PBX.

The advantages of this option are that existing PBX users are not affected during the Skype for Business Server 2015 implementation and configuration tasks can usually be done during business hours without impacting telephony availability.

Enabling users for Skype for Business Enterprise Voice requires coordinated action on both the PBX and Skype for Business Server 2015. On the Skype for Business Server 2015 side, the user has to be enabled for Enterprise Voice, while on the PBX side, the user's phone number has to be set to either forward or simultaneously ring the Skype for Business number. This allows users to use both their existing PBX phone and Skype for Business devices at the same time.

Another thing to consider is the ultimate goal for Enterprise Voice in the office/company. If the long-term goal is to replace the PBX with Skype for Business Server 2015, then there will come a time when something will have to be done to directly connect Skype for Business Server 2015 to the PSTN, which will incur additional time and cost. The pros and cons are shown in Table 33.1.

TABLE 33.1 Pros and Cons of Skype for Business Server 2015 Behind the PBX

Pros	Cons
Low impact on existing PBX users.	Complex work required on PBX to function.
Work can be done during business hours in most cases.	Additional PBX hardware may be required.
Lower initial costs.	Availability of qualified PBX administrators.
	Still requires labor/hardware if Skype for Business Server 2015 becomes the primary voice solution.

Skype for Business Server 2015 in Front of the PBX

If Skype for Business Server 2015 will ultimately replace the existing PBX, then it can make more sense to plan ahead and place Skype for Business Server 2015 in front of the PBX, as shown in Figure 33.6. Skype for Business Server 2015 is attached directly to the PSTN, which would be the final configuration.

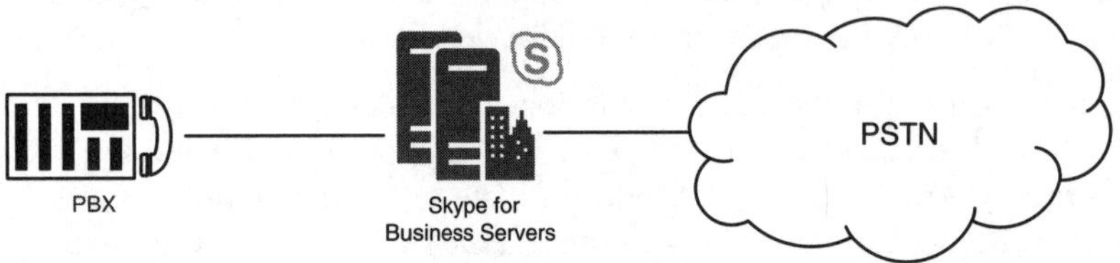

FIGURE 33.6 Skype for Business in front of PBX.

This option can obviously impact existing PBX functionality because a PSTN gateway needs to be inserted in front of the PBX. The gateway will require twice as many interfaces as there are attached to the PBX. For example, if there are two T1/E1 lines coming into the PBX, then the gateway will have to have four (two inbound from the PSTN, two outbound to the PBX). Careful planning and after-hours testing has to be done to ensure this will not impact the existing solution.

The PSTN gateway can be configured to route calls to either Skype for Business Server 2015 or the PBX (or both). This solution requires very little change to the PBX and is highly advantageous if PBX administrative and hardware support is limited.

Once this setup is in place, migration to Skype for Business Server 2015 is vastly simplified, and when migration is complete, the PBX is simply turned off and decommissioned. This is shown in Table 33.2

TABLE 33.2 Pros and Cons of Skype for Business Server 2015 in Front of the PBX

Pros	Cons
Skype for Business is in its final position at the beginning of the migration.	Potential connectivity impact to existing PBX users.
No change to PBX infrastructure required.	Higher gateway costs for additional PSTN interfaces.

Skype for Business Server 2015 Parallel to the PBX

Instead of attempting to integrate with an existing PBX, administrators can elect to build Skype for Business Server 2015 in parallel to the PBX, with no connectivity, as illustrated in Figure 33.7. This is often done in cases where the office is small enough for a flash cutover over a weekend or if the site will be replacing its traditional telephony infrastructure with a SIP trunk and doesn't require any direct connectivity to the PBX. The benefits and challenges are shown in Table 33.3.

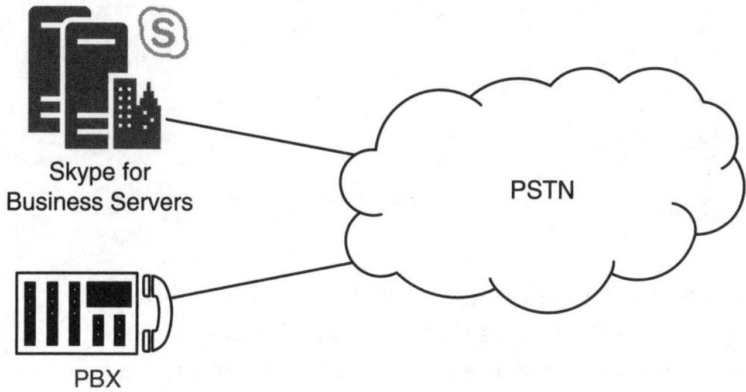

FIGURE 33.7 Skype for Business beside PBX.

TABLE 33.3 Pros and Cons of Skype for Business Server 2015 in Parallel with the PBX

Pros	Cons
Skype for Business is in its final position at the beginning of the migration.	No connectivity between Skype for Business and the PBX.
No change to the PBX infrastructure required.	Cost and management overheard to support multiple PSTN interfaces for a period of time, if not cutting over all at once.

Active Directory Phone Number Configuration

Skype for Business Server 2015 displays phone numbers stored in Active Directory user and contact accounts and can be selected in drop-down boxes for click-to-dial. As such, it is important to use a consistent format throughout the company.

While administrators can theoretically use any numbering scheme they desire, it is highly recommended to follow internationally set standards. The internationally recognized format for telephone numbers is called the *E.164* standard, published by the Telecommunication Standardization Sector of the International Telecommunication Union, or ITU-T for short.

An E.164 number has to be globally unique and follow specific formatting rules. E.164 numbers starts with a plus sign, then a one-to-three digit country code, followed by an area code in most countries (national destination code or NDC) and then the subscriber number.

The following example shows E.164 formatted numbers for Toronto, Canada and London, UK. The U.S., Canada, and most of the Caribbean are all part of the North American Numbering Plan (NANP, which is managed by the NANP Association, or NANPA), and use 1 as the country code. The United Kingdom's country code is 44. One of several area codes for Toronto is 416, while London's city code is 20. Subscriber numbers in the U.S. and Canada are seven digits long, whereas UK numbers are eight digits long. Other countries may or may not have area/city codes, and subscriber number length can vary wildly, even within the same country. An example is shown in Figure 33.8.

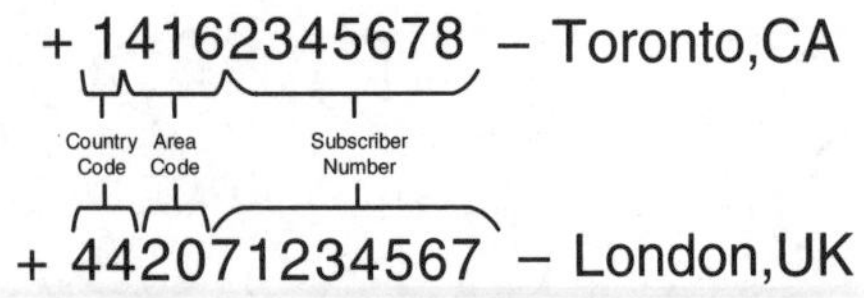

+ 14162345678 – Toronto,CA

Country Code
Area Code
Subscriber Number

+ 442071234567 – London,UK

FIGURE 33.8 E.164 numbering examples.

To work with click-to-dial in Skype for Business, phone numbers in Active Directory should be formatted to E.164 standards, but if they cannot match this format for some reason, administrators can use the PowerShell commands `*-CsAddressBookNormalizationConfiguration` and `*-CsAddressBookNormalizationRule` to normalize to the E.164 format. This allows non-E.164 AD phone numbers to appear in Skype for Business and work with click-to-dial. Skype for Business Server 2015 comes with a default set of rules that will normalize most numbers to E.164, but it is always a good idea to verify this in advance.

Active Directory phone numbers can have separators to enhance readability, such as +1 (416) 234-5678 and +44.20.7123.4567. Use whatever format is familiar to users, but inserting country-specific prefixes should be avoided, as in the UK, where numbers are often formatted like +44 (0) 20.7123.4567. Also, do not add country-specific routing codes for international numbers in Active Directory, such as 011 and 00. These routing codes are not part of the E.164 standard.

For companies that use extension dialing, use the appropriate main office number as the main part of the E.164 phone number, followed by x or X for maximum compatibility, as in +1 (416) 234-5678 x234.

It's important to use E.164 formatting, even if the company only has a single office. When federating with another company, its entirely likely they won't be able to click-to-dial published non–Skype for Business numbers if E.164 formatting isn't used, simply because the other company can't anticipate the internal numbering scheme used.

Skype for Business Phone Number Configuration

Each Enterprise Voice–enabled user has to have a unique line URI assigned. A *line URI* is the user's phone number formatted according to RFC 3966, published by the Internet Engineering Task Force (IETF) and shown in Figure 33.9.

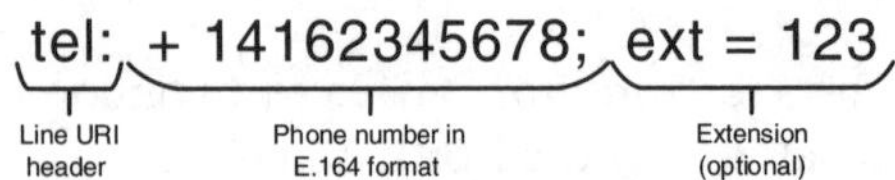

FIGURE 33.9 Tel URI formatting example.

A line URI must start with the `tel:` header, followed by a plus sign (not enforced but recommended), then any number of digits, then any extra optional attributes separated by a semicolon. The most commonly used attribute in Skype for Business Server 2015 is the `;ext=` attribute, which signifies an extension.

A user's line URI *should* match up to their E.164-formatted office number as defined in Active Directory. E.164 formatting isn't enforced, however, and Skype for Business Server 2015 will allow administrators to create line URIs that follow any format. A line URI like `tel:245` would be acceptable in Skype for Business Server 2015, but should not be used due to its lack of scalability and incompatibility with other federated customers' dial plans.

DIDs

In many companies, users are assigned directly dialable numbers, which are known as *Direct Inward Dialing* (DID) numbers or *Direct Dial-In* (DDI) numbers. External users don't have to dial a central number to speak to a receptionist (or auto-attendant) to reach the target user. At minimum, the line URI in Skype for Business Server 2015 should be similar to this (using London, UK as an example):


```
tel:+442031234567
```

This example is the bare minimum required for a Skype for Business Server 2015 line URI. However, even if a user has a direct number, the line URI should include the extension attribute to allow users to use a short number of digits to identify themselves when dialing in to conferences from a non-Skype for Business phone. Skype for Business Server 2015 dial-in conferencing uses the extension attribute for this purpose. If the extension isn't a part of the line URI, users would have to enter their entire phone number when identifying themselves to a Skype for Business Server 2015 dial-in conference.

```
tel:+442031234567;ext=4567
```

NOTE

Administrators do not have to formulate any special dialing rules to account for the extension when the main part of the line URI is unique across the enterprise.

Extensions

For cost, business, or technical reasons, a company may not use DIDs for their internal users. Instead, everyone may use an internal extension. Following best practices, each user should be assigned a valid E.164 phone number with an RFC 3966–formatted extension. The following example shows how to formulate line URIs for an office whose main number is +1 (212) 333-4444 and use three-digit extensions starting with 2:

```
tel:+12123334444;ext=201
tel:+12123334444;ext=202
```

Although not strictly required, every number in a given office should have the same E.164 main number, followed by a unique extension. This makes normalization and routing much simpler. Avoid assigning "tel" URIs made solely up with the extension. This will not scale well when dealing with multiple locations and special routing scenarios.

Ideally, each office should use a unique extension range, even if it is technically allowed to use the same extension (assuming the main number is different for each site).

The following example is allowed because the entire phone number is unique, even though the extensions are the same:

Joe at Waterloo Office: `+15197778888;ext=345`

Lara at Toronto Office: `+14163334444;ext=345`

However, this is less than ideal because it will be more difficult to create global extension dialing rules that work the same across all locations. In cases where there are overlapping extensions, it's best to add one or more site identification digits to the beginning of the extension to make dial plan management easier, as shown here:

Joe at Waterloo Office: `+15197778888;ext=`**`2`**`345`

Lara at Toronto Office: `+14163334444;ext=`**`3`**`345`

One thing to stress is that you cannot use the main office number alone without an extension for any purpose in Skype for Business Server 2015 if that number is being used for extensions. If `tel:+14163334444;ext=3xxx` is assigned to users, then `tel:+14163334444` cannot be used by itself for an Exchange auto-attendant or response group. If so, all inbound calls will fail with a "485 Ambiguous" error that only shows itself during a call trace. Auto-attendants and response groups should either use a different DID or be assigned an extension off the main number like the other users.

Gateways and Trunks

Before diving into creating dial plans and voice policies, the connections to the PSTN have to be defined in Skype for Business Server 2015 Topology Builder as gateways and trunks. A PSTN connection can be a PSTN gateway, a Session Border Controller (SBC), an IP-PBX, or a Direct SIP connection to a third-party SIP provider. Each physical connection is defined as a *gateway,* and logical connections to different IP ports on the gateway are defined as *trunks.*

A gateway consists of only the FQDN or IP address where the gateway can be reached, as shown in Figure 33.10. The trunk consists of the listening port and protocol (TCP or TLS) of the gateway and the Mediation Server name and port that will be used to make the connection, like in Figure 33.11. The trunk name does not have to correlate with the physical name of the associated trunk; it can be whatever makes sense to the administrator. Each gateway must have one or more associated trunks. The Mediation Server port must be within the range defined for the Mediation Server, as shown in Figure 33.12. It is the trunk that is used in Skype for Business Server 2015 routes, which are described later in this chapter.

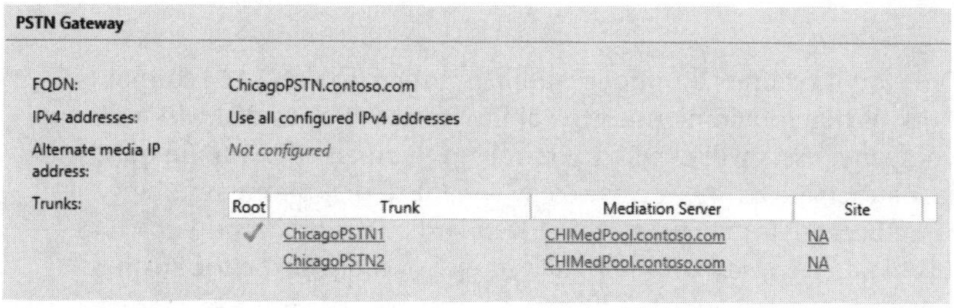

PSTN Gateway
FQDN: ChicagoPSTN.contoso.com
IPv4 addresses: Use all configured IPv4 addresses
Alternate media IP address: Not configured
Trunks:
Root | Trunk | Mediation Server | Site
✓ ChicagoPSTN1 CHIMedPool.contoso.com NA
ChicagoPSTN2 CHIMedPool.contoso.com NA

FIGURE 33.10 PSTN gateway.

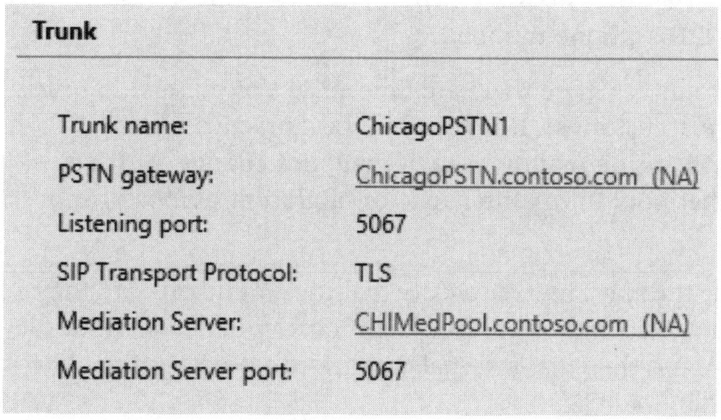

Trunk
Trunk name: ChicagoPSTN1
PSTN gateway: ChicagoPSTN.contoso.com (NA)
Listening port: 5067
SIP Transport Protocol: TLS
Mediation Server: CHIMedPool.contoso.com (NA)
Mediation Server port: 5067

FIGURE 33.11 PSTN trunk.

General
FQDN: CHIMedPool.contoso.com
IPv4 addresses: Use all configured IPv4 addresses
Associations
Edge pool (for media): Not associated
Note: To view the federation route, use the site property page.
Next hop selection
Next hop pool: ChicagoSFBPool.contoso.com (NA)
Mediation Server PSTN gateway
TLS listening port: 5067 - 5068
TCP listening port: Not configured
Trunks:
Default | Trunk | Gateway | Site
ChicagoPSTN1 ChicagoPSTN.contoso.com NA
ChicagoPSTN2 ChicagoPSTN.contoso.com NA

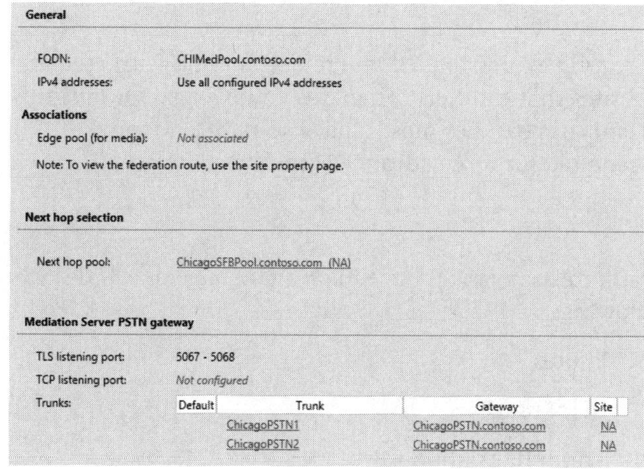

FIGURE 33.12 Mediation Server properties.

Dial Plans

Ensuring Active Directory and line URI phone numbers adhere to the E.164 format is only part of the story. While providing users the ability to use click-to-dial will work for users within the company, users will expect to be able to manually dial phone numbers. Administrators must anticipate all the ways users will want to dial phone numbers and ensure those numbers are formatted to E.164 standards. This process is known as *normalization* and is handled by *normalization rules* in one or more Skype for Business Server 2015 dial plans.

A *dial plan* is a collection of normalization rules that can be applied at either the global, Skype for Business Server 2015 site (not a physical site), server pool, user, or even PSTN gateway level. A dial plan should ensure that no matter what a user dials, it will be formatted to a properly formatted E.164 phone number.

A dial plan should exist for every country where there are Enterprise Voice users, so users are able to dial numbers as they are accustomed. It is generally best practice to assign user-level dial plans because this will ensure dialing behavior will not change for users should they have to move to another pool for maintenance or migration purposes, and it provides maximum flexibility.

Administrators have to think about the ways users typically dial their numbers. Are they used to excluding the 1 for local calls? Do they dial seven-digit local numbers without the area code for their specific location? Do they dial internal extensions? What do they have to dial to make a national or international call?

Administrators also have to consider how any PBX that exists in the environment sends numbers to Skype for Business Server 2015. Is it capable of sending full E.164-formatted phone numbers, or can it only send extensions? A PSTN gateway-level dial plan may be necessary in these cases.

Normalization rules are built using regular expressions. If you're not familiar with regular expressions, there are numerous websites that can help. Thankfully, the Skype for Business Server 2015 Control Panel has a wizard that handles most typical scenarios. Manual regular expression building is only required for more advanced scenarios.

Naming Conventions

When deploying Enterprise Voice, administrators will have to create names for a wide variety of objects, including the following:

Dial plans	Routes
Normalization rules	PSTN usages
Voice policies	Trunk translation rules

Skype for Business Server 2015 doesn't enforce any kind of naming convention, but it's best to decide on one early on and never deviate from it. There are no hard-and-fast rules here. The size, complexity, and geographic scope of the Enterprise Voice deployment should be considered.

In companies that span multiple countries, or even states/provinces in a single country, it is recommended that you use a naming convention that makes objects easy to identify. Consider using a two-letter country code and/or state/province abbreviation as a starting point, separated by a dash. Then add other identifiers for city, office location, or some other name that is easily identifiable. Finally, use something that signifies the calling class of the object, such as "Local," "National," or "International." Here are some examples for what could be normalization rules, or routes or PSTN usages:

US-WA-Seattle-National	US-NewYork-Tollfree
CA-BC-Vancouver-International	UK-London-Mobile
ES-Madrid-Local	SG-Singapore-AllCalls

Using a consistent naming convention makes it much easier to find or sort objects. PowerShell scripting is also much easier.

Normalization Basics

Let's start with a rule that normalizes an NANP 10-digit number to a properly formatted E.164 number:

```
^(\d{10})$  →  +1$1
```

A regular expression should start with `^`, which means to look for a match starting at the beginning of the string, and end with `$`, which means to stop looking at the end. The `\d` is regex code for "a single digit." A number surrounded by curly braces means the preceding element should be counted that many times. So, `\d{10}` means "10 digits." A matched number within the round brackets is accessible as a variable: `$1`. If there are more than one set of brackets, then each bracket set is represented by `$1`, `$2`, `$3`, and so on. Nothing special is required to account for things like dashes, brackets, and periods in the dialed number. These are automatically removed by Skype for Business Server 2015 prior to normalization.

The right side of the arrow shows what the final normalized number will look like. The preceding example starts with +1 and insert the digits represented by the variable `$1`. So, if someone dials 3124448888, the rule `^(\d{10})$` is matched, since it's a 10-digit number. The normalization rule simply places a +1 in front, and the final result is the E.164-formatted number +13124448888. If someone dials either 9 or 11 or more digits, this pattern won't be matched since the `^` and `$` symbols at the beginning and end mean that the number has to be an exact match for the pattern to work.

Advanced Normalization

Although the preceding example will work for that one specific scenario, it's best to try to deal with any possible way to dial numbers in a single rule. Look at the following NANP example:

```
^1? ([2-9]\d\d [2-9]\d{6}) \d* (\D+\d+)?$ → +1$1
 ❶    ❷          ❸          ❹    ❺
```

- The `?` after the first `1` means the preceding number can be either present or not for a match. This allows for users to dial either 10- or 11-digit North American numbers and be matched by the same rule.
- The `[2-9]` means "match any single digit between 2 and 9." Then there are two single digits, represented by `\d\d`. Together, this indicates a North American area code, which can be any number from 200–999.
- The `[2-9]\d{6}` represents the subscriber number, which is seven digits long but has to start with 2–9.
- `\d*` means "0 or more digits," which is useful to include to allow for "overdialing," where a user may dial more numbers than are actually allowed.
- `(\D+\d+)?` simply means "one or more non-digits followed by one or more digits may or may not be present." This is handy for accepting phone numbers from users' Outlook contacts, which could have some phone numbers with oddly formatted extensions at the end, like "ext 443" or "x443". The expression will drop the extension from the number.

The end result is a single normalization rule that will accept a wide variety of dialed numbers and return a nicely formatted E.164 phone number. If the user enters **12125551111** or **2125551111** or **2125551111 extension num 59** (from Outlook, for instance), it will be normalized as +12125551111.

Each country will have its own conventions for dialing phone numbers. Administrators can either use local knowledge, Wikipedia, national telephony regulator websites, or the Skype for Business–specific Skype Optimizer website (www.skypeoptimizer.com) to determine the dial rules for any given country.

International Normalization

For international numbers, users should be forced to dial their usual international routing code (like 00 for a good part of the world or 011 for NANP) to make sure they really want to dial an international number. Otherwise, users could accidentally dial internationally when they intended to dial locally. If someone intended to dial a Vancouver, Canada number by dialing 6046551111, it could end up routing to Penang, Malaysia by accident (60 is Malaysia's country code, and 46 is the city code for Penang). To avoid this, force users to dial their country's international access code (011 or 00 or similar) before they enter an international number. This rule takes care of that for NANP:

```
^011([2-9]\d{6,14})(\D+\d+)?$  →  +$1
```

And this rule is for a country like the UK:

```
^00((1[2-9]\d\d[2-9]\d{6})|([2-9]\d{6,14}))(\D+\d+)?$  →  +$1
```

The latter example is a bit different from the NANP example, because the first normalization rule expects a country code that starts with a number between 2 and 9. NANP is the only country code that starts with a 1, and all NANP numbers are the same length and format, so we can build a more specific rule for that portion and separate the sections with a regex OR symbol (|).

So, with the first rule described here, when a user dials 6046551111, the number is normalized to +16046551111. If they meant to dial Penang, Malaysia, they'd have to dial 0116046551111 (or 006046551111 from the UK), which would normalize to +6046551111.

Internal Extensions

Skype for Business Server 2015 makes it easy to not have to know someone's specific phone number in order to reach them. Just look up their name and click the dial icon. However, old habits die hard, and many organizations will demand the ability to dial by extension as they did on the old PBX. Fortunately, these sorts of demands can be accommodated quite easily with normalization rules, when planned properly.

The easiest case is if all internal extensions map directly and consistently to external phone numbers (DIDs). For example, if four-digit extensions that start with seven all map to DIDs that are in the +13125557xxx range, then the corresponding normalization rule will look like this:

```
^(7\d{3})  →  +1312555$1
```

If users don't have a DID, then a rule similar to the following will work well, assuming the main office number is 1 (416) 222-1111:

```
^(5\d{3}) → +14162221111;ext=$1
```

Of course, users' tel URIs must follow the format of `tel:+1416222111;ext=5xxx` for this to work. The same rules for tel URI formatting also apply to Exchange auto-attendants and response group workflows. At no point can the main office number be used by itself for any purpose, or else all calls will fail with a "485 Ambiguous" error.

For incoming calls to the main number, the administrator must create a normalization rule that takes the main office number and routes it to either an Exchange auto-attendant or response group at an unused extension, such as `tel:+14162221111;ext=0000`, or it could be routed to a dedicated receptionist extension. When someone calls the main office number, the phone call will be routed to the proper location.

This works fine in many deployments, but in situations where the incoming phone number is already formatted in E.164 (as with many SIP providers), the process breaks down. When Skype for Business Server 2015 sees a number that starts with a plus sign, it assumes the number is normalized properly and does not apply normalization rules. Users get a busy signal and the dreaded "485 Ambiguous" error will show up in a log trace. Skype for Business Server 2015 sees many users with the same base phone number and doesn't know where to send the call.

If one is used, the PSTN gateway or SBC can be easily configured to drop the plus sign on incoming calls. If connecting directly to a SIP provider, they may be convinced to drop the plus from incoming calls. If neither of those options is available, then the only real option is to apply MSPL scripting to reroute the incoming call to the appropriate destination. See Ken's UC Blog at http://ucken.blogspot.com/2012/02/re-routing-incoming-calls-to.html for a sample script.

In some unfortunate scenarios, users may have DIDs with internal extensions that do not have anything in common with their DID. For example, User A has a DID of +4420322225555 and the extension 205. User B has a DID of +4420378901234 and the extension 206. This can happen when DIDs are purchased piecemeal instead of in large blocks and extensions are handed out on the old PBX in numerical order.

There is no way to create a single normalization rule that will allow users to dial 2xx and reach what is essentially a random DID. In that case, administrators will have to either create one normalization rule for each user (time consuming and not scalable) or more likely abandon the idea of extension dialing. Once users are more familiar with Skype for Business, they will likely realize that extension dialing is not nearly as critical as with a traditional PBX.

External Access Prefixes

A lasting legacy of the PBX era is the concept of dialing an external access prefix to make a call to the outside world. In many deployments, users have to dial a 9 or 8 or some other digit to open a line to the PSTN. In some systems, when you press 9, you can hear the change in dial tone as you actually open a connection to the PSTN.

The main reason for using an external access prefix is to provide a clear demarcation between internal and external calls. When dialing "off-hook"—meaning the user picks up a handset, hears a dial tone, and then starts dialing the number on the keypad—the PBX needs to know where to send the call based on the digits entered on the keypad. This might sound obvious, but if someone punched in the digits 2-1-2-3, the PBX needs to know if that person wants to connect to someone at extension 2123, or if they're just in the process of dialing an external New York number that happens to start with 2123. If the user meant to reach extension 2123, then the PBX will connect the call to that extension and the call is connected as expected. But if the user meant to dial New York number 2123334444, then they will be understandably frustrated they were connected to extension 2123 instead.

The external access prefix deals with this issue in a neat and tidy way. When the user is dialing off-hook, if the external access prefix is pressed before the number is dialed, the PBX will not attempt to connect to an internal extension once enough digits are entered. So, when the user dials **9** 2123, the PBX won't attempt to route the call to extension 2123, and will instead wait for the user to enter the remaining digits necessary to complete a call on the PSTN.

To support external access prefixes in Skype for Business Server 2015 dial plans, simply place the desired external access prefix in the External Access Prefix entry field within a dial plan, as shown in Figure 33.13.

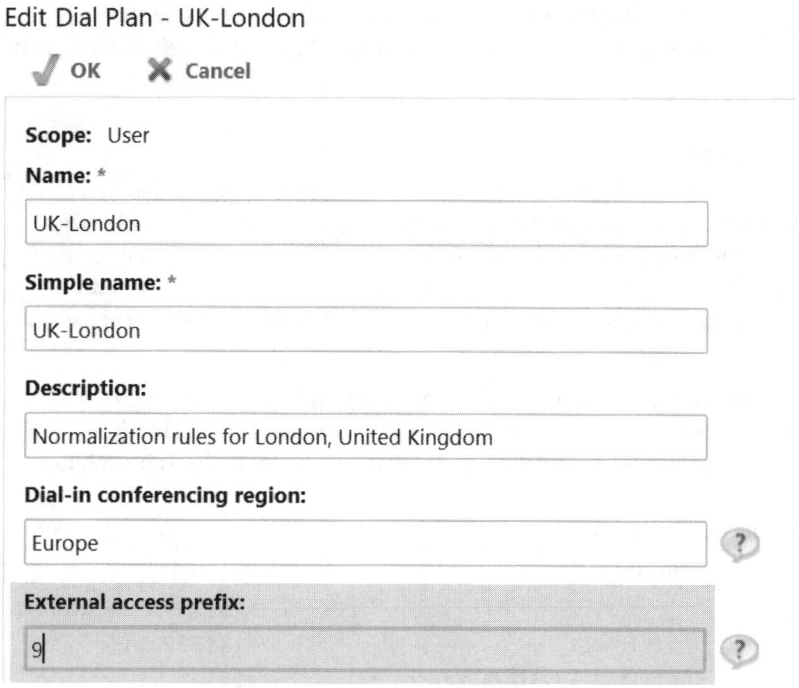

Edit Dial Plan - UK-London

OK Cancel

Scope: User

Name: *

UK-London

Simple name: *

UK-London

Description:

Normalization rules for London, United Kingdom

Dial-in conferencing region:

Europe

External access prefix:

9

FIGURE 33.13 External Access Prefix.

Then on any extension-specific normalization rules, check the Internal Extension box.

Combined, these options do several things. First, they allow people to dial phone numbers in Skype for Business the same way they're accustomed to on the PBX without having to adjust normalization rules. It also makes a Skype for Business desk phone work the same way a PBX phone works when the user is dialing off-hook. Unlike with a traditional PBX, users aren't forced to enter a 9, but if they habitually dial off-hook, then they'll have the same experience as before, while avoiding any misdialed numbers.

Inbound Normalization

Inbound phone calls to Skype for Business Server 2015 should be normalized to E.164 just like any other dialed number; otherwise, calls won't get sent to users. This can be done in one of two ways:

- A site-level dial plan, which applies to all users and objects in a given site. This includes inbound calls coming through a gateway or PBX.
- A pool-level dial plan associated with a specific trunk/gateway.

Using a pool-level trunk is beneficial if there are specific normalization rules that need to be applied to one gateway but not another. Otherwise, site-level dial plans are generally sufficient.

One issue to watch out for with incoming calls is numbers that are already formatted for E.164 when the company uses extensions for user phone numbers. This is often seen with third-party SIP providers.

Putting It All Together

Skype for Business Server 2015 evaluates normalization rules in an assigned dial plan from top to bottom. To minimize processing time and to avoid surprises, put rules with a narrower scope and more frequent use at the top of the list. If a phone number can be matched by more than one rule, put the more restrictive rule first. Don't put PBX access codes such as 9 in normalization rules. These are better handled via external access prefixes (as described in the previous section).

When a user dials a number, Skype for Business Server 2015 will start at the top of the normalization rule list and works its way down until it finds a match. The final normalization rules for a simple North American dial plan might look like Table 33.4.

TABLE 33.4 North American Dial Plan

Name	Pattern	Translation
US-Chicago-5xxx-Ext	`^(5\d{3})$`	+13125551111;ext=$1
CA-Toronto-7xxx-Ext	`^(7\d{3})$`	+1416222$1
NA-National	`^1?([2-9]\d\d[2-9]\d{6})\d*(\D+\d+)?$`	+1$1
NA-Service	`^([2-9]11)$`	$1
NA-International	`^011([2-9]\d{6,14})(\D+\d+)?$`	+$1

And a similar one for Berlin, Germany is shown in Table 33.5.

TABLE 33.5 Berlin, Germany Dial Plan

Name	Pattern	Translation
DE-Berlin-Local	`^([2-9]\d{4,8})$`	+4930$1
DE-TollFree	`^0(800\d{7,12})\d*$`	+49$1
DE-Premium	`^0(900\d{7})$`	+49$1
DE-Mobile	`^0(1[567]\d{8,9})$`	+49$1
DE-National	`^0((180\d{5,7}|[2-7]\d{5,}|[89][1-9]\d{5,10}|90[1-9]\d{4,8}))\d*(\D+\d+)?$`	+49$1
DE-Service	`^(11\d{1,4}|911)$`	$1
DE-International	`^00((1[2-9]\d\d[2-9]\d{6})|([2-9]\d{6,14}))(\D+\d+)?$`	+$1

Because everything is normalized to a unique and standardized E.164 phone number, it's much easier to modify at the gateway level to comply with local PSTN or PBX requirements. This is accomplished with trunk translation rules, which will be discussed later.

Instead of having a detailed normalization rule for each specific call class (toll-free, national, mobile, and so on), everything could be simplified down to a single normalization rule that accepts any string of digits and prepends the relevant country code, but it is best practice to validate user input as early in the dialing process as possible. With detailed normalization rules, users will have visual feedback they entered a valid number because the client will add the + sign and country code indicating it has been successfully normalized.

Sharp-eyed readers may notice that the NA-Service and DE-Service normalization rules do not place a plus sign before the number. The reasoning behind this is that numbers such as 911 are not E.164-formatted numbers. They do not start with the country code, nor are they dialable from outside the country. While highly unlikely, there's a chance that a service number in one country might conflict with a valid E.164 phone number in another country.

One last thing to remember is that any incoming number that starts with a + sign is assumed to be already formatted for E.164, and no normalization rules will apply. It will be dialed as is. Keep this in mind when formatting phone numbers in Active Directory.

Voice Policies and Voice Routing

Skype for Business Server 2015 *voice policies* define the set of calling features available to users and what types of calls they are authorized to make. Voice policies are assigned at either the user, site, or global level. As with dial plans, it is usually best to assign user-level voice policies so if users have to be moved to another pool in a different site during maintenance, their calling behavior won't change.

Calling features are configured from the Skype for Business Server 2015 Control Panel (or PowerShell) and are generally self-explanatory. For most companies, the defaults are acceptable, as shown in Figure 33.14.

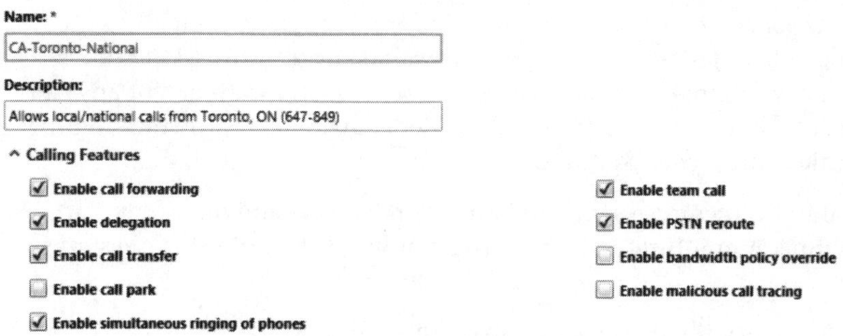

FIGURE 33.14 Default calling feature settings.

Determining the types of calls available to members of a given voice policy is accomplished through a set of administrator-defined ordered *PSTN usages*, which are simply collections of one or more voice routes.

A *voice route* defines the actual path a call takes on its way out to the PSTN via a Skype for Business Server 2015 topology defined trunk. A voice route consists of a regular expression that specifies what phone numbers are allowed as well as the PSTN gateway/trunk to send the call to. A call will only use a route if the normalized dialed number matches the regular expression associated with that route.

Each voice policy can contain multiple PSTN usages. The PSTN usages assigned to a given voice policy determine what numbers a user is allowed to dial. With proper PSTN usage assignment, users can be limited to calling whatever phone numbers the administrator deems acceptable. For example, one voice policy may allow only local dialing (useful for common area phones), while another may allow calls to a specific set of countries.

Routes and PSTN usages should follow the same naming convention as determined when creating dial plans. The recommended format is `<2-LetterCountryCode>-<State/Prov (optional)>-<Location>-<CallClass>`, as shown the Table 33.6.

TABLE 33.6 PSTN Usage Table

US-NewYork-National	IT-Rome-Premium
UK-London-AllCalls	AU-Sydney-Mobile
US-FL-Miami-Local	DE-Munich-International

The order of PSTN usages within a voice policy is critical. When a call is made, Skype for Business Server 2015 will evaluate routes from within PSTN usages starting at the top and working its way down until a match is found. If the first match isn't available, Skype for Business Server 2015 will continue evaluating PSTN usages and routes until it runs out of assigned PSTN usages.

Conversely, do not count on route ordering within a PSTN usage to control routing preference. If there are two matching routes within a PSTN usage, Skype for Business Server 2015 may use either one of the routes to complete the call.

PSTN usages can be as generic or as specific as required. For instance, a company with a single PSTN gateway and no desire for call restrictions could create a single PSTN usage with a single route that has a matching pattern of `^\+\d+$` (which means accept any call starting with + and at least one digit). This is the simplest way to deal with voice routing, but provides very little control over voice traffic.

Most companies will want to enforce some limitations on its users and more granular control over call routing. Administrators should ask themselves the following questions prior to voice policy design:

- Do you want to control the types of calls that users can make?
- Do you want to prevent long-distance, premium number, and/or international calls to a subset of users?
- Do you want to limit call forwarding to costly long-distance or international numbers?
- Do you want to use least-cost routing either within a single country or between countries?

If the answer to these questions is no, then it may be best to keep things simple by using a single catch-all PSTN usage/route combination for each PSTN gateway in the environment. For others, a more detailed approach can provide near limitless call-routing possibilities.

Basic Voice Policy Design

For each location that requires them, create voice policies named to describe the types of calls that are allowed through that policy. Separate voice policies should exist for each class of call that is expected to be deployed to users. For instance, US-Miami-Local, US-Miami-National, and US-Miami-International are voice policies that allow members to call phone numbers scoped at the local, national, and international levels, respectively. The Local policy may be used for common-area phones, the National one for general usage, and International for executives.

In the US-Miami-Local voice policy, a PSTN usage called US-Miami-Local should be created with routes that only allow local and toll-free calls. A PSTN usage called US-Miami-Service should also be created that allows x11 type calls.

The US-Miami-National voice policy should have a PSTN usage called US-Miami-National that allows calls to other U.S. area codes, U.S./Canada area codes, or anywhere in the North American Numbering Plan, along with the US-Miami-Service PSTN usage.

Finally, the US-Miami-International voice policy should contain the US-Miami-National and US-Miami-International PSTN usages.

The final voice policy/PSTN usage/route breakdown will look similar to Tables 33.7, 33.8, and 33.9.

TABLE 33.7 Miami Local PSTN Usage Table

Voice Policy	PSTN Usage	Route	Route Pattern	Gateway
US-Miami-Local	US-Miami-Local	US-Miami-Local	`^\+1(305|754|786|954)[2-9]\d{6}$`	USGW1
		US-Miami-TollFree	`^\+18(00|8\d|77|66|55|44|33|22)\d{7}$`	USGW1
	US-Miami-Service	US-Miami-Service	`^[2-9]11$`	USGW1

TABLE 33.8 Miami National PSTN Usage Table

Voice Policy	PSTN Usage	Route	Route Pattern	Gateway
US-Miami-National	US-Miami-National	US-Miami-National	`^\+1[2-9]\d\d[2-9]\d{6}$`	USGW1
	US-Miami-Service	US-Miami-Service	`^[2-9]11$`	USGW1

TABLE 33.9 Miami International PSTN Usage table

Voice Policy	PSTN Usage	Route	Route Pattern	Gateway
US-Miami-International	US-Miami-National	US-Miami-National	`^\+1[2-9]\d\d[2-9]\d{6}$`	USGW1
	US-Miami-Service	US-Miami-Service	`^[2-9]11$`	USGW1
	US-Miami-International	US-Miami-International	`^\+[2-9]\d{6,14}$`	USGW1

Users who are assigned to one of these policies will be limited to calling numbers that match routes assigned to PSTN usages within their respective voice policy. Users assigned to the US-Miami-Local voice policy can only dial within the Miami area. Users assigned to US-Miami-National can call anywhere in North America and the Caribbean. Users assigned to the US-Miami-International voice policy are able to call anywhere in the world.

Least-Cost Routing

PSTN usages can be ordered in such a way to route phone calls through gateways that reduce call costs for a company. This is called *least-cost routing* (or *tail-end hop-off*). Imagine a company with locations in Miami, U.S. and London, UK. Companies can save money by sending calls from the U.S. bound for the UK across the corporate WAN through the UK PSTN gateway (and vice versa). Assuming it is allowed by the telcos, this practice can save companies from paying high international toll costs.

To add least-cost routing to voice policies, add the appropriate "–Local" and "–National" PSTN usages for the other country (or countries) below the corresponding PSTN usages for the first country, as shown in Tables 33.10, 33.11, and 33.12.

TABLE 33.10 Miami Local PSTN Usage Table with Least-Cost Routing

Voice Policy	PSTN Usage	Route	Route Pattern	Gateway
US-Miami-Local	US-Miami-Local	US-Miami-Local	`^\+1(305|754|786|954)[2-9]\d{6}$`	USGW1
		US-Miami-TollFree	`^\+18(00|8\d|77|66|55|44|33|22)\d{7}$`	USGW1
	UK-London-Local	UK-London-Local	`^\+4420([378]\d{7})$`	UKGW1
		UK-London-TollFree	`^\+44(80(0\d{6,7}|8\d{7}|01111)|500\d{6})$`	UKGW1
	US-Miami-Service	US-Miami-Service	`^[2-9]11$`	USGW1

TABLE 33.11 Miami National PSTN Usage Table with Least Cost Routing

Voice Policy	PSTN Usage	Route	Route Pattern	Gateway
US-Miami-National	US-Miami-National	US-Miami-National	`^\+1[2-9]\d\d[2-9]\d{6}$`	USGW1
	UK-London-National	UK-London-National	`\+44\d{9,11}$`	UKGW1
	US-Miami-Service	US-Miami-Service	`^[2-9]11$`	USGW1

TABLE 33.12 Miami International PSTN Usage Table with Least Cost Routing

Voice Policy	PSTN Usage	Route	Route Pattern	Gateway
US-Miami-International	US-Miami-National	US-Miami-National	`^\+1[2-9]\d\d[2-9]\d{6}$`	USGW1
	UK-London-National	UK-London-National	`\+44\d{9,11}$`	UKGW1
	US-Miami-Service	US-Miami-Service	`^[2-9]11$`	USGW1
	US-Miami-International	US-Miami-International	`^\+[2-9]\d{6,14}$`	USGW1

Each of the original policies now uses least-cost routing to UK-bound phone calls through the UK gateway. It's important to note that in the US-Miami-International policy, the UK-London-National PSTN usage must be above the US-Miami-International usage. Otherwise, calls to the UK would route through the U.S. gateway because any UK-bound call would match the International route and route out the U.S. gateway before the UK-London-National usage was evaluated.

Failover/Resiliency Routing

The idea behind failover or resiliency routing is to use a particular PSTN gateway for normal day-to-day call routing, but have a backup PSTN trunk ready in case the primary one is down. This is different from load-balanced routing, where the goal is to evenly spread call traffic between two or more trunks.

For example, imagine a Skype for Business Server 2015 deployment in Boston and another in Seattle. If call cost isn't a factor, it's best to route all calls from Boston users out the Boston PSTN gateway to reduce WAN traffic and call latency. If the Boston trunk is down, calls should fail over to the Seattle PSTN trunk (and vice versa).

A common error people make in an attempt to make things simple and easier to manage is to create a single route for all calls, and place both the Boston and Seattle trunks inside that route. Because the Boston trunk was added first, it appears first in the list, and administrators are lulled into thinking that calls will always use the Boston trunk unless its down, at which point the Seattle trunk is used.

In actual fact, calls will load-balance themselves between the Boston and Seattle trunks. If the other site is in a different country, the result could be very high international toll charges because half the national calls would be routed out the other country's gateway as an international call, like in Table 33.13.

TABLE 33.13 Gateway Routing

Voice Policy	PSTN Usage	Route	Trunks
Global	AllCalls	AllCalls	BostonGW SeattleGW

The proper way to achieve failover routing is via *PSTN Usage ordering*, as shown in Table 33.14. Instead of creating a single route with multiple gateways inside it, create a Boston PSTN usage with a route to the Boston PSTN gateway, and another Seattle PSTN usage with a route to the Seattle gateway. In the voice policy assigned to Boston users, add both the Boston and Seattle PSTN usages, ensuring the Boston one is above the Seattle one. For the Seattle voice policy, put Seattle first.

TABLE 33.14 Gateway Failover Routing

Voice Policy	PSTN Usage	Route	Trunks
US-Boston	US-Boston-AllCalls	US-Boston-AllCalls	BostonGW1
	US-Seattle-AllCalls	US-Seattle-AllCalls	SeattleGW1

This will achieve true failover routing. For Boston users, all calls will route out the Boston trunk, unless it is down. The same thing works for Seattle users.

Incidentally, putting multiple trunks in a single route does have its uses. If multiple PSTN gateways exist within the same data center for redundancy, putting multiple trunks within a route will load-balance calls between all the trunks, skipping any gateways marked as down. This can be called *round-robin* or *load-balanced* routing.

Both load-balancing and failover routing can be easily accomplished by structuring the voice policies as in Table 33.15.

TABLE 33.15 Routing for Failover and Load Balancing

Voice Policy	PSTN Usage	Route	Trunks
US-Boston	US-Boston-AllCalls	US-Boston-AllCalls	BostonGW1 BostonGW2
	US-Seattle-AllCalls	US-Seattle-AllCalls	SeattleGW1 SeattleGW2

Calls will preferentially use the two Boston gateways unless both are down, at which point they will use both of the Seattle gateways.

Location-Based Routing

Countries such as India have rather strict telecom laws saying any calls that exit the country must exit via the PSTN and cannot use the corporate WAN for toll-bypass/least-cost routing. For instance, imagine a company with a Skype for Business Server 2015 deployment in India and the U.S. A user sitting in India is not allowed to call a U.S. PSTN number and route the call to the U.S. via the corporate WAN and exit to the PSTN via the American Skype for Business Server 2015 deployment. This scenario can be easily dealt with via judicial application of PSTN usages in the appropriate voice policies, as described in previous sections.

However, if an American user travels to India, their American voice policy would still apply (unless the administrator moved the user temporarily to the India Skype for Business server). Their PSTN calls would route over the WAN to the American Skype for Business server, which is not allowed by India telecom rules.

Location-based routing is designed to deal with this problem. *Voice-routing policies* (different from voice policies) can be created and applied to Skype for Business Server 2015 sites so that calls will route according to the user's physical location, rather than their assigned voice policy. Location-based routing can only be configured via PowerShell using the following general steps:

1. Ensure that all sites/subnets to use location-based routing are defined in Skype for Business Server 2015 (see the section "Network Configuration" later in this chapter for more information).
2. Use `New-CSVoiceRoutingPolicy` to create a voice routing policy. Assign the appropriate PSTN usages that will ensure all calls will route via the local PSTN gateway.
3. Use `Set-CSNetworkSite` to enable location-based routing for the desired site via `-EnableLocationBasedRouting:$TRUE` and to assign the previously created voice routing policy.
4. Use `Set-CSTrunkConfiguration` to assign network sites and enable routing restrictions on the PSTN trunk, using `-EnableRoutingRestriction:$TRUE`.
5. Use `Set-CSVoicePolicy` to enable location-based routing for the users assigned to that policy, using `-PreventPSTNTollBypass:$TRUE`.

If the hypothetical American user travels to the India office, their calls will use the India Skype for Business Server 2015 deployment, rather than use the WAN for least-cost routing. Inbound calls to the user's American phone number will go to voicemail, because letting them take the call via the WAN would run afoul of India's dial rules.

Location-based routing can also be used outside of countries such as India without the restrictions on inbound calls coming over the WAN. This can be very desirable in situations where a significant portion of the workforce moves from office to office, especially in environments where bandwidth back to the user's home pool is lacking. To configure location-based routing without restrictions, follow the preceding instructions, but leave out the `-EnableLocationRestriction:$TRUE` setting when running `Set-CSTrunkConfiguration`.

Keep in mind that location-based routing is a purely PowerShell-managed solution. There are very few indicators in the Skype for Business Server 2015 Control Panel that will alert administrators to this being in place, which can make troubleshooting call-routing issues more difficult. Documentation is extremely important in this situation.

Trunk Configuration

With the voice policy/PSTN usages/routes all set up, calls should be routed to the proper gateway for sending out to the PSTN. Additional configuration may be required, depending on the type of connection. If connecting through a certified PSTN gateway, Session Border Controller, or SIP provider, there should be documentation advising what configuration is necessary. For example, many SIP providers don't support REFER, and it should be set to None, or else there will be issues with transferring or forwarding calls.

In terms of number formatting, if the connection to the PSTN is done through a SIP provider, its very likely they accept E.164-formatted phone numbers and nothing else needs to be done. If connecting via traditional methods, the local PSTN provider will have their own formatting rules for calls that may not be compatible with E.164. For example, national calls in many parts of the world have to be prepended with 0. International calls require 00, 000, 011, or something else, entirely depending on the country and the specific phone provider.

To accommodate these requirements, trunk translation rules are used to add or remove digits from E.164-formatted phone numbers before sending the call out to the PSTN. For instance, a Chicago gateway to the PSTN might need to strip the +1 from local calls, strip the + from long distance calls, and add 011 to international calls. An example for Chicago would look something like Table 33.16.

TABLE 33.16 International Translation Rule

Trunk Translation Rule Name	Pattern	Translation	E.164	Sent to GW
US-Chicago-Local	`^\+1((312|773|872)\d{7})`	$1	+13125551111	3125551111
US-Chicago-National	`^\+(1[2-9]\d\d[2-9]\d{6})$`	$1	+16045551111	16045551111
US-Chicago-International	`^\+([2-9]\d{6,14})$`	011$1	+442055551111	011442055551111
US-Chicago-Service	`^([2-9]11)$`	$1	411	411

If calls route through a PBX before going to the PSTN, the necessary external access prefix can be added here, and phone numbers can be stripped down to extensions for PBX-bound calls. An example (using 9 as the external access prefix) is shown in Table 33.17.

TABLE 33.17 Stripping an External Dial Prefix

Trunk Translation Rule Name	Pattern	Translation	E.164	Sent to GW
US-Chicago-Internal	`^\+1312555(2\d{3})$`	$1	+13125552705	2705
US-Chicago-Local	`^\+1((312|773|872)\d{7})`	9$1	+13125551111	93125551111
US-Chicago-National	`^\+(1[2-9]\d\d[2-9]\d{6})$`	9$1	+16045551111	916045551111
US-Chicago-International	`^\+([2-9]\d{6,14})$`	9011$1	+442055551111	9011442055551111
US-Chicago-Service	`^([2-9]11)$`	9$1	411	9411

Inter-trunk Routing

Inter-trunk routing is a feature that allows Skype for Business Server 2015 to be the central call processor for a multi-PBX deployment. Using inter-trunk routing, Skype for Business Server 2015 can pass inbound phone calls on to a different destination, which could be another PBX system or even back out to the PSTN.

This is accomplished by assigning PSTN usages to a trunk using the Associated PSTN Usages dialog box, as shown in Figure 33.15.

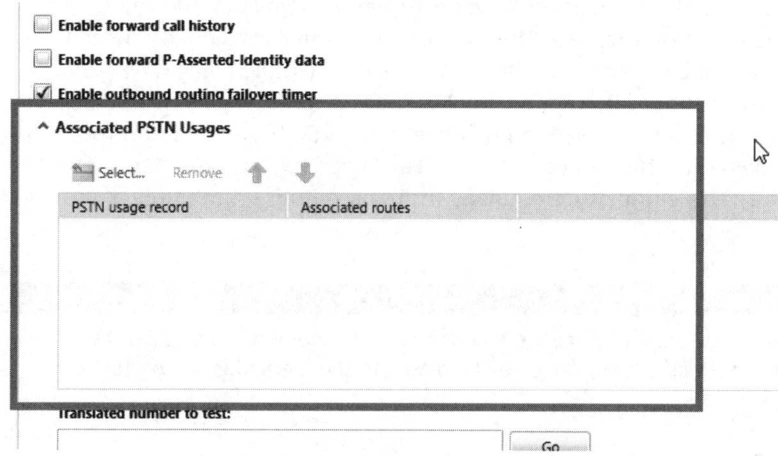

FIGURE 33.15 Associated PSTN Usages dialog box.

Normally, when Skype for Business Server 2015 receives an incoming call, it will first look to see if there is an internal user or service assigned to that number. If there isn't a match, Skype for Business Server 2015 will return a fast busy signal to the caller.

Using inter-trunk routing, if that unmatched number matches a route within any PSTN usage assigned to the incoming trunk, it will route the call to the destination gateway/PBX assigned to that route.

This is done by creating a PSTN usage containing routes for all numbers that should be routed to other systems, as shown in Table 33.18.

TABLE 33.18 PSTN Usage for Inter-trunk Routing

PSTN Usage	Route Name	Route Pattern	Trunks
US-InterTrunkRouting	US-Seattle-PBX	`^\+12065552\d{3}$`	US-Seattle-GW1
	US-NewYork-PBX	`^\+12125557\d{3}$`	US-NewYork-GW1

The PSTN usage is assigned to the Associated PSTN Usages dialog box on the trunk that will receive inbound calls to those numbers. If the incoming call doesn't match an existing user or service, and does match one of the routes in the PSTN usage, it will route out the assigned gateway.

NOTE

If inter-trunk routing is not being used in the environment, do not place any PSTN usages here. Call looping may result.

Media Bypass

One of the main purposes of the Mediation Server is to transcode media into the G.711 format required by the next-hop gateway. This is a processor-intensive activity, which impacts the total number of calls that a Mediation Server can handle. Many Skype for Business Server 2015–compatible gateways or IP-PBXs support *media bypass*, where instead of sending phone audio through the Mediation Server, the audio bypasses it and routes directly between the client and the gateway/IP-PBX. The Skype for Business client sends the media encoded as G.711, eliminating the need for transcoding. An example is shown in Figure 33.16.

NOTE

In a non-media-bypass environment, if network conditions are deemed acceptable, the Skype for Business client will actually send G.711 media to the Mediation Server to reduce transcoding overhead.

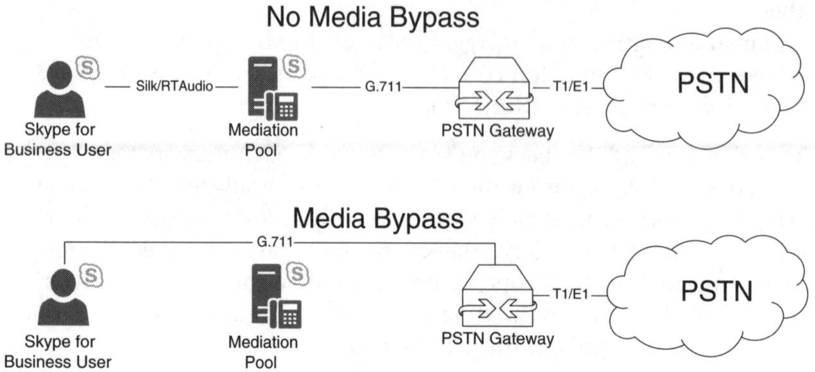

FIGURE 33.16 Media bypass.

Enabling media bypass has several benefits. First, it reduces processor utilization on Mediation Servers, which has an important effect on overall server sizing and capacity planning. Second, media bypass allows for a significant reduction in the overall number of Mediation Servers required, especially when remote sites with local PSTN gateways are concerned. Without media bypass, it's important to keep media paths as short as possible to reduce overall network traffic and latency. This requires placing Mediation Servers close to the next-hop gateways; otherwise, media would have to flow across the WAN from the client to the Mediation Server, then back to the local gateway. If media can flow directly from Skype for Business clients to the gateway without involving a Mediation Server, then it is no longer necessary to have Mediation Servers in the same site as the gateways. Mediation Servers can be centralized because call setup and other related signaling are not nearly as bandwidth intensive or time sensitive as media.

Media bypass has to be centrally enabled via either PowerShell or Skype for Business Server 2015 Control Panel. There are two options: either enable media bypass globally for all calls or use site/region information to determine if media bypass should be used.

Media bypass uses the concept of bypass IDs to determine suitability for media bypass. When a call is made, Skype for Business does a check to see if the bypass ID assigned to the subnet where the client is situated matches the one assigned to the site. If they match, then media bypass will be attempted.

When media bypass is enabled globally, a single bypass ID is generated for the entire Skype for Business Server 2015 deployment. Because there's a single bypass ID, every call will attempt to use media bypass. This is generally not desirable across WAN links because G.711 encoded audio is not as efficient or resilient to changing network conditions as other codecs used by Skype for Business such as RTAudio or Silk.

To use media bypass effectively, it should be enabled using sites and region information entered as part of a full call admission control setup.

Network Configuration

Media bypass, call admission control, and emergency services location policies all rely on a properly described network to function correctly. In Skype for Business Server 2015, the network is broken down into several distinct components:

- **Regions**—Network regions are the backbone of a network. Each network region must be associated with a Skype for Business Server 2015 central site (where Skype for Business Front End Servers are deployed) defined within the topology. Network regions are typically a hub where many other network sites are connected. Examples of regions are North America and Europe, or even areas on a smaller scale such as West Coast and East Coast. In a typical MPLS-type mesh WAN architecture, a single region should be created to represent the MPLS cloud.

- **Sites**—Each network region consists of at least one site and possibly many more. Sites are offices or locations that are part of a network region. In other words, all the offices or locations that have users homed in the central site for the region should be created as sites. A network site object should also be created for the central site, which might seem redundant, but there is no automatic mapping of a site within the topology to a site in the network configuration.

- **Subnets**—Each subnet used at a site should be entered and associated with the correct site. Skype for Business endpoints are associated with a site and region by being matched to a subnet defined here. The Call Admission Control and Media Bypass features rely on matching the subnet of the media gateway to callers, so be sure to include the subnets used for voice hardware. It is important to use the actual subnet/mask combination that is assigned to devices; otherwise, media bypass won't function correctly because it relies on the subnet/mask combination for determining bypass IDs.

- **Bandwidth policy profiles**—Bandwidth policy profiles define a network link speed and the available bandwidth for audio or video calls. The individual, one-way session limit can be specified, as well as the total amount of bandwidth used for audio and video traffic. Bandwidth policy profiles are associated with a site or region link. Sites do not require a bandwidth policy profile to be assigned. In fact, if sites within a region are not bandwidth constrained, no profile should be assigned. Assign bandwidth policy profiles only to sites that require limits on their audio and video WAN usage.

- **Region link**—When multiple regions exist, region links should be defined that identify the amount of bandwidth available between two geographic regions. An example would be a North American region and a European region, each with a central site and multiple branch sites associated. A region link defines the bandwidth available between any North American site and a European site.

- **Region route**—A region route specifies how two regions should be connected. In many cases, a region route mimics a region link and can just be between two different regions. In other cases where two regions are not directly connected but share a link to a common region, a region route defines how these regions must traverse the common region to communicate. In that case, two different region links must be crossed, which might each have a different bandwidth policy profile.

- **Site link**—The final component of the network configuration is a site link. In most cases, sites are connected to a network region directly, which acts as a hub for the users. There might be instances where in addition to a connection to the network region central site, sites have a direct connection to each other that bypasses the central site. Site links are used to create these objects that can then have a bandwidth policy profile associated.

Call Admission Control

Planning to deploy Call Admission Control (CAC) features in Skype for Business Server 2015 depends greatly on the network configuration discussed in the preceding section. CAC relies on determining an endpoint's site and region through the network subnet. Call Admission Control in Skype for Business Server 2015 applies to both audio and video traffic, but organizations can specify different limits for each type of traffic. Both a session limit (one-way traffic) and a total limit for all sessions can be specified.

The key to successful Call Admission Control deployment is to correctly define and associate the bandwidth policy profiles to sites and links by completing the following steps:

1. Identify the connection speed of each WAN link to sites that are bandwidth constrained.
2. Define the maximum audio and video session and total bandwidth limits to be used by Skype for Business endpoints associated with site and policy. These limits vary based on the desired traffic type and the different audio codecs used.
3. Evaluate the site and make some estimates on the type of audio codecs used to create an appropriate limit. For example, if users make several point-to-point calls, RTAudio or Silk is predominantly used. If most calls are conferences, Siren or G.722 audio might be more prevalent.

It is also important to note that Call Admission Control applies only to Skype for Business endpoints traversing a WAN link. Other applications transmitting data on the same WAN link are not affected by Call Admission Control policies. Organizations can define a bandwidth limit for Skype for Business traffic and still see that WAN link become saturated due to other applications. In this scenario, it makes sense to enforce QoS policies on the WAN link to ensure that Skype for Business endpoint calls are prioritized over other traffic. These QoS reservations should ideally match the CAC bandwidth limits.

Bandwidth Estimates Table 33.19 defines the various bandwidth estimates for each protocol, with all values represented in Kbps. This table is useful for configuring bandwidth policy profiles. The typical bandwidth usage values can normally be used for planning purposes. Forward Error Correction (FEC) is enabled when Skype for Business clients detect poor network connectivity, and it attempts to provide a more resilient voice connection to compensate for network jitter or latency. Capacity planning numbers are shown in this table.

TABLE 33.19 Bandwidth Planning by Audio Codec

Codec	Typical Bandwidth (Kbps)	Maximum Bandwidth Without FEC (Kbps)	Maximum Bandwidth with FEC (Kbps)
RTAudio (P2P Narrowband)	29.3	44.8	56.6
RTAudio (P2P Wideband)	39.8	62.0	91.0
SILK (P2P Wideband)	44.3	69	105
G.722 (Conferencing)	46.1	100.6	164.6
Siren (Conferencing)	25.5	52.6	68.6
G.711 (PSTN)	64.8	97.0	161.0

CAC Internet Rerouting When a bandwidth policy limit is exceeded by a user, Call Admission Control will attempt to reroute the call. First, the call attempts to be directed over the Internet if both sites have an Edge Server. Instead of using the WAN link, the call traverses the Internet and is relayed between the Edge Servers in each site. If that is not possible or fails, the call can reroute across the PSTN. Whether this is allowed depends on whether the voice policy assigned to the user allows this feature. If neither Internet nor PSTN rerouting is possible, the call attempts to be sent directly to voicemail. Lastly, if voicemail is unavailable, the call simply fails.

TIP

The public IP address of the A/V Edge roles must be entered in the network configuration with a 32-bit mask and associated to the appropriate sites for Edge reroute to work properly.

Emergency Services

An important consideration in any company is how to deal with emergency calls. Almost every country in the world has a short number (or numbers) that can be dialed to reach various emergency services. In countries the U.S., Canada, and a good part of the Caribbean, 911 is used for any emergency service. A large number of other countries use 112, while other countries may have different numbers for police, ambulance, and fire.

At the most basic level, emergency numbers can be normalized and routed as with any other phone number. Although this will work, it has a big limitation that is important to recognize.

First, with normal behavior, Skype for Business Server 2015 voice policies "follow" the user, no matter what location they are in. A user in Chicago could be configured to route all calls out the Chicago PSTN gateway. If that user travels to the New York office and dials 911, the call will continue to use the Chicago PSTN gateway and emergency services will be delayed, which can be a dangerous situation.

Location Policies

Location policies can be used in Skype for Business Server 2015 so that emergency calls will route depending on the user's current location, regardless of the settings in their voice policy. Location policies work in conjunction with Skype for Business Server 2015 sites and subnets. While the policy entries seem to indicate it is for E911 purposes only (a purely U.S.-focused concept), it will work with emergency services anywhere in the world.

For location policies to work for emergency services numbers, follow these steps and refer to Figure 33.17 for an example:

1. Define a user-level location policy for every site where there is a connection to the PSTN.

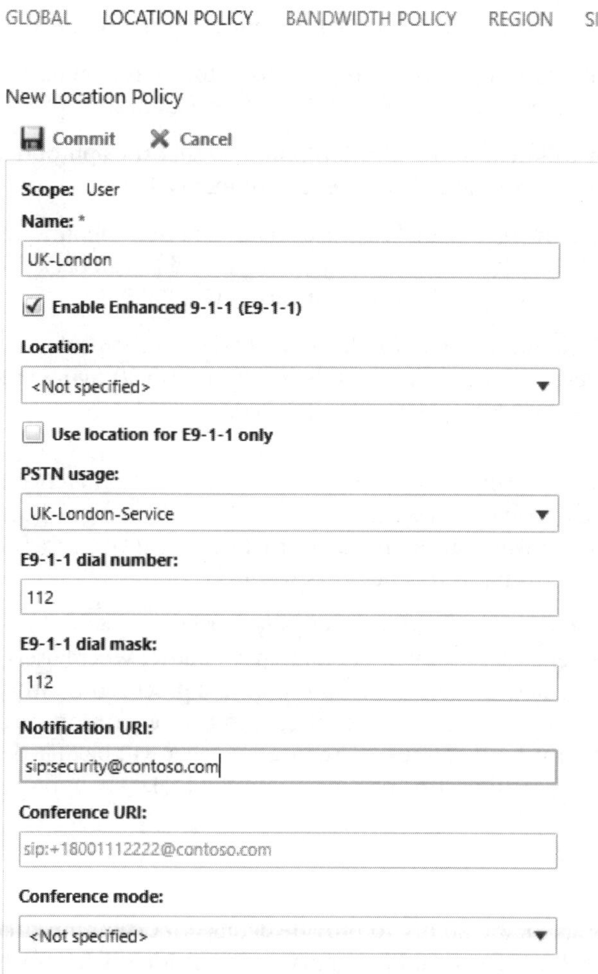

FIGURE 33.17 New location policy.

2. Check the Enable Enhanced 911 box (again, ignore the 911 bit, as this will work anywhere in the world).
3. Don't change Location, unless using E911 in the United States.
4. Assign a PSTN usage that will route the call out to the PSTN at that specific location. If the advice for creating PSTN usages and routes has been followed, this should be a "–Service" PSTN usage (as in UK-London-Service).
5. Define the emergency dial string and mask. The dial string is the actual emergency number that will be used for location services. The mask is an alternative number that can be dialed and will be translated to the main dial string.
6. Assign the location policy to the appropriate Skype for Business Server 2015 network site object.

Although not strictly necessary, the following additional best practices should be followed:

- Assign the appropriate default location policy to every user, to act as a fallback in case they are outside a Skype for Business Server 2015–defined subnet.
- Configure the notification URI field in the location policy so that the appropriate people are aware whenever the configured emergency number is dialed.
- If using analog gateways for emergency dialing only, make sure that inbound calls route to the appropriate person, should emergency services need to call back (ideally the same person who has been assigned to the notification URI field).
- Consider populating the location information database (LIS) even if outside the U.S., because this can help whoever has been assigned the notification URI figure out where the person who called emergency services is located.

A special note about the conferencing URI fields: Note the field labeled "Conference URI," which implies someone can be conferenced in when someone else dials the emergency number. Unfortunately, this doesn't work unless an E911 provider in the U.S. is being used. Outside the U.S., entering anything in this field has no effect.

Assuming location policies have been configured for every site in the company, this will ensure that the proper emergency services will be notified no matter where users happen to be within the corporate network. Keep in mind that this process only works for users *within the corporate network*. Users outside the office won't have location-specific policies applied to them, and their default emergency services number will be dialed. Administrators should review these factors with their legal team and take the appropriate action.

Enhanced 911 (E911)

Skype for Business Server 2015 has the capability to provide detailed location information to an Emergency Services Service Provider or an Emergency Location Identification Number (ELIN) gateway through a location information database. This is known as Enhanced 911, or E911 for short.

NOTE

E911 in Skype for Business Server 2015 is supported only within the United States.

Location Information Database

Skype for Business Server 2015 identifies an endpoint's physical location by examining the network subnet, switch, and wireless access point the client uses. This collection of network objects is referred to as the Location Information Service (LIS) database and must be populated by administrators in advance of enabling E911. The LIS database is completely separate from the Skype for Business Server 2015 network configuration of sites and subnets discussed separately. The LIS database function is only to provide a mapping of network objects to physical addresses that can be sent to the service provider or ELIN gateway.

This database can be populated manually or can be linked to a secondary location information database if one already exists. For Skype for Business Server 2015 to use a secondary location information database, the service must adhere to the Skype for Business Server 2015 Request/Response schema.

If you are manually populating the location database, start by identifying each of the network access points, switches, and subnets within the organization and the physical location associated with each object. When determining an endpoint's location, Skype for Business Server 2015 first uses the wireless access point, and then the switch ID, and lastly a subnet to determine location. This is because each of these items can potentially span multiple rooms or floors in a building, so none is an exact location.

After the location information database is populated, it should be validated with the Emergency Services Service Provider. This validation process compares the addresses associated to each network object with the database maintained by the provider to ensure that each location entered in the LIS database can be correctly routed to a Public-Safety Answering Point (PSAP) that can respond to the request. Alternatively, any ELINs must be entered in the telephony provider's Automatic Location Identification (ALI) database.

SIP Trunk Service Provider

The Emergency Services Service Provider is a third-party service that acts as a liaison between a Skype for Business Server 2015 deployment and the PSAP via SIP trunk. It is important to clarify that Skype for Business Server 2015 does not natively contact a Public Safety Access Point directly. Instead, it is the responsibility of the Emergency Services Service Provider to route the emergency calls to the correct PSAP.

Skype for Business Server 2015 provides an endpoint's location to the Emergency Services Service Provider using the PIDF-LO format, which is really an XML BLOB containing all the detailed address information.

When planning for Enhanced 911 services, an organization must first identify where E911 will be deployed. This might be only within a primary site, in multiple sites, or extended to branch sites. When planning E911 for branch sites, be sure to consider scenarios in which a WAN link is unavailable. It is possible that branch or remote sites will not be able to provide location information or even contact an Emergency Services Service Provider without a resilient WAN link.

The connection to the Emergency Services Service Provider is accomplished through a dedicated SIP trunk. When the SIP trunk is being provisioned, a VPN tunnel to the Emergency Services Service Provider is created using an existing Internet connection, or a dedicated connection can be provisioned to separate and isolate the emergency calls.

An advantage to the service provider method is that it can also serve remote users signed in through an Edge Server. The addresses entered by remote users won't be validated in advance through a master database, but the service provider can answer the call, confirm the address delivered by the Skype for Business client's PIDF-LO data, and then route to an appropriate PSAP for the remote user.

The final consideration with the SIP trunk is to recognize that it does not bypass Call Admission Control policies. If a bandwidth policy is exceeded by an emergency call, the call will not succeed. When planning for E911, be sure to consider the effects of Call Admission Control on where SIP trunks to an Emergency Services Service Provider are placed. For example, in a site where WAN bandwidth is constrained, it might make sense to deploy a local Mediation Server and SIP trunk to a provider to ensure that Call Admission Controls never prevent an emergency call across the WAN link.

Emergency Location Identification Number

Another method for providing detailed address information is through the use of Emergency Location Identification Numbers. Consider an organization that has multiple floors in a single building, and a single PRI circuit for phone calls. When an emergency call is placed, the PSAP can see the physical address for the organization based on the circuit, but no information is passed about which floor the emergency responders should go to. The PSAP has a main number that can be called back, but that number might route to a receptionist who has no idea someone in the building has tried calling emergency services.

An ELIN is a unique phone number that identifies a particular Emergency Response Location (ERL). An ERL could be a floor, a wing, or another arbitrary location within a building. Each ERL is then assigned an ELIN so that if the PSAP sees a call from a particular ELIN, the PSAP should know exactly what area or floor of building has requested help.

Within the LIS database, the ELIN is actually entered in the Company field. When the gateway receives the call and the PIDF-LO information, it places a call using the discovered ELIN as the *called* party, which is then routed to the PSAP and answered.

The other feature of ELIN is that it provides a mapping back to the original caller. The PSAP can be connected to the original caller through that ELIN. The media gateways that support ELIN keep a temporary table of callers who dialed each ELIN so that when a call comes back from the PSAP, it can be properly routed.

Response Groups

Before configuring response groups in Skype for Business Server 2015, an organization should run through a number of planning steps to ensure that the workflow creation is as easy as possible. When a workflow diagram and configuration are created in advance, the actual creation of the workflow in Skype for Business Server 2015 can be completed quickly.

The following steps ease the process of creating workflows:

1. Begin by developing a diagram of the desired workflow. This should include all the possible call flows that a user can be routed through. Also be sure to include scenarios for what happens when a caller becomes unresponsive or does not press a DTMF (Dual-Tone Multi-Frequency) key.

2. Document the exact text that is played to callers so that it is available for text-to speech translation or to be read for an audio recording.

3. If using audio files, identify a user who is responsible for the recording or hire a professional agency to create the recording.

4. Identify the queues required within the workflow. The queue planning phase should include specifying how many concurrent calls can exist within a queue and what action should be taken when the queue reaches capacity. If sending calls to a voicemail box, be sure that the mailbox is monitored in some way so that callers leaving a message receive a response.

5. Identify the different agent groups that will belong to the queues and the individual agents. Ensure that agents are aware they belong to an agent group and are trained on how to handle calls. If using formal groups, make sure that agents understand how to log in and out of the group to take calls.

6. Identify what business hours and holiday schedules will affect the workflow.

7. After collecting all the required information, proceed with creating the agent groups, queues, and workflow objects.

8. Thoroughly test the response group workflow. This should involve traversing every possible option within the workflow to ensure that callers are routed correctly and are never unexpectedly disconnected.

9. Perform any adjustments necessary to the workflow before placing it in production and allowing external callers to reach the workflow.

Summary

Getting voice working in Skype for Business Server 2015 isn't terribly difficult; however, getting it right is. This chapter serves as a how-to guide and offers a number of best practices based on years of experience. Most enterprise voice issues are often misconfiguration issues. Making sure the basic configuration is correct in the beginning will save you hours of troubleshooting later after multiple layers of complexity are piled on. Unified communications is a journey. Take your time and make sure each step is done the best it can be.

Index

Symbols

A

B

C

D

E

F

G

H

I

J

K

L

M

N

O

P

Q

R

S

T

U

V

W